Your Class.
Their Career.
Everyone's Future.

PEARSON
myeducationlab™
Where the Classroom Comes to Life

Helping today's students become the teachers of tomorrow.

"Teacher educators who are developing pedagogies for the analysis of teaching and learning contend that analyzing teaching artifacts has three advantages: it enables new teachers time for reflection while still using the real materials of practice; it provides new teachers with experience thinking about and approaching the complexity of the classroom; and in some cases, it can help new teachers and teacher educators develop a shared understanding and common language about teaching. . . ."[1]

As Linda Darling-Hammond and her colleagues point out, grounding teacher education in real classrooms—among real teachers and students and among actual examples of students' and teachers' work—is an important, and perhaps even an essential, part of training teachers for the complexities of teaching today's students in today's classrooms. For a number of years, we have heard the same message from many of you as we sat in your offices learning about the goals of your courses and the challenges you face in teaching the next generation of educators. Working with a number of our authors and with many of you, we have created a website that provides you and your students with the context of real classrooms and artifacts that research on teacher education tells us is so important. Through authentic in-class video footage, interactive simulations, rich case studies, examples of authentic teacher and student work, and more, **MyEducationLab** offers you and your students a uniquely valuable teacher education tool.

MyEducationLab is easy to use! Wherever the **MyEducationLab** logo appears in the margins or elsewhere in the text, you and your students can follow the simple link instructions to access the **MyEducationLab** resource that corresponds with the chapter content. These include:

VIDEO ■ Authentic classroom videos show how real teachers handle actual classroom situations.

HOMEWORK & EXERCISES ■ These assignable activities give students opportunities to understand content more deeply and to practice applying content.

BUILDING TEACHING SKILLS ■ These assignments help students practice and strengthen skills that are essential to quality teaching. By analyzing and responding to real student and teacher artifacts and/or authentic classroom videos, students practice important teaching skills they will need when they enter real classrooms.

CASE STUDIES

A diverse set of robust cases drawn from some of our best-selling books further expose students to the realities of teaching and offer valuable perspectives on common issues and challenges in education.

SIMULATIONS

Created by the IRIS Center at Vanderbilt University, these interactive simulations give hands-on practice at adapting instruction for a full spectrum of learners.

STUDENT & TEACHER ARTIFACTS

Authentic student and teacher classroom artifacts are tied to course topics and offer practice in working with the actual types of materials that teachers encounter every day.

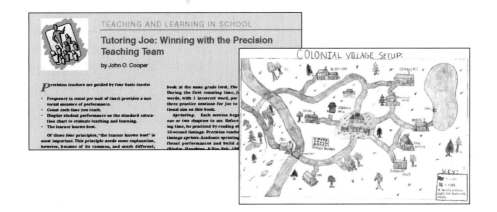

INDIVIDUALIZED STUDY PLAN

Your students have the opportunity to take pre- and post-tests before and after reading each chapter of the text. Their test results automatically generate a personalized study plan, identifying areas of the chapter they must reread to fully understand chapter concepts. They are also presented with interactive multimedia exercises to help ensure learning. The study plan is designed to help your students perform well on exams and to promote deep understanding of chapter content.

READINGS ■ Specially selected, topically relevant articles from ASCD's renowned *Educational Leadership* journal expand and enrich students' perspectives on key issues and topics.

Other Resources

LESSON & PORTFOLIO BUILDERS ■ With this effective and easy-to-use tool, you can create, update, and share standards-based lesson plans and portfolios.

NEWS ARTICLES ■ Looking for current issues in education? Our collection offers quick access to hundreds of relevant articles from the *New York Times* Educational News Feed.

MyEducationLab is easy to assign, which is essential to providing the greatest benefit to your students. Visit **www.myeducationlab.com** for a demonstration of this exciting new online teaching resource.

[1] Darling-Hammond, L., & Bransford, J., Eds. (2005). *Preparing Teachers for a Changing World.* San Francisco: John Wiley & Sons.

PEARSON
myeducationlab™
Where the Classroom Comes to Life

ELEVENTH EDITION

Exceptional Learners

An Introduction to Special Education

Daniel P. Hallahan
University of Virginia

James M. Kauffman
University of Virginia

Paige C. Pullen
University of Virginia

Boston • New York • San Francisco • Mexico City
Montreal • Toronto • London • Madrid • Munich • Paris • Hong Kong
Singapore • Tokyo • Cape Town • Sydney

Executive Editor: *Virginia Lanigan*
Editorial Assistant: *Matthew Buchholz*
Developmental Editor: *Alicia Reilly*
Senior Marketing Manager: *Kris Ellis-Levy*
Production Editor: *Gregory Erb*
Editorial Production Service: *Progressive Publishing Alternatives*
Composition Buyer: *Linda Cox*
Manufacturing Buyer: *Megan Cochran*
Electronic Composition: *Progressive Information Technologies*
Interior Design: *Denise Hoffman*
Photo Researcher: *Sarah Evertson*
Cover Designer: *Linda Knowles*

For related titles and support materials, visit our online catalog at
www.pearsonhighered.com

Between the time website information is gathered and then published, it is not unusual
for some sites to have closed. Also, the transcription of URLs can result in typographical
errors. The publisher would appreciate notification where these errors occur so that they
may be corrected in subsequent editions.

Library of Congress Cataloging-in-Publication Data
Hallahan, Daniel P., 1944–
   Exceptional learners : an introduction to special education / Daniel P. Hallahan, James
M. Kauffman. —11th ed.
      p. cm.
   Includes bibliographical references and index.
   ISBN-13: 978-0-205-57104-8 (hardcover)
   ISBN-10: 0-205-57104-2 (hardcover)
  1.   Special education—United States.   I. Kauffman, James M.   II. Title.

   LC3981.H34 2009
   371.90973—dc22

                                    2007049100

Printed in the United States of America

10 9 8 7 6 5 4 3 2 1   RRD-OH   12 11 10 09 08

Credits appear on page 632, which constitutes an extension of the copyright page.

Allyn & Bacon
is an imprint of

        ISBN-10: 0-205-57104-2
        ISBN-13: 978-0-205-57104-8

About the Authors

Daniel P. Hallahan is the Charles S. Robb Professor of Education at the University of Virginia. He was the inaugural occupant of the Virgil S. Ward Professor of Education Endowed Chair from 1996 to 1998 and was appointed to the university's Cavaliers' Distinguished Teaching Professorship from 2002 to 2004. He received the University of Virginia Outstanding Teaching Award in 1998. In 2003, he was one of ten recipients of the State Council of Higher Education for Virginia's Outstanding Faculty Award. He has served on numerous editorial boards and was the inaugural editor of *Exceptionality*. He is a past president of the Division for Learning Disabilities of the Council for Exceptional Children (CEC), and in 2000 he received the CEC Career Research Award. He has contributed over 100 journal articles and co-authored or co-edited 17 books. In addition to *Exceptional Learners*, his most recent Allyn & Bacon books are Hallahan, Lloyd, Kauffman, Weiss, & Martinez (2005), *Learning Disabilities: Foundations, Characteristics, and Effective Teaching* (3rd ed.) and Kauffman, J. M., & Hallahan, D. P. (2005), *Special Education: What It Is and Why We Need It*.

James M. Kauffman is Professor Emeritus of Education at the University of Virginia, where he held both the William Clay Parrish chair (1992–1994) and the Charles S. Robb chair (1999 until retirement in 2003) in education. In 2007, his former students edited a book in his honor, Crockett, J. B., Gerber, M. M., & Landrum, T. J. (Eds.), *Achieving the Radical Reform of Special Education: Essays in Honor of James M. Kauffman*. Among his other honors and awards are the 2006 Award for Effective Presentation of Behavior Analysis in the Mass Media from the Society for Applied Behavior Analysis, the 2002 Outstanding Leadership Award from the Council for Children with Behavioral Disorders, the 1997 Outstanding Faculty Award from the Curry School of Education Foundation, and the 1994 Research Award from the Council for Exceptional Children. He is a past president of the Council for Children with Behavioral Disorders (CCBD) and a former teacher in both general elementary and special education for students with emotional or behavioral disorders. He is author or co-author of more than 100 journal publications in special education and author or co-author or co-editor of numerous books, including the following: Kauffman, J. M., & Landrum, T. J., *Characteristics of Emotional and Behavioral Disorders of Children and Youth* (9th ed.); Kauffman, J. M. & Landrum, T. J., *Children and Youth with Emotional and Behavioral Disorders: A History of Their Education*; and Stichter, J. P., Conroy, M. A., & Kauffman, J. M., *An Introduction to Students with High-Incidence Disabilities*.

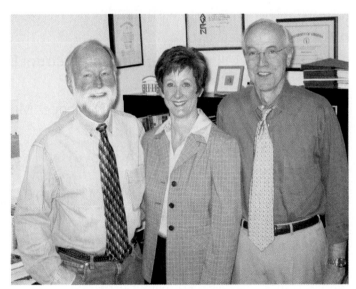

Paige C. Pullen is an associate professor of special education at the University of Virginia. Dr. Pullen teaches courses in reading methods for students with reading disabilities and reading diagnosis and remediation. She has served as an investigator on several large-scale projects funded by the NICHD and OSEP. Her primary area of interest and research is early literacy development and the prevention of reading disabilities. Paige has also worked extensively with schools and serves as a consultant for the Eastern Regional Reading First Technical Assistance Center (ERRFTAC). She is the co-author of *Phonological Awareness Assessment and Instruction*, with Dr. Holly Lane, and *Students with Learning Disabilities*, with Dr. Cecil Mercer.

Jim   *Paige*   *Dan*

Brief Contents

Chapter 1   Exceptionality and Special Education   2

Chapter 2   Integration, Inclusion, and Support of Positive Outcomes   42

Chapter 3   Multicultural and Bilingual Aspects of Special Education   84

Chapter 4   Parents and Families   114

Chapter 5   Learners with Intellectual and Developmental Disabilities   142

Chapter 6   Learners with Learning Disabilities   182

Chapter 7   Learners with Attention Deficit Hyperactivity Disorder   222

Chapter 8   Learners with Emotional or Behavioral Disorders   260

Chapter 9   Learners with Communication Disorders   300

Chapter 10   Learners Who Are Deaf or Hard of Hearing   336

Chapter 11   Learners with Blindness or Low Vision   376

Chapter 12   Learners with Autism Spectrum Disorders   420

Chapter 13   Learners with Low-Incidence, Multiple, and Severe Disabilities   456

Chapter 14   Learners with Physical Disabilities and Other Health Impairments   492

Chapter 15   Learners with Special Gifts and Talents   528

Contents

Preface   xvii

Chapter 1   Exceptionality and Special Education   2

Getting Oriented to Exceptionality and Special Education   5
- Reasons for Optimism   5
- The Importance of Abilities   6
- "Disability" Versus "Handicap"   6
- Disability Versus Inability   7

Educational Definition of Exceptional Learners   8

Prevalence of Exceptional Learners   11
- High-Incidence and Low-Incidence Categories   11

Definition of Special Education   12

Providing Special Education   13

Teachers' Roles   17
- Relationship Between General and Special Education   18
- Special Education and Students at Risk   18

- The Inclusion Controversy   18
- Expectations for All Educators   19
- Expectations for Special Educators   22

History and Origins of Special Education   24
- People and Ideas   25
- Council for Exceptional Children (CEC) and Development of the Profession   27
- Parents and Other Professional Organizations   27

Legislation and Litigation   28
- IDEA, ADA, and NCLB   28
- *Rowley* and Other Court Cases   30

The Intent of Special Education Law: Individualized Education for Students with Disabilities   32

The Progress of Special Education   37

Summary   38

Chapter 2   Integration, Inclusion, and Support of Positive Outcomes   42

Integration of People with Disabilities into the Larger Society   46
- Normalization   47
- Deinstitutionalization   49
- Self-Determination   50
- Universal Design and Universal Design for Learning   51
- Use of New Technologies   52

Inclusion in Schools   53
- Full Inclusion   53
- Differentiated Instruction   60

- Prereferral Teams and Response to Intervention   61
- Other Models of Collaboration with General Education   63

Assessments of Progress   65
- Progress Monitoring   66
- Outcome Measures   66
- Testing Accommodations   66

Special Education in the Context of NCLB   67
- Can We Solve the Dilemma of Standards and Disability?   68

Early Intervention   69
- Consensus on Early Intervention, or How to Do It Best   70
- Are We Ready to Face the Demands of Prevention?   72

Transitions to Adulthood and Employment   73
- Making Transition Fit Level of Need   76
- What Should Be Taught When?   77

Zero Tolerance, PBS, PBIS, and Other Issues of Discipline   77
- Supports for Desired Behavior   78
- How Functional Are Supports?   79

Concluding Thoughts Regarding Trends and Issues   80

Summary   81

Chapter 3   Multicultural and Bilingual Aspects of Special Education   84

America and Multiculturalism   88

Education and Cultural Diversity   91

Multicultural and Bilingual Special Education   94

Identification and Classification of Disabilities   97
- Response to Intervention   97
- Issues in the Identification of Special Gifts and Talents   98

Assessment of Progress   98
- Progress Monitoring   98
- Outcome Measures   99
- Testing Accommodations   100

Instruction in Multicultural and Bilingual Special Education   100
- Teaching Tolerance and Appreciation   102
- Working with Families   103
- Improving Instruction for Language-Minority Students   103
- Adopting Effective Teaching Practices   104
- Identifying and Implementing Effective Reading Instruction   105
- Socialization   108

Summary   111

Chapter 4   Parents and Families   114

Professionals' Changing Views of Parents and Families   118

The Effects of a Child with a Disability on the Family   119
- Parental Reactions   120
- Parental Adjustment   122
- Sibling Reactions   124
- Siblings' Adjustment   125

Family Involvement in Treatment and Education   125
- Family Systems Theory   127
- Social Support for Families   132
- Positive Behavioral Intervention and Support for Challenging Behaviors   132
- Communication Between Parents and Professionals   133
- Parent Advocacy   137

In Conclusion   138

Summary   139

Chapter 5   Learners with Intellectual and Developmental Disabilities   142

What's in a Name? *Mental Retardation* **Versus** *Intellectual and Developmental Disabilities*   **145**

Definition   146
- The AAIDD Definition   147
- Classification of Intellectual Disabilities   149

Prevalence   149

Causes   150
- Prenatal Causes   151
- Perinatal Causes   154
- Postnatal Causes   155

Identification   156
- Intelligence Tests   156
- Adaptive Behavior   157

Psychological and Behavioral Characteristics   157
- Linking Genetic Syndromes to Particular Behavioral Phenotypes   158

Educational Considerations   161
- Systematic Instruction   162
- Instruction in Real-Life Settings with Real Materials   163
- Functional Behavioral Assessment and Positive Behavioral Intervention and Support   163
- Service Delivery Models   164

Assessment of Progress   165
- Progress Monitoring   165
- Outcome Measures   167
- Testing Accommodations and Alternate Assessment   167

Early Intervention   168
- Early Childhood Programs Designed for Prevention   168
- Early Childhood Programs Designed to Further Development   169

Transition to Adulthood   170
- Self-Determination   171
- Community Adjustment   173
- Employment   174
- Prospects for the Future   176

Summary   178

Chapter 6   Learners with Learning Disabilities   182

Definition   185
- The Federal Definition   187
- The National Joint Committee on Learning Disabilities Definition   187

Identification   189
- Achievement-Ability Discrepancy   189
- Response to Intervention or Response to Treatment   189

Prevalence   191
- Increase in Prevalence   192
- Gender Differences   192

Causes   193
- Genetic Factors   194
- Teratogenic Factors   194
- Medical Factors   195

Psychological and Behavioral Characteristics   195
- Interindividual Variation   195
- Intraindividual Variation   195
- Academic Achievement Problems   195
- Perceptual, Perceptual-Motor, and General Coordination Problems   199
- Disorders of Attention and Hyperactivity   199

- Memory and Metacognitive Problems   200
- Social-Emotional Problems   201
- Motivational Problems   202
- The Child with Learning Disabilities as an Inactive Learner with Strategy Deficits   202

Educational Considerations   202
- Cognitive Training   203
- Content Enhancement   205
- Direct Instruction   205
- Peer Tutoring   206
- Service Delivery Models   207

Assessment of Progress   209
- Progress Monitoring   209
- Outcome Measures   212
- Testing Accommodations   213

Early Intervention   214

Transition to Adulthood   215
- Factors Related to Successful Transition   216
- Secondary Programming   217
- Postsecondary Programming   217

Summary   219

Chapter 7   Learners with Attention Deficit Hyperactivity Disorder   222

Brief History   225
- Still's Children with "Defective Moral Control"   225
- Goldstein's Brain-Injured Soldiers of World War I   226
- The Strauss Syndrome   227
- Cruickshank's Work   227
- Minimal Brain Injury and Hyperactive Child Syndrome   227

Definition   228

Prevalence   228

Identification   231

Causes   232
- Areas of the Brain Affected: Prefrontal Lobes, Basal Ganglia, Cerebellum, and Corpus Callosum   232
- Neurotransmitters Involved: Dopamine and Norepinephrine   234
- Hereditary Factors   234
- Toxins and Medical Factors   235

Psychological and Behavioral Characteristics   235
- Barkley's Model of ADHD   235
- Adaptive Behavior   237
- Problems Socializing with Peers   238
- Coexisting Conditions   240

Educational Considerations   241
- Classroom Structure and Teacher Direction   241
- Functional Behavioral Assessment and Contingency-Based Self-Management   242
- Service Delivery Models   247

Medication Considerations   247
- Opposition to Ritalin   249
- The Research Evidence   250
- Cautions Regarding Medication   250
- Medication Versus Behavior Management   251

Assessment of Progress   251
- Progress Monitoring   251
- Outcome Measures   253
- Testing Accommodations   253

Early Intervention   253

Transition to Adulthood   254
- Diagnosis in Adulthood   254
- Adult Outcomes   255
- Importance of Coaching   257

Summary   257

Chapter 8   Learners with Emotional or Behavioral Disorders   260

Terminology 264

Definition 265
- Definitional Problems 265
- Current Definitions 266

Classification 268

Prevalence 269

Causes 270
- Biological Factors 271
- Family Factors 272
- School Factors 272
- Cultural Factors 274

Identification 275

Psychological and Behavioral Characteristics 277
- Intelligence and Achievement 277
- Social and Emotional Characteristics 278

Educational Considerations 285
- Balancing Behavioral Control with Academic and Social Learning 285
- Importance of Integrated Services 286
- Strategies That Work 286
- Service Delivery 287
- Instructional Considerations 288
- Disciplinary Considerations 290

Assessment of Progress 291
- Progress Monitoring and Outcome Measures 291
- Testing Accommodations 293

Early Intervention 294

Transition to Adulthood 296

Summary 297

Chapter 9   Learners with Communication Disorders   300

Definitions 303

Prevalence 305

Communication Variations 306

Language Disorders 307
- Classification of Language Disorders 310

Speech Disorders 314
- Phonological Disorders 314
- Articulation Disorders 315
- Voice Disorders 316
- Fluency Disorders 317
- Motor-Speech Disorders 318

Educational Considerations 319
- Facilitating the Social Use of Language 320
- Question-Asking Strategies 320

- Teaching Literacy: Reading and Written Expression 323

Assessment of Progress 324
- Progress Monitoring 325
- Outcome Measures 325
- Accommodations 325

Early Intervention 326
- Early Development and Early Intervention 326
- Early Intervention in Delayed Language Development 327
- Involvement of Families 328

Transition to Adulthood 330

Summary 333

Chapter 10 Learners Who Are Deaf or Hard of Hearing 336

Definition and Classification 339

Prevalence 341

Anatomy and Physiology of the Ear 342
- The Outer Ear 342
- The Middle Ear 343
- The Inner Ear 343

Identification of Hearing Impairment 344
- Screening Tests 344
- Pure-Tone Audiometry 344
- Speech Audiometry 345
- Tests for Young and Hard-to-Test Children 345

Causes 346
- Conductive, Sensorineural, and Mixed Hearing Impairment 346
- Hearing Impairment and the Outer Ear 346
- Hearing Impairment and the Middle Ear 346
- Hearing Impairment and the Inner Ear 346

Psychological and Behavioral Characteristics 347
- Spoken Language and Speech Development 347
- Sign Language 348

- Intellectual Ability 349
- Academic Achievement 350
- Social Adjustment 351

Educational Considerations 355
- Oral Approaches: The Auditory-Verbal Approach and the Auditory-Oral Approach 356
- Total Communication 358
- The Bicultural-Bilingual Approach 360
- Technological Advances 360
- Service Delivery Models 363

Assessment of Progress 364
- Progress Monitoring 364
- Outcome Measures 366
- Testing Accommodations 368

Early Intervention 368

Transition to Adulthood 369
- Postsecondary Education 370
- Family Issues 371

Summary 372

Chapter 11 Learners with Blindness or Low Vision 376

Definition and Classification 380
- Legal Definition 380
- Educational Definition 381

Prevalence 382

Anatomy and Physiology of the Eye 383

Identification of Visual Impairment 384

Causes 384
- Causes Affecting Children and Adults 384
- Causes Primarily Affecting Children 387

Psychological and Behavioral Characteristics 388
- Language Development 388

- Intellectual Ability 388
- Orientation and Mobility 389
- Academic Achievement 391
- Social Adjustment 391

Educational Considerations 394
- Braille 395
- Use of Remaining Sight 400
- Listening Skills 401
- Orientation and Mobility (O & M) Training 401
- Technological Aids 404

Service Delivery Models 408

Assessment of Progress   410
- Progress Monitoring   410
- Outcome Measures   411
- Testing Accommodations   411

Early Intervention   412

Transition to Adulthood   412
- Independent Living   412
- Employment   415

Summary   416

Chapter 12   Learners with Autism Spectrum Disorders   420

Historical Context: Kanner's and Asperger's Papers   423
- Kanner's Paper   423
- Asperger's Paper   424

Definition of Autism Spectrum Disorders   424
- Autism Defined   425

Asperger Syndrome Defined   425

Prevalence   425

Causes   426
- Early Causal Theories   427
- Today's Causal Theories   428

Identification   431

Psychological and Behavioral Characteristics   433
- Autism   433
- Asperger Syndrome   435
- Attempts to Construct a Unifying Theory of Autism Spectrum Disorders   437

Educational Considerations   439
- Educational Programming Principles for Students with Autism Spectrum Disorders   439
- Educational Strategies for Teaching Social Skills to Students with Asperger Syndrome   440
- Service Delivery Models   441

Assessment of Progress   444
- Progress Monitoring   445
- Outcome Measures   449
- Testing Accommodations and Alternate Assessments   449

Early Intervention   449

Transition to Adulthood   450
- Transition Programming for People with Autism   450
- Transition Programming for People with Asperger Syndrome   450

Summary   453

Chapter 13   Learners with Low-Incidence, Multiple, and Severe Disabilities   456

Definition and Prevalence   459

Traumatic Brain Injury   460
- Definition and Characteristics   460
- Prevalence   462
- Causes   463
- Educational Considerations   463

Deaf-Blindness   467
- Definition   467
- Prevalence   468
- Causes   468
- Psychological and Behavioral Characteristics   471
- Educational Considerations   472

Considerations for Many Students with Low-Incidence, Multiple, and Severe Disabilities 476
- Augmentative or Alternative Communication 476
- Behavior Problems 482

- Early Intervention 484
- Transition to Adulthood 487

Summary 489

Chapter 14 Learners with Physical Disabilities and Other Health Impairments 492

Definition and Classification 495

Prevalence and Need 497

Neuromotor Impairments 497
- Cerebral Palsy 498
- Seizure Disorder (Epilepsy) 500
- Spina Bifida and Other Spinal Cord Injuries 502

Orthopedic and Musculoskeletal Disorders 503

Other Conditions Affecting Health or Physical Ability 504

Prevention of Physical Disabilities 507

Psychological and Behavioral Characteristics 508
- Academic Achievement 508
- Personality Characteristics 509

Prosthetics, Orthotics, and Adaptive Devices for Daily Living 511

Educational Considerations 513
- Individualized Planning 514
- Educational Placement 514
- Educational Goals and Curricula 516
- Links with Other Disciplines 519

Early Intervention 520

Transition 522
- Choosing a Career 523
- Sociosexuality 524

Summary 525

Chapter 15 Learners with Special Gifts and Talents 528

Definition 531

Prevalence 536

Origins of Giftedness 536

Identification of Giftedness 538

Psychological and Behavioral Characteristics 539

Cultural Values Regarding Students with Special Gifts and Talents and Their Education 541

Neglected Groups of Students with Special Gifts and Talents 543
- Underachievers with Special Gifts and Talents 543
- Students Low in Socioeconomic Status and Those Living in Remote Areas 544

- Students with Special Gifts from Cultural- and Ethnic-Minority Groups 544
- Students with Disabilities and Special Gifts and Talents 545
- Females with Special Gifts and Talents 547

Educational Considerations 549
- Acceleration 552
- Enrichment 554
- Early Intervention 554
- Transition to Adulthood 556

Summary 559

**Appendix: CEC Content Standards
and INTASC Core Principles**   562

Glossary   565

References   577

Author Index   613

Subject Index   620

Special Features

Casebook Reflections

- Least Restrictive for Whom?   14, 134, 339, 363
- Should I Take Juanita Pope?   11, 17, 163, 189
- The Red Belt   56, 275
- What Do We Do with Jim?   78, 87, 291
- The Reluctant Collaborator   134, 407, 408
- Who Will Help Patrick?   104, 155, 312, 460, 483, 486
- More Than LD   214, 217, 228, 241, 249, 256

- Never Give Up   240, 543
- How Did We Miss Jack All These Years?   284
- Albert Says What?   319, 325, 326, 329, 332
- Getting to Know Chase   433, 440, 443, 484, 487
- Praying for a Miracle   497, 511, 517, 519, 523
- Filling Mr. K's Shoes—Not!   539, 547

FOCUS ON Concepts

- Teachers' Roles: What Should I Do Before I Make a Referral?   21
- Major Provisions of IDEA   29
- GLSEN in Tough Times: Training Educators About LGBT Issues in a Challenging Political, Economic, and Educational Climate   103
- A Common Sense of Urgency   108
- Facilitating Involvement of Culturally and/or Linguistically Diverse Families   129
- Homework: Tips for Teachers and Administrators   135
- The Human Genome Project: Ethical Issues Pertaining to Intellectual Disabilities   150
- Down Syndrome and Alzheimer's Disease   152
- The Nature—Nurture Controversy   156
- Gullibility as the Hallmark of Mild Intellectual Disability   159
- AAIDD Self-Determination Policy Statement   173
- Dyslexia: Same Brains, Different Languages   198
- How Many Students with ADHD Are Served in Special Education?   230
- Controversial Causal Theories of ADHD   233
- Definitions of the American Speech-Language-Hearing Association   305

- Types of Language Disorders   310
- Identifying Possible Language Problems Related to Transition   332
- Deafness: Disability or Cultural Difference?   342
- The Birth and Evolution of Nicaraguan Sign Language   350
- Tips for Working with Sign Language Interpreters   371
- A Skills Definition of Blindness   382
- Signs of Possible Eye Trouble in Children   385
- Have Advances in Technology Contributed to Illiteracy in Braille?   398
- Touch the Universe   403
- Is There a Link Between Vaccinations and Autism?   428
- Theory of Mind: The Sally and Anne Experiment   438
- Judging the Scientific Basis of Interventions for Autism Spectrum Disorders   442
- The Genetics of Usher Syndrome and Its Geographic Distribution   470
- Simplified Sign Language   477
- First Aid for Epileptic Seizures   502
- One Failure and One Success in Prevention   508
- Prosthetics   513

MAKING IT WORK

Collaboration and Co-Teaching of Students with Disabilities   20

Collaboration and Co-Teaching with Teachers of Students with Intellectual and Developmental Disabilities   177

Collaboration and Co-Teaching for Students with Learning Disabilities   210

Collaboration and Co-Teaching for Students with ADHD   248

Collaboration and Co-Teaching of Students with Emotional or Behavioral Disorders   289

Collaboration and Co-Teaching of Students with Communication Disorders   323

Collaboration and Co-Teaching with Students Who Are Deaf or Hard of Hearing   365

Collaboration and Co-Teaching with Teachers of Students with Blindness or Low Vision   409

Collaboration and Co-Teaching with Teachers of Students with Autism Spectrum Disorder   448

Collaboration and Co-Teaching of Students with Low-Incidence, Multiple, and Severe Disabilities   464

Collaboration and Co-Teaching of Students with Physical Disabilities and Other Health Impairments   515

Collaboration and Co-Teaching of Students with Special Gifts and Talents   553

Personal PERSPECTIVES

- Blair Smith: A Teen with Physical Disabilities Focuses on Her Abilities   9
- An IEP for Alice: What Can Happen When Special Education Works   10
- Kathy Koons: A 19-Year-Old Woman Strives for a Successful Transition to Independence   48
- Parents' Thoughts on Inclusion of Their Children with Severe Disabilities   57
- Desegregation and Degeneration   90
- In Living Black and White   91
- Lessons from My Brother   126
- Advocacy in Action: You Can Advocate for Your Child   138
- Williams Syndrome: An Inspiration for Some Pixie Legends?   160
- Self-Determination: Too Much of a Good Thing?   174
- Learning Disabilities and the Pain of Rejection   201
- Ms. Lopez Conducts an Error Analysis   212
- An Adult with ADHD: Ann's Story   255
- Family Factors   273
- Suggestions for Talking with Students   324
- Gallaudet's Deaf President Now and Unity for Gallaudet Movements   353
- Social Interaction with People Who Are Blind: Points of Etiquette   381
- Stephen Kuusisto's Sensory World   390
- Captain Charles Barbier de la Serre and Louis Braille   396
- Mike May: An Adventure into the World of Sight   406
- Children's Book Author Kathy Hoopmann Addresses Asperger Syndrome   436
- Youth Uses Web to Help Others on "Wrong Planet"   452
- TBI: Often a Hidden Disability   462
- Laura Bridgman and Her Teacher, Samuel Gridley Howe   473
- Life with Cerebral Palsy   480
- Student with Cerebral Palsy Challenges Perspectives   496
- The Importance of Family and School in Coping with Asthma   505
- Weighing the Issue of Placement: One Student's Perspective   517
- Geoff Gallante: A Child Prodigy on Trumpet   542
- Rhodes Scholar Overcomes Disabilities   548
- Child Prodigy Now U.Va. Grad Student   558

Responsive Instruction

Special Education Means Special Instruction   25

Meeting the Needs of English Language Learners
with Special Needs

- Concept Mapping to Improve Achievement   106

Meeting the Needs of Students
with Intellectual Disabilities

- Classwide Peer-Tutoring   166
- Computer-Based Video to Teach Grocery Shopping   175

Meeting the Needs of Students
with Learning Disabilities

- Mnemonics   206
- Direct Instruction   208
- Testing Accommodations   214

Meeting the Needs of Students with Attention Deficit
Hyperactivity Disorder

- Task Switching: Preparing Students with ADHD
  for Change   236
- Planning for Students with ADHD in the General
  Education Classroom   244
- The Benefits of Self-Monitoring and Group
  Contingency   246

Meeting the Needs of Students with Emotional
or Behavioral Disorders

- Strategies for Students with Oppositional Defiant
  Disorder   282
- Approaches to Reducing Bullying in Schools   283
- Functional Behavior Assessments   292

Meeting the Needs of Students
with Communication Disorders

- Working with the Speech-Language Pathologist   322
- Collaboration in an Inner-City Classroom   331

Meeting the Needs of Students Who Are
Deaf or Hard of Hearing

- Assistive Technology   361
- Teaching Phonics   366

Meeting the Needs of Students
with Visual Impairments

- Braille Literacy Instruction   399

Meeting the Needs of Students with Blindness
or Low Vision

- Strategies for Working with Young Children   413

Meeting the Needs of Students with Autism
Spectrum Disorders

- Picture Exchange Communication System (PECS)   446
- Social Stories   447

Meeting the Needs of Students with Low-Incidence,
Multiple, and Severe Disabilities

- The Importance of Establishing Structured Routines   474
- Positive Behavioral Support   485

Meeting the Needs of Students with Physical
Disabilities and Other Health Impairments

- Adapted Physical Education   516
- Integrating Physical and Occupational Therapy in General
  Education Settings   518

Meeting the Needs of Students with Special
Gifts and Talents

- Strategies for the Indentification and Instruction of Twice
  Exceptional Students   546
- Acceleration: A Nation Deceived Report   556

Success Stories

Intensive, relentless, and specific special education makes the difference for struggling learners   13

Early intervention services and community resources prepare Nolan for first grade   170

Hard work at home and school helps Randy read on grade level   196

Developing his self-advocacy skills to get needed accommodations will be key to Josh's success in college   238

Chrissy succeeds in middle school through social skills instruction, positive behavioral supports, and academic interventions   280

Through coordination of medical and educational services, Ryan moves from rehabilitation to school reentry successfully   312

Bailea, a kindergartener with a cochlear implant, benefits from early intervention and co-teaching   356

Patrick prepares for transition from high school through functional academics and vocational education   392

Intensive and early applied behavior analysis prepare Wesley for his general education kindergarten class   444

David gains independence and academic achievement through assistive technology and professional collaboration   478

Danielle prospers due to intensive early intervention and intra-professional and parental communication   520

Noshua excels in a residential acceleration program   550

Preface

Exceptional Learners: An Introduction to Special Education, Eleventh Edition, is a general introduction to the characteristics of exceptional learners and their education. (Exceptional is the term that traditionally has been used to refer to people with disabilities as well as to those who are gifted.) This book emphasizes classroom practices as well as the psychological, sociological, and medical aspects of disabilities and giftedness.

We've written this text with two primary audiences in mind: those individuals who are preparing to be special educators and those who are preparing to be general educators. Given the federal legislative mandates for including students with disabilities in general education classrooms whenever possible, general educators must be prepared to understand this special student population and be ready to work with special educators to provide appropriate educational programming for these students. This book also is appropriate for professionals in other fields who work with exceptional learners (e.g., speech-language pathologists, audiologists, physical therapists, occupational therapists, adapted physical educators, counselors, and school psychologists).

We believe that we've written a text that reaches the heart as well as the mind. It is our conviction that professionals working with exceptional learners need to develop not only a solid base of knowledge, but also a healthy attitude toward their work and the people whom they serve. Professionals must constantly challenge themselves to acquire a solid understanding of current theory, research, and practice in special education and to develop an ever more sensitive understanding of exceptional learners and their families.

What Is New to This Edition?

Like all of our previous revisions, we've approached this current revision with an eye toward providing the reader with the latest, cutting-edge information on research and best practices in special education. Our deletion of over 328 references from the previous edition, coupled with the addition of over 600 new references speaks to our commitment to bringing the freshest perspectives to bear on the ever increasing complexity of educating students with disabilities in today's schools.

Of particular importance in the content revisions made to this edition is **greatly expanded coverage of the assessment of progress of students with disabilities**. In 10 of the chapters, we have included a major section on assessement of progress, including (1) progress monitoring, (2) outcome measures, and (3) testing accommodations. We've renamed and reorganized Chapter 2 to highlight the federal mandates' (e.g., NCLB's, IDEA's) current focus on **student outcomes**. Also in accordance with changes to federal law, we provide **expanded and updated information on response-to-intervention (RTI)** in Chapter 2 as well as Chapter 6.

Recurring Features

Casebook Reflections

The outstanding *Cases for Reflection and Analysis* booklet accompanies every new copy of this text, and illustrates the specific ways in which special education theories, concepts, and practices play out in the lives and education of real students, their teachers, and their families. At several points in each of the main chapters, connections (contributed

> **Casebook Reflections**
>
> REFER TO THE CASE *Should I Take Juanita Pope?* in your booklet. Consider the factors that might contribute to Juanita's failure in school. In what ways does Juanita fit the description of a child who is at risk? ●

by Dr. E. Stephen Byrd, Elon University) are made to various cases in the booklet.

Success Stories: Special Educators at Work

Special educators work in a variety of settings, ranging from general education classrooms to residential institutions. Although their main function involves teaching, these professionals also engage in a variety of activities, such as counseling, collaborating, and consulting. To illustrate this variety, each of the eleven categorical chapters (Chapters 5–15) includes an example of a special educator at work. Written by Dr. Jean B. Crockett of the University of Florida, an experienced special education administrator and teacher educator, each story focuses on a special educator's work with an individual student and shows readers the wide range of challenges faced by special educators, the dynamic nature of their positions, and the competent, hopeful practice of special education. This feature emphasizes the importance of education for students with special needs that is intensive, relentless, and specific, and includes questions for students that relate to CEC Standards.

Focus on Concepts

These features stimulate critical thinking about current research and special topics that are of interest to all educators.

Personal Perspectives

These features present the human side of having a disability, showing how text topics affect the personal lives of students, teachers, parents, and others.

Responsive Instruction: Meeting the Needs of Students

It's our firm belief that most students with disabilities require intensive instruction in order to maximize their potential. Located throughout the text are boxed features, authored by Dr. Kristin Sayeski of the University of Nevada, Las Vegas, that feature a variety of sound, research-based strategies (e.g., mnemonics, self-monitoring and group contingency, class-wide peer tutoring, computer-based video instruction, functional behavioral assessment, testing accommodations) for teaching students with disabilities. Although these strategies can't possibly take the place of a full-blown course and text in teaching methods, we think they offer practical suggestions for meeting the needs of exceptional learners through intensive instruction. In keeping with this era of accountability, these boxes stress teaching practices that have a sound research base.

FOCUS ON Concepts

A Common Sense of Urgency

We need to exercise caution with well-intended but general concepts, for much very poor instruction has occurred as a result of [...] that good [...] for their [...] would dis [...] ends to e [...] cultural e [...] the other [...] elementa [...] ingful inst [...] incapacit [...] according [...] sense of [...] ing each [...] time is n [...] gies that [...]

remedial actions are taken when needed, and there is the clear expectation that all children can and will meet mastery.

Personal PERSPECTIVES

Gallaudet's Deaf President Now and Unity for Gallaudet Movements

Deaf President Now Movement

A prominent and historic example of Deaf activism occurred in the 1980s at Gallaudet University, a liberal arts college for the deaf and hard of hearing, when students and faculty protested the board of trustees' selection of a hearing president. Since its founding in 1864, Gallaudet had never had a deaf president. But when on March 6, 1988 the trustees announced the appointment of yet another hearing president, faculty and students took to the streets and halls in protest. Having successfully shut down the university, organizers of the Deaf President Now Movement issued four demands:

1. that a deaf president be named immediately;
2. that the chair of the board resign;
3. that the board, which consisted of seventeen hearing and four deaf members, be reconfigured to include a majority of deaf members; and
4. that there be no reprisals.

After eight days of protest, the board acceded to all four demands, the most significant of which was the naming of a long-time faculty member who was deaf: I. King Jordan as president of the university.

Unity for Gallaudet Movement

Upon Jordan's retirement, the board announced on May 1, 2006, the appointment of the vice president of the university, Jane K. Fernandes, to be Jordan's successor. Students and faculty once again protested, holding rallies and blocking entrances to the school. The protests continued during the Fall semester, with over a hundred students being arrested for blocking entrances.

Given that Fernandes is also deaf, accounts vary as to why there was such a negative reaction (Tapper & Sandell, 2006; Takrui, 2006). Some cited what they considered a flawed, noninclusive selection process, but many pointed to concerns that Fernandes was not "deaf enough." They objected to her having stated that she wanted to be more inclusive by admitting more students with cochlear implants as well as those who had not grown up learning sign language. (Fernandes herself reportedly grew up using speech and speechreading and didn't learn sign language until she was in her 20s.)

In October 2006, Fernandes was removed as president by the board. In December, 2006, the board named Robert Davila as interim president for two years. Deaf since the age of eight, Davila has previously served in a number of high-level government and university positions.

Responsive Instruction

Special Education Means Special Instruction

[It special education] is empirically supported practice, drawn from research. To provide special education means to set priorities and select carefully what needs to be taught. It means teaching something special and teaching it in a special way. (Zigmond, 1997, pp. 384–385)

Classwide peer tutoring, community-based instruction, mnemonics, direct instruction, self-monitoring, behavioral assessment, instructional adaptations, and adapted physical education—all are research-based practices that are used in today's classrooms. Research in special education has come a long way in the past twenty years (Gersten, Schiller, & Vaughn, 2000). There is now a more substantial research base of effective practices for use with students with disabilities. As in all endeavors, the current research base has limitations, and knowledge is added to it daily. That, combined with many other factors, makes it difficult for teachers to stay current in their knowledge of appropriate instructional practices (Schiller & Malouf, 2000).

Because we believe that effective, empirically supported practice is essential for teachers who work with students with disabilities, we have included a special feature in each disability chapter entitled Responsive Instruction. This feature describes a research-based practice in relative detail, what implications it has for the classroom, and where a teacher can get more information. The practices described within the Responsive Instruction boxes coincide with the CEC Standards for new special educators and provide valuable information for general educators as well. The purpose of the Responsive Instruction boxes is to assist students in connecting the theoretical information provided in the text with current, best-practices in the classroom. For students who are in the early stages of their special education preparation, the feature provides an example of a practical application; for students who are currently teaching or engaged in fieldwork, the feature can direct them to strategies or curricula for classroom use or further exploration.

Making it Work: Collaboration and Co-Teaching

Each of the categorical chapters (Chapter 5–15) includes a feature, authored by Dr. Margaret Weiss of Virginia Tech University, devoted to co-teaching and collaboration among special and general education teachers, families, and other professionals. Because we believe that it's important for all teachers to understand what expertise special educators can contribute to collaborative, general education classrooms, the first section of each box includes information about knowledge and skills special educators should possess as they enter the field, as identified by the Council for Exceptional Children (CEC) in its Performance-Based Professional Standards (2001). The second section contains examples of research-based instructional practices that teachers can use when collaborating or descriptions of successful collaborations in real classrooms. Each box contains specifics about how to get more information about the strategy or classroom described.

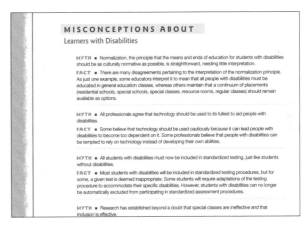

Chapter Preview and Review Features

- **Misconceptions about Exceptional Learners: Myths and Facts Boxes**. We start each chapter with a feature that juxtaposes several myths and facts about the subject of the chapter. This popular feature, familiar to longtime users of previous editions, serves as an excellent advance organizer for the material to be covered.

- **Chapter-Opening Quotes.** Going back to our first edition is the practice of opening each chapter with an excerpt from literature or song. Students continue to tell us that they find these quotes to be effective at grabbing their attention and leading them into some of the issues contained in the text.

- **Questions to Guide Your Reading of This Chapter.** This feature introduces each chapter by highlighting in question form the major topics to be covered.

- **Chapter Summary**. The summary uses the chapter opening questions to structure a streamlined, efficient reference for chapter review.

CEC Standards and INTASC Principles

The Council for Exceptional Children (CEC) Knowledge and Skills Standards and the Interstate New Teacher Assessment and Support Consortium (INTASC) Core Principles provide a framework for all general and special educators. Dr. Elizabeth Martinez, formerly of the Council for Exceptional Children, and currently a supervisor of special education for Loudoun County Public Schools in Virginia, has selected the appropriate standards and principles and has noted their application to content in each chapter. The specific relevance of these standards and principles is highlighted in every chapter of this text via the following features, which together serve as a great reference for students to keep as future teachers and use in preparation for licensure exams such as PRAXIS II.

- *Standards and Principles in This Chapter* Each chapter concludes with a review of CEC Standards (the responsibilities of special educators) and INTASC Principles (the responsibilities of all educators) that are most relevant to the preceding chapter.

Applying the STANDARDS and PRINCIPLES

■ DESCRIBE at least two ways to enhance the integration of students with disabilities into general education classrooms. (CEC Content Standard #1 & INTASC Principle #1)

■ DESCRIBE the pros and cons of child-directed and adult-directed programs for young children with disabilities. (CEC Content Standard #4 & INTASC Principle #4)

■ DESCRIBE ways in which teachers can collaborate with each other, with other professionals, and with families to ensure that students with disabilities are valued members of society. (CEC Content Standard #10 & INTASC Principle #10)

- *Applying the Standards and Principles* This feature asks readers to apply their understanding of chapter material with questions and activities meant to show the practical relevance of the standards.

- *Standards Appendix* This appendix at the end of the book is an easy reference to the CEC Core Content Standards and INTASC Core Principals.

- *Understanding the Standards and Principles* These questions, located in the margins, highlight key connections between text discussions and standards and principles.

UNDERSTANDING THE STANDARDS AND PRINCIPLES Why are members of minority groups more apt to be identified as disabled? (CEC Knowledge and Skill Standard CC1K5)

Council for Exceptional Children

Margin Notes

- **Margin Glossary:** Key Terms are boldfaced in the text when they're first introduced, and defined briefly in the adjacent margin, for reinforcement of concepts while reading, and for convenient reference during studying and review.

- **Internet Resources**: Websites that provide useful and interesting information relevant to text discussions are identified.

INTERNET RESOURCES

Disability rights issues are discussed in an online magazine called Ragged Edge, which can be found at www.ragged-edge-mag.com

- **MyEducationLab**: Brief notes prompt readers to access self-tests, assignments, videos, and many other resources available online at the MyEducationLab Website created specifically for this text.

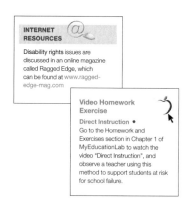

Video Homework Exercise

Direct Instruction ●
Go to the Homework and Exercises section in Chapter 1 of MyEducationLab to watch the video "Direct Instruction", and observe a teacher using this method to support students at risk for school failure.

Supplements for Hallahan, Kauffman, Pullen
Exceptional Learners: An Introduction to Special Education, Eleventh Edition

The following supplements provide an outstanding array of resources that facilitate learning about students with disabilities and their families. For more information, ask your local Pearson Higher Education sales representative, or contact the Allyn & Bacon Merrill Faculty Field Support Department at 1-800-526-0485. For technology products, please contact technical support directly at 1-800-677-6337 or http://247.pearsoned .com. To view our online product catalogs go to www.pearsonhighered.com.

Resources for Instructors

INSTRUCTOR'S RESOURCE MANUAL. The Instructor's Resource Manual includes a wealth of interesting ideas and activities designed to help instructors teach the course. Each chapter includes a chapter-at-a-glance grid that correlates all instructor and student supplementary material to the text outline, a chapter outline, a chapter overview, and an annotated outline wherein the major headings of the chapter are summarized in detail. Included in the annotated outline are key terms, discussion points, suggestions for lecture ideas, and activities. The IRM also keys each chapter to appropriate videos and transparencies available with this text. Also included are references to related media, journals, and Websites. (Please request this item from your local Pearson Higher Education sales representative; also available for download from the Instructor Resource Center at www.pearsonhighered.com/irc.)

TEST BANK. The Test Bank includes more than 1,400 questions, including multiple choice, short answer/essay, true/false, and interpretive exercises. The interpretive exercises present case descriptions or scenarios involving individuals with special needs, followed by questions that require students to apply, analyze, evaluate, or synthesize concepts from the text. Page references to the main text, suggested answers, and skill types, as well as correlation to the CEC Standards and the Praxis principles, have been added to each question to help instructors create and evaluate student tests. (Please request this item from your local Pearson Higher Education sales representative; also available for download from the Instructor Resource Center at www.pearsonhighered.com/irc.)

COMPUTERIZED TEST BANK. The printed Test Bank is also available electronically through the Allyn & Bacon computerized testing system, TestGen. Instructors can use TestGen to create exams in just minutes by selecting from the existing database of questions, editing questions, and/or writing original questions. (Please request this item from your local Pearson Higher Education sales representative; also available for download from the Instructor Resource Center at www.pearsonhighered.com/irc.)

POWERPOINT™ PRESENTATION. Ideal for lecture presentations or student handouts, the PowerPoint™ Presentation created for this text provides dozens of ready-to-use graphic and text images. (Available for download from the Instructor Resource Center at www.pearsonhighered.com/irc.)

ALLYN & BACON TRANSPARENCIES FOR SPECIAL EDUCATION, 2008. A set of 100 acetate transparencies related to topics in the text. (Please request this item from your local Pearson Higher Education sales representative; also available for download from the Instructor Resource Center at www.pearsonhighered.com/irc.)

VIDEOTAPES FOR LECTURE PRESENTATION. These videos help humanize course concepts and provide context to lecture points.

- *Snapshots: Inclusion Video* (22 minutes in length) profiles three students of differing ages with various levels of disability in inclusive class settings. In each case, parents, classroom teachers, special education teachers, and school administrators talk about the steps they have taken to help the students succeed in inclusive settings.

- *Snapshots II: Learning Disabilities, Mental Retardation, Emotional or Behavioral Disorders* and *Snapshots II: Hearing Impairment, Visual Impairment, Traumatic Brain Injury* (20–25 minutes in length) is a two-video set of six segments designed specifically for use in college classrooms. Each segment profiles three individuals, their families, teachers, and experiences. These programs are of high interest to students. Instructors who have used the tapes in their courses have found that they help in disabusing students of stereotypical viewpoints and put a "human face" on the course material.

- *Professionals in Action Videotape: Teaching Students with Special Needs* (120 minutes in length) consists of five 15–30 minute modules presenting viewpoints and approaches to teaching students with various disabilities, in general education classrooms, separate education settings, and various combinations of the two. Each module explores its topic via actual classroom footage and interviews with general and special education teachers, parents, and students themselves.

Resources for Students

STUDY GUIDE. The Study Guide allows students to practice and apply what they have learned in the text through a mix of activities. The Study Guide contains the following sections for every chapter: learning objectives, reflection questions, key terms, practice tests, crossword puzzles, enrichment activities, further activities, and more.

MyEducationLab (www.myeducationlab.com) is a research-based learning tool that brings teaching to life. Through authentic in-class video footage, interactive simulations, rich case studies, examples of authentic teacher and student work, and more, MyEducationLab prepares you for your teaching career by showing what quality instruction looks like.

MyEducationLab is easy to use! In the textbook, look for the MyEducationLab logo in the margins and follow the simple link instructions to access the multimedia "**Homework & Exercises**" and "**Building Teaching Skills**" assignments in MyEducationLab that corresponds with the chapter content. Homework & Exercises offer opportunities to understand content more deeply and to practice applying content. Building Teaching Skills assignments help you practice and strengthen skills that are essential to quality teaching through your analysis and response to student and teacher instructional encounters and artifacts.

The rich, thoughtful and interactive elements you will encounter throughout MyEducationLab include:

- **Individualized Study Plan**: You have the opportunity to take pre- and post-tests before and after reading each chapter of the text. The test results automatically generate a personalized study plan for you, identifying areas of the chapter that you should reread to fully understand chapter concepts. You are also presented with interactive multimedia exercises to help ensure your learning. The study plan is designed to help you perform well on exams and to promote deep understanding of chapter content.

- **Video**: The authentic classroom videos in MyEducationLab show how real teachers handle actual classroom situations.

- **Case Studies**: A diverse set of robust cases illustrate the realities of teaching and offer valuable perspectives on common issues and challenges in education.

- **Simulations**: Created by the IRIS Center at Vanderbilt University, these interactive simulations give you hands-on practice at adapting instruction for a full spectrum of learners.

- **Readings**: Specially selected, topically relevant articles from ASCD's renowned *Educational Leadership* journal expand and enrich your perspectives on key issues and topics.

- **Student & Teacher Artifacts**: Authentic preK-12 student and teacher classroom artifacts are tied to course topics and offer you practice in working with the actual types of materials you will encounter daily as teachers.

- **Lesson & Portfolio Builders**: With this effective and easy-to-use tool, you can create, update, and share standards-based lesson plans and portfolios.

- **News Articles**: Looking for current issues in education? Our collection offers quick access to Link Library, an extensive collection of research and news articles supported by interactive pedagogy.

Acknowledgments

We are grateful to those individuals who provided valuable comments on the tenth edition and drafts of our eleventh edition chapters:

Bill Barfoot, University of Texas at Dallas

Joe M. Blackbourn, University of Mississippi

Deborah Childs, University of St. Louis

Jaime D. Christensen, University of Memphis

Patricia Clark, University of Maine, Augusta

Raymond J. Dalfonso, Kutztown University

Janice Ferguson, Western Kentucky University

Cecil Fore III, University of Georgia

Barbara L. Govendo, Lesley University

Barbara Green, University of Central Oklahoma

Joy Hines, Southeastern Louisiana University

Sharon Ishii-Jordan, Creighton University

Randall E. Jedele, Des Moines Area Community College

Donna Kearns, University of Central Oklahoma

Colleen Klein-Ezell, University of Central Florida

Marcel Lebrun, Plymouth State University

Maribeth Montgomery Kasik, Governors State University

Chris O'Brien, University of North Carolina – Charlotte

Holly Pae, University of South Carolina Upstate

Diana Rogers-Adkinson, University of Wisconsin – Whitewater

Jacques Singleton, University of Memphis

Terry E. Spigner, University of Central Oklahoma

We thank Beth Tuckwiller, currently a doctoral student at the University of Virginia, who oversaw the tedious task of securing permissions for quoted material. We are once again thankful for the wonderful support and assistance we received from the folks at Allyn and Bacon. Alicia Reilly, our Developmental Editor, continues to amaze us with her ability to balance family responsibilities while attending to all the details of our book. We simply can't thank her enough for all she does for us. She is a gem. Greg Erb, a new Production Editor for this edition, brought all the complex pieces of the project to completion flawlessly. Thanks to Jeff Houck, the book's project manager from Progressive Information Technologies—his calm and self-assured demeanor kept us confident that even last minute author changes would be dealt with seamlessly. Editorial Assistant Matt Buchholz's responsiveness to our e-mails and phone calls was critical to meeting deadlines. Thanks to Kris Ellis-Levy, Senior Marketing Manager, for once again taking such a sincere interest in the success of our text and for understanding the need for translating research into practice. Our copy editor, Lorraine Sobson of Reilly/Sobson did a terrific job of keeping us stylistically and grammatically correct. We thank Sarah Evertson, Photo Researcher, for such a splendid job of finding just the right photos. We're sure readers will agree that the extra attention you gave to the project has paid off—the photos are terrific. And finally, Virginia Lanigan, Executive Editor, continues to possess that rare combination of competence, professionalism, sensitivity, and a sense of humor. She's "all business" but with a heart. Thank you, Virginia.

Some Final Thoughts

Finally, for this edition, we have added a new author—Dr. Paige Pullen—who broadens and freshens the book's perspective. Her extensive experience as both a general education and special education teacher add invaluable insights for practitioners.

Given that this is the eleventh edition, some readers might legitimately be wondering whether the first two authors have lost any enthusiasm for the sometimes tedious task required to produce a thorough, up-to-date revision. We assure you that we didn't approach this edition any differently than we did the first. For those loyal users of previous editions, we assure you that we weighed carefully each change or update. We hope you agree that our revisions reflect the myriad changes in the field of special education over the past few years as well as the information explosion brought about by ever more accessible computer databases and the Internet. We also hope you'll agree that we haven't failed in our continuing commitment to bring you the best that research has to offer with regard to educating exceptional learners.

DPH

JMK

PCP

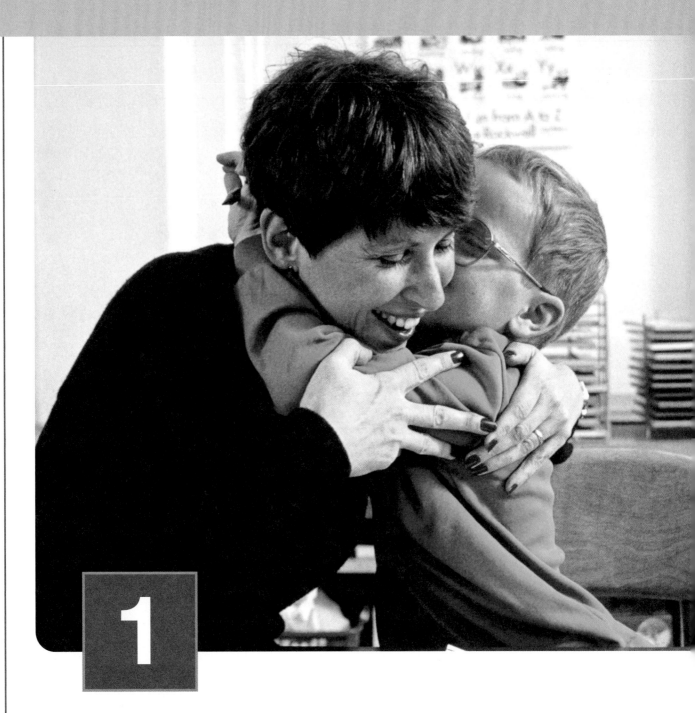

1

Exceptionality
and Special Education

Only the brave dare look
upon the gray—
upon the things which
cannot be explained easily,
upon the things which often
engender mistakes,
upon the things whose cause
cannot be understood,
upon the things we must
accept and live with.
And therefore only the brave
dare look upon difference
without flinching.

—Richard H. Hungerford, "On Locusts"

QUESTIONS **to guide your reading of this chapter . . .**

- How can we get oriented to exceptionality and special education?

- What is the educational definition of "exceptional learners"?

- What is the prevalence of exceptional learners?

- What is the definition of "special education"?

- How is special education provided?

- What are teachers' roles in special education?

- What are the origins of special education?

- What legislation and litigation have affected special education?

- How is the intent of special education law implemented in individualized education for students with disabilities?

- What is our perspective on the progress of special education?

MISCONCEPTIONS ABOUT
Exceptional Learners

MYTH ■ Public schools may choose not to provide education for some students with disabilities.

FACT ■ Federal legislation specifies that to receive federal funds, every school system must provide a free, appropriate public education (FAPE) for every student regardless of any disabling condition.

MYTH ■ By law, the student with a disability must be placed in the least restrictive environment (LRE). The LRE is always the regular classroom.

FACT ■ The law does require that schools place students with disabilities in the LRE. However, the LRE is not always the regular classroom. What LRE means is that the student shall be separated as little as possible from home, family, community, and the regular class setting while appropriate education is provided. In some but not all instances, this will mean placement in the regular classroom.

MYTH ■ The causes of most disabilities are known, but little is known about how to help individuals overcome or compensate for their disabilities.

FACT ■ In most cases, the causes of disabilities are not known, although progress is being made in pinpointing why many disabilities occur. More is known about the treatment of most disabilities than about their causes.

MYTH ■ People with disabilities are just like everyone else.

FACT ■ First, no two people are exactly alike. People with disabilities are unique individuals, just like everyone else. In most cases, most of their abilities are much like those of the average person who is not considered to have a disability. Nevertheless, a disability is a characteristic that is not shared by most people. It is important that disabilities be recognized for what they are, but individuals with disabilities must be seen as having many abilities—other characteristics that they share with the majority of people.

MYTH ■ A disability is a handicap.

FACT ■ A disability is an inability to do something, the lack of a specific capacity. A handicap, on the other hand, is a disadvantage that is imposed on an individual. A disability might or might not be a handicap, depending on the circumstances. For example, the inability to walk is not a handicap in learning to read, but it can be a handicap in getting into the stands at a ball game. Sometimes handicaps are needlessly imposed on people with disabilities. For example, a student who cannot write with a pen but can use a typewriter or word processor would be needlessly handicapped without such equipment.

The study of exceptional learners is the study of differences. The exceptional learner is different in some way from the average. In very simple terms, such a person might have problems or special talents in thinking, seeing, hearing, speaking, socializing, or moving. More often than not, he or she has a combination of special abilities or disabilities. Today, over six million such different learners have been identified in public schools throughout the United States. More than one out of every ten students in the U.S. who is of school age is considered exceptional. The fact that even many so-called normal students have school-related problems makes the study of exceptionality very demanding.

The study of exceptional learners is also the study of similarities. Exceptional individuals are not different from the average in every way. In fact, most exceptional learners are average in more ways than they are not. Until recently, professionals—and laypeople as well—tended to focus on the differences between exceptional and nonexceptional learners, almost to the exclusion of the ways in which all individuals are alike. Today, we give more attention to what exceptional and nonexceptional learners have in common—to similarities in their characteristics, needs, and ways of learning. As a result, the study of exceptional learners has become more complex, and many so-called facts about children and youths with disabilities and those who have special gifts or talents have been challenged.

Getting Oriented to Exceptionality and Special Education

Students of one of the hard sciences might boast about the difficulty of the subject matter because of the many facts they must remember and piece together. Students of special education face quite different problems. To be sure, they study facts, but the facts they must master are relatively few compared to the unanswered questions or ambiguities with which they must deal. Any study of human beings must take into account inherent ambiguities, inconsistencies, and unknowns. In the case of the individual who deviates from the norm, we must multiply all the mysteries of normal human behavior and development by those pertaining to the person's exceptionalities. Because there is no single accepted theory of normal development, it is not at all surprising that relatively few definite statements can be made about exceptional learners and many controversies remain (Kauffman, in press).

Reasons for Optimism

There are patches of sunshine in the bleak gray painted by Hungerford (1950) in his classic but still highly relevant poem (see the excerpt on p. 3). In the vast majority of cases, we are unable to identify the exact reason *why* a person is exceptional, but progress is being made in determining the causes of some disabilities. In Chapter 5, for example, we discuss the detection of causal factors in **Down syndrome**, a condition that results in the largest number of children classified as having moderate intellectual disabilities (mental retardation). Likewise, the incidence of **retinopathy of prematurity**, at one time a leading cause of blindness, has been greatly reduced since the discovery of its cause. The metabolic disorder **phenylketonuria (PKU)** was discovered decades ago, and now infants are routinely tested for PKU soon after birth, so that this type of intellectual disability can be prevented. More recently, the gene responsible for **cystic fibrosis**, an inherited condition characterized by chronic respiratory and digestive problems, has been identified. Advances in drug treatments appear to hold the potential for a cure for **muscular dystrophy**, another inherited disorder characterized by progressive degeneration of muscles (Welch et al., 2007). In the future, the specific genes governing many

■ **Down syndrome**
A condition resulting from an abnormality with the twenty-first pair of chromosomes; the most common abnormality is a triplet rather than a pair (the condition sometimes referred to as trisomy 21); characterized by intellectual disability and such physical signs as slanted-appearing eyes, hypotonia, a single palmar crease, shortness, and a tendency toward obesity.

■ **Retinopathy of prematurity (ROP)**
A condition resulting from administration of an excessive concentration of oxygen at birth; causes scar tissue to form behind the lens of the eye.

■ **Phenylketonuria (PKU)**
A metabolic genetic disorder caused by the inability of the body to convert phenylalanine to tyrosine; an accumulation of phenylalanine results in abnormal brain development.

■ **Cystic fibrosis**
An inherited disease affecting primarily the gastrointestinal (GI) tract and respiratory organs; characterized by thick, sticky mucous that often interferes with breathing or digestion.

■ **Muscular dystrophy**
A hereditary disease characterized by progressive weakness caused by degeneration of muscle fibers.

■ **Hydrocephalus**
A condition characterized by
enlargement of the head because
of excessive pressure of the
cerebrospinal fluid.

**Video Homework
Exercise**

Direct Instruction ●
Go to the Homework and
Exercises section in Chapter 1 of
MyEducationLab to watch the
video "Direct Instruction", and
observe a teacher using this
method to support students at risk
for school failure.

other diseases and disorders will also likely be found. Scientific advances raise the possibility of medications or gene therapies to prevent or correct many disabling conditions. Surgery to correct some identifiable defects can now sometimes be done on a fetus before birth (in utero), completely avoiding some conditions, such as **hydrocephalus** (an accumulation of fluid around the brain that can cause mental or physical disabilities if not corrected). And before long, research might lead to the ability to grow new organs from tissues taken from a person or from stem cells, perhaps allowing a poorly functioning lung, pancreas, or other internal organ to be replaced and the associated physical disabilities to be avoided. Advances in reproductive technology also hold promise for preventing many disabilities (Kauffman & Hallahan, 2007).

Besides these and other medical breakthroughs, research is enhancing understanding of the ways in which the individual's psychological, social, and educational environments are related to learning. For example, special educators, psychologists, and pediatricians are increasingly able to identify environmental conditions that increase the likelihood that a child will have learning or behavior problems (see Bolger & Patterson, 2001; Hallahan, Lloyd, Kauffman, Weiss, & Martinez, 2005; Hart & Risley, 1995; Kauffman, 2005; Walker & Sprague, 2007).

Educational methodology has also made strides. In fact, compared to current knowledge about causes, a lot is known about how exceptional learners can be taught and managed effectively in the classroom. Although special educators lament that not all the questions have been answered, considerably more is known today about how to educate exceptional learners than was the case ten or fifteen years ago (e.g., Hallahan et al., 2005; Heward, 2003; Lloyd, Forness, & Kavale, 1998; Stichter, Conroy, & Kauffman, 2008).

Before moving to the specific subject of exceptional learners, we must point out that we vehemently disagree with Hungerford on an important point: We all must certainly learn to live with disabling exceptionalities, but we must never accept them. We prefer to think there is hope for the eventual eradication of many of the disabling forms of exceptionality. In addition, we believe that it is of paramount importance to realize that even individuals whose exceptionalities are extreme can be helped to lead fuller lives than they would without appropriate education.

The Importance of Abilities

Many people with disabilities have abilities that go unrecognized because their disabilities become the focus of concern and limit attention to what the individual can do. We must study the disabilities of exceptional children and youths if we are to learn how to help them make maximum use of their abilities in school. Some students with disabilities that are not obvious to the casual observer need special programs of education and related services to help them live full, happy, productive lives. However, we must not lose sight of the fact that the most important characteristics of exceptional learners are their abilities, not their disabilities.

"Disability" Versus "Handicap"

Some historians suggest that the idea of disability is a social construction, whereas impairment is not (e.g., Holmes, 2004; Metzler, 2006). There is, indeed, an important distinction between disability and handicap: A disability is an inability to do something, a diminished capacity to perform in a specific way (an impairment); a handicap, however, is a disadvantage imposed on an individual. Thus, a disability might or might not be a handicap, depending on the circumstances. Likewise, a handicap might or might not be caused by a disability. For example, blindness is a disability that can be anything but a handicap in the dark. In fact, in the dark, the person who has sight is the one who is handicapped. Needing to use a wheelchair might be a handicap in certain circumstances,

**INTERNET
RESOURCES**

You can visit the site of the virtual
world congress and exposition on
disability at www.vwcdexpo.com
   For news about special education, see www.specialednews.com

We must not let people's disabilities keep us from recognizing their abilities, or allow their disabilities to become so much the focus of our concern that we overlook their capabilities.

but the disadvantage may be caused by architectural barriers or other people's reactions, not the inability to walk. Other people can handicap those who differ from themselves (in color, size, appearance, language, and so on) by stereotyping them or not giving them opportunities to do the things they are able to do. When working and living with exceptional individuals who have disabilities, we must constantly strive to separate their disabilities from the handicaps. That is, our goal should be to confine their handicaps to those characteristics and circumstances that can't be changed and to make sure that we impose no further handicaps by our attitudes or our unwillingness to accommodate their disabilities.

Disability Versus Inability

Another important distinction is that between inability and disability. All disabilities are an inability to do something. However, not every inability to do something is a disability. That is, disability is a subset of inability: "A disability is an inability to do something that most people, with typical maturation, opportunity, or instruction, can do" (Kauffman & Hallahan, 2005a, p. 30; see also Stichter et al., 2008). Consider age and ability. Most six-month-old infants cannot walk or talk, but they are not thought of as having a disability because their inability is age-appropriate. However, if that inability extends well past the time that most children learn to walk and talk, then we consider their inability a disability. Consider the role of instruction. An adult's inability to read is not a reading disability if she or he has not had reading instruction. Weigh the factor of typical adult human abilities. A typical adult male might not be able to lift 400 pounds, but this isn't considered a disability because most men simply can't lift 400 pounds. Judging inability in the context of old age, the average seventy-year-old can't run ten miles, but most seventy-year-olds can walk a considerable distance. Not being able to run ten miles is not considered a disability for a seventy-year-old, but being unable to walk at all is. The point is, simply, that disability is a significant difference from what we expect most people to be able to do, given their age, opportunities, and instruction.

Educational Definition of Exceptional Learners

UNDERSTANDING THE STANDARDS AND PRINCIPLES What distinguishes exceptional learners from typical learners? (CEC Knowledge and Skills Standards CC2K1 & CC2K5)

Council for Exceptional Children

For purposes of education, exceptional learners are those who require special education and related services if they are to realize their full human potential (Kauffman & Hallahan, 2005a). They require special education because they are markedly different from most students in one or more of the following ways: They may have intellectual disabilities, learning or attention disabilities, emotional or behavioral disorders, physical disabilities, disorders of communication, autism, traumatic brain injury, impaired hearing, impaired sight, or special gifts or talents. The chapters that follow define as exactly as possible what it means to have an exceptionality.

Two concepts are important to this educational definition of exceptional learners: (1) diversity of characteristics and (2) need for special education. The concept of diversity is inherent in the definition of exceptionality; the need for special education is inherent in an educational definition. Exceptional learners differ from most (typical or average) individuals in a particular way that is relevant to their education. Their particular educationally relevant difference demands instruction that is different from what most (typical or average) learners require (Kauffman & Hallahan, 2005a; Kauffman & Konold, 2007; Stichter et al., 2008).

Consider the case described in the Personal Perspectives on page 9. The story illustrates a matter discussed further in Chapter 2: how the focus on persons with disabilities must be on what they can do and how they should be integrated into the larger society as much as possible.

Blair Smith typically, but not always, uses a wheelchair because of a physical disability. However, that doesn't stop her from being a high school cheerleader or from being included with her peers in many typical teenage activities. For her, "appropriate education" requires a few reasonable accommodations that enable access to places and activities. Most of all, she needs—and receives—an attitude of acceptance on the part of teachers and peers.

Sometimes seemingly obvious disabilities are never identified, and the consequences for the person and his or her family, as well as for the larger society, are tragic. Sometimes disabilities are identified but special education is not provided, and opportunities for the child's development are thus squandered. Although early identification and intervention hold the promise of preventing many disabilities from becoming worse, preventive action often is not taken (Kauffman, 1999b, 2005b; Stichter et al., 2008).

Consider the case of author Martha Randolph Carr (Carr, 2004). She describes her son's learning disability (related to his attention deficit/hyperactivity disorder) and her own inability, until he was in high school, to see the disability. Her unwillingness to see his disability was motivated by the typical objections: labels and self-image.

> When Louie was in first grade it became obvious to me that he was having difficulty reading. To avoid labels being placed on my young son, I did what I thought was best: I started reading to Louie. . . . Through elementary and middle school, Louie grew into a thoughtful, intelligent, articulate boy who earned mostly Bs, but who had trouble comprehending the little he could read. No one else knew, and Louie and I rarely talked about it.
>
> His reading difficulty was the only problem I saw, and I accepted that everything else was fine. I told myself that I was doing the right thing because Louie might feel badly about himself if he thought there was something wrong and because mainstream colleges wouldn't accept a kid with learning disabilities. Fortunately, time and high school caught up with both of us.

Finally, in high school, Mrs. Carr and Louie could no longer cover up his disability. But his response to recognizing his disability—to its finally being diagnosed—was very different from what she had anticipated.

Personal PERSPECTIVES

Blair Smith

Blair Smith is different . . . Her legs look like they could snap beneath her at any moment, and she is so short that her perspective barely changes when she rises from her wheelchair.

Still, she always rises.

Smith is among the 20,000 to 50,000 people in the United States with the bone disorder osteogenesis imperfecta (OI). She is also a relentlessly giddy cheerleader at Monticello High School.

There are at least four forms of OI, representing extreme variations in severity from one individual to another. Smith's case falls somewhere in the fairly severe category. OI has rendered her bones soft and brittle, leaving her literally fragile. When she walks, she relies on the support of her crutches and leg braces to keep from breaking a leg or two. Her growth was stunted drastically. . . .

As a ninth-grader at Albemarle High School, Smith cheered from the stands like most of the other Patriot students. But for her sophomore year, she moved to brand-new Monticello . . . and joined the junior varsity team for the Mustangs.

Blair Smith—just another young girl full of life.

And as a junior this past fall, Smith made the varsity squad, serving as a headliner for Monticello's act from September to February. She takes the floor in her wheelchair—Smith's parents had to solicit the aid of [her physical education teacher] to make her use the chair—and participates in the routines in her own way. Stunts are definitely out, but Smith manages to make her indelible mark on the show without the tools of gymnastic display. . . .

"It's been unbelievable," Debbie Smith [Blair's mother] said. "The kids have just been wonderful. They have been wonderful the whole time she has been in school about accepting her for the way she is."

Added Ralph Smith [Blair's father]: "People are always pushing her forward and letting her do things and not putting her in a shell." . . .

She is just another young girl full of life.

That is all. And that makes you want to stand up and cheer.

Source: "Something to Cheer About" by Tom Gresham, *The Daily Progress*, May 7, 2000, pp. E1, E6, Charlottesville, VA. Reprinted with permission.

When I told Louie about the diagnosis, he didn't look hurt or confused. Instead, his face relaxed and he shouted, "You mean I'm not stupid?!" I was so taken aback that I started to cry. Louie said, still very relieved, "Were you worried, too?" I cried harder.

By denying the truth to myself and thus keeping it from Louie, I had left him with the only other plausible answer that he could come up with as to why he always worked so much harder than his friends and didn't get the same grades.

Special education does not always work as it should, but when it does, a student's disability is identified early and effective special education is provided in the least restrictive environment. The student's parents are involved in the decision about how to address the student's needs, and the outcome of special education is the student's improved achievement and behavior. Consider the case of Alice, presented in the Personal Perspectives on page 10.

Students with exceptionalities are an extraordinarily diverse group in comparison to the general population, and relatively few generalizations apply to all exceptional individuals. Their exceptionalities can involve sensory, physical, cognitive, emotional, or communication abilities or any combination of these. Furthermore, exceptionalities may vary greatly in cause, degree, and affect on educational progress, and the effects may vary greatly depending on the individual's age, sex, and life circumstances. Any individual presented as an example of an "exceptional learner" is likely to be representative of exceptional learners in some respects but unrepresentative in others.

Reading Homework Exercise

Labeling ● Go to the Homework and Exercises section in Chapter 1 of MyEducationLab and click on the weblink to read an article that offers a special education teacher's point of view about labeling.

Personal PERSPECTIVES

An IEP for Alice: What Can Happen When Special Education Works

Alice's first-grade teacher called about five minutes after the educational planner left my room. Both the first-grade teacher and the educational planner informed me that at the eligibility meeting the day before, it was determined that Alice qualified for services in my class for children with mild mental retardation [intellectual disabilities].

"It would be great if you could write the IEP for Alice soon, so we could have her start right after Christmas," her teacher suggested. "She cries so much. I feel so bad for her. She's no problem, but she just can't do the work." . . .

The father flatly refused to have her placed in my class. "Alice can do the work. I know she can," he said.

So Alice started out the year with new clothes, a smile, and the fine-motor skills of a two-year-old. And although she was from a loving, attentive family that read to her and paid a lot of attention to her, her skills were seriously delayed compared to the other students in the first grade. It wasn't that she didn't learn. She just took so much longer than the other children in her class. Even though Alice participated in the resource program, the speech program, the occupational therapy program (all done in the general education classroom and including other classmates in her lessons), she could not keep up with even the slowest group in her class.

It wasn't long before Alice was asking her mother, "Why can't I do what the other kids do? I want to do it." Motivation did not seem to be a problem initially, but after a few months, Alice decided not to try. Can't say that I much blame her. After a while, she made her misery known to all, both at home and at school. She became a helpless blob that cried most of the time.

Her teacher said, "As far as I know, no one in my class has ever been mean to Alice. She just purely hates school now," she sighed. Alice's mother agreed with the teacher. "I've asked her over and over again if anyone has been mean to her. She says no, and I believe her." After reading her folder and talking with teachers who worked with Alice, I felt bad for her too.

The parents and I wrote an educational plan for Alice, stating that she would begin attending my class after Christmas. Dad still wasn't so sure that he approved, but knew that something had to be done. "But you have to promise to push her. She can be really manipulative," he warned.

After a few weeks of Alice's placement in my room, the parents and I met again. They seemed much happier. "Alice enjoys coming to school now," they let me know. The dad, much to his credit, wished that he had not denied her services in the fall. "She feels so much better about herself now," he said.

Two years later, Alice's father and I talked about his reaction to the eligibility meeting (the one deciding that Alice qualified for my services). "There were so many people," he said, "and they were all saying that there was something terribly wrong with my daughter. I wondered who in the hell they were talking about! My pretty little girl is so loving and funny. How could they say she was retarded?"

"Does it matter what label they put on her? Isn't she still a pretty, funny, loving little girl?"

"Yeah," he laughed. "Except now she can read!"

Source: Kauffman, J. M., & Pullen, P. L. (1996). Eight myths about special education. *Focus on Exceptional Children, 28*(5), 7–8. Reprinted with permission.

UNDERSTANDING THE STANDARDS AND PRINCIPLES What special services must be provided when a student is identified with a disability? (CEC Knowledge and Skills Standard CC1K6)

Council for Exceptional Children

The typical student who receives special education has no immediately obvious disability. He (more than half of the students served by special education are males) is in elementary or middle school and has persistent problems in learning and behaving appropriately in school. His problems are primarily academic and social or behavioral, and may not be apparent to many teachers until they have worked with him for a period of weeks or months. His problems persist despite teachers' efforts to meet his needs in the regular school program in which most students succeed. He is most likely to be described as having a learning disability or to be designated by an even broader label indicating that his academic and social progress in school is unsatisfactory owing to a disability.

By federal law, schools should not identify these exceptional students as eligible for special education until careful assessment indicates that they are unable to make satisfactory progress in the regular school program without special services designed to meet their extraordinary needs (Huefner, 2006). Federal special education laws and regulations include definitions of several conditions (categories such as learning disability, autism, and hearing impairment) that might create a need for special education. These laws and regulations require that special services be provided to meet whatever special needs are created by a disabling condition and can't be met in the regular educational program. The law doesn't require that special education be provided simply because a student has a disability.

> **Casebook Reflections**
>
> REFER TO THE CASE *Should I Take Juanita Pope?* in your booklet. Many critics of special education say that too many students are identified for services. What characteristics make you think that Juanita has a disability? ●

Prevalence of Exceptional Learners

Prevalence refers to the percentage of a population or number of individuals having a particular exceptionality. The prevalence of intellectual disability, for example, might be estimated at 2.3 percent, which means that 2.3 percent of the population, or twenty-three people in every thousand, are assumed to have intellectual disabilities. If the prevalence of giftedness is assumed to be between 3 percent and 5 percent, somewhere between thirty and fifty people in a sample of a thousand would have special gifts of some kind. Obviously, accurate estimates of prevalence depend on the ability to count the number of people in a given population who have a certain exceptionality.

The task of determining the number of students with exceptionalities might appear simple enough, yet the prevalence of most exceptionalities is uncertain and a matter of considerable controversy. A number of factors make it hard to say with great accuracy and confidence just how many exceptional individuals there are, including vagueness in definitions, frequent changes in definitions, and the role of schools in determining exceptionality—matters that we discuss in later chapters (see also Kauffman & Hallahan, 2005a).

Government figures show that about ten students out of every hundred were receiving special education in the early twenty-first century (U.S. Department of Education, 2005). Beginning in the mid-1970s, there was steady growth in the number of students served by special education, from about 3.75 million in 1976 to more than 6 million by the early twenty-first century. Most of the children and youths who are served by special education are between the ages of six and seventeen. Although preschoolers and youths ages eighteen to twenty-one are being identified with increasing frequency as having disabilities, school-age children and youths in their early teens make up the bulk of the identified population.

The percentage of the special education population identified as having certain disabilities has changed considerably over several decades. For example, the number of students identified as having learning disabilities has more than doubled since the mid-1970s; these students now make up about half of the number of students receiving special education. In contrast, the percentage of students whose primary disability is speech or language impairments declined substantially (but is growing again), and the percentage identified as having intellectual disabilities is now about half of what it was in 1976. No one has an entirely satisfactory explanation of these changes. However, they might in part reflect alterations in definitions and diagnostic criteria for certain disabilities and the social acceptability of the "learning disability" label. In subsequent chapters, we discuss the prevalence of specific categories of exceptionality.

INTERNET RESOURCES

For additional information about annual reports to Congress on IDEA, see www.ed.gov/about/reports/annual/osep/index.html?

High-Incidence and Low-Incidence Categories

Some disabilities occur with a relatively high frequency, and are called *high-incidence disabilities* because they are among the most common. Learning disabilities, communication (speech and language) disorders, emotional disturbance, and mild intellectual disabilities are among those usually considered high-incidence (Stichter et al., 2008). Other disabilities (such as

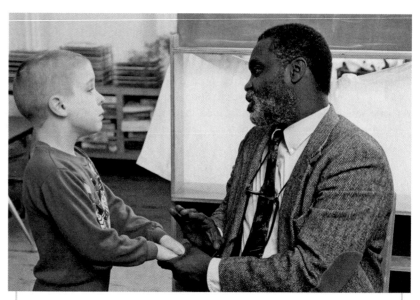

There has been a dramatic increase in the identification of **autism** or **autistic spectrum disorder**, probably representing improved identification procedures and identification of milder cases of autism, not an epidemic.

■ **Autism or autistic spectrum disorder**
A pervasive developmental disability characterized by extreme withdrawal, cognitive deficits, language disorders, self-stimulation, and onset before the age of thirty months.

■ **Traumatic brain injury (TBI)**
Injury to the brain (not including conditions present at birth, birth trauma, or degenerative diseases or conditions) resulting in total or partial disability or psychosocial maladjustment that affects educational performance; may affect cognition, language, memory, attention, reasoning, abstract thinking, judgment, problem solving, sensory or perceptual and motor disabilities, psychosocial behavior, physical functions, information processing, or speech.

UNDERSTANDING THE STANDARDS AND PRINCIPLES How do special education teachers know which instructional strategies and materials to use with their students? (INTASC 1.08)

INTASC

low vision and blindness, deafness, deaf-blindness, and severe intellectual disabilities) occur relatively rarely and are considered low-incidence disabilities.

Although the rates of occurrence of most of the high-incidence disabilities have remained relatively stable in the early twenty-first century, there have been dramatic increases in some of the low-incidence categories. For example, there has been a dramatic increase in the identification of **autism** or **autistic spectrum disorder** since about 1995, a matter discussed further in Chapter 12 (see also Stichter et al., 2008). Other low-incidence categories showing substantial increases in numbers include **traumatic brain injury (TBI)** and orthopedic impairments—much of this due to increases in spinal cord injury and in survival of severe physical trauma owing to better medical care.

Much of the increase in diagnosis of autism probably represents improved identification procedures and identification of milder cases of autism, not an epidemic (National Research Council, 2001). Although some of the increase in TBI might represent better diagnosis, it might also reflect actual increases in brain injuries, as we will discuss in Chapter 13. Increases in orthopedic impairments might reflect the increasing survival rate of infants born with significant physical anomalies and children who have been involved in accidents. Increases in hearing and vision impairments might represent better diagnosis of these disabilities, too.

Definition of Special Education

Special education means specially designed instruction that meets the unusual needs of an exceptional student (see Huefner, 2006), and which might require special materials, teaching techniques, or equipment and/or facilities. Students with visual impairments might require reading materials in large print or braille; students with hearing impairments might require hearing aids and/or instruction in sign language; those with physical disabilities might need special equipment; those with emotional or behavioral disorders might need smaller and more highly structured classes; and students with special gifts or talents might require access to working professionals. Related services—special transportation, psychological assessment, physical and occupational therapy, medical treatment, and counseling—might be necessary if

Intensive, relentless, and specific special education makes the difference for struggling learners

Molly, a student with mental retardation, is a student council representative at her school. Eliot, a student with a learning disability, is finally learning how to read. Josh, a student with attention deficit/hyperactivity disorder, hopes to play football at a Division I school. Through the use of technology, David, a quadriplegic who relies on a ventilator, participates in every aspect of his special school.

These are the stories of success in special education. The critics of special education abound, and we are sure you have heard many of them (e.g., Bolick, 2001; Finn & Rotherham, 2001; Fisher, 2001). Reform movements in the 1980s and 1990s cited a parallel system that was failing students and that needed radical reform (Stainback & Stainback, 1984; Will, 1986). We disagree (e.g., Crockett, 1999–2000; Hockenbury, Kauffman, & Hallahan, 1999–2000; Kauffman, Bantz, & McCullough, 2002; Kauffman & Hallahan, 2005a). Our view of special education is one of challenge and one of the individual, much as Zigmond described:

Special education is, first and foremost, instruction focused on individual need. It is carefully planned. It is intensive, urgent, relentless, and goal-directed. (Zigmond, 1997, pp. 384–385)

We include a Success Stories box in each disability chapter to highlight the intensive, relentless, and specific instruction that is necessary to bring about change in individuals with disabilities. In addition, we include questions at the end of each story that ask you to reflect on your professional development and your beliefs about students with disabilities. Finally, the Success Stories boxes include a section entitled "Using the CEC Standards" to help you integrate the major concepts of the chapters and the Success Stories with the professional requirements of new special educators. Our intent is to provide you with examples of how special education that includes high-quality instruction, hard work, and appropriate collaboration can make for student success.

---

special education is to be effective. The single most important goal of special education is finding and capitalizing on exceptional students' abilities. The Success Stories included in each chapter highlight successes in special education. See introduction above.

The best general education cannot replace special education; special education is more precisely controlled in pace or rate, intensity, relentlessness, structure, reinforcement, teacher-pupil ratio, curriculum, and monitoring or assessment (Kauffman & Hallahan, 2005a; Kauffman & Landrum, 2007). We think it's a good idea to improve the education of all children, an objective of the federal **No Child Left Behind Act (NCLB)** of the early twenty-first century. However, good or reformed general education does not and cannot replace special education for those students at the extremes of the range of disabilities (Kauffman & Hallahan, 2005a; Kauffman & Konold, 2007; Kauffman & Wiley, 2004; Zigmond, 2007).

Video Homework Exercise

Teacher Roles ●
Go to the Homework and Exercises section in Chapter 1 of MyEducationLab to watch videos 1 and 2, about the different roles that special education teachers play in the lives of students with special needs.

Providing Special Education

Several administrative plans are available for the education of exceptional learners, ranging from a few special provisions made by the student's general education teacher to twenty-four-hour residential care in a special facility. Who educates exceptional students and where they receive their education depend on two factors: (1) how and how much the student differs from average students and (2) what resources are available in the school and community. Administrative plans for education vary according to the degree of physical integration—the extent to which exceptional and nonexceptional students are taught in the same place by the same teachers.

Beginning with the least specialized environment, the general education teacher who is aware of the individual needs of students and is skilled at meeting them may be able to acquire appropriate materials, equipment, and/or instructional methods. This level might not require the direct services of specialists; the expertise of the general education

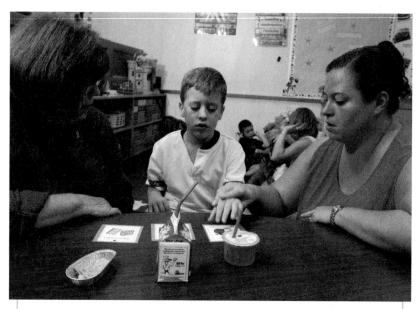

General education teachers often consult with a special educator or other professional who can provide resources and demonstrate the use of equipment or specialized methods of instruction for students in inclusive classrooms.

might meet the student's needs. Some students with disabilities can be accommodated in this way; no truly special education is required to meet their needs.

Alternatively, the general education teacher might need to *consult* with a special educator or other professional (e.g., the school psychologist) in addition to acquiring the special materials, equipment, or methods. The special educator might instruct the general education teacher, refer the teacher to other resources, or demonstrate the use of materials, equipment, or methods. Alternatively, the general and special educators might *co-teach*, with each providing instruction and the special educator emphasizing instruction of the exceptional student(s).

Sometimes a special educator provides *itinerant* services to the exceptional student and/or the general education teacher. The itinerant teacher establishes a consistent schedule, working in a variety of schools and visiting classrooms to instruct students individually or in small groups. This teacher provides materials and teaching suggestions for the general education teacher to carry out and consults with the regular teacher about special problems. This level of specialization is still not high.

A *resource teacher* provides services for students and teachers in a single school. The students being served are enrolled in the general education classroom and work with the specially trained teacher for a length of time and at a frequency determined by the nature and severity of their particular problems. The resource teacher continually assesses the needs of the students and their teachers and usually works with students individually or in small groups in a special *resource room* where special materials and equipment are available. Typically, the resource teacher also serves as a consultant to the classroom teacher, advising on how to instruct and manage the student in the classroom and perhaps demonstrating instructional techniques. The flexibility of the plan and the fact that the student remains with nondisabled peers most of the time have traditionally made this a particularly attractive and popular alternative.

Casebook Reflections

REFER TO THE CASE *Least Restrictive for Whom?* in your booklet. A hearing-impaired teacher of students with hearing impairments in high school, Andy commented on Brian's situation: "How can you consider this [the general education classroom] the least restrictive environment for Brian when he can only communicate with one person in the whole school?" How should one interpret the notion of "least restrictive environment" in Brian's case? Does his case make understanding the concept more difficult? ●

One of the most visible—and, in recent years, controversial—service alternatives is the special *self-contained class*. Such a class typically enrolls fifteen or fewer exceptional students with particular characteristics or needs. The teacher ordinarily has been trained as a special educator and provides all or most of the instruction, assisted by an aide. The students assigned to such classes usually spend most or all of the school day separated from their nondisabled peers. Often, students with disabilities are included with non-disabled students during part of the day (perhaps for physical education, music, or some other activity in which they can participate well).

Special *day schools* provide an all-day special placement for exceptional learners who need this level of specialization or dedication to their needs. The day school usually is organized for a specific category of exceptional students and may contain special equipment necessary for their care and education. These students return to their homes during nonschool hours.

Hospital or homebound instruction is most often required by students who have physical disabilities, although it's sometimes an option for those with emotional or behavioral disorders or other disabilities when no alternative is readily available. Typically, the youngster is confined to the hospital or the home for a relatively short time, and the hospital or homebound teacher maintains contact with the general classroom teacher.

In a *residential school*, exceptional students receive twenty-four-hour care away from home, often at a distance from their communities. This is the highest level of specialization or dedication on the continuum of alternative placements required by the Individuals with Disabilities Education Act (IDEA). These students might make periodic visits home or re-turn each weekend, but during the week, they are residents of the institution, where they receive academic instruction in addition to management of their daily living environment.

Figure 1.1 illustrates the idea of variation in the separation of children from their gen-eral education classrooms and peers. It also illustrates the increasing specialization of envi-ronments. As Kauffman and Hallahan (2005a) point out, the degree to which education is "special" is a continuum. That is, education can be "sort of" special or very, very specialized.

Many school systems, in the process of trying to find effective and economical ways of serving exceptional students, combine or alter these alternatives and the roles special educators and other professionals play in service delivery. There are wide variations among school systems in the kinds of placements made for particular kinds of students.

As we noted earlier, special education law requires placement of the student in the **least restrictive environment (LRE)**, which usually means that the student should be separated from nondisabled classmates and from home, family, and community as little as possible. That is, the student's life should be as normal as possible, and the intervention should be consistent with individual needs and not interfere with individual freedom any more than is absolutely necessary. For example, students should not be placed in special

FIGURE 1.1   Continuum of placement options showing hypothetical relationship between degree of separateness from general education classroom peers and degree of specialness of education

classes if they can be served adequately by resource teachers, and they should not be placed in a residential school if a special class will serve their needs just as well.

Although placement of exceptional students in the least restrictive environment is laudable, the definition of *least restrictive* is not as simple as it seems. Years ago, Cruickshank (1977) pointed out that greater restriction of the physical environment does not necessarily mean greater restriction of psychological freedom or human potential (see also Bateman, 2007; Crockett & Kauffman, 1999, 2001). In fact, it is conceivable that some students could be more restricted in the long run in a general education class where they are rejected by others and fail to learn necessary skills than in a special class or day school where they learn happily and well (Gliona, Gonzales, & Jacobson, 2005; Kauffman, Bantz, & McCullough, 2002; Warnock, 2005). Over half a century ago, Stullken stated, "School administrators should realize that an exceptional child may be more harmfully segregated when kept in a regular class which does not meet his needs than when assigned to a special class which meets his needs much better" (1950, p. 299).

It is important to keep our ultimate goals for the students in mind and to avoid letting the term *least restrictive* become a hollow slogan that results in shortchanging them in their education (Crockett & Kauffman, 1999, 2001; Huefner, 2006; Kauffman, 1995; Kauffman, McGee, & Brigham, 2004). As Morse noted many years ago, "The goal should be to find the most productive setting to provide the maximum assistance for the child" (1984, p. 120). Gliona and colleagues (2005) have suggested that the term *segregated* not be used to describe the necessary and helpful placement of students in environments that are dedicated to highly specialized education, as it is neither accurate nor appropriate for describing the placement of students in the specialized environments they need. The term *dedicated*, they explain, is much more accurate. Gliona and colleagues also suggest a "direct access model" for conceptualizing LRE. As depicted in Figure 1.2, the student is at the center and can access any of the placement options that meet his or her needs. Figure 1.2 shows LRE choices for two different students. In the first case, the student's LRE has been determined to be a special school. In the second case, the student's LRE has been determined to be a combination of resource room services and regular class placement with consultation.

Since the late 1980s, there has been a steady trend toward placing more students with disabilities in general education classes and a corresponding trend toward placing fewer students with disabilities in resource rooms, separate classes, and separate facilities (U.S. Department of Education, 1995, 1997, 2005). Placing more students in general education classes and schools reflects an aim of educational reform, a topic to which we return in Chapter 2.

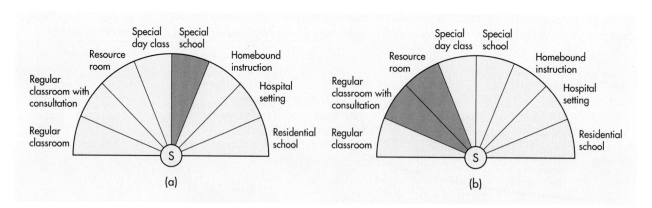

FIGURE 1.2 Direct access model of placement in the least restrictive environment (LRE). (a) a student whose LRE is a special school. (b) a student whose LRE is a combination of programs

Source: Gliona, M. F., Gonzales, A. K., & Jacobson, E. S. (2005). Dedicated, not segregated: Suggested changes in thinking about instructional environments and in the language of special education. In J. M. Kauffman & D. P. Hallahan (Eds.), *The illusion of full inclusion: A comprehensive critique of a current special education bandwagon* (2nd ed., p. 144). Austin, TX: Pro-Ed. Reprinted by permission.

There is considerable variation in the placement of students with disabilities from state to state and among school systems within a given state. However, most exceptional students are now educated in general education classes. Nationwide, nearly 50 percent of exceptional children and youths are now served primarily in general education classes. Relatively few students with disabilities are placed outside of regular schools. Figure 1.3 shows the approximate percentage of students served in each type of placement in the early twenty-first century.

Children under the age of six less often receive education in general education classes and more often attend separate schools than do school-age children. Special classes, separate schools, and other environments such as homebound instruction are used more often for older teenagers and young adults than for students in elementary and high schools. We can explain these differences with several facts:

- Preschoolers and young adults who are identified for special education tend to have more severe disabilities than do students in kindergarten through grade 12.

- Some school systems do not have general education classes for preschoolers and young adults; therefore, placements in other than general education classes are typically more available and more appropriate.

- Curriculum and work-related educational programs for older teens and young adults with disabilities are frequently offered off the campuses of general education high schools.

The least restrictive environment depends in part on the individual's exceptionality. There is almost never a need to place in a separate class or separate school a student whose primary disability is a speech impairment. Likewise, most students with learning disabilities can be appropriately educated primarily in general education classes. On the other hand, the resources that are needed to teach students with severe hearing and vision impairments might require that these students attend separate schools or classes for at least part of their school careers.

FIGURE 1.3 Approximate percentages of students with disabilities in various placement options in the early twenty-first century

Source: Data from the annual reports of the U.S. Department of Education to Congress on Implementation of the Individuals with Disabilities Education Act.

Teachers' Roles

We have noted that most students in public schools who have been identified as exceptional are placed in general education classrooms for at least part of the school day. Furthermore, there is good reason to believe that a large number of public school students who have not been identified as disabled or gifted share many of the characteristics of those who are exceptional. Thus, all teachers must be prepared to deal with exceptional students, although it's unreasonable to expect all teachers to teach all exceptional students (Kauffman & Hallahan, 2005a; Mock & Kauffman, 2002; Zigmond, 2007).

The roles of general and special education teachers are not always clear in a given case. Sometimes, uncertainty about the division of responsibility can be extremely stressful; teachers may feel uneasy because it's not clear whose job it is to make special adaptations for a pupil or just what they are expected to do in cooperating with other teachers.

Casebook Reflections

REFER TO THE CASE *Should I Take Juanita Pope?* in your booklet. Consider the factors that might contribute to Juanita's failure in school. In what ways does Juanita fit the description of a child who is at risk? ●

Relationship Between General and Special Education

During the 1980s, the relationship between general and special education became a matter of increasing concern to policymakers, researchers, and advocates for exceptional children. Radical reformers have recommended that special education be eliminated as a separate, identifiable part of education, calling for a single, unified educational system in which all students are viewed as unique, special, and entitled to the same quality of education. Although many of the suggested reforms have great appeal and some could produce benefits for exceptional students, the basis for integration of special and general education and the ultimate consequences this might bring have been questioned (e.g., Bateman, 2007; Crockett & Kauffman, 1999, 2001; Fuchs & Fuchs, 1994; Hockenbury, Kauffman, & Hallahan, 1999–2000; Kauffman, 1995, 1999–2000; Kauffman & Hallahan, 2005a, 2005b; Martin, 1995; Mock & Kauffman, 2002, 2005; Warnock, 2005; Zigmond, 2007).

Special Education and Students At Risk

One motivation behind reform proposals is concern for pupils considered to be at risk. The term *at risk* is often not clearly defined, but generally refers to students who perform or behave poorly in school and appear likely to fail or fall far short of their potential. Some advocates of reform suggest that at-risk students cannot be or should not be distinguished from those with mild disabilities. Others argue that the problems of at-risk students tend to be ignored because special education siphons resources from general education. Should special education and general education merge for the purpose of making general education better able to respond to students who are at risk? Or should special education maintain its separate identity and be expanded to include these students? Should general education be expected to develop new programs for at-risk students without merging with special education?

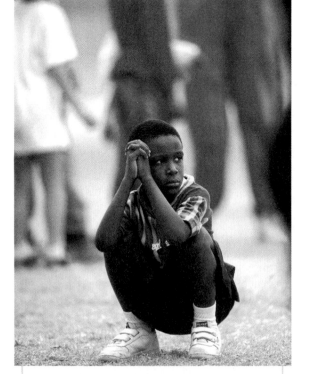

The term *at risk* is often not clearly defined, but it generally refers to students who perform or behave poorly in school and appear likely to fail or fall far short of their potential. Should special education be expanded to include these students?

There are no ready answers to these and other questions about the education of students who are at risk. Regardless of where one draws the line separating those who are considered to be at risk from those with disabilities, the line is arbitrary and leads to doubts about some students. In other words, there is no entirely clear distinction between "at risk" and disability because educational achievement and social competence can vary from a little to a lot, and there is no sudden, dramatic break in people's level of attainment (Boardman & Vaughn, 2007; Kauffman & Hallahan, 2005a; Kauffman & Konold, 2007).

The Inclusion Controversy

The term *inclusion* is often used to describe teaching students with disabilities in the same environment as their age peers who don't have disabilities. Inclusion is now an issue in education worldwide (e.g., Simpson & Kauffman, 2007; Warnock, 2005; see also Chapter 2 for a more in-depth discussion). Regardless of one's views, the controversy about the relationship between special and general education has made teachers more aware of the problems of deciding just which students should be taught specific curricula, which students should receive special attention or services, and where and by whom these should be provided (Crockett & Kauffman, 1999, 2001; Kauffman & Hallahan, 1997, 2005b; Kauffman, Mock, Tankersley, & Landrum, 2008; Mock & Kauffman, 2005).

Expectations for All Educators

Although there are no pat answers to the questions about how special and general education should work together to ensure that every student receives an appropriate education, it's clear that the relationship must be one of cooperation and collaboration. Even though there should not be independent or mutually exclusive educational tracks, general and special educators have somewhat different roles to play. A special feature called Making It Work addresses specific issues of inclusion for each disability area throughout this book; an introductory sample appears on page 20.

One limitation of all teachers is that they cannot accomplish the miracles portrayed in the popular media, even if they are very good at what they do (Moore, 2007). Real teachers can't be as perky, self-sacrificing, idealistic, and influential as those shown in films, nor can most teachers achieve the same results as those who win awards for exceptional performance. Moreover, too many good general education teachers give little or no acknowledgment to special education or the students it is designed to serve. Award-winning general education teacher Rafe Esquith makes no mention whatever of special education or students with disabilities in his popular book, *Teach Like Your Hair's on Fire* (Esquith, 2007).

True, competent teachers can make a significant difference in the lives of the children with whom they work, but the expectations set up by media portrayals—and too often by government or the general public—are unrealistic. Teachers, like those employed in other lines of work, must do the best they can with the resources at their disposal. Striving for excellence is admirable, but recognizing one's real-world limitations, keeping one's duties and accomplishments in perspective, and being happy with the best one can do, even if it's less than perfection, is as important for teachers as it is for students.

Regardless of whether a teacher is specifically trained in special education, he or she may be expected to participate in educating exceptional students in any one of the following ways:

1. *Make maximum effort to accommodate individual students' needs.* Teaching in public schools requires dealing with diverse students in every class. All teachers must make an effort to meet the needs of individuals who might differ in some way from the average or typical student. Flexibility, adaptation, accommodation, and special attention are to be expected of every teacher. Special education should be considered necessary only when a teacher's best efforts to meet a student's individual needs aren't successful.

2. *Evaluate academic abilities and disabilities.* Although a psychologist or other special school personnel might administer a student formal standardized tests in academic areas, adequate evaluation requires the teacher's assessment of the student's performance in the classroom. Teachers must be able to report specifically and precisely how students can and cannot perform in all academic areas for which they are responsible.

3. *Refer for evaluation.* By law, all public school systems must make extensive efforts to screen and identify all children and youths of school age who have disabilities. Teachers must observe students' behavior and refer those they suspect of having disabilities for evaluation by a multidisciplinary team. A student shouldn't be referred for special education unless extensive and unsuccessful efforts have been made to accommodate the student's needs in regular classes. Before referral, school personnel must document the strategies that have been used to teach and manage the student in gen-

Video Homework Exercise

The Inclusive Classroom ● Go to the Homework and Exercises section in Chapter 1 of MyEducationLab to watch the video "The Inclusive Classroom", which demonstrates aspects of the least restrictive environment.

UNDERSTANDING THE STANDARDS AND PRINCIPLES Why is it important for all teachers to have basic understanding of ways in which disabilities impact learning and development? (INTASC 2.01)

INTASC

Teachers of Students with Disabilities

Collaboration and Co-Teaching

According to the *17th Annual Report to Congress*, about 41% of students with disabilities in the United States were served in general education classrooms (U.S. Department of Education, 1995). Ten years later, the *27th Annual Report to Congress* reported that about half of all students with disabilities spent less than 21% of their school time outside of the general education classroom, the most inclusive category reported (U.S. Department of Education, 2005). With an increasing number of students with disabilities in general education classrooms, teachers must collaborate with special educators to meet the needs of the students in their classes. This collaboration can take many forms, such as collaborative consultation (general education teacher getting support from the special educator outside of direct classroom instruction), working with itinerant teachers or paraprofessionals (general education teacher working with a traveling special educator or paraprofessional either within classroom instruction or not), and co-teaching (general and special education teachers working together in direct classroom instruction).

"Making It Work" addresses the issues of collaboration, providing "how-tos" and "cautions." The first section of the feature (What does it mean to be a teacher of students with. . . .) includes information about the knowledge and skills special educators should possess as they enter the field, as identified in the Council for Exceptional Children's (CEC) performance-based professional standards (2003). CEC is the largest professional organization for special educators and is composed of smaller divisions representing professionals and parents from all disability categories. We believe it is important for all teachers to understand what expertise special educators can contribute to collaborative classrooms. For more information, try www.cec.sped.org.

The second section (Strategies in Co-Teaching or Collaboration) provides descriptions of successful collaborations in real classrooms or descriptions of how a strategy can be incorporated into a co-taught classroom. Our hope is that this feature will bring to life the concept of working together to meet the needs of students with disabilities.

eral education. Referral is justified only if these strategies have failed (see Focus on Concepts, p. 21).

4. *Participate in eligibility conferences.* Before a student is provided special education, an interdisciplinary team must determine his or her eligibility. Therefore, teachers must be ready to work with other teachers and with professionals from other disciplines (e.g., psychology, medicine, or social work) in determining a student's eligibility for special education.

5. *Participate in writing individualized education programs.* Every student identified with a disability and receiving special education must have a written individualized education program (IEP). Teachers must be ready to participate in a meeting (possibly including the student and/or parents as well as other professionals) to develop the program.

6. *Communicate with parents or guardians.* Parents (sometimes surrogate parents) or guardians must be consulted during the evaluation of the child's eligibility for special education, formulation of the IEP, and reassessment of any special program that may be designed. Teachers must contribute to the school's communication with parents about the child's problems, placement, and progress.

7. *Participate in due process hearings and negotiations.* Parents, guardians, or students with disabilities themselves who are dissatisfied with the school's response to educational needs may request a due process hearing or negotiations regarding appropriate services. Teachers might be called on to offer observations, opinions, or suggestions in such hearings or negotiations.

8. *Collaborate with other professionals in identifying and making maximum use of exceptional students' abilities.* Finding and implementing solutions to the challenges of educat-

FOCUS ON **Concepts**

Teachers' Roles: What Should I Do Before I Make a Referral?

If you're thinking about referring a student, probably the most important thing you should do is contact the student's parents. If you can't reach them by phone, try a home visit or ask the visiting teacher (or school social worker, psychologist, or other support personnel) to help you set up a conference. It's very important that you discuss the student's problems with the parents before you refer. Parents should never be surprised to find that their child has been referred; they should know well in advance that their child's teachers have noticed problems. One of the most important things you can do to prevent conflict with parents is to establish and maintain communication with them regarding their child's progress.

Before making a referral, check all the student's school records. Look for information that could help you understand the student's behavioral or academic problems. Has the student ever:

■ Had a psychological evaluation?
■ Qualified for special services?
■ Been included in other special programs (e.g., programs for disadvantaged children or speech or language therapy)?
■ Scored far below average on standardized tests?
■ Been retained?

Do the records indicate:

■ Good progress in some areas and poor progress in others?
■ Any physical or medical problem?
■ That the student is taking medication?

Talk to the student's other teachers and professional support personnel about your concern for him or her. Have other teachers:

■ Also had difficulty with the student?
■ Found ways of dealing successfully with the student?

The analysis of information obtained in these ways can help you to teach and manage the student successfully or help you justify to the parents why you believe their child might need special education.

Before making a referral, you'll be expected to document the strategies that you've used in your class to meet the student's educational needs. Regardless of whether the student is later found to have a disabling condition, your documentation will be useful in the following ways:

■ You'll have evidence that will be helpful to or required by the committee of professionals who will evaluate the student.
■ You'll be better able to help the student's parents understand that methods used for other students in the class aren't adequate for their child.
■ You'll have records of successful and/or unsuccessful methods of working with the student that will be useful to you and any other teacher who works with the student in the future.

Your documentation of what you've done might appear to require a lot of paperwork, but careful record keeping will pay off. If the student is causing you serious concern, then you'll be wise to demonstrate your concern by keeping written records. Your notes should include items such as the following:

■ Exactly what you're concerned about
■ Why you're concerned about it
■ Dates, places, and times you've observed the problem
■ Precisely what you've done to try to resolve the problem
■ Who, if anyone, helped you devise the plans or strategies you've used
■ Evidence that the strategies have been successful or unsuccessful

In summary, make certain that you've accomplished the following before you make a referral:

■ Held at least one conference to discuss your concerns with the parents (or made extensive and documented efforts to communicate with the parents)
■ Checked all available school records and interviewed other professionals involved with the child
■ Documented the academic and behavioral management strategies that you've tried

Remember that you should refer a student only if you can make a convincing case that the student might have a disability and probably can't be served appropriately without special education. Referral for special education begins a time-consuming, costly, and stressful process that is potentially damaging to the student and has many legal ramifications.

ing exceptional students is not the exclusive responsibility of any one professional group. General and special education teachers are expected to share responsibility for educating students with special needs. In addition, teachers might need to collaborate with other professionals, depending on the given student's exceptionality. Psychologists, counselors, physicians, physical therapists, and a variety of other specialists might need teachers' perspectives on students' abilities and disabilities, and often rely on teachers to implement critical aspects of evaluation or treatment.

A high level of professional competence and ethical judgment is required to conform to these expectations. Teaching demands a thorough knowledge of child development and expertise in instruction. Furthermore, teachers are sometimes faced with serious professional and ethical dilemmas in trying to serve the needs of students and their parents, on the one hand, and in attempting to conform to legal or administrative pressures, on the other (Crockett & Kauffman, 1999; Howe & Miramontes, 1992; Kauffman & Hallahan, 2007). For example, when there are indications that a student might have a disability, should the teacher refer the student for evaluation and possible placement in special education, knowing that only inadequate or inappropriate services will be provided? Should a teacher who believes strongly that teenage students with mild intellectual disabilities need sex education refrain from giving students any information because sex education isn't part of the prescribed curriculum and is frowned on by the school board?

Expectations for Special Educators

In addition to being competent enough to meet the expectations for all teachers, special education teachers must attain special expertise in the following:

1. *Instructing students with learning problems.* The majority of students with disabilities have more difficulty learning academic skills than do those without disabilities. This is true for all categories of disabling conditions because sensory impairments, physical disabilities, and intellectual or emotional disabilities all tend to make academic learning more difficult. Often, the difficulty is slight; sometimes it is extreme. Special education teachers must have more than patience and hope, though they do need these qualities; they must also have the technical skill to present academic tasks so that students with disabilities will understand and respond appropriately. Exceptional instruction is the key to improving special education (Kauffman & Hallahan, 2005a; Kauffman & Landrum, 2007). Eight dimensions of instruction that make special education special are listed in Table 1.1—although these dimensions are not unique to special education. That is, they are not dimensions of instruction that *only* special educators know about or use. They are modifications or alterations of instructional processes that all teachers use in some way (Kauffman, in press). What makes special education special is not the instruction alone but instruction that is altered to meet the needs of exceptional learners. General education teachers may not be skilled in these instructional alterations to the extent that special educators are, or they may be unable to modify them in a class of typical students to the extent necessary to meet the needs of exceptional learners. Kauffman and Hallahan (2005a) point out that general education may be sort of special; Zigmond (2007) concludes it often takes special education teachers to make it as special as it should be.

General and special education teachers are expected to share responsibility for educating students with special needs and might need to collaborate with other professionals, depending on students' needs or disabilities.

TABLE 1.1	Dimensions of Special Education That Can Make It Truly Special	
Dimension of Instruction	**Definition**	**Alteration of Instruction**
1. Pace (Rate)	Speed of lesson; speed of introducing new concepts	Made slower or faster to meet student characteristics
2. Intensity	Demandingness; difficulty; complexity	Size of steps in learning, number of trials, frequency of reviews adjusted to fit learner
3. Relentlessness or Persistence	Insistence; tenacity; Stick-to-it-iveness	Repeated attempts, using different methods as required
4. Structure	Explicitness, predictability, teacher direction, tolerance, immediacy of consequences	Adjusted (tightened or loosened) to fit individual student
5. Reinforcement	Reward for desired behavior	Increased, made more frequent, immediate, and explicit or tangible as necessary
6. Pupil:Teacher Ratio (Class Size)	Number of students per teacher	Smaller, more individual
7. Curriculum	Content of instruction, purpose of activity	Determined by individual need
8. Monitoring (Assessment)	Keeping track of progress	Daily or near daily checking (testing) of achievement of specific tasks and goals

Source: Kauffman, J. M. & Hallahan, D. P. (2005). *Special education: What it is and why we need it.* Boston: Allyn & Bacon.

2. *Managing serious behavior problems.* Many students with disabilities have behavior problems in addition to their other exceptionalities. Some, in fact, require special education primarily because of their inappropriate or disruptive behavior. Special education teachers must be able to deal effectively with more than the usual troublesome behavior of students. Besides having understanding and empathy, special education teachers must master techniques to draw out particularly withdrawn students, control those who are hyperaggressive and persistently disruptive, and teach critical social skills. Positive, proactive behavior intervention plans are essential for all students who receive special education and exhibit serious behavior problems, regardless of their diagnostic label or classification (Kauffman, Mostert, Trent, & Pullen, 2006; Landrum & Kauffman, 2006).

3. *Evaluating technological advances.* Technology is increasingly applied to the problems of teaching exceptional students and improving their daily lives. New devices and methods are rapidly being developed, particularly for students with sensory and physical disabilities. Special education teachers need more than mere awareness of available technology; they also must be able to evaluate its advantages and disadvantages for teaching the exceptional children and youths with whom they work.

4. *Knowing special education law.* For good or ill, special education today involves many details of law. The rights of students with disabilities are spelled out in considerable detail in federal and state legislation. These laws, as well as the rules and regulations that accompany them, are constantly being interpreted by new court decisions, some of which have widespread implications for the practice of special education. Special educa-

tion teachers don't need to be lawyers, but they do need to be aware of legal requirements and prohibitions if they are to be adequate advocates for students with disabilities (Bateman, 2007; Huefner, 2006; Yell, 2006).

The knowledge and skills that every special education teacher is expected to master have been detailed by the primary professional organization of special educators, the Council for Exceptional Children (1998). We caution here that the specific day-to-day expectations for special education teachers vary from school system to school system and from state to state. These are general expectations and areas of competence with which every special educator will necessarily be concerned; however, special educators have a responsibility to offer not just good instruction but instruction that is highly individualized, intensive, relentless, urgent, and goal-directed (Hallahan, 2007; Kauffman & Hallahan, 2005a; Kauffman & Landrum, 2007; Zigmond, 1997, 2003, 2007). To this end, the special feature Responsive Instruction: Meeting the Needs of Students in each chapter (see introduction, p. 25) provides information about research-based practices to help make instruction intensive, relentless, and goal-directed.

History and Origins of Special Education

There have always been exceptional learners, but there haven't always been special educational services to address their needs (see Holmes, 2004; Metzler, 2006). During the closing years of the eighteenth century, following the American and French Revolutions, effective procedures were devised for teaching children with sensory impairments (i.e., those who were blind or deaf; Winzer, 1986, 1993, 1998). Early in the nineteenth century, the first systematic attempts were made to educate "idiotic" and "insane" children—those who today are said to have **intellectual disabilities** and **emotional or behavioral disorders** (or **emotional disturbance**; Kauffman & Landrum, 2006; Stichter et al., 2008).

In the prerevolutionary era, the most society had offered most children with disabilities was protection—asylum from a cruel world into which they didn't fit and in which they couldn't survive with dignity, if they could survive at all. But as the ideas of democracy, individual freedom, and egalitarianism swept across America and France, there was a change in attitude. Political reformers and leaders in medicine and education began to champion the cause of children and adults with disabilities, urging that these "imperfect" or "incomplete" individuals be taught skills that would allow them to become independent, productive citizens. These humanitarian sentiments went beyond a desire to protect and defend people with disabilities. The early leaders sought to normalize exceptional people to the greatest extent possible and confer on them the human dignity they presumably lacked.

Contemporary educational methods for exceptional children can be traced directly to techniques that were pioneered during the early 1800s. Many (perhaps most) of today's vital, controversial issues have been issues ever since the dawn of special education. Some contemporary writers believe that the history of special education is critically important to understanding today's issues and should receive more attention because of the lessons we can learn from our past (e.g., Kauffman, 1999a; Kauffman & Landrum, 2006; Smith, 1998a, 1998b). In our discussion of some of the major historical events and trends since 1800, we comment briefly on the history of people and ideas, the growth of the discipline, professional and parent organizations, and legislation.

UNDERSTANDING THE STANDARDS AND PRINCIPLES Trace the historical roots of special education practice (CEC Knowledge and Skill Standard CC1K1)

Council for Exceptional Children

Special Education Means Special Instruction

It [special education] is empirically supported practice, drawn from research. To provide special education means to set priorities and select carefully what needs to be taught. It means teaching something special and teaching it in a special way. (Zigmond, 1997, pp. 384–385)

Classwide peer tutoring, community-based instruction, mnemonics, direct instruction, self-monitoring, behavioral assessment, instructional adaptations, and adapted physical education—all are research-based practices that are used in today's classrooms. Research in special education has come a long way in the past twenty years (Gersten, Schiller, & Vaughn, 2000). There is now a more substantial research base of effective practices for use with students with disabilities. As in all endeavors, the current research base has limitations, and knowledge is added to it daily. That, combined with many other factors, makes it difficult for teachers to stay current in their knowledge of appropriate instructional practices (Schiller & Malouf, 2000).

Because we believe that effective, empirically supported practice is essential for teachers who work with students with disabilities, we have included a special feature in each disability chapter entitled Responsive Instruction. This feature describes a research-based practice in relative detail, what implications it has for the classroom, and where a teacher can get more information. The practices described within the Responsive Instruction boxes coincide with the CEC Standards for new special educators and provide valuable information for general educators as well. The purpose of the Responsive Instruction boxes is to assist students in connecting the theoretical information provided in the text with current, best-practices in the classroom. For students who are in the early stages of their special education preparation, the feature provides an example of a practical application; for students who are currently teaching or engaged in fieldwork, the feature can direct them to strategies or curricula for classroom use or further exploration.

People and Ideas

Most of the originators of special education were European physicians. They were primarily young, ambitious people who challenged the wisdom of the established authorities, including their own friends and mentors (Kanner, 1964; see also Kauffman & Landrum, 2006; Stichter et al., 2008; Winzer, 1998).

Most historians trace the beginning of special education as we know it today to Jean-Marc-Gaspard Itard (1775–1838), a French physician who was an authority on diseases of the ear and on the education of deaf students. In the early years of the nineteenth century, this young doctor began to educate a boy of about 12 years of age who had been found roaming naked and wild in the forests of France (sometime referred to as the "wild child" or the "wild boy of Avyron"). Itard's mentor, Philippe Pinel (1745–1826), a prominent French physician who was an early advocate of humane treatment of "insane" people, advised Itard that his efforts would be unsuccessful because the boy, Victor, was a "hopeless idiot." But Itard persevered. He did not eliminate Victor's disabilities, but he did dramatically improve the wild child's behavior through patient, systematic educative procedures (Itard, 1962).

One of Itard's students, Édouard Séguin (1812–1880), immigrated to the United States in 1848. Séguin had become famous as an educator of so-called idiotic children, even though most thinkers of the day were convinced that such children could not be taught anything of significance.

The ideas of the first special educators were truly revolutionary for their times. These are a few of the revolutionary ideas of Itard, Séguin, and their successors that form the foundation for present-day special education:

- *Individualized instruction*, in which the child's characteristics, rather than prescribed academic content, provide the basis for teaching techniques

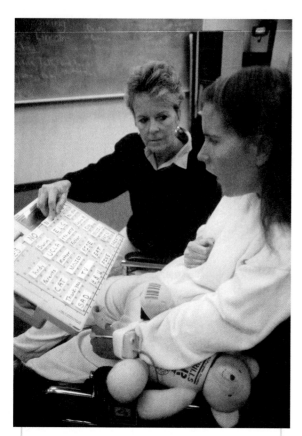

Special educators have the responsibility to offer not just good instruction, but also instruction that is highly individualized, intensive, relentless, urgent, and goal directed.

- *A carefully sequenced series of educational tasks*, beginning with tasks the child can perform and gradually leading to more complex learning

- *Emphasis on stimulation and awakening of the child's senses*, the aim being to make the child more aware of and responsive to educational stimuli

- *Meticulous arrangement of the child's environment*, so that the structure of the environment and the child's experience of it lead naturally to learning

- *Immediate reward for correct performance*, providing reinforcement for desirable behavior

- *Tutoring in functional skills*, the desire being to make the child as self-sufficient and productive as possible in everyday life

- *Belief that every child should be educated to the greatest extent possible*, the assumption being that every child can improve to some degree

So far, we've mentioned only European physicians who figured prominently in the rise of special education. Although much of the initial work did take place in Europe, many U.S. researchers contributed greatly during those early years. They kept informed of European developments as best they could, some of them traveling to Europe for the specific purpose of obtaining firsthand information about the education of children with disabilities.

Among the young U.S. thinkers who were concerned with the education of students with disabilities was Samuel Gridley Howe (1801–1876), an 1824 graduate of Harvard Medical School. Besides being a physician and an educator, Howe was a political and social reformer, a champion of humanitarian causes and emancipation. He was instrumental in founding the Perkins School for the Blind in Watertown, Massachusetts, and also taught students who were deaf and blind. His success in teaching Laura Bridgman, who was deaf and blind, greatly influenced the education of Helen Keller. In the 1840s, Howe was also a force behind the organization of an experimental school for children with intellectual disabilities [mental retardation] and was personally acquainted with Séguin.

When Thomas Hopkins Gallaudet (1787–1851), a minister, was a student at Andover Theological Seminary, he tried to teach a girl who was deaf. He visited Europe to learn about educating the deaf and in 1817 established the first American residential school, in Hartford, Connecticut, for students who were deaf (now known as the American School of the Deaf). Gallaudet University in Washington, D.C., the only liberal-arts college for students who are deaf, was named in his honor.

The early years of special education were vibrant with the pulse of new ideas. It isn't possible to read the words of Itard, Séguin, Howe, and their contemporaries without being captivated by the romance, idealism, and excitement of their exploits. The results they achieved were truly remarkable for their era. Today, special education remains a vibrant field in which innovations, excitement, idealism, and controversies are the norm. Teachers of exceptional children—and that includes all teachers, as noted previously—must understand how and why special education emerged as a discipline (Kauffman & Hallahan, 2005a).

Council for Exceptional Children (CEC) and Development of the Profession

Special education didn't suddenly spring up as a new discipline, nor did it develop in isolation from other disciplines. The emergence of psychology and sociology and especially the beginning of the widespread use of mental tests in the early years of the twentieth century had enormous implications for the growth of special education. Psychologists' study of learning and their prediction of school failure or success by means of tests helped to focus attention on children with special needs. Sociologists, social workers, and anthropologists drew attention to the ways in which exceptional children's families and communities responded to them and affected their learning and adjustment. Anecdotal accounts of intellectual disabilities or mental disorders can be found in the nineteenth-century literature, but they are not presented within the conceptual frameworks that we recognize today as psychology, sociology, and special education (see, for example, Hallahan & Kauffman, 1977; Kauffman & Landrum, 2006; Richards & Singer, 1998). Even in the early twentieth century, the concepts of disability seem crude by today's standards (see Trent, 1998).

As the education profession itself matured and as compulsory school attendance laws became a reality, there was a growing realization among teachers and school administrators that a large number of students must be given something beyond the ordinary classroom experience. Elizabeth Farrell, a teacher in New York City in the early twentieth century, was highly instrumental in the development of special education as a profession. She and the New York City superintendent of schools attempted to use information about child development, social work, mental testing, and instruction to address the needs of children and youths who were being ill served in or excluded from regular classes and schools. Farrell was a great advocate for services for students with special needs (see Safford & Safford, 1998). Her motives and those of the teachers and administrators who worked with her were to see that every student—including every exceptional child or youth—had an appropriate education and received the related health and social services necessary for optimum learning in school (Hendrick & MacMillan, 1989; MacMillan & Hendrick, 1993). In 1922, Farrell and a group of other special educators from across the United States and Canada founded the Council for Exceptional Children, which is still the primary professional organization of special educators.

Contemporary special education is a professional field with roots in several academic disciplines—especially medicine, psychology, sociology, and social work—in addition to professional education. It's a discipline that is sufficiently different from the mainstream of professional education to require special training programs but sufficiently like the mainstream to maintain a primary concern for schools and teaching.

Parents and Other Professional Organizations

Individuals and ideas have played crucial roles in the history of special education, but it's accurate to say that much of the progress that has been made over the years has been achieved primarily by the collective efforts of parents and professionals. Professional groups were organized first, beginning in the nineteenth century. Effective national parent organizations have existed in the United States only since about 1950.

Parent organizations, though offering membership to individuals who may not have exceptional children, primarily comprise parents who do have such children and concentrate on issues that are of special concern to them. Parent organizations have typically served three essential functions: (1) providing an informal group for parents who understand one another's problems and needs and help one another deal with anxieties and frustrations, (2) providing information regarding services and potential resources, and (3) providing the structure for obtaining needed services for their children. Some of

UNDERSTANDING THE STANDARDS AND PRINCIPLES How did Itard, Séguin, Howe, and Gallaudet shape the field of special education? (CEC Knowledge and Skills Standard GC1K3)

INTERNET RESOURCES

You might want to explore the Website of the Council for Exceptional Children at www.cec.sped.org
For more information about the history of special education, see www.npr.org/programs/disability and www.disabilityhistory.org

Video Homework Exercise

Least Restrictive Environment • Go to the Homework and Exercises section in Chapter 1 of MyEducationLab to watch the video "The Inclusive Classroom," which demonstrates aspects of the least restrictive environment.

the organizations that came about primarily as the result of parents' efforts include the ARC (formerly the Association for Retarded Citizens), the National Association for Gifted Children, the Learning Disabilities Association, the Autism Society of America, and the Federation of Families for Children's Mental Health.

Legislation and Litigation

Much of the progress in meeting the educational needs of children and youths with disabilities is attributable to laws requiring states and localities to include students with special needs in the public education system (Bateman, 2007; Bateman & Linden, 2006; Huefner, 2006). We focus here on recent legislation that represents a culmination of decades of legislative history. However, litigation (lawsuits or court decisions) has also played a major role in special education.

IDEA, ADA, and NCLB

■ **Education for All Handicapped Children Act** Also known as Public Law 94-142, which became law in 1975 and is now known as the Individuals with Disabilities Education Act (IDEA).

A landmark federal law was passed in 1975: the **Education for All Handicapped Children Act**, commonly known as P.L. 94–142.* In 1990, this law was amended to become the **Individuals with Disabilities Education Act (IDEA)**. In 1997, the law was amended again, but its name was not changed (see Bateman & Linden, 2006; and Yell, 2006, for details). The law was reauthorized again in 2004, as the Individuals with Disabilities Education Improvement Act (IDEIA; see Huefner, 2006 for details). The 2004 reauthorization is sometimes referred to as IDEA 2004 (Stichter et al., 2008), but for the sake of simplicity we refer to it more simply as IDEA, as the basic requirements of the law have not changed. The federal law known as IDEA ensures that all children and youths with disabilities have the right to a free, appropriate public education.

■ **Individuals with Disabilities Education Act (IDEA)** The Individuals with Disabilities Education Act was enacted in 1990 and reauthorized in 1997 and 2004; it replaced PL 94-142, enacted in 1975. This federal law requires that to receive funds under the act, every school system in the nation must provide a free, appropriate public education for every child between the ages of three and twenty-one, regardless of how or how seriously he or she may be disabled.

Another landmark federal law, enacted in 1990, is the **Americans with Disabilities Act (ADA)**. ADA ensures the right of individuals with disabilities to nondiscriminatory treatment in other aspects of their lives; it provides protections of civil rights in the specific areas of employment, transportation, public accommodations, state and local government, and telecommunications.

IDEA and another federal law focusing on intervention in early childhood (P.L. 99-457) mandate a free, appropriate public education for every child or youth between the ages of three and twenty-one regardless of the nature or severity of the disability. P.L. 99-457 also provides incentives for states to develop early intervention programs for infants with known disabilities and those who are considered to be at risk. Together, these laws require public school systems to identify all children and youths with disabilities and to provide the special education and related services to these students.

■ **Americans with Disabilities Act (ADA)** Civil rights legislation for persons with disabilities ensuring nondiscrimination in a broad range of activities.

The federal law we now know as IDEA was revolutionary because it was the first federal law mandating free, appropriate public education for all children with disabilities. Its basic provisions are described in the Focus on Concepts on p. 29.

Historically, legislation has been increasingly specific and mandatory. Beginning in the 1980s, however, a renewed emphasis on states' rights and local autonomy plus a political strategy of federal deregulation led to attempts to repeal some of the provisions of IDEA (then still known as P.L. 94-142) and loosen federal rules and regulations. Federal disinvestment in education and deregulation of special education programs remain popular ideas. It's not surprising that federal mandates for special education have come under fire. Dissatisfaction with federal mandates is due in part to the fact that the federal government

---

*Legislation is often designated PL (for public law), followed by a hyphenated numeral, the first set of digits representing the number of the Congress that passed the bill and the second set representing the number of that bill. Thus, PL 94-142 was the 142nd public law passed by the 94th Congress.

FOCUS ON **Concepts**

Major Provisions of IDEA

Each state and locality must have a plan to ensure*:

Identification	Extensive efforts to screen and identify all children and youths with disabilities.
Free, Appropriate Public Education (FAPE)	Every student with a disability has an appropriate public education at no cost to the parents or guardian.
Due Process	The student's and parents' rights to information and informed consent before the student is evaluated, labeled, or placed, and the right to an impartial due process hearing if they disagree with the school's decisions.
Parent/Guardian Surrogate Consultation	The student's parents or guardian are consulted about the student's evaluation and placement and the educational plan; if the parents or guardian are unknown or unavailable, a surrogate parent must be found to act for the student.
Least Restrictive Environment (LRE)	The student is educated in the least restrictive environment consistent with his or her educational needs and, insofar as possible, with students without disabilities.
Individualized Education Program (IEP)	A written individualized education program is prepared for each student with a disability, including levels of functioning, long-term goals, extent to which the student will *not* participate in the general education classroom and curriculum, services to be provided, plans for initiating and evaluating the services, and needed transition services (from school to work or continued education).
Nondiscriminatory Evaluation	The student is evaluated in all areas of suspected disability and in a way that is not biased by his or her language or cultural characteristics or disabilities. Evaluation must be by a multidisciplinary team, and no single evaluation procedure may be used as the sole criterion for placement or planning.
Confidentiality	The results of evaluation and placement are kept confidential, though the student's parents or guardian may have access to the records.
Personnel Development, Inservice	Training for teachers and other professional personnel, including inservice training for general education teachers, in meeting the needs of students with disabilities.

*Detailed federal rules and regulations govern the implementation of each of these major provisions.

contributes relatively little to the funding of special education. Although the demands of IDEA are detailed, state and local governments pay most of the cost of special education programs. Some have characterized the legal history of special education as a "long, strange trip" (Yell, Rogers, & Rogers, 1998, p. 219).

Special education law is highly controversial, and battles over IDEA are ongoing. The amendment and continuation of IDEA in 1997 and 2004 represented a sustained commitment to require schools, employers, and government agencies to recognize the abilities of people with disabilities, but the extent to which the 2004 revision of the law represents actual improvement is debatable (Turnbull, 2007; Vitello, 2007). IDEA and ADA require reasonable accommodations that will allow those who have disabilities to participate to the fullest extent possible in all the activities of daily living that individuals without disabilities take for granted. The requirements of ADA are intended to grant equal opportunities to people with disabilities in employment, transportation, public accommodations, state and local government, and telecommunications.

INTERNET RESOURCES

You can access current information about IDEA at: www.ideapractices .org and at www.ed.gov/inits/ commissionsboards/ whspecialeducation/index.html

In the early twenty-first century, under the administration of President George W. Bush, the federal No Child Left Behind Act (NCLB) became a major factor in the focus of public schooling, including special education (see Huefner, 2006; Yell & Drasgow, 2005). NCLB was an attempt to improve the academic performance of all students, including those with disabilities. In fact, under NCLB and IDEA, most students with disabilities are expected to take standard tests of academic achievement and to achieve at a level equal to that of students without disabilities. Moreover, NCLB included the requirement that eventually all teachers be "highly qualified," a designation that leaves much to interpretation (Gelman, Pullen, & Kauffman, 2004). Some have noted that core requirements of NCLB are neither reasonable nor achievable, particularly with reference to special education (Kauffman, 2004, 2005; Kauffman & Konold, 2007; Rothstein, Jacobsen, & Wilder, 2006).

Rowley and Other Court Cases

Laws often have little or no effect on the lives of individuals with disabilities until courts interpret exactly what the laws require in practice. Exceptional children, primarily through the actions of parent and professional organizations, have been getting their day in court more frequently since IDEA and related federal and state laws were passed. Therefore, we must examine litigation to complete the picture of how the U.S. legal system may safeguard or undermine appropriate education for exceptional children.

Zelder (1953) noted that in the early days of public education, school attendance was seen as a privilege that could be awarded to or withheld from an individual child at the discretion of local school officials. During the late nineteenth and early twentieth centuries, the courts typically found that disruptive children or those with mental retardation [intellectual disabilities] could be excluded from school for the sake of preserving order, protecting the teacher's time from excessive demands, and sparing children the discomfort of seeing others who are disabled. In the first half of the twentieth century, the courts tended to defend the majority of schoolchildren from a disabled minority. But now the old excuses for excluding students with disabilities from school are no longer thought to be valid.

Today, the courts must interpret laws that define school attendance as the right of every child, regardless of his or her disability. Litigation is now focused on ensuring that every child receives an education that is appropriate for his or her individual needs. As some legal scholars have pointed out, this doesn't mean that laws or litigation support full inclusion of all children with disabilities in general education (Bateman, 2007; Dupre, 1997; Huefner, 1994, 2006).

Litigation may involve legal suits filed for either of two reasons: because special education services aren't being provided for students whose parents want them or because students are being assigned to special education when their parents believe that they shouldn't be. Suits for special education have been brought primarily by parents whose children are unquestionably disabled and are being denied any education at all or are being given very meager special services. The parents who file these suits believe that the advantages of their children's identification for special education services clearly outweigh the disadvantages. Suits against special education have been brought primarily by parents of students who have mild or questionable disabilities and who are already attending school. These parents believe that their children are being stigmatized and discriminated against rather than helped by special education. Thus, the courts today are asked to make decisions in which individual students' characteristics are weighed against specific educational programs.

Parents want their children with disabilities to have a free public education that meets their needs but doesn't stigmatize them unnecessarily and that permits them to

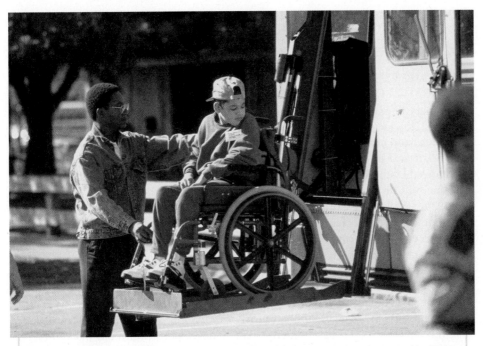

The Individuals with Disabilities Education Act (IDEA), passed in 1990 and renewed in 1997 and 2004, requires public schools to provide equal educational opportunities for all students with disabilities.

be taught in the general education classroom as much as possible. The laws governing education recognize parents' and students' rights to such an education. In the courts today, the burden of proof is ultimately on local and state education specialists, who must show in every instance that the student's abilities and disabilities have been completely and accurately assessed and that appropriate educational procedures are being employed. Much of the special education litigation has involved controversy over the use of intelligence (IQ) and other standardized testing to determine students' eligibility for special education. Although there has been much acrimony in the debate about IQ tests, some scholars have found that IQ scores themselves haven't been the primary means of classifying children as eligible for special education (MacMillan & Forness, 1998).

One historic court case of the 1980s deserves particular consideration. In 1982, the U.S. Supreme Court made its first interpretation of PL 94-142 (now IDEA) in *Hudson v. Rowley*, a case involving Amy Rowley, a child who was deaf (*Board of Education of Hendrick Hudson v. Rowley* 484 US 176, 1982). The Court's decision was that appropriate education for a deaf child with a disability does not necessarily mean education that will produce the maximum possible achievement. Amy's parents had contended that she might be able to learn more in school if she were provided with a sign language interpreter. But the Court decided that because the school had designed an individualized program of special services for Amy and she was achieving at or above the level of her nondisabled classmates, the school system had met its obligation under the law to provide an appropriate education. Future cases will undoubtedly help to clarify what the law means by "appropriate education" and "least restrictive environment" (Bateman, 2007; Crockett & Kauffman, 1999; Huefner, 1994, 2006; Yell, 2005).

INTERNET RESOURCES

For updates on legal issues in special education, see the Website maintained by legal expert Dixie Snow Huefner and click on "Chapter Updates" www.ed.utah .edu/~huefner/sped-law/ spdlawlbk.htm

Reading Homework Exercise

Hudson v. Rowley ● Go to the Homework and Exercises section in Chapter 1 of MyEducationLab to read the opinion of the U.S. Supreme Court in the *Board of Education of Hendrick Hudson v. Rowley.*

The Intent of Special Education Law: Individualized Education for Students with Disabilities

■ **Individualized education program (IEP)**
IDEA requires an IEP to be drawn up by the educational team for each exceptional child; the IEP must include a statement of present educational performance, instructional goals, educational services to be provided, and criteria and procedures for determining that the instructional objectives are being met.

Teacher Artifact Homework Exercise

IEP's ● Go to the Homework and Exercises section in Chapter 1 of MyEducationLab to gain familiarity with some of the primary components of an IEP.

The primary intent of the special education laws passed since 1975 has been to require educators to focus on the needs of individual students with disabilities. The **individualized education program (IEP)** is the most important aspect of this focus; it spells out how a school plans to meet an exceptional student's needs, and the plan must be approved by the student's parents or guardian. IEPs vary greatly in format and detail from one child to another and from one school district to another. Guides for help in writing IEPs are available (e.g., Gibb & Dyches, 2007).

Some school districts use computerized IEP systems to help teachers determine goals and instructional objectives and to save time and effort in writing the documents. Legally, such cut-and-paste IEPs might be questionable because they lack sufficient attention to the particular needs of individuals (see Bateman, 2007; Bateman & Linden, 2006). Many school systems, however, still rely on teachers' knowledge of students and curriculum to complete handwritten IEPs on a district's forms.

Federal and state regulations don't specify exactly how much detail must be included in an IEP, only that it must be a written statement developed in a meeting of a representative of the local school district, the teacher, the parents or guardian, and (whenever appropriate) the child, and that it must include certain elements (see Table 1.2 for reminders and tips). Moreoever, IDEA now allows experimentation with multi-year IEPs under certain circumstances (see Huefner, 2006).

TABLE 1.2   **IEP Reminders and Tips**

1. Because the IEP is at the core of the substantive requirements of IDEA, *all* teachers—including general education teachers, not just special educators—must be trained to understand its purpose and function. General educators who are responsible for implementing any portion of a child's IEP must have access at least to that portion and should be informed of their responsibilities.

2. General educators should see their increased role in IEP development as an opportunity to solicit the program supports needed to make the general education classroom appropriate for children with disabilities. "Dumping" a child into a general classroom without the necessary program supports and supplementary services is unacceptable under IDEA, and general educators have leverage to see that it does not happen.

3. Teachers need to work more closely than ever with parents. Requirements to issue periodic progress reports and to revise IEPs to address lack of progress encourage parental involvement on a regular and continuing basis.

4. Special and general education teachers must balance students' need for achievement in the general curriculum with their need for a specialized curriculum in other areas. Functional curriculum needs should not be sacrificed to the academic curriculum.

5. School officials should be aware that hearing officers and courts are permitted to determine that procedural violations of the IEP process constitute a denial of free, appropriate public education (FAPE) if (1) they impeded the child's right to FAPE, (2) significantly impeded the parents' opportunity to participate in the FAPE decision-making process, or (3) caused a deprivation of educational benefits. If the procedural violations did not produce these substantive violations, they will be considered harmless.

Source: Huefner, D. S. (2006). *Getting comfortable with special education law: A framework for working with children with disabilities* (2nd ed. pp. 192–193). Norwood, MA: Christopher-Gordon, Reprinted by permission.

Individualized Education Program

Student: __Curt_____ Age: __15_____ Grade: __9_____ Date: __1998_____

Unique educational needs, characteristics, and measured present levels of academic achievement and functional performance (PLOPs) *(including how the disability affects the student's ability to participate & progress in the general curriculum)*	Special education, related services and supplemental aids and services, (based on peer-reviewed research to the extent practicable); assistive technology and modifications or personnel support *(including anticipated starting date, frequency, duration, and location for each)*	Measurable annual goals and short-term objectives (progress markers),[1] including academic and functional goals to enable students to be involved in and make progress in the general curriculum and to meet other needs resulting from the disability *(including progress measurement method for each goal)*

Present Level of Social Skills:
 	
Curt lashes out violently when not able to complete work, uses profanity, and refuses to follow further directions from adults.[2]
 	
Social Needs:
 	
• To learn anger management skills, especially regarding swearing
 	
• To learn to comply with requests
	1. Teacher and/or counselor consult with behavior specialist regarding techniques and programs for teaching skills, especially anger management.
	
	2. Provide anger management for Curt.
	
	  Services 3 times/week, 30 minutes.
	
	3. Establish a peer group which involves role playing, etc., so Curt can see positive role models and practice newly learned anger management skills.
	
	  Services 2 times/week, 30 minutes.
	
	4. Develop a behavioral plan for Curt which gives him responsibility for charting his own behavior.
	
	5. Provide a teacher or some other adult mentor to spend time with Curt (talking, game playing, physical activity, etc.).
	
	  Services 2 times/week, 30 minutes.
	
	6. Provide training for the mentor regarding Curt's needs/goals.
		Goal: During the last quarter of the academic year, Curt will have 2 or fewer detentions for any reason.
		
		Obj. 1: At the end of the 1st quarter, Curt will have had 10 or fewer detentions.
		
		Obj. 2: At the end of the 2nd quarter, Curt will have had 7 or fewer detentions.
		
		Obj. 3: At the end of the 3rd quarter, Curt will have had 4 or fewer detentions.
		
		Goal: Curt will manage his behavior and language in an acceptable manner as reported by all of his teachers.
		
		Obj. 1: At 2 weeks, asked at the end of class if Curt's behavior and language were acceptable or unacceptable, 3 out of 6 teachers will say "acceptable."
		
		Obj. 2: At 6 weeks, asked the same question, 4 out of 6 teachers will say "acceptable."
		
		Obj. 3: At 12 weeks, asked the same question, 6 out of 6 teachers will say "acceptable."

[1]For students who take an alternative assessment and are assessed against other than grade level standards, the IEP **must** include short-term objectives (progress markers). For other students, the IEP **may** include short-term objectives. The IEP **must** for all students clearly articulate how the student's progress will be measured, and that progress must be reported to parents at designated intervals.
[2]This PLOP would be more useful if it were qualified, e.g., more than 4 times daily.

FIGURE 1.4   Sample IEP for Curt

Source: Reprinted with permission from Bateman, B. D., & Linden, M. A. (2006). *Better IEPs: How to develop legally correct and educationally useful programs* (4th ed.). Verona, WI: Attainment Company, Inc.

The IEP that is written in most schools contains much information related to the technical requirements of IDEA in addition to the heart of the plan: its instructional components. Figure 1.4 shows what an IEP might look like. Curt "is a ninth-grade low achiever who was considered by the district to be a poorly motivated disciplinary problem student with a 'bad attitude.' His parents recognized him as a very discouraged, frustrated

Unique educational needs, characteristics, and measured present levels of academic achievement and functional performance (PLOPs)	Special education, related services and supplemental aids and services, (based on peer-reviewed research to the extent practicable); assistive technology and modifications or personnel support	Measurable annual goals and short-term objectives (progress markers),[1] including academic and functional goals to enable students to be involved in and make progress in the general curriculum and to meet other needs resulting from the disability
(including how the disability affects the student's ability to participate & progress in the general curriculum)	*(including anticipated starting date, frequency, duration, and location for each)*	*(including progress measurement method for each goal)*

Study Skills/ Organizational Needs:
 	
• How to read text
• Note taking
• How to study notes
• Memory work
• Be prepared for class, with materials
• Lengthen and improve attention span and on-task behavior
 	
Present Level:
 	
Curt currently lacks skill in all these areas.
	1. Speech/lang. therapist, resource room teacher, and content area teachers will provide Curt with direct and specific teaching of study skills, i.e.
	
	  • Note taking from lectures
	  • Note taking while reading text
	  • How to study notes for a test
	  • Memorization hints
	  • Strategies for reading text to retain information
	
	2. Assign a "study buddy" for Curt in each content area class.
	
	3. Prepare a motivation system for Curt to be prepared for class with all necessary materials.
	
	4. Develop a motivational plan to encourage Curt to lengthen his attention span and time on task.
	
	5. Provide aide to monitor on-task behaviors in first month or so of plan and teach Curt self-monitoring techniques.
	
	6. Provide motivational system and self-recording form for completion of academic tasks in each class.
		Goal: At the end of academic year, Curt will have better grades and, by his own report, will have learned new study skills.
		
		Obj. 1: Given a 20–30 min. lecture/oral lesson, Curt will take appropriate notes as judged by that teacher.
		
		Obj. 2: Given 10–15 pgs. of text to read, Curt will employ an appropriate strategy for retaining info.—i.e., mapping, webbing, outlining, notes, etc.—as judged by the teacher.
		
		Obj. 3: Given notes to study for a test, Curt will do so successfully as evidenced by his test score.

[1]For students who take an alternative assessment and are assessed against other than grade level standards, the IEP **must** include short-term objectives (progress markers). For other students, the IEP **may** include short-term objectives. The IEP **must** for all students clearly articulate how the student's progress will be measured, and that progress must be reported to parents at designated intervals.

FIGURE 1.4 *(Continued)*

student who had learning disabilities, especially in language arts" (Bateman & Linden, 2006, p. 150).

As mentioned earlier, there is no standard IEP format used by all schools. An entire IEP might be a document of ten pages or more, depending on the format and the extent and complexity of the student's disabilities. The emphasis should be on writing an IEP that is clear, useful, and legally defensible, not on the IEP format (Bateman & Linden, 1998; Huefner, 2006). Clear and explicit relationships among IEP components are

Unique educational needs, characteristics, and measured present levels of academic achievement and functional performance (PLOPs)	Special education, related services and supplemental aids and services, (based on peer-reviewed research to the extent practicable); assistive technology and modifications or personnel support	Measurable annual goals and short-term objectives (progress markers),[1] including academic and functional goals to enable students to be involved in and make progress in the general curriculum and to meet other needs resulting from the disability
(including how the disability affects the student's ability to participate & progress in the general curriculum)	*(including anticipated starting date, frequency, duration, and location for each)*	*(including progress measurement method for each goal)*
Academic Needs/ Written Language: Curt needs strong remedial help in spelling, punctuation, capitalization, and usage. Present Level: Curt is approximately 2 grade levels behind his peers in these skills.	1. Provide direct instruction in written language skills (punctuation, capitalization, usage, spelling) by using a highly structured, well-sequenced program. Services provided in small group of no more than four students in the resource room, 50 minutes/day. 2. Build in continuous and cumulative review to help with short-term rote memory difficulty. 3. Develop a list of commonly used words in student writing (or use one of many published lists) for Curt's spelling program.	*Goal:* Within one academic year, Curt will improve his written language skills by 1.5 or 2 full grade levels to a 6.0 grade level as measured by a standardized test. Obj. 1: Given 10 sentences of dictation at his current level of instruction, Curt will punctuate and capitalize with 90% accuracy (checked at the end of each unit taught). Obj. 2: Given 30 sentences with choices of usage, at his current instructional level, Curt will make the correct choice in 28 or more sentences. Obj. 3: Given a list of 150 commonly used words in 6th grade writing, Curt will spell 95% of the words correctly.

Adaptations to Regular Program:

- In all classes, Curt should sit near the front of the class.
- Curt should be called on often to keep him involved and on task.
- All teachers should help Curt with study skills as trained by spelling/language specialist and resource room teacher.
- Teachers should monitor Curt's work closely in the beginning weeks/months of his program.

[1]For students who take an alternative assessment and are assessed against other than grade level standards, the IEP **must** include short-term objectives (progress markers). For other students, the IEP **may** include short-term objectives. The IEP **must** for all students clearly articulate how the student's progress will be measured, and that progress must be reported to parents at designated intervals.

FIGURE 1.4 *(Continued)*

required to make sure that the focus of the individualized program—special, individually tailored instruction to meet unique needs—is not lost. In Curt's IEP (Figure 1.4), the relationships among the components are maintained by the alignment of information across columns. Reading across the form, we find first a description of the unique characteristic or need and present level of performance, then the special services and modifications that are needed to address that need, and then the annual goals and objectives or benchmarks related to the need. Under IDEA, not all IEPs must include short-term objectives; if the student is participating in standard (not alternate) assessments of academic achievement required by NCLB, the IEP doesn't have to include short-term objectives.

The process of writing an IEP and the document itself are perhaps the most important features of compliance with the spirit and letter of IDEA. Table 1.3 (page 36) summarizes what educators should and shouldn't do in writing IEPs. Bateman and Linden

UNDERSTANDING THE STANDARDS AND PRINCIPLES Who should be involved in the development of a student's IEP? (INTASC 1.11)

INTASC

TABLE 1.3 Do's and Don'ts for Individualized Education Programs (IEPs)

Do	Don't
Guarantee full and equal parent participation	Fail to individualize the program to fit the student
Truly individualize instruction to fit the student	Fail to address all the student's needs
Make sure present levels of performance (PLOPs), needs, and characteristics are carefully specified	Fail to describe sufficiently and specify all necessary services
Fully detail all services, modifications, and supports to meet the student's needs	Fail to write clear, objective, meaningful, and reasonable PLOPs, objectives, and goals
Make certain that goals and objectives are measurable, real, and taken seriously	

Source: From Information contained in Bateman, B. D., & Linden, M. A. (2006). *Better IEPs: How to develop legally correct and educationally useful programs* (4th ed.). Verona, WI: Attainment Company, Inc.

Building Teaching Skills Exercise

IEP Writing ● Go to the Building Teaching Skills section in Chapter 1 of MyEducationLab to access a Website that offers a useful and thorough web-based tutorial about the IEP process.

(2006) summarize compliance with both the spirit and the letter of the law. When the IEP is prepared as intended by the law, it means that:

- The student's needs have been carefully assessed.
- A team of professionals and the parents have worked together to design a program of education to best meet the student's needs.
- Goals and objectives are clearly stated so that progress in reaching them can be evaluated.

A major problem is that the IEP is often written at the wrong time and for the wrong reason (Bateman & Linden, 2006). As Figure 1.5 (below) illustrates, the legal IEP is written after evaluation and identification of the student's disabilities and before a placement decision is made; what the student needs is determined first, and then a decision is made about placement in the least restrictive environment in which the needed services can be provided. Too often, we see the educationally wrong (and illegal) practice of basing the IEP on an available placement; that is, a student's IEP is written after available placements and services have been considered.

FIGURE 1.5 The right and wrong routes to placement

Source: Adapted by permission from Bateman, B. D., & Linden, M. A. (2006). *Better IEPs: How to develop legally correct and educationally useful programs* (4th ed.). Verona, WI: Attainment Company, Inc.

Legislation and litigation were initially used in the 1960s and 1970s to include exceptional children in public education with relatively little regard for the quality of the education. Since the 1980s, laws and lawsuits have been used to try to ensure individualized education, cooperation, and collaboration among professionals; parental participation; and accountability of educators for providing high-quality, effective programs.

IDEA, for example, is noteworthy for its expansion of the idea of individualized planning and collaboration among disciplines. P.L. 99-457 mandated an **individualized family service plan (IFSP)** for infants and toddlers with disabilities (Stichter et al., 2008). An IFSP is similar to an IEP in that it requires assessment and statement of goals, needed services, and plans for implementation. As we will discuss in Chapter 2, an IFSP also requires more involvement of the family, coordination of services, and plans for making the transition to preschool. IDEA mandates the inclusion of plans for transition from school to work for older students as part of their IEPs. Other provisions of IDEA are intended to improve the quality of services received by children and youths with disabilities.

In the early twenty-first century, some people expressed considerable unhappiness with the results of federal legislation and litigation. Critics have charged that laws that were intended to ensure the appropriate education of students with disabilities have gone awry and that new legislation and federal rules are required (e.g., Finn, Rotherham, & Hokanson, 2001). Others have suggested that the right instruction is actually the key to improving special education (e.g., Kauffman, 2002; Kauffman & Hallahan, 2005a; Kauffman & Landrum, 2007; Zigmond, 2003, 2007).

■ **IFSP**
A plan mandated by P.L. 99-457 to provide services for young children with disabiities (under age 3) and their families.

The Progress of Special Education

Special education has come a long way since it was introduced into U.S. public education over a century ago. It has become an expected part of the public education system, a given rather than an exception or an experiment. Much progress has been made since IDEA was enacted over a quarter century ago. Now parents and their children have legal rights to free, appropriate education; they aren't powerless in the face of school administrators who don't want to provide appropriate education and related services. The enactment of IDEA was one of very few events in the twentieth century that altered the power relationship between schools and parents (Sarason, 1990). The basic points about IEPs are reviewed in Table 1.4 on page 38.

Although IDEA and related laws and court cases have not resulted in flawless programs for exceptional children, they have done much to move U.S. public schools toward providing better educational opportunities for those with disabilities (Bateman, 2007). Laws enacted in the twentieth century helped to ensure that all infants and toddlers with disabilities receive early intervention. Laws such as ADA help to ensure that children and adults with disabilities won't be discriminated against in U.S. society. Laws and court cases can't eliminate all problems in our society, but they can certainly be of enormous help in our efforts to equalize opportunities and minimize handicaps for people with disabilities. But more than law is required to give children with disabilities the education they need. Special education also depends on guidance from other concepts and perspectives, specifically the emphasis on prevention, early intervention, and effective treatment based on scientific thinking that modern medicine seeks to offer (Kauffman & Hallahan, 1974; Kauffman, 2007).

We have made much progress in special education, but making it all that we hope for is—and always will be—a continuing struggle. In Chapter 2, we discuss current trends and issues that highlight dissatisfaction with the way things are and represent hope for what special education and related services might become.

TABLE 1.4 **Answers to Three Basic Questions about IEPs**

1. What must be included in an IEP?

   An IEP must include the following:

   (a) the child's present levels of academic achievement and functional performance;

   (b) measurable annual academic and functional goals that address the child's special education needs relating to both the general curriculum and areas independent of the general curriculum;

   (c) how progress toward the goals will be measured and when periodic reports of progress toward the goals will be issued;

   (d) the specific special education and related services, supplementary aids and services, and program modifications or staff supports to be provided;

   (e) the extent to which the child will not be participating with nondisabled children in the regular class and in extracurricular and nonacademic activities;

   (f) appropriate accommodations, if any, in the administration of state or district-wide assessments of achievement (or statements about the child's alternative assessments);

   (g) the anticipated frequency, duration, and location of services and program modifications; and

   (h) transition goals and services beginning by the time of the first IEP that is in effect when the child is 16 years old.

2. Who should be on the IEP team?

   IEP team members include the parent(s), at least one special educator (or provider of special education), and, in most instances, a general education teacher of the child. An official representative of the LEA [local education agency] and someone who can interpret the instructional implications of evaluation results must also be on the team, but the special or general educator might be able to serve in these positions. The child and others who have "knowledge or special expertise" regarding the child may also be on the team, as appropriate.

3. What are some of the reasons that development of an IEP is so crucial to the effective implementation of IDEA?

   It is the best means of developing home-school cooperation in the education of a child with a disability, it is the basis for determining the appropriate placement, and it is the primary mechanism for determining whether FAPE is being provided.

Source: Huefner, D. S. (2006). *Getting comfortable with special education law: A framework for working with children with disabilities* (2nd ed.). Norwood, MA: Christopher-Gordon, pp. 193–194. Reprinted by permission.

Summary

How can we get oriented to exceptionality and special education?

▶ Exceptionality involves similarities and differences.

▶ Reasons for optimism include better treatment and education, medical breakthroughs, and prevention.

▶ Abilities as well as disabilities must be recognized.

▶ A disability is an inability to do something; a handicap is a limitation that is imposed on someone.

▶ Not all inabilities are disabilities; a disability is an inability to do something that most people, with typical maturation, opportunity, or instruction, can do.

What is the educational definition of exceptional learners?

▶ *Exceptional learners* are those who require special education to reach their full potential.

▶ Many individuals with disabilities require special education, but some do not.

What is the prevalence of exceptional learners?

▶ About 10 students in every 100 (about 10 percent of the student population) are identified as exceptional for special education purposes.

- Some categories of disability are considered high-incidence because they are found relatively frequently (e.g., learning disabilities, communication disorders, emotional or behavioral disorders).

- Some categories of disability are considered low-incidence because they occur relatively rarely (e.g., blindness, deafness, deaf-blindness).

What is the definition of special education?

▶ *Special education* means specially designed instruction that meets the unusual needs of an exceptional student. It may include special materials, teaching techniques, or equipment and/or facilities.

How is special education provided?

▶ Special education may range from a few special provisions made by the student's regular teacher to twenty-four-hour residential care in a special facility. The plan that is chosen depends on two factors:
  - How and how much the student differs from average students
  - What resources are available in the school and community

▶ Different placement options include the following, plus combinations:
  - General education placement with the teacher making accommodations
  - General education with consultation
  - Itinerant services from a specialist
  - Resource room services
  - Special self-contained class
  - Special day school
  - Hospital or homebound instruction
  - Residential school

▶ Federal law (IDEA) calls for placement in the least restrictive environment (LRE) that is compatible with the student's individual needs.

▶ The trend is toward placement in environments closest to the general education classroom in format, especially for younger children.

What are teachers' roles in special education?

▶ All teachers must be prepared to work with exceptional learners.

▶ The relationship between general and special education is becoming closer.

▶ Students who are at risk are becoming an increasingly important issue.

▶ Inclusion is a controversial and important issue.

▶ All educators are expected to do the following:
  - Make maximum effort to accommodate individual students' needs
  - Evaluate academic abilities and disabilities

  - Refer students for further evaluation when appropriate
  - Participate in eligibility conferences
  - Participate in writing individualized education programs
  - Communicate with parents or guardians
  - Participate in due process hearings and negotiations
  - Collaborate with other professionals in identifying and making maximum use of exceptional students' abilities

▶ In addition, special educators are expected to provide or be expert in:
  - Academic instruction of students with learning problems
  - Management of serious behavior problems
  - Technological advances
  - Special education law

What are the history and origins of special education?

▶ Special education became common in institutions and in major cities' public education in the nineteenth century.

▶ Physicians and psychologists played important roles in the early formation of special education.

▶ The Council for Exceptional Children (CEC) and many important parent and professional organizations were formed in the twentieth century.

What legislation and litigation have affected special education?

▶ The primary federal law affecting special education is the Individuals with Disabilities Education Act (IDEA), enacted in the 1970s and reauthorized by the U.S. Congress in 2004.

▶ Also important is the Americans with Disabilities Act (ADA), which prohibits discrimination against persons with disabilities in employment and communications.

▶ In the twenty-first century, the No Child Left Behind Act (NCLB) also is important in the education of exceptional learners.

▶ Lawsuits (litigation) have added to interpretation of the meaning and application of the law.

▶ Some parents sue to keep their children from being identified for special education or to have them educated in less atypical situations; others sue because they want their children to be identified for special education or placed in more specialized environments.

How is the intent of special education law implemented in individualized education for students with disabilities?

▶ The primary concern of the law (IDEA) is that every child with a disability be given a free, appropriate public education.

▶ The primary instrument for achieving this is the individualized education program or IEP.

▶ The IEP is an attempt to make certain a program has been written for each child with a disability and that:
- The student's needs have been carefully assessed
- A team of professionals and the parents have worked together to design a program of education to best meet the student's needs

■ Goals and objectives are clearly stated so that progress in reaching them can be evaluated

What is our perspective on the progress of special education?

▶ Special education has made great progress, but making it better is a continuing struggle.

STANDARDS and PRINCIPLES in this Chapter

SPECIAL EDUCATORS . . .

■ understand the field as an evolving and changing discipline based on philosophies, evidence-based principles and theories, relevant laws and policies, diverse and historical points of view, and human issues that have historically influenced and continue to influence the field of special education and the education and treatment of individuals with exceptional needs both in school and society (from CEC Content Standard #1).

■ understand the similarities and differences in human development and the characteristics between and among individuals with and without exceptional learning needs (from CEC Content Standard #2).

■ realize that individualized decision making and instruction are at the center of special education practice; develop long-range individualized instructional plans anchored in both general and special education curricula, and, in addition systematically translate these individualized plans into

carefully selected shorter-range goals and objectives taking into consideration an individual's abilities and needs, the learning environment, and a myriad of cultural and linguistic factors (from CEC Content Standard #7).

ALL TEACHERS . . .

■ understand the central concepts, tools of inquiry, structures of the discipline(s) he or she teaches and can create learning experiences that make these aspects of subject matter meaningful for students (INTASC Principle #1).

■ understand how children learn and develop, and can provide learning opportunities that support the intellectual, social and personal development of each learner (INTASC Principle #2).

■ plan instruction based on knowledge of subject matter, students, the community and curriculum goals (INTASC Principle #7).

Applying the STANDARDS and PRINCIPLES

■ HOW has the history of special education shaped the field today? Identify and describe at least one current theory, law, point of view, or human issue [refer to Chapter 2] and explain how it might affect the future of special education. (CEC Content Standard #1)

■ IDENTIFY and describe major laws and policies that support students with disabilities. (INTASC 1.04 & 1.12)

■ WHAT distinguishes special educators from general educators? (CEC Content Standard #2 & INTASC Principle #2)

■ WHAT are the components of an individualized education program (IEP)? (CEC Content Standard #7)

■ WHICH specific areas should special educators consider when planning instruction for students with disabilities? (INTASC Principle #7)

Now go to the Hallahan/Kauffman, Eleventh Edition MyEducationLab course at www.myeducationlab.com to:

- take a Pretest to assess your initial comprehension of the chapter content;
- study chapter content with your Individualized Study Plan;
- take a Posttest to assess your understanding of chapter content;
- engage in multimedia exercises to help you build a deeper and more applied understanding of chapter content.

2

Integration, Inclusion, and Support of Positive Outcomes

Come writers and critics
Who prophesize with your pen
And keep your eyes wide,
The chance won't come again.
And don't speak too soon
For the wheel's still in spin
And there's no tellin' who
That it's namin'
For the loser now
Will be later to win
For the times they are a-changin'.

QUESTIONS to guide your reading of this chapter . . .

- What are the trends and issues in integrating people with disabilities into the larger society?

- What are the trends and issues related to normalization and deinstitutionalization?

- What are the trends and issues in self-determination, universal design, and new technologies?

- What are the trends and issues in integrating students with exceptionalities into schools?

- What are the main arguments for and against full inclusion?

- What are the trends and issues in collaboration and response to intervention?

- What are the trends and issues in student participation in progress assessments?

- What are the trends and issues in early intervention and transition?

- What are the trends and issues in discipline of students with disabilities?

- What are our concluding thoughts about trends and issues?

MISCONCEPTIONS ABOUT
Learners with Disabilities

MYTH ■ Normalization, the principle that the means and ends of education for students with disabilities should be as culturally normative as possible, is straightforward, needing little interpretation.

FACT ■ There are many disagreements pertaining to the interpretation of the normalization principle. As just one example, some educators interpret it to mean that all people with disabilities must be educated in general education classes, whereas others maintain that a continuum of placements (residential schools, special schools, special classes, resource rooms, regular classes) should remain available as options.

MYTH ■ All professionals agree that technology should be used to its fullest to aid people with disabilities.

FACT ■ Some believe that technology should be used cautiously because it can lead people with disabilities to become too dependent on it. Some professionals believe that people with disabilities can be tempted to rely on technology instead of developing their own abilities.

MYTH ■ All students with disabilities must now be included in standardized testing, just like students without disabilities.

FACT ■ Most students with disabilities will be included in standardized testing procedures, but for some, a given test is deemed inappropriate. Some students will require adaptations of the testing procedure to accommodate their specific disabilities. However, students with disabilities can no longer be automatically excluded from participating in standardized assessment procedures.

MYTH ■ Research has established beyond a doubt that special classes are ineffective and that inclusion is effective.

FACT ■ Research comparing special versus general education placement is inconclusive because most of these studies have been methodologically flawed. Researchers are now focusing on finding ways of making inclusion work more effectively.

MYTH ■ Professionals agree that labeling people with disabilities (e.g., "mentally retarded," "blind," "behavior disordered") is more harmful than helpful.

FACT ■ Some professionals maintain that labels help them to communicate, explain the atypical behavior of some people with disabilities to the public, and spotlight the special needs of people with disabilities for the general public.

MYTH ■ Everyone agrees that teachers in early intervention programs need to assess parents as well as their children.

FACT ■ Some authorities now believe that although families are an important part of intervention programming and should be involved in some way, special educators should center their assessment efforts primarily on the child, not the parents.

MYTH ■ Everyone agrees that good early childhood programming for students with or without disabilities should be the same.

FACT ■ There is considerable disagreement about whether early intervention programming for children with disabilities should be child-directed, as is typical of regular preschool programs, or more teacher-directed.

MYTH ■ Professionals agree that all students with disabilities in secondary school should be given a curriculum focused on vocational preparation.

FACT ■ Professionals are in conflict over how much vocational versus academic instruction students with mild disabilities should receive.

MYTH ■ There are completely different rules of discipline for students with disabilities.

FACT ■ In most cases, the same discipline rules apply to students with and without disabilities. However, the law does not allow discontinuation of education for a student with a disability. Even if the student is not allowed to return to the school, education must be provided in an alternative setting.

Bob Dylan could have written "The Times They Are A-Changin'" (see the excerpt on p. 43) for special education, which has a rich history of controversy and change. Controversy and change make teaching and studying disabilities challenging and exciting. The history of special education is replete with unexpected twists and turns. Many developments in the past have had unanticipated consequences, and many of today's events and conditions will undoubtedly have consequences that we don't foresee.

Since the 1980s, especially dramatic changes have occurred in the education of people with disabilities, and current thinking indicates that the field is poised for still more changes in the next decade (Lloyd & Hallahan, 2007). One critically important trend and issue for the twenty-first century is the movement toward multicultural special education—the subject of Chapter 3. In this chapter, we explore other major trends in responding to the needs of individuals with disabilities. Specifically, we look at the following:

1. Integration of people with disabilities into society
   a. Normalization
   b. Deinstitutionalization
   c. Self-determination
   d. Universal Design and Universal Design for Learning
   e. Use of new technologies
2. Inclusion of students with disabilities in schools
   a. Full inclusion
   b. Differentiated instruction
   c. Collaboration with general education
   d. Response to intervention
   e. Assessments of academic progress and student outcomes
3. Early intervention with children who have disabilities
   a. Consensus on early intervention
   b. The demands of prevention
4. Transitions to adulthood and employment for students with disabilities
   a. Making transition fit level of need
   b. What should be taught when?

Late actor Christopher Reeve won praise from many for his tireless efforts in the pursuit of a cure for spinal cord injuries, but was also criticized by some disability rights advocates, who disagreed with his definition of "normal."

5. Zero tolerance, PBS(positive behavioral supports), PBIS(positive behavioral intervention and support), and other discipline issues
   a. Supports for desired behavior
   b. How functional are supports?

INTERNET RESOURCES

You can search major newspaper Websites for articles about issues in special education. The New York Times site is www.nytimes.com and the Washington Post site is www.washingtonpost.com

The trend of integrating people with disabilities into the larger society began many decades ago and is stronger than ever today. Champions of integration are proud that they've reduced the number of people who live in institutions and the number of students who attend special schools and special classes. Schools are a part of society, but they aren't miniature reproductions of the larger society (Warnock, 2005). This is why we discuss two different types of integration: One having to do with integration into the larger society, the other having to do more specifically with inclusion in schools.

We also note that many of the issues we discuss overlap. For example, Universal Design for Learning, differentiated instruction, and inclusion are not completely separate or distinct issues. Self-determination is often seen as part of transition planning for adolescents and young adults with disabilities. The integration and inclusion of individuals with disabilities into society and school are multifaceted issues, and our discussion is organized around major themes in these processes.

INTERNET RESOURCES

Community integration and educational inclusion are topics with many associated Websites, including www.normemma.com/index.htm and www.dssc.org

Integration of People with Disabilities into the Larger Society

Some of the radical proponents of integration will not be satisfied until virtually all institutions, special schools, and special classes are eliminated. They recommend keeping all individuals with disabilities in the community and placing all students with disabilities in general education classes. Even today's more conservative advocates of integration recommend much greater interaction between individuals with and without disabilities than was imagined in the 1960s and 1970s.

Normalization

A key principle behind the trend toward more integration of people with disabilities into society is **normalization** (not to be confused with normalization of data bases). Normalization is the philosophy that we should use "means which are as culturally normative as possible, in order to establish and/or maintain personal behaviors and characteristics which are as culturally normative as possible" (Wolfensberger, 1972, p. 28). The idea is that the barriers to participation of people with disabilities in normal life should be broken down; both the means and the ends of education for students with disabilities should be as much like those for nondisabled students as possible. Regarding the means, for example, the idea of normalization is that we should use treatment approaches that are as close as possible to the ones we use with the rest of the population. Regarding the ends, we should strive to weave people with disabilities into the larger fabric of society.

RECOGNIZING POSITIVES AND NEGATIVES IN NORMALIZATION   Normalization continues to be a goal in special education and all other aspects of responding to disability. Consider the case of Kathy Koons, described in the Personal Perspectives feature on p. 48. She's a young woman with a physical disability and relatively low tested intelligence who is anticipating making the transition to independent living in the community. For her, normalization of personal relationships, employment, and community living are important goals.

In every way feasible, those who work with individuals who have disabilities are trying to make the experience of home, school, work, play, and community indistinguishable from those without disabilities. However, people are also more than ever willing to look at the limitations and the downside of normalization.

HOW FAR SHOULD NORMALIZATION BE TAKEN?   Although normalization seems simple enough in principle, it has sparked numerous controversies. Many of these controversies have involved deinstitutionalization, self-determination, and—particularly important for teachers—full inclusion. We discuss a few of the more hotly contested issues.

The phrase "as culturally normative as possible" (Wolfensberger, 1972, p. 28) is open to interpretation. The originators of the normalization principle saw the need for a variety of service delivery options, including residential institutions, special schools, and special classes; more recently, some have interpreted normalization to mean abolishing all such separate settings.

Some groups of people with disabilities are leery about being too closely integrated into nondisabled society. For example, some people who are deaf, because of their difficulty in communicating with the hearing world, prefer associating with other people who are deaf. For them, normalization does not translate into integration into the larger society. (We discuss this further in Chapter 10.) Others have pointed out that a diversity of settings and groupings of people is itself normal in most societies and that schools are not microcosms of society (Kauffman & Hallahan, 1997; Kauffman, Landrum, Mock, Sayeski, & Sayeski, 2005; Kauffman, Mock, Tankersley, & Landrum, 2008; Warnock, 2005).

Some disability rights advocates suggest that the assessment of normalization is wrongheaded, as it begins with the idea that nondisabled people should be seen as the norm to which those with disabilities are compared. For example, a representative of the organization Disabled People's International has called for "the elimination of the value concept of normalization as a measurement and the use of non-disabled people as the norm" (Mathiason, 1997, p. 2). Additionally, issues surrounding human

Personal PERSPECTIVES

Kathy Koons

Kathy is a 19-year-old young woman with **spina bifida**. She has an electric wheelchair that she can control in a very limited way. An instructional assistant works with Kathy to ensure that she is able to get around the school and to assist her with classroom activities. She requires assistance in writing and getting her supplies ready for class, getting her lunch and feeding herself, and controlling her wheelchair.

Kathy is a middle child; she has an older, married sister and a brother who is age 14. Her father is an electrician and her mother does not work outside of the home. The family lives in a very nice house, which has had some modifications made for the wheelchair.

Her school attendance has been very poor. Mrs. Koons has kept Kathy at home for extended periods of time throughout the years, stating that Kathy was not well enough to attend school. The family was told that Kathy would not live to be 5 years old and they have taken care of her every need. The mother does many things that Kathy could do on her own, but would take her a long time to get done. When Kathy is at home, she spends the majority of the time in her wheelchair in front of the TV or stretched out on a blanket on the floor. There is nothing that Kathy does at home for herself or the family.

Kathy is in four resource classes (math, language arts, social studies, and vocational exploration), is in two regular education classes (computers and home economics), and spends one hour a day with an instructional assistant working on daily living and functional living skills. Kathy is working on grooming skills, kitchen skills, making change, telling time, and mobility. She has good verbal skills, but has very limited written language skills because of her limited mobility. She is learning to use a computer so that she can increase her written expressive skills. Kathy has indicated an interest in doing a job that would utilize telephone skills, which is something she feels she could learn to do. She has several friends at school. She says that she would like to have a boyfriend and talks about relationships quite often. She is very concerned about not having someone to marry, being able to leave home, and living on her own.

Kathy's Verbal Scale IQ is 84, Performance Scale IQ is 64, and Full Scale IQ is 75. Curriculum-based assessment results indicate skills functioning at the 7.5 grade level in reading and at the 6.8 grade level in math. She is aware of her academic limitations, but wants to do something with her life. Kathy indicates that she wants to learn to live more independently and to develop job skills. She is older than most of the students in the high school and plans are being made for her to go to a residential independent living center for young adults with physical disabilities, where she will have the opportunity to learn many of the things needed to allow her to live in a group home and have a job. Kathy is very excited about these plans, but her parents are somewhat hesitant.

Source: Sitlington, P. L., & Clark, G. M. (2006). *Transition education and services for students with disabilities* (4th ed., p. 83). Boston: Allyn & Bacon. Reprinted with permission.

---

reproduction seem very likely to spark more controversy around ideas of what should be seen as "normal" and what constitutes "disability" (Kauffman & Hallahan, 2007).

Breaking down barriers to participation of people with disabilities in activities with nonhandicapped individuals can be very controversial. For example, Tatyana McFadden, a young woman who uses a wheelchair because her legs are paralyzed, wants to participate with normal runners in high school track events. (Ms. McFadden has **spina bifida**, a **congenital** condition involving the spinal cord and often resulting in paralysis of the lower extremities—see our chapter on physical disabilities for further discussion.) She recognizes that people who use wheelchairs can't be allowed to participate in some sports with nondisabled athletes (basketball, for example) but argues that she has a legal right to race on the high school track alongside nonparalyzed runners (Saslow, 2007). Her quest for normalization became an extraordinary controversy in her high school in 2007. McFadden is not the only athlete to bring controversy to participation in sport. As we discuss further in Chapter 14, a South African runner, Oscar Pistorius, who races on artificial legs, makes the Olympic

■ **Spina bifida**
A congenital midline defect resulting from failure of the bony spinal column to close completely during fetal development.

■ **Congenital**
A characteristic or condition that is present at birth; might or might not be due to genetic factors.

Committee and others question where to draw the line, if one should be drawn, on allowing people with disabilities to compete with others who don't have those disabilities (see Goodman, 2007; Longman, 2007).

Deinstitutionalization

At one time, it was common to place nearly all children and adults with mental retardation (now often referred to as intellectual disability) and/or mental illness in residential institutions. In the 1960s and 1970s, systematic efforts were made to move people out of institutions and back into closer contact with the community. This movement, referred to as **deinstitutionalization**, led to more children with disabilities being raised by their families, and resulted in the closure of many institutions regardless of the nature of the problems of the people involved. That is, "deinstitutionalization" applies to both institutions for people with intellectual disabilities and to mental hospitals for those with mental illnesses.

COMMUNITY-BASED SERVICES Today, smaller facilities within local neighborhoods are common. Halfway houses exist for individuals with emotional difficulties, who no longer are thought to need the more isolated environment of a large institution. As we discuss in Chapter 5, group homes for people with intellectual disabilities house small numbers of individuals whose disabilities may range from mild to severe. More people with disabilities are now working, with assistance from a **job coach**, in competitive employment situations (Stroman, 2003), and many more are living in communities outside institutions (Saunders, 2007).

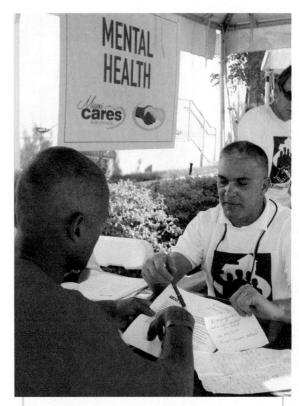

Despite the good intentions and successes of deinstitutionalization, much still needs to be done to improve the quality of life for some people with disabilities who have been released from institutions.

WHAT PROBLEMS DOES DEINSTITUTIONALIZATION SOLVE? Some have asserted that in certain cases, deinstitutionalization has been implemented without much forethought. They maintain that although deinstitutionalization has the potential to improve the quality of life for most people who in previous generations would have lived in institutions, it has failed because of poor planning. They argue that institutions can be humane, effective alternative placements for some individuals. In fact, some people with disabilities have been turned out of institutions onto the streets or into assisted living facilities that are every bit as abusive as larger institutions. Moreover, economic recessions often result in reduced funding, and important research on how institutions can be made most effective has been neglected (Saunders, 2007). In spite of media reporting and public promises to reform the way in which local communities respond to people with intellectual disabilities and other disabilities, the most vulnerable individuals in our society remain at high risk of abuse and neglect (see "Still Failing the Vulnerable," 2007).

A review of research on deinstitutionalization between 1980 and 1999 suggested that many people with intellectual disabilities improved their adaptive behavior by moving into small community homes (University of Minnesota, 1999). However, research also indicates that much still needs to be done to improve the quality of life for some people with disabilities who have been released from institutions. In fact, many people who were or formerly would have been in institutions are now homeless or in jail (see Earley, 2006; Goin, 2007; Lamb & Weinberger, 2001; Torrey & Zdandowic, 1999).

Although deinstitutionalization has its champions and institutions, like communities, can become places of neglect and abuse, some people have pointed out that because so many institutions have been closed there is no place for individuals and families with

■ **Deinstitutionalization**
A social movement of the 1960s and 1970s whereby large numbers of persons with intellectual disabilities and/or mental illness were moved from large mental institutions into smaller community homes or into the homes of their families; recognized as a major catalyst for integrating persons with disabilities into society.

■ **Job coach**
A person who assists adult workers with disabilities (especially those with intellectual disabilities), providing vocational assessment, instruction, overall planning, and interaction assistance with employers, family, and related government and service agencies.

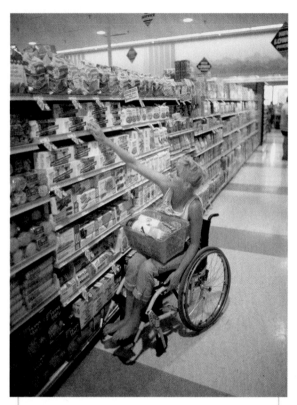

A key goal for individuals with disabilities is learning skills that allow them self-determination.

serious mental health problems to go in times of crisis. Streets and jails have become the default placements for many mentally ill persons in the absence of mental hospitals, and people with severe mental illness are often neglected until they commit criminal acts. As Earley (2006) and Nomani (2007) have observed, deinstitutionalization has resulted in many states requiring that a person be judged dangerous before he or she can be hospitalized for mental illness.

There is no inexpensive or easy way to provide humane care for people with disabilities. However, it seems clear from exposés and research that simply changing the locale of people from institutions to communities does little or nothing to improve the quality of their lives.

Self-Determination

Deinstitutionalization has fostered increasing recognition that people with and without disabilities have a right to exercise **self-determination**—the right to make one's own decisions about important aspects of one's life, including where to work and live, with whom to become friends, and what education to pursue. Nearly every book about students with disabilities moving toward adulthood and community living now discusses self-determination (e.g., Brolin & Loyd, 2004; Greene & Kochhar-Bryant, 2003; Sitlington & Clark, 2006). Moreover, many publications now express the sentiment that "promoting and enhancing the self-determination of youth with disabilities has become best practice in transition services" (Wehmeyer & Powers, 2007, p. 1).

■ **Self-determination**
The ability to make personal choices, regulate one's own life, and be a self-advocate; a prevailing philosophy in education programming for people with intellectual disabilities; having control over one's life, not having to rely on others for making choices about one's quality of life; develops over one's life span.

■ **Person-centered planning**
Planning for a person's self-determination; planning activities and services based on a person's dreams, aspirations, interests, preferences, strengths, and capacities.

Reading Homework Exercise

Self Determination • Go to the Homework and Exercises section in Chapter 2 of MyEducationLab to access reading materials and relevant questions about why self-determination for people with disabilities must be considered within an appropriate environmental and cultural context.

TAKING CHARGE OF ONE'S LIFE "*Self-determination* might be defined by students as 'making our own decisions'" (Sitlington & Clark, 2006, p. 238). Schwartz, Jacobson, and Holburn (2000) suggest that the primary hallmark of **person-centered planning** is that "the person's activities, services and supports are based upon his or her dreams, interests, preferences, strengths, and capacities" (p. 238). The main idea is that people with disabilities should exercise personal control of their lives (Brolin & Loyd, 2004; Chambers et al., 2007; Greene & Kochhar-Bryant, 2003; Powers et al., 2007); other people—such as psychologists, counselors, physicians, parents, teachers, and administrators—should not make decisions for people with disabilities.

Making schools places where all children have a significant voice or say in important decisions is seen as critical. There is growing recognition that self-determination is learned and should be taught in schools, even in the elementary grades (Browder, Wood, Test, Karvonen, & Algozzine, 2001; Hughes, Wood, Konrad, & Test, 2006; Jones, 2006; Palmer & Wehmeyer, 2003).

In general, self-determination means taking charge of one's life. Teachers can play an important role in promoting the abilities and attitudes students will need to take charge of their lives, through providing instruction in self-determination skills and creating environments where these skills can be practiced. Some professional organizations have policy statements regarding self-determination. We discuss self-determination further in Chapter 5.

DOES SELF-DETERMINATION FIX DISABILITIES? The idea of self-determination, like so many other concepts related to ability and disability, is culturally embedded. In working toward self-determination, as well as any other goal, we must be aware of environmental and cultural differences in the meaning of self, independence, and success (see also

Cronin, 2000; Shogren et al., 2007; Sitlington & Clark, 2006). For some disabilities, such as severe mental illness, making decisions about one's own treatment may be perpetuating human degradation (Earley, 2006). Thus what may seem to be a universally accepted idea may, in fact, apply only within narrow cultural traditions or environmental circumstances or depend on the nature of the disability.

Also at issue is whether person-centered planning, as part of self-determination, represents a false hope rather than a tested and proven strategy for integrating people with developmental disabilities into the larger society. Osborne (2005), for example, states:

> I have argued that PCAs [person-centered approaches] . . . are the latest in a long line of *faux fixes*, all purportedly techniques to deal with persons who have developmental disabilities. A *faux fixe* is literally a false fix of a problem. Usually it is politically correct (for the moment at least) procedure or movement in the social sciences, of which there is uncritical adoption . . . in the face of difficult-to-solve problems. (p. 318)

When labels take precedence over recognizing individual characteristics, labels themselves become disabling.

Universal Design and Universal Design for Learning

Based on the architectural principles of **universal design, Universal Design for Learning (UDL)** serves the general purpose of making learning accessible to more students in inclusionary programs. The idea is that with modifications of *representation* (materials), *expression* (methods of communication), and *engagement* (how students respond to curriculum) a much wider range of students can be included in typical classroom instruction (Spooner, Baker, Harris, Ahlgrim-Delzell, & Browder, 2007).

MAKING THINGS USABLE BY MORE PEOPLE   Access to the World Wide Web by people with disabilities is a current trend with significant implications for design. Section 508 of the Rehabilitation Act requires that federal agencies must ensure equal access by those with and without disabilities to new electronic and information technology as well as information and services. Furthermore, the **Individuals with Disabilities Education Improvement Act (IDEA)** urges educators to consider the use of assistive technology in servicing students with disabilities, to allow a greater diversity of students to be accommodated in typical classrooms (Spooner et al., 2007).

DOES UNIVERSAL DESIGN ELIMINATE THE NEED FOR CUSTOM DESIGN?   One continuing issue is when to assume that the limits of universal design have been reached and go ahead with production. Inventors and designers may do their best to be "smart from the start" (Pisha & Coyne, 2001), but perhaps no one can be certain that no potential user's needs have been overlooked. At some point, someone decides to put a gadget or technology into production under the assumption that the design is as universal as it can be made at that time.

Modifications of instruction used in UDL can make lessons appropriate for a wider range of students than has typically been the case. Thus, teachers must not overlook the possibility that they could be designing lesson plans that are appropriate for a greater variety of students.

Perhaps the term *universal*, like the term *all*, should not be taken too literally, or it becomes self-defeating. Very likely, there will always be the need to "customize" for individuals. Even in instruction, some special education researchers note that students with

■ **Universal design**
The design of new buildings and tools to make them usable by the widest possible population of potential users.

■ **Universal Design for Learning (UDL)**
Designing lessons that are appropriate for all learners.

INTERNET RESOURCES

Issues related to accessibility of the World Wide Web to people with disabilities are found at www.seriweb.com

■ **Individuals with Disabilities Education Improvement Act (IDEA)**
The Individuals with Disabilities Education Act was enacted in 1990 and reauthorized in 1997 and 2004; it replaced PL 94-142, enacted in 1975. This federal law requires that to receive federal funds, every school system in the nation must provide a **free, appropriate public education (FAPE)** for every child between the ages of three and twenty-one, regardless of how or how seriously he or she may be disabled.

▪ **Free, appropriate public education (FAPE)**
The primary intent of federal special education law, that the education of all children with disabilities will in all cases be free of cost to parents (i.e., at public expense) and appropriate for the particular student.

INTERNET RESOURCES

For information about universal design, see www.cec.sped.org/ spotlight/udl/ and http://www. cast.org

There is a push today to make computer programs and the World Wide Web accessible to people with disabilities. For some, this means adaptations that allow a person to use a keyboard or mouse or read a visual display.

disabilities need individualized instruction that is not most appropriate for students without disabilities (e.g., Zigmond, 2007).

Building Teaching Skills Exercise

What is Universal Design for Learning? ● Go to the Building Teaching Skills section in Chapter 2 of MyEducationLab and access the article "What is Universal Design for Learning?", which includes a link to a lesson plan in which the principles of UDL are applied.

▪ **Cochlear implantation**
A surgical procedure that allows people who are deaf to hear some environmental sounds; an external coil fitted on the skin by the ear picks up sound from a microphone worn by the person and transmits it to an internal coil implanted in the bone behind the ear, which carries it to an electrode implanted in the cochlea of the inner ear.

Use of New Technologies

As technology becomes ever more sophisticated, the issue of independence will become ever more important. One general guideline might be that if the technology allows people with disabilities to do something they couldn't do without it, then the technology is in their best interest. However, if it allows them to do something new or better but at the same time imposes new limitations, then one might need to rethink the technology's benefits.

Technological advances of all types can have implications for people with disabilities. Advances in three technologies stand out as particularly important: (a) medical treatment, (b) human reproduction, and (c) communication. Some of these advances, particularly those in medical treatment and human reproduction, are very controversial. The controversy is typically about whether something that *can* be done *should* be done, and may involve two or three of the technologies we discuss. For example, should **cochlear implantations**—artificial inner ears, which we discuss further in Chapter 10—be used to allow deaf children to hear whenever possible? This issue involves both medical treatment and communication, and it could involve human reproduction as well. Should disabilities be corrected surgically before birth (in utero), if that is possible? Should the findings of fetal stem cell research be applied to cure or correct physical disabilities if possible? What characteristics of their children should parents be allowed to choose? These are some of the controversial ethical issues that we discuss in later chapters.

Some have seen technological advancements as being the solution to nearly all problems. Educational technology, for example, might involve universal design of lessons to accommodate greater variation among learners. Education has also looked to computer-based technologies as ways of closing gaps in achievement under the No Child Left Behind Act of 2002 (NCLB). However, the mere use of computer technology doesn't appear to produce better learning (Paley, 2007).

THE UPSIDE AND THE DOWNSIDE OF TECHNOLOGY   As the pace of technology quickens, so do applications of these technologies to the daily lives of people with disabilities. In many ways, technologies expand the abilities of people with or without disabilities to access information, communicate, travel, and accomplish many other everyday tasks. Technological applications can also allow some people with disabilities to function like those without disabilities.

One of the major issues concerning technologies is cost. Technologically advanced equipment or surgical procedures typically are very costly at first. Their immediate application to people of any description is beyond the financial reach of most consumers. However, as technological advances become incorporated into everyday life and mass-produced, their cost typically falls dramatically.

Other downsides are dependence on technology and the problem of reliability. People tend to rely on whatever technology they use rather than learn how to do things in alternative ways, so they have no idea how to do things the "old-fashioned" way when a gadget malfunctions.

SHOULD WE DO SOMETHING BECAUSE WE CAN?   An issue that is likely to become more controversial is whether we *should* do all the things that we *can* with new technologies. The moral and ethical dilemmas created by the availability of means to eliminate limitations, whether they are considered disabilities or not—for example, being unable to hear, see, walk, or communicate—will increase in years to come. Particularly troubling will be the issue of whether we *should* allow parents to create "designer babies" to any extent that we *can*. For example, should we allow parents to create children with or without what most people consider disabilities? The ability to select embryos (or create them) with or without certain characteristics (e.g., deafness, dwarfism, diabetes, tendency toward schizophrenia or depression), in addition to presenting ethical dilemmas, raises difficult issues about the definition and meaning of disability (Kauffman & Hallahan, 2007).

Inclusion in Schools

The most controversial issue about integrating students with disabilities into schools is that of inclusion. Especially controversial is what is known as **full inclusion**. Actually, integration or inclusion has been an issue with all exceptional students, including those with special gifts or talents. Here, we discuss integration related to disabilities. We discuss inclusion of gifted and talented students further in Chapter 15.

Full Inclusion

Writers have different ideas about exactly what *full inclusion* means (Kauffman & Hallahan, 2005b; Stainback & Stainback, 1992; Warnock, 2005). However, most definitions contain the following key elements:

- *All* students with disabilities—regardless of the type or severity of disability—attend only general education classes. In other words, there are no separate special education classes.

- *All* students with disabilities attend their neighborhood schools (i.e., the ones they would go to if they had no disabilities).

- General education, not special education, assumes primary responsibility for *all* students with disabilities.

■ **Full inclusion**
All students with disabilities are placed in their neighborhood schools in general education classrooms for the entire day; general education teachers have the primary responsibility for students with disabilities.

Educational programming for students with disabilities has historically been built on the assumption that a variety of service delivery options need to be available (Crockett & Kauffman, 1999, 2001; Kauffman et al., 2008). As we mentioned in Chapter 1, federal special education law (i.e., IDEA), stipulates that schools place students with disabilities in the **least restrictive environment (LRE)**, which is to be chosen from a **continuum of alternative placements (CAP)**.

Most people have conceptualized LRE as involving only a physical location, with alternatives along a continuum of restrictiveness ranging from residential institutions on one end to general education classes on the other (see Figure 1.1 on page 15). Others have suggested that the restrictiveness of an environment is not simply a matter of location, but also includes what is taught and how it is presented—the instructional and social contexts of a place (e.g., Bateman, 2007; Crockett & Kauffman, 2001; Cruickshank, 1977; Rueda, Gallego, & Moll, 2000). The argument can then be made that some special classes or schools are, for *some* students, less restrictive of their academic, emotional, and social development than a general education classroom would be (e.g., Gliona, Gonzales, & Jacobson, 2005; Kauffman, Bantz, & McCullough, 2002; Kauffman et al., in press; Mock & Kauffman, 2002, 2005).

ARGUMENTS FOR AND AGAINST FULL INCLUSION

Labeling Some people fear that a "special education" label can cause a child to feel unworthy or to be viewed by the rest of society as deviant and hence grow to feel unworthy. This fear isn't entirely unfounded. Disabilities are conditions that most people would rather avoid; they aren't seen by most people as good things to have (Kauffman, 2003; Kauffman et al., 2008). Consequently, being described as having a disability can lower a person's self-esteem or cause others to behave differently toward him or her.

Research on the effects of labeling has been inconclusive. On the one hand, studies indicate that people tend to view labeled individuals differently from nonlabeled ones. People are more likely both to expect deviant behavior from labeled individuals and to see abnormality in nondisabled individuals if told (incorrectly) that nondisabled people are deviant. On the other hand, labels can also make nondisabled people more tolerant of those with disabilities. That is, labels can provide explanations or justifications for differences in appearance or behavior for which the person with a disability otherwise might be blamed or stigmatized. For example, it is probably fairly common for the nondisabled adult to tolerate a certain degree of socially immature behavior in a child with an intellectual disability (mental retardation) while finding the same behavior unacceptable in a nondisabled child.

In addition to serving as an explanation for unusual behavior, the use of labels is defended on other grounds by some special educators. First, they argue that eliminating one set of labels would only prompt development of another set. Second, they contend that labels help professionals communicate with one another. In talking about a research study, for example, it helps to know the type of population. Third, they assert that labels help to spotlight the special needs of people with disabilities for the general public. Finally, some people have pointed out that any time we use an intervention that is not universal—used with all students regardless of their characteristics—we automatically apply a label. That is, labels are an inescapable part of preventive practices unless those practices are universal—applied to all children without regard to their individual characteristics. The decision, then, is whether we will recognize and talk about the differences we call "disabilities" or

### Sidebar (left margin)

■ **Least restrictive environment (LRE)**
A legal term referring to the fact that exceptional children must be educated in as normal an environment as possible.

■ **Continuum of alternative placements (CAP)**
The full range of alternative placements, from those assumed to be least restrictive to those considered most restrictive; the continuum ranges from general education classrooms in neighborhood schools to resource rooms, self-contained classes, special day schools, residential schools, hospital schools, and home instruction.

UNDERSTANDING THE STANDARDS AND PRINCIPLES What is your opinion about full inclusion? (CEC Knowledge and Skills Standard CC1S1)

Council for Exceptional Children

Labels are misused when they overshadow a person's other attributes. For example, this person's blindness and physical disabilities aren't her defining attributes.

ignore them (Kauffman, 2003, 2005a, 2005b, 2007; Kauffman & Hallahan, 2005a; Kauffman & Konold, 2007).

Separate Special Education   Some special educators assert that research shows separate **pull-out programs** to be ineffective. These educators maintain that students with disabilities have better, or at least no worse, scores on cognitive and social measures if they stay in general education classes than if they're put in special education for all (self-contained classes) or part (resource rooms) of the school day. Adding fuel to this argument are studies showing that sometimes students receive inadequate instruction in pull-out programs (e.g., Vaughn, Moody, & Schumm, 1998). On the other hand, some studies show that some students with disabilities make better progress in more specialized settings, and that full inclusion does not serve all children best (see Mock & Kauffman, 2005).

Research and opinion on inclusion is currently debated in nations other than the United States (see Begeny & Martens, 2007; Warnock, 2005). Research findings and logical analysis challenge the idea that full inclusion is best for *all* students (Kauffman & Hallahan, 2005a, 2005b). The place where the child is taught shouldn't be seen as more important than meeting the child's needs (Warnock, 2005; Zigmond, 2003).

People with Disabilities As a Minority Group   Advocates of full inclusion tend to see people with disabilities as members of a minority group rather than as individuals who have difficulties as an inherent result of their disabilities (Stainback & Stainback, 1992). Thinking of people with disabilities as a minority is consistent with the views of disability rights activists. These activists are a part of the **disability rights movement**, which is patterned after the civil rights movement of the 1960s. Disability activists claim that they, like African Americans and other ethnic minority groups, are an oppressed minority. They have coined the term **handicapism**, a parallel of *racism*.

The disability rights movement is international and addresses a wide range of issues. It includes a spectrum of views on controversial topics; not every statement of every person with a disability is representative of the majority of people with disabilities (Michalko, 2002; Simpson & Kauffman, 2007; Switzer, 2003; Tregaskis, 2004; Warnock, 2005). For example, whereas some express negative sentiments about finding a cure for spinal cord injuries that would allow people with paralysis to walk, others find optimism about reversing the effects of spinal cord injuries laudable and heartening (Groopman, 2003; Kastor, 1997).

Many critics of full inclusion do not deny that in many ways, people with disabilities have been treated similarly to oppressed minority groups such as African Americans, Hispanics, and women: They have experienced discrimination on the basis of their disability and therefore can be considered an oppressed minority group. However, people with disabilities are an incredibly heterogeneous population. General goals can be the same for all people with disabilities, but specific needs vary greatly. Clearly, the particular problems that an adolescent with severe intellectual disabilities and blindness faces are considerably different from those of a combat veteran who has lost the use of his or her legs. Although activists admit that it would not be good for the public to believe that all people with disabilities are alike (any more than they already do), this heterogeneity makes it difficult for people with disabilities to join forces on specific issues.

Critics don't see that the minority group of people with disabilities translates into the same educational placement decisions as it does for African Americans, Hispanics, and women (Bateman, 2007; Dupre, 1997; Gliona et al., 2005; Hallahan & Kauffman, 1994; Kauffman & Hallahan, 1993; Kauffman & Lloyd, 1995). They argue that separation of students with disabilities from the mainstream can be defended on educational grounds. Students with disabilities are sometimes placed in special classes or resource rooms to better accommodate their educational needs. Placement in separate educational environments is inherently unequal, these critics maintain, when it is done for factors that are irrelevant to learning (e.g., skin color), but such placements may result in equality

UNDERSTANDING THE STANDARDS AND PRINCIPLES   Why is it important to preserve the continuum of services? (CEC Knowledge and Skill Standard GC1K5)

Council for Exceptional Children

■ **Pull-out programs**
Special education programs in which students with disabilities leave the general education classroom for part or all of the school day (e.g., to go to a special class or resource room).

■ **Disability rights movement**
Patterned after the civil rights movement of the 1960s, this is a loosely organized effort to advocate for the rights of people with disabilities through lobbying legislators and other activities. Members view people with disabilities as an oppressed minority.

■ **Handicapism**
A term used by activists who fault the unequal treatment of individuals with disabilities. This term is parallel to the term *racism*, coined by those who fault unequal treatment based on race.

INTERNET RESOURCES

The National Public Radio Show "This American Life" broadcast a show, "Special Ed," that explored how students labeled as disabled handled their labels. To hear this show go to http://www.thislife.org/Default.aspx and go to the archive for the show on 7/20/07. You might also go to www.howsyournews.com to see news reported by people with disabilities.

UNDERSTANDING THE STANDARDS AND PRINCIPLES
Do you agree with full-inclusion proponents who favor full inclusion on ethical grounds?
(CEC Knowledge and Skill Standard CC1S1)

Council for Exceptional Children

Reading Homework Exercise

Integration • Go to the Homework and Exercises section in Chapter 2 of MyEducationLab to access a web article that discusses handicapism and steps school systems can take to integrate students with disabilities into the mainstream.

Reading Homework Exercise

Labels • Go to the Homework and Exercises section in Chapter 2 of MyEducationLab to access a web article that provides a different perspective about the use of labels for students who have learning disabilities.

when done for instructionally relevant reasons (e.g., the student's ability to learn, difficulty of material being presented, preparation of the teacher).

Finally, critics of full inclusion argue that the most important civil right of students with disabilities and their parents is the right to choose where to be taught. That is, IDEA gives parents—and students themselves, when appropriate—the right to choose the environment they, not advocates of full inclusion, consider most appropriate and least restrictive (Crockett & Kauffman, 1998, 1999, 2001; Gliona et al., 2005).

Ethics Versus Empirical Evidence Full-inclusion proponents emphasize discrimination against people with disabilities, tending to approach integration from an ethical perspective without considering evidence. For them, empirical data on the comparative effectiveness of full inclusion versus separate programs are irrelevant. Apparently, even if well controlled research shows that separate programs lead to better academic and social outcomes than do full-inclusion programs, these advocates would still favor full inclusion on ethical grounds (see Kavale & Forness, 2000; Kavale, Mostert, & Kauffman, 2008; Mostert, Kavale, & Kauffman, 2008b; Sasso, 2001 for comment on this tactic).

The rationale for full inclusion is based on presumptive moral values, not research data. However, the presumed moral values are not based on realities, making the assumed values meaningless (see Kauffman & Landrum, 2005; Mock & Kauffman, 2005; Warnock, 2005). The ideology of full inclusion suggests that this equal access can be achieved only when each and every student is included in neighborhood schools and general education classes, taking his or her rightful places alongside age peers who have not been identified as having disabilities.

Unfortunately, full inclusion ignores the considerable evidence that children and adults need affiliation, for at least some of the time, with others like themselves (Hall, 2002). Some professionals see as folly the disregard of empirical evidence espoused by some proponents of full inclusion (Fuchs & Fuchs, 1991; Kauffman, 1989, 1999a, 2002; Kauffman & Hallahan, 1997, 2005b; Kauffman, Lloyd, Hallahan, & Astuto, 1995; Kavale & Forness, 2000; Mock & Kauffman, 2005). Although believing that ethical actions are always of the utmost importance, they assert that decisions about what is ethical should be informed by research. Some critics maintain that proponents of full inclusion have resorted to rhetoric rather than reason, and have traded in their credentials as scientific researchers in favor of becoming advocates and lobbyists (see Mostert, Kauffman, & Kavale, 2003; 2008a; Sasso, 2001).

On the basis of research to date, we conclude that many students with disabilities need intensive instruction if they are to make substantial progress (Zigmond, 2003, 2007). Such intensive instruction will sometimes need to be delivered in separate special education settings such as special classes or resource rooms. Unfortunately, teachers in general education classrooms often find it difficult to provide enough intensive instruction, even with supports that are intended to help students survive the general education curriculum.

The current structure of resource room programs, in which teachers have heavy caseloads and cannot provide the instruction students need, is a setup for failure (Moody, Vaughn, Hughes, & Fischer, 2000). As Zigmond (2003) suggests, asking where students should be taught is the wrong question; asking how well they're taught should be the focus of special education (Kauffman & Hallahan, 2005a; Kauffman & Landrum, 2007). Peer attitudes are critical, and research does not indicate clearly that full inclusion, at least of students with intellectual disabilities (mental retardation), is perceived as appropriate by most peers or increases the social acceptance of students with such disabilities (see Siperstein, Parker, Bardon, & Widaman, 2007).

Casebook Reflections

REFER TO THE CASE *The Red Belt* in your booklet. Because Tyler is extremely explosive and verbally abusive, what are the arguments for and against including him in the general education class for mathematics? How can the present debate on inclusion and the reality of Tyler's needs be resolved? ●

Continuum of Placements   Repeated polls, surveys, and interviews have indicated that the vast majority of students with disabilities and their parents are satisfied with the special education system and placement options (e.g., Guterman, 1995). Many students say that they prefer separate classes (Klinger, Vaughn, Schumm, Cohen, & Forgan, 1998). Parents have banded together to keep special schools open for their children (Gliona et al., 2005). Although many students are no doubt unhappy with the stigma of the label "learning disabilities," the majority seems not to regret that they aren't educated in general education classes. As one student summed up:

> [Full inclusion] would make it worse. Basically it would be embarrassing for that person [a student with learning disabilities]. [An inclusive classroom] would be egging it more. People would be getting into a lot more fights because somebody is always going to joke around and say something like, "He's a retard." (Guterman, 1995, p. 120)

Palmer and colleagues reviewed the comments of parents of children with severe disabilities about inclusion, finding that although some were supportive of inclusion, others were skeptical. Consider the varied responses of parents in the Personal Perspectives below. There is obviously a range of opinions on the matter; it's not surprising to encounter the argument that those who push hardest for full inclusion have ignored parental perceptions.

Personal PERSPECTIVES

Parents' Thoughts on Inclusion of Their Children with Severe Disabilities

Parents of children with severe disabilities cite the following reasons for supporting inclusion:

1. The child acquires more academic or functional skills because of the higher expectations and greater stimulation in the general education classroom.
2. Nondisabled students benefit by learning to know children with disabilities; they become more sensitive to people with disabilities.
3. Being around "normal" kids helps students with disabilities acquire social skills.
4. Siblings with and without disabilities go to the same school.
5. Segregation of any kind is morally wrong; inclusion is morally right.

Parents of children with severe disabilities have mentioned the following reasons for not supporting inclusion:

1. The type or severity of the child's disability precludes benefits from inclusion.
2. Inclusion would overburden or negatively affect regular classroom teachers and students.
3. The curriculum of the general education classroom doesn't match the needs of the child.

4. The child does not get the needed teacher attention or services in general education.
5. The child is unlikely to be treated well by nondisabled children in the regular classroom.
6. The child is not likely to benefit but is likely to be overwhelmed by the surroundings in the regular classroom.
7. The child is too young (and needs more supervision or structure) or too old (having become used to a special class) to benefit from inclusion.
8. The child needs to be around other children with similar disabilities; he or she fits in better, feels less stigmatized or different, and has more real friends in a special setting.
9. The child is too disruptive or aggressive or has too many behavior problems for a regular class.
10. Teachers and others in general education don't have the appropriate training for dealing with the child's needs.

Source: From Taking sides: Parent's views on inclusion for their children with severe disabilities by D.S. Palmer, K. Fuller, T. Arora, & M. Nelson. *Exceptional Children,* 67, 2001, 467–484. Copyright © 2001 by the Council for Exceptional Children. Reprinted by permission.

Critics of full inclusion argue that, given the empirical evidence, it is wise to be cautious about trying to change current options too quickly or drastically. They admit that there are problems with current special education and that there might even be a need for more integration of students with disabilities, including inclusion of some. They're leery, however, of eliminating the range of service delivery options currently available to school personnel and parents (Crockett & Kauffman, 1999, 2001; Gliona et al., 2005; Martin, 1994; Kauffman, McGee, & Brigham, 2004; Vaughn, Elbaum, & Boardman, 2001).

One group of advocates has suggested a change in thinking and talking about special education placements (Gliona et al., 2005). Whereas it has been common to refer to any placement outside the general education classroom as *segregated*, Gliona and colleagues suggest using the word *dedicated* in referring to such placements. There is no heirarchy of placements: Any one or a combination of alternative placements should be seen as equally appropriate, depending on the student's needs. Gliona and colleagues also point out that "every option on the continuum of alternative placements is some child's least restrictive environment" (p. 138).

The objective of any service-delivery model should be to provide the most effective service for the student involved. Based on their review of evidence-based practices, Kauffman et al. (2008) concluded:

> The most effective service delivery system probably cannot be defined totally in the abstract, for it likely depends on the characteristics of the student (e.g., age, type and severity of disability), the qualifications of the teacher(s) who will provide instruction, other students with whom a student will be grouped, and features of the placement. Our view is that there is probably not a single, best delivery system, but a variety of arrangements suited to make maximum use of the student's abilities. Those who propose a single best solution in all cases (e.g., self-contained special class, inclusion in general education with collaboration and consultation of all concerned parties) are in our opinion misguided. (p. 372)

Opinions and attitudes differ regarding what degree of inclusion is ideal, but most agree that providing the greatest benefit to the individual student should be the goal.

Attitudes of General Educators   General educators' attitudes toward students with disabilities don't suggest the wisdom of full inclusion (e.g., Cook, 2004; Cook, Cameron, & Tankersley, 2007; Cook, Semmel, & Gerber, 1999; Cook, Tankersley, Cook, & Landrum, 2000; Siperstein, Norins, & Mohler, 2007). Most critics of full inclusion sympathize with the classroom teacher's already arduous job. Although some critics blame teachers for their unwillingness to accommodate more students with disabilities, many agree that their hesitation to do so is justified and that training all teachers to be able to meet the needs of all students with disabilities is simply impossible from a practical standpoint (see Kauffman & Landrum, 2007; Lieberman, 1992; Mock & Kauffman, 2002, 2005; Palmer, Fuller, Arora, & Nelson, 2001).

A logical analysis of the problem of full inclusion indicates its infeasability because of the demands on general education teachers. As Zigmond (2003) summarized:

> General educators cannot imagine focusing intensively on individual students to the extent that different instructional activities for different students are being implemented at the same time. This is simply impractical in a classroom of 25 to 35 students. Moreover, special education's most basic article of faith, that instruction must be individualized to be truly effective, is rarely contemplated, let alone observed in most general education classrooms. Mainstream teachers must consider the good of the group and the extent to which the learning activities they present maintain classroom flow, orderliness, and cooperation. In addition, they generally formulate teaching plans that result in a productive learning environment for 90% or more of their students. General education settings are best for learning what most students need to learn.
>
> For many of the remaining 10% of students, however, a different orientation will probably be needed. These students need to learn something different because they are clearly not learning what everyone else is learning. Interventions that might be effective for this group of students require a considerable investment of time and effort, as well as extensive support. (p. 197)

IS INSTRUCTION OR PLACE MORE IMPORTANT?   As the twenty-first century unfolds, the full-inclusion controversy is sharpened, especially by the higher standards that all students are expected to meet. The direction the controversy will take is anyone's guess (see Hoover & Patton, 2004; Kauffman, 1999a, 1999–2000, 2004; Kauffman et al., in press; Kauffman & Hallahan, 2005b; Kauffman & Konold, 2007; Kauffman & Wiley, 2004; Warnock, 2005). However, three dimensions of the controversy appear likely to dominate.

First, there's the question of the legitimacy of atypical placements: Do resource rooms, special classes, and special schools have a legitimate, defensible place in the alternatives that are provided to students with disabilities at public expense? If the answer to this question is "yes," then we are likely to see renewed emphasis on the advantages that such special placements offer.

Second, if a student is not able to function adequately in the general education curriculum, achieving what is judged to be "success" in general education, then should that student remain in the general education environment or be taught in an alternative place with other students who have similar learning needs? If the answer to this question is "remain in the general education environment," then ways must be found to remove the stigma of failure in that environment from both the student and the teacher, who might be judged to have failed to measure up to expectations.

Third, for students who are placed in alternative environments, increasing attention must be given to the quality of instruction provided there (Kauffman & Landrum, 2007; Warnock, 2005; Zigmond, 2007). Vaughn and colleagues (1998) and Moody and colleagues (2000) found that the instruction offered in the resource rooms they studied was not the intensive, individualized, relentless, and effective instruction that should characterize special education.

The critical problem of today's special education might not be that students with disabilities are sometimes taught in separate settings but that special education teachers too seldom use the opportunity of such settings to offer the instruction that students need (Kauffman & Hallahan, 2005a; Kauffman & Landrum, 2007; Kauffman et al., in press; Zigmond, 2003, 2007). We can't overemphasize the importance of intensive instruction in meeting the needs of children with disabilities. In our opinion, children with disabilities should be placed where such instruction is most likely to be provided.

Differentiated Instruction

■ **Differentiated instruction**
Instruction varied to meet the needs of all students.

Some educators suggest that variation among learners must be matched by variation in instruction (e.g., Carolan & Guinn, 2007). Frequently, educators suggest that instruction must be different for students with different learning styles, different brains, or different levels of ability (e.g., Wormeli, 2006; Zull, 2004). Exactly what **differentiated instruction** means in practice is often not clear or is a matter of interpretation of the views of its proponents. The overriding idea, however, is that instruction in a general education classroom can be varied or "differentiated" to make it appropriate for all learners (Tomlinson, 1999). Differentiated instruction could also be considered a way of implementing universal design for learning—making instruction engaging and appropriate for all.

MATCHING TEACHING TO STUDENTS *Differentiated instruction* has several current meanings. As Wormeli (2006) explains it, "Teachers who differentiate instruction simply do what's fair and developmentally appropriate for students when the 'regular' instruction doesn't meet their needs" (p. 14). One line of definitions and suggestions for teaching refers to "learning styles." Another is related to "brain-based" learning and suggests varying what students are presented or asked to do so that the best part of their brains (or their whole brains; see Zull, 2004) are engaged in the activity. Or the suggestion may be that assignments should be varied to accommodate students' "multiple intelligences." Still another has to do with the type and level of a student's response to a lesson. In essence, differentiated instruction is sometimes proposed as a way of including students

Differentiated instruction might be considered a way of implementing universal design for learning—making instruction engaging and appropriate for all.

with disabilities in regular classroom work by asking them to be part of a learning team or by requiring them to do a simpler or parallel task. In some cases, it's used to mean that a teacher can vary instruction to meet the needs of gifted students in the context of a general education classroom (e.g., Betts, 2004; Smith & Weitz, 2003; Tomlinson, 2004).

UNDER WHAT CIRCUMSTANCES IS DIFFERENTIATED INSTRUCTION DEFENSIBLE? Nearly everyone understands that learners are not all alike. However, there is considerable disagreement about the basis for differentiating instruction. Although the idea that instruction must differ for different students is neither new nor questionable, two basic questions need answers:

- What is the basis for varying instruction?
- How much variation in instruction can a teacher be expected to offer without significant loss of instructional focus?

The ideas that "learning styles," "types of brains," "types of intelligence," and so on can be identified and that instruction should be differentiated by these characteristics remain popular. However, evidence that instruction can become more effective if it is differentiated on some basis other than a student's prior learning is lacking (cf. Hyatt, 2007; Lloyd & Hallahan, 2007). Furthermore, even if the basis for differentiation of instruction is defensible, the extent to which teachers can accomplish it in a group of students with very diverse learning needs is questionable. As the diversity of learning needs in a class becomes greater, the problem of differentiation increases as well. The idea is a good one if the basis for differentiation is sound, but like other good ideas in education it can be taken to an unreasonable extreme.

Prereferral Teams and Response to Intervention

Groups of professionals (e.g., special education teachers, counselors, administrators, psychologists) sometimes work with general education teachers to help identify alternative educational strategies for students who are struggling in the classroom before a referral for special education evaluation is made. As the name implies, when a **prereferral team (PRT)** is consulted, the student has not yet been identified as a student with a disability. A teacher usually asks for help when he or she's exhausted her own bag of tricks for helping a difficult-to-teach student. The team reviews the information about a student that the teacher brings to the group and then offers suggestions about what the teacher might try to do to help the student.

One of the primary goals of PRTs is to establish the general education classroom teacher's ownership of a student's education. In other words, PRTs try to keep down the number of referrals to special education by encouraging general educators to try as many alternative strategies as possible before deciding that difficult-to-teach students need to become the primary responsibility of special educators. Although PRTs have become popular, there has been little research on their effectiveness (see Hallahan, Lloyd, Kauffman, Weiss, & Martinez, 2005).

In the most recent reauthorization of IDEA, Congress included an additional option for determining eligibility for special education in the case of suspected learning disabilities that forces varying levels of support in general education before referral to special education. The regulations say that "in determining whether a child has a specific learning disability, states may rely on a process that determines whether the child responds to scientific, research-based intervention as a part of the evaluation." In practice, this concept has been termed **response to intervention (RTI).**

In some ways similar to the concept of the PRT, RTI usually provides for three standard levels of intervention for students who are experiencing difficulties (Boardman & Vaughn, 2007). There are varying forms, but generally the first level includes verification

■ **Prereferral teams (PRTs)**
Teams composed of a variety of professionals, especially general and special educators, who work with general education classroom teachers to come up with strategies for teaching difficult-to-teach children. Designed to influence general educators to take ownership of difficult-to-teach students and to minimize inappropriate referrals to special education.

■ **Response to intervention (RTI)**
(Also called response-to-treatment approach.) A way of determining whether a student has a learning disability; increasingly intensive levels of instructional intervention are delivered, and if the student does not achieve, at some point he or she is determined to have a learning disability or is referred for special education evaluation.

Video Homework Exercise

Collaboration ● Go to the Homework and Exercises section in Chapter 2 of MyEducationLab to access the video "The Collaborative Process", in which a general education teacher and a special education teacher work together to facilitate learning in an inclusive classroom.

of quality, research-based instruction with some standard changes and various other supports for a student in the general education classroom. The teacher monitors the student's progress in the curriculum and in relation to peers. If the student's achievement improves, no other action is taken. If the student's performance doesn't improve, the student moves to Level 2. Level 2 usually includes individual or peer instruction in the areas of difficulty (e.g., reading or writing) or some other form of remediation. If the student's performance doesn't improve at this level, the student moves to Level 3, which is often a referral to special education services.

RTI is usually associated with learning disabilities and academic learning. However, it has implications for students with any disability and is not confined to academic learning but can be applied to social behavior as well (Fairbanks, Sugai, Guardino, & Lathrop (2007). Throughout the RTI process, professionals monitor the student's progress in the curriculum, and these results (with other information) are used to determine special education eligibility (Boardman & Vaughn, 2007; Vaughn & Fuchs, 2003). The difference between RTI and PRTs is that in RTI, students move through predetermined steps and their progress is monitored closely, whereas in PRTs, interventions are determined on an individual basis and a student's progress might or might not be as closely monitored.

PRT, RTI, OR BOTH?   Advocates of RTI claim that it should be the primary activity of the PRT, claiming it will reduce the number of referrals for special education and provide more options for students with disabilities to participate in general education classrooms. The argument is that because high-quality instruction is provided at every level, RTI helps to determine whether a student is truly a student with a disability and not a student who has been subjected to poor or missing instruction (see Boardman & Vaughn, 2007). Unfortunately, little research evidence is available to determine whether RTI is effective. It has been used on a wide scale in only a few school districts in the country (Fuchs, Mock, Morgan, & Young, 2003). Nevertheless, IDEA gives schools the option of using RTI for identification of learning disabilities, as well as a means of improving instruction for all students. Some have argued that although RTI is defensible as a way of improving early

Effective collaboration among general educators, special educators, and other professionals is a key ingredient in the successful participation of students with disabilities in general education classrooms.

intervention and instruction for struggling learners, its use as a means of identifying disabilities is questionable (Boardman & Vaughn, 2007; Kavale, Kauffman, & Bachmeier, 2007). We discuss these issues further in our chapter on learning disabilities.

Other Models of Collaboration with General Education

Whether or not one supports the concept of full inclusion, the fact is that most educators are in favor of some degree of integration of students with disabilities with nondisabled students. There are generally five other methods of helping students with disabilities to participate in the general education classroom:

1. Collaborative consultation
2. Cooperative teaching and other team arrangements
3. Curricula and instructional strategies
4. Accommodations and adaptations
5. Training general education teachers to accommodate diversity

The current trend is toward a variety of collaborative arrangements. All are intended to increase the cooperation between general and special education for the benefit of students with disabilities.

COLLABORATIVE CONSULTATION   Once it has been determined that a student is in fact a student with a disability, he or she may receive special education services within the general education classroom through **collaborative consultation**. In collaborative consultation, the special education teacher or psychologist acts as an expert who provides advice to the general education teacher. The special educator might suggest changes to instruction or additional supports, such as behavior plans or school-home notes. This special educator might see the student with a disability in a resource room or other special education setting also, or the student might receive all of his or her instruction in the general education class. Much remains unknown about what makes this plan work.

CO-TEACHING   Sometimes referred to as collaborative teaching or **cooperative teaching**, co-teaching takes mutuality and reciprocity in collaborative consultation one step further (see Scruggs, Mastropieri, & McDuffie, 2007; Walsh & Jones, 2004). **Co-teaching** between general and special educators means "two or more professionals delivering substantive instruction to a diverse, or blended, group of students in a single physical space" (Cook & Friend, 1998, p. 454).

There are many forms of co-teaching in schools, but the most common appears to be for one teacher to instruct and the other to assist in some way (Scruggs et al., 2007). Sometimes, teachers find it very effective and workable. Other times, co-teaching can present incredible challenges to teachers and to students. Unfortunately, research on cooperative teaching is lacking (Zigmond, 2007).

CURRICULA AND INSTRUCTIONAL STRATEGIES   In addition to teacher cooperation, there are curricula and instructional strategies that help in making some students with disabilities successful in the general education classroom. **Cooperative learning** is an instructional strategy that many proponents of inclusion believe is an effective way of integrating students with disabilities into groups of nondisabled peers. In cooperative learning, students work together in heterogeneous small groups to solve problems or practice responses.

▪ **Collaborative consultation**
An approach in which a special educator and a general educator collaborate to identify teaching strategies for a student with disabilities. The relationship between the two professionals is based on the premises of shared responsibility and equal authority.

▪ **Cooperative teaching**
An approach in which general educators and special educators teach together in the general classroom; it helps the special educator know the context of the general education classroom better.

▪ **Co-Teaching**
A special educator working side-by-side with a general educator in a classroom, both teachers providing instruction to the group.

UNDERSTANDING THE STANDARDS AND PRINCIPLES   Describe at least two curricula and instructional strategies. (INTASC 4.10)

INTASC

▪ **Cooperative learning**
A teaching approach in which the teacher places students with heterogeneous abilities (for example, some might have disabilities) together to work on assignments.

■ **Peer-mediated instruction**
The deliberate use of a student's classroom peer(s) to assist in teaching an academic or social skill.

■ **Peer tutoring**
A method that can be used to integrate students with disabilities in general education classrooms. Based on the notion that students can effectively tutor one another, the role of learner or teacher is assigned to either the student with a disability or the nondisabled student.

■ **Peer confederates**
Peers who assist the teacher.

■ **Classwide peer tutoring (CWPT)**
An instructional procedure in which all students in the class are involved in tutoring and being tutored by classmates on specific skills as directed by their teacher.

■ **Partial participation**
An approach in which students with disabilities, while in the general education classroom, engage in the same activities as nondisabled students but on a reduced basis; the teacher adapts the activity to allow each student to participate as much as possible.

■ **Modifications**
Changes made in instruction or assessment to make it possible for a student with a disability to respond more normally.

■ **Accommodations**
Changes in the delivery of instruction, type of student performance, or method of assessment which do not significantly change the content or conceptual difficulty of the curriculum.

■ **Adaptations**
Changes in curricular content or conceptual difficulty or changes in instructional objectives and methods.

■ **Tiered assignments**
Assignments varying in difficulty but on a single topic.

Another research-based instructional strategy to enhance the integration of students with disabilities is **peer-mediated instruction** (Fuchs et al., 2001; Gardner et al., 2001; Maheady, Harper, & Mallette, 2001; see also Fulk & King, 2001 and the Websites they list). Peer-mediated instruction may refer to **peer tutoring**, the use of **peer confederates** in managing behavior problems, or any other arrangement in which peers are deliberately recruited and trained to help teach an academic or social skill to a classmate (Falk & Wehby, 2001).

When the whole class is involved, the strategy is referred to as **classwide peer tutoring (CWPT)**. In this procedure, peer tutoring is routinely done by all students in the general education classroom for particular subject matter, such as reading or math (Greenwood, Arrega-Mayer, Utley, Gavin, & Terry, 2001; Kourea, Cartledge, & Musti-Rao, 2007). CWPT doesn't mean that the teacher provides no instruction. On the contrary, teachers must provide instruction in how to do peer tutoring and in the content of the tutoring sessions. Peers tutor each other to provide drill and practice of skills they already have.

Partial participation, another instructional strategy, means having students with disabilities participate, on a reduced basis, in virtually all activities experienced by all students in the general education classroom. It questions the assumption that including students with severe mental and physical limitations is a waste of time because they cannot benefit from the activities in the same way that nondisabled students can. Whether partial participation actually achieves these goals to the benefit of students is an open question.

INSTRUCTIONAL ACCOMMODATIONS AND ADAPTATIONS Instruction may be modified for learners with disabilities. **Modifications** usually take the form of amended materials or assignments and are different from changes in curricula or instructional strategies. **Accommodations** include changes in instruction that don't significantly change the content or conceptual difficulty level of the curriculum. Alternatively, **adaptations** generally involve more significant modifications of instruction than accommodations (Miller, 2002).

Tiered assignments (Tomlinson, 2001) are an example of adaptations, wherein teachers provide choices for assignments on a single topic that vary in difficulty. For example, when studying a novel, some students might write paragraphs that identify and describe the characters; others might write paragraphs or papers that analyze the traits of each character, using examples from the book. In this case, both the assignment and the subsequent grading are different.

TRAINING GENERAL EDUCATION TEACHERS One point of view is that both general education and special education teachers are necesssary, and that they should work together, but that they have distinct roles to play. Zigmond (2007) describes teaching students with disabilities as a two-person job, meaning that truly effective special education requires both a general education teacher and a special education teacher trained to do different things, not merely to work together with a common purpose. In the press for inclusion and collaboration, Zigmond suggests, perhaps the primary role and function of the special education teacher has gotten lost. In her words:

> I propose that a "special education coach" be assigned to each school building to provide consultation and job-embedded staff development that helps build capacity among general education teachers for meeting the needs of diverse learners in their content classes. (p. 130)

Zigmond (2007) argues that the popular co-teaching model of collaboration can't provide the kind of intensive instruction that students with learning disabilities and behavior disorders (and, presumably, many students with other disabilities as well) require if they are to make adequate progress. Moreover, she argues that special education teachers need special expertise in teaching specialized and individualized curricula. General education teachers are content specialists and should be trained by the "special education coach" to address a wider range of instructional needs than they otherwise would have, but they can't take the place of special education teachers.

WHO SHOULD DO WHAT?   The roles of general and special education teachers continue to be debated. One perspective is that all general education teachers should be equipped, at least with special educators as co-teachers, to teach all students, including those with every kind of disability. This suggestion seems infeasible for a variety of reasons (see Kauffman & Hallahan, 2005a). A competing perspective is that although general education teachers need to be taught how to include a wide range of learners in their classrooms, special education teachers are needed to work specifically and intensively with students who have disabilities (e.g., Zigmond, 2007).

Another issue that continues to bedevil education, both general and special, is the preparation that teachers should have and what "highly qualified," as required by NCLB, should be taken to mean (Gelman, Pullen, & Kauffman, 2004). Various alternative routes to teacher certification have been offered, and in general education "highly qualified" usually has been taken to mean that the teacher is well prepared in a content area. However, some have argued that special education teachers need expertise that goes beyond content. Zigmond (2007) observed that special education teachers may need training in general education before they receive training in special education, just as other professionals typically add specialization to their general preparation:

> I do not take issue with the possibility that as a profession, we should require that special education be a second certificate that adds specialization to the general training provided to general education teachers at the elementary or secondary levels (on the medical model of the general practitioner who then specializes). (p. 119)

Zigmond (2007) also noted that students with learning and behavior disorders are often overwhelmed, disorganized, and frustrated in school and lack many important learning strategies. In preparing teachers, she suggested:

> The job of the special education teacher should be to find the time and resources to teach students with [learning and behavior disorders] all the skills NOT taught in the general education curriculum. (p. 127)

It seems highly likely that for decades to come, there will be controversy about what makes a good teacher. There will also be continuing debate about the working relationship between general and special education teachers, regardless of judgments of their quality.

Assessments of Progress

In the 1990s, state and federal policymakers became concerned about what they perceived as a general decline in students' educational achievement. As a result, they emphasized "standards-based" reforms. These reforms involve setting standards of learning that are measured by standardized tests. The reformers believed that teachers' expectations have been too low and that all students should be held to higher standards (see Finn, Rotherham, & Hokanson, 2001; Hoover & Patton, 2004; Pugach & Warger, 2001; Thurlow, 2000; Thurlow, Nelson, Teelucksingh, & Draper, 2001).

Concerns of special educators were expressed primarily in the 1997 amendments to IDEA. Concerns of general educators were expressed primarily in NCLB, which was actually a reauthorization of the Elementary and Secondary Education Act (Yell & Drasgow, 2005). Both laws had the intention of improving the instruction of students with disabilities by

Simulation Homework Exercise

Instructional Accomodations ● Go to the Homework and Exercises section in Chapter 2 of MyEducationLab and complete the simulation exercise titled "Instructional Accommodations."

Federal law now requires that the inclusion of students with disabilities in assessments of progress in the general education curriculum must be addressed in every individualized education program (IEP).

making sure that these students are included in the assessments of educational progress demanded of all students. NCLB requires that the average scores of various subgroups of students be reported and that all groups, including students with disabilities, show progress. NCLB also requires that gaps in the performance of various groups be closed so that the averages for the various subgroups are not significantly different. Although this objective appears to be impossible to achieve in the case of students with disabilities, it is nonetheless an assumption of NCLB, IDEA, and the President's Commission on Excellence in Special Education, which was appointed in 2001 by President George W. Bush and that submitted its report in 2002 (see Kauffman, 2004; Kauffman & Konold, 2007; Kauffman & Wiley, 2004).

Progress Monitoring

■ **Progress monitoring**
Brief, frequent measures of performance used to determine whether a student is learning as expected; if student isn't learning as expected, the teacher can make changes to the instruction.

Progress monitoring assessments are frequent, quick-and-easy measures that are administered at regular intervals and provide information on whether or not a student is learning as expected. The purpose of progress monitoring instruments is to determine whether current instructional practices are appropriate for individual students and to identify instructional needs.

Outcome Measures

Measures of student achievement, or outcome measures, are standardized measures administered in group settings. These measures compare a student's performance with other students, or compare a state's or district's performance with other states or districts. Measures of student outcomes are often used for systems of accountability, including a student's promotion to the next grade level. As a result of IDEA and NCLB, students with disabilities are included in these assessments along with their peers without disabilities.

Testing Accommodations

Accommodations for evaluation procedures might involve altering setting, the presentation format, or the response format. Setting or scheduling accommodations alter the setting or time of the assessment, such as small-group administration and extended time.

Presentation accommodations alter the way the assessment is presented to the student, such as having problems and directions read aloud. Response accommodations alter the way in which the student answers questions on the assessment, such as oral or typed responses. Accommodations can make a significant difference in how students with some disabilities are able to perform on standardized tests. Therefore, making sure that students are assessed with appropriate accommodations for their disabilities is extremely important when they are included in evaluations of progress. However, inappropriate accommodations merely undercut reasonable expectations for students with disability and misrepresent students' true capabilities (Kauffman et al., 2004; Pierangelo & Giuliani, 2006).

UNDERSTANDING THE STANDARDS AND PRINCIPLES Why has the standards-based reform movement generated controversy? (CEC Knowledge and Skill Standard GC1K3)

Special Education in the Context of NCLB

The standards-based reform movement of the late twentieth and early twenty-first centuries brought with it a heavy emphasis on access to the general education curriculum for students with disabilities (Hoover & Patton, 2004; Pierangelo & Giuliani, 2006; Zigmond, 2007). The curriculum for students with disabilities often has been different from the curriculum in general education. Failure to teach students with disabilities the same things that are taught in general education has been interpreted to mean that the expectations for these students are lower, resulting in their low achievement and failure to make a successful transition to adult life.

Understandably, the standards-based reform movement has generated much controversy: What constitutes curriculum? What should be the curriculum? What should the standards be (just how high should they be, and in what areas of the curriculum should they be set)? Who should set the standards? How should achievement of or progress toward the standards be measured? What should be the consequences for students—and for schools or states—if standards aren't met? What should be given up in music, art, poetry, physical education, and other areas to ensure progress on standardized tests in core curriculum areas of reading and math?

These are not trivial questions for general or special educators. Dobbs (2004) reported that some schools are indeed dropping classes in art, foreign language, and other electives to give more time and attention to the standards required by NCLB. Another writer complained that his poetry-writing class in a Washington, DC, middle school was eliminated because of NCLB standards (Grim, 2004).

For students with disabilities, additional questions arise: Should all standards apply to all students, regardless of disability? What should be the consequences of failing to meet a given standard if the student has a disability? Under what circumstances are alternative standards appropriate? Under what circumstances should special accommodations be made in assessing progress toward a standard? Answering questions like these requires professional judgment in the individual case, and such judgment is required by law (see Bateman, 2007; Huefner, 2006; Johns, 2003; Kauffman & Hallahan, 2005a; Thurlow, 2000; Yell, 2006). Moreover, assuming that IDEA and NCLB require the same things of students with disabilities is erroneous (Johns), and expecting students with disabilities to score the same, on average, as students without disabilities is expecting the impossible (Kauffman, 2004; Kauffman & Konold, 2007; Kauffman & Wiley, 2004). As Melissa Gogel, a sixth-grade special education teacher, said, "We [special educators and their students] will always fail. . . . The government is trying to put everybody in one melting pot and say that everybody has to pass the same test" (Dobbs, 2004, p. A12).

We might ask what NCLB is actually interpreted to mean. Is the same level of performance expected of all students? Following is one educational consultant's view:

Teachers say they have to teach the students where they are, which means at sixth-grade level in high school if they can't read well. Their attitude may be compassionate, but it is misguided. There's ample evidence that accelerating instruction works better than retarding it in the name of remediation. Observations made in the Dallas Unified School District show that students who score well have teachers who cover the curriculum appropriate to the grade level. These teachers spend little time on drill and practice, and don't remediate in the classroom but rather get help for students outside of class. (Mitchell, 2004, p. A21)

If this view is taken as defensible, then what happens to remedial programs and to special education during the school day? Is it a good idea to provide instruction that is beyond the student's level of ability to understand and perform successfully? One noted special educator said that in her opinion, Mitchell's educational philosophy could be stated in a nutshell: "Teach the best and shoot the rest" (Janet Lerner, personal communication, April 27, 2004; see also Kauffman, 2005c; Kauffman & Konold, 2007; Kauffman & Landrum, 2006). The issue is of obvious importance to general education, but it is of particular concern to special education for two reasons: First, federal regulations allow only a small minority of students with disabilities to be excluded from the same testing as students without disabilities; NCLB allows states to exempt 2 percent of the population from standard assessment procedures (U.S. Department of Education, 2007). Second, some of the programs that are being eliminated (e.g., art, music, physical education, and other "noncore" or extracurricular activities) are those in which students with disabilities are most likely to experience success and be successfully included in general education (see Siperstein, Parker, et al., 2007).

Can We Solve the Dilemma of Standards and Disability?

In any area of performance, setting a standard that very few individuals fail will eventually be perceived as "low." Setting a standard that many individuals cannot reach will be perceived, at least after a time, as "high." The idea of universal proficiency is, simply put, not rational (Rothstein, Jacobsen, & Wilder, 2006).

Who will be blamed for a given person's failure to meet a standard and who will be congratulated when someone meets or exceeds a standard depend on our assessment of the effort expended by teacher and student. However, one thing seems certain: Standards will not homogenize achievement or expectations. The consequences of standards-based reform such as NCLB for students with and without disabilities will become clearer as reforms are implemented and standards are set. Some commentators have noted that the basic premises and language of NCLB are seductive. It is "an idea that seems so right you wonder how any decent-minded legislator could oppose it" (Raspberry, 2004, p. A21). Yet, Raspberry also notes, the law has a fatal flaw, which is its focus on punishing those who do not meet its standards: "its underlying assumption that school failure is willful, and that if you put the fear of God in the people who run the schools, they'll do their jobs a lot better" (p. A21).

Requiring all students with disabilities, and those for whom the tests are inappropriate for other reasons, to take state exams is considered by some to be cruel to both students and teachers (Kauffman, 2002, 2004; Kauffman & Konold, 2007; Kauffman & Wiley, 2004). However, testing to determine outcomes is necessary if we want to know whether programs for students with disabilities are "working" (Kauffman & Konold). Standardized tests have a legitimate place in assessing outcomes, and demonizing the tests themselves is not helpful. However, it is important to understand that "testing is useful only if you make the right comparisons for the right reasons" (Kauffman, 2002, p. 240). When it comes to special education, it's wrong to compare outcomes for students with disabilities to outcomes for students without disabilities. The right comparisons are contrasting students with disabilities who receive special education (or any given treatment) to those who don't receive it, or comparing students with disabilities before and after they receive special education (Kauffman, 2004; Kauffman & Hallahan, 2005a).

Federal law requires that a variety of early intervention services be available to all infants and toddlers identified as having disabilities. Such services include special education instruction, physical therapy, speech and language therapy, and medical diagnostic services.

Early Intervention

Many educators and social scientists believe that the earlier in life a disability is recognized and a program of education or treatment is started, the better the outcome will be for the child (e.g., Gargiulo & Kilgo, 2005; Howard, Williams, & Lepper, 2005; Noonan & McCormick, 2006; Stichter, Conroy, & Kauffman, 2008; Walker, Ramsey, & Gresham, 2004; Walker & Sprague, 2007). They also see an important federal role in ensuring early intervention. Three basic arguments underlie early intervention:

1. A child's early learning provides the foundation for later learning, so the sooner a special program or intervention is begun, the further the child is likely to go in learning more complex skills.

2. Early intervention is likely to provide support for the child and family that will help prevent the child from developing additional problems or disabilities.

3. Early intervention can help families adjust to having a child with disabilities; give parents the skills they need to handle the child effectively at home; and help families find the additional support services they may need, such as counseling, medical assistance, or financial aid.

Children whose disabilities are diagnosed at a very young age tend to be those with specific syndromes (e.g., Down syndrome) or obvious physical disabilities. Many have severe and multiple disabilities. Throughout the primary grades, children with disabilities may be categorized under the broad label **developmental delay** rather than identified as having a more specific disability (e.g., a federal special education category such as autism, learning disability, or emotional disturbance). Typically, such a child's needs cannot be met by a single agency or intervention, so many professionals must work

Video Homework Exercise

Early Intervention • Go to the Homework and Exercises section in Chapter 2 of MyEducationLab and watch the video "Early Intervention", about the benefits of preschool for young children with special needs.

▪ **Developmental delay**
A term often used to encompass a variety of disabilities of infants or young children indicating that they are significantly behind the norm for development in one or more areas such as motor development, cognitive development, or language.

together closely and with parents if the child is to be served effectively (Gallagher, Rhodes, & Darling, 2004; Noonan & McCormick, 2006). If the child's disabilities are recognized at an early age and intervention by all necessary professionals is well coordinated, the child's learning and development can often be greatly enhanced.

In the area of emotional and behavioral disorders, particularly those involving children who are highly oppositional or disobedient and aggressive from a young age, early intervention shows enormous promise (Walker & Sprague, 2007). Long-term follow-up data suggest that the life course of children who are at high risk for becoming aggressive and disruptive can be changed dramatically through early behavioral intervention (Strain & Timm, 2001).

Federal laws now require that a variety of early intervention services be available to all infants and toddlers who are identified as having disabilities. Such services include special education instruction, physical therapy, speech and language therapy, and medical diagnostic services. In addition, laws require the development of an **individualized family service plan (IFSP)**. As we discussed in Chapter 1, an IFSP is similar to an IEP for older children, but it broadens the focus to include the family as well as the child. In fact, federal regulations stipulate that the family be involved in the development of the IFSP. Table 2.1 shows how an IFSP is compared to a young student's IEP. As Noonan and McCormick (2006) note, an IFSP may be written for children up to six years of age, but usually an IFSP is written for infants and children up to three years of age, with the IEP being more common for children three and older.

One common way of categorizing the variety of early intervention programs is to consider whether the primary location of the services is in a center, a home, or a combination of the two. The earliest early intervention programs for children with disabilities were center-based. In **center-based programs**, the child and the family come to the center for training and/or counseling. One advantage of center-based programs is that center staff can see more children. Furthermore, some professionals believe that this program allows center staff to have more influence over what goes on in the interaction between parent and child.

In more recent years, authorities have advocated **home-based programs** or a combination of center- and home-based approaches. There are several advantages to approaches that take place in the home. A couple of the most important are that (1) with the increase in mothers working outside the home and single-parent families, home-based programs are more convenient for more family members, and (2) skills and techniques learned by children and adults at the center need to be transferred to the home, but when these skills are learned in the natural environment—that is, the home—this transfer is not necessary.

As preschool programs and daycare become more pervasive, more and more young children with disabilities are being included in "natural" environments with their nondisabled or typically developing peers. The integrated or inclusionary daycare or preschool program is thus another type of program.

Consensus on Early Intervention, or How to Do It Best

Compared to most of special education, that for infants, toddlers, and preschoolers has had few controversial issues. This is probably because so many professionals have fought for so long to get the needs of very young children recognized that they have not had time to engage in many debates about specific details involved in early intervention. In a sense, early childhood special educators have been bound together by the common goal of securing legislation and programming for young children with disabilities. Nevertheless, there have been and continue to be some areas of disagreement among early childhood special education professionals. Three of the most compelling issues are the following:

■ **Individualized family service plan (IFSP)**
A plan mandated by PL 99-457 to provide services for young children with disabilities (under three years of age) and their families; drawn up by professionals and parents; similar to an IEP for older children.

■ **Center-based program**
A program implemented primarily in a school or center, not in the student's home.

■ **Home-based programs**
Programs delivered primarily in a student's home rather than in a school or center.

1. The appropriate role of the family in early intervention
2. Whether it is better to have a child- or an adult-directed curriculum
3. Whether full inclusion is best for all young children.

We devote all of Chapter 4 to family issues, so we discuss only the second and third issues here.

CHILD-DIRECTED VERSUS ADULT-DIRECTED PROGRAMS   Tension exists between early childhood educators who are concerned with nondisabled populations and those who are focused on children with disabilities over the degree of adult direction that is most appropriate, whether the adult is a parent or teacher. Heavily influenced by the theories of the

INTERNET RESOURCES

Resources for Early Childhood Special Education has a useful site at www.mcps.k12.md.us/curriculum/pep/pz.html
The National Information Center for Children and Youth with Disabilities has a useful Website at www.nichcy.org

---

TABLE 2.1   **Comparison of IDEA Requirements for the IFSP and the IEP**

An IFSP must include

A statement of the child's present level of development in these areas: physical (including vision, hearing, and health status), cognitive, communication, psychosocial, and adaptive behavior.

A statement of family strengths, resources, concerns, and priorities related to the child's development.

A statement of the major outcomes expected to be achieved for the child and family.

A statement of the frequency, intensity, and method of delivering the early intervention services necessary to produce desired outcomes for the child and family.

A statement of the natural environments where services will be provided or a statement explaining why services will not be provided in natural environments.

Projected dates for the initiation of services and anticipated duration of services.

The name of a service coordinator responsible for implementation of the IFSP and coordination with other agencies/professionals.

Steps to be implemented to ensure successful transition (a transition plan) to preschool services provided by the public schools.

Written consent from the parents or legal guardian.

An IEP must include

A statement of the child's present levels of educational performance. For preschool children, a description of how the disability affects the child's participation in age-appropriate activities.

A statement of annual goals and short-term objectives detailing what the child is expected to learn over a specific time with criteria to determine if the goals/objectives have been achieved.

A statement of the special education and related services to be provided to help the child reach the goals and objectives.

The extent of time to which the child will participate with nondisabled peers in the general education setting, including district and state assessments and an explanation of the time the student will *not* participate with nondisabled peers.

Projected dates that the special education program and other services will begin and anticipated duration of services.

A transition plan (at age 14) stating the student's needs and agency responsibilities.

Date for evaluation of performance (review at least annually or as often as progress is reported for children without disabilities).

Source: Noonan, M. J., McCormick, L. (2006). *Young children with disabilities in natural environments: Methods and procedures* (p. 56). Baltimore: Paul H. Brookes. Reprinted by permission.

noted Swiss psychologist Jean Piaget, most early childhood teachers are oriented toward a curriculum that allows children to explore their environment relatively freely. These teachers advocate a developmental approach, assuming that children's development will unfold naturally with encouragement, guidance, and support from the teacher.

Many early interventionists, on the other hand, come from a tradition that assumes that children with disabilities need a heavy dose of direction from adults if they are to learn the skills they lack. Furthermore, early childhood special educators have generally had a greater focus on individualizing instruction for preschoolers through task analysis, adaptation of materials and activities, and systematic assessment (Bowe, 2004; Deiner, 2004; McLean, Wolery, & Bailey, 2004; Noonan & McCormick, 2006; Wilson, 2003). As more and more children with disabilities have been integrated with nondisabled preschoolers, the issues of adult direction and individualization have come to the fore.

A major task facing early childhood special educators is to reach agreement with mainstream early childhood educators on programming for preschoolers with disabilities. Both sides can undoubtedly learn from each other. On the one hand, researchers have known for a long time that preschoolers with disabilities do better in highly structured, teacher-directed, individualized programs (Abt Associates, 1976–1977). On the other hand, authorities have noted that moving from a highly structured preschool intervention program to a traditional kindergarten can present problems of transition (Noonan & McCormick, 2006).

UNDERSTANDING THE STANDARDS AND PRINCIPLES What are some trends and issues in early childhood education and early childhood special education? (CEC Knowledge and Skill Standard EC1K2)

INCLUSIVE EDUCATION   Virtually all early childhood educators suggest that children with identifiable disabilities and those who are considered at risk for school failure should be included in programs that are designed to serve diverse groups of learners, including young children without disabilities. In fact, most preschoolers with disabilities now receive their education totally or primarily in general education classrooms. However, the extent to which the practices in programs for typically developing young children are appropriate for children with disabilities has been a matter of considerable controversy (Noonan & McCormick, 2006; Odom, 2000).

A radical philosophy of inclusive education will not necessarily serve all young children well. However, some research has suggested that with proper adjustment for the individual needs of children, inclusion of young children with disabilities is always or nearly always beneficial (Noonan & McCormick, 2006; Odom, 2000; Strain, 2001). Certainly, there is more evidence supporting the inclusion of very young children in groups with typically developing students than there is supporting the inclusion of older students.

Are We Ready to Face the Demands of Prevention?

We hope that early childhood education will continue to play an important role in eliminating and lessening the impact of disability on children and their families. We caution, however, not to assume that early intervention alone will mean fewer children with disabilities (see Kauffman, 2005b). Although educators are devising more effective programs of early intervention, the number of children with disabilities is increasing. The reasons for this increase are many and complex and are related to changes in economic and social conditions in the United States, including these twenty-first-century factors:

- A high percentage of young children and their mothers live in poverty, have poor nutrition, and are exposed to environmental conditions likely to cause disease and disability.
- Many babies are born to teenage mothers.
- Many babies are born to mothers who receive inadequate prenatal care, have poor nutrition during pregnancy, and abuse substances that can harm the fetus.
- Many babies are born with a low birth weight.

Students with disabilities must have preparation for life after high school, including further education, work, and independent living. Working with a job coach and with the cooperation of a local business, a student is integrated into this work staff.

- Environmental hazards, both chemical and social, are increasing.
- Millions of children are subjected to abuse and to environments in which violence and substance abuse are pervasive.
- Substantial cuts in, and revisions of, social programs have widened the gap between needs and the availability of social services.

Early intervention seems to hold great promise for prevention of disabilities, but there are strong forces working against prevention, including the revulsion many people feel for labels and the propositions of education reformers that work against identifying problems early and intervening to stop them from getting worse (Kauffman, 1999b, 2005a, 2005b; Kauffman & Konold, 2007). Besides prevention, other continuing issues include assessment of infants and toddlers, the use of computer technology with young children, the changing roles of special educators, emerging philosophies of early childhood education, cultural and linguistic diversity, and access to community resources (see McLean et al., 2004; Noonan & McCormick, 2006).

Transitions to Adulthood and Employment

Most students complete high school and find jobs, enter a vocational training program, or go to college without experiencing major adjustment difficulties. We know that dropout and unemployment rates are far too high for all youths, especially in economically depressed communities, but the outlook for students with disabilities is perhaps even worse.

Published figures on dropout rates must be viewed with caution because there are many different ways of defining the term *dropout* and computing the statistics. Studies of what happens to students with disabilities during and after their high school years strongly suggest, however, that a higher percentage of them, compared to students without disabilities, have difficulty in making the transition from adolescence to adulthood

UNDERSTANDING
THE STANDARDS AND
PRINCIPLES   What should
professionals and parents consider
when planning students' transition
to adulthood? (CEC Knowledge
and Skill Standard GC10S4)

Council for
Exceptional
Children

■ **Supported employment**
A method of integrating people
with disabilities who cannot work
independently into competitive
employment; includes use of an
employment specialist, or job
coach, who helps the person with
a disability function on the job.

**INTERNET
RESOURCES**

Information about disability related
to jobs, shopping, and other issues
can be found at www.wemedia.org

■ **Job coach**
A person who assists adult workers
with disabilities (especially those
with intellectual disabilities), providing vocational assessmment, instruction, overall planning, and
interaction assistance with employers, family, and related government
and service agencies.

and from school to work. Many students with disabilities drop out of school, experience
great difficulty in finding and holding jobs, do not find work that is suited to their
capabilities, do not receive further training or education, or become dependent on their
families or public assistance programs. Thus, transition to work and adulthood is an
ongoing issue of great importance and is related to self-determination (Brolin & Loyd,
2004; Greene & Kochhar-Bryant, 2003; Sitlington & Clark, 2006; Wehmeyer, Palmer,
Soukup, Garner, & Lawrence, 2007).

Federal laws, including IDEA, require attention to transition plans for older students, and these must be incorporated in students' IEPs. Transition services include
a coordinated set of outcome-oriented activities that promote movement from school
to postsecondary education, vocational training, integrated employment (including
supported employment), continuing adult education, adult services, independent
living, or community participation. Typical services are described in Table 2.2.

IDEA requires that each student's IEP contain a statement of needed transition services,
beginning no later than fourteen years of age and annually thereafter. (For students for
whom it is appropriate or deemed at risk of failure, the statement is to be included in the IEP
at a younger age.) In addition, the IEP must include a statement of the linkages and/or
responsibilities of each participating agency before the student leaves the school setting.

An important aspect of this legislation is that it recognizes that transition
involves more than just employment. Many authorities have applauded this broad
emphasis on independent living, community adjustment, and so forth. For example,
some have championed the idea that transition programming should be aimed at
improving the quality of life for people with disabilities. Although quality of life is
difficult to define precisely, personal choice is one of its underlying principles (see
Eisenman, 2007). However, maintaining physical and material well-being, adopting
adult roles such as those required for employment and appropriate leisure activities,
building satisfying interpersonal relationships, assuming social responsibilities, and
finding personal fulfillment are clearly aspects of a desirable quality of life.

An increase in supported employment has come with the federal mandate for transition
services. **Supported employment** is designed to assist people with disabilities who cannot
function independently in competitive employment, and it has been particularly helpful in
vocational preparation and employment of people with severe disabilities (Brolin & Loyd,
2004). It's a method of ensuring that they are able to work in integrated work settings alongside people without disabilities. In a typical supported employment situation, an employment specialist, or **job coach**, places the individual in a job with a business. The job coach
then provides on-site training that is gradually reduced as the worker is able to function more
independently on the job. A job coach may be known by a variety of titles, including coordinator, but regardless of the title the idea is that it refers to a professional who places and
supervises students in the workplace (Sitlington & Clark, 2006). Competitive employment is
usually defined as working at least twenty hours per week at a type of job usually filled by a
person without disabilities. We discuss supported employment further in Chapter 5.

Preparing students for continued education, adult responsibilities, independence,
and employment has always been a goal of public secondary education. However, schools
are increasingly recognizing that preparation for a work career is something that must
begin in the early grades and be taught specifically along with other skills. Those who
study transition are also increasingly recognizing the importance of family in making
career choices (Lindstrom, Doren, Metheny, Johnson, & Zane, 2007).

How much of the curriculum should be devoted to occupational skills at each level of
schooling, from the primary grades through high school? This question has been
addressed by numerous experts in transition programming. Figure 2.1 on page 75 shows
the relative curriculum emphasis recommended by Brolin and Loyd (2004). They suggest
that for many students with disabilities occupational skills become increasingly important
as the child ages and should dominate the curriculum in the senior high school.

TABLE 2.2	**Typical Adult Service and Community Employment Alternatives**

1. Competitive (unsupported) employment—on company payroll with benefits and without trainer or support from a human services agency.

2. Job placement, or transitional support into regular employment—short-term help from an agency, such as the state vocational rehabilitation agency, in finding and getting adjusted to a job.

3. Supported employment—job placement, training, and continuing support for as long as necessary in an integrated community business. Supported employment can be in the form of an individual placement or a group model of several workers, such as an enclave or mobile work crew. Workers earn minimum wage or better.

4. Volunteer work—unpaid work that is preferred or chosen by an individual for reasons other than "daily support." This is usually done for community service organizations, such as the SPCA, a hospital, or the National Cancer Society. Labor laws define what types of work are considered volunteer. Workers with disabilities cannot volunteer to do work that would pay a wage to employees without disabilities.

5. Sheltered work—work done in a sheltered workshop where the majority of workers are disabled and earn subminimum wages. Sheltered workshops can offer a variety of employment and evaluation services, such as work activity, work adjustment training, vocational evaluation, long-term sheltered employment, and work activity programs.

6. Work activity center-based or nonintegrated day programs—focus on "prevocational" skills, such as motor tasks or self-care skills.

7. Day activity or adult day care center—based, nonintegrated programs—usually have a therapeutic or nonvocational emphasis, depending on the funding source.

Source: Moon, M. S., & Inge, K. (2000). Vocational preparation and transition. In M. E. Snell & F. Brown (Eds.), *Instruction of students with severe disabilities* (5th ed., p. 595). Upper Saddle River, NJ: Merrill. Reprinted with permission.

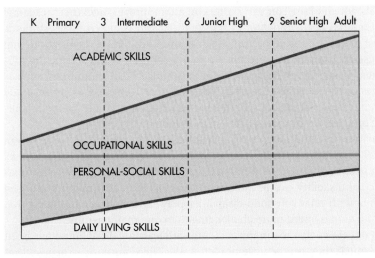

FIGURE 2.1	Suggested curriculum for career development at various

grade levels

Source: Brolin, D. E., & Loyd, R. J. (2004). *Career development and transition services: A functional life-skills approach* (4th ed., p. 430). Upper Saddle River, NJ: Prentice Hall. Reprinted with permission.

Making Transition Fit Level of Need

As with early intervention programming, little controversy surrounds the basic premise of transition programming for students as they move from secondary school to work or postsecondary education. All special educators agree that transition programming is critical for the successful adjustment of adults with disabilities. However, there is some controversy about the specifics of transition. Much of this has to do with trying to meet the diverse requirements of the federal mandate. A few states have achieved a high degree of compliance with federal law and have implemented excellent transition policies, but many others have not. Many IEPs are in technical compliance with the IDEA mandate for transition but lack key elements, reflecting a lack of thoughtful planning.

Some professionals are debating how best to build a curriculum that covers education, employment, independent living, and community participation. This concern for meeting the diverse needs of students is manifested somewhat differently for students with more severe disabilities than for those with milder disabilities.

STUDENTS WITH LOW-INCIDENCE DISABILITIES For students with severe or low-incidence disabilities, much of the concern focuses on the coordination and linkage of the many agencies outside the school setting (Moon & Inge, 2000; Sitlington & Clark, 2006). Many special education personnel are unaccustomed to working with nonschool agencies. For example, the relationship between vocational and special education has traditionally been ambiguous. Federal regulations, however, now require that special education work with vocational education as well as with other agencies in the community.

Special educators at the secondary level have been moving toward more involvement in the community, but the federal transition mandate has hastened the need for these outreach efforts. Approaches such as supported employment, for example, require that special educators work with local employers in establishing training and working environments for students with disabilities. Not all special educators have been trained for this expanded role, however. We're still in the infancy stage of knowing how best to accomplish this interface between the school and community environments. Experimentation is needed with approaches to educating special educators for this broader role.

STUDENTS WITH HIGH-INCIDENCE DISABILITIES For students with milder or high-incidence disabilities, much of the concern centers on attempting to meet their academic as well as their vocational needs (Stichter et al., 2008). Teachers of secondary students are constantly faced with the decision of how much to stress academics versus vocational preparation. Because their disabilities are milder, many children with learning disabilities, for example, may be able to go on to postsecondary educational institutions, such as community colleges or universities. It's often difficult to tell as early as tenth grade (when such decisions need to be made) whether to steer students with learning disabilities toward college preparatory or more vocationally oriented curricula.

It might seem intuitive that successful transition for young people with severe disabilities is harder to achieve than for young people with relatively mild disabilities. However, this isn't necessarily the case. Finding employment at which people with relatively mild intellectual disability can be successful is not as easy as it might seem (see Leahy, 2004). People with relatively mild disabilities may have multiple problems that make their successful employment more challenging than one might assume.

Some authorities believe that too many students with learning disabilities have been sold short on how much they can achieve academically. These authorities believe that such students are written off as academic failures who can never achieve at the college level. This diminished expectation for academic success translates into a curriculum that makes few academic demands on students.

Other authorities maintain that an overemphasis on academics leaves many students with learning disabilities unprepared to enter the world of work on leaving school. They believe that the learning problems of students with learning disabilities tend to be minimized. They assert that just because students with learning disabilities are characterized as having mild disabilities, they do not necessarily have insignificant learning impairments.

Along these same lines, some professionals think that far too few support services are available to students with high-incidence disabilities. Whereas transition services such as supported employment are available to people with severe disabilities, individuals with milder disabilities are often left to fend for themselves once they graduate from secondary school.

What Should Be Taught When?

It's still too early to tell how much effect the emphasis on standards-based reform and the inclusion of students with disabilities in general education curriculum and assessment procedures (as mandated by NCLB and IDEA) will have on students with disabilities. However, despite some of the unresolved issues, we can be encouraged by all the attention that special educators have given to the area of transition. A variety of transition opportunities are available now that were unavailable just a few years ago. It is increasingly clear that successful transition takes early and sustained effort, but it is not clear just how such support can best be provided (see Moon & Inge, 2000; Peck, 2004; Sitlington, Clark, & Kolstoe, 2000; Sitlington & Clark, 2006). Figure 2.2 shows the overarching concern for transition, even in an era emphasizing academic standards. Standards of academic learning are important, as are outcomes of other types, and students must have opportunities for both. Transition is the key element in bringing standards, alternative outcomes, and opportunities together.

In considering transition issues, it's helpful to keep in mind that a smooth and successful transition to adult life is difficult for any adolescent. Individuals find many different routes to adulthood, and we would be foolish to prescribe a single pattern of transition. Our goal must be to provide the special assistance needed by adolescents and young adults with disabilities that will help them to achieve the most rewarding, productive, independent, and integrated adult lives possible. This goal cannot be achieved by assuming that all adolescents and young adults with disabilities, or even all individuals who fall into a given special education category, will need the same special transition services or that all will achieve the same level of independence and productivity. One of education's great challenges is to devise an effective array of programs that will meet the individual needs of students on their paths to adulthood.

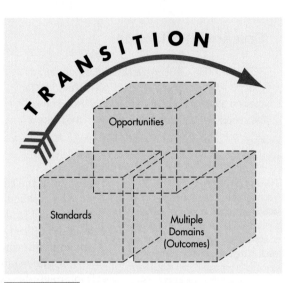

FIGURE 2.2 Transition in relation to standards, opportunities, and multiple domains (outcomes)

Source: Greene, G., & Kochhar-Bryant, C. A. (2003). *Pathways to successful transition for youth with disabilities* (p. 447). Upper Saddle River, NJ: Prentice Hall. Reprinted with permission.

Zero Tolerance, PBS, PBIS, and Other Issues of Discipline

Classroom management and discipline is recognized as among the most difficult problems of teachers, both general and special education (Evertson & Weinstein, 2006; Kauffman, Mostert, Trent, & Pullen, 2006). Teachers and school administrators are often unsure of just what freedom and constraints the law allows them in disciplining students with disabilities. They must struggle with balancing the rights of students with disabilities against the common good of maintaining a safe and orderly school environment (McCarthy & Soodak, 2007).

Reading Homework Exercise

Zero Tolerance • Go to the Homework and Exercises section in Chapter 2 of MyEducationLab and read the fact sheet "Zero Tolerance" for a broader perspective on the issues related to the 1994 initiative.

Casebook Reflections

REFER TO THE CASE *What Do We Do with Jim?* in your booklet. Jim was leaving school in handcuffs for shoving the psychologist into the door. How should the school handle Jim's instruction with the present zero-tolerance policy for school discipline? ●

■ **Zero tolerance**
A school policy, supported by federal and state laws, that having possession of any weapon or drug on school property will automatically result in a given penalty (usually suspension or expulsion) regardless of the nature of the weapon or drug or any extenuating circumstances.

One of the most dramatic and controversial measures involving discipline for serious offenses is known as **zero tolerance** (Skiba & Rausch, 2006). School administrators and teachers have been assumed to abuse their discretion in determining the punishment for certain serious offenses, such as bringing a weapon to school. Therefore, higher authorities (e.g., boards of education) in many cases removed discretion from the hands of teachers and lower administrators. The higher authorities prescribed a given punishment such as long-term suspension or expulsion for a particular offense, regardless of the circumstances surrounding the act. For example, an elementary school child who accidentally takes a paring knife to school in her lunch box might be expelled. A high school student who forgets to remove a roofing knife from his pocket and turns it in at the office because he knows he should not have it in school might be expelled. A student with intellectual disability who brings a toy gun to school, even though he does not understand that a gun is a weapon and even toy weapons are forbidden in school, might be expelled. The zero-tolerance rationale does not allow any exceptions for extenuating circumstances.

Violence, disorder, and drugs in schools are serious problems that must be addressed. However, zero tolerance and standardization of penalties present particular problems for special education. All educators recognize the need for schoolwide discipline that brings a high degree of uniformity to consequences for particular acts (e.g., Fenning & Bohanon, 2006; Liaupsin, Jolivette, & Scott, 2004; Martella, Nelson, & Marchand-Martella, 2003). Special educators also argue for exceptions based on the relevance of the student's disability to the event in question, and note that zero tolerance has not made schools safer places (see Skiba & Peterson, 2000; Skiba & Rausch, 2006).

Supports for Desired Behavior

The discipline of students with disabilities is highly controversial, and many teachers and school administrators are confused about what is legal. Special rules apply to managing some of the serious misbehavior of students who are identified as having disabilities. In some cases, the typical school rules apply, but in others, they do not (see Bateman & Linden, 2006; Huefner, 2006; Yell, 2006; Yell, Rozalski, & Drasgow, 2001). In any case, much of the special education advocacy regarding discipline is based on finding alternatives to suspension and expulsion for bringing weapons or drugs to school or for endangering others, as keeping students out of school is not an effective way of helping them learn to behave acceptably.

Three concepts and related procedures provide the basis for much of the controversy surrounding the discipline of students with disabilities:

1. Determining whether the behavior is or is not a manifestation of the student's disability,
2. Providing an alternative placement for the student's education for an interim period if temporary removal from the student's present placement is necessary, and
3. Developing positive, proactive behavior intervention plans.

We discuss these issues further in Chapter 8, as they most frequently arise in the case of students with emotional or behavioral disorders.

■ **Manifestation determination**
Determination whether a student's misbehavior is a manifestation of a disability.

Deciding whether a student's misbehavior is or is not a manifestation of disability is called a **manifestation determination**, based on the idea that it would be unfair to punish a student for engaging in a misbehavior that is part of his or her disability. However, if the misbehavior is not a manifestation of disability, then the usual punishment for students without disabilities should apply. For example, if a misbehavior is the result of a seizure or other neurological disorder or a manifestation of intellectual incapacity or emotional disturbance, then the student should not be punished for it.

The manifestation determination is a highly controversial issue, and some writers believe that it is more political than educational in purpose (Dupre, 2000; Katsiyannis & Maag, 2001). Some people argue that the process actually undermines fairness because the rules or procedures for the manifestation determination are not entirely objective, requiring subjective judgment about the causes of misbehavior.

Perhaps the most critical part of the discipline provisions of IDEA is the requirement that schools must devise **positive behavioral intervention plans** for students with disabilities who have behavior problems. The emphasis of this requirement is on creating proactive and positive interventions and avoiding punishment. When discipline is involved, the school must reevaluate the student's IEP and make efforts to address the misconduct that led to the problem, using positive (nonpunitive) means to the greatest extent possible. Also required is a **functional behavioral assessment (FBA)**, in which educators attempt to determine and alter the factors that account for the student's misconduct. The intent of the legal requirement is to encourage proactive problem solving rather than reactive punishment of misconduct.

Positive behavioral supports (PBS) are procedures required under IDEA to help students behave as desired (Bradley, 2001). It suggests exclusive use of positive (rewarding) consequences for appropriate behavior rather than punishment for misbehavior. Supposedly, PBS uses systemic and individualized positive-only strategies to prevent problem behavior and achieve positive social and learning outcomes. Positive-only behavior management practices have high emotional appeal, but reliable evidence does not support them (Kauffman et al., 2006; Lloyd & Hallahan, 2007).

An approach with more support from research is **PBIS (positive behavioral intervention and support)**. It integrates valued outcomes, the science of human behavior, validated procedures, and systems change to enhance quality of life and reduce problem behavior. Its primary goal is to improve the link between research-validated practices and the environments in which teaching and learning occur. This behaviorally based systems approach enhances the capacity of schools, families, and communities to design effective teaching and learning environments that improve lifestyle results (personal, health, social, family, work, recreation, etc.) for all children and youth. These environments apply contextually and culturally appropriate interventions to make problem behavior less effective, efficient, and relevant and to make desired behavior more functional (Sugai, Sprague, Horner, & Walker, 2000). However, it does recognize the value of nonviolent negative consequences (punishment) in managing behavior.

IDEA includes allowances for schools to use an **interim alternative educational setting (IAES)** in the discipline of a student with disabilities who can not be managed satisfactorily in the general education classroom or regular school. For example, an IAES might be a separate special school serving students with behavior problems, a separate arrangement within the public school similar to in-school suspension, or a self-contained classroom. IAES is intended to encourage schools to use such alternatives rather than suspension or expulsion. The law doesn't define what an IAES must be, but only what it must provide: a continuation of education and modifications spelled out in the IEP. The IAES must also include specific programming to address and prevent the recurrence of the behavior that prompted the placement in the first place. Such settings might be used for students with serious behavior problems as a way of preserving order and manageability of the typical classroom and school.

How Functional Are Supports?

The struggle to resolve discipline issues involving students with disabilities is ongoing. On the one hand, school administrators want the highest possible degree of uniformity of expectations (i.e., the same high expectations for all students). On the other hand,

UNDERSTANDING THE STANDARDS AND PRINCIPLES What does the law say with respect to discipline of students with disabilities? (CEC Knowledge and Skill Standard CC1K2)

Council for Exceptional Children

▪ **Positive behavioral intervention plans**
A plan for changing behavior with an emphasis on positive reinforcement (rewarding) procedures.

▪ **Functional behavior assessment (FBA)**
Evaluation that consists of finding out the consequences (what purposes the behavior serves), antecedents (what triggers the behavior), and setting events (contextual factors) that maintain inappropriate behaviors.

▪ **Positive behavioral support (PBS)**
Positive reinforcement (rewarding) procedures intended to support a student's appropriate or desirable behavior.

▪ **Positive behavior intervention and support (PBIS)**
Systematic use of the science of behavior to find ways of supporting desirable behavior rather than punishing the undesirable behavior; positive reinforcement (rewarding) procedures that are intended to support a student's appropriate or desirable behavior.

▪ **Interim alternative educational setting (IAES)**
A temporary placement outside general education for students whose behavior is extremely problematic, but in which their education is continued.

INTERNET RESOURCES

For updates on legal issues in special education, see the Website maintained by legal expert Dixie Snow Huefner and click on "Chapter Updates": www.ed.utah .edu/~huefner/sped-law/spdlawbk .htm or www.wrightslaw.com

special educators and other advocates for students with disabilities see the uniformity of disciplinary rules as failure to accommodate students' individual abilities and needs. The legal requirements regarding discipline, including suspension and expulsion, will continue to evolve as educators find more productive ways of dealing with serious misconduct. It is difficult to determine whether misbehavior is a function of a child's disability, and manifestation determinations will continue to be a matter of controversy for as long as the law requires them.

What are the components of a useful functional analysis of behavior? Can classroom teachers conduct such analyses without help from others? Some suggest that the FBA is considerably more complicated than many people think and that the law (IDEA) may have gotten considerably ahead of teachers' ability to do the necessary analyses. Although the idea is good and a few educators may be able to perform a useful FBA, many functional analyses are poorly done (see Fox & Gable, 2004; Landrum & Kauffman, 2006; Sasso, Conroy, Stichter, & Fox, 2001).

PBS is also a controversial issue. Many special educators recommended it as an approach, and it has the backing of federal law. Although PBS appeals to instincts to respond humanely to problem behavior, it has its critics. For example, Mulick and Butter (2005) state that "PBS fails as a science because it does not indicate how to differentiate reality from desire" (p. 400). They argue that PBS is not actually a new science and that it unrealistically assumes that positive supports alone can be effective in correcting misbehavior. Evidence supporting the idea of discipline that is "all positive all the time" is lacking, but evidence does support the judicious use of punishing consequences in the context of predominantly positive support (Kauffman & Landrum, 2006; Lloyd & Hallahan, 2007).

The use of any interim alternative setting, meaning that the student is placed outside the general education classroom, is also a controversial issue. IAES involves separation of the student from the mainstream, which is objectionable to those who see inclusion in general education as more important than anything else.

Concluding Thoughts Regarding Trends and Issues

It is understandable to feel overwhelmed by the controversial nature of special education; there are a number of unanswered questions facing our field. It seems that just as we find what we think are the right answers to a certain set of questions about how to educate students with disabilities, more challenging questions emerge.

It would be easy to view this inability to reach definitive conclusions as indicative of a field in chaos. We disagree. This constant state of questioning is a sign of health and vigor, an indication that special education is based on scientific understanding, not on philosophy or mere speculation. Far from seeking and providing final answers, science thrives on the unknown and on controversy. True, there are rules for how to figure things out: science is all about examining the most reliable information (see Kauffman & Sasso, 2006a, 2006b; Mostert, Kavale, & Kauffman, 2008b; Sasso, 2001, 2007).

The controversial nature of special education makes it exciting and challenging. We would be worried (and we believe people with disabilities and their families would be worried, too) if there were suddenly complete agreement on all important issues in the field. We should constantly be striving to find better ways to provide education and related services for people with disabilities based on the best evidence we can obtain (Lloyd & Hallahan, 2007). In doing this, it's inevitable that there will be differences of opinion.

Summary

What are the trends and issues in integrating people with disabilities into the larger society?

▶ The major trends and issues involve normalization, deinstitutionalization, self-determination, universal design, and the use of new technologies.

What are the trends and issues in normalization?

▶ *Normalization* dictates that both the means and the ends of education for people with disabilities should be as normal as possible.

▶ Normalization is difficult to define precisely in practice, and some people with disabilities do not wish to be "normalized."

What are the trends and issues in deinstitutionalization?

▶ *Deinstitutionalization* refers to placing people with disabilities in smaller community settings rather than in large, centralized institutions; it is a continuing trend.

▶ Some researchers question the wisdom of complete deinstitutionalization, as some people who return to community placements do not fare well.

What are the trends and issues in self-determination?

▶ Self-determination is based on the philosophy that people with disabilities should make decisions about their own lives.

▶ Some see certain aspects of self-determination, such as person-centered planning, as lacking research support.

What are the trends and issues in universal design?

▶ Universal design refers to the principle that a device or program should be workable for as many potential users as possible.

▶ Although devices and programs may be designed for a wide variety of users, few can be made useable by literally all, and custom designs are probably always going to be necessary for some users.

What are the trends and issues in the use of technologies?

▶ The major technologies that are controversial for people with disabilities involve medical advances, human reproduction, and communications.

▶ There is controversy about whether we *should* do something just because we *can*.

What are the trends and issues in integrating students with exceptionalities into schools?

▶ The major issues involve full inclusion, collaboration with general education, response to intervention, participation in assessments of educational progress, early intervention, transition, and discipline.

What are the trends and issues in full inclusion?

▶ Full inclusion is very controversial; it is based on four assumptions:
  ■ Labeling of people is harmful.
  ■ Special education pull-out programs have been ineffective.
  ■ People with disabilities should be viewed as a minority group.
  ■ Ethics should take precedence over empiricism.

▶ Opponents of full inclusion put forth the following arguments:
  ■ Professionals and parents are largely satisfied with the current level of integration.
  ■ General educators are unwilling and/or unable to cope with all students with disabilities.
  ■ Although equating disabilities with minority group status is in many ways legitimate, there are limitations in translating it into educational programming recommendations.
  ■ An unwillingness to consider empirical evidence is professionally irresponsible.
  ■ Available empirical evidence does not support full inclusion.
  ■ In the absence of data to support one service delivery model, special educators must preserve the continuum of placements.

What are the trends and issues in collaboration with general education?

▶ *Collaboration* with general education means that special educators and general educators work together in arrangements such as prereferral teams, consultation, and co-teaching.

▶ Some question the effectiveness of popular forms of collaboration such as co-teaching and recommend that special education teachers be involved either in training general education teachers to accommodate a wider range of students or in actually teaching students with disabilities.

What are the trends and issues in response to intervention?

▶ *Response to intervention* refers to students' response to scientific, research-based instruction.

► Although response to intervention has been suggested as a means of identifying students with learning disabilities, some question its usefulness as an identification tool.

What are the trends and issues in participation in assessments of educational progress?

► Both IDEA and NCLB require the participation of most students with disabilities in general assessments of educational progress.

► Proponents of participation suggest that special education has not been held accountable for students' progress.

► Some educators point out that the average achievement of students with disabilities will always be—even with good instruction—lower than the average for students without disabilities.

What are the trends and issues in early intervention?

► Early intervention is now mandated by law; a cornerstone of early intervention is the individualized family service plan (IFSP).

► There are three issues pertaining to early childhood intervention:
  ■ The appropriate role of the family
  ■ Whether the curriculum should be teacher centered or child centered
  ■ Whether full inclusion is best for all young children

What are the trends and issues in transitions to adulthood and employment?

► Issues focus largely on coordinating and linking the many agencies outside the school setting.

► Transition is defined as including a variety of postschool activities, including postsecondary education, vocational training, integrated employment, continuing and adult education, adult services, independent living, or community participation.

► The IEPs of students with disabilities must, by law, incorporate transition plans.

► Interventions often involve supported employment or job coaches.

What are the trends and issues in the discipline of students with disabilities?

► Concern for safe and orderly schools resulted in controversial policies related to the discipline of students with disabilities.

► Much of the controversy regarding discipline has to do with zero tolerance for certain behaviors, such as bringing a weapon or drugs to school.

► Disciplinary action the school may take might depend on determining whether the student's misbehavior was or was not a manifestation of his or her disability.

► In most cases, the same rules of discipline apply to students with disabilities as apply to all other students.

What are our concluding thoughts about trends and issues?

► We believe controversy indicates that the field of special education is alive and well.

► We should be constantly striving to make special education better.

STANDARDS and PRINCIPLES in this Chapter

SPECIAL EDUCATORS . . .

■ understand the field as an evolving and changing discipline based on philosophies, evidence-based principles and theories, relevant laws and policies, diverse and historical points of view, and human issues that have historically influenced and continue to influence the field of special education and the education and treatment of individuals with exceptional needs both in school and society (from CEC Content Standard #1).

■ possess a repertoire of evidence-based instructional strategies to individualize instruction (from CEC Content Standard #4).

■ use collaboration to facilitate the successful transitions of individuals with exceptional learning needs across settings and services (from CEC Content Standard #10).

ALL TEACHERS . . .

■ understand the central concepts, tools of inquiry, structures of the discipline(s) he or she teaches and can create learning experiences that make these aspects of subject matter meaningful for students (INTASC Principle #).

■ understand and use a variety of instructional strategies to encourage students' development of critical thinking, problem solving, and performance skills (INTASC Principle #4).

■ foster relationships with school colleagues, families, and agencies in the larger community to support students' learning and well being (INTASC Principle #10).

Applying the STANDARDS and PRINCIPLES

- DESCRIBE at least two ways to enhance the integration of students with disabilities into general education classrooms. (CEC Content Standard #1 & INTASC Principle #1)

- DESCRIBE the pros and cons of child-directed and adult-directed programs for young children with disabilities. (CEC Content Standard #4 & INTASC Principle #4)

- DESCRIBE ways in which teachers can collaborate with each other, with other professionals, and with families to ensure that students with disabilities are valued members of society. (CEC Content Standard #10 & INTASC Principle #10)

PEARSON
myeducationlab
Where the Classroom Comes to Life

Now go to the Hallahan/Kauffman, Eleventh Edition MyEducationLab course at www.myeducationlab.com to:

- take a Pretest to assess your initial comprehension of the chapter content;
- study chapter content with your Individualized Study Plan;
- take a Posttest to assess your understanding of chapter content;
- engage in multimedia exercises to help you build a deeper and more applied understanding of chapter content.

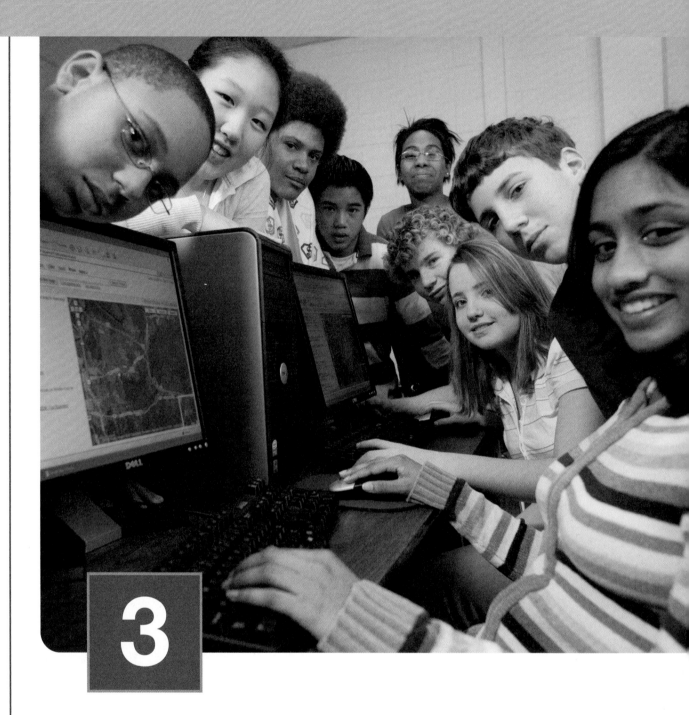

3

Multicultural and Bilingual Aspects of Special Education

I think schools are a crucial—probably the most crucial—site for inviting us to view ourselves in a different mirror. I think schools have the responsibility to teach Americans about who we are and who we have been. This is where it's important for schools to offer a more accurate, a more inclusive multicultural curriculum. The classroom is the place where students who come from different ethnic or cultural communities can learn not only about themselves but about one another in an informed, systematic and non-intimidating way. I think the schools offer us our best hope for working it out. I would be very reluctant to depend upon the news media or the entertainment media, which do not have a responsibility to educate.

—Ronald Takaki
"Reflections from a Different Mirror"

QUESTIONS to guide your reading of this chapter . . .

- In what ways do we see universality of cultural pride and shame?
- What is American about multiculturalism?
- What are the important concepts about cultural diversity for education?
- What are the most important aspects of multicultural and bilingual special education?

Multicultural and Bilingual Aspects of Special Education

MYTH ■ Multicultural education addresses the concerns of ethnic minorities who want their children to learn more about their history and the intellectual, social, and artistic contributions of their ancestors.

FACT ■ This is a partial truth. In fact, multicultural education seeks to help the children of all ethnic groups appreciate their own and others' cultural heritages—plus our common American culture that sustains multiculturalism.

MYTH ■ Everyone agrees that multicultural education is critical to our nation's future.

FACT ■ Some people, including some who are members of ethnic minorities, believe that multicultural education is misguided and diverts attention from our integration into a distinctive, cohesive American culture.

MYTH ■ Implementing multicultural education is a relatively simple matter of including information about all cultures in the curriculum and teaching respect for them.

FACT ■ Educators and others are struggling with how to construct a satisfactory multicultural curriculum and multicultural instructional methods. Nearly every aspect of the task is controversial: which cultures to include, how much attention to give to each, and what and how to teach about them.

MYTH ■ Multiculturalism includes only the special features and contributions of clearly defined ethnic groups.

FACT ■ Ethnicity is typically the focal point of discussions of multiculturalism, but ethnicity is sometimes a point of controversy if it is defined too broadly (for example, by lumping all Asians, all Africans, or all Europeans together). Besides ethnic groups, other groups and individuals—such as people identified by gender, sexual orientation, religion, and disability—need consideration in a multicultural curriculum.

MYTH ■ Disproportionate representation of ethnic minorities in special education is no longer a problem.

FACT ■ Some ethnic minorities are still underrepresented or overrepresented in certain special education categories. For example, African American students, especially males, are overrepresented in programs for students with emotional disturbance and underrepresented in programs for gifted and talented students.

MYTH ■ Disability is never related to ethnicity.

FACT ■ Some disabilities are genetically linked and therefore more prevalent in some ethnic groups. For example, sickle-cell disease (a severe, chronic, hereditary blood disease) occurs disproportionately in children with ancestry from Africa, Mediterranean and Caribbean regions, Saudi Arabia, and India.

MYTH ■ If students speak English, there is no need to be concerned about bilingual education.

FACT ■ Conversational English is not the same as the more formal and sometimes technical language used in academic curriculum and classroom instruction. Educators must make sure that students understand the language that is used in teaching, not just informal conversation.

Many nations and regions are splintered into factions, clans, tribes, and gangs. In some cases, this splintering has been accompanied by extreme cruelty of individuals or groups toward others. Differences—especially those of national origin, religion, ethnic origin, color, custom, sexual orientation, social class, and disability—are too often the basis for viciousness.

No personal characteristic of skin color, ethnic identity, sexual identity, nationality, religion, disability—or any other cultural marker—immunizes anyone against the mistreatment of others. This remains a central problem of humankind. In the early twenty-first century, slavery is still practiced in some nations of the world, and "civilized" people mistreat prisoners who might or might not differ from their guards in nationality, ethnicity, religion, or other cultural features. Suicide bombers kill and maim others. Terrorists kill, maim, and threaten, and acts of war do the same. Not so long ago, systematic efforts were made in a highly "civilized" society to exterminate people with disabilities, and we would be wise to learn the lessons history can teach us about our personal and collective capacity for brutality (Mostert, 2002).

Despite the ongoing mistreatment of others based on cultural difference, few of us would want to live in a world without diversity. Cultural diversity should be a valued component in the human experience; it is one that has sparked periods of advancement/change throughout history. The adventures of Marco Polo in China brought about changes in Italian culture and eventually the entire European continent. Similarly, when African slaves in America encountered European music they blended it with their African music to create the spirituals, and out of the spirituals grew other musical genres such as blues, jazz, and gospel (Gardner, Ohio State University). There are countless examples throughout history of cultures learning from each other; unfortunately, there are also countless examples of people of one culture devaluing individuals from another.

All cultures and ethnic groups of the world can take pride in much of their heritage, but all also bear a burden of indignity because at some time they have engaged in the ruthless treatment or literal enslavement of others. Sometimes this treatment has extended to minority members of their own larger group whose differences have been viewed as undesirable or intolerable. Not only is religion the basis for conflict (in places such as Northern Ireland and Iraq), but just the appearance of being different or assumptions about appearances have been sufficient to trigger discrimination. For example, in his memoir *Angela's Ashes*, Frank McCourt (1996) describes how in the mid-twentieth century, some Catholics in Ireland looked askance at what they called "Protestant hair":

> Come here till I comb your hair, said Grandma. Look at that mop, it won't lie down. You didn't get that hair from my side of the family. That's that North of Ireland hair you got from your father. That's the kind of hair you see on Presbyterians. If your mother had married a proper decent Limerickman you wouldn't have this standing up, North of Ireland, Presbyterian hair. (p. 128)

In virtually every nation, society, religion, ethnic group, tribe, or clan, discrimination exists against those who are different. It's therefore critically important that we learn to accept the principle that those who differ from us are equals as human beings. Furthermore, all educators need to understand the purpose of **multicultural education**, which aims for educational institutions and curricula that provide equal educational opportunities to students regardless of their gender, social class, ethnicity, race, disability, or other cultural identity. It also seeks to socialize students to a multicultural norm: acceptance of and respect for those whose culture is different

---

Casebook Reflections

REFER TO THE CASE *What Do We Do with Jim?* in your booklet. Jim's mother claims that the reason he doesn't do well "is because he is African-American and the teachers are prejudiced." In what way(s) do you think the issues about Jim's behavior are culturally based or are related to cultural diversity? What else might be the case? ●

Video Homework Exercise

The Importance of Culture ● Go to the Homework and Exercises section in Chapter 3 of MyEducationLab to watch the video "The Importance of Culture" for another perspective on multicultural education.

■ **Multicultural education** Aims to change educational institutions and curricula so they will provide equal educational opportunities to students regardless of their gender, social class, ethnicity, race, disability, or other cultural identity.

It's common to dwell on the problems associated with cultural differences. However, a world void of diversity would be bland and uneventful. Multiculturalism is an intricate component to the human experience and the advancement of societies.

from one's own and knowledge of our shared history. Schools play a central role in multicultural education, as Takaki notes in his comments on page 85.

Multiculturalism also involves the specter of collective versus individual pride and guilt in behavior. Is the entire group of people that compose a culture justified in taking pride in the fact that one of their group has accomplished something notable? Is an entire group of people—perhaps a nation—guilty for the acts of some of its members? Clearly, the assignment of collective guilt is a convenient, time-honored way of perpetuating discrimination, ethnic cleansing, genocide, and other acts of violence. Collective pride can blind people to the faults of members of a group and create a false sense of worthiness.

America and Multiculturalism

Nothing in this world reflects diversity more than nature. The landscape of Earth is an intricate mix of shapes, forms, and colors each with its own identity and spirit, separate, and yet a piece of a whole. The land we live in probably best reflects this notion. The landscape of the United States, a quilt woven of dramatically different terrains, is populated by people equally as unique and diverse. Glancing over the entire country from the Pacific to the Atlantic, you see many different environments coexisting: warm deserts, snowcapped mountains, golden plains, green valleys, lush marshlands, sandy beaches, and bustling cities. All are different, yet one: the United States. No less than its geography, the people who inhabit the United States also exemplify nature's diversity (De Melendez & Beck, 2007, p. 4).

America is an increasingly diverse country, as De Melendez and Beck (2007) eloquently describe. Our desire as Americans should be to build a diverse but just society in which the personal freedom and pride of all cultural groups and respect for others' cultural heritage are the norm, a society in which fear, hate, and abuse are eliminated and in which guilt or accomplishment is not determined by association. Working toward this ideal demands a multicultural perspective, one from which we can simultaneously accomplish two tasks. First, we must renew our efforts to achieve social justice and take specific steps to understand and appreciate one another's cultures. Second, in doing so, we must pledge our first loyalty to common cultural values that make diversity a strength rather than a fatal flaw. We seek a commitment to our common humanity and to democratic ideals that bind people together for the common good and give all of them freedom for the rightful honoring of their heritage.

Multicultural education has its critics, some of whom see it as eroding the moral foundations of society and undermining the central purpose of schooling: ensuring the academic competence of students. Multiculturalism is sometimes distorted into indefensible ideology (Ravitch, 2003); we don't understand how the multicultural education that we advocate can be anything but helpful in students' academic learning and socialization to American ideals.

Since the civil rights movement of the 1960s, educators have become increasingly aware of the extent to which differences among cultural and ethnic groups affect children's schooling. Gradually, educators and others are coming to understand that the cultural diversity of the United States and the world demands multicultural education. Progress in constructing multicultural education has been slow, however, in part because of the way in which all cultural groups tend to view themselves as the standard against which others should be judged.

Education that takes full advantage of the cultural diversity in our schools and the larger world requires much critical analysis and planning. It can be very difficult for all cultural or ethnic groups to find common satisfaction in any specific curriculum, even if they are all seeking what they consider the multicultural ideal. Moreover, some argue that the more important goal is finding the common American culture and ensuring that our children have a common cultural literacy (Ravitch, 2003). Even the metaphors that we use for dealing with cultural diversity and cultural unity are points of controversy. The United States has often been called a "cultural melting pot," but some now reject the notion of total melding or amalgamation—they reject the metaphor of an alloy in which metals are dissolved in each other and fused into a new substance. Those who reject the alloy or melting pot metaphor want each identifiable group to be recognized as separate, distinct, and legitimate in its own right.

That racism and discrimination remain serious problems in the United States and most other nations and societies of the world is obvious. People of every cultural description struggle with the meaning of differences that might seem trivial or superficial to some but elicit powerful emotional responses and discrimination from others. As Anne Lewis points out on page 90, the problems of desegregating schools have remained in the face of the May 1954 *Brown vs. Board of Education* Supreme Court decision that ended legal racial segregation (Lewis, 2004). The No Child Left Behind Act of 2002 (NCLB) can be seen as another law making "white flight" and segregation of school possible (see Kauffman & Konold, 2007).

Misunderstanding and suffering are still often associated with differences in color as well as gender, religion, sexual orientation, family affiliation, abilities and disabilities, and political beliefs. Antisemitism and other racist attitudes still exist in all regions of America as well as in all nations of the world, and no cultural group is entirely free of prejudice and other racist sentiments. Consider the experience of Susie Kay, a Jewish teacher in a Washington, DC, high school where all the students are African American:

> Kay's students say they know about white culture mainly from television shows; hardly any interact regularly with whites—"Caucasians," as they call them. Most have never met a Jewish person, except for Miss Kay, who wears her Star of David necklace every day. Prompting students to ask, "Isn't that the star of the Devil?"

Video Homework Exercise

Brown v. Board of Education • Go to the Homework and Exercises section in Chapter 3 of MyEducationLab to watch the video "Brown v. Board of Education", about the landmark court decision and the current state of racial segregation in the U.S.

Effective multicultural education promotes among all students pride in their own cultures, understanding and appreciation of different cultures, and ensures equal educational opportunities for all students, regardless of cultural background.

UNDERSTANDING THE STANDARDS AND PRINCIPLES What challenges might educators face in striving to accomplish the general purposes of multicultural education? (CEC Knowledge and Skill Standard CC6K2)

"And what's the difference between a white person and a Jew anyway?" asks another. Both are rich, right? (Horwitz, 1998, p. F1)

The solution is not as simple as becoming sensitized to differences. Too often, Eurocentrism is met with Europhobia, Afrocentrism with Afrophobia, homocentrism with homophobia, sensitivity to difference with hypersensitivity about being different. Nor is the solution to become "blind" to difference (see Hicks, 2005). The simple reality is that we cannot accept or accommodate what we do not see and label (Kauffman, 2001, 2003; Kauffman & Hallahan, 2005). Perhaps the solution includes both engendering sensitivity to differences and building confidence that one's own differences won't be threatened by others. The solution might also require helping students learn how to view themselves and others from different perspectives.

We're optimistic about multicultural education because it's an opportunity to face our nation's shared problems squarely and to extract the best human qualities from each cultural heritage. It provides the opportunity to develop an appreciation of our individual and shared cultural treasures and to engender acceptance, if not love, of all differences that are not destructive of the human spirit. The best antidote for cultural insularity is inclusiveness. Insularity will be overcome by adherence to truly American values of multiculturalism.

Multiculturalism is now a specialized field of study and research in education, and its full exploration is far beyond the scope of this chapter. Of particular concern to special educators is how exceptionalities are related to cultural diversity and the way in which special education fits within the broader general education context in a multicultural society. Cultural diversity presents particular challenges for special educators in three areas: assessment of abilities and disabilities, instruction, and socialization. Before discussing each of these challenges, we summarize some of the major concepts about education and cultural diversity that set the context for multicultural and bilingual special education.

Personal PERSPECTIVES

Desegregation and Degeneration

With a shortage of smart teachers (and any teachers in some areas), it is not surprising that the least experienced and lowest-scoring teachers are teaching the neediest students. Districts want to keep middle-class parents and good teachers happy, so they rarely challenge union seniority policies that allow the best teachers to clump together in less needy schools. When resources are scarce, the least powerful get the least.

Choice is the new euphemism for white flight. Now that those who desire schools that enroll "our kind" have pushed suburban sprawl to its limit, they have turned to parental choice, including vouchers, as a way to use public funds for private purposes. The parental choice provisions of the No Child Left Behind (NCLB) act were almost an afterthought in many urban school districts, which already catered to primarily middle-class parents through extensive choice programs. Charters are another form of separation, as a recent study found in Boston: no English-language learner was enrolled in a charter school, only half of the charter school students were low-income compared to three-fourths in the traditional Boston schools, and only one in 10 had a disability. Charter schools now seem to offer a new haven for the advantaged.

Source: Lewis, A. C. (2004). Desegregation and degeneration. *Phi Delta Kappan, 85,* 643–644. Reprinted by permission.

Personal PERSPECTIVES

In Living Black and White

My son used to attend a small nursery school. Over the course of a year, three different teachers in his school assured me that he was colorblind. Resigned to this diagnosis, I took my son to an ophthalmologist who tested him and pronounced his vision perfect. I could not figure out what was going on until I began to listen carefully to what he was saying about color.

As it turned out, my son did not misidentify color. He resisted identifying color at all. "I don't know," he would say when asked what color the grass was; or, most peculiarly, "It makes no difference." This latter remark, this assertion of the greenness of grass making no difference, was such a precociously cynical retort that I began to suspect some social complication in which he somehow was invested.

The long and short of it is that the well-meaning teachers at his predominantly white school had valiantly and repeatedly assured their charges that color makes no difference. "It doesn't matter," they told the children, "whether you're black or white or red or green or blue." Yet upon further investigation, the very reason that the teachers had felt it necessary to impart this lesson in the first place was that it did matter, and in predictably cruel ways: Some of the children had been fighting about whether black people could play "good guys."

My son's anxious response was redefined by his teachers as physical deficiency—illustrative, perhaps, of the way in which the liberal ideal of colorblindness is too often confounded. That is to say, the very notion of blindness about color constitutes an ideological confusion at best, and denial at its very worst. I recognize, certainly, that the teachers were inspired by a desire to make whole a division in the ranks. But there is much overlooked in the move to undo that which clearly and unfortunately matters just by labeling it that which "makes no difference." The dismissiveness, however unintentional, leaves those in my son's position pulled between the clarity of their own experience and the often alienating terms in which they must seek social acceptance.

Source: Excerpt from "The Emperor's New Clothes" From *Seeing a Color-Blind Future: The Paradox of Race* by Patricia Williams. Copyright © 1997 by Patricia J. Williams. Reprinted with permission of Farrar, Strauss & Giroux, Inc.

Education and Cultural Diversity

Culture has many definitions. However, most definitions include the following elements:

1. Values and typical behavior
2. Languages or dialects
3. Nonverbal communication
4. Awareness of one's cultural identity
5. World views or general perspectives

These elements can together make up a national or shared culture. Within the larger culture are many **subcultures** that share the common characteristics of the larger culture. The term *subculture* shouldn't be interpreted to mean anything other than a part (not the total) of the larger or general culture. Subculture doesn't mean lesser in importance, nor does it indicate that one group is dominated by another. We prefer the term subculture to microculture simply because "sub" can mean associated with or part of whereas "micro" means small. Some subcultures aren't small and may, in fact, be the majority group in a given region, state, organization, or other group. European Americans are a subculture in the United States of America, although they have to date been the majority of Americans. But, of course, European Americans can be considered as subcultures described by their region or nation of origin, as well as by other categories.

Subcultures include all of the various subcategories of citizens that one might name, including various political parties, ethnic identities, gender, sexual orientation, age, and disability (and subcultures include the largest subgroup in any given area, which, although

■ Subculture

A culture that is associated with or part of a larger culture; a culture that is not the entire culture of a nation or other entity. Sometimes called "microculture," but a subculture is not necessarily small or a minority of a larger culture.

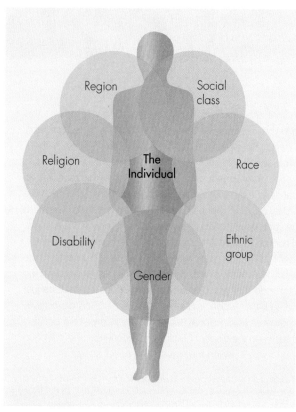

FIGURE 3.1 Individuals belong to many different subculture groups

Source: From J. A. Banks, *Cultural diversity and education: Foundation, curriculum, and teaching* (p. 76). Copyright © 1994 by Allyn & Bacon. Reprinted/adapted with permission.

UNDERSTANDING THE STANDARDS AND PRINCIPLES How might a student's subculture affect his/her school performance? (INTASC 3.08 & 3.09)

INTASC

perhaps the largest in its region, is not all of the larger culture). Subcultures may have unique values, behavior, languages or dialect, nonverbal communication, awareness, identity, and views. Some subcultures are voluntary (e.g., religion, political party), and some are involuntary (e.g., skin color, gender). Figure 3.1 illustrates that an individual might identify with the larger, general culture and also belong to many different subcultures. The variety of subcultures to which a person belongs affects his or her behavior. The larger, general culture in the United States consists of certain overarching values, symbols, and ideas, such as justice, equality, and human dignity. Within the United States, subcultures might share these common values but differ in many other ways.

The number of subcultures represented in U.S. schools has increased in recent decades because of the variety of immigrants from other countries, particularly Southeast Asia. However, it has also increased because of greater recognition of and sensitivity to subcultures, such as those represented by disability, age, sexual orientation, religion, and so on.

Many American children live in poverty. Poverty clearly places children at higher risk of disability compared to children who are reared in conditions of economic advantage (Fujiura & Yamaki, 2000). Many urban children spend a great deal of time on the streets or are homeless (Walker, 2000). Thus, the United States in the twenty-first century is more diverse than ever in the subcultures it includes—diverse in ethnic groups, economic status, lifestyles, and disabilities.

Students from some subcultures in U.S. society do extremely well in school, but others don't. The factors accounting for the school performance of subcultures are complex, and social scientists are still searching for the attitudes, beliefs, traditions, and opportunities that foster the success of specific cultural groups. Although there is considerable evidence that various ethnic minority communities have a strong influence on students' achievement and school behavior, we offer three cautions. First, we need to guard against stereotypes—assumptions that one's cultural identity is sufficient to explain academic achievement or economic success. The "Doonesbury" cartoon on page 93 makes this point rather well. Second, the fact that some minority communities may have a strong influence on school success doesn't relieve schools of the obligation to provide a multicultural education. All students need to feel that they and their cultural heritage are included in the mainstream of American culture and schooling. Third, unless teachers and other school personnel value minority students—see value and promise in them and act accordingly by setting challenging but not unreachable expectations—the support of families and the minority community may be insufficient to improve the academic success of minority students. Too often, minority students are devalued in school, regardless of their achievements and behaviors.

The general purposes of multicultural education are to promote pride in the positive aspects of one's own cultural heritage and understanding of cultures that are different from one's own, foster positive attitudes toward cultural diversity, and ensure equal educational opportunities for all students. These purposes cannot be accomplished unless students develop an understanding and appreciation of their own cultural heritage, as well as an awareness and acceptance of cultures different from their own. Understanding and appreciation are not likely to develop automatically through unplanned contact with members of other cultures. Rather, teachers must plan experiences that teach about culture and provide models of cultural awareness and acceptance and the appreciation of cultural diversity.

Doonesbury

BY GARRY TRUDEAU

On the surface, teaching about cultures and engendering an acceptance and appreciation of cultural diversity appear to be simple. However, two questions immediately complicate things: Which cultures shall we include? What and how shall we teach about them? The first question demands that we consider all the cultures that might be represented in the school and the difficulties inherent in including them all. In some urban school districts with large numbers of immigrant children, more than twenty different languages may be spoken in students' homes. If any subgroup is not represented in any given class or school activity or if the proportion of students in any given class or school activity isn't the same as the proportion of that group in the student body, then some people will consider it to be segregated. Answering the second question is also problematic because it's often difficult to know what to teach and how. Some cultural groups find the traditions, ceremonies, values, holidays, and other characteristics of other cultures unacceptable or even offensive. That is, when it comes to what and how to teach about other cultures, the stage may be set for conflict. Treating all cultures with equal attention and respect can present substantial or seemingly insurmountable logistical and interpersonal problems.

Ethnic or national origin is only one dimension of cultural diversity, one branch of many in the multicultural program. Ethnicity isn't the only representation of culture, and there is much variation of culture within any ethnic group (Keogh, 2003). In fact, assuming that all individuals of a particular racial, ethnic, disability, or other cultural group have the same values and perspectives is a form of stereotyping (see Kauffman, Conroy, Gardner, & Oswald, 2008).

One of the most controversial aspects of multicultural education is the use of language. For instance, is it appropriate to refer to a minority or minorities when the group to which we refer constitute half or more of the population in a given school, district, region, or state? What labels and terms are acceptable for designating various groups? What languages or dialects should be used for instruction? With the arrival of many immigrants to the United States, the issue of bilingual education and its relationship to multiculturalism has become increasingly important. As we discuss later, bilingual education is of even greater concern when children with disabilities are considered (Gersten & Baker, 2000).

Given the multiplicity of subcultures, each wanting—if not demanding—its precise and fair inclusion in the curriculum, it isn't surprising that educators sometimes feel caught in a spiral of factionalism and feuding. Additional questions about cultural values inevitably must be addressed: Which cultural values and characteristics should we embrace? Which, if any, should we shun? Would we, if we could, fully sustain some cultures, alter some significantly, and eliminate others? Consider, for example, cultures in which women are treated as chattel, as well as the drug culture, the culture of street gangs, and a culture that tolerates slavery. To what extent does every culture have a right to perpetuate itself? How should we respond to some members of the Deaf culture, for example, who reject the prevention of deafness or procedures and devices that enable deaf children to hear, preferring deafness to

INTERNET RESOURCES

For more information about bilingual education and linguistic diversity in education, see www.ed.gov/about/offices/list/oela/index.html?src=mr

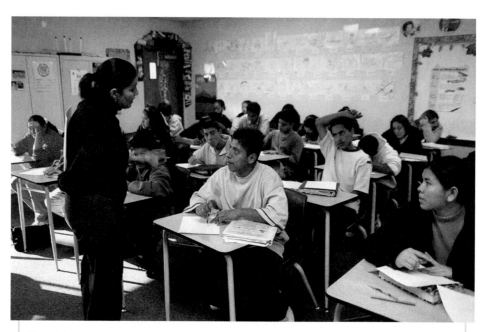

One of the most controversial aspects of multicultural education is the use of language. With the arrival of many immigrants to the United States, the issue of bilingual education has become increasingly important.

UNDERSTANDING THE STANDARDS AND PRINCIPLES Why are members of minority groups more apt to be identified as disabled? (INTASC 3.09)

INTASC

hearing and wishing to sustain the Deaf culture deliberately (see Kauffman & Hallahan, 2005; Mundy, 2002)? How should educators view and react to subcultures that reject studying and school achievement (see Welsh, 2004)?

Depending on how we define culture, the values of our own cultural heritage, and our role in multicultural education, we might find ourselves embroiled in serious cultural conflicts. No wonder that some describe the late twentieth and early twenty-first centuries as an era of "culture wars." To deal effectively with the multicultural challenge, we must focus on the challenges that are most pertinent to special education.

Multicultural and Bilingual Special Education

The subcultures that are of particular importance for special education are ethnic groups and exceptionality groups. Banks and Banks (2007) note that an *ethnic group* has a common historic origin and a shared identity, heritage, and tradition. It has value orientations, behavioral patterns, and often political and economic interests that differ from those of other groups in the larger society. An ethnic group may be a majority or a minority of people in a given country or region. We define an *exceptionality group* as a group sharing a set of specific abilities or disabilities that are especially valued or that require special accommodation within a given subculture. Thus, a person may be identified as exceptional in one ethnic group (or other subculture defined by gender, social class, religion, etc.) but not in another. The inability to read or speak standard English, for example, may identify a student as having a disability in an English-speaking culture, but the same student would not be considered disabled in a culture in which English-language skills are unimportant.

What is the best way to train teachers to be aware of their own cultural histories and biases? Because of the relatively poor performance of many students of color in schools, many parents and policymakers, as well as teacher educators, see better teacher education as critically important. Making certain that every classroom is staffed by a "highly qualified" teacher is one of the objectives of NCLB, but "highly qualified" is a concept that is open to question (Gelman, Pullen, & Kauffman, 2005).

Part of the better training of teachers is helping them to be more knowledgeable about and responsive to both their own and their students' cultures. Some teacher educators suggest that this can be accomplished only if teachers understand their own culture's history of community, rules, ways of handling tasks, language, and values related to people and outcomes (Artiles, Trent, Hoffman-Kipp, & Lopez-Torres, 2000; Osher et al., 2004).

Ethnicity and exceptionality are distinctly different concepts. In fact, multicultural special education must focus on two primary objectives that go beyond the general purposes of multicultural education:

1. Ensuring that ethnicity is not mistaken for educational exceptionality

2. Increasing understanding of the subculture of exceptionality and its relationship to other cultures

Ethnicity can be mistaken for exceptionality when one's own ethnic group is viewed as setting the standard for all others. For example, patterns of eye contact, physical contact, use of language, and ways of responding to people in positions of authority vary greatly among ethnic groups. Members of each ethnic group must realize that what they see as deviant or unacceptable in their own group might be normal and adaptive in another ethnic group. That is, we must not mistakenly conclude that a student has a disability or is gifted just because he or she is different.

Students may be particularly likely to be identified or not identified as having certain disabilities depending on their gender and ethnicity. For example, a recent study examining the influence of race and ethnicity on psychiatric diagnoses found that adolescents of color were more likely to be identified with disruptive behavior disorders than their Caucasian peers (Nguyen, Huang, Arganza, & Liao, 2007). In the same study, males and children living in poverty were also more likely to be identified as having a behavior disorder. This disproportional representation of males and ethnic minority students in special education is a problem of long standing. Boys make up considerably more than half of the students with certain disabilities (e.g., about 75 percent of those with emotional disturbance [NICHY, 2003]), and the percentage of students with certain disabilities who are ethnic minorities is disproportionately high—or, in some cases, disproportionately low. Table 3.1 shows the discrepancies between the percentages of all public school students who are white, black, Asian/Pacific Islander, Hispanic, and American Indian and the percentages of these minorities who are identified as having certain disabilities.

Notice that white, Asian/Pacific Islander, and Hispanic students receive special education at percentages somewhat below their representation in the general population, whereas black and American Indian students are overrepresented in special education. One has to be careful not to misinterpret these figures. For example, a common misinterpretation is that 20 percent of black students are receiving special education (Reschly, 2001). Such misinterpretations demean the image of minority students and may undermine the

**Video & Article
Homework Exercise**

**Perspective
Taking** ● Go to the Homework and Exercises section in Chapter 3 of MyEducationLab and read the article by Harvard professor Dr. Gehlbach exploring individuals' abilities to take the perspectives of others. The video at the end of the article allows you to test your own ability to consider the social perspective of others.

TABLE 3.1 **Percentage of Students of Various Ethnic Groups in the Total School Population and the Percentage of Those Receiving Special Education**

	White	Black	Asian/Pacific Islander	Hispanic	American Indian
Percent of total school population	66.2	14.8	3.8	14.2	1.0
Percent of those receiving special education	61.3	19.9	1.9	15.3	1.4

Source: U.S. Department of Education (2004). *Twenty-sixth annual report to Congress on the implementation of the Individuals with Disabilities Education Act.* Washington, DC: Author.

seriousness of the problem of overrepresentation. The actual meaning of the figures shown in Table 3.1 is that about 20 percent of the students receiving special education are black, a far different matter than the common misinterpretation.

It's also important to recognize that disproportionality is not an equal problem in all special education categories, schools, localities, or states for any given ethnic group. The problem of overrepresentation varies with ethnic group and the proportion of the school population that is minority (see Coutinho & Oswald, 2000; Osher et al., 2004; Oswald & Coutinho, 2001).

Important civil rights are involved in the issue of disproportional representation in special education. On the one hand, children with disabilities have a right to appropriate education regardless of their ethnicity, even if their ethnic group is statistically over-represented in special education. On the other hand, children also have a right to free-dom from discrimination and segregation. The disproportional placement of ethnic minority students in special education strongly suggests that in some cases, students are misidentified and wrongly placed (and stigmatized and segregated) in special education, whereas in other cases, ethnic minority students' disabilities are ignored (and the students are therefore denied appropriate education).

The reasons for the disproportional representation of certain groups in special education might involve assessment of students' abilities, but other factors such as com-munity standards and resources might be implicated as well. There is little argument that children of color disproportionately experience poverty or that poverty is a risk fac-tor for disability. Moreover, data suggest that low academic achievement is a significant predictor of identification for special education, and it is well recognized that dispropor-tionate numbers of children of color receive substandard schooling and score relatively low on tests of academic achievement (Hosp & Reschly, 2004). However, the problem of disproportionality is very complex and there are no simple solutions (Oswald & Coutinho, 2001). The Individuals with Disabilities Education Improvement Act (IDEA) directs schools to address the problem but does not say precisely how.

The complexity of this issue requires an integrated and multifaceted effort to promote greater educational access and excellence for racial/ethnic minority students that involves policymakers, educators, researchers, parents, advocates, students, and community rep-resentatives. The disproportionate representation of racial/ethnic minority students in special education programs and classes points to the need to do the following:

1. Have available strong academic programs that foster success for all students in general and special education
2. Implement effective, appropriate special education policies and procedures for early intervention, referral, assessment, eligibility, classification, placement, and reevaluation
3. Increase the level of home, school, and community involvement in education
4. Use diverse community resources to enhance and implement educational programs for all students

Disproportionality isn't the only multicultural issue in special education. People with certain exceptionalities can develop their own subcultures (Gollnick & Chinn, 2006). Those with severe hearing impairments, for example, are described by some as belonging to a Deaf culture that is not well understood by most normally hearing people and that results in feel-ings of isolation or separation from people with normal hearing. An important aspect of multicultural special education is developing an increased awareness, understanding, and appreciation of cultural differences involving disabilities. Multicultural special education is not merely a matter of overcoming students' prejudice and stereotyping. We must also edu-cate ourselves as teachers to improve methods of assessment, provide effective instruction, and foster appropriate socialization.

Identification and Classification of Disabilities

Assessment is a process of collecting information about individuals or groups for the purpose of making decisions. In education, assessment ordinarily refers to testing, interviewing, and observing students. Assessment serves various purposes, including **screening** (quick measures to determine who may need further assessment), diagnosis (measures to identify specific problems), progress monitoring (frequent measures to help guide instruction), and outcomes measures (assessments to determine the effectiveness of educational programming). Clearly, assessment often results in important decisions about people's lives. Therefore, in the U.S. culture, there is great concern for accuracy, justice, and fairness.

> ▪ **Screening**
> Quick measures administered to determine who may need further assessment.

Unfortunately, the accuracy, justice, and fairness of many educational assessments, especially those involving special education, are open to question (McDonnell, McLaughlin, & Morison, 1997; Utley & Obiakor, 2001b). Particularly when ethnic subcultures are involved, traditional assessment practices have frequently violated the U.S. ideals of fairness and equal opportunity regardless of ethnic origin, gender, or disability. That is, the assessment practices of educators and psychologists have frequently come under attack as being biased, resulting in misrepresentation of the abilities and disabilities of ethnic minorities and exceptional students, resulting in classification and overrepresentation in special education rather than improved educational programming (Artiles, Rueda, Salazar, & Higareda, 2005; Macswan & Rolstad, 2006). Even prereferral practices, in which the objective is to find solutions to educational problems before referral for evaluation, are subject to bias.

The problems in assessing students are numerous and complex, and there are no simple solutions (Thurlow, Nelson, Teelucksingh, & Draper, 2001; Utley & Obiakor, 2001b). Many of the problems are centered on traditional standardized testing approaches to assessment that have serious limitations: (1) They don't take cultural diversity into account, (2) they focus on deficits in the individual alone, and (3) they don't provide information useful in teaching. Although these problems haven't been entirely overcome, awareness of them and the use of more appropriate assessment procedures for diverse learners are increasing. Assessment must not result in the misidentification of children whose language or other characteristics are merely different, but it must identify those whose differences represent disabilities.

Response to Intervention

Concerns about appropriate assessment for classifying a student with a disability are not unique to racial and ethnic minorities. The traditional methods used for identifying students with learning disabilities have been a controversial topic in special education in recent years. IQ-achievement discrepancy formulae (a student who is not achieving to his or her potential as measured by a discrepancy in the IQ and achievement test scores) have been the primary means for identifying students with learning disabilities. As a result of concern that this may not be the best way to identify students for special education services, IDEA provides an alternative method that states may use to identify students with learning disabilities. This method, called **response to intervention (RTI)**, bases identification on whether or not a child responds to effective intervention. If a student responds to intervention that is typically effective, he would not receive special education services. On the other hand, a student who does not respond to what is typically effective intervention would receive special education services. IQ-achievement discrepancy and RTI are discussed fully in Chapter 6.

> ▪ **Response to intervention**
> or response-to-treatment approach. A way of determining whether a student has a learning disability; increasingly intensive levels of instructional intervention are delivered, and if the student does not achieve at some point, he or she is determined to have a learning disability or is referred for special education services.

RTI is being used more widely to identify students with disabilities, although the research that supports its use as an effective method is based on monolingual students. In addition, the effective interventions on which RTI is based, particularly for identifying

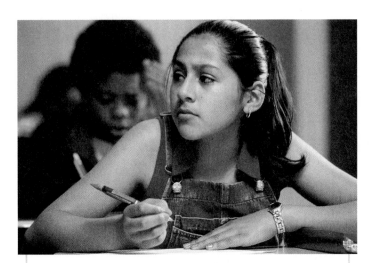

Traditional assessment practices have frequently been viewed to be in violation of the American ideas of fairness and equal opportunity regardless of culture, ethnicity, gender, or disability.

students with reading disability, have been validated only with monilingual, English-speaking students (Linan-Thompson, Vaughn, Prater, & Cirino, 2006). Although there are concerns about the use of RTI, this method also has positive implications for culturally diverse students. RTI models that rely on quality instruction prior to identification may prevent students from culturally diverse groups from falling behind and thus being identified for special education (Klingner & Edwards, 2006). Thus, like other areas of assessment and instruction, more research is needed to determine whether RTI methods are appropriate for use with English language learners and other minority populations.

Issues in the Identification of Special Gifts and Talents

Finally, we note that fair and accurate assessment is an issue in identifying special gifts and talents as well as disabilities. Too often, the extraordinary abilities of students of color or other ethnic difference and students with disabilities are overlooked because of bias or ignorance on the part of those responsible for assessment. Currently, alternative methods for identifying students for gifted and talented programs are being investigated. In one study (Pierce et al., 2007), an alternative identification procedure resulted in an increased representation of Hispanic and English language learners in a gifted program. In Chapter 1, we emphasized the importance of identifying the abilities as well as the disabilities of students. To that, we add the importance of being aware of culturally relevant gifts and talents and recognizing and valuing the abilities of minority students.

Assessment of Progress

Progress Monitoring

Methods to monitor student progress in interventions have become more common as a result of current legislation (i.e., NCLB and IDEA). The increase in informal measures to assess student progress is particularly beneficial to students from diverse populations. Progress monitoring assessments may be less biased than traditional standardized tests.

■ **Curriculum-based measurement**
A formative evaluation method designed to evaluate performance in the curriculum to which students are exposed; usually involves giving students a small sample of items from the curriculum in use in their schools; proponents argue that CBM is preferable to comparing students with national norms or using tests that do not reflect the curriculum content learned by the students.

One specific approach to monitoring progress is **curriculum-based measurement** (CBM; Fuchs & Fuchs, 1997; Jones, 2001a, 2001b), which contrasts sharply with traditional testing in which students are tested infrequently and may never before have seen the specific items on the test. CBM involves students' responses to their usual instructional materials; it entails direct and frequent samples of performance from the curriculum in which students are being instructed. CBM measures are used commonly as a way to determine students' responsiveness to RTI models (Fuchs, Fuchs, & Compton, 2004; Fuchs et al., 2007). This form of assessment is thought to be more useful for teachers than traditional testing and to decrease the likelihood of cultural bias. Recent studies have demonstrated that reading CBMs are effective in detecting changes in performance over time for English language learners (Gunn, Smolkowski, Biglan, Black, & Blair, 2005; Linan-Thompson, Vaughn, Hickman-Davis, & Kouzekanani, 2003; Ramirez & Shapiro, 2006).

Although some evidence on the efficacy of CBM for students of minority cultures is available, more research is needed to understand the factors related to optimal administration of these measures (Colon & Kranzler, 2007), particularly with diverse populations. We discuss CBM in more detail in Chapter 6.

Outcome Measures

Standardized tests may be biased because most of the test items draw on specific experiences that students from different subcultures may not have had. Tests may, for example, be biased in favor of the likely experiences of white, middle-class students or be couched in language that is unfamiliar to members of a certain subculture (Singh, Baker, Winton, & Lewis, 2000). Tests may be administered in ways that penalize students with impaired vision, hearing, or ability to answer in a standard way. Because test scores are often the basis for deciding that a student qualifies for special education, many scholars suspect that test bias accounts for the disproportionate representation of certain groups in special education (especially males and children of color), and the neglect of many children of color who are gifted.

At best, test scores represent a sample of an individual's ability to respond to a standard set of questions or tasks; they don't tell us all the important things an individual has learned or how much he or she can learn. Controversy over the biases inherent in standardized tests and the search for so-called culture-free and culture-fair tests is long standing (Taylor, 1997). Three cautions are in order:

1. Tests give only clues about what a student has learned.
2. Test scores must be interpreted with recognition of the possible biases the test contains.
3. Testing alone is an insufficient basis for classifying a student or planning an instructional program.

Traditional assessment procedures focus on the student, not on the environment in which he or she is being taught. Critics of traditional assessment have decried the assumption that any deficit that is identified is necessarily a deficit of the student. So, in addition to assessing the student's behavior or performance, many educators now suggest assessing the instructional environment. This might involve classroom observation and interviews with the student and teacher. It focuses on such items as whether instruction is presented clearly and effectively, the classroom is effectively controlled, the teacher's expectations are appropriate, appropriate curriculum modifications are made, thinking skills are being taught, effective motivational strategies are used, the student is actively engaged in academic responding and given adequate practice and feedback on performance, and progress is directly and frequently evaluated. The purpose of assessing the instructional environment is to make sure that the student is not mistakenly identified as the source of the learning problem (see Hallahan, Lloyd, Kauffman, Weiss, & Martinez, 2005; Utley & Obiakor, 2001b). An underlying assumption is that this approach will decrease the likelihood that cultural differences will be mistaken for disabilities.

Traditional assessment procedures result in test scores that may be useful in helping to determine a student's eligibility for special education or other special services. These testing procedures don't, however, typically provide information that is useful in planning for instruction. A variety of alternative assessment procedures were devised in the late 1980s and early 1990s that focus on students' performance in the curriculum or on tasks in everyday contexts, rather than on how well they did on standardized tests (see Rueda & Kim, 2001). The intent of these procedures is to avoid the artificiality and biased nature of traditional testing and obtain a more fair and

UNDERSTANDING THE STANDARDS AND PRINCIPLES How might RTI and CBM reduce the likelihood of cultural bias? (INTASC 3.09)

INTASC

Reading Homework Exercise

Assessment of the Classroom Environment ● Go to the Homework and Exercises section in Chapter 3 of MyEducationLab and read the discussion of "Assessment of the Classroom Environment", about the importance of assessing the entire instructional environment to make sure that students are not identified as the source of a learning problem when the culprit is actually cultural differences.

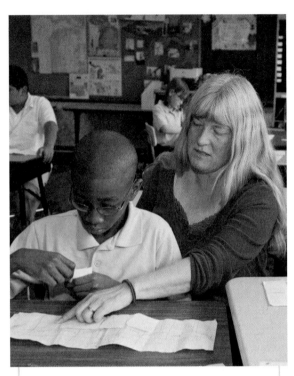

Multicultural education must balance goals that on the surface might appear to be at odds: Equalizing opportunity and achievement for all learners while differentiating instruction to accommodate learner differences.

instructionally useful assessment of students' abilities. These procedures can be useful in some respects, but they are not a solution to all problems of assessment (Terwilliger, 1997; Utley & Obiakor, 2001b).

Testing Accommodations

Testing accommodations are provided to students with limited English proficiency and students with disabilities for the purpose of assessing student knowledge on an equal basis as students without disabilities, and for whom English is a first language. Accommodations should not give an advantage to students, but provide students an equal opportunity to demonstrate knowledge and skills.

Testing accommodations for English language learners should reduce the language barriers that may interfere with assessment results (Albus, Thurlow, Liu, & Bielinski, 2005). The most common accommodations include administration modifications (e.g., extended time, small-group and individual administration) and the use of a bilingual dictionary. Translation of tests to the student's **native language** and bilingual versions of tests are also used, but not as common (Abedi, Hofstetter, & Lord, 2004). Unfortunately, empirical evidence isn't available on the efficacy of these accommodations. A study on the efficacy of using an English dictionary during testing did not demonstrate an advantage for students using this accommodation (Albus et al., 2005).

■ **Native-language emphasis**
An approach to teaching language-minority pupils in which the students' native language is used for most of the day and English is taught as a separate subject.

UNDERSTANDING THE STANDARDS AND PRINCIPLES What are some challenges associated with addressing the differing ways in which students from culturally diverse backgrounds learn? (CEC Knowledge and Skill Standard CC3K5)

Council for Exceptional Children

Instruction in Multicultural and Bilingual Special Education

A major objective of multicultural education is ensuring that all students are instructed in ways that do not penalize them because of their cultural differences and that, in fact, capitalize on their cultural heritage (see Council for Exceptional Children, 2000). The methods that are used to achieve this objective are among the most controversial topics in education today. All advocates of multicultural education are concerned with the problem of finding instructional methods that help to equalize educational opportunity and achievement for all cultural groups—that is, methods that break down the inequities and discrimination that have been part of the U.S. public education system and which IDEA seeks to eliminate. Yet there is considerable debate over the question of what instructional methods are most effective in achieving this goal.

If students' differences are ignored, then students will probably receive instruction not suited to their needs. They will likely fail to learn many skills, which will in turn deny them power and opportunity in the larger culture. For example, if we ignore non-English-speaking students' language and cultural heritage and force them to speak English, they may have great difficulty in school.

However, the answer to this problem is not necessarily recognition of students' differences, for instruction that is geared to individual students' subculture might teach only skills that are valued by the subculture. Because the larger or more general culture does not value these skills, the students' difference will be perpetuated. For example, if non-English-speaking students are taught in their native language and are not required to learn English, then their progress in the English-speaking society will be slowed.

Should a student who speaks no English be forced to give up his or her native language in school and learn to use only English (ignoring the cultural-linguistic difference)? Or should the student's native language be used as the primary vehicle of instruction, and English taught as a second language (acknowledging the cultural-linguistic difference)? We could pose similar questions for students with severe hearing impairments: Should we teach them by using primarily sign language or spoken language? The same dilemma appears in providing instruction for students with other disabilities: To what extent should they be treated as different and provided with special accommodations, and to what extent should they be treated just like everyone else (Kauffman, McGee, & Brigham, 2004)?

Clearly, the problem of instruction in multicultural education isn't easily resolved, especially for bilingual students in special education (Gersten & Baker, 2000). Most authorities now agree, however, that accepting and fostering cultural diversity must not be used as an excuse for not teaching students the skills they need to survive and prosper in the larger context of American culture.

Many call for instructional practices that are culturally sensitive or culturally responsive, meaning attuned to the particular cultural characteristics of learners (e.g., McIntyre, 2007; Shealey & Callins, 2007; Sleeter, 1999; Villegas & Lucas, 2007). The assumption underlying many assertions about culturally sensitive or culturally responsive instruction is that students with different cultural backgrounds need to be taught differently, that certain aspects of a student's cultural heritage determine to a significant extent how he or she learns best. Perhaps it's understandable that when emphasis is placed on differences in the ways in which students learn, there is also emphasis on devising special programs and schools that cater to these differences. Furthermore, the greater the diversity of cultural backgrounds of students in one class, the greater the difficulty in teaching all students effectively—if we assume that cultural background determines how students are best taught.

If children from a particular culture learn better when taught in a certain way, then it may be extremely difficult to teach multicultural groups of students. Which is the lesser evil: grouping students for instruction based on their cultural affiliation, or short-changing some by using a particular instructional method? Can either evil be avoided entirely? Do students learn best when they are taught by someone who shares their cultural heritage? If so, what does that mean for recruiting and assigning teachers, and what does it mean for grouping students for instruction? How do we best address the problem of increasing the cultural and linguistic diversity of special education teachers (see Kauffman et al., 2008; Tyler, Yzquierdo, Lopez-Reyna, & Flippin, 2004)? Which is more important in a teacher: instructional competence or cultural affiliation? If neither is more important than the other, how should teachers be recruited and trained?

Of course, we might hypothesize that certain methods of instruction are equally effective for all students in a culturally diverse group (see Council for Exceptional Children, 2000; Kauffman et al., 2008). That is, some instructional approaches (e.g., Direct Instruction, cooperative learning, peer tutoring, and cross-age grouping) allow teachers to provide culturally sensitive instruction to all members of a diverse group at once. **Classwide peer tutoring** may, in fact, be particularly useful in helping children at the elementary school level who are not proficient in English to learn English more efficiently (Fulk & King, 2001; Greenwood, Arrega-Mayer, Utley, Gavin, & Terry, 2001). Evidence also suggests that peer tutoring is effective for improving important reading skills (i.e., DIBELS Nonsense Word Fluency and Phonemic Segmentation Fluency; Good & Kaminski, 2002) of Hispanic students (Calhoon, Al Otaiba, Greenberg, King, & Avalos, 2006). One group of researchers concluded that "Specific teacher behaviors (e.g., positive reinforcement, questioning techniques) have been shown to

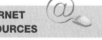

INTERNET RESOURCES

For more information about bilingual education and linguistic diversity in education, see www.ed.gov/about/offices/list/oela/index.html?src=mr

■ **Classwide peer tutoring**
An instructional procedure in which all students in the class are involved in tutoring and being tutored by classmates on specific skills as directed by their teacher.

lead to better student outcomes, and we assume that the absence of these behaviors has a deleterious effect on student learning" (Tyler et al., 2004, pp. 27–28). Sensitivity to individuals, regardless of their culture, and effective instruction are essential elements of multicultural education worthy of the name. Kauffman et al. (2008) concluded:

> All things considered, we believe that we can be passionately committed to education as a science while maintaining sensitivity to the cultural differences of individual children and their families. However, first and foremost we must recognize that the most culturally responsive practices are empirically validated instructional strategies (Heward, 2003). At this point the data seem to suggest that this applies to all children, regardless of their ethnicity . . .
>
> In short, we believe that cultural sensitivity in education is based on scientifically grounded regard for the individual student. In our opinion, it's impossible for educators to be sensitive to the needs of a student while being insensitive to that student's culture. Ultimately, ineffective [instructional] procedures are insensitive to both the needs of the student and to his or her culture in spite of any attempts to cast them as "culturally responsive." In all cases, cultural sensitivity requires using the most effective acceptable means to help students achieve socially validated objectives.

Both special and general education must adopt instructional programs that value all students and help all to be as successful as possible in American society, regardless of their specific cultural heritage. This is supported by both research and by our common commitment to the American values of equality of opportunity and fairness for all, and is contained in five instructional goals:

1. Teaching tolerance and appreciation of difference
2. Working cooperatively with families
3. Improving instruction for language-minority students
4. Adopting effective teaching practices
5. Identifying and implementing effective reading instruction for English language learners

Teaching Tolerance and Appreciation

INTERNET RESOURCES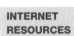

Teaching Tolerance magazine and teaching ideas can be found at www.tolerance.org/teach and the Gay, Lesbian and Straight Network (GLSEN) can be found at www.glsen.org

---

UNDERSTANDING THE STANDARDS AND PRINCIPLES How can special educators teach students to appreciate those who are different from themselves? (CEC Knowledge and Skill Standard CC5K7)

Council for Exceptional Children

By tolerance, we don't mean merely toleration of others who are seen as undesirable, nor does the publication *Teaching Tolerance* mean such toleration. Our definition of *tolerance* is an appreciation and valuing—the opposite of rejection, denigration, or toleration of a necessary evil. It means working for equity and fair treatment, seeing those who are different in culture as equal. Still, mere toleration would be a step away from the hostile rejection, ridicule, and subjugation that intolerance breeds.

Noted historian Ronald Takaki (1994), interviewed for an article in *Teaching Tolerance*, recalls that his grandparents were Japanese immigrant plantation laborers in Hawaii. Nobel laureate and author Elie Wiesel (2004), writing in the Sunday magazine *Parade*, recalls his rescue from a concentration camp. Both suggest that the American promise of equality and fairness can become a reality only if we free ourselves from a legacy of racism and prejudice. We can do so by acknowledging the reality of our past and learning more about ourselves and our heritage.

Overcoming prejudice and teaching students to appreciate those who are different from themselves is by no means easy. Moreover, this is not an area in which research can provide definitive guidelines. Yet proposed methods for how teachers can help students learn both self-esteem and tolerance of difference seem promising (Banks & Banks, 2007; Utley & Obiakor, 2001a). Some schools focus on incorporating diversity by design or organizing anti-bias clubs that encourage understanding and tolerance of others (e.g., Bennett, 2000; Collins, 2000; McAfee, 2000).

Teaching tolerance and appreciation of difference is not, of course, limited to ethnic, regional, sexual orientation, or language differences but includes differences of all types, including disabilities.

Working with Families

Schools have always depended, in part, on family involvement and support for their success. Because working with families is so important, we have devoted Chapter 4 to the topic.

Different cultural traditions mean that parents have different views of exceptionality and disability and different ways of accommodating these differences in their children (Cho, Singer, & Brenner, 2000; Pullen, 2004). An understanding of the cultural basis for parents' attitudes and wishes, particularly for families that have recently come to the United States, is therefore critical. When combined with other differences, difficulties for students with disabilities are increased, as pointed out in the description of GLESN below.

Improving Instruction for Language-Minority Students

Students for whom English is a second language face the simultaneous demands of learning a new language and mastering traditional subject matter. Those who also have disabilities encounter a third demand of coping with the additional hurdles imposed by their exceptionalities. Bilingual special education is therefore particularly controversial, presenting difficult dilemmas and paradoxes. Moreover, NCLB's demand that students who aren't fluent in English score, on average, the same as those who are fluent in English has created extraordinary controversy about language learning.

Reading & Classroom Activity Homework

Teaching Tolerance ● Go to the Homework and Exercises section in Chapter 3 of MyEducationLab and access the weblink to classroom activities. Find an activity that is related to your field of study and summarize the main points, including whether it promotes the view of *Teaching Tolerance*.

UNDERSTANDING THE STANDARDS AND PRINCIPLES What are some challenges associated with addressing the differing ways in which students from culturally diverse backgrounds learn? **(CEC Knowledge and Skill Standard CC3K5)**

Council for Exceptional Children

FOCUS ON **Concepts**

GLSEN in Tough Times
Training Educators about LGBT Issues in a Challenging Political, Economic, and Educational Climate

Teachers of today's youth must be especially aware of the individual needs that each child brings to the classroom, and develop strategies to make the classroom a safe environment in which to address these needs. Among the youth in each class, an unknown population are lesbian, gay, bisexual or transgender (LGBT), and they bring special concerns to school similar to other students who experience harassment and acts of violence because they are different. According to the 2003 National School Climate Survey by the Gay, Lesbian and Straight Education Network, or GLSEN, harassment continues at unacceptable levels and is too often ignored: 84% of LGBT students report being verbally harassed because of their sexual orientation and 82.9% of students report that faculty never or rarely intervene when present. The survey also found that unchecked harassment correlates with poor performance and diminished aspirations: LGBT youth who report significant verbal harassment are twice as likely to report they do not intend to go to college and their GPAs are significantly lower. When youths with behavior disorders are also LGBT, their personal and school-related problems are likely to be compounded while their ability to deal effectively with these problems is diminished.

Source: Bell, K. (2004). GLSEN in tough times: Training educators about LGBT issues in a challenging political, economic, and educational climate. *Beyond Behavior,* *13*(2), 29–30.

Casebook Reflections

REFER TO THE CASE *Who Will Help Patrick?* in your booklet. Margaret's approach to parenting is shouting, fear, and intimidation. Is socioeconomic status also a cultural issue in this case? To what extent might Margaret's attitudes and discipline of Patrick be explained by cultural factors? Could Margaret's approach to dealing with Patrick be justified as culturally acceptable and appropriate? ●

■ **Sheltered-English approach**
A method in which language-minority students are taught all their subjects in English at a level that is modified constantly according to individuals' needs.

UNDERSTANDING THE STANDARDS AND PRINCIPLES Describe six components of effective teaching. (INTASC 5.06)

INTASC

One approach to teaching language-minority students is to emphasize use of their native languages. In this approach, all academic instruction is initially provided in each student's native language, and English is taught as a separate subject. Later, when the student has demonstrated adequate fluency in English, he or she makes the transition to instruction in English in all academic subjects.

Another approach is to offer content-area instruction in English from the beginning of the student's schooling but at a level that is "sheltered," or constantly modified to make sure the student understands it. The goal of this approach is to help the student learn English while learning academic subjects as well.

In the first approach—native-language emphasis—students are taught for most of the day in their native languages and later make a transition to English. In the **sheltered-English approach**, students receive instruction in English for most of the school day from the beginning of their schooling. The question as to which approach is better for students with disabilities has not been answered, although it's clear that changing from one approach to the other when students change schools creates particular difficulties (Gersten & Baker, 2000; Gersten & Woodward, 1994).

Another issue for language-minority instruction is whether an emphasis on the natural uses of language or, alternatively, on skills such as vocabulary and pronunciation is most effective. However, this controversy might be based on a false dichotomy. What students need is an effective balance between skill building and language that is meaningful and relevant to their lives and interests (Gersten & Baker, 2000). Moreover, instruction of language-minority students needs to be consistent with effective teaching.

Adopting Effective Teaching Practices

In a sense, effective multicultural education requires only that we implement what we know about effective instruction. Effective teaching practices are sensitive to each individual student's cultural heritage, sense of self, view of the world, and acquired knowledge

Video Homework Exercise

A Bilingual Navajo School ● Go to the Homework and Exercises section in Chapter 3 of MyEducationLab to watch the video "A Bilingual Navajo School" and its depictions of the broader issues related to bilingual education.

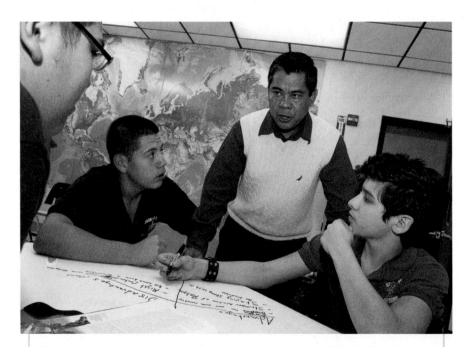

Educational programming must challenge all learners to stretch their abilities. History warns teachers not to "underteach" minority learners.

and skills. Teaching about various cultures, individual differences, and the construction of knowledge should permeate and transform the curriculum (Banks & Banks, 2007). Nonetheless, for language-minority students—indeed, for all students—we can articulate more specific components of effective teaching (see Kauffman et al., 2008). Gersten, Brengelman and Jimenez (1994) outlined six components of effective teaching:

1. *Scaffolding and strategies.* Students learn more efficiently when they are provided a scaffold, or structure, for ideas and strategies for problem solving. In **scaffolded instruction**, the teacher assists the student in learning a task and then phases out the help as the student learns to use the strategy independently. (See Chapter 6 for further discussion.) Means of helping students learn more easily include stories, visual organizers (e.g., pictures, diagrams, outlines), **mnemonics** (tactics that aid memory, such as rhymes or images), and **reciprocal teaching** (in which the student sees the teacher use a learning strategy and then tries it out).

2. *Challenge.* Too much of education, even special education, is not appropriately challenging for students. All students—including those who are from cultural minorities, who are at high risk for failure, and who have disabilities—need to be given challenging tasks. Appropriately challenging tasks are those that a given student finds just manageable. Although these tasks are not impossible, they do require serious effort and stretch the student's capabilities. Too often, teachers underestimate the capabilities of minority and exceptional students and underteach them.

3. *Involvement.* Students must be engaged in extended conversations, in which they use complex linguistic structures. Verbal exchanges between teachers and pupils must not always be short, simple, and direct (although such exchanges have their place). Rather, teachers must probe with questions, share experiences, and elicit from pupils the kind of language that demonstrates their active involvement in learning.

4. *Success.* Students who are at the highest risk of failure and dropping out are those who have low rates of success in daily school activities. All students need to experience frequent success, and teachers must present challenging tasks at which the student can be successful. Failure should not be perpetuated.

5. *Mediation and feedback.* Too often, students work for long periods without receiving feedback, or are given feedback that is not comprehensible, or are asked for rote responses to which they attach little or no meaning. Providing frequent, comprehensible feedback on performance is vital to effective teaching, as is focusing on the meanings of responses—how evidence and logic are used to construct questions and their answers.

6. *Responsiveness to cultural and individual diversity.* The content of instruction must be related to students' experiences, including those as individuals and as members of various cultural groups. The issues of cultural and individual diversity cannot be adequately considered in a few special lessons; rather, they must be included routinely in all curriculum areas. (p. 9)

■ **Scaffolded instruction**
A cognitive approach to instruction in which the teacher provides temporary structure or support while students are learning a task; the support is gradually removed as the students are able to perform the task independently.

■ **Mnemonics**
Techniques that aid memory, such as using rhymes, songs, or visual images to remember information.

■ **Reciprocal teaching**
A method in which students and teachers are involved in a dialogue to facilitate learning.

Identifying and Implementing Effective Reading Instruction

Of all academic skills, reading is most important. It's a skill that is necessary for school and life success, and reading instruction should be based on the best scientific evidence possible (Reyna, 2004).

Reading may be the most important skill for academic and life success. Federally funded research on teaching reading skills to English language learners indicates that intensive intervention produces significant improvements.

Meeting the Needs of English Language Learners with Special Needs

Concept Mapping to Improve Achievement

WHAT THE RESEARCH SAYS

In order to create educational environments conducive to academic success for English language learners, it is important to understand the range of challenges schools can pose to such students. Cloud (2002) identifies five areas through which teachers can address the needs of English language learners and create culturally responsive environments: (1) curriculum and materials, (2) classroom interactions, (3) teaching approaches, (4) resource management, and (5) counseling and parent outreach. By selecting material that is relevant to the students' experience, establishing classroom interactions that are comfortable to the student (e.g., some students may prefer more peer-to-peer interactions whereas others prefer more teacher-directed instruction), and engaging in effective instructional strategies that promote vocabulary and language development, teachers create classroom environments that support academic success.

Concept mapping is a particular teaching approach demonstrated in the research to be effective for both English language learners and students with special needs (Chularut & DeBacker, 2003; Gersten & Baker, 2000). Concept mapping applications can be created using culturally relevant materials and designed to enhance vocabulary and concept development.

RESEARCH STUDY

Chularut and DeBacker (2003) investigated the influence of concept mapping on the academic achievement of English language learners. Concept maps are instructional tools that promote learning through the use of visual representation of related topics. Concept maps allow students to see how concepts are related within a network of relationships (see Figure A for an example).

For their study, the researchers randomly assigned two groups of English language learners ($n = 79$) to either concept map instruction or individual study plus discussion. The four-week research study consisted of pretesting, five study sessions on five different reading passages that included work with concept maps or individual study plus discussion, and posttesting. The concept map group received instruction and daily practice in creating concept maps. Instructors monitored the development of the maps and provided instructional feedback. The instructors did not, however, read or interpret the content.

The individual study plus discussion group was provided the same reading materials as the concept map group. The individual study group, however, also received supplemental vocabulary pages that contained definitions of challenging words or concepts. After studying the passages independently (asking for assistance when needed), the students participated in an instructor-led whole-group discussion on the meaning and implications of the passage. Both groups were aware that they would be tested on the material.

RESEARCH FINDINGS

The results of the posttest showed that students in the concept map group scored higher than students in the individual study plus discussion group. In addition, within the concept map group, students who had higher English proficiency made greater gains than students in the lower English-proficiency group. The results demonstrated that although both groups benefited from the opportunity to study the passages individually, greater benefit was derived from working with the concept maps. Therefore, the construction of the concept maps led to greater retention of the material and increased understanding of the content. These findings support the use of concept maps

However, students who are English language learners often have difficulty learning to read (McCardle, McCarthy, & Leos, 2005; Pollard-Durodola, Mathes, Vaughn, Cardenas-Hagan, Linan-Thompson, 2006; Vaughn, Mathes, Linan-Thompson, & Francis, 2005). Fortunately, recent funding by the federal government has provided for extensive research on teaching reading skills to English language learners (McCardle & Leung, 2006). Researchers are currently examining whether methods that are effective with monolingual students at risk for reading disability are also effective for non-English speakers. One early finding of this research program was that interventions that are comprehensive (i.e., including explicit instruction in phonemic awareness, alphabetic principle, fluency, vocabulary, comprehension) produced significant improvements for these students (Linan-Thompson et al., 2006; Vaughn, Cirino, et al., 2006; Vaughn, Linan-Thompson, et al., 2006; Vaughn, Mathes, et al., 2006). Less comprehensive interventions did not produce significant results (Denton et al., with English language learners at a range of proficiency and skill levels.

APPLYING THE RESEARCH TO TEACHING

Teachers implement concept mapping in their classrooms either by providing teacher-created maps or by having students generate their own maps. Research has shown that both uses have educational benefit, but greater gains are found when students generate the maps themselves (Ruzic & O'Connell, 2001). Concept maps can be used to help students brainstorm ideas for writing, communicate or represent complex ideas, link prior knowledge with new information, or assess understanding or misunderstanding.

Steps for creating concept maps include:

1. Gather research and drawing materials. If students are creating their own maps, identify and collect the relevant possible resources (i.e., textbooks, reference materials, teacher-selected Websites, photos, graphs). Drawing materials may include colored pencils and shape stencils.
2. Select one of the concept map formats. There are a variety of different types of concept maps—spider maps, hierarchy maps, and flowchart maps to name a few. The topic selected will influence the type of map needed.
3. In the standard concept map (Novak & Gowin, 1984) concepts are circled and links drawn to connect these concepts. The links are then labeled to explain the relationship between or among the concepts. Concepts should only be listed once on the map (Ahlberg, 2004).
4. Generate the map by brainstorming concepts related to the overall question or theme of the map. Connect the concepts and label the relationships.
5. Revise and refine the maps. Typically, final maps should be the result of several drafts.

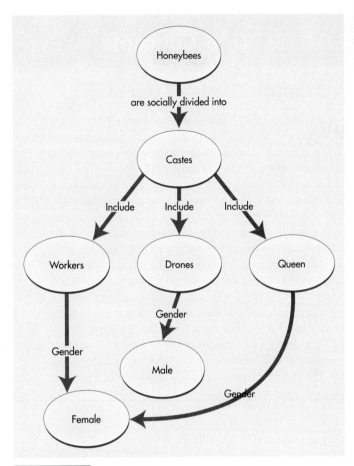

FIGURE 3.2 Figure A Concept Map: Honeybees

Sutphin, M. (2007, January). *Mapping concepts from the classroom to the computer: Instructors hope to combine concept maps and the Internet to test agriculture students.* Blacksburg, VA: Virginia Technical University College of Agriculture and Life Sciences. Reprinted with permission.

● *By Kristin L. Sayeski*

2004). With this increased emphasis on reading intervention research for non-English speakers, educators may soon have empirically validated methods for teaching effectively. For example, the responsive instruction feature on page 106 provides an empirically validated strategy.

For young children in particular, research increasingly points to the importance of an environment in which children have the opportunity to listen to reading, examine books, engage in activities such as saying nursery rhymes, writing, and seeing and talking about printed materials (Hammill, 2004; Peck & Scarpati, 2004). This means encouraging such literacy-related activities in the home, which cannot occur unless the teacher is competent in addressing cultural differences among families. It also means teaching with a sense of urgency, as described on page 108, and understanding that effective instruction is special education's bottom line (Kauffman & Hallahan, 2005; Kauffman et al., 2008).

FOCUS ON **Concepts**

A Common Sense of Urgency

We need to exercise caution with well-intended but general concepts, for much very poor instruction has occurred as a result of misguided interpretations. To illustrate, we often stress that good teachers should care about and demonstrate concern for their students. One teacher who was brought to my attention would display very caring behaviors by taking time on her weekends to expose some of her poor urban students to community cultural events such as art shows, museums, and libraries. On the other hand, extensive observations in her general education elementary classroom revealed constant chaos and little meaningful instruction. Although she wanted to be effective, she was incapacitated by her lack of skill, and her students suffered accordingly. To be specific, I would propose that a school with a sense of community is one that is united in the urgency of helping each child master the grade-level curriculum. Classroom time is not wasted, teachers are well trained in teaching strategies that work, children's progress is monitored constantly,

remedial actions are taken when needed, and there is the clear expectation that all children can and will meet mastery.

Schools with underachieving culturally diverse students clearly need this common sense of urgency. Most educators will say that they care about their students and have no racial or cultural animus, but relatively few teachers are aware that one of the best examples of the absence of bias is to teach with this sense of urgency, fully expecting children to learn. Schools that fail to be alarmed when two thirds to three quarters of their students are two to three grades behind academically are consciously or unconsciously subscribing to this bias.

Source: Cartledge, G. (2004). Another look at the impact of changing demographics on public education for culturally diverse learners with behavior problems: Implications for teacher preparation. In L. M. Bullock & R. A. Gable (Eds.), *Quality personnel preparation in emotional/behavioral disorders: Current perspectives and future directions* (pp. 64–69). Denton, TX: Institute for Behavioral and Learning Differences at the University of North Texas. Reprinted with permission.

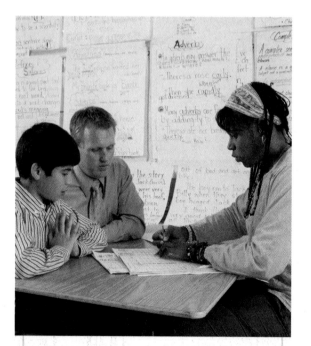

Of all the academic skills, reading is most important. Teachers should encourage literacy-related activities in the home, so they must be aware of and competent in addressing cultural differences among families.

A viable multicultural curriculum cannot be created and simply handed out to teachers (Banks & Banks, 2007). Teachers must be invested in the endeavor, as their values, perspectives, and teaching styles will affect what is taught and how. The effective implementation of a multicultural curriculum requires teaching strategies that are involvement oriented, interactive, personalized, and cooperative.

This perspective applies to our own teaching and writing as well. In any textbook, the adequate treatment of multicultural issues cannot be confined to a single chapter. A chapter like this one—devoted specifically to multicultural education—may be necessary to ensure that the topic is given sufficient focused attention. Our intention in this book, however, is to prompt consideration of multicultural issues in every chapter.

Socialization

Academic instruction is one of two primary purposes of education. The other, socialization, involves helping students develop appropriate social perceptions and interactions with others and learn how to work for desirable social change. Socializing the student does not mean that any kind of behavior or attitude is acceptable in school; nor does it mean ignoring the student's cultural heritage. Commonalities among children are greater than their differences (Cushner, McClelland, & Safford, 2006), but cultural and linguistic differences nonetheless pose significant challenges for teachers,

FOR BETTER OR FOR WORSE LYNN JOHNSTON

Source: FOR BETTER OR FOR WORSE © (1992) Lynn Johnston Productions. Distributed by Universal Press Syndicate. Reprinted with permission. All rights reserved.

who must make the classroom an affirming place for students (Cartledge and Loe, 2001; see also Osher et al., 2004).

In some cases, helping children learn appropriate social skills might require helping parents learn how to teach their children (Elksnin & Elksnin, 2000). This requires understanding the cultural and linguistic diversity of families. Destructive and stereotypic social perceptions and interactions among differing subcultural groups are long-standing problems in schools and communities in the United States, particularly when there are cultural differences among students in language and social behavior (Osher et al., 2004). The cartoon above illustrates how stereotypes have affected the way we think about people and the ideas that are embedded in our language. Part of the process of multicultural socialization is giving students experiences that make them question the way we think about other cultures.

The most obvious examples involve racial discrimination, although sex discrimination and discrimination against people of differing religions and disabilities are also common in our society. Consider the case of Adelaide Ruffner, a woman with cerebral palsy, who was considered not acceptable as a teacher in the 1960s but went on to earn a master's degree and to be recognized for her extraordinary work with children with disabilities and their families. In a report of Ruffner's award-winning work, Dadurka (2004) related:

> Though her family was supportive, others were not always so accepting. When Ruffner began her student-teaching term at Johnson Elementary in the 1960s, she was let go after six weeks.
> "The parents complained. Back then you were judged by your exterior. . . . People were scared," she said. "It was like segregation." (p. A2)

There is no guarantee that discrimination such as that experienced by Adelaide Ruffner will not be encountered today. Teachers and teacher educators must become keenly aware of their own cultural heritages, identities, and biases before they can help their students deal with cultural diversity in ways that enhance democratic ideals, such as human dignity, justice, and equality (Banks & Banks, 2007). Becoming comfortable with one's own identity as a member of subcultural groups is an important objective for both teachers and students. Depending on the cultural context, accepting and valuing one's identity can be quite difficult.

Teaching about different cultures and their value may be important in reducing racial and ethnic conflict and promoting respect for human differences. Equally important, however, is structuring classroom interactions to promote the understanding and appreciation of others. One of the most effective ways of breaking down prejudice and encouraging appropriate interaction among students with different characteristics is **cooperative learning**. In cooperative learning, students of different abilities and cultural characteristics work together as a team, fostering interdependence.

Teachers of exceptional children and youths must be aware of the potential variety of subcultural identities of their students. Review the multiple aspects of cultural identity

Reading Homework Exercise

Cooperative Learning ●
Go to the Homework and Exercises section in Chapter 3 of MyEducationLab to access the reading "Cooperative Learning in Multicultural Education Programs", about the benefits of cooperative learning.

■ **Cooperative learning**
A teaching approach in which the teacher places students with heterogeneous abilities (for example, some might have disabilities) together to work on assignments.

suggested by Figure 3.1 (page 92) and reflect on the combinations of these and other subcultures that a given student might adopt. One of the cultural identities that is not included in Figure 3.1 is sexual orientation, yet many children and adolescents, including many with educational exceptionalities, experience serious difficulties with what some have called the "invisible" culture of gay and lesbian youth. Students who are "straight" might struggle with their own prejudices against homosexuals, prejudices that are all too often fostered by both their peers and adults and sometimes given justification by identification with a religious or political subculture. Gay and lesbian students are often harassed and abused verbally and physically in school and may suffer from serious depression or other psychological disorders as a result; even the appearance or assumption of being gay can lead to abuse (see Associated Press, 2004; Bell, 2004). Gay students need to be able to be themselves without fear of harassment or discrimination (Elliot, 2000). Consider also that a student might be both gay or lesbian and gifted, physically disabled, intellectually disabled, or have another educational exceptionality.

Our point is that the task of socialization in a multicultural society demands attention to the multitude of identities that students may assume. It also demands an awareness that any of these identities may carry the consequence of social rejection, isolation, and alienation. Many children with disabilities are lonely and need to develop friendships (Pavri, 2001). Our task as educators is to promote understanding of cultural differences and acceptance of individuals whose identities are different from one's own. Building pride in one's cultural identity is a particular concern in teaching exceptional students. As we have noted elsewhere, many people in the Deaf community prefer to be called the Deaf, which runs contrary to the current use of terms such as hearing impaired. Deaf people and blind people have begun to express pride in their identities and cultures and, at the same time, foster multicultural experiences involving other languages and customs (Gallucci, 2000). In fact, for increasing numbers of people with disabilities, labels are to be embraced, not hidden.

People from many segments of society—such as parents of children with disabilities, senior citizens, religious groups, and recovering alcoholics—find that congregating for mutual support and understanding enhances their feelings of self-worth. Educators need to consider the possible value of having students with disabilities congregate for specific purposes.

By trying to avoid labels and insisting that students with disabilities always be placed with those who do not have disabilities, perhaps we risk giving the message that those who have disabilities are less desirable or even not fit to associate with as peers. Bateman (1994) suggests that "something is terribly and not very subtly insulting about saying a bright learning disabled student ought not attend a special school with other students who have learning disabilities because he needs to be with non-disabled students" (p. 516). In striving for true multicultural awareness, we might learn that it's more productive in the long run to embrace identities associated with exceptionalities, while working to increase tolerance and understanding of differences, than it is to avoid labels or refrain from congregating students with specific characteristics.

One of the most difficult tasks of teaching is socializing students through classroom discipline—that is, through the management of classroom behavior. Managing classroom behavior presents a serious challenge for nearly all teachers and a particularly difficult challenge for most special education teachers (see Evertson & Weinstein, 2006; Kauffman, Mostert, Trent, & Pullen, 2006). Two considerations are critical: the relationship between the teacher's approach to classroom discipline and the parents' child-rearing practices and the teacher's sensitivity to cultural differences in responses to discipline.

Teachers might have an approach to classroom discipline that they consider effective and humane but that differs radically from some cultures' accepted child-rearing practices. Educators, like everyone else, are often ethnocentric, believing that their views are right and those of others are wrong based on cultural values. In a given case, they might be right, in that their view is more humane or effective, but they might also be insensitive to the values of students and their families. Teachers must be sensitive to individuals and families, but that sensitivity does not allow ignoring what reliable research tells us about human behavior (Kauffman et al., 2008).

In the case of discipline involving students of culturally diverse backgrounds, the teacher might face difficult ethical decisions about child abuse or neglect. When do one's own beliefs about the treatment of children demand that a culturally condoned disciplinary practice be confronted as abuse or neglect? Answering this question is not easy.

Finally, we note that education should not merely socialize students to fit into the existing social order. The goals of multicultural education include teaching students to work for social change, which entails helping students who are members of oppressed minorities become advocates for themselves and other members of their subcultures (Banks & Banks, 2007; Utley & Obiakor, 2001c).

Summary

In what ways do we see universality of cultural pride and shame?

▶ People of every identity take justifiable pride in aspects of their heritage.

▶ People of every identity have conducted themselves in ways that bring shame to their group.

▶ Collective guilt and collective pride are problems for every group.

What is American about multiculturalism?

▶ The United States is a very diverse society that seeks justice for all.

▶ Ideally, American culture is one that celebrates diversity within a framework of clearly defined common values.

What are the important concepts about cultural diversity for education?

▶ American society is made of many subcultures (cultures that are a part, not all, of the larger societ(y), each of which is characterized by:
  ■ Values and typical behavior
  ■ Language or dialects
  ■ Nonverbal communication
  ■ Awareness of one's cultural identity
  ■ World views or general perspectives

▶ Special education must foster achievement in the context of cultural diversity.

What are the most important aspects of multicultural and bilingual special education?

▶ Assessment that honors the student's cultural heritage and does not penalize the student.

▶ Instruction that uses the student's cultural strengths and that involves teaching tolerance and appreciation of culture, working with families, improving language instruction for language-minority students, improving literacy instruction for language-minority students, and adopting effective teaching practices

▶ Socialization to multicultural norms

STANDARDS and PRINCIPLES in this Chapter

SPECIAL EDUCATORS . . .

■ are active and resourceful in seeking to understand how primary language, culture, and familial backgrounds interact with the individual's exceptional condition to impact the individual's academic and social abilities, attitudes, values, interests, and career options (from CEC Content Standard #3).

■ foster environments in which diversity is valued and individuals are taught to live harmoniously and productively in a culturally diverse world (from CEC Content Standard #5).

■ match their communication methods to an individual's language proficiency and cultural and linguistic differences; provide effective language models; and use communication strategies and resources to facilitate understanding of subject matter for individuals with exceptional learning needs whose primary language is not English (from CEC Content Standard #6).

ALL TEACHERS . . .

■ understand how students differ in their approaches to learning and create instructional opportunities that are adapted to diverse learners (INTASC Principle #3).

■ use an understanding of individual and group motivation and behavior to create a learning environment that encourages positive social interaction, active engagement in learning, and self-motivation (INTASC Principle #5).

■ use knowledge of effective verbal, nonverbal, and media communication technologies to foster active inquiry, collaboration, and supportive interaction in the classroom (INTASC Principle #6).

Applying the STANDARDS and PRINCIPLES

■ DESCRIBE ways in which students from culturally diverse backgrounds might differ in the ways they learn. What strategies might a special educator use to address those differences? (CEC Content Standard #3)

■ HOW might a lack of attention to cultural, ethnic, gender, and linguistic differences affect the identification of students for special services? (INTASC 3.04 & 3.09)

■ HOW might having a child with disabilities influence a family's view of themselves as caregivers and as members of their communities? (INTASC 3.06)

■ HOW can special educators foster environments in which diversity is valued and individuals are taught to live harmoniously and productively in a culturally diverse world? (CEC Content Standard #5)

Now go to the Hallahan/Kauffman, Eleventh Edition MyEducationLab course at www.myeducationlab.com to:

- take a Pretest to assess your initial comprehension of the chapter content;
- study chapter content with your Individualized Study Plan;
- take a Posttest to assess your understanding of chapter content;
- engage in multimedia exercises to help you build a deeper and more applied understanding of chapter content.

4

Parents and Families

I am often asked to describe the experience of raising a child with a disability—to try to help people who have not shared that unique experience to understand it, to imagine how it would feel. It's like this. . . .

When you're going to have a baby, it's like planning a fabulous vacation trip—to Italy. You buy a bunch of guide books and make your wonderful plans. The Coliseum. The Michelangelo David. The gondolas in Venice. You may learn some handy phrases in Italian. It's all very exciting.

After months of eager anticipation, the day finally arrives. You pack your bags and off you go. Several hours later, the plane lands. The stewardess comes in and says, "Welcome to Holland."

"Holland?!?" you say. "What do you mean Holland?? I signed up for Italy! I'm supposed to be in Italy. All my life I've dreamed of going to Italy."

But there's been a change in the flight plan. They've landed in Holland and there you must stay.

The important thing is that they haven't taken you to a horrible, disgusting, filthy place, full of pestilence, famine and disease. It's just a different place.

So you must go out and buy new guide books. And you must learn a whole new language. And you will meet a whole new group of people you would never have met.

It's just a different place. It's slower-paced than Italy, less flashy than Italy. But after you've been there for a while and you catch your breath, you look around. . . . and you begin to notice that Holland has windmills. . . . and Holland has tulips. Holland even has Rembrandts.

But everyone you know is busy coming and going from Italy . . . and they're all bragging about what a wonderful time they had there. And for the rest of your life, you will say "Yes, that's where I was supposed to go. That's what I had planned."

And the pain of that will never, ever, ever, ever go away . . . because the loss of that dream is a very very significant loss.

But . . . if you spend your life mourning the fact that you didn't get to Italy, you may never be free to enjoy the very special, the very lovely things . . . about Holland.

—Emily Perl Kingsley
"Welcome to Holland"

QUESTIONS to guide your reading of this chapter . . .

- How have professionals' views of parents changed?
- What are the effects of a child with a disability on the family?
- What are the best ways for families to be involved in treatment and education?

MISCONCEPTIONS ABOUT

Parents and Families of Persons with Disabilities

MYTH ■ Professionals need to focus their intervention efforts only on the parents, especially the mother, of children with disabilities.

FACT ■ Professionals now believe that the family (including extended family) as well as friends should be included in intervention programming for children with disabilities.

MYTH ■ Parents are to blame for many of the problems of their children with disabilities.

FACT ■ Parents can influence their children's behavior, but so, too, can children affect how their parents behave. Research shows that some children with disabilities are born with difficult temperaments, which can affect parental behavior.

MYTH ■ Parents must experience a series of reactions—shock and disruption, denial, sadness, anxiety and fear, and anger—before adapting to the birth of a child with a disability.

FACT ■ Parents don't go through emotional reactions in lockstep fashion. They may experience some, or all, of these emotions but not necessarily in any particular order.

MYTH ■ Many parents of infants with disabilities go from physician to physician, "shopping" for an optimistic diagnosis.

FACT ■ Just the opposite is often true. Parents frequently suspect that something is wrong with their baby but are told by professionals not to worry—that the child will outgrow the problem. Then they seek another opinion.

MYTH ■ The father is unimportant in the development of the child with a disability.

FACT ■ Although they are frequently ignored by researchers and generally do experience less stress than mothers, fathers can play a critical role in the dynamics of the family.

MYTH ■ Parents of children with disabilities are destined for a life of stress and misery.

FACT ■ Some parents experience high degrees of disruption and stress, but over time many come to learn to cope. And some actually gain unanticipated positive benefits from having a child with a disability.

MYTH ■ Siblings are usually unaffected by the addition of a child with a disability to the family.

FACT ■ Siblings often experience the same emotional reactions as parents do, and their lack of maturity can make coping with these emotions more difficult.

MYTH ■ The primary role of the early intervention professional should be to provide expertise for the family.

FACT ■ Many authorities now agree that professionals should help parents become more involved in making decisions for the family.

MYTH ■ The typical family in the United States has two parents, is middle class, and has only the father working outside the home.

FACT ■ Demographics are changing rapidly. There are now many more families with both parents working outside the home as well as more single-parent families and families living in poverty.

MYTH ■ Parents who elect not to be actively involved in their child's education and treatment are neglectful.

FACT ■ Although it's desirable for parents to be involved, it is sometimes very difficult for them to do so because of their commitments to other family functions (e.g., work and child care).

MYTH ■ Professionals are always in the best position to help families of people with disabilities.

FACT ■ Informal sources of support, such as extended family and friends, are often more effective than formal sources of support, such as professionals and agencies, in helping families adapt to a family member with a disability.

MYTH ■ Teachers should respect the privacy of parents and communicate with them only when absolutely necessary—for example, when their child has exhibited serious behavior problems.

FACT ■ Teachers should initiate some kind of contact with parents as soon as possible, so that if something like a serious behavior infraction does occur, some rapport with the parents will already have been established.

As Emily Perl Kingsley—the mother of a child with Down syndrome—points out (see p. 115), the birth of a child with a disability can have a profound effect on the family. But the exact nature of the effect is not always certain. Reactions of family members to the individual with a disability can run the gamut from absolute rejection to complete acceptance, from intense hate to intense love, from total neglect to overprotection. But most important, a child with disabilities does not always threaten the family's well-being. In fact, some parents and siblings testify that having a family member with a disability has strengthened the family bonds.

In this chapter, we explore the dynamics of families with children with disabilities and discuss parental involvement in treatment and education. Before proceeding further,

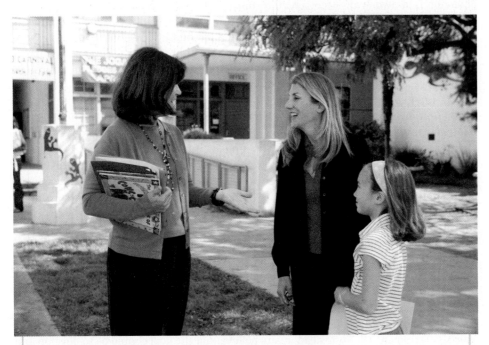

The prevailing philosophy now dictates that whenever possible, professionals should seek the special insights that parents can offer by virtue of living with their children.

however, we present a historical perspective of the role of parents and families of children who are disabled.

Professionals' Changing Views of Parents and Families

Today, knowledgeable professionals who work with exceptional learners are aware of the importance of the family; importantly, most recognize that it's families and not just parents who are crucial for successful outcomes for persons with disabilities. As one influential team of family intervention advocates has put it:

> Until early intervention developed a family-centered approach, almost all emphasis was on parents and not on families. . . . Policy makers and professionals now recognize that partnerships should not be limited to parents only (especially to mothers only). Partnerships can and should involve relationships between professionals and other family members, such as fathers, grandparents, brothers and sisters, and even close family friends. Each of these people can support and enhance the educational outcomes for students with exceptionalities. (Turnbull, Turnbull, Erwin, & Soodak, 2006)

Even though we now recognize how crucial it is to consider the concerns of parents and families in treatment and educational programs for individuals who are disabled, this was not always the case. Professionals' views of the role of parents have changed dramatically. In the not too distant past, some professionals pointed to the parents as the primary cause of the child's problems or as a place to lay blame when practitioners' interventions were ineffective. For at least two reasons, we now know that automatically holding parents responsible for their children's problems is inappropriate.

First, research has shown that the direction of causation between child and adult behavior is a two-way street (Bell & Harper, 1977; Collins, Maccoby, Steinberg, Hetherington, & Bornstein, 2000; Mangelsdorf & Schoppe-Sullivan, 2007). Sometimes the parent changes the behavior of the child or infant. However, sometimes the reverse is true. Research over several years has confirmed that the behaviors of individuals with a wide variety of disabilities ranging in age from infancy through adolescence can affect the behavior of their parents toward them (Brooks-Gunn & Lewis, 1984; Mahoney & Robenalt, 1986; Orsmond, Seltzer, Greenberg, & Krauss, 2006; Slonims & McConachie, 2006). For example, some infants who are disabled are relatively unresponsive to stimulation from their parents, making it more difficult to interact with these children. With an understanding of the reciprocal nature of parent–child interaction, we are more likely to sympathize with a mother's frustration in trying to cuddle an infant with severe developmental disabilities or a father's anger in attempting to deal with his teenager who has an emotional or behavioral disorder.

Second, researchers have found that the family can have a positive influence on the educational process. Although many authorities used to think that parents needed training to achieve a positive effect on their children, more and more educators now have recognized that parents often have as much or more to offer than professionals regarding suggestions for the treatment of their children. The prevailing philosophy now dictates that whenever possible, professionals should seek the special insights that parents can offer. Furthermore, authorities today are less likely to view the purpose of early intervention to be training parents to assume the role of quasi-therapist or quasi-teacher (Berry & Hardman, 1998). Instead, many believe that the goal should be to develop and preserve the natural parent–child relationship as much as possible. In sum, a healthy parent–child relationship is inherently beneficial.

TABLE 4.1	Importance of Families to Teachers and Teachers to Families

Families . . .

- Provide teachers with personal information that can explain why certain students' behaviors are occurring in the classroom.

- Provide background information and medical histories to teachers and to the school that can help teachers understand why a student behaves or learns in certain ways.

- Reinforce directives that teachers give their students, especially on homework assignments.

- Support teachers by serving as chaperones or volunteers in the classroom.

- Help teachers determine students' interests so that long-term education or vocation goals can be established.

- Tell teachers about which types of discipline and learning strategies work best with their children.

- Help teachers determine each student's strengths and needs so that appropriate instructional goals are created.

Teachers . . .

- Provide families with documented evidence of their children's progress and successes.

- Help families become more actively involved in their children's education.

- Help families determine where a student's interests lie so that appropriate long-term goals can be established.

- Teach and reinforce social skills that are needed for students to be successful, contributing members of the communities in which families live.

- Tell families when their children exhibit inappropriate behaviors or academic needs in the classroom.

- Provide important educational and community data to help families stay current and knowledgeable about opportunities available for children.

- Lend a helping hand, a supportive ear, and a friendly face to all families served.

Source: Adapted from O'Shea, D. J., & O'Shea, L. J. (2001). Why learn about students' families? In D. J. O'Shea, L. J. O'Shea, R. Algozzine, D. J. Hammitte (Eds.), *Families and teachers of individuals with disabilities: Collaborative orientations and responsive practices* (pp. 5–24). Austin: Pro-Ed, Inc. Copyright © 2001. Adapted by permission of Pro-Ed, Inc.

The fact is that parents and teachers have a symbiotic relationship. Each group can benefit enormously from the other. (See Table 4.1.)

Recognizing the importance of the family, Congress has passed several federal laws stipulating that schools make a concerted effort to involve parents and families in the education of their children with disabilities. Current law mandates that schools attempt to include parents in crafting their children's individualized education programs (IEPs; see Chapter 1). In the case of children under three years of age, schools must involve parents in developing **individualized family service plans (IFSPs)**. The focus of the IFSP is family-centered; it not only addresses the needs of the individual child who has a disability, but also focuses on the child's family by specifying what services the family needs to enhance the child's development.

■ **Individualized family service plan (IFSP)**
A plan for services for young children with disabilities (under three years of age) and their families; drawn up by professionals and parents; similar to an IEP for older children; mandated by PL 99-457.

The Effects of a Child with a Disability on the Family

The birth of any child can have a significant effect on the dynamics of the family. The parents and other children must undergo a variety of changes to adapt to the presence of a new member. The effects on the family of the birth of a child with a disability can be even more profound.

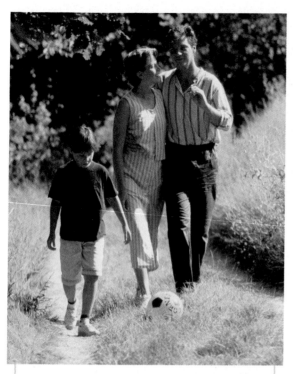

The birth of any child has a profound effect on his or her family, and when the child is born with a disability, the effect is even more so.

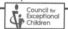
The everyday routines that most families take for granted are frequently disrupted in families with children who are disabled (Keogh, Garnier, Bernheimer, & Gallimore, 2000; Stoneman & Gavidia-Payne, 2006). For example, the child with a disability might require alterations in housing (e.g., the family might decide to move closer to therapists), household maintenance schedules (e.g., chores might not be done as quickly because of lack of time), and even parents' career goals (e.g., a parent might pass up a promotion to spend more time with the child).

In addition to affecting family dynamics, a child with a disability can influence family members' employment. One survey of families with children with disabilities, for example, found that over half reported that one or more family members altered their work hours, worked fewer hours, changed jobs, or quit working altogether because of having a child with a disability (Anderson, Larson, Lakin, & Kwak, 2002).

It's important to note that the child with a disability can have an impact on both parents and siblings, and in different ways.

Parental Reactions

A STAGE THEORY APPROACH   Traditionally, researchers and clinicians have suggested that parents go through a series of stages after learning they have a child with a disability. Some of these stages parallel the proposed sequence of responses that accompany a person's reactions to the death of a loved one. Based on interviews of parents of infants with serious physical disabilities, a representative set of stages includes shock and disruption, denial, sadness, anxiety and fear, anger, and finally adaptation (Drotar, Baskiewicz, Irvin, Kennell, & Klaus, 1975).

Several authorities have questioned the wisdom of this stage approach in understanding parental reactions. One argument against a strict stage model comes from the fact that many parents report that they don't engage in denial. In fact, they're often the first to suspect a problem. It's largely a myth that parents of children who are disabled go from physician to physician, "shopping" for a more favorable diagnosis. In fact, all too frequently, they have to convince the doctor that there is something wrong with their child.

Although parents might not go through these reactions in a rigid fashion, some do experience some or all these emotions at one time or another. Another commonly reported reaction is guilt.

THE ROLE OF GUILT   The parents of a child with a disability frequently wrestle with the feeling that they are in some way responsible for their child's condition. Even though there is absolutely no basis for such thoughts in the vast majority of cases, guilt is one of the most commonly reported feelings of parents of exceptional children.

The high prevalence of guilt is probably due to the fact that the primary cause of so many disabilities is unknown. Uncertainty about the cause of the child's disability creates an atmosphere that is conducive to speculation by the parents that they themselves are to blame. Mothers are particularly vulnerable. As Featherstone (1980), the mother of a boy who was blind and had hydrocephaly, severe intellectual disability, cerebral palsy, and seizures, described it:

> Our children are wondrous achievements. Their bodies grow inside ours. If their defects originated in utero, we blame our inadequate bodies or inadequate caution. If . . . we accept credit for our children's physical beauty (and most of us do, in our hearts), then inevitably we assume responsibility for their physical defects.

The world makes much of the pregnant woman. People open doors for her, carry her heavy parcels, offer footstools and unsolicited advice. All this attention seems somehow posited on the idea that she is creating something miraculously fine. When the baby arrives imperfect, the mother feels she has failed not only herself and her husband, but the rest of the world as well.

Soon this diffuse sense of inadequacy sharpens. Nearly every mother fastens on some aspect of her own behavior and blames the tragedy on that. (pp. 73–74)

DEALING WITH THE PUBLIC   In addition to ambivalence about the cause of the child's disability, parents can feel vulnerable to criticism from others about how they deal with their child's problems. Parents of children with disabilities sometimes sense, correctly or not, that others are scrutinizing their decisions about their child's treatment, educational placement, and so forth.

The public can sometimes be cruel in their reactions to people with disabilities. People with disabilities—especially those with disabilities that are readily observable—are inevitably faced with inappropriate reactions from those around them. And understandably, parents often assume the burden of responding to inappropriate or even cruel reactions from the public. The following experience of the mother of a child with autism is illustrative:

Worn out, I toss my purse under the seat and look absently out the window onto the dark tarmac. Last to board, a woman and a girl of about ten struggle to get into the small, crowded plane. The girl flaps her hand frantically near her face. The pair move in a sort of lunging, shuffling duet. The mother's eyes are firmly fixed toward the rear of the plane and her hand is vise-gripped to the girl's wrist. I know this scenario: mother and child with autism traveling. Small world.

Loud guttural sounds, almost a moan, almost a scream, come from the girl. Her first utterance causes the people near me to shift around in their seats and nervously clear their throats. . . .

The girl's sounds begin to escalate as the plane hits some turbulence. Fellow passengers murmur. To me, of course, this feels like home. . . .

More NOISE. The child is obviously upset and uncomfortable. At least that's obvious to me. The pressure in her ears is probably giving her excruciating pain. I am jarred from my internal reflection by a man's cold remark.

"Why can't she make her be quiet?" the passenger behind me complains loudly.

"Why the hell did she bring her on a plane," hisses the other. Passengers in the seats next to them chuckle.

It's all I can do not to turn around and shout, "Be glad that you aren't that uncomfortable. Be glad that you aren't that child's caretaker, having to dread taking a short, forty-minute flight because of cutting remarks from jerks like you. Aren't you glad she isn't your child because if she was you couldn't just get off a plane and walk away from her!" But I stew in silence.

The plane is descending. We will touch ground soon. The people behind me will get off the plane and glide down to their baggage and their cars. Perhaps they will stop for a martini before they go home, with only themselves to worry about.

The mother in the rear of the plane will wait until everyone else is off, struggle down the rickety steps, carrying too many bags and trying to keep her grip on the tired, crotchety girl. A week from now the others will not even remember this flight or the girl who was making so much noise. I will not be able to forget her. (Gerlach, 1999, pp. 108–110)

Reading Homework Exercise

Parenting a Child with Special Needs ● Go to the Homework and Exercises section in Chapter 4 of MyEducationLab to read the fact sheet "Parenting a Child with Special Needs", reviewing the experiences of parents as they find out that their child has special needs.

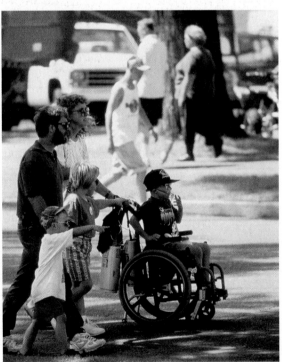

People with disabilities are inevitably faced with inappropriate reactions from those around them, and parents often must help their children respond to such behavior.

DEALING WITH THE CHILD'S FEELINGS   In addition to dealing with the public's reactions to their child's disability, parents face the delicate task of talking with the child about his or her disability. This can be a difficult responsibility because parents need to address the topic without making the disability seem more important than it actually is. In other words, parents don't want to alarm the child or make the child more concerned about the disability than is necessary.

Nevertheless, the child with a disability usually has questions about it: How did I get it? Will it go away? Will it get worse? Will I be able to live independently as an adult? If possible, parents should wait for the child to ask specific questions to which they can respond, rather than lecture about generalities. However, it is a good idea for parents to talk honestly with the child at as early an age as possible, especially before the teenage years, when so many parents and children have problems communicating.

Parental Adjustment

There is abundant evidence that parents of children with disabilities undergo more than the average amount of stress (Lessenberry & Rehfeldt, 2004). The stress is usually not the result of major catastrophic events but rather the consequence of daily responsibilities related to child care. A single event, such as a family member coming down with a serious illness, can precipitate a family crisis, but its effects will be even more devastating if the family was already under stress because of a multitude of daily hassles.

PARENTAL REACTION TO STRESS   Contrary to what one might think, stress doesn't appear to be strongly linked to the severity of the child's disability. For example, parents of children with more severe disabilities might have greater child-care burdens, but parents of children with milder disabilities might be more likely to experience additional stress related to that felt by parents of children without disabilities (e.g., stress pertaining to school achievement, dating, driving a car). Stress, however, does appear to be linked to the types of behavioral problems the child might have, with more strain being created by children who exhibit socially offensive and disruptive behaviors (Hastings, Daley, Burns, & Beck, 2006; Orsmond et al., 2006).

The factors that appear to be most predictive of how parents will cope with the stress are their prior psychological makeup and marital happiness and the quality and degree of informal support they receive from others. Although there are exceptions, it's fair to say that parents who were well adjusted and happily married before the birth of the child have a better chance of coping with the situation than do those who were having psychological or marital problems.

Social support that parents receive from each other, extended family members, friends, and others can be critical in helping them cope with the stress of raising a child with a disability (Duis, Summers, & Summers, 1997; Gavidia-Payne & Stoneman, 1997; Singer, 2002). The support can be physical, such as offering child care, or it can be psychological. Just having someone to talk to about problems can be helpful.

CHANGING VIEWS OF PARENTAL ADJUSTMENT   At one time, most professionals assumed that parents of children with disabilities were destined for a life of stress and misery. Whereas at one time it was popular to blame parents for their children's disabilities, it then became commonplace to go overboard in assuming that children with disabilities almost invariably caused parents to become dysfunctional or depressed (Ferguson, 2002). Across several studies, researchers found that mothers of children with developmental disabilities are at an increased risk of experiencing depression (Singer, 2006). Twenty-nine percent of these mothers experienced depression.

The figure of 29 percent certainly signals that mothers of these children are vulnerable to depression, but it's important to keep in mind that it also means that 71 percent did not become depressed. It's also important to keep in mind that the population studied was mothers, not fathers, and it was for children with developmental disabilities (a category used for young

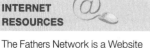

INTERNET RESOURCES

The Fathers Network is a Website devoted to information for fathers of children with disabilities and special health needs: www.fathersnetwork.org

children who usually end up being categorized as intellectually disabled at school age). Much more research is needed on fathers as well as other disabilities and other age groups.

Given the research available, professionals should have a heightened sensitivity to the possibility that parents of children with disabilities may experience varying levels of depression. At the same time, there are many who cope very well. In addition, there are numerous anecdotal accounts of some parents who report that adding a child with a disability to the family actually has some unanticipated positive results (Ferguson, 2002; Scorgie & Sobsey, 2000; Skinner, Bailey, Correa, & Rodriguez, 1999). They report undergoing life-changing experiences, which include becoming:

- More tolerant of differences in other people
- More concerned about social issues
- Better parents
- A closer-knit family
- More philosophical or spiritual about life

Elizabeth King Gerlach's (1999) philosophical outlook on society's obsession with normalcy was undoubtedly shaped by her having a child with a disability:

Society views disability as a "tragedy." In fact, the greater tragedy is society's larger and erroneous view that there is such a state as "normal." . . .

"Normal" does exist, but you have to look for it. It is a place that is somewhere between the middle of two extremes. For instance, [a] good example of normal can be found on my clothes dryer, between "fluff," and "shrink it." This area is marked "normal." I use this setting because it is the closest to normal that my life usually gets.

The truth is, "normal" is not a word that should apply to the human condition. People are different, and they constantly change. A close approximation to "normal" might be "balanced." . . . And some of us endeavor to maintain a balanced state within ourselves,

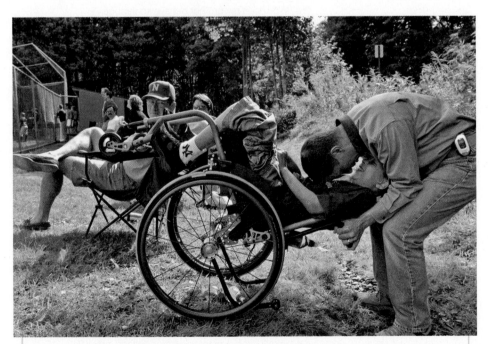

Some parents report that having a child with a disability in the family has unanticipated positive results, including greater tolerance of differences in other people, being better parents, and having a closer-knit family.

UNDERSTANDING THE
STANDARDS AND
PRINCIPLES What can special
educators do to address concerns
siblings of a student with a disability
may have? (CEC Knowledge and
Skill Standard CC10K3)

Council for
Exceptional
Children

INTERNET
RESOURCES

Author Brady Udall has written a
short story that poignantly explores
the feelings of a sibling toward his
brother with a disability. You can read
it at http://www.thegodparticle
.com/2004_02/01Udall.html.
You can also listen to or download
a podcast of Udall reading the
story. It's the third act of the "In Dog
We Trust"10/29/07 episode of
This American Life.
http://www.thislife.org/

our families, and our communities. We have to discover what this means for ourselves, and this too changes over time.

I used to think there was such a thing as a "normal, happy family" and that it was something attainable. I hadn't experienced that as a child, so I set out to create it as an adult. Autism bombed that notion. Just as well. I'm not pretending that autism, in its varying degrees of severity, isn't painful in many ways for everyone involved. It is. I'm simply saying that some of that pain is relieved with understanding and acceptance. Having a child with a disability has shown me how precious life really is and that being human means learning to love. The simplicity and complexity of this understanding never cease to amaze me. (pp. 4–6)

This is not to minimize the fact that the added stress a child with a disability often brings can have a devastating impact on the stability of the family. It's dangerous to assume, though, that the birth of a child with a disability automatically spells doom for the psychological well-being of the parents or for the stability of their marriage.

Sibling Reactions

Although a relatively large body of literature pertains to parental reactions, much less information is available about siblings of people with disabilities. What is available, however, indicates that siblings can and frequently do experience the same emotions—fear, anger, guilt, and so forth—that parents do. In fact, in some ways, siblings might initially have an even more difficult time than their parents in coping with some of these feelings, especially when they are younger. Being less mature, they might have trouble putting some of their negative thoughts into proper perspective. And they might be uncomfortable asking their parents the questions that bother them. Table 4.2 provides examples of sibling concerns.

TABLE 4.2	**Sibling Concerns About . . .**
Their sibling with a disability	• What caused the disability?
	• Why does my brother behave so strangely?
	• Will my sister ever live on her own?
Their parents	• Why do they let my brother get away with so much?
	• Why must all their time be given to my sister?
	• Why do they always ask me to babysit?
Themselves	• Why do I have such mixed feelings about my sister?
	• Will I catch the disability?
	• Will we have a normal brother–sister relationship?
Their friends	• How can I tell my best friend about my brother?
	• Will my friends tell everyone at school?
	• What should I do when other kids make fun of people with disabilities?
Their school and community	• What happens in special education classes?
	• Will I be compared with my sister?
	• What should I tell strangers?
Adulthood	• Will I be responsible for my brother when my parents die?
	• Do I need genetic counseling?
	• Should I join a parents' and/or siblings' group?

Source: Adapted from *Brothers & sisters—A special part of exceptional families* (3rd ed.), by P. A. Gallagher, T. H. Powell, & C. A. Rhodes, 2006, Baltimore, MD: Paul H. Brookes. Reprinted by permission.

Although some feelings about their siblings' disabilities might not appear for many years, a substantial number of accounts indicate that nondisabled siblings are aware at an early age that their brothers or sisters are different in some way. As nondisabled siblings grow older, their concerns often become focused on how society views them and their siblings who are disabled. Adolescence can be a particularly difficult period. Teens, fearing rejection by peers, often don't want to appear different, and having a sibling with a disability can single a person out.

Siblings' Adjustment

Children, like parents, can adapt well or poorly to having family members with disabilities. Not much research exists in this area. The little solid research evidence that does exist is in the area of intellectual disabilities and suggests that, although siblings are at a slightly elevated risk, they are at lower risk than parents of experiencing depression and anxiety (Rossiter & Sharpe, 2001). But, as is the case with parents, some people report having benefited from having a sibling with a disability; see the Personal Perspectives on p. 126.

Why some siblings respond negatively whereas others do not isn't completely understood. Although not definitive, there is some evidence that birth order, gender, and age differences between siblings have some bearing on adjustment (Berry & Hardman, 1998). A nondisabled sister who is older than her sibling who has a disability, for example, might have a negative attitude when she reaches adolescence because she often has to shoulder child-care responsibilities (Burke, 2004).

Siblings of the same gender and siblings who are close in age are more likely to experience conflicts. At older ages, however, when siblings are adults, there is evidence that women show more favorable attachments than men do to their sibling with a disability, and adults who are of the same gender as their sibling with a disability experience more favorable emotional responses (Orsmond & Seltzer, 2000).

Access to information is one key to adjustment for siblings of children with disabilities. As is noted in Table 4.2, siblings have myriad questions pertaining to their sibling's disability. Straightforward answers to these questions can help them to cope with their fears.

Teachers, as well as parents, can provide answers to some of these questions. Teachers, for example, can talk with students about the materials and contents of programs for their siblings with disabilities (Gallagher, Powell, & Rhodes, 2006). Another excellent resource for providing information and support to siblings are the **sibshops** workshops (Meyer & Vadasy, 1994) specifically designed to help siblings of children with disabilities.

Siblings of children with disabilities often recount being aware at a very early age that something was different about their brothers or sisters. Siblings' attitudes change at different stages of their lives; for example, adolescents become more concerned about public perception of themselves and their siblings with disabilities.

INTERNET RESOURCES

The Sibling Support Project (http://www.siblingsupport.org) provides extensive resources about sibshops.

■ **Sibshops**
Workshops for siblings of children with disabilities; designed to help siblings answer questions about the disability and learn to adjust to having a sister or brother with a disability.

Family Involvement in Treatment and Education

As we noted earlier, today's professionals are more likely to recognize the positive influence parents can have on their exceptional children's development. This more positive attitude toward parents is reflected in how parents are now involved in the treatment and education of their children.

At one time, most early intervention programs for families of children with disabilities operated according to the philosophy that the professionals had the expertise and

Personal PERSPECTIVES

Lessons from My Brother

I never actually thought about how much or if my younger brother's Down syndrome affected my decision to become a doctor until the question was posed recently. After much introspection, I finally decided that my experience with my brother did not influence the decision to practice, but the way I practice medicine. The skills learned while participating in his care have served me well in my dual roles as physician and mother.

His short sixteen years of life had a lasting effect on my life and my view of others. Carlton taught me patience, attentive listening, never to underestimate or allow myself to be underestimated, it's never too late to learn, and the enjoyment of simple pleasures of life. All aspects of my life were changed by the brief time he spent with us, and I am just realizing all he taught. . . .

At the age of sixteen he appeared to be a three-and-a-half foot, thin baby. Carlton remained a "baby" for the rest of his life; wearing diapers, crawling everywhere only able to walk if supported and was carted about with long legs dangling from my petite mother's hips like extra appendages.

He would periodically press his protruding eyes further out of their sockets with his thumbs for some optical pleasure known only to him. As a little girl, in trying to understand why he performed the only activity that could even be considered self-inflicted harm, I tried this maneuver myself, although not as aggressively. Seeing only a few scattered bursts of light, I gave

up and chalked it up to different wiring in our brains. Even then, Carlton was teaching me to at least try to see things from another's perspective. The lesson learned in the literal was later easily expanded to the figurative and empathy was the result.

After watching someone with a toddler's mentality for over a decade bask happily in the sun or laugh ecstatically in a mass of squirming puppies, a newfound recognition and appreciation of all things simple cannot help but develop. . . .

Watching my mother care for an exceptional child with limited resources and my brother thrive despite all that was lacking sowed the seeds of fortitude that I would need to succeed in my medical career. I now recognize that the odds were stacked against this poor African American girl from rural Alabama ever becoming a physician. I never even saw the long line of hurdles as a whole and simply took them one at a time; failure was not an option. Because of Carlton I never learned to underestimate others or myself.

Dr. Valencia Clay is a graduate of the University of Alabama School of Medicine. She is board certified in Internal Medicine, works as a medical director for a disability insurance company and a hospice medical consultant.

Source: Clay, V. (2006). Lessons from my brother. *Exceptional Parent, 36*(12), 24–25. Reprinted by permission.

■ **Family-centered model**
A consumer-driven model that encourages the family to make its own decisions with respect to services while mobilizing resources and supports for the family's goals.

that the families needed that expertise to function. Most authorities today, however, advocate a **family-centered model** (Blue-Banning, Summers, Frankland, Nelson, & Beegle, 2004; Dunst, 2002; Mangelsdorf & Schoppe-Sullivan, 2007). According to these authorities, the family-centered model encourages the family to make its own decisions with respect to services while mobilizing resources and supports for the family's goals. Another way of describing the family-centered approach is to say that it is a model in which the professionals work *for* the family.

Family-centered models reflect a change from viewing parents as passive recipients of professional advice to viewing them as equal partners in the development of treatment and educational programs for their children. The notion is that when professionals do not just provide direct services but also encourage the family to help themselves and their children, the family assumes control over their own lives and avoids the dependency that is sometimes associated with typical professional–family relationships.

Achieving the right balance between offering assistance and allowing families to make independent decisions can be challenging. For example, interviews with parents have resulted in the following recommendations:

- Be direct—but don't tell us what to do.
- Tell the truth and be honest—but also be hopeful and encouraging.

TABLE 4.3 **Suggestions for Teachers to Involve Families in Class and School Activities**

- Empathize with students and family members to understand what they may be experiencing and act according to their needs instead of personal needs.

- Value individual families, cultures, and their uniqueness instead of trying to categorize and stereotype families.

- Take time each morning to speak with students. Communicate regularly with family members.

- Allow options when communicating with families. Use a variety of contacts, including phone, face to face, notebook, or home visits. Determine the school professional with whom the family members may feel most comfortable.

- Communicate with both households when there is a joint custody arrangement. Don't assume that the information from school is reaching both parents.

- Be considerate of home arrangement facts when assigning homework. There might be no one at home to help with projects or difficult assignments that would need adult supervision.

- Plan alternative conference times in addition to school hour conferences. Think convenience for the families instead of teachers only. Hold conferences frequently. Avoid talking over or under the parents' heads: Avoid educational jargon.

- Make every conference meaningful and productive. Include the student in some of the conferences. Begin and end every conference, conversation, meeting, with a positive fact or work sample.

- Invite families into the classroom as much as possible. Value any and all contributions or suggestions family members make. Use lessons to incorporate family customs, rituals, and traditions.

- Value the diversity of all students and their family compositions. Even though a family composition might seem unstructured or confusing, there are lessons and a contribution they can make to the class. Set up programs that benefit all students and all types of households.

Source: Adapted from O'Shea, D. J., & Riley, J. E. (2001). Typical families: Fact or fiction? In D. J. O'Shea, L. J. O'Shea, R. Algozzine, D. J. Hammitte (Eds.), *Families and teachers of individuals with disabilities: Collaborative orientations and responsive practices* (pp. 25–50). Austin: Pro-Ed, Inc. Copyright © 2001. Adapted by permission of Pro-Ed, Inc.

- Be knowledgeable—but admit when you don't know the answer.
- Don't overwhelm—but don't hold back information. (Meadow-Orlans, Mertens, & Sass-Lehrer, 2003)

Table 4.3 lists several tips for teachers that are consistent with a family-centered approach.

The effort to build professional–parent partnerships is consistent with the thinking of child development theorists who stress the importance of the social context within which child development occurs. The renowned child development and family theorist Urie Bronfenbrenner (1979, 1995) was influential in stressing that an individual's behavior cannot be understood without understanding the influence of the family on that behavior. Furthermore, the behavior of the family cannot be understood without considering the influence of other social systems (e.g., the extended family, friends, and professionals) on the behavior of the family. The interaction between the family and the surrounding social system is critical to how the family functions. A supportive network of professionals (and especially friends) can be beneficial to the family of a child with a disability.

UNDERSTANDING THE STANDARDS AND PRINCIPLES
How can teachers better communicate with families? (CEC Knowledge and Skill Standards CC7S2 & CC7S3)

Council for Exceptional Children

Family Systems Theory

The emphasis on the individual's behavior being understood in the context of the family and the family's behavior being understood in the context of other social systems is the basic principle underlying **family systems theory** (Lambie, 2000). There are several family system theories, all of which assume that the more treatment and educational

■ **Family systems theory** Stresses that the individual's behavior is best understood in the context of the family and the family's behavior is best understood in the context of other social systems.

programs take into account the relationships and interactions among family members, the more likely it is they will be successful. One model developed specifically with people with disabilities in mind includes four interrelated components: family characteristics, family interaction, family functions, and family life cycle (Turnbull et al., 2006).

FAMILY CHARACTERISTICS   **Family characteristics** include basic information about the family, such as the type and severity of the disability, the family's size, cultural background, socioeconomic status, coping styles, and special conditions (e.g., spousal abuse, maternal depression). Family characteristics help to determine how family members interact with each other and with others outside the family. For example, it could make a difference whether the child is learning disabled or deaf, is an only child or has five siblings, is of the upper middle class or lives in poverty, and so forth.

Recent trends in U.S. society make it even more important to take into account family characteristics. In particular, teachers should be attentive to the expanding ethnic diversity in the United States. (See the Focus on Concepts on p. 129 for suggestions on facilitating involvement of culturally and linguistically diverse families in the education of their children; see also Chapter 3.) In addition to wider ethnic diversity, there are also increases in the number of families in which both parents work outside the home, single-parent families, same-sex unions, and families living in poverty. Families particularly vulnerable to the stresses of raising a child with disabilities are those facing additional struggles arising from poverty or single-parent status. Unfortunately, a higher prevalence of disabilities exists in single-parent families and families in poverty (Fujiura & Yamaki, 2000).

Another group on the rise in numbers and who face considerable challenges raising children with disabilities are military families. The changing demographics of those in the military have contributed to these problems. An increasing number of low-income women are looking to the military for career opportunities; more than 80 percent of the military are married with children; and the military is the United States' largest employer of single parents (Taylor et al., 2005). Perhaps the biggest change in recent years has been the additional stresses associated with the separation of soldiers from their families due to deployment to Iraq. This stress has been difficult not only for the spouse of a soldier, but it has been especially difficult when the mother, herself, is a soldier. As one team of researchers concluded after in-depth interviews with low-income mothers in the military who were attempting to raise a child or children with disabilities:

> Although the women in our study entered the military as a career and felt very positively about the opportunities it could offer them when they enlisted, once they became mothers of a child with disabilities, the economic hardship and inflexibility in the workplace proved incompatible with successfully parenting a child with a disability. (Taylor et al., 2005, p. 96)

Coupled with these demographic changes—and to a certain extent influenced by them—families today live under a great deal more stress than they did in previous decades. Adding to this stress is the threat of terrorism subsequent to the attacks on the World Trade Center and the Pentagon on September 11, 2001. On the one hand, children need attention and reassurance more than ever; but on the other hand, because of pressures to earn a living, parents have fewer resources to draw on to provide comfort to their children.

These dramatic societal changes present formidable challenges in working with families of children with disabilities. As family configurations change, professionals need to alter their approaches. For example, approaches that are successful with two-parent families might not be suitable for single mothers. Also, professionals need to understand that today's parent is living under increasing stress and might find it correspondingly difficult to devote time and energy to working on behalf of his or her child.

■ **Family characteristics**
A component of the Turnbulls' family systems model; includes type and severity of the disability as well as such things as size, cultural background, and socioeconomic background of the family.

INTERNET RESOURCES

Fiesta Educativa is a project focused on providing information for Spanish-speaking families that have a child with a disability: www.fiestaeducativa.org

FOCUS ON **Concepts**

Facilitating Involvement of Culturally and/or Linguistically Diverse Families

The increasing ethnic diversity of schools in the United States has resulted in a wider mismatch between the ethnicities of teachers and students, especially students in special education. One of the difficulties facing many special education teachers, who are often white, is knowing how to involve families from a different culture. Howard Parette and Beverly Petch-Hogan (2000), two professors at Southeast Missouri State University, offer several suggestions.

Contacts with Families

- *Problem:* Families from culturally and/or linguistically diverse backgrounds often defer to professionals as the "experts." *Possible solution*: Do not assume that school personnel should always take the lead in providing information or contacting families.
- *Problem:* Some families mistrust school personnel. *Possible solutions*: Identify trusted people in the community (e.g., a minister, physician, retired teacher) to contact the family; establish a Family Advisory Council where parents can present issues; make use of interpreters in the case of parents who are English language learners.

Location of Meetings

- *Problem:* Meetings typically take place in a school building, which can present problems for parents without transportation and may be perceived as aversive or intimidating. *Possible solutions*: Provide transportation, or hold the meeting at a neutral site, e.g., neighborhood church or community center.

Supports During the Meeting

- *Problem:* Child care for families can make it difficult to attend a meeting. *Possible solution*: Provide child care.

Provision of Information/Training

- *Problem:* Professionals often deliver information to families via lectures and printed materials. *Potential solution*: Consider that culturally and linguistically diverse families are often more comfortable obtaining information in less formal settings, such as parent support groups.
- *Problem:* Typically, parents alone are the targets of information and training. *Potential solution*: Consider involving siblings or extended family members because they often assume significant responsibility for childcare.

Knowledge of Family Priorities, Needs, Resources

- *Problem:* Some families may find the implementation of intervention programs results in too much stress for the family. *Potential solution*: Be sensitive to families' desire not to get involved too deeply in intervention efforts.
- *Problem:* Some families do not view time in the same way as many professionals do. *Potential solution*: Be flexible in scheduling meeting times and consider video-or audio-taping parts of meetings missed by families.

Source: Parette, H. P., & Petch-Hogan, B. (2000). Approaching families: Facilitating culturally/linguistically diverse family involvement. *Teaching Exceptional Children, 33*(2), 4–10. Reprinted by permission.

FAMILY INTERACTION   Family members can have a variety of functional and dysfunctional ways of relating to one another. The more the parent responds appropriately to the young child's body language, gestures, facial expressions, and so forth, the more the child's development will flourish.

In the Turnbulls' model, **family interactions** reflect family cohesion and adaptability, important determinants of the "health" of a family. In general, families are healthier if they have moderate degrees of cohesion and adaptability.

Cohesion   Cohesion refers to the degree to which an individual family member is free to act independently of other family members. An appropriate amount of family cohesion permits the individual to be his or her own person while at the same time drawing on other family members for support as needed. Families with low cohesion might not offer the child with a disability the necessary support, whereas the overly cohesive

■ **Family interaction**
A component of the Turnbulls' family systems model; refers to how cohesive and adaptable the family is.

Adults with intellectual disabilities, especially those who live at home, often have special problems finding the right degree of independence from their families. When they do live away from home, parents are often concerned about providing enough support so their children don't become socially isolated.

family might be overprotective. Research suggests that good cohesion has positive benefits for the child as well as other family members (Howell, Hauser-Cram, & Kersh, 2007; Magana, Schwartz, Rubert, & Szapocznik, 2006).

It's often difficult for otherwise healthy families to find the right balance of cohesion. They sometimes go overboard in wanting to help their children and, in so doing, limit their children's independence. Adolescence can be a particularly stressful time, when it's normal for teenagers to loosen their familial bonds. What makes the situation difficult for many families of children with disabilities is that because of the disability, by necessity the child has often been more protected. In fact, there is research to suggest that in the early years, the more supportive the parent is with the child, the better. In one study, mothers of toddlers with Down syndrome who engaged in more helpful behaviors during play, such as steadying objects and otherwise making it more likely that the children would experience success, had children who were more likely to play and vocalize (Roach, Barratt, Miller, & Leavitt, 1998).

Cohesion can also be an issue for adults with disabilities. Current thinking dictates that people with disabilities should live in the community, but many will need support from their families to do this successfully. Living in the community demands a number of daily living skills—such as managing personal finances, keeping to a work schedule, and planning and preparing meals—that don't always come easily even to nondisabled young adults. Finding the right degree of independence from the family for young adults with disabilities can be a significant challenge. As one mother explained about future living arrangements for her daughter with severe intellectual disabilities:

> I would like to see her live fairly close. . . . She's going to have to have some support, I know that. . . . And I would like to see her close enough so that we always have the constant, not constant, [sic] but we will always be there if she needs us. And both Tim and I agree that that's something we will always do. We will be here. But, on the other hand, if we want to go away for a month, we'll know there are other people that can be called upon to give her the support she needs. (Lehmann & Baker, 1995, p. 30)

Adaptability   Adaptability refers to the degree to which families are able to change their modes of interaction when they encounter unusual or stressful situations. Some families are so chaotic that it's difficult to predict what any one member will do in a given situation. In such an unstable environment, the needs of the family member who is disabled might be overlooked or neglected. At the other end of the continuum are families characterized by extreme rigidity. Each family member has his or her prescribed family role. Such rigidity makes it difficult to adjust to the addition of a new family member, especially one with a disability. For example, the mother's involvement in transporting the child with a disability to therapy sessions might necessitate that the father be more involved taking care of the other children.

▪ **Family functions**
A component of the Turnbulls' family systems model; includes such things as economic, daily care, social, medical, and educational needs.

FAMILY FUNCTIONS   **Family functions** are the numerous routines in which families engage to meet their many and diverse needs—economic, daily care, social, medical, and educational.

An important point for teachers to consider is that education is only one of several functions in which families are immersed. For some students, especially those with multiple disabilities, several professionals might be vying for the parents' time. It's natural, of course, for teachers to want to involve parents as much as possible. Positive benefits can occur when parents are part of the treatment program. At the same time, however, teachers need to respect the fact that education is just one of the many functions to which families must attend.

Several authorities have reported that some families of students with disabilities prefer a passive, rather than an active, degree of involvement in their children's education (Turnbull & Turnbull, 2006). There are often legitimate reasons for playing a more passive role. For example, in some cultures it's customary for parents to refrain from interfering with the roles of school personnel in educational matters. Furthermore, some parents might simply be so busy attending to other family functions that they are forced to delegate most of the educational decisions to teachers. Teachers should respect the parents' desire to play a relatively passive role in their child's education.

FAMILY LIFE CYCLE   Several family theorists have noted that the impact of a child with a disability on the family changes over time (Berry & Hardman, 1998; O'Shea, O'Shea, Algozzine, & Hammitte, 2001), and that there is value in looking at families of children with disabilities from a **family life cycle** perspective. Most family theorists consider four stages in the lives of families: early childhood, childhood, adolescence, and adulthood.

Transitions between life cycle stages are often stressful for families, especially families with children who are disabled. We've already mentioned the difficulties facing families at the transition point when their child, as an adult, moves into more independent work and living settings. A particularly difficult issue for some parents of children with disabilities who are entering adulthood is that of mental competence and guardianship. Parents who decide that their children are not competent to make rational choices without endangering themselves can go through legal channels to obtain guardianship of their children. **Guardianship** means that one person has the authority, granted by the courts, to make decisions for another person. Guardianship can range in degree from total to more limited or temporary authority to make decisions.

Another particularly troublesome transition can be from the relatively intimate confines of an infant or preschool program to the larger context of a kindergarten setting, which requires more independence on the part of the child. As one parent relates:

> As my daughter's third birthday approached, I lived in dread. . . . The infant program had become home away from home for me. It was supportive and intimate. I had made some lifelong friendships, as well as having established a comfortable routine in our lives. I saw making the transition to a preschool program in the school district as an extremely traumatic experience, second only to learning of Amy's diagnosis. . . .
>
> First, I was concerned that my husband and I, along with professionals, would be deciding the future of our child. How could we play God? Would our decisions be the right ones? Second, I feared loss of control, as I would be surrendering my child to strangers— first to the school district's intake assessment team and then to the preschool teacher. The feeling of being at the mercy of professionals was overwhelming. In addition, I had more information to absorb and a new system with which to become familiar. . . . (Hanline & Knowlton, 1988, p. 116)

Transitions between stages are difficult because of the uncertainty that each new phase presents to the family. One of the reasons for the uncertainty pertains to replacements of the professionals who

Web Research Homework Exercise

Supporting Families • Go to the Homework and Exercises section in Chapter 4 of MyEducationLab to search for Websites that offer support to families for various disabilities.

■ **Family life cycle**
A component of the Turnbulls' family systems model; consists of birth and early childhood, childhood, adolescence, and adulthood.

■ **Guardianship**
A legal term that gives a person the authority to make decisions for another person; can be full, limited, or temporary; applies in cases of parents who have children who have severe cognitive disabilities.

There is evidence in ethnic minority families of familial and religious support of members with disabilities.

work with the child who is disabled. In particular, parents of a child with multiple disabilities, who requires services from multiple professionals, can be anxious about the switches in therapists and teachers that occur many times throughout the child's life, especially at transition points.

Social Support for Families

■ **Social support**
Emotional, informational, or material aid provided to a person or a family; this informal means of aid can be very valuable in helping families of children with disabilities.

Authorities now recognize that families can derive tremendous benefit from social support provided by others (Lenhard et al., 2007; Singer, 2002). **Social support** refers to emotional, informational, or material aid that is provided to persons in need. In contrast to assistance that comes from professionals and agencies, social support is informal, coming from such sources as extended family, friends, church groups, neighbors, and social clubs.

ETHNICITY AND SOCIAL SUPPORT   There is evidence of familial and religious support in ethnic minority families (Harry, 2002; Magana et al., 2006). The values of some minority groups place heavy emphasis on caring for one's own family members, disabled or not. The family's church plays a major social support role for many minorities, again regardless of whether they are disabled or not.

PARENTAL SUPPORT GROUPS   One common type of social support, especially for parents of recently diagnosed children, is parental support groups that consist of parents of children with the same or similar disabilities. Such groups can be relatively unstructured, meeting infrequently with unspecified agendas, or they can be more structured. They serve as a means for parents to share their experiences, thus providing educational and emotional support. Parental support groups, however, are not of benefit to everyone. Some parents actually experience more stress from sharing problems and listening to the problems of others (Berry & Hardman, 1998).

INTERNET RESOURCES FOR PARENTS   The Internet is an excellent resource for parents of children with disabilities. Dozens of electronic mailing lists, newsgroups, blogs, and World Wide Web sites are now devoted to disability-related topics. Through these means, parents of children with disabilities can communicate with each other, with people who have disabilities, and with professionals concerning practical as well as theoretical issues. There are lists and newsgroups for specific disabilities (e.g., Down syndrome, attention deficit/hyperactivity disorder, cerebral palsy, cystic fibrosis) as well as more general ones.

INTERNET RESOURCES @

There are several projects, many of which are funded by the federal government, focused on providing information and support to families of children with disabilities. Following are some examples:
   PACER Center: www.pacer.org
   Beach Center: www.beachcenter.org
   Federation for Children with Special Needs: www.fcsn.org
   Family Village of the Waisman Center, U of Wisconsin: www.familyvillage.wisc.edu/index.htmlx
   Through the Looking Glass: www.lookingglass.org
   National Center for Infants, Toddlers and Families: Zero to Three: www.zerotothree.org
   Exceptional Parent is a magazine focused on families with children with disabilities. It also provides useful information on its Website: www.eparent.com

PARENT CENTERS   The U. S. Department of Education has established over 100 Parent Training and Information Centers and Community Parent Resource Centers—each state has at least one of these centers. The Technical Assistance Alliance for Parent Centers (www.taalliance.org) assists and coordinates the work of these centers. The general purpose of the centers is to help parents of children with disabilities to (1) understand their children's special needs; (2) communicate with professionals; (3) participate in educational decision-making, such as IEP and IFSP meetings; and (4) obtain information about services, programs, and resources. A national report from the Technical Assistance Alliance for Parent Centers indicated that parents have found these centers valuable (Turnbull et al., 2006).

Positive Behavioral Intervention and Support for Challenging Behaviors

Some children with disabilities engage in behaviors that are particularly challenging for professionals and family members alike. Children with emotional or behavioral disorders and those with autism, for example, sometimes exhibit outbursts of aggressive or

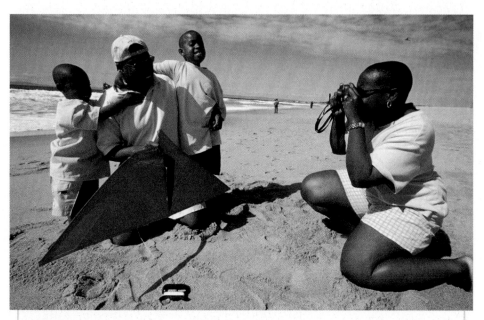

Positive behavioral intervention and support (PBIS) for families might include mealtimes, seasonal celebrations, visits to relatives, etc. as opportunities for reinforcing positive or appropriate behavior.

self-injurious behavior. As one team of researchers documented, such behaviors can have a profound impact on the family:

> The families we interviewed described a family life that was deeply and pervasively affected. . . . The entire family system was engaged in multiple accommodations in response to the child's problem behavior. . . . These families were changed as a result of the persistent and overwhelming demands of physically intervening with their child or worrying about their child's problem behavior. As researchers, we found it difficult to construct the prose that would adequately convey the emotional, physical, and structural impact of problem behavior on family life. Problem behavior relentlessly affected family relationships, physical circumstances, social networks, and daily activities. (Fox, Vaughn, Wyatte, & Dunlap, 2002, p. 448)

Such extreme behaviors often require more than just social support from friends and the community. In such cases, professionals may need to help families apply behavioral principles in interacting with their child. In Chapter 2, we discussed **positive behavioral and intervention supports (PBIS)**, contextually and culturally appropriate interventions that emphasize rewarding positive behavior to make problem behavior less effective, efficient, and relevant and to make desired behavior more functional.

In applying PBIS with families, the focus is on **family activity settings**, routines that families engage in, such as mealtimes, seasonal celebrations, visits to relatives, shopping, going on vacations, and eating in restaurants (Lucyshyn, Horner, Dunlap, Albin, & Ben, 2002; Singer, Goldberg-Hamblin, Peckham-Hardin, Barry, & Santarelli, 2002). Under the guidance of professionals, families typically begin by concentrating on just one or two settings before expanding to more.

Communication Between Parents and Professionals

Virtually all family theorists agree that no matter what particular approach one uses to work with parents, the key to the success of a program is how well parents and professionals are able to work together. Even the most creative, well-conceived

■ **Positive behavioral and intervention supports (PBIS)** Systematic use of the science of behavior to find ways of supporting desirable behavior rather than punishing undesirable behavior; positive reinforcement (rewarding) procedures that are intended to support a student's appropriate or desirable behavior.

■ **Family activity settings** Activities that families routinely engage in, such as mealtimes and seasonal celebrations; can be focal points for the implementation of PBIS.

UNDERSTANDING THE STANDARDS AND PRINCIPLES Why is it important to involve families? (CEC Knowledge and Skill Standards CC10K2, CC10K3, CC10S2, CC10S3, & CC10S4)

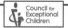

Casebook Reflections

REFER TO THE CASE *The Reluctant Collaborator* in your booklet. There is no mention of Peter's parents in this case. How might this information be relevant in deciding what to do on his behalf? ●

Building Teaching Skills Exercise

Conferences ● Go to the Building Teaching Skills section in Chapter 4 of MyEducationLab to access Websites offering information about conducting successful parent-teacher conferences, both from a teacher's and a parent's perspective.

UNDERSTANDING THE STANDARDS AND PRINCIPLES How can teachers learn more about parents' perspectives? (CEC Knowledge and Skill Standard CC10S5)

Council for Exceptional Children

Casebook Reflections

REFER TO THE CASE *Least Restrictive for Whom?* in your booklet. At the first meeting with Brian's parents, they were angry when Mary suggested that they consider placement in a residential institution for the deaf. How might Mary have communicated with Brian's parents so that this meeting would have been more cordial and constructive? What do you think the parents thought Mary was communicating about them as parents? ●

model is doomed to fail if professionals and parents are unable to communicate effectively.

Unfortunately, such communication doesn't come easily—not too surprising, considering the ingredients of the situation. On the one hand are the parents, who are trying to cope with the stresses of raising a child with a disability in a complex and changing society. On the other hand, there are the professionals—teachers, speech therapists, physicians, psychologists, physical therapists, and so forth—who might be frustrated because they don't have all the answers to the child's problems.

One of the keys to avoiding professional–parent misunderstandings is communication (Kauffman, Mostert, Trent, & Pullen, 2006). It's critical that teachers receive information *from* parents as well as provide information *to* them. The parents have spent considerably more time with the child and have more invested in the child emotionally; they can be an invaluable source of information about the child's characteristics and interests. By keeping parents informed of what is going on in class, teachers can foster a relationship in which they can call on parents for support should the need arise.

Homework is one area in particular that is often a source of misunderstanding and conflict and that requires parental cooperation. The Focus on Concepts on p. 135 offers some strategies for enhancing the homework experience for students with disabilities.

Most authorities agree that the communication between the teacher and parents should start as soon as possible and that it should not be initiated only by negative behavior on the part of the student. Parents, especially those of students with behavior disorders, often complain that the only time they hear from school personnel is when their child has misbehaved. To establish a degree of rapport with parents, some teachers make a practice of sending home a brief form letter at the beginning of the school year, outlining the goals for the year. Others send home periodic newsletters or make occasional phone calls to parents. By establishing a line of communication with parents early in the year, the teacher is in a better position to initiate more intensive and focused discussions should the need arise. Three such methods of communication are parent–teacher conferences, home-note programs, and traveling notebooks.

PARENT–TEACHER CONFERENCES Parent–teacher conferences can be an effective way for teachers to share information with parents. Likewise, they are an opportunity for teachers to learn more about the students from the parents' perspective. In addition to regularly scheduled meetings open to all parents, teachers might want to hold individual conferences with the parents of particular students. Planning is key to conducting successful parent–teacher conferences. How the teacher initiates the meeting, for example, can be crucial. Table 4.4 presents questions teachers should ask themselves in order to facilitate their parent–teacher conferences.

If the focus of the meeting is the student's poor work or misbehavior, the teacher will need to be as diplomatic as possible. Most authorities recommend that the teacher find something positive to say about the student while still providing an objective account of what the student is doing that is troubling. The teacher needs to achieve a delicate balance of providing an objective account of the student's transgressions or poor work while demonstrating advocacy for the student. If parents detect that the teacher is angry, this can make them apprehensive about the treatment the child might be receiving. Conveying only good news can also lose the parents' sense of trust. If the parents only hear good news, then they will be taken by surprise if a serious incident does occur.

FOCUS ON **Concepts**

Homework
Tips for Teachers and Administrators

Give Clear and Appropriate Assignments

If the homework is too hard, is perceived as busy work, or takes too long to complete, students might tune out and resist doing it. Never send home any assignment that students cannot do. Homework should be an extension of what students have learned in class.

- Make sure students and parents have information regarding the policy on missed and late assignments, extra credit, and available adaptations. . . .
- Remind the students of due dates periodically.
- Coordinate with other teachers to prevent homework overload.
- Establish a routine at the beginning of the year for how homework will be assigned.
- Assign homework at the beginning of class. . . .
- Explain how to do the homework, provide examples, and write directions on the chalkboard.
- Have students begin the homework in class, check that they understand, and provide assistance as necessary.

Make Homework Accommodations

- Provide additional one-on-one assistance to students. . . .
- Allow alternative response formats (e.g., allow the student to audiotape an assignment).
- Adjust the length of the assignment.
- Provide a peer tutor or assign the student to a study group.
- Provide learning tools (e.g., calculators).
- Adjust evaluation standards.
- Give fewer assignments. . . .

Ensure Clear Home–School Communication

Recommended ways in which teachers can improve communications with parents include

- Providing a list of suggestions on how parents might assist with homework. For example, ask parents to check with their children about homework daily.
- Providing parents with frequent written communication about homework.

Ways in which administrators can support teachers in improving communication include

- Supplying teachers with the technology needed to aid communication (e.g., telephone answering systems, e-mail, homework hotlines).
- Providing incentives for teachers to participate in face-to-face meetings with parents (e.g., release time, compensation).
- Suggesting that the school district offer after school and/or peer tutoring sessions to give students extra help with homework.

Resources

Bryan, Nelson, & Mathur (1995); Bryan & Sullivan-Burstein (1997); Epstein, Munk, Bursuck, Polloway, & Jayanthi (1999); Jayanthi, Bursuck, Epstein, & Polloway (1997); Jayanthi, Sawyer, Nelson, Bursuck, & Epstein (1995); Klinger & Vaughn (1999); Polloway, Bursuck, Jayanthi, Epstein, & Nelson (1996).

Source: Adapted from Warger, C. (2001, March). *Five homework strategies for teaching students with disabilities.* ERIC Clearinghouse on Disabilities and Gifted Education. Retrieved May 14, 2007, from www.erichoagiesgifted.org/e608.html. Reprinted by permission.

HOME-NOTE PROGRAMS Sometimes referred to as home-contingency programs, home-note programs are a way of communicating with parents and having them reinforce behavior that occurs at school (Kelley, 1990; Kelley & McCain, 1995). By having parents dispense the reinforcement, the teacher takes advantage of the fact that parents usually have a greater number of reinforcers at their disposal than do teachers.

Teachers can choose from several types of home notes. A typical one consists of a simple form on which the teacher records "yes," "no," or "not applicable" to certain categories of behavior (e.g., social behavior, homework completed, homework accurate, in-class academic work completed, in-class academic work accurate). The form also may contain space for the teacher and the parents to write a few brief comments. The student takes the form home, has his or her parents sign it, and returns it the next day. The parents deliver reinforcement for the student's performance. The teacher often starts out sending a note home each day and gradually decreases the frequency until the notes are being sent once a week.

■ **Home-note program**
A system of communication between the teacher and parents; the teacher evaluates the behavior of the student using a simple form, the student takes the form home, gets the parents' signatures, and returns the form the next day.

TABLE 4.4	Questions Teachers Should Ask Themselves About Parent-Teacher Conferences

Have you done your homework?

- Reviewed the student's cumulative records
- Consulted with other professionals
- Documented the student's academic and behavioral progress
- Established rapport with the parents before the conference
- Familiarized yourself with the student and family's culture

Have you involved the parents *before* the conference?

- Discussed the goals of the meeting with the parents and solicited their input
- Involved the student, as appropriate
- Scheduled a mutually convenient day and time for the meeting
- Provided written notice prior to the meeting

How do you involve the parents *during* the meeting?

- Welcome the parents and speak informally with them before the beginning
- Reiterate the goals of the meeting
- Begin with a discussion of the child's strengths
- Support your points with specific examples and documentation
- Encourage parents to share insights
- Ask open-ended questions
- Avoid jargon
- Practice active listening. Remember, one of your big jobs is to listen to parents
- Review the main points of the meeting and determine a course of action
- Provide additional resources (e.g., support groups, family resource centers, Websites)

What do you do *after* the meeting?

- Document the results of the meeting
- Share results with colleagues who work with the student
- Follow up with the parents as needed to discuss changes.

Source: Kauffman, J. M., Mostert, M. P., Trent, S. C., & Pullen, P. L. (2006). *Managing classroom behavior: A reflective case-based approach.* Boston: Allyn & Bacon, p. 149. Reprinted with permission.

Video Homework Exercise

Parents as Child Advocates ● Go to the Homework and Exercises section in Chapter 4 of MyEducationLab to access the video "Parents as Child Advocates", which describes actions parents can take to support the learning of their children with special needs.

■ **Traveling notebook**
A system of communication in which parents and professionals write messages to each other by way of a notebook or log that accompanies the child to and from school.

For home-notes to work, it's important that both teachers and parents agree philosophically with a behavioral approach to managing student behavior. If either is opposed to using reinforcement as a means of shaping behavior, the home-note program is unlikely to succeed.

TRAVELING NOTEBOOKS **Traveling notebooks**, which go back and forth between school and home, are less formal than home notes and particularly appropriate for students who see multiple professionals. The teacher and other professionals, such as speech and physical therapists, can write brief messages to the parents and vice versa. In addition, a traveling notebook allows the different professionals to keep track of what each is doing with the student. Figure 4.1 provides excerpts from a traveling notebook of a two-year-old with cerebral palsy.

Sara,   9/15

We witnessed an apparently significant moment in her oral communication: She'll try to say "all done" after a meal. The execution is imperfect, to say the least, but she gets an "A" for effort. Could you please reinforce this after snack? Just ask her, "What do you say after you finish your snack?"

Thanks,
Lynn

9/28

Lauren had an esp. good day! She was jabbering a lot! Being very expressive with her vocalness & jabbering. I know she said "yes," or an approximate thereof, several times when asked if she wanted something. She was so cute with the animal sounds esp. pig & horse — she was really trying to make the sounds. It was the first time we had seen such a response. Still cruising a lot! She walked with me around the room & in the gym. She used those consonant and vowel sounds: dadada, mamama — her jabbering was just so different & definitely progressive.

Sara

9/29

I want to bring in some different spoons next week to see if she can become more independent in scooping with a large handle spoon or a spoon that is covered.

Joan

Joan –   10/1

Although Lauren would very much approve of your idea for making her more independent during feeding, we'd rather not initiate self-feeding with an adaptive spoon at this time. Here's why:

1. When I feed Lauren or get her to grip a spoon and then guide her hand, I can slip the entire bowl of the spoon into her mouth and get her to close her lips on it. When Lauren uses a spoon without help, she turns it upside-down to lick it or inserts just the tip of it into her mouth and then sucks off the food ...

2. Lauren has always been encouraged to do things "normally." She never had a special cup or a "Tommy Tippee," for instance. Of course it took a year of practice before she could drink well from a cup, and she still dribbles a little occasionally; but she's doing well now. We really prefer to give Lauren practice in using a regular spoon so that she doesn't get dependent on an adaptive utensil.

Lynn

2/26

Good news! Lauren walked all the way from the room to the gym & back — She also walked up & down the full length of the gym!

Several other teachers saw her and were thrilled. She fell maybe twice! But picked herself right up —

Sara

3/2

Lauren had a great speech session! We were playing with some toys and she said "I want help" as plain as day. Later she said "I want crackers" and at the end of the session, she imitated "Cindy, let's go." Super!

Marti

FIGURE 4.1   A traveling notebook. These short excerpts are taken at random from a notebook that accompanies 2-year-old Lauren, who has cerebral palsy, back and forth to her special class for preschoolers. The notebook provides a convenient mode for an ongoing dialogue among her mother Lynn; her teacher, Sara; her occupational therapist, Joan; and her speech therapist, Marti. As you can see from this representative sample, the communication is informal but very informative in a variety of items relating to Lauren.

Parent Advocacy

Another important way that parents and other family members can become involved in treatment and education is through advocacy. **Advocacy** is action that results in benefit to one or more persons (Alper, Schloss, & Schloss, 1996). Advocacy can foster needed or improved services for children while helping parents gain a sense of control over outcomes for their children. Although sometimes associated with the notion of confrontations between parents and professionals, advocacy need not be adversarial. In fact, ideally, parents and professionals work together in their advocacy efforts.

Parents can focus their advocacy on helping their own children as well as other people with disabilities. The latter might involve volunteering for advisory posts with schools and agencies as well as political activism—for example, campaigning for school board members who are sympathetic to educational issues pertinent to students with disabilities. The Personal Perspectives on p. 138 offers suggestions on how parents can prepare themselves to advocate for their child.

■ **Advocacy**
Action that is taken on behalf of oneself or others; a method parents of students with disabilities can use to obtain needed or improved services.

Personal PERSPECTIVES

Advocacy in Action: You Can Advocate for Your Child

Get All the Information You Can

The first step to successful advocacy is to gather information. Learn what is happening in the school, . . . and talk with your child's teacher to learn his or her view of areas of concern.

You should also learn about special education law and its protections. You can obtain this information from the school's special education or guidance director, state departments of education, or parent information and training centers, as well as organizations such as CEC (Council for Exceptional Children). . . .

Talk with your child to learn his or her view of the situation and what he or she thinks will help. Even young children have a keen sense of their stress points and what could be done to make it easier for them to succeed.

What Do You Want the School to Do?

As your child's advocate, you need to be clear about what you want the school to do. Be able to explain what you are happy with, unhappy with, what you want changed, and how you want it changed.

Be a Good Communicator

Communicating well with your child's teacher and other school personnel is essential to your advocacy efforts. . . . Be honest and develop a positive relationship with the teacher and other staff. Start where the concern is, usually the classroom teacher. Only move up the chain of command if you must.

Being diplomatic can be hard when you are concerned about your child's welfare—you want to get feisty. But get feisty only if that is what it takes.

Bring a Companion to Meetings

. . . This person can help you listen, take notes so you are free to concentrate on what is happening, and help you understand what happened afterwards. In addition, your companion can help slow you down if things get too emotional.

Don't Be Afraid to Say No

Don't be pressured into making a bad decision. You can always say no, ask for more information, or for more time to consider a proposed solution. Take the time to consult with experts and people you trust. . . .

Making Your Voice Stronger

One of the best ways to make your voice stronger is to band together with other parents facing similar situations. . . .

When you meet with other parents, share your experiences. As a group, develop some proposals to solve the problem. The parents should then meet with the individual(s) who will be affected. For example, a group of parents who wanted to get computers in the resource room would meet first with the resource room teacher. . . . Then teachers and parents can build an alliance, which can be particularly effective in creating change.

Source: Osher, T. (1997). Advocacy in action: You can advocate for your child! *CEC Today,* 4(4), 4. Reprinted by permission.

INTERNET RESOURCES

The National Information Center for Children and Youth with Disabilities, funded by the U.S. Department of Education's Office of Special Education Programs, has information on the IEP process that parents should find valuable: www.nichcy.org/basicpar.htm

There are now several Websites focused on helping parents and advocates understand special education and the law. Following are some examples:

www.reedmartin.com
www.wrightslaw.com
www.edlaw.net
www.specialedlaw.net/index.mv
www.cleweb.org

As important as advocacy is, not all parents have the personalities or the time to engage in such activities. Also, engaging in advocacy may be more or less suitable to some parents at various stages in their child's development. For example, some parents might be heavily involved in such efforts when their children are young but become exhausted over the years and reduce their involvement. Likewise, some parents might not see the need for intervening on behalf of their children until they encounter problems later on—for example, in transition programming in the teenage years. The best advice for teachers is to encourage parents to be advocates for their children but respect their hesitancy to take on such responsibilities.

In Conclusion

Today's knowledgeable educators recognize the tremendous impact a child with a disability can have on the dynamics of a family. They appreciate the negative as well as the positive influence such a child can exert. Today's knowledgeable educators also realize that the family of a child with a disability can be a bountiful reservoir of support for the child as well as an invaluable source of information for the teacher. Although tremendous advances have been made, we are just beginning to tap the potential that families have for contributing to the development of their children with disabilities. We are just beginning to enable families to provide supportive and enriching environments for their children. And we are just beginning to harness the expertise of families so we can provide the best possible programs for their children.

Summary

How have professionals' views of parents changed?

► Professionals' views of parents are more positive than they once were for at least two reasons:
  ■ Not only can parent behavior influence child behavior, but the reverse can also occur.
  ■ The family can have a positive effect on the educational process.

► Congress has recognized the potentially positive influence by passing legislation mandating that families be involved in developing IEPs and IFSPs.

What are the effects of a child with a disability on the family?

► The addition of a child with a disability to a family can have significant effects on family dynamics and work patterns.

► Parental reactions to the birth of a child with a disability can involve a variety of reactions; guilt (even though unfounded) tends to be one that is frequent.

► Parents must also deal with public reactions to their child as well as the child's feelings about having a disability.

► There is substantial research to show that parents of children with disabilities undergo a great deal of stress.
  ■ How parents deal with the stress is dependent on their prior psychological makeup and marital happiness as well as the quality and quantity of social support they receive.
  ■ Current research indicates that many parents adjust well to having a child with a disability; some even benefit from the experience.

► Siblings of children with disabilities often experience some of the same emotions as the parents.
  ■ Siblings of the same gender and those who are close in age tend to have more conflicts, and at older ages, there is some evidence that women have a closer attachment to their sibling with a disability.
  ■ Having access to accurate information helps siblings to achieve a more positive adjustment.

What are the best ways for families to be involved in treatment and education?

► Most authorities advocate a family-centered model, whereby the families assume more decision making and professionals provide supports for families to achieve their goals.

► Most authorities also stress family systems theory. One such model (the Turnbulls') is composed of family characteristics, family interaction, family functions, and family life cycle.

► Social support, which involves emotional, informational, or material aid provided by nonprofessionals, is important for families.
  ■ There is evidence suggesting that some ethnic minority groups provide especially good social support.
  ■ Two common types of social support are parental support groups and Internet sites devoted to parents of children with disabilities.

► Positive behavioral intervention and supports, the use of positive reinforcement, is an important tool for parents who have children with challenging behavior problems.

► Communication between professionals and families is critical to involving families.
  ■ Parent–teacher conferences are an important means of communication, and preparation is a key to making them successful.
  ■ Home-note programs are a means for communication and a way for teachers to encourage parents to reinforce behavior that occurs at school.
  ■ Traveling notebooks are a way for one or more professionals to communicate with parents.

► Parent advocacy is an important way for families to become involved in the treatment and education of their children.
  ■ Advocacy need not be confrontational.
  ■ A common way to advocate is through active involvement in IEP meetings.
  ■ Teachers should encourage parent advocacy but respect parents who do not wish to be involved in this way.

STANDARDS and PRINCIPLES in this Chapter

SPECIAL EDUCATORS

■ facilitate instructional planning in a collaborative context including the individuals with exceptionalities, families, professional colleagues, and personnel from other agencies as appropriate (from CEC Content Standard #7).

■ routinely and effectively collaborate with families, other educators, related service providers, and personnel from community agencies in culturally responsive ways (from CEC Content Standard #10).

ALL TEACHERS

■ plan instruction based on knowledge of subject matter, students, the community and curriculum goals (INTASC Principle #7).

■ foster relationships with school colleagues, families, and agencies in the larger community to support students' learning and well being (INTASC Principle #10).

Applying the STANDARDS and PRINCIPLES

■ HOW might teachers encourage parents to maintain an active role in their child's education? (CEC Content Standard #7 & INTASC Principle #7)

■ WHAT do you think are the keys to effective collaboration with parents? (CEC Content Standard #10 & INTASC Principle #10)

Now go to the Hallahan/Kauffman, Eleventh Edition MyEducationLab course at www.myeducationlab.com to:

- take a Pretest to assess your initial comprehension of the chapter content;
- study chapter content with your Individualized Study Plan;
- take a Posttest to assess your understanding of chapter content;
- engage in multimedia exercises to help you build a deeper and more applied understanding of chapter content.

5

Learners with Intellectual and Developmental Disabilities

Whenever I step back and consider how "normal" . . . Nicole's life is, I am struck by how different her adulthood is from what Matt and I had thought it would be. [Recently] I paid a visit to the Regional Center. . . .

What a different world it is out there these days, I mused. Parents of a baby or child who is identified as having—or even at risk of having—developmental delays can turn to the Regional Center system for assessments, counseling, intervention therapies, respite care, and a host of other programs for both family and child. . . .

A mother with a crying baby entered the library. As I watched her trying to talk with the volunteer over the din, I thought of the things that haven't changed at all: the gut-wrenching adjustment to the actuality of giving birth to an "imperfect" infant, the exhaustion of caring for the vulnerable son or daughter. . . .

I followed [Colleen Mock] upstairs. . . . She segued into an explanation of the current perspective among professionals. . . . Professionals try to regard children or adults they see as whole people, capable of making decisions for themselves about things that affect their lives. Consumers . . . are encouraged— are empowered—to set goals and make choices. . . . When the appropriate supports are in place as a child grows older, his or her role as the determiner of what is wanted supplants the parents' function as advocate. Support services continue, but consumers are encouraged to use community resources to solve problems that arise, the rationale being that the process of engaging "natural supports"—family members, friends, neighbors, or fellow employees—is controlled by the consumer and integrates him or her in the community far more than dependence on service personnel.

—Sandra Z. Kaufman
Retarded Isn't Stupid, Mom!

QUESTIONS to guide your reading of this chapter . . .

- Why are many professionals now using the term intellectual disabilities instead of mental retardation?

- How do professionals define intellectual disabilities?

- What is the prevalence of intellectual disabilities?

- What causes intellectual disabilities?

- What methods of assessment are used to identify individuals with intellectual disabilities?

- What are some of the psychological and behavioral characteristics of learners with intellectual disabilities?
- What are some educational considerations for learners with intellectual disabilities?
- How do professionals assess students with intellectual disabilities' academic progress, adaptive behavior, and quality of life?
- What are some things to consider with respect to early intervention for learners with intellectual disabilities?
- What are some things to consider with respect to transition to adulthood for learners with intellectual disabilities?

MISCONCEPTIONS ABOUT

Learners with Intellectual and Developmental Disabilities

MYTH ■ Professionals are in agreement about the definition of intellectual disabilities.

FACT ■ There is considerable disagreement about definition, classification, and terminology.

MYTH ■ Once diagnosed as intellectually disabled, a person retains this classification for life.

FACT ■ A person's level of intellectual functioning doesn't necessarily remain stable; this is particularly true for those individuals who are mildly intellectually disabled. With intensive educational programming, some persons can improve to the point that they are no longer intellectually disabled.

MYTH ■ Intellectual disability is defined by how a person scores on an IQ test.

FACT ■ The most commonly used definition specifies that an individual must meet two criteria in order to be considered intellectually disabled: (1) low intellectual functioning and (2) low adaptive skills.

MYTH ■ In most cases, it's easy to identify the cause of intellectual disability.

FACT ■ Although the mapping of the human genome has increased our knowledge about causes of intellectual disabilities, it's still difficult to pinpoint the cause of intellectual disabilities in many people, especially those with mild intellectual disabilities.

MYTH ■ Psychosocial factors are the cause of the vast majority of cases of mild intellectual disabilities.

FACT ■ Exact percentages aren't available, but researchers are finding more and more genetic syndromes that result in mild intellectual disabilities; hereditary factors are also involved in some cases.

MYTH ■ It's possible to determine how much of a person's intelligence is determined by heredity versus the environment.

FACT ■ Most authorities now agree that heredity and the environment don't combine in an additive way, making it futile to come up with precise percentages that each contributes.

MYTH ■ The teaching of vocational skills to students with intellectual disabilities is best reserved for secondary school and beyond.

FACT ■ Many authorities now believe it appropriate to introduce vocational content in elementary school to students with intellectual disabilities.

MYTH ■ When workers with intellectual disabilities fail on the job, it's usually because they don't have adequate job skills.

FACT ■ When they fail on the job, it's more often because of poor job responsibility (poor attendance and lack of initiative) and social incompetence (interacting inappropriately with co-workers) than because of incompetence in task production.

MYTH ■ People with intellectual disabilities should not be expected to work in the competitive job market.

FACT ■ More and more people who are intellectually disabled hold jobs in competitive employment. Many are helped through supportive employment situations, in which a job coach helps them and their employer adapt to the workplace.

As Sandra Kaufman (1999) points out (see p. 143), compared to just a few years ago, there's a world of difference in the quantity and quality of services for people with intellectual and developmental disabilities (also known as mental retardation). At the same time, though, she poignantly reminds us that some things related to intellectual disabilities are likely never to change. For parents, having a child with intellectual disabilities means facing a set of lifelong challenges. The main difference today is that although these parents are very likely to feel overwhelmed initially, they can look around and see signs of hope. They can see examples of adults with intellectual disabilities who lead relatively independent lives, and hold jobs in competitive or semi-competitive work environments.

As Mock explained to Kaufman, much of the success being achieved by people with intellectual disabilities is attributed to a change in philosophy that includes respecting their rights to be a part of decisions affecting their lives and emphasizing the use of natural supports. Later in the chapter, we discuss the important philosophical changes that have brought about the emphasis on self-determination and **natural supports**.

It takes more than well-intentioned philosophies to ensure that people with intellectual disabilities reach their full potential with respect to independent employment and community living. It often takes years of intensive instruction from special educators, working in tandem with other professionals, including general educators, to put the philosophies of self-determination and natural supports into effect.

There have been other changes, too, that have had a profound effect on the field of intellectual disabilities in the past several years. Among the most significant is the fact that this field is in the midst of a name change from *mental retardation* to *intellectual and developmental disabilities*.

■ **Natural supports**
Resources in a person's environment that can be used for support, such as friends, family, co-workers.

What's in a Name? *Mental Retardation* Versus *Intellectual and Developmental Disabilities*

In January 2007, the major professional organization for people with significant cognitive or intellectual disabilities—the American Association on Mental Retardation (AAMR)—changed its name to the American Association on Intellectual and

Developmental Disabilities (AAIDD). To understand the reasons for this change, one needs to appreciate that throughout history people with subaverage intellectual abilities have been the subject of ridicule and scorn. Whatever name that has been applied to them by professionals has ended up being used pejoratively by the public. For example, it's probably surprising to many that as late as the early 1900s the terms "idiot," "imbecile," and "moron" were perfectly acceptable labels for those who, today, would be referred to as having severe, moderate, or mild intellectual disability or mental retardation, respectively. In fact, they were the "official" terms used by professionals and sanctioned by professional organizations. Today, of course, very few would accuse someone of being overly politically correct if he or she viewed these terms as totally inappropriate and demeaning. A somewhat similar history has accompanied the term *mentally retarded*. Over the years it, too, especially its shortened form, *retard*, has come to be used as an insult.

The growing negativity associated with the term *mentally retarded*, coupled with other factors, such as the nearly worldwide acceptance of the term *disability* to describe a variety of limitations, created the climate for the name change to AAIDD. *Intellectual* disability connotes limitations in thinking. *Developmental* disability connotes that the limitations interfere with normal development of functions. In practice, most professionals simply use the shorter term *intellectual disability*.

It's important to stress that, although the AAIDD has considerable credibility, there are others, both outside and inside the organization, who don't share its concern about the label *mental retardation*. Pointing to the historical use and abuse of terms such as *idiot*, some argue that trying to find a "slur-proof" term is fruitless. Others argue that, unlike *idiot*, the term *mentally retarded* has not become a slur except in its shortened form *retard*.

Without taking sides on an issue that appears not to have a "right" answer, in this chapter we've chosen to go with the prevailing view. What's perhaps most important is that the term *intellectual disability* is at least as accurate as *mentally retarded* in describing the primary limitations of this group of individuals. One can also make the argument that *intellectual* is more accurate than *mental* because the latter is often used to refer to emotions, e.g., *mental illness* (Glidden, 2006).

Definition

The issue of defining intellectual disabilities or mental retardation has been contentious. Over the past several years it has become much more difficult to designate someone as intellectually disabled. Today, professionals are more reluctant to apply the label of intellectual disability or mental retardation than they once were. At least three reasons account for this more cautious attitude:

1. Professionals became concerned about the misdiagnosis of children from ethnic minority groups as intellectually disabled. Twenty to thirty years ago, it was much more common for children from ethnic minorities, especially African American and Hispanic students, to be labeled mentally retarded because they did not achieve well in school and they scored poorly on intelligence tests.

2. Some people believe that the diagnosis of mental retardation or intellectual disability results in a stigma that causes children to have poor self-concepts and to be viewed negatively by others.

3. Some professionals now believe that to a certain extent, intellectual disability is a socially constructed condition. For example, AAIDD conceives of intellectual disability not as a trait residing in the individual but as the product of the interaction between a person and his or her environment.

The last point has not gone uncontested. Some authorities think that AAIDD has gone too far in denying the existence of intellectual disability as an essential feature *within* a person (Baumeister, 2006).

A more conservative approach to identifying students as intellectually disabled is reflected in changes in definition that have occurred over the years. Since 1950, the AAIDD has endorsed seven official definitions of mental retardation or intellectual disability.

The AAIDD Definition

The current AAIDD definition reads as follows:

> [Intellectual disability] is a disability characterized by significant limitations both in intellectual functioning and in adaptive behavior as expressed in conceptual, social, and practical adaptive skills. This disability originates before age 18. (AAMR Ad Hoc Committee on Terminology and Classification, 2002, p. 1)

AAIDD also states that the following five assumptions are essential to the application of the definition:

1. Limitations in present functioning must be considered within the context of community environments typical of the individual's age peers and culture.
2. Valid assessment considers cultural and linguistic diversity as well as differences in communication, sensory, motor, and behavioral factors.
3. Within an individual, limitations often coexist with strengths.
4. An important purpose of describing limitations is to develop a profile of needed supports.
5. With appropriate personalized supports over a sustained period, the life functioning of the person with mental retardation [intellectual disability] generally will improve. (AAMR Ad Hoc Committee on Terminology and Classification, 2002, p. 1)

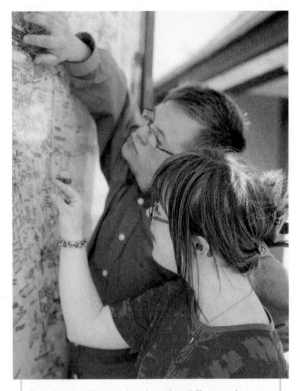

Practical intelligence involves the ability to solve everyday problems, such as preparing meals, using transportation systems, making change, using the Internet, and solving problems that are associated with particular job situations.

The AAIDD definition underscores two important points: Intellectual disability involves problems in adaptive behavior not just intellectual functioning, and the intellectual functioning and adaptive behavior of a person with intellectual disabilities can be improved.

ADAPTIVE BEHAVIOR   At one time, it was common practice to diagnose individuals as mentally retarded (intellectually disabled) solely on the basis of an IQ score. Today, we recognize that IQ tests are far from perfect and that they are but one indication of a person's ability to function. Professionals came to consider **adaptive behavior** in addition to IQ in defining intellectual disability because they began to recognize that some students might score poorly on IQ tests but still be "streetwise"—able to cope, for example, with the subway system, with an after-school job, with peers.

There is no universally accepted definition of adaptive behavior. One that many authorities see as theoretically sound is based on the notion that adaptive behavior consists of **social intelligence** and **practical intelligence** (Greenspan, 1999, 2006b). Social intelligence involves understanding and interpreting people and social interactions, such

UNDERSTANDING THE STANDARDS AND PRINCIPLES   Why are professionals generally more cautious about identifying students as having an intellectual disability? (CEC Knowledge and Skill Standard MR1K1)

Council for Exceptional Children

■ **Adaptive behavior**
Social and practical intelligence that people have learned so that they can function in their everyday lives; along with intellectual functioning, are considered in making a determination of mental retardation/intellectual disability.

■ **Social intelligence**
Ability to understand and interpret people and social interactions.

■ **Practical intelligence**
Ability to solve everyday problems.

Reading Homework Exercise

Mental Retardation/Intellectual Disability ● Go to the Homework and Exercises section in Chapter 5 of MyEducationLab to read the article titled "Mental Retardation/ Intellectual Disability", about expected acquisition of adaptive life skills based on the level of intellectual disability.

■ **Supports**
Resources and strategies that promote a person's development, education, interests, and personal well-being; critical to AAIDD's conceptualization of intellectual disabilities.

■ **Levels of support**
The basis of the AAIDD classification scheme; characterizes the amount of support needed for someone with intellectual disability to function as competently as possible as (1) intermittent, (2) limited, (3) extensive, or (4) pervasive.

as being able to "read" when someone is angry and not being gullible or easily tricked or manipulated. (We discuss gullibility in more detail later.) Practical intelligence involves the ability to solve everyday problems, such as preparing meals, using transportation systems, making change, using the Internet, and solving problems that are associated with particular job situations.

PEOPLE WITH INTELLECTUAL DISABILITIES CAN IMPROVE   In the past, many authorities held little hope for significantly enhancing the functioning of people with intellectual disabilities; they essentially believed intellectual disability to be incurable. Today, however, the prevailing opinion is that the functioning of virtually all people with intellectual disabilities can be improved and that a very few, especially those with very mild intellectual disabilities, can eventually improve to the point at which they are no longer classified as intellectually disabled.

In agreement with the notion that intellectual disability is improvable, the developers of the current AAIDD definition hold that how well a person with intellectual disabilities functions is directly related to the amount of support he or she receives from the environment.

The concept of supports is integral to the AAIDD's conceptualization of intellectual disabilities. They define **supports** as

resources and strategies that aim to promote the development, education, interests, and personal well-being of a person and that enhance individual functioning (AAMR Ad Hoc Committee on Terminology and Classification, 2002, p. 151).

According to AAIDD, sources of supports can be either natural or service-based. Natural supports are those that typically occur in one's environment, such as oneself, family members, or friends. Service-based supports are those provided by professionals, such as teachers, counselors, psychologists. Table 5.1 lists the various **levels of support** that people with intellectual disabilities might need.

TABLE 5.1	**Levels of Support for People with Intellectual Disabilities**

Intermittent

Supports on an as-needed basis, characterized by their episodic (the person does not always need the supports) or short-term nature (supports are needed during life-span transitions, e.g., job loss or acute medical crisis). Intermittent supports may be high or low intensity when provided.

Limited

An intensity of supports characterized by consistency over time, time-limited but not of an intermittent nature, may require fewer staff members and less cost than more intense levels of support (e.g., time-limited employment training or transitional supports during the school-to-adult period).

Extensive

Supports characterized by regular involvement (e.g., daily) in at least some environments (e.g., school, work, or home) and not time-limited nature (e.g., long-term support and long-term home living support).

Pervasive

Supports characterized by their constancy, high intensity, provision across environments, potentially life-sustaining nature. Pervasive supports typically involve more staff members and intrusiveness than do extensive or time-limited supports.

Source: Adapted from AAMR Ad Hoc Committee on Terminology and Classification. (2002). Mental retardation: Definition, classification, and systems of supports (10th ed., p. 152). Washington, DC: American Association on Mental Retardation. Reprinted by permission.

Classification of Intellectual Disabilities

Most school systems classify students with intellectual disabilities according to the severity of their condition. Although AAIDD does not advocate such a classification scheme, two other prominent professional organizations do (the American Psychological Association and the American Psychiatric Association). Most school systems use the American Psychological Association's classifications of **mild** (IQ of about 50 to 70), **moderate** (IQ of about 35 to 50), **severe** (IQ of about 20 to 35), and **profound (IQ below about 20) mental retardation or intellectual disabilities**, or a close approximation.

Prevalence

The average (mean) score on an IQ test is 100. Theoretically, we expect 2.27 percent of the population to fall two standard deviations (IQ = 70 on the Wechsler Intelligence Scale for Children, Fourth Edition, WISC-IV) or more below this average. This expectation is based on the assumption that intelligence, like so many other human traits, is distributed along a normal curve. Figure 5.1 shows the hypothetical normal curve of intelligence. This curve is split into eight areas by means of standard deviations. One standard deviation equals 15 IQ points; 2.14 percent of the population scores between 55 and 70, and 0.13 percent scores below 55. Thus, it would seem that 2.27 percent should fall between 0 and 70. (See p. 156 for more on intelligence tests.)

However, the actual prevalence figures for students who are identified as intellectually disabled are much lower. In recent years, they have been somewhere around 1 percent. Authorities surmise that this lower prevalence figure is due to school personnel considering adaptive behavior or a broader definition of intelligence in addition to an IQ score to diagnose intellectual disabilities. There is also evidence that in cases in which the student's IQ score is in the 70s, thus making identification as mentally retarded or intellectually disabled a close call, parents and school officials might be more likely to identify children as learning disabled because it's perceived as a less stigmatizing label (MacMillan, Gresham, Bocian, & Lambros, 1998).

■ **Mild mental retardation or intellectual disability** A classification used to specify an individual whose IQ is approximately 50–70.

■ **Moderate mental retardation or intellectual disability** A classification used to specify an individual whose IQ is approximately 35–50.

■ **Severe mental retardation or intellectual disability** A classification used to specify an individual whose IQ is approximately 20–35.

■ **Profound mental retardation or intellectual disability** A classification used to specify an individual whose IQ is below approximately 20.

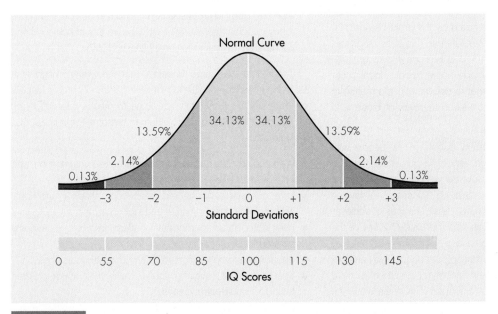

FIGURE 5.1 Theoretical distribution of IQ scores based on normal curve

INTERNET RESOURCES

To see the complete address of Sharon Davis, a representative from the Arc, regarding the Human Genome Project, visit www.ornl .gov/hgmis/resource/arc.html

INTERNET RESOURCES

For further information on the Human Genome Project visit www.ornl.gov/sci/techresources/ Human_Genome/home.shtml

Causes

As recently as the mid-1990s, most experts estimated that the cause of intellectual disabilities was known in only about 10 to 15 percent of cases. However, the mapping of the human genetic code by the Human Genome Project has provided a wealth of information related to causes of intellectual disabilities. (These advances have also engendered a number of thorny issues; see the Focus on Concepts below.) However, not all causes of intellectual disabilities are genetically related, so there still remains a large percentage of cases (probably over 50 percent) in which we can't pinpoint the cause of a child's intellectual disabilities.

A common way of categorizing causes of intellectual disabilities is according to the time at which the cause occurs: **prenatal** (before birth), **perinatal** (at the time of birth), and **postnatal** (after birth).

FOCUS ON **Concepts**

The Human Genome Project: Ethical Issues Pertaining to Intellectual Disabilities

Started in 1990 and completed in 2003, the U.S. Human Genome Project's goals have been to

- *identify* all the approximately 20,000–25,000 genes in human DNA,
- *determine* the sequences of the three billion chemical base pairs that make up human DNA,
- *store* this information in data bases,
- *improve* tools for data analysis,
- *transfer* related technologies to the private sector, and
- *address* the ethical, legal, and social issues that may arise from the project. (Human Genome Project, 2006a)

One of the practical benefits noted by the project's administrators is the development of revolutionary ways to diagnose, treat, and eventually prevent genetic conditions. However, such potential breakthroughs have made some people uneasy. For example, some have asserted that to use genetic information to prevent intellectual disabilities devalues the lives of those who are intellectually disabled:

Then, in a world where disability is not valued, people with disabilities are also not valued, rendering our efforts towards "normalization" impossible. How do we cope with a culture that teaches us, with an emphasis on "success," to devalue individuals whose disabilities render their chances of achievement, in its usual meaning, as less than likely? What of the ethical issues surrounding potential genetic therapies that may eventually "cure" mental retardation? Do people with disabilities lead fulfilling lives with their disability or in spite of it? How do professionals . . . assist and support individuals when the

shifting climate indicates more than ever their worth, or lack thereof, in society? (Kuna, 2001, pp. 159–160)

On the other hand,

the major argument in favor of gene therapy is based on its potential for treating individuals severely affected by their condition. A perfect example is Lesch-Nyhan disease, which is characterized by communication deficits, writhing movements, and involuntary self-injurious behavior. Males who have this disorder have to be restrained constantly to prevent them from inflicting severe damage on themselves. Most have their teeth removed to keep from biting their lips off. If we have a new medical technology that will cure this condition, don't we have an obligation to use it? (Davis, 1997)

The Human Genome Project's Website (www.ornl.gov/sci/ techresources/Human_Genome/elsi/elsi.shtml) contains papers on several ethical issues of relevance to mental retardation, as well as other areas of disability (Human Genome Project, 2006b), including:

- Who should have access to personal genetic information, and how will it be used?
- How does personal genetic information affect an individual and society's perceptions of that individual?
- How does genomic information affect members of minority communities?
- Should testing be performed when no treatment is available?
- Should parents have the right to have their minor children tested for adult-onset diseases?

Prenatal Causes

We can group prenatal causes into (1) **chromosomal disorders**, (2) inborn errors of metabolism, (3) developmental disorders affecting brain formation, and (4) environmental influences.

CHROMOSOMAL DISORDERS   As noted above, scientists are making great strides in identifying genetic causes of intellectual disabilities. At least 1,000 genetic syndromes have been identified as causes of intellectual disabilities (Hodapp & Dykens, 2007). A few of the most common of these genetic syndromes are Down syndrome, Williams syndrome, Fragile X syndrome, and Prader-Willi syndrome.

Down Syndrome   Many, but not all, genetic syndromes are transmitted hereditarily. In fact, by far the most common of these syndromes, **Down syndrome**, is usually not an inherited condition. Down syndrome involves an anomaly at the twenty-first pair of **chromosomes**. In the vast majority of cases of Down syndrome, the twenty-first set of chromosomes (the normal human cell contains twenty-three pairs of chromosomes) is a triplet rather than a pair; hence, Down syndrome is also referred to as **trisomy 21**. Down syndrome is the most common form of intellectual disability that is present at birth (Beirne-Smith, Patton, & Kim, 2006).

Down syndrome is associated with a range of distinctive physical characteristics that vary considerably in number from one individual to another. People with Down syndrome may have thick epicanthal folds in the corners of the eyes, making the eyes appear to slant upward slightly. Other common characteristics include small stature, decreased muscle tone (hypotonia), hyperflexibility of the joints, a small oral cavity that can result in a protruding tongue, short and broad hands with a single palmar crease, heart defects, and susceptibility to upper respiratory infections (Taylor, Richards, & Brady, 2005). There is also evidence of a link between Down syndrome and Alzheimer's disease (see the Focus on Concepts on p. 152.)

By far the most common genetic syndrome, Down syndrome, is usually not an inherited condition, but, rather, an anomaly at the twenty-first pair of **chromosomes**. Also referred to as **trisomy 21**, Down syndrome is the most common form of intellectual disability that is present at birth.

UNDERSTANDING THE STANDARDS AND PRINCIPLES   What do we know about the causes of intellectual disabilities? (CEC Knowledge and Skill Standards MR2K1 & MR2K2)

■ **Prenatal causes of intellectual disabilities**
Causes occurring during fetal development; some examples include chromosomal disorders, inborn errors of metabolism, developmental disorders affecting brain formation, and environmental influences.

■ **Perinatal causes of intellectual disabilities**
Causes at birth; some examples are anoxia, low birthweight, and infections such as syphilis and herpes simplex.

■ **Postnatal causes of intellectual disabilities**
Causes occurring after birth; can be biological (e.g., traumatic brain injury, infections) or psychosocial (an unstimulating environment).

■ **Chromosomal disorder**
Any of several syndromes resulting from abnormal or damaged chromosome(s); can result in intellectual disability.

■ **Down syndrome**
A condition resulting from an abnormality with the twenty-first pair of chromosomes; the most common abnormality is a triplet rather than a pair (the condition sometimes referred to as trisomy 21); characterized by intellectual disability and such physical signs as slanted-appearing eyes, hypotonia, a single palmar crease, shortness, and a tendency toward obesity.

■ **Chromosome**
A rod-shaped entity in the nucleus of the cell; contains genes, which convey hereditary characteristics; each cell in the human body contains 23 pairs of chromosomes.

■ **Trisomy 21**
A type of Down syndrome in which the twenty-first chromosome is a triplet, making forty-seven, rather than the normal forty-six, chromosomes in all.

FOCUS ON **Concepts**

Down Syndrome and Alzheimer's Disease

It has been well over a century since researchers first noted a high prevalence of senility in persons with Down syndrome (Fraser & Mitchell, 1876, cited in Evenhuis, 1990). In the early twentieth century, postmortem studies of the brains of people with Down syndrome revealed neuropathological signs similar to those of people with Alzheimer's disease (Carr, 1994). It was not until the 1980s and 1990s, however, that scientists started to address this correlation seriously.

Postmortem studies of the brains of people with Down syndrome indicate that virtually all who reach the age of thirty-five have brain abnormalities very similar to those of persons with Alzheimer's disease (Hof et al., 1995; Wisniewski, Silverman, & Wegiel, 1994). And behavioral signs of dementia, or mental deterioration, occur in more than half of people with Down syndrome over fifty years of age.

Findings that link Down syndrome to Alzheimer's disease have made researchers optimistic about uncovering the genetic underpinnings of both conditions. For example, researchers have found that some types of Alzheimer's disease are related to mutations of the twenty-first pair of chromosomes (Bush & Beail, 2004). And there is suggestive evidence that a particular protein may be the key to the rapid onset of Alzheimer's in people with Down syndrome (Tansley et al., 2007).

■ **Maternal serum screening (MSS)**
A method of screening the fetus for developmental disabilities such as Down syndrome or spina bifida; a blood sample is taken from the mother and analyzed; if it is positive, a more accurate test such as amniocentesis or CVS is usually recommended.

■ **Spina bifida**
A congenital midline defect resulting from failure of the bony spinal column to close completely during fetal development.

■ **Amniocentesis**
A medical procedure that allows examination of the amniotic fluid around the fetus; sometimes recommended to determine the presence of abnormality.

■ **Chorionic villus sampling (CVS)**
A method of testing the unborn fetus for a variety of chromosomal abnormalities, such as Down syndrome; a small amount of tissue from the chorion (a membrane that eventually helps form the placenta) is extracted and tested; can be done earlier than amniocentesis but the risk of miscarriage is slightly higher.

The degree of intellectual disability varies widely among people with Down syndrome; most individuals fall in the moderate range. In recent years, more children with Down syndrome have achieved IQ scores in the mildly intellectually disabled range than previously, presumably because of intensive special education programming. The likelihood of having a child with Down syndrome increases with the age of the mother (Beirne-Smith et al., 2006). In addition to the age of the mother, researchers point to other variables as possible causes, such as the age of the father, exposure to radiation, and exposure to some viruses. Research on these factors is still preliminary, however.

Methods are available for screening for Down syndrome and some other birth defects, including:

- **Maternal serum screening (MSS)**, in which a blood sample is taken from the mother and screened for the presence of certain elements that indicate the possibility of **spina bifida** or Down syndrome. If the results are positive, the physician can recommend a more accurate test, such as amniocentesis or CVS.

- **Amniocentesis**, where the physician takes a sample of amniotic fluid from the sac around the fetus and analyzes the fetal cells for chromosomal abnormalities. In addition, the amniotic fluid can be tested for the presence of proteins that may have leaked out of the fetus's spinal column, indicating the presence of spina bifida (a condition in which the spinal column fails to close properly).

- **Chorionic villus sampling (CVS)**, in which the physician takes a sample of villi (structures that later become the placenta) and tests them for chromosomal abnormalities. One advantage of CVS is that it can be done earlier than amniocentesis.

- **Nuchal translucency sonogram**, which aids in analyzing fluid from behind the fetus's neck and protein from the mother's blood.

Williams Syndrome **Williams syndrome** is caused by the absence of material on the seventh pair of chromosomes. People with Williams syndrome have intellectual disabilities in the mild to moderate range (Mervis & Becerra, 2007). In addition, they often have heart defects, an unusual sensitivity to sounds, and "elfin" facial features.

Fragile X Syndrome   **Fragile X syndrome** is the most common known hereditary cause of intellectual disabilities (Abbeduto, Brady, & Kover, 2007). In association with intellectual disabilities, it occurs in 1 in 4,000 males and 1 in 6,000 females (Meyer & Batshaw, 2002). In association with milder cognitive deficits, such as learning disabilities, the prevalence may be as high as 1 in 2,000 (Hagerman, 2001). It is associated with the X chromosome in the twenty-third pair of chromosomes. In males, the twenty-third pair consists of an X and a Y chromosome; in females, it consists of two X chromosomes. This disorder is called Fragile X syndrome because in affected individuals, the bottom of the X chromosome is pinched off in some of the blood cells. Fragile X occurs less often in females because they have an extra X chromosome, giving them better protection if one of their X chromosomes is damaged. People with Fragile X syndrome may have a number of physical features, such as a large head; large, flat ears; a long, narrow face; a prominent forehead; a broad nose; a prominent, square chin; large testicles; and large hands with nontapering fingers. Although this condition usually results in moderate rather than severe intellectual disabilities, the effects are highly variable, some people having less severe cognitive deficiencies and some, especially females, scoring in the normal range of intelligence (Dykens, Hodapp, & Finucane, 2000).

Prader-Willi Syndrome   People with **Prader-Willi syndrome** have inherited from their father a lack of genetic material on the fifteenth pair of chromosomes (Dykens et al., 2000). There are two distinct phases to Prader-Willi. Infants are lethargic and have difficulty eating. Starting at about one year of age, however, they become obsessed with food. In fact, Prader-Willi is the leading genetic cause of obesity. Although a vulnerability to obesity is usually their most serious medical problem, people with Prader-Willi are also at risk for a variety of other health problems, including short stature due to growth hormone deficiencies; heart defects; sleep disturbances, such as excessive daytime drowsiness and **sleep apnea** (cessation of breathing while sleeping); and **scoliosis** (curvature of the spine). The degree of intellectual disability varies, but the majority fall within the mildly intellectually disabled range, and some have IQs in the normal range (Taylor et al., 2005).

Inborn Errors of Metabolism   **Inborn errors of metabolism** result from inherited deficiencies in enzymes used to metabolize basic substances in the body, such as amino acids, carbohydrates, vitamins, or trace elements (Thomas, 1985). One of the most common of these is **phenylketonuria (PKU)**. PKU involves the inability of the body to convert a common dietary substance—phenylalanine—to tyrosine; the consequent accumulation of phenylalanine results in abnormal brain development. All states routinely screen babies for PKU before they leave the hospital. Babies with PKU are immediately put on a special diet, which prevents the occurrence of intellectual disabilities. At one time, it was thought that the diet could be discontinued in middle childhood. However, authorities now recommend that it be continued indefinitely, for two important reasons: Those who stop the diet are at risk for developing learning disabilities or other behavioral problems, and women with PKU who go off the diet are at very high risk of giving birth to children with PKU.

Developmental Disorders of Brain Formation   There are a number of conditions, some of which are hereditary and accompany genetic syndromes and some of which are caused by other conditions such as infections, that can affect the structural development of the brain and cause intellectual disabilities. Two examples are microcephalus

■ **Nuchal translucency sonogram**
A method of screening for Down syndrome; fluid from behind the fetus's neck and protein from the mother's blood are analyzed.

■ **Williams syndrome**
A condition resulting from deletion of material in the seventh pair of chromosomes; often results in mild to moderate intellectual disabilities, heart defects, and elfin facial features; people affected often display surprising strengths in spoken language and sociability while having severe deficits in spatial organization, reading, writing, and math.

■ **Fragile X syndrome**
A condition in which the bottom of the X chromosome in the twenty-third pair of chromosomes is pinched off; can result in a number of physical anomalies as well as intellectual disabilities; occurs more often in males than females; thought to be the most common hereditary cause of intellectual disability.

■ **Prader-Willi syndrome**
Caused by inheriting from one's father a lack of genetic material on the fifteenth pair of chromosomes; leading genetic cause of obesity; degree of intellectual disability varies, but the majority fall within the mildly intellectually disabled range.

■ **Sleep apnea**
Cessation of breathing while sleeping.

■ **Scoliosis**
Curvature of the spine.

■ **Inborn errors of metabolism**
Deficiencies in enzymes used to metabolize basic substances in the body, such as amino acids, carbohydrates, vitamins, or trace elements; can sometimes result in intellectual disability; PKU is an example.

■ **Phenylketonuria (PKU)**
A metabolic genetic disorder caused by the inability of the body to convert phenylalanine to tyrosine; an accumulation of phenylalanine results in abnormal brain development.

We're well aware of the harmful effects of toxic agents such as cocaine and heroin and more subtle potential poisons such as tobacco and alcohol. **Fetal alchohol spectrum disorders (FASD)** include a range of disorders in children born to women who have consumed excessive amounts of alcohol while pregnant.

■ **Microcephalus**
A condition causing development of a small, conical-shaped head; proper development of the brain is prevented, resulting in intellectual disabilities.

■ **Hydrocephalus**
A condition characterized by enlargement of the head because of excessive pressure of the cerebrospinal fluid.

■ **Fetal alcohol spectrum disorders (FASD)**
A range of disorders in children whose mothers consumed large quantities of alcohol during pregnancy; not itself a clinical diagnostic category, but it includes FAS, which is a clinical diagnostic category.

and hydrocephalus. In **microcephalus**, the head is abnormally small and conical in shape. The intellectual disability that results usually ranges from severe to profound. There is no specific treatment for microcephaly, and life expectancy is short (National Institute of Neurological Disorders and Stroke, 2007).

Hydrocephalus results from an accumulation of cerebrospinal fluid inside or outside the brain. The blockage of the circulation of the fluid results in a buildup of excessive pressure on the brain and enlargement of the skull. The degree of intellectual disability depends on how early the condition is diagnosed and treated. Two types of treatment are available: surgical placement of a shunt (tube) that drains the excess fluid away from the brain to abdomen or insertion of a device that causes the fluid to bypass the obstructed area of the brain.

Environmental Influences There are a variety of environmental factors that can affect a woman who is pregnant and thereby affect the development of the fetus she is carrying. One example is maternal malnutrition. If the mother-to-be doesn't maintain a healthy diet, fetal brain development might be compromised.

We're also now much more aware of the harmful effects of a variety of substances, from obvious toxic agents, such as cocaine and heroin, to more subtle potential poisons, such as tobacco and alcohol. In particular, **Fetal alchohol spectrum disorders (FASD)** include a range of disorders in children born to women who have consumed excessive amounts of alcohol while pregnant. One of the most severe of those disorders is **fetal alcohol syndrome (FAS)**. Children with FAS are characterized by a variety of abnormal facial features and growth retardation, as well as intellectual disabilities (Centers for Disease Control and Prevention, 2006).

The hazards of radiation to an unborn fetus have been recognized for some time. For example, physicians are cautious not to expose pregnant women to X-rays unless absolutely necessary, and the public has become concerned over the potential dangers of radiation from improperly designed or supervised nuclear power plants.

Infections in the mother-to-be can also affect the developing fetus and result in intellectual disabilities. **Rubella (German measles)**, in addition to being a potential cause of blindness, can also result in intellectual disabilities. Rubella is most dangerous during the first trimester (three months) of pregnancy.

Perinatal Causes

A variety of problems occurring while giving birth can result in brain injury and intellectual disabilities. For example, if the child is not positioned properly in the uterus, brain injury can result during delivery. One problem that sometimes occurs because of difficulty during delivery is **anoxia** (complete deprivation of oxygen).

Low birthweight (LBW) can result in a variety of behavioral and medical problems, including intellectual disabilities (Taylor, Klein, Minich, & Hack, 2000). Because most babies with LBW are premature, the two terms—*LBW* and *premature*—are often used synonymously. LBW is usually defined as 5.5 pounds or lower, and it is associated with a number of factors: poor nutrition, teenage pregnancy, drug abuse, and excessive cigarette smoking. In addition, LBW is more common in mothers living in poverty.

Infections such as **syphilis** and **herpes simplex** can be passed from mother to child during childbirth. These venereal diseases can potentially result in intellectual disabilities.

(Herpes simplex, which shows as cold sores or fever blisters, is not usually classified as a venereal disease unless it affects the genitals.)

Postnatal Causes

We can group causes of intellectual disabilities occurring after birth into two very broad categories: those that are biological in nature and those that are psychosocial in nature.

BIOLOGICAL POSTNATAL CAUSES   Examples of biological postnatal causes are **traumatic brain injury (TBI)**, infections, malnutrition, and toxins. TBI refers to head injuries that result from such things as blows to the head, vehicular accidents, or violent shaking. (We discuss TBI in more detail in Chapter 12.) **Meningitis** and **encephalitis** are two examples of infections that can cause intellectual disabilities. Meningitis is an infection of the covering of the brain that may be caused by a variety of bacterial or viral agents. Encephalitis, an inflammation of the brain, results more often in intellectual disabilities and usually affects intelligence more severely. One of the toxins, or poisons, that has been linked to intellectual disabilities is lead. Although lead in paint is now prohibited, infants still become poisoned by eating lead-based paint chips, particularly in impoverished areas. The effect of lead poisoning on children varies; high lead levels can result in death.

PSYCHOSOCIAL POSTNATAL CAUSES   Children who are raised in poor environmental circumstances are at risk for intellectual disabilities. It should be obvious that extreme cases of abuse, neglect, or understimulation can result in intellectual disabilities. However, most authorities believe that less severe environmental factors, such as inadequate exposure to stimulating adult-child interactions, poor teaching, and lack of reading materials, also can result in intellectual disabilities, especially mild intellectual disability. For example, in one large-scale study of 267,277 children, those who were born to teenage mothers who had fewer than twelve years of education were at increased risk for mild and moderate intellectual disabilities (Chapman, Scott, & Mason, 2002).

Although environmental causes of mild intellectual disabilities are undeniable, heredity can also play a role. For example, in a major study of heredity and mild intellectual disabilities, researchers looked at the degree of similarity in intellectual performance of monozygotic twins versus similarity in performance of dizygotic twins (Spinath, Harlaar, Ronald, & Plomin, 2004). Monozygotic, or identical, twins come from the same egg and have the same genetic makeup. Dizygotic, or fraternal, twins come from separate eggs. In those who scored in the mildly intellectual disability range, the degree of similarity was much higher in monozygotic twins than in dizygotic twins, thus indicating high heritability.

It is important to point out that even though it's tempting to ask how much a person's intelligence is due to the environment versus heredity, it's virtually impossible to disentangle the influence of one from that of the other. (See the Focus on Concepts on p. 156)

For many years, it's been assumed that psychosocial factors are the cause of the vast majority of cases of mild intellectual disabilities whereas organic, or biological, factors are the cause of more severe intellectual disabilities. In recent years, however, authorities are beginning to suspect that many cases of mild intellectual disabilities might be caused by specific genetic syndromes (Dykens et al., 2000; Hodapp & Dykens, 2007). They point to the many cases of people with Prader-Willi syndrome and Williams syndrome, as well as females with Fragile X syndrome, who have mild intellectual disabilities, and they speculate that in the near future, new genetic syndromes will be discovered as causes of mild intellectual disabilities.

Casebook Reflections

REFER TO THE CASE *Who Will Help Patrick?* in your booklet. Patrick's mother abused alcohol and drugs during her pregnancy, and Patrick was moved to a foster home when he was 6 months old. For the past three years of preschool, he has demonstrated a variety of troubling academic and social problems. Patrick is currently identified as developmentally delayed and impaired in speech language. Do you think he will later be identified as a student with intellectual disabilities? Why or why not? ●

■ **Fetal alcohol syndrome (FAS)**
Abnormalities associated with the mother's drinking alcohol during pregnancy; defects include brain damage, facial deformities, growth deficits, and a variety of physical and mental abnormalities.

■ **Rubella (German measles)**
A serious viral disease, which, if it occurs during the first trimester of pregnancy, is likely to cause deformity in the fetus.

■ **Anoxia**
Deprivation of oxygen; can cause brain injury.

■ **Low birthweight (LBW)**
Babies who are born weighing less than 5.5 pounds; usually premature; at risk for behavioral and medical conditions, including intellectual disabilities.

■ **Syphilis**
A venereal disease that can cause mental subnormality in a child, especially if it is contracted by the mother-to-be during the latter stages of fetal development.

■ **Herpes simplex**
A viral disease that can cause cold sores or fever blisters; if it affects the genitals and is contracted by the mother-to-be in the later stages of fetal development, it can cause mental subnormality in the child.

FOCUS ON **Concepts**

The Nature–Nurture Controversy

For many years, theoreticians tended to view the nature–nurture issue from an either/or perspective: Either you believed that heredity held the key to determining intellectual development or you believed that the environment was the all-important factor. Today, however, most authorities believe that both heredity and the environment are critical determinants of intelligence. Some scientists have tried to discover how much of intelligence is determined by heredity and how much by the environment, but many view this quest as futile. They assert that heredity and environment do not combine in an additive fashion to produce intelligence. Instead, the interaction between genes and environment results in intelligence.

The following exchange between a professor of biopsychology and his student points out the importance of viewing intelligence in this way—that is, as the result of an interaction between genetics and experience and not a simple addition of the two:

One of my students told me that she had read that intelligence was one-third genetic and two-thirds experience, and she wondered whether this was true. She must have been puzzled when I began my response by describing an alpine experience. "I was lazily wandering up a summit ridge when I heard an unexpected sound. Ahead, with his back to me, was a young man sitting on the edge of a precipice, blowing into a peculiar musical instrument. I sat down behind him on a large sun-soaked rock, and shared his experience with him. Then, I got up and wandered back down the ridge, leaving him undisturbed.

I put the following question to my student: "If I wanted to get a better understanding of the music, would it be reasonable for me to begin by asking how much of it came from the musician and how much of it came from the instrument?"

"That would be dumb," she said, "The music comes from both; it makes no sense to ask how much comes from the musician and how much comes from the instrument. Somehow the music results from the interaction of the two, and you would have to ask about the interaction."

"That's exactly right," I said. "Now, do you see why . . ."

"Don't say any more," she interrupted. "I see what you're getting at. Intelligence is the product of the interaction of genes and experience, and it is dumb to try to find how much comes from genes and how much comes from experience." (Pinel, 2003, p. 23)

■ **Traumatic brain injury (TBI)**
Injury to the brain (not including conditions present at birth, with trauma, or degenerative diseases or conditions) resulting in total or partial disability or psychosocial maladjustment that affects educational performance; may affect cognition, language, memory, reasoning, abstract thinking, judgment, problem solving, sensory or perceptual and motor abilities, psychosocial behavior, physical functions, information processing, or speech.

■ **Meningitis**
A bacterial or viral infection of the linings of the brain or spinal cord.

■ **Encephalitis**
An inflammation of the brain; can affect the child's mental development adversely.

Identification

Two major areas are assessed to determine whether a person is intellectually disabled: intelligence and adaptive behavior.

Intelligence Tests

There are many types of IQ tests. Because of their accuracy and predictive capabilities, practitioners prefer individually administered tests to group tests. One of the most commonly used IQ tests for children is the WISC-IV (Wechsler, 2003). The WISC-IV consists of a Full-Scale IQ, as well as four composite scores: Verbal Comprehension, Perceptual Reasoning, Working Memory, and Processing Speed.

Although not all IQ tests call for this method of calculation, we can get a rough approximation of a person's IQ by dividing **mental age** (the age level at which a person is functioning) by **chronological age** and multiplying by 100. For example, a 10-year-old student who performs on an IQ test as well as the average 8-year-old (and thus has a mental age of eight years) would have an IQ of 80.

Compared to many psychological tests, IQ tests such as the WISC-IV are among the most valid: the instrument measures what it is supposed to measure. A good indicator of the validity of an IQ test is the fact that it is generally considered the best single index of how well a student will do in school. It's wise to be wary, however, of placing too much faith in a single score from any IQ test. There are at least four reasons for caution:

1. An individual's IQ can change from one testing to another, and although not common, sometimes the change can be dramatic.

2. All IQ tests are culturally biased to a certain extent. Largely because of differences in language and experience, people from minority groups are sometimes at a disadvantage in taking such tests.

3. The younger the child, the less validity the test has. Infant intelligence tests are particularly questionable.

4. IQ tests are not the absolute determinant when it comes to assessing a person's ability to function in society. A superior IQ does not guarantee a successful and happy life, nor does a low IQ doom a person to a miserable existence. Other variables are also important determinants of a person's coping skills in society. That is why, for example, professionals also assess adaptive behavior.

Adaptive Behavior

The basic format of instruments used to measure adaptive behavior requires that a parent, teacher, or other professional answer questions related to the person's ability to perform adaptive skills. We discuss some of these measures later in the section on Progress Monitoring of Adaptive Behavior Skills.

Psychological and Behavioral Characteristics

Some of the major areas in which people with intellectual disabilities are likely to experience deficits are attention, memory, language, self-regulation, motivation, and social development. In considering their psychological and behavioral characteristics, we hasten to point out that a given individual with intellectual disabilities may not display all of these characteristics.

The importance of attention for learning is critical. A person must be able to attend to the task at hand before she or he can learn it. For years, researchers have posited that we can attribute many of the learning problems of persons with intellectual disabilities to attention problems (Tomporowski & Tinsley, 1997). Often attending to the wrong things, they have difficulty allocating their attention properly.

One of the most consistent research findings is that people with intellectual disabilities have difficulty remembering information. Their deficits are widespread, but they often have particular problems with working memory (Conners, 2003; Rosenquist, Conners, & Roskos-Ewoldsen, 2003). **Working memory** involves the ability to keep information in mind while simultaneously doing another cognitive task. Trying to remember an address while listening to instructions on how to get there is an example of working memory.

Virtually all persons with intellectual disabilities have limitations in language comprehension and production. The exact types of problems are largely dependent on the cause of their intellectual disabilities (Abbeduto, Keller-Bell, Richmond, & Murphy, 2006).

Self-regulation is a broad term referring to an individual's ability to regulate his or her own behavior. People who are intellectually disabled also have difficulties with metacognition, which is closely connected to the ability to self-regulate (Bebko & Luhaorg, 1998). **Metacognition** refers to a person's awareness of what strategies are

Children with intellectual disabilities may have problems making and keeping friends, but positive social interactions are certainly achievable and should be nurtured and encouraged.

Video Homework Exercise

Functional Curriculum ●
Go to the Homework and Exercises section in Chapter 5 of MyEducationLab to watch the video "Functional Curriculum" in order to gain a further understanding of how students with intellectual disabilities benefit from functional academics.

■ **Gullibility**
An inclination to believe highly questionable statements or claims, despite scanty evidence; considered by some to be a key characteristic of persons with intellectual disabilities, especially those who are mildly intellectually disabled.

needed to perform a task, the ability to plan how to use the strategies, and the evaluation of how well the strategies are working. Self-regulation is thus a component of metacognition. (We discuss metacognition again in Chapter 6.)

A key to understanding the behavior of persons with intellectual disabilities is to appreciate their problems with motivation (Switsky, 2006). Having usually experienced a long history of failure, they are likely to believe that they have little control over what happens to them. Therefore, they tend to look for external rather than internal sources of motivation.

People with intellectual disabilities are prime candidates for a variety of social problems. As we noted earlier in our discussion of adaptive behavior, they have limited social intelligence that makes it difficult for them to interpret social interactions. For example, they often have problems making and keeping friends for at least two reasons: First, they often have difficulties striking up social interactions with others, and this difference is evident as early as preschool (Kasari & Bauminger, 1998). Second, even when not attempting to interact with others, they may exhibit behaviors that put their peers off. For example, they display higher rates of inattention and disruptive behavior than their nondisabled classmates do.

Some researchers have pointed to a particular type of social problem as being especially characteristic of persons with intellectual disabilities, especially those who are mildly intellectually disabled—gullibility. **Gullibility** can be defined as the "tendency to believe something, usually a highly questionable statement or claim, despite scanty evidence" (Greenspan, Loughlin, & Black, 2001, p. 102). See the Focus on Concepts on p. 159.

Linking Genetic Syndromes to Particular Behavioral Phenotypes

Until recently, most authorities paid little attention to the type of intellectual disability a person had in considering behavioral characteristics. However, researchers have begun

FOCUS ON **Concepts**

Gullibility as the Hallmark of Mild Intellectual Disability

Stephen Greenspan, a prominent researcher in the field of intellectual disabilities, has made a strong case for social intelligence, gullibility in particular, as being the hallmark of intellectual disability, especially in those who are mildly intellectually disabled (Greenspan, 1999, 2004, 2006a, 2006b; Greenspan et al., 2001). Greenspan holds that gullibility likely results from a combination of cognitive and personality factors, with the cognitive limitation being the inability to determine when something is a deceptive claim, and the personality factors relating to an over-reliance on external motivational sources. Greenspan points to main character Pinocchio from the classic 19th-century Italian children's novel of the same name as the perfect example of someone who is mildly intellectually disabled by virtue of his gullibility:

Source: Collodi. (1883). *Pinocchio: The adventures of a puppet.* (1930, Translated by M. A. Murray), New York: A. L. Burt Co.

> Pinocchio was a marionette made of wood who yearned to be a real boy, and who engaged in a long series of adventures seeking to reunite with his "father/creator," the lonely old man Gepetto. As a result of a series of encounters with manipulators and deceivers, Pinocchio is repeatedly duped and sidetracked from attaining his goal. Finally, with the help and forgiveness of the "Fairy with Blue Hair," Pinocchio develops both the social intelligence and moral backbone to survive and prevail in a world of swindlers and con artists, and becomes reunited with Gepetto and turned into a real boy. (Greenspan, 2004, p. 123)

That gullibility has implications for real people with intellectual disabilities (not just wooden marionettes from a children's tale) is demonstrated in *The Collector of Bedford Street*, winner of 19 awards and an Academy Award nominee for Best Documentary Short (Elliott, 2005). The kindly Larry Selman, who is mildly intellectually disabled, is the subject of the film. Over the years, he has single-handedly "collected" thousands of dollars in donations for various charitable initiatives in his Greenwich Village, New York, neighborhood. However, his gullibility has become a cause for concern. Numerous homeless vagrants have taken advantage of his gullibility and talked him into allowing them to take up residence in his apartment. They've begun to steal from him and others in the neighborhood and destroy property. The neighbors come together to help Larry, in the process setting up a trust fund so that he can have some degree of financial independence.

That gullibility has ramifications for life-and-death decisions is borne out by legal decisions regarding the death penalty. After several years of debate in the courts, in 2002 the U. S. Supreme Court in *Atkins v. Virginia* ruled against the use of the death penalty for persons who are intellectually disabled. Many of the arguments in favor of this decision focused on gullibility. Experts argued that, among other things, gullibility made such individuals vulnerable to being tricked into committing crimes without realizing their ramifications or to confessing to crimes that they had not actually committed (Patton & Keyes, 2006). The *Atkins* decision has also reinforced the claims of Greenspan and others that adaptive behavior, gullibility in particular, should figure more prominently in any future changes to the definition of intellectual disabilities (Greenspan & Switsky, 2006).

---

to find general patterns of behavioral characteristics, or **behavioral phenotypes**, associated with some of the genetic syndromes.

Researchers have identified the four genetic syndromes that we discussed under prenatal causes of intellectual disabilities—Down syndrome, Williams syndrome, Fragile X syndrome, and Prader-Willi syndrome—as being ones that have relatively distinctive behavioral phenotypes (Abbeduto et al., 2007; Abbeduto et al., 2003, 2006; Dykens, 2001; Dykens et al., 2000; Fidler, Hepburn, Most, Philofsky, & Rogers, 2007; Hatton et al., 2003; Hodapp & Fidler, 1999; Mervis & Becerra, 2007; Moldavsky, Lev, & Lerman-Sagie, 2001; Roberts, Price, & Malkin, 2007). For example, people with Down syndrome often have significant impairments in language and grammar compared to visual-spatial skills; for individuals with Williams syndrome, the reverse is often true.

■ **Behavioral phenotype**
A collection of behaviors, including cognitive, language, and social behaviors as well as psychopathological symptoms, that tend to occur together in people with a specific genetic syndrome.

In fact, the storytelling ability of the latter, including their ability to modulate the pitch and volume of their voices to interject emotional tone in their stories, together with their sociability and elflike faces, have led to some speculation that the pixies, elves, or fairies depicted in folktales were people with Williams syndrome. (See the Personal Perspectives below.)

Table 5.2 lists some of the major behavioral characteristics associated with Down syndrome, Williams syndrome, Fragile X syndrome, and Prader-Willi syndrome. Although much research has been done to link these behavioral phenotypes with each of the syndromes, there is far from a one-to-one correspondence between the diagnosis and the characteristics. Not all individuals with each of these conditions will have all of the symptoms. In other words, not all people who have a syndrome are exactly alike.

Personal PERSPECTIVES

Williams Syndrome: An Inspiration for Some Pixie Legends?

Folktales from many cultures feature magical "little people"—pixies, elves, trolls, and fairies. A number of physical and behavioral similarities suggest that at least some of the fairies in the early tales might have been modeled on people who had Williams syndrome. Such a view is in keeping with the contention of historians that a good deal of folklore and mythology is based on real life.

The facial traits of Williams people are often described as pixielike. In common with pixies in folklore and art, many people with Williams syndrome have small, upturned noses, a depressed nasal bridge, "puffy" eyes, oval ears, and broad mouths with full lips accented by a small chin. Indeed, those features are so common that Williams children tend to look more like one another than their relatives, especially as children. The syndrome also is accompanied by slow growth and development, which leads most Williams individuals to be relatively short.

The "wee, magical people" of assorted folktales often are musicians and storytellers. Fairies are said to "repeat the songs they have heard" and can "enchant" humans with their melodies. Much the same can be said of people with Williams syndrome, who in spite of typically having subnormal IQs, usually display vivid

The children in the photograph, who are unrelated, display elfin facial features that clinicians associate with Williams syndrome.

narrative skills and often show talent for music. (The large pointed ears that are so often associated with fairies might symbolically represent the sensitivity of those mythical individuals—and of Williams people—to music and to sound in general.)

As a group, Williams people are loving, trusting, caring, and extremely sensitive to the feelings of others. Similarly, elves are frequently referred to as the "good people" or as kind and gentle-hearted souls. Finally, Williams individuals, much like the fairies of legend, require order and predictability. In Williams people, this need shows up as rigid adherence to daily routines and a constant need to keep abreast of future plans.

In the past, storytellers created folktales about imaginary beings to help explain phenomena that they did not understand—perhaps including the distinguishing physical and behavioral traits of Williams syndrome. Today researchers turn to Williams people in a quest to understand the unknown, hoping to decipher some of the secrets of how the brain functions.

Source: Adapted from article. Williams syndrome and the brain by Howard M. Lenhoff, Paul P. Wang, Frank Greenberg, & Ursula Bellugi (1997 December) p. 73. Copyright © 1997 by Scientific American, Inc. All rights reserved. Adapted with permission.

TABLE 5.2	Links between Genetic Syndromes and Behavioral Phenotypes	
Genetic Syndrome	**Behavioral Phenotype**	
	Relative Weaknesses	Relative Strengths
Down syndrome	Receptive and expressive language, especially grammar Problems interpreting facial emotions Cognitive skills tend to worsen over time Early onset of Alzheimer's disease	Visual-spatial skills Visual short-term memory
Williams syndrome	Visual-spatial skills Fine-motor control Anxieties, fears, phobias Overly friendly	Expressive language, vocabulary Verbal short-term memory Imitation of emotional responses Facial recognition and memory Musical interests and skills
Fragile X syndrome	Short-term memory Sequential processing Repetitive speech patterns Social anxiety and withdrawal	Receptive and expressive vocabulary Long-term memory Adaptive behavior
Prader-Willi syndrome	Auditory processing Feeding problems in infancy Overeating, obesity in childhood and adulthood Sleep disturbances Obsessive-compulsive behaviors	Relatively high IQ (average about 70) Visual processing Facility with jigsaw puzzles

Source: Based on Abbeduto et al., 2003, 2006, 2007; Belser & Sudhalter, 2001; Dimitropoulos, Feurer, Butler, & Thompson, 2001; Dykens et al., 2000; Fidler et al., 2007; Fidler, Hodapp, & Dykens, 2002; Hodapp & Dykens, 2007; Hatton et al., 2003; Kasari, Freeman, & Hughes, 2001; Mervis & Becerra, 2007; Mervis, Klein-Tasman, & Mastin, 2001; Moldavsky et al., 2001; Roberts et al., 2007.

INTERNET RESOURCES

The National Association for Down Syndrome (NADS), was founded in 1961 by a group of parents. Its Website at www.nads.org provides information on resources as well as links to other sites devoted to Down syndrome.

The Williams Syndrome Association is devoted to providing information to affected families: www.williams-syndrome.org

The National Fragile X Foundation is devoted to providing information to affected families: www.fragilex.org/html/home.shtml

The Prader-Willi Association (USA) is devoted to providing information to affected families: www.pwsausa.org/

INTERNET RESOURCES

The propensity for those with Prader-Willi to crave food has raised ethical issues pertaining to allowing them to eat and the concept of least restrictive environment. The Prader-Willi Association (USA) has issued a policy statement on the subject. See: www.pwsausa.org/postion/ps002.htm

Educational Considerations

In general, the focus of educational programs varies according to the degree of the student's intellectual disability or how much support the student requires. For example, the lesser the degree of intellectual disability, the more the teacher emphasizes academic skills; the greater the degree of intellectual disability, the more stress there is on self-help, community living, and vocational skills. In practice, however, all students who are intellectually disabled, no matter the severity level, need some instruction in academic, self-help, community living, and vocational skills. We focus on the elementary school level here; we discuss preschool and secondary programming in later sections.

A major issue facing special educators is how to ensure that students with intellectual disabilities have access to the general education curriculum, as dictated by the Individuals with Disabilities Education Act (IDEA; see Chapter 1), while still being taught functional skills. The more severe the level of intellectual disability, the more this is an issue. Authorities recommend that there be a merger of functional and academic curricular standards. This notion of blending academics and functional skills is embodied in **functional academics**, teaching academics in the context of daily living skills (Drew & Hardman, 2004). Whereas the nondisabled child is taught academics (such as reading), to learn other academic content (such as history), the child with

UNDERSTANDING THE STANDARDS AND PRINCIPLES What educational approaches are most appropriate for students with intellectual disabilities? (CEC Knowledge and Skill Standards MR4K1 & MR7S1)

Council for Exceptional Children

■ **Functional academics** Practical skills (e.g., reading a newspaper or telephone book) rather than academic learning skills.

intellectual disabilities is often taught reading to learn to function independently. In functional reading, the child learns academics to do such things as read a newspaper, read the telephone book, read labels on goods at the store, and fill out job applications. Examples of functional math, taken from Colorado's performance indicators, are as follows:

> "make and read simple graphs representing meaningful information and relationships," demonstrate a beginning sense of measurement (e.g., big, little, heavy, light, etc.)," "match number symbols with appropriate amount," and "find months and dates on the calendar." (Browder et al., 2004, p. 216)

Educational programming for students with intellectual disabilities, especially those with more severe intellectual disabilities, often includes the following three features: systematic instruction, instruction in real-life settings with real materials, and functional behavioral assessment and positive behavioral intervention and support.

Systematic Instruction

■ **Systematic instruction**
Teaching that involves instructional prompts, consequences for performance, and transfer of stimulus control; often used with students with intellectual disabilities.

Effective teaching of students with intellectual disabilities involves **systematic instruction:** the use of instructional prompts, consequences for performance, and strategies for the transfer of stimulus control (Davis & Cuvo, 1997). Students who are intellectually disabled often need to be prompted or cued to respond in the appropriate manner. These prompts can be verbal, gestural, or physical, or modeling may be used (Davis & Cuvo, 1997). A verbal prompt can be a question such as "What do you need to do next?" or a command such as "Put your socks in the top dresser drawer." A gestural prompt might involve pointing to the socks and/or the dresser drawer while stating the question or the command. Taking the student's hand and placing it on the socks and/or drawer would be an example of a physical prompt. The adult might also model putting the socks in the drawer before then asking the student to do it.

Research shows that students who are positively reinforced for correct responses learn faster. For students with severe intellectual disabilities in particular, the more immediate the reinforcement, the more effective it is.

With respect to consequences, research has consistently shown that students who are positively reinforced for correct responses learn faster. Positive reinforcers range from verbal praise to tokens that can be traded for prizes or other rewards. For students with severe intellectual disabilities in particular, the more immediate the reinforcement, the more effective it is. Once the student demonstrates the desired behavior consistently, the goal is to wean the student from reliance on external reinforcers as soon as possible. The goal is to reach a point at which the student doesn't have to rely on prompts and can be more independent. To transfer the control away from the prompts to more naturally occurring stimuli, several techniques are used, including delaying the time between a request and the prompt (Kaiser & Grim, 2006; Wolery & Schuster, 1997). For example, with **constant time delay**, the adult starts by making a request ("Please put your clothes away") and giving a prompt simultaneously ("Put your clothes in the top dresser drawer"). On subsequent occasions, the adult might wait a set period of time (e.g., five seconds) between the request and the prompt. With **progressive time delay**, the adult also starts with a simultaneous prompt and request, but the latency period between the two is then increased gradually.

Instruction in Real-Life Settings with Real Materials

Instruction can take place in the classroom, under simulated conditions, or in real-life settings. It's generally better to teach daily living skills to students with intellectual disabilities in the actual settings where they will be using these skills. Because it's easier to hold instruction in classrooms than in real-life settings, the teacher might start out with instruction in the classroom and then supplement it with instruction in real-life situations. For example, the teacher might use worksheets and photos of various shopping activities in class or set up a simulated store with shelves of products and a cash register (Morse & Schuster, 2000). These classroom activities could then be supplemented with periodic visits to real grocery stores. Likewise, it's preferable to use real cans of food and real money in teaching students to read product labels and to make change.

Functional Behavioral Assessment and Positive Behavioral Intervention and Support

One of the major reasons some students with intellectual disabilities have difficulty being included in general education classrooms is that they sometimes exhibit inappropriate behavior, such as hitting, biting, or screaming. Authorities recommend that teachers use a combination of **functional behavioral assessment (FBA)** and **positive behavioral intervention and support (PBIS)** to reduce or eliminate these behaviors. FBA involves determining the consequences, antecedents, and setting events that maintain such behaviors (Horner, Albin, Sprague, & Todd, 2000). *Consequences* refer to the purpose the behavior serves for the person. For example, some students behave inappropriately to gain attention. *Antecedents* refer to things that trigger the behavior. For example, the student might become aggressive only toward certain peers. Setting events take into account broader contextual factors. For example, the student might be more likely to exhibit inappropriate behavior when sick or in hot, humid weather. On the basis of a functional assessment, the teacher can make changes in consequences, antecedents, and/or contextual factors and monitor the effectiveness of these changes.

On the basis of results from the FBA, teachers can develop a PBIS plan for students. As we discussed in Chapters 2 and 4, PBIS involves using contextually and culturally

■ **Constant time delay**
An instructional procedure whereby the teacher makes a request while simultaneously prompting the student and then over several occasions makes the same request and waits a constant period of time before prompting; often used with students with intellectual disabilities.

■ **Progressive time delay**
An instructional procedure whereby the teacher makes a request while simultaneously prompting the student and then over several occasions gradually increases the latency between the request and the prompt; often used with students with intellectual disabilities.

■ **Functional behavioral assessment**
Evaluation that consists of finding out the consequences (what purpose the behavior serves), antecedents (what triggers the behavior), and setting events (contextual factors) that maintain inappropriate behavior.

■ **Positive behavioral intervention and support (PBIS)**
Systemtic use of the science of behavior to find ways of supporting desirable behavior rather than punishing undesirable behavior; positive reinforcement (rewarding) procedures that are intended to support a student's appropriate or desirable behavior.

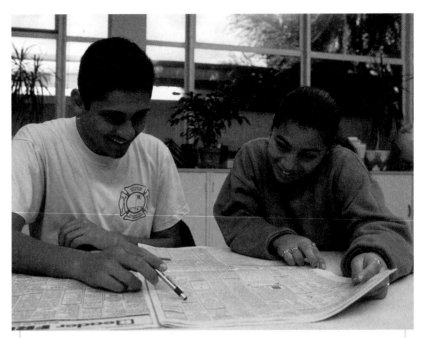

When students with intellectual disabilities are included in general education classes, special and general educators must plan ways to make the experience successful. Without this planning they are likely to be inattentive and socially isolated. Designating general education peers as "buddies" has been found to be a promising way to increase social interactions.

Building Teaching Skills Video Exercise

Science Cooperative Learning ● Go to the Building Teaching Skills section in Chapter 5 of MyEducationLab to watch the video "Science Cooperative Learning", in which students with and without disabilities work cooperatively to conduct a science experiment in plant growth.

appropriate interventions, with an emphasis on rewarding positive behavior, to make problem behavior less effective, efficient, and relevant—and to make desired behavior more functional. PBIS focuses on the total environment of the student, including instruction. Some proponents of PBIS place an emphasis on implementing schoolwide plans to promote positive behavior in all students, not just those with disabilities (Sugai et al., 2000). Under such a plan, all school personnel are prepared to deliver positive reinforcement for appropriate behavior in virtually all settings: classrooms, cafeteria, hallways, playground, school buses, and so on.

Service Delivery Models

Placements for school-age students with intellectual disabilities range from general education classes to residential facilities. Although special classes for these students tend to be the norm, more and more students with intellectual disabilities are being placed in more integrated settings. The degree of integration tends to be determined by the level of severity, students who are less severely intellectually disabled being the most integrated.

However, as we discussed in Chapter 2, some professionals believe that all students with intellectual disabilities should be educated in the general education classroom and that schools should provide the necessary support services (e.g., a special aide or special education teacher) in the class. Researchers have found classwide peer tutoring to be an effective technique for helping to integrate students with intellectual disabilities into general education classrooms. (See the Responsive Instruction on p. 166.)

Although not all authorities agree on how much inclusion should be practiced, virtually all agree that placement in a self-contained class with no opportunity for interaction with nondisabled students is inappropriate. At the same time, even parents who favor integrated settings often believe that it is good for their children to interact with other children with disabilities too and that being the only student in the class with a disability has its drawbacks (Guralnick, Connor, & Hammond, 1995).

When students with intellectual disabilities are included in general education classes, it's important that special and general educators work together to come up with ways to make the experience successful. Without this planning the students are likely to be inattentive and to be socially isolated (Carter, Hughes, Guth, & Copeland, 2005; Kemp & Carter, 2006). Designating general education peers as "buddies" can be a promising way to increase social interactions (Carter et al.); similarly, the Best Buddies College Program (through Best Buddies International, a nonprofit organization) has been found beneficial for both the students with intellectual disabilities and the college students who serve as "Buddies" (Hardman & Clark, 2006).

> **INTERNET RESOURCES**
>
> For more information on Best Buddies, see www.bestbuddies.org

Assessment of Progress

Assessment of students with intellectual disabilities should focus on a variety of domains. In particular, the special educator or other professional should assess the student's academic skills, adaptive behavior skills, and quality of life. In the following sections, we provide examples of assessments that are appropriate for monitoring student progress and assessing student outcomes, along with a discussion of appropriate accommodations and alternate assessment methods.

Progress Monitoring

PROGRESS MONITORING OF ACADEMIC SKILLS **Curriculum-based measurement (CBM)**, which we discussed in Chapter 3, is an appropriate method for monitoring the progress of students with intellectual disabilities who are participating in the general education curriculum. Oral reading fluency is measured in a one-minute reading sample; the instructor graphs the number of correct words read orally in one minute. Teachers assess students once or twice weekly to determine growth and adjust instruction to ensure that goals are met (Stecker, Fuchs, & Fuchs, 2005). The maze procedure is a three-minute CBM task to measure reading comprehension. In a maze procedure, a passage at the student's grade level is provided with every seventh word left out. For each missing word the student selects one of three word choices to complete the passage. The maze procedure is implemented at intervals between one to three months to assess reading growth (Shin, Deno, & Espin, 2000).

Students' progress in mathematics can also be measured with CBM procedures. CBM can be used to measure concepts and application; however, it's best applied to computation problems (Fuchs et al., 2007). For students with intellectual disabilities, appropriate mathematics skills are selected based on the student's curriculum. The teacher presents a certain number of problems to the student (e.g., basic computation facts or mixed computational skills by grade level) and then records the number of correct digits per minute (Stecker et al., 2005).

PROGRESS MONITORING OF ADAPTIVE BEHAVIOR SKILLS Most measures of adaptive behavior are standardized and don't lend themselves well to **progress monitoring**. However, adaptive behavior assessment should be integrated with interventions such that services are provided in a data-based decision framework. Interviews, observations, and

> **UNDERSTANDING THE STANDARDS AND PRINCIPLES** Discuss ways in which special educators can appropriately assess the academic progress, adaptive behavior, and quality of life of students with intellectual disabilities. (CEC Knowledge and Skill Standards CC8S8, MR8K3, & MR8S1)
>
> Council for Exceptional Children
>
> ■ **Curriculum-based measurement (CBM)**
> A formative evaluation method designed to evaluate performance in the curriculum to which students are exposed; usually involves giving students a small sample of items from the curriculum in use in their schools; proponents argue that CBM is preferable to comparing students with national norms or using tests that do not reflect the curriculum content learned by the students.
>
> ■ **Progress monitoring**
> Brief, frequent measures of performance used to determine whether a student is learning as expected; if student isn't learning as expected, the teacher can make changes to the instruction.

Meeting the Needs of Students with Intellectual Disabilities

Classwide Peer-Tutoring

WHAT THE RESEARCH SAYS

In an effort to meet the instructional needs of students with mild intellectual disabilities within inclusive settings, researchers have explored instructional methods that provide the necessary structure, individualization, and level of corrective feedback critical for success for this population. One such method is classwide peer tutoring (CWPT) (Delquadri, Greenwood, Stretton, & Hall, 1983). CWPT involves the use of peers to provide instruction and feedback in a reciprocal format. That is, paired students have the opportunity to serve as a tutor and as a tutee during each session. CWPT procedures were designed to address the need for higher levels of active, academic engagement for all students, but particularly for students with the greatest academic deficits (Greenwood, 1991).

RESEARCH STUDY

A team of researchers conducted a study to examine the effectiveness of CWPT on the spelling performance of eight students (four students with mild intellectual disabilities and four nondisabled students) participating in a general education class (Mortweet et al., 1999). The students with mild intellectual disabilities were included in general education classrooms for spelling, a social activity period, and lunch. The CWPT model was compared to traditional teacher-led instruction during the spelling period. The investigators used the following structure for the CWPT sessions:

1. Each student with mild intellectual disabilities was paired with a nondisabled peer.
2. Tutoring sessions occurred four times a week for twenty minutes per day.
3. Tutoring materials included the list of spelling words, point sheets, and practice sheets.
4. The teacher assigned each pair to one of two competing classroom teams. (Points earned by the pairs contributed to daily team point totals.) Partners and teams were reassigned on a weekly basis.
5. During each session, students served as the tutor for ten minutes and as the tutee for the other ten minutes.
6. Instruction consisted of the tutor reading the spelling word to the tutee. The tutee wrote the spelling word while saying each letter aloud. If the word was spelled correctly, the tutor awarded the tutee two points; if the word was

spelled incorrectly, the tutor spelled the word correctly and the tutee wrote the word three times while naming each letter. The tutee could receive one point for correctly spelling the practice word. After ten minutes, the roles were reversed.
7. The teacher assigned bonus points for pairs that were working cooperatively and following the instructional protocol.
8. When the twenty-minute session was over, the teacher calculated team points on the basis of partner points. The winning team received such privileges as lining up for recess first.
9. Modifications made for the students with mild intellectual disabilities included: shortened word lists, enlarged practice sheets, and tutee reading of words when the student with mild intellectual disabilities was the tutor and was unable to read the word.

RESEARCH FINDINGS

When compared to the teacher-led condition, the CWPT resulted in improved academic performance for all students, increased amount of engaged academic time (approximately five to ten minutes more per student per session), and positive acceptance from the teachers and students. Thus, CWPT provides teachers with a flexible instructional strategy to meet the varying needs of an inclusive classroom.

APPLYING THE RESEARCH TO TEACHING

Given the effectiveness of CWPT, teachers can establish similar procedures in their classes. Tasks such as math facts, spelling, letter sounds, and word identification make great CWPT topics. Following the model established in the study, teachers can create their own tutoring materials. Key features of CWPT include partnering of a higher and lower skilled student, explicit instruction in the tutoring activities (i.e., ample training prior to independent partner work), structured tasks for the tutor to guide the tutee in completing, reciprocal roles so the tutee has the opportunity to be a tutor, and use of points to reward desired behavior.

● *By Kristin L. Sayeski*

self-report techniques can be helpful in monitoring students' progress in adaptive skills (Harrison & Boney, 2002). The Vineland Adaptive Behavior Scale (discussed as an outcome measure) has a short version called a *screener*, which monitors students' progress in the domain of adaptive behavior.

Outcome Measures

OUTCOME MEASURES OF ACADEMIC SKILLS   Several standardized measures of academic achievement are commonly used to assess students with intellectual disabilities. The Woodcock-Johnson III Tests of Achievement (WJ-III; Woodcock, Schrank, Mather, & McGrew, 2007) is an example of a comprehensive standardized measure of academic achievement. The WJ-III measures achievement in reading, mathematics, spelling, written expression, social studies, science, and humanities. The Kaufman Test of Educational Achievement (KTEA; Kaufman & Kaufman, 2004) also assesses academic achievement in the areas of mathematics, reading, and spelling.

Some students with intellectual disabilities may participate in an alternative curriculum that focuses on functional academics, such as reading cooking recipes or making change. Functional reading and mathematics focuses on the skills that are required in daily activities. The Kaufman Functional Academic Skills Test (K-FAST; Kaufman & Kaufman, 1994) is a standardized measure of functional arithmetic and reading for adolescents and adults with intellectual disabilities.

OUTCOME MEASURES OF ADAPTIVE BEHAVIOR SKILLS   Typically, special educators or other professionals measure adaptive behavior indirectly, in that an "informant" provides information on a rating scale or interview (Venn, 2007). The informant should be intimately familiar with the student; it is usually a parent, grandparent, teacher, or other primary caregiver. The Vineland Adaptive Behavior Scale-Second Edition (Vineland-II; Sparrow, Chicchetti, & Balla, 2005) is a popular measure of adaptive behavior for individuals from birth to eighteen years. It includes several domains: communication, daily living skills, socialization, motor skills, and maladaptive behavior.

OUTCOME MEASURES OF QUALITY OF LIFE SKILLS   With the current emphasis on self-determination (which we discussed in Chapter 4 and discuss later in this chapter), more and more professionals are concerned with measuring persons with intellectual disabilities' quality of life. However, measuring quality of life presents a challenge in that a particular individual's perceived quality of life may differ from that of larger society (Brown & Brown, 2005; Cummins, 2005a). Consequently, outcome measures should include both objective and subjective measures that consider society's view of quality of life along with an individual's perceived level of satisfaction.

One measure commonly used to assess adolescents and adults with intellectual disabilities is the Quality of Life Questionnaire (QOL-Q, Schalock & Keith, 1993), which can be used with both English- and Spanish-speaking populations (Caballo, Crespo, Jenaro, Verdugo, & Martinez, 2005). It addresses five factors: satisfaction, well-being, social belonging, dignity, and empowerment/control (Schalock et al., 2002). A more objective scale is the Life Experiences Checklist (LEC; Ager, 1990), which measures the extent to which an individual has ordinary life experiences. It comprises five areas including home, relationships, freedom, leisure, and opportunities for self-enhancement (Cummins, 2005b).

Testing Accommodations and Alternate Assessment

Accommodations for students with intellectual disabilities on standardized tests can include modifications in scheduling, presentation format, and response format. Common scheduling accommodations include extended or unlimited time, or breaking the assessment into smaller, more manageable portions over several days. A typical presentation

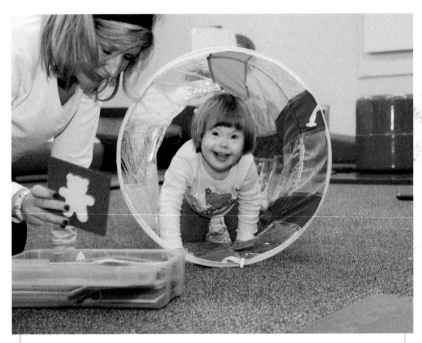

Successful early intervention programs for children with intellectual disabilities often involve parents as much as possible.

accommodation involves reading directions and problems to the student. Some students with intellectual disabilities may have physical difficulties and require response accommodations. For example, a student may dictate responses or use a word processor.

Alternate assessments are for students who can't be tested using traditional methods, even if accommodations are provided. Students with intellectual disabilities participating in an alternate curriculum (e.g., life skills, vocational skills) may participate in alternate assessments. Alternate assessments should measure authentic skills, cover a variety of domains, and include multiple measures across time (Ysseldyke & Olsen, 1999). They can include direct observations of specific behaviors, checklists, rating scales, and curriculum-based measures. Several domains should be covered, for example, functional literacy, communication, leisure-recreation skills, domestic skills, and vocational skills (Spinelli, 2006).

Early Intervention

We can categorize preschool programs for children with intellectual disabilities as those whose purpose is to prevent intellectual disabilities or those that are designed to further the development of children who have already been identified as intellectually disabled. In general, the former address children who are at risk for mild intellectual disabilities, and the latter are for children with more severe intellectual disabilities.

Early Childhood Programs Designed for Prevention

Toward the end of the 20th century, the federal government provided funding for several infant and preschool programs for at-risk children and their families, with the goal being to research their effects. Three such projects were the Perry Preschool Project, the Chicago Child-Parent Center (CPC) Program, and the Abecedarian Project. The first two focused on preschool children from low-income environments who were at risk for a variety of negative outcomes, including intellectual disabilities. Both have demonstrated that early intervention can have positive long-term effects on participants, including reduction in rates of intellectual disabilities. In the case of the Perry Preschool Project (Schweinhart & Weikart, 1993), when students who had received preschool intervention were studied again at age 27, a number of differences favored them over those who had not received the intervention:

- More had completed the twelfth grade
- Fewer had been arrested
- More owned their own homes
- Fewer had ever been on welfare
- They had a lower teenage pregnancy rate
- They earned a better-than-average income
- Classification as intellectually disabled was less likely

Furthermore, a cost-benefit analysis that took into account such things as costs of welfare and the criminal justice system and benefits of taxes on earnings showed a return of $7.16 for every dollar invested in the Perry Preschool Project.

The most recent follow-up of participants in the CPC Program at age twenty indicates similar results: higher school completion rates, lower juvenile arrest rates, and lower rates of grade retention and identification for special education. In fact, the rate of identification for special education was almost half that of the comparison group, which had not received early intervention (Reynolds, Temple, Robertson, & Mann, 2001).

One of the best-known infant stimulation programs is the Abecedarian Project (Ramey & Campbell, 1984, 1987). Participants were identified before birth by selection of children from a pool of pregnant women living in poverty. After birth, the infants were randomly assigned to one of two groups: half to a day-care group that received special services and half to a control group that received no such services. The day-care group participated in a program that provided experiences to promote perceptual-motor, intellectual, language, and social development. The families of these children also received a number of social and medical services. Results of the Abecedarian Project, reported through the age of twenty, indicate that the infants from the day-care group have attained better scores on intellectual and academic measures and are more likely to have attended a four-year college (Campbell, Ramey, Pungello, Sparling, & Miller-Johnson, 2002).

Early Childhood Programs Designed to Further Development

Early childhood programs designed to enhance the development of children already identified with intellectual disabilities place a great deal of emphasis on language and conceptual development. Because these children often have multiple disabilities, other professionals—for example, speech therapists and physical therapists—are frequently involved in their education. Also, many of the better programs include opportunities for parent involvement. Note in the Success Stories on p. 170, for example, how much Nolan Smith's parents have collaborated with Nolan's teachers and therapists. Through practice with their children, parents can reinforce some of the skills that teachers work on. For example, parents of infants with physical disabilities, such as cerebral palsy, can

Video Homework Exercise

Beyond School Rachel ●
Go to the Homework and Exercises section in Chapter 5 of MyEducationLab to watch the video "Beyond School Rachel", which addresses the importance of transition and self-determination for individuals with intellectual disabilities.

INTERNET RESOURCES

"The Teaching of Jon" is a documentary that chronicles the life of a man with Down Syndrome from birth to adulthood. To find out more about his life visit http://www .teachingsofjon.com/.index.html.

Success Stories

Early intervention services and community resources prepare Nolan for first grade

Special Educator Suzanne Knowlton: "Look past appearances to see the child, not the disability."

Six-year-old Nolan Patrick Smith attends Sunflower Elementary School in Kansas.

These are the keys to his success:
- intensive communication and extended time
- relentless pursuit of community resources
- specific goals and practical supports

Special educator Suzanne Knowlton is tutoring Nolan Smith so he'll be ready for first grade. "He's so much fun to work with and he's such a hard worker," she says. "What his parents have done through early intervention has made a world of difference." Nolan, who has Down syndrome, is the second oldest of Kris Kohnke's and Sean Smith's four children. Since he was an infant, Nolan has gained from intensive, relentless, and specific special education.

● **Intensive Communication and Extended Time** Within three weeks of his birth Nolan started intensive speech and language therapy. Now he knows most of his upper and lower case letters, but still has problems counting. Nolan has a broad range of cognitive abilities that are not easily summarized by a single score. He loves to sing and to play sports. "He knows the name of everybody in kindergarten," says Kris. "He also knows their mommies and daddies," adds Sean. Nolan is very social and verbal, but he's hard to understand because of his poor articulation. Intensive speech therapy four days a week and systematic prompts continue to be important to his success.

Remembering information is difficult for Nolan and he gets easily distracted. With frequent and systematic prompts he has better recall and pays closer attention. Nolan learns well through repetition and he needs extra time to practice new skills. The inclusive kindergarten program at Sunflower Elementary School is only half-day, but Nolan's parents asked if he could return for the afternoon session several days a week. The IEP team agreed he could benefit from additional time for specialized instruction, as well as for speech, occupational, and physical therapies. This year, Suzanne Knowlton came to his classroom toward the end of the school day. "We worked on reinforcing or learning skills while the other children were doing activities he'd already done in the morning." Advocating for a flexible schedule worked well for Nolan. "If we hadn't asked about the possibility of a longer day," says Sean, "he probably would have had to attend the half-day program."

● **Relentless Pursuit of Community Resources** Much of Nolan's success depends on asking questions and looking for support within the community. "When Nolan was 3 years old, we realized we weren't doing enough for him. He needed more than speech therapy, and we've pushed hard for him to receive occupational therapy (OT) and physical therapy (PT)," says Kris. "School districts have limited funds and personnel, so we've looked close to home for extra resources," says Sean. Living near a university makes it easier to tap into local

learn from physical therapists the appropriate ways of handling their children to further their physical development. Similarly, parents can learn appropriate feeding techniques from speech therapists.

UNDERSTANDING THE STANDARDS AND PRINCIPLES Transition programming for individuals with intellectual disabilities involves what two related areas? (CEC Knowledge and Skill Standards MR7K1 & MR10S1)

Transition to Adulthood

Most authorities agree that, although the degree of emphasis on transition programming should be greater for older than for younger students, such programming should begin in the elementary years. Table 5.3 depicts some examples of curriculum activities pertaining to domestic, community living, leisure, and vocational skills.

clinics and student internships. The Down Syndrome Clinic at Children's Mercy Hospital in Kansas City specializes in Nolan's health issues, and student interns in speech pathology and special education from the University of Kansas offer home-based services beyond his IEP. Nolan's parents also pursued federal and state funds for respite and other services. "We are able to access about $500 in family grants every six months," says Kris.

● **Specific Goals and Practical Supports** Kris Kohnke and Sean Smith are strong advocates. "We really want Nolan's goals to be practical for him and functional in building real-life skills," says Sean. Since counting is hard, Suzanne Knowlton charts his progress daily as Nolan counts his stickers to earn a weekly prize. (See section on Progress Monitoring on p. 165.) As first grade gets closer, he practices putting sounds together to make words. Suzanne knows this task is hard for Nolan and he'll need more time and repetitions to master this goal. He also needs to communicate his thoughts so that others can understand him.

Nolan's social skills and motor skills are immature, and many goals in these areas are addressed on the playground that he loves so much. "We've had access to good therapists who spot problems and create solutions wherever they're needed," says Kris. "Nolan's OT ordered inserts for his shoes that help him run better and climb stairs more quickly. His PT knows he can't play a game without being taught explicitly how to move his body." This summer, Suzanne Knowlton and Nolan Smith will be working together two days a week to strengthen his academic, social, and motor skills. For the last 30 minutes of each session, one of Nolan's friends will come to play with him on the monkey bars. "He'll be going to first grade with good friends," says Suzanne, "and with teachers who will look past appearances to see the child, not the disability."

CEC'S STANDARDS: PAVING THE WAY TO SUCCESS

ASSESS YOUR STEPS TO SUCCESS in meeting the CEC Knowledge and Skill Base for All Beginning Special Education Teachers of Students with Mental Retardation/Developmental Disabilities. Use the following questions to reflect on the growth of your own professional knowledge, skills, and dispositions.

REFLECTING ON YOUR OWN PROFESSIONAL DEVELOPMENT

If you were Nolan's teacher . . .

■ What are some areas about educating students with intellectual disabilities that you would need to know more about?

■ What are some specific skills that would help you address his academic and behavioral challenges?

■ What personal dispositions do you think are most important for you to develop in teaching students with limited cognitive abilities?

Using the CEC Standards . . .

■ What are some behavioral problems associated with individuals with intellectual disabilities? MR1K6

■ What approaches could you use to create positive learning environments for individuals with intellectual disabilities? MR5K1

■ What are some ways to foster respectful and beneficial relationships between families and professionals? CC10S3

● *By Jean B. Crockett*

Self-Determination

A major goal of transition programming is to help persons with intellectual disabilities to achieve as much self-determination as possible. Although most professionals recommend that emphasizing self-determination should begin as early as possible in elementary school, the focus becomes even greater in adolescence and adulthood. Because people with intellectual disabilities have reduced cognitive capacity, professionals and parents alike have traditionally considered them incapable of making decisions on their own. In a sense, this paternalistic attitude often resulted in a self-fulfilling prophecy by not providing persons with intellectual disabilities an opportunity to take more control over their lives. However, as we noted in Chapter 2, many professionals and parents now champion the notion of promoting self-determination in persons who are intellectually disabled. In

TABLE 5.3 Examples of Curriculum Activities Across the School Years for Domestic, Community Living, Leisure, and Vocational Skills

Skill Area			
Domestic	Community Living	Leisure	Vocational
Elementary school student: Tim			
Washing dishes	Eating meals in a restaurant	Climbing on swing set	Picking up plate, silverware, and
Dressing	Using restroom in a local	Playing board games	glass after a meal
Grooming	restaurant	Playing tag with neighbors	Returning toys to appropriate
Toileting skills	Giving the clerk money for item	Tumbling activities	storage space
Sorting clothes	he wants to purchase	Running	
Junior high school student: Mary			
Washing clothes	Crossing streets safely	Taking aerobics classes	Waxing floors
Cooking a simple hot meal	Purchasing an item from	Playing checkers with a friend	Hanging and bagging clothes
(soup, salad, and sandwich)	a department store	Playing miniature golf	Bussing tables
Raking leaves	Using local transportation	Cycling	Operating machinery (such as
Purchasing items from a list	system to get to and from	Attending high school or	dishwasher, buffer, etc.)
Vacuuming and dusting living	recreational facilities	local college basketball	Following a job sequence
room		games	
High school student: Sandy			
Cleaning all rooms in place	Utilizing bus system to move	Jogging	Performing required janitorial
of residence	about the community	Archery	duties at J.C. Penney
Developing a weekly budget	Depositing checks into bank	Watching college basketball	Performing laundry duties at
Cooking meals	account	Video games	Moon's Laundromat
Maintaining personal needs	Using community health	Card games (Uno)	Performing photography at
Caring for and maintaining	facilities (physician,	Athletic club swimming class	Virginia National Bank
clothing	pharmacist)	Gardening	Headquarters

Source: Adapted from P. Wehman, M. S. Moon, J. M. Everson, W. Wood, & J. M. Barcus. (1988). *Transition from school to work: New challenges for youth with severe disabilities* (Baltimore: Paul H. Brookes), pp. 140–142. Reprinted with permission.

■ **Self-determination**
The ability to make personal choices, regulate one's own life, and be a self-advocate; a prevailing philosophy in education programming for people with intellectual disabilities. Having control over one's life, not having to rely on others for making choices about one's quality of life; develops over one's life span.

■ **Learned helplessness**
A motivational term referring to a condition wherein a person believes that no matter how hard he or she tries, failure will result.

■ **Person-centered planning**
A type of transition model; consumer-driven in that professionals are viewed as working for individuals.

fact, the major parent organization in the field, The Arc, and the major professional organization, AAIDD, have adopted position statements supporting the idea of self-determination. (See the Focus on Concepts on p. 173 for an excerpt from AAIDD's policy.)

Self-determination is the ability to act autonomously, be self-regulated, act in a psychologically empowered manner, and act in a self-realized manner (Wehmeyer & Mithaug, 2006). *Acting autonomously* means behaving according to one's own preferences without dependency on others. Being *self-regulated* means evaluating and revising one's own behavior. Being *psychologically empowered* is believing that one has control over events such that one will be able to influence desired outcomes. Being *self-realized* connotes knowing and accepting one's own strengths and weaknesses and using that knowledge to attain goals.

We shouldn't assume that self-determination will develop on its own in people who are intellectually disabled. On the basis of our previous discussion of their history of learning deficits and vulnerability for developing **learned helplessness**, it should be obvious that people with intellectual disabilities will find it difficult to become self-determined. Investigators have just begun to look into ways of fostering self-determination (e.g., Wehmeyer, Garner, Yeager, Lawrence, & Davis, 2006; Wehmeyer, Palmer, Agran, Mithaug, & Martin, 2000), but much more research is needed to determine the best ways to cultivate self-determination in students with intellectual disabilities.

In keeping with the philosophy of self-determination programming, many professionals are now recommending that transition planning be person-centered. **Person-centered planning** is similar to family-centered planning, which we discussed in Chapter 4, except that it is focused more on the individual than on the family. In other words, person-centered planning is a consumer-driven model that

FOCUS ON Concepts

AAIDD Self-Determination Policy Statement

The following are excerpts from the AAIDD Self-Determination Policy Statement:

Position

■ AAMR [AAIDD] will uphold the right to self-determination as the right to act as the primary causal agent in one's life, to pursue self-defined goals and to participate fully in society. Self-determining individuals control their lives, make choices and decisions based on their interests, abilities, and preferences, and take responsibility for their lives.

■ People with mental retardation [intellectual disabilities] must have the opportunity to advocate for themselves, without fear of punishment, and with the knowledge that their demands and suggestions will be heard and given fair consideration.

■ AAMR [AAIDD] recognizes and supports the right of individuals with mental retardation [intellectual disabilities] to self-determination in every aspect of decision making that affects them as individuals, including living arrangements, work, religious participation, personal relationships, and control of their private funds and public funds designated for the purchase of services for them as individuals. . . .

Source: AAMR. (2000). *Self-determination policy statement* (Rev.). Reprinted by permission.

---

encourages the individual to make his or her own decisions with respect to services while mobilizing resources and supports to meet the person's goals.

Perhaps the most important issue pertaining to self-determination involves deciding just how far to go in allowing people with disabilities to make decisions solely on their own. Some believe that the notion of self-determination can be carried too far. (See the Personal Perspectives on p. 174. Also, as we discussed in Chapter 3, we need to keep in mind that self-determination will be defined differently depending on the particular culture of the individual. Some cultures are more oriented toward valuing individuality and autonomy; others are less so. For example, there is some evidence that Latina mothers of students with intellectual disabilities are less concerned with their children attaining independence as young adults because they value having them close to the family (Rueda, Monzo, Shapiro, Gomez, & Blacher, 2005).

Transition programming for individuals with intellectual disabilities involves two related areas: community adjustment and employment.

Community Adjustment

For people with intellectual disabilities to adjust to living in the community, they need to acquire a number of skills, many of which are in the area of self-help. For example, they need to be able to manage money, use public transportation, and keep themselves well groomed and their living quarters well maintained. They also need to have good social skills so that they can get along with other people in the community. In general, research has shown that attempts to train for community survival skills can be successful, especially when the training occurs within the actual setting in which the individuals live. The Responsive Instruction on p. 175 provides a specific example of the "survival skill" of shopping for groceries.

Although large residential facilities for people with intellectual disabilities still exist, they are fast disappearing. There is a trend toward smaller **community residential facilities (CRFs)**; Lakin, Prouty, & Coucouvanis, 2006; Prouty, Coucouvanis, & Lakin, 2007). Between 1977 and 2005, the number of residents with intellectual disabilities in CRFs of six or fewer increased from 20,400 to 291,000; during this same period, those

INTERNET RESOURCES

"The Collector of Bedford Street" is an excellent documentary about Larry Selman, a man with intellectual disabilities, and how his neighbors banded together to help him. Visit the film's website to learn about Larry and his struggle for self-determination: http://www .thecollectorofbedfordstreet.com

■ **Community residential facility (CRF)**
A place, usually a group home, in an urban or residential neighborhood where about three to ten adults with intellectual disabilities live under supervision.

Personal PERSPECTIVES

Self-Determination: Too Much of a Good Thing?

Some people are beginning to question seriously whether self-determination can be carried too far. For example, some see it as a way to save resources:

> Call it "self-determination," call it "choice," but call it "less." That creative service coordinators can do more with less given enough flexibility is an attractive but fanciful notion when presented as a system-wide solution. The idea has been oversold through the use of success stories involving exceptionally supportive families, friends, and/or communities. How many people or their families really want to, or are really capable of, managing all their supports? A large segment of the population in public service are adults with families whose time is already taxed to the hilt. They live in disinterested communities. . . .
>
> It is time to wake up to the fact that self-determination is increasingly being used to cover for cutbacks in funding where it can be least afforded—among the front-line agencies upon which consumers depend. (Ashbaugh, 2002, pp. 416–417)

Others see it as an impractical panacea that promises too much:

> Human decency and so-called natural law . . . inform us that impaired people need to have competent advocates at their side who, if the occasion requires it, are willing and able to make wise decisions on their behalf, even if these do not always please a person of limited, disturbed, or diminished mentality. (Wolfensberger, 2002b, p. 257)

In response to those who would question the utility of self-determination practices, some have evoked ethical principles:

> Ashbaugh . . . pointed to the lack of empirical evidence supporting many of the basic assumptions offered in arguments for self-determined systems of support. . . . Certainly, we do not need research to tell us what is moral and ethical: People with disabilities should be in charge of their own life. How to best position service delivery systems to make this a reality is, however, in our opinion, still in need of empirical demonstration. (Romer, Richardson, Aigbe, & Porter, p. 293)

---

living in CRFs of 16 or more decreased from 207,400 to 67,100. CRFs, group homes, accommodate small groups (three to ten people) in houses under the direction of "house parents." Placement can be permanent, or it can serve as a temporary arrangement to prepare the individuals for independent living. In either case, the purpose of the CRF is to teach independent living skills in a more normal setting than a large institution offers.

Some professionals question whether CRFs go far enough in offering opportunities for integration into the community. They recommend **supported living**, in which persons with intellectual disabilities receive supports to live in more natural, noninstitutional settings, such as their own home or apartment. There is some evidence that supported living arrangements lead to a higher level of self-determination in people with intellectual disabilities than do CRFs (Stancliffe, Abery, & Smith, 2000).

More and more authorities point to the family as a critical factor in determining whether persons with intellectual disabilities will be successful in community adjustment and employment. Even though many hold up supported living as an ideal, the fact is that the vast majority of adults with intellectual disabilities live with their families (MR/DD Data Brief, 2001). Even for those who live away from home, the family can still be a significant source of support for living in the community and finding and holding jobs.

Employment

Surveys show that adults with intellectual disabilities have high rates of unemployment (National Organization on Disability & Harris, 2000). Even though employment statistics for workers who are intellectually disabled have been discouraging, most professionals working in this area are optimistic about the potential for providing training programs that will lead to meaningful employment for these adults. Research indicates that with appropriate training, individuals with intellectual disabilities can hold down jobs with a

■ **Supported living**
An approach to living arrangements for those with intellectual disabilities that stresses living in natural settings rather than institutions, big or small.

UNDERSTANDING THE STANDARDS AND PRINCIPLES Transition programming for individuals with mental retardation involves what two related areas? (CEC Knowledge and Skills Standards MR7K1 & MR10S1)

Meeting the Needs of Students with Intellectual Disabilities

Computer-Based Video to Teach Grocery Shopping

For many individuals with moderate intellectual disabilities, the focus of their transition plan is on increased independence. For some, this goal might come in the form of independent or semi-independent living. Grocery shopping can be a key skill that leads to greater self-sufficiency and autonomy. The freedom to make choices about which foods are purchased and the ability to locate and retrieve those items from the store can dramatically influence a person's self-determination.

OVERVIEW OF THE STUDY

Many studies have been conducted to determine efficient and effective strategies for teaching individuals with intellectual disabilities to shop for groceries. An example is a study that explored the use of computer-based video to assist students in locating items in a grocery store (Mechling, Gast, & Langone, 2002). In this study, Mechling and colleagues used a computer-based video to teach students how to read words found on grocery store aisle markers and to locate particular items within the corresponding aisle. Four students (ages 9–17) with moderate intellectual disabilities learned to touch aisle sign words on the computer screen and then to select target items from the aisle (again by touching the screen). A system of least prompts was employed to teach the students the steps and reinforce correct responses. Least prompts procedures involve moving from less intrusive to more intrusive guiding. In this study, the least prompt was a command to touch the aisle sign word that corresponded to the student's list (e.g., "Touch potato chip"). If the student did not respond after five seconds, the next level prompt was employed (e.g., a repeat of the command with a gesture toward the screen). The final and most intrusive prompt was to physically guide the student's hand to the screen paired with the command. This least prompts instructional procedure has been demonstrated through research to be very effective in teaching new skills to students who are intellectually disabled. Correct selection of the words on aisle signs were followed by praise and a ten-second video clip of scanning the aisle and viewing the item on the shelf. The computer-based instruction occurred in three phases. During each phase, four additional items were added to the list (i.e., four words for phase 1, eight words for phase 2, and twelve words for phase 3). After the computer-based training in each phase, the teacher took the students to a grocery store, where they were asked to locate all twelve items.

RESEARCH FINDINGS

All four students were able to generalize the reading of aisle sign markers and locating items from the computer session to the grocery store probes. In addition, parents noted that their children tended to locate those items independently when shopping after the study had concluded. The researchers believe that teaching students to make use of the aisle markers enhances grocery-shopping efficiency when compared to traveling up and down all aisles to locate items.

APPLYING THE RESEARCH TO TEACHING

Teachers whose students have transition IEP goals that are community focused can use the tools employed in the study: computer-based video training linked with community-based practice. The researchers created the computer-based video by using Hyperstudio and importing still photos of aisle marker signs and short video clips of scanning and walking down the aisles. The researchers were able to create training videos of three different grocery stores. Frequently, restraints such as scheduling difficulties, time limitations, and access limit a teacher's ability to provide community-based instruction in more than one setting (Mechling et al., 2002). The computer-based training allowed the researchers to include greater variation into the instruction. In addition, the use of the computer allowed for more teaching opportunities without having to go out into the community to provide that support. In summary, the use of computer-based simulations can be a powerful way for teachers to enhance their community-based instruction.

● *By Kristin L. Sayeski*

good deal of success, measured by such things as attendance, employer satisfaction, and length of employment (McDonnell, Hardman, & McDonnell, 2003).

When people with intellectual disabilities are not successful on the job, the cause more often involves behaviors related to job responsibility and social skills than job performance per se (Butterworth & Strauch, 1994; Heal, Gonzalez, Rusch, Copher, & DeStefano, 1990; Salzberg, Lignugaris/Kraft, & McCuller, 1988). In other words, the problem is not so much that people with intellectual disabilities can't perform the job as it is that they have difficulty with such issues as attendance, initiative, responding to criticism, and interacting socially with coworkers and supervisors. This latter problem—social interaction—most consistently distinguishes workers who are intellectually disabled from those who are not.

INTERNET RESOURCES

The Arc has also issued a policy statement on self-determination: www.thearc.org/posits/2002positions.doc

■ **Sheltered workshop**
A facility that provides a structured environment for persons with disabilities in which they can learn skills; can be either a transitional placement or a permanent arrangement.

A variety of vocational training and employment approaches for individuals with intellectual disabilities are available. Most of these are subsumed under two very different kinds of arrangements: the **sheltered workshop** and supported competitive employment.

SHELTERED WORKSHOPS   The traditional job-training environment for adults with intellectual disabilities, especially those who are classified as more severely intellectually disabled, has been the sheltered workshop. A sheltered workshop is a structured environment in which a person receives training and works with other workers with disabilities on jobs requiring relatively low skills. This can be either a permanent placement or a transitional placement before a person obtains a job in the competitive job market.

More and more authorities are voicing dissatisfaction with sheltered workshops. Among the criticisms are the following:

1. Workers make very low wages because sheltered workshops rarely turn a profit. Usually managed by personnel with limited business management expertise, they rely heavily on charitable contributions.

2. There is no integration of workers who are disabled with those who are nondisabled. This restricted setting makes it difficult to prepare workers who are intellectually disabled for working side by side with nondisabled workers in the competitive workforce.

3. Sheltered workshops offer only limited job-training experiences. A good workshop should provide opportunities for trainees to learn a variety of new skills. All too often, however, the work is repetitive and doesn't make use of current industrial technology.

■ **Competitive employment**
A workplace that provides employment that pays at least minimum wage and in which most workers are nondisabled.

■ **Supported competitive employment**
A workplace where adults who are disabled earn at least minimum wage and receive ongoing assistance from a specialist or job coach; the majority of workers in the workplace are nondisabled.

■ **Job coach**
A person who assists adult workers with disabilities (especially those with intellectual disabilities), providing vocational assessment, instruction, overall planning, and interaction assistance with employers, family, and related government and service agencies.

SUPPORTED COMPETITIVE EMPLOYMENT   In contrast to sheltered employment, **competitive employment** is an approach that provides jobs for at least the minimum wage in integrated work settings in which most of the workers are not disabled. In **supported competitive employment**, the person with intellectual disabilities has a competitive employment position but receives ongoing assistance, often from a **job coach**. In addition to on-the-job training, the job coach might provide assistance in related areas, such as finding an appropriate job, interactions with employers and other employees, use of transportation, and involvement with other agencies.

Although more research is needed, thus far research indicates that supported competitive employment leads to better employment outcomes (McDonnell et al., 2003). Although the ultimate goal for some adults with intellectual disabilities might be competitive employment, many will need supported employment for some period of time or even permanently.

In comparison to sheltered workshops, supported competitive employment is more in keeping with the philosophy of self-determination. However, to achieve the goal of self-determination, it's important that clients not become too dependent on their job coach. For this reason, the role of the job coach has been changing in recent years. Many now advocate that the job coach involve co-workers of persons with intellectual disabilities as trainers and/or mentors (Mank, Cioffi, & Yovanoff, 2003). After a period of time, the worker can be weaned from relying on the job coach and can learn to use more natural supports. Recall the quotation at the beginning of the chapter (p. 143), in which Sandra Kaufman talks about the change in philosophy toward the use of natural supports in the form of relatives, neighbors, friends, and coworkers rather than social agency personnel.

Prospects for the Future

Current employment figures and living arrangements for adults with intellectual disabilities might look bleak, but there is reason to be optimistic about the future. Outcomes for adults with intellectual disabilities are improving, albeit slowly, with respect to employment and living arrangements (Frank & Sitlington, 2000). As Kaufman noted at the

Collaboration and Co-Teaching with Teachers of Students with Intellectual and Developmental Disabilities

"Why should this student be in my classroom?"

WHAT DOES IT MEAN TO BE A TEACHER OF STUDENTS WITH INTELLECTUAL DISABILITIES?

Collaboration for students with intellectual disabilities can include general and special educators and, often, other related service personnel and parents. Coordinating all of these participants is the responsibility of the special educator and requires both management and interpersonal skills. Teachers of students with intellectual disabilities are expected to:

1. Develop and implement comprehensive, longitudinal individualized programs in collaboration with team members.
2. Incorporate and implement instructional and assistive technology into the educational program.
3. Select, adapt, and use instructional strategies and materials according to characteristics of the individual with exceptional learning needs.
4. Use performance data and information from all stakeholders to make or suggest modifications in learning environments.
5. Design, implement, and evaluate instructional programs that enhance social participation across environments (Council for Exceptional Children, 2003).

SUCCESSFUL STRATEGIES FOR COLLABORATION

Pat Daniels is the mother of Will, a high school student with Down syndrome. Will's high school education required collaboration between parents, general educators, special educators, and coaches. In the end, Will received his special education diploma and was awarded one of the school's ten Faculty Awards. Pat describes their experiences.

Open lines of communication between the teachers and the parent were extremely important. I made a point to meet each teacher before the school year began. French was one of the more successful classes. The teacher was unaware of what she was getting with Will, but she was willing and eager to learn. She began by getting to know him, not his weaknesses. She let him try activities, putting him in situations where he was successful and challenged. He had a textbook and did homework with the class, taking tests aimed at what he had learned. She

helped find a volunteer 'study-buddy.' This teacher understood that he was working at his own level but she, like others, was often surprised and delighted by his contributions to the class.

The general education teachers and I communicated most frequently about tests and special projects. For example, one history teacher would call me before a test and we would generate specific review questions. Another teacher would send the class's study sheets home with specific items highlighted. Phone calls by teachers describing class projects helped establish exactly what Will was expected to accomplish (Will was not always accurate about the specific instructions given orally in class). When the special education teachers knew of a project, they incorporated time to work on that project into Will's special classes.

Will's drama class was also successful. The teacher let him participate as he was able, even performing at a teachers' meeting. Students' positive attitudes were important to both the French and drama classes. These teachers set the example. Will sat among other students, teachers called upon him, and they assigned him to teams to participate in activities. Will's participation was valued, as was every other student's.

Will was also the manager for two girls' varsity teams and was a member of the track team. The special education teacher was the assistant coach of the volleyball team so she was able to work with the coach to teach Will the duties of a manager. The basketball coach saw Will in action and asked for his help. The coaches expected Will to do what any manager would do, including filling in at practice for missing players and riding the bus to away games. The coaches would communicate with me and I would discuss any of Will's frustrations with them. The coaches made decisions based on Will's abilities, resulting in two 'good finishes' each meet. At many track meets, the encouragement to "RUN" came from teammates and from participants and spectators from the opposing team. Our collaboration with coaches encouraged a student with a hearing impairment and his interpreter to join the team!

● By Margaret P. Weiss

beginning of the chapter, with the development of innovative transition programs, many people with intellectual disabilities are achieving levels of independence in community living and employment that were never thought possible. Most of this success requires the collaboration of parents, students, and many professionals. The Making It Work above describes a successful program from a parent's perspective.

Summary

Why are many professionals now using the term *intellectual disabilities*?

▶ *Intellectual disabilities* is now used by many to refer to persons who, in the past, would have been designated as mentally retarded.

▶ The switch from *mental retardation* to *intellectual disabilities* is primarily due to the fact that the former, especially its shortened form, *"retard,"* has become a slur.

How do professionals define intellectual disabilities?

▶ The American Association on Intellectual and Developmental Disabilities defines intellectual disability as "a disability characterized by significant limitations both in intellectual functioning and in adaptive behavior as expressed in conceptual, social, and practical adaptive skills. This disability originates before age 18."

▶ The definition reflects two principles: (1) Intellectual disability involves problems in adaptive behavior, not just intellectual functioning, and (2) persons with intellectual disability can improve.

▶ Most schools and several professional organizations use the following classifications: mild (IQ of about 50 to 70), moderate (IQ of about 35 to 50), severe (IQ of about 20 to 35), and profound (IQ below about 20).

What is the prevalence of intellectual disabilities?

▶ From a purely statistical-theoretical perspective and relying only on scores on IQ tests, 2.27 percent of the population would be intellectually disabled; however, only about 1 percent of the school-age population is identified as intellectually disabled.

▶ The reason for the lower prevalence in the schools is probably due to (1) schools using low adaptive behavior as well as low IQ as criteria and (2) a preference by some to identify students as learning disabled rather than intellectually disabled because they perceive a learning disability to be less stigmatizing.

What causes intellectual disabilities?

▶ Prenatal causes include (1) chromosomal disorders, (2) inborn errors of metabolism, (3) developmental disorders affecting brain formation, and (4) environmental influences. Chromosomal disorders include Down syndrome, Williams syndrome, fragile X syndrome, and Prader-Willi syndrome.
  ■ Down syndrome results from chromosomal abnormalities; Fragile X syndrome and Prader-Willi syndrome are inherited.
  ■ Phenylketonuria (PKU) is an example of a cause of intellectual disabilities due to an inborn error of metabolism.

  ■ Microcephalus and hydrocephalus are examples of disorders of brain formation.
  ■ Prenatal environmental influences include maternal malnutrition, fetal alcohol syndrome, and rubella (German measles).
  ■ Prenatal screening for Down syndrome and other conditions is available.

▶ Perinatal causes include anoxia (lack of oxygen), low birthweight, and infections such as syphilis and herpes simplex.

▶ Postnatal causes include those that are biologically or psychologically based.
  ■ Biological causes include traumatic brain injury and infections such as meningitis and encephalitis.
  ■ Psychosocial causes (e.g., unstimulating adult–child interactions) can also cause mild intellectual disabilities.
  ■ Although environmental causes of mild intellectual disabilities are undeniable, heredity can also play a role. Most authorities now believe that heredity and environment interact to determine intelligence.
  ■ Recent research suggests that many cases of mild intellectual disabilities are caused by specific genetic syndromes.

What methods of assessment are used to identify individuals with intellectual disabilities?

▶ Individual IQ tests are used to assess intelligence. The following cautions are important: (1) An individual's IQ score can change; (2) all IQ tests are culturally biased to some extent; (3) the younger the child, the less valid are the results; and (4) a person's ability to live a successful and fulfilling life does not depend solely on his or her IQ.

▶ Adaptive behavior measures usually involve a parent, teacher, or other professional answering questions related to the person's independence and daily living skills and maladaptive behavior.

What are some of the psychological and behavioral characteristics of learners with intellectual disabilities?

▶ Major areas of problems for people with intellectual disabilities are attention, memory (especially working memory), language, self-regulation, motivation and social development.
  ■ Some have pointed to gullibility as an area of social development that is particularly limited in persons with intellectual disabilities, especially mild intellectual disabilities.

▶ Researchers are beginning to link genetic syndromes to particular behavioral patterns, or phenotypes.
  ■ Down syndrome is linked to relatively low expressive language, relatively high visual-spatial skills.

- Williams syndrome is linked to relatively low visual spatial skills, relatively high expressive language.
- Fragile X syndrome is linked to relatively low short-term memory, relatively high adaptive behavior.
- Prader-Willi syndrome is linked to relatively low auditory processing and compulsive eating, relatively high visual processing.

What are some educational considerations for learners with intellectual disabilities?

▶ The lesser the degree of intellectual disability, the more the teacher emphasizes academic skills; and the greater the degree of intellectual disability, the more stress there is on self-help, community living, and vocational skills.

▶ Authorities recommend a merger of functional and academic curricular standards, which can be accomplished by teaching functional academics.

▶ Effective teaching of students with intellectual disabilities involves *systematic instruction*: instructional prompts, consequences for performance, and strategies for the transfer of stimulus control.

▶ With respect to behavioral problems, authorities recommend using functional behavioral assessment (FBA) and positive behavioral intervention and support (PBIS).

▶ Although special classes for these students tend to be the norm, more and more students with intellectual disabilities are being placed in more integrated settings.

How do professionals assess students with intellectual disabilities' academic progress, adaptive behavior, and quality of life?

▶ Curriculum-based measurement can be used to monitor academic progress.

▶ Most measures of adaptive behavior are standardized and don't lend themselves to progress monitoring.

▶ Outcome measures for students include standardized achievement tests and standardized test of functional academics.

▶ There are several standardized outcome measures for adaptive behavior and quality of life.

What are some things to consider with respect to early intervention for learners with intellectual disabilities?

▶ Preschool programs differ in their goals according to whether they are aimed at preventing intellectual disabilities or furthering the development of children who have already been identified as intellectually disabled.

▶ In general, prevention programs are aimed at children who are at risk of developing mild intellectual disabilities, whereas programs for children who have been identified as intellectually disabled focus on children with more severe intellectual disabilities.

▶ Research supports the clear link between such interventions and success later in life.

What are some things to consider with respect to transition to adulthood for learners with intellectual disabilities?

▶ Promoting self-determination has become a major guiding principle in educating persons with intellectual disabilities.

▶ Transition programming involves two related areas: community adjustment and employment.
- Community survival skills include such things as managing money, using public transportation, and maintaining living environments. Large residential institutions are fast disappearing in favor of smaller community residential facilities (CRFs). Some people favor supported living, whereby people with intellectual disabilities live in their own apartment or home, over CRFs.
- Two common types of employment models are the sheltered workshop and supported competitive employment. Sheltered workshops offer structured training with other workers with disabilities on jobs requiring relatively low skills. Supported competitive employment involves receiving at least minimum wage in settings in which most of the workers are not disabled, accompanied by ongoing assistance from a job coach.

STANDARDS and PRINCIPLES in this Chapter

SPECIAL EDUCATORS . . .

- understand the field as an evolving and changing discipline (from CEC Content Standard #1).

- understand the similarities and differences in human development and the characteristics [of] individuals with and without exceptional learning needs (from CEC Content Standard #2).

- possess a repertoire of evidence-based instructional strategies (from CEC Content Standard #4).

- develop a variety of individualized transition plans (from CEC Content Standard #7).

- use the results of assessments to help identify exceptional learning needs (from CEC Content Standard #8).

- use collaboration to facilitate the successful transitions of individuals with exceptional learning needs (from CEC Content Standard #10).

ALL TEACHERS . . .

- understand the central concepts, tools of inquiry, structures of the discipline(s) they teach and can create learning experiences that make these aspects of subject matter meaningful (INTASC Principle #1).

- understand how children learn and develop, and can provide learning opportunities that support the . . . development of each learner (INTASC Principle #2).

- understand and use a variety of instructional strategies to encourage students' development of critical thinking, problem solving, and performance skills (INTASC Principle #4).

- plan instruction based on knowledge of subject matter, students, the community and curriculum goals (INTASC Principle #7).

- understand and use formal and informal assessment strategies to evaluate and ensure the continuous intellectual, social and physical development of the learner (INTASC Principle #8).

- foster relationships with school colleagues, families, and agencies in the larger community (from INTASC Principle #10).

Applying the STANDARDS and PRINCIPLES

- ONE of your colleagues, whose background is in general education, asks, "What does it really mean to have intellectual disability?" How would you respond? (CEC Content Standard #1 & #2; INTASC Principle #1 & #2)

- HOW should teachers determine what instructional methods to use with students with intellectual disabilities? (CEC Content Standard #4 & INTASC Principle #4)

- IS it prudent to rely heavily on IQ test results to gauge how well a student with intellectual disabilities will do in school? Why or why not? (CEC Content Standard #8 & INTASC Principle #8)

- HOW would you respond to parents who approach you expressing concern about the future of their high school student with intellectual disability? (CEC Content Standard #7 & #10; INTASC Principle #7 & #10)

Now go to the Hallahan/Kauffman, Eleventh Edition MyEducationLab course at www.myeducationlab.com to:

- take a Pretest to assess your initial comprehension of the chapter content;
- study chapter content with your Individualized Study Plan;
- take a Posttest to assess your understanding of chapter content;
- engage in multimedia exercises to help you build a deeper and more applied understanding of chapter content.

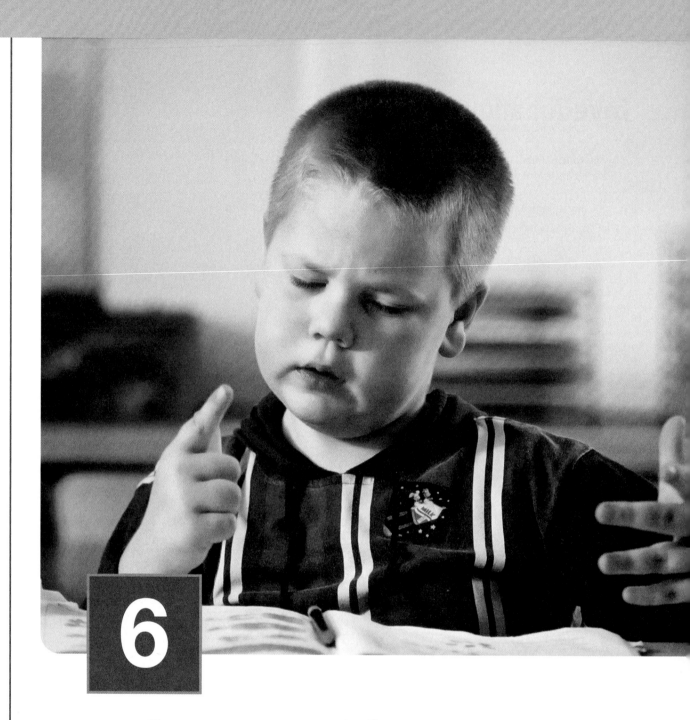

6

Learners with Learning Disabilities

As much as I want to find the perfect words to express what it is like to be dyslexic, I cannot. I can no more make you understand what it is like to be dyslexic than you can make me understand what it is like not to be. I can only guess and imagine. For years, I have looked out, wanting to be normal, to shed the skin that limits me, that holds me back. All the while, others have looked upon me, as well. There were those who have pitied me and those who have just given up on me, those who stood by, supporting me and believing in me, and those who looked at me as if I were an exhibit in a zoo. But, in general, people have shown a desire to understand what dyslexia is and how to teach those afflicted with it. Each side, it seems, longs to understand the other.

—Lynn Pelkey
"In the LD Bubble"

QUESTIONS to guide your reading of this chapter . . .

- How do professionals define learning disabilities?
- How do professionals identify students with learning disabilities?
- What is the prevalence of learning disabilities?
- What causes learning disabilities?
- What are some of the psychological and behavioral characteristics of learners with learning disabilities?
- What are some educational considerations for learners with learning disabilities?
- How do professionals assess students with intellectual disabilities' academic progress?
- What are some things to consider with respect to early intervention for learners with learning disabilities?
- What are some things to consider with respect to transition to adulthood for learners with learning disabilities?

MISCONCEPTIONS ABOUT
Learners with Learning Disabilities

MYTH ■ IQ–achievement discrepancy is a straightforward, error-free way of determining whether a student has a learning disability.

FACT ■ There are numerous conceptual problems in using an IQ–achievement discrepancy.

MYTH ■ Response to intervention (RTI) has been documented to be an error-free way of determining whether a student has a learning disability.

FACT ■ Little research exists on RTI, especially when implemented on a large scale; therefore, many questions remain regarding how best to implement it.

MYTH ■ All students with learning disabilities are brain damaged.

FACT ■ Many authorities now refer to students with learning disabilities as having central nervous system (CNS) dysfunction, which suggests a malfunctioning of the brain rather than actual tissue damage.

MYTH ■ The fact that so many definitions of learning disabilities have been proposed is an indicator that the field is in chaos.

FACT ■ Although at least eleven definitions have been proposed at one time or another, professionals have settled on two: the federal definition and the National Joint Committee on Learning Disabilities definition. And although they differ in some ways, these two definitions have a lot in common.

MYTH ■ The rapid increase in the prevalence of learning disabilities is due solely to sloppy diagnostic practices.

FACT ■ Although poor diagnostic practices may account for some of the increase, there are plausible social/cultural reasons for the increase. In addition, there is evidence that school personnel may "bend" the rules to identify students as learning disabled instead of the more stigmatizing identification of "mentally retarded."

MYTH ■ We know very little about what causes learning disabilities.

FACT ■ Although there is no simple clinical test for determining the cause of learning disabilities in individual cases, recent research strongly suggests causes related to neurological dysfunction possibly resulting from genetic, teratogenic, or medical factors.

MYTH ■ Math disabilities are relatively rare.

FACT ■ Math disabilities may be just as prevalent (or close to it) as reading disabilities.

MYTH ■ We needn't be concerned about the social-emotional well-being of students with learning disabilities because their problems are in academics.

FACT ■ Many students with learning disabilities also develop problems in the social-emotional area.

MYTH ■ Most children with learning disabilities outgrow their disabilities as adults.

FACT ■ Learning disabilities tend to endure into adulthood. Most individuals with learning disabilities who are successful must learn to cope with their problems and make extraordinary efforts to gain control of their lives.

MYTH ■ For persons with learning disabilities, IQ and achievement are the best predictors of success in adulthood.

FACT ■ The best predictors of success for adults with learning disabilities are perseverance, goal-setting, realistic acceptance of weaknesses and ability to build on strengths, exposure to intensive and long-term educational intervention, and especially the ability to take control of their lives.

Lynn Pelkey's (2001) comment about having dyslexia, or reading disability (see p. 183), should provide some degree of solace to researchers, teachers, parents, and policymakers, who have struggled to define learning disabilities since its formal recognition by the federal government in the 1960s. Pelkey has one specific (albeit the most common) form of learning disabilities: a reading disability. Yet even after living with the condition for thirty-five years, she is still unable to articulate its essence.

That she and the best of theoreticians and practitioners are unable to define learning disabilities in precise language, however, doesn't mean that her disability isn't real. If you were to go on to read the rest of her story, you would find that like millions of others who have learning disabilities, she faced tremendous challenges not only academically but also socially. You would also find that Pelkey was able eventually to overcome her feelings of rejection, successfully hold a job, and receive an associate's degree with honors from a community college. Her success, however, came not only from hard work and the support of others (as she notes in the quote on p. 183), but also from coming to terms with her learning disability: "Not long ago, it became very clear to me that I would have to come face-to-face with my feelings about being stupid if I was going to find peace within myself" (Pelkey, 2001, p. 27). As we discuss later in this chapter, being able to take control of one's life is what often separates people with learning disabilities who function successfully as adults from those who do not.

The struggle to elucidate the nature of learning disabilities has traditionally led to professional turmoil over the best ways to educate such students. Although the field of learning disabilities has had to struggle to overcome its penchant for questionable practices and to survive the intense scrutiny of professionals and the lay public, most who work within this field are happy to be part of it. For them, controversy and ambiguity only add excitement to the already challenging task of educating students with learning disabilities. As the field has matured, much more consensus has developed about key issues, such as how to define and identify learning disabilities, what causes learning disabilities, and the best educational treatment approaches.

But even though consensus has been reached, there is by no means unanimity on some of these issues. For example, healthy disagreements still exist with respect to the related issues of definition and identification.

INTERNET RESOURCES

For first-person accounts of having a learning disability, visit www.ldonline.org/first_person/first_person_archives.html

This is a page contained on the LD-Online Website, which is a service of the Learning Project of WETA in Washington, DC. Visit the LD-Online home page for more information on learning disabilities: www.ldonline.org

UNDERSTANDING THE STANDARDS AND PRINCIPLES Why has defining the term *learning disabilities* been so controversial? (CEC Knowledge and Skill Standards CC1K5 & LD1K5)

Council for Exceptional Children

Definition

At a parents' meeting in the early 1960s, Samuel Kirk (1963) proposed the term *learning disabilities* as a compromise because of the confusing variety of labels that were then being used to describe the child with relatively normal intelligence who was having

Educators have struggled to formulate a clear and comprehensive definition of the term *learning disability*, which generally describes children of seemingly normal intelligence who, nevertheless, have learning problems.

learning problems. Such a child was likely to be referred to as *minimally brain injured, a slow learner, dyslexic,* or *perceptually disabled.*

Many parents as well as teachers believed the label "minimal brain injury" to be problematic. **Minimal brain injury** refers to individuals who show behavioral but not neurological signs of brain injury. They exhibit behaviors (e.g., distractibility, hyperactivity, and perceptual disturbances) similar to those of people with real brain injury, but their neurological examinations are indistinguishable from those of nondisabled individuals. Historically, the diagnosis of minimal brain injury was sometimes dubious because it was based on questionable behavioral evidence rather than on more solid neurological data. Moreover, minimal brain injury was not an educationally meaningful term because such a diagnosis offered little real help in planning and implementing treatment. The term *slow learner* described the child's performance in some areas but not in others—and besides, intelligence testing indicated that the ability to learn existed. *Dyslexic,* too, fell short as a definitive term because it described only reading disabilities, and many of these children also had problems in other academic areas, such as math. To describe a child as *perceptually disabled* just confused the issue further, for perceptual problems might be only part of a puzzling inability to learn. So the parents' group finally agreed on the educationally oriented term *learning disabilities.* Accordingly, they founded the Association for Children with Learning Disabilities, now known as the Learning Disabilities Association of America. A few years later, following the lead of the parents, professionals and the federal government officially recognized the term.

The interest in learning disabilities evolved as a result of a growing awareness that a large number of children were not receiving needed educational services. Because they tested within the normal range of intelligence, these children didn't qualify for placement in classes for children with intellectual disabilities. And although many of them exhibited inappropriate behavior disturbances, some of them didn't. Therefore, placement in classes for students with emotional disturbance was thought to be inappropriate. Parents of children who weren't achieving at their expected potential—children who are learning disabled—wanted their children's academic achievement problems corrected.

Eleven different definitions of learning disabilities have enjoyed some degree of acceptance since the field's inception in the early 1960s (Hammill, 1990). Created by individual professionals and committees of professionals and lawmakers, each definition provides a slightly different slant. The two most influential definitions have been

■ **Minimal brain injury**
A term used to describe a child who shows behavioral but not neurological signs of brain injury; the term is now out of favor, primarily because of its lack of diagnostic utility (i.e., some children who learn normally show signs indicative of minimal brain injury).

INTERNET RESOURCES

The Learning Disabilities Association of America remains the major parent organization for learning disabilities. Its Website at www.ldanatl.org contains a variety of information on learning disabilities for parents and professionals.

the federal definition and the definition of the National Joint Committee on Learning Disabilities (NJCLD).

The Federal Definition

The majority of states use a definition that is based on the federal government's definition. This definition, first signed into law in 1975, was—with a few minor wording changes—adopted again in 1997 by the federal government and reauthorized in 2004. As we discuss in the next section, changes have occurred in identification procedures. However, the 2004 reauthorization of the Individuals with Disabilities Education Act (IDEA) did not change the definition contained in the 1997 reauthorization:

> GENERAL—The term "specific learning disability" means a disorder in one or more of the basic psychological processes involved in understanding or in using language, spoken or written, which disorder may manifest itself in an imperfect ability to listen, think, speak, read, write, spell, or do mathematical calculations.
>
> DISORDERS INCLUDED—Such term includes such conditions as perceptual disabilities, brain injury, minimal brain dysfunction, dyslexia, and developmental aphasia.
>
> DISORDERS NOT INCLUDED—Such term does not include a learning problem that is primarily the result of visual, hearing, or motor disabilities, of mental retardation, of emotional disturbance, or of environmental, cultural, or economic disadvantage. (Individuals with Disabilities Education Act Amendments of 1997, Sec. 602(26), p. 13)

The National Joint Committee on Learning Disabilities Definition

The NJCLD, composed of representatives of the major professional organizations involved with students with learning disabilities, came up with an alternative definition. They deemed it necessary to present their own definition because of their dissatisfaction with the following factors in the federal definition:

1. *Reference to psychological processes.* Many of the early pioneers in the learning disabilities field believed that the processing of visual and auditory information, or the making sense of this information (as distinct from visual and auditory acuity problems of those identified as blind or deaf), was the underlying cause of academic problems, such as reading disabilities. Furthermore, they believed that training students in visual- and auditory-processing skills in isolation from academic material would help them conquer their reading problems (Frostig & Horne, 1964; Kephart, 1971; Kirk & Kirk, 1971). Researchers ultimately determined that these perceptual and perceptual-motor exercises did not result in benefits for students' reading achievement (see Hallahan, 1975, and Hallahan & Cruickshank, 1973, for reviews). It was in reaction to the widespread adoption of unproven perceptual training programs that the NJCLD objected to the "basic psychological processes" phrase.

2. *Omission of the intrinsic nature of learning disabilities.* The federal definition makes no mention of causal factors, but the NJCLD considered learning disabilities to be due to central nervous system dysfunction within the individual.

3. *Omission of adults.* The NJCLD responded to the growing awareness that learning disabilities is not just a disability of childhood. It's a lifelong condition.

4. *Omission of self-regulation and social interaction problems.* The NJCLD responded to the growing awareness that students with learning disabilities often experience difficulties in self-regulation and social interaction.

Reading Homework Exercise

Who Is Learning Disabled? Go to the Homework and Exercises section in Chapter 6 of MyEducationLab and read the article "Who Is Learning Disabled?", which provides an overview of two prevailing schools of thought in the psychological community regarding the use of I.Q.-achievement discrepancy in the identification of students with learning disabilities.

5. *Inclusion of terms difficult to define.* The NJCLD believed that the federal definition was confusing because of its inclusion of terms such as *perceptual handicaps, dyslexia,* and *minimal brain dysfunction,* which have been so difficult to define (Hammill, Leigh, McNutt, & Larsen, 1981).

6. *Confusion about the exclusion clause.* The federal definition excludes a learning problem that is primarily due to other disabling conditions, such as mental retardation (intellectual disabilities), but it's vague with respect to whether one could have both a learning disability and another disability. The NJCLD preferred to be explicit about the possibility that someone with another disabling condition, such as intellectual disability, could also have a learning disability.

7. *Inclusion of spelling.* The NJCLD believed that there was no need to mention spelling because it thought it to be included in writing.

On the basis of these seven purported weaknesses of the federal definition, the NJCLD proposed the following definition:

> Learning disabilities is a general term that refers to a heterogeneous group of disorders manifested by significant difficulties in the acquisition and use of listening, speaking, reading, writing, reasoning, or mathematical abilities. These disorders are intrinsic to the individual, presumed to be due to central nervous system dysfunction, and may occur across the life span. Problems in self-regulatory behaviors, social perception and social interaction may exist with learning disabilities but do not by themselves constitute a learning disability.
>
> Although learning disabilities may occur concomitantly with other handicapping conditions (for example, sensory impairment, mental retardation, serious emotional disturbance) or with extrinsic influences (such as cultural differences, insufficient or inappropriate instruction), they are not the result of those conditions or influences. (National Joint Committee on Learning Disabilities, 1989, p. 1)

INTERNET RESOURCES

To see an executive summary of papers from the Learning Disabilities Summit, as well as videos of the presenters, visit www.air.org/LDsummit/default.htm

The full papers, as well as those of respondents, are included in Danielson, L., Bradley, R., & Hallahan, D. P. (Eds.), (2002). *Identification of learning disabilities: Research to practice.* Mahwah, NJ: Lawrence Erlbaum Associates.

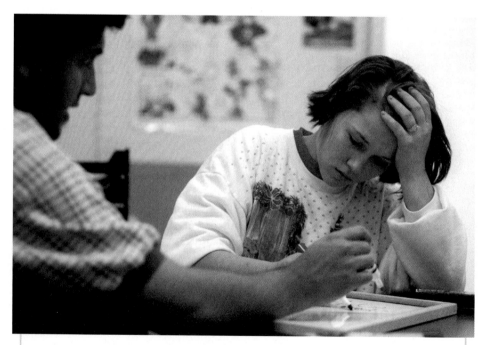

The fact that students with learning disabilities have apparently normal intelligence but still experience learning problems can be frustrating for them, as well as teachers and parents.

Identification

Identification procedures for learning disabilities are currently in a state of transition. As we noted in Chapter 2, the federal government reauthorized the Individuals with Disabilities Education Act (IDEA) in 2004. With this reauthorization the way in which students may be found eligible for special education services as learning disabled has changed dramatically. In this chapter, we discuss achievement–ability discrepancy—the traditional approach to identifying learning disabilities. Then we discuss response to intervention (RTI)—the federally preferred way of identifying learning disabilities contained in the reauthorization. We say "federally preferred" because, even though the law allows for either one of these methods to be used, the wording of the law, as well as the research priorities of the federal government, definitely favor the use of RTI. For example, the law insists that states *must not require* the use of a severe discrepancy between intellectual ability and achievement. And it specifically requires that states *must permit* the use of RTI.

Achievement–Ability Discrepancy

Shortly after presenting its definition in 1977, the federal government published regulations on how to identify students with learning disabilities. The key element in these regulations was that to be identified as learning disabled, the student needed to exhibit a "severe discrepancy between achievement and intellectual ability." In other words, a child who was achieving well below his or her potential would be identified as learning disabled.

The federal government left it up to individual states to decide precisely how they determined whether a student had a severe discrepancy. Most states relied on an **IQ–achievement discrepancy**—a comparison between scores on standardized intelligence and achievement tests. Many states adopted different statistical formulas for identifying IQ–achievement discrepancies. Over the years, however, considerable objection to the use of such formulas developed. Some of the formulas are statistically flawed and lead to inaccurate judgments, and those that are statistically adequate are difficult and expensive to implement. Furthermore, they give a false sense of precision. That is, they tempt school personnel to reduce to a single score the complex and important decision of identifying a learning disability.

In addition to the problem of using formulas, some authorities have objected to using an IQ–achievement discrepancy to identify learning disabilities on other conceptual grounds (Fletcher et al., 2002). For example, some authorities have pointed out that IQ is not a very strong predictor of reading ability. Furthermore, IQ scores of students with learning disabilities are subject to underestimation because performance on IQ tests is dependent on reading ability, to some extent. In other words, students with poor reading skills have difficulty expanding their vocabularies and learning about the world. As a result, they get lower-than-average scores on IQ tests, which lessen the discrepancy between IQ and achievement. Finally, and perhaps most important, some educators have pointed out that the idea of discrepancy is practically useless in the earliest elementary grades. In the first or second grade, a child is not expected to have achieved very much in reading or math, so it's difficult to find a discrepancy. Because of this delay in identification, the IQ–achievement discrepancy approach has been called a "wait-to-fail" model.

Response to Intervention or Response to Treatment

On the basis of the above-mentioned criticisms of IQ–achievement discrepancy, researchers proposed an alternative means of identifying students as learning disabled. Referred to as a **response-to-intervention (RTI)** or **response-to-treatment approach**, this way of

■ **IQ–achievement discrepancy**
Academic performance markedly lower than would be expected on the basis of a student's intellectual ability.

Reading Homework Exercise

Response to Intervention ●
Go to the Homework and Exercises section in Chapter 6 of MyEducationLab and read the article "Historical Perspective", then access the "Structure and Components" sections of the article at the Website titled "Responsiveness to Intervention and Learning Disabilities".

■ **Response-to-intervention (RTI) or response-to-treatment approach**
A way of determining whether a student has a learning disability; increasingly intensive levels of instructional intervention are delivered, and if the student does not achieve, at some point, he or she is determined to have a learning disability or is referred for special education evaluation.

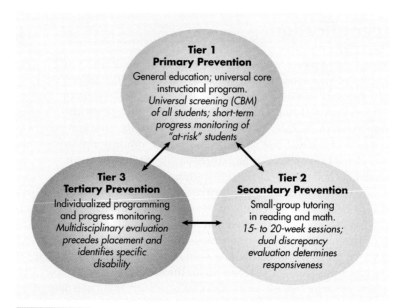

FIGURE 6.1 Fuchs' three-tiered model of response to intervention (RTI)

Source: From Fuchs, L. S., & Fuchs, D. (2007). A model for implementing responsiveness to intervention. *Teaching Exceptional Children, 39*(1), 14–20.

determining a learning disability is based on a multi-tiered model of prevention. There is no universally accepted RTI model. They vary with respect to such things as the number of tiers, the types of interventions used, the criteria used for movement from one tier to the next, and the roles of the special education versus the general education teacher. Virtually all models developed thus far focus on the early elementary grades and on the academic area of reading. Following is a description of the RTI model advocated by Lynn and Doug Fuchs (2007). It involves three tiers of intervention, with each successive tier providing more intensive instruction. See Figure 6.1.

TIER 1: PRIMARY PREVENTION   The first tier implements a core instructional program found by research to be effective for most students in general education. The use of research-based instruction is based on growing complaints from researchers and policy makers that some students are identified as learning disabled because their teachers aren't using high quality instructional techniques. In other words, some students may be victims of "teaching disabilities," not learning disabilities.

Before receiving the core instructional program, all students in the school are screened at the beginning of the school year using **curriculum-based measurement (CBM)**. (We discuss CBM more fully later in the chapter.) With respect to reading, for example, students read aloud a brief passage at their grade level, and the teacher or aide records the number of words read correctly. Teachers then use **progress monitoring** with those "at-risk" students who've done poorly on the brief screening. As discussed in earlier chapters, progress monitoring involves using CBM frequently, e.g., at least once a week. After five weeks, those continuing to struggle on these CBM measures move into Tier 2.

TIER 2: SECONDARY PREVENTION   The second tier involves small-group tutoring by a teacher or highly trained teacher assistant three to four times a week, forty-five minutes per day, for fifteen to twenty weeks. Teachers again monitor student progress frequently using CBM. (The graph in Figure 6.2 is an example of student progress monitoring.) Two criteria are used to assess students' responsiveness. In reading, for example, the dual criteria are (1) the final level reached on the number of words read aloud correctly on the reading passage and (2) the rate of improvement over the fifteen to twenty weeks in the number of words read correctly. Students falling one standard deviation below their classmates on two criteria are referred for multidisciplinary evaluation using a comprehensive battery of

■ **Curriculum-based measurement (CBM)**
A formative evaluation method designed to evaluate performance in the curriculum to which students are exposed; usually involves giving students a small sample of items from the curriculum in use in their schools; proponents argue that CBM is preferable to comparing students with national norms or using tests that do not reflect the curriculum content learned by the students.

■ **Progress monitoring**
Brief, frequent measures of performance used to determine whether a student is learning as expected; if student isn't learning as expected, the teacher can make changes to the instruction.

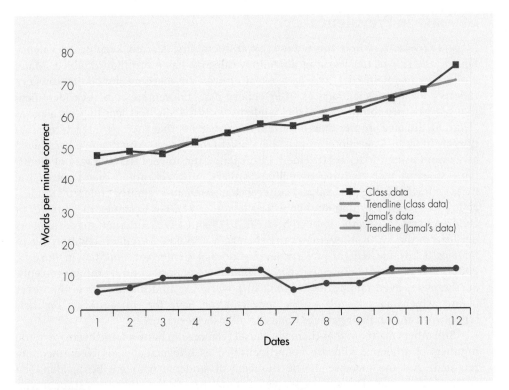

FIGURE 6.2 Example of curriculum-based measurement of reading rate. Jamal, a first grader with learning disabilities, was asked to read from his basal reader for one minute 12 times over three weeks. His rate of reading, as well as his growth rate (trend line) over this period were well below that of his class as whole.

Source: Adapted from Hallahan, D. P., Lloyd, J. W., Kauffman, J. M., Weiss, M. P., & Martinez, E. A. [2005]. *Learning disabilities: Foundations, characteristics, and effective teaching.* Boston: Allyn & Bacon.

standardized tests. Based on this evaluation, the multidisciplinary team determines whether the student is learning disabled or has some other disability, such as intellectual disabilities (mental retardation), before recommending them for Tier 3.

TIER 3: TERTIARY PREVENTION Students entering Tier 3 are formally identified as needing special education. In this tier, students are provided with even more intensive, individualized programming and progress monitoring from special education teachers. Student grouping is even smaller (perhaps even one-on-one), and instructional sessions may be every day for up to 1.5 hours per day.

It's important to keep in mind that, even though the Fuchs' model is perhaps the one that is based on the most rigorous field testing, it is not the only one being used. Much research still remains to be done on how best to implement RTI on a large scale. It's instructive that even the Fuchs have cautioned that RTI is a work in progress (D. Fuchs, Fuchs, McMaster, Yen, & Svenson, 2004; D. Fuchs, Mock, Morgan, & Young, 2003; L. S. Fuchs, 2003; Vaughn & Fuchs, 2003). The federal government has made the funding of research on RTI a high priority over the next several years.

Prevalence

According to U.S. government figures, public schools have identified as learning disabled between 5 and 6 percent of students between six and seventeen years of age. Learning disabilities is by far the largest category of special education. About half of all students identified by the public schools as needing special education are learning disabled.

Video Homework Exercise

Learning Disabilities ●
Go to the Homework and
Exercises section in Chapter 6
of MyEducationLab to watch the
video titled "Learning Disabilities",
in which a teenager discusses
perceptions of her disability.

Increase in Prevalence

Since 1976–1977, when the federal government first started keeping prevalence figures, the size of the learning disabilities category has more than doubled. Many authorities maintain that the rapid expansion of the learning disabilities category reflects poor diagnostic practices. They believe that children are being overidentified, that teachers are too quick to label students with the slightest learning problem as "learning disabled" rather than entertain the possibility that their own teaching practices are at fault. As we noted above, that's one of the reasons why the field has moved away from using the IQ-achievement discrepancy and toward RTI as a way of identifying students with learning disabilities. Others, however, argue that some of the increase might be due to social and cultural changes that have raised children's vulnerability to develop learning disabilities (Hallahan, 1992). For example, the number of children living in poverty doubled between 1975 and 1993. Although these numbers declined in the 1990s, they are on the rise again. Close to 13 million children live in families below the federal poverty level (National Center for Children in Poverty, 2006), and poverty is associated with higher rates of social and learning problems. Furthermore, even families who aren't in poverty are under more stress than ever before, which takes its toll on the time children have for concentrating on their schoolwork and on their parents' ability to offer social support.

Still others maintain that there is a causal relationship between the decrease in the numbers of students who are being identified as intellectually disabled (mentally retarded) and the increase in the numbers of students who are being identified as learning disabled. There is suggestive evidence that when faced with a student who could qualify as intellectually disabled, school personnel often bend the rules to apply the label of "learning disabilities" rather than the more stigmatizing label of "mental retardation" (MacMillan, Gresham, & Bocian, 1998; MacMillan & Siperstein, 2002).

An MRI of a human head displays a normal brain with color coded regions. In recent years researchers have focused on technological assessments of brain activity in search of CNS dysfunction as a basis for learning disabilities, rather than just behavioral symptoms.

Gender Differences

Boys outnumber girls by about three to one in the learning disabilities category. Some researchers have suggested that the prevalence of learning disabilities among males is due to their greater biological vulnerability. The infant mortality rate for males is higher than that for females, and males are at greater risk than females for a variety of biological abnormalities. Other researchers have contended, however, that the higher prevalence of learning disabilities among males might be due to referral bias. They suggest that academic difficulties are no more prevalent among boys than among girls but that boys are more likely to be referred for special education when they do have academic problems because of other behaviors that bother teachers, such as hyperactivity. Research on this issue is mixed (Clarizio & Phillips, 1986; Leinhardt, Seewald, & Zigmond, 1982; S. E. Shaywitz, Shaywitz, Fletcher, & Escobar, 1990). So at this point, it's probably safest to conclude that

some bias does exist but that the biological vulnerability of males also plays a role. For example, the federal government's figures indicate that all disabilities are more prevalent in males, including conditions that are difficult to imagine resulting from referral or assessment bias, such as hearing impairment (53% are males), orthopedic impairment (54% are males), and visual impairment (56% are males). (Hallahan, Lloyd, Kauffman, Weiss, & Martinez, 2005, p. 35)

Causes

For years, many professionals suspected that neurological factors were a major cause of learning disabilities. Many of the theoretical concepts and teaching methods associated with the field of learning disabilities grew out of work done in the 1930s and 1940s with children who were intellectually disabled and brain injured (Werner & Strauss, 1941; see Hallahan & Mercer, 2002, for a review). When the field of learning disabilities was emerging, professionals noted that many of these children displayed behavioral characteristics (e.g., distractibility, hyperactivity, language problems, perceptual disturbances) similar to those exhibited by people who were known to have brain damage, such as those who had suffered a stroke or a head wound.

In the case of most children with learning disabilities, however, there's little neurological evidence of actual *damage* to brain tissues. Therefore, today, the term *dysfunction* has come to replace injury or damage. A child with learning disabilities is now often referred to as having central nervous system (CNS) dysfunction rather than brain injury. Dysfunction does not necessarily mean tissue damage; instead, it signifies a malfunctioning of the brain or central nervous system.

At one time, there was little evidence, other than behavioral symptoms, that children with learning disabilities actually had CNS dysfunction. However, in recent years, researchers have begun to harness advanced technology to assess brain activity more accurately. The most recent technology being used by researchers to document neurological dysfunction in some people with learning disabilities includes **magnetic resonance imaging (MRI), functional magnetic resonance imaging (fMRI), functional magnetic resonance spectroscopy (fMRS)**, and **positron emission tomography (PET) scans.**

- An MRI sends magnetic radio waves through the head and creates cross-sectional images of the brain.
- fMRI and fMRS are adaptations of the MRI. Unlike an MRI, they are used to detect changes in brain activity while a person is engaged in a task, such as reading.
- A PET scan, like an fMRI or fMRS, is used while the person is performing a task. The subject is injected with a substance containing a low amount of radiation, which collects in active neurons. Using a scanner to detect the radioactive substance, researchers can tell which parts of the brain are actively engaged during various tasks.

Using these neuroimaging techniques, researchers have accumulated evidence for structural and functional differences between the brains of those with and without learning disabilities, especially reading disabilities. *Structural differences* refer to such things as the size of the various areas of the brain. *Functional* refers to activity in the brain. Findings from these neuroimaging studies have been relatively consistent in pointing to the **left temporal lobe** and areas around it as being structurally and/or functionally different in persons with dyslexia (Arduini, Capellini, & Ciasca, 2006; Brunswick, McCrory, Price, Frith, & Frith, 1999; Flowers, 1993; Flowers, Wood, & Naylor, 1991; Geogiewa et al., 1999; Hagman et al., 1992; Hoeft et al., 2006; Kibby & Hynd, 2001; McCrory, Frith, Brunswick, & Price, 2000; Paulesu et al., 2001; Pugh et al., 2000; Richards, 2001; Rumsey et al., 1999; Simos et al., 2007; B. A. Shaywitz et al., 2007; S. E. Shaywitz et al., 1998). See Figure 6.3.

Taken as a whole, these studies are not definitive evidence of a neurological basis for all students who are identified as learning disabled. Some researchers have noted that for the most part, the studies have been conducted on individuals with *severe* reading disabilities. However, the results have turned many people who were formerly skeptical into believers that CNS dysfunction could be the cause of many, if not most, cases of learning disabilities.

Even in cases in which one can be fairly certain that the person with learning disabilities has neurological dysfunction, the question still remains: How did the person

■ **Magnetic resonance imaging (MRI)**
A neuroimaging technique whereby radio waves are used to produce cross-sectional images of the brain; used to pinpoint areas of the brain that are dysfunctional.

■ **Functional magnetic resonance imaging (fMRI)**
An adaptation of the MRI used to detect changes in the brain while it is in an active state; unlike a PET scan, it does not involve using radioactive materials.

■ **Functional magnetic resonance spectroscopy (fMRS)**
An adaptation of the MRI used to detect changes in the brain while it is in an active state; unlike a PET scan, it does not involve using radioactive materials.

■ **Positron emission tomography (PET) scans**
A computerized method for measuring bloodflow in the brain; during a cognitive task, a low amount of radioactive dye is injected in the brain; the dye collects in active neurons, indicating which areas of the brain are active.

■ **Left temporal lobe**
An area on the left side of the brain; neuroimaging studies indicate it is responsible for speech, language, and reading abilities and is dysfunctional in persons with reading disabilities.

FIGURE 6.3 The left temporal lobe of the brain and some areas around it are closely associated with reading disabilities.

■ **Familiality studies**
A method of determining the degree to which a given condition is inherited; looks at the prevalence of the condition in relatives of the person with the condition.

■ **Heritability studies**
A method of determining the degree to which a condition is inherited; a comparison of the prevalence of a condition in identical (i.e., monozygotic, from the same egg) twins versus fraternal (i.e., dizygotic, from two eggs) twins.

■ **Teratogens**
Agents, such as chemicals, that can disrupt the normal development of the fetus; a possible cause of learning disabilities and other learning and behavioral problems.

■ **Fetal alcohol syndrome (FAS)**
Abnormalities associated with the mother's drinking alcohol during pregnancy; defects range from mild to severe.

come to have the neurological dysfunction? Possible reasons fall into three general categories: genetic, teratogenic, and medical factors.

Genetic Factors

Over the years, evidence has accumulated that learning disabilities can be inherited. The two most common types of studies that are used to look at the genetic basis of learning disabilities are familiality studies and heritability studies.

Familiality studies examine the degree to which a certain condition, such as a learning disability, occurs in a single family (i.e., the tendency for it to "run in a family"). Researchers have found that about 35 to 45 percent of first-degree relatives of individuals with reading disabilities—that is, the immediate birth family (parents and siblings)—have reading disabilities (Hallgren, 1950; Olson, Wise, Conners, Rack, & Fulker, 1989; Pennington, 1990; Schulte-Korne et al., 2006), and the risk for having reading disabilities goes up for children who have both parents with reading disabilities (Raskind, 2001). The same degree of familiality has also been found in families of people with speech and language disorders (Beichtman, Hood, & Inglis, 1992; Lewis, 1992; Schulte-Korne et al., 2006) and spelling disabilities (Schulte-Korne, Deimel, Muller, Gutenbrunner, & Remschmidt, 1996; Schulte-Korne et al., 2006).

The tendency for learning disabilities to run in families may also be due to environmental factors. For example, it's possible that parents with learning disabilities will pass on their disabilities to their children through their child-rearing practices. Given this, a more convincing method of determining whether learning disabilities are inherited is **heritability studies**—comparing the prevalence of learning disabilities in identical (monozygotic, from the same egg) versus fraternal (dizygotic, from two eggs) twins. Researchers have found that identical twins are more concordant than are fraternal twins for reading disabilities, speech and language disorders, and math disabilities (DeFries, Gillis, & Wadsworth, 1993; DeThorne et al., 2006; Lewis & Thompson, 1992; Reynolds et al., 1996; Shalev, 2004). In other words, if an identical twin and a fraternal twin each has a learning disability, the second identical twin is more likely to have a learning disability than the second fraternal twin.

With the rapid advances in molecular genetics, there is an expanding body of research attempting to pinpoint the genes involved in learning disabilities. Virtually all geneticists agree that no single gene causes a learning disability. Thus far, at least four genes have been identified as candidates for being connected in some way with learning disabilities (Fisher & Francks, 2006; Galaburda, LoTurco, Ramus, Fitch, & Rosen, 2006; McGrath, Smith, & Pennington, 2006; Plomin & Kovas, 2005; Smith, 2007). And, interestingly, evidence suggests that some of these genes are associated with more than one type of learning disability. In other words, the same genes are linked to reading, math, and spelling disabilities (Plomin & Kovas, 2005).

It's important to keep in mind that, as exciting as these genetics findings are, just as was the case for intellectual disabilities (discussed in Chapter 5), the environment also plays an important role in learning disabilities. This is especially true in the early stages of learning, e.g., early reading skills (Petrill, Deater-Deckard, Thompson, DeThorne & Schatschneider, 2006).

Teratogenic Factors

Teratogens are agents that can cause malformations or defects in the developing fetus. In Chapter 5, we discussed **fetal alcohol syndrome (FAS)** and **fetal alcohol spectrum disorders** and lead as potential causes of intellectual disabilities. Authorities have also speculated that some people may be exposed to levels of these substances that are not high enough to result in intellectual disabilities/mental retardation but are high enough to cause learning disabilities.

Medical Factors

There are several medical conditions that can cause learning disabilities. Many of these can also result in intellectual disabilities, depending on the severity of the condition. For example, premature birth places children at risk for neurological dysfunction, and pediatric AIDS can result in neurological damage such that learning disabilities result.

■ **Fetal alcohol spectrum disorders**
A range of disorders whose mothers consumed large quantities of alcohol during pregnancy.

Psychological and Behavioral Characteristics

Before discussing some of the most common characteristics of people with learning disabilities, we point out two important features of this population: People with learning disabilities exhibit a great deal of both interindividual and intraindividual variation.

Interindividual Variation

In any classroom of students with learning disabilities, some will have problems in reading, some will have problems in math, some will have problems in spelling, some will be inattentive, and so on. One term for such interindividual variation is *heterogeneity*. Although heterogeneity is a trademark of children from all the categories of special education, the old adage "No two are exactly alike" is particularly appropriate for students with learning disabilities. This heterogeneity makes it a challenge for teachers to plan educational programs for the diverse group of children they find in their classrooms.

UNDERSTANDING THE STANDARDS AND PRINCIPLES What should teachers know about the psychological, social, and emotional characteristics of individuals with learning disabilities? (CEC Knowledge and Skill Standard LD2K3)

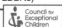

Intraindividual Variation

In addition to differences among one another, children with learning disabilities also tend to exhibit variability within their own profiles of abilities. For example, a child might be two or three years above grade level in reading but two or three years behind grade level in math. Such uneven profiles account for references to *specific* learning disabilities in the literature on learning disabilities.

Some of the pioneers in the field of learning disabilities alerted colleagues to what is termed *intraindividual* variation. Samuel Kirk was one of the most influential in advocating the notion of individual variation in students with learning disabilities. He developed the Illinois Test of Psycholinguistic Abilities (Kirk, McCarthy, & Kirk, 1967), which purportedly measured variation in processes important for reading. Researchers ultimately found that Kirk's test didn't measure processes germane to reading (Hallahan & Cruickshank, 1973; Hammill & Larsen, 1974), and the test is rarely used today. Nonetheless, most authorities still recognize intraindividual differences as a feature of many students with learning disabilities.

We now turn to a discussion of some of the most common characteristics of persons with learning disabilities.

Academic Achievement Problems

Academic deficits are the hallmark of learning disabilities. By definition, if there is no academic problem, a learning disability does not exist.

Video Homework Exercise

Individual Reading ● Go to the Homework and Exercises section in Chapter 6 of MyEducationLab and watch the video titled "Individual Reading", in which a teacher helps a student struggling with decoding and fluency.

Success Stories

Hard work at home and school helps Randy read on grade level

Special Educator Celia Gottesman: "Unless you work harder, faster, and more intensively, they won't catch up."

Ten-year-old Randy Daniels is reading on grade level as he starts fifth grade at Lake Forest Elementary School in Florida.

These are the keys to his success:

- Intensive instruction in reading and math
- Relentless progress monitoring
- Specific incentives and parental support

Randy Daniels ended third grade reading at a second grade level, one year behind many of his classmates. This year he has caught up, and he is proud of it. "I did it! I did it! I did it!" he said when he heard the good news. "Randy moved two years ahead in reading in one year with two intensive summer school experiences, and that's a tremendous achievement" says special educator Dr. Celia Gottesman. Hard work at home and at school helped Randy achieve success through intensive, relentless, and specific special education.

● **Intensive Instruction in Reading and Math** Randy Daniels loves football and he likes to do his best, but last year he struggled to keep up in his regular class. In summer school Randy received intensive instruction for 90 minutes every day in a resource classroom with Celia Gottesman and Waltraud Schmid. Known to their students as Dr. G. and Ms. Schmid, these special educators strengthened Randy's academic skills using a combination of formative assessment, direct instruction, and cognitive strategy training. "We also provided lots of positive reinforcement and personal attention," says Celia. The effective team of Gottesman and Schmid gets results, and this year their high-poverty school met its goals for adequate yearly progress

(AYP). Celia Gottesman teaches reading and math to exceptional learners at Lake Forest Elementary. Waltraud Schmid also taught special education at the school before she retired. As a school volunteer she now helps Celia plan and deliver systematic instruction five days a week. For Celia, teaching students with learning disabilities means accelerating progress as quickly as possible. "We assess frequently to see where students are, what academic and social skills they need, and how fast we can push them—and I'm a pusher," she says. She speaks candidly as the mother of three college graduates who have learning disabilities: "Unless you work harder, faster, and more intensively, they won't catch up."

To improve Randy's reading fluency and comprehension, Celia modified the pace of instruction, and taught him in small groups with other students who struggled with similar concepts and vocabulary. She also taught evidence-based learning strategies to help him anchor academic content. In addition Randy received supplemental one-on-one instruction daily from Waltraud Schmid who inventoried his skill levels and charted his progress. "Mrs. Schmid was a pharmacist in her first career," says Celia, "and you can be sure she knows the importance of collecting data."

■ **Decoding**
The ability to convert print to spoken language; dependent on phonemic awareness and understanding of the alphabetic principles; a significant problem for many people with reading disabilities.

■ **Phonological awareness**
The ability to understand that speech flow can be broken into smaller sound units such as words, syllables, and phonemes; generally thought to be the reason for the reading problems of many students with learning disabilities.

READING   Reading poses the most difficulty for most students with learning disabilities. Students with reading disabilities are likely to experience problems with three aspects of reading: decoding, fluency, and comprehension (Hallahan et al., 2005). **Decoding** is the ability to convert print to spoken language, and is largely dependent on phonological awareness and phonemic awareness. **Phonological awareness** is the understanding that speech consists of small units of sound, such as words, syllables, and phonemes (Pullen, 2002; Troia, 2004). Phonemic awareness is particularly important (Blachman, 2001; Boada & Pennington, 2006). Children with **phonemic awareness** understand that words are made up of sounds, or phonemes. For example, the word *bat* consists of three phonemes: *b, a, t.*

Interestingly, there is suggestive evidence that readers of English are more susceptible to problems with phonological awareness than are readers of some other languages. Some have speculated that this is why reading disabilities are more prevalent in English-speaking countries than in some other countries (see the Focus on Concepts on p. 198).

● **Relentless Progress Monitoring** Celia Gottesman bases instruction on multiple assessments. "We start the year with so much diagnostic information," she says. "We use many sources of data to plan our teaching and to monitor progress including scores on state tests, reading inventories, and curriculum based measurement." In Randy's case Mrs. Schmid used classroom materials to test his reading fluency and math facts. She graphed the number of words he read per minute and charted the number of correct and incorrect math facts daily across a six-week period. This careful progress monitoring helped Celia guide Randy's instruction. "We have a mastery level in mind for each child based on their beginning scores. We isolate the skill we want to teach, we use validated methods to teach that skill, and then we measure the student's response to our instruction," says Celia. "We expected a 75 point increase for Randy on state achievement tests, but he made over 100 points in reading and over 200 points in math."

● **Specific Incentives and Parental Support** According to his teachers, much of the credit for Randy's success goes to his mother, Leann Lee, who makes sure that he practices reading at home. "I don't want my son to become a statistic because he's a black male," says Mrs. Lee. "I want him to learn that he can succeed if he works hard." Mrs. Lee scheduled free tutoring after school, and asked for Reading Mastery workbooks so she could help Randy. "I said to Dr. G, 'I need you to teach me how to teach Randy, so I can teach him at home.'" Leann Lee started an incentive program to raise his reading scores, and Randy is expected to read at least 30 minutes each day. His reward is playing in a local Pop Warner football league and his step-father, Raymond Lee, is now the team coach. Randy has two younger sisters and his parents both work full-time. Their efforts to help him succeed have not been easy but they have been worthwhile. "He's a busy little boy," says Leann. "Rewards motivate him and what he's accomplished is awesome."

CEC'S STANDARDS: PAVING THE WAY TO SUCCESS

Assess your steps to success in meeting the CEC Knowledge and Skill Base for All Beginning Special Education Teachers of Students with Learning Disabilities. Use the following questions to reflect on the growth of your own professional knowledge, skills, and dispositions.

REFLECTING ON YOUR OWN PROFESSIONAL DEVELOPMENT

If you were Randy's teacher . . .

■ What are some areas about educating students with learning disabilities that you would need to know more about?

■ What are some specific skills that would help you address his learning disabilities?

■ What personal dispositions do you think are most important for you to develop in teaching students with learning disabilities to be successful in mastering new skills?

Using the CEC Standards:

■ What are some procedures you might use to identify young children who may be at risk for learning disabilities? (LD8K3)

■ What are some instructional methods you would use with students with learning disabilities to strengthen and compensate for deficits in perception, comprehension, memory, and retrieval? (LD4S5)

■ What are some sources of specialized curricula, materials, and resources for individuals with learning disabilities? (LD7K2)

● *By Jean B. Crockett*

Students who have difficulty decoding invariably have problems with fluency. **Reading fluency** refers to the ability to read effortlessly and smoothly. Recall that Figure 6.2 showed the reading rate for one student compared to the reading rates of his classmates. Reading rate and the ability to read with appropriate expression are components of reading fluency.

Problems with reading fluency are a major reason why students have difficulties with reading comprehension (Good, Simmons, & Kame'enui, 2001). **Reading comprehension** refers to the ability to gain meaning from what one has read. In other words, reading too slowly or in a halting manner interferes with a person's ability to comprehend text.

WRITTEN LANGUAGE People with learning disabilities often have problems in one or more of the following areas: handwriting, spelling, and composition (Hallahan et al., 2005). Although even the best students can have less-than-perfect handwriting, the

▶ **Phonemic awareness**
One's ability to understand that words are made up of sounds, or phonemes.

■ **Reading fluency**
The ability to read effortlessly and smoothly; consists of the ability to read at a normal rate and with appropriate expression; influences one's reading comprehension.

■ **Reading comprehension**
The ability to understand what one has read.

FOCUS ON **Concepts**

Dyslexia: Same Brains, Different Languages

Pity the poor speakers of English. New research suggests that they may be especially prone to manifest dyslexia, the language disorder that makes reading and writing a struggle, simply because their language is so tricky.

The distinctive pattern of spelling and memory problems that characterizes dyslexia has a strong genetic basis, suggesting that some neurological oddity underlies the disorder. But there appears to be a cultural component to the [condition] as well, because dyslexia is more prevalent in some countries than others; for instance, about twice as many people fit the definition of dyslexic in the United States as in Italy. Researchers have suspected that certain languages expose the disorder while others allow dyslexics to compensate. Now a brain imaging study backs this theory up.

A multinational team of researchers used positron emission tomography (PET) scans to observe brain activity in British, French, and Italian adults while they read [Paulesu et al., 2001]. Regardless of language, . . . people with symptoms of dyslexia showed less neural activity in a part of the brain that's vital for reading.

"Neurologically, the disease looks very much the same" in people who speak different languages, says neurologist Eraldo Paulesu of the University of Milan Biocca in Italy. "Therefore, the difference in prevalence of clinical manifestations [among different countries] must be attributed to something else." The researchers

blame language. English consists of just 40 sounds, but these phonemes can be spelled, by one count, in 1120 different ways. French spelling is almost as maddening. Italian speakers, in contrast, must map 25 different speech sounds to just 33 combinations of letters. Not surprisingly, Italian schoolchildren read faster and more accurately than do those in Britain. And it's no surprise that people have a harder time overcoming reading disorders if their language, like English or French, has a very complex, arbitrary system for spelling. . . . Compared to normal readers, dyslexics from all three countries showed less activation in parts of the [left] temporal lobe while reading. [See Figure 6.3 on page 194.] The underutilized areas are familiar to neurologists: Patients with strokes in this area often lose the ability to read and spell, even though they still speak fluently. . . .

This research doesn't supply ready solutions for how to help dyslexic students overcome their reading disability, Paulesu says, short of moving to Italy, Turkey, or Spain, where spelling is simple and straightforward. So sympathize when English- or French-speaking students complain about having to memorize arbitrarily spelled words; they're right to feel wronged.

Source: Reprinted with permission from Helmuth, L. (2001). Dyslexia: Same brains, different languages. *Science,* 291, 2064–2065. Copyright © 2001 by American Association for the Advancement of Science.

INTERNET RESOURCES

To see the full text for the Helmuth article from *Science,* see www.sciencemag.org/ content/vol291/issue5511/ index.shtml

■ **Syntax**
The way words are joined together to structure meaningful sentences (i.e., grammar).

■ **Semantics**
The study of the meanings attached to words.

■ **Phonology**
The study of how individual sounds make up words.

kinds of problems that some students with learning disabilities exhibit are much more severe. These children are sometimes very slow writers, and their written products are sometimes illegible. Spelling can be a significant problem because of the difficulty (noted in the previous section) in understanding the correspondence between sounds and letters.

In addition to the more mechanical areas of handwriting and spelling, students with learning disabilities frequently have difficulties in the more creative aspects of composition (Graham & Harris, 2002; Montague & Graves, 1992). For example, compared to nondisabled peers, students with learning disabilities use less complex sentence structures; include fewer types of words; write paragraphs that are less well organized; include fewer ideas in their written products; and write stories that have fewer important components, such as introducing main characters, setting scenes, and describing a conflict to be resolved (Hallahan et al., 2005).

SPOKEN LANGUAGE   Many students with learning disabilities have problems with the mechanical and social uses of language. Mechanically, they have trouble with **syntax** (grammar), **semantics** (word meanings), and, as we have already noted, **phonology** (the ability to break words into their component sounds and blend individual sounds together to make words).

With regard to social uses of language—commonly referred to as **pragmatics**—students with learning disabilities are often inept in the production and reception of discourse. In short, they're not very good conversationalists. They are unable to engage in the mutual give-and-take that conversations between individuals require. For instance, conversations of individuals with learning disabilities are frequently marked by long silences because they don't use the relatively subtle strategies that their nondisabled peers do to keep conversations going. They're not skilled at responding to others' statements or questions and tend to answer their own questions before their companions have a chance to respond. They tend to make task-irrelevant comments and make those with whom they talk uncomfortable. In one often cited study, for example, children with and without learning disabilities took turns playing the role of host in a simulated television talk show (Bryan, Donahue, Pearl, & Sturm, 1981). In contrast to nondisabled children, children with learning disabilities playing the host role allowed their nondisabled guests to dominate the conversation. Also, their guests exhibited more signs of discomfort during the interview than did the guests of nondisabled hosts.

MATH   Although disorders of reading, writing, and language have traditionally received more emphasis than problems with mathematics, the latter are now gaining a great deal of attention. Authorities now recognize that math disabilities may be just as prevalent as or at least a close second to reading disabilities (Kunsch, Jitendra, & Sood, 2007; Swanson & Jerman, 2006). The types of problems these students have include difficulties with computation of math facts (Cawley, Parmar, Yan, & Miller, 1998) as well as word problems (Woodward & Baxter, 1997); trouble with the latter is often due to the inefficient application of problem-solving strategies.

Perceptual, Perceptual-Motor, and General Coordination Problems

Studies indicate that some children with learning disabilities exhibit visual and/or auditory perceptual disabilities (see Hallahan, 1975, and Willows, 1998, for reviews). A child with visual perceptual problems might have trouble solving puzzles or seeing and remembering visual shapes, for example, or he or she might have a tendency to reverse letters (e.g., mistake a *b* for a *d*). A child with auditory perceptual problems might have difficulty discriminating between two words that sound nearly alike (e.g., *fit* and *fib*) or following orally presented directions.

Teachers and parents have also noted that some students with learning disabilities have difficulty with physical activities involving motor skills. They describe some of these children as having "two left feet" or "ten thumbs." The problems may involve both fine motor (small motor muscles) and gross motor (large motor muscles) skills. Fine motor skills often involve coordination of the visual and motor systems.

Disorders of Attention and Hyperactivity

Students with attention problems display such characteristics as distractibility, impulsivity, and hyperactivity. Teachers and parents of these children often characterize them as being unable to stick with one task for very long, failing to listen to others, talking nonstop, blurting out the first things on their minds, and being generally disorganized in planning their activities in and out of school.

Individuals with learning disabilities often have attention problems (Kotkin, Forness, & Kavale, 2001), often severe enough to be diagnosed as **attention deficit hyperactivity disorder (ADHD)**. ADHD, characterized by severe problems of inattention, hyperactivity, and/or impulsivity, is a diagnosis made by a psychiatrist or psychologist, using criteria established by the American Psychiatric Association (2000; we discuss

■ **Pragmatics**
The study within psycholinguistics of how people use language in social situations; emphasizes the functional use of language, rather than mechanics.

■ **Attention deficit hyperactivity disorder (ADHD)**
A condition characterized by severe problems of inattention, hyperactivity, and/or impulsivity; often found in people with learning disabilities.

ADHD more fully in Chapter 7). Although estimates vary, researchers have consistently found an overlap of 10–25 percent between ADHD and learning disabilities (Forness & Kavale, 2002).

Memory and Metacognitive Problems

Memory and metacognitive problems are closely related. A person who has problems in one of these areas is likely to have problems in at least one of the other components as well.

MEMORY   Parents and teachers are well aware that students with learning disabilities have problems remembering such things as assignments and appointments. In fact, these adults often exclaim in exasperation that they can't understand how a child who is so smart can forget things so easily. Furthermore, early researchers in learning disabilities documented that many students with learning disabilities have a real deficit in memory (Hallahan et al., 2005; Swanson, 2005).

Students with learning disabilities have at least two types of memory problems: **short-term memory (STM)** and **working memory (WM)**. STM problems involve difficulty recalling information shortly after having seen or heard it. WM problems affect a person's ability to keep information in mind while simultaneously doing another cognitive task (Swanson, 2005). Many researchers have found WM deficits in students with reading disabilities (Cohen-Mimran & Sapir, 2007; Gathercole, Alloway, Willis, & Adams, 2005) and students with math disabilities (Geary, Hoard, Byrd-Craven, Nugent, & Numtee, 2007; Swanson & Jerman, 2006). In the case of the latter, it's easy to see how doing math computation often requires being able to hold certain facts or calculations in mind in order to do further calculations to arrive at an answer.

Researchers have found that one of the major reasons that children with learning disabilities perform poorly on memory tasks is that, unlike their nondisabled peers, they don't use strategies. For example, when presented with a list of words to memorize, most children will rehearse the names to themselves. They'll also make use of categories by rehearsing words in groups that go together. Students with learning disabilities are unlikely to use these strategies spontaneously. However, they can be taught memory strategies, such as rehearsal, which research indicates can enhance their academic performance.

METACOGNITION   **Metacognition** has at least three components: the ability to (1) recognize task requirements, (2) select and implement appropriate strategies, and (3) monitor and adjust performance (Butler, 1998).

Regarding the first component—ability to recognize task requirements—students with learning disabilities frequently have problems judging how difficult tasks can be. For example, they might approach the reading of highly technical information with the same level of intensity as when reading for pleasure.

An example of problems with the second component—ability to select and implement appropriate strategies—occurs when students with learning disabilities are asked questions such as "How can you remember to take your homework to school in the morning?" they don't come up with as many strategies (e.g., writing a note to oneself, placing the homework by the front door) as students without disabilities do.

An example of the third component of metacognition—ability to monitor or adjust performance—is comprehension monitoring. **Comprehension monitoring** refers to the abilities employed while one reads and attempts to comprehend textual material. Many students with reading disabilities have problems, for example, in being able to sense when they are not understanding what they are reading (Butler, 1998). Good readers are able to sense this and make necessary adjustments, such as slowing down and/or rereading difficult passages. Students with reading problems are also likely to have problems in picking out the main ideas of paragraphs.

■ **Short-term memory (STM)**
The ability to recall information after a short period of time.

■ **Working memory (WM)**
The ability to remember information while also performing other cognitive operations.

■ **Metacognition**
One's understanding of the strategies available for learning a task and the regulatory mechanisms needed to complete the task.

■ **Comprehension monitoring**
The ability to keep track of one's own comprehension of reading material and to make adjustments to comprehend better while reading; often deficient in students with learning disabilities.

Social-Emotional Problems

Although not all, perhaps not even a majority, of children with learning disabilities have significant social-emotional problems, they do run a greater risk than do their nondisabled peers of having these types of problems. For example, they are at a greater risk for depression, social rejection, suicidal thoughts, and loneliness (Al-Yagon, 2007; Bryan, Burstein, & Ergul, 2004; Daniel et al., 2006; Maag & Reid, 2006; Margalit, 2006). For those who experience behavioral problems, the effects can be long-lasting and devastating. In adulthood, the scars from years of rejection can be painful and not easily healed (McGrady, Lerner, & Boscardin, 2001). See the Personal Perspectives below for testimony to the depth of the emotional scars experienced by some people with learning disabilities.

One plausible reason for the social problems of some students with learning disabilities is that these students have deficits in social cognition. That is, they misread social cues and may misinterpret the feelings and emotions of others. Most children, for example, can tell when their behavior is bothering others. Students with learning disabilities sometimes act as if they are oblivious to the effect their behavior is having on their peers. They also have difficulty taking the perspective of others, of putting themselves in someone else's shoes.

Researchers have noted that problems with social interaction tend to be more evident in children who also have problems in math, visual-spatial tasks, tactual tasks, and self-regulation and organization (Rourke, 1995; Worling, Humphries, & Tannock, 1999). In laypersons' terms, such children are sometimes described as "spacey" or "in a fog." Individuals who exhibit this constellation of behaviors are referred to as having **nonverbal learning disabilities**. However, the term is somewhat of a misnomer because these people often exhibit subtle problems in using language, especially in social situations. Researchers have speculated that nonverbal learning disabilities are caused by malfunctioning of the right half of the brain because of known linkages of math, visual-spatial, and tactual skills to the right cerebral hemisphere. There is also evidence that

■ **Nonverbal learning disabilities**
A term used to refer to individuals who have a cluster of disabilities in social interaction, math, visual-spatial tasks, and tactual tasks.

Personal PERSPECTIVES

Learning Disabilities and the Pain of Rejection

The following excerpt from the autobiography of a 34-year-old man with learning disabilities poignantly illustrates how difficult it can be for some people with learning disabilities to make and keep friends:

> Making new friends was a most difficult process, one I rarely attempted. I had been so shy in the first grade that the other kids saw me as a freak and avoided contact with me. I was socially blackballed from the get-go. When my father, a man without many friends, heard of my social problems he passed along some less than sage advice. He said, "If they don't like you, dazzle them with bullshit." Once I was clear on what bullshit was, I embarked on a destructive path that ruined my prospects of making true friends. In order to keep people interested in maintaining a friendship, I jazzed myself up. When given the opportunity to advance my image in someone else's eyes, I leapt on it, no matter how outrageous the lie. . . .

> All too soon, the practice began to backfire as my peers, not nearly as stupid as I believed, began to challenge my lies. For a while, I stood by my stories, unable to address why I told them or the effect they might have on others. But time and the constant doubt of my classmates eventually wore me down. By the third grade, I was beaten, defenseless, and had nowhere to retreat, so I publicly recanted. After that, word of my confession spread like pink eye through the school yard, and I was left alone. No one at school would befriend the known liar, the boy who could not tell the truth. As my peers rolled down the path of socialization, I was left standing in their dust. Early on, I had tried being myself and it had gotten me alienated. I tried being everything to everyone, and it cost me any hope of social acceptance. I was left with nothing, both socially and emotionally. (Queen, 2001, p. 5)

individuals with nonverbal learning disabilities are at risk for depression, presumably because of the social rejection and isolation they may experience. In extreme cases, they have an increased risk of suicide (Bender, Rosenkrans, & Crane, 1999).

Motivational Problems

Another source of problems for many people with learning disabilities is their motivation, or feelings about their abilities to deal with many of life's challenges and problems. People with learning disabilities may appear content to let events happen without attempting to control or influence them. These individuals have what is referred to as an external, rather than an internal, **locus of control**. In other words, they believe that their lives are controlled by external factors such as luck or fate rather than by internal factors such as determination or ability (Hallahan et al., 2005). People with this outlook sometimes display **learned helplessness**: a tendency to give up and expect the worst because they think that no matter how hard they try, they will fail.

What makes these motivational problems so difficult for teachers, parents, and individuals with learning disabilities to deal with is the interrelationship between learning and motivational problems (Morgan & Fuchs, 2007). A vicious cycle develops: The student learns to expect failure in any new situation on the basis of past experience. This expectancy of failure, or learned helplessness, might then cause the student to give up too easily when faced with a difficult or complicated task. As a result, not only does the student fail to learn new skills; she or he also has another bad experience, reinforcing feelings of helplessness and even worthlessness—and so the cycle goes.

The Child with Learning Disabilities as an Inactive Learner with Strategy Deficits

Many of the psychological and behavioral characteristics we've described can be summed up by saying that the student with learning disabilities is an *inactive learner*, lacking in strategies for attacking academic problems (Hallahan et al., 2005). Specifically, research describes the student with learning disabilities as someone who doesn't believe in his or her own abilities (learned helplessness), has an inadequate grasp of what strategies are available for problem solving (poor metacognitive skills), and has problems producing appropriate learning strategies spontaneously.

The practical implication of this constellation of characteristics is that students with learning disabilities can have difficulties working independently. They're not likely to be "self-starters." Assignments or activities requiring them to work on their own may cause problems unless the teacher carefully provides an appropriate amount of support. As we discussed in Chapter 4, homework is a major problem for many students with disabilities; this is especially true for those with learning disabilities (Bryan & Sullivan-Burstein, 1998; Epstein, Munk, Bursuck, Polloway, & Jayanthi, 1998). Students' difficulties range from failing to bring home their homework to being distracted while doing homework to forgetting to turn in their homework.

Educational Considerations

In this section, we consider four major instructional approaches to alleviating the academic problems of students with learning disabilities: cognitive training, content enhancement, direct instruction, and peer tutoring. Although we look at these approaches individually, in practice they are often combined.

Cognitive Training

Cognitive training involves three components: (1) changing thought processes, (2) providing strategies for learning, and (3) teaching self-initiative. Whereas behavior modification focuses on modifying observable behaviors, cognitive training is concerned with modifying unobservable thought processes, prompting observable changes in behavior. Cognitive training has proven successful in helping a variety of academic problems for many students with learning disabilities (Hallahan et al., 2005).

There are at least two reasons why cognitive training is particularly appropriate for students with learning disabilities—namely, it aims at helping them overcome

1. Metacognitive problems, by providing them with specific strategies for solving problems; and
2. Motivational problems of passivity and learned helplessness, by stressing self-initiative and involving them as much as possible in their own treatment.

A variety of specific techniques fall under the heading of cognitive training. We briefly discuss four: self-instruction, self-monitoring, scaffolded instruction, and reciprocal teaching.

SELF-INSTRUCTION   The purpose of **self-instruction** is to make students aware of the various stages of problem-solving tasks while they are performing them and to bring behavior under verbal control. Typically, the teacher first models the use of the verbal routine while solving the problem. Next, the teacher closely supervises the students using the verbal routine while doing the task. Then the students do it on their own.

One study using self-instruction as an integral feature of instruction involved fifth- and sixth-grade students with learning disabilities solving math word problems (Case, Harris, & Graham, 1992). The five-step strategy that the students learned to use involved saying the problem out loud, looking for important words and circling them, drawing pictures to help explain what was happening, writing the math sentence, and writing the answer. Furthermore, students were prompted to use the following self-instructions:

1. *Problem definition:* "What do I have to do?"
2. *Planning:* "How can I solve this problem?"
3. *Strategy use:* "The five-step strategy will help me look for important words."
4. *Self-evaluation:* "How am I doing?"
5. *Self-reinforcement:* "Good job. I got it right."

SELF-MONITORING   **Self-monitoring** involves students keeping track of their own behavior and often consists of two components: self evaluation and self-recording. The student evaluates his or her behavior and then records whether the behavior occurred. Students can be taught to self-monitor a variety of academic behaviors. For example, after working on several math problems, the student can check his or her answers and then record on a graph how many of the answers were correct. After several days, the student and teacher have an observable record of the student's progress.

In addition to monitoring academic performance, students can also monitor their on- and off-task behavior. In one study, the teacher instructed students to ask themselves "Was I paying attention?" every time they heard a tone on a tape recorder. (The tones occurred randomly every thirty to ninety seconds.) Not only did the students' on-task behavior increased, but their academic productivity also increased (Lloyd, Hallahan, Kauffman, & Keller, 1998; Mathes & Bender, 1997).

■ **Cognitive training**
A group of training procedures designed to change thoughts or thought patterns.

■ **Self-instruction**
A type of cognitive training technique that requires individuals to talk aloud and then to themselves as they solve problems.

■ **Self-monitoring**
A type of cognitive training technique that requires individuals to keep track of their own behavior.

■ **Scaffolded instruction**
A cognitive approach to instruction in which the teacher provides temporary structure or support while students are learning a task; the support is gradually removed as the students are able to perform the task independently.

SCAFFOLDED INSTRUCTION   In **scaffolded** instruction, assistance is provided to students when they are first learning tasks and then is gradually reduced so that eventually students do the tasks independently. For example, in one study, the teacher modeled a three-step strategy for writing, saying the steps aloud:

1. *Think*, who will read this, and why am I writing it?
2. *Plan* what to say using TREE (note Topic sentence, note Reasons, Examine reasons, note Ending).
3. *Write* and *Say More*. (Sexton, Harris, & Graham, 1998, p. 300)

While modeling the strategy, the students and teacher discussed various aspects of it, and the students gradually memorized the strategy and implemented it on their own.

■ **Reciprocal teaching**
A cognitive teaching strategy whereby the student gradually assumes the role of co-instructor for brief periods; the teacher models four strategies for the students to use: (1) predicting, (2) questioning, (3) summarizing, and (4) clarifying.

RECIPROCAL TEACHING   Like scaffolded instruction, **reciprocal teaching** involves an interactive dialogue between the teacher and students in which the teacher–student relationship is similar to that of an expert (teacher) and an apprentice (student). The teacher gradually relinquishes her or his role as the sole instructor and allows the student to assume the role of co-instructor for brief periods. The teacher models and encourages the students to use strategies. For example, in reading,

Reading Homework Exercise

Reciprocal Teaching • Go to the Homework and Exercises section in Chapter 6 of MyEducationLab and read the article titled "Reciprocal Teaching" in which this approach is used to facilitate an improved understanding of reading content.

teachers begin reading selections by having students make predictions based on story titles, headings, or other appropriate passage features. In this way, students are encouraged to activate background knowledge and information and to set a purpose for reading. Teachers then foster practice of good questioning strategies by requiring students to ask "teacher-like" questions rather than fill-in-the-blank questions. In addition, if students are unable to ask a question, the teacher might provide an appropriate question word as a prompt. Summarizing strategies for students include finding the main idea and supporting details and stating this information in their own words without looking at the text. Students are

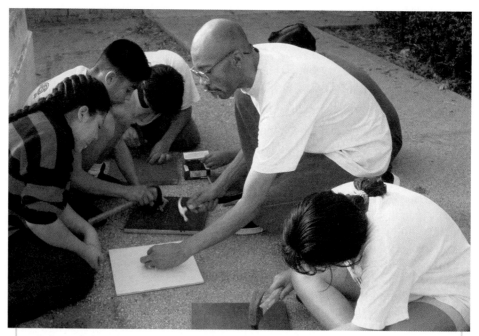

In scaffolded instruction, assistance is provided to students when they are first learning tasks and then is gradually reduced, so that eventually students perform tasks independently.

told to look for a topic sentence or to give a name to a list of items as ways to identify main ideas. Finally, students point out information that is unclear or unknown as they clarify new vocabulary, unfamiliar expressions, or ambiguous information. (Meese, 2001, p. 318)

Content Enhancement

Researchers have also found that enhancing the content of material can help students with learning disabilities (Gajria, Jitendra, Sood, & Sacks, 2007). **Content enhancement** can take many forms. It's a way of making materials more salient or prominent. Two particularly effective ways of enhancing content are graphic organizers and mnemonics. **Graphic organizers** "are visual devices that employ lines, circles, and boxes to organize information: hierarchic, cause/effect, compare/contrast, and cyclic or linear sequences" (Ellis & Howard, 2007, p. 1). **Mnemonics** involve using pictures and/or words to help remember information. For a description of mnemonics and how it can be used in the classroom, see the Responsive Instruction feature on p. 206.

Direct Instruction

Direct instruction (DI) focuses on the details of the instructional process. Advocates of DI stress a systematic analysis of the concept to be taught, rather than analysis of the characteristics of the student. A critical component of DI is task analysis. **Task analysis** involves breaking down academic problems into their component parts so that teachers can teach the parts separately and then teach the students to put the parts together in order to demonstrate the larger skill.

Originally pioneered by Sigfried Engelmann and the late Wesley C. Becker, a variety of DI programs are commercially available for reading and math. They consist of precisely sequenced, fast-paced lessons that are taught to small groups of four to ten students. There is a heavy emphasis on drill and practice. The teacher teaches from a

INTERNET RESOURCES

For more information on DI, visit the Association for Direct Instruction Website: www.adihome.org

Direct Instruction programs, which consist of precisely sequenced, fast-paced lessons taught to small groups of four to ten students, may bring both immediate and long-term academic gains in students with learning disabilities.

Meeting the Needs of Students with Learning Disabilities

Mnemonics

WHAT ARE MNEMONICS?

The term *mnemonic* comes from the name of the Greek goddess of memory, Mnemosyne. Mnemosyne's name was derived from mnemon, meaning mindful. Today, a mnemonic refers to any memory-enhancing strategy. Almost everyone has used a mnemonic at one time or another. To remember the order of the planets, many students learn the phrase "My Very Educated Mother Just Served Us Nine Pizzas." Music students trying to remember scales learn "Every Good Boy Deserves Fudge." Rhymes are another form of mnemonic— "I before E, except after C, or when pronounced as A as in neighbor and weigh." Mnemonics come in a variety of forms, but what defines a mnemonic is its ability to aid in the retention of certain information.

WHAT THE RESEARCH SAYS

It is well documented that many students with learning disabilities have difficulty remembering information and do not spontaneously engage in memory-enhancing strategies, such as rehearsal (Mastropieri & Scruggs, 1998). By the early 1980s, researchers had begun to conduct studies to identify strategies that would address these deficit areas. Although rehearsal was found to be an effective tool for increasing the retention of information, researchers found that memory strategies involving

pictures and elaboration had greater potential (Mastropieri & Scruggs, 1998). Using mnemonic strategies to help children with memory problems remember curriculum content, the teacher transforms abstract information into a concrete picture that depicts the material in a more meaningful way.

Researchers have studied mnemonics and students with learning disabilities in both laboratory settings (i.e., one-to-one with trained experimenters rather than classroom teachers) and classroom settings. Findings from these studies reveal the following gains made by students who were taught using mnemonics:

- Mnemonic keyword method resulted in increased recall of information.
- Small groups of students with learning disabilities could be taught using a variety of mnemonic strategies over a period of days without diminishing the effectiveness of the specific mnemonics.
- Mnemonic pictures aided in the comprehension and recall of information presented in science and history texts.
- Students with learning disabilities could be taught to create their own mnemonics and apply them successfully.
- Students with learning and behavior disorders benefited from teacher-created mnemonics and were able to retain the information longer than students who were not provided mnemonics.

---

well-rehearsed script, and pupils follow the lead of the teacher, who often uses hand signals to prompt participation. The teacher offers immediate corrective feedback for errors and praise for correct responses. See Responsive Instruction on page 208 for more information about DI in the classroom.

DI programs are among the best-researched commercial programs available for students with learning disabilities. Use of these programs not only results in immediate academic gains, but also may bring long-term academic gains (Ellis & Fouts, 1997; Tarver, 1999).

Peer Tutoring

Several types of peer tutoring arrangements have been used successfully with students with learning disabilities. Two examples are classwide peer tutoring and peer assisted learning. In Chapter 5, we discussed the use of classwide peer tutoring for students with intellectual disabilities. (See Responsive Instruction on p. 166 in Chapter 5.) **Classwide peer tutoring (CWPT)** has also been extensively documented as effective for students with learning disabilities or those at risk for learning disabilities (Kourea, Cartledge, & Musti-Rao, 2007; Maheady, Harper, & Mallette, 2003). Classwide peer tutoring consists of "students who are taught by peers who are *trained* and *supervised* by classroom teachers" (Maheady et al., p. 1). "Trained" and "supervised" are emphasized because it's imperative that the teachers carefully structure the tutoring experience. In other words, the instruction isn't just turned over to the students.

Video Homework Exercise

Peer Tutoring • Go to the Homework and Exercises section in Chapter 6 of MyEducationLab to watch the video "Peer Tutoring", in which elements of the tutoring strategies described by your authors are demonstrated.

- **Classwide peer tutoring (CWPT)**
An instructional procedure in which all students in the class are involved in tutoring and being tutored by classmates on specific skills as directed by their teacher.

Franklin Pierce (purse)
14 (forking)

FIGURE A Mnemonic representation of Franklin Pierce, fourteenth president of the United States

Source: Adapted from Mastropieri, M. A., Scruggs, T. E., & Whedon, C. (1997). Using mnemonic strategies to teach information about U.S. Presidents: A classroom-based investigation. *Learning Disability Quarterly, 20,* 13–21. Copyright 1994 by Thomas E. Scruggs and Margo A. Mastropieri.

■ Mnemonics appeared to result in increased motivation, efficacy, and willingness to learn. (Mastropieri & Scruggs, 1998)

IMPLEMENTING MNEMONICS IN THE CLASSROOM

Two effective mnemonic techniques are the keyword and pegword methods (Lasley, Matczynski, & Rowley, 2002). When using a keyword approach, students are taught how to transform an unfamiliar word to a familiar word. For example, the word accolade could be associated with the keyword Kool-Aid. To associate Kool-Aid with the definition of accolade, students can think of someone making a toast to a guest of honor with a cup of Kool-Aid. Thus, the definition "giving praise" will be closely associated with accolade (Levin, 1993).

To use the pegword strategy, students learn to correlate numbers with familiar rhyming words. The teacher creates a picture that incorporates the pegword along with the content associations. Teachers use this strategy when students need to remember the order of information or when there is a number association with the fact. For example, a student who is trying to remember that Monroe was the fifth president could combine the keyword money for Monroe and the pegword hive for five. The image of bees carrying money to a hive would be the mnemonic (Mastropieri & Scruggs, 1998).

Teachers working in inclusive settings find that mnemonics can be a useful strategy for both their special needs and general education students (see Mastropieri, Sweda, & Scruggs, 2000 for examples of inclusive classroom implementations).

EXAMPLE MNEMONIC

Figure A is an example of a mnemonic based on the keyword purse for Franklin Pierce and the pegword forking for fourteen. The "action" of the fork piercing the purse reinforces the connection between the two items and enhances the association students will need to recall.

● *By Kristin L. Sayeski*

Peer-assisted learning strategies (PALS) is based on research-proven, best practices in reading, such as phonological awareness, decoding, and comprehension strategies (D. Fuchs & Fuchs, 2005; D. Fuchs, Fuchs, & Burish, 2000). PALS involves the pairing of a higher performing student with a lower performing student, with the pairs then participating in highly structured tutoring sessions. The students take turns being the "coach" (tutor) and the "reader" (tutee).

INTERNET RESOURCES @

For more information on PALS, visit their Website: www.kc.vanderbilt.edu/kennedy/pals

Service Delivery Models

For many years, the most common form of educational placement for students with learning disabilities was the special education resource room. In the mid-1990s, however, in keeping with the trend toward inclusion, the general education classroom surpassed the resource room as the most popular placement. In addition, the number of placements in separate classrooms has gradually diminished. Forty-nine percent of students with learning disabilities between the ages of six and twenty-one are educated primarily in the regular classroom, with 37 percent being educated in resource rooms and 13 percent in separate classrooms (U.S. Department of Education, 2005).

As we discussed in Chapter 2, more and more schools are moving toward some kind of cooperative teaching arrangement, in which general and special education teachers work together in the general education classroom. Some advocates believe that this model is particularly appropriate for students with learning disabilities, since it allows them to stay in the

Meeting the Needs of Students with Learning Disabilities
Direct Instruction

WHAT IS DIRECT INSTRUCTION?

Direct instruction (DI) is a highly structured, teacher-directed method of instruction. The main features of DI programs are as follows:

- Field-tested, scripted lesson plans
- Curriculum based upon the theory of mastery learning (i.e., students do not move on until they have mastered the concept)
- Rapid pace of instruction highly dependent upon frequent teacher questioning and student response
- Achievement grouping
- Frequent assessments

Siegfried Englemann developed DI in the 1960s on the basis of studies of beginning reading. Since the development of his early DI programs such as DISTAR (Direct Instructional System for Teaching and Remediation), published in 1968, DI programs have been developed in the areas of reading, language arts, mathematics, science, and social studies. One of the defining features of DI programs is that virtually every aspect of instruction undergoes careful evaluation before it is approved for inclusion in the program. Researchers evaluate everything from group size to teacher directions to method of student response to achieve optimal effectiveness. As a result, DI programs have received the highest ranking for program effectiveness in an independent analysis of instructional programs (Ellis, 2001).

WHAT THE RESEARCH SAYS

To obtain an idea of the overall effectiveness of a program, researchers conduct what is called a meta-analysis. To conduct a meta-analysis, researchers identify all studies that have been conducted on a specific technique or program and statistically determine how effective the technique is as a whole. Since the inception of DI, several of these comprehensive evaluations have been conducted in regard to DI curriculum. A recent meta-analysis made over 173 comparisons between DI and other programs. Results showed that (1) 64 percent of the comparisons resulted in statistically significant differences in favor of the groups using DI, (2) 35 percent of the comparisons showed no differences among programs, and (3) 1 percent showed differences in favor of programs other than DI (Adams & Englemann, 1996). In short, the overall effectiveness of DI programs is among the highest in the field of education.

IMPLEMENTING THE CURRICULUM

To implement DI, teachers need to receive training in the program. Because of the highly structured nature of DI materials, many educators and administrators incorrectly assume that DI is "teacher-proof"; that is, anyone could be effective using the materials. Nothing could be further from the truth. Using the materials with ease, understanding the rationale for each component and therefore being able to communicate that to students, and pacing the instruction to meet the unique needs of a group of students requires teaching skills that cannot come from a script. After initial training, coaches or facilitators provide ongoing support for teachers who use DI programs to ensure that teachers are maximizing the effectiveness of the curriculum.

WHAT DOES DI LOOK LIKE?

The sample exercise in Figure A is an excerpt from Corrective Reading, an accelerated reading program for students in grades 3.5 through 12 who have not mastered the basics of decoding and comprehension. In this decoding lesson, students work on phonemic awareness, letter–symbol identification, and sounding out words. The use of choral response increases opportunities for student engagement, and individual questioning ensures individual mastery.

EXERCISE 3

Say the Sounds

Note: **Do not write the words on the board. This is an oral exercise.**

1. Listen: ffféēē. (Hold up a finger for each sound.)
2. Say the sounds in (pause) ffféēē. Get ready. (Hold up a finger for each sound.) ffféēē. (Repeat until the students say the sounds without stopping.)
3. Say it fast. (Signal.) Fee.
4. What word? (Signal.) Fee. Yes, fee.
5. (Repeat steps 2–4 for if, fish, sam, at, me, rim, she, we, ship, fat, miff.)

FIGURE A

● *By Kristin L. Sayeski*

general education classroom for all or almost all of their instruction. However, the research base for cooperative teaching is still in its infancy (Murawski & Swanson, 2001). See Making It Work on p. 210 for a description of a co-teaching situation in an 8th grade Algebra class.

Because students with learning disabilities make up the largest category of special education students and because their academic and behavioral problems are not as severe as those of students with intellectual disabilities or behavior disorders, they are often candidates for full inclusion. However, all the major professional and parent organizations have developed position papers against placing all students with learning disabilities in full-inclusion settings. Research on the effectiveness of inclusion for students with learning disabilities also argues against using full inclusion for *all* students with learning disabilities (Klingner, Vaughn, Hughes, Schumm, & Elbaum, 1998; Vaughn, Elbaum, & Boardman, 2001). Evidence indicates that the legal mandate of IDEA requiring the availability of a full continuum of placements is sound policy for students with learning disabilities.

Assessment of Progress

Assessment of students with learning disabilities typically focuses on academic skills. The following sections provide examples of assessments that are appropriate for monitoring student progress and assessing student outcomes in the areas of reading, mathematics, and written expression, each of which is an area of concern for many students with a learning disability. In addition, we discuss appropriate testing accommodations for students with learning disabilities.

Progress Monitoring

The notion of using assessment information to help plan educational strategies has gained much of its popularity from professionals working in the area of learning disabilities. For example, Curriculum Based Measurement (CBM) was developed largely by Deno and his colleagues (Deno, 1985; L. S. Fuchs, Deno, & Mirkin, 1984) of the University of Minnesota Institute for Research on Learning Disabilities (IRLD). Teachers of students with learning disabilities are using CBM increasingly as a means to monitor progress in academic subjects. In addition to CBM, teachers may administer other forms of informal assessments to monitor students' progress and make instructional decisions. This section provides a brief overview of CBM and other informal measures to monitor progress in the areas of mathematics, reading, and written expression.

CURRICULUM BASED MEASUREMENT **Curriculum Based Measurement (CBM)** involves direct and frequent samples of performance on items from the curriculum in which students are being instructed. Each curriculum-based measure has multiple forms of equivalent difficulty that are administered at regular intervals to determine whether a student is making progress toward a specified goal (McMaster & Espin, 2007). The measures are implemented as short probes that require only minutes to administer.

In reading, for example, CBM typically focuses on oral reading fluency (i.e., the number of words read correctly per minute on a graded passage). In order to monitor progress toward a specified goal, the teacher first gathers data to determine the student's current CWPM. This information is used to calculate a **baseline data point**. Using data of **expected growth norms** (see e.g., L. S. Fuchs, Fuchs, Hamlett, Walz, & Germann, 1993; Hosp, Hosp, & Howell, 2007), he or she establishes a goal for the student and creates an **aim line** on a graph to depict where the student should be performing at a given point in time. The teacher assesses the students reading on a CBM probe two or more times each week and graphs the data to determine if the student is on target to reach the specified goal.

Case Study Homework Exercise

Access to General Curriculum ● Go to the Homework and Exercises section in Chapter 6 of MyEducationLab to read a case study about one student's experiences with obtaining access to the general education system.

UNDERSTANDING STANDARDS AND PRINCIPLES What measures can teachers use to monitor student progress and plan for instruction? (CEC Knowledge and Skill Standards CC8S6, CC8S8, & LD8S1)

Council for Exceptional Children

■ **Curriculum-based measurement (CBM)**
A formative evaluation method designed to evaluate perfomance in the curriculum to which students are exposed; usually involves giving students a small sample of items from the curriculum in use in thier schools; proponents argue that CBM is preferable to comparing students with national norms or using tests that do not reflect the curriculum content learned by the students.

■ **Baseline data point**
Used in CBM; the beginning score gathered before an intervention begins, e.g., the number of correct words per minute that a student reads before receiving a fluency intervention.

■ **Expected growth norms**
Used with CBM; the rate at which the average student is expected to learn given typical instruction.

■ **Aim line**
Used in CBM; based on expected growth norms, a line drawn from the baseline data point to the anticipated end of instruction.

Collaboration and Co-Teaching for Students with Learning Disabilities

"How can she help me if she doesn't know algebra like I do?"

How can co-teaching with a special educator to meet the needs of students with learning disabilities work if the special educator is not as much of a content area specialist as the general educator? Though you might think that would mean an end to equal collaboration in, say, a biology or advanced literature course, teachers of students with learning disabilities have knowledge about learning that can help make them an active part of any co-teaching team.

WHAT DOES IT MEAN TO BE A TEACHER OF STUDENTS WITH LEARNING DISABILITIES?

Most programs for teachers of students with learning disabilities focus on the learning process and effective strategies for learning across the content areas. Specifically, the Council for Exceptional Children (2003) states that teachers of students with learning disabilities should be able to:

1. Use methods for teaching individuals to independently use cognitive processing to solve problems.
2. Use methods for guiding individuals in identifying and organizing critical content.
3. Use methods for ensuring individual academic success in one-to-one, small-group, and large-group settings.
4. Use instructional methods to strengthen and compensate for deficits in perception, comprehension, memory, and retrieval.
5. Identify and teach essential concepts, vocabulary, and content across the general curriculum.

SUCCESSFUL STRATEGIES FOR CO-TEACHING

Joan Hamilton is a former special educator who co-taught with general educators at the middle and high school level. She describes a situation in which she was not the content specialist but was able to provide explicit strategy instruction to all students because of a successful co-teaching arrangement.

I was originally certified to teach social studies from 8th–12th grades. When I began working in those classrooms, I realized that there were several students who really struggled to read the textbook I was using and I became interested in learning disabilities.

After earning a Masters in Special Education, one of my first positions required co-teaching in an 8th grade pre-Algebra classroom. I knew the material but wasn't as confident that I knew the best way to teach it. My co-teacher and I ended up with a class of eighteen students, eleven of whom were identified with disabilities (nine with learning disabilities) and the rest had done poorly in their previous math courses. The textbook prescribed a rigid plan for the classroom: review homework, teach the next lesson, do some practice problems. The pacing guide provided by the district (and part of my co-teacher's evaluation criteria) did not leave many opportunities for creativity in instruction. Though we were both on the same 8th grade team, we could use very little of the team meeting time to plan together. So, after many philosophical discussions, we plunged into the course. After a few weeks, we found a rhythm that seemed to work with the students.

First, my co-teacher taught the lesson as I took notes on the overhead for the students. I would often create a circle on the overhead with the example problem in the middle. As we worked the problem in the middle of the circle, I would use words to describe the step on the outside of the circle (see Rooney, 1998). This helped me understand how my co-teacher would teach the concept. And it provided the students with an annotated example problem.

Next, we both moved around the room to help students as they completed practice problems.

The next day, I did the homework review. This gave me the opportunity to return to the graphic organizers for review and to re-teach the steps of the problem as necessary (as my co-teacher had taught it earlier). It also allowed my co-teacher to circulate and to help individual students.

This co-teaching plan is probably a combination of the structures described in articles and books about co-teaching. It provided us with what we felt was the best support for our students, given the conditions of the classroom and curriculum. We had a few students fail the course because they just didn't even attempt to do much of the work. The majority, however, made it through the material and on to algebra with a basic understanding of the concepts and of how to structure their notes and ask questions.

● By Margaret P. Weiss

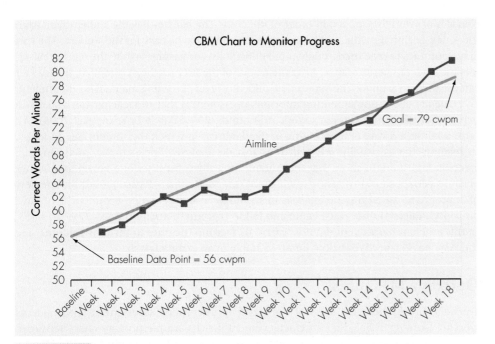

FIGURE 6.4 CBM chart to monitor progress. This graph is an example of progress monitoring using curriculum-based measurement on oral reading fluency for Billy, a fourth grader with a learning disability. Billy's teacher calculated his oral reading rate in correct words per minute at the beginning of the semester to determine his baseline data point (56 cwpm). Based on expected growth rates, she established a goal (79 cwpm) and created a graph with an aim line. The graph illustrates his average cwpm on probes throughout the semester. Billy's teacher was able to adjust instruction after week 8 of instruction and he exceeded his goal, reading 82 cwpm by the end of the semester

Figure 6.4 illustrates a CBM graph for a student, Billy, a fourth grader with learning disability. Billy's teacher had gathered the baseline data point and determined that he read 56 CWPM. She then created an aim line for eighteen weeks of instruction (one semester). Based on expected growth norms (L. S. Fuchs et al., 1993; Hosp et al., 2007) and his baseline data point for CWPM, his teacher determined that Billy should be reading seventy-nine correct words per minute by the end of the semester. After the first five weeks of instruction, Billy was on track to reach his goal by the end of the semester. However, during weeks 6 through 8, his CWPM began to decline such that it looked like he wouldn't be able to reach his goal. At this point, the teacher adjusted her instruction, by adding fifteen minutes per day of peer tutoring, two times a week. From that point on, Billy improved and actually exceeded his goal by the end of the semester.

Although oral reading fluency probes are the most common form of CBM, additional methods are used to monitor student progress in other areas of reading (e.g., phonemic awareness, decoding, and comprehension), mathematics, spelling, and writing. In mathematics, CBMs have been developed that span topics in early mathematics through secondary skills. As early as pre-kindergarten, students may participate in CBM to demonstrate their knowledge of mathematics through various tasks (e.g., circling numbers to demonstrate numeral identification; Foegen, Jiban, & Deno, 2007). For school-age students most CBMs focus on basic operations; however, CBM may be used for computation as well as conceptual knowledge.

INFORMAL ASSESSMENT   In addition to CBM, teachers may also use other informal measures to monitor student progress and plan for instruction. In the area of reading, for example, teachers can use an **informal reading inventory (IRI)**, a series of reading

■ **Informal reading inventory (IRI)**
A method of assessing reading in which the teacher has the student read progressively more difficult series of word lists and passages; the teacher notes the difficulty level of the material read and the types of errors the student makes.

passages or word lists graded in order of difficulty. The teacher has the student read from the series, beginning with a list or passage that is likely to be easy for the student. The student continues to read increasingly more difficult lists or passages while the teacher monitors the student's performance. After the results of the IRI have been compiled, the teacher can use them to estimate the appropriate difficulty level of reading material for the student.

One benefit of implementing informal assessment is that the teacher can also do an **error analysis** of the student's work (Riccomini, 2005; Salvia & Ysseldyke, 2004). An error analysis is a way of pinpointing particular areas in which the student has difficulty. In reading, this is usually referred to as miscue analysis. For example, analyzing the errors in an IRI might show that the student typically substitutes one vowel for another or omits certain sounds when reading aloud (see McKenna & Picard [2006] for a review of appropriate use of miscue analysis in reading). In mathematics, a student may have difficulty understanding place value and fail to regroup in addition (e.g., 27 + 14 = 33; In this problem the student did not "carry" or regroup the ones to the tens column). See the Personal Perspectives below for an example of an error analysis.

Outcome Measures

Teachers and psychologists use **standardized achievement assessment** with students who are learning disabled because achievement deficits are the primary characteristic of these students. Historically, standardized assessments have been administered to identify discrepancies between achievement and ability. Currently, standardized achievement tests are being administered for another purpose: documenting student outcomes. In this era of high-stakes testing and teacher accountability, it's necessary for teachers to document students' academic progress.

Several comprehensive standardized achievement tests used currently for this purpose assess multiple academic areas. For example, the Woodcock Johnson III Tests of Achievement (WJ-III; Woodcock, McGrew, & Mather, 2001) includes subtests in Letter-Word Identification, Reading Fluency, Passage Comprehension, Story Recall, Understanding

---

■ **Error analysis**
An informal method of teacher assessment that involves the teacher noting the particular kinds of errors a student makes when doing academic work.

■ **Standardized achievement assessment**
A method of evaluating a person that has been applied to a large group so that an individual's score can be compared to the norm, or average.

Personal P E R S P E C T I V E S

Ms. Lopez Conducts an Error Analysis

Teachers often use curriculum-based assessment and student work samples to analyze student errors and plan for instruction. Let's listen to a conversation in Ms. Lopez's room during a spelling lesson with Travis:

Ms. Lopez: Travis, let's look at the work you completed yesterday in spelling.

Travis: Okay.

Ms. Lopez: It looks like you had some trouble with the new vowel pattern we've been working on this week. What is your new vowel pattern?

Travis: Uh . . . the "ay?"

Ms. Lopez: That's right. Tell me the rule for the "ay" pattern.

Travis: Um . . . a long /a/ sound is spelled A-Y.

Ms. Lopez: Travis, a long /a/ sound at the end of a one-syllable word is spelled A-Y.

Travis: Oh yeah!

Ms. Lopez: Tell me some words on the list that have the "ay" pattern.

Travis: Um . . . "hay" and "play."

Ms. Lopez: Good. Those are some of the words with the "ay" pattern. Let's look through your spelling list again. The "ay" words are the only words that gave you trouble. I think you've figured out the "ee" words pretty well. We'll do a practice activity tomorrow on just the "ay" words, and I'll test you on just those words before we do the whole spelling list again. Okay, now let's take another look at those tricky "ay" words. . . .

Source: Meese, R. L. (2001). Teaching learners with mild disabilities: Integrating research and practice (2nd ed., p. 137). Stamford, CT: Wadsworth.

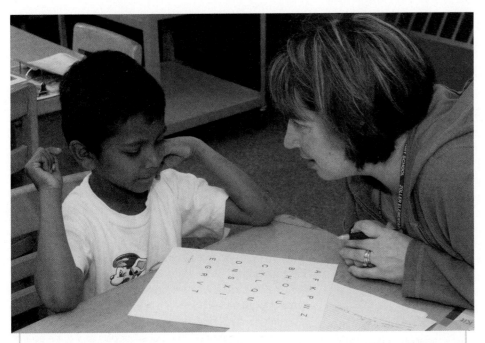

Formative assessments focus on how students perform in light of their abilities, rather than as compared with other students.

Directions, Calculation, Math Fluency, Applied Problems, Spelling, Writing Fluency, Writing Samples, Story Recall-Delayed, and Handwriting Legibility. Other achievement tests focus on specific areas, among them the KeyMath-3 (Pearson, 2007), the Test of Word Reading Efficiency (TOWRE; Torgesen, Wagner, & Rashotte, 1999), and the Test of Written Language, Third Edition (TOWL-III; Hammill & Larsen, 1996).

One limitation of most standardized instruments is that they can't be used to gain much insight into why students have difficulty. Teachers and clinicians use these tests primarily to identify students with learning problems and to provide gross indicators of academic strengths and weaknesses. However, these instruments do provide a means of documenting a student's abilities at a given point in time, for example, at the conclusion of a long-term intervention to demonstrate the efficacy of the instruction.

Testing Accommodations

Accommodations for students with learning disabilities are similar to those for students with intellectual disabilities as presented in Chapter 5. Many students with learning disabilities are provided accommodations on standardized tests that alter scheduling, presentation format, and response format. The most common accommodations for students with learning disabilities are extended time and small group setting administration. Some students with learning disabilities also receive accommodations such as dividing the assessment into multiple sessions and individual assessment. These accommodations are typically considered standard and do not alter the scoring of the test. Students with learning disabilities may also receive accommodations that are considered nonstandard and affect the scoring of the assessment. An example of a presentation accommodation for a student with a learning disability is to have directions read aloud. If reading is not the construct being tested, the problems may also be read aloud. For example, on an assessment of mathematics, a student may be able to have word problems read aloud.

Although testing accommodations are common for students with learning disabilities, particularly extended time, research is not clear on the effectiveness of testing accommodations. For example, it's not clear whether accommodations provide an

UNDERSTANDING THE STANDARDS AND PRINCIPLES Describe the features of the four general types of assessments that practitioners use with students with learning disabilities. (CEC Knowledge and Skills Standards CC8K1)

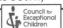

Meeting the Needs of Students with Learning Disabilities

Testing Accommodations

RATIONALE FOR TESTING ACCOMMODATIONS

The majority of individualized education programs (IEPs) developed for students with learning disabilities include testing accommodations. The rationale for providing test accommodations is twofold. First, testing accommodations should increase the participation of students with disabilities in standardized tests. Participation in statewide testing results in greater accountability in regard to the quality of instruction received as well as provides access to the "by-products" of testing such as placement in advanced classes, eligibility for awards or honors, etc. In other words, denying students with disabilities access to standardized testing can have the unanticipated result of lowering expectations and impeding desirable options.

The second reason for providing testing accommodations is to increase the likelihood that the resulting test scores are true indicators of what the student with the disability knows rather than a reflection of the disabling condition. One example of this is providing a test in braille for a student who is blind. With the braille accommodation, the resulting test score reflects what the student knows, not his or her lack of access to reading print.

RESEARCH ON TESTING ACCOMMODATIONS AND DIFFERENTIAL BOOST

Although testing accommodations for students with learning disabilities have become standard practice, there has not been extensive research on this issue (L. S. Fuchs, Fuchs, & Capizzi, 2005). The research that does exist, however, raises important questions related to their wholesale use. Specifically, if testing accommodations are designed to simply "level the playing field" for students with disabilities, then we would expect that giving accommodations to students *without* disabilities would not "boost" their scores. Yet, research on testing accommodations such as extended time (one of the most common accommodations provided) shows benefits for both students with disabilities and students without disabilities (Elliot & Marquart, 2004).

Some have described the desired accommodation effect in terms of a "differential boost" (Phillips, 1994). That is, if the same accommodation is given to students with disabilities and students without disabilities, the "boost" or gain should be evident in the scores of the students with disabilities to a marked degree over the scores of the students without disabilities. This idea that an accommodation should only benefit students with disabilities is also referred to as the "interaction hypothesis." (Sireci, Li, & Scarpati, 2003)

RESEARCH STUDY

A team of researchers set out to identify a set of accommodations for students with reading disabilities that would support the

opportunity for students to demonstrate their knowledge without unfair advantage, or whether the accommodations actually boost their performance. Likewise, more research is needed to determine how to best match testing accommodations for specific students. The Responsive Instruction Box above provides a brief overview of research findings on testing accommodations for students with learning disabilities.

Early Intervention

Casebook Reflections

REFER TO THE CASE *More Than LD* in your casebook. Her academic problems in school began immediately. Could more have been done to prevent her failure earlier? Why or why not? ●

Very little preschool programming is available for children with learning disabilities because of the difficulties in identification at such a young age. When we talk about testing preschool children for learning disabilities, we're really talking about *prediction* rather than *identification* because, strictly speaking, they haven't had much exposure to academics such as reading or math. Unfortunately, all other things being equal, prediction is always less precise than identification. In addition, in the preschool years some children do experience interaction hypothesis (Fletcher et al., 2006). They randomly assigned third graders with and without word-decoding reading disabilities to take a statewide Grade 3 reading test in either a standard or nonstandard administration.

Students in the nonstandard administration group received the following set of accommodations: (1) dividing the test session into 2 blocks of time, (2) reading the proper nouns to students, and (3) reading of question stems and possible responses. These accommodations were selected because they each address a particular characteristic of a student with word decoding difficulties. Breaking the test into two periods reduced testing fatigue. Similarly, decoding proper nouns for students with reading disabilities can be time consuming and frustrating. Therefore, reading proper nouns and reading the possible responses should offset those challenges but not place these students at an advantage over the students in the standard administration. The standard administration group were read the directions and monitored but they didn't receive any other interactive support.

RESEARCH FINDINGS

Test results indicated a significant improvement in the performance of the students with reading disabilities who received the accommodations package. Of particular interest to the researchers was the fact that the set of accommodations had no effect on the students without disabilities. Thus, this study appears to support the interaction hypothesis. In their summary, the researchers stated: "There was no effect of accommodations on the performance of the comparison group of average decoders, suggesting that the accommodations were specific to the students with poor decoding" (Fletcher et al., 2006, p. 146).

APPLYING THE RESEARCH TO TEACHING

The findings from this study demonstrate that it's possible to identify accommodations that are disability-specific and don't introduce an unfair advantage or mask a student's true knowledge and skills. Unfortunately, research has shown that teachers aren't very effective when choosing accommodations. In particular, they sometimes fail to select accommodations that result in benefit for the student (L. S. Fuchs et al., 2005). In many of these cases, the teachers fail to select disability-specific accommodations and simply choose accommodations from a generic list. One way for teachers to improve their selections is to apply various accommodations with the student and measure the effects. Teachers can use the *Dynamic Assessment of Test Accommodations™* (*DATA*) (L. S. Fuchs, Fuchs, Eaton, & Hamlett, 2003) to aid in the process of selecting valid accommodations (L. S. Fuchs et al., 2005). Whether teachers use a formal tool such as *DATA* or test various accommodations more informally, IEP teams should approach the process of selecting accommodations with the same care that is applied to the selection of IEP goals and objectives.

● *By Kristin L. Sayeski*

developmental delays. Some nondisabled children show slow developmental progress at this young age but soon catch up with their peers.

Even though it's wise to be cautious in identifying preschool children as learning disabled, researchers have determined that there are several risk factors that are relatively good predictors of later learning disabilities. Table 6.1 provides a list of developmental milestones parents and teachers should monitor in the preschool years.

Transition to Adulthood

At one time, professionals thought that children outgrew their learning disabilities by adulthood. We now know that this is far from the truth. Although the long-term prognosis for individuals with learning disabilities is generally more positive than that for children with some other disabilities (e.g., behavior disorders), there is still the potential for difficulty. Although the majority of students with learning disabilities don't drop out of school, they are at a higher risk than nondisabled students for dropping out. Also, many adults with learning disabilities have persistent problems in learning, socializing, holding jobs, and living independently (Blackorby & Wagner,

UNDERSTANDING STANDARDS AND PRINCIPLES What can individuals with learning disabilities expect as they transition to adulthood? (CEC Knowledge and Skill Standards TS5K1, CC3K1, & LD10K2)

Council for Exceptional Children

TABLE 6.1	Important Developmental Milestones

- Delay in comprehension and/or expression of spoken language
  - Limited receptive vocabulary
  - Reduced expressive vocabulary ("late talkers")
  - Difficulty understanding simple (e.g., one-step) directions
  - Monotone or other unusual prosodic features of speech
  - Reduced intelligibility
  - Infrequent or inappropriate spontaneous communication (vocal, verbal, or nonverbal)
  - Immature syntax

- Delay in emergent literacy skills
  - Slow speed in naming objects and colors
  - Limited phonological awareness (e.g., rhyming, syllable blending)
  - Minimal interest in print
  - Limited print awareness (e.g., book handling, recognizing environmental print)

- Delay in perceptual-motor skills
  - Problems in gross- or fine-motor coordination (e.g., hopping, dressing, cutting, stringing beads
  - Difficulty in coloring, copying, and drawing

Source: Adapted from National Joint Committee on Learning Disabilities. (2006). *Learning disabilities and young children: Identification and intervention.* Retrieved July 27, 2007 from the World Wide Web. http://www.ldonline.org/article/11511

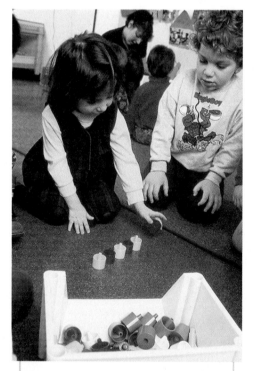

Some of the most accurate predictors of learning problems in preschool that may show up later are emergent literacy skills, such as counting and identifying letters, numbers, shapes, and colors.

1997; Gerber, 1997; Goldstein, Murray, & Edgar, 1998; Witte, Philips, & Kakela, 1998). Even those individuals who are relatively successful in their transition to adulthood often must devote considerable energy to coping with daily living situations.

Factors Related to Successful Transition

How any particular adult with learning disabilities will fare depends on a variety of factors and is difficult to predict. Several researchers have addressed the topic of what contributes to successful adjustment of adults with learning disabilities (Bear, Kortering, & Braziel, 2006; Gerber, Ginsberg, & Reiff, 1992; Kavale, 1988; Lindstrom & Benz, 2002; Raskind, Goldberg, Higgins, & Herman, 1999; Reiff, Gerber, & Ginsberg, 1997; Spekman, Goldberg, & Herman, 1992). Although it would seem that IQ and achievement would be the best predictors of success, according to successful adults with learning disabilities, the things that set them apart from those who are not as successful are the following:

- An extraordinary degree of perseverance
- The ability to set goals for oneself
- A realistic acceptance of weaknesses coupled with an attitude of building on strengths
- Access to a strong network of social support from friends and family
- Exposure to intensive and long-term educational intervention
- High quality on-the-job or postsecondary vocational training
- A supportive work environment
- Being able to take control of their lives

The last attribute, in particular, is a consistent theme among the successful. They have not let their disability rule them; rather, they have taken the initiative to control their own destiny. As one adult remarked, on looking back at his days in secondary school:

> Having an LD is much akin to being blind or losing the use of an appendage; it affects all aspects of your life. In dealing with this, you have two choices. One, you can acknowledge the parasitic relationship the LD has with you and consciously strive to excel despite its presence. . . . The other path let[s] the LD slowly dominate you and become[s] the scapegoat for all your failings. Can't find a good job? Must be the LD. Relationships always fail? It's the LD. If you follow this destructive path, you spend the remainder of your life being controlled by your LD. (Queen, 2001, p. 15)

Secondary Programming

Approaches to educating students with learning disabilities at the secondary level differ, depending on whether the goal is to prepare students for college or work. Students whose goal is to enter work after high school are taught basic academic skills in math, language arts, and reading. They're also taught functional skills, such as on-the-job behavior, filling out job applications, and balancing a checkbook. It's often combined with work-study—supervised work experiences during the school day. Ideally, the student is able to explore a variety of jobs that might be of interest to her or him.

Those students intending to pursue college work are provided with continued support in their academic subjects. Compared to elementary school, the role of the special education teacher typically shifts even more to one of consultation with the general education teachers in the content areas (e.g., math, history, science). The general education teacher teaches the content, and the special education teacher recommends modifications to the format of the content and teaches the student strategies for learning. For example, the learning strategies model developed at the University of Kansas Center for Research on Learning focuses on teaching students to overcome their metacognitive deficits by using learning strategies (Deshler et al., 2001). The Kansas group has developed a variety of strategies that students can use to help them organize information and learn it more efficiently.

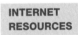

INTERNET RESOURCES

For more information on the University of Kansas Center for Research on Learning, visit www.ku-crl.org

Postsecondary Programming

Postsecondary programs include vocational and technical programs as well as community colleges and four-year colleges and universities. More and more individuals with learning disabilities are enrolling in colleges and universities, and more and more universities are establishing special programs and services for these students. In the 1990s, for example, the percentage of entering first-year college students with learning disabilities nearly tripled—from 1.2 percent to 3.5 percent (Henderson, 1999, as cited in Hitchings et al., 2001).

Secondary school teachers should prepare their students to make the right choices of colleges and help them to delineate what accommodations they will need in their programs. Students and their families may take advantage of published guides to college programs for students with learning disabilities (Cobb, 2003; Peterson, 2003; Wax & Kravets, 2003). Also, students can avail themselves of the special accommodations available for students who are learning disabled when they take the Scholastic Aptitude Test (SAT) and the American College Test (ACT).

In selecting a college, students and their families should explore what kinds of student support services are offered. Section 504 of the Vocational Rehabilitation Act of 1973 (Public Law 93–112) requires that colleges make reasonable accommodations for students with disabilities so that they will not be

Casebook Reflections

REFER TO THE CASE *More Than LD* in your casebook. Shannon wants to be a teacher or work for a TV station. What supports might be available to her in college to help her be more successful? ●

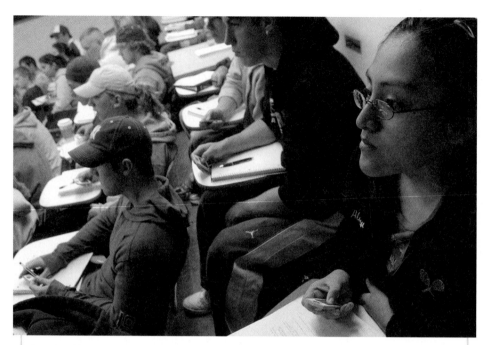

A major difficulty faced by students with learning disabilities in the transition from high school to college is the decrease in the amount of guidance provided by adults, and the greater demand on self-discipline.

discriminated against because of their disabilities. Some typical accommodations are extended time on exams, allowing students to take exams in a distraction-free room, providing tape recordings of lectures and books, and assigning volunteer note-takers for lectures. In addition, two key ingredients are *comprehensiveness* and *individualization*.

> With these support services in mind, there are two overall considerations in selecting a college program: comprehensiveness and individualization. The prospective student should consider the comprehensiveness of services offered. A service plan that includes some type of summer orientation and training program, tutoring in various classes, assessment as needed, emotional support, and accommodations in program planning should meet the needs of most students. However, even when comprehensive services are provided, an individually tailored program is critical. Students should not settle for a program that attempts to fit all students with learning disabilities into one standard program. Rather, case managers should meet with the student with learning disabilities to individually plan appropriate services. (Bender, 2004, p. 384)

A potentially useful skill for college students with learning disabilities is *self-advocacy*: the ability to understand one's disability, be aware of one's legal rights, and communicate one's rights and needs to professors and administrators (Hitchings et al., 2001). Although ideally self-advocacy skills should be taught to students with learning disabilities in secondary school, many students come to college in need of guidance in how to advocate for themselves in a confident but nonconfrontational manner.

There is little doubt that much remains to be learned about programming effectively for students with learning disabilities at the postsecondary level. However, the field has made great strides in opening windows of opportunity for these young adults. Authorities have noted that many college applicants with learning disabilities try to hide their disabilities for fear that they will not be admitted (Gerber, 2006). If the burgeoning interest in postsecondary programming for individuals who are learning disabled continues, we may in the near future see the day when students and colleges routinely collaborate to use information about students' learning disabilities in planning their programs.

Summary

How do professionals define learning disabilities?

▶ The most common definition is that of the federal government, which has been in effect since 1977 (with a few minor wording changes in 1997).

▶ The National Joint Committee on Learning Disabilities presented a definition that differs from the federal government's with respect to (1) no reference to psychological processes, (2) inclusion of intrinsic nature of learning disabilities, (3) inclusion of adults, (4) inclusion of self-regulation and social interaction problems, (5) omission of terms difficult to define, (6) purportedly less confusion regarding the exclusion clause, and (7) omission of spelling.

How do professionals identify students with learning disabilities?

▶ Since the late 1970s, the major method of identifying learning disabilities has been by looking for an IQ–achievement discrepancy.

▶ More recently, professionals have proposed that a response-to-intervention (RTI) approach be used.
  ■ RTI is based on a multi-tiered model of prevention.
  ■ A variety of RTI models have been proposed and implemented.
  ■ Many questions still remain regarding large-scale implementation of RTI.

What is the prevalence of learning disabilities?

▶ Between 5 and 6 percent of school-age students are identified as learning disabled, making learning disabilities the largest category of special education by far.

▶ The prevalence of learning disabilities has more than doubled since the late 1970s.
  ■ Some believe this increase reflects poor diagnostic practices.
  ■ Some believe that some of the increase may be due to social and cultural changes as well as reluctance to label students "mentally retarded."

▶ Boys with learning disabilities outnumber girls about 3 to 1.
  ■ Some believe that this is due to gender bias in referrals.
  ■ Some believe that this is partly due to boys being more vulnerable biologically.

What causes learning disabilities?

▶ With the advance of neuroimaging techniques, most authorities now believe that central nervous system dysfunction underlies learning disabilities.

▶ There is strong evidence that many cases of learning disabilities are inherited.

▶ Teratogens (e.g., fetal alcohol syndrome) and medical factors (premature birth) can also result in learning disabilities.

What are some of the psychological and behavioral characteristics of learners with learning disabilities?

▶ Persons with learning disabilities exhibit interindividual and intraindividual variability.

▶ Academic deficits are the hallmark of learning disabilities.
  ■ Reading disabilities are the most common form of academic disability and can be manifested in decoding, fluency, and comprehension problems.
    ■ Phonological awareness, the understanding that speech consists of units of sound (words, syllables, phonemes), underlies the ability to decode.
    ■ Phonemic awareness—understanding that words are made up of sounds or phonemes—is particularly important for learning to decode.
  ■ Writing disabilities, including handwriting, spelling and composition, are common in students with learning disabilities.
  ■ Spoken language disabilities include problems with syntax (grammar), semantics (word meanings), phonology, and pragmatics (social uses of language).
  ■ Math disabilities include problems with computation and word problems.

▶ Some students with learning disabilities experience problems with perceptual, perceptual-motor, and general coordination.

▶ Many students with learning disabilities have problems with attention, and there is an overlap of 10 to 25 percent between learning disabilities and attention deficit hyperactivity disorder (ADHD).

▶ Memory problems include problems with short-term memory and working memory.

▶ Metacognitive problems include deficits in recognizing task requirements, selecting and using appropriate strategies, and monitoring and adjusting performance.

▶ Social-emotional problems include peer rejection, poor self-concept, and poor social cognition.
  ■ Problems with social interaction are more prevalent in students with problems with math, visual-spatial and tactual tasks, and self-regulation; such students are sometimes referred to as having nonverbal learning disabilities.
  ■ Motivational problems can include having an external locus of control and learned helplessness.
  ■ Some authorities believe that a composite of many of the preceding characteristics indicates that many students with learning disabilities are passive rather than active learners.

What are some educational considerations for learners with learning disabilities?

▶ Cognitive training focuses on (1) changing thought processes, (2) providing strategies for learning, and (3) teaching self-initiative.
  - *Self-instruction* involves having students say out loud what it is they are to do.
  - *Self-monitoring* involves having students self-evaluate and self-record while they are doing academic work.
  - *Scaffolded instruction* involves providing students with teacher support while they perform academic work.
  - *Reciprocal teaching* involves teacher modeling correct performance and then having the student assume the role of co-teacher while using four strategies: predicting, questioning, summarizing, and clarifying.

▶ *Content enhancement* involves increasing the saliency of instructional materials.

▶ *Direct Instruction* (DI) focuses even more directly on academics than does cognitive training; a critical component of DI is task analysis, as well as the following:
  - Field-tested scripted lessons
  - Curricula based on mastery learning
  - Rapid instructional pace
  - Achievement grouping
  - Frequent assessments

▶ Peer tutoring involves students with learning disabilities being tutored by nondisabled classmates who are supervised and trained by the teacher.

▶ With respect to service delivery models, available research evidence indicates that a full continuum of placements is sound policy for students with learning disabilities.

How do professionals assess students with intellectual disabilities' academic progress?

▶ Curriculum-based measurement (CBM) (brief samplings of academic performance) can be used to assess progress.
  - In reading, CBM typically focuses on correct words read per minute.
  - CBM involves comparing the student's performance relative to a baseline point and an aim line based on expected growth norms.

▶ Informal reading inventories can be used to assess progress.

▶ Accommodations on standardized tests can included changes in scheduling and presentation and response formats.

What are some things to consider with respect to early intervention for learners with learning disabilities?

▶ Little preschool programming exists for children with learning disabilities because it's so hard to predict at that age which children will later develop academic problems.

▶ Even though prediction is not perfect, there are several developmental milestones related to comprehension or expression of spoken language, emergent literacy skills, and perceptual skills that indicate risk for having learning disabilities.

What are some things to consider with respect to transition to adulthood for learners with learning disabilities?

▶ Factors related to successful transition include the following:
  - Extraordinary perseverance
  - Setting goals
  - Acceptance of weaknesses, combined with building on strengths
  - Strong network of social support
  - Intensive and long-term educational intervention
  - High-quality on-the-job or postsecondary vocational training
  - Supportive work environment
  - Taking control of one's life

▶ Secondary programming varies according to whether the goal is to prepare for work or college after graduation.
  - Those preparing for work receive training in basic academic skills, functional skills, and supervised work experiences.
  - Those preparing for college receive further academic training with support services from a special educator.

▶ Postsecondary programs include vocational and technical programs as well as community colleges and four-year colleges and universities.

▶ More and more students with learning disabilities are attending college; two key components to look for in college programs are comprehensiveness and individualization.

STANDARDS and PRINCIPLES in this Chapter

SPECIAL EDUCATORS . . .

■ understand how changes in the field of special education influence professional practice, including assessment, instructional planning, implementation, and program evaluation (from CEC Content Standard #1).

■ understand the similarities and differences in human development and the characteristics between and among individuals with and without exceptional learning needs (from CEC Content Standard #2).

■ possess a repertoire of evidence-based instructional strategies to individualize instruction for individuals with exceptional learning needs (from CEC Content Standard #4).

■ use the results of assessments to help identify exceptional learning needs and to develop and implement individualized instructional programs, as well as to adjust instruction in response to ongoing learning progress (from CEC Content Standard #8).

ALL TEACHERS. . .

■ understand the central concepts, tools of inquiry and structures of the discipline(s) they teach and can create learning experiences that make these aspects of subject matter meaningful for students (INTASC Principle #1).

■ understand how children learn and develop, and can provide learning opportunities that support the intellectual, social, and personal development of each learner (INTASC Principle #2).

■ understand and use a variety of instructional strategies to encourage students' development of critical thinking, problem solving, and performance skills (INTASC Principle #4).

■ understand and use formal and informal assessment strategies to evaluate and ensure the continuous intellectual, social, and physical development of the learner (INTASC Principle #8).

Applying the **STANDARDS** and **PRINCIPLES**

■ ONE of your colleagues, whose background is in general education, asks, "What does it really mean to have a learning disability?" How would you respond? (CEC Content Standard #1 & #2; INTASC Principle #1 & #2)

■ WHICH procedure (i.e., IQ-achievement discrepancy or response to intervention) do you think should be used to identify learning disabilities? Explain. (CEC Content Standard #8 & INTASC Principle #8)

■ THE parent of a second grader with a learning disability approaches you to discuss her son's difficulties in reading. "My son doesn't seem to understand that words are made up of sounds. What approaches would work with him?" How would you respond? (CEC Content Standard #4 & INTASC Principle #4)

Now go to the Hallahan/Kauffman, Eleventh Edition MyEducationLab course at www.myeducationlab.com to:

- take a Pretest to assess your initial comprehension of the chapter content;
- study chapter content with your Individualized Study Plan;
- take a Posttest to assess your understanding of chapter content;
- engage in multimedia exercises to help you build a deeper and more applied understanding of chapter content.

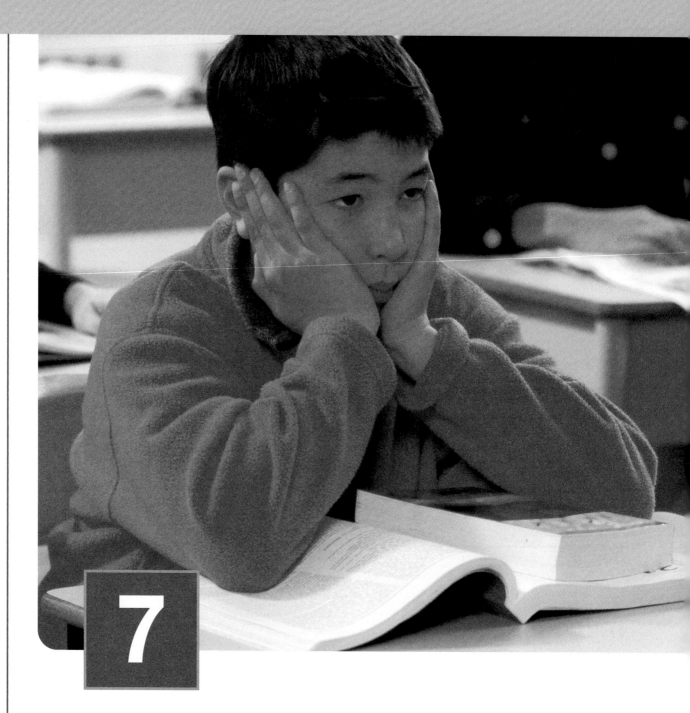

7

Learners with Attention Deficit Hyperactivity Disorder

L et me see if Philip can
Be a little gentleman.
Let me see, if he is able
To sit still for once at table;
Thus Papa bade Phil behave;
And Mamma look'd very grave.
But fidgety Phil,
He won't sit still;
He wriggles
And giggles,
And then, I declare
Swings backwards and forwards
And tilts up his chair,
Just like any rocking horse;
"Philip! I am getting cross!"

—Heinrich Hoffmann
"The Story of Fidgety Philip"

QUESTIONS to guide your reading of this chapter . . .

- What are the historical origins of ADHD?

- What is the current definition of ADHD?

- What is the prevalence of ADHD?

- What methods of assessment are used to identify individuals with ADHD?

- What causes ADHD?

- What are some of the psychological and behavioral characteristics of learners with ADHD?

- What are some educational considerations for learners with ADHD?

- What are some medication considerations for learners with ADHD?

- How do professionals assess students with ADHD's academic, attention, and behavioral progress?

- What are some things to consider with respect to early intervention for learners with ADHD?

- What are some things to consider with respect to transition to adulthood for learners with ADHD?

MISCONCEPTIONS ABOUT

Learners with Attention Deficit Hyperactivity Disorder

MYTH ■ All children with ADHD are hyperactive.

FACT ■ Psychiatric classification of ADHD includes (1) ADHD, Predominantly Inattentive Type, (2) ADHD, Predominantly Hyperactive-Impulsive Type, or (3) ADHD, Combined Type. Some children with ADHD exhibit no hyperactivity and are classified as ADHD, Predominantly Inattentive.

MYTH ■ The primary symptom of ADHD is inattention.

FACT ■ Although the psychiatric classification includes an Inattentive Type, recent conceptualizations of ADHD place problems with behavioral inhibition, executive function, time awareness and management, and goal-directed behavior as the primary behavioral problems of ADHD.

MYTH ■ ADHD is a fad, a trendy diagnosis of recent times in the United States with little research to support its existence.

FACT ■ Reports of cases of ADHD go back to the mid-nineteenth century and the beginning of the twentieth century. Serious scientific study of it began in the early and mid-twentieth century. There is now a firmly established research base supporting its existence. And the prevalence of ADHD in several other countries is at least as high as it is in the United States.

MYTH ■ ADHD is primarily the result of minimal brain injury.

FACT ■ In most cases of ADHD there is no evidence of actual damage to the brain. Most authorities believe that ADHD is the result of neurological dysfunction, which is often linked to hereditary factors.

MYTH ■ The social problems of students with ADHD are due to their not knowing how to interact socially.

FACT ■ Most people with ADHD know how to interact, but their problems with behavioral inhibition make it difficult for them to implement socially appropriate behaviors.

MYTH ■ Using psychostimulants, such as Ritalin, can easily turn children into abusers of other substances, such as cocaine and marijuana.

FACT ■ There is no evidence that using psychostimulants for ADHD leads directly to drug abuse. In fact, there is evidence that those who are prescribed Ritalin as children are less likely to turn to illicit drugs as teenagers. However, care should be taken to make sure that children or others do not misuse the psychostimulants prescribed for them.

MYTH ■ Psychostimulants have a "paradoxical effect" in that they subdue children rather than activate them. Plus, they have this effect only on those with ADHD.

FACT ■ Psychostimulants, instead of sedating children, actually activate parts of the brain responsible for behavioral inhibition and executive functions. In addition, this effect occurs in persons without ADHD, too.

MYTH ■ Because students with ADHD react strongly to stimulation, their learning environments should be highly unstructured in order to take advantage of their natural learning styles.

FACT ■ Most authorities recommend a highly structured classroom for students with ADHD, especially in the early stages of instruction.

Fidgety Phil, the character in the poem by the German physician Heinrich Hoffmann (1865) (see p. 223), is generally considered one of the first allusions in Western literature to what today is referred to as attention deficit hyperactivity disorder (ADHD) (Barkley, 2006c). Phil's lack of impulse control bears an uncanny similarity to today's conceptualization of ADHD as less a matter of inattention than a matter of regulating one's behavior. We discuss this conceptualization more fully later, but it's also important to point out here that Phil's excessive motor activity, or hyperactivity, may be characteristic of many children with ADHD but not all. Interestingly, Hoffman also wrote another poem, "The Story of Johnny Head-in-Air," about a child who fits to a T children with ADHD who do not have problems with hyperactivity.

The fact that the condition was recognized as early as the mid-nineteenth century, albeit only in the form of a "poetic case study," is important. Today, ADHD is often the subject of criticism, being referred to as a phantom or bogus condition—sort of a fashionable, trendy diagnosis for people who are basically lazy and unmotivated. Such thinking is probably one of the reasons why ADHD is not recognized as its own separate category (as are learning disabilities, deafness, blindness, and so forth) by the U.S. Department of Education (USDE); according to the USDE, students with ADHD are to be served by special education under the category of "other health impaired."

Although there are undoubtedly a few people who hide behind an inappropriate diagnosis of ADHD, evidence indicates that the condition is extremely real for those who have it. And, as we point out in the next section, ADHD is not a recently "discovered," trendy diagnosis.

Brief History

In addition to Hoffmann's mid-nineteenth century account of Fidgety Phil, there is evidence of a more scientific nature of the existence of ADHD, dating back to the beginning of the twentieth century.

Still's Children with "Defective Moral Control"

Dr. George F. Still, a physician, is credited as one of the first authorities to bring the condition we now call ADHD to the attention of the medical profession. Still delivered three lectures to the Royal College of Physicians of London in 1902 in which he described cases of children who displayed spitefulness, cruelty, disobedience, impulsivity, and problems of attention and hyperactivity. He referred to them as having "defective moral control" (Still, 1902, p. 1008). In the language of his day, what Still was essentially saying was that these children were lacking in their ability to inhibit or refrain from engaging impulsively in inappropriate behavior. See Figure 7.1.

Although Still's words are more than a century old, they still hold currency; one of the most influential current psychological theories is based on the notion that an essential impairment in ADHD is a deficit involving behavioral inhibition (Barkley, 1997, 2000a, 2000b, 2006e). Still's cases were also similar to today's population of persons with ADHD in at least five ways:

1. Still speculated that many of these children had mild brain pathology.
2. Many of the children had normal intelligence.
3. The condition was more prevalent in males than females.
4. There was evidence that the condition had a hereditary basis.
5. Many of the children and their relatives also had other physical or psychological problems, such as depression and tics.

INTERNET RESOURCES

You can see the "Fidgety Philip" and "Johnny-Head-in-Air" nursery rhymes complete with illustrations at www.fln.vcu.edu/struwwel/guck_e.html and www.fln.vcu.edu/struwwel/philipp_e.htm

INTERNET RESOURCES

In 1998, The National Institutes of Health brought together a panel of experts from a variety of disciplines, including medicine, psychology, and special education, to arrive at consensus regarding identification and treatment of ADHD. Although they concluded that more research was needed on various issues, they affirmed the validity of ADHD: "Although an independent diagnostic test for ADHD does not exist, there is evidence supporting the validity of the disorder." (Diagnosis and Treatment of Attention Deficit Hyperactivity Disorder. NIH Consensus Statement Online 1998, Nov. 16–18). To see the complete NIH consensus statement, go to http://consensus.nih .gov/1998/1998AttentionDeficit-HyperactivityDisorder110html.htm

> ## The Goulstonian Lectures
>
> ON
>
> SOME ABNORMAL PSYCHICAL CONDITIONS IN CHILDREN.
>
> *Delivered before the Royal College of Physicians of London on March 4th, 6th, and 11th, 1902.*
>
> BY GEORGE F. STILL, M.A., M.D. CANTAB., F.R.C.P. LOND.,
>
> ASSISTANT PHYSICIAN FOR DISEASES OF CHILDREN, KING'S COLLEGE HOSPITAL;
>
> ASSISTANT PHYSICIAN TO THE HOSPITAL FOR SICK CHILDREN, GREAT ORMOND-STREET.
>
> ### LECTURE I.
>
> *Delivered on March 4th.*
>
> MR. PRESIDENT AND GENTLEMEN,—The particular psychical conditions with which I propose to deal in these lectures are those which are concerned with an abnormal defect of moral control in children. Interesting as these disorders may be as an abstruse problem for the professed psychologist to puzzle over, they have a very real practical— shall I say social?—importance which I venture to think has been hardly sufficiently recognised. For some years past I have been collecting observations with a view to investigating the occurrence of defective moral control as a morbid condition in children, a subject which I cannot but think calls urgently for scientific investigation.
>
> *Source:* Still, G. F. (1902). Some abnormal psychical conditions in children. *The Lancet, 1,* 1008–1012.

FIGURE 7.1 A reproduction of Dr. George Still's opening remarks for his classic lectures on children with "defective moral control."

■ **Conduct disorder**
A disorder characterized by overt, aggressive, disruptive behavior or covert antisocial acts such as stealing, lying, and fire setting; may include both overt and covert acts.

We return later to Barkley's theory and to these five points. Suffice it to say here that Still's children with "defective moral control" today would very likely be diagnosed as having ADHD by itself or ADHD with **conduct disorder**. Conduct disorder, which we discuss more fully in Chapter 8, is characterized by a pattern of aggressive, disruptive behavior.

Goldstein's Brain-Injured Soldiers of World War I

■ **Perseveration**
A tendency to repeat behaviors over and over again; often found in people with brain injury, as well as those with ADHD.

Kurt Goldstein reported on the psychological effects of brain injury in soldiers who had suffered head wounds in combat in World War I. Among other things, he observed in his patients the psychological characteristics of disorganized behavior, hyperactivity, **perseveration**, and a "forced responsiveness to stimuli"(1936, 1939). Perseveration, the tendency to repeat the same behaviors over and over again, is often cited today by clinicians as a characteristic of persons with ADHD. Goldstein found that the soldiers' forced responsiveness to stimuli was evident in their inability to concentrate perceptually on the "figure" without being distracted by the "ground." For example, instead of focusing on a task in front of them (the figure), they were easily distracted by objects on the periphery (the background).

The Strauss Syndrome

Goldstein's work laid the foundation for the investigations of Heinz Werner and Alfred Strauss in the 1930s and 1940s. Having emigrated from Germany to the United States after Hitler's rise to power, Werner and Strauss teamed up to try to replicate Goldstein's findings. They noted the same behaviors of distractibility and hyperactivity in some children with mental retardation (intellectual disabilities).

In addition to clinical observations, Werner and Strauss used an experimental task consisting of figure/background slides that were presented at very brief exposure times. The slides depicted figures (e.g., a hat) embedded in a background (e.g., wavy lines). Werner and Strauss found that the children with supposed brain damage, when asked what they saw, were more likely than those without brain damage to say that they had seen the background (e.g., "wavy lines") rather than the figure (e.g., "a hat") (Strauss & Werner, 1942; Werner & Strauss, 1939, 1941). After these studies, professionals came to refer to children who were apparently hyperactive and distractible as exhibiting the **Strauss syndrome**.

Cruickshank's Work

William Cruickshank and colleagues, using Werner and Strauss's figure/background task, found that children with cerebral palsy were also more likely to respond to the background than to the figure (Cruickshank, Bice, & Wallen, 1957). There were two important ways in which this research extended the work of Werner and Strauss. First, whereas Werner and Strauss had largely assumed that their children were brain damaged, Cruickshank's children all had **cerebral palsy**, a condition that's relatively easy to diagnose. Cerebral palsy is characterized by brain damage that results in impairments in movement (see Chapter 13). Second, the children Cruickshank studied were largely of normal intelligence, thus demonstrating that children without mental retardation (intellectual disabilities) could display distractibility and hyperactivity.

Cruickshank is also important historically because, as we discuss later in this chapter, he was one of the first to establish an educational program for children who today would meet the criteria for ADHD. At the time (the late 1950s), however, many of these children were referred to as "minimally brain injured."

Minimal Brain Injury and Hyperactive Child Syndrome

At about the same time as Cruickshank's extension of Werner and Strauss's work with children of normal intelligence, the results of a now classic study were published (Pasamanick, Lilienfeld, & Rogers, 1956). This study of the aftereffects of birth complications revived Still's (1902) notion that subtle brain pathology could result in behavior problems, such as hyperactivity and distractibility. Professionals began to apply the label of **minimal brain injury** to children of normal intelligence who were inattentive, impulsive, and/or hyperactive. Although popular in the 1950s and 1960s, the "minimal brain injury" label fell out of favor as professionals pointed out that it was difficult to document actual tissue damage to the brain (Birch, 1964).

"Minimal brain injury" was replaced in the 1960s by the label "hyperactive child syndrome" (Barkley, 2006c). **Hyperactive child syndrome** was preferred because it was descriptive of behavior and didn't rely on vague and unreliable diagnoses of subtle brain damage. This label's popularity extended into the 1970s. By the 1980s, however, it too had fallen out of favor as research began to point to inattention, not hyperactivity, as the major behavioral problem experienced by these children. In fact, some exhibited attention problems without excessive movement.

■ **Strauss syndrome**
Behaviors of distractibility, forced responsiveness to stimuli, and hyperactivity; based on the work of Alfred Strauss and Heinz Werner with children with mental retardation (intellectual disabilities).

■ **Cerebral palsy**
A condition characterized by paralysis, weakness, incoordination, and/or other motor dysfunction because of damage to the brain before it has matured.

■ **Minimal brain injury**
A term used to refer to children who exhibit inattention, impulsivity, and/or hyperactivity; popular in the 1950s and 1960s.

■ **Hyperactive child syndrome**
A term used to refer to children who exhibit inattention, impulsivity, and/or hyperactivity; popular in the 1960s and 1970s.

This recognition of inattention as more important than hyperactivity is reflected in the current definition of ADHD and its immediate predecessors. However, as we discuss later, some authorities are now recommending that deficits in behavioral inhibition replace inattention as the primary deficit in ADHD. In any case, most authorities do not view hyperactivity as the primary deficit in ADHD.

Definition

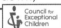

UNDERSTANDING THE STANDARDS AND PRINCIPLES Briefly describe the diagnostic criteria for attention deficit hyperactivity disorder as outlined in the Diagnostic and Statistical Manual of Mental Disorders. (CEC Knowledge and Skill Standard GC1K1)

Most professionals rely on the American Psychiatric Association's (APA's) *Diagnostic and Statistical Manual of Mental Disorders* (*DSM*) criteria to determine whether an individual has ADHD. Over the years, researchers and practitioners have debated whether ADHD is a single syndrome or whether there are subtypes. Partly as a result of this debate, the name for the condition has changed over time. For example, for several years, the APA used the general term *attention deficit disorder* (ADD) to refer to all people with the condition. It then allowed for the subtypes of ADD with Hyperactivity and ADD without Hyperactivity.

The current *DSM* uses ADHD as the general term and subdivides individuals into (1) ADHD, Predominantly Inattentive Type; (2) ADHD, Predominantly Hyperactive-Impulsive Type; and (3) ADHD, Combined Type (American Psychiatric Association, 2000). See Table 7.1.

Prevalence

INTERNET RESOURCES

Adults and children with ADHD, as well as parents of children with ADHD, can find a wealth of useful information from organizations devoted to ADHD. The oldest organization devoted to ADHD is the Children and Adults with Attention-Deficit/Hyperactivity Disorder (CHADD). A more recent organization is the National Attention Deficit Disorder Association (National ADDA). Their respective Websites are www.chadd.org and www.add.org

ADHD is widely recognized as one of the most frequent reasons, if not the most frequent reason, children are referred for behavioral problems to guidance clinics. One-third to one-half of cases referred to guidance clinics are for ADHD (Richters et al., 1995). Most authorities estimate that from 3 to 7 percent of the school-age population have ADHD (Barkley, 2006d). However, because the U.S. Department of Education does not recognize ADHD as a separate category of special education, it's difficult to estimate how many students with ADHD are served in special education. (See Focus on Concepts on p. 230.)

ADHD occurs much more frequently in boys than girls, with estimates being about 3 to 1 in community-based samples (Barkley, 2006d). Some have speculated that boys are identified more often than girls because boys tend to exhibit the highly noticeable hyperactive or impulsive type of ADHD, whereas girls are more likely to exhibit the inattentive type. Some gender bias in referral may exist, but our best research evidence suggests that it's not enough to account for the wide disparity in prevalence rates between boys and girls. Gender differences are likely due to constitutional, or biological, differences.

Some critics have asserted that ADHD is primarily a U.S. phenomenon, a result of our society's emphasis on achievement and conformity. However, statistics do not bear this out. Although it's difficult to compare prevalence rates cross-culturally because of differing diagnostic criteria, sampling techniques, and cultural expectations, the evidence strongly suggests that prevalence rates at least as high as those in the United States are found in several other countries, including Canada, Australia, New Zealand, Germany, Japan, China, Brazil, the Netherlands, and Qatar (Baumgaertel, Wolraich, & Dietrich, 1995; Bener, Al Qahtani, & Abdelaal, 2007; Esser, Schmidt, & Woerner, 1990; Fergusson, Horwood, & Lynskey, 1993; Graetz, Sawyer, Hazell, Arney, & Baghurst, 2001; Kanbayashi, Nakata, Fujii, Kita, & Wada, 1994; Kroes et al.,

Casebook Reflections

REFER TO THE CASE *More Than LD* in your booklet. Shannon's diagnosis of ADHD did not come until she was in the sixth grade. We know from research that girls can be overlooked for having ADHD. Why do you think that is? ●

TABLE 7.1 **Diagnostic Criteria for Attention Deficit Hyperactivity Disorder**

A. Either (1) or (2):

   1. six (or more) of the following symptoms of inattention have persisted for at least 6 months to a degree that is maladaptive and inconsistent with developmental level:

Inattention

   (a) often fails to give close attention to details or makes careless mistakes in schoolwork, work, or other activities

   (b) often has difficulty sustaining attention in tasks or play activities

   (c) often does not seem to listen when spoken to directly

   (d often does not follow through on instructions and fails to finish schoolwork, chores, or duties in the workplace (not due to oppositional behavior or failure to understand instructions)

   (e) often has difficulty organizing tasks and activities

   (f) often avoids, dislikes, or is reluctant to engage in tasks that require sustained mental effort (such as schoolwork or homework)

   (g) often loses things necessary for tasks or activities (e.g., toys, school assignments, pencils, books, or tools)

   (h) is often easily distracted by extraneous stimuli

   (i) is often forgetful in daily activities

   2. six (or more) of the following symptoms of hyperactivity-impulsivity have persisted for at least 6 months to a degree that is maladaptive and inconsistent with developmental level:

Hyperactivity

   (a) often fidgets with hands or feet or squirms in seat

   (b) often leaves seat in classroom or in other situations in which remaining seated is expected

   (c) often runs about or climbs excessively in situations in which it is inappropriate (in adolescents or adults, may be limited to subjective feelings of restlessness)

   (d) often has difficulty playing or engaging in leisure activities quietly

   (e) is often "on the go" or often acts as if "driven by a motor"

   (f) often talks excessively

Impulsivity

   (g) often blurts out answers before questions have been completed

   (h) often has difficulty awaiting turn

   (i) often interrupts or intrudes on others (e.g., butts into conversations or games)

B. Some hyperactive-impulsive or inattentive symptoms that caused impairment were present before age 7 years.

C. Some impairment from the symptoms is present in two or more settings (e.g., at school [or work] and at home).

D. There must be clear evidence of clinically significant impairment in social, academic, or occupational functioning.

E. The symptoms do not occur exclusively during the course of a Pervasive Developmental Disorder, Schizophrenia, or other Psychotic Disorder and are not better accounted for by another mental disorder (e.g., Mood Disorder, Anxiety Disorder, Dissociative Disorder, or a Personality Disorder).

Code based on type

● Attention-Deficit/Hyperactivity Disorder, Combined Type: if both Criteria A1 and A2 are met for the past 6 months

● Attention-Deficit/Hyperactivity Disorder, Predominantly Inattentive Type: if Criterion A1 is met but Criterion A2 is not met for the past 6 months

● Attention-Deficit/Hyperactivity Disorder, Predominantly Hyperactive-Impulsive Type: if Criterion A2 is met but Criterion A1 is not met for the past 6 months

Coding note: For individuals (especially adolescents and adults) who currently have symptoms that no longer meet full criteria, "In Partial Remission" should be specified.

Source: Reprinted with permission from the *Diagnostic and Statistical Manual of Mental Disorders,* Fourth Edition, text revision, pp. 92–93. Copyright © 2000 American Psychiatric Association.

FOCUS ON Concepts

How Many Students with ADHD Are Served in Special Education?

Because ADHD is such a prevalent condition, one would think that it would be relatively easy to find out how many students with ADHD receive special education services. Federal law, after all, requires that schools report how many students with a given disability have been identified for special education services. However, when Public Law 94–142 (the Education for All Handicapped Children Act) was passed in 1975, ADHD was not included as one of the separate categories of special education. This was due in part to two interrelated factors: (1) The research on this condition was still in its infancy, and (2) the advocacy base for children with ADHD was not yet well developed. For example, the *Diagnostic and Statistical Manual of Mental Disorders* in use at the time (the *DSM-II*, published in 1968) was vague in its criteria for identifying children with these problems. And the major advocacy organization for people with ADHD, CHADD (Children and Adults with Attention Deficit Disorder), was not founded until 1987.

By the time of the reauthorization of the law as the Individuals with Disabilities Education Act (IDEA) in 1990, however, there was substantial research on ADHD, and CHADD's membership was well on its way to its present level of 20,000 members. CHADD lobbied hard for ADHD to be considered a separate category, arguing that children with ADHD were being denied services; they could qualify for special education only if they also had another disability, such as learning disabilities or emotional disturbance. Their lobbying was unsuccessful. However, in 1991, the U.S. Department of Education determined that students with ADHD would be eligible for special education under the category "other health impaired" (OHI) "in instances where the ADD is a chronic or acute health problem that results in limited alertness, which adversely affects educational performance." Students with ADHD can also qualify for accommodations under another law: Section 504 of the Rehabilitation Act of 1973.

Many professionals are still disappointed with the decision not to include ADHD as a separate category; they say that using the OHI category is too roundabout a means of identification, and Section 504 is not completely satisfactory because it doesn't require an individualized education program (IEP; see Chapter 1 pp. 32–37).

However, the growth of the OHI category since 1991 suggests that more and more students with ADHD are being identified as OHI (see Figure A). Although numbers in the OHI category have multiplied by almost nine times in just under fifteen years, the 0.88 percent reported for 2003–2004 is still well below the prevalence estimates of 3 to 7 percent. Many authorities think that fewer than half of students with ADHD are receiving special education services. As long as ADHD is not recognized as a separate category of special education, however, it will be virtually impossible to know exactly how many school-age children with ADHD are receiving special education services.

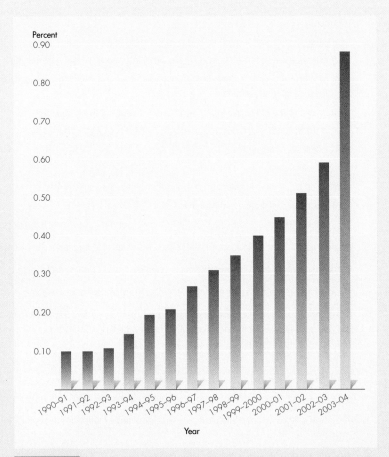

FIGURE A Percentage of students aged 6 to 21 receiving special education services in the category of "other health impaired."

Source: U.S. Department of Education. (1992–2005). *Fourteenth through twenty-seventh annual reports to Congress on the implementation of the Individuals with Disabilities Education Act.* Washington, DC; Author.

2001; Leung et al., 1996; Rohde et al., 1999; Schaughency, McGee, Raja, Freehan, & Silva, 1994; Szatmari, 1992; Wilens, Biederman, & Spencer, 2002).

Some critics have also suggested that African American children, especially boys, are diagnosed disproportionately as ADHD. Unfortunately, there are no definitive, large-scale epidemiological studies on this topic. What scanty evidence does exist suggests that they are no more likely to be formally identified as ADHD than their white peers (Rowland et al., 2001). However, there is some suggestive evidence that some cultural bias exists in how teachers view inattentive and hyperactive behaviors in children. For example, in one study, white teachers were more likely than African American teachers to rate African American students as highly inattentive and hyperactive (Reid, Casat, Norton, Anastopoulos, & Temple, 2001). In another study, compared to White teachers, Hispanic teachers were more likely to rate Hispanic, but not White children, as more hyperactive and impulsive (DeRamirez & Shapiro, 2005).

Video Homework Exercise

ADHD ● Go to the Homework and Exercises section in Chapter 7 of MyEducationLab to watch the video "ADHD", in which teachers and resource providers discuss the progress of their students with ADHD.

Identification

It's because of findings like the ones above, showing that teachers and other professionals may not always be accurate in their ratings of attention and hyperactivity, that authorities stress the importance of using several sources of information before arriving at a determination that an individual is ADHD. Most authorities agree that there are four important components to assessing whether a student has ADHD: a medical examination, a clinical interview, teacher and parent rating scales, and behavioral observations. The medical examination is necessary to rule out medical conditions, such as brain tumors, thyroid problems, or seizure disorders, as the cause of the inattention and/or hyperactivity (Barkley & Edwards, 2006).

The clinical interview of the parent(s) and the child provides information about the child's physical and psychological characteristics, as well as family dynamics and interaction with peers. Although the interview is essential to the diagnosis of ADHD, clinicians

In addition to medical exams and clinical interviews, rating scales filled out by teachers, parents, and in some case children, can help quantify the process of identifying children who might have ADHD.

need to recognize the subjective nature of the interview situation. Some children with ADHD can look surprisingly "normal" in their behavior when in the structured and novel setting of a doctor's office.

In an attempt to bring some quantification to the identification process, researchers have developed rating scales to be filled out by teachers, parents, and, in some cases, the child. Some of the most reliable and popular are the Conners Rating Scales-Revised (CRS-R; Conners, 2001) and the ADHD Rating Scale-IV (DuPaul, Power, Anastopoulos, & Reid, 1998), based on the *DSM-IV* criteria. Raters, who can be either parents or teachers, rate the child on items pertaining to each of the eighteen criteria listed in the *DSM-IV* (see Table 7.1). For example, for the first item, "Fails to give close attention to details or makes careless mistakes in his/her work," they rate 0 (never or rarely), 1 (sometimes), 2 (often), or 3 (very often), and so forth. Assessment scales for adults (for example, the Conners Adult ADHD Rating Scales; Conners, Erhardt, & Sparrow, 2000) are more recent.

Whenever possible, the clinician should observe the student. This can be done in the classroom; clinicians who specialize in diagnosing and treating children with ADHD sometimes have specially designed observation rooms in which they can observe the child while he or she performs tasks requiring sustained attention. In addition, professionals can use a **continuous performance test (CPT)** in the clinic. A typical CPT consists of stimuli (e.g., *X*'s and *O*'s) presented one at a time on a screen rapidly (about one per second), with the individual pressing a button every time a particular stimulus (e.g., *X*) appears or a particular sequence (e.g., *O* followed by *X*) appears. The computer keeps track of the number of correct responses, failures to respond to a correct stimulus (omission errors), and incorrect responses or responses to the wrong stimulus (commission errors).

■ **Continuous performance test (CPT)**

A test measuring a person's ability to sustain attention to rapidly presented stimuli; can help in the diagnosis of ADHD.

UNDERSTANDING THE STANDARDS AND PRINCIPLES What do we know about the causes of ADHD? (CEC Knowledge and Skill Standard GC2K3)

Council for Exceptional Children

Causes

Probably because there is no simple diagnostic test, such as a blood test, for ADHD, there has been much controversy over what actually causes ADHD and a history of questionable causal theories. (See Focus on Concepts on p. 233.) We now know, however, that there's strong evidence linking neurological abnormalities to ADHD.

As we noted earlier, authorities in the early and middle parts of the twentieth century attributed problems of inattention and hyperactivity to neurological problems resulting from brain damage. When researchers were unable to verify actual tissue damage in cases of ADHD, many professionals soured on the idea that ADHD was neurologically based. However, as we noted in our discussion of learning disabilities in Chapter 6, the development of neuroimaging techniques such as MRIs, PET scans, and fMRIs in the 1980s and 1990s allowed scientists for the first time to obtain more detailed and reliable measures of brain functioning. Using these techniques, researchers have made great strides in documenting the neurological basis of ADHD. As is the case with learning disabilities, research indicates that ADHD most likely results from neurological dysfunction rather than actual brain damage. Again, like learning disabilities, evidence points to heredity as playing a very strong role in causing the neurological dysfunction, with teratogenic and other medical factors also implicated to a lesser degree.

Reading Homework Exercise

Brain Research • Go to the Homework and Exercises section in Chapter 7 of MyEducationLab and read the article "Attention Loss: ADHD May Lower Volume of Brain", in which differences in the brain sizes of children with and without ADHD are reported.

Areas of the Brain Affected: Prefrontal Lobes, Frontal Lobes, Basal Ganglia, Cerebellum, and Corpus Callosum

Using neuroimaging techniques, several teams of researchers (Nigg, 2006; Voeller, 2004) have found consistent abnormalities in three areas of the brain in people with ADHD: the prefrontal lobes, frontal lobes, basal ganglia (specifically, the caudate and the globus pallidus), cerebellum, and corpus callosum (see Figure 7.2). Specifically, researchers have

FIGURE 7.2 Areas of the brain (frontal lobes, prefrontal lobes, cerebellum, globus pallidus and caudate of the basal ganglia, corpus callosum) that some researchers have identified as abnormal in people with ADHD.

FOCUS ON Concepts

Controversial Causal Theories of ADHD

Over the years, a number of myths have sprung up about what causes hyperactive behavior or ADHD. Most of these have little if any substantial scientific support. A good example is sugar. Parents and teachers have often complained that young children become more hyperactive when they ingest sugar in the form of soft drinks, cakes, and candies. However, careful research has demonstrated that this is not the case (Wolraich, Wilson, & White, 1995). The mistaken notion that sugar causes hyperactivity probably originated from the observation that children are hyperactive in situations in which sweets are served. Being relatively stimulating and unstructured, these situations, such as parties, are likely to elicit hyperactive behavior.

Another example is that of television and video games. Many people in the general public believe that by watching too much television or playing too many video games, children will become ADHD. One study did find that children who watch more television as preschoolers are rated as more inattentive at seven years of age (Christakis, Zimmerman, DiGiuseppe, & McCarty, 2004). However, this isn't proof that watching television causes ADHD or even higher rates of inattention. It could be that attention problems, themselves, cause children to want to watch more television. Or it could be that parents find that one way to control their child's hyperactive behavior, at least for a short period of time, is to put them in front of a TV. Or it could be that parents who let their children watch more television contribute in some other ways to their children's

inattentive behavior. Perhaps they provide less supervision generally.

Other environmental agents that some believe cause ADHD are artificial food colorings and additives. The original proponent of this theory was Benjamin Feingold, a pediatric allergist (Feingold, 1975) who proposed a strict diet devoid of these additives. Although substantial research has shown that this diet is not beneficial for all children with ADHD (Kavale & Forness, 1983), a recent research study presents some provocative data suggesting that when young children are on a diet containing food colorings and additives, their parents rate them higher in inattention and hyperactivity than when they are on a diet free of colorings and additives (Bateman et al., 2004). A particular strength of this study is that the parents were "blind" to when the children's diet did or did not contain colorings and additives. However, a major caveat is that the children's behavior didn't differ with or without the diet on arguably more objective measures of inattention and hyperactivity administered by researchers in the clinic.

Another caveat is that this study still falls short of demonstrating a causal link between diet and formal ADHD diagnosis. Further research is definitely warranted to determine whether there might be a subgroup of children with ADHD, however small, who might benefit from a diet restricting certain food additives and colorings. In the meantime, there's no support for automatically placing all children with ADHD on such restricted diets.

■ **Frontal lobes**
Two lobes located in the front of
the brain; responsible for executive
functions; site of abnormal
development in people with ADHD.

■ **Prefrontal lobes**
Two lobes located in the very front
of the frontal lobes; responsible
for executive functions; site of
abnormal development in people
with ADHD.

■ **Basal ganglia**
A set of structures within the brain
that include the caudate, globus
pallidus, and putamen, the first two
being abnormal in people with ADHD;
generally responsible for the coordination and control of movement.

■ **Caudate**
A structure in the basal ganglia of the
brain; site of abnormal development
in persons with ADHD.

■ **Globus pallidus**
A structure in the basal ganglia
of the brain; site of abnormal
development in people with ADHD.

■ **Cerebellum**
An organ at the base of the brain
responsible for coordination and
movement; site of abnormal development in persons with ADHD.

■ **Corpus callosum**
A part of the brain, consisting of
millions of fibers connecting the left
and right hemispheres; responsible
for communication between the
two hemispheres; site of abnormal
development in persons with ADHD.

■ **Neurotransmitters**
Chemicals involved in sending messages between neurons in the brain.

■ **Dopamine**
A neurotransmitter, the levels of
which may be abnormal in people
with ADHD.

■ **Norepinephrine**
A neurotransmitter, the levels of
which may be abnormal in people
with ADHD.

■ **Molecular genetics**
The study of the organization of
DNA, RNA, and protein molecules
containing genetic information.

found that the size of each of these areas is smaller in children and adults with ADHD than in those who are nondisabled. Although not always consistent, several of the studies point to the abnormality occurring on the right side of the brain, especially the right basal ganglia (Castellanos, 1997). In addition, PET scans suggest reduced metabolic activity in the frontal lobes and basal ganglia in people with ADHD (Lou, Henriksen, & Bruhn, 1984; Lou, Henriksen, Bruhn, Borner, & Nielsen, 1989; Vance et al., 2007; Volkow et al., 2007).

PREFRONTAL, FRONTAL LOBES   Located in the front of the brain, the **frontal lobes**—and especially the very front portion of the frontal lobes, the **prefrontal lobes**—are responsible for what are referred to as *executive functions*. Among other things, executive functions involve the ability to regulate one's own behavior. (We discuss executive functions more fully later.)

BASAL GANGLIA   Buried deep within the brain, the **basal ganglia** consist of several parts, the **caudate** and the **globus pallidus** being the structures that are abnormal in persons with ADHD. The basal ganglia are responsible for the coordination and control of motor behavior (Pinel, 2006).

CEREBELLUM   The **cerebellum** is also responsible for the coordination and control of motor behavior. Although it's relatively small, constituting only about 10 percent of the mass of the brain, the fact that it contains more than half of all the brain's neurons attests to its complexity (Pinel, 2006).

CORPUS CALLOSUM   The **corpus callosum** consists of millions of fibers that connect the left and right hemispheres of the brain. Being responsible for communication bet-ween the hemispheres, it's important for a variety of cognitive functions.

Neurotransmitters Involved: Dopamine and Norepinephrine

Much exciting research is being conducted on what neurotransmitter abnormalities might cause ADHD. **Neurotransmitters** are chemicals that help in the sending of mes-sages between neurons in the brain. Researchers have found that abnormal levels of two neurotransmitters—**dopamine** and **norepinephrine**—appear to be involved in ADHD (Barkley, 2006b; Solanto, 2002; Volkow et al., 2007).

Hereditary Factors

Most authorities agree that there's a hereditary basis to ADHD. Evidence for the genetic transmission of ADHD comes from at least three sources: family studies, twin studies, and molecular genetic studies.

FAMILY STUDIES   Generally, studies indicate that if a child has ADHD, the chance of his or her sibling having ADHD is about 32 percent (Barkley, 2006b). Children of adults with ADHD run a 57 percent risk of having ADHD (Biederman et al., 1995). In addition, sev-eral studies demonstrate that parents of children with ADHD are two to eight times more likely to also be ADHD than are parents of non-ADHD children (Faraone & Doyle, 2001).

TWIN STUDIES   Several researchers have compared the prevalence of ADHD in identical (monozygotic, from the same egg) versus fraternal (dizygotic, from two eggs) twins, when one of the members of the pair has ADHD. These studies consistently show that if an iden-tical twin and a fraternal twin each have ADHD, the second identical twin is much more likely to have ADHD than is the second fraternal twin (Levy & Hay, 2001; Nigg, 2006).

MOLECULAR GENETIC STUDIES   With the mapping of the human genome have come advances in **molecular genetics**, the study of the molecules (DNA, RNA, and protein) that regulate genetic information. Molecular genetic research on ADHD is in its early stages, but it's safe to say that in the vast majority of cases there is no one single gene that causes ADHD. Several genes contribute to ADHD. In particular, genes that are involved in regulating dopamine have been implicated in persons with ADHD (Barkley, 2006b; Nigg, 2006).

Toxins and Medical Factors

In Chapters 5 and 6, we discussed **toxins**—agents that can cause malformations in the developing fetus of a pregnant woman—as the cause of some cases of intellectual disabilities or learning disabilities. Although the evidence for toxins is not as strong as that for heredity, some of these same substances have been shown to be related to ADHD. For example, exposure to lead and the abuse of alcohol or tobacco (Faraone & Doyle, 2001) by pregnant women does place the unborn child at increased risk of developing ADHD.

Other medical conditions may also place children at risk for having ADHD. Again, the evidence is not as strong as it is for heredity, but complications at birth and low birthweight are associated with ADHD (Levy, Barr, & Sunohara, 1998; Milberger, Biederman, Faraone, Guite, & Tsuang, 1997). Smoking during pregnancy is associated with having babies of low birthweight; there's also suggestive evidence that smoking by mothers-to-be can result in their children who are genetically susceptible based on their dopamine-related genes being at risk for ADHD (Neuman et al., 2007).

Psychological and Behavioral Characteristics

The *DSM-IV* criteria discussed earlier (see Table 7.1) provides a sense of some of the typical behaviors of students with ADHD. Although most people think that inattention is the key characteristic of ADHD, there's a growing consensus that inattention, hyperactivity, and impulsivity are actually the result of problems in behavioral inhibition.

Barkley's Model of ADHD

There's an abundance of research pointing to problems with behavioral inhibition in people with ADHD (Barkley, 1997, 2000a, 2006e; Semrud-Clikeman et al., 2000; Schachar, Mota, Logan, Tannock, & Klim, 2000; Willcutt, Pennington, et al., 2001). As we noted earlier, Russell Barkley, in particular, has proposed a model of ADHD in which behavioral inhibition is key. In its simplest form, this model proposes that problems in behavioral inhibition set the stage for problems in executive functions and time awareness and management, which then disrupt the person's ability to engage in persistent goal-directed behavior.

BEHAVIORAL INHIBITION **Behavioral inhibition** involves the ability to:

1. delay a response,
2. interrupt an ongoing response, if one detects that the response is inappropriate because of sudden changes in the demands of the task, or
3. protect a response from distracting or competing stimuli (Lawrence et al., 2002).

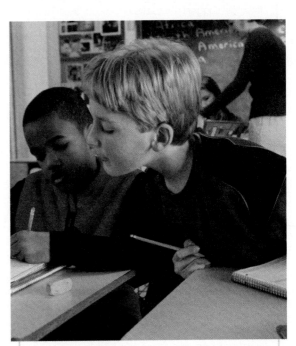

Students with ADHD may experience difficulties with behavioral inhibition, including the ability to wait one's turn, recognize inappropriate responses, or resist distractions.

Responsive Instruction

Meeting the Needs of Students with Attention Deficit Hyperactivity Disorder

Task Switching: Preparing Students with ADHD for Change

WHAT THE RESEARCH SAYS

Many researchers contend that the primary deficit of students with ADHD is deficient behavioral inhibition (see p. 235). In other words, once a student with ADHD begins a task, it is difficult for him or her to mentally switch to a new activity. Researchers hypothesize that the executive controls needed to "inhibit" the current activity and "start up" the next are different for students with ADHD compared to students who do not have ADHD.

RESEARCH STUDY

A group of researchers examined task-switching ability of students with and without ADHD (Cepeda, Cepeda, & Kramer, 2000). Results from the study indicated that clear performance deficits existed for unmedicated students with ADHD in the first trial after a task switch, even when the tasks were considered compatible, such as both tasks involving numbers. All students with ADHD, unmedicated or medicated, had higher "switch costs"—increased response time—when the new task was incompatible with the old task (e.g., switching from a number-identification task to a word-identification task). This type of task required the inhibition of thinking about numbers and the preparation for thinking about letters and sounds. The findings suggest that differences do exist between students

with and without ADHD in the ability to efficiently and effectively task switch.

APPLYING THE RESEARCH TO TEACHING

Studies such as the one presented here indicate the need to support students with ADHD as they transition from one activity to another. Cognitive support for such transitions can include the following:

- Allowing for time between asking a student to do or say something and expecting the response (i.e., increasing wait time)
- Avoiding overloading a students' working memory (Barkley, Murphy, & Kwasnik, 1996) by limiting the number of steps or sequence of procedures a student must keep in working memory or by providing a visual for students to refer to
- Creating routinized procedures for daily transitions
- Preparing students for the type of response that will be required when asking a question
- Dividing instruction into consistent, predictable sequences throughout the day

● *By Kristin L. Sayeski*

Problems in behavioral inhibition can be reflected in the ability to wait one's turn, to refrain from interrupting conversations, to resist potential distractions while working, or to delay immediate gratification to work for larger, long-term rewards (Tripp & Alsop, 2001). In addition, there's evidence that problems with behavioral inhibition in children with ADHD is related to abnormalities of the caudate in the brain (Semrud-Clikeman et al., 2000). In the classroom, difficulties with behavioral inhibition can present themselves during task switching or transitions. See the Responsive Instruction above for a description of research on this topic and how to apply this research to the classroom.

EXECUTIVE FUNCTIONS   The delay allowed by behavioral inhibition permits the individual to self-regulate his or her behavior. This ability to engage in a variety of self-directed behaviors involves what are referred to as **executive functions**. The fact that there is a wealth of evidence that executive functions are controlled by the prefrontal and frontal lobes of the brain fits nicely with the neuroimaging studies pointing to these areas of the brain being abnormal in persons with ADHD.

In Barkley's model, persons with ADHD can exhibit problems with executive function in four general ways. First, they often have problems with working memory (WM). As we noted in Chapter 5, WM refers to a person's ability to keep information in mind that "can be used to guide one's actions either now or in the near future" (Barkley &

■ **Executive functions**
The ability to regulate one's behavior through working memory, inner speech, control of emotions and arousal levels, and analysis of problems and communication of problem solutions to others; delayed or impaired in people with ADHD.

Murphy, 1998, p. 2). In the case of students with ADHD, deficiencies in WM can result in forgetfulness, a lack of hindsight and forethought, and problems with time management.

Second, people with ADHD frequently have delayed inner speech. **Inner speech** is the inner "voice" that allows people to "talk" to themselves about various solutions when in the midst of solving a problem. Students with ADHD who have deficient inner speech have problems in guiding their behavior in situations that demand the ability to follow rules or instructions.

Third, children and adults with ADHD have problems controlling their emotions and their arousal levels. They often overreact to negative or positive experiences. On hearing good news, for example, children with ADHD might scream loudly, unable to keep their emotions to themselves. Likewise, they are often quick to show their temper when confronted with frustrating experiences.

Fourth, children and adults with ADHD have difficulty analyzing problems and communicating solutions to others. They're less flexible when faced with problem situations, often responding impulsively with the first thing that comes to mind. Josh, the student described in the Success Stories on p. 238, has many of the executive function difficulties we've just discussed. He has problems with completing homework, solving problems, and organizing himself to keep up with his work. Josh hopes to play sports in college, so he must figure out how to organize and study to get better grades.

TIME AWARENESS AND MANAGEMENT   Barkley (2000a) sees the deficit in time awareness and management shown by people with ADHD as crucial:

> Understanding time and how we organize our own behavior within and toward it is a major key to the mystery of understanding ADHD. . . . I now believe that the awareness of themselves across time is the ultimate yet nearly invisible disability afflicting those with ADHD. (p. 30)

PERSISTENT GOAL-DIRECTED BEHAVIOR   The many problems with executive functions experienced by people with ADHD lead to deficits in engaging in sustained goal-directed activities:

> The poor sustained attention that apparently characterizes those with ADHD probably represents an impairment in goal- or task-directed persistence arising from poor inhibition and the toll it takes on self-regulation. And the distractibility ascribed to those with ADHD most likely arises from poor interference control that allows other external and internal events to disrupt the executive functions that provide for self-control and task persistence. The net effect is an individual who cannot persist in effort toward tasks that provide little immediate reward and who flits from one uncompleted activity to another as disrupting events occur. The inattention in ADHD can now be seen as not so much a primary symptom as a secondary one; it is the consequence of the impairment that behavioral inhibition and interference control create in the self-regulation or executive control of behavior. (Barkley, 1997, p. 84)

With diminished self-regulation or executive control abilities, students with ADHD find it exceedingly difficult to stay focused on tasks that require effort or concentration but which are not inherently exciting (e.g., many school-related activities). There is substantial evidence that students with ADHD, indeed, have lower academic achievement than those without disabilities (Frazier, Youngstrom, Glutting, & Watkins, 2007).

Adaptive Behavior

The concept of **adaptive behavior skills** (e.g., self-help, community use, home use, and so forth) has traditionally been associated with the area of mental retardation or intellectual disabilities. The American Association on Intellectual and Developmental Disabilities' definition, for example, stipulates that intellectual disabilities be defined as impairments in intelligence

■ **Inner speech**
An executive function; internal language used to regulate one's behavior; delayed or impaired in people with ADHD.

Reading Homework Exercise

Barkley's Characteristics ●
Go to the Homework and Exercises section in Chapter 7 of MyEducationLab and read the section "Major Characteristics" within the article "About ADHD: A Fact Sheet by Dr. Barkley", in which Dr. Barkley lists eight characteristics of students with ADHD and the symptomology of ADHD.

■ **Adaptive skills**
Skills needed to adapt to one's living environment (e.g., communication, self-care, home living, social skills, community use, self-direction, health and safety, functional academics, leisure, and work); usually estimated by an adaptive behavior survey; one of two major components (the other is intellectual functioning) of the AAMR definition.

Developing his self-advocacy skills to get needed accommodations will be key to Josh's success in college

Josh: "It's not like the work is hard; it's just getting it done!"

High school sophomore Josh Bishop hopes to play football on a team in the National Collegiate Athletic Association's Division I, despite his struggles with organization and time management.

These could be the keys to his success:

● Intensive classroom structure and consistent expectations
● Relentless positive reinforcement and behavioral support
● Specific accommodations and self-advocacy

Special educator Jane Warner coordinates services for college students with disabilities at the university where Josh Bishop hopes to play football. She guides many students like Josh and encourages incoming freshmen with ADHD to begin their self-advocacy early. Josh doesn't find schoolwork hard to do, but he finds it hard to get done. Although her son does not receive special education services, Josh's mother, Joni Poff, encourages him to seek out structures and supports so that he can meet his future goals.

● **Intensive Classroom Structure and Consistent Expectations**   Josh is a successful athlete, but in the classroom, he faces challenges. "I never have been very organized. I got by in elementary school, but middle school was a real wake-up call. In sixth grade, I'd get all my homework done in class. In seventh grade, I had homework due for every class."

Josh keeps an assignment book but admits that he doesn't use it faithfully. "When I've missed a deadline, sometimes I don't turn the work in at all. I know I need to do homework and I keep saying I'm going to do it, and then I don't turn it in and I get a zero. I can get work done at school, but I just can't get it done at home." According to his mother, "Josh does better with shorter time segments in a more structured setting. At home, he has trouble following through with sustained work. His pediatrician told me to back off. Josh takes medication during the day, and it's harder for him to concentrate in the evening."

Josh mentioned his medication but did not refer to his difficulties with completing written work, organizational skills, or attentiveness as being out of the ordinary. He would rather not be treated differently from other students, but he says that only a few teachers have provided the classroom structure that he needs. His mother thinks that the most successful teachers for Josh have been those who were very organized and made their expectations very clear. "They weren't wishy-washy. They were sympathetic that some things were difficult for Josh. They understood that he wasn't being purposefully lazy or disrespectful, but they still held high expectations for him."

● **Relentless Positive Reinforcement and Behavioral Support**   Josh was diagnosed by his pediatrician with ADHD when he was 7 years old. "Josh always had a high activity level," recalls his mother. "In kindergarten, he was put on a behavior

and adaptive behavior (see Chapter 5). In recent years, authorities in the ADHD field have discovered that many children and adults with ADHD also have difficulties in adaptive behavior (Barkley, 2006a; Whalen et al., 2006). A good example is that they have more problems related to driving as adolescents and young adults: more accidents and traffic violations (Cox, Merkel, Kovatchev, & Seward, 2000; Fischer, Barkley, Smallish, & Fletcher, 2007; Woodward, Fergusson, & Horwood, 2000). It's logical to assume that poor behavioral inhibition would lead to driving problems, and there's evidence that it may also be related to poor anger control (Richards, Deffenbacher, Rosen, Barkley, & Rodricks, 2007).

Problems Socializing with Peers

Compared to their nondisabled classmates, students with ADHD are rejected more often by their peers, have fewer close friends, and are disliked by students who enjoy high social status (Hoza, 2007). Some authorities have even argued that the social problems that students with ADHD experience are so common that they should be considered the contract with stickers as positive reinforcement, but his first grade teacher didn't follow through with his behavior management." By second grade, medication was recommended. Josh's family moved to a small school district where the local high school he attends has only 650 students. Contact between home and school has been close. But as he has matured and the academic demands have increased, says his mother, "high school has been difficult for Josh. Recently, I asked him to take advantage of a tutor or some structured support to help reinforce his behavior, but he seems determined to do it alone."

● **Specific Accommodations and Self-Advocacy**   Doing it alone is not always the answer, says Jane Warner. Students with ADHD frequently need support when they move from high school to college. "Study skills and time management are troublesome for students with ADHD. Things can start to fall apart. Students might miss several classes and think they can never go back, so they just sit out and their grades go down, their self-esteem starts to slip, and they hit the wall." Warner encourages students to disclose their learning needs confidently and make the primary contact with the office for disability services on campus. Students with ADHD who have not received special services in high school are advised to get the documentation they need for colleges to provide them with appropriate accommodations. "We prefer comprehensive evaluations that have been done by a qualified professional within the previous three years," says Warner. "IEPs are part of the puzzle but IEPs can't be used as the only documentation for post-secondary accommodations."

Warner points out that current evaluations provide a clear picture of strengths and weaknesses, especially if the evaluator explains what the results mean in lay terms and makes specific educational recommendations. "Sometime between now and high school graduation," she says, "getting a current clinical evaluation will be a very important strategy for developing his self-advocacy and for moving Josh closer to reaching his goals."

CEC'S STANDARDS: PAVING THE WAY TO SUCCESS

Assess your steps to success in meeting the CEC Knowledge and Skill Base for All Beginning Special Education Teachers. Use the following questions to reflect on the growth of your own professional knowledge, skills, and dispositions.

REFLECTING ON YOUR OWN PROFESSIONAL DEVELOPMENT

If you were Josh's teacher . . .

■ What are some areas about educating students with ADHD about which you would need to know more?

■ What are some specific skills that would help you to address his academic and behavioral challenges?

■ What personal dispositions do you think are most important for you to develop in teaching students with challenging behaviors posed by ADHD?

Using the CEC Standards

■ How would you describe the psychological and social-emotional characteristics of individuals with ADHD? (GC2K4)

■ What are the effects of various medications on individuals with ADHD? (CC2K7)

■ What type of procedures would you use to increase self-awareness, self-management, self-control, self-reliance, and self-esteem in a student with ADHD? (CC4S5)

● *By Jean B. Crockett*

---

defining characteristic of the condition (Landau, Milich, & Diener, 1998). Although the evidence might not warrant asserting that all persons with ADHD experience problems getting along with others, it's probably safe to say that the majority experience significant problems in peer relations. In fact, it usually doesn't take long for others to find students with ADHD uncomfortable to be around. For example, one team of researchers found that after just one day in a summer camp, many children with ADHD were rejected by other campers (Erhardt & Hinshaw, 1994).

Unfortunately, the negative social status experienced by students with ADHD is difficult to overcome and is usually long lasting. The enduring nature of social rejection leads easily to social isolation. The result is that many children and adults with ADHD have few friends, even though they may desperately want to be liked. This can set up a vicious circle in which they attempt to win friends by latching onto the least chance for interaction with others. But their frantic need for friendship, coupled with their deficient impulse control, ends up leading them to bother or pester the very people they are trying to befriend.

UNDERSTANDING THE STANDARDS AND PRINCIPLES   Describe the social status experienced by many students with ADHD. (CEC Knowledge and Skill Standard CC3K1)

239

Given the problems in behavioral inhibition, it's not surprising that so many children and adults with ADHD end up socially ostracized. Unable to regulate their behavior and emotions, they are viewed as rude by others. It isn't that they don't know how to behave appropriately so much as that they are unable to do so (Landau et al., 1998). In other words, if asked what the appropriate behavior in a given situation should be, they can often give the socially acceptable answer. But when faced with choices in the actual situation, their deficits in behavioral inhibition lead them to make choices impulsively and to overreact emotionally.

Coexisting Conditions

ADHD often occurs simultaneously with other behavioral and/or learning problems, such as learning disabilities or emotional or behavioral disorders. In addition, persons with ADHD run a higher risk than the general population for substance abuse.

LEARNING DISABILITIES   Studies using careful diagnostic criteria have found an overlap of 10 to 25 percent between ADHD and learning disabilities (Forness & Kavale, 2002). Some authorities maintain that the relationship is strongest for students who have ADHD, Predominantly Inattentive Type (Marshall, Hynd, Handwerk, & Hall, 1997; Willcutt, Chhabildas, & Pennington, 2001).

EMOTIONAL OR BEHAVIORAL DISORDERS   Estimates of the overlap with ADHD vary widely, but it's safe to say that 25 to 50 percent of people with ADHD also exhibit some form of emotional or behavioral disorder (Hallahan & Cottone, 1997; Forness & Kavale, 2002). Some people with ADHD can exhibit aggressive, acting-out behaviors, whereas others can have the types of withdrawn behaviors that accompany anxiety or depression. In fact, anxiety is evident in between 15 to 35 percent of children with ADHD and they are especially vulnerable to having multiple anxiety disorders compared with nondisabled children (Schatz & Rostain, 2007).

Children with ADHD who also have externalizing types of behavior disorders are especially vulnerable for early drug use.

SUBSTANCE ABUSE   Adolescents with ADHD are more likely to experiment prematurely with alcohol, tobacco, or illicit drugs (Molina et al., 2007), and adults with ADHD are about twice as likely as the general population to abuse alcohol or to become dependent on drugs, such as cocaine (Biederman, Wilens, Mick, Faraone, & Spencer, 1998; Lambert & Hartsough, 1998). Children with ADHD who also have externalizing types of behavior disorders or who have the ADHD, Predominantly Hyperactive-Impulsive type are especially vulnerable for early drug use (Chilcoat & Breslau, 1999). In addition, a strong association exists between having ADHD in adolescence and adulthood and cigarette smoking (Lambert & Hartsough, 1998; Tercyak, Lerman, & Audrain, 2002). Some reports in the popular media have claimed that the treatment of ADHD with psychostimulants such as Ritalin leads children to take up the use of illegal substances. However, there is very little research to back up this claim (Connor, 2006).

> **Casebook Reflections**
>
> REFER TO THE CASE *More Than LD* in your booklet. Her parents thought that they saw signs of something more than a learning disability. How does this comment reflect the difficulty of separating learning disabilities and ADHD? ●

Exactly why ADHD co-occurs with so many other learning and behavioral disabilities is unclear. Researchers are just beginning to tease out which of several possibilities are the most likely reasons for so much overlap between ADHD and other disabilities. For example, does having ADHD put one at risk for developing another disability, such as learning disabilities or depression? Or do ADHD and the other disability occur independent of each other? Is there a genetic basis to the coexistence of so many of these conditions? Research over the next few years should begin to provide more definitive answers to these questions.

Educational Considerations

In this section, we consider two aspects of effective educational programming for students with ADHD:

- Classroom structure and teacher direction
- Functional behavioral assessment and contingency-based self-management

Reading Homework Exercise

Supporting Learners ●
Go to the Homework and Exercises section in Chapter 7 of MyEducationLab and read the article "Helping the Student with ADHD in the Classroom: Strategies for Teachers", then compare and contrast several strategies that support learners with ADHD.

Classroom Structure and Teacher Direction

As noted earlier, William Cruickshank was one of the first to establish a systematic educational program for children who today would meet the criteria for ADHD. Two hallmarks of Cruickshank's program were reducing stimuli irrelevant to learning and enhancing materials important for learning, and a structured program with a strong emphasis on teacher direction.

Because Cruickshank assumed that children with attention problems were susceptible to distraction, irrelevant stimuli were reduced as much as possible. For example, students' workspaces consisted of three-sided cubicles to reduce distractions. On the other hand, teachers were encouraged to use attractive, brightly colored teaching materials. The structure came in the form of a systematic schedule of activities for each child for virtually each minute of each day (Cruickshank, Bentzen, Ratzeburg, & Tannhauser, 1961).

It's rare today to see teachers using all the components of Cruickshank's program, especially the cubicles. Many authorities now believe that not all children with ADHD are distracted by things in their environment. For those who are distractible, however, some authorities recommend the use of such things as cubicles to reduce extraneous stimulation.

The degree of classroom structure and teacher direction advocated by Cruickshank is also rarely seen today. First, this intensity of structure could be achieved only in a self-contained classroom; most students with ADHD today are in general education settings.

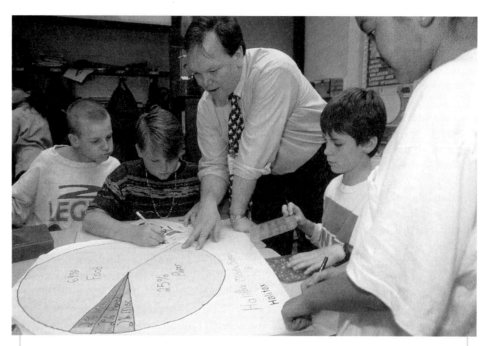

Teacher-directed general education classes, with colorful visual aids, enclosed teaching areas, and proximity to the teacher have been successful learning environments for students with ADHD.

Second, most authorities today believe that a structured program is important in the early stages of working with many students with ADHD but that these students gradually need to learn to be more independent in their learning. Nevertheless, many of Cruickshank's ideas are still alive in the educational recommendations of today's professionals. For example:

> All children, and particularly, those with ADHD, benefit from clear, predictable, uncomplicated routine and structure. It helps if the day is divided into broad units of time and if this pattern is repeated daily. Within each block of lesson time there should be a similar breaking down of tasks and activities into subtasks/activities. Presenting the student with an enormously detailed list of tasks and subtasks should be avoided. An important goal should be to create a simple overarching daily routine that the student will eventually learn by heart. The number of tasks should be kept small and tight timelines should be avoided. Complexities of timetabling and working structures merely confuse students with ADHD, because a major difficulty that goes with this condition is a poorly developed ability to differentiate between and organize different bits of information. This clearly makes the formal curriculum difficult to manage, without having to struggle with the organizational arrangements that surround the curriculum. Once a workable daily timetable has been established this should be publicly displayed and/or taped to the student's desk or inside his or her homework diary. (Cooper, 1999, p. 146)

For more specifics about planning for students with ADHD in the classroom, see Responsive Instruction on page 244. For recommendations on how to introduce, conduct, and conclude lessons see Table 7.2.

Functional Behavioral Assessment and Contingency-Based Self-Management

As we noted in Chapter 5, **functional behavioral assessment (FBA)** is an important aspect of dealing with behavioral problems of students with intellectual disabilities.

▪ **Functional behavioral assessment (FBA)** Evaluation that consists of finding out the consequences (what purpose the behavior serves), antecedents (what triggers the behavior), and setting events (contextual factors) that maintain inappropriate behavior.

| TABLE 7.2 | **Introducing, Conducting, and Concluding Lessons** |

Introducing Lessons

- *Provide an advance organizer.* Prepare students for the day's lesson by quickly summarizing the order of various activities that are planned.

- *Review previous lessons.* Review information about previous lessons on this topic.

- *Set learning expectations.* State what students are expected to learn during the lesson. For example, explain to students that a language arts lesson will involve reading a story about Paul Bunyan and identifying new words in the story.

- *State needed materials.* Identify all materials that the children will need during the lesson rather than leaving them to figure out on their own the materials required. For example, specify that children will need their journals and pencils for journal writing or their crayons, scissors, and colored paper for an art project.

- *Explain additional resources.* Tell students how to obtain help in mastering the lesson. For example, refer children to a particular page in the textbook for guidance on completing a worksheet.

- *Simplify instructions, choices, and scheduling.* The simpler the expectations communicated to an ADHD student, the more likely it is that he or she will comprehend and complete them in a timely and productive manner.

Conducting Lessons

- *Be predictable.* Structure and consistency are very important for children with ADHD; many do not do well with change. Minimal rules and minimal choices are best for these children. They need to understand clearly what is expected of them, as well as the consequences for not adhering to expectations.

- *Support the student's participation in the classroom.* Provide students with ADHD with private, discreet cues to stay on task and advance warning that they will be called on shortly. Avoid bringing attention to differences between ADHD students and their classmates. At all times, avoid the use of sarcasm and criticism.

- *Check student performance.* Question individual students to assess their mastery of the lesson. For example, you can ask students who are doing seatwork to demonstrate how they arrived at the answer to a problem, or you can ask individuals to state, in their own words, how the main character felt at the end of the story.

- *Perform ongoing student evaluation.* Identify students who need additional assistance. Watch for signs of lack of comprehension, such as daydreaming or visual or verbal indications of frustration. Provide these students with extra explanations, or ask another student to serve as a peer tutor for the lesson.

- *Follow-up directions.*
  - *Oral directions.* After giving directions to the class as a whole, provide additional oral directions for a child with ADHD. For example, ask the child if he or she understood the directions and repeat the directions together.
  - *Written directions.* Provide follow-up directions in writing. For example, write the page number for an assignment on the chalkboard and remind the child to look at the chalkboard if he or she forgets the assignment.

- *Divide work into smaller units.* Break down assignments into smaller, less complex tasks. For example, allow students to complete five math problems before presenting them with the remaining five problems.

- *Eliminate or reduce frequency of timed tests.* Tests that are timed might not allow children with ADHD to demonstrate what they truly know owing to their potential preoccupation with elapsed time.

Concluding Lessons

- *Provide advance warnings.* Provide advance warning that a lesson is about to end. Announce five or ten minutes before the end of the lesson (particularly for seatwork and group projects) how much time remains. You might also want to tell students at the beginning of the lesson how much time they will have to complete it.

- *Check assignments.* Check completed assignments for at least some of the students. Review what they have learned during the lesson to get a sense of how ready the class was for the lesson and how to plan the next lesson.

- *Preview the next lesson.* Instruct students on how to begin preparing for the next lesson. For example, inform the students that they need to put away their textbooks and come to the front of the room for a large-group spelling lesson.

Source: Adapted from U.S. Department of Education, Office of Special Education and Rehabilitative Services, Office of Special Education Programs. (2004). Teaching Children with Attention Deficit Hyperactivity Disorder: Instructional Strategies and Practices.

Meeting the Needs of Students with Attention Deficit Hyperactivity Disorder

Planning for Students with ADHD in the General Education Classroom

WHAT THE RESEARCH SAYS

The majority of students with ADHD are served in general education classrooms. Through adding key modifications or supports to their traditional instructional routines, teachers can address the needs of students with ADHD without taking away from the instruction of students without disabilities in their class.

The following lesson sequence includes a description of research-supported supports that can be provided at each stage of instruction and a rationale for how those supports meet the needs of students with ADHD.

APPLYING THE RESEARCH TO TEACHING

Stage 1: Pre-planning—Divide Instruction into Meaningful "Chunks"

Description   Before instruction, break your instructional sequence into meaningful chunks or steps (Rosenshine, 1995). By dividing your instructional sequence into small, meaningful sections, you ensure that all students do not move on until they understand and that ample practice and teacher feedback has been provided at each step (Hudson, 1997).

Rationale   Long tasks can be overwhelming for students with ADHD. Chunking allows for shorter periods of focused attention, activity changes as you move through the instructional sequence, focused practice, and reduced reliance on working memory (Kemp, Fister, & McLaughlin, 1995).

Stage II: Introduction

Description   During this stage, the teacher introduces the day's instructional objectives. Information or activities that should be included in the introduction are (1) a rationale for the lesson, (2) an explanation or presentation of a model of what the end result of the lesson will be, and (3) an advance organizer that informs students of the sequence of instructional activity (Allsopp, 1999).

Rationale   These activities provide a "road map" for students to follow. For students with ADHD who have difficulty focusing on the main task or goal (Barkley, 1997), explicit identification of lesson goals or outcomes and clearly delineated steps create an external goal-setting guide.

Stage III: Instruction and Modeling

Description   After the teacher has set the stage for learning, the instructional part of the lesson begins. During this stage, a teacher might demonstrate a procedure or phenomenon, present students with a problem scenario to be solved, or have students engage in an activity that will then be linked to key instructional concepts. Regardless of the particular method the teacher is using to teach, students should have a clear understanding of what the teacher is doing and what they should be doing in response. Strategies for effective teaching include the teacher (1) thinking aloud as he or she presents the initial part of the lesson, (2) modeling the exact steps the students will complete, and (3) soliciting feedback from students during the instructional phase (Mercer & Mercer, 1998).

It's also extremely useful in educational programming for students with ADHD. FBA involves determining the consequences, antecedents, and setting events that maintain inappropriate behaviors (Horner & Carr, 1997). Examples of typical functions of inappropriate behavior of students with ADHD are to avoid work and to gain attention from peers or adults (DuPaul & Ervin, 1996).

■ **Contingency-based self-management**
Educational techniques that involve having students keep track of their own behavior, for which they then receive consequences (e.g., reinforcement).

Contingency-based self-management approaches usually involve having people keep track of their own behavior and then receive consequences, usually in the form of rewards, based on their behavior (Davies & Witte, 2000; Shapiro, DuPaul, & Bradley-Klug, 1998). For example, the teacher might have students use self-monitoring to record how many times they left their seats during a class period. For directions about how to use self-monitoring in the classroom, see Responsive Instruction on page 246 and Chapter 6.

A combination of FBA and contingency-based self-management techniques has proven successful in increasing appropriate behavior of elementary and secondary students with ADHD (DuPaul, Eckert, & McGoey, 1997; Ervin, DuPaul, Kern, & Friman, 1998; Shapiro et al., 1998). In one study, for instance (Ervin et al., 1998), a combination

Rationale A student with ADHD might have difficulty making connections between the instructional phase of a lesson and the activity, assignment, or worksheet that follows. By providing a clear model of what needs to be done, demonstrating the type of inner speech that should be guiding their thinking (via the think-aloud), and checking students for understanding, the teacher increases the likelihood of students making connections between the instruction and the practice or application of the concept (Kucan & Beck, 1997).

Stage IV: Guided Practice

Description The guided practice (GP) stage is the critical transition stage between instruction and independent practice (IP). During GP, students have the opportunity to practice or work with the concept being taught while the teacher is actively providing feedback (Allsopp, 1999; Kemp et al., 1995). GP can consist of students working several problems at the board or on whiteboards at their desks, students explaining (in their own words) to the class what was previously presented, or groups of students doing the first part of a task and reporting their work to the class. The key element of GP is that the teacher has the opportunity to correct or reteach before students are engaged in IP.

Rationale The GP stage provides an important bridge for students with ADHD who may need to be actively engaged in the task to be receptive to instructional guidelines or recommendations provided during instruction (Kemp et al., 1995). GP also provides an opportunity for positive reinforcement as the student makes initial attempts at understanding. Given the chunking of the lesson, teachers could go through the Instruction/Modeling and GP stages two to three times during a given lesson. Providing frequent shifts in activity creates additional support for such ADHD characteristics as short attention span, task-completion difficulty, and short-term memory problems (Rooney, 1995).

Stage V: Independent Practice

Description Independent practice (IP) comes in many forms, ranging from individual to pair or small-group work to homework. The purpose of IP is for students to apply what was taught. At this point in the instructional sequence, students should understand the task requirements and be able to perform the task with competence (Rosenshine, 1995).

Rationale Work presented at students' frustration level can be a trigger for common ADHD behaviors—out of seat or verbal or physical disruptions. By establishing clear expectations for IP, ensuring students are capable of the work, and providing support, teachers increase the likelihood of meaningful student engagement.

Stage VI: Closure and Review

Description At the end of every lesson, time should be permitted to "recap" the main ideas of the lesson. For closure, teachers can review key vocabulary, have students state something they learned, or have students complete a brief journal activity. During closure, the lesson's "big idea" should be reinforced as well as connections made to past and future learning (Kameenui & Carnine, 1998).

Rationale Students with ADHD may have difficulty with synthesizing information (Barkley, 1994). Providing closure at the end of a lesson creates the support necessary for students to make connections among the day's concepts (Rosenshine, 1995).

In summary, teachers can serve many students with ADHD effectively within the general education setting, providing the instruction is responsive to their unique needs.

● *By Kristin L. Sayeski*

of FBA and contingency-based self-management increased the on-task behavior of two adolescents with ADHD. For one of the students, the FBA interviews with the teacher and observations in the classroom led the researchers and teachers to conclude that the adolescent boy's disruptive behavior was a function of gaining peer attention. They based this assumption on evidence that the antecedents to his inattentive behavior consisted of such things as peers looking his way, calling out his name, and making gestures toward him and that the consequences of his inattention were such things as the peers laughing or returning comments to him.

The contingency-based self-management phase involved the student evaluating his on-task behavior on a five-point scale (0 = unacceptable to 5 = excellent) at the end of each math class. The teacher also rated the student's behavior, and the student was awarded points based on how closely the ratings matched. During writing class, the teacher awarded negative or positive points to members of the class depending on whether or not they responded to attention-seeking behaviors from any member of the class. In both classes, the points could be used for privileges.

Meeting the Needs of Students with Attention Deficit Hyperactivity Disorder

The Benefits of Self-Monitoring and Group Contingency

WHAT THE RESEARCH SAYS

Many students with ADHD lack the ability to self-monitor. Self-monitoring requires the ability to appraise a situation and consider alternative ways of responding as well as possible outcomes associated with the various forms of responding (Shapiro, DuPaul, & Bradley-Klug, 1998). This inability to think before acting creates problems for students with ADHD in the areas of paying attention in class, responding to social situations appropriately, and finishing assigned tasks. To address these issues, teachers can help students learn to use self-management procedures to monitor, record, analyze, and reinforce their own behavior (Davies & Witte, 2000). Many studies have repeatedly demonstrated the effectiveness of teaching students such strategies (Cobb, Sample, Alwell, & Johns, 2006; Harris, Friedlander, Saddler, Frizzelle, & Graham, 2005; Lloyd, Hallahan, Kauffman, & Keller, 1998; Reid & Lienemann, 2006; Reid, Trout, & Schartz, 2005).

Although teaching self-management to students with ADHD has been proven to be effective, many teachers prefer whole-class or group-contingency plans. Within a group-contingency model, the behavior of one student is tied to the outcome of the whole group. Group-contingency models promote interdependence, as group members must work together to meet a goal (Tankersley, 1995). Under a group contingency, teachers can use the same behavior management approach for all students and don't have to differentiate their treatment of the few students who need help with self-management. Thus, group contingencies can be very effective for general education teachers whose classrooms include students with ADHD.

RESEARCH STUDY

One study examined the effects of a management program with third-graders on the behaviors of students with ADHD in a general education classroom (Davies & Witte, 2000). All students—those with ADHD as well as nondisabled students—were responsible for monitoring their own behavior, and contingencies were established for group performance. Procedures for the group intervention were:

1. If any student displayed the target behavior [inappropriate verbalizations], she or he moved one dot from his/her group's chart from the green section into the blue section. If the child did not move the dot after about ten seconds, then the teacher moved a dot into the red section of the chart.

2. The rewards a group received were related to how many dots the group had in the green section of their chart at the end of the intervention period. Each group needed to have at least one dot left in the green section at the end of the intervention period to receive the reinforcer. [Each group started with five dots.] (Davies & Witte, 2000, p. 141)

RESEARCH FINDINGS

Results from the study demonstrated a decrease in talking out of turn for the four students with ADHD. In addition, there was no evidence of possible negative side effects of peer pressure, such as threats or negative verbal comments (Davies & Witte, 2000).

APPLYING THE RESEARCH TO TEACHING

Findings from this study demonstrate the effectiveness of using self-management within the context of a group contingency. Teachers can implement similar management strategies through (1) targeting specific undesirable behaviors to be eliminated or specific desirable behaviors to be reinforced, (2) creating a chart for students to use for self-management, (3) communicating the procedures for recording behaviors on the chart (e.g., "If you do X, mark your chart" or "When the beeper beeps, check to see if you are doing X, then mark your chart accordingly"), or (4) connecting the self-management procedures to a group contingency (e.g., "If all students get over X points during the lesson, all students will get a homework pass").

● *By Kristin L. Sayeski*

THE ROLE OF REINFORCEMENT   Authorities have pointed to the crucial role that contingency plays in contingency-based self-management: reinforcement of some kind, such as social praise or points that can be traded for privileges, is especially important for self-management techniques to be effective. For example, an extensive review of research found that contingency-based self-management strategies were more effective than self-management strategies without contingencies in leading to positive behavioral changes in students with ADHD (DuPaul & Eckert, 1997).

Although the use of behavioral procedures such as reinforcement and punishment is somewhat controversial—there are those who are opposed to their use (Kohn, 1993)—many authorities consider them almost indispensable in working with students

TABLE 7.3	Pfiffner, Barkley, and DuPaul's Intervention Principles for ADHD

1. Rules and instructions must be clear, brief, and often delivered through more visible and external modes of presentation.

2. Consequences must be delivered swiftly and immediately.

3. Consequences must be delivered more frequently [than for students without ADHD].

4. The types of consequences must often be of a higher magnitude, or more powerful [than for students without ADHD].

5. An appropriate and often richer degree of incentives must be provided.

6. Reinforcers, or particularly, rewards must be changed or rotated more frequently.

7. Anticipation is the key. Teachers must be mindful of planning ahead, particularly during phases of transition across activities or classes, to ensure that the children are cognizant of the shift in rules (and consequences) that is about to occur.

Source: Condensed from Pfiffner, L. J., Barkley, R. A., & DuPaul, G. J., Treatment of ADHD in school settings. In R. A. Barkley, *Attention-deficit hyperactivity disorder: A handbook for diagnosis and treatment* (3rd ed.). New York: Guilford Press, 2006, pp. 554–555. Adapted with permission.

with ADHD. For example, they're an integral part of a set of intervention principles advocated by one team of authorities (see Table 7.3).

Service Delivery Models

Because the U.S. Department of Education doesn't recognize ADHD as a separate special education category, we don't have statistics on how many of these students are served in different classroom environments. It's safe to assume, however, that one can find students with ADHD across the entire continuum, from residential schools to full inclusion in general education classrooms. But because, as we noted earlier, there is reason to believe that fewer than half receive any special education services (Forness & Kavale, 2002), it's logical to assume that most students with ADHD spend most of their time in general education classrooms. Making It Work on page 248 describes different ways to use co-teaching to help meet the needs of these students, whether they receive special education services or not.

As with all students with disabilities, the best placement for students with ADHD should be determined on an individual basis. Although full inclusion in a general education classroom might be appropriate for some students with ADHD, the estimate that over half don't receive any special education services should be viewed with some concern. This is especially true in light of the fact that studies have shown that positive behavioral changes in students with ADHD are much more likely to occur in special education than in general education settings (DuPaul & Eckert, 1997).

Medication Considerations

One of the most controversial topics in all of special education is the treatment of ADHD with medication. **Psychostimulants**, which stimulate or activate neurological functioning, are by far the most frequent type of medication prescribed for ADHD. The most common stimulant prescribed for ADHD is methylphenidate, or **Ritalin**. **Adderall** is another stimulant that is sometimes prescribed. The fact that physicians would prescribe a psychostimulant for someone who exhibits hyperactivity is, at first blush, counterintuitive. In fact, for years professionals referred to the **paradoxical effect of Ritalin** because its effects appeared to be the opposite of those one would expect in the case of

UNDERSTANDING THE STANDARDS AND PRINCIPLES Describe effective educational programming for students with ADHD. (CEC Knowledge and Skill Standards CC4S3 & CC4S5)

Council for Exceptional Children

■ **Psychostimulants**
Medications that activate dopamine levels in the frontal and prefrontal areas of the brain that control behavioral inhibition and executive functions; used to treat persons with ADHD.

■ **Ritalin**
The most commonly prescribed psychostimulant for ADHD; its generic name is methylphenidate.

■ **Adderall**
A psychostimulant for ADHD.

■ **Paradoxical effect of Ritalin**
The now discredited belief that Ritalin, even though a stimulant, acts to subdue a person's behavior and that this effect of Ritalin is evident in people with ADHD but not in those without ADHD.

Collaboration and Co-Teaching for Students with ADHD

"How can I get this student focused?!"

WHAT DOES IT MEAN TO BE A TEACHER OF STUDENTS WITH ATTENTION DEFICIT HYPERACTIVITY DISORDER?

Currently, the Council for Exceptional Children doesn't have specific competencies for teachers of students with Attention Deficit Hyperactivity Disorder (ADHD). As you read in this chapter, ADHD isn't recognized as a separate special education category by the U.S. Department of Education. These students, however, often have additional disabling conditions and are served by teachers with expertise in those areas. That expertise may include:

1. Understanding educational implications of characteristics of various exceptionalities.
2. Understanding the effects of various medications on individuals with exceptional learning needs.
3. Using procedures to increase the individual's self-awareness, self-management, self-control, self-reliance, and self-esteem.

SUCCESSFUL STRATEGIES FOR CO-TEACHING

Co-teaching classroom configurations come in many forms and all give teachers "more hands" to meet the needs of students with ADHD. Vaughn, Schumm, and Arguelles (1997) describe five basic models of co-teaching that provide co-teachers with opportunities to use the instructional strategies described in this chapter and in Table 7.3 on p. 247.

One Teach, One Drift

In this model, one teacher is responsible for instruction and the other teacher drifts, monitoring students. This model allows the drifting teacher to redirect students who may be off task, to observe and mark student monitoring forms, to provide feedback on individual student's attention and participation, and to deliver reinforcers or consequences on a frequent basis.

Station Teaching

In station teaching, co-teachers split content into two parts and students into three groups. Each teacher teaches one of the two content pieces at a station to a small group of students and the other group works independently. The student groups rotate between stations. Teachers can break content down into smaller tasks that maintain the attention of all students. Each teacher is able to work with a small group of students, making it easier to ensure that they

Case Study Homework Exercise

Discipline • Go to the Homework and Exercises section in Chapter 7 of MyEducationLab and read the case study "He Just Needs a Little Discipline", which addresses the importance of teachers and families working together when designing and implementing interventions for students with ADHD.

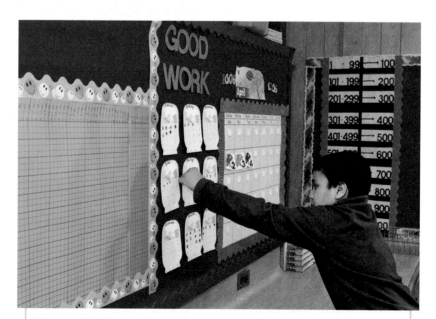

Programs that allow students to monitor their own behavior and performance may encourage them to maintain appropriate behavior at school.

are focused and learning. It is also easier to help students work together and to provide reinforcers and consequences more frequently. The difficulty lies in making sure that students with ADHD can work appropriately in the independent station.

Parallel Teaching

In parallel teaching, the two teachers split the class into two groups and teach the same content to a smaller group of students. This model provides the same opportunities as station teaching, along with the chance to modify the instructional delivery of the same content material to meet the needs of the student.

Alternative Teaching

The alternative teaching model includes content instruction by one teacher to a large group of students and remedial or supplementary instruction by the other teacher to a small group of students. The teacher of the small group can modify delivery of content, control the delivery of consequences and rewards, and closely monitor and observe students. In addition, the teacher of the small group can incorporate instruction in strategies such as self-monitoring.

Team Teaching

In team teaching, co-teachers alternate or "tag team" in delivering instruction to the entire class. In this model, co-teachers can both be on the lookout for misconceptions, confusion, inattention, and disruption. These can then be addressed in the flow of instruction rather than afterward or on an individual basis. In addition, co-teachers can work together to both present content and learning strategies in unison to better meet the needs of all students.

In All Models

Teachers working together can discuss and better evaluate whether rules and instructions are clear, brief, and delivered in appropriate formats for students with ADHD. Co-teachers can also work together to better anticipate "rough spots" for students with ADHD, particularly during transition times, changes in routines, or complex tasks (see Table 7.3). The varying models of co-teaching provide the flexibility for teachers to adjust instructional delivery to meet the objectives of the teachers and the needs of the students with ADHD.

Cautionary Note

All too often, co-teachers fall into the habit of using one model to the exclusion of others. This is unfortunate in that it may mean that one teacher doesn't participate actively in instruction and/or planning. This nonparticipation can lead to a lack of interest on the teacher's part and a disregard for that teacher on the students' part. The models of co-teaching were developed to match the needs of instruction. Both teachers should participate in instruction in a way that matches their expertise.

● *By Margaret P. Weiss*

someone who does not have ADHD. Researchers have concluded, however, that Ritalin influences the release of the neurotransmitters dopamine and norepinephrine, thus enabling the brain's executive functions to operate more normally (Connor, 2006). Furthermore, it's now believed that Ritalin has the same chemical and behavioral effect on people who don't have ADHD as it does on those with ADHD (Solanto, 1998).

Ordinarily, Ritalin takes about one hour to take effect, the optimal effect occurring at about two hours. The effects of Ritalin usually wear off after about four hours. Responsiveness to Ritalin is highly individual, so the dosage level and number of doses per day vary from person to person.

More recently, the U.S. Food and Drug Administration has approved **Strattera**, a nonstimulant, for use with ADHD. Compared to the stimulants, much less research has been conducted on Strattera, but that which has been done indicates it can be effective for some children and adults.

■ **Strattera**
A nonstimulant medication for ADHD; affects the neurotransmitter norepinephrine.

Opposition to Ritalin

Not all professionals, parents, and laypeople are in favor of using pyschostimulants for ADHD. In fact, Ritalin has been the subject of numerous assaults in the media. Critics have appeared on nationally broadcast television shows such as *Oprah, Geraldo,* and *20/20,* as well as evening and morning news shows. The Church of Scientology's objection to Ritalin has received much publicity due to Hollywood actor Tom Cruise's criticisms of

Casebook Reflections

REFER TO THE CASE *More Than LD* in your booklet. After Shannon's teachers had made several modifications for instruction, Mrs. Morgan recommended talking to Dr. Rodriguez about putting Shannon on medicine. Do you think that was an appropriate suggestion? Why or why not? ●

Ritalin. Although some criticisms have been relatively mild, others have ranged from assertions that ADHD is a bogus diagnosis to claims that professionals are trying to control children with medication and make them overly docile.

The Research Evidence

Over the last 30 to 40 years, dozens of research teams around the world have studied the effects of several medications on ADHD. Most of this research has focused on the psychostimulant, Ritalin.

EFFECTIVENESS   Despite all the negative publicity in the media, most ADHD authorities are in favor of Ritalin's use. After hundreds of studies, the research is overwhelmingly positive on its effectiveness in helping students to have more normalized behavioral inhibition and executive functioning (Connor, 2006). Moreover, Ritalin not only leads to better results on parent and teacher rating scales, but also leads to improved academic achievement as well as classroom behavior such as better note-taking, on-task behavior, quiz scores, homework completion, and written-language work (Evans et al., 2001).

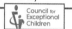

UNDERSTANDING THE STANDARDS AND PRINCIPLES   What are the pros and cons of treating ADHD with medication? (CEC Knowledge and Skill Standard CC2K7)

Council for Exceptional Children

NONRESPONDERS AND SIDE EFFECTS   Even though research has demonstrated the general effectiveness of Ritalin, it's important to point out that it's not effective for everyone. Somewhere around 30 percent of those who take Ritalin do not have a favorable response (Barbaresi et al., 2006). In addition, some side effects are possible, including insomnia, reduction in appetite, abdominal pain, headaches, and irritability. There has also been speculation on the possibility that in a very small number of cases, Ritalin causes tics or increases their intensity in those who already have tics (DuPaul, Barkley, & Connor, 1998). There have been many anecdotal reports of a "rebound effect," in which a child exhibits irritability as the Ritalin wears off. In most cases, these side effects are mild and can be controlled. For example, in the case of the two most common side effects—insomnia and reduction in appetite—care should be taken not to take the Ritalin too close to mealtime or bedtime. In the case of the rebound effect, some physicians recommend using a time-release form of Ritalin.

DRUG ABUSE   A popular misconception is that by taking Ritalin, children with ADHD are more likely to become abusers of drugs such as marijuana or cocaine as adolescents or young adults. There is little if any documented evidence that this occurs (Connor, 2006). In fact, there is suggestive evidence that those with ADHD who are prescribed Ritalin as children are less likely to turn to illicit drugs as teenagers (Biederman, Wilens, Mick, Spencer, & Faraone, 1999). Some have speculated that perhaps those who are not medicated with Ritalin turn to other drugs to try to find "peace of mind" or to "chill out."

Cautions Regarding Medication

Although the research is overwhelmingly positive on the effectiveness of medication for increasing appropriate behavior, there are still a number of cautions:

Psychostimulants, especially Ritalin, have sparked a national controversy over the treatment of ADHD. Although Ritalin is not effective for everyone and can have side effects, the bulk of research evidence supports its effectiveness.

- Medication should not be prescribed at the first sign of a behavior problem. Only after careful analysis of the student's behavior and environment should medication be considered. The use of psychostimulants for ADHD in the United States increased approximately eight-fold from the 1970s to the 1990s (Wilens & Biederman, 1992), and in the first five years of the twenty-first century, the rate has approximately doubled (Castle, Aubert, Verbrugge, Khalid, & Epstein, 2007). Although much of this increase in recent years can be attributed to an increase in prescriptions for females and adults coincident with the increase in diagnosis in these populations, it still should alert us to turning too quickly to medication as *the* answer to ADHD.

- Although research has demonstrated the effectiveness of medication on behavioral inhibition and executive functions, the results for academic outcomes have not been as dramatic. Although important academic measures, such as work completed or accuracy on assignments, have shown substantial improvement, the impact on achievement tests has been less (Forness, Kavale, & Crenshaw, 1999). Thus, teachers shouldn't assume that medication will take care of all the academic problems these students face.

- Parents, teachers, and physicians should monitor dosage levels closely so that the dose used is effective but not too strong. Proper dosage levels vary considerably.

- Teachers and parents shouldn't lead children to believe that the medication serves as a substitute for self-responsibility and self-initiative.

- Teachers and parents shouldn't view the medication as a panacea; they, too, must take responsibility and initiative in working with the child.

- Parents and teachers should keep in mind that psychostimulants are a controlled substance. There is the potential for siblings, peers, or the child himself or herself, to attempt to experiment with them.

- The final key to the effective use of medication is communication among parents, physicians, teachers, and the child.

Medication Versus Behavior Management

Over the years, parents and professionals have considered the question of whether medication is more, less, or equally effective as behavior management. Unfortunately, research thus far hasn't provided a definitive answer. The National Institute of Mental Health launched a large-scale study to address the question (MTA Cooperative Group, 1999). After fourteen months of treatment, combining medication and behavior management was the most effective, followed by medication alone. Behavior management, while effective for some students, was a distant third. However, three years after the treatment groups were formally discontinued, leaving it to families and schools to decide whether to use medication and/or behavior management, there were no differences among the treatments—children from all three of the original treatment groups fared better than those with no treatment at all (Jensen et al., 2007). Based on these results and others (Fabiano et al., 2007; Majewicz-Hefley & Carlson, 2007), it appears that the best course of action is to first try a combination of medication and behavior management. But one can take comfort in knowing that medication alone or behavior management alone is also effective.

Assessment of Progress

Assessment of students with ADHD includes procedures for evaluating social and emotional behaviors and academic skills. Many of the procedures described in Chapter 6 on learning disabilities are also appropriate for students with ADHD. In the following sections we discuss methods for monitoring student progress, measuring student outcomes, and providing appropriate testing accommodations.

Progress Monitoring

MONITORING ACADEMIC PROGRESS   Students with ADHD often experience difficulties with academic tasks as a result of inattention, impulsivity, and/or poor executive

Reading Homework Exercise

Medication for Preschoolers? ● Go to the Homework and Exercises section in Chapter 7 of MyEducationLab and read the article "Med-start Kids: Pros, Cons of Ritalin for Preschool ADHD", which addresses the controversial topic of medication for preschoolers with ADHD.

Reading Homework Exercise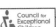

Relevance of Diet? ● Go to the Homework and Exercises section in Chapter 7 of MyEducationLab and read the article "The Feingold Diet: Dubious Benefits, Subtle Risks." Evaluate the claims and "success stories" presented in the article.

UNDERSTANDING THE STANDARDS AND PRINCIPLES   Describe ways teachers can monitor the academic and behavioral progress of students with ADHD. (CEC Knowledge and Skill Standards CC8S8 & GC8S1)

Council for Exceptional Children

skills functioning. In addition, students with ADHD are commonly diagnosed with a second disorder such as a learning disability (DuPaul & Stoner, 2003, Mayes, Calhoun, & Crowell, 2000) or intellectual disability (Abikoff, 2002). Thus, the importance of monitoring their progress in academic skills can't be overstated.

Curriculum-based measurement (CBM), introduced in Chapter 3 and described in more detail in Chapter 6, is an appropriate method for monitoring academic progress for students with ADHD. An advantage of CBM for students with ADHD is that the measures take very little time to administer and are focused on a particular task. CBM should be implemented with students with ADHD to ensure that academic progress is adequate. Monitoring progress on academic tasks should be accompanied by methods for monitoring students' attention and academic engaged time.

MONITORING OF ATTENTION AND BEHAVIOR   Two methods are used commonly to assess a student's attention to tasks and social/emotional behavior: rating scales and direct observation. The Conners Rating Scales-Revised (CRS-R; Conners, 2001) can be used for measuring student outcomes or to monitor student progress. Sample scale items comprise measures of opposition, inattention, anxiety, and social problems. An advantage of the CRS-R over other rating scales is its Treatment Progress ColorPlot form, designed to monitor treatment effects over time (Taylor, 2006).

Teachers can directly observe students on a regular schedule to monitor attention, academic engaged time, and disruptive behavior. Behavioral recording systems provide a framework to conduct systematic observations. For example, **momentary time sampling** allows the teacher to conduct brief observations and collect data on a specific set of behaviors. In momentary time sampling, the observer determines the length of the observation and divides it into intervals (e.g., fifteen minutes may be divided into fifteen intervals of one minute each). At the beginning of each interval, the observer records whether the student is exhibiting the behavior of interest and then does not observe the student until the beginning of the next interval.

Figure 7.3 below provides an example of a momentary time sampling chart for a student, Susie, who is working to increase her time on task. The observation lasted for fifteen minutes. The observer placed a check mark in the box if Susie was attending to the task at the time sampled, and an X if she was not attending. At the end of the observation period, Susie was on-task ten out of the fifteen intervals, or 67 percent of the time. Susie's teacher may use the momentary time sampling procedure at regular intervals to monitor her attention to tasks and modify interventions as needed.

Margin notes

■ **Curriculum-based measurement (CBM)**
A formative evaluation method designed to evaluate performance in the curriculum to which students are exposed; usually involves giving students a small sample of items from the curriculum to use in their schools; proponents argue that CBM is preferable to comparing students with national norms or using tests that do not reflect the curriculum content learned by the students.

■ **Momentary time sampling**
An interval recording procedure used to capture a representative sample of a target behavior over a specified period of time.

Student Name: *Susie*
Date: *3/10/2008*
Setting: *Small group reading lesson*
Time of day: *9:30 a.m. – 9:45 a.m.*

	1	2	3	4	5	6	7	8	9	10	11	12	13	14	15
Attending to Task	✓	X	✓	✓	X	X	✓	✓	X	✓	✓	✓	X	✓	✓

10 /15 intervals = *67%*

FIGURE 7.3   Momentary time sampling is an interval recording procedure to capture a representative sample of a target behavior over a specified period of time. Susie's teacher observed her for fifteen minutes, glancing at her at the beginning of each minute. If Susie was on-task, her teacher put a check mark in the corresponding box for that interval, or an X if she was not on task. At the end of the observation period, she calculated the number of intervals she was on-task to determine a percentage of on-task behavior for the fifteen-minute time period.

Outcome Measures

Outcome measures for students with ADHD focus on both social/emotional behavior and academics. Rating scales are commonly used to measure behavioral outcomes (Taylor, 2006). Academic outcome measures typically include standardized measures of academic achievement, just as for students with learning disabilities.

Several commercial rating scales are available in addition to the CRS-R. The Diagnostic Assessment Scale for Attention/Deficit Hyperactivity Disorder (Ryser & McConnell, 2001) is appropriate for individuals ages five to eighteen years old. This scale evaluates inattention, hyperactivity, and impulsivity. Like many rating scales, different versions are available for use with parents and teachers.

A unique measure of student outcomes is the Telephone Interview Probe (TIP) (Corkum, Andreou, Schachar, Tannock, & Cunningham, 2007). This instrument uses brief telephone interviews of parents and teachers for the purpose of determining the effects of interventions for students with ADHD. It's particularly useful for evaluating the effects of psychostimulant medications on an individual at a specific time of day or setting. Many common rating scales are limited to broader time frames and don't provide the specificity required to make decisions in regard to treatment. The TIP provides ratings of inattention, impulsiveness, hyperactivity, oppositional behavior, and problem situations for three time points during the day (i.e., morning, afternoon, evening).

Testing Accommodations

Accommodations for students with ADHD typically include setting and accommodations such as small-group or individual administration in a quiet location to minimize possible distractions and testing schedule modifications such as extended time and frequent breaks. In one study of accommodations for students with ADHD, 81 percent of the students received additional time to complete tests (Schnoes, Reid, Wagner, & Marder, 2006). In addition, students with ADHD who also exhibit learning difficulties may receive modifications to presentation format and response format, similar to those for students with learning disabilities.

Early Intervention

Diagnosis of young children with ADHD is particularly difficult because many young children who don't have ADHD tend to exhibit a great deal of motor activity and a lack of impulse control. For the very reason that excessive activity and impulsivity are relatively normal for young children, preschoolers with ADHD can be particularly difficult to manage. Thus, those preschoolers who really do have ADHD are a great challenge to parents and teachers.

Because of the severity of the symptoms of preschoolers who've been diagnosed with ADHD, the importance of the educational principles of classroom structure, teacher direction, functional behavioral assessment, and contingency-based self-management that we discussed above are all the more important. Given that even young children who don't have ADHD lack fully developed self-management skills, most recommend an even stronger emphasis on the use of contingencies in the form of praise, points, and tangible rewards.

Research has shown that providing parents of preschool children with ADHD with intensive, structured methods of applying behavior management procedures can be successful in improving behavior and pre-academic skills (Kern et al., 2007). However, in the case of preschoolers with ADHD and high rates of aggression, even implementing very intensive early intervention procedures (including highly structured classrooms with strong contingencies) leads only to limited behavioral and academic improvements that do not endure (Shelton et al., 2000). In other words, even high-quality early intervention is not likely to remediate completely the symptoms of children with ADHD and severe aggression. Such children need long-term programming.

Building Teaching Skills Lesson Planning Exercise

Planning for Learners with ADHD • Go to the Building Teaching Skills section in Chapter 7 of MyEducationLab and refer to the Responsive Instruction feature in the chapter titled "Planning for Students with ADHD in the General Education Classroom."

Transition to Adulthood

Not too long ago, most professionals assumed that ADHD diminished in adolescence and usually disappeared by adulthood. Authorities now recognize about two thirds of individuals who are diagnosed with ADHD in childhood will continue to have significant symptoms in adulthood (Faraone & Doyle, 2001). The Personal Perspectives on p. 255 relates an example of ADHD's effects on an adult . With the greater recognition of ADHD by the scientific community as well as by the popular media, many people are being diagnosed with ADHD in adulthood. Several studies indicate a prevalence rate of about 4 to 5 percent (Barkley, 2006d; Kessler et al., 2006), similar to the rate for children.

Diagnosis in Adulthood

The diagnosis of ADHD in adults is controversial. Because of the long-held assumption that ADHD did not persist into adulthood, there isn't a very long history of research on ADHD in adults. In recent years, however, professionals have begun to make progress in identifying and treating ADHD in adults. Because there's no test for ADHD, most authorities hold that the person's **history** is of utmost importance. As one authoritative team has put it:

▪ **History**
A patient's "story" of his or her functioning in life with respect to strengths and weaknesses; considered crucial by many physicians in the diagnosis of ADHD.

> Taking a history both from the identified patient (child or adult) and from someone else (parents, spouse, or significant other) constitute the crux of the evaluation. Although not usually considered a test, the history is the best method of assessment that we have. Sometimes it is the only "test" that will be needed. . . .
>
> The most common misconception about how to diagnose [ADHD], a misconception subscribed to by most schools and many professionals, is that there is a "test" for [ADHD], a psychological test or brain scan, that absolutely pins down the diagnosis. But there is no such test. The closest we have to it is the history. The history is more valuable than any paper-pencil test or brain scan.
>
> It is the individual's own story—what we doctors call the history—that makes or breaks the diagnosis of [ADHD]. (Hallowell & Ratey, 2006, pp. 117–118)

For learners with ADHD, coaching beyond high school, through either a job coach, therapist, or teacher-counselor is highly recommended.

Personal PERSPECTIVES

An Adult with ADHD: Ann's Story

I grew up not feeling very good about myself. In school, it was hard for me to stay on the subject or to finish anything. . . . Teachers would be on my back. They said I was such a good child—they couldn't understand it. And I tried so hard. I just couldn't finish anything. . . . I was distracted very easily by practically everything. If someone sneezed, I'd look at him and my mind would go off in a million directions. I'd look out the window, wondering why he had sneezed. . . .

The situation has persisted into adulthood. I'm very disorganized. Take housekeeping, for example. After dinner, when I start the dishes, I'll wash a little, then run and wipe off the table, wipe the cabinet, talk on the phone, and never get anything completed. I have to really concentrate and tell myself "You are going to get the dishes done." Then they get done, but I still get the urge to stop and go wash off the dining room table. Just like someone is pulling me. My closet and drawers are still a mess, just like when I was a kid. What's really hard is to stay with any kind of paper work—bills, for example. It's my husband's job to do the bills. If it were mine, we'd probably be in jail. . . . Only recently at age forty-five have I been able to sit down and write a letter. I usually write small postcards.

I'm the most impulsive person in the world. It gets me in trouble. If I see something I know I shouldn't buy, I'll buy it anyway.

Or, I'll say something that I know the minute it comes out of my mouth I'm going to regret. . . .

I wish I could just slow down and relax. I have problems sitting still. . . . People say I make them nervous, but I don't even realize I'm doing anything. That hurts my feelings. I don't want to be different.

My dream has always been to be some kind of counselor, but I felt like I wasn't college material, so I got married and had two children. I have a real estate license now. I don't know how I passed the test. I must have guessed right. What I like about selling is that I'm always on the move and I love people. I'm tuned into them. But I'm too sensitive to have a sense of humor. I think I have a thin skin. I get my feelings hurt easily. When that happens, I cry and go into my shell.

My mood swings from high to low. I either feel very good or very down. I feel up if the house looks good. If I get everything done that I think I should, it makes me feel good about myself. I feel responsible for a lot of people. If my husband is in a bad mood, or if things aren't going right for my kids, my mother, or my sister, I feel bad. I don't know what's wrong with me.

● *Ann Ridgley*

Source: Weiss, L. (1992). Attention deficit disorder in adults (pp. 11–14). Lanham, MD: Taylor Publishing Co. Reprinted by permission.

As crucial as the history is, however, its subjective nature does make it vulnerable to misinterpretation. Therefore, clinicians have come up with guidelines for diagnosis. Table 7.4 contains a set of suggested diagnostic criteria for adults.

Adult Outcomes

Many adults with ADHD also have antisocial, anxiety, and depression disorders and more school failure experience and employment problems than adults who don't have ADHD (Barkley & Murphy, 2007; Rucklidge, Brown, Crawford, & Kaplan, 2007; Weyandt & DuPaul, 2006). Those who have a coexisting condition such as depression or aggression tend to have less positive outcomes than those who do not. Although people with ADHD are at risk for poorer outcomes, it's important to point out that there are many adults with ADHD who have highly successful careers and jobs, and many have happy marriages and families.

EMPLOYMENT   Adults with ADHD are more apt than their nondisabled peers to experience problems on the job with respect to getting along with others, being bored, and being disciplined by supervisors (Murphy & Barkley, 2007). One of the keys to successful employment, especially for persons with ADHD, is to select a job or career that maximizes the individual's strengths and minimizes her or his weaknesses. Success is often dependent on pursuing a job that fits a person's needs for structure versus independence. It is

UNDERSTANDING THE STANDARDS AND PRINCIPLES   What do we know about transition to adulthood for students with ADHD? (CEC Knowledge and Skill Standards CC10K2 & CC10K3)

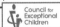
Council for Exceptional Children

TABLE 7.4	**Suggested Diagnostic Criteria for Attention Deficit Disorder in Adults**

Note: Consider a criterion met only if the behavior is considerably more frequent than that of most people of the same mental age.

A. A chronic disturbance in which at least twelve of the following are present:

- A sense of underachievement, of not meeting one's goals (regardless of how much one has actually accomplished).
- Difficulty getting organized.
- Chronic procrastination or trouble getting started.
- Many projects going simultaneously; trouble with followthrough.
- A tendency to say what comes to mind without necessarily considering the timing or appropriateness of the remark.
- A frequent search for high stimulation.
- An intolerance of boredom.
- Easy distractibility, trouble focusing attention, tendency to tune out or drift away in the middle of a page or a conversation, often coupled with an ability to hyperfocus at times.
- Often creative, intuitive, highly intelligent.
- Trouble in going through established channels, following "proper" procedure.
- Impatient; low tolerance of frustration.
- Impulsive, either verbally or in action, as in impulsive spending of money, changing plans, enacting new schemes or career plans, and the like; hot-tempered.
- A tendency to worry needlessly, endlessly; a tendency to scan the horizon looking for something to worry about, alternating with inattention to or disregard for actual dangers.
- A sense of insecurity.
- Mood swings, mood lability, especially when disengaged from a person or a project.
- Physical or cognitive restlessness.
- A tendency toward addictive behavior.
- Chronic problems with self-esteem.
- Inaccurate self-observation.
- Family history of ADD or manic-depressive illness or depression or substance abuse or other disorders of impulse control or mood.

B. Childhood history of ADD. (It may not have been formally diagnosed, but in reviewing the history, one sees that the signs and symptoms were there.)

C. Situation not explained by other medical or psychiatric condition.

Source: From *Driven to distraction: Recognizing and coping with attention deficit disorder from childhood through adulthood.* by Edward M. Hallowell, M.D. and John J. Ratey, M.D., copyright © 1994 by Edward H. Hallowell, M.D. and John J. Ratey, M.D. Used by permission of Pantheon Books, a division of Random House, Inc.

recommended that those who work best with structure look for jobs with organizations that have a clear mission and lines of authority, with an emphasis on oversight from supervisors who have an understanding of ADHD. Those who find formal structures too confining should look for work environments that are flexible, have variety, and allow one to be independent (Hallowell & Ratey, 2006).

MARRIAGE AND FAMILY Given some of the behavioral characteristics of ADHD, it's not surprising that husbands and wives of people with ADHD frequently complain that their spouse is a poor listener, preoccupied, forgetful, unreliable, messy, and so forth. A person's ADHD can have a negative impact on the entire family. Parents who have ADHD may find it difficult to manage the daily lives of their children. As one parent put it, "I couldn't remember to brush my teeth when I was a kid, and now I can't remember to tell my kid to brush his teeth" (Weiss, Hechtman, & Weiss, 2000, p. 1060).

Casebook Reflections

REFER TO THE CASE *More Than LD* in your booklet. After the consultation with their doctor, Shannon's father felt that he had had the same problems in school: lack of attention, disorganization, problems keeping up with schoolwork. Do you think he had ADHD but was never diagnosed? What do these remarks reveal? ●

Many authorities recommend that the first step to treatment is to have all family members become educated about the facts associated with ADHD. Because ADHD is a family issue, they also recommend that all members of the family should be partners in its treatment.

Importance of Coaching

One highly recommended therapeutic technique is coaching (Hallowell & Ratey, 2006). **Coaching** involves identifying someone whom the person with ADHD can rely on for support. The coach, who can be a therapist or a friend, is someone who can regularly spend a few minutes to help keep the person with ADHD focused on his or her goals. The coach provides the structure needed to plan for upcoming events and activities and heaps on praise when tasks are accomplished.

■ **Coaching**
A technique whereby a friend or therapist offers encouragement and support for a person with ADHD.

Although ADHD is a lifelong struggle for most people with the condition, with the appropriate combination of medical, educational, and psychological counseling, satisfactory employment and family adjustment are within the reach of most people with ADHD. Now that most authorities recognize that ADHD often continues into adulthood, more and more research will be focused on treatment of ADHD in adults. With this research should come an even more positive outlook for adults with ADHD.

Summary

What are the historical origins of ADHD?

▶ In the mid-nineteenth century, Dr. Heinrich Hoffman wrote nursery rhymes about "Fidgety Phillip" and "The Story of Johnny Head-in-Air."

▶ In 1902, Dr. George F. Still reported on children whom he referred to as having "defective moral control."

▶ In the 1930s, Kurt Goldstein reported on soldiers who had head wounds in World War I.

▶ In the 1930s and 1940s, Heinz Werner and Alfred Strauss reported on children with mental retardation (intellectual disabilities) who were assumed to be brain-injured, referred to as having the "Strauss syndrome."

▶ In the 1950s, William Cruickshank extended Werner and Strauss's work to children with normal intelligence.

▶ In the 1950s and 1960s, the term *minimal brain injury* was used to refer to children who were of normal intelligence but who were inattentive, impulsive, and/or hyperactive.

▶ In the 1960s and 1970s, the term *hyperactive child syndrome* was popular.

What is the current definition of ADHD?

▶ Most professionals rely on the American Psychiatric Association's Diagnostic and Statistical Manual of Mental Disorders, which uses ADHD as the general term and subdivides individuals into (1) ADHD, Predominantly Inattentive Type; (2) ADHD, Predominantly Hyperactive-Impulsive Type; and (3) ADHD, Combined Type.

What is the prevalence of ADHD?

▶ The best estimates are that 3 to 7 percent of the school-age population has ADHD.

▶ Boys with ADHD outnumber girls, most likely owing to biological differences and perhaps some referral bias.

What methods of assessment are used to identify individuals with ADHD?

▶ Professionals usually use four methods of assessment: (1) a medical examination, (2) a clinical interview, (3) teacher and parent rating scales, and (4) behavioral observations. The behavioral observations can be done in the classroom and/or in the clinician's office.

What causes ADHD?

▶ Neuroimaging studies have identified five areas of the brain that might be affected in people with ADHD: the prefrontal lobes, the frontal lobes, the basal ganglia, the cerebellum, and the corpus callosum.
  ■ The prefrontal and frontal lobes are responsible for executive functions, or the ability to regulate one's behavior.
  ■ The basal ganglia and cerebellum are involved in coordination and control of motor behavior.
  ■ The corpus callosum connects the left and right hemispheres of the brain and serves as a pathway for nerve signals between the two.

▶ Research has identified an imbalance in each of two neurotransmitters: dopamine and norepinephrine.

▶ Family studies, twin studies, and molecular genetic studies indicate that heredity may also be a significant cause of ADHD.

▶ Exposure to toxins such as lead and abuse of alcohol and tobacco, as well as medical factors such as complications at birth and low birth weight, can also be a cause of ADHD.

What are some of the psychological and behavioral characteristics of learners with ADHD?

▶ Barkley's theory of ADHD points to problems with (1) behavioral inhibition, (2) executive functioning, (3) time awareness and management, and (4) persistent goal-directed behavior.

▶ People with ADHD also often experience problems in adaptive behavior and in their relationships with peers.

▶ Several conditions often co-exist with ADHD: learning disabilities and emotional-behavioral problems, such as depression and anxiety; people with ADHD are also at risk for substance abuse problems.

What are some educational considerations for learners with ADHD?

▶ Good educational programming for students with ADHD involves a high degree of classroom structure and teacher-directed activities.

▶ Good educational programming for students with ADHD involves functional assessment and contingency-based self-management.
  ■ Functional behavioral assessment involves determining the consequences, antecedents, and setting events that maintain inappropriate behaviors.
  ■ Such approaches might also include self-monitoring or self-management programs, wherein students record their own behaviors.

What are some medication considerations for learners with ADHD?

▶ Psychostimulants, such as Ritalin, are prescribed most often; Strattera, a nonstimulant, has recently been introduced.

▶ Scientific studies (including a large-scale study sponsored by the National Institute for Mental Health) support the effectiveness of medication, and most authorities on ADHD favor its use.

▶ Some cautions about medication are that some people are non-responders, dosage levels should be monitored closely, some people experience side effects (although these usually are not serious), children should not be encouraged to see the medication as a replacement for self-initiated behavioral control, and medication should not be the first response to problem behavior.

How do professionals assess students with ADHD's academic, attention, and behavioral progress?

▶ Curriculum-based measurement can be used to assess progress in academics and attention and behavior.
  ■ Momentary time sampling is particularly useful for assessing behavioral progress.

▶ Testing accommodations often include small-group or individual administration in a quiet location, extended time, and frequent breaks.

What are some things to consider with respect to early intervention for learners with ADHD?

▶ Diagnosing ADHD in early childhood is difficult, partly because very young children typically have short attention spans and are motorically active.

▶ Principles of classroom structure, teacher direction, functional behavioral assessment, and contingency-based self-management are important for preschoolers with ADHD.

▶ Because young children typically do not have strong self-management skills, contingencies in the form of praise, points, and tangible rewards are important.

What are some things to consider with respect to transition to adulthood for learners with ADHD?

▶ A thorough clinical history is critical in diagnosing ADHD in adults.

▶ Although exceptions exist, adults with ADHD tend to have less positive outcomes than the general population in terms of employment, marriage and family, and general social well-being.

▶ Coaching is a therapeutic technique often recommended for adults with ADHD.

STANDARDS and PRINCIPLES in this Chapter

SPECIAL EDUCATORS . . .

■ understand the field as an evolving and changing discipline (from CEC Content Standard #1).

■ understand the similarities and differences in human development and the characteristics between and among individuals with and without exceptional learning needs (from CEC Content Standard #2).

■ understand the effects that an exceptional condition can have on an individual's learning in school and throughout life (from CEC Content Standard #3).

- possess a repertoire of evidence-based instructional strategies (from CEC Content Standard #4).

- use the results of assessments to help identify exceptional learning needs (from CEC Content Standard #8).

- use collaboration to facilitate the successful transitions of individuals with exceptional learning needs across settings and services (from CEC Content Standard #10).

ALL TEACHERS . . .

- understand the central concepts, tools of inquiry, structures of the discipline(s) they teach and can create learning experiences that make these aspects of subject matter meaningful (INTASC Principle #1).

- understand how children learn and develop and can provide learning opportunities that support the intellectual, social, and personal development of each learner (INTASC Principle #2).

- understand how students differ in their approaches to learning and create instructional opportunities that are adapted to diverse learners (INTASC Principle #3).

- understand and use a variety of instructional strategies to encourage students' development of critical thinking, problem solving, and performance skills (INTASC Principle #4).

- understand and use formal and informal assessment strategies to evaluate and ensure the continuous intellectual, social, and physical development of the learner (INTASC Principle #8).

- foster relationships with school colleagues, families, and agencies in the larger community to support students' learning and well-being (INTASC Principle #10).

Applying the **STANDARDS** and **PRINCIPLES**

- ONE of your colleagues, whose background is in general education, asks, "What does it really mean to have ADHD?" How would you respond? (CEC Content Standard #1 & #2; INTASC Principle #1 & #2)

- WHAT should teachers know about the psychological and behavioral characteristics of students with ADHD? (CEC Content Standard #3 & INTASC Principle #3)

- HOW should teachers determine what instructional methods to use with students with ADHD? (CEC Content Standard #4 & INTASC Principle #4)

- HOW easy or difficult is it to identify ADHD? (CEC Content Standard #8 & INTASC Principle #8)

- HOW would you respond to parents who approach you expressing concern about the future of their high school student with ADHD? (CEC Content Standard #10 & INTASC Principle #10)

Now go to the Hallahan/Kauffman, Eleventh Edition MyEducationLab course at www.myeducationlab.com to:

- take a Pretest to assess your initial comprehension of the chapter content;
- study chapter content with your Individualized Study Plan;
- take a Posttest to assess your understanding of chapter content;
- engage in multimedia exercises to help you build a deeper and more applied understanding of chapter content.

8

Learners with Emotional or Behavioral Disorders

It has always been hard for me to have friends. I want friends, but I don't know how to make them. I always think people are being serious when they are just joking around, but I don't figure that out until a lot later. I just don't know how to adapt.

I get into fights with people all the time. I take their teasing seriously and get into trouble. I don't remember having as much trouble getting along with kids when I was little. They seemed to feel sorry for me or thought I was weird. I used to run away from kids and hide in the bathroom at school or under my desk.

After I got back from the hospital, I really couldn't get along with anyone. That was when kids first began calling me "retard." I am not retarded, but I get confused and can't figure out what is going on. At first I couldn't figure out what they were saying to me. Finally one girl in my special education class became my friend. She kind of took care of me. I had another friend in junior high who was also nice and kind to me. But my best friend is my dog Cindie. Even though I give her a hard time, she is always ready to love me.

I like to play by myself best. I make up stories and fantasies. My mother says it is too bad I have such a hard time writing, because with my imagination and all the stories I have created in my mind I could write a book.

—Anonymous

QUESTIONS to guide your reading of this chapter . . .

- What terminology is used to describe emotional or behavioral disorders?
- What is the definition of emotional or behavioral disorder?
- How are emotional or behavioral disorders classified?
- What is the prevalence of emotional or behavioral disorders?
- What are the causes of emotional or behavioral disorders?
- How are emotional or behavioral disorders identified?
- What are the major educational considerations regarding emotional or behavioral disorders?
- How do professionals assess the progress of students with emotional or behavioral disorders?
- What are important considerations in early intervention for learners with emotional or behavioral disorders?
- What are important considerations in transition to adulthood for learners with emotional or behavioral disorders?

Learners with Emotional or Behavioral Disorders

MYTH ■ Most children and youths with emotional or behavioral disorders are not noticed by people around them.

FACT ■ Although it is difficult to identify the types and causes of problems, most children and youths with emotional or behavioral disorders, whether aggressive or withdrawn, are quite easy to spot.

MYTH ■ Students with emotional or behavioral disorders are usually very bright.

FACT ■ Relatively few students with emotional or behavioral disorders have high intelligence; in fact, most have below-average IQs.

MYTH ■ Most students who are seen by their teachers as a "pain in the neck" are not disturbed; they are disturbing to others, but they are not disturbed.

FACT ■ Most students who are disturbing to others are also disturbed. One of the signs of emotional health and good adjustment is behaving in ways that do not cause others concern, being neither unusually aggressive and disruptive nor overly reticent and socially withdrawn.

MYTH ■ Students with emotional or behavioral disorders exhibit problematic behavior constantly.

FACT ■ Most students with emotional or behavioral disorders often exhibit typical behavior most of the time.

MYTH ■ Most students with emotional or behavioral disorders receive special education and/or mental health services.

FACT ■ The vast majority of students with emotional or behavioral disorders are not identified and served in a timely fashion by either mental health or special education. Only a small percentage (perhaps 20 percent) are recognized as having an emotional or behavioral impairment.

MYTH ■ Youngsters who exhibit shy, anxious behavior are more seriously impaired than those whose behavior is hyperaggressive.

FACT ■ Youngsters with aggressive, acting-out behavior patterns have less chance for social adjustment and mental health in adulthood. Neurotic, shy, anxious children and youths have a better chance of getting and holding jobs, overcoming their problems, and staying out of jails and mental hospitals, unless their withdrawal is extreme. This is especially true for boys.

MYTH ■ Most students with emotional or behavioral disorders need a permissive environment, in which they feel accepted and can accept themselves for who they are.

FACT ■ Research shows that a firmly structured and highly predictable environment is of greatest benefit for most students.

MYTH ■ Only psychiatrists, psychologists, and social workers are able to help children and youths with emotional or behavioral disorders overcome their problems.

FACT ■ Most teachers and parents can learn to be highly effective in helping youngsters with emotional or behavioral disorders, sometimes without extensive training or professional certification. Many of these children and youths do require services of highly trained professionals as well.

MYTH ■ Undesirable behaviors are only symptoms; the real problems are hidden deep in the individual's psyche.

FACT ■ There is no sound scientific basis for belief in hidden causes; the behavior and its social context are the problems. Causes may involve thoughts, feelings, and perceptions.

MYTH ■ Juvenile delinquency and the aggressive behavior known as conduct disorder can be effectively deterred by harsh punishment if children and youths know that their misbehavior will be punished.

FACT ■ Harsh punishment, including imprisonment, not only does not deter misbehavior, but also creates conditions under which many individuals become even more likely to exhibit unacceptable conduct.

Children and youths who have emotional or behavioral disorders aren't typically good at making friends. Their most obvious problem is failure to establish close and satisfying emotional ties with other people who can help them. As the youth in the excerpt on page 261 describes, it can be easier for these individuals to hide, both physically and emotionally. If they do develop friendships, it's often with deviant peers (Farmer, 2000; Farmer, Quinn, Hussey, & Holahan, 2001; Kauffman & Landrum, 2009a; Walker, Ramsey, & Gresham, 2004).

Some of these children are withdrawn. Other children or adults might try to reach them, but these efforts are usually met with fear or disinterest. In many cases, quiet rejection continues until those who are trying to make friends give up. Because close emotional ties are built around reciprocal social responses, people lose interest in others who do not respond to social overtures.

Many other children with emotional or behavioral disorders are isolated from others not because they withdraw from friendly advances but because they strike out with hostility and aggression. They're abusive, destructive, unpredictable, irresponsible, bossy, quarrelsome, irritable, jealous, defiant—anything but pleasant. Naturally, most other children and most adults choose not to spend time with children like this unless they have to. Some strike back at youngsters who show these characteristics. It's no wonder that these children and youths seem to be embroiled in a continuous battle with everyone. The reaction of most other children and adults is to withdraw to avoid battles, but rejected children then do not learn to behave acceptably. Teachers and well-behaved peers naturally tend to withdraw from them or avoid them, which reduces their opportunities to learn both academic and social skills.

The opinion that children with emotional or behavioral disorders aren't really disturbed, just a pain in the neck, is typically based on a serious misunderstanding. Students can be both disturbed *and* disturbing, have an emotional or behavioral disorder *and* irritate the teacher. True, some irritating students don't have an emotional or behavioral disorder. However, most children with an emotional or behavioral disorder are irritating to teachers, whereas most children are neither irritating nor have such a disorder. Moreover, a student who's consistently irritating is at high risk of acquiring an emotional or behavioral disorder if he or she doesn't already have one or to encourage such disorders in others, simply because the reactions of teachers and peers are likely to be negative and hostile.

Another widespread misunderstanding is that children and youths with emotional or behavioral disorders exhibit the problematic behavior all the time—24/7. Most people don't seem to understand the fact that such disorders tend to be episodic, highly variable, and sometimes situation-specific (for example, only when demands are placed on them to perform or only outside their home or family). People often don't understand the fact

Video Homework Exercise

Interventions ● Go to the Homework and Exercises section in Chapter 8 of MyEducationLab to watch the video "Behavior Disorder", which demonstrates how intervention can help students with EBD.

Research Article Homework Exercise

Inclusion Issues ● Go to the Homework and Exercises section in Chapter 8 of MyEducationLab to access a research article that explores the exclusion of children with EBD from receiving special education services.

that their own observation may catch the student at a time when the impairment is *not* being exhibited. Many people also don't seem to realize that a parent who is psychologically impaired himself or herself may be a very poor or unreliable reporter of the student's behavior at home. Understanding the on-again, off-again nature of these disorders is critical. Expecting someone with an emotional or behavioral disorder to exhibit problem behavior all the time is somewhat like expecting a person with a seizure disorder to have seizures all the time. Emotional or behavioral disorders are not exhibited as consistently as is intellectual disability or cerebral palsy.

Where does the problem start? Does it begin with behavior that frustrates, angers, or irritates other people? Or does it begin with a social environment so uncomfortable or inappropriate that the child can only withdraw or attack? These questions can't be answered fully on the basis of current research. The best thinking today is that the problem isn't always just in the child's behavior or just in the environment. The problem arises because the social interactions and transactions between the child and the social environment are inappropriate. This is an ecological perspective—an interpretation of the problem as a negative aspect of the child and the environment in which the child lives. And there are two equally serious mistakes people can make: First, assuming that the problem is merely in the child who exhibits inappropriate behavior; second, assuming that the child's behavior is not the problem, only the context in which it occurs.

UNDERSTANDING THE STANDARDS AND PRINCIPLES Why has defining emotional and behavioral disorders always been problematic? (CEC Knowledge and Skill Standards CC1K5 & BD1K1)

Council for Exceptional Children

Terminology

Many different terms have been used to designate children who have extreme social-interpersonal and/or intrapersonal problems, including *emotionally handicapped, emotionally impaired, behaviorally impaired, socially/emotionally handicapped, emotionally conflicted,* and *seriously behaviorally disabled*. These terms don't designate distinctly different types of disorders; that is, they don't refer to clearly different types of children and youths. Rather, the different labels appear to represent personal preferences for terms and slightly different theoretical orientations. The terminology of the field is so variable and confusing that it's possible to pick a label of choice simply by choosing one or more of the overlapping terms from Figure 8.1's set A and combining it with one of those from set B (and, if it seems appropriate, adding other qualifiers, such as *serious* or *severe*). Thus, one could have emotional disturbance, behavioral disorder, emotional or behavioral disorder, social disability, and so on.

Until 1997, *seriously emotionally disturbed* was the term used in federal special education laws and regulations. *Seriously* was dropped from the terminology in 1997. *Emotionally disturbed* is the term used in the Individuals with Disabilities Education Act (IDEA) and reports on its implementation (e.g., U.S. Department of Education, 2005), but it has been criticized as inappropriate. *Behaviorally disordered* is consistent with the name of the Council for Children with Behavioral Disorders (CCBD, a division of the Council for Exceptional Children) and has the advantage of focusing attention on the clearly observable aspect of these children's problems: disordered behavior. Many authorities favor terminology indicating that these children may have emotional or behavioral problems or both (Cullinan, 2004, 2006; Kauffman & Landrum, 2009a; Kavale, Forness, & Mostert, 2005).

In 1990, the National Mental Health and Special Education Coalition, representing over thirty professional and advocacy groups, proposed the term *emotional or behavioral disorder* to replace *emotional disturbance* in federal laws and regulations (Forness & Knitzer, 1992). *Emotional or behavioral disorder* could become the generally accepted terminology of the field, although changes in federal and state laws and regulations may be slow in coming.

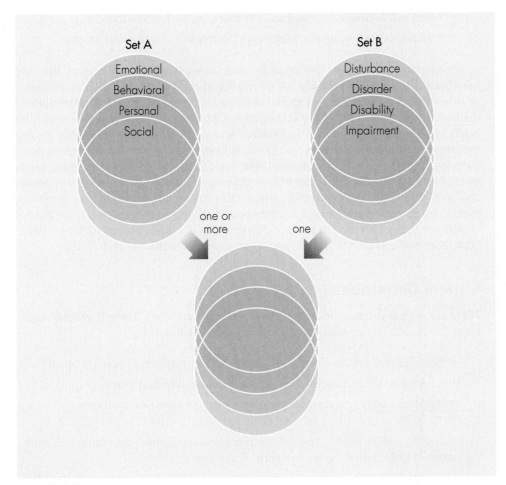

FIGURE 8.1 Possible combinations of terms. Choose one or more in set A combined with one in set B.

Definition

Defining emotional and behavioral disorders has always been problematic. Professional groups and experts have felt free to construct individual working definitions to fit their own professional purposes (Cullinan, 2004; Kauffman, Brigham, & Mock, 2004; Kauffman & Landrum, 2006, 2009a; Landrum & Kauffman, 2003). Until recently, no one has come up with a definition that a majority of professionals understand and accept.

Definitional Problems

Defining emotional and behavioral disorders is somewhat like defining a familiar experience—anger, loneliness, or happiness, for example. We all have an intuitive grasp of what these experiences are, but forming objective definitions of emotional or behavioral disorders is difficult for the following reasons:

- We lack precise definitions of mental health and normal behavior.
- There are substantial differences among conceptual models.
- Measurement of emotions and behavior is imprecise.

- Emotional or behavioral disorders often overlap with other disabilities.
- Professionals who diagnose and serve children and youths often disagree.

Consider each of these problems in turn. Mental health and normal behavior have been hard to define precisely. It's no wonder, then, that the definition of emotional or behavioral disorder presents a special challenge. Conceptual models—assumptions or theories about why people behave as they do and what we should do about it—may offer conflicting ideas about just what the problem is (Kauffman & Landrum, 2009a, 2009b). Emotional or behavioral disorders tend to overlap a great deal with other disabilities, especially learning disabilities and intellectual disability. Finally, each professional group has its own reasons for serving individuals with emotional or behavioral disorders. For example, clinical psychologists, school psychologists, social workers, teachers, and juvenile justice authorities all have their particular concerns and language. Differences in the focuses of different professions tend to produce differences in definition as well (Cullinan, 2004, 2006; Forness & Kavale, 1997; Kauffman & Landrum, 2009a; Kavale et al., 2005).

Current Definitions

There are several common features among current definitions. There is general agreement that emotional or behavioral disorder refers to the following:

- Behavior that goes to an extreme—not just slightly different from the usual
- A problem that is chronic—one that does not quickly disappear
- Behavior that is unacceptable because of social or cultural expectations

THE FEDERAL DEFINITION   The federal rules and regulations governing the implementation of IDEA define the term *emotionally disturbed* as follows:

i. The term means a condition exhibiting one or more of the following characteristics over a long period of time and to a marked extent, which adversely affects educational performance:
   A. An inability to learn that cannot be explained by intellectual, sensory, or health factors;
   B. An inability to build or maintain satisfactory relationships with peers and teachers;
   C. Inappropriate types of behavior or feelings under normal circumstances;
   D. A general pervasive mood of unhappiness or depression; or
   E. A tendency to develop physical symptoms or fears associated with personal or school problems.
ii. The term includes children who are schizophrenic. The term does not include children who are socially maladjusted unless it is determined that they are emotionally disturbed. (45 C. F. R. 121a5[b][8][1978])

These inclusions and exclusions (in ii above) are unnecessary (Bower, 1982; Kauffman & Landrum, 2009a). Bower's five criteria (A–E above) for emotional disturbance indicate that schizophrenic children must be included and that socially maladjusted children cannot be excluded. Furthermore, the clause "which adversely affects educational performance" makes interpretation of the definition impossible, unless the meaning of educational performance is clarified. Does educational performance refer only to academic achievement? If so, then children with other listed characteristics who achieve on grade level are excluded.

UNDERSTANDING THE STANDARDS AND PRINCIPLES   Why has the federal definition of the term *emotionally disturbed* been widely criticized? (CEC Knowledge and Skill Standards CC1K5 & BD1K1)

Council for Exceptional Children

Developing objective criteria for defining emotional and behavioral disorders can be problematic, partly because feelings of unhappiness or anger are familiar– or "normal"– to all people.

One of the most widely criticized and controversial aspects of the definition is its exclusion of children who are socially maladjusted but not emotionally disturbed. Some states and localities have started to interpret social maladjustment as **conduct disorder**— aggressive, disruptive, antisocial behavior. The American Psychological Association and the CCBD have condemned this practice, which has no empirical basis (Costenbader & Buntaine, 1999; Kauffman & Landrum, 2009a).

AN ALTERNATIVE TO THE FEDERAL DEFINITION   The National Mental Health and Special Education Coalition proposed an alternative definition in 1990. The coalition's proposed definition is as follows:

i. The term emotional or behavioral disorder means a disability characterized by behavioral or emotional responses in school so different from appropriate age, cultural, or ethnic norms that they adversely affect educational performance. Educational performance includes academic, social, vocational, and personal skills. Such a disability:

   A. is more than a temporary, expected response to stressful events in the environment;

   B. is consistently exhibited in two different settings, at least one of which is school-related; and

   C. is unresponsive to direct intervention in general education, or the child's condition is such that general education interventions would be insufficient.

ii. Emotional and behavioral disorders can co-exist with other disabilities.

iii. This category may include children or youths with schizophrenic disorders, **affective disorder, anxiety disorder**, or other sustained disorders of conduct or adjustment when they adversely affect educational performance in accordance with section (i). (Forness & Knitzer, 1992, p. 13)

■ **Conduct disorder**
A disorder characterized by overt, aggressive, disruptive behavior or covert antisocial acts such as stealing, lying, and fire setting; may include both overt and covert acts.

INTERNET RESOURCES

The Council for Children with Behavioral Disorders (CCBD) maintains a Website at www.ccbd.net

■ **Affective disorder**
A disorder of mood or emotional tone characterized by depression or elation.

■ **Anxiety disorder**
A disorder characterized by anxiety, fearfulness, and avoidance of ordinary activities because of anxiety or fear.

Advantages of the proposed definition over the federal definition include the following:

- It uses terminology that reflects current professional preferences and concern for minimizing stigma.
- It includes both disorders of emotions and disorders of behavior, and recognizes that they may occur either separately or in combination.
- It is school-centered but acknowledges that disorders exhibited outside the school setting are also important.
- It is sensitive to ethnic and cultural differences.
- It does not include minor or transient problems or ordinary responses to stress.
- It acknowledges the importance of prereferral interventions but does not require slavish implementation of them in extreme cases.
- It acknowledges that children and youths can have multiple disabilities.
- It includes the full range of emotional or behavioral disorders of concern to mental health and special education professionals without arbitrary exclusions.

■ **Externalizing**
Acting-out behavior; aggressive or disruptive behavior that is observable as behavior directed toward others.

■ **Internalizing**
Acting-in behavior; anxiety, fearfulness, withdrawal, and other indications of an individual's mood or internal state.

Classification

Researchers have identified two broad, pervasive dimensions of disordered behavior: **externalizing** and **internalizing**. Externalizing behavior involves striking out against others (see Furlong, Morrison, & Jimerson, 2004). Internalizing behavior involves mental or emotional conflicts, such as depression and anxiety (see Gresham & Kern, 2004). Some researchers have found more specific disorders, but all of the more specific disorders can be located on these two primary dimensions.

Researchers differentiate between the externalizing and internalizing dimensions of behavioral disorders. Externalizing behavior refers to striking out against others, damaging property, and other disruptive actions.

Individuals may show behaviors characteristic of both dimensions; the dimensions are not mutually exclusive. A child or youth might exhibit several behaviors associated with internalizing problems (e.g., short attention span, poor concentration) and several of those associated with externalizing problems as well (e.g., fighting, disruptive behavior, annoying others). Actually, **comorbidity**—the co-occurrence of two or more conditions in the same individual—is not unusual (Cullinan, 2004; Tankersley & Landrum, 1997). Few individuals with an emotional or behavioral disorder exhibit only one type of maladaptive behavior.

Children may exhibit characteristic types of behavior with varying degrees of intensity or severity. That is, either dimension of behavior may be exhibited to a greater or lesser extent; the range may be from normal to severely disordered. For example, an individual might have a severe conduct disorder, an externalizing problem defined by overt, aggressive, disruptive behavior or covert antisocial acts such as stealing, lying, and fire setting. Severe emotional or behavioral disorders include the extremes of any externalizing or internalizing problem. Individuals with **schizophrenia** have a severe disorder of thinking. They might believe that they are controlled by alien forces or might have other delusions or hallucinations. Typically, their emotions are inappropriate for the actual circumstances, and they tend to withdraw into their own private worlds. Childhood schizophrenia is a disorder that typically begins after a normal period of development during early childhood.

■ **Comorbidity**
Co-occurrence of two or more conditions in the same individual.

■ **Schizophrenia**
A disorder characterized by psychotic behavior manifested by loss of contact with reality, distorted thought processes, and abnormal perceptions.

Prevalence

Credible studies in the United States and many other countries have consistently indicated that at least 6 to 10 percent of children and youths of school age exhibit serious and persistent emotional/behavioral problems (Kauffman and Landrum, 2009a). However, less than 1 percent of schoolchildren in the United States are identified as emotionally disturbed for special education purposes (U.S. Department of Education, 2005). A report on children's mental health from the U.S. Surgeon General has also indicated that a very small percentage of children with serious emotional or behavioral disorders receive mental health services (U.S. Department of Health and Human Services, 2001). More recent studies confirm the Surgeon General's report (e.g., Costello, Egger, & Angold, 2005, 2006). Costello et al. (2005) concluded:

> Substantively, we can say with certainty that only a small proportion of children with clear evidence of functionally impairing psychiatric disorder receive treatment. Once upon a time, when effective treatments for child and adolescent psychiatric disorders were rare, this was regrettable but not a major public health issue. Now it is. The tragedy is compounded by powerful evidence that most psychiatric disorders have their origins early in life: risk even for adult-onset disorders is often increased by childhood adversities, and disorders manifesting themselves in the early years often recur in adulthood. So the public health directive to intervene early is clear. . . , but the reality is different. (p. 982)

There is a huge gap between estimates of prevalence and services, either by mental health or special education, as indicated by Costello et al. (2006), Kauffman and Landrum (2009a), and Kauffman, Mock, and Simpson (in press). However, misunderstanding of this fact is common. For example, Harry and Klingner stated incorrectly that "the risk of identification [for emotional or behavioral disorders] increased from just over 1 percent in 1974 to just over 5 percent in 1998" (2006, p. 4) and that students served as having emotional or behavioral disorders "grew by 500 percent between 1974 and 1998, from just over 1 percent in 1974 to just over 5 percent in 1998" (2007, p. 18). The National

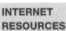

INTERNET RESOURCES

The U.S. Surgeon General's 2001 report on children's mental health is found at www.surgeongeneral.gov/topics/cmh

INTERNET RESOURCES

For a site with links to articles about children's health, including emotional and behavioral problems, see www.mcleanhospital.org

Viewpoints differ as to whether juvenile delinquent youths should automatically be considered to have emotional or behavioral disorders.

Research Council (Donovan & Cross, 2002) reported that special education for students in this category grew from less than 0.5 percent in 1974 to less than 1 percent in 1998, and the U.S. Department of Education (2005) reported that in 2002 the percent served was still lower than 1 percent.

The most common types of problems exhibited by students who are placed in special education for emotional or behavioral disorders are externalizing—aggressive, acting-out, disruptive behavior. Boys outnumber girls in displaying these behaviors by a ratio of five to one or more. Overall, boys tend to exhibit more aggression than girls do, although antisocial behavior in girls is an increasing concern (Furlong et al., 2004; Schaffner, 2006; Talbott & Callahan, 1997).

Juvenile delinquency and the antisocial behavior known as conduct disorder present particular problems in estimating prevalence. Disabling conditions of various kinds are much more common among juvenile delinquents than among the general population (Nelson, Leone, & Rutherford, 2004; O'Mahony, 2005). Moreover, the social and economic costs of delinquency and antisocial behavior are enormous. Adolescent males account for a disproportionately high percentage of serious and violent crime in U.S. society. Those who exhibit serious antisocial behavior are at high risk for school failure as well as other negative outcomes (Kauffman & Landrum, 2009a; Walker et al., 2004).

UNDERSTANDING THE STANDARDS AND PRINCIPLES Briefly describe four major factors to which the causes of emotional or behavioral disorders have been attributed. (CEC Knowledge and Skill Standards BD2K1)

Council for Exceptional Children

Causes

The causes of emotional or behavioral disorders have been attributed to four major factors:

1. Biological disorders and diseases
2. Pathological family relationships
3. Undesirable experiences at school
4. Negative cultural influences

Although in the majority of cases, there is no conclusive empirical evidence that one of these factors is directly responsible for the disorder, some factors might give a child a predisposition to exhibit problem behavior, and others might precipitate or trigger it. That is, some factors, such as genetics, influence behavior over a long time and increase the likelihood that a given set of circumstances will trigger maladaptive responses. Other factors (such as observing one parent beating the other) might have a more immediate effect and might trigger maladaptive responses in an individual who is already predisposed to problem behavior.

Another concept that is important in all theories is the idea of contributing factors that heighten the risk of a disorder. It's extremely unusual to find a single cause that has led directly to a disorder. Usually, several factors together contribute to the development of a problem. In almost all cases, the question of what specifically has caused the disorder can't be answered because no one really knows. However, we often do know the factors that place children at risk—the circumstances or conditions that increase the chances that a child will develop the disorder. Figure 8.2 illustrates how risk factors accumulate

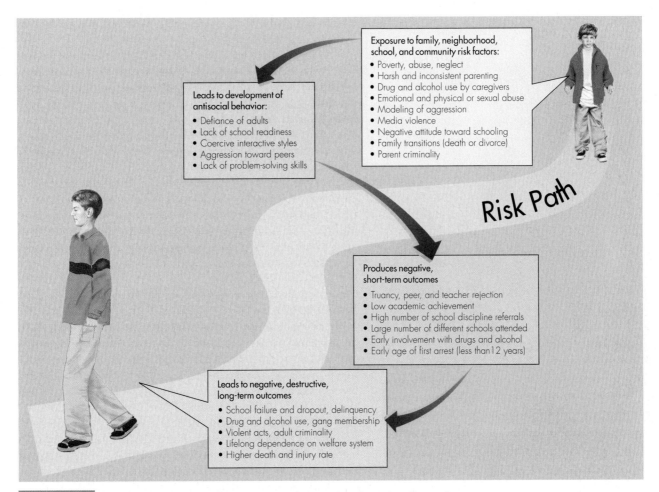

FIGURE 8.2 Risk pathway to antisocial and violent behavior. It reflects the effects of exposure to known risk factors and developmental outcomes.

Source: From Early identification and intervention for youth with antisocial and violent behavior by Jeffrey Sprague and Hill Walker. *Exceptional Children, 66,* p. 371. Copyright © by the Council of Exceptional Children. Reprinted with permission.

to place children and youths at risk for antisocial and violent behavior—often called conduct disorder—which is one of the most common and troubling emotional-behavioral problems of young people (see also Kazdin, 1997).

Biological Factors

Behaviors and emotions may be influenced by genetic, neurological, or biochemical factors, or by combinations of these. Certainly, there is a relationship between body and behavior, and it would therefore seem reasonable to look for a biological causal factor of some kind for certain emotional or behavioral disorders (Cooper, 2005; Forness & Kavale, 2001). We do know, for example, that prenatal exposure to alcohol can contribute to many types of disability, including emotional or behavioral disorders. But only rarely is it possible to demonstrate a relationship between a specific biological factor and an emotional or behavioral disorder.

For most children with emotional or behavioral disorders, there simply is no real evidence that biological factors alone are at the root of their problems. For those with severe and profound disorders, however, there is evidence to suggest that biological factors may contribute to their conditions. Moreover, there is increasing evidence that medications are helpful in addressing the problems of many or most students with

Research Article Homework Exercise

Childhood Schizophrenia
● Go to the Homework and Exercises section in Chapter 8 of MyEducationLab to access a research article that addresses the biology of childhood schizophrenia.

Substance abuse may contribute to emotional and behavioral problems, but it is difficult to determine when or whether it is the direct cause.

emotional or behavioral disorders if they receive state-of-the-art psychopharmacology (Konopasek & Forness, 2004).

All children are born with a biologically determined behavioral style, or temperament. Although children's inborn temperaments may be changed by the way they are reared, some people have long believed that children with so-called difficult temperaments are predisposed to develop emotional or behavioral disorders. There is no one-to-one relationship between temperament and disorders, however. A difficult child might be handled so well or a child with an easy temperament so poorly that the outcome will be quite different from what one would predict on the basis of initial behavioral style (Keogh, 2003). Other biological factors besides temperament—disease, malnutrition, and brain trauma, for example—can predispose children to develop emotional or behavioral problems. Substance abuse also can contribute to emotional and behavioral problems. Except in rare instances, it is not possible to determine that these factors are direct causes of problem behavior (see Kauffman & Landrum, 2009a).

Emotional and behavioral disorders are, in essence, social phenomena, whether they have biological causes or not. The causes of emotional and behavioral disorders are seldom exclusively biological or psychological. Once a biological disorder occurs, it nearly always creates psychosocial problems that then also contribute to the emotional or behavioral disorder. Medication may be of great benefit, but it is seldom the only intervention that is needed (Forness & Beard, 2007; Forness & Kavale, 2001; Forness, Kavale, Sweeney, & Crenshaw, 1999; Konopasek & Forness, 2004). The psychological and social aspects of the disorder must also be addressed.

Family Factors

Even in cases of severe emotional or behavioral disorders, it is not possible to find consistent and valid research findings that allow the blame for the children's problem behavior to be placed primarily on their parents (Kauffman & Landrum, 2009a). Very good parents sometimes have children with very serious emotional or behavioral disorders, and incompetent, neglectful, or abusive parents sometimes have children with no significant emotional or behavioral disorders. The relationship between parenting and emotional or behavioral disorders isn't simple, but some parenting practices are definitely better than others.

Educators must be aware that most parents of youngsters with emotional or behavioral disorders want their children to behave more appropriately and will do anything they can to help them. These parents need support resources—not blame or criticism—for dealing with very difficult family circumstances. The Federation of Families for Children's Mental Health was organized in 1989 to help provide such support and resources, and parents are organizing in many localities to assist each other in finding additional resources (Jordan, Goldberg, & Goldberg, 1991). In the Personal Perspectives on page 273, one of the founding members shares her perspective on why parents are so often blamed for their children's emotional or behavioral disorders.

INTERNET RESOURCES

The home page of the PACER (Parent Advocacy Coalition for Educational Rights) Center is www.pacer.org
For the Federation of Families for Children's Mental Health, see www.ffcmh.org

School Factors

Some children already have emotional or behavioral disorders when they begin school; others develop such disorders during their school years, perhaps in part because of damaging experiences in the classroom itself. Children who exhibit disorders when they

Personal PERSPECTIVES

Family Factors

Dixie Jordan is the parent of a 19-year-old son with an emotional and behavioral disorder. She is director of the Families and Advocates Partnership for Education at the PACER Center in Minneapolis (a resource center for parents of children with disabilities) and a founding member of the Federation of Families for Children's Mental Health. She is also a Systems of Care coach for Four Directions Consulting.

Why do you think there is such a strong tendency to hold parents responsible for their children's emotional or behavioral disorders?

I am the parent of two children, the younger of which has emotional and behavioral problems. When my firstborn and I were out in public, strangers often commented on what a "good" mother I was, to have such an obedient, well-behaved, and compliant child. Frankly, I enjoyed the comments and really believed that those parents whose children were throwing tantrums and generally demolishing their environments were simply not very skilled in child-rearing. I recall casting my share of reproachful glances in those days and thinking with some arrogance that raising children should be left to those of us who knew how to do it well. Several years later, my second child and I were on the business end of such disdain, and it was a lesson in humility that I shall never forget. Very little that I had learned in the previous three years as a parent worked with this child; he was neurologically different, hyperactive, inattentive, and noncompliant even when discipline was consistently applied. His doctors, his neurologist, and finally his teachers referred me to parenting classes, as though the experiences I had had with my older child were nonexistent; his elementary principal even said that there was nothing wrong that a good spanking wouldn't cure. I expected understanding that this was a very difficult child to raise, but the unspoken message was that I lacked competence in basic parenting skills, the same message that I sent to similarly situated parents just a few years earlier.

Most of us in the world today are parents. The majority of us have children who do not have emotional or behavioral problems. Everything in our experience suggests that when our children are successful and obedient, it is because of our parenting.

We are reinforced socially for having a well-behaved child from friends, grandparents, even strangers. It makes sense, then, to attribute less desirable behaviors in children to the failure of their parents to provide appropriate guidance or to set firm limits. Many parents have internalized that sense of responsibility or blame for causing their child's emotional problems, even when they are not able to identify what they might have done wrong. It is a very difficult attitude to shake, especially when experts themselves cannot seem to agree on causation. With most children, the "cause" of an emotional or behavioral disorder is more likely a complex interplay of multiple factors than "parenting styles," "biology," or "environmental influences" as discrete entities, but it is human nature to latch onto a simple explanation—and inadequate parenting is, indeed, a simple explanation. When systems blame parents for causing their child's emotional or behavioral disorders, the focus is no longer on services to help the child learn better adaptive skills or appropriate behaviors, but on rationalizing why such services may not work. When parents feel blamed, their energies shift from focusing on the needs of their child to defending themselves. In either instance, the child is less well served.

Another reason that people hold parents responsible for their children's emotional or behavioral disorders is that parents may be under such unrelenting stress from trying to manage their child's behavior that they may resort to inappropriate techniques because of the failure of more conventional methods. A parent whose 8-year-old hyperactive child smashes out his bedroom window while being timed out for another problem may know that tying the child to a chair is not a good way to handle the crisis, but may be out of alternatives. It may not have been the "right" thing for the parent to do, but [he or she] is hardly responsible for causing the child's problems in the first place. It would be a mistake to attribute the incidence of abuse or neglect as "causing" most emotional or behavioral disorders without consideration that difficult children are perhaps more likely to be abused due to their noncompliant or otherwise difficult behaviors.

Source: Reprinted with the permission of Merrill Prentice Hall from *Characteristics of emotional and behavioral disorders of children and youth* (9th ed.), by James M. Kauffman and Timothy J. Landrum. Copyright © 2009 by Pearson Education, Inc.

enter school may become better or worse according to how they are managed in the classroom (Furlong, Morrison, & Fisher, 2005; Kauffman & Landrum, 2009a; Walker, 1995; Walker et al., 2004). School experiences are no doubt of great importance to children, but as with biological and family factors, we cannot justify many statements about how such experiences contribute to the child's behavioral difficulties. A child's temperament and social competence can interact with the behaviors of classmates and teachers in contributing to emotional or behavioral problems.

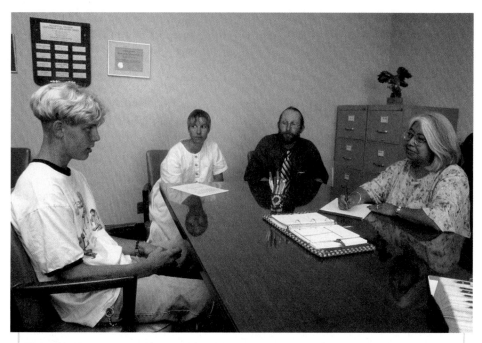

There is a danger that a child who exhibits problem behavior may become trapped in a spiral of negative interactions, resulting in worsening problems with teachers and peers.

There is a very real danger that a child who exhibits problem behavior will become trapped in a spiral of negative interactions, in which he or she becomes increasingly irritating to and irritated by teachers and peers. In considering how they might be contributing to disordered behavior, teachers must ask themselves questions about their academic instruction, expectations, and approaches to behavior management. Teachers must not assume blame for disordered behavior to which they are not contributing, yet it is equally important that teachers eliminate whatever contributions they might be making to their students' misconduct (see Kauffman & Landrum, 2009a; Kauffman, Mostert, Trent, & Pullen, 2006).

Cultural Factors

Children, their families, and schools are embedded in cultures that influence them (Walker et al., 2004). Aside from family and school, many environmental conditions affect adults' expectations of children and children's expectations of themselves and their peers. Values and behavioral standards are communicated to children through a variety of cultural conditions, demands, prohibitions, and models. Several specific cultural influences come to mind: the level of violence in the media (especially television and motion pictures), the use of terror as a means of coercion, the availability of recreational drugs and the level of drug abuse, changing standards for sexual conduct, religious demands and restrictions on behavior, and the threat of nuclear accidents or war. Peers are another important source of cultural influence, particularly after the child enters the upper elementary grades (Farmer, 2000; Farmer et al., 2001).

Although we know much about what heightens risk or puts children on the path to emotional and behavioral disorders, we also know what helps children and puts them on the path to success at school. Figure 8.3 depicts circumstances and life events that lower risk and help children achieve success at school.

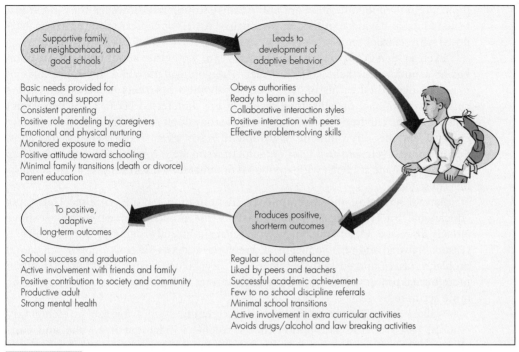

FIGURE 8.3 Path to success at school.

Source: Reprinted with the permission of Merrill Prentice Hall from *An introduction to students with high incidence disabilities*, by J. P. Stichter, M. A. Conroy, & J. M. Kauffman. Copyright © 2008 by Pearson Education, Inc.

Identification

It's much easier to identify disordered behaviors than it is to define and classify their types and causes. Most students with emotional or behavioral disorders do not escape the notice of their teachers. Occasionally, such students don't bother anyone and thus are invisible, but it is usually easy for experienced teachers to tell when students need help. Teachers often fail to assess the strengths of students with emotional or behavioral disorders. However, it's important to include assessment of students' emotional and behavioral competencies, not just their weaknesses or deficits (Epstein & Sharma, 1997; Jones, Dohrn, & Dunn, 2004).

The most common type of emotional or behavioral disorder—conduct disorder, an externalizing problem—attracts immediate attention, so there is seldom any real problem in identification. Students with internalizing problems might be less obvious, but they aren't difficult to recognize. Students with emotional or behavioral disorders are so readily identified by school personnel, in fact, that few schools bother to use systematic screening procedures. Also, the availability of special services for those with emotional or behavioral disorders lags far behind the need—and there is not much point in screening for problems when there are no services available to treat them. Children with schizophrenia are seldom mistaken for those who are developing normally. Their unusual language, mannerisms, and ways of relating to others soon become matters of concern to parents, teachers, and even many casual observers. Children with schizophrenia are a very small percentage of those with emotional or behavioral disorders, and

Casebook Reflection

REFER TO THE CASE *The Red Belt* in your booklet. Tyler acts out when he is frustrated and unable to do his work. He also is explosive and verbally aggressive. How do Tyler's characteristics fit the description of a student with attention deficit/hyperactivity disorder, and in what ways does his behavior match the characteristics of a student with emotional or behavioral disorders? ●

problems in their identification are not usually encountered. However, they might first be identified as having another disorder, such as ADHD or depression, and later be diagnosed with schizophrenia.

Even so, don't conclude that there is never any question about whether a student has an emotional or behavioral disorder. The younger the child, the more difficult it is to judge whether his or her behavior signifies a serious problem. And some children's emotional or behavioral disorders are undetected because teachers aren't sensitive to the children's problems or because they don't stand out sharply from other children in the environment who might have even more serious problems. Furthermore, even sensitive teachers sometimes make errors of judgment. Also keep in mind that some students with emotional or behavioral disorders don't exhibit problems at school.

Formal screening and accurate early identification for the purpose of planning educational intervention are complicated by the problems of definition we have already discussed. In general, however, teachers' informal judgments have served as a reasonably valid and reliable means of screening students for emotional or behavioral problems (as compared with judgments of psychologists and psychiatrists). When more formal procedures are used, teachers' ratings of behavior have turned out to be quite accurate.

Walker and his colleagues devised a screening system for use in elementary schools, based on the assumption that a teacher's judgment is a valid and cost-effective (though greatly underused) method of identifying children with emotional or behavioral disorders (Walker & Severson, 1990; Walker, Severson, & Feil, 1994; see also Walker, Ramsey, & Gresham, 2003–2004a; Walker et al., 2004). Although teachers tend to over-refer students who exhibit externalizing behavior problems (i.e., those with conduct disorders), they tend to under-refer students with internalizing problems (i.e., those characterized by anxiety and withdrawal). A three-step process ensures that children aren't overlooked in screening but that time and effort are not wasted:

1. The teacher lists and ranks students with externalizing and internalizing problems. Those who best fit descriptions of students with externalizing problems and those who best fit descriptions of those with internalizing problems are listed in order from most like to least like the descriptions.

2. The teacher completes two checklists for the three highest-ranked pupils on each list. One checklist asks the teacher to indicate whether each pupil exhibited specific behaviors during the past month (such as "steals," "has tantrums," "uses obscene language or swears"). The other checklist requires the teacher to judge how often (never, sometimes, frequently) each pupil shows certain characteristics (e.g., "follows established classroom rules" or "cooperates with peers in group activities or situations").

3. Pupils whose scores on these checklists exceed established norms are observed in the classroom and on the playground by a school professional other than the classroom teacher (a school psychologist, counselor, or resource teacher). Classroom observations indicate the extent to which the pupil meets academic expectations; playground observations assess the quality and nature of social behavior. These direct observations of behavior, in addition to teachers' ratings, are then used to decide whether the child has problems that warrant classification for special education. Such carefully researched screening systems can lead to improved services for children with emotional or behavioral disorders. Systematic efforts to base identification on teachers' judgments and careful observation should result in services being directed to those students who are most clearly in need.

A teacher's judgment usually is a valid and cost-effective method of identifying children with emotional or behavioral disorders.

Psychological and Behavioral Characteristics

Describing the characteristics of children and youths with emotional or behavioral disorders is an extraordinary challenge because disorders of emotions and behaviors are extremely varied. Individuals may vary markedly in intelligence, achievement, life circumstances, and emotional and behavioral characteristics.

Intelligence and Achievement

The idea that children and youths with emotional or behavioral disorders tend to be particularly bright is a myth. Research clearly shows that the average student with an emotional or behavioral disorder has an IQ in the dull–normal range (around 90) and that relatively few score above the bright-normal range. Compared to the normal distribution of intelligence, more children with emotional or behavioral disorders fall into the ranges of slow learner and mild intellectual disability. On the basis of a review of the research on the intelligence of students with emotional or behavioral disorders, Kauffman and Landrum (2009a) hypothesized distributions of intelligence as shown in Figure 8.4.

There are pitfalls in assessing the intellectual characteristics of a group of children by examining the distribution of their IQs. Intelligence tests aren't perfect instruments for measuring what we mean by intelligence, and it can be argued that emotional or behavioral difficulties might prevent children from scoring as high as they are capable of scoring. Still, the lower-than-normal IQs for these students do indicate lower ability to perform tasks that other students perform successfully, and the lower scores are consistent with impairment in other areas of functioning (e.g., academic achievement and social skills). IQ is a relatively good predictor of how far a student will progress academically and socially, even in cases of severe disorders.

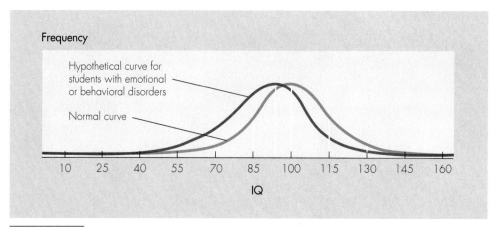

FIGURE 8.4 Hypothetical frequency distribution of IQ for students with emotional or behavioral disorders as compared to a normal frequency distribution.

Source: Reprinted with permission of Merrill Prentice Hall from *Characteristics of emotional and behavioral disorders of children and youth* (9th ed.) by James M. Kauffman and Timothy J. Landrum. Copyright © 2009 by Pearson Education, Inc.

Most students with emotional or behavioral disorders are also underachievers at school, as measured by standardized tests (Kauffman & Landrum, 2009a). A student with an emotional or behavioral disorder does not usually achieve at the level expected for his or her mental age; seldom are such students academically advanced. In fact, many students with severe disorders lack basic reading and arithmetic skills, and the few who seem to be competent in reading or math are often unable to apply their skills to every-day problems.

Social and Emotional Characteristics

Previously, we described two major dimensions of disordered behavior based on analyses of behavior ratings: externalizing and internalizing. The externalizing dimension is characterized by aggressive, acting-out behavior; the internalizing dimension is characterized by anxious, withdrawn behavior and depression. Our discussion here focuses on these two types.

A given student might, at different times, show both aggressive and withdrawn or depressed behaviors. Remember that most students with emotional or behavioral disorders have multiple problems (Tankersley & Landrum, 1997; Walker et al., 2004). At the beginning of this chapter, we said that most students with emotional or behavioral disorders aren't well liked or identify with deviant peers. Studies of the social status of students in regular elementary and secondary classrooms indicate that those who are identified as having emotional or behavioral disorders may be socially rejected. Early peer rejection and aggressive behavior place a child at high risk for later social and emotional problems (Ialongo, Vaden-Kiernan, & Kellam, 1998). Many aggressive students who aren't rejected affiliate primarily with others who are aggressive (Farmer, 2000; Farmer, Farmer & Gut, 1999, 2001). The relationship between emotional or behavioral disorders and communication disorders is increasingly clear (Rogers-Adkinson & Griffith, 1999). Many children and youths with emotional or behavioral disorders have great difficulty in understanding and using language in social circumstances. Chrissy, the middle school student with emotional or behavioral disorders described in the Success Stories on page 280, has great difficulty understanding language. Her teachers focused on positive behavioral supports and increasing her vocabulary to help improve her social skills.

AGGRESSIVE, ACTING-OUT BEHAVIOR (EXTERNALIZING)   As we noted earlier, conduct disorder is the most common problem exhibited by students with emotional or behavioral disorders. Hitting, fighting, teasing, yelling, refusing to comply with requests, crying, destructiveness, vandalism, extortion—these behaviors, if exhibited often, are very likely to earn a child or youth the label "disturbed." Normal children cry, scream, hit, fight, become negative, and do almost everything else children with emotional or behavioral disorders do, but not as impulsively and not as often. Youngsters of the type we are discussing here drive adults to distraction. These youths aren't popular with their peers either, unless they are socialized delinquents who don't offend their delinquent friends. They typically don't respond quickly and positively to well-meaning adults who care about them and try to be helpful. The Responsive Instruction on page 282 provides strategies for classroom teachers who deal with students with oppositional and defiant behavior.

Aggression has been analyzed from many viewpoints. The analyses that have the strongest support in empirical research are those of social learning theorists, such as Bandura (1973, 1986), and behavioral psychologists, such as Colvin, Patterson, and others (Colvin, 2004; Patterson et al., 1992; Walker et al., 2004). Their studies take into account the child's experience and his or her motivation, based on the anticipated consequences of aggression. In brief, they view aggression as learned behavior and assume that it is possible to identify the conditions under which it will be learned.

Children learn many aggressive behaviors by observing parents, siblings, playmates, and people portrayed on television and in movies. Individuals who model aggression are more likely to be imitated if they are high in social status and are observed to receive rewards and escape punishment for their aggression—especially if they experience no unpleasant consequences or obtain rewards by overcoming their victims. If children are placed in unpleasant situations and they cannot escape from the unpleasantness or obtain rewards except by aggression, they are more likely to be aggressive, especially if this behavior is tolerated or encouraged by others. Aggression is encouraged by external rewards

UNDERSTANDING THE STANDARDS AND PRINCIPLES   What do we know about the social characteristics of individuals with emotional or behavioral disorders? (CEC Knowledge and Skill Standard BD2K3)

Council for
Exceptional
Children

■ **Aggression**
Behavior that intentionally causes others harm or that elicits escape or avoidance responses from others.

Children who act out aggressively or impulsively with frequent negative confrontations often are not well liked by their peers.

Success Stories

Chrissy succeeds in middle school through social skills instruction, positive behavioral supports, and academic interventions

School principal Teresa Zutter: "Chrissy, I've called you to my office because you are a star!"

Fourteen-year-old Christina Isaacs attends a special public middle school program for students with emotional and behavioral disorders. These are the keys to her success:

- Intensive instruction in social skills and academics
- Relentless positive behavioral support
- Specific interventions for academic achievement, reducing reliance on adults, building friendships, and increasing her self-confidence

Special educator and school principal Teresa Zutter praised eighth grader Chrissy Isaacs for making progress toward her annual goals. Chrissy is included daily in general classes for physical education and teen life, and she sings every afternoon with the middle school chorus. "I want to do well in regular classes because I want to be a cheerleader and get a regular high school diploma," she says with pride. Chrissy started seventh grade as a girl in distress—physically frail and frightened—but she prospered from intensive, relentless, and specific special education.

● **Intensive Instruction: Social Skills and Academics** The Herndon Center serves sixty students in grades seven and eight with emotional and behavioral disorders. These students need close attention, and the program offers a small student–teacher ratio. In addition to Zutter, there are thirteen teachers and a psychologist, a social worker, a guidance counselor, a health awareness monitor, and a conflict resolution teacher. Weekly clinical staff meetings address students' needs and provide a forum for educators and support staff to discuss problems. "This is such a spirited staff," says Zutter. "We laugh a lot and take care of each other."

Each classroom is equipped with a hot-line telephone connected to the main office. A carpeted quiet room serves as a time-out area for angry students. Zutter works closely with parents, alerting them to misbehaviors and sometimes calling them to take their sons or daughters home. Rules and policies are clear for students, teachers, and families. Gaining trust is critical. For these students, "there is an absolute need for structure and for individualization," says Zutter. "We have so many people here to help and to talk to students that no one has to hit to communicate."

● **Relentless Positive Behavioral Support: Coping with Stress** The center's treatment model assumes that students thrive on positive reinforcement. Nonphysical punishment is used on occasion, but only to the degree necessary, and students are taught mechanisms to cope with their anxieties. "Girls and boys who are stressed can be made to feel better," says Zutter. "They are not just ED for a while but have entrenched behaviors; it's a life struggle. They won't be okay without interventions and without being taught how to cope with stress."

(social status, power, suffering of the victim, obtaining desired items), vicarious rewards (seeing others obtain desirable consequences for their aggression), and self-reinforcement (self-congratulation or enhancement of self-image). If children can justify aggression in their own minds (by comparison to the behaviors of others or by dehumanizing their victims), they are more likely to be aggressive. Punishment can actually increase aggression under some circumstances: when it is inconsistent or delayed, when there is no positive alternative to the punished behavior, when it provides an example of aggression, or when counterattack against the punisher seems likely to be successful.

Teaching aggressive children to be less so is no simple matter, but social learning theory and behavioral research do provide some general guidelines. In general, research doesn't support the notion that it is wise to let children act out their aggression freely. The most helpful techniques include providing examples (models) of nonaggressive responses to aggression-provoking circumstances, helping the child rehearse or role-play

Chrissy is a good example. When she started seventh grade, she was out of touch with reality, staring at her own reflection whenever she could and slipping into the protection of fantasy. She was socially awkward and needed to learn how to act in various situations. When she was lost in her own thoughts, she would throw tantrums or provoke fights without seeing the impact her behaviors had on her relationships. She was also becoming oppositional.

As long as she is confronted gently and is not embarrassed in front of other students, Chrissy is responsive to correction. She takes pride in her appearance and musical talents. Socially, she tries to be everybody's friend, but peers are still afraid of her erratic and aggressive behaviors. "Chrissy tends to be overly sensitive to what others are saying, whether it relates to her or not," says her mother. When she is angry, Chrissy resorts to profanity and physical threats. This year she managed to develop some stable and cherished friendships with a few girls.

● **Specific Interventions: Vocabulary Development, Increased Adult Attention, and Homework Accommodations** Chrissy started seventh grade below grade level in most areas. She could decode words, but she couldn't comprehend what she read. She couldn't organize her thoughts. With frequent reassurance and lots of help to stay on task, Chrissy made gains and performed at grade level in all classes by the end of the year. Speech therapy helped Chrissy to develop vocabulary and use words with multiple meanings, like those in the jokes and riddles she couldn't understand. Accommodations included extra adult attention, additional time to complete class work and tests, shortened assignments, peer/work helpers, and directions stated several times. Although she daydreamed, Chrissy was willing to work hard and to focus when she was provided with support. She is now described as a conscientious student who worries about the quality of her work. According to Zutter,

"Chrissy will always have some difficulties, but with help, she can be eased from her world of fantasy. Hopefully, she'll value herself and stay in reality."

CEC'S STANDARDS: PAVING THE WAY TO SUCCESS

ASSESS YOUR STEPS TO SUCCESS in meeting the CEC Knowledge and Skill Base for All Beginning Special Education Teachers of Students with Emotional and Behavioral Disorders. Use the following questions to reflect on the growth of your own professional knowledge, skills, and dispositions.

REFLECTING ON YOUR OWN PROFESSIONAL DEVELOPMENT

If you were Chrissy's teacher . . .

■ What are some areas about educating students with emotional or behavior disorders that you would need to know more about?

■ What are some specific skills that would help you address her academic and behavioral challenges?

■ What personal dispositions do you think are most important for you to develop in teaching students with challenging behaviors?

Using the CEC Standards

■ What are some functional classroom designs for students with emotional/behavioral disorders? (BD5K2)

■ How would you identify realistic expectations for Chrissy's personal and social behavior in various settings? (CC5S2)

■ What are some professional organizations relevant to the field of emotional/behavioral disorders and how could you participate in their activities? (BD91, BD9S1)

● *By Jean B. Crockett*

---

nonaggressive behavior, providing reinforcement for nonaggressive behavior, preventing the child from obtaining positive consequences for aggression, and punishing aggression in ways that involve as little counteraggression as possible (e.g., using time-out or brief social isolation rather than spanking or yelling; Colvin, 2004; Kauffman et al., 2006; Walker et al., 2003–2004b, 2004). The Responsive Instruction box on page 283 provides a description of a schoolwide strategy to reduce aggression and bullying.

The seriousness of children's aggressive, acting-out behavior shouldn't be underestimated. It was believed for decades that although these children cause a lot of trouble, they aren't as seriously disabled as are children who are shy and anxious. Research has exploded this myth. When combined with school failure, aggressive, antisocial behavior in childhood generally predicts a gloomy future in terms of social adjustment and mental health, especially for boys (Ialongo et al., 1998). When we consider that conduct disorders and delinquency are highly correlated with school failure, the importance of

Meeting the Needs of Students with Emotional or Behavioral Disorders

Strategies for Students with Oppositional Defiant Disorder

UNDERSTANDING ODD

Some children continually act out in specifically defiant ways, such as willfully disobeying an adult's request or blaming others for their poor decision making. Often these children are angry and have a difficult time making friends or receiving positive regard from adults. Such behaviors are associated with the psychological category of oppositional defiant disorder (ODD) (American Psychiatric Association, 1994). Obviously, the acting out (externalizing) behaviors associated with ODD place children in a position to have difficulty in school, and many of these children would be considered to have a behavioral disorder.

To be diagnosed with ODD, children must exhibit at least four of the following behaviors for at least six months: "often loses temper, often argues with adults, often actively defies or refuses to comply with adults' request or rules, often deliberately annoys people, often blames others for his or her mistakes or misbehavior, is often touchy or easily annoyed by others, is often angry and resentful, and is often spiteful or vindictive" (Knowlton, 1995, p. 6). It is important for teachers to recognize that all children will go through periods of defiance in the natural course of development. What differentiates children with ODD from their typically developing peers is the persistent nature of the opposition. Many children will experiment with being defiant—having a temper tantrum in response to an undesirable situation or choosing not to comply with an adult request. These children eventually abandon the disobedience with more adaptive strategies for getting their needs met (Knowlton, 1995). Children with ODD, on the other hand, continue to use maladaptive responses with adults and their peers even though it leads to alienation and rejection.

BEHAVIOR MANAGEMENT AND ODD

Ironically, many of the behavior management strategies that a teacher would employ with most students do not meet the unique needs of students with ODD. One of the most effective behavior management techniques, positive reinforcement, is one such strategy that can have the opposite effect on students with ODD. The following story illustrates this:

Billy has always had problems walking down the hall. . . . he continually pulls down papers or pictures that other classes have displayed on the walls. Even though he has received several verbal reminders from me and the principal and has as a consequence spent some recess time inside, he continues to exhibit this behavior. On this particular day . . . [w]e walked all the way to the gym without Billy pulling down a single picture. . . . I turned to the group and said to Billy that I was very proud of him. . . . Billy immediately ran to the closest wall and pulled down several pictures. (Knowlton, 1995, pp. 7–8)

CLASSROOM SUGGESTIONS

As you can see from this example, Billy's desire not to be controlled and to do the opposite of what was expected resulted in positive reinforcement failing. Thus, interventions with students who are oppositional must take into consideration the primary response system for ODD students: public opposition. Knowlton (1995) suggests these indirect reinforcement techniques when working with oppositional students:

1. The "walk-by" reinforcement: A brief positive comment or tap as the teacher walks by. This minimizes the need for the student to publicly respond and reduces the chance of the student negatively engaging the teacher.
2. Whispering: Providing the student with a private, positive message gives the student the opportunity not to respond.
3. Leaving notes: Similar to the other strategies, leaving a note in the student's desk reduces the likelihood of getting a negative response from the student.
4. Providing rewards: Like all indirect methods, rewards can be delivered but should be done without any amplification or excessive praise. Responses that are delivered in a matter-of-fact manner can remove the emotion that an oppositional student desires.

Other suggestions include avoiding arguing; reducing perceived teacher control through establishing standardized procedures; offering students choices; anticipating problems; allowing appropriate outlets for anger such as physical, noncompetitive activities; clearly identifying consequences; and providing counseling support from a therapist or trained counselor. The goal of all of these strategies is to retrain the student's negative pattern of interacting so that someday traditional positive reinforcement is just that—positive.

● *By Kristin L. Sayeski*

Meeting the Needs of Students with Emotional or Behavioral Disorders

Approaches to Reducing Bullying in Schools

UNDERSTANDING BULLYING

Recent school tragedies directly or indirectly tied to bullying have resulted in increased attention on the part of administrators, teachers, and students to the issue of bullying in schools. One program recommended by researchers addresses bullying through involving key people who can help the aggressor learn more appropriate behaviors and help the victim learn options for responding. In addition to bringing all stakeholders together, the program addresses the issue from several vantage points (Garrity, Jens, Porter, Sager, & Short-Camilli, 1996, 2000).

A COMPREHENSIVE APPROACH TO REDUCING BULLYING

Garrity and colleagues' program involves the entire school (students, teachers, administrators, staff) as well as students' families. Staff members receive training in response procedures, and then teachers implement the program within their classes. A summary of this model follows.

WHO SHOULD BE INVOLVED?

1. *Teachers and other staff members.* All school personnel need to be informed of standard procedures and be willing to act. Students, including both the bully and the victim, must know that teachers and staff will respond.
2. *The caring majority.* The caring majority are those students who neither bully nor are bullied. These students know the bullying is occurring but often do not know whether or how to respond.
3. *The bullies.* The bullies need to be addressed in ways that stop their aggression toward other students and direct their need for power into more prosocial directions.
4. *The victims.* Victims need protection and support, but they also need the social and interpersonal skills critical for seeking outside and internal support.
5. *Parents.* Parents should be made aware of school policies and procedures. Informed parents will feel more secure about sending their child to school and know the type of response that will occur when their child is either the bully or the victim.

WHAT IS INVOLVED?

1. *Staff training.* All school personnel are involved in staff training, including bus drivers, after-school workers, media specialists, and others. During staff training, faculty members learn about the different manifestations of bullying (e.g., physical aggression, name calling, gossiping, intimidating phone calls, verbal threats, and locking in confined spaces); explore ways to address both the victim and bully; role-play conflict resolution, particularly how to address the bully in a firm, no-nonsense manner; generate an antibullying curriculum, such as selecting literature on bullies and victims or creating skits or artwork with similar themes; and develop a comprehensive school plan for addressing instances of bullying.
2. *Classroom intervention.* Within the classroom, students are taught rules to eliminate bullying, strategies for reacting to bullying, and steps to follow if they see bullying occurring.

The following rules, strategies, and steps are recommended by Garrity and colleagues (1996, 2000):

a. Rules for Bully-Proofing Our Classroom:
   i. We will not bully other students.
   ii. We will help others who are being bullied by speaking out and by getting adult help.
   iii. We will use extra effort to include all students in activities at our school.
b. What I Can Do if I Am Being Bullied:
   i. HA = Help and assert
   ii. HA = Humor and avoid
   iii. SO = Self-talk and own it
c. What I Can Do if I See Someone Being Bullied:
   i. Creative problem solving
   ii. Adult help
   iii. Relate and join
   iv. Empathy

Finally, Garrity and colleagues suggest the following strategies for empowering victims: (1) Teach a repertoire of friendship-making skills, (2) develop an understanding that self-esteem affects friendships and how one handles bullying, and (3) teach skills that help victims to feel empowered and better able to handle bullies.

● *By Kristin L. Sayeski*

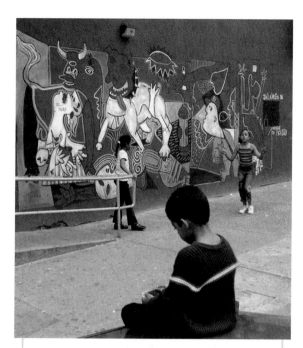

A particularly important aspect of immature, withdrawn behavior is depression, which has been recognized as a serious and widespread problem among children and adolescents.

■ **Enuresis**
Urinary incontinence; wetting oneself.

■ **Encopresis**
Bowel incontinence; soiling oneself.

Casebook Reflection

REFER TO THE CASE *How Did We Miss Jack All These Years?* in your booklet. Jack's situation is very sad because of the problems in his family and with his brother. Jack seems to be internalizing all of his problems. Should Jack have been identified as having a disability? If you think so, at what point in his school career do you think the disability could have been identified? ●

meeting the needs of acting-out and underachieving children is obvious (Kauffman & Landrum, 2009a; Walker et al., 2004).

IMMATURE, WITHDRAWN BEHAVIOR AND DEPRESSION (INTERNALIZING) In noting the seriousness of aggressive, acting-out behavior, we don't intend to downplay the disabling nature of immaturity and withdrawal or depression. Such disorders not only have serious consequences for individuals in their childhood years, but also carry a very poor prognosis for adult mental health. The child whose behavior fits a pattern of extreme immaturity and withdrawal or depression cannot develop the close and satisfying human relationships that characterize normal development. Such a child will find it difficult to meet the pressures and demands of everyday life. The school environment is the one in which anxious and withdrawn adolescents in particular experience the most distress (Masia, Klein, Storch, & Corda, 2001).

As in the case of aggressive, acting-out behavior, withdrawal and depression can be interpreted in many different ways. Proponents of the psychoanalytic approach are likely to see internal conflicts and unconscious motivations as the underlying causes. Behavioral psychologists tend to interpret such problems in terms of failures in social learning; this view is supported by more empirical research data than other views (Kauffman & Landrum, 2009a). A social learning analysis attributes withdrawal and immaturity to an inadequate environment. Causal factors may include overrestrictive parental discipline, punishment for appropriate social responses, reward for isolated behavior, lack of opportunity to learn and practice social skills, and models (examples) of inappropriate behavior. Immature or withdrawn children can be taught the skills they lack by arranging opportunities for them to learn and practice appropriate responses, showing models engaging in appropriate behavior, and providing rewards for improved behavior.

A particularly important aspect of immature, withdrawn behavior is depression. Only relatively recently have mental health workers and special educators begun to realize that depression is a widespread and serious problem among children and adolescents (Kaslow, Morris, & Rehm, 1997; Sheras, 2001). Today, the consensus of psychologists is that the nature of depression in children and youths is quite similar in many respects to that of depression in adults. The indications of depression include disturbances of mood or feelings, inability to think or concentrate, lack of motivation, and decreased physical well-being. A depressed child or youth might act sad, lonely, and apathetic; exhibit low self-esteem, excessive guilt, and pervasive pessimism; avoid tasks and social experiences; and/or have physical complaints or problems in sleeping, eating, or eliminating. Sometimes depression is accompanied by such problems as bed-wetting (nocturnal **enuresis**), fecal soiling (**encopresis**), extreme fear of or refusal to go to school, failure in school, or talk of suicide or suicide attempts. Depression also frequently occurs in combination with conduct disorder.

Suicide is among the leading causes of death among young people ages fifteen to twenty-four. Depression, especially when severe and accompanied by a sense of hopelessness, is linked to suicide and suicide attempts. Therefore, it is important for all those who work with young people to be able to recognize the signs. Substance abuse is also a major problem among children and teenagers and may be related to depression.

Depression sometimes has a biological cause, and antidepressant medications have at times been successful in helping depressed children and youths to overcome their problems

(Konopasek & Forness, 2004). In many cases, however, no biological cause can be found. Depression can also be caused by environmental or psychological factors, such as the death of a loved one, separation of one's parents, school failure, rejection by one's peers, or a chaotic and punitive home environment. Consider the boy's experience in the following account:

> One terrible morning at my house, my mother woke up next to my father, who had died in his sleep. It was Dec. 5, 1989, the day before my fourth birthday. . . . My dad's death hit us hard. My mother was left alone with two energetic little boys. She tried to be cheerful, but I knew she was crying every night, and I ached to be the man of the house. Within a few years, I had plunged into a massive depression. I didn't want to live. I couldn't get out of bed, and I stopped eating and playing. A couple of hospitalizations and a long recovery awaited me. (Godwin, 2004, p. C10)

Often, just having someone with whom to build a close relationship—in the case just described, a "big brother" volunteer—can be an important key in recovery from depression. Also, interventions based on social learning theory—instructing children and youths in social interaction skills and self-control techniques and teaching them to view themselves more positively, for example—have often been successful in such cases (Gresham & Kern, 2004).

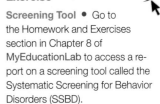

Reading Homework Exercise

Screening Tool • Go to the Homework and Exercises section in Chapter 8 of MyEducationLab to access a report on a screening tool called the Systematic Screening for Behavior Disorders (SSBD).

Educational Considerations

Students with emotional or behavioral disorders typically have low grades and other unsatisfactory academic outcomes, have higher dropout rates and lower graduation rates than other student groups, and are often placed in highly restrictive settings. Moreover, these students are disproportionately from poor and ethnic-minority families and frequently encounter the juvenile justice system (Coutinho, Oswald, Best, & Forness, 2002; Oswald, Coutinho, Best, & Singh, 1999). Consequently, their successful education is among the most important and challenging tasks facing special education today (Landrum, Tankersley, & Kauffman, 2003). Finding a remedy for the disproportionate representation of ethnic minorities in programs for students with emotional or behavioral disorders is a critical issue. However, finding effective intervention strategies for diverse students is equally important (Ishii-Jordan, 2000; Landrum & Kauffman, 2003).

Unfortunately, there has never been a consensus among special educators about how to meet the challenge of educating students with emotional or behavioral disorders. Although a national agenda has been written for improving services to students with emotional or behavioral disorders, it is so vaguely worded that it is of little value in guiding the design of interventions (Kauffman & Landrum, 2006, 2009a).

Several different conceptual models of education have been described over the decades (Kauffman & Landrum, 2006). A combination of models guides most educational programs today (see Kauffman & Landrum, 2009a, 2009b, for a description and case illustrations of models.) All credible conceptual models have two objectives: (1) controlling misbehavior and (2) teaching students the academic and social skills they need. They don't focus on one objective to the exclusion of the other, and recognize the need for integrating all the educational, psychological, and social services these students require.

Balancing Behavioral Control with Academic and Social Learning

Some writers have suggested that the quality of educational programs for students with emotional or behavioral disorders is often dismal. The focus is often said to be on external control of students' behavior, and academic instruction and social learning are too often secondary or almost entirely neglected. Teachers might not have knowledge and skills in teaching basic skills such as reading (Coleman & Vaughn, 2000). Although the quality of instruction is undoubtedly low in too many programs, examples can be found of effective academic and social instruction for students at all levels (Kauffman, Bantz, & McCullough, 2002; Peacock Hill Working Group, 1991; Walker, Forness, et al., 1998).

Behavioral control strategies are an essential part of educational programs for students with externalizing problems (Colvin, 2004). Without effective means of controlling disruptive behavior, it's extremely unlikely that academic and social learning will occur. Excellent academic instruction will certainly reduce many behavior problems as well as teach important academic skills (Falk & Wehby, 2001; Kauffman et al., 2006; Stein & Davis, 2000; Sutherland & Wehby, 2001). Nevertheless, even the best instructional programs won't eliminate the disruptive behaviors of all students. Teachers of students with emotional or behavioral disorders must have effective control strategies, preferably involving students as much as possible in self-control. In addition, teachers must offer effective instruction in academic and social skills that will allow their students to live, learn, and work with others (Farmer et al., 2001; Walker et al., 2004). Teachers must also allow students to make all the choices they can—manageable choices that are appropriate for the individual student (Jolivette, Stichter, & McCormick, 2002; Kauffman et al., 2006).

Importance of Integrated Services

Children and youths with emotional or behavioral disorders tend to have multiple and complex needs. For most, life is coming apart in more ways than one. In addition to their problems in school, they typically have family problems and a variety of difficulties in the community (e.g., engaging in illegal activities, an absence of desirable relationships with peers and adults, substance abuse, difficulty finding and maintaining employment). Thus, children or youths with emotional or behavioral disorders might need, in addition to special education, a variety of family-oriented services, psychotherapy or counseling, community supervision, training related to employment, and so on. No single service agency can meet the needs of most of these children and youths, but it is clear that school plays an important role (Farmer & Farmer, 1999; Kauffman & Landrum, 2009a). Integrating these needed services into a more coordinated and effective effort is now seen as essential.

Strategies That Work

Building Teaching Skills Teacher Artifact Exercise

Self-Management ● Go to the Building Teaching Skills section in Chapter 8 of MyEducationLab in which a strategy called Self-Management is described for use with students with emotional behavioral disorders.

Regardless of the conceptual model that guides education, we can point to several effective strategies. Successful strategies at all levels, from early intervention through transition, balance concern for academic and social skills and provide integrated services. These strategies include the following elements (Peacock Hill Working Group, 1991; see also Walker, Forness, et al., 1998; Kauffman & Landrum, 2009a):

- *Systematic, data-based interventions*—interventions that are applied systematically and consistently and that are based on reliable research data, not unsubstantiated theory
- *Continuous assessment and monitoring of progress*—direct, daily assessment of performance, with planning based on this monitoring
- *Provision for practice of new skills*—skills are not taught in isolation but are applied directly in everyday situations through modeling, rehearsal, and guided practice
- *Treatment matched to the problem*—interventions that are designed to meet the needs of individual students and their particular life circumstances, not general formulas that ignore the nature, complexity, and severity of the problem
- *Multicomponent treatment*—as many different interventions as are necessary to meet the multiple needs of students (e.g., social skills training, academic remediation, medication, counseling or psychotherapy, and family treatment or parent training)

- *Programming for transfer and maintenance*—interventions designed to promote transfer of learning to new situations, recognizing that quick fixes nearly always fail to produce generalized change

- *Commitment to sustained intervention*—interventions designed with the realization that many emotional or behavioral disorders are developmental disabilities and will not be eliminated entirely or cured.

Service Delivery

Only a relatively small percentage of children and youths with emotional or behavioral disorders are officially identified and receive any special education or mental health services (Costello et al., 2005). Consequently, the individuals who do receive special education tend to have very serious problems, although most (along with those who have mild intellectual disability or learning disabilities) have typically been assumed to have only mild disabilities. That is, the problems of the typical student with an emotional or behavioral disorder who is identified for special education are often more serious than many people have assumed. The term *severe* doesn't apply only to schizophrenia; a child can have a severe conduct disorder, for example, and its disabling effects can be extremely serious and persistent (Farmer et al., 2001; Kauffman & Landrum, 2009a; Kazdin, 1997; Patterson et al., 1992).

Compared to students with most other disabilities, a higher percentage of students with emotional or behavioral disorders are educated outside regular classrooms and schools, probably in part because students with these disorders tend to have more serious problems before they are identified. Emotional or behavioral disorders include many different types of behavioral and emotional problems, which makes it hard to make generalizations about how programs are administered.

TRENDS TOWARD INCLUSION   Even so, the trend in programs for students with emotional or behavioral disorders is toward integration into regular schools and classrooms. Even when students are placed in separate schools and classes, educators hope for reintegration into the mainstream. Integration of these students is typically difficult and requires intensive work on a case-by-case basis (Fuchs, Fuchs, Fernstrom, & Hohn, 1991; Kauffman, Lloyd, Baker, & Riedel, 1995; Walker & Bullis, 1991). Furthermore, some educators, researchers, and parents have made the case that students with emotional or behavioral disorders who are at high risk for continued problems need the structure and support of a special class; that being in a separate class can be better than being included in general education (Farmer et al., 2001; Kauffman et al., 2006; Kauffman, Mock, Tankersley, & Landrum, in 2008). Making It Work on page 289 provides suggestions as to how teachers can collaborate to implement positive behavioral supports for students with emotional or behavioral disorders in the general education classroom.

DIFFERENT NEEDS REQUIRE DIFFERENT PLACEMENTS   Placement decisions for students with emotional or behavioral disorders are particularly problematic (Kauffman, Lloyd, Hallahan, & Astuto, 1995). Educators who serve students with the most severe emotional or behavioral disorders provide ample justification for specialized environments for these children and youths. That is, it's impossible to replicate in the context of general education in a neighborhood school the intensive, individualized, highly structured environments with very high adult–student ratios offered in special classes and facilities (see Brigham & Kauffman, 1998; Farmer et al., 2001; Kauffman, Landrum, Mock, Sayeski, & Sayeski, 2005; Kauffman & Hallenbeck, 1996).

Hence, it's extremely important that the full continuum of placement options be maintained for students with emotional or behavioral disorders and that placement decisions be made on an individual basis after designing an appropriate program of education and related services. Students must not be placed outside general education classrooms and schools unless their needs require it. The IDEA mandate of placement in the least restrictive environment applies to students with emotional or behavioral disorders as well as those in all other

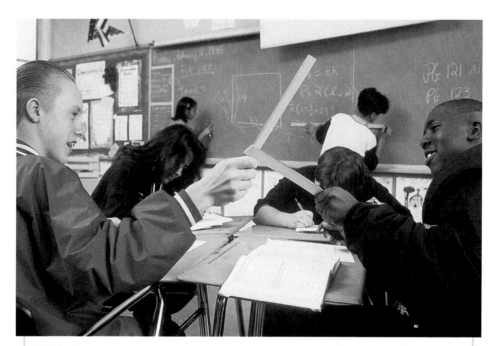

Including students with emotional and behavioral disorders in general education classrooms may sometimes be problematic since social interactions are a primary area of concern.

categories: They are to be taught in general education with their nondisabled peers to the extent that doing so is consistent with their appropriate education. However, students' needs for appropriate education and safety take priority over placement in a less restrictive environment (Bateman & Linden, 2006; Bateman & Chard, 1995; Crockett & Kauffman, 1999).

Because delinquency is a legal term, not an educational distinction, educational arrangements for juvenile delinquents are not always well delineated.

Instructional Considerations

Before being identified for special education, many students with emotional or behavioral disorders have been in general education where they could observe and learn from appropriate peer models. In reality, though, these students usually fail to imitate these models. They are unlikely to benefit merely from being with other students who have not been identified as disabled, as incidental social learning is insufficient to address their difficulties (Colvin, 2004; Hallenbeck & Kauffman, 1995; Kauffman & Pullen, 1996; Rhode, Jensen, & Reavis, 1992). For students with emotional or behavioral disorders to learn from peer models of appropriate behavior, most will require explicit, focused instruction about whom and what to imitate. In addition, they might need explicit and intensive instruction in social skills, including when, where, and how to exhibit specific types of behavior (Walker et al., 2004).

The academic curriculum for most students with emotional or behavioral disorders parallels that for most students. The basic academic skills have a great deal of survival value for any individual in society who is capable of learning them; failure to teach a student to read, write, and perform basic arithmetic deprives that student of any reasonable chance for successful adjustment to the everyday demands of life. Students who don't acquire academic skills that allow them to compete with their peers are likely to be socially rejected (Kauffman & Landrum, 2009a; Walker, 1995).

Collaboration and Co-Teaching of Students with Emotional or Behavioral Disorders

"I Don't Want Him in My Classroom if He Can't Follow the Rules!"

Statewide standards to improve educational outcomes and policies of zero tolerance to increase the safety of public schools have placed increased pressure on all teachers. These two issues, combined with the fact that many general educators do not receive training in more than routine classroom management, often make a teacher hesitant to collaborate with special educators to include students with emotional/behavioral disorders, even though many students who create discipline problems are not identified as having a disability. The increase in disciplinary concerns in schools is actually a great reason for general educators to collaborate with teachers skilled in assessing and managing behavior.

WHAT DOES IT MEAN TO BE A TEACHER OF STUDENTS WITH EMOTIONAL OR BEHAVIORAL DISORDERS?

The expertise of a teacher of students with emotional or behavioral disorders includes understanding, assessing, and managing behavior to promote learning across the content areas. Specifically, the Council for Exceptional Children (2001) has identified the following as those skills necessary for beginning teachers of students with emotional/behavioral disorders:

1. Know prevention and intervention strategies for individuals who are at risk of emotional or behavioral disorders.
2. Use a variety of nonaversive techniques to control targeted behavior and maintain attention of individuals with emotional or behavioral disorders.
3. Establish a consistent classroom routine, and use skills in problem solving and conflict resolution.
4. Plan and implement individualized reinforcement systems and environmental modifications at levels equal to the intensity of the behavior.
5. Integrate academic instruction, affective education, and behavior management for individuals and groups.
6. Assess appropriate and problematic social behaviors of individuals.

SUCCESSFUL STRATEGIES FOR CO-TEACHING

Recent research has validated the use of positive behavioral supports (PBS) for students with chronically challenging behaviors. Lewis (2000) identifies six steps in developing PBS plans for individual students in any classroom. These steps provide a unique opportunity for collaboration among general and special education faculty. Special and general educators can work together on each step to lighten the workload, provide different perspectives, and improve consistency.

The first step is to define the behavior operationally. Each teacher can provide feedback to the other to pinpoint exactly what the student is doing in the classroom, not just stating, "He's disruptive." Step 2 includes conducting a functional behavioral assessment (FBA). FBAs are time-consuming and include observing, analyzing, and hypothesizing about the behavior. Two (or more) teachers working together can observe the student at different times and in different situations, using both formalized and informal observation systems, without losing time with the rest of the class. They can also analyze data together to move to step 3: developing a hypothesis about why the student engages in the behavior. Step 4 is targeting a replacement behavior—What do the teachers want the student to do instead of the unwanted behavior? Teachers who know the student well then work together to identify this behavior, analyze it, and describe what skills the student has and does not have in order to set up a teaching scheme for this new behavior (step 5). Next, the teachers work together to teach the student the new behavior, reinforce it in the classroom, and verify that it is achieving the goals for both student and teachers. The last step is to modify the environment enough that the previous inappropriate behavior does not result in the same outcome. This can be the most difficult part and require the greatest amount of teamwork. The student will probably still try the old behavior. Teachers will hope to not see it again and can get discouraged if they do. It is at this point that teachers working together will need to support one another and to enlist other collaborators, such as administrators, parents, and other teachers, to keep the plan going. More information about positive behavioral supports is available at the Office of Special Education Program's Technical Assistance Center on Positive Behavioral Interventions and Supports at www.pbis.org/english/index.html

● *By Margaret P. Weiss*

NEED FOR SOCIAL SKILLS   Students with emotional or behavioral disorders might need specific instruction in social skills as well. We emphasize two points: (1) Effective methods are needed to teach basic academic skills, and (2) social skills and affective experiences are as crucial as academic skills. How to manage one's feelings and behavior and how to get along with other people are essential features of the curriculum for many students with emotional or behavioral disorders. These children cannot be expected to learn such skills without instruction, for the ordinary processes of socialization obviously have failed (Walker et al., 2004). Enlisting the help of peers—including peers with emotional or behavioral disorders who have learned important social skills themselves—can be an effective strategy in some cases (Blake, Wang, Cartledge, & Gardner, 2000; Farmer et al., 2001; Presley & Hughes, 2000; Stichter, Conroy, & Kauffman, 2008).

Students with schizophrenia and other major psychiatric disorders vary widely in the behaviors they exhibit and the learning problems they have. Some might need hospitalization and intensive treatment; others might remain at home and attend regular public schools. Again, the trend today is away from placement in institutions or special schools and toward inclusion in regular public schools. In some cases, students with major psychiatric disorders who attend regular schools are enrolled in special classes.

NEEDS OF JUVENILE DELINQUENTS   Educational arrangements for juvenile delinquents are hard to describe in general terms because *delinquency* is a legal term, not an educational distinction, and because programs for extremely troubled youths vary so much among states and localities. Special classes or schools are sometimes provided for youths who have histories of threatening, violent, or disruptive behavior. Some of these classes and schools are administered under special education law, but others aren't because the pupils assigned to them aren't considered emotionally disturbed. In jails, reform schools, and other detention facilities that house children and adolescents, wide variation is found in educational practices. Education of incarcerated children and youths with disabilities is governed by the same laws that apply to those who are not incarcerated, but the laws aren't always carefully implemented. Many incarcerated children don't receive assessment and education appropriate for their needs because of lack of resources, poor cooperation among agencies, and the attitude that delinquents and criminals are not entitled to the same educational opportunities as law-abiding citizens (Katsiyannis & Archwamety, 1999; Kauffman & Landrum, 2009a; Nelson et al., 2004).

SPECIAL CHALLENGES FOR TEACHERS   Given all this, it is clear that teachers of students with emotional or behavioral disorders need to be able to tolerate a great deal of unpleasantness and rejection without becoming counteraggressive or withdrawn. These students have been rejected by others; if kindness and concern were the only things they needed, they probably wouldn't be considered to have disabilities. Teachers cannot expect caring and decency always to be returned, and must be sure of their own values and confident of their teaching and living skills. They must be able and willing to make wise choices for students who choose to behave unwisely (Kauffman & Landrum, 2009a; Kauffman et al., 2006; Kerr & Nelson, 2006).

Disciplinary Considerations

Discipline is a controversial topic, especially for students with disabilities, as we discussed in Chapter 2. Many teachers and school administrators are confused about what's legal. Special rules do apply in some cases to students who have been identified as having disabilities. In some instances, the typical school rules apply; in others, they don't, under the 2004 reauthorization of IDEA. The issues are particularly controversial for students with emotional or behavioral disorders because, although their behavior might be severely problematic, the causes of their misbehavior are often difficult to determine.

INTERNET RESOURCES @

For information about juvenile justice and education, see www.edjj.org

Reading Homework Exercise

FBA Strategies ● Go to the Homework and Exercises section in Chapter 8 of MyEducationLab to review a summary of Functional Behavioral Assessment (FBA) strategies and answer relevant questions.

Uncertainty or controversy usually surrounds a change in a student's placement or suspension or expulsion due to very serious misbehavior such as bringing a weapon or illegal drugs to school. IDEA discipline provisions for students with disabilities are intended to maintain a safe school environment without violating the rights of students with disabilities to fair discipline, taking the effects of their disability into consideration.

In 2001, the reauthorization of the Elementary and Secondary Education Act (ESEA) allowed local school officials to discipline a student with disabilities just as they discipline students without disabilities when it comes to suspension and expulsion. ESEA does not require that schools suspend or expel children with disabilities as they would those without disabilities, but it does allow it. ESEA gave states and localities the option of following the IDEA rules and continuing the education of a student whose placement is changed to an alternative setting. IDEA also allows suspension and expulsion under some conditions (see Huefner, 2006).

FUNCTIONAL BEHAVIORAL ASSESSMENT AND POSITIVE BEHAVIORAL INTERVENTION AND SUPPORTS   IDEA calls for **functional behavioral assessment (FBA)** if the student's behavior is persistently a problem, but the meaning of *functional asessment* isn't entirely clear in the context of the law. You might recall from Chapter 1 that FBA assists educators in determining and altering the factors that account for a student's misconduct. Nevertheless, precisely what the law now requires of special educators and other school personnel is uncertain (Landrum, 2000; Mueller, Edwards, & Trahant, 2003; Sasso, Conroy, Stichter, & Fox, 2001; Sugai & Horner, 1999–2000). Apparently, the intent of the law is to require teachers to assess student behavior in ways that lead to the selection of effective intervention strategies. The Responsive Instruction feature on page 292 offers suggestions about how teachers can use FBA in figuring out how best to manage problem behavior.

There is now great emphasis on positive behavioral supports and behavior intervention plans for students with emotional and behavioral disorders. Increasingly, researchers recognize that problem behavior occurs less frequently in the classroom when the teacher is offering effective instruction (Kauffman et al., 2006).

Assessment of Progress

Just as educational considerations for students with emotional or behavioral disorders (EBD) must include controlling misbehavior and teaching students academic and social skills, assessment must also address these areas. Teachers should engage in methods to determine whether social/emotional and academic needs of students with (EBD) are being met. In addition to FBAs, assessing students with EBD includes monitoring student progress to plan instruction and measuring student outcomes to document the success of both social and academic interventions.

Progress Monitoring and Outcome Measures

EVALUATING THE PROGRESS AND OUTCOMES OF BEHAVIORAL INTERVENTIONS   The ongoing assessment program for students with EBD should include measures that address several domains of social-emotional behavior that influence academic learning, including interpersonal skills, study skills, motivation, and engagement (DiPerna, 2006). Two methods that may be employed to monitor the behavioral progress are rating scales and direct observation. Direct observation is often implemented through FBAs.

Casebook Reflection

REFER TO THE CASE *What Do We Do With Jim?* in your booklet. Jim came off nine days of suspension from school. The administration believed that he would not do well in the self-contained class for SED with the "streetwise guy." The principal suggested placing him in the resource room with Frieda, who has her teaching credential in SED. In what ways was this action appropriate, and in what ways was it problematic? ●

UNDERSTANDING THE STANDARDS AND PRINCIPLES   What should teachers know about assessment of behavior? (CEC Knowledge and Skill Standards BD8S1 & BD8S2)

Council for Exceptional Children

■ **Functional behavioral assessment (FBA)**
Evaluation that consists of finding out the consequences (what purpose the behavior serves), antecedents (what triggers the behavior), and setting events (contextual factors) that maintain inappropriate behavior.

INTERNET RESOURCES

Resources for positive behavior management are increasingly available on the World Wide Web. Many sites are being developed, and most provide links to other sites. Following are some that you might want to access:

The National Center on Education, Disability and Juvenile Justice at www.edjj.org

The Oregon Social Learning Center at www.oslc.org

The Technical Assistance Center on Positive Behavioral Interventions and Supports at www.pbis.org

Meeting the Needs of Students with Emotional or Behavioral Disorders

Functional Behavioral Assessments

WHAT THE RESEARCH SAYS

Functional behavioral assessments (FBAs) have become standard practice in the development of Individualized Education Programs (IEPs), particularly the behavior intervention plan (BIP) component, for students with emotional or behavioral disabilities. Under IDEA, school districts are required to conduct a FBA/BIP for any student who receives disciplinary action that results in more than ten days' suspension or a change in placement due to disciplinary issues. Unfortunately, the implementation of these assessments varies greatly—as does, then, the efficacy of the tool (Fox & Davis, 2005; Sasso, Conroy, Stichter, & Fox, 2001). When implemented correctly, research clearly demonstrates the effectiveness of the interventions employed based upon FBAs (Fox & Davis). Thus, the burden is upon school districts to ensure FBAs are implemented to the empirical standards established in the research.

RESEARCH STUDY

Van Acker and colleagues (Van Acker, Boreson, Gable, & Patterson, 2005) conducted an analysis of FBAs and BIPs created across a state to determine the prevalence of "best practices"

in implementation. This analysis followed a three-year effort on behalf of the state to provide FBA training to teachers in the form of one- and two-day workshops. Over two hundred school districts and intermediary agencies participated in the training. It is important to note that many schools sent limited representatives to the state training. These representatives would then return to their home school and provide information to fellow IEP team members who had not attended the training. Upon completion of the training sessions, seventy-one IEP teams voluntarily submitted their FBA/BIPs for review for the study. Each FBA/BIP was scored using a standard rating scale.

RESEARCH FINDINGS

Despite the statewide initiative related to high quality FBA/BIP development, the majority of plans reviewed exhibited serious flaws. The most prevalent issues were:

1. *Failure to identify specific target behaviors.* The overarching goal of a FBA/BIP is to reduce, eliminate, or replace challenging behaviors; thus, the failure to identify a clearly measurable target behavior results in an unfocused plan or a plan that was not directly connected to the

■ **Curriculum-based measurement (CBM)**
A formative evaluation method designed to evaluate performance in the curriculum to which students are exposed; usually involves giving students a small sample of items from the curriculum in use in their schools; proponents argue that CBM is preferable to comparing students with national norms or using tests that do not reflect the curriculum content learned by the students.

Several rating scales are available to assess students' social skills. The School Social Behavior Scales (SSBS-2; Merrell, 2002) evaluates social competence and antisocial behavior and should be completed by teachers or other school personnel. Each of the two scales comprises thirty-two items divided into the following subscales: Peer Relations, Self-Management-Compliance, Academic Behavior, Hostile-Irritable, Anitsocial-Aggressive, and Defiant-Disruptive.

The Learning and Study Strategies Inventory (Weinstein, Palmer, & Schulte, 2002) is a self-report instrument appropriate for high school (LASSI-HS) and college students (LASSI) to assess learning and study strategies. LASSI scales include measures of attitude, motivation, time management, anxiety, concentration, study aids, and test strategies.

MEASURING PROGRESS AND OUTCOMES IN ACADEMIC SKILLS   Students with EBD often have difficulty with academic tasks and fail to make adequate progress in school. Ongoing assessment for these students should be implemented to ensure that they are making sufficient progress toward academic goals and to plan instruction. The methods for monitoring progress for students with EBD would be the same as those for students with learning disabilities and ADHD described in Chapters 6 and 7 respectively. For example, **curriculum-based measurement (CBM)** in mathematics, reading, and spelling are behavior(s) of concern. A related flaw was to assume that a cluster of behaviors (e.g., hitting, swearing, and non-compliance) all related to the same function and therefore, different assessments for each behavior were not conducted.

2. *Failure to verify the hypothesized function of the behavior.* As teams are developing the FBA, they hypothesize the function of behavior of concern. In other words, they generate a hypothesis as to *why* the student is behaving in an undesirable manner. Teams can test the hypothesis through variable manipulation (e.g., if the hypothesized function was teacher attention, teacher attention could be removed to see if the behavior escalated). Similarly, teams could use data triangulation—the use of more than one data source in order to support the hypothesis. Teams typically did not show evidence of attempting to verify hypotheses prior to developing interventions.

3. *Failure to connect the function of the behavior to the specific interventions identified in the BIP.* In the study, the most significant (and problematic) flaw was that the BIPs failed to directly address the issues identified in the FBA. Only twenty-five of the interventions could be clearly linked to the function of the behavior and the promotion of desirable and appropriate behaviors. Ideally, BIPs are created using the principles of positive behavioral intervention and support—creating environmental conditions and reinforcers to promote desired behaviors. In contrast to positive intervention and behavioral support, fifty-six of the plans submitted include over reliance on aversive consequences.

In some cases, these aversive consequences served the *same function* as the undesirable behavior. For example, if the FBA indicated that a student skipped class (i.e., "escaped") due to a skill deficit, the BIP would then call for suspension as the aversive consequence in response to skipping. Clearly, this consequence has the capacity to increase rather than decrease the undesired behavior!

APPLYING THE RESEARCH TO TEACHING

To avoid falling into the same pitfalls identified in their study, Van Acker and colleagues (2005) created the following checklist for teams to self-evaluate their plans:

1. Clearly identified target behavior.
2. Verification of hypothesized target behavior function.
3. Clear BIP indicating function of the behavior met through alternative, desirable behavior.
4. Positive behavioral supports indicated.
5. Modification of physical or social context as a part of BIP.
6. Plan for monitoring and evaluating BIP.

As a final note, Van Acker and colleagues did find that the higher quality FBA/BIPs were those submitted by teams who had at least one member of the group with significant training (e.g., coursework in applied behavior analysis, district or state training in FBA). Thus, school districts and school personnel should actively seek out training and support for all IEP members.

● *Kristin L. Sayeski.*

---

widely implemented for such students. CBM has a significant research base to support its use, particularly with students with high incidence disabilities. Likewise, standardized measures of academic skills to measure student outcomes are readily available. These assessments were described in Chapter 6 on learning disabilities.

The Academic Competence Evaluation Scales (ACES; DiPerna & Elliott, 2000) is a measure that assesses both academic skills as well as social and behavioral skills that lead to academic success. The academic components of the ACES are reading and language arts, mathematics, and critical thinking. In addition to the academic skills, ACES measures motivation, engagement, study skills, and interpersonal skills. It's appropriate for students in K–12 settings as well as college students. A "goal attainment scale" specifically measures the progress of students and helps evaluate the effects of an intervention.

Testing Accommodations

Students with EBD are typically included in standardized assessments of academic outcomes, and many benefit from testing accommodations. The most common accommodations are scheduling and presentation accommodations. Fortunately, most students (about 75 percent) receive extended time for tests (Wagner et al., 2006). Fewer students with EBD receive presentation accommodations (e.g., having the test or directions read aloud).

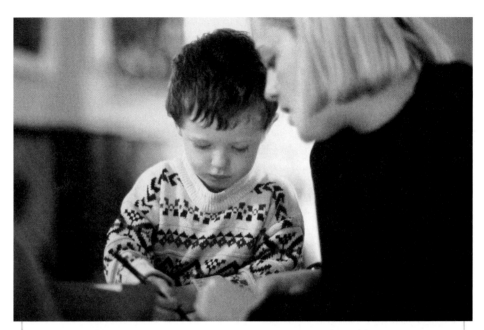

Preschool intervention for children with emotional or behavioral disorders has been quite effective in preventing or reducing subsequent problems. However, identifying these disorders between 3 and 5 years can be difficult.

UNDERSTANDING THE STANDARDS AND PRINCIPLES What interventions might be effective for a preschooler who is exhibiting overly aggressive or withdrawn behavior? (CEC Knowledge and Skill Standard BD4K4)

Video Homework Exercise

Positive Behavior Supports Go to the Homework and Exercises section in Chapter 8 of MyEducationLab to watch the video "Teacher Praise." How does the description of Positive Behavioral Supports described by the authors compare to the classroom management approach in the video?

Although many students are receiving testing accommodations, research isn't clear on which accommodations are most useful to students with EBD (Gunter, Denny, & Venn, 2000).

Early Intervention

Early identification and prevention are basic goals of intervention programs for any category of disability (Bowe, 2004; Gargiulo & Kilgo, 2005; Noonan & McCormick, 2006; Sprague & Walker, 2000). For students with emotional or behavioral disorders, these goals present particular difficulties—yet also hold particular promise (Dunlap et al., 2006; Walker & Sprague, 2007). The difficulties are related to the definition and measurement of emotional or behavioral disorders, especially in young children; the particular promise is that young children's social-emotional behavior is quite flexible, so preventive efforts seem to have a good chance of success (Kaiser, 2000; Kamps, Tankersley, & Ellis, 2000; Kauffman, 1999, 2005).

As Thomas and Guskin remarked, "Diagnosis of disruptive behaviors in very young children is challenging because they appear to respond to a variety of risk factors with similar hyperactive, aggressive, and defiant behaviors (2001, p. 50). Nevertheless, early identification and prevention of EBD—or, what some have termed "challenging behavior"—is possible (Qi & Kaiser, 2003). Table 8.1 suggests three ways in which such behavior might be prevented.

The patterns of behavior that signal problems for the preschool child are those that bring them into frequent conflict with, or keep them aloof from, their parents or caretakers and their siblings or peers. Many children who are referred to clinics for disruptive behavior when they are seven to twelve years of age showed clear signs of behavior problems by the time they were three or four—or even younger (Loeber, Green, Lahey, Christ, & Frick, 1992; Shaw, Owens, Giovannelli, & Winslow, 2001; Walker et al., 2004). Infants or toddlers who exhibit a very "difficult temperament"—who are irritable; have irregular patterns of sleeping, eating, and eliminating; have highly intense responses to many stimuli and negative reactions toward new situations—are at risk for developing serious behavior problems

TABLE 8.1   **Prevention of Challenging Behavior**

1. Children and their families who access mental and physical care are less likely to have behavioral and social problems.

2. Nurturing and positive parenting is associated with children who have healthy relationships and reduced challenging behavior.

3. High quality early education environments and caregiver interactions are associated with fewer behavior problems and the development of social competence.

Source: From Prevention and intervention with young children's challenging behavior: Perspectives regarding current knowledge. by G. Dunlap, P. S. Strain, L. Fox, J. J. Carta, M. Conroy, B. J. Smith, et al. *Behavioral Disorders, 32*, 29–45. Table 1, p. 33. Copyright © 2008 by the Council for Exceptional Children. Reprinted with permission.

unless their parents are particularly skillful at handling them. Children of preschool age are likely to elicit negative responses from adults and playmates if they are much more aggressive or much more withdrawn than most children their age. (Remember the critical importance of same-age comparisons. Toddlers frequently grab what they want, push other children down, and throw things and kick and scream when they don't get their way; toddlers normally don't have much finesse at social interaction and often hide from strangers.)

Because children's behavior is quite responsive to conditions in the social environment and can be shaped by adults, the potential for primary prevention—preventing serious behavior problems from occurring in the first place—would seem to be great. If parents and teachers could be taught effective child management skills, perhaps many or most cases could be prevented (Dunlap et al., 2006; Ialongo et al., 1998; Walker et al., 2004; Walker, Kavanagh, et al., 1998; Walker & Sprague, 2007). Furthermore, one could imagine that if parents and teachers had such skills, children who already have emotional or behavioral disorders could be prevented from getting worse (secondary prevention). But as Bower (1981) notes, the task of primary prevention is not that simple. For one thing, the tremendous amount of money and personnel that are needed for training in child management are not available. For another, even if the money and personnel could be found, professionals would not always agree on what patterns of behavior should be prevented or on how undesirable behavior could be prevented from developing (Kauffman, 1999, 2005; Kazdin, 1995).

If overly aggressive or withdrawn behavior is identified in a preschooler, what kind of intervention program is most desirable? Behavioral interventions are highly effective (see Peacock Hill Working Group, 1991; Strain & Timm, 2001; Strain et al., 1992; Walker, Forness, et al., 1998; Walker et al., 2004; Walker & Sprague, 2007). A behavioral approach implies defining and measuring the child's behaviors and rearranging the environment (especially adults' and other children's responses to the problem child) to teach and support more appropriate conduct. In the case of aggressive children, social rewards for aggression should be prevented. For example, hitting another child or throwing a temper tantrum might result in brief social isolation or time-out instead of adult attention or getting one's own way.

In summary, it is possible to identify at an early age those children who are at high risk for emotional or behavioral disorders (Dunlap et al., 2006; Farmer et al., 2001; Walker, Kavanagh, et al., 1998; Walker et al., 2004; Walker & Sprague, 2007; Wehby, Dodge, & Valente, 1993). These children exhibit extreme aggression or social withdrawal and may be socially rejected or identify with deviant peers. They should be identified as early as possible, and their parents and teachers should learn how to teach them essential social skills and how to manage their problem behavior using positive, nonviolent procedures. If children with emotional or behavioral disorders are identified very early and intervention is sufficiently comprehensive, intense, and sustained, then there's a good chance that they can recover and exhibit developmentally normal patterns of behavior (Strain & Timm, 2001; Timm, 1993; Walker et al., 2004; Walker & Sprague, 2007).

Nevertheless, research suggests that in practice early intervention typically doesn't occur (Dunlap et al., 2006). In fact, intervention usually doesn't begin until the child has

Case Study Homework Exercise

Interventions • Go to the Homework and Exercises section in Chapter 8 of MyEducationLab to read the case study "Eric's Last Stand", which offers a depiction of some of the EBD characteristics and interventions you've read about in this chapter.

exhibited an extremely disabling pattern of behavior for several years (Duncan, Forness, & Hartsough, 1995). The primary reasons given as to why early, comprehensive, intense, and sustained intervention is so rare include worry about labeling and stigma, optimism regarding the child's development (i.e., the assumption that he or she will "grow out of it"), lack of resources required to address the needs of any but the most severely problematic children, and ignorance about the early signs of emotional or behavioral problems (Kauffman, 1999, 2004, 2005).

Transition to Adulthood

Programs designed for adolescents with emotional or behavioral disorders vary widely in aims and structure (Cheney & Bullis, 2004; Maag & Katsiyannis, 1998; Nelson et al., 2004). Nelson and Kauffman (1977) describe the following types, which remain the basic options today:

- Regular public high school classes
- Consultant teachers who work with general education teachers to provide individualized academic work and behavior management
- Resource rooms and special self-contained classes to which students may be assigned for part or all of the school day
- Work-study programs in which vocational education and job experience are combined with academic study
- Special private or public schools that offer the regular high school curriculum in a different setting
- Alternative schools that offer highly individualized programs that are nontraditional in both setting and content
- Private or public residential schools

Incarcerated youths with emotional or behavioral disorders are an especially neglected group in special education (Nelson et al., 2004). The special educational needs of many (or most) of these teenagers who are in prison might be neglected because incarcerated youths are defined as socially maladjusted rather than emotionally disturbed. The current federal definition appears to allow denial of special education services to a large number of young people who exhibit extremely serious misbehaviors and have long histories of school failure.

It is difficult to design special education programs at the secondary level for students with emotional or behavioral disorders; this category of youths is so varied. Adolescents categorized for special education purposes as emotionally disturbed may have behavioral characteristics ranging from extreme withdrawal to aggressive delinquency, intelligence ranging from severely disabled to highly gifted, and academic skills ranging from preschool to college level. It's hardly realistic to suggest that any single type of program or model will be appropriate for all such youths. In fact, youths with emotional or behavioral disorders, perhaps more than any other category of exceptionality, need a highly individualized, creative, and flexible education. Programs may range from teaching daily living skills in a sheltered environment to advanced placement in college, from general education placement to hospitalization, and from the traditional curriculum to unusual and specialized vocational training (see Brolin & Loyd, 2004; Sitlington & Clark, 2006).

Transition from school to work and adult life is particularly difficult for adolescents with emotional or behavioral disorders. Many of them lack the basic academic skills necessary for successful employment. In addition, they often behave in ways that prevent them from being accepted, liked, and helped by classmates, employers, coworkers, and neighbors. It is not surprising that students with emotional or behavioral disorders are among the most likely to drop out of school and among the most difficult to train in transition programs (Cheney & Bullis, 2004; Edgar & Siegel, 1995; Malmgren, Edgar, & Neel, 1998; Sitlington & Clark, 2006).

Brolin and Loyd (2004) provide a case example of a student with "emotional/behavioral disturbance":

> Stephen is a 16-year-old boy who has difficulty building and maintaining satisfactory relationships with his peers and teachers. In most of his general education classes, he is inattentive and fails to complete class assignments, which has resulted in a lack of academic progress. Stephen functions at the eighth grade level in both reading and mathematics. Sometimes Stephen appears to be depressed and unhappy. His behavior in class and in nonacademic settings is often inappropriate and immature. (p. 240)

Many children and youths with emotional or behavioral disorders grow up to be adults who have real difficulties leading independent, productive lives. The outlook is especially grim for children and adolescents with conduct disorders. Contrary to popular opinion, the child or youth who is shy, anxious, or neurotic is not the most likely to have psychiatric problems as an adult. Rather, it is the conduct-disordered (hyperaggressive) child or youth whose adulthood is most likely to be characterized by socially intolerable behavior and lack of social competence (Kazdin, 1995, 1997; Walker & Stieber, 1998; Walker et al., 2004). About half the children who are hyperaggressive will have problems that require legal intervention or psychiatric care when they are adults.

Successful transition to adult life is often complicated by neglectful, abusive, or inadequate family relationships. A high percentage of adolescents with conduct disorder have family relationships of this nature. However, the emphasis on punishment and imprisonment, particularly of African American males, appears to be counterproductive. The emphasis on punishment contributes to family deterioration and harsh conditions of life that perpetuate undesirable conduct (Miller, 1997).

Examples of relatively successful high school and transition programs are available, most of which employ a behavioral approach (Cheney & Bullis, 2004; Edgar & Siegel, 1995; Peacock Hill Working Group, 1991). However, it is important to stress the term *relatively* because many adolescents and young adults with severe conduct disorder appear to have a true developmental disability that requires intervention throughout their life span (Wolf, Braukmann, & Ramp, 1987). By the time these antisocial youths reach high school, the aim of even the most effective program is to help them accommodate their disabilities. Rather than focusing on remediation of academic and social skills, these programs attempt to teach youths the skills they will need to survive and cope in school and community, to make a transition to work, and to develop vocations (Walker et al., 2004). Well-planned alternative schools appear to offer important options to students at high risk, including those with emotional or behavioral problems (Duke, Griesdorn, & Kraft, 1998; Tobin & Sprague, 1999).

INTERNET RESOURCES

For more information about antisocial children and youth and their management, see www.oslc.org

Summary

What terminology is used to describe emotional and behavioral disorders?

▶ The current term in federal laws is *emotionally disturbed*.

▶ The terminology of various states and localities is varied and sometimes confusing; it includes a variety of combinations of terms such as emotional disturbance, behavioral disorder, and social maladjustment.

What is the definition of *emotional and behavioral disorder*?

▶ Any definition generally refers to behavior that goes to an extreme, a problem that is chronic, and behavior that is unacceptable because of social or cultural expectations.

▶ The current federal definition lists five characteristics, any one of which must be exhibited to a marked extent and over a period of time and adversely affect educational performance:
  ■ Inability to learn
  ■ Inability to establish satisfactory relationships
  ■ Inappropriate behavior
  ■ Pervasive unhappiness or depression
  ■ Physical symptoms, pains, or fears

▶ The major points of the definition of the National Mental Health and Special Education Coalition are that the behavior:
  ■ Is more than a temporary, expected response to stressful events in the environment
  ■ Is consistently exhibited in two different settings, at least one of which is school
  ■ Is unresponsive to direct intervention in general education, or the child's condition is such that general education interventions would be insufficient.

How are emotional and behavioral disorders classified?

▶ Psychiatric classifications are not very useful to teachers.

▶ The most useful and reliable classifications are based on the primary dimensions of externalizing (acting against others) and internalizing (acting against self).

What is the prevalence of emotional and behavioral disorders?

▶ Most studies suggest that 5–10 percent of the child population have such disorders.

▶ Special education and mental health serve only a fraction of those needing help for serious disorders (i.e., about 1 percent of the child population).

What are the causes of emotional and behavioral disorders?

▶ Causes are multiple and complex, and seldom can a single cause be identified.

▶ Major causal factors include biology, family, school, and culture.

How are emotional and behavioral disorders identified?

▶ Teacher judgment plays the most significant role.

▶ Most students are below average in tested intelligence and academic achievement.

▶ Students exhibit externalizing (aggressive toward others) or internalizing (immature, withdrawn, depressed) behavior or a combination of the two.

What are the major educational considerations regarding emotional and behavioral disorders?

▶ A balance between behavioral control and academic instruction is required.

▶ Integrated services are important.

▶ Strategies that work best include the following:
  ■ Systematic, data-based interventions
  ■ Continuous assessment and monitoring of progress
  ■ Provision for practice of new skills
  ■ Treatment matched to the problem
  ■ Multicomponent treatment
  ■ Programming for transfer and maintenance
  ■ Commitment to sustained intervention

▶ Service delivery emphasizes inclusion when appropriate and the importance of a full continuum of alternative placements.

▶ Instruction should be highly structured and relevant to the student's life.

▶ Special disciplinary considerations include functional behavioral assessment and positive behavioral support.

How do professionals assess the progress of students with emotional or behavioral disorders?

▶ Professionals may use a variety of standardized scales and observations to assess behavior; curriculum-based measurement is recommended for assessing academic progress.

▶ Testing accommodations might involve alterations in scheduling, such as extended time, or presentation, such as having directions read aloud.

What are important considerations in early intervention for learners with emotional or behavioral disorders?

▶ Early intervention is often suggested but seldom practiced.

What are important considerations in transition to adulthood for learners with emotional or behavioral disorders?

▶ Transition is difficult but particularly important because the long-term and employment outcomes for most students are not good.

STANDARDS and PRINCIPLES in this Chapter

SPECIAL EDUCATORS . . .

■ understand the field as an evolving and changing discipline (from CEC Content Standard #1).

■ understand the similarities and differences in human development (from CEC Content Standard #2).

- possess a repertoire of evidence-based instructional strategies (from CEC Content Standard #4).

- actively create learning environments for individuals with exceptional learning needs that foster cultural understanding, safety and emotional well-being, positive social interactions, and active engagement (from CEC Content Standard #5).

- use the results of assessments to help identify exceptional learning needs (from CEC Content Standard #8).

- use collaboration to facilitate the successful transitions of individuals with exceptional learning needs across settings and services (from CEC Content Standard #10).

ALL TEACHERS . . .

- understand the central concepts, tools of inquiry, structures of the discipline(s) they teach and can create learning experiences that make these aspects of subject matter meaningful for students (INTASC Principle #1).

- understand how children learn and develop (from INTASC Principle #2).

- understand and use a variety of instructional strategies (from INTASC Principle #4).

- use an understanding of individual and group motivation and behavior to create a learning environment that encourages positive social interaction, active engagement in learning, and self-motivation (INTASC Principle #5).

- understand and use formal and informal assessment strategies to evaluate and ensure the continuous intellectual, social, and physical development of the learner (INTASC Principle #8).

- foster relationships with school colleagues, families, and agencies in the larger community to support students' learning and well-being (INTASC Principle #10).

Applying the **STANDARDS** and **PRINCIPLES**

- ONE of your colleagues, whose background is in general education, asks, "What does it really mean to have an emotional or behavioral disorder?" How would you respond? (CEC Content Standard #1 & #2; INTASC Principle #1 & #2)

- HOW should teachers determine what instructional methods to use with students with emotional or behavioral disorders? (CEC Content Standard #4 & INTASC Principle #4)

- WHAT is your opinion with respect to where students with emotional or behavioral disorders should be taught? (CEC Content Standard #5 & INTASC Principle #5)

- HOW easy or difficult is it to identify an emotional or behavioral disorder? (CEC Content Standard #8 & INTASC Principle #8)

- HOW would you respond to parents who approach you expressing concern about the future of their high school student with an emotional or behavioral disorder? (CEC Content Standard #4 & #10; INTASC Principle #4 & #10)

Now go to the Hallahan/Kauffman, Eleventh Edition MyEducationLab course at www.myeducationlab.com to:

- take a Pretest to assess your initial comprehension of the chapter content;
- study chapter content with your Individualized Study Plan;
- take a Posttest to assess your understanding of chapter content;
- engage in multimedia exercises to help you build a deeper and more applied understanding of chapter content.

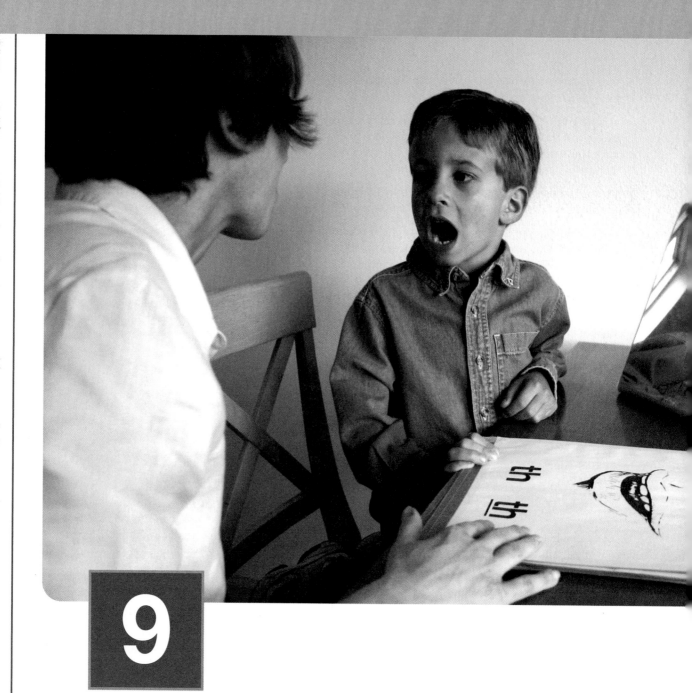

9

Learners with Communication Disorders

*S*tutterers have a tendency to generalize their fear of one word that begins with a particular sound to a fear of all words that begin with the same sound. In the space of the summer I'd effectively eliminated every *F* from my vocabulary, with the exception of the preposition, "for," which for the time being was too small to incite terror. A few weeks later, my fear of *F* ended when another letter—I think it was *L*—suddenly loomed large.

—David Shields
Dead Languages

QUESTIONS **to guide your reading of this chapter . . .**

- How are communication disorders defined?
- What is the prevalence of communication disorders?
- What is the difference between communicative differences and disorders?
- What are the major disorders of language?
- What are the major disorders of speech?
- What are the main educational considerations for communication disorders?
- What are the major features of assessment of progress for students with communication disorders?
- What are the major aspects of early intervention for communication disorders?
- What is emphasized in transition for students with communication disorders?

MISCONCEPTIONS ABOUT

Learners with Communication Disorders

MYTH ■ Children with language disorders always have speech difficulties as well.

FACT ■ It is possible for a child to have good speech yet not make any sense when he or she talks; however, most children with language disorders have speech disorders as well.

MYTH ■ Individuals with communication disorders always have emotional or behavioral disorders or intellectual disabilities.

FACT ■ Some children with communication disorders are normal in cognitive, social, and emotional development.

MYTH ■ How children learn language is now well understood.

FACT ■ Although recent research has revealed quite a lot about the sequence of language acquisition and has led to theories of language development, exactly how children learn language is still unknown.

MYTH ■ Stuttering is primarily a disorder of people with extremely high IQs. Children who stutter become stuttering adults.

FACT ■ Stuttering can affect individuals at all levels of intellectual ability. Some children who stutter continue stuttering as adults; most, however, stop stuttering before or during adolescence with help from a speech-language pathologist. Stuttering is primarily a childhood disorder, found much more often in boys than in girls.

MYTH ■ Disorders of phonology (or articulation) are never very serious and are always easy to correct.

FACT ■ Disorders of phonology can make speech unintelligible; it is sometimes very difficult to correct phonological or articulation problems, especially if the individual has cerebral palsy, intellectual disabilities, or emotional or behavioral disorders.

MYTH ■ There is no relationship between intelligence and communication disorders.

FACT ■ Communication disorders tend to occur more frequently among individuals of lower intellectual ability, although they may occur in individuals who are extremely intelligent.

MYTH ■ There is not much overlap between language disorders and learning disabilities.

FACT ■ Problems with verbal skills—listening, reading, writing, speaking—are often central features of learning disabilities. The definitions of language disorders and several other disabilities are overlapping.

MYTH ■ Children who learn few language skills before entering kindergarten can easily pick up all the skills they need, if they have good peer models in typical classrooms.

FACT ■ Early language learning is critical for later language development; a child whose language is delayed is unlikely to learn to use language effectively merely by observing peer models. More explicit intervention is typically required.

MYTH ■ English language learners who have acquired proficient social language will also succeed in academic tasks.

FACT ■ Basic Interpersonal Communication Skills (BICS) do not ensure students' academic success. Students require proficiency in more advanced language skills, referred to as Cognitive Academic Language Proficiency (CALP) to be successful in academic areas.

Communication is such a natural part of our everyday lives that we seldom stop to think about it. Social conversation with families, friends, and casual acquaintances is normally so effortless and pleasant that it is hard to imagine having difficulty with it. Consider the following description of speech by Hulit and Howard (2006):

> Speech is so much a part of the human experience that we truly take it for granted, but it is a wondrous human gift. The next time you engage in a conversation with one or more people, consider the speech chains that connect speakers to listeners. Marvel at the speed involved in the sending and receiving of messages (p. 14).

Most of us have feelings of uncertainty about the adequacy of our speech or language only in stressful or unusual social situations, such as talking to a large audience or being interviewed for a job. If we always had to worry about communicating, we would worry about every social interaction we had.

For some people, however, communication is not effortless and pleasant. Their communication may take great effort. For instance, some individuals have serious problems producing a sufficiently clear voice quality, described as a *voice disorder*, and other individuals are unable to comprehend the language that others produce, described as a *receptive language disorder*. The young man David Shields (see page 301) was unable to produce fluent speech, or speech of an appropriate rhythm and rate; this is a *fluency disorder*, or stuttering.

Not all communication disorders involve disorders of speech. Not all speech disorders are as handicapping in social interactions as stuttering, nor is stuttering the most common disorder of speech. Stuttering affects only about one person in twenty during childhood, and only about one in a hundred people stutter throughout their lives. Most cases of childhood stuttering are resolved by adulthood (Owens, Metz, & Haas, 2007; Yairi & Ambrose, 2004).

Today, difficulty such as that described by Shields is viewed within the broad context of communication disorders because of the obstacle it presents to social interaction, which is the major purpose of language. The young man's stuttering resulted in an inability to convey his thoughts and feelings, not just a problem of being fearful and unable to say certain words. In thinking about communication disorders, three elements of communication must be considered: the contexts in which communication occurs (e.g., in a group, in the classroom), the functions expressed by communication or the reasons one communicates (e.g., to request, to comment, to reason), and the actual execution of communication comprehension and expression.

INTERNET RESOURCES

An important Website to visit for more information about communication disorders is the home page of the American Speech–Language–Hearing Association at www.asha.org

Definitions

Speech and language are tools used for communication. **Communication** is the process of sharing information and involves many **communicative functions**, such as seeking social interaction, requesting objects, sharing ideas, and rejecting an object or interaction. It requires sending messages in understandable form (encoding) and receiving and understanding messages (decoding). It always involves a sender and a receiver of messages, but

■ **Communication**
The process of sharing information.

■ **Communicative function**
Acts of communication, such as requesting, rejecting, commenting, arguing, and reasoning.

■ **Communication disorders**
Impairments in the ability to use speech or language to communicate.

■ **Language**
An arbitrary code or system of symbols to communicate meaning.

■ **Expressive language**
Encoding or sending messages in communication.

■ **Receptive language**
Decoding or understanding messages in communication.

■ **Speech**
The formation and sequencing of oral language sounds during communication.

■ **Augmentative or alternative communication (AAC)**
Alternative forms of communication that do not use the oral sounds of speech or that augment the use of speech.

■ **Speech disorders**
Oral communication that involves abnormal use of the vocal apparatus, is unintelligible, or is so inferior that it draws attention to itself and causes anxiety, feelings of inadequacy, or inappropriate behavior in the speaker.

■ **Language disorders**
Oral communication that involves a lag in the ability to understand and express ideas, putting linguistic skill behind an individual's development in other areas, such as motor, cognitive, or social development.

■ **Phonology**
The study of how individual sounds make up words.

■ **Morphology**
The study within psycholinguistics of word formation; how adding or deleting parts of words changes their meaning.

■ **Syntax**
The way words are joined together to structure meaningful sentences; grammar.

■ **Semantics**
The study of the meanings attached to words and sentences.

it does not always involve oral language. Communication can also be nonverbal—in fact, much of the meaningful interaction among humans occurs nonverbally (Owens et al., 2007). Language (both verbal and nonverbal) and speech are important tools for human communication. A **communication disorder** impairs the ability to transmit or receive ideas, facts, feelings, and desires and may involve language or speech or both, including hearing, listening, reading, or writing.

Language is the communication of ideas—sending and receiving them—through an arbitrary system of symbols used according to certain rules that determine meaning. Encoding or sending messages is referred to as **expressive language**. Decoding or understanding messages is referred to as **receptive language**. When people think of language, they typically think of oral language. **Speech**—the neuromuscular activity of forming and sequencing the sounds of oral language—is the most common symbol system used in communication between humans. Without the rule-governed symbol system that we call language, we would have only grunts and groans, not speech.

Some languages, however, are not based on speech. For example, American Sign Language (ASL) does not involve speech sounds; it is a manual language used by many people who cannot hear speech. **Augmentative or alternative communication (AAC)** for people with disabilities involving the physical movements of speech may consist of alternatives to the speech sounds of oral language (e.g., picture boards, ASL, gestures, and electronic devices that produce speech; see the discussion of AAC in Chapter 13).

The American Speech–Language–Hearing Association (ASHA) provides definitions of disorders of communication, including speech disorders, language disorders, and variations in communication (differences or dialects and augmentative systems) that are not disorders (see the Focus on Concepts on page 305). **Speech disorders** are impairments in the production and use of oral language. They include disabilities in making speech sounds, producing speech with a normal flow, and producing voice.

Language disorders include problems in comprehension and expression. Remember that language is governed by rules. The problems—rule violations—may involve the form (phonology, morphology, syntax), content (semantics), or use of language (pragmatics).

- **Phonology** refers to the rules governing speech sounds—the particular sounds and how they are sequenced.
- **Morphology** refers to the rules that govern alterations of the internal organization of words, such as adding suffixes and other grammatical inflections to make proper plurals, verb tenses, and so on.
- **Syntax** refers to the rules of organizing sentences that are meaningful, including subject and predicate and placing modifiers correctly, for example.
- **Semantics** refers to the rules about attaching meanings and concepts to words.
- **Pragmatics** refers to the rules about using language for social purposes.

Language disorders may involve any one or a combination of these five subsystems of language. Differences in speech or language that are shared by people in a given region, social group, or cultural/ethnic group should not be considered disorders. For example, African American English (Ebonics or Black English Vernacular), Appalachian English, and the Cajun dialect are varieties of English, not disorders of speech or language. These differences are governed by their own rules and reflect the cultural and linguistic diversity of North America. As long as speech and language are guided by consistent rules of a language community, they are not disorders, although they may differ from what we are accustomed to hearing and saying.

Similarly, the use of AAC systems does not imply that a person has a language disorder. Rather, such systems support people who have temporary or permanent inabilities to use speech satisfactorily for communication. Those who use AAC systems might or might not have language disorders in addition to their inability to use speech.

FOCUS ON **Concepts**

Definitions of the American Speech–Language–Hearing Association

I. A communication disorder is an impairment in the ability to receive, send, process, and comprehend concepts or verbal, nonverbal, and graphic symbol systems. A communication disorder may be evident in the processes of hearing, language, and/or speech. A communication disorder may range in severity from mild to profound. It may be developmental or acquired. Individuals may demonstrate one or any combination of communication disorders. A communication disorder may result in a primary disability or it may be secondary to other disabilities.

A. A speech disorder is an impairment of the articulation of speech sounds, fluency, and/or voice.

1. An articulation disorder is the atypical production of speech sounds characterized by substitutions, omissions, additions, or distortions that may interfere with intelligibility.

2. A fluency disorder is an interruption in the flow of speaking characterized by atypical rate, rhythm, and repetitions in sounds, syllables, words, and phrases. This may be accompanied by excessive tension, struggle behavior, and secondary mannerisms.

3. A voice disorder is characterized by the abnormal production and/or absences of vocal quality, pitch, loudness, resonance, and/or duration, which is inappropriate for an individual's age and/or sex.

B. A language disorder is impaired comprehension and/or use of spoken, written, and/or other symbol systems. The disorder may involve (1) the form of language (phonology, morphology, syntax), (2) the content of language (semantics), and/or (3) the function of language in communication (pragmatics) in any combination.

1. Form of Language

a. Phonology is the sound system of a language and the rules that govern the sound combinations.

b. Morphology is the system that governs the structure of words and the construction of word forms.

c. Syntax is the system governing the order and combination of words to form sentences, and the relationships among the elements within a sentence.

2. Content of Language

a. Semantics is the system that governs the meanings of words and sentences.

3. Function of Language

a. Pragmatics is the system that combines the above language components in functional and socially appropriate communication.

II. Communication Variations

A. Communication difference/dialect is a variation of a symbol system used by a group of individuals that reflects and is determined by shared regional, social, or cultural/ethnic factors. A regional, social, or cultural/ethnic variation of a symbol system should not be considered a disorder of speech or language.

B. Augmentative/alternative communication systems attempt to compensate and facilitate, temporarily or permanently, for the impairment and disability patterns of individuals with severe expressive and/or language comprehension disorders. Augmentative/alternative communication may be required for individuals demonstrating impairments in gestural, spoken, and/or written modalities.

Source: American Speech-Language-Hearing Association. (1993). Definitions of communication disorders and variations. *ASHA, 35* (Suppl. 10), pp. 40–41. Reprinted with permission.

Prevalence

Establishing the prevalence of communication disorders is difficult because they are extremely varied, sometimes difficult to identify, and often occur as part of other disabilities (e.g., intellectual disabilities, brain injury, learning disability, or autism). About a million children—approximately one-fifth of all children who are identified for special education—receive services primarily for language or speech disorders. Speech-language

■ **Pragmatics**
The study within psycholinguistics of how people use language in social situations; emphasizes the functional use of language, rather than mechanics.

UNDERSTANDING THE STANDARDS AND PRINCIPLES Are cultural and linguistic differences necessarily related to language disorders? Why or why not? (CEC Knowledge and Skill Standard CC6K1)

Council for Exceptional Children

therapy is one of the most frequently provided related services for children with other primary disabilities (e.g., intellectual disabilities or learning disability).

It's probably reasonable to estimate that about 10 to 15 percent of preschool children and about 6 percent of students in elementary and secondary grades have speech disorders; about 2 to 3 percent of preschoolers and about 1 percent of the school-age population have language disorders. Communication disorders of all kinds are predicted to increase during the coming decades, as medical advances preserve the lives of more children and youths with severe disabilities that affect communication. Therefore, there is a need for more speech-language pathologists in the schools as well as for greater knowledge of communication disorders by special and general education teachers and greater involvement of teachers in helping students learn to communicate effectively.

Communication Variations

The fact that a student doesn't use the speech or language that is expected in school does not necessarily mean that she or he has a language disorder. The more important question is whether the student is an effective communicator in his or her speech and language community (see Goldstein & Iglesias, 2004; Justice, 2006; Owens, 2004). Someone with a language difference that is also a disorder has difficulty communicating in every language environment, including his or her home language community.

■ **Dialect**
Systematic language variations that are rule-governed. Typically, a dialect refers to a language variation of a particular group of speakers of a particular language (i.e., regional or cultural differences in language patterns).

Systematic language variations that are rule-goverened are considered **dialects** (Vinson, 2007). A dialect may lead to a misdiagnosis of a language disorder. The speech or language of African American children, for example, might mistakenly be judged to indicate disorder when it is merely different from standard American English. Although a language variation or dialect does not constitute a language disorder, an individual may both have a language disorder and exhibit a variation that is not a disorder. Such an individual will be unable to communicate effectively even with others who use the same language variation.

Encouraging the communication of children whose cultural heritage or language patterns are not those of the professional's subculture is of increasing concern to classroom teachers and speech-language clinicians (see Chapter 3). On the one hand, care must be taken not to mistake a cultural or ethnic difference for a disorder; on the other hand, disorders that exist in the context of a language difference must not be overlooked. When assessing children's language, the professional must be aware of the limitations of normative tests and sources of potential bias.

A child might not have a language disorder yet have a communicative difference that requires special teaching to promote academic achievement and social communication. Children of nondominant cultures must be taught the rules for effective communication in the dominant culture. However, professionals must also understand and accept the effectiveness of a child's home language in its cultural context. Failure to teach children the skills they need to communicate effectively according to the rules of the dominant culture will deny them many opportunities. In effect, children of minority language groups might need to learn to live in two worlds: one in which their home language is used and one in which school language is used.

Many students for whom language difference is an issue do not speak entirely different languages, but variations peculiar to certain groups of speakers—that is, dialects. For example, one dialect that is different from standard English (and is not a language disorder) is Appalachian English. People in Appalachia speak a variation of English with features that are not shared by other English dialects. Teachers must understand—and help their students understand—that other dialects are not inferior or limited language systems. Furthermore, cultural differences must be recognized regardless of the communication device being used. Multicultural issues arise in all communication interactions, including those in which AAC is used (Goldstein & Iglesias, 2004).

Families differ greatly in the ways they talk to children and in the language they expect children to use. Although students might not have language disorders, their language variations could put them at a disadvantage in using language in an academic context. Consequently, some people have suggested that children who come to school without mastery of the English of their textbooks should be taught it directly and consistently (e.g., Raspberry, 2001). Among the recommendations of Goldstein and Iglesias (2004, pp. 368–369) are the following:

- Taking the student's cultural values and learning style into account
- Asking for help from colleagues, parents, and others, if necessary
- Viewing the student in the naturalistic context of the classroom
- Knowing the features of the community's dialects
- Taking the student's dialect into account
- Using the least biased tools for assessment

A major concern today in both special and general education is teaching children who are learning English as a second language, who are non-English proficient, or who have limited English proficiency. Bilingual education is a field of concern and controversy because of the rapidly changing demographics in many American communities. Spanish-speaking children make up a rapidly growing percentage of the students in many school districts. Moreover, a large number of children from various nations who do not speak English have immigrated to the United States during the past decade. Many of these children have no proficiency or limited proficiency in English, and some have disabilities as well. Bilingual special education is still a developing field. As we discussed in Chapter 3, finding the best way to teach children to become proficient in English, particularly when they have disabilities as well as language differences, is a special challenge for the twenty-first century.

A child may not have a language disorder yet have a communication difference that demands special teaching. Such differences might be related to culture and/or disability.

Language Disorders

Communication disorders cannot be understood without knowledge of normal language development. So before discussing the disorders of language and speech, we provide a brief description of normal language development. Language disorders are discussed first and more extensively than speech disorders, because the primary focus of speech-language pathologists and other specialists in communicative disorders has shifted from speech to language during the evolution of special education and related services (Owens, Evans, & Haas, 2000).

The newborn makes few sounds other than cries. Within a few years, however, the human child can form the many complex sounds of speech, understand spoken and written language, and express meaning verbally. The major milestones in this ability to use language are fairly well known by child development specialists, although the underlying mechanisms that control the development of language are still not well understood. What parts of the process of learning language are innate, and what parts are controlled by the environment? What is the relationship between cognitive development and language

Video Homework Exercise

Supporting Students ●
Go to the Homework and Exercises section in Chapter 9 of MyEducationLab to watch the video "Communication Disorders–George's Support", about a non-typically developing student.

TABLE 9.1 **Development of Speech, Language, and Communication**

Age	Accomplishments
Newborn	Prefers human face and voice Able to discriminate loudness, intonation, and phonemes
3 months	Begins babbling Responds vocally to partner
6 months	Begins reduplicated babbling "Ba-ba-ba"
8 months	Begins gesturing Begins variegated babbling Imitates tonal quality of adult speech, called jargon
10 months	Adds phonetically consistent forms
12 months	First word spoken. Words fill intentions previously signaled by gestures.
18 months	Begins combining words on the basis of word-order rules
2 years	Begins adding bound morphemes. Average length or mean length of utterance (MLU) is 1.6–2.2 morphemes.
3 years	More adultlike sentence structure. Mean length of utterance (MLU) is 3.0–3.3 morphemes.
4 years	Begins to change style of talking to fit conversational partner. Mean length of utterance (MLU) is 3.6–4.7 morphemes.
5 years	Ninety percent of language form learned
6 years	Begins to learn visual mode of communication with writing and reading
8 years	All American English speech sounds acquired
Adolescence	Able to competently participate in conversations and telling of narratives Knows multiple meanings of words and figurative language Uses a gender style, or genderlect, when talking
Adult	Vocabulary has expanded to 30,000–60,000 words Specialized styles of communicating with different audiences and for diverse purposes

Source: Owens, R. E., Jr., Evans, D. E., & Haas, B. A. (2000). *Introduction to communication disorders: A life span perspective.* Boston: Allyn & Bacon.

development? These and many other questions about the origins and uses of language cannot yet be answered definitively.

Table 9.1 describes typical development of speech, language, and communication. The child with a language disorder may eventually reach many or most of the milestones shown for normal development, but at a later age than typically developing children. It is important to note that children sometimes seem to "catch up" in language development, only to fall behind typical development again at a later age.

No one knows exactly how children learn language, but we do know that language development is related in a general way to physical maturation, cognitive development, and socialization. The details of the process—the particulars of what happens physiologically, cognitively, and socially in the learning of language—are still being debated. Nelson (1998) discusses six theories of language that have dominated the study of human communication at various times. The six theories and research based on them have established the following:

1. Language learning depends on brain development and proper brain functioning. Language disorders are sometimes a result of brain dysfunction, and ways to compensate for the dysfunction can sometimes be taught. The emphasis is on biological maturation.

2. Language learning is affected by the consequences of language behavior. Language disorders can be a result of inappropriate learning, and consequences can sometimes be arranged to correct disordered language. The emphasis is on behavioral psychology.

3. Language can be analyzed as inputs and outputs related to the way information is processed. Faulty processing may account for some language disorders, and more effective processing skills can sometimes be taught. The emphasis is on information processing.

4. Language is acquired by a biological process that dictates rules governing the form, content, and use of language. Language disorders are the result of a failure to acquire or employ rule-governed aspects of language, and these disorders may be overcome by helping an individual induce or learn these rules. The emphasis is on a linguistic or nativist perspective.

5. Language is one of many cognitive skills. Language disorders reflect basic problems in thinking and learning, and sometimes these disorders can be addressed effectively by teaching specific cognitive skills. The emphasis is on cognitive development.

6. Language arises from the need to communicate in social interactions. Language disorders are a breakdown in ability to relate effectively to one's environment, and the natural environment can sometimes be arranged to teach and support more effective interaction. The emphasis is on social interaction.

All these theories contain elements of scientific truth, but none is able to explain the development and disorders of language completely. Each of the six theories has advantages and disadvantages for assessing language disorders and devising effective interventions. Advances in neurological imaging technology may lead to better understanding of the biological bases of language (Foundas, 2001). However, pragmatic or social interaction theory is widely viewed as having the most direct implications for speech-language pathologists and teachers because it focuses most directly on how communication skills can be fostered through adult–child interaction (Owens, 2004).

Language involves listening and speaking, reading and writing, technical discourse, and social interaction. Language problems are therefore basic to many of the disabilities discussed in this book, especially hearing impairment, intellectual disabilities, traumatic brain injury, autistic spectrum disorder, and learning disability.

UNDERSTANDING THE STANDARDS AND PRINCIPLES How is language development related to physical maturation, cognitive development, and socialization? (CEC Knowledge and Skill Standard GC2K1 & GC6K3; INTASC 2.06)

Council for Exceptional Children

INTERNET RESOURCES

For information about normal speech and language development and the difference between speech disorder and language disorder, visit the Speech-Language Pathology site at home.ica.net/~fred

No one knows exactly how or why children learn language, but we do know language development is related in a general way to physical maturation, cognitive development, and socialization.

Classification of Language Disorders

Language disorders can be classified according to two primary dimensions: domain (subsystem or type) and etiology (cause). The ASHA definitions in the Focus on Concepts on page 305 suggest a classification scheme involving five subsystems or types of language: phonological (sounds), morphological (word forms), syntactical (word order and sentence structure), semantic (word and sentence meanings), and pragmatic (social use of language). Difficulty with one of these dimensions of language is virtually certain to be accompanied by difficulty with one or more of the others. However, children with language disorders often have particular difficulty with one dimension. Language disorders involving these subsystems are illustrated in the Focus on Concepts below.

Another way of classifying language disorders is based on the presumed cause (etiology) or related conditions. Classification by etiology provides two subtypes: primary and

FOCUS ON Concepts

Types of Language Disorders

Disorders can affect any one or a combination of the form (phonology, morphology, or syntax), content (semantics), or use (pragmatics) of language. Following are illustrations of each of five types of disorders. Remember that in judging what is a disorder, one must keep in mind the individual's age, culture, and linguistic community so that normal development and differences are not mistakenly considered disorders.

Phonological Disorder

An elementary student might pronounce words with certain sounds omitted or distorted. For example, the student might say *boo* for the color *blue*, *dat* for *that*, *tee* for *teeth*, and *wabba* for *rubber* and in other ways fail to communicate effectively because the sounds of many words are omitted, distorted, or substituted. This same student might also have little awareness of the phonological structure of language, so the student is unable to identify the sounds that make up a word (e.g., the word *bag* contains three sounds). This difficulty has posed problems for the student's reading development, specifically learning the relationship between letters and sounds.

Morphological and Syntactical (or Morphosyntactic) Disorder

Problems with morphology and syntax tend to occur together. A school-age child or older person with morphological difficulties may have problems inflecting words using suffixes (e.g., making a plural by adding *s*, constructing the present progressive by adding *ing*). The person might not understand how to make the past tense of the word *hide* (say *hided* instead of *hid*) or how to contract auxiliary verbs (e.g., *is, am, are*) to make contracted verbs (e.g., *she's going, I'm waiting, we're going*). The school-age child

with syntactic difficulties might leave out important grammatical markers, such as articles (*a, an, the*) and might have problems using pronouns correctly (e.g., say *her did it* instead of *she did it*).

Semantic Disorder

A school-age child or older person might have a difficult time learning new words or using new words when appropriate. For instance, after hearing the word *rumpus* five times in the story *Where the Wild Things Are*, the child might still react to this word in the future as if he or she has never heard it before. Or when faced with a situation that has rumpus-like characteristics, the child would not be able to use the word to describe the situation. The individual might not be able to make sense of stories, retell them in ways that make sense to listeners, or say things to which others can attach meaning. For example, instead of "On Christmas, we sing songs and open presents and have special things to eat," the person might say, "Sing Merry Christmas, presents, eating lots of stuff."

Pragmatic Disorder

A school-age child or older person might not understand how to use language in social situations. For example, the person might start a conversation with a complete stranger by saying something like "I like planes a lot, and I like to watch them" or say something offensive, such as "You sure are fat!" or, in response to an invitation to take a turn in conversation (e.g., "Burt, what do you think?") give an inappropriate response (e.g., "No! You say."). Individuals with pragmatic language disorders may not know how to make their needs clear to others or know how to use language for practical purposes (e.g., asking someone to call 911 in an emergency).

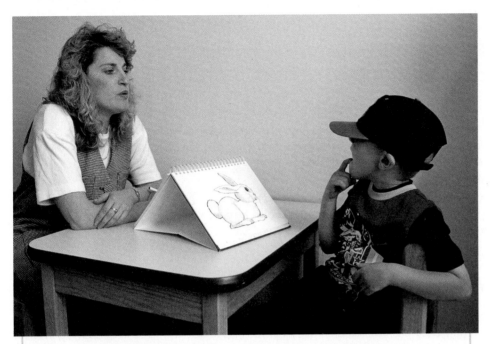

Children with language disorders often have particular difficulty with one dimension of language, be it phonology, morphology, syntax, semantics, or pragmatics.

secondary. A **primary language disorder** has no known cause. A **secondary language disorder** is caused by another condition, such as intellectual disabilities, hearing impairment, autistic spectrum disorder, cerebral palsy, or traumatic brain injury.

A scientific approach to problems demands classification, but human beings and their language are very difficult to categorize. Therefore, all classification systems contain ambiguities, and none can account for all cases. In a textbook devoted to language disorders, Owens (2004) notes:

> Many children with [language impairments] cannot be described easily by any of the categories discussed in this chapter. Such children may have either more than one primary diagnostic category or characteristics that do not fit into any category. Each child represents a unique set of circumstances, so language assessment and intervention should be individualized. (p. 20)

Ryan, the student described in the Success Stories on page 312, is a perfect example of this concept. He suffered a brain injury and, with the help of his family and involved professionals, he learned to communicate again. Ryan was fortunate enough to experience a full recovery but his struggles with communication are fresh in his mind.

PRIMARY LANGUAGE DISORDERS   **Specific language impairment (SLI)** refers to a language disorder that has no identifiable cause; it is an unexpected and unexplained variation in the acquisition of language (Silliman & Scott, 2006). These disorders result in significant limitations in language and are not due to intellectual disabilities, the perceptual problems that characterize language learning disability, hearing problems, and so on (Owens et al., 2007). Often, SLI involves multiple aspects of language. Academic problems, particularly in the areas of reading and writing, are common for children with SLI (Choudhury & Benasich, 2003; Kohnert, Windsor, & Yim, 2006).

■ **Primary language disorder**
A language disorder that has no known cause.

■ **Secondary language disorder**
A language disorder that is caused by another disorder or disability, such as intellectual disabilities, hearing impairment, or brain injury.

■ **Specific language impairment (SLI)**
A language disorder with no identifiable cause; language disorder not attributable to hearing impairment, intellectual disabilities, brain dysfunction, or other plausible cause; also called specific language disability.

Success Stories

Through coordination of medical and educational services, Ryan moves from rehabilitation to school reentry successfully

Ryan: "When I look back, I realize how slow I was as a result of the head injury."

College student Ryan McGarr was severely injured in a Thanksgiving Day car wreck during his junior year in high school. An innovative traumatic brain injury project provided a bridge between his rehabilitation services and school reentry.

These are the keys to his success:

● Intensive coordination of services and supports

● Relentless instruction in academics and vocabulary development

● Specific goals for compensatory strategies and teacher training

Special Educator Nancy Maher-Maxwell directed a specialized traumatic brain injury (TBI) Project for the Nassau County Board of Cooperative Educational Services in New York. When Ryan was injured, she coordinated his medical and educational services. She also trained his teachers to meet his individual needs as he reentered school after the accident. Ryan remained in a coma for three days and his residual difficulties in language and cognitive processing presented academic challenges. He credits his success to intensive, relentless, and specific special education along with spontaneous neurological recovery and a strong desire to achieve.

● **Intensive Coordination of Services and Supports** Kathy McGarr was grateful that someone at the hospital told her about the TBI project: "Just the trauma, and trying to take care of your other children—the whole family tends to fall apart. I didn't have the concentration or anything to deal with this." According to Maher-Maxwell, "research suggests that kids who have this connection between rehabilitation and school reentry, along with ongoing staff support once they've returned, have greater success rates than those who don't."

Ryan returned to school part-time in April of his junior year. He went to an outpatient rehabilitation center for therapies in the

---

■ **Early expressive language delay (EELD)**
A significant lag in the development of expressive language that is apparent by age 2.

■ **Language-based reading impairment**
A reading problem that is based on a language problem.

Early expressive language delay (EELD) refers to a significant lag in expressive language (i.e., the child doesn't have a fifty-word vocabulary or use two-word utterances by age two) that the child won't outgrow. About half the children whose language development is delayed at age two will gradually catch up developmentally with their age peers; however, the other half will not catch up and will continue to have language problems throughout their school years.

Language-based reading impairment involves a reading problem based on a language disorder. This disorder cannot be identified until the child begins learning to read and has problems. Research of such abilities as phonological awareness, alphabet knowledge, and grammatical speech have helped in identifying children who are vulnerable to this kind of disorder (Justice & Schuele, 2004; Vellutino, Fletcher, Snowling, & Scanlon, 2004). A significant percentage of children who show language impairments in kindergarten will have obvious reading problems by second grade (Catts, Adlof, Hogan, & Ellis Weismer, 2005; Catts, Fey, Zhang, & Tomblin, 2001; Sawyer, 2006). Although **phonological awareness** has garnered attention for the past two decades, a new area of language is coming to the forefront. Newer research is providing some evidence that syntactic and semantic knowledge is predictive of later reading comprehension (Catts et al., 2001; Muter, Hulme, Snowling, & Stevenson, 2004; Silliman & Scott, 2006), again indicating significant risk for children with language impairment.

Casebook Reflection

REFER TO THE CASE *Who Will Help Patrick?* in your booklet. Patrick is labeled as developmentally delayed. Do you foresee him also being labeled with a speech language disorder? Why or why not? What makes this decision difficult? ●

morning and then to his local public high school in the afternoon for English, social studies, art, and resource room. He returned full-time for his senior year, carrying a full program of academic courses with resource room support for 45 minutes daily.

● **Relentless Instruction in Academics and Vocabulary Development** Nancy Maher-Maxwell remembers that when she met Ryan six weeks after the accident, he was determined to graduate with his class and wanted tutoring. "The psychologist at the hospital, who evaluated him nine weeks after the accident, told me Ryan would probably never finish school and that I was overwhelming him with academics," says Mrs. McGarr, "but it was what he wanted, and I had to let him try to do it." To start the process, Maher-Maxwell contacted Ryan's school district. His former English teacher agreed to be his home tutor. With Maher-Maxwell's help, her lessons were individualized, concentrating on vocabulary and word meanings. She used flashcards and together with Ryan made up funny sentences using mnemonics to help him remember information. Instead of giving him a chapter to read in history, she chunked material to be learned by breaking it up into smaller units.

● **Specific Goals for Compensatory Strategies and Teacher Training** The TBI Project coordinated Ryan's reentry into the regular educational environment by providing workshops as well as ongoing support for his teachers. Training emphasized Ryan's need to take in new information in a variety of ways. Teachers learned techniques to reinforce study skills, such as taking notes, outlining chapters, and organizing projects. "Often the typical high school teacher will lecture on the subject, expect the kids to take good notes, and evaluate them on a test. Because of the disruptions in the learning systems of students with TBI, there may be a slower rate in processing, so extended time is often necessary both in teaching and in testing," Nancy Maher-Maxwell says.

His mother recalls that it was hard to tell whether Ryan would regain his language abilities. "In speech therapy, he had a terrible time with categorization skills. His therapist asked him to name five green vegetables, and he couldn't do it! What was even more surprising was that he couldn't imagine that anyone could!"

TBI is an acquired injury that demands new adjustments. "If I hadn't spoken with Nancy," says Mrs. McGarr, "I wouldn't have known to put Ryan in a resource room, since he never needed special education before." Head injuries can also make the future harder to predict. "That early neuropsychological evaluation that said he could forget about his academic aspirations never took into account Ryan's determination and the compensatory strategies that special education could provide," says Maher-Maxwell.

Ryan still finds that he is more easily distracted than he used to be, and he continues to need extended time on some college exams. He remains confident about the future, saying, "I'll succeed in the world doing whatever I want to do. I have no doubts about that."

● *By Jean B. Crockett*

SECONDARY LANGUAGE DISORDERS The literature on language disorders often includes discussion of the particular communication impairments of individuals with other specific disabling conditions, such as intellectual disabilities or autistic spectrum disorder (e.g., Owens, 2004). Difficulty in using language in social interactions and relationships is now seen as a basic problem in many disorders.

Emotional and behavioral disorders, for instance, may range from social reticence or withdrawal to severe acting out and aggression (McCabe & Marshall, 2006; Rogers-Adkinson & Griffith, 1999). Young children who have language disorders might have special difficulty in developing skills in social interaction because they do not interpret social circumstances correctly and have difficulty expressing themselves. Donahue, Hartas, and Cole (1999) provide an example.

In a kindergarten classroom, there are two adjacent (unisex) bathroom doors, each sporting almost identical pumpkin face posters. Almost invisible to the adult eye, one pumpkin has the faintest suggestion of eyelashes (instead of triangle eyes, this pumpkin has rectangles with a jagged top). A boy identified as having a language disorder comes out of this bathroom and goes to his table. Another boy approaches him, saying:

Why did you go to the girls' bathroom? (pointing to the pumpkin face)

Huh?

You went to the girls' bathroom.

No—no—. That not girls'.

Yes it is.

Reading Homework Exercise

Facts and Figures ●
Go to the Homework and Exercises section in Chapter 9 of MyEducationLab to view some facts and figures regarding the types of communication disorders most often seen in school-age children.

No way—boys can too. (voice rising)

Yeah, there's a girl pumpkin on it.

But—but . . . that not a girl! (getting angry)

Yeah, look at those eyelashes.

But—but . . . NOT! (Splutters, jumps up and shoves the other boy. The teacher intervenes, and gives the child with the language disorder a time-out for fighting. He sits angrily, muttering to himself, "not a girl!") (p. 72)

Speech Disorders

UNDERSTANDING THE STANDARDS AND PRINCIPLES Describe the educational implications of at least two major speech disorders (CEC Knowledge and Skill Standard CC2K1)

Council for Exceptional Children

■ **Phonological disorders**
A phonological disorder is a disorder that occurs in children who are younger than 9 years old. The disorder results in the impaired ability to produce sounds in his or her own language.

Speech disorders are very heterogeneous. That is, there are many different types, degrees, and combinations of them. Speech disorders pose a wide variety of challenges to the communication abilities of school children.

We provide only brief descriptions of the major disorders affecting the speech of school-age children. Most speech disorders are treated primarily by a speech-language pathologist, not by a classroom teacher. However, both general and special education teachers are expected to work collaboratively with speech-language pathologists in assessment and intervention.

Phonological Disorders

Phonological disorders occur in children younger than nine years of age. They do not include the normally developing young child's inability to say words correctly. The cause of the disorder is often unknown, but for some reason the child does not understand the rules for producing the sounds of his or her language. The child's speech sound production is different from age-appropriate, culturally based expectations. The child doesn't

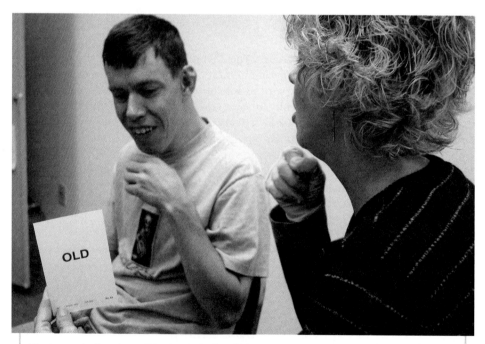

Most speech disorders will be treated primarily by speech-language pathologists, not classroom teachers. Teachers should be aware of possible speech disorders in order to be able to refer students properly.

seem to understand how to differentiate and produce the phonemes or sounds of language to construct intelligible words. This disorder occurs in about four or five in one hundred children, somewhat more often in boys than in girls.

Phonological disorders are difficult to distinguish conceptually from articulation disorders (Owens et al., 2007). A child with an articulation disorder simply has trouble producing sounds correctly. In contrast, the child with a phonological disorder seems to have a poor inner representation of the sounds of language. He or she might not understand the contrasts between or the distinctiveness of sound, which results in problems with how speech sounds are produced. For instance, the child who does not have an internal representation of consonants at the end of words produces *hat* as *ha* and *dog* as *do*.

Phonology is critical to literacy. Learning to read requires an understanding of the alphabetic principle—that letters work systematically to represent sounds, and these sounds can be blended together to form words (Lane & Pullen, 2004). **Phonological awareness** is an understanding of the sound structure of language; it includes the abilities to blend sounds into words, to segment words into sounds, and to otherwise manipulate the sounds of spoken language. Without phonological awareness, a student is unable to make sense of the alphabetic principle, which results in an inability to decode words. Some, but not all, children with phonological disorders lack phonological awareness. Some have serious problems with verbal working memory (remembering what was said or what they want to say) or word learning and word retrieval. Deficits in working memory and word retrieval are considered a phonological processing disorder.

Phonological disorders may occur with a variety of other disorders (Justice, 2006). There are many different theories of phonology and alternative classification systems that are beyond our scope here (see Justice, 2006; Kent, 2004; Vihman, 2004); suffice to say that phonological disorders represent a failure of the child to understand the sound system of language at an age-appropriate level and in a culturally appropriate way. This disorder of the phonological system of language affects speech sound production and often affects literacy as well.

■ **Phonological awareness**
The ability to understand that speech flow can be broken into smaller sound units such as words, syllables, and phonemes; lack of such awareness is generally thought to be the reason for the reading problems of many students with learning disabilities.

Articulation Disorders

Articulation disorders involve errors in producing sounds. The problem is not an underlying phonological problem but a disorder in which the individual omits, substitutes, distorts, or adds speech sounds. Lisping, for example, involves a substitution or distortion of the /s/ sound (e.g., *thunthine* or *shunshine* for *sunshine*). Missing, substituted, added, or poorly produced word sounds can make a speaker difficult to understand or even unintelligible. Such errors in speech production may also carry heavy social penalties, subjecting the speaker to teasing or ridicule.

When are articulation errors considered a disorder? That depends on a clinician's subjective judgment, which will be influenced by her or his experience, the number and types of errors, the consistency of these errors, the age and developmental characteristics of the speaker, and the intelligibility of the person's speech (see Bernthal & Bankson, 2004).

Young children make frequent errors in speech sounds when they are learning to talk. Many children do not learn to produce all the speech sounds correctly until they are eight or nine years old. Furthermore, most children make frequent errors until after they enter school. The age of the child is thus a major consideration in judging the adequacy of articulation. Another major consideration is the characteristics of the child's language community, because children learn speech largely through imitation. For instance, a child who is reared in the Deep South might have speech that sounds peculiar to residents of Long Island, but this does not mean that the child has a speech disorder. Remember that there are differences that are not disorders.

The number of children who have difficulty producing word sounds decreases markedly during the first three or four years of elementary school. Among children with other disabilities, especially intellectual disabilities and neurological disorders such as cerebral palsy, the prevalence of articulation disorders is higher than that in the general population.

Lack of ability to articulate speech sounds correctly can be caused by biological factors. For example, brain damage or damage to the nerves controlling the muscles that are used in speech may make it difficult or impossible to articulate sounds (Bernthal & Bankson, 1998; Cannito, Yorkston, & Beukelman, 1998). Furthermore, abnormalities of the oral structures, such as a cleft palate, can make normal speech difficult or impossible. Relatively minor structural changes, such as loss of teeth, can produce temporary errors. Poor articulation may also result from a hearing loss.

The parents of a preschool child might refer the child for assessment if he or she has speech that is really difficult to understand. Most schools screen all new pupils for speech and language problems, and in most cases, a child who still makes many articulation errors in the third or fourth grade will be referred for evaluation. Older children and adults sometimes seek help on their own when their speech draws negative attention. Speech-language pathologists assess not only articulation but also social and developmental history, hearing, general language ability, and speech mechanisms.

Although speech-language pathologists' interest in articulation disorders has appeared to decrease in recent years, with more attention being given to language and phonology, persistent articulation disorders may have serious long-term consequences. The decision about whether to include a child in an intervention program depends on the child's age, other developmental characteristics, and the type and consistency of the articulation errors (Williams, 2001).

Articulation disorders are often accompanied by other disorders of speech or language; therefore, the child might need intervention in multiple aspects of communication (Bauman-Waengler, 2000; Hodson & Edwards, 1997; Nelson, 1998). The decision to include or not include a child in speech-language therapy also depends on the pathologist's assessment of the likelihood that the child will self-correct the errors and of the social penalties, such as teasing and shyness, the child is experiencing. If the child misarticulates only a few sounds but does so consistently and suffers social embarrassment or rejection as a consequence, an intervention program is usually called for.

Voice Disorders

People's voices are perceived as having pitch, loudness, and quality. Changes in pitch and loudness are part of the stress patterns of speech. Vocal quality is related not only to production of speech sounds, but also to the nonlinguistic aspects of speech. Voice disorders, though difficult to define precisely, are characteristics of pitch, loudness, and/or quality that are abusive of the **larynx**; hamper communication; or are perceived as markedly different from what is customary for someone of a given age, sex, and cultural background (Robinson & Crowe, 2001).

Voice disorders can result from a variety of causes and can be grouped into three primary categories including functional disorders, organic disorders, and neurological disorders (Anderson & Shames, 2006). Disorders that are a result of damage to the larynx (i.e., trauma) are considered functional disorders. A physical condition including growths in the larynx (e.g., nodules, polyps, or cancerous tissue) that has affected the structure or function of the larynx are considered organic disorders. Disorders that are a result of nervous system dysfunction are considered neurological disorders.

Misuse or abuse of the voice also can lead to a quality that is temporarily abnormal. High school cheerleaders, for example, frequently develop temporary voice disorders due to the formation of nodules (calluses) on their vocal cords (Campbell, Reich, Klockars, & McHenry, 1988). The same kind of problem can be caused by a child's screaming. Teachers and others who constantly use a very loud voice, whether expressing passionate beliefs, talking over noisy conditions, or speaking in a room with poor acoustics, may also develop voice problems.

■ **Larynx**

The structure in the throat containing the vocal apparatus (vocal cords); laryngitis is a temporary loss of voice caused by inflammation of the larynx.

Disorders resulting from misuse or abuse of the voice can damage the tissues of the larynx. So can smoking or inhaling substances that irritate the vocal folds. Sometimes a person has psychological problems that lead to a complete loss of voice (**aphonia**) or to severe voice abnormalities.

Voice disorders having to do with **resonance**—vocal quality—may be caused by physical abnormalities of the oral cavity (such as **cleft palate**) or damage to the brain or nerves controlling the oral cavity. Infections of the tonsils, adenoids, or sinuses can also influence how the voice is resonated. Most people who have severe hearing loss typically have problems in achieving a normal or pleasingly resonant voice. Finally, sometimes a person simply has not learned to speak with an appropriately resonant voice. There are no biological or deep-seated psychological reasons for the problem; rather, it appears that she or he has learned faulty habits of positioning the organs of speech.

Teachers need to observe children for common symptoms of voice disorders, such as hoarseness, aphonia, breathiness, odd pitch (voice too high or too low pitched), or an inappropriately loud or soft voice. A teacher who notes possible problems should ask a speech-language pathologist to conduct an evaluation. Teachers should also monitor their own voices for indications of vocal stress.

Fluency Disorders

Normal speech is characterized by some interruptions in speech flow. Especially when a child is learning to talk, we can expect normal **dysfluencies**. These are the hesitations, repetitions, and other interruptions of normal speech flow that are entirely normal parts of learning to use language. All of us occasionally get speech sounds in the wrong order (e.g., saying *revalent* for *relevant*), speak too quickly to be understood, pause at the wrong place in a sentence, use an inappropriate pattern of stress, or become dysfluent—that is, stumble and backtrack, repeating words or phrases, and fill in pauses with *uh* while trying to think of how to finish what we have to say. It is only when the speaker's efforts are so intense or the interruptions in the flow of speech are so frequent or pervasive that they keep him or her from being understood or draw extraordinary attention that they are considered disorders. Besides, listeners have a greater tolerance for some types of dysfluencies than others. Most of us will more readily accept speech-flow disruptions that we perceive as necessary corrections of what the speaker has said or is planning to say than disruptions that appear to reflect the speaker's inability to proceed with the articulation of what she or he has decided to say (Robinson & Crowe, 2001).

The most frequent type of fluency disorder is stuttering. **Stuttering** is different from normal dysfluency in both the rate and the type of dysfluency. Children who stutter produce dysfluencies at a greater rate than children who do not stutter, with dysfluencies making up more than 10 percent of speech (Guitar, 1998). Also, children who stutter produce part-word repetitions ("I wa-wa-want . . ."), sound prolongations ("It is at my hhhhhouse . . ."), and sound blocks ("My name is M#ike . . ."), all of which are types of dysfluencies not normally seen in young children. About 1 percent of children and adults are considered stutterers. More boys than girls stutter. Many children quickly outgrow their childhood dysfluencies. These children generally use regular and effortless dysfluencies, appear to be unaware of their hesitancies, and have parents and teachers who are unconcerned about their speech patterns. Those who stutter for more than a year and a half or two appear to be at risk for becoming chronic stutterers (Conture, 2001).

Stuttering is actually not always just dysfluency. It often consists of repetitions, prolongations of sounds, and blocks in which the person seems unable to make the intended sound, which are the core behaviors of stuttering. But it can also consist of related secondary behaviors that are intended to avoid or escape the dysfluency, such as gestures, head nods, eye blinks, and so on. It also includes negative feelings about communication on the part of those who stutter.

■ **Aphonia**
Loss of voice.

■ **Resonance**
The quality of the sound imparted by the size, shape, and texture of the organs in the vocal tract.

■ **Cleft palate**
A condition in which there is a rift or split in the upper part of the oral cavity; may include the upper lip (cleft lip).

INTERNET RESOURCES

For information about cleft lip, cleft palate, and other cranio-facial deformities and effects on speech, see SMILES at www.cleft.org

■ **Dysfluencies**
Hesitations, repetitions, and other disruptions of normal speech flow.

■ **Stuttering**
Speech characterized by abnormal hesitations, prolongations, and repetitions; may be accompanied by grimaces, gestures, or other bodily movements indicative of a struggle to speak, anxiety, blocking of speech, or avoidance of speech.

INTERNET RESOURCES

More information about stuttering is available at the following sites: National Center for Stuttering at www.stuttering.com and the Stuttering Foundation of America at www.stuttersfa.org

**Video Homework
Exercise**

Stuttering • Go to the
Homework and Exercises section
in Chapter 9 of MyEducationLab
to watch the video "Stuttering: By
Kids, For Kids", in which students
"overcome their stuttering and do
not let stuttering overcome them."

■ **Dysarthria**
A condition in which brain damage
causes impaired control of the
muscles used in articulation.

■ **Apraxia**
The inability to plan and coordinate
speech.

**Reading Homework
Exercise**

Dysarthria and Apraxia •
Go to the Homework and
Exercises section in Chapter 9
of MyEducationLab to read
additional information about
dysarthria and apraxia.

A child who is thought to stutter should be evaluated by a speech-language pathologist. Early diagnosis is important if the development of chronic stuttering is to be avoided. Unfortunately, many educators and physicians do not refer potential stutterers for in-depth assessment because they are aware that dysfluencies are a normal part of speech-language development. Some experts also advocate a "wait and see" approach (Curlee & Yairi, 1997). But nonreferral is extremely detrimental to children who are at risk for stuttering. Persistent stuttering that goes untreated can result in a lifelong disorder that affects the ability to communicate, develop positive feelings about oneself, and pursue certain educational and employment opportunities (Conture, 2001; Curlee & Siegel, 1997).

Motor-Speech Disorders

The muscles that make speech possible are under voluntary control. When there is damage to the areas of the brain that control these muscles or to the nerves leading to the muscles, there is a disturbance in the ability to speak normally. These disorders may involve controlling speech sounds (**dysarthria**) or planning and coordinating speech (**apraxia**). Both dysarthria and apraxia affect the production of speech, slow its rate, and reduce intelligibility (Owens et al., 2000). Keep in mind, too, that dysarthria and apraxia are not mutually exclusive. That is, an individual can have both problems. Because these disorders are caused by a neurological problem, they are often called neurogenic disorders of speech.

By listening to the person's speech and inspecting his or her speech mechanism, the speech-language pathologist assesses the ability of the person with a motor-speech disorder or neurogenic speech disorder to control breathing, phonation, resonation, and articulatory movements. Medical, surgical, and rehabilitative specialists in the treatment of neurological disorders also must evaluate the person's problem and plan a management strategy. In cases in which the neurological impairment makes the person's speech unintelligible, an AAC system might be required.

There are several ways in which damage to the areas of the brain controlling the muscles used for speech create a disturbance in the ability to speak normally.

DYSARTHRIA   Difficulties in speaking may occur because the muscles controlling breathing, the larynx, the throat, the tongue, the jaw, and/or the lips cannot be controlled precisely. Depending on the nature of the injury to the brain, perceptual and cognitive functions may also be affected; the individual may have a language disorder in addition to a speech disorder.

Dysarthria is characterized by slow, labored, slurred, and imprecise speech. As a result of brain injury, the person's respiratory support for making speech sounds is affected, and his or her speech may be characterized by shallow breathing, hoarseness, and reduced loudness. The person might not be able to produce speech sounds precisely because of muscle weakness.

Probably the condition that most frequently accounts for dysarthria in children is **cerebral palsy**—brain injury before, during, or after birth that results in muscular weakness or paralysis. Among the many causes of brain injury are physical trauma, oxygen deprivation, poisoning, diseases, and strokes. Vehicular accidents are a frequent cause of traumatic brain injury in adolescence and young adulthood. Anything that causes brain injury can cause dysarthria.

APRAXIA   Apraxia is characterized by a disruption of motor planning and programming so that speech is slow, effortful, and inconsistent. A person with this disorder may recognize that he or she is making errors and try to correct them, but the attempts at correction make it even harder to understand what the person intends to say. Owens et al. (2000) provide the following example of the speech of someone with apraxia:

> O-o-on . . . on . . . on cavation, cavation, cacation . . . oh darn . . . vavation, of, you know, to Ca-ca-caciporenia . . . no, Lacifacnia, vafacnia to Lacifacnion . . . On vacation to Va-cafornia, no darn it . . . to Ca-caliborneo . . . not bornia . . . fornia, Bornfifornia . . . no, Balliforneo, Ballifornee, Balifornee, Californee, California. Phew, it was hard to say Cacaforneo. Oh darn. (p. 416)

Developmental apraxia is a disorder of motor planning that emerges as the child develops speech and language skills. Children with this disorder show significant delays in the ability to produce speech sounds and to organize sounds into words for effective communication. **Acquired apraxia** has similar symptoms but it occurs because of a stroke or other type of brain damage after learning speech. Usually, the person with apraxia knows that he or she is making errors, wants to correct them, knows what he or she wants to communicate, but simply cannot do so. Consequently, apraxia is an unusually frustrating disorder for the speaker.

■ **Cerebral palsy**
A condition characterized by paralysis, weakness, lack of coordination, and/or other motor dysfunction; caused by damage to the brain before it has matured.

■ **Developmental apraxia**
A disorder of speech or language involving problems in motor planning such that the child has difficulty in producing speech sounds and organizing words and word sounds for effective communication. The cause may be unknown.

■ **Acquired apraxia**
As in developmental apraxia, there are problems in motor planning such that the child has difficulty in producing speech sounds and organizing words and word sounds for effective communication. However, the problem is known to be caused by neurological damage.

Educational Considerations

Children with all types of disabilities are increasingly placed in general education classrooms. This means that all teachers must become aware of how they can address language problems in the classroom (Owens, 2004; Throneburg, Calvert, Sturm, Paramboukas, & Paul, 2000). Helping children overcome speech and language disorders is not the responsibility of any single professional. Rather, identification is the joint responsibility of the classroom teacher, the speech-language pathologist, and parents. The teacher can carry out specific suggestions for individual cases. By listening attentively and empathetically when children speak, providing appropriate models of speech and language for children to imitate, and encouraging children to use their communication skills appropriately, the

Casebook Reflection

REFER TO THE CASE *Albert Says What?* in your booklet. In the case of Albert, the speech-language pathologist works with Albert using sign language, but to no avail. What other approaches might be used? ●

classroom teacher can help not only to improve speech and language, but also to prevent some disorders from developing in the first place.

Facilitating the Social Use of Language

In considering language development, the primary role of the classroom teacher is to facilitate the social use of language. The fact that a student has a language or speech disorder does not necessarily mean that the teacher or clinician must intensify efforts to teach the student about the form, structure, or content of language. Rather, language must be taught as a way of solving problems by making oneself understood and making sense of what other people say.

The classroom offers many possibilities for language learning. It should be a place in which there are almost continuous opportunities for students and teachers to employ language and obtain feedback in constructive relationships. Language is the basic medium through which most academic and social learning takes place in school. Nevertheless, the language of school, in both classrooms and textbooks, is often a problem for students and teachers.

School language is more formal than the language many children use at home and with playmates. It is structured conversation, in which listeners and speakers or readers and writers must learn to be clear and expressive, to convey and interpret essential information quickly and easily. Without skill in using the language of school, a child is certain to fail academically and virtually certain to be socially unsuccessful as well.

Teachers need the assistance of speech-language specialists in assessing their students' language disabilities and in devising interventions. Specifics about how speech-language pathologists work to meet the needs of students with communication disorders is the topic of the Making It Work on page 323. Part of the assessment and intervention strategy must also examine the language of the teacher. Problems in classroom discourse involve how teachers talk to students as well as how students use language. Learning how to be clear, relevant, and informative and how to hold listeners' attention are not only problems for students with language disorders but also problems for their teachers. The Personal Perspectives on page 324 offers some general guidelines for how teachers should talk with students. Likewise, the Responsive Instruction feature on p. 322 provides a strategy for promoting social communication.

Question-Asking Strategies

One example of the role of the teacher's language in classroom discourse is asking questions. Teachers often ask students too many questions in areas of their identified weaknesses, thereby inadvertently curtailing the students' use of expressive language. For example, a teacher might ask a preschooler who does not know colors to identify colors repeatedly. Or a teacher may overuse yes/no questions (e.g., "Is this blue?" "Are you finished?"), which curtail the child's engagement in extended dialogues or provocative conversations. Unfortunately, teachers might not know how to modify their questions to teach concepts effectively, so their questions merely add to children's confusion.

Alternative question-asking strategies can be used to help students think through problems successfully. When a student fails to answer a higher-order question because it is beyond his or her level of information or skill, the teacher should reformulate the problem at a simpler level. After the intermediate steps are solved, the teacher can return to the question that was too difficult at first.

Teachers sometimes do not clearly express their intent in questioning students or fail to explicitly delimit the topic of their questions. For example, a teacher might ask, "What are you going to tell me?" (not being clear about intention) or "How have you been

UNDERSTANDING THE STANDARDS AND PRINCIPLES How can teachers help students improve their speech and language? (CEC Knowledge and Skill Standard CC4S3)

Council for Exceptional Children

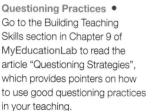

Building Teaching Skills Reading Exercise

Questioning Practices ● Go to the Building Teaching Skills section in Chapter 9 of MyEducationLab to read the article "Questioning Strategies", which provides pointers on how to use good questioning practices in your teaching.

The classroom offers many possibilities for language learning and should provide almost continuous opportunities for students and teachers to employ language and obtain feedback in constructive relationships.

feeling recently?" (asking a question that is too general or not sufficiently focused). Consequently, students become confused. Teachers must learn to clarify the problems under such circumstances. Teachers must also give unambiguous feedback to students' responses to their questions. Too often, teachers do not tell students explicitly that their answers are wrong, for fear of showing nonacceptance. Lack of accurate, explicit feedback, however, prevents students from learning the concepts involved in instruction. Our points here are these:

- The teacher's role is not merely to instruct students about language but also to teach them how to use it. More specifically, the teacher must help students learn how to use language in the context of the classroom.

- The teacher's own use of language is a key factor in helping students learn effectively, especially if students have language disorders.

Teachers need to keep in mind, too, that language disorders can change with a child's development. Just because a child has receptive or expressive language within the normal range at one age doesn't mean that it will be within the same range at a later age. Figure 9.1 depicts changes with age for Troy, a child whose language problems are shown at various ages (Plante & Beeson, 2004). Language intervention can change the nature and course of a child's language abilities, but even with therapy, a child might have language problems that are persistent. Notice that Troy, who received speech-language services, did not achieve expressive language abilities close to the normal range until age fourteen, and only then did his expressive language ability exceed his receptive ability.

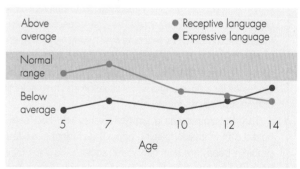

FIGURE 9.1 For children with developmental language disorders, the components of language can change over time. Here we can see how a single child's receptive and expressive language skills shift over time relative to typically developing peers.

Source: Plante, E., & Beeson, P. M. (2004). *Communication and communication disorders: A clinical introduction*. Boston: Allyn & Bacon, p. 182. Copyright © 2004. Reprinted/adapted by permission of Allyn & Bacon.

Meeting the Needs of Students with Communication Disorders as a Result of Fetal Alcohol Spectrum Disorders

Social Communication

WHAT THE RESEARCH SAYS

Social communication is vital for all individuals. The ability to engage others, understand other people's perspectives, display cause-and-effect reasoning, and use language to meet one's needs are important aspects of social communication. A high proportion of students with Fetal Alcohol Spectrum Disorders (FASD) experience difficulties with social communication (Coggins, Olswang, Olson, & Timler, 2003). One of the roles of a speech-language pathologist is to address these types of deficits (see Chapter 5 for more information on FASD).

Two intriguing lines of research that have been targeted to address the social communication needs of students with FASD are "theory of mind" studies and social-communication skill training (Timler et al., 2005). Theory of mind refers to the ability to understand and predict others' mental state (see *Focus on Concepts: Theory of Mind* p. 438). Many researchers account for students' with FASD difficulties in social communication to a theory of mind deficit. Theory of mind studies attempt to teach students how to interpret and predict others' expriences in order to avoid the "false beliefs" these students typically hold. Research on social communication, on the other hand, attempts to improve communication by directly teaching the skills needed through techniques such as modeling, role-playing, use of scripts, checklists, and self monitoring (Timler et al., 2005).

RESEARCH STUDY

In their study, Timler and colleagues (2005) attempted to create a clinical intervention for a student with fetal alcohol syndrome that combined the practices associated with theory of mind research with the practices of direct teaching. The intervention for the study included two aspects. The first aspect addressed the theory of mind deficit by teaching the student verbs that are used to refer to another's mental state (e.g., think, know, guess). The second aspect assisted the student in generating numerous strategies for addressing a social situation and then selecting the optimal strategy to employ.

The participant was a girl (9.8 years) who had been diagnosed with fetal alcohol syndrome. The student exhibited many problem behaviors and had fewer social skills then other kids her age. She had difficulty making friends and did not engage in socially acceptable ways when interacting with peers. She also demonstrated difficulty with memory—a particular problem in social situations that often require one to remember prior information in order to respond appropriately.

For the intervention, the student would role-play (along with 2 other students participating in the program) using social scripts and a checklist to guide the routine. The checklist questions prompted the students to think about what they knew and what others knew about this situation (e.g., What do I know? What does he know? What do they think?), how to generate and select an appropriate response (e.g., Do I know what I need to do? What do you think I could do? What do I think is the BEST choice?), and how to evaluate the response (e.g., What do I think happened? How do I know this? What do others think happened?). During the 2-hour session, the students would run through 3–5 scripts, stop the action within the scripts, and respond to the checklist questions. The researchers measured the student's use of mental state verbs, strategies for obtaining a goal, and generation of appropriate consequence for an action.

RESEARCH FINDINGS

Prior to the intervention, baseline data showed that the student produced zero mental state verbs. During the intervention and after the intervention, the student began to use mental state verbs and longer, more complex responses to the justification questions (e.g., Why? How?). The student's social cognitive skills were measured by the number of possible strategies generated and her evaluation of the possible consequence. The number of strategies increased from two to four by the end of week 4 but her first strategy generated was consistently the least appropriate. In addition, she required prompting to develop the additional strategies. The student's judgment of the consequences remained self-focused (e.g., "to not get in trouble") rather than other-focused (e.g., "because that would make her happy"). In conclusion, the researchers found that the use of a checklist was a promising way to increase the student's ability to think about others and generate strategies.

APPLYING THE RESEARCH TO TEACHING

In addition to creating a specific pullout intervention, such as the one developed for their study, the researchers encourage the use of question checklists in other settings (e.g., the classroom, at home). Timler and colleagues (2005) also recommend prompting students to use the checklist during "on-the-spot" social situations to encourage generalization and promote internalization of the questions. In general, however, classroom teachers should promote thinking about other people's perspectives and use mental state verbs to elicit students' evaluation of social interactions in order to improve the social communication of students.

Collaboration and Co-Teaching of Students with Communication Disorders

"Answer me, Amanda. What? Has the cat got your tongue?"

Although throwaway lines like the one in the title might seem harmless, to some students with communication disorders, such statements bring on feelings of fear, shame, and anxiety. Simple misunderstandings during discussion, reluctance to respond to questions for which they have the answers, and an inability to interpret directions are all problems students might have if they have communication disorders. These characteristics might be incorrectly interpreted by the general classroom teacher. The teacher might think that the student is disrespectful, is "not getting it," or "hears when he wants to." Language delays are a thread that run through many disabilities, not just communication disorders (B. Lubker, personal communication). For these reasons, collaboration with a speech-language pathologist or language interventionist is very important for students with communication disorders and their teachers.

WHAT DOES IT MEAN TO BE A TEACHER OF STUDENTS WITH COMMUNICATION DISORDERS?

What is a speech-language pathologist? According to the American Speech-Language-Hearing Association (ASHA), speech-language pathologists help people to develop their communication abilities and treat speech, language, and voice disorders. The services of a speech-language pathologist include prevention, identification, evaluation, treatment, and rehabilitation of communication disorders.

ASHA is the professional organization that oversees the certification of speech-language pathologists. This organization has established a set of standards for the newly trained pathologist. The Certificate of Clinical Competence (CCC) is given only to those with a master's or doctoral degree. The CCC includes requirements in basic science courses, professional coursework, 375 clock hours of supervised clinical observation/practice, a clinical fellowship, and a national examination. This is a tremendous amount of coursework in the basics of physiology and audiology, evaluation, and remediation of speech problems.

SUCCESSFUL STRATEGIES FOR COLLABORATION

Speech-language pathologists are encouraged to participate in a variety of collaborative structures, such as co-teaching and collaborative consultation. The general education classroom is one of the environments in which students with language problems must generalize the individual skills they are taught by speech language pathologists, whether they receive instruction in these skills in that classroom or in separate settings. Therefore, the speech-language pathologist can work with the general education teacher, quite often through the special education teacher, to let that teacher know the specific implications of the speech or language disorder for a student's performance in the classroom. The pathologist can also provide guidance in identifying components of a general educator's instruction that may be causing problems and can help modify those components. Finally, the speech language pathologist can work with the general educator to monitor a student's progress, celebrate victories, and work toward a student's independence. For more information, see the American Speech–Language–Hearing Association Website at www.asha.org.

● *By Margaret P. Weiss*

Teaching Literacy: Reading and Written Expression

Developing literacy is a special problem for many students with speech and language disorders. As noted earlier in this chapter, students with language impairments often have reading deficits in both word recognition skills and comprehension. It is less common for individuals who have pure speech disorders to have difficulties with reading, but those with language, or language and speech problems are indeed at significant risk for reading disability (Snowling & Hayiou-Thomas, 2006). In particular, students who have poor phonological awareness are typically unable to learn how to decode without intervention. **Decoding** refers to the ability to transfer the written words into speech. For those students with language impairments who learn how to decode, many will still have difficulty with reading comprehension. Thus, it is critical for the classroom teacher, speech-language pathologist, and special education teacher

■ **Decoding**
The ability to convert print to spoken language; dependent on phonemic awareness and understanding of the alphabetic principles; a significant problem for many people with reading disabilities.

Personal PERSPECTIVES

Suggestions for Talking with Students

■ Choose a topic of interest to the student. Comment on the student's thinking, feelings, and experiences, as he or she describes them by providing models of other words or phrases.

■ After initiating the conversation, let the student take the lead. Show interest in and, if appropriate, excitement about what the student says.

■ Try not to ask lots of questions, and when you do ask questions, ask open-ended ones for which explanations are appropriate.

■ Use appropriate wait-time with your questions; don't demand an immediate response, but give the student enough time to formulate an answer. Be comfortable with some open or empty spaces in the conversation; don't rush.

■ Encourage question-asking in return, and give honest and open answers (except, of course, decline politely to answer inappropriate or highly personal questions).

■ Keep your voice at an appropriate level, keep your pace moderate, and keep the conversation light and humorous unless the topic of conversation is serious and humor is inappropriate.

■ Avoid being judgmental or making snide remarks about the student's language, because if the student thinks you are judgmental or you correct every error he or she will stop talking to you. Demonstrate acceptance of the student's language.

■ Do not interrupt the student when he or she is talking, and listen attentively to the student's ideas; show respect.

■ Provide as many opportunities as you can for the student to use language in social situations, and respond appropriately to the student's attempts to use language to accomplish his or her goals.

to work together to provide explicit and systematic intervention in reading for children with language impairments.

In addition to reading problems, students with language impairment also have difficulty with written expression. As students progress through the grades, written language takes on increasing importance. Students are expected to read increasingly complex and difficult material and understand its meaning. In addition, they are expected to express themselves more clearly in writing. The interactions teachers have with students about their writing—the questions they ask to help students understand how to write for their readers—are critical to overcoming disabilities in written language (Graham, Harris, MacArthur, & Schwartz, 1998).

Finally, we note that intervention in language disorders employs many of the same strategies used in intervention in learning disabilities. Metacognitive training, strategy training, and other approaches discussed in Chapter 6 are typically appropriate for use with students who have language disorders (see also Hallahan, Lloyd, Kauffman, Weiss, & Martinez, 2005; Mercer & Pullen, 2009).

Assessment of Progress

UNDERSTANDING THE STANDARDS AND PRINCIPLES Describe two methods for monitoring the progress of students with language impairments (CEC Knowledge and Skill Standard CC8S8)

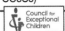

A primary purpose of language assessment is to inform instruction. An intervention plan based on assessment must consider the content, form, social context, and use of language. That is, it must consider the following:

● What the child talks about and should be taught to talk about

● How the child talks about things and how he or she could be taught to speak of those things more intelligibly

- How the child functions in the context of his or her linguistic community

- How the child uses language and how the child's language use could be made to serve the purposes of communication and socialization more effectively

After the intervention plan has been developed, an ongoing assessment plan is implemented to monitor progress and outcome measures are identified to ensure programmatic goals are met.

> **Casebook Reflection**
>
> REFER TO THE CASE *Albert Says What?* in your booklet. Albert understands what his teachers and mother are saying but is unable to communicate verbally or intelligibly. What assessments might be used to understand his disability? ●

Progress Monitoring

Methods for monitoring the progress of students with language impairments may use a system of dynamic assessment that involves a cycle of teaching, followed by testing, and then reteaching as necessary (Ehren & Nelson, 2005). **Dynamic assessments** are administered during the learning process and the **speech-language pathologist (SLP)** determines how the student performs with and without support (Anderson & Shames, 2006). This information guides intervention as the SLP establishes what the student is able to do and where further intervention is required. Dynamic assessments can be used in the context of an Response to Intervention (RTI) program by SLPs (Ehren & Nelson).

 Curriculum-based language and communication assessment (CBLA) can also be used to monitor students' progress. CBLA differs from curriculum-based measurement (CBM) discussed in earlier chapters in that it measures a student's speech, language, and communication skills that are required to learn the school curriculum (Staskowski & Nelson, 2007). CBLA generally measures the communications skills required to participate in the school curriculum and the strategies the student employs to conduct curricular tasks. Based on the observations related to these two areas, the SLP then determines what skills the student needs to acquire and how to modify the task to ensure success.

■ **Dynamic assessments**
Dynamic assessment is an approach to assessment and intervention that is interactive. The speech-language pathologist tests a student, uses the results to guide instruction, and then tests the student again. This cycle is continued throughout the intervention process.

■ **Speech-language pathologist**
A speech-language pathologist (SLP) is a specialist in the assessment, treatment, and prevention of communication disorders.

■ **Curriculum-based language and communication assessment (CBLA)**
Curriculum-based language assessment is a method of evaluating the speech and language skills that a student needs to be successful in the school curriculum.

Outcome Measures

As in other areas of education, the current trend requires that service providers demonstrate the value of communication intervention in terms of student outcomes. Although myriad formal assessments are available that provide data in all of the language domains, these measures may not illustrate the improvements in the daily life of the individual with a disability. New measures that evaluate the individual's success in the daily environment, school performance, and emotional well-being are needed (Lubinski & Golper, 2007).

 Currently, SLPs may rely on the National Outcomes Measurement System (NOMS) to measure the outcomes of students in communication interventions. In an effort to assist SLPs in documenting treatment outcomes, the American Speech Language Hearing Association formed the National Center for Treatment Effectiveness in Communication in the early 1990s (Mullen, 2003). A result of these efforts is the NOMS, an online database assessment system. The SLP uses a series of scales that measure functional communication. These data, along with demographic and diagnostic data, are used to generate a report of outcomes based on the individual's intervention plan.

Accommodations

Many students with communication disorders participate in statewide standardized assessments with accommodations. Accommodations for students with communication

Casebook Reflection

REFER TO THE CASE *Albert Says What?* in your booklet. Although Albert does not have expressive language, he demonstrates normal receptive language. He is also able to write his name, to understand his assignments, and to make good grades in school. In light of these factors, what type of placement do you foresee as the least restrictive environment for him? What about in the future? ●

disorders will be similar to those for students with learning disabilities. Frequently, students with communication disorders receive setting or scheduling accommodations including small-group administration and extended time. Students with more significant communication disorders may require communication devices in response and presentation accommodations. Communication devices include speech output (translating text to speech) and speech recognition systems. Most states that allow these accommodations consider them to be nonstandard, and thus the scoring of the assessment is altered (Lazarus, Thurlow, Lail, Eisenbraun, & Kato, 2006).

Early Intervention

Early intervention is critically important for two primary reasons:

1. The older the child is when intervention is begun, the smaller the chance that he or she will acquire effective language skills (other things being equal).
2. Without having functional language, the child cannot become a truly social being (Warren & Abbaduto, 1992). Of all the skills in which a child may be lagging, language—communication—is the most important, as it is the foundation of academic and social learning.

Early Development and Early Intervention

The study of children's early development has shown that the first several years of life are a truly critical period for language learning. We have known for a long time that much of children's language, literacy, and social development depends on the nature and quantity of the language interactions they have with parents or other caregivers. In the homes of children who come to school ready to learn, the language interactions between parents and children have typically been frequent, focused on encouragement and affirmation of the children's behavior, emphasized the symbolic nature of language, provided gentle guidance in exploring things and relationships, and demonstrated the responsiveness of adults to children. By contrast, children who enter school at a disadvantage tend to have experienced much lower rates of language interaction; to have heard primarily negative, discouraging feedback on their behavior; and to have heard language that is harsh, literal, and emotionally detached.

In a now classic study, Hart and Risley (1995) compared the language experiences of children of professional parents, working-class parents, and parents on welfare. The contrasts in language experiences and the effects observed in children's academic achievement and behavior are stark, but the differences are unrelated to income or ethnicity. Rather, the differences are related to how and how much the parents talked to their children. As summed up by the authors:

> Our data showed that the magnitude of children's accomplishments depends less on the material and educational advantages available in the home and more on the amount of experience children accumulate with parenting that provides language diversity, affirmative feedback, symbolic emphasis, gentle guidance, and responsiveness. By the time children are 3 years old, even intensive intervention cannot make up for the differences in the amount of such experience children have received from their parents. If children could be given better parenting, intervention might be unnecessary. (p. 210)

Thus, it appears that the key to preventing many disabilities related to language development is to help parents improve how they relate to their children when they are infants and toddlers. Nevertheless, for many young children, intervention in the preschool and primary grades will be necessary. But such intervention must be guided by understanding of children's families, particularly the primary caretaker's, usually the mother's, views of language development (Hammer & Weiss, 2000). Preschoolers who require intervention for a speech or language disorder occasionally have multiple disabilities that are sometimes severe or profound.

Language is closely tied to cognitive development, so impairment of general intellectual ability is likely to have a retarding influence on language development. Conversely, lack of language can hamper cognitive development. Because speech is dependent on neurological and motor development, any neurological or motor problem might impair ability to speak. Normal social development in the preschool years also depends on the emergence of language, so a child with language impairment is at a disadvantage in social learning. Therefore, the preschool child's language is seldom the only target of intervention.

Early Intervention in Delayed Language Development

Children with language disorders may follow the same sequence of development as most children but achieve each skill or milestone at a later-than-average age. Some children with language disorders reach final levels of development that are significantly below those of their peers who don't have disabilities. Still other children may be generally delayed in language development but show great discrepancies in the rate at which they acquire certain features of language.

Some children develop speech late but will eventually develop age-appropriate speech and language (Vinson, 2007). Yet many children whose language development is delayed show a developmental lag that they won't outgrow (Owens, 2004). They are frequently diagnosed as having intellectual disabilities or another developmental disability. Sometimes these children come from environments where they have been deprived of many experiences, including the language stimulation from adults that is required for normal language development, or they have been severely abused or neglected. Regardless of the reasons for a child's delayed language, however, it's important to understand the nature of the delay and to intervene to give him or her the optimal chance of learning to use language effectively.

Some children three years of age or older show no signs that they understand language and do not use language spontaneously. They might make noises, but they use them to communicate in ways that may characterize the communication of infants and toddlers before they have learned speech. In other words, they may use **prelinguistic communication**. For example, they may use gestures or vocal noises to request objects or actions from others, to protest, to request a social routine (e.g., reading), or to greet someone.

■ **Prelinguistic communication** Communication through gestures and noises before the child has learned oral language.

When assessing and planning intervention for children with delayed language, it is important to consider what language and nonlanguage behaviors they imitate, what they comprehend, what communication skills they use spontaneously, and what part communication plays in their lives. It's also important, particularly with young children, to provide intervention in contexts in which language is used for normal social interaction. For example, parents or teachers may use a milieu teaching approach, "a naturalistic language intervention designed to teach functional language skills" (Kaiser, Hemmeter, Ostrosky, Alpert, & Hancock, 1995, p. 40). In this approach, teaching is built around the child's interests. When the child requests some action, object, or activity from the adult, the adult prompts the child's language and makes access to

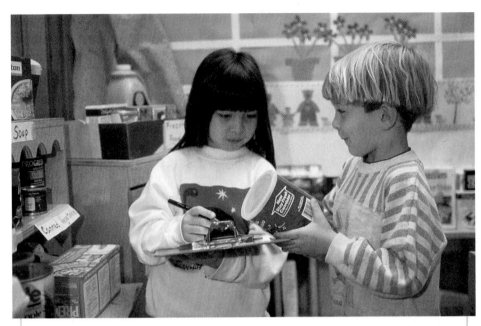

Milieu teaching is an approach that uses naturalistic language to teach functional language skills. In this approach, teaching is built around the child's interests.

■ **Milieu teaching**
A naturalistic approach to language intervention in which the goal is to teach functional language skills in a natural environment.

what is requested contingent on an attempt to communicate. **Milieu teaching** is a naturalistic approach, in that it encourages designing interventions that are similar to the conversational interactions that parents and children ordinarily have. Prelinguistic communication may be a good indication of a child's later ability to use language (Calandrella & Wilcox, 2000). The effectiveness of a milieu teaching approach may depend, at least to some extent, on mothers' responsiveness to their children's prelinguistic communication (Yoder & Warren, 2001).

Involvement of Families

Intervention Guidelines Homework Exercise

Early Intervention ● Go to the Homework and Exercises section in Chapter 9 of MyEducationLab to access a Website that provides the New York State guidelines in best practices for providing early intervention to children with communication disorders.

Researchers have become increasingly aware that language development has its beginning in the earliest mother–child interactions. Concern for the child's development of the ability to communicate can't be separated from concern for development in other areas. Therefore, speech-language pathologists are a vital part of the multidisciplinary team that evaluates an infant or young child with disabilities and develops an individualized family service plan (IFSP; see Chapters 2 and 4). Early intervention programs involve extending the role of the parent. This means a lot of simple play with accompanying verbalizations. It means talking to the child about objects and activities in the way most mothers talk to their babies. But it also means choosing objects, activities, words, and consequences for the child's vocalizations with great care so the chances that the child will learn functional language are enhanced (Fey, Catts, & Larrivee, 1995).

Early childhood specialists now realize that prelinguistic intervention is critical for language development—that is, intervention should begin before the child's language emerges. The foundations for language are laid in the first few months of life through stimulating experiences with parents and other caretakers (Koury, 2007). In the early years of implementing IFSPs, emphasis was placed on assessing families' strengths and needs and training parents how to teach and manage their children. More recently, professionals have come to understand that assessing

The first several years of life are truly critical for language learning.

families in the belief that professionals know best is often misguided. Parents can indeed be helped by professionals to play an important role in their children's language development. But the emphasis today is on working with parents as knowledgeable and competent partners whose preferences and decisions are respected (Hammer & Weiss, 2000; see also discussion in Chapter 4).

Intervention in early childhood is likely to be based on assessment of the child's behavior related to the content, form, and especially the use of language in social interaction. For the child who has not yet learned language, assessment and intervention will focus on imitation, ritualized and make-believe play, play with objects, and functional use of objects. At the earliest stages in which the content and form of language are interactive, it is important to evaluate the extent to which the child looks at or picks up an object when it is referred to, does something with an object when directed by an adult, and uses sounds to request or refuse things and call attention to objects. When the child's use of language is considered, the earliest objectives involve the child looking at the adult during interactions; taking turns in and trying to prolong pleasurable activities and games; following the gaze of an adult and directing the behavior of adults; and persisting in or modifying gestures, sounds, or words when an adult does not respond. In the preschool, teaching discourse (conversation skills) is a critical focus of language intervention. In particular, emphasis is placed on teaching children to use the discourse that is essential for success in school. Children must learn, for example, to report their experiences in detail and to explain why things happen, not just add to their vocabularies. They must learn not only word forms and meanings, but also how to take turns in conversations and maintain the topic of a conversation or change it in an appropriate way. Preschool programs in which such language teaching is the focus may include teachers' daily individualized conversations with children, daily reading to individual children or small groups, and frequent classroom discussions.

Casebook Reflection

REFER TO THE CASE *Albert Says What?* in your booklet. We know nothing from the case about his early developmental history except that his mother took certain pieces out of his school file. What do you think might have been some of the early signs or symptoms of Albert's communication disorder? ●

Current trends are directed toward providing speech and language interventions in the typical environments of young children. This means that classroom teachers and speech-language pathologists must develop a close working relationship. The speech-language pathologist might work directly with children in the classroom and advise the teacher about the intervention that he or she can carry out as part of the regular classroom activities. Alternatively, the speech-language pathologist might work with the teacher directly to help her incorporate effective instructional practices for these students. The Responsive Instruction on page 331 provides an example of one successful collaboration. The child's peers may also be involved in intervention strategies. Because language is essentially a social activity, its facilitation requires involvement of others in the child's social environment—peers as well as adults (Audet & Tankersley, 1999; Fey et al., 1995; Prizant, 1999).

Normally developing peers have been taught to assist in the language development of children with disabilities by doing the following during playtimes: establishing eye contact; describing their own or others' play; and repeating, expanding, or requesting clarification of what the child with disabilities says. Peer tutors can help in developing the speech and language of their classmates who may use different dialects (McGregor, 2000). Another intervention strategy involving peers is sociodramatic play. Children are taught in groups of three, including a child with disabilities, to act out social roles such as those people might take in various settings (e.g., a restaurant or shoe store). The training includes scripts that specify what each child is to do and say, which the children can modify in creative ways.

Transition to Adulthood

In the past, adolescents and adults in speech and language intervention programs generally fell into three categories: (1) the self-referred, (2) those with other health problems, and (3) those with severe disabilities. Adolescents or adults might refer themselves to speech-language pathologists because their phonology, voice, or stuttering is causing them social embarrassment and/or interfering with occupational pursuits. These are generally people with long-standing problems who are highly motivated to change their speech and obtain relief from the social penalties their differences impose.

Adolescents and adults with other health problems might have experienced damage to speech or language capacities as a result of disease or injury, or they might have lost part of their speech mechanism through injury or surgical removal. Treatment of these individuals always demands an interdisciplinary effort. In some cases of progressive disease, severe neurological damage, or loss of tissues of the speech mechanism, the outlook for functional speech is not good. However, surgical procedures, medication, and prosthetic devices are making it possible for more people to speak normally. Loss of ability to use language is typically more disabling than loss of the ability to speak. Traumatic brain injury may leave the individual with a seriously diminished capacity for self-awareness, goal setting, planning, self-directing or initiating actions, inhibiting impulses, monitoring or evaluating one's own performance, or problem solving. Recovering these vital language-based skills is a critical aspect of transition of the adolescent or young adult from hospital to school and from school to independent living (Klein & Moses, 1999).

Individuals with severe disabilities might need the services of speech-language pathologists to help them achieve more intelligible speech. They might also need to be taught an alternative to oral language or given a system of augmented communication. One of the major problems in working with adolescents and adults who have severe

Responsive Instruction

Meeting the Needs of Students with Communication Disorders
Collaboration in an Inner-City Classroom

WHAT THE RESEARCH SAYS

Research on early language ability has demonstrated a correlation between early language development and later reading ability (Snow, Burns, & Griffin, 1998). Children from low income homes, with identified language impairments, or who have difficulty speaking English face considerable challenges in learning to read (Snow et al., 1998; Stothard, Snowling, Bishop, Chipchese, & Kaplon, 1998; Walker, Greenwood, Hart, & Carta, 1994).

Given the fact that many inner-city school districts have disproportionately high numbers of students who fall into one of the above "risk factors," school personnel are constantly seeking ways to reduce these risks. Recommendations from professional organizations encourage collaboration among professionals in order to capitalize on specific areas of strength and provide connected interventions across settings. In the area of language, the American Speech–Language–Hearing Association, the professional organization of speech-language pathologists, recommends that speech-language pathologists and the classroom teachers collaborate to intensify language instruction within general education classrooms (American Speech–Language–Hearing Association, 1991).

RESEARCH STUDY

One team of researchers explored the effectiveness of a collaborative, classroom-based intervention to improve the vocabulary and phonological awareness of inner-city kindergartners and first graders (Hadley, Simmerman, Long, & Luna, 2000). Eighty-three percent of the students in this school district were eligible for free or reduced-cost lunch—a marker for low socioeconomic status. In addition, 28 percent of the students were considered limited English proficient. For the study, four general education classrooms were selected. Two classrooms served as the control groups (i.e., received no intervention) and two served as the experimental groups (i.e., received the intervention). The intervention consisted of the speech-language pathologist teaching language-related lessons two and a half days per week and regularly collaborating with the general education teacher to develop other language-based activities to integrate throughout the day. The control classes followed standard instructional practices with no collaboration or teaching from the speech-language pathologist.

RESEARCH FINDINGS

Following the six-month intervention, students in the experimental groups demonstrated greater gains in the areas of receptive vocabulary, expressive vocabulary, beginning sound awareness, and letter-sound associations when compared to students in the control group. Additionally, the findings demonstrated that both native English speakers and students with normative backgrounds benefited from the intensive vocabulary and phonemic awareness instruction. The study demonstrated the ability of speech-language pathologists to collaborate successfully with general education teachers. This collaboration facilitated the teaching of explicit skills within educationally relevant communication and curricular activities.

APPLYING THE RESEARCH TO TEACHING

The results of this study demonstrate potential benefits of collaboration between speech-language pathologists and general educators. Critical are:

- Creating time for joint planning so that intervention activities are planned and roles are clearly established;
- Identifying specific goals to be addressed and allocating intervention activities by expertise;
- Modeling on the part of the speech-language pathologist so that the classroom teacher can use the strategies throughout the day, not just when the speech-language pathologist is present. (Hadley et al., 2000)

● *By Kristin L. Sayeski*

disabilities is setting realistic goals for speech and language learning. Teaching simple, functional language—such as social greetings, naming objects, and making simple requests—may be realistic goals for some adolescents and adults.

A major concern of transition programming is ensuring that the training and support provided during the school years are carried over into adult life. To be successful, the transition must include speech-language services that are part of the natural

Casebook Reflection

REFER TO THE CASE *Albert Says What?* in your booklet. The story of Albert ends with his mother stating that her brother has the same condition but is able to conduct a normal life. What does this piece of information say about Albert's transition to adulthood? ●

UNDERSTANDING THE STANDARDS AND PRINCIPLES What speech-language services should teachers keep in mind when planning students' transition programming? (CEC Knowledge and Skill Standard GC7K2)

Council for Exceptional Children

environment. That is, the services must be community based and integrated into vocational, domestic, recreational, consumer, and mobility training activities. Speech-language interventions for adolescents and young adults with severe disabilities must emphasize functional communication—understanding and making oneself understood in the social circumstances that are most likely to be encountered in everyday life (Justice, 2006). Developing appropriate conversation skills (e.g., establishing eye contact, using greetings, taking turns, and identifying and staying on the topic), reading, writing, following instructions related to recreational activities, using public transportation, and performing a job are examples of the kinds of functional speech-language activities that may be emphasized.

Today, much more emphasis is being placed on the language disorders of adolescents and young adults who do not fit into other typical categories of disabilities. Many of these individuals were formerly seen as having primarily academic and social problems that were not language related. But now it is understood that underlying many or most of the school and social difficulties of adolescents and adults are basic disorders of language. These language disorders are a continuation of difficulties experienced earlier in the person's development.

Classroom teachers are in a particularly good position to identify possible language-related problems and request help from a communication specialist. The Focus on Concepts below describes for teachers several characteristics exhibited by older children and adolescents that may indicate a need for consultation and intervention. Addressing problems like these as early and effectively as possible is important in helping youngsters make successful transitions to more complex and socially demanding environments.

Some adolescents and adults with language disorders are excellent candidates for strategy training, which teaches them how to select, store, retrieve, and process information (see Hallahan et al., 2005; see also Chapter 6). Others, however, don't have the required reading skills, symbolic abilities, or intelligence to benefit from the usual training in cognitive strategies. Whatever techniques are chosen for adolescents and older students, the teacher should be aware of the principles that apply to intervention with these individuals.

FOCUS ON **Concepts**

Identifying Possible Language Problems Related to Transition

Older children and adolescents may need help from a communication specialist if they:

- Fail to understand instructions in typical situations
- Cannot use language effectively to meet their daily living needs

- Frequently violate social rules involving politeness and interpersonal interactions
- Do not have the ability to read important signs and symbols, complete forms, and write simple reports
- Have problems speaking so that others understand

Summary

How are communication disorders defined?

▶ Communication involves sharing information between two individuals or among more than two individuals.

▶ Communicative functions include requesting, rejecting, commenting, arguing, reasoning, and so on.

▶ Communication disorders may involve language or speech or both, and they impair communicative functions.
  ■ Language is sending and receiving ideas—expression and reception—through an arbitrary system of symbols used according to rules.
  ■ Speech is the neuromuscular activity of forming and sequencing the sounds of oral language.

What is the prevalence of communication disorders?

▶ Reasonable estimates are that about 10 to 15 percent of preschool children and about 6 percent of students in elementary and secondary grades have speech disorders.

▶ Probably about 2 to 3 percent of preschoolers and about 1 percent of the school-age population have language disorders.

What is the difference between communicative differences and disorders?

▶ Differences include dialects, regional differences, language of ethnic minority groups, and nondominant languages.

▶ An individual with a difference that is not a disorder is an effective communicator in his or her language community, whereas someone with a disorder has impaired communication in all language environments.

What are the major disorders of language?

▶ There are many different theories of language development and the disorders of language.

▶ Language disorders may be primary (no known cause) or secondary (attributable to another condition or disability).

▶ Primary language disorders include specific language impairment (SLI), early expressive language delay (EELD), and language-based reading impairment.

▶ Secondary language disorders include those related to emotional or behavioral disorders or any other disability, such as intellectual disabilities or autistic spectrum disorder.

What are the major disorders of speech?

▶ Speech disorders are a very heterogeneous group of problems related to the production of oral language, including the following:
  ■ *Phonological disorders*—problems in understanding the sound system of language
  ■ *Articulation disorders*—problems in producing correct speech sounds
  ■ *Voice disorders*—problems in producing voice with appropriate pitch, loudness, or quality
  ■ *Fluency disorders*—problems in maintaining speech flow
  ■ *Motor-speech*—problems in speaking due to neuromotor damage, including the following:
    ■ *Dysarthria*—problems in controlling the production of speech sounds
    ■ *Apraxia*—problems in planning and coordinating speech

What are the main educational considerations for communication disorders?

▶ The classroom teacher needs to work with others in three main areas:
  ■ Facilitating the social uses of language
  ■ Question-asking
  ■ Teaching literacy: Reading and written language

What are the major features of assessment of progress for students with communication disorders?

▶ A primary purpose of language assessment is to inform instruction.

▶ Assessment for intervention requires attention to the following:
  ■ What the child talks about and should be taught to talk about
  ■ How the child talks about things and how he or she could be taught to speak of those things more intelligibly
  ■ How the child functions in the context of his or her linguistic community
  ■ How the child uses language and how his or her use of it could be made to serve the purposes of communication and socialization more effectively

▶ Progress monitoring assessments are dynamic and should follow a cycle of teaching, testing, and reteaching.

▶ Progress monitoring assessments include curriculum-based language assessment (CBLA).

▶ Assessment of student outcomes should be implemented to confirm that learning has occurred.

What are the major aspects of early intervention for communication disorders?

▶ Early intervention is based on early language development.

▶ Early intervention usually involves working with delayed language.

▶ Early intervention requires working with families.

What is emphasized in transition for students with communication disorders?

▶ Transition involves helping students use the language demanded for successful employment.

STANDARDS and PRINCIPLES in this Chapter

SPECIAL EDUCATORS . . .

■ understand the similarities and differences in human development and the characteristics between and among individuals with and without exceptional learning needs (from CEC Content Standard #2).

■ possess a repertoire of evidence-based instructional strategies to individualize instruction for individuals with exceptional learning needs (from CEC Content Standard #4).

■ understand typical and atypical language development and the ways in which exceptional conditions can interact with an individual's experience with and use of language (from CEC Content Standard #6).

■ develop a variety of individualized transition plans, such as transitions from preschool to elementary school and from secondary settings to a variety of postsecondary work and learning contexts (from CEC Content Standard #7).

ALL TEACHERS . . .

■ understand how children learn and develop and can provide learning opportunities that support the intellectual, social, and personal development of each learner (INTASC Principle #2).

■ understand and use a variety of instructional strategies to encourage students' development of critical thinking, problem solving, and performance skills (INTASC Principle #4).

■ use knowledge of effective verbal, nonverbal, and media communication technologies to foster active inquiry, collaboration, and supportive interaction in the classroom (INTASC Principle #6).

■ plan instruction based on knowledge of subject matter, students, the community, and curriculum goals (INTASC Principle #7).

Applying the STANDARDS and PRINCIPLES

■ ONE of your colleagues, whose background is in general education, asks, "What does it really mean to have a language disorder?" How would you respond? (CEC Content Standard #2 & INTASC Principle #2)

■ WHAT can teachers do to help students overcome speech and language disorders? (CEC Content Standard #4 & INTASC Principle #4)

■ WHY are language differences sometimes mistaken for language disorders? (CEC Content Standard #6 & INTASC Principle #6)

■ WHAT language-related problems might older children and adolescents exhibit that may indicate a need for consultation and intervention? (CEC Content Standard #7 & INTASC Principle #7)

Now go to the Hallahan/Kauffman, Eleventh Edition MyEducationLab course at www.myeducationlab.com to:

- take a Pretest to assess your initial comprehension of the chapter content;
- study chapter content with your Individualized Study Plan;
- take a Posttest to assess your understanding of chapter content;
- engage in multimedia exercises to help you build a deeper and more applied understanding of chapter content.

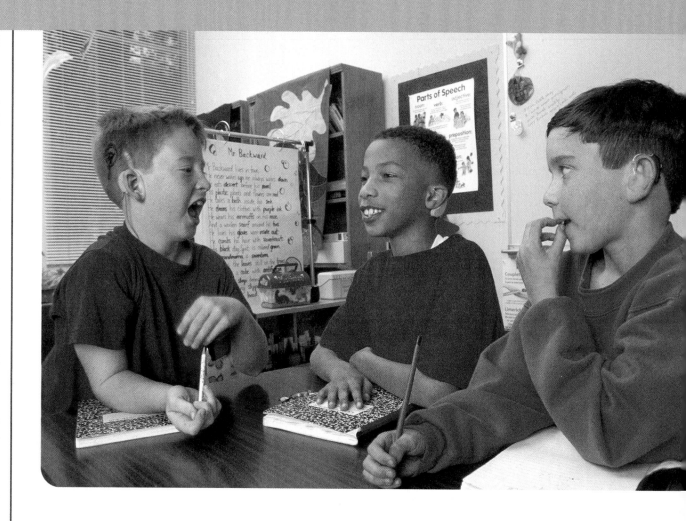

10

Learners Who Are Deaf or Hard of Hearing

Upon transitioning to high school, friends dispersed into separate crowds. The new school was much bigger. . . . I found myself becoming increasingly isolated. One afternoon . . . , I sat on the sofa . . . having a mutually desired but laborious conversation with my mother. . . . I asked her why I didn't have as many friends as the other kids. . . . She looked at me with a surprised expression on her face.

"You don't know why?" she asked.

"No."

"It's because you can't hear, and they don't understand that."

That was a revelation and turning point in my life. Until that moment, I had only understood my deafness in a blur. I had never understood this difference between myself and others to be such a determining factor in my life. . . . But still I did not realize all the implications regarding relationships, my future, language, and education. I did not know this wasn't just a hearing problem. The difficulties I faced were not because I had a hearing problem, but because the often-cruel world around me was full of barriers. That understanding was a long way off.

—Martha Sheridan
Inner Lives of Deaf Children: Interviews and Analysis

QUESTIONS to guide your reading of this chapter . . .

- How do professionals define and classify individuals who are deaf or hard of hearing?

- What is the prevalence of hearing impairment?

- How is hearing impairment identified?

- What causes hearing impairments?

- What are some psychological and behavioral characteristics of learners with hearing impairments?

- What are some educational considerations for learners with hearing impairments?

- How do professionals assess the academic progress of students with hearing impairments?

- What are some things to consider with respect to early intervention for learners with hearing impairments?

- What are some things to consider with respect to transition to adulthood for learners with hearing impairments?

MISCONCEPTIONS ABOUT
Learners Who Are Deaf or Hard of Hearing

MYTH ■ People who are deaf are unable to hear anything.

FACT ■ Most people who are deaf have some residual hearing.

MYTH ■ Deafness is not as severe a disability as blindness.

FACT ■ Although it's impossible to predict the exact consequences of a disability on a person's functioning, in general, deafness poses more difficulties in adjustment than does blindness. This is largely due to the effects hearing loss can have on the ability to understand and speak oral language.

MYTH ■ It's unhealthy for people who are deaf to socialize almost exclusively with others who are deaf.

FACT ■ Many authorities now recognize that the phenomenon of a Deaf culture is natural and should be encouraged. In fact, some are worried that too much mainstreaming will diminish the influence of the Deaf culture.

MYTH ■ In learning to understand what is being said to them, people with a hearing impairment concentrate on reading lips.

FACT ■ Lipreading refers only to visual cues arising from movement of the lips. Some people who have a hearing impairment not only read lips but also take advantage of a number of other visual cues, such as facial expressions and movements of the jaw and tongue. They are engaging in what is referred to as speechreading.

MYTH ■ Speechreading is relatively easy to learn and is used by the majority of people with a hearing impairment.

FACT ■ Speechreading is extremely difficult to learn, and very few people who have a hearing impairment actually become proficient speechreaders.

MYTH ■ American Sign Language (ASL) is a loosely structured group of gestures.

FACT ■ ASL is a true language in its own right, with its own set of grammatical rules.

MYTH ■ People within the Deaf community are in favor of mainstreaming students who are deaf into general education classes.

FACT ■ Some within the Deaf community have voiced the opinion that general education classes are not appropriate for many students who are deaf. They point to the need for a critical mass of students who are deaf in order to have effective educational programs for these individuals. They see separate placements as a way of fostering the Deaf culture.

MYTH ■ Families in which both the child and the parents are deaf are at a distinct disadvantage compared to families in which the parents are hearing.

FACT ■ Research has demonstrated that children who are deaf who have parents who are also deaf fare better in a number of academic and social areas. Authorities point to the parents' ability to communicate with their children in ASL as a major reason for this advantage.

To be deaf, or even hard of hearing, often places a person in a difficult place somewhere between the world of the hearing and the world of the Deaf. Martha Sheridan's (2001) words (see p. 337) reflect the isolation that can accompany a hearing impairment—an isolation caused primarily by communication problems. As we see in this chapter, even if the hearing impairment isn't severe enough for a child to be classified as "deaf," but rather as "hard of hearing," the child with a hearing impairment is at a distinct disadvantage in virtually all aspects of English language development. The importance of the English language in U.S. society, particularly in school-related activities, is obvious. Many of the problems that people with hearing impairment have in school are due primarily to their difficulties in English. We explore this issue in some depth in this chapter.

A related controversy inherent in Martha Sheridan's (2001) words is the debate about whether the child who is deaf should be educated to communicate orally or through manual sign language. Sheridan is typical of the approximate 95 percent of those who are deaf, in that both her parents are hearing (Mitchell & Karchmer, 2004) and had chosen not to learn sign language. Also common, unfortunately, is the difficulty that Sheridan had learning to speechread, or to use visual information (including lip movements) from a number of sources, to understand what is being said.

Again, like others in the same situation, Sheridan eventually went on to immerse herself in the Deaf community. She found her identity as a Deaf person through her experiences at Gallaudet University, the primary postsecondary institution for students with hearing impairment:

> Gallaudet was a major gateway for me. It was the pot of gold at the end of my search for self, and it represented the beginning of the rest of my life. It was at Gallaudet that I discovered what it means to be deaf. . . . Here, and with sign language, my love for learning blossomed. (Sheridan, 2001, pp. 7–8)

But not all people who are deaf elect to join the Deaf community. Some become fluent enough in spoken English to function in mainstream society. Others are able to straddle both the world of the hearing and the Deaf. But no matter what the outcome, virtually all people who are deaf, as well as their parents, struggle with critical choices about oral versus manual modes of communication and cultural identity. With respect to the latter, in fact, many members of the Deaf community consider themselves part of a cultural minority rather than disabled.

All of these thorny issues make deafness one of the most challenging fields of study in all of special education. As you would surmise from our discussion of other special education areas, this challenge is evident in attempts to arrive at a definition of hearing impairment.

Casebook Reflection

REFER TO THE CASE *Least Restrictive for Whom?* in your booklet. Mary Scanlon had learned in a Characteristics of Persons with Disabilities course that "deafness was probably the most difficult disability with which to live." Do you agree with this assessment? Why or why not?   ●

Video Homework Exercise

Classroom Aides ●
Go to the Homework and Exercises section in Chapter 10 of MyEducationLab to watch the video "Hearing Impairment", which depicts the services of an aide in a general education classroom.

Definition and Classification

By far the most common way of classifying hearing impairment is the division between *deaf* and *hard of hearing*. Although it's common to think that being deaf means not being able to hear anything and that being hard of hearing means being able to hear a little bit, this is generally not true. Most people who are deaf have some residual hearing. Complicating things is the fact that different professionals define the two categories differently. The extreme points of view are represented by those with a physiological orientation versus those with an educational orientation.

■ **Decibels**
Units of relative loudness of sounds; zero decibels (0 dB) designates the point at which people with normal hearing can just detect sound.

UNDERSTANDING THE STANDARDS AND PRINCIPLES What is the distinction between deaf and hard of hearing? (CEC Knowledge and Skill Standard DH1K1)

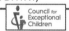

■ **Congenitally deaf**
Deafness that is present at birth; can be caused by genetic factors, by injuries during fetal development, or by injuries occurring at birth.

■ **Adventitiously deaf**
Deafness that occurs through illness or accident in an individual who was born with normal hearing.

■ **Prelingual deafness**
Deafness that occurs before the development of spoken language, usually at birth.

■ **Postlingual deafness**
Deafness occurring after the development of speech and language.

Those who maintain a strictly physiological viewpoint are interested primarily in the measurable degree of hearing impairment. Children who can't hear sounds at or above a certain intensity (loudness) level are classified as "deaf"; others with a hearing impairment are considered "hard of hearing." Hearing sensitivity is measured in **decibels** (units of relative loudness of sounds). Zero decibels (0 dB) designates the point at which the average person with normal hearing can detect the faintest sound. Each succeeding number of decibels that a person cannot detect indicates a certain degree of hearing impairment. Those who maintain a physiological viewpoint generally consider people with hearing impairments of about 90 dB or greater to be deaf and people with impairments at lower decibel levels to be hard of hearing. For comparison purposes, 90 dB is the approximate loudness of a lawn mower (American Academy of Otolaryngology—Head and Neck Surgery, 2007).

People with an educational viewpoint are concerned with how much the hearing impairment is likely to affect the child's ability to speak and develop language. Because of the close causal link between hearing impairment and delay in language development, these professionals categorize primarily on the basis of spoken language abilities. *Hearing impairment* is a broad term that covers individuals with impairments ranging from mild to profound; it includes those who are deaf or hard of hearing. Following are commonly accepted, educationally oriented definitions for *deaf* and *hard of hearing*:

- A deaf person is one whose hearing disability precludes successful processing of linguistic information through audition, with or without a hearing aid.
- A person who is hard of hearing generally, with the use of a hearing aid, has residual hearing sufficient to enable successful processing of linguistic information through audition (Brill, MacNeil, & Newman, 1986, p. 67).

Educators are extremely concerned about the age of onset of hearing impairment. Again, the close relationship between hearing impairment and language delay is the key. The earlier the hearing impairment occurs in life, the more difficulty the child will have developing the language of the hearing society (e.g., English). For this reason, professionals frequently use the terms **congenitally deaf** (those who are born deaf) and **adventitiously deaf** (those who acquire deafness at some time after birth).

Two other frequently used terms are even more specific in pinpointing language acquisition as critical: **Prelingual deafness** refers to deafness that occurs at birth or early in life before speech and language develop. **Postlingual deafness** is deafness that occurs after the development of speech and language. Experts differ about the dividing point between prelingual and postlingual deafness. Some believe that it should be at about eighteen months; others think it should be lower, at about twelve months or even six months (Meadow-Orlans, 1987).

Some professionals find it useful to classify according to hearing threshold levels, such as mild (26–40 dB), moderate (41–55 dB), moderate-severe (56–70 dB), severe (71–90 dB), and profound (91 dB and above; Andrews, Leigh, & Weiner, 2004). These levels of loss of hearing sensitivity cut across the broad classifications of deaf and hard of hearing, which stress the degree to which speech and language are affected rather than being directly dependent on hearing sensitivity.

Some authorities object to adhering too strictly to any of the various classification systems. Because these definitions deal with events difficult to measure, they're not precise. Therefore, it is best not to form any hard-and-fast opinions about an individual's ability to hear and speak solely on the basis of a classification of his or her hearing disability.

In considering issues of definition, it's important to point out that there is growing sentiment among people who are deaf that deafness should not even be considered a disability (Padden & Humphries, 2005). In the Focus on Concepts on p. 342, note that Lane at times uses the term Deaf with a capital *D* and at other times does not. Although there

A current issue in defining deafness is that many people in the Deaf community do not want to be considered as having a disability. Instead, they want to be thought of as members of a cultural group with its own language—American Sign Language (ASL).

is some variance, the following is the distinction that is often used by those who view deafness as a cultural difference rather than as a disability:

> The lowercase "deaf" refers to those for whom deafness is primarily an audiological experience. It is mainly used to describe those who lost some or all of their hearing in early or late life, and who do not usually wish to have contact with signing Deaf communities, preferring to try to maintain their membership in the majority society in which they were socialized.
>
> "Deaf" refers to those born Deaf or deafened in early (sometimes late) childhood, for whom the sign languages, communities and cultures of the Deaf collective represents their primary experience and allegiance, many of whom perceive their experience akin to other language minorities. (Ladd, 2003, p. xvii)

Later in the chapter, we discuss more thoroughly the nature and purpose of the Deaf culture. For now, it's enough to be aware of the challenges that have been raised to the very notion of considering deafness a disability.

Prevalence

Estimates of the number of children with hearing impairment vary considerably, due to such factors as differences in definition, populations studied, and accuracy of testing. The U.S. Department of Education's statistics indicate that the public schools identify about 0.13 percent of the population from six to seventeen years of age as deaf or hard of hearing. Although the Department of Education doesn't report separate figures for the categories of deaf versus hard of hearing, there is strong evidence that students who are hard of hearing are far more prevalent than those who are deaf (Meadow-Orlans, Mertens, & Sass-Lehrer, 2003). Furthermore, some authorities believe that many children who are hard of hearing who could benefit from special education are not being served.

FOCUS ON **Concepts**

Deafness: Disability or Cultural Difference?

For the vast majority of society, it seems fairly obvious that deafness is a disability. However, it is far from obvious to many people who are deaf, who argue that instead of being considered disabled, people who are deaf should be considered a cultural minority with a language of their own: sign language (Ladd, 2003; Lane, 2002; Padden & Humphries, 1988). As Harlan Lane puts it:

> What is the source of the belief that being a Deaf person entails an inherent biological limitation? Why is deaf associated with loss rather than difference or gain (different language, different culture, etc.)? I submit that it is because the society that has elaborated the concept of deaf is largely hearing and conceptualizes deaf as a loss of hearing. Indeed, the difference in hearing of a person born Deaf and one born hearing is called "hearing loss," although the Deaf person didn't lose anything. (Lane, 2002, p. 366)

Knowing that some within the Deaf community do not believe that deafness is a disability presents an interesting and challenging problem for educators and other professionals. Should their wishes be honored? Special educators, in particular, are trained to help remediate differences and to try to make people with such differences as "normal" as possible. Would it be professionally irresponsible not to find students who are deaf eligible for special education services?

One team of authorities has acknowledged that there has been a history of viewing some behaviors, such as very expressive facial expressions and overt methods of getting someone's attention, of people who are deaf as pathological when, in fact, they are merely cultural differences (Andrews, Leigh, & Weiner, 2004). However, they also note that many within the Deaf community were advocates for equal rights protections under the Americans with Disabilities Act. They further state:

> The point to be made is that the hearing population, including professionals, need to focus on and recognize the . . . positive aspects of deaf people. . . . The pendulum has swung from the time when deafness was viewed as a pathology so severe that Alexander Graham Bell, in a paper published by the prestigious National Academy of Science, proposed that stringent eugenics should be applied to eradicate deafness through genetic and reproductive restrictions (Bell, 1883). This bears testimony to the conditions and attitudes deaf people have faced in the past. It makes understandable their desire to have their culture respected and the focus placed on their abilities, not limitations. (Andrews et al., 2004, p. 12)

An important statistic is that close to 25 percent of students who are deaf in the United States come from Hispanic-speaking homes (Gallaudet Research Institute, 2005). In addition, there are relatively large numbers of other non-English-speaking immigrants who are deaf. The relatively high numbers of students who are deaf who come from non-English-speaking families creates significant challenges for the schools. Deafness by itself makes spoken language acquisition in the native language very difficult, let alone deafness plus attempting to learn a second language.

Anatomy and Physiology of the Ear

The ear is one of the most complex organs of the body. The many elements that make up the hearing mechanism are divided into three major sections: the outer, middle, and inner ear. The outer ear is the least complex and least important for hearing; the inner ear is the most complex and most important for hearing. Figure 10.1 shows these major parts of the ear.

The Outer Ear

The outer ear consists of the auricle and the external auditory canal. The canal ends with the **tympanic membrane (eardrum)**, which is the boundary between the outer and middle ears. The **auricle** is the part of the ear that protrudes from the side of the head.

■ **Tympanic membrane (eardrum)**
The anatomical boundary between the outer and middle ears; the sound gathered in the outer ear vibrates here.

■ **Auricle**
The visible part of the ear, composed of cartilage; collects the sounds and funnels them via the external auditory canal to the eardrum.

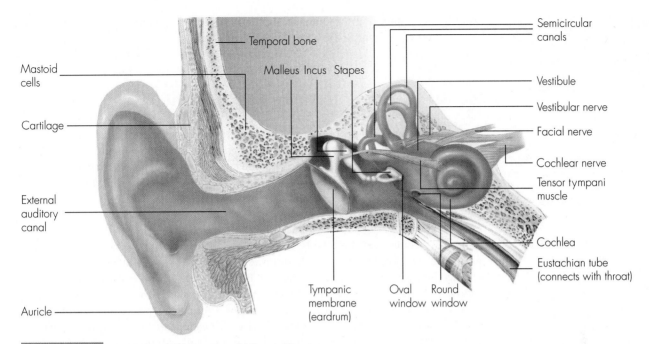

Mastoid cells

Cartilage

External auditory canal

Auricle

Temporal bone

Malleus Incus Stapes

Tympanic membrane (eardrum)

Oval window

Round window

Semicircular canals

Vestibule

Vestibular nerve

Facial nerve

Cochlear nerve

Tensor tympani muscle

Cochlea

Eustachian tube (connects with throat)

FIGURE 10.1   Illustration of the outer, middle, and inner ear.

The part that the outer ear plays in the transmission of sound is relatively minor. Sound is collected by the auricle and is funneled through the external auditory canal to the eardrum, which vibrates, sending the sound waves to the middle ear.

The Middle Ear

The middle ear comprises the eardrum and three very tiny bones (**ossicles**) called the **malleus** (hammer), **incus** (anvil), and **stapes** (stirrup), which are contained within an air-filled space. The chain of the malleus, incus, and stapes conducts the vibrations of the eardrum along to the **oval window**, which is the link between the middle and inner ears. The ossicles function to create an efficient transfer of energy from the air-filled cavity of the middle ear to the fluid-filled inner ear.

The Inner Ear

About the size of a pea, the inner ear is an intricate mechanism of thousands of moving parts. Because it looks like a maze of passageways and is highly complex, this part of the ear is often called a *labyrinth*. The inner ear is divided into two sections according to function: the vestibular mechanism and the cochlea. These sections, however, do not function totally independently of each other.

The **vestibular mechanism**, located in the upper portion of the inner ear, is responsible for the sense of balance. It's extremely sensitive to such things as acceleration, head movement, and head position. Information about movement is fed to the brain through the vestibular nerve.

By far the most important organ for hearing is the **cochlea**. Lying below the vestibular mechanism, this snail-shaped organ contains the parts necessary to convert the mechanical action of the middle ear into an electrical signal in the inner ear that is transmitted to the brain. In the normally functioning ear, sound causes the malleus, incus, and stapes of the middle ear to move. When the stapes moves, it pushes the oval window in and out, causing the fluid in the cochlea of the inner ear to flow. The movement of the fluid in turn causes a complex chain of events in the cochlea, ultimately

■ **Ossicles**
Three tiny bones (malleus, incus, and stapes) that together make possible an efficient transfer of sound waves from the eardrum to the oval window, which connects the middle ear to the inner ear.

■ **Malleus**
The hammer-shaped bone in the ossicular chain of the middle ear.

■ **Incus**
The anvil-shaped bone in the ossicular chain of the middle ear.

■ **Stapes**
The stirrup-shaped bone in the ossicular chain of the middle ear.

■ **Oval window**
The link between the middle and inner ears.

■ **Vestibular mechanism**
Located in the upper portion of the inner ear; consists of three soft, semicircular canals filled with a fluid; sensitive to head movement, acceleration, and other movements related to balance.

■ **Cochlea**
A snail-shaped organ that lies below the vestibular mechanism in the inner ear; its parts convert the sounds coming from the middle ear into electrical signals that are transmitted to the brain.

■ **Otoacoustic emissions**
Low-intensity sounds produced by the cochlea in response to auditory stimulation; used to screen hearing problems in infants and very young children.

■ **Audiologist**
An individual trained in audiology, the science dealing with hearing impairments, their detection, and remediation.

■ **Pure-tone audiometry**
A test whereby tones of various intensities and frequencies are presented to determine a person's hearing level.

■ **Hertz (Hz)**
A unit of measurement of the frequency of sound; refers to the highness or lowness of a sound.

resulting in excitation of the cochlear nerve. With stimulation of the cochlear nerve, an electrical impulse is sent to the brain, and sound is heard.

Identification of Hearing Impairment

There are four general types of hearing tests: screening tests, pure-tone audiometry, speech audiometry, and specialized tests for very young children. Depending on the characteristics of the examinee and the use to which the results will be put, the audiologist may choose to give any number of tests from any one or a combination of these four categories.

Screening Tests

There are screening tests for infants and screening tests for school-age children. An initiative by the American Academy of Pediatricians has resulted in 93% of all newborns being screened for hearing (American Academy of Pediatrics, 2007). Some of these tests involve computer technology to measure **otoacoustic emissions**. The cochlea not only receives sounds, but also emits low-intensity sound when stimulated by auditory stimuli. These sounds emitted by the cochlea are known as otoacoustic emissions, and they provide a measure of how well the cochlea is functioning (Campbell & Mullin, 2006).

Many schools have routine screening programs in the early elementary grades. These tests, especially those that are group rather than individually administered, are less accurate than tests done in an **audiologist**'s office. Children detected through screening as having possible problems are referred for more extensive evaluation.

Pure-Tone Audiometry

Pure-tone audiometry is designed to establish the individual's threshold for hearing at a variety of different frequencies. Frequency, measured in **hertz (Hz)** units, has to do with the number of vibrations per unit of time of a sound wave; the pitch is higher with more vibrations, lower with fewer. A person's threshold for hearing is simply the level at which he or she can first detect a sound; it refers to how intense a sound must be before the person detects it. As mentioned earlier, hearing sensitivity, or intensity, is measured in decibels (dB).

Pure-tone audiometers present tones of varying intensities, or decibel levels, at varying frequencies, or pitch (hertz). Audiologists are usually concerned with measuring sensitivity to sounds ranging from 0 to about 110 dB. A person with average-normal hearing is barely able to hear sounds at a sound-pressure level of 0 dB. The zero decibel level is frequently called the zero hearing-threshold level, or **audiometric zero**. Because the decibel scale is based on ratios, each increment of 10 dB is a tenfold increase in intensity. This means that 20 dB is ten times more intense than 10 dB, and 30 dB is one hundred times more intense than 10 dB. Whereas a leaf fluttering in the wind registers about 0 dB, normal conversation is about 60 dB, and, as we stated earlier, a power lawnmower is about 90 dB (American Academy of Otolaryngology—Head and Neck Surgery, 2007).

Hertz are usually measured from 125 Hz (low pitch) to 8,000 Hz (high pitch). Frequencies in speech range from 80 to 8,000 Hz, but most speech sounds have energy in the 500- to 2,000-Hz range.

Testing each ear separately, the audiologist presents a variety of tones within the range of 0 to about 110 dB and 125–8,000 Hz until she or he establishes at what level of intensity (dB) the individual can detect the tone at a number of frequencies—125 Hz, 250 Hz, 500 Hz, 1,000 Hz, 2,000 Hz, 4,000 Hz, and 8,000 Hz. For each frequency, there is a measure of degree of hearing impairment. A 50-dB hearing impairment at 500 Hz, for example, means the individual is able to detect the 500-Hz sound when it is given at an intensity level of 50 dB, whereas the average person would have heard it at 0 dB.

Speech Audiometry

Because the ability to understand speech is of prime importance, audiologists use **speech audiometry** to test a person's detection and understanding of speech. The **speech reception threshold (SRT)** is the decibel level at which one is able to understand speech. One way to measure the SRT is to present the person with a list of two-syllable words, testing each ear separately. The dB level at which he or she can understand half the words is often used as an estimate of SRT level.

Tests for Young and Hard-to-Test Children

A basic assumption for pure-tone and speech audiometry is that the individuals tested understand what is expected of them. They must be able to comprehend the instructions and show with a head nod or raised hand that they have heard the tone or word. None of this might be possible for very young children (under about four years of age) or for children with certain disabilities.

Audiologists use a number of different techniques to test the hearing of young and hard-to-test children. For example, some use the otoacoustic emission testing mentioned earlier. Others use **play audiometry**. Using pure tones or speech, the examiner teaches the child to do various activities whenever he or she hears a signal. The activities are designed to be attractive to the young child. For example, the child might be required to pick up a block, squeeze a toy, or open a book. In **tympanometry**, a rubber-tipped probe is inserted in the ear, sealing the ear canal, and the effects of pressure and sound are then measured to assess the functioning of the middle ear. Still another method is **evoked-response audiometry**, which measures changes in brain wave activity by using an electroencephalograph (EEG). It can be used during sleep, and the child can be sedated and thus not be aware that he or she is being tested.

■ **Audiometric zero**
The lowest level at which people with normal hearing can hear.

■ **Speech audiometry**
A technique that tests a person's detection and understanding of speech, rather than using pure tones to detect hearing loss.

■ **Speech reception threshold (SRT)**
The decibel level at which a person can understand speech.

■ **Play audiometry**
Use of a game-like format to test hearing of young and hard-to-test children; the examiner teaches the child to respond to sounds.

■ **Tympanometry**
A method of measuring the middle ear's response to pressure and sound.

■ **Evoked-response audiometry**
A technique involving electro-encephalograph measurement of changes in brain wave activity in response to sounds.

Tympanometry is used to assess the middle ear's response to pressure and sound.

■ **Conductive hearing
impairment**
A hearing impairment, usually mild,
resulting from malfunctioning along
the conductive pathway of the ear
(i.e., the outer or middle ear).

■ **Sensorineural hearing
impairment**
A hearing impairment, usually
severe, resulting from
malfunctioning of the inner ear.

■ **Mixed hearing impairment**
A hearing impairment resulting from
a combination of conductive and
sensorineural hearing impairments.

■ **External otitis**
An infection of the skin of the
external auditory canal; also called
swimmer's ear.

■ **Otitis media**
Inflammation of the middle ear.

Causes

We discuss causes with respect to the type of hearing impairment (conductive, sensorineural, and mixed) as well as the location of the hearing impairment (outer, middle, or inner ear).

Conductive, Sensorineural, and Mixed Hearing Impairment

Professionals classify causes of hearing impairment on the basis of the location of the problem within the hearing mechanism. There are three major classifications: conductive, sensorineural, and mixed hearing impairments. A **conductive hearing impairment** refers to an interference with the transfer of sound along the conductive pathway of the middle or outer ear. A **sensorineural hearing impairment** involves problems in the inner ear. A **mixed hearing impairment** is a combination of the two. Audiologists attempt to determine the location of the dysfunction. The first clue may be the severity of the loss. A general rule is that hearing impairments greater than 60 or 70 dB usually involve some inner-ear problem. Audiologists use the results of pure-tone testing to help determine the location of a hearing impairment, converting the results to an audiogram— a graphic representation of the weakest (lowest-decibel) sound the individual can hear at each of several frequency levels. The profile of the audiogram helps to determine whether the loss is conductive, sensorineural, or mixed.

Hearing Impairment and the Outer Ear

Although problems of the outer ear are not as serious as those of the middle or inner ear, several conditions of the outer ear can cause a person to be hard of hearing. In some children, for example, the external auditory canal does not form, resulting in a condition known as atresia. Children may also develop **external otitis**, or "swimmer's ear," an infection of the skin of the external auditory canal. Tumors of the external auditory canal are another source of hearing impairment.

Hearing Impairment and the Middle Ear

Although abnormalities of the middle ear are generally more serious than problems of the outer ear, they, too, usually result in a classification as hard of hearing rather than deaf. Most middle-ear hearing impairments occur because the mechanical action of the ossicles is interfered with in some way. Unlike inner-ear problems, most middle-ear hearing impairments are correctable with medical or surgical treatment.

The most common problem of the middle ear is **otitis media**—an infection of the middle-ear space caused by viral or bacterial factors, among others. Otitis media is common in young children—50% are diagnosed with it before their first birthday, and 80% by their third birthday (Cook & Walsh, 2005). It is linked to abnormal functioning of the eustachian tubes. If the eustachian tube malfunctions because of a respiratory viral infection, for example, it cannot do its job of ventilating, draining, and protecting the middle ear from infection. Otitis media can result in temporary conductive hearing impairment, and even these temporary losses can make the child vulnerable for having language delays (Feldman et al., 2003). If untreated, otitis media can lead to rupture of the tympanic membrane.

Hearing Impairment and the Inner Ear

The most severe hearing impairments are associated with the inner ear. In addition to problems with hearing sensitivity, a person with inner-ear hearing impairment can have additional problems, such as sound distortion, balance problems, and roaring or ringing in the ears.

Causes of inner-ear disorders can be hereditary or acquired. Genetic or hereditary factors are a leading cause of deafness in children. In fact, over 400 different varieties of hereditary deafness have been identified (Arnos, 2002). Scientists have recently identified mutation in the **connexin-26 gene** as the most common cause of congenital deafness, accounting for about 20 percent of childhood deafness (National Center for Biotechnology Information, 2007).

Acquired hearing impairments of the inner ear include those due to bacterial infections (e.g., meningitis, the second most frequent cause of childhood deafness), prematurity, viral infections (e.g., mumps and measles), anoxia (deprivation of oxygen) at birth, prenatal infections of the mother (e.g., maternal rubella, congenital syphilis, and cytomegalovirus), Rh incompatibility (which can now usually be prevented with proper prenatal care of the mother), blows to the head, side effects of some antibiotics, and excessive noise levels.

Two of the above conditions deserve special emphasis because of their relatively high prevalence. **Congenital cytomegalovirus (CMV)**, a herpes virus, deserves special mention because it's the most frequent viral cause of deafness in newborns. CMV can result in a variety of conditions, such as intellectual disabilities, visual impairment, and especially hearing impairment. In addition, repeated exposure to such things as loud music, gunshots, or machinery can result in gradual or sudden hearing impairment.

■ **Connexin-26 gene**
A gene, the mutation of which causes deafness; the leading cause of congenital deafness in children.

■ **Congenital cytomegalovirus (CMV)**
The most frequently occurring viral infection in newborns; can result in a variety of disabilities, especially hearing impairment.

Psychological and Behavioral Characteristics

Hearing impairment can have profound consequences for some aspects of a person's behavior and little or no effect on other characteristics. Consider this question: If you were forced to choose, which would you rather be—blind or deaf? On first impulse, most of us would choose deafness, probably because we rely on sight for mobility and because many of the beauties of nature are visual. But in terms of functioning in an English language-oriented society, the person who is deaf is at a much greater disadvantage than is someone who is blind.

Spoken Language and Speech Development

By far the most severely affected areas of development in the person with a hearing impairment are the comprehension and production of the English language. We stress English because it is the predominant language in the United States of those who can hear. In other words, people who are hearing impaired are generally deficient in the language used by most people of the hearing society in which they live. The distinction is important, because people who are hearing impaired can be expert in their own form of language: sign language.

Nevertheless, it's an undeniable fact that individuals with hearing impairment are at a distinct disadvantage. This is true in terms of language comprehension, language production, and speech. Speech intelligibility is linked to (1) degree of hearing impairment and (2) the age of onset of the hearing impairment. Even after intensive speech therapy, it's rare for children with prelingual profound deafness to develop intelligible speech (Marschark, 2002). Infants who are able to hear their own sounds and those of adults before becoming deaf have an advantage over those born deaf. Children who are deaf are handicapped in learning to associate the sensations they feel when they move their jaws, mouths, and tongues with the auditory sounds these movements produce. In addition, these children have a difficult time hearing adult speech, which nonimpaired children can hear and imitate.

UNDERSTANDING THE STANDARDS AND PRINCIPLES What should teachers know about the psychological and behavioral characteristics of individuals who are deaf or hard of hearing? (CEC Knowledge and Skill Standards DH2K1, DH3K3, & DH3K4)

Council for Exceptional Children

TABLE 10.1 Degrees of Hearing Impairment and Impact on Communication

Hearing Level	Descriptor	Impact on Communication
10 to 15 dB	Normal	No impact on communication
16 to 25 dB	Slight	In quiet environments, the individual has no difficulty recognizing speech, but in noisy environments, faint speech is difficult to understand.
26 to 40 dB	Mild	In quiet conversational environments in which the topic is known and vocabulary is limited, the individual has no difficulty in communicating. Faint or distant speech is difficult to hear even if the environment is quiet. Classroom discussions are challenging to follow.
41 to 55 dB	Moderate	The individual can hear conversational speech only at a close distance. Group activities, such as classroom discussions, present a communicative challenge.
56 to 70 dB	Moderate-Severe	The individual can hear only loud, clear conversational speech and has much difficulty in group situations. Often, the individual's speech is noticeably impaired though intelligible.
71 to 90 dB	Severe	The individual cannot hear conversational speech unless it is loud and even then, cannot recognize many of the words. Environmental sounds can be detected, though not always identified. The individual's speech is not altogether intelligible.
91 dB +	Profound	The individual may hear loud sounds but cannot hear conversational speech at all. Vision is the primary modality for communication. The individual's own speech, if developed at all, is not easy to understand.

Source: From Schirmer, B. R. (2001). *Psychological, social, and educational dimensions of deafness.* Boston: Allyn & Bacon. Reprinted/adapted with permission.

Table 10.1 provides general examples of the effects that various degrees of hearing impairment can have on English language development. This is only a general statement of these relationships, because many factors interact to influence language development in the child with hearing impairment.

Sign Language

Although children who are deaf face extraordinary challenges in learning a spoken language, with exposure they can easily learn **sign language**. However, historically, sign language has suffered from several misconceptions, including the belief that it is not a true language. The notion that sign language is simply a primitive, visual representation of oral language similar to mime was first challenged by the pioneering work of William Stokoe at Gallaudet University. A linguist, Stokoe submitted that, analogous to the phonemes of spoken English, each sign in ASL consists of three parts: handshape, location, and movement (Stokoe, 1960; Stokoe, Casterline, & Croneberg, 1976). For many years, Stokoe's colleagues scoffed at him, but research in several areas has proved that he was correct in asserting that sign language is a true language.

GRAMMATICAL COMPLEXITY OF SIGN LANGUAGE   Researchers have continued to refine Stokoe's (1960) work on sign language grammar, confirming its complexity. For example, like spoken language, sign language has grammatical structure at the sentence level (syntax) as well as the word or sign level (Goldin-Meadow, 2003). Handshapes, location, and movement are combined to create a grammar every bit as complex as that of spoken language.

NONUNIVERSALITY OF SIGN LANGUAGE   Contrary to popular opinion, there's not a single, universal sign language. Just as geographical or cultural separations result in different spoken languages, they also result in different sign languages. For example, people who are deaf in France communicate in French Sign Language, and those in the United States use American Sign Language (ASL). A person who is deaf visiting a foreign country has difficulties communicating with others who are deaf, much as a hearing person does. This is because sign languages, like spoken languages, evolve over time through common usage. In other words, sign language was not invented by any one person or a committee of people. The eighteenth-century French clergyman Charles-Michel de l'Eppe is often referred to as the "father of sign language." On hearing this, some people assume that de l'Eppe invented sign language. However, what he did was to take French Sign Language, which already existed within the Deaf community, and promote its usage. This is not to diminish his profound impact on advocating for using sign language in educating students with hearing impairments.

There have been several studies verifying the evolutionary aspect of sign languages. For example, twins who are deaf born to hearing parents soon begin to develop a signing system to communicate with each other. However, even after several years of such communication, their means of communication is still extremely rudimentary and nowhere near as sophisticated as ASL. The Nicaraguan Sign Language Study has also documented how sign languages change over time. (See Focus on Concepts on p. 350.)

DEVELOPMENTAL MILESTONES OF SIGN LANGUAGE   Considerable evidence indicates that children who are deaf reach the same language development milestones in sign as nondisabled children do in spoken language, and do so at about the same time (Emmorey, 2002; Goldin-Meadow, 2003). For example, they manually "babble" at about the same time as hearing infants verbally babble. And infants who are deaf sign their first words and two-word phrases at about the same time that hearing infants verbalize their first words and two-word phrases.

NEUROLOGICAL FOUNDATIONS OF SIGN LANGUAGE   Further evidence that sign language is a true language comes from studies showing that sign language has the same neurological underpinnings as does spoken language. In Chapter 6, we noted that areas within the left cerebral hemisphere of the brain are primarily responsible for language. However, we were referring to spoken language. Interestingly, using neuroimaging techniques, there is substantial evidence that the left hemisphere of the brain is also the primary site responsible for sign language acquisition and use (Campbell & MacSweeney, 2004; Emmorey, 2002; Waters et al., 2007). Also, stroke patients who are deaf are more likely to have deficits in signing if the stroke is to the left hemisphere than if the right hemisphere is damaged.

Intellectual Ability

For many years, professionals believed that the spoken language of individuals who are deaf was a sign that they also had intellectual deficiencies. As was noted earlier, however, we now know that they might not have a spoken language such as English, but if they use American Sign Language, they are using a true language with its own rules of grammar.

Any intelligence testing of people who are hearing impaired must take their English language deficiency into account. Performance tests, rather than verbal tests, especially if they are administered in sign, offer a much fairer assessment of the IQ of a person with

Reading Homework Exercise

Civil Rights Guidelines ● Go to the Homework and Exercises section in Chapter 10 of MyEducationLab and read "Deaf Students Education Services", an article provided by the Office of Civil Rights (OCR). The article offers additional policy guidance to educators of students who are deaf or hard of hearing.

FOCUS ON Concepts

The Birth and Evolution of Nicaraguan Sign Language

For years researchers have claimed that sign languages evolve naturally over time wherever there is a critical mass of persons who are deaf. Their need to communicate is a driving force in the development of their sign language. Although these scholars' conclusions were compelling, much of their work was based on retrospective analyses of sign languages that were already in existence. However, beginning in the 1970s, researchers were presented with a rare opportunity to study and document the evolution of sign language in Nicaragua:

> Before the 1970s, there was no deaf community in Nicaragua. Deaf people were largely isolated from each other, and used simple home sign systems and gesture ('mímicas') to communicate with their families and friends. The conditions necessary for a language to arise occurred in 1977, when a center for special education established a program initially attended by 50 young deaf children. The number of students at the school . . . grew to 100 by 1979, the year of the Sandinista revolution.

> In 1980, a vocational school for adolescent deaf children was opened. . . . By 1983 there were over 400 deaf students enrolled in the two schools. Initially, the language program emphasized spoken Spanish and lipreading, and the use of signs by teachers limited to fingerspelling (using simple signs to sign the alphabet). The program achieved little success, with most students failing to grasp the concept of Spanish words. However, while the children remained linguistically disconnected from their teachers, the schoolyard, the street, and the bus to and from school provided fertile ground for them to communicate with each other, and by combining gestures and elements of their home-sign systems, a pidgin-like form, and then a creole-like language rapidly emerged. They were creating their own language. This "first-stage" pidgin . . . is still used by many of those who attended the school at this time.

> Staff at the school, unaware of the development of this new language, saw the children's gesturing as mime, and as a failure to acquire Spanish. Unable to understand what the children were saying to each other, they asked for outside help, and in June 1986, the Nicaraguan Ministry of Education contacted

Judy Kegl, an American Sign Language linguist from Northeastern University. As Kegl and other researchers began to analyze the language, they noticed that the young children had taken the pidgin-like form of the older children to a higher level of complexity, with verb agreement and other conventions of grammar. This more complex sign language is now known as *Idioma de Señas de Nicaragua* (ISN). (*Nicaraguan Sign Language*, 2007)

One surprising finding has been that over time, the youngest signers have been the ones who have been most influential in changing the grammar of ISN (Kegl, Senghas, & Coppola, 1999). However, the complete development and perpetuation of ISN is dependent on a complex interplay between the generations (Senghas, 2003). The bottom line is that sign language, like spoken language, changes over time based on intergenerational interactions among users of the language.

a hearing impairment. When these tests are used, there is no difference in IQ between those who are deaf and those who are hearing (Prinz et al., 1996).

Academic Achievement

Unfortunately, most children who are deaf have large deficits in academic achievement. Reading ability, which relies heavily on English language skills and is probably the most important area of academic achievement, is most affected. For example, the average student who is hearing impaired leaves school with a deficit of at least five years in reading (Kyle & Harris, 2006). Even in math, their best academic subject, students with hearing impairment trail their hearing peers by substantial margins.

Several studies have demonstrated that children who are deaf who have parents who are deaf have higher reading achievement and better language skills than do those who have hearing parents. There is not universal agreement on why this is the case (Powers, 2003). However, many authorities speculate that it's because of the positive influence of sign language. Parents who are deaf might be able to communicate better with their children through the use of ASL, providing the children with needed support. In addition, children who have parents who are deaf are more likely to be proficient in ASL, and ASL can aid these children in learning written English and reading.

A supportive home environment is associated with higher achievement in students who are deaf. Families that are more involved in their child's education, seek knowledge about their child's condition to provide guidance, have high expectations for achievement, don't try to overprotect their child, and participate along with their child in the Deaf community are likely to have higher-achieving children (Schirmer, 2001).

Social Adjustment

Social development and personality development in the hearing population depend heavily on communication, and the situation is no different for those who are deaf. The hearing person has little difficulty finding people with whom to communicate. The person who is deaf, however, can face problems in finding others with whom he or she can converse. Studies have demonstrated that many students who are deaf are at risk for loneliness (Cambra, 1996; Charlson, Strong, & Gold, 1992). Two factors are important in considering the possible isolation of students who are deaf: inclusion and hearing status of the parents.

Researchers have shown that in inclusionary settings, very little interaction typically occurs between students who are deaf and those who are not (Kluwin, Stinson, & Colarossi, 2002). Furthermore, in inclusionary settings, students who are deaf feel more emotionally secure if they have other students who are deaf with whom they can communicate (Stinson & Whitmire, 1992). This is not always possible, however, because of the low prevalence of hearing impairment. Some interventions using cooperative learning have been successful in increasing the interactions between students who are deaf and their hearing peers (Kluwin et al., 2002).

Some authorities believe that the child who is deaf and has hearing parents runs a greater risk of being unhappy than the child who has parents who also are deaf. This is because many hearing parents, as well as hard-of-hearing parents, don't become proficient in ASL (Mitchell & Karchmer, 2005) and are unable to communicate with their children easily. Given that about 95 percent of children who are deaf have hearing parents (Mitchell & Karchmer, 2004), this problem in communication might be critical.

The need for social interaction is probably most influential in leading many people with hearing impairment to associate primarily with others with hearing impairment. If their parents are deaf, children who are deaf are usually exposed to other deaf families from an early age. Nonetheless, many people who are deaf end up, as adults, socializing predominantly with others who are deaf, even if they have hearing parents and even if they didn't come into contact as children with many other children who were deaf. This phenomenon of socializing with others who are deaf is attributable to the influence of the Deaf culture.

THE DEAF CULTURE   In the past, most professionals viewed isolation from the hearing community on the part of many people who are deaf as a sign of social pathology. Now most professionals agree with the many people who are deaf who believe in the value of having their own Deaf culture. They view this culture as a natural condition emanating from the common bond of sign language.

Reading Homework Exercise

Deaf Culture ● Go to the Homework and Exercises section in Chapter 10 of MyEducationLab and read the article "Comparative Chart: Deaf and Ethnic Cultures", which poses several questions about Deaf culture.

UNDERSTANDING THE STANDARDS AND PRINCIPLES   How might a family's strong belief in Deaf culture positively or negatively affect the education of a student who is deaf or hard of hearing? (CEC Knowledge and Skill Standards DH1K2 & DH1K4)

Council for Exceptional Children

Whereas professionals once viewed isolation from the hearing community as a sign of social pathology, many now recognize the value of having a Deaf culture.

The unifying influence of sign language is the first of six factors noted by Reagan (1990) as demarcating the Deaf community as a true culture:

1. *Linguistic differentiation* is at the heart of Deaf culture; many within the Deaf community view themselves as bilingual, with individuals possessing varying degrees of fluency in ASL and English (Ladd, 2003; Padden & Humphries, 2005). People who are deaf continually shift between ASL and English as well as between the Deaf culture and that of the hearing (Padden, 1996).

2. *Attitudinal deafness* refers to whether a person thinks of himself or herself as deaf. It might not have anything to do with a person's hearing acuity. For example, a person with a relatively mild hearing impairment might think of herself or himself as deaf more readily than does someone with a profound hearing impairment.

3. *Behavioral norms* within the Deaf community differ from those in hearing society. A few examples of these norms, according to Lane, Hoffmeister, and Bahan (1996), are that people who are deaf value informality and physical contact in their interactions with one another, often giving each other hugs when greeting and departing, and their leave-takings often take much longer than those of hearing society. Also, they are likely to be frank in their discussions, not hesitating to get directly to the point of what they want to communicate.

4. *Endogamous marriage* patterns are evident from surveys showing rates of ingroup marriage as high as 90 percent. The Deaf community tends to frown on "mixed marriages" between people who are deaf and those who are hearing.

5. *Historical awareness* of significant people and events pertaining to people who are deaf permeates the Deaf community. They are often deferential to elders and value their wisdom and knowledge pertaining to Deaf traditions.

6. *Voluntary organizational networks* are abundant in the Deaf community. Some examples are the National Association of the Deaf, the World Games for the Deaf (Deaf Olympics), and the National Theatre of the Deaf.

INTERNET RESOURCES

Visit the National Theatre of the Deaf's Website to look for upcoming performances in your area: www.NTD.org

CONCERN FOR THE EROSION OF DEAF CULTURE   Many within the Deaf community and some professionals are concerned that the cultural status of children who are deaf is in peril (Lane et al., 1996; Padden & Humphries, 2005). They believe that the increase in inclusion is eroding the cultural values of the Deaf culture. In the past, much of Deaf culture was passed down from generation to generation through contacts made at residential schools, but if they attend local schools, today's children who are deaf may have little contact with other children who are deaf. Many authorities now recommend that schools involve members of the Deaf community in developing classes in Deaf history and culture for students who are deaf who attend local schools.

DEAF ACTIVISM: THE GALLAUDET EXPERIENCE   Considering all groups with exceptionalities, those who are deaf have been one of the most, if not the most, outspoken about their rights. Even though some might think that the Deaf community is in peril of losing its identity, it's still very active in advocating a variety of social, educational, and medical policies. Two good examples of this activism are Gallaudet's Deaf President Now and Unity for Gallaudet Movements (see the Personal Perspectives below) and the debate over cochlear implants.

INTERNET RESOURCES

Two examples of publications devoted to issues of concern to the Deaf community are the magazines *Silent News* and *Deaf Life*. The former also has a Web version (www.silentnews.com/index.html). On the site, it presents itself as "a good glimpse into the Deaf community." Deaf Life's Website at www.deaflife.com has chat rooms for adults and just for children.

Personal PERSPECTIVES

Gallaudet's Deaf President Now and Unity for Gallaudet Movements

Deaf President Now Movement

A prominent and historic example of Deaf activism occurred in the 1980s at Gallaudet University, a liberal arts college for the deaf and hard of hearing, when students and faculty protested the board of trustees' selection of a hearing president. Since its founding in 1864, Gallaudet had never had a deaf president. But when on March 6, 1988 the trustees announced the appointment of yet another hearing president, faculty and students took to the streets and halls in protest. Having successfully shut down the university, organizers of the Deaf President Now Movement issued four demands:

1. that a deaf president be named immediately;
2. that the chair of the board resign;
3. that the board, which consisted of seventeen hearing and four deaf members, be reconfigured to include a majority of deaf members; and
4. that there be no reprisals.

After eight days of protest, the board acceded to all four demands, the most significant of which was the naming of a long-time faculty member who was deaf: I. King Jordan as president of the university.

Unity for Gallaudet Movement

Upon Jordan's retirement, the board announced on May 1, 2006, the appointment of the vice president of the university, Jane K. Fernandes, to be Jordan's successor. Students and faculty once again protested, holding rallies and blocking entrances to the school. The protests continued during the Fall semester, with over a hundred students being arrested for blocking entrances.

Given that Fernandes is also deaf, accounts vary as to why there was such a negative reaction (Tapper & Sandell, 2006; Takruri, 2006). Some cited what they considered a flawed, noninclusive selection process, but many pointed to concerns that Fernandes was not "deaf enough." They objected to her having stated that she wanted to be more inclusive by admitting more students with cochlear implants as well as those who had not grown up learning sign language. (Fernandes herself reportedly grew up using speech and speechreading and didn't learn sign language until she was in her 20s.)

In October 2006, Fernandes was removed as president by the board. In December, 2006, the board named Robert Davilla as interim president for two years. Deaf since the age of eight, Davilla has previously served in a number of high-level government and university positions.

INTERNET RESOURCES

The National Association of the Deaf had for years been opposed to cochlear implants. However, in the fall of 2000, it issued a policy statement that was much more neutral in tone; see www.nad.org/ ciposition

The Public Broadcasting Service (PBS) has established an excellent Website focused on the documentary "Sound and Fury": www.pbs. org/wnet/soundandfury

Although the site focuses on the issue of cochlear implants, it also contains useful information pertaining to the Deaf culture and links to other interesting Websites.

■ **Cochlear implantation**
A surgical procedure that allows people who are deaf to hear some environmental sounds; an external coil fitted on the skin by the ear picks up sound from a microphone worn by the person and transmits it to an internal coil implanted in the bone behind the ear, which carries it to an electrode implanted in the cochlea of the inner ear.

DEAF ACTIVISM: THE COCHLEAR IMPLANT DEBATE   Deaf activists have also been aggressive in attacking what they consider an oppressive medical and educational establishment. An example of just how much this segment of the Deaf community is at odds with many professionals is its opposition to the medical procedure of cochlear implantation. This procedure involves surgically implanting electronic elements under the skin behind the ear and in the inner ear. A small microphone worn behind the ear picks up sounds and sends them to a small computerized speech processor worn by the person. The speech processor sends coded signals to an external coil worn behind the ear, which sends them through the skin to the implanted internal coil. The internal coil then sends the signals to electrodes implanted in the inner ear, and these signals are sent on to the auditory nerve. (See Figure 10.2.)

Ever since the U.S. Food and Drug Administration approved the use of cochlear implants for young children in 1990, there have been thousands of operations both in the United States and the rest of the world, especially Australia. The technology is advancing rapidly, but not everyone with hearing impairment is a candidate for implantation. Generally, it is recommended for those who have a severe to profound sensorineural loss in both ears. In children, most implants occur between the ages of two and six years (National Institute on Deafness and Other Communication Disorders, 2006). The Food and Drug Administration has not approved cochlear implants for children under the age of twelve months.

Although the manufacturers of these devices, as well as many within the medical community, view cochlear implants as miraculous, many within the Deaf community oppose them, viewing the process as physically and culturally invasive:

> I expect that most Americans would agree that our society should not seek the scientific tools or use them, if available, to change a child biologically so he or she will belong to the majority rather than the minority—even if we believe that this biological engineering might reduce the burdens the child will bear as a member of a minority. Even if we could take children destined to be members of the African American, or Hispanic American, or Native American, or Deaf American communities and convert them with bio-power into white, Caucasian, hearing males—even if we could, we should not. We should likewise refuse cochlear implants for young deaf children even if the devices were perfect. (Lane, 1992, p. 237)

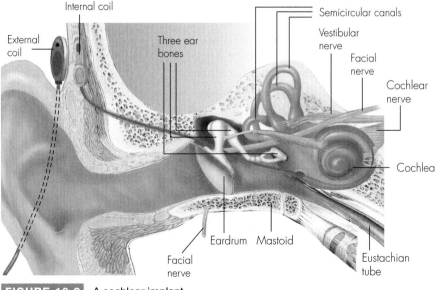

FIGURE 10.2   A cochlear implant

The Deaf community has not had to confront the issue raised by Lane: whether to have the surgery even if it were to result in perfect hearing. Although perfect hearing through cochlear implants might not be just around the corner, enormous strides in technology have resulted in many more cases than ever before of greatly improved hearing for people with implants. These more positive results are making it more difficult for those who are deaf, or their parents, to decide whether to choose cochlear implantation. One problem is that in order to reap the benefits of improved hearing from the implant, many professionals recommend intensive oral instruction. As we discuss later, many within the Deaf community favor manual (ASL) over oral teaching methods. So they are concerned that those with implants may not gain enough exposure to sign language. Also, results still vary enormously from individual to individual. (See the Success Stories on pp. 356–357 for an example of a child whose cochlear implant has been relatively successful.) In the case of children, research shows that the earlier the transplant takes place, the better the resulting ability to hear and speak (Nicholas & Geers, 2006; Spencer, 2004). But the majority of children with implants still don't attain hearing and speaking skills within the range of hearing children (Spencer). Again, this is a far cry from a cure, but for some, it's enough of an improvement to elect to undergo the surgery.

DEAF ACTIVISM: THE GENETIC ENGINEERING DEBATE   Ironically, deaf activists can also put scientific discoveries to use to help sustain the Deaf culture but not without facing thorny ethical concerns (Johnston, 2005; Moores, 2002). Earlier, we noted the discovery of the mutation of the connexin-26 gene as the leading cause of deafness in children. Parents could use such information to increase their chances of having a baby who is deaf. (Contrary to what many in hearing society assume, when both parents are deaf, they usually would prefer to have a baby who is deaf.) For example, they could use **in vitro fertilization**, a procedure that is usually used to help infertile couples, whereby egg cells from the mother are fertilized in the laboratory and then placed in the mother's uterus. Parents who are deaf could choose to retain only fertilized eggs that have the connexin-26 mutation. Another option that actually has been used by deaf couples is artificial insemination by a donor who has a high probability of carrying genes leading to deafness (Mundy, 2002; Sanghavi, 2006).

■ **In vitro fertilization**
The procedure of removing eggs from the mother, fertilizing them with the father's sperm in a laboratory, then returning them to the mother's uterus; used to help infertile couples conceive.

Educational Considerations

Formidable problems face the educator who works with students who are deaf or hard of hearing. As we would expect, one major problem is communication. Dating back to the sixteenth century, there has been a raging debate about how individuals who are deaf should converse (Lane, 1984). This controversy is sometimes referred to as the **oralism–manualism debate**, to represent two very different points of view: oralism favors teaching people who are deaf to speak; manualism advocates the use of some kind of manual communication. Manualism was the preferred method until the middle of the nineteenth century, when oralism began to gain predominance. Currently, most professionals recommend both oral and manual methods in what is referred to as a **total communication approach** (Andrews et al., 2004). However, many within the Deaf community believe that even the total communication approach is inadequate, and they advocate for a **bicultural-bilingual approach**, which promotes ASL as a first language and instruction in the Deaf culture.

We first discuss the major techniques that make up the oral approach and the oral portion of the total communication approach; then we explore total communication, followed by a discussion of the bicultural-bilingual approach.

■ **Oralism–manualism debate**
The controversy over whether the goal of instruction for students who are deaf should be to teach them to speak or to teach them to use sign language.

■ **Total communication approach**
An approach for teaching students with hearing impairment that blends oral and manual techniques.

■ **Bicultural-bilingual approach**
An approach for teaching students with hearing impairment that stresses teaching American Sign Language as a first language and English as a second language and promotes the teaching of Deaf culture.

Success Stories

Bailea, a kindergartener with a cochlear implant, benefits from early intervention and co-teaching

Special Educator Heather Miles: "Set expectations high and really work to meet them."

Five-year-old Bailea Kohler uses a cochlear implant in an inclusive kindergarten class.

These are the keys to her success:
- intensive early intervention and structured routines
- relentless focus on teamwork
- specific interventions in auditory-verbal learning

"I just love Bailea," says special educator Heather Miles. "She's strong willed and very curious about things." Bailea's father says she's an energetic and happy five-year-old. "She always has bumps and bruises from trying to keep up with her older sister, Madison." Bailea was born deaf to hearing parents, Stacia and Mike Kohler. She has a cochlear implant and she has benefited from intensive, relentless, and specific special education.

● **Intensive Early Intervention and Structured Routines** At first Bailea's doctors predicted her hearing would improve. "When she failed to hear doors slam or dogs bark, I reached out to everybody I could to find the best for her," says Stacia. When she was twelve months old Bailea started intensive speech and language services three days a week at the Saginaw Hearing Center, in Saginaw, Michigan. An audiologist recommended a cochlear implant, but before surgery Bailea was required to wear hearing aids for six months. "It was a constant fight and she tried to pull them out," recalls Stacia. "Bailea had surgery to implant the cochlear device when she was nineteen months old. Her hearing specialist drove three hours to the University of Michigan in Ann Arbor, in an ice storm to visit Bailea in the hospital. The professionals who worked with us were like family."

Structured routines have been important. "Bailea likes being in charge," says Heather, and she started kindergarten at age five with temper tantrums when she couldn't make her needs known. Classmates were positive models, but structured interactions and instruction helped her communicate. "We use a picture schedule to provide students with visual supports for learning. We also use tape to assign places for students to sit on the carpet during group time. Bailea's special place is near the front so she can scoot away if she needs to." Bailea's language skills are not strong and her attention span is short in group settings. "Sometimes," says Heather, "the loudness of talking and laughter can get a bit much and she needs to get away."

● **Relentless Focus on Teamwork** Coordinated teamwork is critical to Bailea's success. Heather Miles has collaborated for seven years with Bailea's kindergarten teacher, Mrs. English, who also has experience as a special educator. Their classroom is equipped with a portable FM speaker that amplifies sounds for any of the nineteen students who might benefit. Heather spends two hours daily with Mrs. English, co-teaching reading and language arts in the morning, and writing in the afternoon. Sometimes Bailea joins Heather in a larger group for Direct

---

■ **Auditory-verbal approach**
Part of the oral approach to teaching students who are hearing impaired; stresses teaching the person to use his or her remaining hearing as much as possible; heavy emphasis on use of amplification; heavy emphasis on teaching speech.

■ **Auditory-oral approach**
An oral approach to teaching students who are hearing impaired; like auditory-verbal approach, stresses use of remaining hearing, amplification, and speech, but also includes use of visual cues.

Oral Approaches: The Auditory-Verbal Approach and the Auditory-Oral Approach

THE AUDITORY-VERBAL APPROACH The **auditory-verbal approach** focuses exclusively on using audition to improve speech and language development (Andrews et al., 2004). It assumes that most children with hearing impairment have some residual hearing that can be used to their benefit. It relies heavily on amplification technology, such as hearing aids and cochlear implants, and stresses that this amplification technology should be instituted at as young an age as possible. There is also a heavy emphasis on speech training. Because children with hearing impairments have problems hearing their own speech or that of others and often hear speech in a distorted fashion, they must be explicitly instructed in how to produce speech sounds.

THE AUDITORY-ORAL APPROACH The **auditory-oral approach** is similar to the auditory-verbal approach, but it also stresses the use of visual cues, such as speechreading

Instruction (discussed in Chapter 6), and other times they work together in a separate classroom. Both teachers meet monthly with the speech and hearing specialists to ensure everyone is working toward the same goals. An audiologist sees Bailea weekly in the classroom and regularly attends team meetings. Says Heather, "She makes practical suggestions by telling us where the FM reception is best in the room, and she observes Bailea's behavior to monitor the volume and functioning of the cochlear implant." School personnel aren't responsible for adjusting implanted devices, so Bailea's parents let the medical team at the University of Michigan know about any problems that might be occurring with the implant in the classroom.

● **Specific Interventions for Auditory-Verbal Learning** The Kohlers credit the team with helping Bailea develop the desire to hear. At home eleven-year-old sister Madison patiently helps Bailea to communicate. It hasn't been easy. The fragile cochlear device breaks easily—three times in recent months— but her new implant is smaller and less bulky than the original device. The new technology seems to make a positive difference in her ability to distinguish sounds, says Heather. "When I work with her individually, she can develop a thought and together we stretch the words into a sentence. Now, she can write phonetically in a manner that most people can read." Bailea's language skills are delayed, so Heather monitors the rate with which she speaks and takes extra time to explain things in detail. "Bailea mimics what others are doing but she doesn't always grasp the concept. If directions call for using scissors to cut out three characters and put them in the story order, she would look at others cutting, but not really understand what she's supposed to do next." Heather uses a variety of assessments (see section on progress monitoring on p. 364) at least every two weeks to monitor Bailea's early literacy skills and to chart her progress. "We set expectations high," she says, "and really work to meet them."

CEC'S STANDARDS: PAVING THE WAY TO SUCCESS

ASSESS YOUR STEPS TO SUCCESS in meeting the CEC Knowledge and Skill Base for All Beginning Special Education Teachers of Students Who Are Deaf and Hard of Hearing. Use the following questions to reflect on the growth of your own professional knowledge, skills, and dispositions.

REFLECTING ON YOUR OWN PROFESSIONAL DEVELOPMENT

If you were Bailea's teacher . . .

- What are some areas about educating students who are deaf and hard of hearing that you would need to know more about?
- What are some specific skills that would help you address her academic and behavioral challenges?
- What personal dispositions do you think are most important for you to develop in teaching students with hearing loss?

Using the CEC Standards:

- What are some ways that families influence the overall development of the individual who is deaf or hard of hearing? DH3K3
- How would you design a classroom environment that maximizes opportunities for visual and/or auditory learning for individuals who are deaf or hard of hearing? DH5S5
- What are some sources of specialized materials for individuals who are deaf or hard of hearing? DH4K1

● *By Jean B. Crockett*

---

and cued speech. Sometimes inappropriately called *lipreading*, **speechreading** involves teaching children to use visual information to understand what is being said to them. *Speechreading* is a more accurate term than *lipreading* because the goal is to teach students to attend to a variety of stimuli in addition to specific movements of the lips. For example, proficient speechreaders read contextual stimuli so that they can anticipate certain types of messages in certain types of situations. They use facial expressions to help them interpret what is being said to them. Even the ability to discriminate the various speech sounds that flow from a person's mouth involves attending to visual cues from the tongue and jaw as well as the lips. For example, to learn to discriminate among vowels, the speech-reader concentrates on cues related to the degree of jaw opening and lip shaping.

Cued speech is a way of augmenting speechreading. In cued speech, the individual uses hand shapes to represent specific sounds while speaking. Eight hand shapes are cues for certain consonants, and four serve as cues for vowels. Cued speech helps the speechreader differentiate between sounds that look alike on the lips. Although it has some devoted advocates, cued speech is not used widely in the United States.

■ **Speechreading**
A method that involves teaching children to use visual information from a number of sources to understand what is being said to them; more than just lipreading, which uses only visual clues arising from the movement of the mouth in speaking.

■ **Cued speech**
A method to aid speechreading in people with hearing impairment; the speaker uses hand shapes to represent sounds.

■ **Homophenes**
Sounds that are different but that look the same with regard to movements of the face and lips (i.e., visible articulatory patterns).

■ **Signing English systems**
Used simultaneously with oral methods in the total communication approach to teaching students who are deaf; different from American Sign Language because they maintain the same word order as spoken English.

■ **Fingerspelling**
Spelling the English alphabet by using various finger positions on one hand.

CRITICISMS OF THE ORAL APPROACH   Several authorities have been critical of using an exclusively oral approach with students who have hearing impairment (Lane et al., 1996; Padden & Humphries, 2005). In particular, they object to the deemphasis of sign language in this approach, especially for children who are deaf. These critics assert that it's unreasonable to assume that many children with severe or profound degrees of hearing impairment have enough hearing to be of use. Therefore, denying these children access to ASL is denying them access to a language to communicate.

Critics of the oral approach also point out that speechreading is extremely difficult and that good speechreaders are rare (Andrews et al., 2004). It's easy to overlook some of the factors that make speechreading difficult. For instance, speakers produce many sounds with little obvious movement of the mouth. Another issue is that the English language has many **homophenes**—different sounds that are visually identical when spoken. For example, a speechreader cannot distinguish among the pronunciations of *p*, *b*, and *m*. There is also variability among speakers in how they produce sounds. Finally, such factors as poor lighting, rapid speaking, and talking with one's head turned are further reasons why good speechreading is a rare skill (Menchel, 1988).

Total Communication

As we noted previously, most schools have adopted the total communication approach, a combination of oral and manual methods. Total communication involves the simultaneous use of speech with one of what are known as **signing English systems**—approaches that professionals have devised for teaching people who are deaf to communicate. **Fingerspelling**, the representation of letters of the English alphabet by finger positions, is also used occasionally to spell out certain words (see Figure 10.3).

There has been growing dissatisfaction with total communication among some professionals and by many within the Deaf community. The focus of the criticism has been on the use of signing English systems rather than ASL. Unlike ASL, signing English systems maintain the same word order as spoken English, thereby making it possible to

A total communication approach blends oral and manual methods.

A B C D E F
G H I J K L
M N O P Q R
S T U V W X
Y Z AND

FIGURE 10.3 Fingerspelling alphabet

speak and sign at the same time. Defenders of signing English systems state that the correspondence in word order between signing English systems and English helps students to learn English better. Advocates of ASL assert that the use of signing English systems is too slow and awkward to be of much benefit in learning English. They argue that word order is not the critical element in teaching a person to use and comprehend English.

Advocates of ASL believe that fluency in ASL provides students with a rich background of information that readies them for the learning of English. Furthermore, they argue that ASL is the natural language of people who are deaf and that it should be fostered because it is the most natural and efficient way for students who are deaf to learn about the world. Unlike ASL, signing English systems are not true languages. They have been invented by one or a few people in a short period of time, whereas true sign

UNDERSTANDING THE STANDARDS AND PRINCIPLES What are the pros and cons of the total communication approach? (CEC Knowledge and Skill Standards DH6K4, DH6K5, & DH6K7)

Council for Exceptional Children

languages such as ASL have evolved over several generations of users. Many of the critics of the total communication approach advocate the bicultural-bilingual approach.

The Bicultural-Bilingual Approach

Although there are several variations of the bicultural-bilingual approach, most of them contain these three features (Schirmer, 2001):

1. ASL is considered the primary language, and English is considered the secondary language.
2. People who are deaf play an important role in the development of the program and its curriculum.
3. The curriculum includes instruction in Deaf culture.

Bilingual education for students who are deaf can be structured so that ASL is learned first, followed by English, or the two can be taught simultaneously. In addition, children who are deaf born to hearing parents usually learn English first before they are exposed to ASL in a bilingual program.

Lending credence to those advocating ASL instruction are studies showing a relationship between ASL usage and academic performance in English (Wilbur, 2000). However, research directly bearing on the efficacy of bicultural-bilingual programs is in its infancy. Even though at least one study has found evidence for the effectiveness of bicultural-bilingual programming (Andrews, Ferguson, Roberts, & Hodges, 1997), it is probably safest to conclude that

> No fail-safe, success-guaranteed method exists for educating deaf children, though periodically through the history of deaf education various methods have been proposed as the pedagogical solution. In the 1960s and 1970s, total communication was considered to be the answer. In the 1980s and 1990s, bilingual education was touted as the solution. With the increase in cochlear implants, greater numbers of children are being educated orally/aurally . . . and oral/aural approaches have seen renewed interest. Ultimately, the profession may recognize that only a range of approaches can meet the needs of a range of deaf children. (Schirmer, 2001, p. 203)

Technological Advances

A number of technological advances have made it easier for persons with hearing impairment to communicate with and/or have access to information from the hearing world. This technological explosion has primarily involved five areas: hearing aids, captioning, telephones, computer-assisted instruction, and the Internet. The Responsive Instruction on page 361 provides advice on selecting and integrating assistive technology.

HEARING AIDS   There are three main types of hearing aids: those worn behind the ear, those worn in the ear, and those worn farther down in the canal of the ear. The behind-the-ear hearing aid is the most powerful and is therefore used by those with the most severe hearing impairment. It's also the one that children most often use because it can be used with FM systems that are available in some classrooms. With an FM system, the teacher wears a wireless lapel microphone, and the student wears an FM receiver (about the size of a cell phone). The student hears the amplified sound either through a hearing aid that comes attached to the FM receiver or by attaching a behind-the-ear hearing aid to the FM receiver. Whether a student will be able to benefit from a hearing aid by itself depends a great deal on the acoustic qualities of the classroom.

UNDERSTANDING THE STANDARDS AND PRINCIPLES What are the features of a bicultural-bilingual approach? Does research support its effectiveness? (CEC Knowledge and Skill Standards DH6K4, DH6K5, & DH6K7)

Council for Exceptional Children

Video Homework Exercise

Technology • Go to the Homework and Exercises section in Chapter 10 of MyEducationLab to watch the video "SmartBoards for Students with Hearing Impairments."

Meeting the Needs of Students Who Are Deaf or Hard of Hearing

Assistive Technology

WHAT IS ASSISTIVE TECHNOLOGY?

Assistive technology is defined under IDEA as "any item, piece of equipment or product system, whether acquired commercially off the shelf, modified, or customized, that is used to increase, maintain, or improve the functional capabilities of children with disabilities" (Federal Register, August 19, 1991, p. 41272). For students with hearing impairments, assistive technology can offer support for receptive and expressive communication, access to visual instruction, and individualization of instruction critical for their success. To make the most of assistive technology in the classroom, teachers need to be aware of how the technology can be integrated into the context of instruction.

TYPES OF ASSISTIVE TECHNOLOGY

Students who are deaf or hard of hearing may benefit from the following types of assistive technology:

- Amplification devices such as hearing aids or frequency modulated (FM) systems
- Computer-assisted instruction
- Captioned programming
- Telecommunication devices for the deaf (TDD)
- Speech digitizers and synthesizers

CLASSROOM APPLICATIONS

Before introducing assistive technology in the classroom, the teacher should identify instructional goals for the student. Guiding questions such as "What is it the student cannot do as a result of his or her disability?" and "Would assistive technology enable the student to meet the goal?" facilitate the identification of instructionally relevant technologies (Chambers, 1997).

When selecting technology, teachers should consider whether there is a low-tech alternative that would meet the same instructional goals, the level of support necessary to maintain the technology, the skills required to appropriately use the device, and the potential availability of the technology in other environments outside of the classroom (Garrick-Duhaney & Duhaney, 2000).

Finally, teachers should plan for meaningful integration of the technology into the teaching–learning process. Consideration of environmental demands and task expectations helps teachers to determine where and when to use the technologies. Questions can include the following:

- What is the physical arrangement?
- What is the instructional context?
- What supports already exist in the environment?
- What activities support the student's curriculum?
- What are the critical elements of the instructional activities?
- How might the activities be modified to accommodate the student's needs?
- How might the technology support the student's participation in those activities? (Chambers, 1997)

● *By Kristin L. Sayeski*

Although hearing aids are an integral part of educational programming, some children who are deaf can't benefit from them because of the severity and/or nature of the hearing impairment. Generally, hearing aids make sounds louder, not clearer, so if a person's hearing is distorted, a hearing aid will merely amplify the distorted sound.

It is critical for the student, parents, and teachers to work together to ensure the maximum effectiveness of any device. This means that the teacher should be familiar with its proper operation and maintenance.

TELEVISION, VIDEO, AND MOVIE CAPTIONING At one time, viewers needed a special decoder to access captioned programs. Federal law now requires that TVs over thirteen inches screen size must contain a chip to allow one to view captions without a decoder—and also stipulates that virtually all new programming must be captioned. However, advocates such as the National Association of the Deaf continue to press for more and better captioning. One need only watch a live news show on TV to see how inaccurate some of the captions can be.

Technological advances such as this state of the art video telephone system allow students who are deaf to converse with friends over dedicated ISDN lines using their primary language, American Sign Language.

Many videotapes and DVDs available from rental stores are captioned as well. The most recent innovation in captioning is the Rear Window captioning system, which displays captions on transparent acrylic panels that movie patrons can attach to the cup holders on their seats. The captions are actually displayed in reverse at the rear of the theater, and the viewer sees them reflected on his or her acrylic screen.

TELEPHONE ADAPTATIONS   At one time, people with hearing impairments had problems using telephones, either because their hearing impairment was too great or because of acoustic feedback (noise caused by closeness of the telephone receiver to their hearing aids). However, this has changed since the invention of **text telephones (TT)**, sometimes referred to as TTYs (teletypes) or TDDs (telecommunication devices for the deaf). A person can use a TT connected to a telephone to type a message to anyone else who has a TT, and a special phone adaptation allows someone without a TT to use the pushbuttons on his or her phone to "type" messages to someone with a TT.

The federal government now requires each state to have a relay service that allows a person with a TT to communicate with anyone through an operator, who conveys the message to a person who does not have a TT. The TT user can carry on a conversation with the non-TT user, or the TT user can leave a message.

Another expanding technology is **video relay service (VRS)**. VRS enables people who are deaf to communicate with hearing people through a sign language interpreter serving as an intermediary. For example, the person who is deaf can communicate in sign over television or video camera over the Internet to the interpreter, who then speaks to the hearing caller and also signs the response back to the person who is deaf.

COMPUTER-ASSISTED INSTRUCTION   The explosion of microcomputer and related technology (e.g., DVDs, CD-ROMs) is expanding learning capabilities for people who are deaf and their families. For example, visual displays of speech patterns on a computer screen can help someone with hearing impairment to learn speech. DVD programs showing people sign are also available for use in learning ASL.

■ **Text telephone (TT)**
A device connected to a telephone by a special adapter; allows communication over the telephone between people who are hearing impaired and those with hearing; sometimes referred to as a TTY (teletype) or TDD (telecommunication device for the deaf).

■ **Video relay service (VRS)**
A service, using a sign language interpreter, a video camera or computer, and an Internet connection, that allows persons who are deaf to communicate with those who are hearing.

Another example of computer-based technology is C-Print. With C-Print, a hearing person, using an abbreviation system that reduces keystrokes, transcribes on a computer what is being said by, for example, someone lecturing. The student who is deaf can read a real-time text display on her or his computer as well as receive a printout of the text at a later time.

Researchers are also working on using gesture recognition technology to help young children who are deaf practice ASL skills (Brashear et al., 2006; Lee, Henderson, & Brashear, 2005). The child sits in front of a monitor and wears special wireless gloves whose movement can be monitored by the computer to determine how accurately the child is signing.

THE INTERNET   The information superhighway has opened up a variety of communication possibilities for people who are deaf. For example, electronic mail allows people who are deaf to communicate with one another as well as with hearing individuals. People who are deaf may also subscribe to e-mail lists, connect to newsgroups or Web-based boards, and participate in chat rooms devoted to deafness, along with a multitude of other subjects. The ever-expanding World Wide Web provides access to a multitude of information sources.

In addition to providing people who are deaf with a way to access information, educators can use the Internet to help students who are deaf practice reading and writing skills. For instance, teachers can set up newsgroups, mailing lists, Web boards, or Weblogs through which students can communicate with others in the class, the school, or worldwide.

Service Delivery Models

Students who are deaf or hard of hearing can be found in settings ranging from general education classrooms to residential institutions. Since the mid-1970s, more and more of these students have been attending local schools in self-contained classes, resource rooms, and general education classes. Currently, about 86 percent of students with hearing impairments between the ages of six and twenty-one attend classes in local schools, and 43 percent spend the vast majority of their time in the general education classroom (U.S. Department of Education, 2005). Even though students with hearing impairment are now included to a very high degree in general education classrooms, they are still served in special schools or residential settings more than most other disability categories, with about 7 percent in the former and 7 percent in the latter type of placement.

Many people within the Deaf community have been critical of the degree of inclusion that is occurring (Aldersley, 2002; Lane et al., 1996; Padden & Humphries, 2005; Siegel, 2000). They argue that residential schools (and, to a lesser extent, day schools) have been a major influence in fostering the concept of a Deaf culture and the use of ASL. Inclusion, they believe, forces students who are deaf to lose their Deaf identity and places them in a hearing and speaking environment in which it is almost impossible for them to succeed. In particular, critics of inclusion argue that when a student who is deaf is placed in a setting with nondisabled children, he or she is usually the only student with a hearing impairment in the class. This lack of a "critical mass" of students who are deaf can lead to two interrelated problems: a lack of peers with whom the student who is deaf can communicate and a high degree of social isolation. There is some evidence that this social isolation is experienced most acutely at the middle and high school levels (Oliva, 2004).

Students who are deaf tend to be less socially mature than their hearing peers and find it difficult to interact with their hearing classmates in inclusionary settings (Kluwin et al., 2002). Even though inclusion can present problems for many students who are deaf, by no means is it a negative experience for all students. Research on the effects of integrating students who are deaf with hearing peers has consistently found that social and academic outcomes vary depending on the individual.

Casebook Reflection

REFER TO THE CASE *Least Restrictive for Whom?* in your booklet. Brian's parents had used simple signs with him since he was a little boy. However, he could not communicate or socialize with other students in his school or his parents. How might teachers or support personnel have helped to improve this situation? ●

Although students who are deaf or hard of hearing are included to a very high degree in general education classrooms, they are still served in separate settings more than any other disability category.

UNDERSTANDING THE STANDARDS AND PRINCIPLES How have technological advances helped individuals with hearing impairment communicate? (CEC Knowledge and Skill Standard DH5S3)

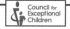

For some, full integration is beneficial; for others, a separate setting is best. Researchers have found that effective inclusive programming for students who are deaf is related to support from the school administration and parents and opportunities for instruction in the general education classroom by special educators trained in deaf education (Schirmer, 2001). For an example of how this can work, read the Making It Work on page 365.

UNDERSTANDING THE STANDARDS AND PRINCIPLES How can special educators assess the academic progress of students who are deaf or hard of hearing? (CEC Knowledge and Skill Standards DH8S1 & DH8S2)

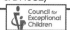

Assessment of Progress

Many children who are deaf or hard of hearing are educated in inclusive settings with their nondisabled peers. However, as we noted earlier, these students characteristically underachieve in academic areas. To ensure that they receive appropriate instruction, it's critical to assess their progress and outcomes in academic subject areas.

Progress Monitoring

Curriculum-based measurement (CBM) can be implemented as a means of monitoring students' with hearing impairments academic progress. Research suggests that CBM may be an appropriate method for measuring reading fluency (i.e., rate) and comprehension (i.e., passage retelling) for students who use sign language (Allinder & Eccarius, 1999). To measure a student's reading fluency, the examiner asks the student to read a passage for a three-minute time period using sign language. The reading rate is then determined by calculating the number of correct words signed per minute. To measure comprehension, the student retells the passage and the examiner determines the number of correct idea units retold. These procedures are similar to those used for hearing students. Mathematics skills may also be monitored using standard CBM methods that are implemented with hearing students.

Collaboration and Co-Teaching of Students Who Are Deaf or Hard of Hearing

"If he can't hear me, how can I teach him?"

Working with a teacher of students who are deaf or hard of hearing may mean learning a new language or how to work with interpreters. This may cause anxiety and initial reluctance on the part of the general education teacher to try to collaborate. In all cases, the general educator who is being asked to collaborate has a right to a thorough understanding of the abilities of the student (not just the disabilities) and of the goals the special educator has set for the collaboration.

WHAT DOES IT MEAN TO BE A TEACHER OF STUDENTS WHO ARE DEAF OR HARD OF HEARING?

The focus of training for teachers of the deaf or hard of hearing is not on content but on the assessment, characteristics, and management of hearing impairments. Again, these teachers have special skills that they can offer the general educator, such as:

1. An understanding of the communication features (e.g., visual cues, accommodations) that are necessary to enhance cognitive, emotional, and social development of students with hearing impairments.

2. An ability to modify incidental language experiences (e.g., communicating with other students and friends when working in groups) to fit the visual and other sensory needs of individuals who are deaf or hard of hearing.

3. A knowledge of strategies to facilitate cognitive and communicative development in individuals who are deaf or hard of hearing. (Council for Exceptional Children, 2003).

Tapping into these areas of expertise will certainly help in a collaborative situation, but it takes more than expertise in a teaching area to make a collaboration work, as evidenced by the following example.

SUCCESSFUL STRATEGIES FOR CO-TEACHING

Cindy Sadonis (a teacher of students who are deaf/hard of hearing) and Connie Underwood (a third-grade teacher) worked collaboratively to include Joe and Brittany. Joe used hearing aids but had language deficits and Brittany had a profound hearing loss and used both sign and oral language.

Cindy: I teach nine students with hearing impairments in grades K through 5. The students receive a range of special education services. All students, however, are mainstreamed for library, music, PE, guidance, and special events.

Connie: I teach a general education third-grade class. There are seventeen students. I had worked with students with hearing impairments in my general education classroom in the past, and although the experiences were positive in many ways, I felt that I was connecting with the students "at a distance."

Cindy: We were both apprehensive despite being friends, co-workers, and experienced teachers. I went into Connie's room and she and her third-grade students came into my room.

Connie: I had three main fears. First, was I going to be able to communicate with Joe and Brittany without an interpreter? Yikes! My signing skills were labored, elementary, and painfully wrong at times. Second, how much more planning and time would this take? When I was lead teacher, Cindy interpreted and observed and was ready the following week with lessons on the same theme. I became a support in her room when she became the lead teacher. Third, I was concerned about student relationships. Without prompting, our students began signing as they tried to communicate, and by the latter part of the year it was amazing how much communication was going on at the lunch table, in PE, and even secretively (or so the kids thought) in the classroom.

There were times when Brittany and Joe still felt different and when my students found it much easier to engage in conversations with their friends without hearing losses.

Cindy: It's important to know that collaborative teaching to this degree is often difficult, largely due to schedule. Positive teacher attitudes are required if inclusion is to succeed. Challenges presented themselves along the way for us, too. Social interaction was always an area of need despite our best efforts. As teachers, we have highs and lows too. Working through them has helped us continue to move in the right direction.

For more information on hearing impairments, visit the National Institute of Deafness and Other Communication Disorders at www.nidcd.nih.gov/health/kids/index.htm

● By Margaret P. Weiss

Meeting the Needs of Students Who Are Deaf or Hard of Hearing

Teaching Phonics

WHAT THE RESEARCH SAYS

Research has demonstrated a direct correlation between the development of phonemic awareness and phonics skills to the development of successful readers (Adams, 1990). For students who are deaf or hard of hearing, phonics instruction is often overlooked or ignored due to the assumption that students who can't hear sound segments (a sensory process) can't learn phonological units (a cognitive process) (Hanson, 1989; Trezek & Malmgren, 2005). Yet research that compares accomplished and average deaf and hard of hearing readers finds that the use of phonological information is a distinguishing variable between the two groups (Hanson & Lichtenstein, 1990). Therefore, the teaching of phonology to students who are deaf or hard of hearing may result in higher levels of reading achievement for this population.

RESEARCH STUDY

Researchers worked with twenty-three middle school students who were deaf or hard of hearing (Trezek & Malmgren, 2005). Students were divided into two groups—a treatment group and the comparison group. The treatment group received instruction using a systematic, explicit remedial phonics program. The comparison group

continued to receive the reading instruction typically provided as a part of the standard curriculum. The purpose of their study was to determine if a prepackaged phonics program could be modified in order to successfully teach deaf or hard of hearing students and to determine if the modified program resulted in the acquisition and generalization of phonics skills.

The phonics program received by the treatment group consisted of three key activities: pronunciations, sound instruction, and word reading. For the pronunciation phase of instruction, modifications included speechreading, articulatory feedback, and the Visual Phonics system. These modifications supported the production of sounds and words that were "reasonable versions" of typical phonetic pronunciation (Trezek & Malmgren, 2005). The ability to understand the subtle differences in sound production creates the foundation for understanding and applying "phonics rules" as students learn to decode.

The Visual Phonics modification, which uses hand cues in conjunction with the generation of a sound, highlights how these subtle differences can be taught to students who are deaf or hard of hearing. These hand cues provided visual feedback about a sound. For example, the position of the mouth is the same for the production of the sounds /d/ and /t/. When

The STAR Reading, Math, and Early Literacy Assessments (Renaissance Learning, 2006) are also useful for monitoring the academic progress of students who are deaf or hard of hearing. These measures are computerized assessment tools that provide immediate information on student skills to assist with instructional planning. The National Center on Student Progress Monitoring evaluated this measure and found that it met high standards of rigor in progress monitoring standards (U.S. Department of Education, National Center on Progress Monitoring, 2006).

Outcome Measures

Performance on measures documenting academic outcomes has significant implications for students; however, these assessments may not be technically appropriate for students who are deaf or hard of hearing. Unfortunately, most standardized assessments are biased toward the majority culture (Mason, 2005). Educators must consider these biases carefully when making decisions as a result of students' outcomes. Despite these concerns it's important to have methods to evaluate students' academic achievement.

Research supports the development of phonics-based reading skills for students who are deaf or hard of hearing (Musselman, 2000; Perfetti & Sandak, 2000; Trezek & Wang, 2006; see the Responsive Instruction above). Consequently, measures to assess reading skills should be similar to those of hearing students: Important outcome skills include word producing the /d/ sound, voice is produced; in contrast, the /t/ sound is unvoiced. Visual Phonics cues allowed the treatment group students to "see" whether a sound is voiced or unvoiced. Students could also touch the teacher's throat to feel the difference between voiced and unvoiced sounds.

The comparison group received the standard reading curriculum. At this school (similar to many schools), the reading curriculum was established/selected by the individual teacher. The comparison teacher for this study used a variety of literature-based reading programs; students would read stories and complete vocabulary or comprehension worksheets based on the stories. The teacher emphasized vocabulary development and comprehension and did not provide explicit phonics instruction.

Both groups received forty-five minutes of instruction daily for a period of eight weeks. The study assessed students' ability to identify sounds in isolation and within words as well as read whole words. A generalization assessment tested students' ability to apply phonics principles to pseudo words.

RESEARCH FINDINGS

Pretest scores were similar for both the treatment and comparison group. The range of scores was 1 to 33 correct for both groups. Across both groups, students with more hearing performed better than those with more significant hearing loss. By the end of the eight-week study, posttest scores for the treatment group jumped to a range of 43 to 45 correct responses, whereas the comparison groups' scores remained the same as

the pretest. These results demonstrated that students with a range of hearing loss could be taught critical phonological skills. The generalization assessment yielded similar results—the treatment group significantly outperforming the control group.

APPLYING THE RESEARCH TO TEACHING

The results from this study should be compelling to teachers who work with students who are deaf or hard of hearing. The study clearly indicates that students with hearing loss can acquire phonics skills and transfer them to reading applications. Narr (2006) recommends the following strategies for teaching phonemic awareness and phonology for students who are deaf and hard of hearing:

1. Use acoustic highlighting, emphasizing target sounds, for students with residual hearing to assist students in distinguishing important differences in sounds.
2. Use strategies such as Visual Phonics or cued speech, which both use hand shapes to represent sound.
3. Use the "sandwich technique." Begin by signing and mouthing (saying) the whole word. Next, fingerspell or write most of the word omitting the target phoneme. Finally, mouth (or say) the phoneme, and then sign and mouth the whole word.
4. Teach syllabication. Syllables can be conveyed through fingerspelling "chunks" of a word in order for students to internalize these phonological representations.

● *By Kristin L. Sayeski*

identification, pseudoword reading, and reading comprehension. The Wechsler Individual Achievement Test-II (WIAT-II; Weschler, 2002) has been used effectively with students who are deaf or hard of hearing to measure these skills. Practitioners administered the WIAT-II to students using speech and sign language simultaneously, and students responded in a manner consistent with their instruction (e.g., signs, fingerspelling, vocalization, and Visual Phonics cues) (Trezek & Wang, 2006). This standardized measure administered with accommodations resulted in student performance that was consistent with the instruction they received, suggesting that the modified assessment was appropriate.

Few standardized measures of reading ability are available for students who are deaf or hard of hearing. The Test of Early Reading Ability-Deaf and Hard of Hearing (TERA-D/HH; Reid, Hresko, Hammill, & Wiltshire, 1991) is one of the only standardized measures that has been designed and normed for students who are deaf. Constructs assessed in the TERA-D/HH are similar to the standard TERA, including knowledge of the alphabet (letter naming and signed reading), print conventions, word recognition, and reading comprehension. An advantage of the TERA-D/HH is that it can be used for both progress monitoring and measuring student outcomes.

A comprehensive standardized achievement test that has been normed for students who are deaf and hard of hearing is the Stanford Achievement Test, Ninth Edition (SAT 9). The content of the SAT-9 includes reading, mathematics, spelling, language, science and social studies. The SAT-9 is one of the most commonly used assessments for academic subjects for students who are deaf or hard of hearing (Luckner & Bowen, 2006).

Testing Accommodations

As students who are deaf or hard of hearing are being included in standardized assessments at higher rates, states are developing guidelines for the use of accommodations (Thompson, Johnston, Thurlow, & Altman, 2005). The most common presentation accommodations for these students are sign interpretation for directions and for test questions. Most states allow signing directions without restriction, but some states consider the accommodation for signing questions nonstandard (Lazarus, Thurlow, Lail, Eisenbraun, & Kato, 2006). A nonstandard accommodation often affects scoring and interpretation of the test. Students who are deaf or hard of hearing also receive response accommodations such as signing responses to an interpreter.

Early Intervention

Education for infants and preschoolers with hearing impairments is of critical importance. Such programs not only can help facilitate the development of the children, but also may be beneficial in reducing parents' stress levels (Lederberg & Golbach, 2002).

Because language development is such an issue for children who are hearing impaired and because early childhood is such an important time for the development of language, it's not surprising that many of the most controversial issues surrounding early intervention in the area of deafness focus on language. As indicated in our earlier discussion of oralism versus manualism, some people maintain that English language should be the focus of intervention efforts, and others hold that ASL should be used starting in infancy.

Children who are deaf who have parents who are deaf are likely to do better than children who are deaf who have hearing parents. For example, in infancy, they develop ASL at a rate similar to the rate at which hearing infants of hearing parents develop English. But infants who are deaf who have hearing parents don't develop either English or ASL at as fast a rate. This may be because day-to-day interactions between mothers and infants are more facilitative and natural when both the infant and parents are deaf than when the infant is deaf and the parents are hearing.

In addition to facility with ASL, parents who are deaf also have the advantage of being better prepared to cope with their infant's deafness (Meadow-Orlans, 1990). Most parents who are hearing are unprepared for the birth of a child with hearing impairment, whereas parents who are deaf can draw on their own experiences in order to offer helpful support to their child who is deaf.

Hearing parents, especially if they want to teach their infants sign language, may need help in understanding the importance of the visual modality in communicating with their infants (Bornstein, Selmi, Haynes, Painter, & Marx, 1999). Hearing parents need to understand, for example, that the eye gaze of the infant who is deaf is extremely important because it's his or her way of expressing interest and motivation.

Hearing parents of children who are deaf face a quandary over how to provide their children with appropriate sign language models. Both signed English and ASL, especially the latter, are difficult to learn to a high degree of fluency in a relatively short time. And like any language, ASL is harder to acquire as an adult and can rarely be learned to the same degree of fluency as that possessed by a native ASL signer.

The fact that over 95 percent of children who are deaf have parents who are hearing underscores the importance of intervention for many infants who are deaf. In fact, many authorities believe that there is a far greater need for early intervention for families with hearing parents of a child who is deaf than for families in which both the parents and the child are deaf (Andrews & Zmijewski, 1997).

Educators have established preschool intervention projects to teach the basics of sign language to the parents of children who are deaf as well as to the children themselves. Such projects are generally successful at teaching the rudiments of sign to parents and

There are now over 100 postsecondary programs in the United States and Canada for students who are deaf or hard of hearing. Many of these students choose to attend traditional colleges and universities as well.

infants. Once the child is ready to progress beyond one- and two-word signed utterances, however, it's important that native signers be available as models. Authorities recommend a practice that is popular in Sweden: that adults who are deaf be part of early intervention efforts because they can serve as sign language models and can help hearing parents form positive expectations about their children's potential (Lane et al., 1996). Even though hearing parents might never be able to communicate fluently in sign language, it is important that they continue to sign with their child. Not only does signing allow parents a means of communicating with their child; it also demonstrates that they value the child's language and the Deaf culture.

Transition to Adulthood

Unemployment and underemployment (being overqualified for a job) have been persistent problems for persons with a hearing impairment, especially women (Punch, Hyde, & Creed, 2004; Schirmer, 2001). There is some evidence, however, that this bleak picture is slowly beginning to change. The primary reason for this change has been the expansion of postsecondary programming for students with hearing impairment. A fifteen-year follow-up of graduates with hearing impairment from two- and four-year colleges found that a college education made a substantial difference in having a satisfying career and life (Schroedel & Geyer, 2000).

The reasons why those who are hearing impaired have a more difficult time finding appropriate and satisfying employment have a lot to do with a poor understanding on the part of the hearing population of what it means to have a hearing impairment and what accommodations they can make in the workplace (Punch, Creed, & Hyde, 2006). Likewise, people with hearing impairments, themselves, often aren't prepared to ask for the right accommodations and have difficulties making good career choices (Punch et al., 2004).

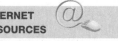

INTERNET RESOURCES

Deafcareers magazine (www.deafcareers.com) offers a forum for practitioners and the Deaf community to address career preparedness.

Postsecondary Education

Before the mid-1960s, the only institution established specifically for the postsecondary education of students with hearing impairment was Gallaudet College (now Gallaudet University). Except for this one institution, these students were left with no choice but to attend traditional colleges and universities. However, traditional postsecondary schools were generally not equipped to handle the special needs of students with hearing impairment. It's little wonder, then, that a study by Quigley, Jenne, and Phillips (1968) was able to identify only 224 people with hearing impairment who were graduates of regular colleges and universities in the United States between 1910 and 1965.

Findings such as these led to the expansion of postsecondary programs. The federal government has funded a wide variety of postsecondary programs for students with hearing impairment. The two best-known ones are Gallaudet University and the National Technical Institute for the Deaf (NTID) at the Rochester Institute of Technology. The NTID program, emphasizing training in technical fields, complements the liberal arts orientation of Gallaudet University. At NTID, some students with hearing impairment also attend classes with hearing students at the Rochester Institute of Technology.

In addition to Gallaudet and NTID, there are now well over 100 postsecondary programs in the United States and Canada for students with hearing impairment. By law, Gallaudet and NTID are responsible for serving students from all fifty states and territories. Others serve students from several states, from one state only, or from specific districts only.

Although many people who are deaf who enroll in higher education choose to attend Gallaudet, NTID, or colleges with special programs, some go to traditional colleges and universities. These students usually take advantage of the expanding roles of university programs that have been established to facilitate the academic experiences of students with disabilities. One of the accommodations often recommended is to provide sign language interpreters in the classes of students with hearing impairment.

SIGN LANGUAGE INTERPRETERS Even though most authorities would agree that having a sign language interpreter is one of the best accommodations, it's important to keep in mind that this is a far cry from leveling the academic playing field for students with hearing impairments. First, there is a national shortage of adequately trained interpreters (Schick, Williams, & Kupermintz, 2006). Even when students with hearing impairment have access to highly trained interpreters, the amount of information they are able to take in falls well below that of their hearing peers. In other words, when hearing students and students who are deaf hear and see (through interpretation) the same lecture, the students who are deaf don't learn as much of the material (Marschark, Pelz, et al., 2005; Marschark, Sapere, Convertino, & Seewagen, 2005; Marschark, Sapere, Convertino, Seewagen, & Maltzen, 2004).

The role of interpreters generates a debate over using ASL versus transliteration. **Transliteration**, which is similar to signed English, maintains the same word order as spoken English. ASL, by contrast, requires the interpreter to digest the meaning of what is said before conveying it through signs. The little research that has been done comparing the two has not provided clear-cut evidence of one being more beneficial than the other.

Most college instructors have limited, if any, experience in working with sign language interpreters. Even so, it is critical that instructors and interpreters work closely together to provide the optimum learning experience for students who are deaf while not disrupting other students in the class (Seal, 2004). The

■ **Transliteration**
A method used by most sign language interpreters in which the signs maintain the same word order as that of spoken English; American Sign Language (ASL) is also used by some interpreters.

FOCUS ON **Concepts**

Tips for Working with Sign Language Interpreters

General Principles

- The interpreter must be certified. (The Americans With Disabilities Act specifies different types of acceptable certification.)
- The interpreter must maintain confidentiality.
- The interpreter should match the needs of the student with respect to preference for such things as ASL versus signed English, transliteration versus interpretation, and use of voice while interpreting.
- The interpreter should be available for all school-related activities.
- If at times the student can interact with peers successfully without the interpreter, then he or she should be allowed to do so.
- The interpreter is there to interpret, not to act as a classroom aide or to teach. (Seal, 2004)

Specifics

- The interpreter should have copies of all handouts and, if possible, copies of the textbooks.
- The instructor and fellow students should talk directly to the student and not to the interpreter.
- In a lecture class, the instructor should be aware of the pace of his or her delivery, perhaps pausing more frequently than usual.
- In a discussion class, participants should try to talk one at a time and account for the time lag between what is spoken and its signed interpretation.
- The instructor might want to request that the interpreter stop the class if something becomes too complicated to interpret. In fact, the interpreter's need to clarify might very well signal that the rest of the students do not understand the information either. (Siple, 1993)

Focus on Concepts above provides some tips for working with sign language interpreters.

Family Issues

With regard to raising a family, people who are deaf often face unique challenges. National statistics indicate that 95 percent of adults who are deaf choose deaf spouses, and 90 percent of the offspring of these marriages have normal hearing (Buchino, 1993). These hearing children often serve as interpreters for their parents. Being called on to interpret for one's parents can help to develop self-confidence around adult authority figures (e.g., doctors, lawyers, insurance agents), but it can also force one to face some unpleasant biases, as the following story from a hearing child of deaf parents demonstrates:

> Curled up in the seat, chin dug into my chest, I noticed there was a lull in the conversation. Dad was a confident driver, but Mom was smoking more than usual.
> "Something happened? That gas station?" Mom signed to me.
> "No, nothing," I lied.
> "Are you sure?"
> "Everything is fine." Dad and I had gone to pay and get directions. The man behind the counter had looked up, seen me signing and grunted, "Huh, I didn't think mutes were allowed to have driver's licenses." Long ago I'd gotten used to hearing those kind of comments. But I never could get used to the way it made me churn inside. (Walker, 1986, p. 9)

These children also sometimes resent that being called on to interpret for their parents has interfered with their social lives (Buchino, 1993).

There has been a long tradition of preparing students who are deaf for manual trades (Lane, 1992). But unskilled and semiskilled trades are fast disappearing from the

UNDERSTANDING THE STANDARDS AND PRINCIPLES What can individuals with hearing impairment expect as they transition to adulthood? (CEC Knowledge and Skill Standards DH7K1, DH10K2, & DH10S2)

INTERNET RESOURCES

Children of Deaf Adults (CODA; www.coda-international.org) is an organization devoted to children of adults who are deaf. As stated on the Website, "CODA is an organization established for the purpose of promoting family awareness and individual growth in hearing children of deaf parents. This purpose is accomplished through providing educational opportunities, promoting self-help, organizing advocacy efforts, and acting as a resource for the membership and various communities."

workforce in favor of jobs requiring higher-level skills. As a result, adults who are deaf face even greater obstacles when they enter the job market.

Although the educational, work, and social opportunities for adults who are deaf are often limited, there are reasons to be optimistic about the future. With the continued expansion of transition programming, postsecondary education, and greater public awareness of the potential of people who are deaf should come a brighter outlook for more adults who are deaf.

Summary

How do professionals define and classify individuals who are deaf or hard of hearing?

▶ Those with a *physiological* perspective use a decibel loss of 90 dB or greater as the cutoff for deafness.

▶ Those with an *educational* perspective classify individuals as deaf if they are unable to process linguistic information, with or without a hearing aid; they classify individuals as hard of hearing if they are able to process this information with the help of a hearing aid.

▶ Congenital versus adventitious deafness refers to being born deaf versus acquiring deafness after birth; prelingual deafness versus postlingual deafness refers to deafness occurring before versus after speech and language development.

▶ There is growing sentiment in the Deaf community that those who are deaf should be considered as a cultural/linguistic minority rather than disabled.

What is the prevalence of hearing impairment?

▶ About 0.13 percent of students from six to seventeen years of age are identified as hearing impaired, with those classified as hard of hearing being more prevalent than those identified as deaf.

▶ Close to 23 percent of students who are deaf come from Hispanic-speaking homes.

What are some basic anatomical and physiological characteristics of the ear?

▶ The outer ear consists of the auricle and external auditory canal.

▶ The middle ear consists of the eardrum and three tiny bones (ossicles): the malleus, incus, and stapes.

▶ The inner ear consists of the vestibular mechanism and the cochlea; the former monitors balance, and the latter is the most important for hearing because it is responsible for sending electrical impulses to the brain via the cochlear nerve.

How is hearing impairment identified?

▶ Screening tests for infants often measure otoacoustic emissions, low-intensity sound emitted from the cochlea when stimulated.

▶ Pure-tone audiometry assesses decibel (intensity) and hertz (frequency) levels.

▶ Speech audiometry assesses the ability to detect and understand speech.

▶ Specialized tests for young children and those who are hard to test include play audiometry, tympanometry, and evoked-response audiometry.

What causes hearing impairments?

▶ Conductive hearing impairments involve the middle or outer ear, sensorineural hearing impairments involve the inner ear, mixed hearing impairments involve both.

▶ Impairments of the outer ear are caused by such things as infections of the external canal or tumors.

▶ Impairments of the middle ear are often due to malfunctioning of the ossicles; otitis media is a common cause of temporary middle-ear hearing problems.

▶ Impairments of the inner ear usually result in greater hearing impairment than do those of the middle or outer ear; impairments of the inner ear can be hereditary or acquired, but the former are much more common. Genetic or hereditary factors are the leading cause of deafness in children, with mutation of the connexin-26 gene now considered the most common cause of congenital deafness.

What are some psychological and behavioral characteristics of learners with hearing impairments?

▶ The most severely affected area is comprehension and production of English.

▶ Sign language is the primary language of most people in the Deaf community.
   ■ Each sign consists of three parts: handshape, location, and movement.

- Sign language is a true language, as evidenced by the facts that sign language is as grammatically complex as spoken language, there is no universal sign language, children who are deaf reach the same language milestones and at the same times as do those who are hearing, the neurological underpinnings of sign are the same as those for spoken language.
▶ Deafness does not affect intelligence.
▶ Most students who are deaf have extreme deficits in academics, especially reading.
  - Students who are deaf who have parents who are deaf do better academically.
  - A supportive home environment is associated with higher achievement.
▶ Students who are deaf might face limited opportunities for social interaction.
  - The inclusion movement can result in students who are deaf not having peers who are deaf with whom to communicate.
  - About 95 percent of children who are deaf have hearing parents, most of whom are not proficient in sign language.
  - Many authorities recognize the Deaf culture as a means of healthy social communication. There is concern that the Deaf culture might be eroding owing to inclusionary programming. Deaf activists have raised issues with respect to cochlear implants and genetic engineering.

What are some educational considerations for learners with hearing impairments?
▶ The oral approach consists of the following:
  - The auditory-verbal approach, which focuses on using audition to improve speech and language development.
  - The auditory-oral approach, which is like the auditory-verbal approach with the addition of using visual cues such as speechreading and cued speech.
▶ The manual approach stresses sign language.
▶ Most educational programs use a total communication approach, a blend of oral and manual techniques, the latter being a type of signing English system in which the English word order is preserved.
▶ Some advocate for a bicultural-bilingual approach, which consists of three features: ASL is considered the primary language, people who are deaf are involved in the development of the program and curriculum, and the curriculum involves instruction in Deaf culture.
▶ Educational placement of students who are deaf includes the full continuum, but more inclusive settings are becoming more and more popular, with about 85 percent of students who are deaf attending classes in regular schools and 40 percent spending the vast majority of their time in

general education classrooms. Many within the Deaf community are concerned that the inclusion movement results in the absence of a "critical mass" of students who are deaf, which can result in social isolation.
▶ Numerous technological advances are occurring in hearing aids; television, video, and movie captioning; text telephone technology; computer-assisted instruction; and the Internet.

How do professionals assess students' with hearing impairments academic progress?
▶ Using sign language, professionals can implement CBM to monitor progress in reading fluency, reading comprehension, and math.
▶ A few standardized tests are available to assess academic outcomes of students with hearing impairments.
▶ One of the most common accommodations for standardized assessments involves the use of sign language both for the delivery of administrator directions/instructions and student responses.

What are some things to consider with respect to early intervention for learners with hearing impairments?
▶ Families of children who are deaf who have hearing parents might be in greater need of early intervention programming than families in which the parents are deaf.
▶ Because it is difficult for hearing parents to become fluent in sign language, native signers are a part of some intervention programs.

What are some things to consider with respect to transition to adulthood for learners with hearing impairments?
▶ In addition to Gallaudet University and the National Technical Institute for the Deaf, there are now several postsecondary programs for students with hearing impairment.
▶ A common accommodation in college is the use of sign language interpreters. Transliteration involves maintaining the same word order as English whereas ASL does not.
▶ Ninety percent of the children of two parents who are deaf have normal hearing. These children often face challenges of negotiating between the Deaf community and hearing society.
▶ There has been a long tradition of preparing many students who are deaf for manual trades; however, these trades are disappearing.
▶ Expanded transition programming, postsecondary education, and public awareness promises a brighter outlook for adults who are deaf.

STANDARDS and PRINCIPLES in this Chapter

SPECIAL EDUCATORS . . .

■ understand the field as an evolving and changing discipline (from CEC Content Standard #1).

■ understand the similarities and differences in human development (from CEC Content Standard #2).

■ understand the effects that an exceptional condition can have on an individual's learning (from CEC Content Standard #3).

■ actively create learning environments . . . that foster cultural understanding, safety and emotional well-being, positive social interactions, and active engagement (from CEC Content Standard #5).

■ use individualized strategies to enhance language development and teach communication skills (from CEC Content Standard #6).

■ develop a variety of individualized transition plans (from CEC Content Standard #7).

■ use the results of assessments to help identify exceptional learning needs (from CEC Content Standard #8).

■ use collaboration to facilitate the successful transitions of individuals with exceptional learning needs (from CEC Content Standard #10).

ALL TEACHERS . . .

■ understand the central concepts, tools of inquiry, structures of the discipline(s) they teach (from INTASC Principle #1).

■ understand how children learn and develop (from INTASC Principle #2).

■ understand how students differ in their approaches to learning and create instructional opportunities that are adapted to diverse learners (INTASC Principle #3).

■ use an understanding of individual and group motivation and behavior to create a learning environment that encourages positive social interaction, active engagement in learning, and self-motivation (INTASC Principle #5).

■ use knowledge of effective verbal, nonverbal, and media communication technologies to foster active inquiry, collaboration, and supportive interaction in the classroom (INTASC Principle #6).

■ plan instruction based on knowledge of subject matter, students, the community, and curriculum goals (INTASC Principle #7).

■ understand and use formal and informal assessment strategies (from INTASC Principle #8).

■ foster relationships with school colleagues, families, and agencies (from INTASC Principle #10).

Applying the STANDARDS and PRINCIPLES

■ WHAT should teachers know about how hearing impairment is defined? (CEC Content Standard #1 & INTASC Principle #1)

■ WHY is it important for teachers to know about the causes of hearing impairment? (CEC Content Standards #1, #2, & #3; INTASC Principles #1, #2, & #3)

■ THE parents of a young child who is hard of hearing ask you to advise them on how their child should be taught to converse. How would you respond? (CEC Content Standards #5 & #6; INTASC Principles #5 & #6)

■ HOW is hearing ability measured? (CEC Content Standard #8 & INTASC Principle #8)

■ HOW would you respond to parents who approach you expressing concern about the future of their deaf high school student? (CEC Content Standards #7 & #10; INTASC Principles #7 & #10)

Now go to the Hallahan/Kauffman, Eleventh Edition MyEducationLab course at www.myeducationlab.com to:

- take a Pretest to assess your initial comprehension of the chapter content;
- study chapter content with your Individualized Study Plan;
- take a Posttest to assess your understanding of chapter content;
- engage in multimedia exercises to help you build a deeper and more applied understanding of chapter content.

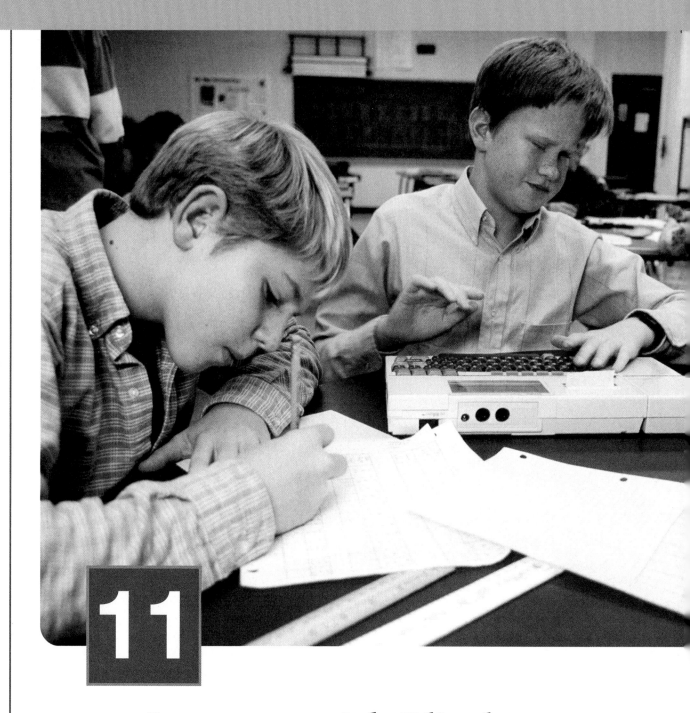

11

Learners with Blindness or Low Vision

Ray, no one knows what it's like to carry water
The way your mother made you carry it—

Even the boy Pharaoh
Wore a yoke on his shoulders

Just to show he was a man.
History doesn't matter much,

At least until your child
"Done gone blind"—your Mama saw it—

"You always got to carry water," she said.
"This ain't no kidding around."

Long time
You carried water

In both hands,
Feeling for the path

With your feet.
Ray, your Mama knew—

A song comes that way—
Or else it never will.

Laugh or cry it's the same.
A Mockingbird listens from a telephone wire.

Long time, water, both hands.

—Stephen Kuusisto
"Elegy for Ray Charles and His Mother"

Source: Stephen Kuusisto, "Elegy for Ray Charles" from *Ragged Edge* (June 2004).
Copyright © 2004 by Stephen Kuusisto. Reprinted with permission of the author.

QUESTIONS to guide your reading of this chapter . . .

- How do professionals define and classify learners with blindness and low vision?

- What is the prevalence of visual impairment?

- What are some basic anatomical and physiological characteristics of the eye?

- How is visual ability measured?

- What causes visual impairments?

- What are some of the psychological and behavioral characteristics of learners with visual impairments?

- What are some educational considerations for learners with visual impairments?

- How do professionals assess students' with visual impairments progress in academic and functional skills?

- What are some things to consider with respect to early intervention for learners with visual impairments?

- What are some things to consider with respect to transition to adulthood for learners with visual impairments?

MISCONCEPTIONS ABOUT
Learners with Blindness or Low Vision

MYTH ■ People who are legally blind have no sight at all.

FACT ■ Only a small percentage of people who are legally blind have absolutely no vision. Many have a useful amount of functional vision.

MYTH ■ People who are blind have an extra sense that enables them to detect obstacles.

FACT ■ People who are blind do not have an extra sense. Some can learn to develop an "obstacle sense" by noting the change in pitch of echoes as they move toward objects.

MYTH ■ People who are blind automatically develop better acuity in their other senses.

FACT ■ Through concentration and attention, individuals who are blind can learn to make very fine discriminations in the sensations they obtain. This is not automatic but rather represents learning to use received sensations better.

MYTH ■ People who are blind have superior musical ability.

FACT ■ The musical ability of people who are blind is not necessarily better than that of sighted people; however, many people who are blind pursue musical careers as one way in which they can achieve success.

MYTH ■ Stereotypic behaviors (e.g., body rocking, head swaying) are always maladaptive and should be totally eliminated.

FACT ■ Although more research is needed, there are some authorities who maintain that these behaviors, except when they are extreme, can help persons who are blind regulate their levels of arousal.

MYTH ■ Braille is not very useful for the vast majority of people who are blind; it should only be tried as a last resort.

FACT ■ Very few people who are blind have learned braille, primarily due to fear that using it is a sign of failure and to a historical professional bias against it. Authorities acknowledge the utility of braille for people who are blind.

MYTH ■ Braille is of no value for those who have low vision.

FACT ■ Some individuals with low vision have conditions that will eventually result in blindness. More and more, authorities think that these individuals should learn braille to be prepared for when they can't read print effectively.

MYTH ■ If people with low vision use their eyes too much, their sight will deteriorate.

FACT ■ Only rarely is this true. Visual efficiency can actually be improved through training and use. Wearing strong lenses, holding books close to the eyes, and using the eyes often cannot harm vision.

MYTH ■ Mobility instruction should be delayed until elementary or secondary school.

FACT ■ Many authorities now recognize that even preschoolers can take advantage of mobility instruction, including the use of a cane.

MYTH ■ The long cane is a simply constructed, easy-to-use device.

FACT ■ The National Academy of Sciences has drawn up specifications for the manufacture of the long cane and its proper use.

MYTH ■ Guide dogs take people where they want to go.

FACT ■ The guide dog does not "take" the person anywhere; the person must first know where he or she is going. The dog is primarily a protection against unsafe areas or obstacles.

MYTH ■ Technology will soon replace the need for braille and for mobility aids such as the long cane and guide dogs. In addition, a breakthrough for restoring complete sight through technology is just around the corner.

FACT ■ As amazing as some of the technology is in the field of vision impairment, it's doubtful that it will be as effective as braille, the long cane, or guide dogs anytime soon. Research on artificial vision is exciting, but it too does not promise to have huge practical benefits for some time.

Stephen Kuusisto, author of the poem reprinted on page 377, was blind from birth but was well into his adult years before he stopped the charade of trying to "pass" as a sighted person. Once at peace with his blindness, he was able to turn his energies to more productive endeavors, such as being a successful author. As Kuusisto acknowledges in his elegy to Ray Charles, people vary in their response to being blind. Some actually gain an inner strength from adversity, for example, "She'd make me cut wood, wash clothes and build a fire under the pot. . . . People thought that was abusive. My mother had the attitude 'He's got to learn, and just because he's blind doesn't mean he's stupid'" (Interview with Ray Charles, reported June 11, 2004 by Reuters UK). However, a major impediment to being able to accept one's blindness is society's reactions to people who are blind. Visual impairments seem to evoke more awkwardness than most other disabilities. Why are we so uncomfortably aware of blindness? For one thing, blindness is visible. We often don't realize that a person has impaired hearing, for example, until we actually talk to him or her. The person with visual impairment, however, usually has a variety of symbols: a cane, thick or darkened glasses, a guide dog.

Another possible reason for being self-conscious around people who are blind is the role that eyes play in social interaction. Poets, playwrights, and songwriters have long recognized how emotionally expressive the eyes can be for people who are sighted. Those of us who are sighted know how uncomfortable it can be to talk with someone who does not make eye contact with us. Think how often we have heard someone say or have ourselves said that we prefer to talk face to face on an important matter, rather than over the telephone.

Another reason we fear loss of vision is that the sense of sight is linked so closely with the traditional concept of beauty. We derive great pleasure from our sight. Our feelings about others are often based largely on physical appearances that are visually perceived. Additionally, our use of language reinforces a negative view of blindness:

> The word blind has always meant more than merely the inability to see. . . . Throughout history of the language and in common usage today, the word [blind] connotes a lack of understanding . . . , a willful disregard or obliviousness, a thing meant to conceal or deceive. In fact, when you stop to listen, the word is far more commonly used in its figurative than its literal sense. And it comes up so often: blind faith, blind devotion, blind luck, . . . blind alley, . . . blind taste test, double-blind study, flying blind, . . . blind submission, blind side, blind spot. . . . Pick up any book or magazine and you will find dozens of similes and metaphors connecting blindness and blind people with ignorance, confusion, indifference, ineptitude. (Kleege, 1999, p. 21)

So although blindness is the least prevalent of all disabilities, at least in children, people dread it. It is reportedly the third most feared condition; only cancer and AIDS outrank it (Jernigan, 1992). With a bit of reflection, however, it becomes obvious that our anxieties about blindness are irrational. Most of our apprehension can be attributed to our lack of experience in interacting with individuals with visual impairment. It's not until we talk to people who are blind or read about their appreciation of sounds, smells, and touch that we begin to realize that sight is not the only sense that enables us to enjoy beauty or interact socially with other people.

Like anyone with a disability, the person who is blind wants to be treated like everyone else. Most people who are blind do not seek pity or unnecessary help. In fact, they can be fiercely protective of their independence. The Personal Perspectives on p. 381 provides etiquette tips on interacting with someone who is blind.

In this chapter, we hope to dispel several myths about blindness. We start by presenting a fact that most sighted people do not know: The majority of people who are blind can actually see.

Video Homework Exercise

Self-Perception • Go to the Homework and Exercises section in Chapter 11 of MyEducationLab to watch the video "Visual Impairment", in which a teenager with a visual impairment discusses his disability.

Definition and Classification

The two most common ways of describing someone with visual impairment are the legal and educational definitions. Laypeople and medical professionals use the former; the latter is the one educators favor. The two major classifications are blindness and low vision.

Legal Definition

■ **Legally blind**
A person who has visual acuity of 20/200 or less in the better eye even with correction (e.g., eyeglasses) or has a field of vision so narrow that its widest diameter subtends an angular distance no greater than 20 degrees.

The legal definition involves assessment of visual acuity and field of vision. A person who is **legally blind** has visual acuity of 20/200 or less in the better eye even with correction (e.g., eyeglasses) or has a field of vision so narrow that its widest diameter subtends an angular distance no greater than 20 degrees. The fraction 20/200 means that the person sees at 20 feet what a person with normal vision sees at 200 feet. (Normal visual acuity is thus 20/20.) The inclusion of a narrowed field of vision in the legal definition means that a person may have 20/20 vision in the central field but severely restricted peripheral vision. Legal blindness qualifies a person for certain legal benefits, such as tax advantages and money for special materials.

Personal PERSPECTIVES

Social Interaction with People Who Are Blind: Points of Etiquette

The following letter to "Dear Abby" from the president of the American Foundation for the Blind lists some appropriate ways that the sighted can interact with those who are blind. Suggestions such as these help to avoid awkward social situations.

Dear Abby:

You recently ran a letter from a woman who gave a few tips on what sighted people should do when they meet a blind person. As president of the American Foundation for the Blind, and a blind person myself, I believe I can add a few more points of etiquette your readers may find helpful.

1. Speak to people who are blind or visually impaired using a natural conversational tone and speed. Do not speak loudly and slowly unless the person also has a hearing impairment.
2. Address blind people by name when possible. This is especially important in crowded places.
3. Immediately greet blind people when they enter a room or service area. This lets them know you are present and ready to assist.

4. Indicate the end of a conversation with a blind person in order to avoid the embarrassment of leaving a person speaking when no one is actually there.
5. Feel free to use words that refer to vision when conversing with blind people. Words such as "look," "see," "watching TV," are part of everyday communication. The words "blind" and "visually impaired" are also acceptable in conversation.
6. Do not leave a blind person standing in "free space" when you serve as a guide. Also, be sure that the person you guide has a firm grasp on your arm or is leaning against a chair or a wall if you have to be separated momentarily.
7. Be calm and clear about what to do if you see a blind person about to encounter a dangerous situation. For example, if the person is about to bump into something, calmly and firmly call out, "Wait there for a moment; there is an obstruction in your path."

Carl R. Augusto, President
American Foundation for the Blind, New York

Source: Letter reprinted with permission of the American Foundation for the Blind.

In addition to this classification of blindness, there is a category referred to as **low vision** (sometimes referred to as partially sighted). According to the legal classification system, persons who have low vision have visual acuity falling between 20/70 and 20/200 in the better eye with correction.

Educational Definition

Many professionals, particularly educators, find the legal classification scheme inadequate. They have observed that visual acuity is not a very accurate predictor of how people will function or use whatever remaining sight they have. Although a small percentage of individuals who are legally blind have absolutely no vision, the majority can see to some degree.

Many who recognize the limitations of the legal definitions of blindness and low vision favor the educational definition, which stresses the method of reading instruction. For educational purposes, individuals who are blind are so severely impaired they must learn to read **braille**, a system of raised dots by which people who are blind read with their fingertips. It consists of quadrangular cells containing from one to six dots whose arrangement denotes different letters and symbols. Alternatively, they use aural methods (audiotapes and records). Those who have low vision can read print, even if they need adaptations such as magnifying devices or large-print books.

■ **Low vision**
A term used by educators to refer to individuals whose visual impairment is not so severe that they are unable to read print of any kind; they may read large or regular print, and they may need some kind of magnification; using the legal/medical system, low vision is acuity between 20/70 and 20/200 in the better eye with correction.

■ **Braille**
A system in which raised dots allow people who are blind to read with their fingertips; each quadrangular cell contains from one to six dots, the arrangement of which denotes different letters and symbols.

FOCUS ON **Concepts**

A Skills Definition of Blindness
Focusing on Skills

Most definitions of disability, including blindness and low vision, focus on what the person *cannot* do. Carol Castellano, the mother of a child who is blind and the first vice president of the National Organization of Parents of Blind Children and president of New Jersey Parents of Blind Children, offers a different perspective. She proposes a *skills* definition of blindness:

I propose that blindness/visual impairment simply means *using alternative skills and tools in place of, or in addition to, eyesight in order to gain information or perform tasks. . . .*

If the task is sorting laundry, the tool might be braille or tactile labels. . . . If the task is reading, the alternative tool might be braille or large print. (Castellano, 2005, p. 16)

Castellano also questions the utility of distinguishing between blindness and low vision, believing that equating blindness with braille reinforces the notion that braille is somehow inferior to visual techniques such as large print.

A skills definition is also reflected in the following statement by a man who lost his sight: "So am I blind? I think so. . . . For me to live my life the way I want to, I must use a combination of blindness skills, alternative techniques, and access technology to accomplish tasks I used to do using vision" (Pare, 2005, p. 412).

A Blindness Skills Quiz

Castellano (2005) notes that one of the challenges for teachers and parents is to identify skills that persons who are blind can use to perform everyday tasks. Here are some examples she uses:

How might a blind person . . .
1. keep track of where his/her toddler is?
2. shop at a supermarket?
3. grill meat on a barbeque?
4. go on the Internet?
5. pour a glass of juice?

Here are some possible solutions.
1. Attach bells to the baby's shoes (as many sighted parents do) or pay attention to the rustle of plastic diapers.
2. Write a shopping list in braille, make use of the store's courtesy service, ask a reader or driver to come along to assist, or shop online.
3. Use long oven mitts and a grilling basket.
4. Use a screen enlarging program or a screen reading program that makes the computer talk.
5. Use the sound of the liquid and the weight of the glass to tell when the glass is getting full, or hook one finger over the edge of the glass and stop pouring when the liquid reaches their finger. (Castellano, 2005, pp. 16–17)

INTERNET RESOURCES

The Website at www.nbp.org/alph. html shows the braille alphabet. This Website, maintained by the National Braille Press, allows the user to type in a word or name and have it translated into braille.

Reading Homework Exercise

Strategies for Young Children • Go to the Homework and Exercises section in Chapter 11 of MyEducationLab and review the suggested strategies to interact with young children who are blind or have low vision.

It is important to note that even though people with low vision can read print, many authorities believe that some of them can benefit from using braille. (We discuss this later in the chapter.) This is why we emphasized above that those who are considered blind must use braille to read.

There are some who think that both the legal definition and the educational definition are flawed because both focus on limitations rather than skills (see the above Focus on Concepts).

Prevalence

Blindness is primarily an adult disability. Most estimates indicate that blindness is approximately one-tenth as prevalent in school-age children as in adults. The federal government classifies only about 0.05 percent of the population ranging from six to seventeen years of age as "visually impaired," which includes those who are blind or who have low vision. This makes visual impairment one of the least prevalent disabilities in children.

Anatomy and Physiology of the Eye

The anatomy of the visual system is extremely complex, so our discussion here will focus only on basic characteristics. Figure 11.1 shows the functioning of the eye. The physical object being seen becomes an electrical impulse that is sent through the optic nerve to the visual center of the brain, the occipital lobes. Before reaching the optic nerve, light rays reflecting off the object being seen pass through several structures within the eye. The light rays do the following:

1. Pass through the **cornea** (a transparent cover in front of the iris and pupil), which performs the major part of the bending (refraction) of the light rays so that the image will be focused

2. Pass through the **aqueous humor** (a watery substance between the cornea and lens of the eye)

3. Pass through the **pupil** (the contractile opening in the middle of the **iris**, the colored portion of the eye that contracts or expands, depending on the amount of light striking it)

4. Pass through the **lens**, which refines and changes the focus of the light rays before they pass through the **vitreous humor** (a transparent gelatinous substance that fills the eyeball between the retina and lens)

5. Come to a focus on the **retina** (the back portion of the eye, containing nerve fibers connected to the **optic nerve**, which carries the information back to the brain)

■ **Cornea**
A transparent cover in front of the iris and pupil in the eye; responsible for most of the refraction of light rays in focusing on an object.

■ **Aqueous humor**
A watery substance between the cornea and lens of the eye.

■ **Pupil**
The contractile opening in the middle of the iris of the eye.

■ **Iris**
The colored portion of the eye; contracts or expands, depending on the amount of light striking it.

■ **Lens**
A structure that refines and changes the focus of the light rays passing through the eye.

■ **Vitreous humor**
A transparent, gelatinous substance that fills the eyeball between the retina and the lens of the eye.

■ **Retina**
The back portion of the eye, containing nerve fibers connected to the optic nerve.

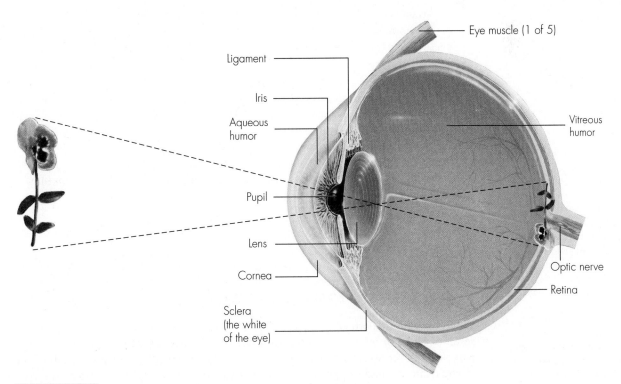

Ligament

Iris

Aqueous humor

Pupil

Lens

Cornea

Sclera (the white of the eye)

Eye muscle (1 of 5)

Vitreous humor

Optic nerve

Retina

FIGURE 11.1   The basic anatomical features of the eye and the visual process.

■ **Visual acuity**

The ability to see fine details; usually measured with the Snellen chart.

■ **Snellen chart**

Used in determining visual acuity; consists of rows of letters or Es arranged in different positions; each row corresponds to the distance at which a normally sighted person can discriminate the letters; does not predict how accurately a child will be able to read print.

■ **Visual efficiency**

A term used to refer to how well one uses his or her vision, including such things as control of eye movements, attention to visual detail, and discrimination of figure from background; believed by some to be more important than visual acuity alone in predicting a person's ability to function visually.

■ **Functional vision assessment**

An appraisal of an individual's use of vision in everyday situations.

INTERNET RESOURCES

Several Websites contain sample Snellen charts. Some examples are: http://en.wikipedia.org/wiki/Snellen_chart http://www.mdsupport.org/snellen.html http://www.i-see.org/eyecharts.html

The Website of Prevent Blindness America contains an example of a Web-based measure of near vision: www.preventblindness.org/eye_tests/near_vision_test.html

Prevent Blindness America, founded in 1908, is a voluntary organization devoted to eye health and safety. Its Website at www.preventblindness.org contains a variety of information on blindness prevention.

■ **Refraction**

The bending of light rays as they pass through the structures (cornea, aqueous humor, pupil, lens, vitreous humor) of the eye.

Identification of Visual Impairment

Visual acuity is most often measured with the **Snellen chart**, which consists of rows of letters (for individuals who know the alphabet). For the very young and or those who cannot read, the chart has rows of the letter *E* arranged in various positions, and the person's task is to indicate in what direction the "legs" of the *E*'s face. Each row corresponds to the distance at which a person with normal vision can discriminate the letters or the directions of the *E*'s. (There are eight rows, one corresponding to each of the following distances: 15, 20, 30, 40, 50, 70, 100, and 200 feet.) People are normally tested at the 20-foot distance. If they can distinguish the letters in the 20-foot row, they are said to have 20/20 central visual acuity for far distances. If they can distinguish only the much larger letters in the 70-foot row, they are said to have 20/70 central visual acuity for far distances.

Although the Snellen chart is widely used and can be very useful, it has at least three limitations:

1. It measures visual acuity for distant but not near objects, which is why it's necessary to report the results in terms of central visual acuity for far distances. Many educational activities, particularly reading, require visual acuity at close distances. A variety of near-vision tests, consisting of cards with different size print or symbols, are available. For example, a person might be asked to name letters that range in size from smaller to larger than the letters on this page on a card that is at a typical reading distance from the person's eyes.

2. Visual acuity, as measured by the Snellen chart, doesn't always correspond with visual efficiency. **Visual efficiency** refers to the ability, for example, to control eye movements and to use visual information quickly and accurately (Barraga & Erin, 2001). Teachers often assess visual efficiency by observing the student performing in a variety of settings or by using an instrument designed for this purpose.

3. Visual acuity doesn't always correspond with how a student actually uses her or his vision in natural settings, which have variable environmental conditions (e.g., fluorescent lighting, windows that admit sunshine, highly reflective tile floors).

To determine how students use their vision in everyday situations, the vision teacher performs a **functional vision assessment**. The vision teacher observes the student in his or her daily activities, taking note of how the student functions under a variety of conditions (e.g., in sunny or cloudy weather) and on a variety of tasks (e.g., reading books, navigating within the classroom or from class to class; Miller, 1999).

As part of this assessment, teachers should be alert to signs that children might have visual disabilities. Prevent Blindness America (2005) has listed a number of signs of possible eye problems on their Website (see the Focus on Concepts p. 385).

Causes

Causes Affecting Children and Adults

When considering both children and adults, the most common visual problems are the result of errors of refraction. **Refraction** refers to the bending of the light rays as they pass through the various structures of the eye. **Myopia** (nearsightedness), **hyperopia** (farsightedness), and **astigmatism** (blurred vision) are examples of refraction errors that affect central visual acuity. Although each can be serious enough to cause significant

FOCUS ON **Concepts**

Signs of Possible Eye Trouble in Children

If one or more of these signs appear, take your child to an eye doctor right away.

What do your child's eyes look like?
- eyes don't line up, one eye appears crossed or looks out
- eyelids are red-rimmed, crusted or swollen
- eyes are watery or red (inflamed)

How does your child act?
- rubs eyes a lot
- closes or covers one eye
- tilts head or thrusts head forward
- has trouble reading or doing other close-up work, or holds objects close to eyes to see
- blinks more than usual or seems cranky when doing close-up work

- things are blurry or hard to see
- squints eyes or frowns

What does your child say?
- "my eyes are itchy," "my eyes are burning" or "my eyes feel scratchy."
- "I can't see very well."
- After doing close-up work, your child says "I feel dizzy," "I have a headache" or "I feel sick/nauseous."
- "Everything looks blurry," or "I see double."

Remember, your child may still have an eye problem even if he or she does not complain or has not shown any unusual signs.

Source: Retrieved December 3, 2007 from the World Wide Web: www.preventblindness. org/children/trouble_signs.html. Reprinted with permission from Prevent Blindness America ®. Copyright © 2005.

impairment (myopia and hyperopia are the most common impairments of low vision), wearing glasses or contact lenses usually can bring vision within normal limits.

Myopia results when the eyeball is too long. In this case, the light rays from the object in Figure 11.2a would be in focus in front of, rather than on, the retina. Myopia affects vision for distant objects, but close vision may be unaffected. When the eyeball is too short, hyperopia (farsightedness) results (see Figure 11.2b). In this case, the light rays from the object in the diagram would be in focus behind, rather than on, the retina. Hyperopia affects vision for close objects, but far vision may be unaffected. If the cornea or lens of the eye is irregular, the person is said to have astigmatism. In this case, the light rays from the object in the figure would be blurred or distorted.

Among the most serious impairments are those caused by glaucoma, cataracts, and diabetes. These conditions occur primarily in adults, but each, particularly the latter two,

■ **Myopia**
Nearsightedness; vision for distant objects is affected; usually results when eyeball is too long.

■ **Hyperopia**
Farsightedness; vision for near objects is affected; usually results when the eyeball is too short.

■ **Astigmatism**
Blurred vision caused by an irregular cornea or lens.

Video Homework Exercise

Echolocation • Go to the Homework and Exercises section in Chapter 11 of MyEducationLab to watch the introductory video about echolocation.

(a)   (b)

FIGURE 11.2 Visual problems: (a) myopia, (b) hyperopia

(a)

(b)

(c)

(d)

(e)

FIGURE 11.3 These are simulations of how people with certain visual impairments see the world: (a) normal vision; (b) glaucoma; (c) cataracts; (d) diabetic retinopathy; (e) retinitis pigmentosa

■ Glaucoma
A condition often, but not always, due to excessive pressure in the eyeball; the cause is unknown; if untreated, blindness results.

■ Optic nerve
The nerve at the back of the eye, which sends visual information back to the brain.

can occur in children. See Figure 11.3 for simulations of how different eye conditions affect how people see.

Glaucoma is actually a *group* of eye diseases that causes damage to the **optic nerve**. At one time, it was thought to be due exclusively to excessive pressure inside the eyeball; we now know that some cases of glaucoma occur with normal pressure (Glaucoma

Research Foundation, 2006). It is referred to as the "sneak thief of sight" because it often occurs with no symptoms. However, glaucoma can be detected through an eye exam; and because it occurs more frequently in older people (and in African Americans), professionals recommend increasingly frequent checkups, starting at age 35 (and even more frequently for African Americans).

Cataracts are caused by a clouding of the lens of the eye, which results in blurred vision. In children, the condition is called congenital cataracts, and distance and color vision are seriously affected. Surgery can usually correct the problems caused by cataracts.

Diabetes can cause **diabetic retinopathy**, a condition that results from interference with the blood supply to the retina.

Causes Primarily Affecting Children

For children, **cortical visual impairment (CVI)** is now the leading cause of visual impairment in the Western world (Edelman et al., 2006). Whereas most causes of visual impairment are due to abnormalities in the eye itself, CVI results from widespread damage to parts of the *brain* responsible for vision (American Printing House for the Blind, 2004). The damage or dysfunction can be the result of a variety of causes, such as a head injury or infection. Although researchers are still refining a description of CVI, there appears to be a unique pattern of visual responses associated with CVI. Some of these responses are an avoidance of looking at new visual information, a preference for looking at near objects, non-purposeful gazing, distinct color preferences, attraction to rapid movements, and abnormal visual reflexes.

Several other visual impairments primarily affect children. These are often due to prenatal causes, many of which are hereditary. We have already discussed congenital (meaning present at birth) cataracts and glaucoma. Another congenital condition is retinitis pigmentosa, a hereditary disease resulting in degeneration of the retina. It can start in infancy, early childhood, or the teenage years. **Retinitis pigmentosa** usually causes the field of vision to narrow (**tunnel vision**) and also affects one's ability to see in low light (**night blindness**). Included in the "prenatal" category are infectious diseases that affect the unborn child, such as syphilis and rubella.

One of the most dramatic medical discoveries of a cause of blindness involved a condition now referred to as **retinopathy of prematurity (ROP)**. ROP, which results in abnormal growth of blood vessels in the eye, began to appear in the 1940s in premature infants. In the 1950s, researchers determined that excessive concentrations of oxygen often administered to premature infants were causing blindness. The oxygen was necessary to prevent brain damage, but it was often given at too high a level. Since then, hospitals have been careful to monitor the amount of oxygen administered to premature infants. Today, with medical advances, many more premature babies are surviving, but they need very high levels of oxygen and are thus at risk for ROP. Furthermore, ROP can result from factors other than excessive oxygen that are related to being born very prematurely (National Eye Institute, 2005).

Strabismus and nystagmus, two other conditions resulting in visual problems, are caused by improper muscle functioning. **Strabismus** is a condition in which one or both eyes are directed inward (crossed eyes) or outward. Left untreated, strabismus can result in permanent blindness because the brain will eventually reject signals from a deviating eye. Fortunately, most cases of strabismus can be corrected with eye exercises or surgery. Eye exercises sometimes involve the person's wearing a patch over the good eye for periods of time to force use of the eye that deviates. Surgery involves tightening or loosening the muscles that control eye movement. **Nystagmus** is a condition in which there are rapid involuntary movements of the eyes, usually resulting in dizziness and nausea. Nystagmus is sometimes a sign of brain malfunctioning and/or inner-ear problems.

■ **Cataracts**
A condition caused by clouding of the lens of the eye; affects color vision and distance vision.

■ **Diabetic retinopathy**
A condition resulting from interference with the blood supply to the retina; the fastest-growing cause of blindness.

■ **Cortical visual impairment (CVI)**
A poorly understood childhood condition that apparently involves dysfunction in the visual cortex; characterized by large day-to-day variations in visual ability.

■ **Retinitis pigmentosa**
A hereditary condition resulting in degeneration of the retina; causes a narrowing of the field of vision and affects night vision.

■ **Tunnel vision**
A condition characterized by problems in peripheral vision, or a narrowing of the field of vision.

■ **Night blindness**
A condition characterized by problems in seeing at low levels of illumination; often caused by retinitis pigmentosa.

■ **Retinopathy of prematurity (ROP)**
A condition resulting in abnormal growth of blood vessels in the eye; caused by factors related to premature birth, including the administration of an excessive concentration of oxygen at birth.

■ **Strabismus**
A condition in which the eyes are directed inward (crossed eyes) or outward.

■ **Nystagmus**
A condition in which there are rapid involuntary movements of the eyes; sometimes indicates a brain malfunction and/or inner-ear problems.

**UNDERSTANDING
THE STANDARDS AND
PRINCIPLES** What should
teachers know about the
psychological and behavioral
characteristics of individuals
who are visually impaired? (CEC
Knowledge and Skill Standards
VI2K4 & VI2K5)

Council for
Exceptional
Children

Psychological and Behavioral Characteristics

Language Development

Most authorities believe that lack of vision does not have a very significant effect on the ability to understand and use language (Rosel, Caballer, Jara, & Oliver, 2005). Because auditory more than visual perception is the sensory modality through which we learn language, it's not surprising that studies have found that people who are blind are not impaired in language functioning. The child who is blind is still able to hear language and might even be more motivated than the sighted child to use language because it's the main channel through which he or she communicates with others.

Intellectual Ability

PERFORMANCE ON STANDARDIZED INTELLIGENCE TESTS   At one time, it was popular for researchers to compare the intelligence of sighted people with that of persons with blindness. Most authorities now believe that such comparisons are virtually impossible because finding comparable tests is so difficult. From what is known, there is no reason to believe that blindness results in lower intelligence.

CONCEPTUAL ABILITIES   It is also very difficult to assess the performance of children with visual impairment on laboratory-type tasks of conceptual ability. Many researchers, using conceptual tasks originally developed by noted psychologist Jean Piaget, have concluded that infants and very young children who are blind lag behind their sighted peers. This is usually attributed to the fact that they rely more on touch to arrive at conceptualizations of many objects, and touch is less efficient than sight. However, these early delays don't last for long, especially once the children begin to use language to gather information about their environment (Perez-Pereira & Conti-Ramsden, 1999). Touch, however, remains a very critical sense throughout life for those who are blind. As one person who is blind described it, he "sees with his fingers" (Hull, 1997).

An important difference between individuals with and without sight is that the latter need to take much more initiative to learn what they can from their environment. Sighted infants and children can pick up a lot of visual information incidentally. In a sense, the world comes to them; children who are visually impaired need to extend themselves out to the world to pick up some of the same information. Exploring the environment motorically, however, doesn't come easily for infants and young children with visual impairment, especially those who are blind. Many have serious delays in motor skills, such as sitting up, crawling, and walking (Celeste, 2002). Therefore, adults should do as much as possible to encourage infants and young children who are blind to explore their environment.

In addition to fostering a sense of exploration in children who are visually impaired, it is critical that teachers and parents provide intensive and extensive instruction, including repetition, in order to help them develop their conceptual abilities:

When a student cannot see, . . . It can be mystifying to comprehend what the front and back of a store are when the student is inside of it.

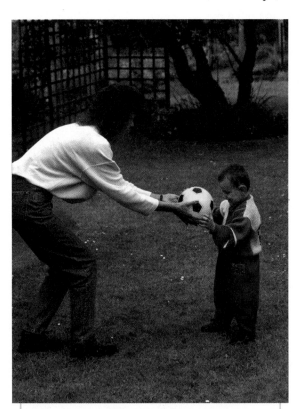

Infants and children who are blind may have serious delays in motor skills, such as sitting up, crawling, and walking. Therefore, adults should do as much as possible to encourage them to explore their environment.

It is especially difficult if the student is thinking of the front and back of his or her own body that, as the student moves, are continually changing relationship to objects and their fronts and backs. . . . A gradual approach to teaching concepts, presenting many repetitions over time and in a variety of situations, with repeated opportunities for tactile exploration, will yield the most detailed mental image and the most thorough understanding. (Knott, 2002, p. 69)

Orientation and Mobility

Orientation and mobility skills are very important for the successful adjustment of people with visual impairment. **Orientation and mobility (O & M)** skills refer to the ability to have a sense of where one is in relation to other people, objects, and landmarks (orientation) and to move through the environment (mobility).

O & M skills depend to a great extent on spatial ability. Authorities have identified two ways in which persons with visual impairment process spatial information: as a sequential route or as a map depicting the general relation of various points in the environment (Webster & Roe, 1998). The latter method, referred to as **cognitive mapping**, is preferable because it offers more flexibility in navigating. Consider three sequential points—A, B, and C. A sequential mode of processing spatial information restricts a person's movement so that the person can move from A to C only by way of B. But a person with a cognitive map of points A, B, and C can go from A to C directly without going through B. Although not impossible, it is more difficult for people who are blind to build these cognitive maps. Vision allows us to

> construct a coherent sense of the physical environment and our place in it, without struggling to remember. On entering an unfamiliar classroom, a sighted child is able to take in something of the whole at a glance, and perhaps work out the overall position of the room in relation to more familiar places, such as the library, computer room. . . . For the child with a visual impairment, constructing an inner map of this new classroom presents a problem of synthesizing information from the integration of small, local details to achieve a functional sense of the whole, which must then be largely memorised. (Webster & Roe, 1998, p. 69)

Mobility skills vary greatly among people with visual impairment. It is surprisingly difficult to predict which individuals will be the best travelers. For example, common sense seems to tell us that mobility would be better among those who have more residual vision and those who lose their vision later in life, but this is not always the case. How much motivation and how much proper instruction one receives are critical to becoming a proficient traveler.

OBSTACLE SENSE   Some persons who are blind, when walking along the street seem able to sense objects in their path. This ability has come to be known as the **obstacle sense**—an unfortunate term in some ways, because many laypeople have taken it to mean that people who are blind somehow develop an extra sense. It's easy to see why this misconception exists. Even people who are blind have a very difficult time explaining the phenomenon (Hull, 1997). A number of experiments have shown that with experience, people who are blind come to learn to detect subtle changes in the pitches of high-frequency echoes as they move toward objects. Actually, they are taking advantage of the **Doppler effect**, a physical principle wherein the pitch of a sound rises as a person moves toward its source.

Although obstacle sense can be important for the mobility of someone without sight, by itself it will not make its user a highly proficient traveler. It is merely an aid. Extraneous noises (e.g., traffic, speech, rain, wind) can render obstacle sense unusable. Also, it requires walking at a fairly slow speed to be able to react in time.

Reading Homework Exercise

Achievement Tests • Go to the Homework and Exercises section in Chapter 11 of MyEducationLab and read the article "Blind Student Bucks State Ruling: Test is Unfair Teenager Says", which addresses the issues associated with achievement tests for students who are blind or have low vision.

■ **Orientation and mobility (O & M) skills**
The ability to have a sense of where one is in relation to other people, objects, and landmarks and to move through the environment.

■ **Cognitive mapping**
A nonsequential way of conceptualizing the spatial environment that allows a person who is visually impaired to know where several points in the environment are simultaneously; allows for better mobility than does a strictly sequential conceptualization of the environment.

■ **Obstacle sense**
A skill possessed by some people who are blind, whereby they can detect the presence of obstacles in their environments; research has shown that it is not an indication of an extra sense, as popularly thought; it is the result of learning to detect subtle changes in the pitches of high-frequency echoes.

■ **Doppler effect**
A term used to describe the phenomenon of the pitch of a sound rising as the listener moves toward its source.

THE MYTH OF SENSORY ACUTENESS   Along with the myth that people with blindness have an extra sense comes the general misconception that they automatically develop better acuity in their other senses. However, people who are blind don't have lowered thresholds of sensation in touch or hearing. What they are able to do is make better use of the sensations they obtain. Through concentration and attention, they learn to make very fine discriminations. It's easy to overlook just how much information can be picked up through listening and senses other than sight. The Personal Perspectives below gives an example of how much a person who is blind can appreciate about his or her surroundings through non-visual information.

Personal PERSPECTIVES

Stephen Kuusisto's Sensory World

People who are sighted often miss out on just how much information can be gained through other senses, such as hearing, touch, and smell. People who are blind, however, come to rely on these other senses. And for them, the world can consist of a rich array of sounds, textures, and smells. The following excerpt from Stephen Kuusisto's memoir, *Eavesdropping*, vividly demonstrates just how opulent these non-visual sensations can be:

Stephen Kuusisto and his guide dog Corky.

Maybe it was a Saturday. I remember that my parents were still sleeping. I had a plan and dressed quietly. When I was certain that no one was awake I slipped from the house. I loved to walk in the woods and follow the beams of light or depths of shade that fell between the trees. I remember that on this particular day I got lost while chasing light and found myself standing in front of the university's horse barn. I knew that somewhere in the cool space before me a horse was breathing. I stood in the door and listened to him breathe. He sounded like water going down a drain. Then I took one step forward into a pyramid of fragrances.

What a thing! To be a young boy smelling hay and leather and turds!

From his place in the dark the horse gurgled like water in the back of a boat.

Mice scurried like beaded curtains disturbed by the hand.

I stood in that magical nowhere and listened to a full range of barn sounds.

I was a blind child approaching a horse!

Behind me a cat mewed.

Who would guess that horses sometimes hold their breath?

The horse was eying me from his corner.

Then two cats were talking.

Wind pushed forcefully at the high roof.

Somewhere up high a timber groaned.

My horse was still holding his breath.

When would he breathe again?

Come on boy!

Breathe for me!

Where are you?

I heard him rub his flank against a wall.

Then I heard him breathe again with great deflation!

He sounded like a fat balloon venting in swift circles.

And then I imitated him with my arm pressed to my mouth.

I made great, flatulent noises by pressing my lips to my forearm.

How do you like that, horse?

He snorted.

I noticed a ringing of silence. An insect traveled between our bursts of forced air.

Sunlight warmed my face. I was standing in a wide sunbeam.

I was in the luminous whereabouts of horse! I was a very small boy and I had wandered about a mile from home. Although I could see colors and shapes in sunlight, in the barn I was completely blind.

But I had made up my mind to touch a horse.

Judging by his breathing, his slow release of air, that sound of a concertina, judging by this I was nearly beside him. And so I reached out and there was a great wet fruit of his nose, the velvet bone of his enormous face. And we stood there together for a little while, all alive and all alone. (Kuusisto, 2006, pp. 7–8)

Source: Kuusisto, S. (2006). *Eavesdropping.* New York: W. W. Norton & Company. Reprinted by permission.

Another common belief is that people who are blind automatically have superior musical talent. Some do embark on musical careers, but this is because music is an area in which they can achieve success.

Academic Achievement

Most professionals agree that direct comparisons of the academic achievement of students who are blind with that of sighted students must be interpreted cautiously because the two groups must be tested under different conditions. There are, however, braille and large-print forms of some achievement tests. The few studies that have been done suggest that both children with low vision and those who are blind are sometimes behind their sighted peers (Rapp & Rapp, 1992). Most authorities believe that when low achievement does occur, it is due not to the blindness itself, but to such things as low expectations or lack of exposure to braille. Patrick, the student described in Success Stories on pages 392–393, has begun to learn braille as an older student. He enjoys reading braille instead of holding his book two inches from his right eye and struggling to use his remaining sight.

With respect to reading, we do know that learning to read braille is similar in some important ways to learning to read print. For example, **phonological awareness** (discussed in Chapter 6) is an important component of learning to read print or braille (Barlow-Brown & Connelly, 2002; Gillon & Young, 2002).

Social Adjustment

Most people with visual impairment are socially well adjusted. However, the road to social adjustment for people with visual impairment may be a bit more difficult for two reasons. First, social interactions among the sighted are often based on subtle cues, many of which are visual. Second, sighted society is often uncomfortable in its interactions with those who are visually impaired (Erin, 2006).

SUBTLE VISUAL CUES   Most of us who are sighted take for granted how often we use visual cues to help us in our social interactions. In growing up, we learn most of these cues incidentally by observing others. Thus, children with visual impairment often need to be taught directly how to use these cues (Jindal-Snape, 2005; Sacks, 2006). Facial expressions, such as smiling, are a good example of visual cues that don't come spontaneously for persons who are visually impaired. John M. Hull, whose eyesight deteriorated gradually over several years, kept a diary of his experiences. The following entry pertains to smiling:

> Nearly every time I smile, I am conscious of it. . . . Why is this? It must be because there is no reinforcement. There is no returning smile. . . . Most smiling is responsive. You smile spontaneously when you receive a smile. For me it is like sending dead letters. Have they been received, acknowledged? Was I even smiling in the right direction? (Hull, 1997, p. 30)

SOCIETY'S DISCOMFORT WITH BLINDNESS   Authorities point out that sighted people feel ill at ease in interacting with people with visual impairments, which then interferes with smooth social interaction. Unfortunately, some people who are blind feel that they need to go to great lengths to appear "normal." The following account, written by the National Federation of the Blind's president (himself blind), of one man's attempt not to appear different is humorous but poignant:

> Dr. Schroeder became a teacher and an administrator of public programs of education, but he was still affected by his beliefs about blindness. With the acquisition of the new job, Dr. Schroeder had the money to buy a house. He faced the problem of how to get the lawn

UNDERSTANDING THE STANDARDS AND PRINCIPLES   Does a student's visual impairment necessarily affect his/her academic achievement? Why or why not? (CEC Knowledge and Skill Standards VI2K4 & VI3K3)

Council for Exceptional Children

■ **Phonological awareness** The ability to understand that speech flow can be broken into smaller sound units such as words, syllables, and phonemes; generally thought to be the reason for the reading problems of many students with learning disabilities.

UNDERSTANDING THE STANDARDS AND PRINCIPLES   Discuss some social adjustment challenges individuals with visual impairment may experience. (CEC Knowledge and Skill Standards VI2K5 & CC5S2)

Council for Exceptional Children

Reading Homework Exercise

Promoting Braille • Go to the Homework and Exercises section in Chapter 11 of MyEducationLab and read the list of ways to promote the use of Braille in the community.

Success Stories

Patrick prepares for transition from high school through functional academics and vocational education

Patrick's mother, Audrey Pugh: "All I want anyone to do is give him a fair chance."

Nineteen-year-old Patrick Pugh is a high school junior with impaired vision and multiple disabilities. He is working toward his future with consistent and specialized support.

These are the keys to Patrick's success:

- Intensive instruction from specialized personnel
- Relentless persistence over time
- Specific goals for transition and vocational education

Special educator Ricki Curry, an itinerant teacher of students with visual impairments, has worked closely with Patrick for fourteen years. She credits much of his progress to a key ingredient—time. Since he was 5 years old, she has set high expectations for Patrick, who has no vision in his left eye and only partial sight in his right eye. His speech is slurred, and he does not have functional use of his left arm or leg. "Patrick is eager to learn new things," says Curry, who credits his success to intensive, relentless, and specific special education.

● Intensive Instruction from Specialized Personnel
Patrick started vision and physical therapy when he was 2 years old. Ricki Curry remembers the little boy whose eyes would lift aimlessly to the ceiling, not using what vision he had. "Our basic goal was for Patrick to learn to use his sight by tracking objects and looking at pictures, but as a 5-year-old, he was stubborn, difficult, and noncompliant," she recalls. Despite his reluctance, Patrick successfully learned literal information and concrete routines. He was highly distractible, and progress was very slow.

His parents hoped that all he needed was extra time, so he stayed in a preschool for children with special needs until he was 7 years old.

Patrick spent first grade in a self-contained class for children with learning disabilities in the nearest physically accessible elementary school. Curry continued to provide weekly sessions and to supervise his vision services. He was also given a personal aide to assist with mobility and visual modifications. "In some ways, kids with personal aides never encounter problems, so they don't learn any problem solving skills!" says Curry. "On the other hand, there are some effective strategies that can be used by paraeducators." Patrick's hand use was limited, so his aide assisted him with writing. Math was broken down into small steps, reading was individualized, and he was taught to use a large-print word processor.

● Relentless Persistence over Time Patrick finished elementary school two years older than most of his classmates yet only able to do rote math. His reading skills were also concrete; he could decode text but had limited comprehension. "He

mowed. He thought he might hire somebody to do it, but (he reasoned) if he asked a sighted person to mow his lawn, the neighbors would believe he was not able to do it himself because he was blind. This would reinforce their assessment of him as inferior. However, he was also afraid to mow the lawn himself because the neighbors might watch him do it, and if he missed a patch of grass, they would conclude that he was incompetent. He could, of course, cover the lawn in such a way that he would not miss any grass—going over it repeatedly in narrow strips—but this would look unusual and peculiar to the neighbors.

Dr. Schroeder did not want to look peculiar. He decided that the best solution was for him to mow his lawn when the neighbors were not likely to observe. He decided to cut the grass at night. I cannot say how the neighbors reacted to this plan. However, if the objective is to seem normal, I doubt that mowing the lawn at night is the best way to accomplish this purpose.

The efforts of Dr. Fred Schroeder to avoid looking conspicuous and to appear normal remind me of my own embarrassing experiences. How great a premium there is on seeming normal! (Maurer, 2000, p. 294) could answer factual questions, but he couldn't make that leap to the abstract," recalls Curry. "Patrick was in a middle school science class learning about mitochondria. That's when it really hit me. Sure, he could learn the definition of mitochondria, but was this functional for him? He'd never use this word again!"

Patrick was 13 years old when his mother and the IEP team decided that he needed a class that emphasized functional academics, such as money skills. "At that point, we all knew this was what he needed," says Curry. "Patrick has multiple learning needs, and it takes him a long time to learn; it takes intensive care and a lot of specific teaching. This class gave him the right information at the right pace. We forgot about the mitochondria and were now reading for comprehension."

● **Specific Goals for Transition and Vocational Education**
Patrick started high school at the age of 17, and a creative program was crafted for him blending functional academics, work experience, and independent living skills. He spends his mornings in two periods of functional English and math. He then boards a van for the vocational center three afternoons a week, where he eats lunch with coworkers. Two afternoons are spent at an independent living center learning to clean, shop, and travel around the community.

Patrick Pugh and Ricki Curry work sixty minutes daily on braille skills geared toward his vocational goals. "I think there's a job out there for Patrick," says Curry. "We've got two years to get those skills really sharp." Patrick enjoys reading braille and translating printed sentences with a unimanual brailler. According to Curry, he's exceeding everybody's expectations. "Every time we've taught him something, he's had some success in learning it." This description of Patrick does not surprise Audrey Pugh. "Opportunity is the main thing," she says. "All I want anyone to do is give him a fair chance."

An important point is that it should not be only up to people who are visually impaired to change their ways of interacting socially. Not only might some people with visual impairment profit from instruction in using appropriate visually based cues (e.g., facial expressions, head nods, and gestures), but sighted people also can learn to use their natural telephone skills when communicating with people who are blind. Two sighted people talking on the telephone use a variety of auditory cues to help them communicate, even though they can't see each other (e.g., responding with "uh-hum" or "yeah," asking for more information, adjusting tone of voice (Fichten, Judd, Tagalakis, Amsel, & Robillard, 1991).

STEREOTYPIC BEHAVIORS An impediment to good social adjustment for some students with visual impairment is **stereotypic behaviors**: repetitive, stereotyped movements such as body rocking, poking or rubbing the eyes, repetitive hand or finger movements, and grimacing. These can begin as early as a few months of age. For many years, the term *blindisms* was used to refer to these behaviors because it was thought

■ **Stereotypic behaviors**
Any of a variety of repetitive behaviors (e.g., eye rubbing) that are sometimes found in individuals who are autistic, blind, severely intellectually disabled, or psychotic; sometimes referred to as *stereotypies* or *blindisms*.

A misconception about people who are blind is that they do not adjust well socially.

that they were manifested only in people who are blind; however, they are also sometimes characteristic of children with normal sight who are severely intellectually disabled or autistic.

Several competing theories concern the causes of stereotypic behaviors (McHugh & Lieberman, 2003). Some researchers believe that they are an attempt to provide oneself with more stimulation to make up for a relative lack of sensory or social stimulation. Others believe them to be an attempt to self-regulate one's stimulation in the face of overstimulation. In either case, most authorities believe that these behaviors serve to stabilize the person's arousal level (Warren, 1994).

There is even some disagreement about how much one should intervene to reduce or eliminate stereotypic behaviors. On the one hand, when done to the extreme, these behaviors can interfere with learning and socialization, and can even be physically injurious. On the other hand, if not done to the extreme, such behaviors might help maintain an appropriate level of arousal (Warren, 1994). In addition, some have argued for society's need to be more tolerant of stereotypic behaviors: "As researchers and advocates . . . , let us consider the idea that rocking is simply an idiosyncrasy or individual difference that should be ignored or for which we should demand greater awareness, tolerance, and understanding" (McHugh & Lieberman, 2003, p. 472).

UNDERSTANDING THE STANDARDS AND PRINCIPLES What modifications should teachers consider when working with students with little or no sight? (CEC Knowledge and Skill Standards VI5S1, VI7S1 & VI7S3)

Council for Exceptional Children

Educational Considerations

Lack of sight can severely limit a person's experiences because a primary means of obtaining information from the environment is not available. What makes the situation even more difficult is that educational experiences in the typical classroom are frequently visual. Nevertheless, most experts agree that, in many ways, students who are visually impaired should be educated in the same general way as sighted children. However, teachers need to make some important modifications. The most important

TABLE 11.1 *Dos* and *Don'ts* for Teachers Working with Students with Visual Impairments

Do	Don't
. . . feel comfortable using vision words, such as "look," "see," and "watch."	. . . be afraid to touch the visually impaired student, but tell him/her you are about to touch him/her; respect the student's personal preferences about touching.
. . . use the student's name when calling on him/her.	
. . . read out loud what you are writing on the board.	. . . overprotect; let the student try as many things as possible for him/herself.
. . . encourage independence; the visually impaired student needs to learn to do as much as possible for him/herself.	. . . worry about your initial feelings of awkwardness; remember that you are teaching a *child*—who happens to have a disability.
. . . include the visually impaired student in as many class activities as possible.	
. . . give explicit directions; avoid the words "here" and "there" because they may not give enough information.	. . . be afraid to require a student's best work.
	. . . be afraid to require good behavior; administer the same discipline, if needed, as you would for a sighted child; rules *do* count.
. . . fill in experiential gaps when you discover them.	
. . . allow extra time when needed, for tactual exploration, when appropriate, slower visual/ braille reading, etc.	. . . hesitate to ask the student what something looks like to him/her, it may help you understand the quality of the student's vision.
. . . provide extra storage space for special equipment/materials.	. . . feel you must tolerate unacceptable behavior in the visually impaired student any more than you would in a normally sighted student.
. . . encourage the use of aids/devices (*not* aides).	

Source: Bishop, V. E. (2004). *Teaching visually impaired children* (3rd ed.). Springfield, IL: Charles S. Thomas.

difference is that students with visual impairment have to rely on other sensory modalities to acquire information. See Table 11.1 for do's and don'ts for teachers.

The student with little or no sight will possibly require special modifications in four major areas: (1) braille, (2) use of remaining sight, (3) listening skills, and (4) orientation and mobility training. The first three pertain directly to academic education, particularly reading; the last refers to skills needed for everyday living.

Braille

In nineteenth century France, Louis Braille introduced a system of reading and writing for people who, like him, were blind. Although not the first method that was developed, Braille's was the one that became widely used. Even his system, however, was not adopted for several years after he invented it. (See the Personal Perspectives on p. 396.)

One braille code, called **literary braille**, is used for most everyday situations; other codes are available for more technical reading and writing. The **Nemeth Code**, for example, is used for mathematical and scientific symbols. Some authorities support adoption of **Unified English Braille**, which combines these several codes into one (Jolley, 2006). Proponents argue that Unified English Braille is more efficient in that it unifies literary and technical writing, both of which are increasingly necessary, and it unifies differences in codes between the United States and the United Kingdom. Although gaining some momentum, at this point, Unified English Braille has not been adopted widely.

Building Teaching Skills Reading Exercise

Teaching with Braille ● Go to the Building Teaching Skills section in Chapter 11 of MyEducationLab and read the article titled, "Teaching Reading in Braille."

■ **Literary braille**
Braille symbols used for most writing situations.

■ **Nemeth Code**
Braille symbols used for mathematics and science.

■ **Unified English Braille**
A combination of literary braille and braille codes for technical fields, such as the Nemeth Code for science and mathematics; not yet widely adopted.

Personal PERSPECTIVES

Captain Charles Barbier de la Serre and Louis Braille

The first person to develop a system of reading and writing for persons who are blind was Captain Charles Barbier de la Serre. However, his original reason for inventing the system was for military purposes. Only after his system was rejected by the military establishment did he suggest it as a system for people who are blind. But they, too, turned down his offer. And, ironically, one of his biggest critics was Louis Braille:

In 1822, Captain Charles Barbier de la Serre came to present his night-writing code to the [National Institute for the Young Blind]. He was a career military officer of aristocratic background, presumably full of indignation that his code had been rejected by the army, forcing him to offer it instead to this nearly destitute and decidedly distasteful institution. Children at the institute read texts with embossed Roman characters. Since they had to trace each letter with their fingers, reading was slow and inefficient. Barbier's code used patterns of raised dots to represent phonic units, which would reduce the number of characters required for each word and make reading quicker and more accurate. Among the collection of children selected to test the Barbier system was one skinny, pale, thirteen-year-old boy. . . . This boy, when prodded to speak, not only criticized Barbier's code as inferior to the embossed texts already in use but actually enumerated its flaws.

And Barbier must have been an imposing figure, with a voice accustomed to giving orders. To him, this boy Braille, this son of a saddler, this runty bag of bones was the sort of boy one routinely ignored except to have him stoop to give one a leg up onto a horse.

But Braille spoke up anyway. As he analyzed the flaws in Barbier's code, it set into motion the thought process that would lead to his own code. Two years later Braille perfected his own system. He used six dots instead of Barbier's twelve. He made each character represent a letter in the alphabet so that a child who learned to read would also learn to spell. And he made provisions for punctuation, numbers, and musical notation. When he proposed his code to the institute's director, they rejected it too. They cited the same common objections they had to Barbier's system. . . . What seemed particularly threatening about Braille's code was that he produced it himself. When the blind learned to write at all, they used a sort of stencil to make Roman letters. But they could not read what they wrote. Braille's code was easy to write, requiring only a couple of simple tools. It would allow blind children to send messages to each other and to read them without sighted intervention. To give blind children a method of communication that their sighted custodians would not be able to oversee meant trouble. Who knew what messages those blind children might write . . . ? It was not until 1847 that Braille's code was authorized for use in the institute. During the twenty-three-year interim, students secretly used and trained each other in the forbidden code even though discovery meant punishment, even expulsion.

Source: Kleege, G. (1999). *Sight unseen.* New Haven, CT: Yale University Press, pp. 223–225. Reprinted with permission.

The basic unit of braille is a quadrangular cell, containing from one to six dots (see Figure 11.4). Different patterns of dots represent letters, numbers, and even punctuation marks. Generally, the best method of reading braille involves using both hands:

Both hands start at the top left side of the page. Together they move across the letters until they reach the middle. While the right hand continues across, the left hand moves down a line and orients itself at the beginning of that line. When the right hand is finished with the top line, the left hand immediately begins to read the second line. The right hand joins the left until they reach the middle of the second line of text. (Bailey, 2003, p. 324).

Two basic means of writing in braille are the Perkins Brailler and the slate and stylus. The **Perkins Brailler** has six keys, one for each of the six dots of the cell (see Figure 11.5). When depressed simultaneously, the keys leave an embossed print on the paper. More portable than the Perkins Brailler is the **slate and stylus** (see Figure 11.6). The stylus—a pen-shaped instrument—is pressed through the opening of the slate, which holds the paper between its two halves.

Perhaps the most hotly debated topic in the field of visual impairment concerns whether students who are blind should be taught to use braille or another method of

■ **Perkins Brailler**
A system that makes it possible to write in braille; has six keys, one for each of the six dots of the cell, which leave an embossed print on the paper.

■ **Slate and stylus**
A method of writing in braille in which the paper is held in a slate while a stylus is pressed through openings to make indentations in the paper.

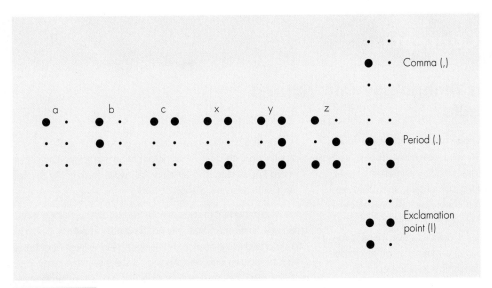

FIGURE 11.4 Examples of symbols from braille

communication, such as a tape recorder or voice-activated computer. At one time, it was fairly common for students with blindness to use braille, but the percentage of students who are blind who use braille has steadily declined since the mid-1960s, when nearly half used braille. Today, authorities estimate that only about 12 percent of school-age children who are blind use braille as their primary method of reading (Raeder, 2006).

Many within the community of people who are blind are alarmed at the reduced availability of braille and assert that it has led to a distressing rate of illiteracy (Castellano, 2005; Schroeder, 2002). For the sighted, literacy involves the ability to read and write printed words. For those who are blind, literacy equates with the ability to read and write braille. They charge that too few sighted teachers are proficient in braille and that they do little to discourage the notion held by some that using braille indicates inferiority. Whether a person is comfortable in identifying himself or herself as blind is critical to whether that person will be motivated to learn braille. Ironically, advances in technology have also contributed to reduction in the use of braille. (See the Focus on Concepts on p. 398.)

Many authorities are concerned that, even when students do receive braille instruction, it is often not intense enough. In a survey of experts on braille usage, the respondents stated

INTERNET RESOURCES

The American Foundation for the Blind has a Website, Braille Bug Site, devoted to encouraging young children to learn braille: www.afb. org/braillebug

FIGURE 11.5 A Perkins Brailler

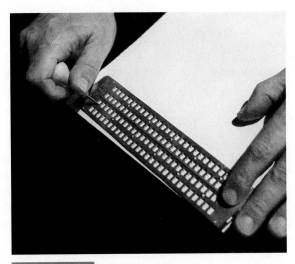

FIGURE 11.6 A slate and stylus in use

FOCUS ON **Concepts**

Have Advances in Technology Contributed to Illiteracy in Braille?

There is no doubt that technology has brought about many positive changes for people who are blind. Today, vast amounts of material can be accessed digitally and electronically. For example, books on tape, talking computers, speech recognition software, and computerized magnification devices have made it ever easier to obtain and produce information. However, the question arises of whether such devices have made it *too* easy to acquire and generate such information. In other words, has easier access served as a disincentive to learning braille. As one reporter has put it:

There are now more ways than ever for the blind to acquire information. Much of the world is moving away from words on a page and toward electronic/digital information. The proliferation of books on tape means blind people no longer have to wait to "read" the latest bestseller. Talking computers have brought the blind to the world and the world to the blind.

These advances have placed a generation of blind young adults and children in an information paradox: They have more knowledge at their disposal, while their ability to read and write declines. (Faherty, 2006)

It's also important to consider that relying on technology sometimes has drawbacks that may not be readily apparent. Consider computerized magnification. Straining to read enlarged print on a computer screen can be fatiguing to the eyes and body, thus reducing one's desire to read for pleasure: "Would you be tempted to read *War and Peace* on a computer screen with letters four inches high?" (Castellano, 2005, p. 25). And consider tape recording class lectures versus note taking in braille: "First of all, it takes too much time; in addition to the reading assignments, the student must also listen to lectures in their entirety in order to study. Second, the student misses the benefits of the note-taking process itself—selecting, organizing, and beginning to analyze and synthesize information" (Castellano, p. 25).

---

that in the early stages of braille acquisition, in particular, students need daily instruction for several years (Koenig & Holbrook, 2000) See the Responsive Instruction on p. 399). The need for intensive braille instruction presents a dilemma for school systems because of the lack of qualified braille instructors.

Advocates of braille also point out that it's essential for most students who are legally blind to learn braille to lead independent lives. Bolstering their argument is research indicating that adults who had learned braille in childhood as their primary medium for reading were employed at almost twice the rate of those who had used print as their primary medium (Ryles, 2000). A way of ensuring that braille becomes more readily available is through **braille bills**, now on the books in most states. Although the specific provisions of these bills vary from state to state, the National Federation of the Blind (NFB), a major proponent of braille bills, has drafted a model bill that specifies two important components:

1. Braille must be available for students if any members of the individualized education program (IEP) team, including parents, indicate that it is needed.

2. Teachers of students with visual impairment need to be proficient in braille.

Federal law now reinforces the first component above. IDEA specifies that braille services and instruction are to be a part of the IEP unless all members of the team, including parents, agree that braille should not be used. To provide a way of determining the braille proficiency of licensed teachers of students who are blind, the NFB is currently field testing a National Literary Braille Competency Test.

Authorities now recommend that some students with low vision who are able to read large print or print with magnification should also be taught braille. There are many students with low vision whose condition dictates that their vision will worsen over the

■ **Braille bills**
Legislation passed in several states to make braille more available to students with visual impairment; specific provisions vary from state to state, but major advocates have lobbied for (1) making braille available if parents want it, and (2) ensuring that teachers of students with visual impairment are proficient in braille.

INTERNET RESOURCES

The National Federation of the Blind is probably the leading organization devoted to advocacy for people who are blind: www.nfb.org

Another important organization is the American Foundation for the Blind: www.afb.org

Meeting the Needs of Students with Visual Impairments
Braille Literacy Instruction

WHAT THE RESEARCH SAYS

For many years, access to high-quality braille literacy programs was hit-or-miss in this country. Barriers such as large caseloads, emphasis on core academic instruction over instruction in braille, lack of adequate assessment materials, and lack of administrative support for this specialized instruction all contributed to the challenge of delivering quality braille instruction (Hatlen, 1998). The 1997 Amendments to the Individuals with Disabilities Education Act (IDEA) sought to change that by requiring all individualized education programs (IEPs) for students with visual impairments to provide for instruction in braille unless an evaluation clearly demonstrates that this is not appropriate for the child's needs both now and in the future.

Empirical research (Ryles, 1997) and professional recommendations (Rex, Koenig, Wormsley, & Baker, 1994) support the need for 1½ to 2 hours of daily braille literacy instruction to foster high literacy levels for students with visual impairments. Braille literacy instruction includes the use of braille as a primary reading medium, particularly during the early elementary years similar to the period of print-literacy development for students without visual impairments, and as a secondary reading medium to supplement or support the use of print.

RESEARCH STUDY

Koenig and Holbrook (2000) designed a study to garner professional consensus related to how braille literacy programs should be delivered. A specific research technique, the Delphi method, provided them with a unique tool for determining consensus. The Delphi method requires surveying the same pool of respondents. In each round of surveys, respondents answer the questions but also provide comments or recommendations on how to change or improve the questions. Each time respondents receive the survey (after the initial round) they are provided with the compiled data and comments from the previous round. Final analysis reflects a minimum of three rounds of survey review and input.

Koenig and Holbrook selected forty professionals for the study based upon experience and expertise in teaching braille. The respondents represented various service delivery options (i.e., resource room, itinerant, and residential schools) and teaching capacities (i.e., those actively teaching and those who are no longer providing direct service but are professionals in the field). Round 1 of the survey included questions related to eleven areas of braille literacy and a "proposed level of service." Respondents indicated agreement or disagreement with the proposed level of service and/or offered alternative recommendations and comments. This process continued for three rounds of surveys.

RESEARCH FINDINGS

Overall, the respondents were able to reach consensus on the factors associated with high quality braille literacy programs. Specific recommendations included:

1. Overwhelming and universal support for daily braille instruction for a period of one to two hours during the early elementary grades (kindergarten through third grade)
2. The need for early intervention, provided in moderate to short sessions, for concept development
3. Pre-braille instruction (e.g., exposure to names in braille, tactile labels, writing experiences) for preschool and kindergarten-age students for periods of thirty minutes to one hour
4. Daily contact for a period of one to two hours for students with print literacy skills who are just learning braille
5. Teaching listening skills such as aural-reading and live-reader skills on a moderate to periodic basis
6. Teaching key-boarding and word processing skills beginning in Grades 1, 2, or 3
7. Braille slate and stylus instruction several days a week for moderate to short time periods beginning in third or fourth grade
8. Teaching students who are blind to write their signatures, spending one to three days per week for short sessions on this task beginning in middle school.

One point of contention was over when and how much time should be devoted to the development of dual media—that is, teaching both print and braille. Some respondents called for teaching both daily and for long sessions; others expressed concern regarding overloading students or the importance of establishing one primary mode. Clearly, this issue requires more research and attention.

APPLYING THE RESEARCH TO TEACHING

The authors of the study, as well as the Council for Exceptional Children's Division on Visual Impairments (DVI), stress that all literacy planning for students with visual impairments should be made on an individual basis (Koenig, Sanspree, & Holbrook, n.d.). The type(s) of reading mediums (print, braille, or both) selected for instruction should be determined after an assessment of the unique needs of the particular student. Thus, no medium is inherently superior, rather, different students will require different supports in order for them to become literate individuals. Therefore, teachers of students with visual impairments should use the above recommendations as a guideline for making individual determinations of services.

● *By Kristin L. Sayeski*

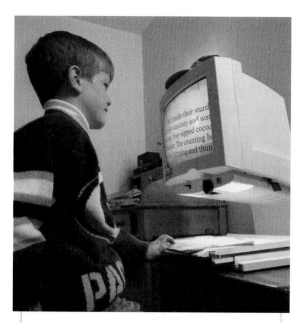

Most professionals agree on the importance of encouraging people with visual impairment to use what sight they do have, but not to the exclusion of braille for those who need it.

■ **Large-print books**
Books having a font size that is larger than the usual 10-point type; a popular size for large-print books is 18-point type.

■ **Magnifying devices**
Often recommended for people with low vision; can be for close vision (e.g., handheld magnifier) or distance vision (e.g., monocular telescope or binocular telescope mounted on eyeglass frames).

years. Learning braille at an early age prepares them for the time when their eyesight no longer allows them to read print.

Use of Remaining Sight

For many years, there was a great deal of resistance to having children with visual impairment use their sight in reading and some other activities. Many myths contributed to this reluctance, including beliefs that holding books close to the eyes is harmful, strong lenses hurt the eyes, and using the eyes too much injures them. It's now recognized that this is true only in very rare conditions. In fact, most agree on the importance of encouraging people with visual impairment to use what sight they do have but not to the exclusion of braille for those who need it.

Two visual methods of aiding children with visual impairment to read print are large-print books and magnifying devices. **Large-print books** are simply books printed in larger-size type. The text in this book, printed primarily for sighted readers, is printed in 10-point type. Figure 11.7 shows print in 18-point type, one of the most popular sizes for large-print materials. Type sizes for readers with visual impairment may range up to 30-point type.

The major difficulty with large-print books is that they are bigger than usual and therefore require a great deal of storage space. In addition, they are of limited availability, although, along with the American Printing House for the Blind, a number of commercial publishers are now publishing and marketing large-print books. Another potential disadvantage is that students who become dependent on large-print books may have difficulties when they encounter situations, such as many jobs, in which large-print materials are unavailable.

With advances in technology, more and more authorities are recommending **magnifying devices** instead of, or in addition to, large-print books (Zimmerman, Zebehazy, & Moon, in press). With respect to reading speed and comprehension, using magnifying devices is at least as effective as using large-print books for many students (Lussenhop & Corn, 2003). Magnifying devices can be for close vision or distance vision. They can be portable, such as handheld magnifiers, monocular telescopes, or binocular telescopes that sit on eyeglass-type frames. Or they can be tabletop closed-circuit television scanners that present enlarged images on a TV screen. Authorities highly recommend that students with low vision receive intensive instruction in the use of magnifying devices rather than being left on their own to use them (Corn & Koenig, 2002).

This is an example of 10-pt. type.

This is an example of 18-pt. type.

This is an example of 24-pt. type.

FIGURE 11.7 Typefaces come in various sizes. Large-print books often use 18-point type and 24-point type.

Listening Skills

The importance of listening skills for children who are blind cannot be overemphasized. There is a tendency to assume that listening skills will develop automatically in children who are blind. However, authorities agree that in most cases these children must be taught how to listen. In addition, teachers should provide a classroom environment as free from auditory distractions as possible.

Listening skills are becoming more important than ever because of the increasing accessibility of recorded material. The American Printing House for the Blind and the Library of Congress are major sources for these materials. Listeners can play the material at normal speed, or they can use a compressed-speech device that allows them to listen at about 250 to 275 words per minute. This method works by discarding very small segments of the speech. Some of the more sophisticated compressed-speech devices use a computer to eliminate those speech sounds that are least necessary for comprehension.

UNDERSTANDING THE STANDARDS AND PRINCIPLES   How can teachers help with the orientation and mobility of students with visual impairment? (CEC Knowledge and Skill Standards VI4K11 & VI7S1)

Council for
Exceptional
Children

Orientation and Mobility (O & M) Training

The importance of O & M training can't be overemphasized. How well the person with a visual disability can navigate her or his environment will greatly determine how independent and socially integrated she or he will be. Societal changes have made being a pedestrian—with or without blindness—even more challenging (Barlow, Bentzen, & Bond, 2005; Huebner & Wiener, 2005; Sauerburger, 2005). Among other things, intersections are wider, often with multiple traffic signals for through-, left-, and right-turn lanes that are set to change based on traffic flow. In addition, cars, especially hybrids, are now quieter and thus more difficult to detect.

There are four general methods to aid the orientation and mobility of people with visual impairment: the long cane, guide dogs, tactile maps, and human guides.

THE LONG CANE   Professionals most often recommend the long cane for those individuals with visual impairments who need a mobility aid. It is called a **long cane** because it's much longer than the canes typically used for support or balance. The optimum length of the cane should be about $1\frac{1}{2}$ inches above the lowest part of the sternum (the vertical bone in the middle of the chest) (Rodgers & Emerson, 2005). Long canes can be straight, folded, or telescopic; the last two types are more compact but not as sturdy as the straight cane (Knott, 2002). The user receives auditory and tactual information about the environment by moving the cane along the ground. It can alert the user to drop-offs such as potholes or stairs, and can help to protect the lower part of the body from collision with objects.

Although watching a skilled user of the long cane can give the impression that it's easy to manipulate, intensive training in its proper use is often required. The traveler holds the butt or crook of the long cane at about the height of the navel and sweeps it in an arc a little wider than shoulder width and about three steps in front of the body, lightly touching the ground in front with the cane tip (Castellano, 2005). Proper touch technique requires considerable coordination between the sweeping of the cane and the movement of the feet.

At one time, O & M teachers thought that young children were not old enough to be taught mobility skills. Some parents, especially sighted parents, saw the use of a cane as too stigmatizing. As one person who is blind said:

> The cane was the thing that my parents put off for as long as they could, and they did it with the support of educators. For them the cane was the symbol. It transformed me from being their blind son—which was okay—to being somebody who might grow up to be a blind man. That wasn't okay. So I didn't see a cane until I was about eleven years old. (Wunder, 1993, p. 568)

Today, however, more and more preschoolers are learning cane techniques.

There has been considerable debate about whether people who are themselves blind should be allowed to be mobility instructors. Those who oppose this practice mainly

■ **Long cane**
A mobility aid used by individuals with visual impairment, who sweep it in a wide arc in front of them; proper use requires considerable training; the mobility aid of choice for most travelers who are blind.

Today, more and more preschoolers are learning cane techniques, though there is considerable debate about whether people who are themselves blind should be used as mobility instructors.

INTERNET RESOURCES

The Website HowStuffWorks.com has a section devoted to guide dogs: www.howstuffworks.com/guide-dog.htm

■ **Guide dogs**
Dogs trained for the purpose of helping people who are blind navigate the environment; generally not recommended for children; they require extensive training for the user.

INTERNET RESOURCES

A number of organizations and companies focus on raising and training guide dogs and helping people who are blind learn to use guide dogs. Following are some examples:

The Seeing Eye, Inc.: www.seeingeye.org

Guide Dogs of America: www.guidedogsofamerica.org

Guiding Eyes for the Blind, Inc.: www.guiding-eyes.org

Guide Dog Foundation for the Blind, Inc.: www.guidedog.org

Guide Dogs for the Blind, Inc.: www.guidedogs.com

focus on safety concerns, asking, for example, whether instructors who are blind would be able to warn their students of potential dangers in the environment such as hanging tree limbs, icy sidewalks, or construction sites (Millar, 1996). Those who favor having instructors who are blind view such concerns as overprotection. They note that such potential dangers are part of the frequently faced realities of cane travel, and that instructors who are blind are more likely to allow their pupils to encounter such obstacles in training and thereby learn to cope with them (Hill, 1997).

GUIDE DOGS   Guide dogs are not as popular an option as most people tend to think. Extensive training is required to learn how to use guide dogs properly. The extended training—as well as the facts that guide dogs are large, walk relatively fast, and need to be cared for—make them particularly questionable for children. Also, contrary to what most people think, the guide dog does not "take" the person who is blind anywhere. The person must first know where he or she is going; the dog is primarily a safeguard against walking into dangerous areas.

For some adults, however, guide dogs have proven to be valuable aides and companions. It's mostly an issue of personal preference, but some users of guide dogs believe that the dogs can alert their owners to potential hazards in the environment—stairways, entrances, exits, and elevators—sooner than can be detected by a cane (Gabias, 1992).

People who are sighted should keep in mind a few guidelines pertaining to guide dogs and their owners (Ulrey, 1994):

1. Although it might be tempting to pet a guide dog, you should do so only after asking the owner's permission. Guide dogs are not just pets; they are working for their owner.

2. If someone with a guide dog appears to need help, approach on the right side (guide dogs are almost always on the left side) to offer assistance.

3. Do not take hold of the dog's harness, as this may confuse the dog and the owner.

TACTILE MAPS **Tactile maps** are embossed representations of the environment. People who are blind can orient themselves to their surroundings by touching raised symbols representing streets, sidewalks, buildings, and so forth. These maps can be displayed in public places, or more portable versions can be made from a type of paper.

Embossment, or raised symbols, has also been used to help people who are blind to appreciate environments that are considerably more vast than what are found locally. (See the Focus on Concepts below.)

■ **Tactile map**
An embossed representation of the environment that people who are blind can use to orient themselves to their surroundings.

FOCUS ON **Concepts**

Touch the Universe

When Noreen Grice was an undergraduate working as an intern at the Boston Museum of Science in the 1980s, she happened to ask some students visiting from the Perkins School for the Blind what they thought of the planetarium show (Chandler, 2003). One youngster straight away spoke up, "That stunk!"

Although no doubt taken aback by the student's honesty, Grice immediately asked:

Why does it have to stink?

She decided to write a brochure that could be produced in braille. "Then, I said, 'Wait a minute. That's not what's missing. The thing that's missing is the pictures.'" (Chandler, 2003, p. 104)

The experience with the Perkins' students served as a catalyst for Grice's search for a method of presenting tactile representations of astronomical objects. Now an astronomer and in charge of the Boston Museum of Science's Planetarium, Grice over the years has experimented with various methods of producing tactile images of heavenly bodies. In 2002, her quest culminated in the publication of *Touch the Universe*. Consisting of photographs, embossed shapes, and a combination of braille and large-print captions, the book presents 14 photos taken with the Hubble Space Telescope. Planets, stars, and galaxies come to life for readers who are visually impaired as well as those with sight. As a fellow astronomer who consulted with Grice on the project puts it:

As a radio astronomer (and the world's only blind one at that), I feel a powerful intuitive connection with the astonishing exotic objects in the distant universe. When I touch the tactile image of the Hubble Northern Deep Field of galaxies in *Touch the Universe*, I am overwhelmed by the same astonishment, a sensory connection with the distant cosmos. It has oft been said that a picture is worth a thousand words. Well, for the first time in my career, I get the picture. (From the back cover of *Touch the Universe*, by Noreen Grice [2002], published by Joseph Henry Press, National Academies Press)

UNDERSTANDING
THE STANDARDS AND
PRINCIPLES What technological
aids are available to address visual
impairments? (CEC Knowledge
and Skill Standard VI7S1)

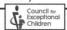

HUMAN GUIDES Human guides undoubtedly enable people with visual impairment to have the greatest freedom in moving about safely. However, most O & M specialists do not recommend that this be the primary means of navigation because it fosters too much dependence on other people. There are times, however, when the use of a human guide is warranted. Most people who are blind who travel unaccompanied don't need help from those around them. However, if a person with visual impairment looks as though he or she needs assistance, you should first ask if help is wanted. If physical guidance is required, allow the person to hold onto your arm above the elbow and to walk a half-step behind you. Sighted people tend to grasp the arms of people with visual impairments and to sort of push them in the direction they are heading. (See Figure 11.8.)

Technological Aids

Visual impairment is perhaps the disability area in which the most technological advances have been made. The infusion of technology has occurred primarily in two general areas: (1) communication and information access and (2) orientation and mobility. In addition, there has been some highly experimental research on artificial vision.

(a) (b) (c)

FIGURE 11.8 Human guide technique. (a) The child maintains a constant grip on the guide's arm while following the guide around obstacles as they travel through the environment. To maintain a grip that allows active participation in travel, the child must grasp the guide's arm so the thumb is placed on the outside, with the remaining fingers gripping the inside of the arm (b). The child is a half-step behind and to the side of the guide.

A common adaptation for smaller students is to have the student grasp the guide's extended fingers, wrist, or forearm rather than maintaining a grip above the elbow (c). Effective guided travel involves a partnership between guide and child with both participants actively involved.

Source: Gense, D. J., & Gense, M. (2000, July, Revised). The importance of orientation and mobility skills for students who are deaf-blind. *DB-LINK Fact Sheet,* retrieved March 22, 2004 from the World Wide Web: http://www.tr.wou.edu/dblink/o&m2.htm. Copyright © 2000 DB-LINK. Reprinted with permission. Figure adapted from illustration by Rebecca Marsh-McCannell.

TECHNOLOGICAL AIDS FOR COMMUNICATION AND INFORMATION ACCESS There are now computers and software available that convert printed material into synthesized speech or braille. One such device is the **Kurzweil 1000™**. The user places the material on a scanner that reads the material with an electronic voice or renders it in braille. The Kurzweil 1000™ can also be used by students with reading disabilities. The machines are compatible with MP3 players and other devices, such as portable braille notetakers, which we discuss next.

Portable **braille notetakers** can serve the same function as the Perkins Brailler or slate and stylus, but offer additional speech-synthesizer and word-processing capabilities. The user enters information with a braille keyboard and can transfer the information into a larger computer, review it using a speech synthesizer or braille display, or print it in braille or text. However, even those who are major proponents of using braille notetakers caution against using them to the exclusion of laptop or desktop computers (Chong, 2004). Computers allow much greater flexibility in producing printed material, and much of what people who are blind produce is for consumption by the sighted community.

Millions of people now own hand-held personal data assistants (PDAs) and cell phones. Some manufacturers have responded to the need to make these accessible for people with disabilities, such as blindness, by developing "talking" cell phones and PDAs. Some additional features they've included are voice recognition, audio cues for main functions, and keys more easily distinguishable by touch.

Two services available for those who are visually impaired are Newsline® and Descriptive Video Service. **NFB-Newsline®**, a free service available through the National Federation of the Blind, allows individuals to access magazines and newspapers twenty-four hours a day from any touch-tone telephone. Over 200 newspapers, including most of the major ones (e.g., *USA Today, The New York Times, The Wall Street Journal, The Washington Post, The Los Angeles Times,* and *The Toronto Globe and Mail*) are now available (National Federation of the Blind, 2006). The user can access the information. **Descriptive Video Service®** inserts a narrated description of key visual features of programs on television. It is also available in some movie theaters as well as some movies on videotape or DVD.

Great strides have been made in recent years to make computers and the World Wide Web more accessible for people with disabilities, including those who have visual impairments. With respect to computer software, there are **screen readers** (such as JAWS® for Windows®) that magnify information on the screen, convert on-screen text to speech, or do both.

Designers of Web pages are also coming to understand that what might be attractive for the sighted can be problematic for those with visual impairments. An article with the clever title "[Image] [Image] [Image] [Link] [Link] [Link]: Inaccessible Web Design from the Perspective of a Blind Librarian" offered the following observations:

> During the past few years, advances in Internet technology have greatly enhanced librarian's access to information. Unfortunately, these same advances have made my job more complicated. Just a few years ago, I could surf the Web . . . without thinking twice. Those were the days when everything was text. . . .
>
> With the increased use of graphics, keyboard commands became beveled buttons or cute icons that could be activated with a click. Boring backgrounds became whimsical wallpapers. Important messages could blink or scroll across the screen. The Web became user-friendly. Unfortunately, this user-friendly Web was not very friendly to me. (Lewis & Klauber, 2002, p. 138.)

However, strides are being made to make the Web more accessible for people with visual impairments. The American Foundation for the Blind has published several suggestions for Web developers (American Foundation for the Blind, 2002). And the

■ **Kurzweil 1000™**
A computerized device that converts print into speech for persons with visual impairment; the user places the printed material over a scanner that then reads the material aloud by means of an electronic voice.

■ **Braille notetakers**
Portable devices that can be used to take notes in braille, which are then converted to speech, braille, or text.

INTERNET RESOURCES

The Cellular Telecommunications & Internet Association has a Website that provides information on cell phone products and features for people with disabilities: www.accesswireless.org

■ **Newsline®**
A service allowing access via touch-tone phone to several national newspapers; available free of charge to those who are visually impaired.

■ **Descriptive Video Service®**
A service for use by people with visual impairment that provides audio narrative by key visual elements; available for several public television programs and some videos of movies.

■ **Screen reader**
Software for computers that magnifies images on the screen, converts text on the screen to speech, or both.

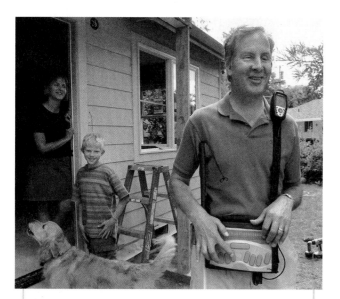

Visual impairment is an area of disability in which technological advances continue to be made. Michael May, blind since the age of three, uses braille GPS equipment to get around.

National Federation of the Blind has established procedures for certifying Websites as being accessible to people who are blind.

TECHNOLOGICAL AIDS FOR ORIENTATION AND MOBILITY Researchers are working on a number of sophisticated electronic devices for sensing objects in the environment, including the laser cane and the Miniguide. These devices operate on the principle that human beings can learn to locate objects by means of echoes, much as bats do. The laser cane can be used in the same way as the long cane or as a sensing device that emits beams of infrared light which are converted into sound after they strike objects in the path of the traveler. The Miniguide is a small (1.8-ounce), hand-held device. Research has shown that the Miniguide is useful for such things as avoiding obstacles, locating doorways, avoiding park benches and poles, and detecting overhanging obstacles (Hill & Black, 2003). However, it doesn't detect drop-offs so it's not meant to be used alone without also using some other aid such as a long cane.

Personal PERSPECTIVES

Mike May: An Adventure into the World of Sight

Founder of the Sendero Group (the manufacturer of the BrailleNote GPS), clocked at sixty-five miles per hour as the world's fastest blind skier, and hired as the first blind political risk analyst for the CIA, Mike May, blind since age three, has never shied away from challenges. But perhaps his biggest challenge was his decision in 1999 to undergo stem cell transplant surgery to restore sight in his one operable eye. And it wasn't just the pain from the surgery or the fact that he might lose the miniscule amount of light perception he had in that eye, it was facing the prospect of leaving the world of blindness to which he had adapted so comfortably and successfully. Even more daunting was the fact that virtually every other known case of individuals who had been blind and then been given sight had resulted in harmful psychological consequences (Kurson, 2005, 2007).

Popular science writer Oliver Sacks (1996) was perhaps the first to introduce the general public to a case of someone whose sight was surgically restored after years of blindness.

Virgil's case was typical of others who had preceded him. Overwhelmed at having to learn to process an entire new sense, he experienced frustration and depression. Virgil eventually lost his sight again, and ironically it seemed to release him from his state of despair:

At the beginning, there was certainly amazement, wonder, and sometimes joy. . . . But then came the problems, the conflicts, of seeing but not seeing, not being able to make a visual world, and at the same time being forced to give up his own. He found himself between two worlds, at home in neither. . . . But then, paradoxically, a release was given, in the form of a second and now final blindness—a blindness he received as a gift. Now, at last, Virgil is allowed not to see, allowed to escape from the glaring, confusing world of sight and space, and to return to his own true being, the intimate, concentrated world of the other senses that had been his home for almost fifty years. (Sacks, 1996, pp. 151–152)

Software is available that allows people who are blind to take advantage of information obtained from the Global Positioning System (GPS). More than two dozen GPS satellites are constantly circling the earth and sending back signals, which can be picked up by hand-held receivers. Combining this information with an expanding data base of several million geographic points in the United States, the GPS allows users to determine their whereabouts with considerable accuracy. The BrailleNote GPS converts the GPS signals to braille. The makers of the BrailleNote GPS have entered twelve million points into the device. In addition, users can enter their own information into the device so that they can plan their routes to and from various destinations.

There has also been remarkable progress in developing an artificial vision system for people who are blind. One such technique involves surgically attaching a digital camera and computer hardware to the visual cortex of the brain (Dobelle, 2000; Groopman, 2003). Another involves implanting stem cells into the cornea. However, these surgeries are extremely complicated and the results are highly variable. Even when the surgery is successful, those who have been blind since birth or from a very young age can find it overwhelming to adjust to the flood of visual sensations. See the Personal Perspectives on p. 406.

> ### Casebook Reflection
>
> REFER TO THE CASE *The Reluctant Collaborator* in your booklet. There is little mention of using technology with Peter. How might he benefit from technological aids? ●

Fortunately, thus far, Mike May has been up to the challenge and has not been driven into the depths of despair experienced by so many before him. His biographer Robert Kurson attributes this to his extraordinarily adventurous attitude toward life. But it's important to note that his vision is still far from what sighted people experience:

> He continued to struggle to see things in three dimensions, and his world stayed much like an abstract painting, a huge collection of colorful, flattened shapes that didn't always make sense. Information flooded his head, a never-ending flow that he could sometimes stem only by closing his eyes. High-speed events, such as the passing of cars and bicycles, became frightening; his brain simply didn't have time to interpret the information. Things often looked very close, scary close. Previous patients had been undone by these kinds of threats. May told himself that this was part of the adventure, that the leap forward wasn't really a leap at all if everything felt safe. (Kurson, 2005)

Kurson notes that scientists using neuron-imaging have studied May's brain and determined that those areas responsible for processing color, motion, and two-dimensional objects appear activated, but those used for spatial perception, judging faces, and processing three-dimensional objects are not. They theorize that this is because the former are more primitive and don't depend as much on experience to develop. What this means is that for May to be able to make sense of much of his world he would need to:

> use cumbersome work-arounds to see much of what sighted people see automatically. He would have to build a database of clues—earrings, long hair, plucked eyebrows—to help determine gender by face. He would have to employ usable context—an orange, round blob on a basketball court is most likely a basketball—to identify simple objects. He would have to spend time thinking about whether a skyscraper was a big thing far away or a little thing close up. All of it would require massive cognitive effort, the prospect of which had been enough to threaten the emotional well-being of May's predecessors. (Kurson, 2005)

Mike May continues to serve as a pioneer in helping scientists and others who are blind understand blindness, sightedness, and the complexity of the human brain and human emotions. For more information on Mike May's fascinating journey into sightedness, see Robert Kurson's *Crashing Through: A Story of Risk, Adventure, and the Man Who Dared to See* (Random House, 2007) and "Into the Light" (*Esquire*, June 2005). There is also a movie based on Kurson's book in production at Fox 2000.

Casebook Reflection

REFER TO THE CASE *The Reluctant Collaborator* in your booklet. Peter's classroom teacher rarely approached Peter. She preferred to talk about any problems to the itinerant teacher for students with impairment. Do you think this attitude would have changed if she had more information about the language development and intellectual ability of students who are blind or visually impaired? ●

CAUTIONS ABOUT TECHNOLOGY   Words of caution are in order in considering the use of computerized and electronic devices. Supporters of braille argue that although tape recorders, computers, and other technological devices can contribute much to reading and acquiring information, these devices cannot replace braille. For example, finding a specific section of a text and "skimming" are difficult with a tape recording, but these kinds of activities are possible when using braille. Taking notes for class, reading a speech, or looking up words in a dictionary is easier when using braille than when using a tape recorder. Braille proponents are especially concerned that the slate and stylus be preserved as a viable method of taking notes. They point out that just as computers have not replaced paper and pen or pencil for people who are sighted, neither can they take the place of the slate and stylus for people who are blind.

Technological devices designed for orientation and mobility also have limitations. They are best viewed as potential secondary O & M aids. They are not appropriate as substitutes for the long cane, for example.

Although technology might not be the answer to all the difficulties faced by people who are blind, there is no doubt that technology can make their lives easier and more productive. And as technologies develop for society in general, it is important that those who are visually impaired be able to take advantage of them.

Service Delivery Models

The four major educational placements for students with visual impairment, from most to least separate, are residential school, special class, resource room, and general education class with itinerant teacher help. In the early 1900s virtually all children who were blind were educated in residential institutions. Today, **itinerant teacher services**, wherein a vision teacher visits several different schools to work with students in their general education classrooms, is the most popular placement for students with visual impairment. The fact is, there are so few students with visual impairment that most schools find it difficult to provide services through special classes or resource rooms. Making It Work on page 409 illustrates how an itinerant teacher supports a general education teacher.

■ **Itinerant teacher services** Services for students who are visually impaired in which the special education teacher visits several different schools to work with students and their general education teachers; the students attend their local schools and remain in general education classrooms.

Residential placement, however, is still a relatively popular placement model compared to other areas of disability. For example, a little over 6 percent of students with visual impairment between the ages of six and twenty-one are placed in a residential institution, whereas only about 0.5 percent of students with intellectual disabilities are so placed. The advantage of residential placement is that services can be concentrated to this relatively low-incidence population. In the past, most children who were blind attended such institutions for several years; today some may attend on a short-term basis (e.g., one to four years). The prevailing philosophy of integrating children with visual impairments into classes with sighted children is also reflected in the fact that many residential facilities have established cooperative arrangements with local public schools wherein the staff of the residential facility usually concentrates on training for independent living skills such as mobility, personal grooming, and home management, whereas local school personnel emphasize academics.

Casebook Reflection

REFER TO THE CASE *The Reluctant Collaborator* in your booklet. Compare Jenny and Ricki's collaboration (see Making It Work on page 409) with the example of Mary Scanlon and Ms. Cunningham. How might Peter's general education and itinerant teachers work more effectively together? How do you think he will fare in the future? ●

Collaborating and Co-Teaching with Teachers of Students with Blindness or Low Vision

"I don't have time to learn braille!"

WHAT DOES IT MEAN TO BE A TEACHER OF STUDENTS WITH VISUAL IMPAIRMENTS?

Collaboration for students with visual impairments often takes the form of working with itinerant special education teachers. This can be frustrating for general educators in that they are left "on their own" when the special educator is at another building. Therefore, in planning for collaboration, it's important that the general educator and itinerant teacher have time to plan for student needs that may arise at any time. Working with the general educator to plan for instruction, the teacher of students with visual impairments can offer expertise in:

1. Strategies for teaching listening and compensatory auditory skills.
2. Techniques for modifying instructional methods and materials.
3. Design of multisensory learning environments that encourage active participation by individuals with visual impairments in group and individual activities.
4. Strategies for teaching basic concepts.
5. Strategies for teaching organization and study skills.
6. Strategies for teaching individuals with visual impairments to use thinking, problem-solving, and other cognitive strategies. (Council for Exceptional Children, 2003)

SUCCESSFUL STRATEGIES FOR CO-TEACHING

Ricki Curry (an itinerant teacher) and Jenny Garrett (a fourth-grade teacher) talk about how they collaborated to fully include Dennis, a student with a severe visual impairment.

Jenny: My fourth-grade class consisted of 23 nine- and ten-year-old students, including two children with learning disabilities, one with severe behavior disorders, and Dennis. They began the year reading anywhere from a first- to a sixth-grade level.

Ricki: Although he has some usable vision, Dennis can see no details from a distance of more than about two feet and uses large-print texts for reading.

Jenny: Dennis has some difficulty making friends because of his immaturity, his compulsive talking, and his inability to listen.

On the other hand, he's got a good sense of humor and is quick with language. Dennis was in my class all day long for every academic subject. Ricki worked with him during language arts block, teaching braille. She would come to school during the last half of my planning period, which gave us a daily opportunity to discuss assignments, homework, curricular adaptations, equipment, and the like. Homework was an enormous issue. Ricki helped him set up a notebook with a homework contract enclosed and a special highlighter, which he used to mark off completed assignments. He had to write down the assignments himself, remember to take the notebook home, complete the assignments, get a parent's signature, and get it back to school.

The hardest part of working with Dennis was the start-up period. I had to get to know him, his visual capabilities, his strengths and weaknesses, his coping strategies. I began adapting my teaching style, using an easel rather than the blackboard so that he could scoot up to it. I had to decide how hard to push, what to expect from his parents, and what to demand from Dennis.

Ricki: I often found myself overwhelmed by the number of things that Jenny and/or Dennis needed help with in the short time that I was in the building. And so many things seemed to go wrong in the time between when I left one day and arrived again the next day! Although I was frustrated by the limitations imposed by time constraints, the beauty of the inclusion model was that I was very aware of the true gestalt of Dennis's program and knew exactly what he was involved in all the time. Had I not had an almost daily view of his classroom performance, I might not have believed how hard it was to integrate this very bright, verbal, personable child into Jenny's class.

Jenny: Collaboration works best when there is a match of personalities as well as energy, enthusiasm for teaching, and professionalism.

More information about visual impairments and their impact on the classroom can be found at the Division for Visual Impairments: www.ed.arizona.edu/dvi/welcome.htm

● *By Margaret P. Weiss*

■ **Curriculum-based management (CBM)**
A formative evaluation method designed to evaluate performance in the curriculum to which students are exposed; usually involves giving students a small sample of items from the curriculum in use in their schools; proponents argue that CBM is preferable to comparing students with national norms or using tests that do not reflect the curriculum content learned by the students.

Assessment of Progress

To assess students' with visual impairments academic progress, one can focus on their braille skills for reading and reading comprehension and Nemeth Code skills for mathematics. O & M skills are important functional skills that can be assessed.

Progress Monitoring

MONITORING ACADEMIC SKILLS Because the use of braille is a critical aspect of academic success for students with blindness or low-vision and IDEA requires that braille instruction be included in the IEP, it's important to monitor the progress these students make in braille skills. **Curriculum-based measurement (CBM)**, introduced in Chapter 3, is an effective method for measuring students' with visual impairments academic progress in the particular curriculum to which they are exposed. Braille versions of CBM reading passages have similar technical adequacy to CBM passages used with sighted readers (Morgan & Bradley-Johnson, 1995). Printed versions of passages can be translated into braille for use in monitoring students' braille reading rate and accuracy. However, standard CBM procedures should be modified for students with visual impairments because reading braille typically takes longer than reading print. For example, rather than the typical one-minute reading sample for sighted readers, CBM samples should be two to three minutes for braille readers. Likewise, the three-second interval provided for self-corrections should be extended to six seconds (Morgan & Bradley-Johnson, 1995).

Mathematics skills can also be monitored using CBM. Proficiency in basic computation of whole numbers is critical to mathematical success (Kilpatrick, Swafford, & Findell, 2001). Commercial CBM measures are available to monitor students' progress in computational fluency, and these measures can be translated into Nemeth Code for use with students with visual impairment. Standard CBM mathematics probes contain multiple items of one type (e.g., two-digit addition problems). A sighted student works for approximately two to four minutes (Thurber, Shinn, & Smolkowski, 2002), and the probe is scored by calculating the number of correct digits per minute. Students with blindness would require longer for the same probes because Nemeth Code is more difficult to read and takes about twice the amount of time as reading standard print. Large-print versions may be used for students with low-vision; additional time may also be needed for these students, however twice the time may not be necessary.

Informal reading inventories provide a method for monitoring students' reading progress. The Basic Reading Inventory: Pre-Primer through Grade Twelve & Early Literacy Assessments (Johns, 2005) has been translated into braille and large print editions. Like informal reading inventories for students with sight, these measures evaluate students' decoding, fluency, and comprehension skills.

Although resources for assessment materials for students with blindness or low-vision are limited, the Texas School for the Blind and Visually Impaired has developed an assessment kit for teachers. This kit includes informal checklists and other informal assessments for a variety of skills including Abacus, braille, calculator, keyboarding, and Nemeth Code. All of these skills are important to the academic success of students with blindness or low vision.

MONITORING FUNCTIONAL SKILLS AND QUALITY OF LIFE O & M skills are critical to the successful adjustment of people with visual impairment, and thus should be the focus of progress-monitoring procedures. Common procedures for assessing O & M skills traditionally have comprised subjective checklists and self-report data. However, emerging technologies currently used for O & M training also offer promise for advancing progress-monitoring procedures. O & M instructors can use Global Positioning Systems (GPSs) as a systematic way for monitoring the travel proficiency of their clients. The addition of **GeoLogger** to a GPS system gathers data such as travel times, travel modes, routes, and trip duration. Evaluating these data frequently can help O & M instructors improve their clients' travel proficiency through data-based planning.

Outcome Measures

High-stakes testing to determine yearly progress has significant implications for students with visual impairments. Until recently, students with blindness or low vision were excluded from standardized testing because of a lack of accessibility to many tests (Bolt & Thurlow, 2004). One concern about including these students on such tests is that the normative data for many standardized tests are based on children without disabilities and aren't representative of students with visual impairment or other disabilities (Hannan, 2007). In addition, the tests must be administered with non-standard presentation accommodations (e.g., braille or large print), which then compromises the standardization process.

OUTCOME-BASED MEASURES FOR ACADEMIC SKILLS   The focus of outcome-based measures for academics is the same as that of progress monitoring. The Neale Analysis of Reading Ability-Braille Version (Greaney, Hill, & Tobin, 1998) is an assessment of reading skills that has been standardized for children with blindness or low-vision (Farrell, 2006). A benefit of this instrument is that it assesses reading rate, accuracy, and comprehension and provides alternate forms for pretest and posttest. A popular assessment to evaluate academic achievement for students with visual impairment is the Brigance Comprehensive Inventory of Basic Skills-Revised (CIBS-R; Brigance, 1999), which is available in braille (Hannan, 2007). It assesses skills in listening comprehension, reading comprehension, math computation and problem solving, mathematical concept knowledge, and written expression.

OUTCOME-BASED MEASURES FOR FUNCTIONAL SKILLS AND QUALITY OF LIFE   A number of instruments (e.g., Visual Disability Assessment, VDA, Pesudovs & Coster, 1998; Activities of Daily Vision Scale, ADVS, Mangione et al., 1992) are available to measure functional outcomes and quality of life for individuals with visual impairment (for a review see Haymes, Johnston, & Heyes, 2001). A simple thirteen-question survey has been developed and validated to measure the functional independence of individuals with blindness or low vision (De l'Aune, Williams, Watson, Schuckers, & Ventimiglia, 2004).

Testing Accommodations

IDEA requires appropriate accommodations or alternate assessments for students with disabilities who need them. Among the most common accommodations for students with blindness and low vision are presentation accommodations (e.g., test in braille, test in regular print with magnification, large print test) and response accommodations (e.g., use of brailler). Scheduling accommodations are also important to students with visual impairments given that students' reading rate in braille is usually slower than that of a sighted student. However, little empirical evidence is available to determine the technical adequacy of these accommodations or alternate assessments for students with disabilities, particularly those with visual impairments (Zebehazy, Hartmann, & Durando, 2006). Furthermore, few states report having a representative on review teams qualified to examine test items to determine sources of potential bias for students with visual impairments (Thompson, Johnston, Thurlow, & Altman, 2005; Thompson & Thurlow, 2003). Despite the concerns with the reliability and validity of measures when accommodations are provided, more states are beginning to provide accommodations for students who are blind or have low vision, and including these students in tests of high-stakes accountability (Lazurus, Thurlow, Lail, Eisenbraun, & Kato, 2006).

■ **GeoLogger**
A multipurpose device for collecting detailed travel data including second-by-second position and speed data. This device works in concert with a GPS system; it has been used for assessment purposes to evaluate the orientation and mobility skills of persons with blindness or low-vision.

Early Intervention

Researchers have documented that immediately after birth infants begin processing a wealth of visual information in their environment (Berk, 2005). This fact makes it easy to understand why intensive intervention should begin as early as possible to help the infant with visual impairment begin to explore the environment. As we noted earlier, many infants who are blind lag behind their peers in motor development. Consequently, O & M training should be a critical component of preschool programming.

Although many people believe that preschoolers with visual impairments should be educated in inclusive settings with sighted children, it is critical that teachers facilitate interactions between the children. Given that the classmates of a student with visual impairment are almost always sighted, there is a potential for social isolation. We know from research that merely placing preschoolers who are visually impaired with sighted preschoolers doesn't lead to their interacting with one another (Celeste, 2006; D'Allura, 2002). Teachers must provide instruction in appropriate interactions (see the Responsive Instruction on p. 413), using active engagement and repeated opportunities for learning.

Most authorities agree that it's extremely important to involve parents of infants with visual impairment in early intervention efforts. Parents can become actively involved in working at home with their young children, helping them with fundamental skills such as mobility and feeding, as well as being responsive to their infants' vocalizations (Chen, 1996). Parents, too, sometimes need support in coping with their reactions to having a baby with visual impairment.

UNDERSTANDING THE STANDARDS AND PRINCIPLES What can individuals with visual impairment expect as they transition to adulthood? (CEC Knowledge and Skill Standards VI7K2 & VI10K1)

Council for Exceptional Children

Transition to Adulthood

Two closely related areas are difficult for some adolescents and adults with visual impairment: independence and employment.

Independent Living

With proper training, preferably starting no later than middle school, most people who are blind can lead very independent lives. However, there is evidence that many students who are blind aren't receiving the necessary training in daily living skills (Lewis & Iselin, 2002; Wolffe et al., 2002). Ironically, some have asserted that the movement toward including students with visual impairment in general education and providing them access to the general education curriculum has led to a diminished emphasis on teaching skills necessary for independence (Spungin, 2003). They say that itinerant teachers often do not have enough time to do much direct teaching of daily living skills.

Many authorities also point out that a major reason why adolescents and adults with visual impairment might have problems becoming independent is because of the way society treats people without sight. A common mistake is to assume that they are helpless. Many people think of blindness as a condition to be pitied. People with visual impairment have a long history of arguing against paternalistic treatment by sighted society, often resisting governmental actions that were presumably designed to help them. For example, the NFB recently passed resolutions opposing the universal installation of accessible pedestrian signals and underfoot raised dome detectable warnings. **Accessible pedestrian signals (APSs)** alert people who are blind to when it is safe to walk across an intersection. The most common types provide

■ **Accessible pedestrian signals (APSs)** Devices for people who are blind to let them know when the "walk" signal is on at intersections; can be auditory, tactile, or both.

Responsive Instruction

Meeting the Needs of Students with Blindness or Low Vision
Strategies for Working with Young Children

WHAT RESEARCH SAYS

Children with blindness or low vision learn best through active engagement with their environment. Because these children do not receive visual stimuli to support what they hear, they depend on tactile interactions to promote learning. Research on infants with visual impairment, however, indicates they spend less time exploring and interacting with the environment than do infants without visual disabilities (Chen, 2001). As a result, natural understanding of people, objects, activities, and the environment is limited.

RESEARCH-BASED RECOMMENDATIONS IN EARLY CHILDHOOD SETTINGS

To promote cognitive skills, children with visual impairment require direct instruction (Chen, 2001). Structured experiences that allow children to have repeated interactions with objects, people, or situations promote understanding of cause and effect. For example, an infant with a visual impairment drops a spoon. If someone were to hand the spoon back to the child, the infant would not understand (1) where the spoon went, (2) how the spoon returned to him or her, and (3) that similar phenomena occur every time something is dropped. Repeated exposure to the act of dropping items and showing the child where the item fell will teach the concept of gravity and reinforce the difficulty involved in locating dropped items!

In addition to systematic, repeated learning opportunities, children with visual impairment should interact with real objects rather than models (Chen & Dote-Kwan, 1999). A child who has not previously developed the concept of a banana will be unable to make the connection between a plastic banana and a real one. Instruction therefore should include opportunities for conceptual development through repeated interactions with real objects.

Concepts involving spatial relationship can be difficult to learn because they are dependent upon a visual reference to a physical object. For example, concepts of "in front of" and "behind" are frequently taught in relationship to one's body. Similarly, understanding of physical characteristics such as color, size, shape, and texture can be challenging without a visual reference. Children with visual impairment will need many opportunities to manipulate objects to reinforce these abstract concepts. Even the concepts of outside and inside can be misunderstood if children are not explicitly exposed to the differentiating characteristics of each (e.g., walls, ceilings, doors, streets, sidewalks, grass) (Chen, 2001).

Although children with visual impairment develop language in a manner similar to that of children without visual impairment, children with visual impairment have greater difficulty mastering nuances of language that are visually dependent, such as pronouns (Chen, 2001). Imagine how difficult it would be to interpret pronouns if you could not see the person talking, what is being talked about, or other people who are being referenced. Again, direct instruction in language skills is recommended.

Finally, much of what young children learn about the world comes from watching and imitation. The development of play, adaptive behaviors, and social interactions is largely dependent on modeling. Hand-over-hand modeling, hand-under-hand modeling, play or social interaction modeling, and participatory modeling all foster social and emotional development.

● *By Kristin L. Sayeski*

auditory or tactile cues or a combination of the two. Some operate all the time—for example, whenever the "walk" signal for sighted pedestrians is lit, an auditory cue such as a chirping noise is activated. Some operate only when a button is pushed. **Raised dome detectable warnings** alert people who are blind to unsafe areas, such as ledges next to tracks in subway stations.

The NFB has stated that APSs might be needed at some complex intersections, but that they are not needed universally (Maurer, 2003). They claim that APSs can be distracting and that continuously operating APSs add to noise pollution, which can

■ **Raised dome detectable warnings**
Bumps in the pavement that are designed to alert people who are blind to unsafe areas.

interfere with the person's hearing traffic flow. The NFB asserts that the raised dome detectable warnings are also not needed in many instances and that they can lead to unstable walking conditions.

Underlying the NFB's objection to both of these travel aids is its concern that sighted society will view people who are blind as needing more accommodations than necessary, thus reinforcing the notion that they're helpless. Whether one agrees with the NFB or believes that it is being overly sensitive, there's no doubt that sighted society is inclined to view people who are blind in a paternalistic manner. The following account of a trip taken by students from the O & M Program of Louisiana Tech University to the World Trade Center in New York City points out—with considerable irony, given the tragedy of September 11, 2001—how misguided special treatment toward those who are blind can be. Presumably because of their blindness, the group experienced lax security in their trip up to the top of the building. Afterwards, in the words of one of the students,

we made jokes about lax security. If you want to bomb the trade center, just walk in with a white cane, and they will welcome you with open arms. There was a bit of irony in this. In 1993 the World Trade Center had been bombed, but at the moment I had forgotten one important detail about that event. . . .

The thing which I had forgotten about that event was brought back to my attention. I don't remember if it was a graduate student, a center student, or a staff member who said it, but as soon as the words were out, a little piece of irony clicked into place. In a federal penitentiary outside my home town of Springfield, Missouri, sits a blind man. His crime? He masterminded the [1993] bombing of the World Trade Center. When will they ever learn?

Society too loses something when it offers undeserved privileges to people it believes inferior. The general public loses the chance to experience the distinctiveness that we can add to society. . . . [T]hese people expect us all to be the same. They cannot tell the good guys from the bad guys in the blind minority. (Lansaw, 2000, pp. 964–965)

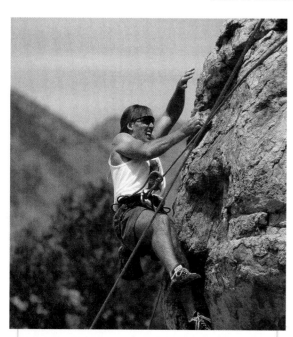

Erik Weihenmayer receives accolades for his mountain climbing, but bristles when praise for the accomplishments of blind persons appears to mask low expectations.

Compounding the problem of paternalism, the public also has a tendency to make superheroes out of people who are blind when they accomplish relatively mundane tasks. Although climbing mountains such as Mount McKinley or Mount Everest are no mundane feats, the sentiments of Erik Weihenmayer point out that the accolades can sometimes be way over the top:

Not all of my time leading up to the climb [of Mount McKinley] was spent on the mountain; as part of their public-education campaign, the [American Foundation for the Blind] asked me to do some TV interviews. One was a cheesy daytime talk show, on which I was showcased among a group of blind people deemed "amazing and inspirational." All the blind people were led onto the stage, canes tapping and dogs' tails wagging, and seated in a row in front of the crowd. I was featured first, and the host opened with, "A blind mountain climber. Isn't that incredible? Even I, who can see just fine, wouldn't think of climbing a mountain." This wasn't the first time I had heard the "even I" statement. It was always meant as a compliment, but it never failed to annoy me. There might be a dozen other factors that prevented the host from excelling in the sport of mountain climbing. She might be fifty pounds overweight, wheezing with every breath, and might never have even set foot on a mountain, but in her mind, success or failure was automatically attributed to one factor: sight or no sight. . . .

Throughout the rest of the segment, I squirmed in my seat. . . . I was simply a blind person who planned to climb a mountain and nothing more. But people sensationalize the lives of blind people when, often, all they did was exhibit a semblance of normalcy. I had been receiving these accolades my whole life: give someone directions to my house—incredible. Make eye contact in a conversation—amazing. Pour a glass of milk without spilling it all over the table—inspiring. Each of us on the panel was being honored for our heroic tales, but the recognition spoke more loudly of low expectations than of accomplishment. My heart burned with the memory of my heroes, people like Helen Keller, who took the world's perceptions about the disabled and shattered them into a million pieces, people whose stories made me hunger for the courage to live in their image. (Weihenmayer, 2001, pp. 166–168)

Even though people who are blind can achieve virtually the same degree of independence as people who are sighted, it would be a mistake to assume that this comes naturally or easily. Many independent living skills that sighted people learn incidentally need to be taught explicitly to those who are visually impaired. The NFB publishes a book that can be useful in this regard (Jernigan, 1994). It has chapters, for example, on cooking, sewing, marking dials, tactile labeling, and shopping ideas.

Employment

Many working-age adults with visual impairment are unemployed, and those who do work are often overqualified for the jobs they hold. For example, surveys indicate that adults who are blind are employed at about half the rate of those who are sighted (Capella-McDonnall, 2005; Houtenville, 2003), and data show that they are paid the lowest average hourly rate of all the disability categories (Kirchner & Smith, 2005). This unfortunate situation is due to a history of inadequate transition programming at the secondary school level rather than to the visual impairment itself. With proper transition programming, students with visual impairment, even those who are totally blind, can go on to hold jobs at every level of preparation—teachers, laborers, physicians, engineers. Proper transition programming, however, must be intensive and extensive, including numerous well-supervised work experiences or internships while still in secondary school.

High on the list of ways to improve employment possibilities for those who are blind are job accommodations. Employees who are blind report that relatively minor adjustments can go a long way toward making it easier for them to function in the workplace. Suggested adaptations include improved transportation (such as car pools), better lighting, tinted office windows to filter light, prompt snow removal, regularly scheduled fire drills to ensure spatial orientation, hallways that are free of obstacles, and computer software (such as screen magnification programs) and reading machines that convert print into braille (Rumrill, Roessler, Battersby-Longden, & Schuyler, 1998; Rumrill, Schuyler, & Longden, 1997).

Visual impairment no doubt poses a real challenge for adjustment to everyday living. However, people with visual impairment have many similarities with people in the rest of society. Special and general educators need to achieve the delicate balance between providing special programming for students with visual impairment and treating them in the same manner as they do the rest of their students.

INTERNET RESOURCES

The American Foundation for the Blind has a Website (http://www.afb.org/Section.asp?SectionID=7) devoted to helping people who are blind find jobs. The site, which also has information for employers, has information on such things as career exploration, finding a job, getting hired, and keeping a job. It also offers a way to link to other workers who are blind and who can serve as mentors.

Summary

How do professionals define and classify learners with blindness and low vision?

▶ Those using a legal definition use visual acuity and field of vision:
- Blindness is visual acuity of 20/200 or less in the better eye with correction; low vision is 20/70 to 20/200.
- Blindness is a field of vision no greater than 20 degrees.

▶ Those using an educational definition use method of reading:
- Blindness is needing to use braille or aural methods.
- Low vision is being able to read print (enlarged or magnified).

▶ Some advocate a skills definition of visual impairment—a focus on what methods other than, or in addition to, sight are needed to gain information or perform tasks.

What is the prevalence of visual impairment?

▶ Blindness is primarily an adult disability.

▶ Fewer than 0.05 percent of students from age 6 to 17 are identified as visually impaired.

What are some basic anatomical and physiological characteristics of the eye?

▶ Objects are seen when an electrical impulse travels from the optic nerve at the back of the eye to the occipital lobes of the brain.

▶ Light rays pass through the cornea, aqueous humor, pupil, lens, vitreous humor, and retina before reaching the optic nerve at the back of the brain.

How is visual ability measured?

▶ Visual acuity for far distances is most often measured by using the Snellen chart.

▶ There are also measures available for measuring visual acuity for near distances.

▶ Visual efficiency, controlling eye movements, and using visual information, is often assessed by teacher observation.

▶ Vision teachers can perform functional assessments to determine how students use their vision in everyday situations.

What causes visual impairments?

▶ The most common visual problems result from errors of refraction:
- Myopia (nearsightedness)
- Hyperopia (farsightedness)
- Astigmatism (blurred vision)

▶ Some conditions affect both adults and children:
- Glaucoma is a group of diseases causing damage to the optic nerve.
- Cataracts cause clouding of the lens of the eye.
- Diabetic retinopathy results from interference of the blood supply to the retina.

▶ Some conditions affect primarily children:
- Retinitis pigmentosa usually causes tunnel vision and night blindness.
- Cortical visual impairment results from brain damage or dysfunction.
- Retinopathy of prematurity can be caused by excessive concentrations of oxygen or other factors.

▶ Improper muscle functioning can cause visual problems:
- Strabismus refers to the eyes being turned inward (crossed eyes) or outward.
- Nystagmus refers to rapid involuntary movements of the eyes.

What are some of the psychological and behavioral characteristics of learners with visual impairments?

▶ Language development is largely unaffected, although there can be subtle developmental delays, especially in infancy.

▶ There may be early delays in conceptual development, which do not last long.

▶ Motor delays in infancy are common; it is important that adults encourage them to explore their environment to help overcome these delays.

▶ Orientation and mobility (O & M) skills depend on spatial abilities:
- People with visual impairment can process spatial information either sequentially or as a cognitive map; the latter is more efficient.
- Some people with visual impairment have the obstacle sense, the ability to detect objects by noting subtle changes in high frequency echoes (the Doppler effect).
- Two myths are that people who are blind have an extra sense and that they automatically develop better acuity in their other senses.

▶ Studies suggest that some students who are blind experience low academic achievement, which is most likely due to low expectations or lack of exposure to braille.

▶ Phonological awareness is important for learning to read print or braille.

▶ The social adjustment problems that people with visual impairment have are largely due to sighted society's reactions to blindness.

▶ Some people with visual impairment engage in stereotypic (repetitive) behaviors.
- Most authorities attribute stereotypic behaviors to an attempt to stabilize arousal levels.
- There is disagreement about whether to intervene with these behaviors.

What are some educational considerations for learners with visual impairments?

▶ The ability to read braille is a crucial skill.
- Many authorities believe that the use of braille has slipped to dangerously low levels.
- Braille bills have helped to ensure that students receive instruction in braille.
- Federal law requires that braille be available if any member of the IEP team, including parents, think it necessary.
- Authorities point out that many people with low vision can benefit from braille instruction.

▶ The use of remaining sight is an important skill.
- Large-print books are useful, although the need for storage space is a drawback.
- Magnifying devices can be used for close or distance vision.

▶ Listening skills are important.

▶ O & M skills are of critical importance.
- Learning to use a long cane is very important.
- Unfortunately, some resist using a long cane because they think it stigmatizing.
- Preschoolers and young children can learn cane techniques.
- There is debate about whether those who are blind can be good mobility instructors.

▶ Some find using a guide dog very helpful.
- Guide dogs are much more practical for adults than for children.
- Guide dogs do not take the person anywhere; instead, they primarily alert the owner to dangerous areas.

▶ Tactile maps can be very helpful.

▶ Human guides, although not recommended as a primary means of mobility, can be helpful at times.

▶ Technological aids are becoming increasingly important.
- There are technological aids for communication and information access, such as braille notetakers, personal data assistants, Newsline®, Descriptive Video Service®, and screen readers for computers.
- There are technological aids for O & M, such as obstacle detection devices and the Global Positioning System (GPS).
- Learners with visual impairments should not become so dependent on technology that they neglect basic techniques, such as braille, the slate and stylus, and the long cane.

▶ Itinerant teacher services is the most common service delivery model, and compared to other areas of disability residential placement is relatively popular.

How do professionals assess students' with visual impairments academic and functional skills?

▶ Teachers can monitor progress in braille skills involved in reading and mathematics using CBM.

▶ O & M instructors can monitor travel skills using GPS devices.

▶ Professionals can assess academic outcomes using braille versions of standardized academic tests.

▶ Testing accommodations often include testing in braille, large-print, or extended time.

What are some things to consider with respect to early intervention for learners with visual impairments?

▶ Intensive intervention should begin as early as possible.

▶ Inclusive settings can be beneficial, but it is important that the teacher facilitate interactions between students with visual impairments and sighted students.

▶ It is important to try to involve parents.

What are some things to consider with respect to transition to adulthood for learners with visual impairments?

▶ Most people who are blind can lead very independent lives.

▶ The current emphasis on inclusion needs to be viewed with caution to make sure it does not come at the expense of learning independent living skills.

▶ Sighted society needs to be careful not to treat those with visual impairments as helpless.

▶ Explicit teaching of independent living skills is essential.

▶ Many working-age adults with visual impairments are unemployed or are overqualified for the jobs they hold.

▶ Transition programming should be intensive and extensive.

▶ Job accommodations are essential.

STANDARDS and PRINCIPLES in this Chapter

SPECIAL EDUCATORS . . .

■ understand the field as an evolving and changing discipline (from CEC Content Standard #1).

■ understand the similarities and differences in human development and the characteristics between and among individuals with and without exceptional learning needs (from CEC Content Standard #2).

■ understand the effects that an exceptional condition can have on an individual's learning in school and throughout life (from CEC Content Standard #3).

■ develop a variety of individualized transition plans (from CEC Content Standard #7).

■ use the results of assessments (from CEC Content Standard #8).

■ use collaboration to facilitate the successful transitions of individuals with exceptional learning needs across settings and services (from CEC Content Standard #10).

ALL TEACHERS . . .

■ understand the central concepts, tools of inquiry, structures of the discipline(s) they teach and can create learning experiences that make these aspects of subject matter meaningful for students (INTASC Principle #1).

■ understand how children learn and develop and can provide learning opportunities that support the intellectual, social, and personal development of each learner (INTASC Principle #2).

■ understand how students differ in their approaches to learning and create instructional opportunities that are adapted to diverse learners (INTASC Principle #3).

■ plan instruction based on knowledge of subject matter, students, the community, and curriculum goals (INTASC Principle #7).

■ understand and use formal and informal assessment strategies to evaluate and ensure the continuous intellectual, social, and physical development of the learner (INTASC Principle #8).

■ foster relationships with school colleagues, families, and agencies in the larger community to support students' learning and well being (INTASC Principle #10).

Applying the STANDARDS and PRINCIPLES

■ WHAT should teachers know about how visual impairment is defined? (CEC Content Standard #1 & INTASC Principle #1)

■ WHY is it important for teachers to know about the causes of visual problems? (CEC Content Standards #1, #2, & #3; INTASC Principles #1, #2, & #3)

■ HOW is visual acuity measured? (CEC Content Standard #8 & INTASC Principle #8)

■ HOW would you respond to parents who approach you expressing concern about the future of their blind high school student? (CEC Content Standards #7 & #10; INTASC Principles #7 & #10)

Now go to the Hallahan/Kauffman, Eleventh Edition MyEducationLab course at www.myeducationlab.com to:

- take a Pretest to assess your initial comprehension of the chapter content;
- study chapter content with your Individualized Study Plan;
- take a Posttest to assess your understanding of chapter content;
- engage in multimedia exercises to help you build a deeper and more applied understanding of chapter content.

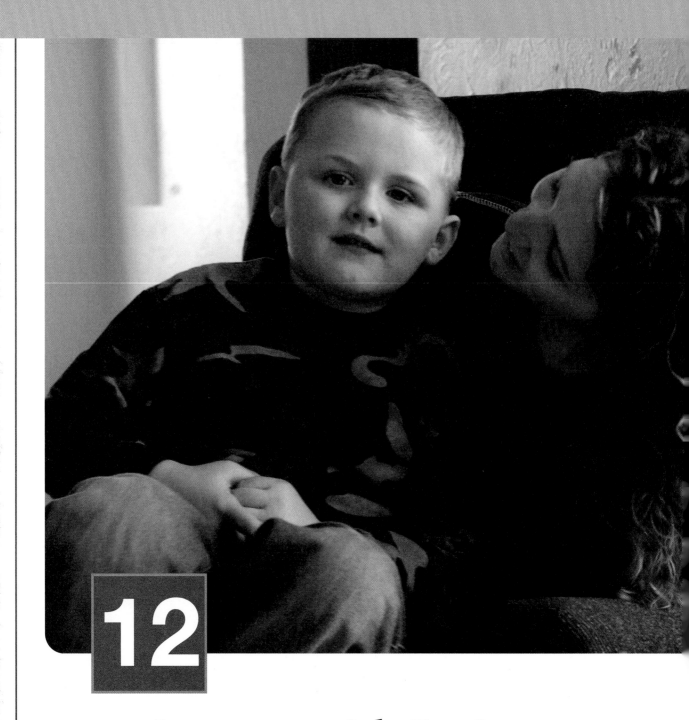

12

Learners with Autism
Spectrum Disorders

A friend published a sweet autobiography entitled "Thank You, Everyone," in which she expressed gratitude to everybody who had influenced her, ranging from Woody Allen to my sister Betsy. If I were to create a similar book, I would call it "Sorry, Everyone," and apologize for my youthful cluelessness: To the girl in seventh grade with the protruding jawbone (it never occurred to me that she would not share by enthusiasm for her unusually simian features). To the boy who came over to my house in the middle of my Caruso[1] phase and endured a precious weekend afternoon comparing recordings of "Celeste Aida." To the perplexed young women from early adolescence who might have become lovers had I understood that their sudden friendship and proximity had any sort of physical impetus. Instead, I chattered on about this and that, rarely making eye contact, and soon they vanished, in search of more game and grounded potential partners. Sorry, everyone. I didn't understand.

—Tim Page
"Parallel Play: A Lifetime of Restless Isolation Explained."
The New Yorker, August 20, 2007, p. 39.

---

[1]Enrico Caruso—the Italian opera singer of the early 20th century, widely acknowledged as one of the most famous tenors.

QUESTIONS to guide your reading of this chapter . . .

- What is the history behind autism spectrum disorders?
- How do professionals define autism spectrum disorders?
- What is the prevalence of autism spectrum disorders?
- What causes autism spectrum disorders?
- What methods are used to identify individuals with autism spectrum disorders?
- What are some of the psychological and behavioral characteristics of learners with autism spectrum disorders?
- What are some educational considerations for learners with autism spectrum disorders?
- How is the progress of students with autism spectrum disorders assessed?
- What are some things to consider with respect to early intervention for learners with autism spectrum disorders?
- What are some things to consider with respect to transition to adulthood for learners with autism spectrum disorders?

MISCONCEPTIONS ABOUT
Learners with Autism Spectrum Disorders

MYTH ■ Autism is a single, well-defined category of disability.

FACT ■ Autism comprises a wide spectrum of disorders and ranges from very severe to very mild.

MYTH ■ People with autism spectrum disorders are intellectually disabled and can't be involved in higher education or professions.

FACT ■ Autism spectrum disorders include people from the full range of intellectual capacity. Although a high percentage do have intellectual disabilities, many with milder forms, such as Asperger syndrome, are highly intelligent, earn graduate degrees, and are successful professionals.

MYTH ■ All people with autism are impaired in some cognitive areas but are highly intelligent or geniuses in other areas.

FACT ■ Only a very few people with autism have extraordinary skills. Called autistic savants, these individuals are not geniuses in the traditional sense, but they possess very highly developed splinter skills—skills that are in isolation from functional skills.

MYTH ■ There is an autism epidemic that must be due to something dangerous in our environment, such as a toxin or virus.

FACT ■ There has undoubtedly been an increase in the number of diagnosed cases of autism. Most authorities assert that this can be accounted for by three things: a widening of the criteria used to diagnose autism, including the recognition of milder forms such as Asperger syndrome; a greater awareness of autism in the general public as well as in the medical, psychological, and educational professions; and diagnosing people as autistic who previously would have received a different diagnosis, e.g., intellectually disabled (mentally retarded).

MYTH ■ The measles, mumps, and rubella (MMR) vaccine causes autism.

FACT ■ The Institute of Medicine of the National Academies commissioned a review of available evidence and concluded that the evidence favors rejection of a causal relationship between MMR vaccine and autism.

MYTH ■ Bad parenting, especially cold, nonresponsive mothering ("refrigerator moms") can cause autism.

FACT ■ There is no evidence that bad parenting can cause autism. Furthermore, even if a parent is relatively unresponsive, this might be in reaction to the infant's low level of arousal or because of parental stress regarding the child's abnormal behavior.

As the poignant words of Tim Page attest (see p. 421), people with autism are often misunderstood. Also as his words attest, this misunderstanding often arises because people with autism don't understand the social cues of others. They are, indeed, clueless about how odd their behavior appears and the effect it can have on others. It's important to point out that the peculiar behavior highlighted by Page—impaired ability to read social cues—is but one of myriad aberrant perceptual, cognitive, linguistic, and social behaviors that individuals with autism might display. And although there are some consistent patterns to the deficits that accompany autism, there is also a great deal of variation in symptoms exhibited by those who are autistic. Not only do the symptoms vary, but the severity of the symptoms can be wide ranging. Some have deficits so severe that communicating with them requires enormous effort. Others, like Page, a Pulitzer Prize-winning music critic for the *The Washington Post*, function in many respects at a very high level. Before turning to the definition of autism and its variants, such as Asperger syndrome, it's helpful to provide some historical context to our discussion.

Historical Context: Kanner's and Asperger's Papers

The seminal work in the field of autism began with two scientific papers published one year apart (1943 and 1944) by physicians working independently: Leo Kanner and Hans Asperger. Interestingly, both were born and raised in Vienna; however, Kanner came to the United States and wrote his historic paper in English. Asperger's work went largely ignored for many years, probably because it was published in German at the time of World War II.

Also interestingly, both Kanner and Asperger used the term *autistic* to refer to the children they were observing. Autism was a label that had been coined earlier in the twentieth century (Bleuler, 1916) and was used to refer to individuals who had an extremely narrow range of personal relationships and restricted interactions with their environment: "a withdrawal from the fabric of social life into the self. Hence the words 'autistic' and 'autism' from the Greek word autos meaning 'self'" (Frith, 2003, p. 5).

Kanner's Paper

Kanner (1943) reported on the cases of eleven children from the Child Psychiatric Unit at Johns Hopkins University. Some of the major characteristics that distinguished these children were:

- An inability to relate to others in an ordinary manner
- An extreme autistic aloneness that seemingly isolated the child from the outside world
- An apparent resistance to being picked up or held by the parents
- Deficits in language including . . . echolalia. . . .
- Extreme fear reactions to loud noises
- Obsessive desire for repetition and maintenance of sameness
- Few spontaneous activities such as typical play behavior
- Bizarre and repetitive physical movement such as spinning or perpetual rocking (Scheuermann & Weber, 2002, p. 2)

A major conclusion that Kanner reached was that these children could be distinguished from children who had **schizophrenia** in at least three ways:

1. The children with schizophrenia tended to withdraw from the world, whereas the children with autism never seemed to have made any social connections to begin with.

■ **Schizophrenia**
A disorder characterized by psychotic behavior manifested by loss of contact with reality, distorted thought processes, and abnormal perceptions.

■ **Echolalia**

The parroting repetition of words or phrases either immediately after they are heard or later; often observed in individuals with autism spectrum disorders.

2. The children with autism exhibited some unique language patterns, such as pronoun reversals (e.g., *I* for *it*, *he* for *she*) and **echolalia**, the repetition of words or phrases.

3. The children with autism did not appear to deteriorate in their functioning over time, as did some children with schizophrenia.

Asperger's Paper

Asperger (1944) reported on four cases of children he observed in summer camp who preferred to play alone and not interact with other children. These children were similar to Kanner's cases with two notable exceptions. First, they had average intelligence—although they seemed to channel their intellectual pursuits into obsessive preoccupation in narrow areas, such as machinery or mathematical calculations. Second, their language was perceived as normal. (Later in this chapter, we'll discuss more recent research suggesting subtle language abnormalities.)

Asperger referred to his cases as having "autistic psychopathy." It was nearly forty years later that his work gained scientific notoriety when Lorna Wing (1981) published a paper that referred to Asperger's original paper and sparked interest in the topic. She was the one who suggested calling the condition *Asperger's syndrome*; it was her paper that drew attention to the condition and was the catalyst for Asperger syndrome's becoming recognized as a condition meriting attention.

■ **Autism spectrum disorders**

Five similar conditions: autism, Asperger syndrome, Rett syndrome, childhood disintegrative disorder, and pervasive developmental disorder not otherwise specified; all involve varying degrees of problems with communication skills, social interactions, and repetitive and stereotyped patterns of behavior.

Definition of Autism Spectrum Disorders

Although autism has been a separate category under the Individuals With Disabilities Education Act (IDEA) since 1990, other disorders similar to it in many ways are now typically collected under a broader term: **autism spectrum disorders**. A similar term is *pervasive developmental disorders*, although most professionals now use the term *autism*

Children with autism spectrum disorders may be distinguished by many characteristics, often including an aversion to interaction with peers.

spectrum disorders. All of the disorders classified as autism spectrum disorders are "characterized by varying degrees of impairment in three areas: (1) communication skills, (2) social interactions, and (3) repetitive and stereotyped patterns of behavior" (Strock, 2004). By far the most prevalent of the disorders on the spectrum are autism and Asperger syndrome. Thus, we confine our discussion to these two conditions.

Autism Defined

Autism, as defined by the Individuals with Disabilities Education Act (IDEA) is

> a developmental disability affecting verbal and nonverbal communication and social interaction, generally evident before age 3, that affects a child's performance. Other characteristics often associated with autism are engagement in repetitive activities and stereotyped movements, resistance to environmental change or change in daily routines, and unusual responses to sensory experiences. The term does not apply if a child's educational performance is adversely affected primarily because the child has serious emotional disturbance. (34 C.F.R., Part 300, 300.7[b][1]) Individuals With Disabilities Education Improvement Act, 2004)

Although not specifically noted in the IDEA definition, autism is also characterized by severe cognitive deficits.

Asperger Syndrome Defined

As we've already discussed, persons with **Asperger syndrome** have higher intelligence and communication skills than those with autism, but they display most, if not all of the other characteristics of autism spectrum disorders, with their primary difficulties being in social interactions. In general, we can think of Asperger syndrome as a milder form of autism.

Prevalence

Several prevalence studies indicate that about 0.6 percent (1 out of 166) of the population has an autism spectrum disorder (Fombonne, 2005). It's unclear how many of these individuals have autism, Asperger syndrome, or one of the other rarer varieties of autism spectrum disorder. However, what data do exist suggest that the majority of these cases are those with autism rather than Asperger syndrome.

Two important points should be noted regarding this prevalence rate of 1 in 166. First, it's far higher than the prevalence rate of students identified as autistic and receiving special education services. The fact that only 0.27 percent (about 1 in 370) of students 6 to 17 years of age are identified as autistic and receiving special education likely means that some students are not receiving the services they need or that some students are being identified as intellectually disabled (mentally retarded) or learning disabled instead of autistic.

Second, the rate of 1 in 166 reflects the fact that the prevalence of autism has increased dramatically over the past thirty to forty years. The first large-scale epidemiological survey of autism (Lotter, 1966) found a prevalence rate of about 0.04 percent (1 out of 2,500). Several other surveys in the 1970s found similar rates (Fombonne, 2005).

Such growth in prevalence statistics for autism has led some to speculate that some mysterious toxin in our environment may be the culprit. Others point to the now

INTERNET RESOURCES

An important and comprehensive report on autism and autistic spectrum disorders is available from the National Academy of Sciences at http://www.nap.edu/catalog.php?record_id=10017

UNDERSTANDING THE STANDARDS AND PRINCIPLES   How is autism defined in the Individuals with Disabilities Education Act? (CEC **Knowledge and Skill Standard CC1K5**)

Council for Exceptional Children

■ **Autism**
One of five autistic spectrum disorders; characterized by extreme social withdrawal and impairment in communication; other common characteristics are stereotyped movements, resistance to environmental change or change in daily routines, and unusual responses to sensory experiences; usually evident before age of 3 years.

■ **Asperger syndrome**
One of five autistic spectrum disorders; a milder form of autism without significant impairments in language and cognition; characterized by primary problems in social interaction.

INTERNET RESOURCES

For a comprehensive overview of Asperger syndrome, including definition, causes, and treatments, see this National Institute of Neurological Disorders and Stroke Website: www.ninds.nih.gov/disorders/asperger/asperger.htm

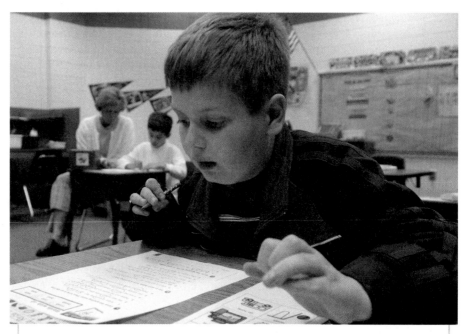

Prevalence estimates for each of the autism spectrum disorders vary considerably, though studies are consistent in pointing to a higher prevalence in males than females, except for Rett syndrome, in which the majority affected are females.

UNDERSTANDING THE STANDARDS AND PRINCIPLES What do we know about the causes of autism? (CEC Knowledge and Skill Standard IC2K3)

Council for
Exceptional
Children

■ **Rett syndrome**
One of five autistic spectrum disorders; normal development for five months to four years, followed by regression and intellectual disabilities (mental retardation); much more prevalent in females.

widespread use of vaccinations for babies and toddlers (see Focus on Concepts on p. 428). Most scientists, however, conclude that there is no epidemic and, in fact, that there is no increase in the number of actual cases (Fombonne, 2001; Frith, 2003; National Research Council, 2001; Shattuck, 2006; Wing & Potter, 2002). Instead, they argue, the reported increase is due to three things:

1. a widening of the criteria used to diagnose autism, including the recognition of milder forms such as Asperger syndrome,

2. a greater awareness of autism in the general public as well as the medical, psychological, and educational professions, and

3. "diagnostic substitution," the phenomenon of persons now being identified as having an autism spectrum disorder who previously would have been diagnosed as mentally retarded (intellectually disabled) or learning disabled.

Studies consistently point to a higher prevalence of autism spectrum disorders in males than females (about 3:1 or 4:1)—with the exception of **Rett syndrome**, in which the vast majority affected are females. (Rett syndrome, a very rare autistic spectrum disorder, is an inherited condition characterized by normal development followed by a severe regression of cognitive abilities.)

Causes

With the rapid increase in autism has come an increase in research into its causes. This research has dramatically altered our understanding of the causes of the condition. Early speculative causal theories have been replaced by a more scientifically based set of theories.

Early Causal Theories

Hans Asperger conjectured that there was a biological and hereditary basis for autism (Hewetson, 2002). Kanner too speculated that the cause of autism was biological, but he also noted that the parents of these children were not "warmhearted":

> In the whole group, there are very few really warmhearted fathers and mothers. . . . Even some of the happiest marriages are rather cold and formal affairs. Three of the marriages were dismal failures. The question arises whether or to what extent this fact has contributed to the condition of the children. The children's aloneness from the beginning of life makes it difficult to attribute the whole picture exclusively to the type of the early parental relations with our patients.
>
> We must then assume that these children have come into the world with innate inability to form the usual, biologically provided affective contact with people. (Kanner, 1943, pp. 42–43.)

Even though Asperger and Kanner came down on the side of a biological basis for autism, the prevailing **psychoanalytic** ideas of the 1960s held sway for several years for professionals who were groping to find an answer to the puzzling condition of autism. One psychiatrist in particular was extremely influential in promoting the idea that parents, especially mothers, were the cause of their children's autism. Perhaps influenced by Kanner's anecdotal reference to a handful of parents as not being warmhearted plus his later statement that "emotional refrigeration has been the common lot of autistic children" (Eisenberg & Kanner, 1956), Bruno Bettelheim (1967) conceived a theory that cold and unresponsive mothers caused autism. Most authorities attribute the term *refrigerator moms* (once used to refer to mothers of children with autism) to Bettelheim.

As we noted in Chapter 4, it wasn't too long ago that it was common to blame parents for the problems of their children, so Bettelheim's ideas were not viewed as radical. We now recognize that the direction of causation between child and adult behavior is a two-way street (Bell & Harper, 1977). It's reasonable to conclude that parents of a relatively unresponsive baby would themselves display behaviors that seemed cold and

■ **Psychoanalytic**
Related to psychoanalysis, including the assumptions that emotional or behavior disorders result primarily from unconscious conflicts and that the most effective preventive actions and therapeutic intervention involve uncovering and understanding unconscious motivations.

Video Homework Exercise

Refrigerator Mothers ●
Go to the Homework and Exercises section in Chapter 12 of MyEducationLab and view several brief film clips regarding Bruno Bettelheim and the concept of the "refrigerator mother" referred to by your authors. Pay special attention to clip number four, "Clips from the Dark Past."

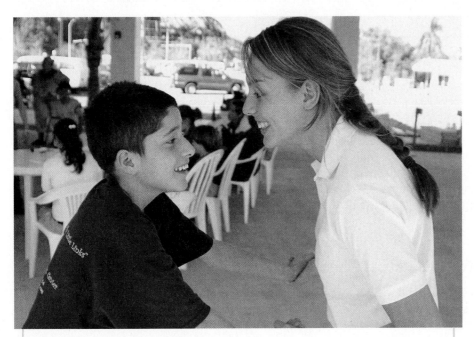

For much of the twentieth century it was widely speculated that parents, especially mothers, were the cause of their children's autism.

FOCUS ON **Concepts**

Is There a Link Between Vaccinations and Autism?

There has been a firestorm of controversy about whether the measles, mumps, rubella (MMR) vaccine can cause autism. In particular, there are assertions that the preservative **thimerosal**, which contains small traces of mercury, is the culprit.* In higher doses, mercury is known to cause neurological deficits. Thus far, evidence strongly indicates no connection between this vaccine and autism. How did this apparently specious theory come to be? How can we explain its influence on the public at large? It's an interesting lesson in how science, the media, public policy, and the legal system sometimes interact.

The Original Wakefield Paper

In 1998, Andrew Wakefield, along with twelve coauthors, published a paper in *The Lancet* on twelve cases of children with autism who had been referred to a clinic in England for **gastrointestinal** problems. Wakefield and colleagues reported two major findings. First, several of the children had a particular form of intestinal lesions. Second, parents or physicians of eight of the children attributed the onset of autistic symptoms to MMR

---

*In 1999, the American Academy of Pediatrics and the U.S. Public Health Service issued a joint statement recommending the removal of thimerosal from vaccines. Since that time, U.S. drug companies have stopped using thimerosal in vaccines, and it is estimated that no MMR vaccinations containing thimerosal since 2001 have been given in the United States.

vaccination; that is, the symptoms suddenly appeared a short time (48 hours to two weeks) after vaccination.

With respect to the latter finding, they concluded: "We did not prove an association between [MMR] vaccine and the syndrome [autism] described. . . . Studies are underway that may help resolve this issue" (Wakefield et al., 1998, p. 641).

In the same issue, the editors of *The Lancet* commissioned a commentary to the Wakefield paper that pointed out its limitations. One of the major limitations was that the onset of symptoms shortly after the immunization could very likely have been coincidental:

> A first dose of MMR vaccine is given to about 600,000 children every year in the UK, most during the second year of life, the time when autism first becomes manifest. Not surprisingly, therefore, some cases will follow MMR vaccination. (Chen & DeStefano, 1998, p. 612)

Public Reaction to the Wakefield Paper

Although Wakefield and colleagues stated that they did not *prove* that the MMR vaccine caused autism and although the commentary cautioned readers against drawing that conclusion, these caveats were lost on much of the public. Once the possible connection between vaccines and autism was reported by the media, public fear spread quickly in Europe as well as North America.

■ **Thimerosal**
A preservative, that up until 1999, was used in vaccines as a preservative; contains small traces of mercury, which in higher doses is known to cause neurological defects.

■ **Gastrointestinal**
Pertaining to the stomach, intestines, and/or other related organs.

distant. Furthermore, we know that the families and parents of children with autism typically experience considerable stress because they are suddenly and unexpectedly confronted by the child's disability. Usually, their child does not look different from the typical child, and often the child has gone through a short period of months or years of apparently normal development before the parents recognize that something is wrong. It's therefore understandable that parents would behave in ways that reflect stress and concern.

Today's Causal Theories

Scientists don't yet know precisely what's wrong with the brain in autism spectrum disorders, but they have established unequivocally that the cause is neurological, not interpersonal (National Research Council, 2001; Muller, 2007; Strock, 2004). Furthermore, they have strong evidence that genetics plays a role in many cases. However, given the range of symptoms and levels of severity of autism spectrum disorders, it's a reasonable guess that there is no single neurological or genetic cause.

This reaction, in turn, provoked concern that the public's loss of faith in the MMR vaccine could lead to an outbreak of measles. Many researchers and physicians wrote letters to the editors of *The Lancet* about this.

The Lancet is a prestigious, peer reviewed journal with high public profile. The profession, journalists, the public, and especially distressed parents of ill children suppose that a publication in this journal will be true. In this example you print a commentary, which if it had been a peer reviewer's report, should have led to the rejection of the paper. (Beale, 1998, p. 906)

We are now at a point when the elimination of measles is a real possibility. If, as a result of this paper, parents reject MMR vaccine, this could lead to a re-emergence of measles infection with the associated deaths and permanent neurological damage among young children, and a resurgence of rubella infection leading to a rise in congenital rubella births and terminations of pregnancies. (Bedford et al., 1998, p. 907)

Several Authors Submit Retraction

Ten of the thirteen authors of the Wakefield paper also voiced concerns about the public reaction and offered a retraction (Murch et al., 2004). They pointed out that the major focus of the paper was on the intestinal abnormalities of the children and that their data were "insufficient" to find a causal link between MMR

vaccinations and autism. Furthermore, in light of the press coverage's potentially negative impact on public health, they considered that "now is the appropriate time that we should together formally retract the interpretation placed upon these findings in the paper" (Murch et al., p. 750).

Institute of Medicine's Commissioned Report

Since publication of the Wakefield paper, there have been several epidemiological studies of the possible autism–MMR vaccine link. In the United States, several federal agencies, including the prestigious Institute of Medicine of the National Academies, commissioned a review of the available evidence. In their third and final report, the committee concluded "that the evidence favors rejection of a causal relationship between MMR vaccine and autism" (Institute of Medicine, 2004, p. 6; bold in the original).

Lawsuits Multiply

Despite overwhelming scientific epidemiological evidence to the contrary, many parents remain unconvinced that MMR vaccinations did not cause their children's autism. For example, as of June, 2007, over 4,800 lawsuits had been filed in the United States alleging that thimerosal had caused autism. Time will tell whether any of these suits are successful. In the meantime, the vast majority of the research community maintains that the MMR vaccine, with or without thimerosal, does not cause autism.

NEUROLOGICAL BASIS OF AUTISM SPECTRUM DISORDERS   That autism spectrum disorders have a neurological basis is suggested by the fact that people with autism have a high incidence of brain seizures and cognitive deficits (Volkmar & Pauls, 2003). Furthermore, postmortem studies and neurological imaging studies, using the same techniques that we discussed in earlier chapters on learning disabilities and attention deficit hyperactivity disorder (ADHD)—e.g., positron emission tomography scans, computerized axial tomographic scans, and magnetic resonance imaging—have implicated a number of areas of the brain (Strock, 2004; Muller, 2007; Volkmar & Pauls, 2003). In fact, because so many areas are affected, many authorities now think that autism is better conceived as a disorder of neural networks rather than as being due to an abnormality in one specific part of the brain. Figure 12.1 depicts some of the major brain structures affected.

Although several areas of the brain appear to be involved in autism spectrum disorders, researchers have found some provocative evidence that a certain type of neuron may be involved in persons with autism spectrum disorders' difficulties in interpreting the emotions of others. **Mirror neurons**, located deep within the brain in and around the amygdala (see Figure 12.1), activate when a person imitates the behavior of another

■ **Mirror neurons**
Neurons that fire when someone imitates or watches another person's behavior; malfunctioning in people with autism spectrum disorders; located deep within the brain in and around the amygdala.

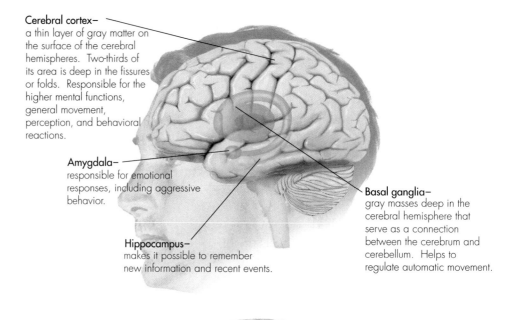

Cerebral cortex–
a thin layer of gray matter on the surface of the cerebral hemispheres. Two-thirds of its area is deep in the fissures or folds. Responsible for the higher mental functions, general movement, perception, and behavioral reactions.

Amygdala–
responsible for emotional responses, including aggressive behavior.

Hippocampus–
makes it possible to remember new information and recent events.

Basal ganglia–
gray masses deep in the cerebral hemisphere that serve as a connection between the cerebrum and cerebellum. Helps to regulate automatic movement.

Corpus callosum–
consists primarily of closely packed bundles of fibers that connect the right and left hemispheres. Allows for communication between the hemispheres.

Brain stem–
located in front of the cerebellum. Serves as a relay station, passing messages between various parts of the body and the cerebral cortex. Primitive functions essential to survival (breathing and heart control) are located here.

Cerebellum–
located at the back of the brain. Fine tunes motor activity. Regulates balance, body movements, coordination, and the muscles used in speaking.

FIGURE 12.1 Major brain structures implicated in autism

Strock, M. (2004). *Autism spectrum disorders (pervasive developmental disorders)*. Bethesda, MD: U.S. Department of Health and Human Services, National Institutes of Health, National Institute of Mental Health. Retrieved December 6, 2007, from www.nimh.nih.gov/publicat/autism.cfm

person. For example, if Person A *imitates* Person B's smile or frown, Person A's mirror neurons fire. Importantly, even if Person A simply *sees* Person B smile or frown, Person A's mirror neurons fire. But if Person A has an autistic spectrum disorder, his or her mirror neurons do not activate when seeing someone else smile or frown (Dapretto et al., 2006). The malfunctioning mirror neurons may be the reason why a person with autism has problems in understanding the emotions of others.

Another interesting line of neurological research involves the brain and head size of people with autism (Courchesne, Carper, & Akshoomoff, 2003; Courchesne et al., 2001; Fombonne, Roge, Claverie, Courty, & Fremoile, 1999; Piven, Arndt, Bailey, & Andreason, 1996; Piven et al., 1995). Studies indicate that the brains and heads of young children with autism tend to grow suddenly and excessively in the first two years of life and then taper off to be about normal in size by adolescence. In his 1943 paper, Kanner noted that many of the children he studied had overly large heads. Since then, large head size has come to be "one of the most replicated neurobiological findings in the disorder" (Lainhart, 2003). Research suggests that their large head size, at least in males, may be due to elevated levels of growth hormones (Mills et al., 2007).

The significance of abnormally high rates of brain growth in the first two years is underscored by the fact that this is a time of critical importance to brain organization:

> The organizational events in the brain during the first two years set the neurodevelopmental stage for the acquisition of language and the capacity for inference, a sense of self-awareness (Herschkowitz, 2000), and, eventually, complex information processing (Minshew, Sweeney, & Luna, 2002). (Lainhart, 2003, p. 394)

GENETIC BASIS OF AUTISM SPECTRUM DISORDERS   Scientific evidence for autism having a hereditary component is very strong (Hoekstra, Bartels, Verweij, & Boomsma, 2007; Strock, 2004; Volkmar & Pauls, 2003). Studies have shown that when one family member is diagnosed with autism, the chances are 50 to 200 times higher that another family member also has autism than in the population as a whole. When a monozygotic (identical, one egg) twin has autism, the chances are much greater that the other twin will also have autism than is the case with dizygotic (fraternal, two eggs) twins. Furthermore, even if they aren't diagnosed as autistic, family members of those with autism are more likely to exhibit autistic-like characteristics at a subclinical level, such as a lack of close friends, a preoccupation with narrow interests, and a preference for routines (Stone, McMahon, Yoder, & Walden, 2007; Volkmar & Pauls, 2003).

In addition to a direct hereditary cause of autism spectrum disorders, there is now evidence that sporadic genetic mutations are involved in some cases. Researchers have found that tiny gene mutations—spontaneous deletions and/or duplications of genetic material—that can result in autism are sometimes passed down to children from one or both parents (Sebat et al., 2007). This is similar to the way children with Down syndrome acquire an anomaly on the 21st chromosome. Also similar to Down syndrome, the frequency of these mutations increases with the age of the parent, especially the mother.

Research has yet to identify all the exact genes involved. However, researchers are overwhelmingly consistent in stating that there is no one "autism gene"—multiple genes are involved and not the same ones are implicated in all people with autism.

Identification

There is no universally used diagnostic test for autism or any of the other disorders in the spectrum. The diagnosis of autism is often made by a psychiatrist using criteria established by the American Psychiatric Association (2000) that focus on communication skills, social interactions, and repetitive and stereotyped patterns of behavior (see Table 12.1). In addition to observing the child in the examining room and taking a detailed history from parents, clinicians can use behavioral observation instruments and ask parents and/or teachers to fill out behavior checklists.

Although the diagnosis of autism might sound somewhat vague, the behavioral symptoms are so severe and striking that it's actually relatively easy to diagnose, at least by the age of three to five years. (Asperger syndrome, by contrast, is somewhat more subjective because the symptoms are milder.) But professionals are hopeful that with more research they may be able to diagnose autism much earlier; there is evidence that parents often start to notice the child with autism's differences (see Table 12.2) well before formal diagnosis, which is usually after the age of three (Gray, Tonge, & Bereton, 2006).

As noted in Table 12.2, an indicator for autism is if a young child loses or regresses in babbling, speech, or social skills. Parents of some children with autism have often claimed that their child was progressing normally for about the first two years and then

■ **Childhood disintegrative disorder**
One of five autistic spectrum disorders; normal development for at least two and up to ten years, followed by significant loss of skills; much more prevalent in males.

■ **Pervasive developmental disorder not otherwise specified (PDD-NOS)**
One of five autistic spectrum disorders; pervasive delay in development that does not fit into any of the other diagnostic categories.

TABLE 12.1	Autism Spectrum Disorders

- *Autism:* extreme social withdrawal and impairment in communication; often includes stereotyped movements, resistance to change, and unusual responses to sensory experiences; usually manifests before three years of age

- *Asperger syndrome (AS) or Asperger disorder:* much like mild autism, but without significant impairments in cognition and language

- *Rett syndrome:* normal development for five months to four years, followed by regression and intellectual disabilities (mental retardation); much more prevalent in females

- *Childhood disintegrative disorder:* normal development for at least two and up to 10 years, followed by significant loss of skills; much more prevalent in males

- *Pervasive developmental disorder not otherwise specified (PDD-NOS):* persons who display behaviors typical of autism but to a lesser degree and/or with an onset later than three years of age

■ **Autistic regression**
Phenomenon whereby a child appears to progress normally until about 16 to 24 months of age and, then, begins to show signs of being autistic and ultimately is diagnosed as autistic.

abruptly began to regress in his or her behavior. Estimates of this **autistic regression** range from about 20 to 47 percent of cases of children with autism (Werner & Dawson, 2005). Researchers have begun to document that these parents' perceptions are, in fact, valid (Landa, Holman, Garrett-Mayer, 2007; Werner & Dawson, 2005). In one study, for example, researchers compared the home videotapes of first-year and second-year birthday parties and found that those whose parents said they had regressed had indeed shown signs of regression (Werner & Dawson, 2005). These findings also help explain why some parents have believed that vaccinations caused their children's autism (See Focus on Concepts on p. 428.)

Video Homework Exercise

Autism Spectrum Disorders ● Go to the Homework and Exercises section in Chapter 12 of MyEducationLab and select several videos to watch, then reflect on the different manifestations of autism in the children profiled.

TABLE 12.2	Early Signs of Autism

6 Months

- No big smiles or other warm, joyful expressions

9 Months

- No back-and-forth sharing of sounds, smiles, or other facial expressions

12 Months

- No consistent response to his/her own name
- No babbling
- No back-and-forth gestures, such as pointing, showing, reaching, waving, or three-pronged gaze (e.g., child looks at adult, looks at toy to indicate interest in it, looks back at adult to communicate something about the toy)

16 Months

- No words

24 Months

- No two-word meaningful phrases (without imitating or repeating)

Any loss of speech or babbling or social skills at any age

Sources: Cadigan & Estrem (2006/07), Rogers (2000), Travis & Sigman (2000).

Psychological and Behavioral Characteristics

As noted earlier, there is some variation in the behavioral characteristics associated with the different autism spectrum disorders. Our discussion focuses on autism and Asperger syndrome.

Autism

We noted that people with autism have deficits in social interaction, communication, and repetitive and stereotyped patterns of behavior. In addition, they display cognitive deficits, and some have abnormal sensory perceptions.

IMPAIRED SOCIAL INTERACTION   Most social interaction problems that individuals with autism exhibit involve deficits in social responsiveness. Parents of children with autism often notice that their babies or toddlers don't respond normally to being picked up or cuddled. The young child with autism might not show a differential response to parents, siblings, or their teachers compared to other strangers. They might not smile in social situations, or they might smile or laugh when nothing appears funny. Their eye gaze often differs significantly from that of others; they sometimes avoid eye contact with others or look out of the corners of their eyes. They might show little or no interest in other people but be preoccupied with objects. They might not learn to play normally. These characteristics persist and prevent the child from developing typical attachments to their parents or friendships with their peers. In fact, they often give the impression that they aren't interested in making friends.

IMPAIRED COMMUNICATION   Most children with autism lack **communicative intent**, or the desire to communicate for social purposes. As many as 50 percent are thought to be **mute**; they use no, or almost no, language (Scheuermann & Webber, 2002). Those who do develop speech typically show abnormalities in intonation, rate, volume, and content of their oral language. Their speech sounds "robotic," or they might exhibit echolalia, parroting what they hear. They might reverse pronouns (e.g., confuse *you* and *I* or refer to themselves as *he* or *she* rather than *I* or *me*). Using language as a tool for social interaction is particularly difficult. If they do acquire language, they might have considerable difficulty using it in social interactions because they're unaware of the reactions of their listeners.

REPETITIVE AND STEREOTYPED PATTERNS OF BEHAVIOR   Many people with autism display **stereotypic behaviors**: repetitive, ritualistic motor behaviors such as twirling, spinning objects, flapping the hands, and rocking, similar to those that are evident in some people who are blind (see Chapter 11). Another characteristic frequently seen in autism and related disorders is extreme fascination or preoccupation with objects and a very restricted range of interests. Children with autism might play ritualistically with an object for hours at a time or show excessive interest in objects of a particular type. They can become upset by any change in the environment (e.g., something out of place or something new in the home or classroom) or any change in routine; some individuals with autism seem intent on the preservation of sameness and have extreme difficulty with change or transition (Adreon & Stella, 2001; Myles & Simpson, 2001).

IMPAIRED COGNITION   Most individuals with autism display cognitive deficits similar to those of people with intellectual

UNDERSTANDING THE STANDARDS AND PRINCIPLES   Describe the social characteristics likely to be exhibited by persons with autism. (CEC Knowledge and Skill Standard IC2K4)

■ **Communicative intent**
The need to communicate for social reasons; thought to be lacking in most children with autism.

■ **Mute**
Possessing no, or almost no, language; characteristic of many with autism.

■ **Stereotypic behaviors**
Any of a variety of repetitive behaviors (e.g., eye rubbing) that are sometimes found in individuals who are autistic, blind, severely mentally retarded, or psychotic; sometimes referred to as stereotypies or blindisms.

Casebook Reflections

REFER TO THE CASE *Getting to Know Chase* in your booklet. Although Chase is able to perform at grade level academically, he engages in person-specific, ritualistic behaviors and rigid associations, and exhibits a fascination with glass. Do his characteristics resemble those of a student with one of the autism spectrum disorders? Why or why not? ●

disabilities. However, there are some cognitive processing problems that seem to be peculiar to autism:

> Children with autism are thought to display difficulty in coding and categorization of information, . . . relying on literal translations, and they seem to remember things by their location in space rather than concept comprehension (Schuler, 1995). For example, "shopping" means going to a particular store on a particular street, rather than the concept of visiting any type of store, browsing around, perhaps buying something . . . or various other aspects of the concept of "shopping." In fact, it has been speculated that individuals with autism employ an "echo box-like memory store" (Grandin, 1995; Hermelin, 1976). This would explain why autistic children may excel at putting puzzles together and building things out of blocks, matching tasks, or drawing replicas. However, they tend to perform poorly on tasks requiring verbal comprehension and expressive language. (Scheuermann & Webber, 2002, p. 9)

The striking difference in favor of visual and spatial abilities relative to language and conceptual abilities has been termed *thinking in pictures* by Temple Grandin, a designer of livestock handling facilities and a Professor of Animal Science at Colorado State University. Although Grandin is more typical of someone with Asperger syndrome, her description of heightened visual-spatial abilities is applicable to some with autism as well as to some with Asperger syndrome:

> I credit my visualization abilities with helping me understand the animals. . . . One of my early livestock design projects was to create a dip-vat and cattle-handling facility for a feed yard. . . . A dip vat is a long, narrow, 7-ft. deep swimming pool through which cattle move in single file. It is filled with pesticide to rid the animals of ticks, lice and other external parasites. . . . The animals often panicked because they were forced into the vat down a steep, slick decline. . . .
>
> The first thing I did when I arrived at the feedlot was put myself inside the cow's head and see with its eyes. Because their eyes are on the sides of their head, cattle have wide-angle vision. Those cattle must have felt as if they were being forced to jump down an airplane escape slide into the ocean.
>
> One of my first steps was to convert the ramp from steel to concrete. If I had a calf's body and hooves, I would be very scared to step on a slippery metal ramp. The final design had a concrete ramp at a 25° downward angle. Deep grooves in the concrete provided secure footing. The ramp appeared to enter the water gradually, but in reality it abruptly dropped away below the water's surface. The animals could not see the drop-off because the dip chemicals colored the water. When they stepped out over the water, they quietly fell in because their center of gravity had passed the point of no return. (Grandin, 2002, p. 56).

There are some individuals with autism who have such extraordinary skills that at first blush, one thinks they are geniuses. These individuals are referred to as autistic savants. An **autistic savant** might have relatively severe autism, in that he or she shows serious developmental delays in overall social and intellectual functioning. However, the person with this condition also shows remarkable ability or apparent talent in particular splinter skills—skills that exist in apparent isolation from the rest of the person's abilities to function. An autistic savant might have extraordinary capabilities in playing music, drawing, or calculating. For example, when given a date that is far into the future, such as September 9, 2016, some autistic savants are immediately able to say that this will be a Friday. The same person, however, might not have the functional mathematical skills to be able to purchase items in a grocery store. The character Raymond, played by Dustin Hoffman, in the movie *Rain Man* (1988) was an autistic savant (see Sacks, 1995, and Treffert, 2006, for other examples).

Temple Grandin credits her visualization abilities for her success in designing feed pens.

INTERNET RESOURCES

The following Website contains a variety of information on autistic savants, including video clip profiles of several autistic savants: http://www.wisconsinmedicalsociety.org/savant_syndrome

■ **Autistic savant**
A person with severe autism whose social and language skills are markedly delayed but who also has advanced skills in a particular area, such as calculation or drawing.

Because the skills of individuals who are autistic savants are so extraordinary, they are often covered in the media. This fact, along with publicity that accompanies such films as *Rain Man* (1988), *Shine* (1996; a film loosely based on the life of pianist David Helfgott), and *Mozart and the Whale* (2005), has led to the misconception in the general public that most, if not all, people with autism have amazing talents. Although we don't have precise figures, most estimates are that only 10 percent of those who are autistic are autistic savants.

ABNORMAL SENSORY PERCEPTIONS   Some people with autism are either hyperresponsive or hyporesponsive to particular stimuli in their environment. For example, some experience hypersensitivity to visual stimuli, such as being overly sensitive to fluorescent lights, and others can be overly sensitive to touch. Interestingly, some people with autism are totally the opposite of hyperresponsive. They are very *un*responsive to auditory, visual, or tactile stimuli. In fact, to the casual observer, some appear to be deaf or blind. Still others have a combination of hypersensitivity and hyposensitivity, for instance, being oblivious to loud noises such as a fire alarm but overreacting to someone whistling at a great distance.

Some people with autism experience a neurological mixing of the senses or synaesthesia. **Synaesthesia** occurs when the stimulation of one sensory or cognitive system results in the stimulation of another sensory or cognitive system. Daniel Tammet, who has Asperger syndrome and has phenomenal savant skills in memory and math—setting a British and European record for reciting Pi from memory, to 22,514 decimal places—describes his synaesthesia in his aptly titled memoir, *Born on a Blue Day*:

> I was born on 31 January 1979—a Wednesday. I know it was a Wednesday, because the date is blue in my mind and Wednesdays are always blue, like the number nine or sound of loud voices arguing. . . .
>
> Numbers are my friends and they are always around me. Each one is unique and has its own personality. Eleven is friendly and five is loud, whereas four is both shy and quiet—its my favorite number, perhaps because it reminds me of myself. Some are big—23, 667, 1179—while others are small: 6, 13, 581. Some are beautiful, like 333, and some are ugly, like 289. . . .
>
> No matter where I go or what I'm doing, numbers are never far from my thoughts. In an interview with chat show host David Letterman in New York, I told David he looked like the number 117—tall and lanky. Later outside, in the appropriately numerically named Times Square, I gazed up at the towering skyscrapers and felt surrounded by nines—the number I most associate with feelings of immensity. (Tammet, 2006, pp. 1–2)

Asperger Syndrome

People with Asperger syndrome are likely to display impairment or abnormalities in the same areas (i.e., social interaction, communication, repetitive and stereotyped patterns of behavior, cognitive processing, sensory perception) as those who have autism, but to a milder degree. We focus our discussion on impairments in social skills and communication skills because research suggests that social interaction is the biggest challenge of those with Asperger syndrome and because problems in communicating contribute to their social ineptitude.

IMPAIRED SOCIAL INTERACTION   A major reason that people with Asperger syndrome have so much difficulty in social interactions is that they aren't adept at reading social cues. In fact, at times, they can appear clueless about what constitutes appropriate social behavior. Because they can be highly verbal and intelligent, others may get the impression that they are willfully disregarding social etiquette. By "turning off" those around them, they become further ostracized from their peer group, making it difficult to

Video Homework Exercise

Autistic Savants ●
Go to the Homework and Exercises section in Chapter 12 of MyEducationLab and view several brief film clips about Daniel, an autistic savant.

■ **Synaesthesia**
A mixing of sensory or cognitive systems whereby stimulation of one elicits stimulation of the other, e.g., numbers or letters are perceived as having inherent colors or different sounds are perceived as having inherent colors.

UNDERSTANDING THE STANDARDS AND PRINCIPLES   Describe the social characteristics likely to be exhibited by persons with Asperger syndrome. (CEC Knowledge and Skill Standard IC2K4)

Personal PERSPECTIVES

Children's Book Author Kathy Hoopmann Addresses Asperger Syndrome

Australian children's book author Kathy Hoopmann is known for her continuing "Asperger Adventure Series" *Blue Bottle Mystery* (2000), *Of Mice and Aliens* (2001), *Lisa and the Lacemaker* (2002), and *Haze* (2003), in which the main character has Asperger syndrome. Unlike her previous books, *All Cats Have Asperger's Syndrome* (2006) appeals to a wide-ranging audience of preschoolers through adults, especially cat-lovers. As one reviewer puts it: "[It's] a great addition for the coffee table for any residence. I would also suggest this for therapist, doctor, and school offices" (Sayers, 2007). Here are a few pages.

Source: Hoopmann, K. (2006). *All cats have Asperger syndrome.* London: Jessica Kingsley Publishers. (pp 3–6). Reprinted by permission.

He likes to be near those he loves, but doesn't want them to hold him,

. . . preferring squishy places to a hug.

Instead of coming to people for comfort, he may be overly attached to a toy . . .

. . . or a pet.

make and keep friends and to interact with others. See Personal Perspectives above for a unique way of helping peers and others understand the unusual characteristics of those with Asperger syndrome.

The essence of the social problems for individuals with Asperger syndrome is captured by the notion of the hidden curriculum (Myles & Simpson, 2001, 2003). The **hidden curriculum** refers to the "dos and don'ts" of everyday living that most people learn incidentally or with very little instruction from others: behaviors or ways of acting that most of us take for granted. Recall Tim Page's "Sorry, Everyone" letter at the beginning of the chapter (see p. 421), in which he referred to commenting on his fellow student's monkey-like (simian) features. For people with Asperger syndrome, these rules of behavior remain hidden. What makes it all the more difficult for the person with Asperger syndrome is that the hidden curriculum can be different for different settings:

> Everyone knows that Mrs. Robbins allows students to whisper in class as long as they get their work done, whereas Mrs. Cook does not tolerate any level of noise in her class. Similarly, everyone knows that Mr. Johnson, the assistant principal, is a stickler for following the rules, so no one curses or even slouches in his presence. Everyone also knows that the really tough guys (the ones who beat up unsuspecting kids) hang out behind the slide, just out of teachers' view—everyone knows these things—everyone, that is, except the student with Asperger syndrome.
>
> Outside of school, the hidden curriculum is an even bigger issue. What is the hidden curriculum for talking to or taking rides from strangers? The bus driver is a stranger, but it is permissible to accept a ride from her. . . . It is okay to accept candy from the distributor who is giving free samples at Toys "R" Us, yet it is not prudent to take candy from a stranger standing on the street corner. (Myles & Simpson, 2003, p. 132)

▪ **Hidden curriculum**
The "dos and don'ts" of social interactions that most people learn incidentally or with little instruction but that remain hidden for those with Asperger syndrome.

Building Teaching Skills

Hidden Curriculum ●
Go to the Building Teaching Skills section in Chapter 12 of MyEducationLab to gain an understanding of the hidden curriculum and the reasons that children with autism have difficulty learning it.

Contributing to their social awkwardness, people with Asperger syndrome also have a tendency to interpret what others say very literally. Stephen Shore (2003) provides examples of his struggles with being overly literal:

> A friend of mine . . . said he felt "like a pizza." "What do you mean—'feel like a pizza'?" And it wasn't until college that I realized, "Oh, he meant he felt like EATING a pizza." At this time, idioms usually go zipping past me but I am often able to "pull them back" for further examination before I say something ridiculous. But it takes some additional thinking on my part, to figure out "Well, what's the meaning? How do I interpret this?" . . .
>
> I remember when I was about nineteen, sitting in a restaurant with my parents, and they said to me, "You know, that girl over there, she's got her eye on you; she's giving you the eye." "WHAT DO YOU MEAN SHE'S GIVING ME THE EYE? I DON'T WANT HER EYE! You need two eyes; you see in stereo. She needs HER two eyes, that's gross and sickening anyway and I won't take it." Idioms like that one got away. (Shore, 2003, p. 198)

IMPAIRED COMMUNICATION SKILLS   According to the American Psychiatric Association's diagnostic criteria, Asperger syndrome doesn't involve "clinically significant general delay in language" (American Psychiatric Association, 2000, p. 84). However, numerous practitioners and researchers have asserted that this statement is misleading (Mesibov, Shea & Adams, 2001). People with Asperger syndrome may be able to express themselves using age-appropriate vocabulary and grammar, but they often exhibit numerous idiosyncratic language and language-related behaviors. They often have problems with **pragmatics**, the social uses of language. For example, they might speak using an abnormal voice inflection, such as a monotone, talk too loudly or too quickly or slowly, not be adept at taking turns talking in a conversation, engage in monologues, or repeat the same thing over and over. In Chapter 6, we noted that people with learning disabilities can also experience problems with pragmatics; however, the deficits in pragmatic skills of those with Asperger syndrome are usually much more severe and pervasive.

The problems with pragmatics of those with Asperger syndrome also extend to nonverbal communication skills

> such as standing closer to another person than is customarily accepted; intensely staring at another person for long periods; maintaining abnormal body posture; failing to make eye contact or displaying an inexpressive face, thereby failing to signal interest, approval, or disapproval; and failing to use or understand gestures and facial expressions. (Myles & Simpson, 2003, p. 9)

■ **Pragmatics**
The study within psycholinguistics of how people use language in social situations; emphasizes the functional use of language rather than the mechanics.

Attempts to Construct a Unifying Theory of Autism Spectrum Disorders

Although a wide variety of psychological and behavioral characteristics have been attributed to individuals with autism spectrum disorders, some researchers have attempted to build theories that can account for many of the behaviors displayed. The three most prominent theories identify the major impairments as being accounted for by problems in (1) executive functions, (2) weak central coherence, or (3) theory of mind (Frith, 2003; National Research Council, 2001; Volkmar & Pauls, 2003). Even though none of these three theories, by itself, can explain all the myriad problems displayed, together they help us begin to build a composite picture of autism spectrum disorders.

EXECUTIVE FUNCTIONS   In Chapter 7, we noted that many people with attention deficit hyperactivity disorder (ADHD) exhibit difficulties in self-directed behaviors. These self-directed behaviors, or **executive functions**, include such things as working memory, self-regulation of emotions, and the ability to plan ahead. Research indicates that

■ **Executive functions**
The ability to regulate one's behavior through working memory, inner speech, control of emotions and arousal levels, and analysis of problems and communication of problem solutions to others; delayed or impaired in those with ADHD and autism spectrum disorders.

many people with autism have difficulties with executive functions (Ozonoff, 1997). These problems are often more severe than those experienced by people with ADHD.

CENTRAL COHERENCE   Some authorities have identified people with autism as having weak **central coherence** (Frith, 2003), the natural inclination for most people to bring order and meaning to information in their environment by perceiving it as a meaningful whole rather than as disparate parts. Individuals with autism, on the other hand, get caught up in details in classic "not being able to see the forest for the trees" fashion.

Interestingly, some people with autism don't seem to recognize that their way of processing information is disjointed, nor do they appear to have any desire or need to bring coherence to their fragmented perceptions:

> A patient exhibiting autistic symptoms from early childhood obsessively collected information about the addresses of juvenile courts. It is unknown how this extremely odd interest arose. However it came about, it would be less odd if it emerged from a general interest in courts, buildings, or town plans. In this case it would not be just a fragment, however well studied, but part of a bigger picture. But this was definitely not the case for this patient. When asked why he did not want to know about the addresses of nonjuvenile courts, he replied, "They bore me to tears." This was not a joke on his part. The remark showed a total lack of understanding that interests are expected to be justified as part of a coherent pattern of likes and dislikes, and not arbitrary. (Frith, 2003, pp. 157–158)

THEORY OF MIND   **Theory of mind** refers to a person's ability to take the perspective of other people. It's the ability to "read" the mind of other people with respect to such things as their intentions, feelings, beliefs, and desires. Earlier, we discussed how difficult it is for many people with Asperger syndrome to read social cues. The reading of social cues is another way of saying that a person can anticipate and understand what another is probably thinking. Most of us are able to infer the emotional state of those with whom we are conversing by interpreting cues, such as tone of voice and facial expressions. We're able to gauge how others are reacting to what we're saying using similar cues.

People with autism spectrum disorders have varying degrees of difficulty inferring the thoughts of others. Some, in fact, don't seem to understand that their thoughts are different from those of others. See Focus on Concepts below for a study demonstrating the theory-of-mind problems exhibited by children with autism.

■ **Central coherence**
The inclination to bring meaning to stimuli by conceptualizing them as a whole; thought to be weak in people with autism spectrum disorders.

■ **Theory of mind**
The ability to take another's perspective in a social exchange; the ability to infer another person's feelings, intentions, desires, etc.; impaired in those with autism spectrum disorders.

UNDERSTANDING THE STANDARDS AND PRINCIPLES   What type of education is likely to be most appropriate for students with autism spectrum disorders? (CEC Knowledge and Skill Standards CC4S3, IC4S1, & CC5K5)

FOCUS ON **Concepts**

Theory of Mind: The Sally and Anne Experiment

In what has become regarded as a classic study of theory-of-mind problems, researchers investigated whether children with autism age six to sixteen years were able to recognize that others can have false beliefs that affect their judgment (Baron-Cohen, Leslie, & Frith, 1985). Using two dolls (Sally and Anne), an investigator acted out the following scenario to three groups of children (autistic, Down syndrome, nondisabled):

> Sally has a basket and Anne has a box. Sally has a marble and she puts it into her basket. She then goes out. Anne takes out Sally's marble and puts it into her box while Sally is away. Now Sally comes back and wants to play with her marble. At this point we ask the critical question: "Where will Sally look for her marble?" The answer is, of course, "In the basket." (Frith, 2003, pp. 82, 84)

The vast majority of the nondisabled children and even the children with Down syndrome answered correctly. However, only a few of the children with autism gave the correct response. They were unable to understand that Sally had no way of knowing that the marble had been switched—that to her way of thinking, the marble was where she had left it.

Educational Considerations

As we have mentioned, the characteristics of autism spectrum disorders are quite varied. When these characteristics are severe, they typically carry a very guarded prognosis, even with early, intensive intervention. A significant percentage of children with severe symptoms are unlikely to recover completely, although they might make substantial progress (Charlop-Christy, Schreibman, Pierce, & Kurtz, 1998; National Research Council, 2001).

Because autism's symptoms are so unusual and so resistant to remediation, it's been fertile ground for faddish and unproven treatment methods. As one authority has put it:

> The ASD [autism spectrum disorders] field is particularly well known for its willingness to embrace and/or maintain a liberal tolerance toward unproven and controversial interventions and treatments. A number of these purportedly effective methods appear to have neither empirical nor logical foundation. (Simpson, 2004, p. 139)

A team of researchers at the University of Kansas (Simpson et al., 2005) critiqued the major approaches to autism spectrum disorders and rated them according to their scientifically based credibility. (See Focus on Concepts on p. 442.)

Educational Programming Principles for Students with Autism Spectrum Disorders

Although educational programming for students with autism spectrum disorders covers a wide variety of areas, there are some guidelines on which most authorities have agreed. First, generally speaking, many believe that the greatest areas of needed instruction are communication skills for those with autism and social skills for those with Asperger syndrome. Also, most agree that educational programming for students with autism spectrum disorders should include (1) direct instruction of skills, (2) behavior management using functional behavioral assessment and positive behavioral intervention and support, and (3) instruction in natural settings. These three elements are evident in the interventions judged as scientifically based. (See Focus on Concepts on p. 442.)

DIRECT INSTRUCTION OF SKILLS   Effective instruction for students with autism spectrum disorders usually requires a highly structured, directive approach that uses basic principles of behavioral psychology for analyzing tasks and how best to teach them. *Direct instruction* means using structured, teacher-led lessons; instruction in small groups or one on one; lessons presented in small steps; frequent use of teacher questions; extensive opportunities for practice; and frequent feedback, reinforcement and correction (Hallahan, Lloyd, Kauffman, Weiss, & Martinez, 2005). Teachers can use direct instruction to teach skills in communication, social interaction, and daily living.

BEHAVIOR MANAGEMENT   Students with autism spectrum disorders, especially those with severe levels of autism, sometimes display highly inappropriate behaviors, such as biting, hitting, or screaming. As we mentioned in our discussion of intellectual disabilities, ADHD, and emotional or behavioral disorders (see Chapters 5, 7, and 8), authorities recommend that a combination of **functional behavioral assessment (FBA)** and **positive behavioral and intervention support (PBIS)** may reduce or eliminate these behaviors. FBA involves determining the consequences, antecedents, and setting events that maintain such behaviors (Horner, Albin, Sprague, & Todd, 2000). *Consequences* refer to the purpose the behavior serves for the person. *Antecedents* refer to things that trigger the behavior. *Setting events* take into account the contextual

Reading Homework Exercise

Controversial Treatment ● Go to the Homework and Exercises section in Chapter 12 of MyEducationLab and read about a controversial treatment called "chelation" that is touted by some as a treatment for autism.

■ **Functional behavioral assessment (FBA)**
Evaluation that consists of finding out the consequences (what purpose the behavior serves), antecedents (what triggers the behavior), and setting events (contextual factors) that maintain inappropriate behaviors.

■ **Positive behavioral intervention and support (PBIS)**
Systematic use of the science of behavior to find ways of supporting desirable behavior rather than punishing undesirable behavior; positive reinforcement (rewarding) procedures that are intended to support a student's appropriate or desirable behavior.

Effective instruction for students with autism spectrum disorders often requires the use of direct instruction in small group or one-on-one settings to teach skills in communication, social interaction, cognition, and functional academics.

factors in which the behavior occurs. For example, the student might be more likely to exhibit inappropriate behavior toward the end of the day when he or she is more tired.

PBIS involves finding ways to support positive behaviors of students rather than punishing negative behaviors. It focuses on the total environment of the student, including instruction.

INSTRUCTION IN NATURAL SETTINGS   Educators of students with autism spectrum disorders are increasingly emphasizing applying behavioral psychology in natural settings and in natural interactions—the kinds of settings and interactions that nondisabled children enjoy. Researchers are constantly trying to make better instructional use of the natural interactions by which children normally learn language and other social skills. The Success Stories feature on pages 444–445 relates how a combination of these strategies (direct instruction, behavior management, and instruction in natural settings) has helped Wesley, a six-year-old with autism, to reach his preschool and kindergarten goals.

Teachers or speech clinicians can also use **augmentative or alternative communication (AAC)** systems (see Chapters 9 and 13) for students with autism who are nonverbal or who have very little functional language. One such system that uses pictures to help students initiate and maintain functional communication is the Picture Exchange Communication System (PECS; see Responsive Instruction on p. 446).

■ **Augmentative or alternative communication (AAC)**
Alternative forms of communication that do not use the oral sounds of speech or that augment the use of speech.

Casebook Reflection

REFER TO THE CASE *Getting to Know Chase* in your booklet. According to the case, Chase's behavior began to improve over the year through the behavior program worked out by his teachers. How do you foresee Chase's future involvement in school, community, and work? ●

Educational Strategies for Teaching Social Skills to Students with Asperger Syndrome

Because the needs of students with Asperger syndrome are primarily focused on social skills and because these students are likely to be the most integrated into general education classrooms, we discuss strategies that focus on social skill development separately.

Students with Asperger syndrome need explicit instruction in social skills that most students pick up through indirect or incidental learning:

> Students with AS are at a disadvantage because they do not understand the hidden curriculum. As a result, they inadvertently break the rules associated with the hidden curriculum and either get in trouble with adults or are further ostracized or hurt by peers. Instruction and interpretation of hidden curriculum items should be an integral part of the education of children and youth with AS. It is through these types of activities that individuals with this exceptionality can learn to understand and function in the world around them. (Myles & Simpson, 2001, p. 285)

Researchers have shown that at least two types of strategies for teaching social skills have been relatively successful: (1) social interpreting and (2) coaching (Myles, 2003).

SOCIAL INTERPRETING   A social interpreter is "someone who can turn a confusing event into a meaningful interaction through explanation and clarification" (Myles, 2003, p. 28). Researchers and practitioners have devised several ways to train social interpreting skills. One such technique is SODA (Stop, Observe, Deliberate, and Act; Bock, 2002), wherein the student is taught self-monitoring questions such as:

> *Stop:* What is the room arrangement?, What is the activity or routine? . . .
> *Observe:* What are the people doing?, What are people saying?, What is the length of a typical conversation . . .?
> *Deliberate:* What would I like to do? What would I like to say? How will I know when others would like to visit longer . . .?
> *Act:* Approach person(s) with whom I'd like to visit. Say, "Hello, how are you?" Listen to person(s) *and* ask related questions. Look for cues that this person would like to visit longer or would like to end this conversation. (Myles, 2003, p. 32)

Another technique similar to social interpreting is social stories (see Responsive Instruction on p. 447).

COACHING   Coaching involves helping persons with Asperger syndrome to prepare ahead of or during a social interaction. For example, the teacher might do the following:

- Point out another child who is alone and might want to interact socially. *"Johnny is standing over there by himself. I think he might want someone to play with. Why don't you go over and talk to him."*
- Provide the child with a sentence or topic he can use in a social exchange. *"Ask Susan if she has seen [a current popular movie]. If she has, you can say 'What did you like about the movie.' If she says that she hasn't seen the movie, say, "What movies have you seen lately?"* (Myles, 2003, p. 37)

People with Asperger syndrome often have a great deal of difficulty initiating conversations. One recommended strategy is to provide them with "conversation starters"—cards that contain topics that might be of interest to same-age and same-sex peers (Myles, 2003).

Service Delivery Models

The U.S. Department of Education (2005) reports that currently, the most popular placement for students with autism is in a self-contained classroom. About 44 percent of school-age students with autism are in separate classes, about 27 percent are primarily in

UNDERSTANDING THE STANDARDS AND PRINCIPLES   Where are most students with autism educated? How should placement decisions be made? (CEC Knowledge and Skill Standard CC1K6)

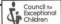

FOCUS ON **Concepts**

Judging the Scientific Basis of Interventions for Autism Spectrum Disorders

A team of researchers at the University of Kansas (Simpson et al., 2005) analyzed the research behind some of the interventions for students with autism spectrum disorders, categorizing them according to how much and how strongly the evidence supported use of these treatments.

Scientifically Based Practice: The interventions and treatments . . . have undergone a substantial amount of rigorous research. The evidence repeatedly and consistently provides similar results that prove children and youth with ASD [autism spectrum disorders] display a significant increase in skill acquisition as a consequence of the intervention.

Promising Practice: Interventions and treatments . . . have (1) been widely used for several years without any or with few adverse outcomes, and/or (2) undergone research that suggests that children and youth with ASD respond favorably and display skill acquisition as a consequence of the intervention. However, these practices require additional scientific evidence to be considered truly scientifically based.

Limited Supporting Information for Practice: Interventions and treatments . . . have been subjected to limited research with children and youth with ASD, are not widely utilized. . . , or reflect a wide range of results (poor to favorable). . . .

Not Recommended: Interventions and treatments . . . have (1) undergone a substantial amount of rigorous research and the evidence proves that the intervention or treatment does not increase skill acquisition or favorable results . . . , and/or (2) there have been serious detrimental effects and outcomes for some children and youth. . . . (Simpson et al., 2005, pp. 10–11)

Table A lists the ratings for the interventions. The researchers classified the interventions according to their focus: interpersonal relationships, skill-based, cognitive, physiological/biological/neurological, other.

It's important to keep in mind that, since the publication of Simpson and colleagues' work, additional research might have resulted in some of these interventions in the "Promising" or "Limited Supporting Information" categories shifting from one rating to another. However, it's more unlikely that those in the "Scientifically Based" or "Not Recommended" categories would markedly change, as there already was a substantial amount of evidence gathered on those interventions.

The intervention with perhaps the strongest scientifically based research support is **applied behavior analysis (ABA)**. ABA is a highly structured approach that focuses on teaching functional skills and continuous assessment of progress. Grounded in behavioral learning theory, ABA emphasizes positive reinforcement or rewarding of desired behaviors. In its original conceptualization, ABA also meant punishing undesired behaviors. Today, many professionals avoid or de-emphasize the use of punishment, and research suggests that this has not resulted in a decrease in effectiveness (Sallows & Graupner, 2005).

■ **Applied behavior analysis (ABA)**
A highly structured approach that focuses on teaching functional skills and continuous assessment of progress; grounded in behavioral learning theory.

general education classrooms, about 18 percent are in resource rooms, about 10 percent are in separate schools, and about 1 percent are in residential facilities.

Partly because of the emphasis on teaching children with autism spectrum disorders in the more naturalistic context of everyday interactions and environments, an increasing percentage of such students are being taught in neighborhood schools and general education classrooms, especially at younger ages. In this model, general educators and special educators work together to meet the individual needs of students with autism. However, there is little research describing how this collaboration should look in the classroom. One promising format might be the Autism Spectrum Disorder Inclusion Collaboration model (Simpson, deBoer-Ott, & Smith-Myles, 2003;

TABLE A	Scientific Basis for Interventions for Autism Spectrum Disorders				
	Interpersonal Relationships	**Skill-Based**	**Cognitive**	**Physiological/ Biological/ Neurological**	**Other**
Scientifically-Based Practice	Applied Behavior Analysis (ABA) Discrete Trial Teaching (DTT) Pivotal Response Training (PRT)	Learning Experiences: An Alternative Program for Preschoolers and Parents (LEAP)			
Promising Practice	Play-Oriented Strategies	Assistive Technology Augmentative Alternative Communication (ACC) Incidental Teaching Joint Action Routines (JARS) Picture Exchange Communication System (PECS) Structured Teaching (TEACCH)	Cognitive behavioral modification Cognitive learning strategies Social decision making Social stories	Pharmacology Sensory Integration (SI)	
Limited Supporting Information for Practice	Gentle teaching option method (Son-Rise program) Floor time Pet/animal therapy Relationship Development Intervention (RDI)	Fast ForWord van Dijk curricular approach	Cartooning Cognitive scripts Power cards	Auditory Integration Training (AIT) Megavitamin therapy Scotopic Sensitivity Syndrome (SSS): Irlen Lenses	Art therapy Candida: Autism connection Feingold diet Herbs & minerals Music therapy
Not Recommended	Holding therapy	Facilitated Communication (FC)			

Source: Adapted from Simpson et al. (2005). *Autism spectrum disorders: Interventions and treatments for children and youth.* Thousand Oaks, CA: Corwin Press. (pp. 9–10)

(see Making It Work on page 448). Nevertheless, some of the effective instruction of children with autism spectrum disorders requires one-on-one teaching or teaching in very small groups, and sometimes this can't be done effectively in the general education classroom.

Even when such intensive instruction is offered in specialized settings, state-of-the-art teaching emphasizes the most natural possible human interactions. At the preschool level, teachers are emphasizing natural interactions with nondisabled peers in general education classrooms. At the elementary level,

Casebook Reflection

REFER TO THE CASE *Getting to Know Chase* in your booklet. Chase is receiving his schooling in a center for students with emotional/behavior disorders, not his local public school. Do you think this is the best placement for him (the least restrictive environment)? Do you think he would be more successful in the general education classroom? ●

Intensive and early applied behavior analysis prepare Wesley for his general education kindergarten class

Mrs Gilmer, Wesley's mother: "His success has helped us feel more encouraged about his future."

Six-year-old Wesley Gilmer has attended a special elementary school program for students with autism. This year, Wesley will participate in the general education kindergarten with specialized supports.

These are the keys to his success:

- intensive, explicit instruction in social skills and academics
- relentless and structured positive behavioral support
- specific interventions for skill acquisition and communication

Special education coordinator Toni Elitharp glows with pride as Wesley Gilmer takes his place as a student in the general education kindergarten program. Wesley has mastered his preschool goals, and he will continue to receive specially designed instruction as he learns the kindergarten curriculum. Wesley doesn't say much about his experiences, but the smile on his face tells the story. Wesley started preschool at three years of age with significant difficulties associated with autism, but he prospered from intensive, relentless, and specific special education.

● **Intensive, Explicit Instruction in Social Skills and Academics** Mountain View Elementary School serves neighborhood students in preschool through fifth grade. The school also provides specialized programming for children with autism who need intensive attention in classes with a small student–teacher ratio. The faculty and staff at Mountain View are active participants in creating a warm, caring, and cooperative climate for learning. "This school is child-centered," says Elitharp, who finds the key to working with students with autism is understanding their unique characteristics.

Toni Elitharp helps teachers learn to use applied behavior analysis (ABA), an educational model that targets individualized skill acquisition and behavior reduction. The ABA approach for teaching children with autism emphasizes the use of task analysis, discrete teaching, positive reinforcement, behavior intervention, and self-monitoring. "Visual strategies are also necessary to guide the students through the daily plan," says Elitharp. "It's a struggle for children with autism to know the sequence of their day without seeing the sequence in a visually explicit way." Mr. Gilmer says, "Wesley is a visual sponge."

● **Relentless and Structured Positive Behavioral Support** According to Elitharp, "children with autism live by rules, routine, and the predictability of their environment." She sees Wesley as an example of a child with autism who has thrived on relentless and structured support in coping with unpredictable events.

When he started preschool, Wesley had no parallel play skills or appropriate social skills for his age. "I knew there were some peculiarities," says Mrs. Gilmer, "but he also had some unique talents." Now, as long as Wesley is shown a picture schedule of

educators are including more children with autism spectrum disorders in cooperative learning groups with their nondisabled peers in general education classrooms.

UNDERSTANDING THE STANDARDS AND PRINCIPLES What can teachers use to monitor the progress of language development and social/adaptive behavior of students with autism spectrum disorder? (CEC Knowledge and Skill Standard CC8S8)

Council for
Exceptional
Children

Assessment of Progress

Two critical areas of assessment for students with autism spectrum disorders are progress in language development and social/adaptive behavior. This section describes measures to monitor student progress and to evaluate student outcomes in these two areas. In addition, we provide information on testing accommodations and alternate assessments for students with autism spectrum disorders.

his day and is made aware of any changes before they occur, he is able to participate in all activities. He now takes pride in his work, interacts with peers and adults, and shows a variety of appropriate emotions.

Wesley started preschool as a developmentally delayed child with autism. His communication skills, social skills, and readiness skills were very limited. Through the use of task analysis for each new skill, a predictable manner of presenting each skill, visual strategies, and consistent positive reinforcement, Wesley was able to make gains and perform above grade level by the end of his preschool career.

● **Specific Interventions: Skill Acquisition and Communication** "ABA helps children learn how to learn," says Elitharp. She shows teachers how to break skills down into smaller units for easier understanding, how to practice the small units with each child, and then how to help the child connect the smaller units to something more meaningful. "The use of physical prompts reinforces correct learning, and then the prompts are gradually reduced until skills are self maintained," she explains.

Elitharp also encourages teachers to use assistive technologies and a variety of communication systems to help children with autism gain the ability to generalize skills. Speech therapy has helped Wesley to develop his expressive vocabulary. "As he developed language, he became a happier little boy," says Mrs. Gilmer. "He is now prompting us to help him learn what he wants to learn."

"When you first learn your child has autism, you want to find out what it means, and it's often discouraging," says Mr. Gilmer. "We tried to find encouraging stories. We had so many questions." Mrs. Gilmer remembers, "We'd set little goals for Wesley, hoping they could be accomplished. They have been accomplished because of the willingness and patience of those who have worked with him." According to Toni Elitharp, Wesley has come far from where he began. "He has worked hard, and he will still have to work hard to progress in a world that is sometimes foreign to him." With continued effort and help from educators trained to provide specialized instruction, he should continue to succeed.

CEC'S STANDARDS: PAVING THE WAY TO SUCCESS

ASSESS YOUR STEPS TO SUCCESS in meeting the CEC Knowledge and Skill Base for All Beginning Special Education Teachers of Students in Individualized General Curriculums and of Students in Individualized Independence Curriculums. Use the following questions to reflect on the growth of your own professional knowledge, skills, and dispositions.

REFLECTING ON YOUR OWN PROFESSIONAL DEVELOPMENT

If you were Wesley's teacher . . .
- What are some areas about educating students with autism that you would need to know more about?
- What are some specific skills that would help you to address his academic and behavioral challenges?
- What personal dispositions do you think are most important for you to develop in teaching students with autism?

Using the CEC Standards
- What are some research-supported methods for teaching individuals with autism? (GC4S1)
- Describe how you might use task analysis in planning instruction for a student with autism. (CC7S5)
- What steps would you take in planning and implementing individualized reinforcement systems and environmental modifications for a student with autism? (IC7S1)

● *By Jean B. Crockett*

Progress Monitoring

MONITORING PROGRESS IN LANGUAGE DEVELOPMENT Teachers can use the MacArthur-Bates Communicative Development Inventory-Second Edition (CDI-II; Fenson et al., 2003) to monitor the progress of language development of very young children with autism spectrum disorder. Although this measure was designed for typically developing children, it's also been validated for children with disabilities, including children with autism spectrum disorders (Luyster, Lopez, & Lord, 2007; Luyster, Qiu, Lopez, & Lord, 2007). The CDI-II is appropriate for children ages eight to thirty months, and the CDI-III (Fenson, 2007) expands the measure for use with children up to thirty-seven months of age.

MONITORING PROGRESS IN SOCIAL/ADAPTIVE BEHAVIOR The PDD Behavior Inventory (PDDBI) (Cohen & Sudhalter, 2005) is designed to monitor the progress in

Meeting the Needs of Students with Autism Spectrum Disorders
Picture Exchange Communication System (PECS)

The National Research Council (2001) estimates that one-third to one-half of children with autism don't use speech functionally. Teachers can use augmentative and alternative communication systems to assist and support these individuals' communication (Mirenda, 2003). Augmentative systems supplement existing communication (e.g., the use of manual signs in addition to limited speech). Alternative systems, by contrast, serve as the primary means of communication (e.g., the use of pictures or line drawings to express communication in the absence of any other speech or communication).

One AAC system is the Picture Exchange Communication System (PECS), originally designed by Bondy and Frost to support the communication of students with autism (Bondy & Frost, 2001; Frost & Bondy, 2002). PECS allows individuals to make requests or demands, choose preferred items, and express feelings by using picture cards. The PECS teaches students to exchange the symbols physically for preferred items and build simple communication sentences through the use of picture cards.

WHAT THE RESEARCH SAYS

Several studies examining the acquisition and impact of PECS found that students were able not only to learn the symbols and use them functionally, but also to replace the use of symbols with spontaneous and imitative speech after an extended period of using the cards (Bondy & Frost, 1994; Charlop-Christy et al., 2002; Schwartz, Garfinkle, & Bauer, 1998). The advantages of PECS for supporting communication of individuals with autism are:

- Greater flexibility owing to the nonelectrical nature of the system
- Ability of students with poor manual fine motor skills to make use of the system, compared to nonaided communication such as manual signs
- Ease of implementation and acquisition
- Communication that is meaningful and naturally reinforcing

- The potential for increased speech development and production concurrent with the use of the aided symbols (Mirenda, 2003)

APPLYING THE RESEARCH TO TEACHING

Implementing the PECS begins with teaching students to exchange a picture for a desired item. They are taught how to discriminate among the symbols and to build communication "sentences." As students progress with the materials, they are also taught to respond to questions and to comment on situations. With PECS, students don't rely on external prompts; rather, they're taught to initiate communication by using the cards. Typically, the PECS is taught in four to six phases:

- Phase I: Teach students to spontaneously request desired items or activities by exchanging a picture card for the item. Students practice with one card at a time. Immediate reinforcement comes from receiving the item or participating in the activity.
- Phase II: Expand the vocabulary of the student by increasing the number of cards used yet still only using one card at a time.
- Phase III: Teach the student to discriminate among many cards to identify the desired card by placing a number of cards on a board.
- Phase IV: Teach basic sentence structure using sentence strips on a board (e.g., "I want" paired with the picture of the desired item).
- Phases V and VI: Add adjectives and other words to expand communication. This includes adding words such as *four*, *red*, *I see*, *I hear*, and *I feel* (Wallin, 2004).

Although PECS was originally designed for preschoolers, research has shown that it can be effective with adolescents and adults. Teachers can learn to use the system by following the PECS Training Manual (Frost & Bondy, 2002).

● *By Kristin L. Sayeski*

social/adaptive behavior of students two to twelve years old. Unlike diagnostic tools, the PDDBI is sensitive to change (Cohen, Schmidt-Lackner, Romanczyk, & Sudhalter, 2003). The PDDBI includes parent and teacher versions and assesses the following domains of maladaptive behavior: (1) sensory/perceptual approach behaviors, (2) ritualisms/resistance to change, (3) social pragmatic problems, (4) semantic/pragmatic problems, (5) arousal regulation problems, (6) specific fears, and (7) aggressiveness. Adaptive behaviors assessed include (1) receptive social communication abilities and (2) expressive social communication abilities (see Cohen, et al., 2003 for a description of the PDDBI).

The Social Responsiveness Scale (SRS) (Constantino & Gruber, 2005) is a parent/teacher scale that may be used to monitor progress in social/adaptive behavior (social awareness,

Meeting the Needs of Students with Autism Spectrum Disorders

Social Stories

WHAT THE RESEARCH SAYS

A salient characteristic of students with autism spectrum disorders is an impairment in social interaction. Social Stories™ (Gray, 2004), an intervention originally developed by Carol Gray in 1991, was designed to help students with autism spectrum disorder "unpack" social situations and scaffold appropriate responses. Students with autism spectrum disorder can become overwhelmed when faced with interacting with others and as a result, can respond in inappropriate ways. Social Stories provide a description of the social interaction of concern (e.g., waiting in line in the cafeteria) and then provide statements of appropriate responses (e.g., thinking of a favorite song while waiting) (Crozier & Sileo, 2005). Some research has suggested the effectiveness of Social Stories for decreasing undesirable behaviors such as aggression, screaming, temper tantrums, and table manners and increasing prosocial responses of students with autism spectrum disorder (Kuoch & Mirenda, 2003; Norris & Dattilo, 1999; Scattone, Wilczynski, Edwards, & Rabian, 2002).

RESEARCH STUDY

One team of researchers investigated the effectiveness of using Social Stories for increasing appropriate social interactions (Scattone, Tingstrom, & Wilczynski, 2006). They selected three boys (two 8-year-olds and one 13-year-old) who didn't initiate or interact with peers appropriately during free-time activities, but who did have intelligible speech and could speak in complete sentences. Each day five minutes prior to the scheduled free time (either lunch or recess depending on the boy), the student would read or be read his Social Story. Each Social Story was written specifically for the individual student for the explicit purpose of increasing the number of appropriate social interactions with peers. Researchers then recorded the number of interactions.

RESEARCH FINDINGS

Prior to introducing the Social Stories, all three boys were observed three days per week for eleven weeks to obtain baseline data. After participating in the Social Story intervention, two of the boys experienced increases in the amount of social interactions. One student had a dramatic rise in the number of social interactions (from an average of 7 percent during baseline to 39 percent after the intervention). The other student had more moderate increases (13 percent to 28 percent postintervention). The final student showed no change after intervention.

Findings from this study indicate that it's possible to use Social Stories to increase peer interactions for some students with autism spectrum disorder. Overall, research suggests the success of Social Stories in reducing inappropriate behaviors and the potential for Social Stories to be used, alone or in combination with other interventions, to increase social interactions.

APPLYING THE RESEARCH TO TEACHING

Teachers and parents can create their own Social Stories to promote the development of new social skills for students with autism spectrum disorder. In general, Social Stories should be written from the student's perspective and include a beginning, middle, and end. Social Stories can use graphics or illustrations to support the text. Social Stories can be paired with "cartooning" (drawing stick figures similar to a comic strip) (Glaeser, Pierson, & Fritschmann, 2003). The emphasis of all Social Stories is on describing actions and events, but other types of sentences should be used to support the description. Gray (2004) defines the seven different possible Social Story sentence types:

1. *Descriptive sentences* objectively describe where, when, who, what, and why.
2. *Perspective sentences* are written from the perspective of others involved in the social situation and provide insight as to how they may think or feel.
3. *Cooperative sentences* provide reminders to adults as to how they can assist the student learn the new skill.
4. *Directive sentences* define the social response to the situation that is desired. These sentences typically begin with "I will try" or "I will work on" statements to indicate some understanding that it will not be every time.
5. *Affirmative sentences* emphasize the tone and directive of the Social Story.
6. *Control sentences* are created by the student to help him or her remember the directive.
7. *Partial sentences* are fill-in-the-blank sentences to be completed by the student.

Once a story is created, teachers can make the story into a book (with one or two sentences per page) and add pictures. Teachers often report that students enjoy their Social Stories books and make them a part of their school routines.

● *By Kristin L. Sayeski*

Collaboration and Co-Teaching with Teachers of Students with Autism Spectrum Disorder

"I don't know anything about students with autism spectrum disorder. How can this work?"

WHAT DOES IT MEAN TO BE A TEACHER OF STUDENTS WITH AUTISM SPECTRUM DISORDER?

The Council for Exceptional Children doesn't identify separate knowledge and skills requirements for teachers of students with autism spectrum disorders. In most cases, a teacher working with these students would be certified to teach in the area of emotional/behavioral disorders, or in either the area of individualized general education or independence curriculum. Though there are no specific guidelines for the preparation of teachers of students with autism spectrum disorders, this is a new and growing area of study and many universities (and other groups) offer specific training programs. The University of North Carolina's Treatment and Education of Autistic and related Communication-handicapped Children (TEACCH) program is but one example.

SUCCESSFUL STRATEGIES FOR COLLABORATION

Collaboration strategies for students with autism spectrum disorders are rather new and few have been tested for effectiveness in the general education classroom. Nevertheless, researchers are working to create models that are effective and support both the general and special educators who are working "by the seat of their pants" at this point. One such model is the Autism Spectrum Disorder Inclusion Collaboration model (Simpson et al., 2003), which "emphasizes shared responsibility and shared decision making among general educators, special educators, and support personnel. The model also permits consideration of both learner behaviors and instructional factors" (p. 117). The model includes five main components: (1) environmental and curricular modifications, general education classroom support, and instructional methods; (2) attitudinal and social support; (3) coordinated team commitment; (4) recurrent evaluation of inclusion procedures; and (5) home–school collaboration. The model isn't prescriptive in its recommendations for how collaboration should look in the classroom, but it does list specific items that should be in place in each component in order for collaboration to work. These items include:

Environmental and Curricular Modifications

- Availability of appropriately trained support personnel
- Inservice training
- Implementation of appropriate instructional methods
- Availability of paraeducators
- Adequate teacher planning time
- Reduced class size

Attitudinal and Social Support

- School administration has positive attitude toward inclusion
- Administrative support for those working to include students with autism spectrum disorders
- Dissemination of information about autism spectrum disorders
- Use of curricula and experiences to facilitate understanding and sensitivity toward students with autism spectrum disorders
- Social interaction training for students with autism spectrum disorders

Coordinated Team Commitment

- Clear definition of roles for service delivery personnel
- Effective communication
- Shared decision making

Recurrent Evaluation of Inclusion Practices

- Evaluating appropriate supplemental aides and services
- Evidence of benefit from participation and education
- Student demonstration of appropriate participation

Home-school Collaboration

- Meaningful participation
- Suitable administrative supports
- School willingness to listen

● *By Margaret P. Weiss*

INTERNET RESOURCES

More information about TEACCH can be found at www.teacch.com.

social information processing, reciprocal social communication, social anxiety, and avoidance). The SRS evaluates the severity of social impairment of individuals with autism spectrum disorders between the ages of four and eighteen.

Outcome Measures

The CDI-II, CDI-III, PDDBI, and SRS can also be used as outcome measures to evaluate the effectiveness of interventions. In addition, teachers can include direct observation in natural settings to evaluate the effectiveness of interventions and services provided for students with autism spectrum disorder. Standardized measures are also available to evaluate program outcomes.

The Autism Social Skills Profile (ASSP) (Bellini & Hopf, 2007) is a standardized outcome measure that examines social skills of children and adolescents with autism spectrum disorder. The ASSP is completed by teachers or parents and includes three subscales: (1) Social Reciprocity, (2) Social Participation/Avoidance, and (3) Detrimental Social Behaviors.

The Childhood Autism Rating Scale (CARS) (Schopler, Reichler, & Renner, 1988) is frequently used for screening and diagnostic purposes, and can also be used to evaluate the effectiveness of interventions (Cohen et al., 2003). CARS focuses on behaviors that deviate from children developing typically and is appropriate for children over two years old.

Testing Accommodations and Alternate Assessments

Accommodations provided to students with autism spectrum disorder vary based on the degree of severity of the disability. Some students with autism spectrum disorders who are high functioning academically may be included on standard assessments of educational progress with basic testing accommodations such as setting, scheduling, presentation format, and response format modifications. Extended time and small-group/individual administration are common modifications to the testing schedule and setting.

Many students with autism spectrum disorders are unable to participate in large-scale standard assessments of educational progress even with accommodations (Vacca, 2007), and require alternate assessment methods. Furthermore, for students receiving a modified or alternate curriculum, the alternate assessment should evaluate their progress in that curriculum. The most common form of alternate assessment is a portfolio (Thompson & Thurlow, 2001). A portfolio is a collection of items (e.g., anecdotal notes, student work samples) to provide evidence of growth on specified goals. For students with autism spectrum disorders, direct observation of behavior can also be an important component of alternate assessments.

Early Intervention

Most early intervention programming focuses on children with relatively severe degrees of autism spectrum disorders, such as autism, rather than milder degrees, such as Asperger syndrome. (As previously noted, Asperger syndrome is usually not diagnosed until the child is beyond the preschool years.)

To be most effective, education and related interventions for students with autism must be early, intensive, and highly structured and should involve families. Early, intensive intervention may produce remarkable gains in many young children with autism spectrum disorders although no intervention yet can claim universal success in enabling these children to overcome their disabilities completely. Education increasingly focuses on using natural interactions to teach students in natural environments, including general education classrooms to the extent possible. The National Research Council (2001)

Video Homework Exercise

Early Detection ●
Go to the Homework and Exercises section in Chapter 12 of MyEducationLab to watch the video "Why Early Detection of Autism is Crucial."

reviewed research and practice and found strong consensus for the following essential features of effective preschool programs for children with autism spectrum disorders:

- Entry into intervention programs as soon as an autism spectrum diagnosis is seriously considered;

- Active engagement in intensive instructional programming for a minimum of the equivalent of a full school day, 5 days (at least 25 hours) a week, with full year programming varied according to the child's chronological age and developmental level;

- Repeated, planned teaching opportunities generally organized around relatively brief periods of time for the youngest children (e.g., 15–20 minute intervals), including sufficient amounts of adult attention in one-to-one and very small group instruction to meet individualized goals;

- Inclusion of a family component, including parent training;

- Low student/teacher ratios (no more than two young children with autistic spectrum disorders per adult in the classroom); and

- Mechanisms for ongoing program evaluation and assessments of individual children's progress, with results translated into adjustments in programming. (p. 175)

Better understanding of the parental role has led to having parents work together with others as "co-therapists" in many treatment programs. If early intervention is to be as intensive and pervasive as required, family involvement is essential. Without parental participation in training, children are unlikely to acquire and maintain the communication and daily living skills they need for social development and eventual independence.

Transition to Adulthood

We discuss transition to adulthood for those with more severe forms of autism spectrum disorders, such as autism, separately from the less severe form of Asperger syndrome.

Transition Programming for People with Autism

Transition programming for people with autism follows virtually the same principles as those for people with intellectual disabilities (see Chapter 5). Transition planning should begin as early as the elementary years and become gradually more intensive in the middle school and secondary years. The current prevailing philosophy is **person-centered planning**, whereby the person with the disability is encouraged to make his or her own decisions as much as possible. More and more people with autism are being integrated into the community in small **community residential facilities** and in **supported living** settings, such as their own homes or apartments. The goal for work settings is for people with autism to be in **competitive employment** or **supported competitive employment** situations.

Transition Programming for People with Asperger Syndrome

As with programming at earlier ages, planning for transition to adulthood for people with Asperger syndrome is largely concerned with issues of social interaction. Research suggests that the social interaction issues for people with Asperger syndrome tend to increase as they reach adolescence and adulthood (Myles & Simpson, 2003). Unfortunately, this increase in difficulties in social interactions works against their achieving success in employment. Research also indicates that when people with Asperger syndrome do experience job difficulties, it usually has something to do with inappropriate social interactions rather than job performance (Gerhardt, 2003).

UNDERSTANDING THE STANDARDS AND PRINCIPLES What do we know about transition to adulthood for students with autism and Asperger syndrome? (CEC Knowledge and Skill Standards CC10K2 & CC10S9)

Council for Exceptional Children

■ **Person-centered planning**
Planning for a person's self-determination; planning activities and services on the basis of a person's dreams, aspirations, interests, preferences, strengths, and capacities.

■ **Community residential facility (CRF)**
A place, usually a group home, in an urban or residential neighborhood where about three to ten adults with disabilities live under supervision.

■ **Supported living**
An approach to living arrangements for those with disabilities that stresses living in natural settings rather than institutions, big or small.

■ **Competitive employment**
A workplace that provides employment that pays at least minimum wage and in which most workers are nondisabled.

■ **Supported competitive employment**
A workplace where adults who are disabled earn at least minimum wage and receive ongoing assistance from a specialist or job coach; the majority of workers in the workplace are nondisabled.

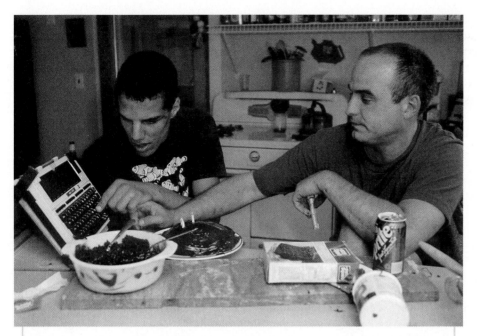

Many persons with autism are being integrated into the community in small residential facilities and supported living settings, such as their own homes or apartments.

One way of approaching deficits in social interaction is to consider a continuum from social survival skills to social competence. The notion here is that therapists or teachers of people with Asperger syndrome should focus first on social survival skills because they are the minimum necessary for independence. Table 12.3 provides examples of social skills on the continuum from survival to competence.

In transition programming for people with any kind of disability, it is always important that employers, college instructors, and those in similar positions have a solid understanding of the nature of the disability. In many cases, the person with Asperger syndrome may be misunderstood because he or she is intelligent but engages in eccentric behaviors.

It is fair to ask just how much the social eccentricities of people with Asperger syndrome should be tolerated or how much these behaviors actually interfere with the culture of the

INTERNET RESOURCES

The following Website has resources specifically for college students with Asperger syndrome: www.users.dircon.co.uk/~cns/

TABLE 12.3 **Toward Promoting Skills from Social Survival to Social Competence**

	Emphasis **Less Competence** **More Survival** **Necessary: Skills upon which independence may depend**	**Preferred: Skills that support independence but may not be critical**	**Emphasis** **Greater Competence** **Less Survival** **Marginal: Skills that, while valuable, may be negotiable**
Riding mass transit	Wait until others get off before you get on	Whenever possible, choose a seat where you are not sitting next to someone	Whenever possible, put a row between you and other passengers
Lunch with coworkers	Eat neatly	Respond to interactions from coworkers	Initiate conversations with coworkers
Job interview	Eye contact	Ask informed questions about the employer	Comment on items in the office that may be relevant (e.g., is the person someone who likes to fish?)

Source: Gerhardt, P. F. (2003). Transition support for learners with Asperger syndrome: Toward a successful adulthood. In R. W. Du Charme & T. P. Gullotta (Eds.), *Asperger syndrome: A guide for professionals and families* (pp. 157–171). New York: Kluwer Academic/Plenum Publishing (p. 161).

workplace. Most people would agree that there is room for improvement in society's attitudes toward those who behave differently from the norm but do not bother or harm others. In many cases, it is probably reasonable to ask how much it matters that an individual employee does not fit in socially with the rest of the workforce if he or she gets the job done. The following quote expresses well the tension between changing the individual with Asperger syndrome and changing society's reaction to people with the condition:

> A sentiment often expressed at the Douglass Group, a support group for adults with AS [Asperger syndrome] that I founded a number of years ago was "If you NTs [neurotypicals—a term coined by those with Asperger syndrome to describe those who do not have neurological disabilities] have all the skills, why don't you adapt for a while?" The perceived professional proclivity to focus solely on somehow "changing" the person with AS was often discussed as similar to expecting a person who is blind to see if only he or she would try harder. Given that, group members instead argued that while the primary focus of intervention should remain on the provision of skills to the learner with AS, the focus should be expanded to include comprehensive community education. (Gerhardt, 2003, p. 158)

Many people with Asperger syndrome, in fact, are becoming advocates for themselves and others who have their condition. For example, numerous Websites, created by individuals with Asperger syndrome, offer information and support (see the Personal Perspectives below).

Personal PERSPECTIVES

Youth Uses Web to Help Others on "Wrong Planet"

People who suffer from Asperger syndrome often feel like they're on the "wrong planet" and don't fit in. One area teen, however, is trying to ensure they don't feel quite so out of this world. Alex Planck, an 18-year-old rising senior at Charlottesville High School, is the cofounder of a new Website for people with Asperger syndrome. . . .

The site, www.wrongplanet.net, was launched last month but already has close to 300 members. It features a chat room, member profiles, articles about Asperger's, personal Web logs, or "blogs," and an online store selling everything from shirts to mouse pads . . . .

"There were other Web sites . . . but they were kind of elitist," he said. His site fosters a sense of community and helps people fit in with society.

"They also didn't have as many features as our site," Planck added.

Creating and maintaining the site has been exciting for Planck. The site has received visits from such far off places as New Zealand, Australia, Denmark, and the Seychelles, a group of islands in the Indian Ocean. . . .

Alex Planck

Although Planck says his greatest passion is learning new things, he confesses that computers are among his most enduring interests.

"It's easy to become obsessed with them because there's so much about them," he explained. Planck's partner in founding the site, Dan Grover, is a 15-year-old from Vermont who has already launched Wonderwarp, his own software group. Planck recently joined the group as a programmer.

Planck's mother, Mary, is a teacher . . . and his father, Doug, . . . is a lawyer.

"I think [the site] is such a neat resource. It's so hard to imagine what these kids deal with," his mother said.

Aside from computers and learning, the teen is also an enthusiastic mountain biker. He's hoping to attend the University of Virginia next year.

"When he wants to do something and he's focused on it, he's amazing," Mary Planck said, "We're proud of him."

Source: Cannon, J. (2004, July 22). Youth uses Web to help others on 'wrong planet.' *Charlottesville Daily Progress.*

Summary

What is the history behind autism spectrum disorders?

▶ In 1943, Leo Kanner reported on cases of children, whom he labeled as "autistic," who had major problems in communication and social interactions, as well as bizarre repetitive movements and an obsessive dislike of change.

▶ In 1944, Hans Asperger reported on cases of children, whom he referred to as having "autistic psychopathy," who he thought had normal intelligence and language but who were socially isolated and had obsessive interests in extraordinarily narrow areas.

How do professionals define autism spectrum disorders?

▶ Autism is characterized by severe deficits in communication, social interaction, and cognitive functioning and often involves repetitive, stereotyped movements, resistance to change, and unusual sensory perceptions.

▶ People who have Asperger syndrome have higher cognitive and language skills than those with classic autism, but they have problems in the other areas, especially social interaction.

What is the prevalence of autism spectrum disorders?

▶ Current estimates are that 1 out of 166 persons have an autism spectrum disorder.

▶ With the exception of Rett syndrome, which occurs primarily in females, males outnumber females 3:1 or 4:1 in autism spectrum disorders.

▶ Prevalence figures have risen dramatically for autism in the past thirty to forty years, leading some to declare an autism "epidemic" and to claim that there must be some mysterious toxin in our environment or that the measles, mumps, rubella (MMR) vaccination may be a cause; the best scientific evidence indicates that the MMR vaccination does not cause autism.

▶ Most authorities maintain that the increase in autism is due to a widening of the criteria for identification as autism, a greater awareness of autism spectrum disorders, and diagnostic substitution (e.g., persons now identified as having an autism spectrum disorder previously might have been identified as intellectually disabled).

What causes autism spectrum disorders?

▶ Early causal theories were influenced by psychoanalytic thinking and blamed parents, often mothers, for causing autism by being too cold and unresponsive.

▶ Today's causal theories point to a neurological and genetic basis for autism.
  - Several areas of the brain are implicated, such as the cerebral cortex, basal ganglia, amygdala, hippocampus, corpus callosum, brain stem, and cerebellum; this has led authorities to view autism spectrum disorders as a disorder of neural networks.
  - Evidence indicates that heredity as well as spontaneous genetic mutations are involved in causing autism.
  - Evidence indicates that there is no single gene that results in autism.

What methods are used to identify individuals with autism spectrum disorders?

▶ There is no universally used diagnostic test for autism spectrum disorders.

▶ For autism, the clinician uses criteria that focus on communication skills, social interactions, and repetitive and stereotyped patterns of behavior.

▶ For Asperger syndrome, the clinician looks for normal or close to normal communication abilities but problems in social interactions and repetitive and stereotyped patterns of behavior, but to a lesser extent than in classic autism.

What are some of the psychological and behavioral characteristics of learners with autism spectrum disorders?

▶ People with autism have deficits in communication, social interaction, and cognition, as well as repetitive and stereotyped patterns of behavior, and some have abnormal sensory perceptions.
  - Most lack communicative intent, the desire to communicate socially.
  - They have cognitive deficits similar to those of people with intellectual disabilities; some have additional peculiarities, such as processing things visually and spatially rather than conceptually or linguistically.
  - Some, who are called autistic savants, have extraordinary splinter skills.
  - Examples of abnormal sensory perceptions are being hyperresponsive, hyporesponsive, or synaesthesia (a mixing of sensory information).

▶ Compared to people with autism, those with Asperger syndrome often display a milder degree of impairments or abnormalities in social interaction, communication, repetitive and stereotyped patterns of behavior, cognitive processing, and sensory perceptions.

- People with Asperger syndrome often have difficulties with social interactions, understanding the hidden curriculum (the dos and don'ts of everyday living), and taking things too literally.
- Another communication challenge in Asperger syndrome is in pragmatics, the social uses of verbal and nonverbal communication skills.

▶ Three theories have been proposed to account for many deficits in autism spectrum disorders. No one of them explains all the deficits of all the disorders, but together they begin to build a composite picture.
- Problems with executive functions include such things as working memory, self-regulation of emotions, and the ability to plan ahead.
- Problems with central coherence involve paying too much attention to details or parts in cognitive processing, thereby leading to impairments in conceptualizing coherent wholes.
- Problems with a theory of mind lead to impairments in taking another person's perspective, or being able to "read" what they might be thinking.

What are some educational considerations for learners with autism spectrum disorders?

▶ The greatest areas of needed instruction are in communication skills (for those with autism) and in social skills (for those with Asperger syndrome).

▶ Educational programming for students with autism spectrum disorders should include (1) direct instruction of skills, (2) behavior management using functional behavioral assessment and positive behavioral support, and (3) instruction in natural settings.
- The intervention with the strongest research support—applied behavior analysis (ABA)—includes these elements.

- Students with Asperger syndrome need explicit instruction in social skills; two general strategies for teaching such skills are social interpreting and coaching.

How do professionals assess the progress of students with autism spectrum disorders?

▶ Progress in language development and social/adaptive behavior can be monitored using one or more scales designed for such purposes.

▶ Standardized scales can be used to assess outcomes.

▶ Students with autism spectrum disorders may receive testing accommodation in such things as setting, scheduling, presentation format, and response format.

What are some things to consider with respect to early intervention for learners with autism spectrum disorders?

▶ The most effective early intervention programs are intensive, highly structured, and involve families.

▶ Early intervention programs often use natural interactions to teach students in natural environments, including general education classrooms to the extent possible.

What are some things to consider with respect to transition to adulthood for learners with autism spectrum disorders?

▶ For those with autism, the emphasis is on person-centered planning, with living arrangements in community residential facilities or supported living settings and placement in competitive employment or supported competitive employment situations.

▶ For those with Asperger syndrome, the focus is often on improving social interactions both in employment and in postsecondary school settings.

STANDARDS and PRINCIPLES in this Chapter

SPECIAL EDUCATORS . . .

- understand the field as an evolving and changing discipline (from CEC Content Standard #1).

- understand the similarities and differences in human development (from CEC Content Standard #2).

- possess a repertoire of evidence-based instructional strategies (from CEC Content Standard #4).

- actively create learning environments for individuals with exceptional learning needs that foster cultural understanding, safety and emotional well-being, positive social interactions, and active engagement of individuals with exceptional learning needs (from CEC Content Standard #5).

- use the results of assessments to help identify exceptional learning needs (from CEC Content Standard #8).

- use collaboration to facilitate the successful transitions of individuals with exceptional learning needs (from CEC Content Standard #10).

ALL TEACHERS . . .

- understand the central concepts, tools of inquiry, structures of the discipline(s) they teach and can create learning experiences that make these aspects of subject matter meaningful (INTASC Principle #1).

- understand how children learn and develop (from INTASC Principle #2).

- understand and use a variety of instructional strategies to encourage students' development of critical thinking, problem solving, and performance skills (INTASC Principle #4).

- use an understanding of individual and group motivation and behavior to create a learning environment that encourages positive social interaction, active engagement in learning, and self-motivation (INTASC Principle #5).

- understand and use formal and informal assessment strategies (from INTASC Principle #8).

- foster relationships with school colleagues, families, and agencies in the larger community to support students' learning and well being (INTASC Principle #10).

Applying the STANDARDS and PRINCIPLES

- HOW easy or difficult is it to identify autism? (CEC Content Standards #1, #2, & #8; INTASC Principles #1, #2, & #8)

- HOW should teachers determine what instructional methods to use with students with autism spectrum disorders? (CEC Content Standards #4 & #5; INTASC Principles #4 & #5)

- HOW would you respond to parents who approach you expressing concern about the future of their high school student with autism? (CEC Content Standard #10 & INTASC Principle #10)

Now go to the Hallahan/Kauffman, Eleventh Edition MyEducationLab course at www.myeducationlab.com to:

- take a Pretest to assess your initial comprehension of the chapter content;
- study chapter content with your Individualized Study Plan;
- take a Posttest to assess your understanding of chapter content;
- engage in multimedia exercises to help you build a deeper and more applied understanding of chapter content.

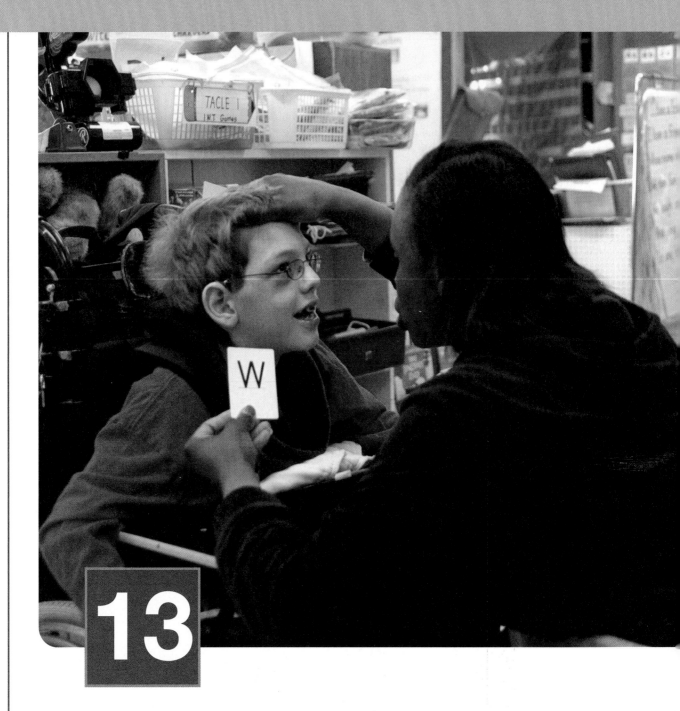

13

Learners with Low-Incidence, Multiple, and Severe Disabilities

Accidents divide things into the great Before and After.

"Even before his brain injury, Alan had a hard time remembering names," I'll say. "Since Daddy's accident, I have to work more," I tell our daughter, Kelly. The brain injury community marks time by asking how long someone has been "out of" injury, the same way bereavement counselors ask how long your loved one has been dead.

Out of what, exactly?

Out of the giant crevice that has been exploded into the bedrock of your life.

Here's how I see it: One day, you and your family are hiking across a long, solid plain, when out of the sky comes a blazing meteor that just happens to hit one family member on the head. The meteor creates a huge rift in the landscape, dragging the unlucky one down to the bottom of the crevice it has made. You spend the next year on a rescue mission, helping him climb to the top, but when he gets up there, you realize that he has been greatly changed by the hardship. He doesn't know a meteor has hit him. He will never know, really. He only knows that he has spent a lot of time in a dark, confusing place. He left a lot of stuff behind, the stuff he was carrying with him, down in the big hole, and it's impossible to get it all back.

—Cathy Crimmins
Where Is the Mango Princess?

QUESTIONS to guide your reading of this chapter . . .

- What is the definition of low-incidence, multiple, and severe disabilities, and what is their prevalence?

- What is traumatic brain injury, and how might it affect education?

- How is deaf-blindness defined, and what are the special educational problems it entails?

- What considerations apply to many students with low-incidence, multiple, and severe disabilities?

MISCONCEPTIONS ABOUT

Learners with Low-Incidence, Multiple, and Severe Disabilities

MYTH ■ People with severe and multiple disabilities have problems so severe that the best they can hope for is employment in a sheltered workshop.

FACT ■ With intensive and extensive instruction, many people with severe and multiple disabilities are now able to be employed in more integrated work settings.

MYTH ■ People with severe and multiple disabilities have problems so severe that the best they can hope for is to live under close supervision in a large residential facility.

FACT ■ With intensive and extensive instruction, many people with severe and multiple disabilities are now able to live independently or semi-independently by themselves or in a small community residential facility (CRF).

MYTH ■ A person with traumatic brain injury (TBI) can be expected, with time, to recover completely and function without disabilities.

FACT ■ Some people with TBI do recover completely, but many do not. Usually, a person with TBI has long-term disabilities that may be compensated for in many ways, but these disabilities don't ordinarily disappear completely, even with the best treatment and rehabilitation.

MYTH ■ For students with Usher syndrome whose vision will deteriorate over time, it's best not to introduce braille and training with the long cane while their vision is still relatively good because to do so stigmatizes them.

FACT ■ Braille and orientation and mobility training should not wait until the later stages of vision loss. Getting a head start on learning these complex skills almost always outweighs any stigmatization that might occur.

MYTH ■ Someone who can't speak will have extreme difficulty making himself or herself understood to others.

FACT ■ With an appropriate augmentative or alternative communication (AAC) system, a person who can't speak will be able to carry on a normal conversation, sometimes very near the rate at which nondisabled speakers talk. The flexibility, speed, and usefulness in communication of AAC are increasing rapidly with new technologies, and they now often allow a user to approximate the typical verbal exchanges between speakers.

MYTH ■ The only really effective way of controlling the undersirable behavior of people with severe and multiple disabilities is to use punishment.

FACT ■ Functional behavioral assessment and positive behavioral supports are finding more and more ways of replacing undesirable with desirable behavior without the use of punishment. Often, the key is finding out what the person with severe and multiple disabilities is trying to communicate and helping him or her find a more effective, efficient way of communicating that to others.

MYTH ■ Braille is only for people who are blind.

FACT ■ It is helpful to teach braille to two groups of individuals who are not blind: (1) those who have visual impairments so severe that they can't read print reliably and (2) those whose condition will worsen with time to the point at which braille will be their only option.

458

The definition of any category of exceptionality is controversial. Low-incidence, severe, and multiple disabilities are no exception. Disabilities of every type are difficult to understand. The causes, meanings, and life course associated with disabilities are often unknown. People may be even more mystified by disabilities that are severe or profound.

Definition and Prevalence

The Association for Persons with Severe Handicaps (TASH) uses the following definition of severe disabilities:

> *individuals with disabilities of all ages, races, creeds, national origins, genders and sexual orientations who require ongoing support in more than one major life activity in order to participate in an integrated community and enjoy a quality of life similar to that available to all citizens. Support may be required for life activities such as mobility, communication, self-care, and learning as necessary for community living, employment, and self-sufficiency. (Snell & Brown, 2006, pp. 69–70, italics in original)*

People with a severe disability in any area typically have more than one disability. Furthermore, a combination of mild disabilities may present severe educational problems (Kauffman, in press). As noted in the Individuals with Disabilities Education Improvement Act of 2004 (IDEA): "Multiple disabilities means concomitant impairments . . . the combination of which causes such severe educational problems that they cannot be accommodated in special education programs solely for one of the impairments" (34 CFR, Sec. 300 (b)(6)). IDEA also states that

> The term "children with severe disabilities" refers to children with disabilities who, because of the intensity of their physical, mental, or emotional problems, need highly specialized education, social, psychological, and medical services in order to maximize their full potential for useful and meaningful participation in society and for self-fulfillment. The term includes those children with severe emotional disturbance (including schizophrenia), autism, severe and profound mental retardation, and those who have two or more serious disabilities, such as deaf-blindness, mental retardation and blindness, and cerebral palsy and deafness. Children with severe disabilities may experience severe speech, language, and/or perceptual-cognitive deprivations, and evidence abnormal behaviors, such as failure to respond to pronounced social stimuli, self-mutilation, self-stimulation, manifestation of intense and prolonged temper tantrums, and the absence of rudimentary forms of verbal control, and may also have intensely fragile physiological conditions. (34 CFR, Sec. 315.4(d))

Low-incidence, severe, and multiple disabilities are often linked conceptually. They occur in only a relatively small percentage of cases of disability (Kauffman, in press). Furthermore, nearly any low-incidence, severe disability will involve extensive and ongoing support in more than one major life activity. That is, low-incidence, severe, and multiple disabilities tend to go together. True, one can find a severe disability that involves a single life activity (e.g., profound deafness that involves only manual-visual rather than vocal-aural communication) or multiple disabilities, none of which is severe (e.g., relatively mild orthopedic impairment, mild visual impairment, and mild intellectual disability). All of the low-incidence, severe, and multiple disabilities that we discuss in the chapter probably affect fewer than 1 percent of the population.

With these considerations in mind, in this chapter, we first discuss the categories and problems of traumatic brain injury and deaf-blindness. Then we discuss issues that apply to all categories of low-incidence, multiple, and severe disabilities: augmentative and

Video Homework Exercise

Student Profile ● Go to the Homework and Exercises section in Chapter 13 of MyEducationLab to watch the video "Who is Star?"

alternative communication, behavior problems, early intervention, and transition to adulthood.

We mentioned severe and profound intellectual disability in Chapter 5 and discussed autistic spectrum disorders in Chapter 12. However, much of what we present in this chapter applies to some individuals with autism and to those with severe or profound intellectual disability as well. Remember, though, that autistic spectrum disorders can range from mild to severe, as is the case in all other categories of disability.

Traumatic Brain Injury

■ **Traumatic brain injury (TBI)**
Injury to the brain (not including conditions present at birth, birth trauma, or degenerative diseases or conditions) resulting in total or partial disability or psychosocial maladjustment that affects educational performance; may affect cognition, language, memory, attention, reasoning, abstract thinking, judgment, problem solving, sensory or perceptual and motor disabilities, psychosocial behavior, physical functions, information processing, or speech.

INTERNET RESOURCES

More information about TBI may be found at the Brain Injury Association of America: www.biausa.org

■ **Open head injury**
A brain injury in which there is an open wound in the head, such as a gunshot wound or penetration of the head by an object, resulting in damage to brain tissue.

■ **Closed head injury**
Damage to the brain that occurs without penetration of the skull; might be caused by a blow to the head or violent shaking by an adult.

Since 1990, when the new IDEA recognized the category of **traumatic brain injury (TBI)**, students may be found eligible for special education and related services. Today, there is much greater understanding of the nature of TBI and the educational needs of students with TBI (Ashley, 2004; for current information, search www.ninds.nih.gov/disorders/tbi/tbi.htm). Unlike cerebral palsy, TBI is brain damage that is acquired by trauma after a period of normal neurological development. As the passage quoted on page 457 suggests, TBI is a life-altering experience. It presents unique educational problems that often have been poorly understood and mismanaged. Recent medical advances have greatly improved diagnosis and treatment.

Historically, recognition and treatment of disabilities are often encouraged by the return of injured soldiers to civilian life. Because TBI is one of the most common injuries of the wars in Iraq and Afghanistan, perhaps the public will become more aware of and demand better treatment of those with TBI.

Definition and Characteristics

Commonly accepted definitions of TBI specify the following:

1. There is injury to the brain caused by an external force.
2. The injury is not caused by a degenerative or congenital condition.
3. There is a diminished or altered state of consciousness.
4. Neurological or neurobehavioral dysfunction results from the injury.

Most definitions also specify that the injury is followed by impairments in abilities required for school learning and everyday functioning.

TBI can result from two categories of injury: open or closed. **Open head injuries** involve a penetrating head wound, from such causes as a fall, gunshot, assault, vehicular accident, or surgery. In **closed head injuries**, there is no open head wound but brain damage is caused by internal compression, stretching, or other shearing motion of neural tissues within the head.

The educational definition of TBI focuses on impairments in one or more areas important for learning. The federal (IDEA) definition of TBI states that it is

an acquired injury to the brain caused by an external physical force, resulting in total or partial functional disability or psychosocial impairment, or both, that adversely affects a child's educational performance. The term applies to open or closed head injuries resulting in impairments in one or more areas, such as cognition; language; memory; attention; reasoning; abstract thinking; judgment; problem-solving; sensory,

Casebook Reflection

REFER TO THE CASE, *Who Will Help Patrick?* in your booklet. We are not told much about Patrick's early development except that his mother was a substance abuser. Nevertheless, in what ways does he demonstrate that he has multiple and severe disabilities? ●

perceptual, and motor abilities; psychosocial behavior; physical functions; information processing; and speech. The term does not apply to injuries that are congenital or degenerative, or brain injuries induced by birth trauma. (34 CFR, Sec. 300.7(6)(12))

TBI is a medical problem; its various consequences create a need for special education. The effects of TBI range from very mild to profound and may be temporary or permanent. Often, the effects are immediate, and these immediate effects set TBI apart from most other disabilities—the child or youth is literally changed overnight (Council for Exceptional Children, 2001). The sudden change presents particular difficulties to families and teachers, not to mention the individual sustaining the injury (Ashley, 2004; Dell Orto & Power, 2000). However, sometimes the effects of TBI are not seen immediately after the injury but appear months or even years afterward. The possible effects of TBI include a long list of learning and psychosocial problems, such as:

Justin Greenwood, who suffered a brain injury during a football game, works on his short-term memory during a therapy session.

- Problems remembering things
- Problems learning new information
- Speech and/or language problems
- Difficulty sequencing things
- Difficulty in processing information (making sense of things)
- Extremely uneven abilities or performance (able to do some things but not others)
- Extremely uneven progress (quick gains sometimes, no gains other times)
- Inappropriate manners or mannerisms
- Failure to understand humor or social situations
- Becoming easily tired, frustrated, or angered
- Unreasonable fear or anxiety
- Irritability
- Sudden, exaggerated swings of mood
- Depression
- Aggression
- Perseveration (persistent repetition of one thought or behavior)

UNDERSTANDING THE STANDARDS AND PRINCIPLES Explain the federal (IDEA) definition of TBI in your own words. (CEC Knowledge and Skill Standard IC1K1)

Council for Exceptional Children

One of the great difficulties with TBI is that it's often "invisible." Like a learning disability, it is not something that one necessarily notices about a person at first. True, in some cases, a person with TBI has paralysis, slurred speech, or some other indicator of brain damage that is quickly apparent. But in many cases, the person with TBI looks just like everyone else. In the Personal Perspectives on page 462, Cathy Crimmins describes one aspect of life following the TBI of her husband, Alan, who acquired his brain injury in a speedboat accident in 1996. (Bill is Alan's counselor from the Office of Vocational Rehabilitation.) Crimmins's book vividly illustrates not only the sudden change in abilities and behavior with which individuals and families must cope, but also the hidden nature of TBI.

Video Homework Exercise

Student Profile—TBI ● Go to the Homework and Exercises section in Chapter 13 of MyEducationLab to watch the video "Traumatic Brain Injury."

Personal PERSPECTIVES

TBI: Often a Hidden Disability

Yesterday Bill and Alan met with Alan's employers at the First Union Bank. All systems seem go for a return to work part-time some time in January, and at this point the folks at the bank say they understand Alan's limitations. Part of Bill's job is to act as an advocate and explain brain injury to Alan's bosses and coworkers. He will also go to work with Alan every day, functioning as a job coach. The biggest accommodation the bank will have to make is to allow Alan to work part-time, at the beginning only twelve hours a week. Alan looks just fine—that's why TBI is often dubbed "the hidden disability"—but everyone must understand why he has to take it slow. The hardest concept to get across is that brain injury is a *physical* condition. "If Alan were in a wheelchair or had a cast on his leg, people would understand that something happened," says Crystal Mangir. "But no one can see a broken brain."

Source: Crimmins, C. (2000). *Where is the mango princess?* (p. 199). New York: Knopf.

Prevalence

The exact prevalence of TBI is difficult to determine, but we do know that TBI occurs at an alarming rate among children and youths. Estimates are that each year about 0.5 percent of school-age children acquire a brain injury. By the time they graduate from high school, nearly 4 percent of students may have TBI. Of about a million children and adolescents who receive head injuries each year, roughly 15,000 to 20,000 will experience lasting effects (Council for Exceptional Children, 2001).

Males are more prone to TBI than females are, and the age range in which TBI is most likely to occur for both males and females is late adolescence and early adulthood

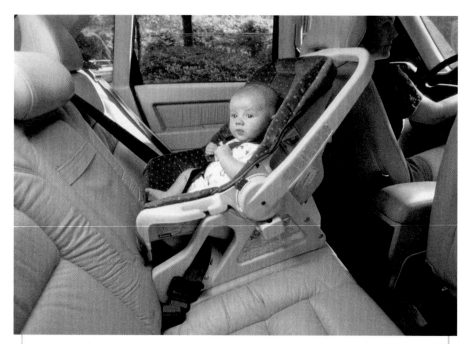

The prevalence of TBI is disconcerting because so many of the causes of TBI are entirely preventable or avoidable by following ordinary safety precautions, such as properly securing infants and children in car safety seats.

(Christensen, 1996). The Council for Exceptional Children (2001) refers to TBI as a "silent epidemic." It's considered an epidemic because of its increasing prevalence; it's "silent" because many serious head injuries are unreported and many cases of TBI go undetected or are mistaken for other disabilities. The prevalence of TBI is disconcerting because so many of the causes of TBI are entirely preventable or avoidable by following ordinary safety precautions. Moreover, the prevalence of TBI has increased so much in recent years that it is now sometimes discussed as a high-incidence (frequent) rather than a low-incidence (uncommon) disability (see Stichter, Conroy, & Kauffman, 2008).

Causes

Under age five, accidental falls are the dominant cause of TBI, with vehicular accidents and child abuse causing substantial injuries as well. After age five, and increasingly through adolescence, vehicular accidents (including accidents involving pedestrians, bicycles, motorcycles, and cars) account for the majority of TBI; assaults and gunshot wounds are increasingly prevalent among youths at older ages. Closed head injuries may be caused by a variety of events besides vehicular accidents, including a fall or abuse such as violent shaking of a child by an adult.

Educational Considerations

The educational implications of TBI are varied and depend on the nature and severity of the injury and the age and abilities of the individual at the time of injury. A significant issue in educating someone who has experienced TBI is helping family members, teachers, and peers to respond appropriately to the sudden and sometimes dramatic changes that may occur in the student's academic abilities, appearance, behavior, and emotional states (Dell Orto & Power, 2000). Both general and special education teachers need training about TBI and its ramifications if students are to be reintegrated successfully into the schools and classrooms they attended before the injury (DePompei & Tyler, 2004; Stichter et al., 2008; Tyler & Mira, 1999). The following characteristics are essential features of appropriate education for students with TBI:

1. Transition from a hospital or rehabilitation center to the school.
2. A team approach involving regular and special educators, other special teachers, guidance counselor, administrators, and the student's family.
3. An individualized education program (IEP) concerned with cognitive, social/behavioral, and sensorimotor domains.
4. Educational procedures to help students solve problems in focusing and sustaining attention for long periods, remembering previously learned facts and skills, learning new things, dealing with fatigue, and engaging in appropriate social behavior.
5. Emphasis on the cognitive processes through which academic skills are learned, not just curriculum content.
6. Plans for addressing long-term needs in addition to immediate and annual IEP goals (DePompei & Tyler, 2004; Savage, 1988; Tyler & Mira, 1999).

TBI is a special case of neurological impairment (discussed further in Chapter 14), in which there's a sudden alteration in abilities; this can often cause frustration for the student and teachers who must cope with this loss. The student must undergo medical treatment to address the biophysical aspects of the injury, and it's critical that educators understand the implications of the injury for structuring the student's psychological and social environments in school (Best, Heller, & Bigge, 2005; Dell Orto & Power, 2000; Tyler & Mira, 1999).

UNDERSTANDING THE STANDARDS AND PRINCIPLES What are some issues special educators should consider when planning instruction for students who have experienced TBI? (CEC Knowledge and Skill Standard CC4S3)

Council for Exceptional Children

Collaboration and Co-Teaching of Students with Low-Incidence, Multiple, and Severe Disabilities

"We may have different goals for students. How can we solve that problem?"

SUCCESSFUL STRATEGIES FOR COLLABORATION

Students with severe disabilities often require a wide range of services at school. Many professionals, including teachers, nurses, and aides, must collaborate to provide those services. With so many people involved in a student's education, problems are likely to arise and everyone should be ready to engage in collaborative problem solving.

Partners in collaborative settings should develop a plan to attack problems before they arise. Problems can be related to the student's response to settings and personnel, the student's environment, differences in professional goals, and discrepancies in professional philosophies. Though the causes might be different, a similar step-by-step process can be used to address each one. Mostert (1998) describes the following steps for successful problem solving:

1. *Is there a problem to solve?* This step involves reflection on these questions: Is there really a problem here? Who owns it? Is the problem solvable?

2. *What is the problem?* Once a problem has been identified, participants define it in specific, objective terms. Statements such as "I don't like her attitude" must be refined to describe the situation specifically; "Sofia makes inappropriate comments about other students when I ask her a question in class." After the problem is defined, partners gather data on the frequency, duration, and degree of the problem in a variety of environments.

3. *How can the problem be solved?* All participants generate solutions to the problem. This is the brainstorming step, so all suggestions should be welcomed.

4. *Which solution or combination is best?* Personnel working together must be able to discuss the solutions presented and evaluate them without emotional attachment. Interventions for students should be judged as to whether there is evidence of previous success (research-based, not anecdotal), whether there are appropriate supports and resources, whether the participants can and will fully implement it, and whether the intervention is truly appropriate for the student. Solutions that do not fit these criteria should be abandoned.

5. *Which solution should we select?* After evaluating all solutions, the partners choose the one to implement.

6. *How will we implement the solution?* This step requires delegating responsibilities for the solution to members of the team. It means specifically stating what the team hopes will happen, setting up how the partners will know if the solution worked, and scheduling a time to reconvene to share data.

7. *Did it work?* This step requires data collection again. Partners must be able to present information as to whether the solution achieved its goals. If not, it is time to start the process again. If the solution worked, the team can move on to another problem!

Problem solving with other professionals requires that participants develop an environment with open communication, overcoming barriers by using effective communication skills. According to Walther-Thomas, Korinek, McLaughlin, and Williams (2000), these skills include the following:

1. *Listening.* Attending to the speaker, paraphrasing content, reflecting feelings, and summarizing.

2. *Repetition.* Sending the same message to partners repeatedly and through different channels.

3. *Empathy.* Making predictions about how a partner will respond to a message you send.

4. *Understanding.* Making sure that the language you use is clear and concise.

When collaborating with other professionals and even with students, there is no way to avoid problems. But to avoid conflict, partners should discuss and set up problem-solving strategies before these situations occur. Problem-solving strategies, along with effective communication skills, will help collaborators to provide continuous, appropriate services to students.

● *By Margaret P. Weiss*

The teacher must focus on helping the student with TBI to recover cognitive abilities, because these are most critical to academic and social progress. The abilities to remember and to make sense of academic information and social circumstances are key to the student's long-term success. The teacher must help the student learn to use coping mechanisms and alternative strategies, such as using a tape recorder, a planner, or other organizational devices and memory aids for whatever abilities cannot be recovered. TBI also presents particular challenges to teachers in areas of assessment and educational planning. As the Council for Exceptional Children has noted,

> the educational needs of the child with TBI will change quickly after the injury. Therefore, the child's IEP goals and objectives must be developed initially for achievement over short periods of time, 4–6 weeks, rather than six months to a year as is traditionally done. Likewise, the child may need more frequent assessments than other children with disabilities. (2001, p. 15)

A major problem in reentry to school after TBI—at least if the consequences are serious—is that the student tends to see himself or herself as not having changed, whereas peers and teachers are likely to notice that the student with TBI is not the same. Dell Orto and Power (2000) note that our societal emphasis on productiveness, organization, independence, and achievement can contribute to negative attitudes toward a student with TBI. "Academic deficits displayed by survivors of TBI conflict with achievement values, not only causing discomfort in teachers, but frustration and perhaps a sense of rejection in the young person" (p. 22). Many teachers apparently don't want students with TBI in their classrooms, probably because these students exhibit characteristics that teachers find troublesome (just consider the bulleted list on p. 461). Thus, a student's returning to school after TBI is a major issue that typically requires a team approach involving a variety of professionals, as we mentioned in our list of essential features of appropriate educational programs. Collaboration and problem solving by this team are essential to the success of the student's reentry. (See Making It Work on page 464 for more on team problem solving.)

The assessment of a student's academic and social skills following TBI is tricky because it's often difficult or impossible to separate physiological causes or reasons for difficulty with a task from other causes. More important than knowing precisely what difficulties have a physiological cause is pinpointing just what the student's academic and social learning difficulties are. Here again, a team approach is essential. Neurologists can often provide information about the consequences of TBI that helps teachers to set reasonable expectations and teach coping skills that help the student to compensate for abilities that will not return.

LANGUAGE DISORDERS   A student with TBI might acquire a language disorder after a period of normal development, or acquire a more severe language disorder than existed before the injury (see Chapter 9). Individuals with TBI are a very diverse population, although a disproportionate number of students with TBI have a pretrauma history of learning problems or delayed speech and language.

Language or speech disorders are the greatest complicating factor in most students' return to school following TBI. A loss of ability to understand and formulate language due to brain injury is sometimes referred to as a **motor-speech disorder**, which we discussed in Chapter 9. The student may have trouble finding or saying words or constructing sentences that are appropriate for the topic of conversation or social context. Problems like these can be a source of frustration, anger, and confusion for students with TBI.

■ **Motor-speech disorder**
Loss or impairment of the ability to understand or formulate language because of accident or illness.

The language problems that are acquired with TBI are primarily related to the cognitive and social demands of communication. The student might have problems with tasks that demand responding quickly, organizing, dealing with abstractions, sustaining attention (especially if there are distractions), learning new skills, responding appropriately in social situations, and showing appropriate affect. In fact, TBI can potentially disrupt all aspects of the give-and-take of social interaction that are required for effective communication.

The effects of TBI on language are extremely variable, and careful assessment of the given individual's abilities and disabilities is critically important. Interventions may range from making special accommodations, such as allowing more response time or keeping distractions to a minimum, to focusing on instruction in the social uses of language.

Depending on the site and degree of brain damage, a person with TBI may have motor control problems that interfere with communication, including the cognitive and social aspects of communication. Some students with TBI cannot communicate orally using the muscles of speech and must rely on alternative or augmentative communication systems, which we describe later in the chapter.

SOCIAL AND EMOTIONAL PROBLEMS   Brain injury may be accompanied by a variety of serious social and emotional effects. We know that TBI can cause violent aggression, hyperactivity, impulsivity, inattention, and a wide range of other emotional or behavioral problems, depending on just what parts of the brain are damaged. The possible effects of TBI include a long list of other psychosocial problems, some of which we listed previously as general characteristics.

The emotional and behavioral effects of TBI are determined by more than the physical damage; they also depend on the student's age at the time of injury and the social environment before and after the injury. Home, community, or school environments that foster misbehavior of any child or youth are known to be associated with increased risk for acquiring TBI. Such environments are extremely likely to worsen any emotional or behavioral problem resulting from TBI. Creating an environment that is conducive to and supportive of appropriate behavior is one of the great challenges of dealing effectively with the results of brain injury.

Many of the typical **behavior modification** or **behavior management** strategies that are used with other students who have emotional or behavioral difficulties are appropriate for use with students who have TBI. Consistency, predictability, and

▪ **Behavior modification**
Systematic control of environmental events, especially of consequences, to produce specific changes in observable responses. May include reinforcement, punishment, modeling, self-instruction, desensitization, guided practice, or any other technique for strengthening or eliminating a particular response.

▪ **Behavior management**
Strategies and techniques used to increase desirable behavior and decrease undesirable behavior. May be applied in the classroom, home, or other environment.

The emotional issues involved in TBI can be especially complex. Eileen Vosper, 12, enjoys holding Kelli, a six-year-old collie who serves in a pet therapy program for children and adults with brain-injury related disabilities. The visits with the dogs are short, but meaningful.

reinforcement (praise, encouragement, and other rewards) are particularly important (Persel & Persel, 2004), as is developing rapport with the student. Developing a good personal relationship with a student with TBI can be particularly challenging, as such students can be unpredictable, irritable, and angry at those who are trying to help (see Kauffman, Mostert, Trent, & Pullen, 2006; Tyler & Mira, 1999).

TBI often shatters an individual's sense of self. Recovering one's identity can require a long period of rehabilitation and can be a painstaking process requiring multidisciplinary efforts (Best et al., 2005; Dell Orto & Power, 2000; Fraser & Clemmons, 2000). Effective education and treatment often require not only classroom behavior management, but also family therapy, medication, cognitive training, and communication training.

INTERNET RESOURCES

For further information, you might want to visit the Websites of the Brain Injury Association of America (www.biausa.org) and the National Institute of Neurological Diseases and Stroke (www.ninds.nih.gov/disorders/tbi/tbi.htm).

Deaf-Blindness

In Chapters 10 and 11, we noted that, depending on the level of severity, blindness or deafness can have a substantial impact on a person's ability to function independently. For those who are both deaf and blind, the impact can be even more profound than simply adding the effects of each disability. Because the primary avenues for receiving information—sight and sound—are limited, those who are deaf-blind are at risk for having extensive problems in communicating and in navigating their environments.

Although being cut off from the sights and sounds of daily life makes deaf-blindness one of the most challenging of all multiple disabilities (Scheetz, 2001), this doesn't mean that a person with deaf-blindness is doomed to a poor-quality life. In general, outcomes for individuals with deaf-blindness depend on at least three things:

1. The quality and intensity of instruction the person receives is critical. Teachers of students with deaf-blindness "must make the most of every opportunity for learning. All interactions with adults and all aspects of the environment will be harnessed to help the child overcome the restrictions imposed by sensory impairments" (Hodges, 2000, p. 167).

2. The degree and type of visual impairment and auditory impairment can vary dramatically in individuals with deaf-blindness. The term *deaf-blindness* covers those with visual impairments ranging from low vision (20/70 to 20/200 in the better eye with correction) to those who are totally blind. Likewise, the term covers those with hearing impairments ranging from mild to profound. Although there are some very notable exceptions, in general, the more severe the impairments, the greater is the impact on a person's ability to adapt.

3. The vast majority of students who are deaf-blind have other disabilities and medical conditions. For example, approximately 11 percent of children between birth and age twenty-two who are deaf-blind also have intellectual disabilities (Hembree, 2000). In general, the more numerous and severe these other disabilities, the greater is the impact on a person's ability to adapt.

INTERNET RESOURCES

A variety of information about deaf-blindness is found at www.deafblind.com and at www.tr.wou.edu/dblink

Building Teaching Skills Exercise

Deaf-Blind Students ● Go to the Building Teaching Skills section in Chapter 13 of MyEducationLab to read the overview of a grant-funded research study on the education of students with deaf-blindness.

Definition

As we discussed in Chapters 10 and 11, there is considerable controversy over the definitions of deafness and blindness. As one might expect, this means that defining deaf-blindness is even more controversial than defining deafness or blindness by itself. The Individuals with Disabilities Education Improvement Act (2004) describes deaf-blindness as an individual

(1) (i) Who has a central visual acuity of 20/200 or less in the better eye with corrective lenses, or a field defect such that the peripheral diameter of visual field subtends an angular

distance no greater than 20 degrees, or a progressive visual loss having a prognosis leading to one or both of these conditions:

(ii) Who has a chronic hearing impairment so severe that most speech cannot be understood with optimum amplification, or a progressive hearing loss having a prognosis leading to this condition; and

(iii) For whom the combination of impairments described in paragraphs (1)(i) and (ii) of this definition causes extreme difficulty in attaining independence in daily life activities, achieving psychosocial adjustment, or obtaining a vocation;

(2) Who, despite the inability to be measured accurately for hearing and vision loss due to cognitive or behavioral constraints, or both, can be determined through functional and performance assessment to have severe hearing and visual disabilities that cause extreme difficulty in attaining independence in daily life activities, or obtaining vocational objectives; or

(3) Who meets any other requirements that the Secretary may prescribe. (34 CFR, Sec. 396.4 (c)(2)

Many states have found this definition too vague and have either developed their own definitions or added other criteria to the federal definition. For example, Alaska has added the following criteria:

Vision: Visual acuity of 20/70 or less in the better eye with correction; visual field restriction of 20 degrees or less; functional vision which is virtually absent or unmeasurable for purposes of learning; need for special services requiring the use of non-standard instructional materials or aids designed to facilitate the child's learning; temporary impairment or loss of vision due to illness, accidents, temporary treatments; a diagnosis of a syndrome or disorder associated with progressive vision loss.

Hearing: Hearing impairment of 30dB or greater unaided in the better ear; recurrent otitis media or documented history of recurrent otitis media affecting language or learning abilities; functional hearing which is absent or unmeasurable for purposes of learning; diagnosis of a syndrome or disorder associated with a progressive hearing loss. (National Information Clearinghouse on Children Who Are Deaf-Blind, 2001)

Prevalence

The fact that definitions and criteria vary from state to state, coupled with the fact that so many students with deaf-blindness also have other disabling conditions, makes it very difficult to get an accurate picture of prevalence rates. However, research indicates that there are about 10,000 individuals from birth to twenty-two years of age who are deaf-blind (Hembree, 2000). The number of adults with deaf-blindness is estimated to be about 35,000–40,000 (Baldwin, 1994, as cited in Miles, 1998).

Causes

Causes of deaf-blindness can be grouped into three broad categories: (1) genetic/chromosomal syndromes, (2) prenatal conditions, and (3) postnatal conditions.

GENETIC/CHROMOSOMAL SYNDROMES   As we discussed in Chapter 5, researchers are making enormous strides in discovering genetic/chromosomal intellectual disability syndromes. Some of these syndromes are inherited, and some result from damaged genetic and/or chromosomal material. This is also the case with respect to deaf-blindness. There are now over fifty genetic/chromosomal syndromes associated with deaf-blindness. The most common are **CHARGE syndrome**, **Usher syndrome**, and **Down syndrome**.

CHARGE Syndrome   CHARGE syndrome is characterized by a number of physical anomalies that are present at birth. The letters in CHARGE refer to some of the most common characteristics of this condition: C = coloboma, cranial nerves; H = heart defects; A = atresia of

---

UNDERSTANDING THE STANDARDS AND PRINCIPLES Do states generally accept the federal government's definition of deaf-blindness? Why or why not? (CEC Knowledge and Skill Standard IC1K1)

Council for Exceptional Children

■ **CHARGE syndrome**
A genetic syndrome resulting in deaf-blindness; characterized by physical anomalies, often including coloboma (abnormalities of the pupil, retina and/or optic nerve), cranial nerves, heart defects, atresia (absence or closure) of the choanae (air passages from nose to throat), retardation in growth and mental development, genital abnormalities, ear malformation and/or hearing loss.

■ **Usher syndrome**
An inherited syndrome resulting in hearing loss and retinitis pigmentosa, a progressive condition characterized by problems in seeing in low light and tunnel vision; there are three different types of Usher syndrome, differing with respect to when it occurs developmentally and the range of the major symptoms of hearing impairment, vision impairment, and balance problems.

■ **Down syndrome**
A condition resulting from a chromosomal abnormality; characterized by intellectual disabilities and such physical signs as slanted-appearing eyes, hypotonia, a single palmar crease, shortness, and a tendency toward obesity; the most common type of Down syndrome is trisomy 21.

the choanae; R = retardation in growth and mental development; G = genital abnormalities; E = ear malformation and/or hearing loss. The exact cause of CHARGE is still being debated, but there is growing evidence that it results from a genetic abnormality (Aitken, 2000; Oley, 2001). The reason for the uncertainty is probably that the condition was not identified in the medical literature until 1979 (Hall, 1979).

Coloboma refers to a condition in which the child is born with an abnormally shaped pupil and/or abnormalities of the retina or optic nerve. Coloboma can result in a variety of visual problems, including deficits in visual acuity and extreme sensitivity to light.

The **cranial nerves** supply information between the brain and various muscles and glands in the body. Individuals with CHARGE syndrome often have paralysis or weakness of facial muscles as well as swallowing problems because of abnormal development of some of the cranial nerves.

The vast majority of children with CHARGE syndrome are born with heart defects. Some of these problems are relatively minor, but some are life threatening and require surgery (CHARGE Syndrome Foundation, 2001).

An **atresia** is the absence or closure of a body opening present at birth. The **choanae** are air passages from the nose to throat. When the choanae are blocked or narrowed, the ability to breathe is affected. Surgery can help to correct these breathing problems.

Most children with CHARGE syndrome are of normal size at birth but may experience growth problems because of nutrition, heart problems, and/or growth hormone abnormalities (CHARGE Syndrome Foundation, 2001). In addition, some are intellectually disabled.

Genital anomalies include incomplete or underdeveloped genitals. This is more common in males than in females (Brown, 1996).

CHARGE syndrome can result in a variety of structural abnormalities of the outer, middle, and/or inner ear. The consequent hearing impairment may be conductive, sensorineural, or mixed (both conductive and sensorineural).

Usher Syndrome   Usher syndrome, an inherited condition, is characterized by hearing impairment and **retinitis pigmentosa**. As mentioned in Chapter 10, retinitis pigmentosa can result in vision problems starting in infancy, early childhood, or the teenage years, with the condition becoming progressively worse. It results in problems in seeing in low light, referred to as **night blindness**, and as it progresses, it results in a narrowing of the field of vision, referred to as **tunnel vision**.

There are three types of Usher syndrome, varying with respect to the type and time of occurrence of the major symptoms of hearing loss, vision loss, and balance problems. For example, depending on the type of Usher syndrome, the person can be born profoundly deaf, hard of hearing, or with normal hearing that deteriorates over time. Some experience night blindness starting in infancy; others have night blindness starting in the teenage years. Some have severe balance problems, due to inner-ear problems, starting in infancy; some have no balance problems; and some are born with normal balance that deteriorates over time.

Genetics research has identified more and more genes that cause the three types of Usher syndrome. As of February 2001, researchers had localized six genes causing six subtypes of Usher I, three genes causing three subtypes of Usher II, and one gene causing Usher III (Boys Town National Research Hospital Genetics Department, 2001).

Although Usher syndrome is one of the most common hereditary conditions causing deaf-blindness, its overall prevalence is very low. There are only about 300 people from birth to age twenty-two who have been identified as having Usher syndromes I–III (Hembree, 2000). However, the genetics of Usher syndrome show an interesting demographic pattern (see Focus on Concepts on p. 470).

Down Syndrome   Most often noted as a cause of intellectual disability (see Chapter 5), Down syndrome is also sometimes associated with deaf-blindness. Unlike Usher syndrome, which is inherited, Down syndrome results from damaged chromosomal material.

■ **Coloboma**
A condition of the eye in which the pupil is abnormally shaped and/or there are abnormalities of the retina or optic nerve; can result in loss of visual acuity and extreme sensitivity to light.

■ **Cranial nerves**
Twelve pairs of nerves that connect the brain with various muscles and glands in the body.

■ **Atresia**
Absence or closure of a part of the body that is normally open.

■ **Choanae**
Air passages from the nose to the throat.

■ **Retinitis pigmentosa**
A hereditary condition resulting in degeneration of the retina; causes a narrowing of the field of vision and affects night vision.

■ **Night blindness**
A condition characterized by problems in seeing at low levels of illumination; often caused by retinitis pigmentosa.

■ **Tunnel vision**
A condition characterized by problems in peripheral vision, or a narrowing of the field of vision.

FOCUS ON **Concepts**

The Genetics of Usher Syndrome and Its Geographic Distribution

About one in seventy-five people carries an Usher gene, but most do not realize that they have it. Usher syndrome is an *autosomal-recessive disorder*, meaning that for a child to have the condition, both parents must be carriers of the gene. And with each such pregnancy, there is a one-in-four chance of the child having Usher syndrome. Thus, the chance of having a child with Usher syndrome is relatively rare even among those who carry the gene, and that is why the prevalence of Usher syndrome is so low. However, the odds of producing an offspring with Usher syndrome rise dramatically among people who are related:

> Each of us, regardless of family history, is thought to silently carry five or more recessive genes that have the potential to cause genetic disorders in the next generation. But the chance of conceiving a child with a recessive disorder is low because most unrelated couples do not carry the exact same recessive genes. Conversely, because members of one's immediate or extended family share a similar genetic makeup, it becomes easier for two autosomal recessive genes to match up to cause a particular disorder. Thus, children conceived by parents who are related to each other are at higher than average risk for being affected by autosomal recessive disorders. And in certain cultures in which marriages between relatives are the norm or in which many people preferentially choose partners with the same inherited trait (e.g., marriage between two people with deafness), recessive conditions occur more commonly than expected. (Dykens, Hodapp, & Finucane, 2000, p. 46)

Unfortunately, social forces have operated historically to make the likelihood of intermarriage higher among a certain cultural group: the Acadian French of south Louisiana. This has resulted in a relatively higher number of people with Usher syndrome in this area of the country. Following is an excerpt from a retired teacher who had worked at the Louisiana School for the Deaf for twenty-seven years:

> To begin with, Usher syndrome among the Acadian French people in south Louisiana was something people knew the "about" of, but not the "what" or "why" of. They knew that generation after generation of children were struck

mysteriously with deafness and eventually with partial-to-full blindness. It was something that was dreaded, but had to be endured. Again and again, cousins, aunts, uncles, and sometimes two or three children in a family were found to have the condition, but no one knew what to do, or what to call it.

> The "what" and "why" of it was that the Acadian parishes of south Louisiana have a far higher percentage of Usher syndrome than anywhere else in the United States. This extraordinarily high percentage has been documented in several studies. . . . For example, [Kloepfer, Laguaite, and McLaurin, 1966] estimated that 30 percent of the deaf population in the parishes of Lafayette, Vermillion, and Acadia had Usher syndrome. The high incidence is a result of several hundred years of intermarriage among this close-knit ethnic group. Inevitably, two individuals, both carrying a recessive gene for Usher syndrome transmitted to them by a common ancestor, marry and have children with this condition.

> The Acadians, or Cajuns, as they are called, were originally from Acadia (Nova Scotia) in Canada. In the 1700s they were expelled from that area by the English. They moved down along the east-coast of America, finally settling along the bayous of several south Louisiana parishes. At first they were not readily accepted by people in the area and were somewhat isolated both by language and by culture. With time, however, the Cajuns came into their own and have won admirers around the world for their music, love of fun, and never-to-be-forgotten cuisine.

> Many students at the Louisiana School for the Deaf (LSD) come from the Acadian parishes resulting in a high incidence of Usher syndrome at the school. . . . Fifteen to twenty percent of children on the Louisiana deaf-blind census for children birth through age 21 are known to have Usher syndrome [Type 1] as compared to an average of 3 percent for all other states in the nation. (Melancon, 2000, p. 1)

The high prevalence of Usher syndrome in south Louisiana is also the subject of a video narrated by the well-known neurologist Oliver Sacks, *The Ragin' Cajun Usher Syndrome,* produced by the British Broadcasting Company.

PRENATAL CONDITIONS   Like Down syndrome, two of the most common types of **prenatal** conditions—**rubella**, sometimes referred to as **German measles**, and **congenital cytomegalovirus (CMV)**—can cause intellectual disability and/or deaf-blindness. When rubella occurs in a pregnant woman, especially in the first trimester, it can lead to a variety of disabilities, including deaf-blindness. Children born with CMV, a herpes virus, are also at risk for a variety of disabilities, including deaf-blindness.

POSTNATAL CONDITIONS   Among the most common **postnatal** conditions that can cause deaf-blindness are **meningitis** and traumatic brain injury (TBI). As we learned in Chapter 5, meningitis, which is an infection of the covering of the brain, can also cause intellectual disability. TBI, as we discussed earlier in this chapter, can result in a variety of other disabilities, as well as deaf-blindness.

Psychological and Behavioral Characteristics

People who are deaf-blind can have significant problems in at least three areas: (1) accessing information, (2) communicating, and (3) navigating the environment (Aitken, 2000).

PROBLEMS ACCESSING INFORMATION   People who are sighted and have hearing are able to access a variety of information about their world, whether it be from the media (e.g., newspapers, television, the Internet) or other people. For people who are deaf-blind, however, access to this information is much harder to obtain. And because communication is largely dependent on the availability of information, restricted access to information can have a negative impact on the ability to communicate:

> The consequence of not being able to access information is that life experiences are reduced. Lack of everyday ordinary experiences—how to make a sandwich, knowing that water comes from a tap—makes it more difficult for the person who is deaf-blind to build up a store of world knowledge. Without that store of world knowledge what is there to communicate about? (Aitken, 2000, p. 3)

PROBLEMS COMMUNICATING   Most authorities agree that the biggest obstacle faced by people with deaf-blindness is communication (Aitken, 2000; Ford & Fredericks, 1995; Miles, 1998). Without a strong commitment by teachers and other professionals and parents to providing a variety of opportunities for communication, the child who is deaf-blind can easily become socially isolated. The pattern for this isolation can begin at birth. The baby

> may not be able to make and sustain eye contact or to respond to a soothing voice. His mother's face may be invisible or only a blur and her speech only a low sound which he cannot pick out from the background of other noises. The deafblind baby may register little of the world around him, or may find it a frightening place full of half-registered shapes and sounds. He will not hold his mother's attention with a ready gaze and will not be able to play the games of sight, sound and movement which other babies enjoy. If his vision and hearing are so seriously damaged that he cannot use visual or auditory cues to warn him that someone is coming to pick him up, or that a particular activity is about to happen, contact with other people may even become threatening. (Pease, 2000, p. 38)

Once this pattern of isolation has been established, it's difficult to reverse. Therefore, it is critical that professionals and parents work together to provide an environment that's as supportive and rich in communication opportunities as possible.

No better example of the importance of providing a language-rich environment exists than the classic case of Helen Keller (1880–1968) and her teacher Annie Sullivan (1866–1936). Popularized by the classic movie *The Miracle Worker* (1962), Helen Keller's accomplishments are now familiar to most of us. Having lost her sight and hearing at the

■ **Prenatal**
Occurring or developing in the fetus before birth.

■ **Rubella (German measles)**
A serious viral disease, which, if it occurs during the first trimester of pregnancy, is likely to cause a deformity in the fetus.

■ **Congenital Cytomegalovirus (CMV)**
The most frequently occurring viral infection in newborns; can result in a variety of disabilities, especially hearing impairment.

■ **Postnatal**
Occurring in an infant after birth.

■ **Meningitis**
A bacterial or viral infection of the linings of the brain or spinal cord; can cause a number of disabilities.

UNDERSTANDING THE STANDARDS AND PRINCIPLES   What should teachers know about the psychological and behavioral characteristics of individuals who are deaf-blind? (CEC Knowledge and Skill Standard IC2K4)

Council for Exceptional Children

INTERNET RESOURCES

For information on Helen Keller, including many of her letters and papers, visit the Website maintained by the American Foundation for the Blind: www.afb.org/section.asp? sectionid=1

age of nineteen months, Keller went on to extraordinary achievements, including graduating cum laude from Radcliffe College in 1904, publishing essays and books (including the much acclaimed *The Story of My Life*, 1905, written while she was in college and available in over fifty languages), touring the country lecturing on blindness, being a spokesperson for women's right to vote, and receiving the Presidential Medal of Freedom, the nation's highest civilian award.

Helen Keller is testimony to the power of the human spirit to overcome overwhelming odds. However, just as important, she is testimony to the power of intensive and extensive special education instruction. As remarkable as she was, it's doubtful that Keller would have conquered her condition without the prolonged instruction from Annie Sullivan, who devoted nearly fifty years to being Keller's teacher and constant companion. Sullivan, herself born blind, had had some of her sight restored through several operations. She arrived at the home of the Kellers in 1887 to meet a not yet seven-year-old Helen, who had some rudiments of communication but who was prone to severe tantrums. Through persistence and intensive instruction, Sullivan was able to set Helen's mind free to learn language and higher concepts.

Sullivan and Keller are not the only famous teacher–student team to demonstrate the importance of intensive instruction of the deaf-blind. See Personal Perspectives on page 473 for the story of Laura Bridgman and Samuel Gridley Howe.

PROBLEMS NAVIGATING THE ENVIRONMENT   As we discussed in Chapter 11, people who are blind or who have low vision can have significant difficulties with mobility. For people who are deaf-blind, these problems are often even more pronounced. Individuals who are blind and hearing are able to pick up auditory cues that help them in navigation. For example, being able to hear approaching traffic can be very helpful when crossing an intersection, and being able to hear such things as buses, trains, and construction noises, can help a person who is blind to identify her or his location. However, people who are both deaf and blind are restricted in their ability to make use of auditory signals for navigating the environment.

Educational Considerations

The major educational needs of infants and preschoolers, as well as of older students, who are deaf-blind fall generally under the categories of communication and orientation and mobility. Both, but especially communication, are required for social interaction. If these skills are taught effectively, then the social interaction of deaf-blind individuals is enhanced considerably (Janssen, Riksen-Walraven, & van Dijk, 2004).

In addressing needs for communication and orientation and mobility, practitioners and parents should keep in mind at least two important principles: the importance of direct teaching and the importance of structured routines.

THE IMPORTANCE OF DIRECT TEACHING   Many students with disabilities (e.g., intellectual disability, learning disabilities, blindness, deafness) are more reliant than those without disabilities on having teachers teach them directly. Whereas students without disabilities can learn a great deal incidentally (e.g., from seeing or hearing things that happen around them), students with disabilities are often in greater need of having material taught to them directly (see Kauffman, 2002; Kauffman & Hallahan, 2005). As we mentioned in connection with Helen Keller and Laura Bridgman, because of their restricted sensory input, this need for direct teaching of information is even more pronounced for students who are deaf-blind than it is for children with other disabilities.

THE IMPORTANCE OF STRUCTURED ROUTINES   To create a successful environment for learning, it's also critical that teachers and other professionals and parents provide a sense of security for students who are deaf-blind. One of the best ways to create this

Personal PERSPECTIVES

Laura Bridgman and Her Teacher, Samuel Gridley Howe

Although most people are familiar with the story of Helen Keller, Laura Bridgman (1829–1889) was actually the first documented case of a deaf-blind person to learn language. Laura was struck at the age of two with scarlet fever and left deaf and blind.

Samuel Gridley Howe (1801–1876) was one of the nineteenth century's most daring social activists, reforming schools, prisons, and mental institutions as well as being a member of the "Secret Six" who lent financial support to John Brown's campaign to end slavery in the United States with his ill-fated launching of the raid at Harper's Ferry in 1859. Howe received his medical degree from Harvard University in 1824. After serving a seven-year stint as a surgeon in the Greek civil conflict, he returned to Boston. In 1832, he was named head of the Perkins Institution and Massachusetts School for the Blind (now named the Perkins School for the Blind).

After reading a newspaper account of Laura, Howe visited her parents and convinced them to send the eight-year-old to Perkins in 1837. There, he and his teachers worked painstakingly with Laura for several years. In addition to the goals of teaching her to communicate, Howe viewed Bridgman as a philosophical and religious experiment. By showing that she could learn to communicate, he was debunking the materialists, who held that sensory input was necessary in order to form concepts: "As Laura reached out to the world around her, Howe thrilled to witness the triumph of mind over matter" (Freeberg, 2001, p. 41). With respect to religion, Howe hoped to show that Laura possessed an innate moral consciousness that was intact despite her sensory losses.

Howe held open houses for the public to see the accomplishments of the students at Perkins. Laura soon became the major attraction, drawing hundreds of onlookers. One of the early visitors was Charles Dickens, whose account of his meeting with Laura, which he described in *American Notes*, further publicized the accomplishments of Howe's work with her.

Howe eventually became discouraged because Laura did not progress as far as he had hoped. Although she was able to

Laura Bridgman with Samuel Gridley Howe.

communicate well, her personality, characterized by immaturity and occasional fits of rage, kept her from becoming the ideal case to prove his philosophical and theological theories.

Although her achievements were not as spectacular as Keller's, Bridgman's accomplishments were extraordinary for the time, a time when many authorities believed that to be deaf-blind was to be mentally retarded. Furthermore, had it not been for Bridgman, Keller might never have received the instruction that unlocked her intellect. Helen's parents were alerted to the potential of teaching their own daughter after reading about Bridgman's accomplishments. Furthermore, Helen's teacher, Annie Sullivan, herself a former student at Perkins, consulted Howe's reports on Laura before embarking on her journey to tutor Helen. Perhaps most important,

Laura Bridgman's dramatic story drew the public's attention to the wider reform movement that was transforming the lives of many disabled people in nineteenth century America. Howe and other educators invented teaching tools, experimented with curriculum, and built new institutions that helped thousands of people with sensory handicaps to overcome the physical barriers that had always deprived them of an education. . . . Chipping away at centuries of accumulated prejudice and misunderstanding, these students and their teachers began to dismantle one of the greatest barriers faced by the blind and the deaf, the deep-rooted misconception that people with sensory handicaps are unreachable and somehow less than fully human. In the crucial early years of this important reform movement, no person did more to challenge those assumptions and inspire new respect for the disabled than Laura Bridgman. (Freeberg, 2001, pp. 220–221)

Source: Reprinted by permission of the publisher from *The Education of Laura Bridgman: First Deaf and Blind Person to Learn Language* by E. Freeberg, Cambridge, MA: Harvard University Press, Copyright © 2001 by the President and Fellows of Harvard College.

Responsive Instruction

Meeting the Needs of Students with Low-Incidence, Multiple, and Severe Disabilities

The Importance of Establishing Structured Routines

WHAT THE RESEARCH SAYS

Researchers and practitioners from Project PLAI* (Promoting Learning Through Active Interaction) have developed several modules for working with infants who have multiple disabilities and their families (Chen, Alsop, & Minor, 2000; Klein, Chen, & Haney, 2000). One of the modules focuses on establishing predictable routines. Specifically, for infants who are deaf-blind, they have recommended the following objectives:

- Create a predictable routine by identifying at least five daily activities that can be scheduled in the same sequence each day.
- Identify predictable sequences within specific activities (i.e., "subroutines").
- Identify and use specific auditory, visual, tactile, olfactory, and kinesthetic cues to help the infant anticipate familiar activities. (Chen et al., 2000, p. 6)

The following describes how they implemented these objectives with fourteen-month-old Michael, his mother, Cecelia, and older sister, Kate. Michael was born prematurely and only weighed one pound, eight ounces at birth. He was diagnosed with severe ROP (retinopathy of prematurity), cerebral palsy, and a hearing loss of undetermined severity.

An early interventionist helped Cecelia realize that Michael could better understand what was going on around him if his daily events were more predictable. In addition to the early morning and evening routines, Cecelia decided to try to increase the predictability of Michael's routines in several ways. After he finished his morning bottle, he would always get a bath. After the bath, Cecelia would put lotion on him and give him a shoulder and back massage. At bedtime, she would give him his bottle and then Kate would rock him while watching TV. Cecelia also realized that she and Michael had developed "subroutines." For example, after removing Michael's diaper and cleaning him, she would blow on his tummy and say, "Okay, all dry. All dry." Then

*Project PLAI was a four-year collaborative project involving California State University-Northridge, SKI-HI Institute at Utah State University, and several early intervention programs, funded by the Office of Special Education Programs, U.S. Department of Education.

she would sprinkle powder and put a new diaper on him, say "All done," and give him a kiss while picking him up.

Other predictable routines and subroutines followed. Before going into Michael's room, Cecelia would always announce loudly, "Here comes Mommy." She would touch his shoulders before picking him up. Before putting him in the bath, she would put his foot in the water a couple of times, which helped him to stop screaming when he was placed in the tub. Before Cecelia gave Michael his back massage, she would rub some lotion on her fingers and let him smell it. (Chen, Alsop, & Minor, 2000, pp. 6–7).

APPLYING THE RESEARCH TO TEACHING

Although the above example pertains to infants, structured routines are no less important for school-age children who have multiple disabilities, including deaf-blindness. School routines are particularly important for the student who is deaf-blind because the only way for that child to learn is by doing. The student will be unable to learn through visually observing or hearing stimuli that will assist her or him in making sense of the world. Therefore, the student will be dependent upon the creation of a safe learning environment and trust with the primary instructor (Moss & Hagood, 1995). School routines that would benefit the student who is deaf-blind are as follows:

- *Turn-taking routines*. By keeping interactions balanced ("me, then you"), the student will consistently know when to respond and be more active in his or her learning.
- *Travel or movement routines*. If the student does not feel comfortable moving around the classroom or school, he or she may choose to not move. Lack of mobility decreases opportunities for exploration, social interaction, and independence.
- *Communication routines*. The student who is deaf-blind will rely on tactile communication. The student will be unable to make connections among input without direct interaction with others. Therefore, it is important to establish routines for communication as the student moves from objects to gestures for communication.

● *By Kristin L. Sayeski*

---

sense of security is through the use of structured routines (Chen, Alsop, & Minor, 2000; Miles, 1998), discussed in detail in the Responsive Instruction above.

COMMUNICATION   The hands play a critical role in communication for most students who are deaf-blind. In effect, the hands become the "voice, or the primary means of expression" (Miles, 1999, p. 1). A number of modes of communication that involve touch are used with people who are deaf-blind. **Braille** is the most obvious one. Some other common tactile learning strategies are **hand-over-hand guidance**, **hand-under-hand guidance**, **adapted signs**, and **touch cues** (Chen, Downing, & Rodriguez-Gil, 2000/2001).

Hand-Over-Hand Guidance   Hand-over-hand guidance involves the adult placing his or her hand(s) over the child's hand(s) while exploring an object or signing. Although this technique may be necessary, especially for children who have physical disabilities that interfere with movement of their hands, it does have some disadvantages (Chen et al., 2000/2001; Miles, 1999). Some children are resistant to this technique, apparently because they do not like the feeling of loss of control over their hands. Furthermore, some children can become too passive, waiting for someone else's hands to be placed over theirs rather than reaching out on their own.

Hand-Under-Hand Guidance   Hand-under-hand guidance is often recommended as an alternative to hand-over-hand guidance. This technique involves the adult gently slipping his or her hand(s) underneath part of the child's hand(s) while the child is exploring an object. It becomes the tactile equivalent to pointing (Miles, 1999). One of the main advantages of hand-under-hand guidance is that it is noncontrolling, and some authorities believe that when children and adults explore objects and movements together it lays a foundation for language (Miles, 1999).

Adapted Signs   Signs used by the Deaf community, such as American Sign Language and signed English, are visually based, which makes them difficult or impossible to use by people who are deaf-blind, depending on the severity of their visual impairment. For this reason, a variety of tactual versions of signing have been created (Chen et al., 2000/2001). For example, for the reception of signs, the person who is deaf-blind can place his or her hands on the hands of the signer; for the expression of signs, the teacher or parent can hold the hands of the person who is deaf-blind and guide him or her to produce signs.

Touch Cues   Touch cues are tactual signals that can convey a number of messages depending on the situation and context. It is important that the touch cues be consistent; a child will not be able to decipher the meaning of a touch cue if different people use it for a variety of messages. For example, patting or tapping a child on the shoulder may express:

- positive feedback ("Great job")
- a request or directive ("Sit down")
- information ("Your turn")
- comfort or reassurance ("Don't cry, you're OK")

Touch cues should be used selectively, conservatively, and consistently so that the child can develop an understanding of what they represent (Chen et al., 2000/2001, p. 3).

ORIENTATION AND MOBILITY   As we learned in Chapter 10, **orientation and mobility (O & M)** training is critical for those who are blind or who have low vision. The more a person with visual impairment is able to navigate the environment, the more independent she or he is able to become. For people who have both visual impairment and hearing impairment, the need for mobility training is even more important because they are at even greater risk of being unable to navigate their environment.

■ **Braille**
A system in which raised dots allow people who are blind to read with their fingertips; each quadrangular cell contains from one to six dots, the arrangement of which denotes different letters and symbols.

■ **Hand-over-hand guidance**
A tactile learning strategy for persons who are deaf-blind; the teacher places his or her hands over those of the person who is deaf-blind and guides them to explore objects.

■ **Hand-under-hand guidance**
A tactile learning strategy for persons who are deaf-blind; the teacher places his or her hands underneath part of the student's hand or hands while the child is exploring objects.

■ **Adapted signs**
Signs adapted for use by people who are deaf-blind; tactually based rather than visually based, such as American Sign Language for those who are deaf but sighted.

■ **Touch cues**
Tactual signals used to communicate with persons who are deaf-blind; can be used to signify a variety of messages.

This blind child is assisted by a teacher who is using the hand-over-hand technique to help him explore a tray of potato sticks.

■ **Assistance card**
A relatively small card containing a message that alerts the public that the user is deaf-blind and needs assistance in crossing the street.

O & M training for people who have both visual and hearing impairment differs in at least two ways from O & M training for those with only visual impairment. First, adaptations are needed to communicate with people with deaf-blindness (Gense & Gense, 2004). The O & M instructor might need to use such adaptations as an interpreter, adapted signs, and/or touch cues to communicate with the student who is deaf-blind.

Second, it's sometimes necessary to alert the public that a traveler is deaf-blind. Even the best travelers with deaf-blindness occasionally become temporarily disoriented and need assistance. Hearing people with visual impairment can ask for assistance relatively easily. However, people who have both hearing and visual impairment may have a more difficult time communicating their needs to the public, and it won't always be obvious to the public that the person has both a visual and hearing impairment. A long cane can signal vision loss, but it does not indicate hearing impairment. Therefore, some professionals advocate the use of assistance cards. **Assistance cards** are usually relatively small (e.g., 3″ × 6″) and can be held up by the person who is deaf-blind at a busy or unfamiliar intersection. The words on the card indicate that the person is asking for assistance—for example, "Please help me to CROSS STREET. I am both DEAF and VISUALLY IMPAIRED, so TAP ME if you can help. Thank you" (Franklin & Bourquin, 2000, p. 175).

SPECIAL CONSIDERATIONS FOR STUDENTS WITH USHER SYNDROME Students with Usher syndrome present some special educational challenges because most of them have progressive visual impairment. They might start out having relatively good vision, but their vision inevitably declines to the point at which they are legally, if not totally, blind. The effects of retinitis pigmentosa, which accompanies Usher syndrome, can sometimes be erratic and change rapidly, thus catching the student and his or her family off guard (Miner & Cioffi, 1999). Even when the deterioration occurs slowly over the course of several years, parents and teachers of children with Usher syndrome might neglect the importance of preparing the child for the fact that he or she will one day have substantial visual impairment. Sometimes, they fear that the early introduction of braille and O&M training will stigmatize the child and damage his or her self-concept. However, most authorities now agree that braille and O & M training should not wait until the student can no longer function as a seeing individual.

Considerations for Many Students with Low-Incidence, Multiple, and Severe Disabilities

Some of the devices and methods that we describe here might apply to any of the disabilities we discuss in this chapter. Communication, behavior management, early intervention, transition, employment, family involvement, and normalization are all concerns that are frequently encountered with any of these disabilities.

Augmentative or Alternative Communication

For some individuals with severe and multiple disabilities, oral language is out of the question; they have physical or cognitive disabilities, usually as a result of neurological damage, that preclude their learning to communicate through normal speech. A system of **augmentative or alternative communication (AAC)** must be designed for them.

AAC includes any manual or electronic means by which such a person expresses wants and needs, shares information, engages in social closeness, or manages social etiquette (Beukelman & Mirenda, 1998; Beukelman, Yorkston, & Reichle, 2000; Gerenser & Forman, 2007; Lloyd, Fuller, & Arvidson, 1997). Students for whom AAC must be designed range in intelligence from highly gifted to profoundly intellectually disabled but they all have one characteristic in common: the inability to communicate effectively through speech because

INTERNET RESOURCES
You might want to Google Augmentative and Alternative Communication and explore various Websites, such as www.isaac-online.org/select_language.html

■ **Augmentative or alternative communication (AAC)**
Alternative forms of communication that do not use the oral sounds of speech or that augment the use of speech.

of a physical impairment. Some of these individuals are unable to make any speech sounds at all; others need a system to augment their speech when they can't make themselves understood because of environmental noise, difficulty in producing certain words or sounds, or unfamiliarity with the person with whom they want to communicate.

Manual signs or gestures are useful for some individuals. But many individuals with severe physical limitations are unable to use their hands to communicate through the usual sign language; they must use another means of communication, usually involving special equipment. However, Nikki Kissane, a University of Virginia undergraduate student who intends to become an orthopedic surgeon, has developed a simplified sign language system. Children and adults with limited speech capabilities can learn and use her simplified signs more easily than traditional signs (see Focus on Concepts below).

> **UNDERSTANDING THE STANDARDS AND PRINCIPLES** What forms of augmentative or alternative communication might be helpful for individuals with severe and multiple disabilities? (CEC Knowledge and Skill Standards CC6S1 & IC6S3)
>
> Council for Exceptional Children

FOCUS ON **Concepts**

Simplified Sign Language

Figuring out how to communicate effectively with simple gestures has not been an easy task for U.Va. student Nikki Kissane. But thanks to her research efforts, mute children and adults or those with limited speech capabilities have a new simplified communication system that is easier to learn, produce, and understand than existing sign languages. . . .

After witnessing her grandfather suffer a series of strokes and seeing the physiological and emotional difficulties he experienced, Kissane approached psychology professor John Bonvillian to see if she could participate in his ongoing research on sign-language communication for nonspeaking but hearing individuals. . . .

Kissane studied more than 20 sign language dictionaries to identify signs that are "iconic," those clearly resembling the object or action they represent, or "transparent," those that easily convey their meaning. To illustrate, cradling one's arms while gently rocking back and forth would be a transparent sign for "baby," whereas gesturing throwing a ball would be an iconic gesture for "throw."

From her research, Kissane identified about 900 signs for such everyday words as "comb," "book" and "reach" that have the potential of being easily understood and communicated through simple hand and arm gestures. She also created numerous new signs to supplement those she found in her search.

To determine if such signs could be incorporated into a simplified system, she had volunteer U.Va. students view different groups of signs to see which ones they could remember and repeat easily. All signs recalled perfectly by at least 70 percent of the participants were added to a lexicon.

Kissane also observed some classes led by her mother, who teaches elementary school art to children, including several with autism. She gained pointers from her mother on how to draw the gestures.

"I observed a few of the classes to see where autistic children struggle in motor and cognitive skills," Kissane said.

Source: Wooten, I. L. (2001, May 18). Student develops new sign language system. *Inside UVA, 31*(18), 12. Reprinted with permission. Photos from The Daily Progress, Charlottesville, VA. Reprinted with permission.

Eye

Celebrate

Sleep

Success Stories

David gains independence and academic achievement through assistive technology and professional collaboration

Mrs. Womack, David's mother: "When some teachers hear that ventilator, their tendency is to pamper the child, but I want him treated like a student."

Sixteen-year-old David Womack attends an academic day school for students with severe physical disabilities.

These are the keys to his success:

- intensive collaboration,
- relentless emphasis on technology,
- specific goals for independence and academic achievement.

On the second day of second grade, seven-year-old David Womack was hit by a car as he stepped off the school bus. The accident injured his spinal cord, leaving him with no movement below his neck and with an inability to breathe on his own. After two years of rehabilitation, David was ready to leave the hospital and reenter school. His parents and other members of the IEP team made the decision to enroll nine-year-old David in a special day school for students with intense medical and physical needs. David's achievements are the result of intensive, relentless, and specific special education.

● Intensive Collaboration David's specialized day school is staffed with medical and therapeutic personnel and with teachers who are dually certified as special and general educators. David was the first student dependent on a ventilator to attend the school. He entered his third-grade classroom in a large electronic sip-and-puff wheelchair that he propelled by blowing air through a strawlike mouthpiece. His life-support system, called "the vent," was mounted on the back of his chair and made a loud rhythmic sound. Never more than several feet away was a private-duty nurse who monitored him at all times. "It was so scary," recalls Mrs. Womack. "I could tell everybody was nervous."

The school's task included helping the Womack family adjust to a different life and stimulating David to discover his new potential. Even though the staff was experienced in dealing with difficult physical issues, David presented a challenge, and the presence of the ventilator and the private nurse emphasized his fragility. Says occupational therapist Ginette Howard, "We had to raise everybody's expectations by treating David like a student instead of a patient!"

The school's technology team supported David's classroom learning. Howard and computer teacher Maryann Cicchillo combined their knowledge of instructional software and sophisticated technologies to provide David with the tools to read, write, and compute. Classroom teachers followed their lead, and so did his nurse, Gail Nolan, who was committed to his academic and social growth. David's progress was built slowly but steadily on a foundation of trust.

● Relentless Emphasis on Technology David was frightened to leave the hospital, so the first task was securing his ventilator equipment for classroom use. "We made sure there was a plastic casing over the dials because he was afraid someone might play with the settings," Howard recalls. The second year, he

The problems to be solved in helping individuals communicate in ways other than signing include selecting a vocabulary and giving them an effective, efficient means of indicating elements in their vocabularies. Although the basic ideas behind AAC are quite simple, selecting the best vocabulary and devising an efficient means of indication for many individuals with severe disabilities are extraordinarily challenging. As one AAC user put it, "The AAC evaluation should be done with the AAC user involved in the process from step one. It is the augmented speaker who will be using the device every day, both personally and professionally, not the AAC specialist" (Cardona, 2000, p. 237).

A variety of approaches to AAC have been developed, some involving relatively simple or so-called low-technology solutions and some requiring complex or high-technology solutions (Lloyd et al., 1997). Many different direct-selection and scanning methods have been devised for AAC, depending on individual capabilities. The system that is used may involve pointing with the hand or a headstick, eye became more confident and more willing to try new technologies. David progressed from being withdrawn and fearful to trusting and to developing an interest in computer applications. Providing him with computer access became the challenge.

"David has chin supports to keep his head erect, and he can move his mouth," says Howard. She and Cicchillo selected a small alternative-access keyboard that was worked by an electronic wand. With much effort, David would clench a mouthstick in his teeth and gently tap the attached wand on the miniature impulse-sensitive keyboard. Cicchillo ensured that appropriate software was available to David's teachers through the school's network. Gradually, David became accustomed to using the mouthstick and to the expectation that he was independently responsible for his school work.

● **Specific Goals for Independence and Academic Achievement** David's technology sessions have increased his independence as a student. He uses a word prediction and abbreviation/ expansion program to reduce the number of keystrokes and to increase his speed in writing assignments. He is eager to try new technologies that challenge his accuracy and increase his speed. "I can't tell you how many times we've explored technology to support homework assignments, to take tests, or complete a paper," says Cicchillo.

"Science is my favorite subject," says David, a quiet young man who speaks in a soft, breathy voice. Dorothy Vann's science lab is fully accessible, with adjustable tables and low sinks. The lab is also equipped with instructional technology that David needs to fully participate. In biology, he views slides through a stereo microscope that utilizes a small attached camera to project video images. "I knew David was capable of doing more than he initially showed us," says Vann.

Working with David has been an evolving process for each of the collaborators. In reflecting on their work with David, Howard and Cicchillo identify a breaking-in period when teachers and the child who is newly ventilator-dependent have to overcome their fears. According to Dorothy Vann, "It takes a while for a child to accept goals for achievement and to believe in his or her own success."

CEC'S STANDARDS: PAVING THE WAY TO SUCCESS

ASSESS YOUR STEPS TO SUCCESS in meeting the CEC Knowledge and Skill Base for All Beginning Special Education Teachers of Students in Individualized Independence Curriculums. Use the following questions to reflect on the growth of your own professional knowledge, skills, and dispositions.

REFLECTING ON YOUR OWN PROFESSIONAL DEVELOPMENT

If you were David's teacher . . .

■ What are some areas about educating students with severe disabilities that you would need to know more about?

■ What are some specific skills that would help you address David's academic and emotional challenges?

■ What personal dispositions do you think are most important for you to develop in teaching students with severe disabilities?

Using the CEC Standards

■ What are some ways in which special educators could select, plan, and coordinate the activities of related services personnel to maximize direct instruction for a student with severe disabilities? (IC10S3)

■ How would you develop a technology plan based on an adaptive technology assessment for a student with a severe disability? (IC8S5)

■ What strategies would help you to identify and prioritize areas of the general curriculum and accommodations for a student with a severe disability? (CC7S1)

● *By Jean B. Crockett*

---

movements, or operation of a microswitch by foot, tongue, or head movement or breath control. Sometimes, the individual can use a typewriter or computer terminal that is fitted with a key guard so that keys are not likely to be pressed accidentally or use an alternative means for selecting keystrokes. See Success Stories above about David, a fourth grader who uses an alternative-access keyboard. Other students use communication boards, which offer an array of pictures, words, or other symbols and can be operated with either a direct-selection or scanning strategy. The content and arrangement of the board will vary, depending on the person's capabilities, preferences, and communication needs.

Speed, reliability, portability, cost, and overall effectiveness in helping a person communicate independently are factors to be considered in designing and evaluating AAC (Beukelman & Mirenda, 1998; Lloyd et al., 1997). Some AAC systems are very slow, unreliable (either because of the equipment or a poor match with the abilities of

INTERNET RESOURCES

Simplified signs are shown at www.simplifiedsigns.org For augmentative and alternative communication, see www.isaac-online.org

the user), cumbersome, or useful only in very restricted settings. Although people typically think of the equipment and material costs that AAC involves, the real costs must include intensive and extensive instruction. A communication board will not necessarily be useful just because it is available. And the most sophisticated technological solution to communication is not always the one that will be most useful in the long run.

Today, researchers are finding increasingly innovative and creative technological solutions to the problem of nonvocal communication. At the same time, they are recognizing the importance of making decisions that are highly individualized and evidence-based (Gerenser & Forman, 2007; Schlosser & Raghenvendra, 2004). No one is well served by AAC that is not highly reliable from a scientific point of view.

Until rather recently, many practitioners saw AAC primarily as a means of allowing users to demonstrate the language skills they have already acquired. But now researchers and practitioners increasingly emphasize how AAC can be a tool for teaching language— for helping AAC users not only to give voice to what they feel and know about specific tasks, but also to acquire increasingly sophisticated language skills (Nelson, 1998; Oken-Fried & Bersani, 2000; Yoder, 2001).

Researchers are attempting to make it possible for young AAC users to talk about the same kinds of things that other youngsters do (Marvin, Beukelman, Brockhaus, & Kast, 1994). Other efforts are directed at training AAC users to tell those with whom they communicate how to interact with them more effectively—that is, to train AAC users in pragmatics. Personal Perspectives below was written by Chris Featherly when he was an eighteen-year-old high school student. His story and others written by AAC users (Oken-Fried & Bersani, 2000) illustrate the value of AAC and issues involved in its use. The fact that Chris Featherly has cerebral palsy, a congenital neurological condition

Personal PERSPECTIVES

Life with Cerebral Palsy

Chris Featherly

My name is Christopher Glen Featherly, and I'm going to try to give you a little overview of life with cerebral palsy as I know it.

I'm 18 years old and was born in Fort Worth, Texas. I'm currently attending Bremen High School in Midlothian, Illinois. . . .

When I came from Texas to live with my grandparents at the age of 5, I only had five generic signs for communication. My grandmom wouldn't put up with that, and so she went to the library for a sign language book. Now she learned that there really was something upstairs! The school system wanted me to use a 48-page, three-ring binder of pictures for my communication. Can you see me, using my right hand, to flip between 48 pages to talk to someone? I don't think so! My grandmom took me to Siegel Institute in downtown Chicago for a speech evaluation. They said, "This kid needs a TouchTalker [an AAC device; see www.prentrom.com for descriptions of other devices]. . . ." Well, guess what! The school speech clinician said, "No. He doesn't have language, and if he has it [Touch

Talker] he won't use his own voice to talk." So guess what grandmom did? She took me to Homewood to see another speech therapist. What do you think she said? You got it! She said, "TouchTalker." So back to school, and again the answer was, "No." Grandmom then told them she was going to take me to Shriners. If they said TouchTalker, that would be the mode of communication I would have. Well, what do you think they said? Yup! It was TouchTalker. Now, we knew how school felt about it, which meant it was in our ball park. It was time to save money and purchase it so that I could get stuff out of my head and stuff into it. By now, do you sorta have an idea what kind of grandmom I have?

[Chris's story goes on to describe software and hardware upgrades that he needed as he progressed, and his use of online resources.]

Source: Featherly, C. (2000). Life with cerebral palsy. In M. Oken-Fried & H. A. Bersani (Eds.), *Speaking up and spelling it out: Personal essays on augmentative and alternative communication* (pp. 189–193). Baltimore: Paul H. Brookes.

that we discuss in Chapter 14, is beside the point here. The important thing is that some people have physical limitations that preclude their efficient use of oral language and need an augmented or alternative means of communicating.

Users of AAC encounter three particular challenges that are not faced by natural communicators:

1. AAC is often much slower than natural communication—perhaps one-twentieth the typical rate of speech. This can result in great frustration for both AAC users and natural communicators.

2. Users of AAC who are not literate must rely on a vocabulary and symbols that are selected by others. If the vocabulary and symbols, as well as other features of the system, are not well chosen, AAC will be quite limited in the learning and personal relationships it allows.

3. AAC must be constructed to be useful in a variety of social contexts, allow accurate and efficient communication without undue fatigue, and support the individual's learning of language and academic skills.

Progress in the field of AAC requires that all of these challenges be addressed simultaneously. AAC is increasingly focused on literacy and the right to use print, including writing, for communication. In many ways the emphasis on basic literacy skills parallels the emphasis on literacy for all students, regardless of disabilities (Yoder, 2001).

The need for AAC is increasing as more people with severe disabilities, including those with TBI and other disabilities, are surviving and taking their places in the community. As more students with severe disabilities are integrated into regular educational programs at all levels, the availability and appropriate use of AAC in such classrooms become more critical issues (Beukelman & Mirenda, 1998; Lloyd et al., 1997). Whatever system of AAC is devised, it must be relatively easy to use, efficient, mechanically reliable, and reliable in communicating the user's thoughts and intentions, not someone else's (Schlosser & Raghenvendra, 2004).

One type of AAC that burst on the scene in the early 1990s is facilitated communication (FC). FC requires that a "facilitator" physically assist the user in typing out messages on a keyboard. Although FC quickly became very popular and still is used by some, it has been called into serious question because it appears to communicate the facilitator's words, not the words of the person with disabilities. In fact, FC appears to have been discredited by research (Jacobson, Foxx, & Mulick, 2005; Kauffman & Sasso, 2006; Mostert, 2001; Mostert, Kavale, & Kauffman, 2008; National Research Council, 2001). Beukelman and Mirenda, noting that a very small number of people around the world appear to be typing independently after being taught with FC, concluded, "we do not believe that FC works for everyone or even with most people" (1998, p. 329). Any AAC device that misrepresents the user's communication demeans the user through pretense. This is not acceptable, as all people with disabilities should be treated with dignity and respect (Kauffman & Sasso, 2006; Yoder, 2001). The goal of AAC should be independent communication in which there is no doubt about the authenticity of the messages, as the National Research Council points out.

The remarkable increase in the power and availability of microcomputers is radically changing the ability to provide AAC and make sure that the user's words are communicated. New applications of microcomputers may lead to breakthroughs that will allow people with severe disabilities to communicate more effectively, even if they have extremely limited muscle control. Furthermore, existing microcomputer software suggests ways of encouraging children to use their existing language skills. Technological developments will no doubt revolutionize AAC within a few years (Oken-Fried & Bersani, 2000). Loncke (2001) predicts that electronic communication will lead to globalization of AAC, which seems consistent with Chris Featherly's online communication (see Personal Perspectives, p. 480).

UNDERSTANDING THE STANDARDS AND PRINCIPLES What can teachers do about behavior problems some individuals with multiple disabilities may exhibit? (CEC Knowledge and Skill Standards CC5K6, CC5S2, CC5S5, CC5S10, & CC5S11)

Council for Exceptional Children

■ **Functional behavioral assessment (FBA)**
Evaluation that consists of finding out the consequences (what purpose the behavior serves), antecedents (what triggers the behavior), and setting events (contextual factors) that maintain inappropriate behaviors.

■ **Positive behavioral support (PBS)**
Positive reinforcement (rewarding) procedures intended to support a student's appropriate or desirable behavior.

■ **Self-stimulation**
Any repetitive, stereotyped activity that seems only to provide sensory feedback.

■ **Self-injurious behavior (SIB)**
Behavior causing injury or mutilation of oneself, such as self-biting or head-banging; usually seen in individuals with severe and multiple disabilities.

Much information about AAC is now available on various Websites. The International Society for Augmentative and Alternative Communication (ISAAC) publishes the professional journal *Augmentative and Alternative Communication* and maintains a Website. Parents need to be aware of the availability of AAC and demand equipment and training that are effective for their child (Snell, 2004).

Behavior Problems

Some individuals who have certain severe or multiple disabilities engage in problematic behaviors such as self-stimulation, self-injury, tantrums, aggression toward others, or some combination of these (Bodfish, 2007; Gardner, 2007; Nezu, Nezu, Klein, & Clair, 2007). In fact the federal IDEA definition recognizes self-stimulation, self-mutilation, tantrums, and failure to respond to social stimuli as prominent features of many severe and multiple disabilities.

We caution that not all people with low incidence, severe, or multiple disabilities exhibit the behavior problems we discuss here. Many people who are deaf-blind and many who have TBI, autism, or other severe or multiple disabilities do not engage in these behaviors. Nevertheless, most of the people who do exhibit these problems to a significant extent have severe and multiple disabilities. Moreover, behaviors of the type that we discuss here add a level of complexity and seriousness to any disability. Thus, finding solutions to these behavior problems is critical to treating the individual with respect and helping the person to participate in typical school and community activities.

There is much controversy regarding behavior problems of people with severe disabilities. Some assume that such problems simply will not occur if appropriate programs of instruction are provided. Others suggest that **functional behavioral assessment (FBA), positive behavioral support (PBS)**, and nonaversive treatments (i.e., treatments in which punishment has no place) will be sufficient in all cases. However, others claim that positive behavioral supports and nonaversive treatments are insufficient in some cases to overcome behavior problems (e.g., Cullen & Mudford, 2005; Mulick & Butter, 2005; Newsom & Kroeger, 2005).

SELF-STIMULATION **Self-stimulation** can be defined as any repetitive, stereotyped behavior that seems to have no immediately apparent purpose other than providing sensory stimulation. Self-stimulation (a form of stereotyped movement) may take a wide variety of forms, such as swishing saliva, twirling objects, hand-flapping, fixed staring, and the like. Repetitive, stereotyped behavior (sometimes called stereotypy) may have multiple causes, including social consequences, in addition to sensory stimulation (Bodfish, 2007; Kennedy, Meyer, Knowles, & Shukla, 2000; Rapp, Miltenberger, Galensky, Ellingson, & Long, 1999).

Nearly everyone sometimes engages in some form of self-stimulation, such as lip-biting, hair-stroking, and nail-biting, but not at the high rate that characterizes a disability. Nondisabled infants engage in self-stimulation, and so do nondisabled adults, particularly when they are tired or bored. Only the high rate, lack of subtlety, and social inappropriateness of such self-stimulation differentiate it from the norm.

Self-stimulation becomes problematic when it occurs at such a high rate that it interferes with learning or social acceptability or when it occurs with such intensity that it does injury. Some individuals with autism or other pervasive developmental disability engage in self-stimulation to the exclusion of academic and social learning. In most of these cases, it appears that only intrusive, directive intervention will be successful in helping the individual learn academic and social skills (Kauffman & Landrum, 2009).

SELF-INJURY **Self-injurious behavior (SIB)** is repeated physical self-abuse, such as biting, scratching, or poking oneself, head-banging, and so on. Unchecked, SIB often results in self-mutilation. Self-stimulation can be so frequent and intense that it becomes SIB. For example, Worsdell, Iwata, Conners, Kahng, and Thompson (2000) studied SIB characterized by hand-biting, head- or body-hitting, hand-mouthing, and skin-picking. Hand-mouthing is self-stimulation of the kind that all infants do; even some nondisabled adults can be seen occasionally mouthing their hands. However, hand-mouthing becomes self-injurious for some people with severe developmental disabilities, resulting in serious skin lesions.

TANTRUMS Severe tantrums can include a variety of behaviors, including self-injury, screaming, crying, throwing or destroying objects, and aggression toward others. Sometimes, the event that sets off a tantrum is unknown, at least to the casual observer. Often, however, a tantrum is precipitated by a request or demand that the individual do something (perhaps a self-care task or some academic work), and the consequence of the tantrum is that the demand is withdrawn, thus reinforcing the tantrum behavior.

Tantrums impose a handicap on the individual who uses them to avoid learning or doing important things. They stymie socialization, as most people want to avoid interacting with someone who is likely to have a tantrum. Teachers and others who work most successfully with individuals who have tantrums do not withdraw reasonable demands for performance. What they do is modify their demand or circumstances in some way or alternate their demands for performance in ways that are less likely to set off a tantrum.

AGGRESSION TOWARD OTHERS Not all aggression toward others is associated with tantrums. Some individuals with severe or multiple disabilities engage in calculated physical attacks that threaten or injure others (Gardner, 2007). Sometimes these attacks come without warning or only after subtle indications of imminent assault that only someone who knows the individual well is likely to perceive. Aggression toward others is disabling because it limits social interactions. For understandable reasons, people tend to avoid those they believe are likely to endanger or hurt them. Research suggests that aggression and other undesirable behavior such as SIB may be followed by attention or other rewarding consequences for individuals with severe and multiple disabilities (Thompson & Iwata, 2001).

LACK OF DAILY LIVING SKILLS Lack of daily living skills refers to the absence or significant impairment of the ability to take care of one's basic needs, such as dressing, feeding, or toileting. Many people with severe and multiple disabilities must be taught the adaptive behavior that is expected of older children and adults. These adaptive behaviors include a wide variety of tasks involving clothing selection and dressing, food preparation and eating, grooming, socializing, using money, using public transportation, playing games or other recreation, and so on (Snell & Brown, 2006).

FUNCTIONAL BEHAVIORAL ASSESSMENT AND POSITIVE BEHAVIORAL INTERVENTION AND SUPPORT Problem behaviors are often related to a brain disorder or brain injury, even if the disorder is not understood. An example is severe autism, which often includes self-stimulation, self-injury, tantrums, or all of these. However, there is increasing emphasis on analyzing and changing the environments in which problem behavior is exhibited, that is, increasing focus on the immediate and alterable influences on behavior rather than on immutable or historical reasons for behavior (Bodfish, 2007; Horner, Albin, Sprague, & Todd, 2000; Snell & Brown, 2006).

In earlier chapters, we introduced the ideas of **functional behavioral assessment (FBA)** and **positive behavioral intervention and support (PBIS)**, primarily as they apply to students with less severe disabilities (see Chapters 2, 5, 7, 8, and 12). However, these procedures may be particularly important for students with severe and multiple

Casebook Reflection

REFER TO THE CASE, *Who Will Help Patrick?* in your booklet. When his special education coordinator worked with him, he threw the pegboard across the room and flailed wildly at her with his fists, which required her to restrain him. His preschool teacher often puts him in a crib for his tantrums. What might be the reasons for this behavior? How much of this behavior can be attributed to his disability? ●

■ **Functional behavioral assessment (FBA)** Evaluation that consists of finding out the consequences (what purpose the behavior serves), antecedent (what triggers the behavior), and setting events (contextual factors) that maintain inappropriate behaviors.

INTERNET RESOURCES

For management of behavior problems, see www.pbis.org

■ **Neonatal intensive care unit (NICU)**
A special unit in a hospital designed to provide around-the-clock monitoring and care of newborns who have severe physical problems; staffed by professionals from several disciplines, such as nursing, social work, occupational therapy, respiratory therapy, and medicine; similar to an intensive care unit for older children and adults.

disabilities. FBA entails finding out why or under what circumstances problem behavior is exhibited, and PBIS involves creating an environment that supports appropriate behavior.

FBA often reveals how a student uses self-stimulation, SIB, tantrums, or aggression against others. A student might behave inappropriately to escape or avoid unpleasant or nonpreferred activities or tasks (see Kauffman & Landrum, 2009). In many instances, researchers and practitioners find that the student has no other effective and efficient means of communication. The task, therefore, is to figure out how the student is using unacceptable communication and teach him or her a more effective and efficient and acceptable means of letting others know what he or she wants or is feeling. FBA has led to the discovery that sometimes people with severe and multiple disabilities use inappropriate behavior to communicate a variety of their wants or needs (e.g., "Pay attention to me," "Let me out of here," "There's nothing to do," "There's too much to do," or "I don't want to do that now").

Positive behavioral intervention and support (PBIS) is the vehicle for teaching a student how to behave more appropriately, making appropriate behavior "work" for their communication. In the case of students with severe and multiple disabilities, making PBIS a part of managing behavior across school, home, neighborhood, and community is particularly important (Families and Disability Newsletter, 2001; Horner et al., 2000). The Responsive Instruction on page 485 provides a more detailed discussion of PBIS for students with multiple or severe disabilities.

Early Intervention

Most children with multiple and severe disabilities are identified at birth or soon thereafter because their disabilities are very noticeable to parents, physicians, and/or nurses. Some newborns with severe and multiple disabilities require extensive medical treatment and therefore are immediately placed in **neonatal intensive care units (NICUs)**. NICUs are the equivalent of intensive care units (ICUs) for older children and adults, providing

Authorities agree that parents should be encouraged to spend as much time as possible with the infants being cared for in neonatal intensive care units (NICUs).

Meeting the Needs of Students with Low-Incidence, Multiple, and Severe Disabilities

Positive Behavioral Support[1]

WHAT IS POSITIVE BEHAVIORAL SUPPORT?

Recent reauthorizations of the Individuals with Disabilities Education Act require teachers, school systems, and those involved with students who exhibit challenging behaviors to approach problematic behavior through a mechanism called "positive behavioral support." Positive behavioral support (PBS) refers to the process of identifying alternative, acceptable ways to communicate through teaching more appropriate behaviors and/or changing the environment to reduce the likelihood of prompting the undesirable behavior (Kogel, Kogel, & Dunlap, 1996). This approach to behavior management differs fundamentally from traditional behavior modification plans that focus on the elimination of target behaviors, yet do not take into account possible environmental or personal triggers when doing so. For example, a student's undesirable behavior of banging his head on his desk might be eliminated by placing a baseball cap on his head. Although this might appear to be an acceptable solution, if the student's banging was a sign of boredom or an anxiety-producing peer in the vicinity, the baseball cap solution does not address the function of the behavior, and it is likely that another behavior will manifest in response to the original source of the behavior.

PBS, by contrast, is guided by two fundamental assumptions: (1) Each behavior carries a communicative intent, and (2) typically, multiple factors influence the presence of specific behavior. Interventions based upon these assumptions, therefore, include a functional behavioral assessment (FBA) (Horner, Vaughn, Day, & Ard, 1996). FBA seeks to identify the purpose of the behavior and supporting environmental conditions. The results of such assessment lead to the development of multifaceted plans that can include changing situational events, altering events that immediately precede the behavior, teaching alternative responses to the situation, and providing meaningful reinforcers to promote acceptable responses (Horner et al., 1996).

[1]May also be called positive behavioral intervention and support (PBIS).

APPLYING THE RESEARCH TO TEACHING

Support strategies such as removing high-frustration activities (e.g., difficult assignments, undesirable directives), selecting functional and meaningful (from the student's perspective) curricula, reducing fear or anxiety about a situation through precorrection (e.g., a teacher might suggest what to do when feeling frustrated), teaching more appropriate ways to make requests or express oneself, using behavior modification to reinforce desired behaviors and communicate nonacceptability, and creating activities that build upon student interest and strength are all a part of implementing PBS.

Based on a synthesis of studies that included PBS, the U.S. Office of Special Education Programs makes the following recommendations to support the behavioral needs of individuals with significant disabilities.

- *Respond to individual needs.* Services and programs should be responsive to the preferences, strengths, and needs of individuals with challenging behavior. In addition, students may benefit from instruction in self-determination skills, social skills, goal-setting, and independent learning skills.
- *Alter environments.* If something in the individual's environment influences the challenging behavior, it is important to organize the environment for success. For example, clearly defined work spaces and quiet work areas may assist a child who is noise-sensitive.
- *Teach new skills to the individual with challenging behavior and members of his or her social network.* Individuals need to be taught alternative, appropriate responses that serve the same purpose as the challenging behavior.
- *Appreciate positive behaviors.* It is important to reinforce and acknowledge all positive behaviors consistently. (U.S. Office of Special Education Programs, 1998, p. 1)

● *By Kristin L. Sayeski*

around-the-clock monitoring of bodily functions. The NICU staff consists of several specialists, often including specially trained nurses, physicians, respiratory care practitioners, occupational therapists, and social workers. Because NICUs are expensive to staff and administer, not all hospitals have them; therefore, newborns are sometimes transported from one hospital to another that has a NICU. Even though the infant is under constant medical supervision, most authorities agree that parents should be allowed to spend as much time as possible with their newborns so that bonding can take place between the parents and infant. Some NICUs allow parents to "room in" with their babies.

Other children with severe and multiple disabilities might seem typical at birth but are recognized as having pervasive developmental disabilities within the first couple of years of their lives. In the case of very serious TBI, an individual might actually be developing normally until the event that severely damages her or his brain. Therefore, early intervention should be seen as having two meanings: (1) early in the child's life and (2) as soon as possible after the disability is detected.

The Division for Early Childhood (DEC) of the Council for Exceptional Children (CEC) recommends practices based on six criteria that are considered essential to early intervention programs in special education: (1) research- or value-based practices, (2) family-centered practices, (3) a multicultural perspective, (4) cross-disciplinary collaboration, (5) developmentally and chronologically age-appropriate practices, and (6) adherence to the principle of normalization (McLean & Odom, 1996; see also Bowe, 2004; Gargiulo & Kilgo, 2005; Howard, Williams, & Lepper, 2005; Noonan & McCormick, 2006).

RESEARCH- OR VALUE-BASED PRACTICES Early intervention programs should be based as much as possible on techniques that research has shown to be effective (Morris & Mather, 2008). Unfortunately, it is not always possible to conduct all the necessary research before an approach or technique is adopted. The CEC task force recommended that when research has not provided definitive evidence of an approach's effectiveness, the approach be based on values held by the early childhood special education community. Some of these value-based practices are providing individualized practices for each child and family, communicating with family members in a nonpaternalistic manner and with mutual respect and caring, making center environments safe and clean, and providing opportunities for families to have access to medical decision making.

FAMILY-CENTERED PRACTICES At one time, the prevailing philosophy in early childhood special education programming ignored parents and families at best or viewed them primarily as potential negative influences on the child with disabilities. When early intervention programs did involve parents, the assumption often was that the parents had little to offer and were in need of training to improve their parenting skills. Although it's true that some parents do need to be educated about how to be better parents, to assume that this is always the case is paternalistic and off-putting to the majority of parents, who are very capable. For this reason, authorities now recommend that one not assume that parents have little or nothing to offer with respect to how to work with their children. Instead, they emphasize that parents, siblings, and extended family can be a valuable and integral part of the educational process for young children with disabilities.

As we discussed in Chapters 1, 2, and 4, IDEA also recognizes that parents and families should be central to the educational process for infants and toddlers. The requirement for individualized family service plans (IFSPs), in fact, dictates that the family be central in the decision-making process for the child. A family-centered philosophy means taking into account the particular priorities and needs of the family when an educational intervention plan for the child is being developed.

MULTICULTURAL PERSPECTIVE Given the changing ethnic demographics in the United States, it is critical that all special education programming be culturally sensitive. It's particularly important that early intervention professionals adopt a multicultural perspective because parents are often still coping with the stress of having had their child diagnosed with a disability (McLean & Odom, 1996; Noonan & McCormick, 2006). Having at least someone in the program who can speak the family's language is important. So is communicating respect, caring, and sensitivity. And it's important to provide

Casebook Reflection

REFER TO THE CASE *Who Will Help Patrick?* in your booklet. Patrick is living with his foster mother; however, the living conditions are very grave. How does the issue of family play a significant part in the success of a child with multiple and severe disabilities? ●

services that are unbiased, nondiscriminatory with regard to disability, gender, race, religion, and ethnic and cultural orientation. Perhaps the most important multicultural factor, however, is providing services that are effective (Kauffman, Conroy, Gardner, & Oswald, in press).

CROSS-DISCIPLINARY COLLABORATION Because infants and young children with multiple and severe disabilities by definition have needs in multiple areas, best practice dictates that professionals from several disciplines should be involved. It is critical that these professionals collaborate in a coordinated way to provide high-quality services. There are different kinds of cross-disciplinary models, but the most essential feature for success is that the professionals in each of the disciplines work collaboratively, not independently. Some authorities also recommend that professionals should be willing to share roles.

DEVELOPMENTALLY AND CHRONOLOGICALLY AGE-APPROPRIATE PRACTICES The term **developmentally appropriate practice (DAP)** was first used by the National Association for the Education of Young Children, an organization that focuses on early childhood education for children without disabilities. DAP refers to the practice of using educational methods that are at the developmental levels of the child and that meet the child's individual needs (Bredekamp & Rosegrant, 1992). Many early childhood special educators are in agreement with the notion of DAP, but they believe that it should be balanced with the need for using educational methods that are also chronologically age appropriate. They believe that young children with disabilities should be educated as much as possible alongside their same-age nondisabled peers rather than with much younger nondisabled peers.

■ **Developmentally appropriate practice (DAP)**
Educational methods for young children that are compatible with their developmental levels and that meet their individual needs; coined by the National Association for the Education of Young Children.

PRINCIPLE OF NORMALIZATION As we discussed in Chapter 2, normalization is the philosophical principle that all people with disabilities should have educational and living environments that are as similar as possible to those of people who do not have disabilities. CEC's DEC has adopted the philosophy of inclusion wholeheartedly in their statement on inclusion:

> Inclusion, as a value, supports the right of all children, regardless of their diverse abilities, to participate actively in natural settings within their communities. A natural setting is one in which the child would spend time had he or she not had a disability. (Division for Early Childhood, 1993, as cited in McLean & Odom, 1996, p. 12)

Transition to Adulthood

Transition to adulthood is a critical time for most people with severe and multiple disabilities. Fortunately, as we noted in Chapter 2, the field of special education has made great strides in developing transition services for people with disabilities. Much of this progress has been made because of a change in philosophy about how people with disabilities are treated, and this change is nowhere more evident than in the treatment of people with severe and multiple disabilities. For example, not too long ago, with respect to employment the best that could be hoped for was to be able to place such individuals in a **sheltered workshop**. Now, however, a much wider range of options is available, including, for some people, **competitive employment** alongside workers who are nondisabled.

■ **Sheltered workshop**
A facility that provides a structured environment for people with disabilities in which they can learn skills; can be either a transitional placement or a permanent arrangement.

■ **Competitive employment**
A workplace that provides employment that pays at least minimum wage and in which most workers are nondisabled.

CHANGING PHILOSOPHY We can point to at least two principles of transition programming that reflect the change in philosophy toward treating people with severe

Casebook Reflection

REFER TO THE CASE *Getting to Know Chase* in your booklet. At the end of this case, Chase is about to enter middle school. How might he benefit from early vocational programming? What might you include in his transition plan? ●

■ **Self-determination**
Having control over one's life, not having to rely on others for making choices about one's quality of life; develops over one's life span.

■ **Person-centered plan**
A method of planning for people with disabilities that places the person and his or her family at the center of the planning process.

■ **Natural supports**
Resources in a person's environment that can be used for support, such as friends, family, and coworkers.

■ **Job coach**
A person who assists adult workers with disabilities (especially those with intellectual disabilities), providing vocational assessment, instruction, overall planning, and interaction assistance with employers, family, and related government and service agencies.

■ **Daily living skills**
Skills required for living independently, such as dressing, toileting, bathing, cooking, and other typical daily activities of nondisabled adults.

■ **Individualized education program (IEP)**
IDEA requires an IEP to be drawn up by the educational team for each exceptional child; the IEP must include a statement of present educational performance, instructional goals, educational services to be provided, and criteria and procedures for determining that the instructional objectives are being met.

disabilities with more dignity (Westling & Fox, 2000). First, there is an emphasis on **self-determination**, which

> has been described as "acting as the primary causal agent in one's life and making choices and decisions regarding one's quality of life, free from undue external influence or interference" (Wehmeyer, 1992, p. 305). Self-determination develops over the life span and is associated with reaching adulthood . . . Issues such as accessibility, employment rights, community living, inclusive schooling, mobility, and personal care assistance all stem from the desire of individuals with disabilities to access the activities and lifestyles they desire. (Westling & Fox, 2000, p. 473)

As part of this emphasis on self-determination, professionals have developed a number of **person-centered plans**, which focus on the student's preferences and those of her or his family in planning for the future (Snell & Brown, 2006). Although person-centered planning is now part of most programs for people with severe disabilities, some have suggested that such plans are not particularly beneficial (e.g., Osborne, 2005).

Second, authorities now recommend that natural supports be an integral part of transition planning. Rather than always creating new services for a person's particular needs, the notion of **natural supports** is to try first to find available resources that already exist in the workplace or the community. With respect to work, this might mean training coworkers to provide assistance rather than immediately assuming that a **job coach** is required. With respect to community living, this might mean having the person with a disability living in an apartment, with assistance in **daily living skills** from a neighbor, family member, or paid attendant, rather than living in a residential facility with attendants.

VOCATIONAL PROGRAMMING   As we stated in Chapter 2, a student's **individualized education program (IEP)** must contain a transition plan, beginning no later than age sixteen (and by age fourteen when appropriate). The transition plan should contain recommendations for how to ready the student for the world of work and/or for postsecondary education or training.

For many students with severe and multiple disabilities, it's advisable that vocational training actually begin in elementary school because it might take several years to

There is a growing range of employment options available to persons with severe and multiple disabilities, including sheltered workshops, but also competitive environments alongside workers who do not have disabilities.

acquire all the skills they'll need to hold down a job successfully. In elementary school, the training might consist of such things as learning to keep on schedule, building social skills, performing worklike tasks (e.g., helping to take attendance, collecting lunch money), and beginning to learn about different types of jobs.

In secondary school, the focus shifts to involving the student in actual work situations in the community with the help of a job coach. The student should be involved in selecting these placements, and there should be enough variety in the jobs that the student gets a good sample of what kinds of jobs are available and what he or she is good at and likes. In the early stages, this might involve the student volunteering in several different types of placements. Later, it is preferable that the student engage in paid work placements. Being paid adds to the reality of the experience and provides an opportunity for the student to learn how to handle finances.

COMMUNITY AND DOMESTIC LIVING SKILLS   As we noted in Chapter 5, community living skills involve such things as using transportation, shopping, using telephones, managing money, and using the Internet. Domestic living skills include such things as preparing meals, doing laundry, housekeeping, yard maintenance, and so forth. At one time, community living skills were taught primarily or solely in classroom settings. In other words, teachers arranged their classroom to simulate a community setting, such as an aisle in a grocery store. Authorities now believe that simulations are much inferior to using real community settings (Westling & Fox, 2000). The best place to teach domestic living skills, however, is not necessarily in the student's home. Because students aren't that far away from the time when they will move out of their parents' home and because teaching domestic skills is often done in small groups, there are some advantages to using a setting other than their own home. Thus, domestic living skills are often taught in a school setting, such as the home economics classroom and the school cafeteria.

Another reason for using the school as the instructional setting some of the time is to ensure that the student with disabilities has a chance to interact with peers who do not have disabilities (Browder & Bambara, 2000; Moon & Inge, 2000; Snell & Brown, 2006). Inclusion in regular school programs provides social opportunities for students, and social skills are critical for successful integration into the community and workplace.

The last thirty to forty years have brought enormous strides in preparing people with multiple and severe disabilities to lead productive lives as adults. It wasn't that long ago that people with multiple and severe disabilities were housed in large residential institutions and had minimal contact with the public. Today, with intensive and extensive instruction and the support of professionals and the community, many of them can aspire to work alongside nondisabled persons and live independently or semi-independently by themselves or in a small **community residential facility (CRF)**.

■ **Community residential facility (CRF)**
A place, usually a group home, in an urban or residential neighborhood where about three to ten adults with intellectual disabilities live under supervision.

Summary

What is the definition of low-incidence, multiple, and severe disabilities, and what is their prevalence?

▶ Low-incidence, multiple, and severe disabilities are those that occur relatively infrequently and require extensive support in more than one major life activity, such as mobility, communication, self-care, independent living, employment, and self-sufficiency. Probably 1 percent or fewer of all learners have such low-incidence, multiple, or severe disabilities.

What is traumatic brain injury, and how might it affect education?

▶ Traumatic brain injury (TBI) is injury to the brain resulting in total or partial disability or psychosocial maladjustment that affects educational performance.

■ It may be the result of closed head injuries or open head injuries.

■ It may affect cognition, language, memory, attention, reasoning, abstract thinking, judgment, problem solving, sensory or perceptual and motor disabilities, psychosocial behavior, physical functions, information processing, or speech, all of which are important in school.

How is deaf-blindness defined, and what are the special educational problems it entails?

▶ Deaf-blindness is defined by significant impairments in both hearing and seeing, although the individual may have some residual hearing or sight.

■ It may be caused by a variety of genetic and chromosomal syndromes, prenatal conditions, and postnatal conditions.

■ The person who is deaf-blind has difficulty accessing information, communicating, and navigating the environment.

■ It requires direct teaching, structured routines, and emphasis on communication and mobility.

What considerations apply to many students with low-incidence, multiple, and severe disabilities?

▶ Communication, behavior management, early intervention, and transition to adulthood are concerns that apply to many learners with these disabilities.

■ Augmentative or alternative communication (AAC) is important for those who can't communicate effectively through speech.

■ Common behavior problems requiring special management include self-stimulation, self-injury, tantrums, aggression toward others, lack of daily living skills, all of which may require functional behavioral assessment and positive behavioral support.

■ Early intervention should be based on both research and values and be family-centered, multicultural, cross-disciplinary, age-appropriate, and feature normalization.

■ Transition to adulthood should honor the concepts of person-centered planning and natural supports, feature vocational programming, and include community and domestic living skills.

STANDARDS and PRINCIPLES in this Chapter

SPECIAL EDUCATORS . . .

■ understand the field as an evolving and changing discipline (from CEC Content Standard #1).

■ understand the similarities and differences in human development and the characteristics between and among individuals with and without exceptional learning needs (from CEC Content Standard #2).

■ possess a repertoire of evidence-based instructional strategies (from CEC Content Standard #4).

■ create learning environments for individuals with exceptional learning needs that foster cultural understanding, safety and emotional well-being, positive social interactions, and active engagement of individuals with exceptional learning needs (from CEC Content Standard #5).

■ are familiar with technologies to support and enhance communication of individuals with exceptional needs (from CEC Content Standard #6).

■ develop a variety of individualized transition plans (from CEC Content Standard #7).

■ use collaboration to facilitate successful transitions of individuals with exceptional learning needs (from CEC Content Standard #10).

ALL TEACHERS . . .

■ understand the central concepts, tools of inquiry, structures of the discipline(s) they teach and can create learning experiences that make these aspects of subject matter meaningful (INTASC Principle #1).

■ understand how children learn and develop and can provide learning opportunities that support the intellectual, social and personal development of each learner (INTASC Principle #2).

■ understand and use a variety of instructional strategies to encourage students' development of critical thinking, problem solving, and performance skills (INTASC Principle #4).

■ use an understanding of individual and group motivation and behavior to create a learning environment that encourages positive social interaction, active engagement in learning, and self-motivation (INTASC Principle #5).

■ use knowledge of effective verbal, nonverbal, and media communication technologies to foster active inquiry, collaboration, and supportive interaction in the classroom (INTASC Principle #6).

■ plan instruction based on knowledge of subject matter, students, the community and curriculum goals (INTASC Principle #7).

■ create a learning environment that encourages positive social interaction, active engagement in learning, and self-motivation (INTASC Principle #10).

Applying the **STANDARDS** and **PRINCIPLES**

- ■ WHAT do you think teachers should be most aware of as they think about implementing instructional strategies to meet the academic needs of students with severe and multiple disabilities? (CEC Content Standards #1, #2, & #3 & INTASC Principles #1, #2, & #3)

- ■ WHAT are the benefits of functional behavioral assessment (FBA) and positive behavior intervention and support (PBIS)? (CEC Content Standard #5 & INTASC Principle #5)

- ■ THE parents of a young child with severe and multiple disabilities express concern about their child's difficulties. They are most concerned about their child's inability to communicate. What would you tell them? (CEC Content Standard #6 & INTASC Principle #6)

- ■ WHAT can individuals with severe and multiple disabilities expect as they transition to adulthood? (CEC Content Standards #7 & #10 & INTASC Principles #7 & #10)

Now go to the Hallahan/Kauffman, Eleventh Edition MyEducationLab course at www.myeducationlab.com to:

- • take a Pretest to assess your initial comprehension of the chapter content;
- • study chapter content with your Individualized Study Plan;
- • take a Posttest to assess your understanding of chapter content;
- • engage in multimedia exercises to help you build a deeper and more applied understanding of chapter content.

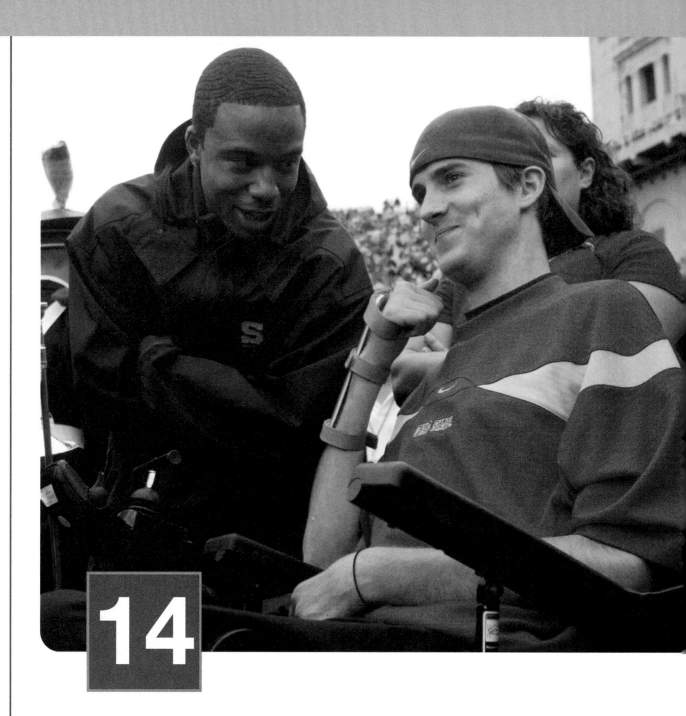

14

Learners with Physical Disabilities and Other Health Impairments

Jim trudged down the steps and across the yard. He felt mad at the world. He was angry at the uncles for bringing him up here, and mad at Mama for letting him come. He thought about going to wait in the truck for the uncles to come back, but his legs wouldn't stop moving down the slope of the yard. Penn had been to the top of the Empire State Building. Penn had been to Independence Hall. Jim had no idea what to say to a boy who had seen the things Penn had seen. And he had no idea what to say to a boy who had polio. When he walked past the rocking chairs, his stomach dropped as if he had jumped off of something high. He took a deep breath and turned around. "Hey, Penn," he said.

"Hey, Jim," said Penn.

The two boys stared at each other and grinned, then shook hands awkwardly, as if a grown-up were making them do it. Jim looked down at Penn's legs before he could stop himself. Penn slapped his right leg twice with an open palm.

"It's this one," he said. "I can't move this one."

"Oh," Jim said. "I'm sorry."

Penn shrugged. "It's okay," he said. "It could've been a lot worse." He kicked his left leg straight out. "This one's fine."

—Tony Earley
Jim the Boy

QUESTIONS to guide your reading of this chapter . . .

- How are physical disabilities defined and classified?
- What is the prevalence of physical disabilities, and what is the need for special education?
- What are some major neuromotor impairments?
- What are some major orthopedic and musculoskeletal disorders?
- What other conditions affect health or physical ability?
- How can physical disabilities be prevented?
- What are the psychological and behavioral characteristics of individuals with physical disabilities?
- What are prosthetics, orthotics, and adaptive devices?
- What are the major educational considerations for students with physical disabilities?
- Why is early intervention important, and on what should it focus?
- What are the major issues in transition for students with physical disabilities?

Learners with Physical Disabilities and Other Health Impairments

MYTH ■ Cerebral palsy is a contagious disease.

FACT ■ Cerebral palsy is not a disease. It's a nonprogressive neurological injury. It's a disorder of muscle control and coordination caused by injury to the brain before or during birth or in early childhood.

MYTH ■ Physical disabilities of all kinds are decreasing because of medical advances.

FACT ■ Because of advances in medical technology, the number of children with severe disabilities is increasing. The number of survivors of serious medical conditions who develop normally or have mild impairments, such as hyperactivity and learning disabilities, is also increasing.

MYTH ■ The greatest educational problem involving children with physical disabilities is highly specialized instruction.

FACT ■ The greatest educational problem is teaching people without disabilities about what it's like to have a disability and how disabilities can be accommodated.

MYTH ■ The more severe a person's physical disability, the lower is his or her intelligence.

FACT ■ A person can be severely physically disabled by cerebral palsy or another condition but have a brilliant mind.

MYTH ■ People with epilepsy are mentally ill.

FACT ■ People with epilepsy (seizure disorder) aren't any more or less disposed to mental illness than are those who don't have epilepsy.

MYTH ■ Arthritis is found only in adults, particularly those who are elderly.

FACT ■ Arthritic conditions are found in people of any age, including young children.

MYTH ■ People with physical disabilities have no need for sexual expression.

FACT ■ People with physical disabilities have normal sexual urges and need outlets for sexual expression.

MYTH ■ Physical disabilities shape people's personalities.

FACT ■ People with physical disabilities have the full range of personality characteristics found among those who don't have physical disabilities. There are no particular personality characteristics associated with physical disability.

MYTH ■ If a child with a physical disability such as cerebral palsy or spina bifida learns to walk as a young child, then he or she will maintain that ability throughout life.

FACT ■ Continuing intervention through adolescence and adulthood—the entire life span—is required in many cases. Unless they have continued support for ambulation, adolescents or adults might find walking much more difficult or give up walking, even if they learned to walk as children.

In Western culture, many people are almost obsessed with their bodies. They don't just want to be healthy and strong; they want to be beautiful—well formed and attractive to others. In fact, some people seem to be more concerned about the impression their bodies make than they are about their own well being. They might even endanger their health in an effort to become more physically alluring. It isn't really surprising, then, that people with physical disabilities must fight two battles: the battle to overcome the limitations imposed by their physical conditions and the battle to be accepted by others.

Individuals with physical disabilities or differences are often stared at, feared, teased, socially rejected, or treated cruelly. This has been the case throughout history, and it remains true today (see Holmes, 2004 and Metzeler, 2006 for historical perspectives). Sometimes people feel embarrassed about someone else's disability, not seeming to understand the feelings of the person who has the disability. Or people might feel that an acquired physical disability must change someone's personality dramatically. In Tony Earley's (2000) story about Jim and his friend Penn, who had polio, we see Jim's mixed feelings of anger and fear when seeing his pal for the first time after Penn was paralyzed (see p. 493). We probably expect Jim's mixture of anger, fear, and inquisitiveness from a ten-year-old—wondering about death, the permanence of disability, how it feels to have the disability, and so on. But most of us have such feelings and questions, regardless of our age. And most people with physical disabilities share Penn's matter-of-factness and eagerness to be accepted and get on with life.

Although polio has been virtually eradicated by vaccination, many other causes of partial paralysis and other physical disabilities haven't been eliminated. Attitudes toward physical disabilities have not changed much in many ways, nor have the problems of having physical disabilities. Consider the Personal Perspectives of Chandler Pascale (page 496). Children with physical disabilities often face more than the problem of acceptance. For many, accomplishing the simple tasks of everyday living seems a minor—or major—miracle.

Video Homework Exercise

Physical Disabilities ● Go to the Homework and Exercises section in Chapter 14 of MyEducationLab to watch the video "Physical Disabilities."

Definition and Classification

In this chapter, we consider children whose primary distinguishing characteristics are health or physical problems. *Children with physical disabilities or other health impairments* are those whose physical limitations or health problems interfere with school attendance or learning to such an extent that special services, training, equipment, materials, or facilities are required. They are also sometimes referred to as "*children with special health care needs*" (Giardino, Kohrt, Arye, & Wells, 2002, p. 707).

Children who have physical disabilities might also have other disabilities of any type or special gifts or talents. Thus, the characteristics of children with physical disabilities are extremely varied. The child's physical condition is the proper concern of the medical profession, but when physical problems have obvious implications for education, teaching specialists are needed. The fact that the primary distinguishing characteristics of children with physical disabilities are medical conditions, health problems, or physical limitations highlights the necessity of interdisciplinary cooperation. There must be communication between physicians and special educators to maintain the child's health and at the same time develop whatever capabilities the child has (Best, Heller, & Bigge, 2005).

Physical disabilities occur with tremendous variety. Children may have **congenital anomalies** (defects they are born with), or they may acquire disabilities through accident or disease after birth. Some physical disabilities are comparatively mild and transitory; others are profound and progressive, ending in total incapacitation and early death. Some are chronic diseases that are increasingly common (DeAngelis, 2007). It is difficult to discuss physical disabilities in general; this chapter is organized around specific conditions that fall into one of three categories: neuromotor impairments, orthopedic and musculoskeletal disorders, and other conditions that affect health or physical ability.

▪ **Congenital anomaly**
An irregularity (anomaly) that is present at birth; might or might not be due to genetic factors.

Personal PERSPECTIVES

Student with Cerebral Palsy Challenges Perspectives
Stung by slights from classmates, teen writes column in response

Associated Press

SPOTSYLVANIA—Chandler Pascale got tired of the nasty comments.

It was bad enough that some students snickered behind his back about the way he walked. But when they yelled at him to get out of the way and called him names like "retard," Chandler did something about it.

The 15-year-old, who moves slower than others because he has cerebral palsy, wrote a column in his school paper.

"Lately, I have heard people laugh at me, mock me, cuss me out [which I may add is an act of the purest cowardice] and plainly insult me right to my face," he wrote. "To stab me in the back when you think I can't hear or see you is like spitting in my face."

The column appeared in the December 2006 issue of the Lightning Bolt, Chancellor High School's newspaper.

It generated a lot of feedback, said adviser Tom Panarese.

Several people wrote letters to the editor, and at least one teacher read the column to all her classes.

Ninth-grader Courtnie Wolfe was among those who showed the story to friends and parents.

"I thought it was heartbreaking," Courtnie said, "I didn't realize it was that bad. It must have taken a lot of courage for him to do that."

Editor-in-chief Phylicia Foster said she always considered Chandler, a sophomore, one of the best writers on staff. She has a new respect for him now.

When classmates said they felt bad for Chandler, Phylicia told them not to feel sorry for him, but to treat him like an individual.

That's all he's ever wanted.

Positive attitude

Chandler was born prematurely with a disease that affects the messages the brain sends to the legs.

Still, he moves through Chancellor's hallways at a good clip without a cane or walker.

He had a key to the school elevator but gave it back. He doesn't ask to leave class a few minutes early to beat the rush, and he won't ride the handicapped bus.

"I want to be like everybody else," Chandler said. "That's extremely important."

When the bell rings for a class change, Chandler waits for the rush to die down before he ventures into the hallways. He usually

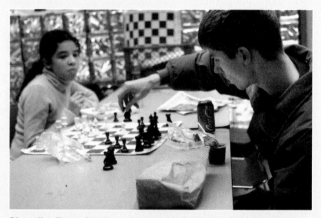

Chandler Pascale plays chess with freshman Maria Valentin during lunch at their Spotsylvania school. Chandler, who moves slower than others because he has cerebral palsy, wrote a column in his school paper about his disability.

packs lunch because school food doesn't appeal to him and to avoid cafeteria lines.

On a recent day, he barely spoke to anyone during or between classes.

He's a hard worker, said Mary Ann Lopez, who taught Chandler Spanish last year.

Uphill battle

He also has faced more than his share of hardships. He's had several painful operations.

His father abandoned him when he was a baby, and his mother died of a brain aneurysm when he was 7.

Chandler lives with his grandparents, Joe and Alice Pascale, in Salem Fields.

Since the column, he believes things have gotten better and people have become more understanding.

"They don't ignore me," Chandler said. "They just leave me be."

That's the way he likes it.

English teacher Lisa McCrary read Chandler's column to her classes and said her students connected to him—for an instant.

"But it's faded," she said, sadly. "I think it did touch them for a moment, a high-school moment."

Source: "Student with cerebral palsy challenges perspectives" by the Associated Press. *Charlottesville Daily Progress,* Charlottesville, VA, March 2, 2007, p. A5. Reprinted with permission.

It's important to make distinctions between conditions that are acute or chronic and between those that are episodic or progressive. An **acute** illness or condition may be very serious or severe, but with treatment (which may include hospitalization or medication) it resolves, and the person recovers. Someone with a serious infection or who has a serious accident may, for example, become acutely ill or be in critical condition for a time but recover. However, a **chronic** condition is ongoing. It does not resolve, even with the best treatment; it is an incurable condition. Cerebral palsy is chronic; it can't be cured. An **episodic** condition is one that recurs, although most of the time the individual can function quite normally. Its occurrence is limited primarily to successive episodes. The episodes don't necessarily become more serious or severe over time. Asthma and seizure disorders (epilepsy), for example, tend to be episodic. However, a **progressive** condition is one that becomes more and more serious or severe over time, usually involving more and more complications or deterioration. Muscular dystrophy is an example of a physical problem that is usually progressive.

Prevalence and Need

About 0.9 percent of the population ages six to seventeen (roughly 435,000 students in U.S. public schools) are being served under two special education categories related to physical disabilities. About 0.14 percent (approximately 70,000) of these have orthopedic disabilities, and 0.76 percent (about 365,000) have other health problems (U.S. Department of Education, 2005). This doesn't include students with traumatic brain injury or multiple disabilities or young children who are said to have a developmental delay. The needs of many students with physical disabilities are unmet because the number of children and youths with such disabilities is growing, and health and social service programs aren't keeping up.

Statistics reported by the U.S. Department of Education (2005) show a dramatic increase from the early 1990s to 2004 in the percentage of the school population served by special education due to health problems. Increases in the prevalence might be due in part to improvements in the identification of, and medical services to, children with certain conditions. Ironically, medical advances have not only improved the chances of preventing or curing certain diseases and disorders, but also assured the survival of more children with severe medical problems—just as improved medical care means that more combat soldiers are surviving grievous wounds. Many children with severe and multiple disabilities and those with severe, chronic illnesses or severe injuries, who in the past wouldn't have survived long, today can have a normal life span. Declining mortality rates don't necessarily mean that there will be fewer individuals with disabilities. Moreover, improvements in medical care might not lower the number of individuals with disabilities unless there is also a lowering of risk factors in the environment—factors such as accidents, toxic substances, poverty, malnutrition, disease, and interpersonal violence.

Neuromotor Impairments

Neuromotor impairment is caused by injury to the brain or spinal cord (neurological damage) that also affects the ability to move parts of one's body (motor impairment). It may be associated with injury to the brain before, during, or after birth. **Traumatic brain injury (TBI)**, which we discussed in Chapter 13, involves brain damage with an identifiable external cause (trauma) after birth. However, brain injury can be acquired from a variety of

---

Casebook Reflections

REFER TO THE CASE *Praying for a Miracle* in your booklet. Peter is very capable academically but suffers from muscular dystrophy. How does his case show the complexities of harmonizing the needs of a child's academic abilities with the needs of a child's disability, which in this case is progressive? ●

■ **Acute**
A serious state of illness or injury from which someone often recovers with treatment.

■ **Chronic**
A permanent condition; not temporary.

■ **Episodic**
Occurring in episodes; a temporary condition that will pass but may recur.

■ **Progressive**
A disease or condition that worsens over time and from which one seldom or never recovers with treatment.

UNDERSTANDING THE STANDARDS AND PRINCIPLES What do we know about the causes and types of neuromotor impairments? (CEC Knowledge and Skill Standard PH2K2)

Council for Exceptional Children

■ **Traumatic brain injury (TBI)**
Injury to the brain (not including conditions present at birth, birth trauma, or degenerative diseases or conditions) resulting in total or partial disability or psychosocial maladjustment that affects educational performance; may affect cognition, language, memory, attention, reasoning, abstract thinking, judgment, problem solving, sensory or perceptual and motor disabilities, psychosocial behavior, physical functions, information processing, or speech.

nontraumatic causes as well: hypoxia (reduced oxygen to the brain, as might occur in near drowning), infection of the brain or its linings, stroke, tumor, metabolic disorder (such as may occur with diabetes, liver disease, or kidney disease), or toxic chemicals or drugs.

In many cases of brain damage, it's impossible to identify the exact cause of the neuromotor impairment. The important point is that when a child's nervous system is damaged, no matter what the cause, muscular weakness or paralysis is almost always one of the symptoms. Because these children can't move about like most others, their education typically requires special equipment, special procedures, or other accommodations for their disabilities.

Cerebral Palsy

Cerebral palsy (CP) is not a disease. It's not contagious, it's not progressive (although improper treatment can lead to complications), and there are no remissions. Martin (2006) offers a succinct definition:

> Cerebral palsy is a disorder of movement and posture. It is caused by a brain injury that occurred before birth, during birth, or during the first few years after birth. The injury hinders the brain's ability to control the muscles of the body properly. The brain tells our muscles how to move and controls the tension of the muscles. Without the proper messages coming from the brain, infants with cerebral palsy have difficulty learning basic motor skills such as crawling, sitting up, or walking. (p. 2)

However, CP is actually more complicated than an impairment of movement and posture, as Martin (2006) and others recognize. For practical purposes, CP can be considered part of a syndrome that includes motor dysfunction, psychological dysfunction, seizures, and emotional or behavioral disorders due to brain damage (see also Pellegrino, 2002).

Some individuals with CP show only one indication of brain damage, such as motor impairment; others show combinations of symptoms. The usual definition of CP refers to paralysis, weakness, lack of coordination, and/or other motor dysfunction because of damage to the child's brain before it has matured. Symptoms can be so mild that they are

■ **Cerebral palsy (CP)**
A condition characterized by paralysis, weakness, lack of coordination, and/or other motor dysfunction; caused by damage to the brain before it has matured.

Reading Homework Exercise

Cerebral Palsy ● Go to the Homework and Exercises section in Chapter 14 of MyEducationLab to access information about a man named Dan Keplinger, an artist with cerebral palsy.

Advances in medical and rehabilitation technology offer increasing hope of overcoming disabilities associated with cerebral palsy.

detected only with difficulty or so profound that the individual is almost completely incapacitated. Because CP includes such a heterogeneous group of children, the label *cerebral palsy* has been called into question by some. Others have noted that the label "defines groups of children who are desperately in need of a service, and this seems an adequate ground" for continuing to use the label (Bax, 2001, p. 75).

Although there is no cure for CP, advances in medical and rehabilitation technology offer increasing hope of overcoming the disabilities resulting from neurological damage. For example, intensive long-term physical therapy in combination with a surgical procedure in which the surgeon cuts selected nerve roots below the spinal cord that cause spasticity in the leg muscles allows some children with spastic CP to better control certain muscles. Such treatment allows some nonambulatory children to walk and helps others to walk more normally. However, the fact that children are enabled to walk doesn't mean that they will be able to walk all their lives. Continued services might be required if they are to continue walking as adults (Bottos, Feliciangeli, Sciuto, Gericke, & Vianello, 2001).

CAUSES AND TYPES   Anything that can damage the brain during its development can cause CP. Before birth, maternal infections, chronic diseases, physical trauma, or maternal exposure to toxic substances or X-rays, for example, can damage the brain of the fetus. During the birth process, the brain can be injured, especially if labor or birth is difficult or complicated. Premature birth, hypoxia, high fever, infections, poisoning, hemorrhaging, and related factors can cause harm after birth. In short, anything that results in oxygen deprivation, poisoning, cerebral bleeding, or direct trauma to the brain can be a possible cause of CP.

Although CP occurs at every social level, it is more often seen in children born to mothers in poor socioeconomic circumstances. Children who live in such circumstances have a greater risk of incurring brain damage because of such factors as malnutrition of the mother, poor prenatal and postnatal care, environmental hazards during infancy, and low birthweight. However, the prevalence of CP in children with very low birthweight has declined in recent years due to better treatment of premature infants (Robertson, Watt, & Yasui, 2007).

The two most widely accepted means of classification specify the limbs that are involved and the type of motor disability. Some individuals have a mixture of various types of CP. Classification according to the extremities involved applies not just to CP but to all types of motor disability or paralysis. The most common classifications are **quadriplegia** (all four limbs are involved) and **paraplegia** (only the legs are involved).

Likewise, classification by type of movement applies not only to CP, but also to other types of neuromotor disabilities. **Spasticity** refers to stiffness or tenseness of muscles and inaccurate voluntary movement. **Choreoathetoid** is the term applied to abrupt, involuntary movements and difficulty maintaining balance. **Atonic** refers to floppiness or lack of muscle tone.

The important point about CP is that the brain damage affects strength and the ability to move parts of the body normally. The difficulty of movement may involve the limbs as well as the muscles involving facial expressions and speech. As a result, someone with CP might have difficulty moving or speaking or might exhibit facial contortions or drooling. But these results of brain damage don't necessarily mean that the person's intelligence or emotional sensitivity has been affected by the damage affecting muscle control (again, consider the Personal Perspectives of Chandler Pascale on p. 496).

ASSOCIATED DISABILITIES AND EDUCATIONAL IMPLICATIONS   CP is a developmental disability—a multidisabling condition that is far more complex than a motor disability alone. When the brain is damaged, sensory abilities, cognitive functions, and emotional responsiveness as well as motor performance are usually affected. A high proportion of children with CP are found to have hearing impairments, visual impairments, perceptual disorders, speech problems, emotional or behavioral disorders, intellectual disability (mental retardation), or some combination of several of these disabling conditions

INTERNET RESOURCES

The United Cerebral Palsy Association provides information and resources for people with CP and their families: www.ucp.org

■ Quadriplegia
 A condition in which all four limbs are paralyzed

■ Paraplegia
 A condition in which both legs are paralyzed.

■ Spasticity
 Characterized by muscle stiffness and problems in voluntary movement; associated with spastic cerebral palsy.

■ Choreoathetoid
 Characterized by involuntary movements and difficulty with balance; associated with choreoathetoid cerebral palsy.

■ Atonic
 Lack of muscle tone; floppiness.

in addition to motor disability. They might also exhibit such characteristics as drooling or facial contortions.

Some individuals with CP have normal or above-average intellectual capacity, and a few test within the gifted range. Nevertheless, the average tested intelligence of children with CP is lower than the average for the general population. We must be very cautious in interpreting the test results of children with CP, however, as many standardized tests of intelligence and achievement might be inappropriate for individuals with special difficulties in perception, movement, or response speed. Furthermore, the movement problems of a child with CP might become more apparent when the child is in a state of emotional arousal or stress; this can complicate using typical testing procedures, which tend to be demanding and stressful.

The educational problems of children who have CP are as multifaceted as their disabilities. Not only do these children need special equipment and procedures because of their physical disabilities, but they often require the same special educational procedures and equipment as children with vision, hearing, or communication disorders, learning disabilities, emotional or behavioral disorders, or intellectual disability. Careful and continuous educational assessment of the individual child's capabilities is particularly important. Teaching the child who has CP demands competence in many aspects of special education and experience in working with a variety of disabling conditions in a multidisciplinary setting (Best et al., 2005; Martin, 2006).

Seizure Disorder (Epilepsy)

▪ **Seizure (convulsion)**
A sudden alteration of consciousness, usually accompanied by motor activity and/or sensory phenomena; caused by an abnormal discharge of electrical energy in the brain.

▪ **Epilepsy**
A pattern of repeated seizures.

INTERNET RESOURCES

More information about epilepsy is available at www.efa.org

A person has a **seizure** when there is an abnormal discharge of electrical energy in certain brain cells. The discharge spreads to nearby cells, and the effect may be loss of consciousness, involuntary movements, or abnormal sensory phenomena. The effects of the seizure depends on the location of the cells in which the discharge starts and how far the discharge spreads.

About one in ten children has a seizure at some time, usually associated with a high fever or serious illness (Weinstein, 2002). However, this does not mean that one in ten children has epilepsy. A person with **epilepsy** has a chronic neurological condition and has *recurrent* seizures (Arzimanoglou, Guerrini, & Aicardi, 2004; Weinstein, 2002). Because seizures reflect abnormal brain activity, it's not surprising that they occur more often in children with developmental disabilities (e.g., intellectual disability or cerebral palsy) than in children without disabilities (Best et al., 2005).

CAUSES AND TYPES Seizures are caused by damage to the brain. As brain imaging and molecular biology advance, scientists are arriving at a better understanding of risk for epilepsy (Avoli, Rogawski, & Avanzini, 2001; Barkovich, 2005). The most common immediate causes include lack of sufficient oxygen (hypoxia), low blood sugar (hypoglycemia), infections, and physical trauma. Certain conditions, such as those just listed, tend to increase the chances that neurochemical reactions will be set off in brain cells (Vining & Freeman, 1996). In many cases, the causes are unknown. Some types of seizures may be progressive; that is, they may damage the brain or disrupt its functioning in such a way that having a seizure increases the probability of having another. Even though the cause of seizures isn't well understood, it's important to note that with proper medication, most people's seizures can be controlled.

Seizures can take many forms; neurologists debate the best way to classify seizures (e.g., Parra, Augustijn, Geerts, & Boas, 2001). However, educators should note that seizures may differ along at least the following dimensions:

- *Duration*: Seizures may last only a few seconds or for several minutes.
- *Frequency*: Seizures may occur as frequently as every few minutes or only about once a year.

- *Onset*: Seizures may be set off by certain identifiable stimuli or be unrelated to the environment, and they may be totally unexpected or be preceded by certain internal sensations.

- *Movements*: Seizures may cause major convulsive movements or only minor motor symptoms (e.g., eye blinks).

- *Causes*: Seizures may be caused by a variety of conditions, including high fever, poisoning, trauma, and other conditions mentioned previously; but in many cases, the causes are unknown.

- *Associated disabilities*: Seizures may be associated with other disabling conditions or be unrelated to any other medical problem or disability.

- *Control*: Seizures may be controlled completely by drugs, so that the individual has no more seizures, or they may be only partially controlled.

EDUCATIONAL IMPLICATIONS   About half of all children with seizure disorders have average or higher intelligence—just as is true for the general population. Among those without intellectual disability, however, there seems to be a higher-than-usual incidence of learning disabilities (Arzimanoglou et al., 2004; Besag, 1995). Although many children who have seizure disorders have other disabilities, some don't. Consequently, both general and special education teachers can expect to encounter children who have seizures (see Spiegel, Cutler, & Yetter, 1996).

Besides obtaining medical advice about management of the child's particular seizure disorder, teachers should know first aid for epileptic seizures (see Focus on Concepts, p. 502). Ignorance about the causes of seizures and about first aid are among the most common misconceptions about epilepsy (Arzimanoglou et al., 2004; Gouvier, Brown, Prestholdt, Hayes, & Apostolas, 1995; Weinstein, 2002).

Seizures are primarily a medical problem and require primarily medical attention; The responsibilities of educators are:

1. General and special education teachers need to help dispel ignorance, superstition, and prejudice toward people who have seizures and provide calm management for the occasional seizure the child may have at school (Spiegel et al., 1996).

2. Special education teachers who work with students with severe intellectual disability or teach children with other severe developmental disabilities need to be prepared to manage more frequent seizures as well as to handle learning problems. The teacher should record the length of a child's seizure and the type of activity the child was engaged in before it occurred. This information will help physicians in diagnosis and treatment. If a student is being treated for a seizure disorder, the teacher should know the type of medication and its possible side effects (Best et al., 2005).

Some children who don't have intellectual disability but have seizures exhibit learning and behavior problems. These problems might result from damage to the brain that causes other disabilities as well, or they might be the side effects of anticonvulsant medication or the result of mismanagement by parents and teachers. Teachers must be aware that seizures of any type can interfere with the child's attention or the continuity of education. Brief seizures might require the teacher to repeat instructions or allow the child extra time to respond. Frequent major convulsions might prevent even a bright child from achieving at the usual rate.

Many students with epilepsy have no learning problems at all. However, some do have learning disabilities, and children with epilepsy have emotional or behavioral disorders more often than those without epilepsy. In fact, *Epilepsia*, the journal of the International League Against Epilepsy, devoted an entire special issue to learning disabilities

FOCUS ON **Concepts**

First Aid for Epileptic Seizures

A major epileptic seizure is often dramatic and frightening. It lasts only a few minutes, however, and does not require expert care. These simple procedures should be followed:

■ Remain calm. You cannot stop a seizure once it has started. Let the seizure run its course. Do not try to revive the individual.

■ If the person is upright, ease him or her to the floor and loosen his or her clothing.

■ Try to prevent the individual from striking his or her head or body against any hard, sharp, or hot objects; but do not otherwise interfere with movement.

■ Turn the individual's face to the side so that saliva can flow out of the mouth.

■ Do not insert anything between the individual's teeth.

■ Do not be alarmed if the individual seems to stop breathing momentarily.

■ After the movements stop and the person is relaxed, allow him or her to sleep or rest if he or she wishes.

■ It isn't generally necessary to call a doctor unless the attack is followed almost immediately by another seizure or the seizure lasts more than ten minutes.

■ Notify the parents, guardians, or next of kin that a seizure has occurred.

■ After a seizure, many people can carry on as before. If, after resting, the individual seems groggy, confused, or weak, it may be a good idea to accompany him or her home.

Source: Courtesy of Epilepsy Foundation of America.

(Ayala, Elia, Cornaggia, & Trimble, 2001). If children with epilepsy do have problems in school, their school adjustment can be improved dramatically if they are properly assessed, placed, counseled, taught about seizures, and given appropriate work assignments. The quality of life of children with epilepsy is related to the same risk factors that affect quality of life for others with disabilities, including problems with **executive function** (see Chapter 7), problems with **adaptive behavior** (see Chapter 5), low IQ, psychosocial difficulties, low family income, and early age of onset (Sherman, Slick, & Eyrl, 2006).

Spina Bifida and Other Spinal Cord Injuries

Neurological damage can involve only the spinal cord, leaving the brain unaffected. Spinal cord injury can occur before or after birth, affecting the individual's ability to move or control bodily functions below the site of the injury (Best et al., 2005).

During early fetal development, the two halves of the embryo grow together or fuse at the midline. Incomplete closure results in congenital midline defects such as cleft lip and cleft palate. **Spina bifida** is a congenital midline defect that results from failure of the bony spinal column to close completely during fetal development. It is one type of **neural tube defect** (a malformation of the spine, spinal cord, or brain; see Barkovich, 2005; Liptak, 2002). The defect may occur anywhere from the head to the lower end of the spine. Because the spinal column is not closed, the spinal cord (nerve fibers) can protrude, resulting in damage to the nerves and paralysis and/or lack of function or sensation below the site of the defect.

Spina bifida is often accompanied by paralysis of the legs and of the anal and bladder sphincters because nerve impulses are not able to travel past the defect. Surgery to close the spinal opening is performed in early infancy, but this doesn't repair the nerve damage. Although spina bifida is one of the most common birth defects resulting in physical disability, its causes are not known.

■ **Executive function**
The ability to regulate one's behavior through working memory, inner speech, control of emotions and arousal levels, and analysis of problems and communication of problem solutions to others; delayed or impaired in people with ADHD.

■ **Adaptive behavior**
The social and practical intelligence used in people's everyday lives; along with IQ, is considered in making a determination of intellectual disability.

■ **Spina bifida**
A congenital midline defect resulting from failure of the bony spinal column to close completely during fetal development.

■ **Neural tube defect**
Any defect involving the spinal cord.

Spinal cord injuries resulting from accidents after birth are also a major cause of paralysis. The basic difference between spina bifida and other spinal cord injuries is that the individual who is injured after birth has gone through a period of normal development and must adjust to an acquired disability.

EDUCATIONAL AND SOCIAL IMPLICATIONS   The extent of the paralysis resulting from a spinal cord injury depends on how high or low on the spinal column the injury is. Some children with spinal cord injuries are able to walk independently, some need braces, and others have to use wheelchairs. Lack of sensation and ability to control bodily functions, too, depends on the nature of the injury. Therefore, the implications for education are extremely varied. However, factors other than muscle weakness or paralysis alone affect a child's ability to walk (Bartonek & Saraste, 2001). Careful analysis of motivation and other environmental inducements to walk are critically important.

Some children will have acute medical problems that might lead to repeated hospitalizations for surgery or treatment of infections. Lack of sensation in certain areas of the skin can increase the risk of burns, abrasions, and pressure sores. The child might need to be repositioned periodically during the school day and monitored carefully during some activities in which there is risk of injury.

Because the student with spina bifida has deficiencies in sensation below the defect, she or he may have particular problems in spatial orientation, spatial judgment, sense of direction and distance, organization of motor skills, and body image or body awareness. Lack of bowel and bladder control in some children will require periodic **catheterization**. Many children can be taught to do the procedure known as clean intermittent catheterization themselves, but teachers should know what to do or obtain help from the school nurse.

Enormous progress has been made in treating spina bifida and in including those who have paralysis as a result of the condition in schools and the larger society. Nevertheless, controversies sometimes arise regarding just what appropriate inclusion in school activities might entail. For example, a high school athlete with spida bifida took legal action to be included with nondisabled runners, even though she had to use a wheelchair on the track because her legs were paralyzed (Saslow, 2007).

Orthopedic and Musculoskeletal Disorders

Some children are physically disabled because of defects or diseases of the muscles or bones. Even though they don't have neurological impairments, their ability to move is affected. Most of the time, muscular and skeletal problems involve the legs, arms, joints, or spine, making it difficult or impossible for the child to walk, stand, sit, or use his or her hands. The problems may be congenital or acquired after birth, and the causes can include genetic defects, infectious diseases, accidents, or developmental disorders.

Two of the most common musculoskeletal conditions affecting children and youths are **muscular dystrophy** and **juvenile rheumatoid arthritis** (Leet, Dormans, & Tosi, 2002). Muscular dystrophy is a hereditary disease that is characterized by progressive weakness caused by degeneration of muscle fibers. No cure exists yet for muscular dystrophy, but advances in pharmacology are promising (Welch et al., 2007). Juvenile rheumatoid arthritis is a potentially debilitating disease in which the muscles and joints are affected; the cause and cure are unknown (Best et al., 2005). It can be a very painful condition and is sometimes accompanied by complications such as fever, respiratory problems, heart problems, and eye infections. Among children with other physical disabilities, such as cerebral palsy, arthritis may be a complicating factor that affects

■ **Catheterization**
The insertion of a tube into the urethra to drain the bladder.

■ **Muscular dystrophy**
A hereditary disease characterized by progressive weakness caused by degeneration of muscle fibers.

■ **Juvenile rheumatoid arthritis**
A systemic disease with major symptoms involving the muscles and joints.

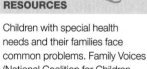

■ **Scoliosis**
An abnormal curvature of the spine.

the joints and limits movement. These and other conditions can significantly affect a student's social and academic progress at school.

A wide variety of other congenital conditions, acquired defects, and diseases also can affect the musculoskeletal system, such as the spinal curvature known as **scoliosis** or missing or malformed limbs (see Best et al., 2005; Heller, Alberto, Forney, & Schwartzman, 1996). In all these conditions, as well as in cases of muscular dystrophy and arthritis, the student's intelligence is unaffected unless there are additional associated disabilities. Regarding the musculoskeletal problem itself, special education is necessary only to improve the student's mobility, to ensure that proper posture and positioning are maintained, to provide for education during periods of confinement to hospital or home, and otherwise to make the educational experience as normal as possible.

Other Conditions Affecting Health or Physical Ability

In addition to those discussed so far, an extremely wide array of diseases, physiological disorders, congenital malformations, and injuries can affect students' health and physical abilities and create a need for special education and related services. Chronic diseases and health conditions of children have increased dramatically during recent decades (Perrin, Bloom, & Gortmaker, 2007). These diseases and health-related conditions include childhood obesity, diabetes, and asthma, for example.

Special educators need to be familiar with the range of physical disabilities and the types of accommodations that might be necessary to provide an appropriate education and related services (see Batshaw, 2002; Best et al., 2005). Moreover, teachers should understand that chronic diseases make many children's lives complicated and difficult because of possible hospitalizations, restrictions of activity, medications, teasing, and other consequences that, essentially, rob children of the experiences most of us associate with being kids (Zylke & DeAngelis, 2007).

Asthma is an increasingly common lung disease characterized by episodic inflammation or obstruction of the air passages such that the person has difficulty in breathing. Usually, the difficulty in breathing is reversible (i.e., is responsive to treatment). Severe asthma can be life-threatening, and in some cases it severely restricts a person's activities. The disease can also get better or worse for poorly understood reasons, and the unpredictability of the condition can be difficult to deal with. In Personal Perspectives on page 505, Kathryn Hegarty describes some of her experiences with asthma. Note that she received important support from both her family and her school. Without the special resource class for students with special needs, which she describes as "The Base," she doesn't think she would have been able to go to school.

Congenital malformations and disorders can occur in any organ system, and they may range from minor to fatal flaws in structure or function. In many cases, the cause of the malformation or disorder is not known; other conditions are

Fetal alcohol syndrome, associated with mothers' alcohol use during pregnancy, results in distinct physical and developmental abnormalities.

Personal PERSPECTIVES

The Importance of Family and School in Coping with Asthma

I was diagnosed with asthma at the age of two so I don't remember what life was like without it. Fortunately, throughout my younger years the illness never affected me significantly and I was able to do everything other children my age did.

I was lucky to have a supportive family, we had always been very close, but things changed when my asthma got worse. My older brother, Andrew, was very protective, although he had quite a tough time as he was always told to look after me. My Mum and Dad were often shouted at when I was feeling fed up or if I was begging them to discharge me from the hospital. It was when I hit puberty that things started to go wrong. I woke up one morning feeling a bit breathless and I found that my inhaler wasn't helping. My Mum took me to hospital where I was put on a nebuliser. It was the same medication as my inhaler but it was delivered through a breathing mask. I soon felt better and was sent home, although it started to become a regular occurrence. I was put on a very high dose of steroids. The list of possible side effects included weight gain, high blood pressure and brittle bones. . . .

Over the following months my asthma got progressively worse, which involved my having short but frequent stays in the hospital. My school had a facility called "The Base" for pupils who needed to work out of their usual class for a variety of reasons. This meant that on days I was not feeling well I could go there and work would be brought down from my classes so that I could work quietly at my own pace. I could also use this facility if the [elevators] were out of use since it was difficult for me to use the stairs around the school as I would become so breathless.

I certainly wouldn't have been at school half as much without "The Base." I became very friendly with one of the teachers who worked there. She provided not only educational support, but emotional support as well. I would often go in feeling fed up and frustrated. She would sit down and listen while I poured my heart out and told her how awful my life was.

Some days, even walking to the bus stop was too much for me, so the school provided a taxi to take me between home and school. It meant that if I was unwell while I was at school, I could telephone the taxi to pick me up early, or if I hadn't been well during the night I could go in to school later. It gave me a lot of freedom but I didn't abuse it. The school knew that I wanted to be there so I didn't have to feel guilty if I was late or even if I didn't go in at all. . . . [Kathryn also describes her worsening condition, some classmates' misunderstanding, and her lack of social life due to her illness.]

I think the fact that I have such a supportive family has kept me going. I am also extremely grateful to my school. If it hadn't been for "The Base" I would hardly have been there at all. I could have given up a long time ago, but I didn't. I am a fighter because I have had to be. I will always have asthma. It is part of my life but, hopefully, I am over the worst of it. From now on things can only get better.

Source: Hegarty, K., Lyke, T., Doherty, R., & Douglas, S. (2000). "I didn't ask to have this": First-person accounts of young people. In A. Closs (Ed.), *The education of children with medical conditions* (pp. 15–17). London: David Fulton. Reprinted by permission.

---

known to be hereditary or caused by maternal infection or substance use by the mother during pregnancy. In Chapter 5, we discussed **fetal alcohol syndrome (FAS)**, which is now one of the most common syndromes involving malformations and intellectual disability, is caused by the mother's use of alcohol during pregnancy. Worldwide, FAS is now seen in about 1 in 1,000 live births, and the prevalence of other disorders related to alcohol use of women during pregnancy is a serious problem (Archibald et al., 2001).

More children die in accidents each year than are killed by all childhood diseases combined. Millions of children and youths in the United States are seriously injured and disabled temporarily or permanently in accidents each year. Many of those who don't acquire traumatic brain injury receive spinal cord injuries that result in partial or total paralysis below the site of the injury. Others undergo amputations or are incapacitated temporarily by broken limbs or internal injuries.

■ **Asthma**
A lung disease characterized by episodic difficulty in breathing, particularly exhaling, due to inflammation or obstruction of the air passages.

■ **Fetal alcohol syndrome (FAS)**
Abnormalities associated with the mother's drinking alcohol during pregnancy; defects range from mild to severe, including growth retardation, brain damage, intellectual disability, hyperactivity, anomalies of the face, and heart failure; also called *alcohol embryopathy*.

■ **Acquired immune deficiency syndrome (AIDS)**
A virus-caused illness resulting in a breakdown of the immune system; currently, no known cure exists.

■ **Human immunodeficiency virus (HIV)**
The virus that leads to AIDS; a type of retrovirus that gradually disables the body's immune system, eventually leading to AIDS. The virus has been detected in the bloodstream of a person who is said to be "HIV positive."

Acquired immune deficiency syndrome (AIDS) is often thought to be a disease that merely makes one susceptible to fatal infections. However, children with AIDS often acquire neurological problems as well, including intellectual disability, cerebral palsy, seizures, and emotional or behavioral disorders. AIDS is caused by the **human immunodeficiency virus (HIV)**. Although HIV infections can be spread in other ways, the primary means of transmission in adolescents and adults is through sexual contact. Infants may contract the disease during the birth process. Although HIV does often result in neurological damage and cognitive impairment, it appears that at least in some cases the damage may be reversible with state-of-the-art drug therapies (Willen, 2006).

Most of the reported new cases of HIV infections are in minority populations, and almost three-fourths of the new infections in the group aged thirteen to nineteen years are in minority populations. It's clear that "HIV infection in American adolescents has not received the attention it merits over the years" (Rogers, 2001, p. 1).

HIV/AIDS still carries considerable stigma in our society (Murphy, Roberts, & Hoffman, 2002). As children and youths with AIDS and other viral and bacterial infections live longer owing to improved medical treatments, there will be an increasing need for special education and related services. Teachers should be aware that if reasonable procedures are followed for preventing infections, there is no serious concern regarding transmission of HIV in the classroom (Ainsa, 2000; Best et al., 2005; Spiegel & Bonwit, 2002).

We have already mentioned fetal alcohol syndrome, which results in disabilities acquired by children of mothers who abuse alcohol during pregnancy. The abuse of other substances by mothers also has negative implications for their children. If the mother is a substance abuser, then there is also a high probability of neglect and abuse by the mother after her baby is born. Many women who are intravenous drug users not only risk chemical damage to their babies, but might also give them venereal diseases such as syphilis, which can result in disabilities. Children of such mothers are also at risk for being born with AIDS. If the number of substance-abusing mothers increases, then the number of infants and young children with severe and multiple disabilities will increase as well. In spite of the multiple causal factors involved, the prospects of effective early intervention with children who are exposed prenatally to drugs are much better than previously thought. Although the consequences of any drug use during pregnancy may be serious, the near hysteria of the 1980s about the irreversible effects of crack cocaine on infants was not justified. True, many children who are exposed prenatally to drugs will have developmental disabilities. Like the developmental disabilities that have other causes, however, those of children who are exposed before birth to drugs are amenable to modification.

Some students have conditions that require particularly careful treatment because seemingly minor mistakes or oversights can have very serious consequences for them. Programs for students who are medically fragile must be particularly flexible and open to revision. Daily health care plans and emergency plans are essential, as are effective lines of communication among all who are involved with the student's treatment, care, and schooling. Decisions regarding placement of these students must be made by a team that includes health care providers and school personnel as well as the student and his or her parents.

An increasing number of children are returning home from hospitalization able to breathe only with the help of a ventilator (a mechanical device that forces oxygen into the lungs through a tube inserted into the trachea). Many of these children are also returning to public schools, sometimes with the assistance of a full-time nurse. Whether it's appropriate for children who are dependent on ventilators or other medical technology to attend general education is debatable. Educators and parents together must make decisions in each individual case, weighing medical judgment about danger to the child as well as the interest of the child in being integrated into as many typical school activities as possible with her or his peers.

Prevention of Physical Disabilities

Although some physical disabilities aren't preventable by any available means, many or most are. For instance, failure to wear seat belts and other safety devices accounts for many disabling injuries. Likewise, driving under the influence of alcohol or other drugs, careless storage of drugs and other toxic substances, careless storage of firearms, use of alcohol and other drugs during pregnancy, and a host of unsafe and unhealthful practices that could be avoided cause many disabilities (Hanson, 1996). For example, lowering the incidence of obesity and increasing healthful diet and healthful physical activity could do much to prevent health complications of children, particularly diabetes (see DeAngelis, 2007).

Teenage mothers are more likely than older women to be physically battered ("Battering and Teen Pregnancy," 2001). Teens are also more likely than older women to give birth to premature or low-birthweight babies, and these babies are at high risk for a variety of psychological and physical problems when they reach school age (Cowden & Funkhouser, 2001). Thus, preventing adolescent pregnancies would keep many babies from being born with disabilities. Inadequate prenatal care, including maternal infections and inadequate maternal nutrition during pregnancy, also contributes to the number of babies born with disabilities. And for young children, immunization against preventable childhood diseases could lower the number of those who acquire disabilities (Hanson, 1996).

Child abuse is a significant contributing factor in creating physical disabilities in the United States, and its prevention is a critical problem. Many thousands of children, ranging from newborns to adolescents, are battered or abused each year. Teachers can play an extremely important role in detecting, reporting, and preventing child abuse and neglect because, next to parents, they are the people who spend the most time with children. If they suspect abuse or neglect, teachers must report it to child protective services under state and local regulations. These vary from one area and state to another, but ordinarily, the teacher is required to report suspected cases of child abuse or neglect to a school administrator, law enforcement officer, or social services official. A professional who fails to report child abuse or neglect may be held legally liable.

Children who are already disabled physically, intellectually, or emotionally are more at risk for abuse than are nondisabled children (Vig & Kaminer, 2002). Because children with disabilities are more vulnerable and dependent, abusive adults find them easy targets. Moreover, some of the characteristics of children with disabilities are sources of additional stress for their caretakers and may be contributing factors in physical abuse. These children often require more time, energy, money, and patience than children without disabilities. Parenting any child is stressful; parenting a child with a disability can demand more than some parents are prepared to give. It isn't surprising that children with disabilities are disproportionately represented among abused children and that the need for training is particularly great for parents of children with disabilities.

We mentioned in Chapters 1 and 5 that **phenylketonuria (PKU)** is now understood to be an inborn metabolic disorder that, untreated with a special diet, causes intellectual disability. PKU is generally thought of as a problem associated with intellectual

■ **Phenylketonuria (PKU)**
A metabolic genetic disorder caused by the inability of the body to convert phenylalanine to tyrosine; an accumulation of phenylalanine results in abnormal brain development.

Teenage girls are more likely than older women to give birth to premature or low-birthweight babies, who will be at high risk for learning problems when they reach school age.

FOCUS ON **Concepts**

One Failure and One Success in Prevention

Lisa was discharged from the hospital at 3 days of age. Her parents were surprised and upset to be called back a week later, after doctors reported that Lisa had a positive PKU screening test. Amino acid studies confirmed the diagnosis, and Lisa was placed on low-phenylalanine formula. Her parents could hardly believe there was a problem because Lisa looked and acted well and achieved her developmental milestones on time. The visits to the metabolism clinic were difficult reminders of her "silent disorder." Once Lisa entered elementary school, she began resisting the restrictions on her diet, and her parents had difficulty maintaining good metabolic control. Lisa was born in 1970, when the importance of strict dietary control was not widely known. She stopped her diet at

seven years of age. Psychometric testing at ten years of age showed that she had an IQ score of 85. Despite learning difficulties in school, she graduated from high school and began a clerical job. She soon became pregnant but was not placed back on a low-phenylalanine diet. Her child was born with microcephaly, and at age five has intellectual disability requiring limited supports. Fortunately, Lisa's younger sister Barbara, who also has PKU, has had a better outcome. Barbara has remained on the low-phenylalanine diet continuously and intends to remain on the diet through her pregnancy.

Source: Batshaw, M. L., & Tuchman, M. (2002). PKU and other inborn errors of metabolism. In M. L. Batshaw (Ed.), *Children with disabilities* (5th ed., pp. 333–345). Baltimore: Paul H. Brookes. Reprinted with permission.

■ **Neurotoxin**
A substance known to damage nerve cells.

disability, but it is also an issue of health and prevention of disabilities. Inborn metabolic disorders can result not only in intellectual disability but in other disabilities associated with brain damage. This is because metabolic disorders may result in the buildup of **neurotoxins**, which can cause any of the disabilities associated with brain damage, including intellectual disability.

PKU isn't the only genetically determined metabolic disorder (see Batshaw & Tuchman, 2002), nor is it simply a metabolic disorder that results in intellectual disability if it is untreated in early childhood. Effective treatment of PKU does require a special diet free of or very low in phenylalanine for the infant, but the individual must remain on such a diet. Furthermore, women must continue the diet during pregnancy to avoid damaging the fetus. The Focus on Concepts feature above illustrates the negative developmental consequences (lack of prevention) resulting from resistance to the special dietary restrictions, as well as a happier case of prevention.

Psychological and Behavioral Characteristics

Academic Achievement

It's impossible to make many valid generalizations about the academic achievement of children with physical disabilities because they vary so widely in the nature and severity of their conditions. The environmental and psychological factors that determine what a child will achieve academically also are extremely varied, and generalizations about academic outcomes aren't possible (see Batshaw, 2002; Best et al., 2005).

Many students with physical disabilities have erratic school attendance because of hospitalization, visits to physicians, bed-rest requirements, and so on. Some learn well with ordinary teaching methods; others require special methods because they have intellectual disability or sensory impairments in addition to physical disabilities. Because of the frequent interruptions in their schooling, some fall considerably behind their age peers in academic achievement, even though they have normal intelligence and motivation. The two major effects of a physical disability, especially if it is severe or prolonged, are that a child might be deprived of educationally relevant experiences and that he or she might not be able to learn to manipulate educational materials and respond to educational tasks the way most children do.

Some children with mild or transitory physical problems have no academic deficiencies at all; others have severe difficulties. Some students who have serious and chronic health problems still manage to achieve at a high level. Usually, these high-achieving children have high intellectual capacity, strong motivation, and teachers and parents who make every possible special provision for their education. Children with neurological impairments are, as a group, most likely to have intellectual and perceptual deficits and therefore to be behind their age peers in academic achievement.

Personality Characteristics

Research does not support the notion that there is a certain personality type or self-concept associated with any physical disability. Children and youths with physical disabilities are as varied in their psychological characteristics as nondisabled children, and they are apparently responsive to the same factors that influence the psychological development of other children. How children adapt to their physical limitations and how they respond to social-interpersonal situations greatly depend on how parents, siblings, teachers, peers, and the public react to the children (Best et al., 2005; Lerner, Lowenthal, & Egan, 1998; Llewellyn & Chung, 1997).

PUBLIC REACTIONS   Public attitudes can have a profound influence on how children with physical disabilities see themselves and on their opportunities for psychological adjustment, education, and employment. If the reaction is one of fear, rejection, or discrimination, these children might spend a great deal of energy trying to hide their stigmatizing differences. If the reaction is one of pity and an expectation of helplessness, people with disabilities will tend to behave in a dependent manner. To the extent that other people can see children with physical disabilities as people who have certain limitations but are otherwise just like everyone else, children and youths with disabilities will be encouraged to become independent, productive members of society (see Nabors & Larson, 2002).

Several factors seem to be causing greater public acceptance of people with physical disabilities. Professional and civic groups encourage support and decrease fear of people who are disabled through information and public education. People with physical disabilities are increasingly visible in the media, and they are often portrayed in a more realistic and positive light. Government insistence on the elimination of architectural barriers that prevent citizens with disabilities from using public facilities serves to decrease discrimination. Programs to encourage hiring workers with disabilities help the public to see those with physical disabilities as constructive, capable people. Laws that protect every child's right to public education bring more individuals into contact with people who have severe or profound disabilities. But there's no doubt that many children with physical disabilities are still rejected, feared, pitied, or discriminated against. The more obvious the physical flaw, the more likely it is that the person will be perceived in negative terms by the public.

Public policy regarding children's physical disabilities has not met the needs of most such children and their families. In particular, as successful medical treatment prolongs the lives of more and more children with severe, chronic illnesses and other disabilities, issues of who should pay the costs of treatment and maintenance (which are often enormous) and which children and families should receive the limited available resources are becoming critical.

CHILDREN'S AND FAMILIES' REACTIONS   As we suggest above, children's reactions to their own physical disabilities are largely a reflection of how others respond to them

Audio Clip Homework Exercise

Cerebral Palsy ● Go to the Homework and Exercises section in Chapter 14 of MyEducationLab to listen to a woman named Vicki Page talk about what it is like to grow up with cerebral palsy.

Children's feelings about their own disabilities are largely a reflection of how they are treated by others, and also of the attitude that their own families take toward them. They are more likely to see themselves as "normal" if they are treated that way, and encouraged to participate in regular activities.

(see Olrick, Pianta, & Marvin, 2002; Singh, 2003). Shame and guilt are learned responses; children will have such negative feelings only if others respond to them by shaming or blaming them (and those who are like them) for their physical differences. Children will be independent and self-sufficient (within the limits of their physical disabilities) rather than dependent and demanding only to the extent that they learn how to take care of their own needs. And they will have realistic self-perceptions and set realistic goals for themselves only to the extent that others are honest and clear in appraising their conditions.

However, certain psychological reactions are inevitable for the child with physical disabilities, no matter how she or he is treated. The wish to be nondisabled and to participate in the same activities as most children and the fantasy that the disability will disappear are to be expected. With proper management and help, the child can be expected eventually to accept the disability and live a happy life, even though he or she knows the true nature of the condition. Fear and anxiety, too, can be expected. It's natural for children to be afraid when they are separated from their parents, hospitalized, and subjected to medical examinations and procedures that might be painful. In these situations, too, proper management can minimize emotional stress. Psychological trauma is not a necessary effect of hospitalization. The hospital environment may, in fact, be better than the child's home in the case of abused and neglected children.

Other important considerations regarding the psychological effects of a physical disability include the age of the child and the nature of the limitation (e.g., whether it is congenital or acquired, progressive or not). But even these factors are not uniform in their effects. A child with a relatively minor and short-term physical disability might become more maladjusted, anxious, debilitated, and disruptive than another child with a terminal illness because of the way the child's behavior and feelings are managed. Certainly, understanding the child's and the family's feelings about the disability is important. But it's also true that managing the consequences of the child's behavior is a crucial aspect of education and rehabilitation. Adolescence is a difficult time for most

UNDERSTANDING THE STANDARDS AND PRINCIPLES What determines how children adapt to their physical limitations and how they respond to social-interpersonal situations? (CEC Knowledge and Skill Standards CC3K3, CC3K4, & PH3K1)

Council for Exceptional Children

parents, and the fact that a child has a physical disability does not necessarily mean that the family will find a youngster's adolescence more difficult or less difficult (Magill-Evans, Darrah, Pain, Adkins, & Kratochvil, 2001).

Family support, school experiences, medical treatment, and attitudes have a very significant effect on the life of a child with a chronic health problem. Besides the school and society at large, the family and its cultural roots are important determinants of how and what children with physical disabilities will learn; therefore, it's important to take cultural values into account in teaching children not only about the academic curriculum but about their disability as well.

Prosthetics, Orthotics, and Adaptive Devices for Daily Living

Many individuals with physical disabilities use prosthetics, orthotics, and other adaptive devices to help them function better on a daily basis. A **prosthesis** is an artificial replacement for a missing body part (e.g., an artificial hand or leg); an **orthosis** is a device that enhances the partial function of a part of a person's body (a brace or a device that allows a person to do something). **Adaptive devices** for daily living include a variety of adaptations of ordinary items found in the home, office, or school—such as a device to aid bathing or hand washing or walking—that make performing the tasks required for self-care and employment easier for the person who has a physical disability.

The most important principles to keep in mind are use of residual function, simplicity, and reliability. For example, the muscles of the arm, shoulder, or back operate an artificial hand. This might be too complicated or demanding for an infant or young child with a missing or deformed upper limb. Depending on the child's age, the length and function of the amputated limb, and the child's other abilities, a passive "mitt" or a variety of other prosthetic devices might be more helpful. Choice of the most useful prosthesis will depend on careful evaluation of each individual's needs. A person without legs may be taught to use his or her arms to move about in a wheelchair or to use his or her torso and arms to get about on artificial legs (perhaps also using crutches or a cane). Again, each individual's abilities and preferences must be evaluated in designing the prosthesis (see Best et al., 2005; Heller et al., 1996).

Two points regarding prosthetics, orthotics, and residual function must be kept in mind:

1. *Residual function is often important even when a prosthesis, orthosis, or adaptive device is not used.* For example, it may be crucial for the child with cerebral palsy or muscular dystrophy to learn to use the affected limbs as well as possible without the aid of any special equipment because using residual function alone will make the child more independent and can help to prevent or retard physical deterioration. Moreover, it's often more efficient for a person to learn not to rely completely on a prosthesis or orthosis, as long as he or she can accomplish a task without it.

2. *Spectacular technological developments often have very limited meaning for the immediate needs of the majority of individuals with physical disabilities.* It might be years before expensive experimental equipment is tested adequately and marketed at a cost that most people can afford, and a given device might be applicable only to a small group of individuals with an extremely rare condition. Even though a device may provide greater ability to participate in ordinary childhood

■ **Prosthesis**

A device designed to replace, partially or completely, a part of the body (e.g., artificial teeth or limbs).

■ **Orthosis**

A device designed to restore, partially or completely, a lost function of the body (e.g., a brace or crutch).

■ **Adaptive devices**

Special tools that are adaptations of common items to make accomplishing self-care, work, or recreation activities easier for people with physical disabilities.

INTERNET RESOURCES

The Northwestern University Prosthetics Research Laboratory and Rehabilitation Engineering Program is dedicated to the improvement of prostheses and orthoses: www.nupoc .northwestern.edu

Rehabilitation tools and assistive devices may be researched at www.rehabtool.com

At Adrian's Adaptive Closet, you will find links to sites that offer clothes adapted for individuals who use wheelchairs: www .adrianscloset.com

The site for Wheelchair Net is a community for people who have a common interest in wheelchair technology and its improvement and successful application: www .wheelchairnet.org

Casebook Reflections

REFER TO THE CASE *Praying for a Miracle* in your booklet. Adaptations are in the planning stages for Peter's house to be made wheelchair accessible. Adjustments have been made for proper equipment to be installed for his bathing and toileting. What other challenges do you foresee? ●

activities, the current cost of some technological devices is clearly a barrier to their widespread use. Common standby prostheses, orthoses, and other equipment adapted to the needs of individuals will continue to be the most practical devices for a long time to come.

We don't mean to downplay the importance of technological advances for people with physical disabilities. Advances in technology and applications have provided extraordinary help for many students with disabilities (Best et al., 2005; DeFord, 1998; Levy & O'Rourke, 2002; Lindsey, 2000). Our point here is that the greatest significance of a technological advance often lies in how it changes seemingly ordinary items or problems. For example, technological advances in metallurgy and plastics have led to the design of much more functional braces and wheelchairs. The heavy metal-and-leather leg braces that were formerly used by many children with cerebral palsy or other neurological disorders—cumbersome, difficult to apply, and not very helpful in preventing deformity or improving function—have been largely supplanted by braces constructed of thermoform plastic. Wheelchairs are being built of lightweight metals and plastics and redesigned to allow users to go places that are inaccessible to the typical wheelchair. And an increasing number of computerized devices are improving the movement and communication abilities of people with disabilities.

The greatest problem today isn't in devising new or more sophisticated assistive technology but rather in accurately evaluating children and youths to determine what would be most useful and then making that technology available. Most schools do not now make maximum use of available technology. Many children and youths who need prostheses or other assistive devices, such as computers, special vehicles, and self-help aids, are not carefully evaluated and provided with the most appropriate equipment.

Two social issues involving prosthetics are social acceptance and participation in sports. Returning war veterans are sure to expose more people than ever to prosthetic limbs (see McGrath, 2007). Furthermore, as a story in the May 13, 2007, issue of *The New York Times* Sunday Style section illustrated, people with disabilities, including those with prosthetic limbs, are increasingly, unashamedly exposing them to the public (Navarro, 2007). In sports, a growing controversy that has become a matter of general public concern (see Goodman, 2007) is whether prosthetic limbs and surgical enhancements—such as Lasik

Rehabilitation engineers are redesigning wheelchairs for use in off-the-street recreational and work environments.

FOCUS ON **Concepts**

Prosthetics

People with disabilities, particularly those with prostheses, are increasingly participating in society without trying to hide their disabilities—even the cartoon Doonesbury features a character who acquired a prosthetic lower limb after his leg was amputated following his injury in the Iraq war. Prosthetics are becoming more stylish as well as more sophisticated and useful with the increasing use of technologies in their design and engineering, and these advances in the development of prosthetics require society to confront new ethical issues.

Some people who rely on prosthetics, such as South African racing phenomenon Oscar Pistorius, who has no lower legs and runs on J-shaped carbon fiber blades known

as Cheetahs, do not think of themselves as disabled (see Goodman, 2007; Longman, 2007). As we mentioned in Chapter 2, and as Goodman discusses, sport regulators such as the Olympics Committee will need to consider not only the possible unfair advantage of people in wheelchairs compared to runners using

their feet but also the possible advantage of those who use Cheetahs or other prostheses rather than natural body parts.

You might consider the competitions under which you would feel a prosthetic device offers an unfair advantage. For example, under what conditions would you consider wrestling unfair, were one of the wrestlers using a prosthesis? Under what conditions would you consider an intellectual competition unfair were a competitor using a form of prosthetic intelligence? These questions and others like them may seem silly at this point, but remember that the questions now being raised about running on prostheses would have seemed silly a few years ago. Ethical issues will grow along with miniaturization of computerized components, new materials, new engineering ideas, new surgical and control techniques, and other advances in prostheses (not to mention more accepting social attitudes). It takes considerable imagination to hypothesize all of the possible issues that society will face in the next few decades (see Cascio, 2007; McGrath, 2007).

surgery and, inevitably, we predict, other prosthetic devices, including artificial computer-operated gadgets of all kinds—give competitors an unfair advantage (Longman, 2007; see also Howe, M., n.d.). In a sense, the controversy may parallel that of performance-enhancing drugs: what is fair and what is not, in athletic competitions? Some of these issues are considered in the Focus on Concepts above.

Educational Considerations

Too often, we think of people who have physical disabilities as being helpless or unable to learn. It's easy to lower our expectations for them because we know that they are indeed unable to do some things. We forget, though, that many people with physical disabilities can learn to do many or all of the things that most nondisabled people do, although sometimes they must perform these tasks in different ways (e.g., a person who does not have the use of the hands might have to use the feet or mouth). Accepting the limitations imposed by physical disabilities without trying to see how much people can learn or how the environment can be changed to allow them to respond more effectively is an insulting and dehumanizing way of responding to physical differences. This is true in academics, but it is also the case in physical education. Adapted physical education is

Building Teaching Skills Lesson Planning Exercise

OHI • Go to the Building Teaching Skills section in Chapter 14 of MyEducationLab to access information and resources to develop a lesson plan designed to educate your students about the different health impairments other students in your school may have.

now a special educational feature of all school programs that make appropriate adaptations for students with disabilities (Auxter, Pyfer, & Huettig, 2005; Sherrill, 2004).

Educating students with physical disabilities isn't so much a matter of special instruction for children with disabilities as it is of educating the nondisabled population (Best et al., 2005; Closs, 2000). People with physical disabilities solve many of their own problems, but their lives are often needlessly complicated because the nondisabled give no thought to what life is like for someone with specific physical limitations. Design adaptations in buildings, furniture, household appliances, and clothing can make it possible for someone with a physical disability to function as efficiently as a nondisabled person in a home, school, or community.

The objectives of educators and other professionals who work with children and youths with physical disabilities should include autonomy and self-advocacy (Best et al., 2005; Bullock & Mahon, 2000). Children with physical disabilities typically want to be self-sufficient, and they should be encouraged and taught the skills they need to take care of themselves to the maximum extent possible. This requires knowledge of the physical limitations created by the disability and sensitivity to the child's social and academic needs and perceptions—understanding of the environmental and psychological factors that affect classroom performance and behavior.

Individualized Planning

Students with complex physical disabilities typically require a wide array of related services as well as special education. The individualized education programs (IEPs) for such students tend to be particularly specific and detailed. The instructional goals and objectives often include seemingly minute steps, especially for young children with severe disabilities (see Best et al., 2005; Hanson, 1996; Heller et al., 1996; Lerner et al., 1998). Many of the children under age three who need special education and related services are children with physical disabilities. These children, under federal law, have an **individualized family service plan (IFSP)** rather than an IEP. The IFSP (see Chapters 1 and 2) must specify how the family will be involved in intervention as well as what other services will be provided.

Some parents of children with chronic health conditions might wish that their children didn't exist, could be cured, or would improve significantly, although their actual expectations are more realistic (Wolman, Garwick, Kohrman, & Blum, 2001).

Educational Placement

Children with physical disabilities may be educated in any one of several settings, depending on the type and severity of the condition, the services available in the community, and the medical prognosis for the condition, but most are in general education settings (Best et al., 2005; Nabors & Lehmkuhl, 2004). If such children ordinarily attend general education classes but must be hospitalized for more than a few days, they may be included in a class in the hospital itself. If they must be confined to their homes for a time, a visiting or homebound teacher can provide tutoring until they can return to general education. In these cases, which usually involve children who have been in accidents or who have conditions that are not permanently and severely disabling, relatively minor, commonsense adjustments are required to continue the children's education and keep them from falling behind their

---

UNDERSTANDING THE STANDARDS AND PRINCIPLES What two objectives should professionals who work with children and youth with physical disabilities keep in mind? (CEC Knowledge and Skill Standards PH4K1, PH4K2, & PH4S1)

Council for Exceptional Children

■ **Individualized family service plan (IFSP)**
A plan mandated by P.L. 99-457 to provide services for young children with disabilities (under three years of age) and their families; drawn up by professionals and parents; similar to an IEP for older children.

Design adaptations in buildings, furniture, household appliances, and clothing can make it possible for someone with a physical disability to function as efficiently as a nondisabled person in a home, school, or community.

Collaboration and Co-Teaching of Students with Physical Disabilities and Other Health Impairments

"But I'm Not a Nurse!"

Students with physical disabilities and other health impairments often require complex systems of care, including services from health care professionals, related service personnel, and special educators. It is easy for everyone to forget about the students' cognitive and social needs because of the day-to-day physical needs. Even though a student with physical disabilities may have a wide range of services, the least restrictive environment for them may be the general education classroom. It is in this situation that collaboration with a special educator is important for the general education teacher to understand and meet the needs of these students.

WHAT DOES IT MEAN TO BE A TEACHER OF STUDENTS WITH PHYSICAL DISABILITIES AND OTHER HEALTH IMPAIRMENTS?

Special educators who work with students with physical disabilities must have skills related to learning and instruction, as well as skills in determining appropriate assistive technology devices, positioning, and socialization. According to the Council for Exceptional Children (2001), they should be adept at:

1. Using adaptations and assistive technology to provide individuals with physical and health disabilities full participation and access to the general curriculum
2. Using techniques of physical management to ensure participation in academic and social environments
3. Integrating an individual's health care plan into daily programming
4. Participating in the selection and implementation of augmentative or alternative communication systems

These skills require a broad range of training for special educators, including medical management and extensive collaboration with health care providers and families. With this knowledge, special educators can collaborate with general education teachers to adjust instruction, change the physical environment of the classroom, and communicate successfully with students.

SUCCESSFUL STRATEGIES FOR CO-TEACHING

Jo is a special education teacher of five- and six-year-olds with cerebral palsy and spina bifida. Charlotte is a general education teacher with a group of twenty-eight kindergarten-aged students, some of whom had never had any school experiences. They describe their collaboration experiences.

Jo: We combined the children into two groups. Each group was made up of half of my children and half of Charlotte's children. We'd occasionally put the two groups together. I became an expert in a certain content area. I taught it to two groups, and Charlotte did the same.

Charlotte: Our classes are scheduled for music together because of our collaboration. We had a music teacher come in who taught music to both classes as a large group; however, Jo and I did stay in the classroom to facilitate management needs because it was such a large group for one teacher to handle. In fact, we had to teach the music teacher some management ideas. It was a good experience for the music teacher; she was able to see how you can work with a range and variety of children. It's important to find someone who has a similar philosophy and treats children the way you do, but it also must be someone you can get along with, who has the same tolerance that you do. Had we not been friendly, liked each other, and respected the way each other did things, Jo and I would not have been successful. We have seen collaborations that were not as successful as ours because they did not develop out of commonalities.

Jo: One of the most demanding things about our collaboration was keeping up with the kids, keeping them on pace, and trying to make it valuable for them educationally. As much as I want this very worthwhile social experience for my special needs kids, am I giving them the multisensory nuts-and-bolts special education that they need? I constantly have to try and strike a balance between the social needs of the children and the intense requirements of their special needs.

Charlotte: The most demanding thing about our collaboration was not working together ourselves, but effectively meeting the needs of the children. That's really the most demanding thing: living up to them.

● *By Margaret P. Weiss*

Meeting the Needs of Students with Physical Disabilities and Other Health Impairments

Adapted Physical Education

WHAT IS ADAPTED PHYSICAL EDUCATION?

Adapted physical education (APE) is an instructional service, not a setting or placement. Students receive APE when their disability necessitates a physical education program different from their peers. The difference can be in the form of an alternative activity, an instructional modification or adaptation, or different criteria for success. APE can be part of an integrated program, for students with and without physical disabilities, or can be a stand-alone program for students with disabilities only.

WHO QUALIFIES FOR ADAPTED PHYSICAL EDUCATION?

Any student with an IEP may be eligible for APE. IDEA requires that "physical education services, specially designed if necessary, must be made available to every child with a disability receiving a free appropriate public education." Necessary adaptations are determined by IEP team members. Any student with gross motor skill deficits or limitations in strength, flexibility, or physical fitness should be considered for APE services.

STRATEGIES FOR MAKING ACCOMMODATIONS

Strategies for making accommodations to general physical education classes include (Auxter, Pyfer, & Huettig, 2001):

- Reducing the size of the playing field through reducing the size of the soccer field, goal area, basketball court, or length of a race
- Changing the size of equipment by using larger or more colorful balls, increasing the size of the bat but decreasing weight, using larger rackets, lighter bows, or scoops for catching
- Reducing the playing area by adding more players to the field or court
- Modifying basic rules such as everyone plays seated, less mobile players get two or three bounces to get to the ball in tennis, rest periods or frequent substitutions are allowed, shorten the game, or partner activities
- Using specialized equipment such as a ramp or bumpers for bowling, a batting tee, or a sit-ski for skiing

The overarching aim for APE is for students to have access to activities that will support physical, recreational, and/or leisure goals. APE should take place in the least restrictive environment (LRE). Determining the LRE involves considerations of safety as well as opportunities for meaningful participation. For many students, the LRE will be the general education physical education class.

● *By Kristin L. Sayeski*

classmates. At the other extreme, usually involving serious or chronic disabilities, the child might be taught for a time in a hospital school or a special public school class designed specifically for children with physical disabilities.

Today, most children with disabilities are being integrated into the public schools because of advances in medical treatment: new developments in bioengineering, allowing them greater mobility and functional movement; decreases in or removal of architectural barriers and transportation problems; and the movement toward public education for all children. Any placement has positive and negative features, and the best decision for a particular child requires weighing the pros and cons. Working with a special educator to better understand a student's needs and how to meet those needs is imperative. For an example of how teachers can work together, read Making It Work on page 515. Sometimes the benefits of a particular type of placement are either greatly exaggerated or almost completely dismissed.

Educational Goals and Curricula

Educational goals and curricula cannot be prescribed for children with physical disabilities as a group because their individual limitations vary so greatly. Even among children with the same condition, goals and curricula must be determined after assessment of each child's intellectual, physical, sensory, and emotional characteristics. A physical disability,

Personal PERSPECTIVES

Weighing the Issue of Placement: One Student's Perspective

There were gains and losses at special school. Some of the positives were small classes and individual tuition to catch up on work I missed when absent, on-site paramedical therapy and medical specialists who visited school, so saving time, energy and having to be off school. There was more specialist equipment available too, some of my own, some for the use of anyone who needed it at any time. The school was fully accessible. I suppose the other thing was that there was less feeling of isolation or difference in relation to being ill or disabled: that was the norm.

On the negative side, special schools then didn't really encourage assertiveness and pride about being disabled, there really was a prevailing medical model of "caring" that could result in childlike dependency. In mainstream schools there is an understanding that kids will experiment with so-called bad habits such as smoking and sex, but staff were horribly shocked and dismayed when I was found smoking. . . . It is ironic that when I was in special school so many of us would have benefited from more liberal and "normal" approaches with opportunities for mainstreaming, but now, when so many of the children who attend special school seem to have far more complex and profound disabilities, they can't take advantage of the progress fully.

Source: Hegarty, K., Lyke, T., Doherty, R., & Douglas, S. (2000). "I didn't ask to have this": First-person accounts of young people. In A. Closs (Ed.), *The education of children with medical conditions* (p. 18). London: David Fulton. Reprinted with permission.

---

especially a severe and chronic one that limits mobility, may have two implications for education: (1) The child might be deprived of experiences that nondisabled children have, and (2) the child might find it impossible to manipulate educational materials and respond to educational tasks the way most children do. For example, a child with severe cerebral palsy can't take part in most outdoor play activities and travel experiences and might not be able to hold and turn pages in books, write, explore objects manually, or use a typewriter without special equipment. Among other things, this student might require adapted physical education. Read Responsive Instruction on page 516 for more about adapted physical education.

For children with an impairment that is only physical, curriculum and educational goals should ordinarily be the same as those for nondisabled children: reading, writing, arithmetic, and experiences designed to familiarize them with the world around them. In addition, special instruction might be needed in mobility skills, daily living skills, and occupational skills; because of their physical impairments, these children might need special, individualized instruction in the use of mechanical devices that will help them to perform tasks that are much simpler for people without disabilities. For children with other disabilities in addition to physical limitations, curricula will need to be further adapted (Best et al., 2005).

Educational goals for students with severe or profound disabilities must be related to their functioning in everyday community environments. Only recently have educators begun to address the problems of analyzing community tasks (e.g., crossing streets, using money, riding public transportation, greeting neighbors) and planning efficient instruction for individuals with severe disabilities. Efficient instruction in such skills requires that teaching occur in the community environment itself.

UNDERSTANDING THE STANDARDS AND PRINCIPLES What should teachers consider when planning educational goals for children with physical disabilities? (CEC Knowledge and Skill Standards PH5K1, PH5K2, & PH5K3)

Council for Exceptional Children

Casebook Reflections

REFER TO THE CASE *Praying for a Miracle* in your booklet. During elementary and middle school, Peter has been taught in a special school for students with physical disabilities and other health impairments. Looking ahead to the transition years, his principal believes that Peter might benefit from being placed in a mainstream program for the gifted and talented in his local high school. What possibilities might this open? What problems? ●

Meeting the Needs of Students with Physical Disabilities and Other Health Impairments

Integrating Physical and Occupational Therapy in General Education Settings

The majority of students with physical disabilities receive related services as a part of their educational program. Related services can include anything from speech-language pathology to counseling to transportation. Two common related services for students with physical disabilities are occupational and physical therapy. Researchers have found that the more integrated these types of services are into education settings, the more effective the outcomes (Karnish, Bruder, & Rainforth, 1995).

PHYSICAL AND OCCUPATIONAL THERAPY

Understanding the differences between physical and occupational therapy can be confusing. Yet a clear understanding of the skills that are supported through these therapies is fundamental for creating the necessary bridge between out-of-class therapy and integrated therapy that supports student learning.

Physical therapy addresses sensory and gross motor functions. Physical therapists can assist students by identifying optimal positions for various tasks; teach students how to move within the classroom and school environment; and develop students' movement, strength, and coordination. Occupational therapists provide support for daily living skills such as dressing, bathing, and toileting as well as fine motor skills (handling small objects, handwriting, oral-motor skills).

CLASSROOM IMPLICATIONS

Despite the different focuses of the two groups, their services can overlap. As a classroom teacher, multidisciplinary collaboration among all services providers is a must. When planning for the integration of physical or occupational services in the classroom, the classroom teacher should consider the following:

■ What are educationally relevant services versus medically relevant services? For example, an educationally relevant service would be to work on transfer and handling techniques with the teacher and paraprofessional to position a student for instruction. A medically relevant therapy would be strength building (Szabo, 2000).

■ What are the educationally relevant IEP goals, and how can therapy support progress toward those goals? For example, mobility independence, ability to operate assistive technology, improved posture, and improved upper extremity coordination are all therapy goals that directly relate to improved educational outcomes.

■ What type of service is necessary: direct, indirect, or both? Direct services involve hands-on treatment provided directly by the therapist. Preferably, these treatments occur within the natural environment (classroom, playground, gym) where the skill is expected. Indirect services, on the other hand, involve consultation or monitoring support. Under a consultation model, the therapist makes recommendations for instructional modifications, activity enhancement, environmental modifications, adaptation of materials, or schedule alterations. It may even include training the classroom teacher in ways to provide direct services. Monitoring involves periodic evaluations of student progress and related training for team members. A combination of direct and indirect services provides both direct services for certain goals or skills and consultation support for others.

■ Is peer support appropriate? As students become more skilled, peer support can be solicited. This reduces the dependence a student has on any one individual and encourages interdependence—an important skill as students get older.

By working with therapists to identify ways to support therapy within the classroom, teachers learn ways to reduce the physical challenges students can encounter within general education settings, while fostering the development of necessary physical and occupational skills.

● *By Kristin L. Sayeski*

The range of educational objectives and curricula for children with physical disabilities is often extended beyond the objectives and curricula typically provided for other students in school. For example, very young children and those with severe neuromuscular problems might need objectives and curricula focusing on the most basic self-care skills (e.g., swallowing, chewing, self-feeding). Older students might need not only to explore possible careers in the way all students should, but also to consider the special accommodations their physical limitations demand for successful performance as well (see Best et al., 2005).

Although all students can profit from a discussion of death and dying, education about these topics might be particularly important in classrooms in which a student has a terminal illness. Teachers should be direct and open in their discussion of death and dying. Death shouldn't be a taboo subject; nor should teachers deny their own feelings or squelch the feelings of others. Confronted with the task of educating a child or youth with a terminal illness, teachers should seek available resources and turn to professionals in other disciplines for help (Heller et al., 1996; Leaman, 2000).

Links with Other Disciplines

Children seldom have a single disability, and many children with physical disabilities have other disabilities as well. Therefore, multiple disciplines are often required, and special education is only one of many services required (see Batshaw, 2002).

Many children with physical disabilities will need the services of a physical therapist and/or occupational therapist. (For a description of classroom implications, see Responsive Instruction on page 518.) Both can give valuable suggestions about helping the child use his or her physical abilities to the greatest possible extent, continuing therapeutic management in the classroom, and encouraging independence and good work habits. The teacher should be particularly concerned about how to handle and position the child so that the risk of further physical disability will be minimized and independent movement and manipulation of educational materials can be most efficiently learned.

Specialists in prosthetics and orthotics design and build artificial limbs, braces, and other devices that help individuals who are physically disabled to function more conventionally. By conferring with such specialists, the teacher will better understand the function and operation of a child's prosthesis or orthosis and know what the child can and cannot be expected to do.

Cooperation with psychologists and social workers can be particularly important in the case of a child with a physical disability. Working with the child's family and community agencies is often necessary to prevent lapses in treatment. The child may also be particularly susceptible to psychological stress, so the school psychologist might need to be consulted to obtain an accurate assessment of intellectual potential.

Speech-language therapists are often called on to work with children with physical disabilities, especially those with cerebral palsy. The teacher will want advice from the speech-language therapist on how to maximize the child's learning of speech and language. Individuals of all ages need access to play and recreation, regardless of their physical abilities. Any adequate program for children or youths with physical disabilities will provide toys, games, and physical exercise to stimulate, amuse, and teach recreation skills and provide the youngster with options for productive leisure (Bullock & Mahon, 2000; Sherrill, 2004). Physical education that is adapted to the abilities and disabilities of students is an important part of every sound school program.

Casebook Reflections

REFER TO THE CASE *Praying for a Miracle* in your booklet. There is no mention of physical or occupational therapists in this case. What might their role be in assisting Peter? What suggestions might they have to make Peter's transition more successful? ●

People with physical disabilities can learn to do many of the things most nondisabled persons do, although sometimes they must perform these tasks in different ways. Educating students with physical disabilities is mostly a matter of educating the nondisabled population of this fact.

Danielle prospers due to intensive early intervention and intra-professional and parental communication

Jennifer Durrance, Danielle's mother: "Her teacher wrote me notes daily because she knew Danielle couldn't tell me about her day."

After three years of early intervention services, four-year-old Danielle Durrance receives early childhood special education in an inclusive preschool program.

These are the keys to her success:

- intensive *early intervention*,
- relentless *communication*,
- specific *goals addressing physical delays and academic readiness*.

Special educator Leigh Anne Williams teaches typically developing youngsters as well as 3- and 4-year-olds with disabilities or developmental delays. Danielle Durrance is the only child in her class who uses a wheelchair. Her mother, Jennifer Durrance, communicates frequently with Williams to ensure that Danielle receives appropriate instruction and related services in her inclusive preschool program. Since she was 9-months-old, Danielle has prospered from intensive, relentless, and specific special education.

● **Intensive Early Intervention** Danielle has cerebral palsy (CP), a neurological condition that limits her mobility, her speech, and her social interactions. On the day before Halloween, she dabbed white finger-painted ghosts and goblins on black paper. Danielle finished her creation at her standing table, a piece of adaptive equipment that provides her with vertical support for up to 60 minutes each day. While her nine classmates washed their hands, Danielle transferred to her wheelchair with the help of one of the classroom's three instructional assistants. "My assistants take turns lifting Danielle and positioning her to use her walker or the vestibular swing that hangs from the classroom ceiling. They also help

with her personal hygiene and we keep a chart on the bathroom door to be sure we're sharing her physical support," says Williams.

Danielle was born prematurely at 34 weeks gestation and experienced a lack of oxygen during delivery. She weighed only 4 pounds, 4 ounces, at birth and spent 11 days in the hospital. When she was 4 months old her mother suspected something was wrong. "She couldn't roll over and find a toy that was near her in the crib. You know how babies look at their hands a lot? Well, she would mostly look at one hand; she kept her other hand down." At 6 months, Danielle was not sitting up and it was clear that her eyes were crossed. When she was 9 months old, developmental tests, including an MRI, confirmed that Danielle had CP and early intervention services began. A special education teacher came to the house to work with Danielle and her parents drove her to physical and occupational therapy several times a week. They also made visits to an ophthalmologist.

● **Relentless Communication** Mrs. Durrance credits effective communication between parents and professionals for Danielle's smooth transition from early intervention services to preschool special education. "At the transition meeting, someone asked if

Early Intervention

All people who work with young children with physical disabilities have two concerns: (1) early identification and intervention and (2) development of communication. Identifying signs of developmental delay so that intervention can begin as early as possible is important in preventing further disabilities that can result from lack of teaching and proper care. Early intervention also maximizes the outcome of therapy (see Conlon, 2002). Communication skills are difficult for some children with physical disabilities, and they are a critical objective of any preschool program (see Chapter 9). See the Success Stories above featuring Danielle, a four-year-old

I had a picture of Danielle with me. I really appreciated that. There was nothing in particular that caused me to feel stressed, but I think teachers should know that many parents feel very nervous at these meetings."

Jennifer Durrance also advises teachers to learn as much as they can about how a child's disability affects her life and her learning:

Know the IEP, especially when a child is served in the regular classroom.

Keep communication a priority. Teachers need to know the parents of the child, too.

Seek information. Know that parents are knowledgeable about their child's disability.

● **Specific Goals Addressing Physical Delays and Academic Readiness** Danielle has attended the Green Valley Preschool Program since August, 1999. According to evaluations using the Carolina Curriculum for Preschoolers with Special Needs, Danielle has progressed in all developmental areas, although her delays in cognition and social adaptation place her approximately 1 year to 1 1/2 years behind her age peers. She remembers objects that have been hidden, understands concepts like empty/full, and add one more. Socially, she follows directions, expresses enthusiasm for work or play, plays games with supervision, and enjoys being with other children. According to her IEP, Danielle's social interactions are limited by her physical delays. Danielle's fine and gross motor skills place her closer to 2 years behind her age peers. She receives occupational and physical therapy to enhance her manipulative and visual motor skills and to improve her mobility and endurance. She also receives speech-language therapy. Receptively, Danielle appears to understand many age-appropriate concepts and vocabulary, but she doesn't often initiate communication, nor does she imitate consistently.

In Spring the IEP team will make decisions for Danielle's programming for the next school year. Together, her parents and her multi-disciplinary team will decide if Danielle should start Kindergarten with her age peers or whether she would benefit more from extended preschool support.

CEC'S STANDARDS: PAVING THE WAY TO SUCCESS

ASSESS YOUR STEPS TO SUCCESS in meeting the CEC Knowledge and Skill Base for All Beginning Special Education Teachers of Students with Physical and Health Disabilities. Use the following questions to reflect on the growth of your own professional knowledge, skills, and dispositions.

REFLECTING ON YOUR OWN PROFESSIONAL DEVELOPMENT

If you were Danielle's teacher . . .

■ What are some areas about educating students with physical disabilities that you would need to know more about?

■ What are some specific skills that would help you address her academic and physical challenges?

■ What personal dispositions do you think are most important for you to develop in teaching students with physical disabilities?

Using the CEC Standards

■ What are the roles and responsibilities of medical and related services personnel in educating students with physical disabilities?

■ What are some frequent concerns of families of students with physical disabilities and what are some strategies to address these concerns?

■ What are some instructional practices, strategies, and adaptations necessary to accommodate the physical and communication characteristics of students with physical disabilities?

● *By Jean B. Crockett*

who has received intensive language instruction as well as other modifications to her environment.

Besides communication, the first concern of teachers of young children with physical disabilities should be handling and positioning. *Handling* refers to how the child is picked up, carried, held, and assisted; *positioning* refers to providing support for the child's body and arranging instructional or play materials in certain ways. Proper handling makes the child more comfortable and receptive to education. Proper positioning maximizes physical efficiency and ability to manipulate materials; it also inhibits undesirable motor responses while promoting desired growth and motor patterns (Best et al., 2005). Proper positioning for one child might not be appropriate for another.

The teacher of young children with physical disabilities must know how to teach gross motor responses—such as head control, rolling over, sitting, standing, and walking—and understand how abnormal reflexes that may be a part of developmental disabilities can interfere with learning basic motor skills. If the child has severe neurological and motor impairments, the teacher might need to begin by focusing on teaching the child to eat (e.g., how to chew and swallow) and to make the oral movements that are required for speech (Best et al., 2005; Martin, 2006). Fine motor skills, such as pointing, reaching, grasping, and releasing, can be critically important. These motor skills are best taught in the context of daily lessons that involve self-help and communication.

Motor skills shouldn't be taught in isolation but as part of daily living and learning activities that will increase the child's communication, independence, creativity, motivation, and future learning. Learning social responsiveness, appropriate social initiation, how to play with others, and problem solving are other important goals for which the teacher must develop instructional strategies.

UNDERSTANDING THE STANDARDS AND PRINCIPLES What do we know about transition to adulthood for students with physical disabilities? (CEC Knowledge and Skill Standards PH10S1 & PH10S4)

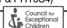
Council for Exceptional Children

Transition

Transition involves a turning point, a change from one situation or environment to another. When special educators speak of transition, they typically refer to change from school to work or from adolescence to adulthood. For children with physical disabilities, however, transition is perhaps a more pervasive concern than it is for children with other disabilities. It may involve discharge from intensive care or transition from hospital to home at any age. In fact, transition begins for some newborns immediately after they have been treated with sophisticated medical procedures. Nevertheless, we focus here on the transition concerns of adolescents and young adults with physical disabilities. Clearly, transition planning for many students with physical disabilities, including those who are supported by medical technology, is inadequate (Morningstar et al., 2001).

Two areas of concern for transition stand out clearly for adolescents and young adults with physical disabilities: careers and sociosexuality. Adolescents begin contemplating and experimenting with jobs, social relations, and sexuality in direct and serious ways. For the adolescent with a physical disability, these questions and trial behaviors are often especially perplexing, not just to themselves but also to their families: Can I get and hold a satisfying job? Can I become independent? Will I have close and lasting friendships? Will anyone find me physically attractive? How can I gratify my sexual needs? Ordinary adolescents have a hard time coming to grips with these questions and the developmental tasks they imply; adolescents with physical disabilities often have an even harder time (see White, Schuyler, Edelman, Hayes, & Batshaw, 2002).

As we pointed out in discussing psychological characteristics, there is no formula for predicting the emotional or behavioral problems a person with a given physical disability might have. Much depends on the management and training the person has received and continues to receive as an adolescent and as an adult. Bottos and colleagues provide the following caution about interventions for cerebral palsy: "Services for individuals with CP should be planned keeping in mind an entire life perspective rather than just the child-focused approach. Reduced contact when children grow up often results in a general deterioration of the quality of life of adults with disabilities and their careers" (2001, p. 526). Andersson and Mattsson (2001) drive the point home: In their study, 35 percent of adults with CP reported decreased walking ability, and 9 percent had stopped walking altogether.

Choosing a Career

In working out an occupational goal for the adolescent or young adult with physical disabilities, it's important to carefully assess the individual's specific abilities, disabilities, and motivation. Postsecondary education must be considered in light of the individual's interests, strengths, demands, and accessibility. Some disabilities clearly rule out certain occupational choices. With other disabilities, high motivation and full use of residual function can make it possible to achieve unusual professional status.

One of the greatest problems in dealing with adolescents who have physical disabilities is helping them to attain a realistic employment outlook. Intelligence, emotional characteristics, motivation, and work habits must be assessed at least as carefully as physical limitations. Furthermore, the availability of jobs and the demands of certain occupations must be taken into account. The child who has moderate intellectual disability and severe spastic quadriplegia, for instance, is highly unlikely to have a career as a lawyer, a laboratory technician, or a clerk-typist. But what of one who has severe spastic quadriplegia and a bright mind? Such a person might well overcome both the physical limitation and the associated social stigma and be successful in a wide variety of fields in which the work is more mental than physical.

There are no simple conclusions regarding the occupational outlook for students with physical disabilities. Those with mild or transitory disabling conditions might not be affected at all in their occupational choices. Yet some with relatively mild physical disabilities might be unemployed or even unemployable because of inappropriate social and emotional behavior or poor work habits; they might need vocational rehabilitation training to function even in a vocation with limited demands. Some people with severe physical disabilities are able to use their intelligence, social skills, and residual physical abilities to the fullest and become competitive employees (or employers) in demanding occupations.

The outlook for employment of students with physical or multiple and severe disabilities has been improved dramatically by legislation and research and demonstration projects. As we mentioned in Chapter 1, the Americans with Disabilities Act of 1990 requires that reasonable accommodations be made to create equal employment opportunities for people with disabilities. More accessible transportation and buildings, increased skill in using technology to allow people to accomplish tasks at work, and greater commitment to preparing people with disabilities for work are resulting in more personal independence, economic self-sufficiency, and social acceptance, which benefit not only people with disabilities, but the economy and society as well.

We now recognize that preparing for work begins in childhood. Long before adolescence, children, including those with physical disabilities, need to be taught about and to explore various careers. They need to be thinking about what they like to do as well as what they are particularly good at and about the demands and rewards of various kinds of jobs. The objective should be to help students select appropriate training and enter a career that makes maximum use of their abilities in ways that they find personally gratifying.

Supported employment for people with severe disabilities is a relatively new concept that is being adopted widely. In this approach, a person with a severe disability works in a regular work setting. He or she becomes a regular employee, performs a

■ **Supported employment**
A method of integrating people with disabilities who cannot work independently into competitive employment; includes use of an employment specialist, or job coach, who helps the person with a disability function on the job.

valued function in the same workplace as nondisabled employees, and receives fair remuneration. Training and continued support are necessary—hence the term *supported employment*. For example, a person with disabilities might be hired as a greeter at a store but needs training and continued support in such skills as making eye contact, smiling, welcoming shoppers to the store, and offering a shopping cart or information to customers. Training and continued support might also be required to help the person with disabilities know when to leave people alone and not insist on providing information or assistance that the customer does not want.

New technologies, especially in computing and other electronic devices, offer great promise for enabling students with physical disabilities to achieve personal independence, to acquire education and training that will make them employable, and to find employment. In some cases, the technology is readily available and educators need only to become aware of the software (e.g., software that allows the functions of keys to be altered), find ways in which keystrokes can be saved through subprogramming routines (e.g., macros or find-and-replace features in word processing), or provide substitutions for physical manipulation of materials (e.g., computer graphics programs as substitutes for paper paste-ups or model construction).

Sometimes an individual's ability to use standard equipment is greatly enhanced by a simple modification such as orientation or location. Simply placing a keyboard in a vertical position over a monitor can enhance the ability of someone who uses a headstick to use a computer. A headstick is an adaptive device that allows someone who can't use his or her hands or feet, but who has control of neck muscles, to use a computer or accomplish other tasks. Teachers must always look for simple, inexpensive or cost-free ways to facilitate the performance of students with disabilities—to prevent an environment designed for people without disabilities from handicapping those who must do things a different way. Overlooking the seemingly obvious is perhaps the way in which we most frequently handicap people with disabilities.

Sociosexuality

Until fairly recently, physical disabilities were assumed to cancel human sexuality. People who were not typical physically, especially if they had limited mobility, were thought of as having no sex appeal for anyone and as having little or no ability or right to function sexually.

Fortunately, attitudes and experiences are changing. It's now recognized that people with disabilities have a right to family life education, including sex education, and to a full range of human relationships, including appropriate sexual expression. Sociosexual education for students with physical disabilities, as with such education for all other children and youths, should begin early, continue through adulthood, and include information about the structures and functions of the body, human relationships and responsibilities, and alternative modes of sexual gratification. Youths with physical disabilities need to experience close friendships and warm physical contact that is not sexually intimate. But it is neither realistic nor fair to expect people with physical disabilities to keep all their relationships platonic or to limit themselves to fantasy. Most physical disabilities, even if severe, don't in themselves kill sexual desire or prevent sexual gratification, nor do they preclude marriage and children. The purpose of special education and rehabilitation is to make exceptional individuals' lives as full and complete as possible. In the case of youths with physical disabilities, this might involve teaching or providing alternative means of sexual stimulation and accepting sexual practices and relationships that are different from the norm. With sensitive education and rehabilitation, satisfying sociosexual expression can be achieved by all but a small minority of people with disabilities.

INTERNET RESOURCES

The Attainment Company creates resources to help people identify the emerging issues in special education and to access the educational materials that will allow them to meet such issues effectively: www .attainmentcompany.com

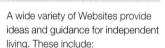

INTERNET RESOURCES

A wide variety of Websites provide ideas and guidance for independent living. These include:

Canine Companions for Independence, a nonprofit organization providing assistance dogs: www.caninecompanions.org

A collection of computer-related products and services available to assist people with disabilities: www.closingthegap.com

The Independent Living Research Utilization Center: www.ilru.org

The Institute on Independent Living: www.independentliving.org

Summary

How are physical disabilities defined and classified?

▶ Physical disabilities are physical limitations or health problems that interfere with school attendance or learning to such an extent that special services, training, equipment, materials, or facilities are required.
   ■ May be congenital or acquired.
   ■ May be acute or chronic, episodic or progressive.
   ■ May be accompanied by other disabilities, such as intellectual disability and emotional or behavioral disorders, or special gifts or talents.

▶ Major categories are neuromotor impairments, orthopedic or musculoskeletal disorders, and other conditions that affect health or physical abilities.

What is the prevalence of physical disabilities, and what is the need for special education?

▶ Less than 0.5 percent of the child population have physical disabilities.
   ■ About half of these have multiple disabilities.
   ■ About one-fourth of these have orthopedic problems.
   ■ About one-fourth of these have chronic health problems.

What are some major neuromotor impairments?

▶ All involve damage to the brain before, during, or soon after birth or damage to the spinal cord.
   ■ Cerebral palsy, characterized by paralysis, weakness, uncoordination, and/or other motor dysfunction, sometimes by intellectual disability or other disabilities
   ■ Seizure disorder, an abnormal electrical discharge in the brain
   ■ Spina bifida, the failure of the spinal column to close during fetal development

What are some major orthopedic and musculoskeletal disorders?

▶ Muscular dystrophy, a degenerative disease causing a progressive weakening and wasting away of muscle

▶ Juvenile rheumatoid arthritis, acute inflammation around the joints that may cause chronic pain and other complications

What other conditions affect health or physical ability?

▶ Fetal alcohol syndrome (FAS), now one of the most common causes of malformation and intellectual disability, caused by the mother's abuse of alcohol during pregnancy

▶ AIDS, a life-threatening viral infection that often involves neurological complications such as intellectual disability, seizures, cerebral palsy, and emotional or behavioral disorders

▶ Accidents

How can physical disabilities be prevented?

▶ Safety prcautions, better health care, prevention of pregnancy in early teens, prevention of child abuse, prevention of conditions that cause brain or spinal injury

What are the psychological and behavioral characteristics of individuals with physical disabilities?

▶ No generalizations are possible.

▶ Much depends on the reactions of family and the public.

What are prosthetics, orthotics, and adaptive devices?

▶ Prosthetics are artificial body parts.

▶ Orthotics enhance the function of a body part.

▶ Adaptive devices aid daily activity.

What are the major educational considerations for students with physical disabilities?

▶ Education must make the most of the student's assets.

▶ Education should be as normal as possible and equip the student for daily living as well as employment or further education.

Why is early intervention important, and on what should it focus?

▶ Early intervention is important in preventing further disability and maximizing the child's development.

▶ Early intervention should focus on communication, handling, positioning, and social skills.

What are the major issues in transition for students with physical disabilities?

▶ Transition may involve movement from one setting to another as well as preparation for adulthood.
   ■ Choice of and preparation for a career are important issues.
   ■ Sociosexuality is another critical issue.

STANDARDS and PRINCIPLES in this Chapter

SPECIAL EDUCATORS . . .

- understand the similarities and differences in human development and the characteristics between and among individuals with and without exceptional learning needs (from CEC Content Standard #2).

- understand the effects that an exceptional condition can have on an individual's learning in school and throughout life (from CEC Content Standard #3).

- possess a repertoire of evidence-based instructional strategies to individualize instruction for individuals with exceptional learning needs (from CEC Content Standard #4).

- actively create learning environments for individuals with exceptional learning needs that foster cultural understanding, safety and emotional well-being, positive social interactions, and active engagement of individuals with exceptional learning needs (from CEC Content Standard #5).

- use collaboration to facilitate the successful transitions of individuals with exceptional learning needs across settings and services (from CEC Content Standard #10).

ALL TEACHERS . . .

- understand how children learn and develop and can provide learning opportunities that support the intellectual, social, and personal development of each learner (INTASC Principle #2).

- understand how students differ in their approaches to learning and create instructional opportunities that are adapted to diverse learners (INTASC Principle #3).

- understand and use a variety of instructional strategies to encourage students' development of critical thinking, problem solving, and performance skills (INTASC Principle #4).

- use an understanding of individual and group motivation and behavior to create a learning environment that encourages positive social interaction, active engagement in learning, and self-motivation (INTASC Principle #5).

- foster relationships with school colleagues, families, and agencies in the larger community to support students' learning and well being (INTASC Principle #10).

Applying the STANDARDS and PRINCIPLES

- DESCRIBE at least two types of physical disabilities (CEC Content Standard #2 & INTASC Principle #2)

- DESCRIBE some effects a physical disability might have on a student's education (CEC Content Standard #3 & INTASC Principle #3)

- HOW should teachers determine what instructional methods to use with students with physical disabilities? (CEC Content Standard #4 & INTASC Principle #4)

- DESCRIBE a learning environment that would be well suited for students with physical disabilities. (CEC Content Standard #5 & INTASC Principle #5)

- HOW would you respond to parents who approach you expressing concern about the future of their high school student with a physical disability? (CEC Content Standard #10 & INTASC Principle #10)

Now go to the Hallahan/Kauffman, Eleventh Edition MyEducationLab course at www.myeducationlab.com to:

- take a Pretest to assess your initial comprehension of the chapter content;
- study chapter content with your Individualized Study Plan;
- take a Posttest to assess your understanding of chapter content;
- engage in multimedia exercises to help you build a deeper and more applied understanding of chapter content.

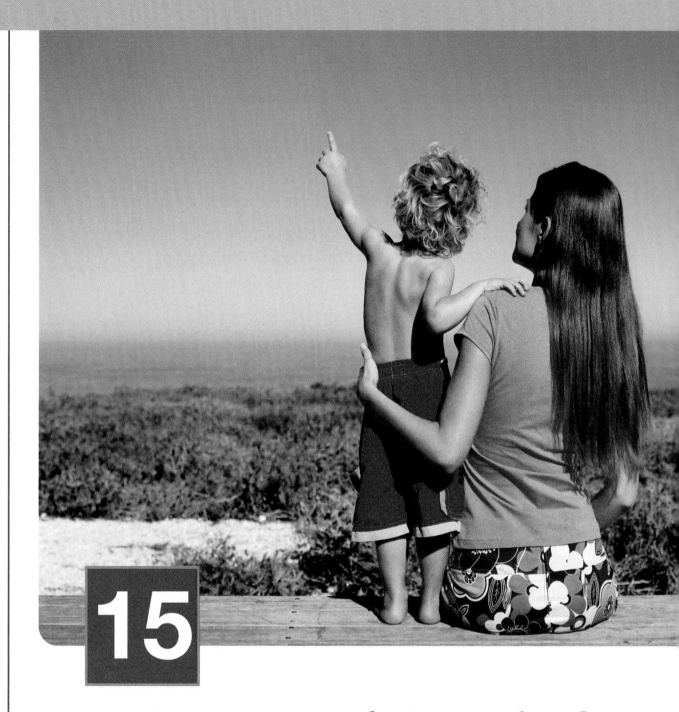

15

Learners with Special Gifts and Talents

A genius is not very likely to ever discover himself; neither is he very likely to be discovered by his intimates; they are so close to him that he is out of focus to them and they can't get at his proportions; they cannot perceive that there is any considerable difference between his bulk and their own. They can't get a perspective on him and it is only by a perspective that the difference between him and the rest of their limited circle can be perceived.

—Mark Twain
The Autobiography of Mark Twain

QUESTIONS to guide your reading of this chapter . . .

- How is giftedness defined?
- What is the prevalence of giftedness?
- What are the origins of giftedness?
- How is giftedness identified?
- What are the psychological and behavioral characteristics of students with special gifts?
- How do cultural values affect the education of students with special gifts?
- What groups of students with special gifts are neglected?
- What are the major educational considerations for students with special gifts?
- What are the major problems of early intervention for children with special gifts?
- What provisions are made for transition of students with special gifts?

MISCONCEPTIONS ABOUT
Learners with Special Gifts and Talents

MYTH ■ People with special intellectual gifts are physically weak, socially inept, narrow in interests, and prone to emotional instability and early decline.

FACT ■ There are wide individual variations, and most individuals with special intellectual gifts are healthy, well adjusted, socially attractive, and morally responsible.

MYTH ■ Those who have special gifts or talents are in a sense superhuman.

FACT ■ People with special gifts or talents are not superhuman; rather, they are human beings with extraordinary gifts in particular areas. And like everyone else, they may have particular faults.

MYTH ■ Children with special gifts or talents are usually bored with school and antagonistic toward those who are responsible for their education.

FACT ■ Most children with special gifts like school and adjust well to their peers and teachers, although some do not like school and have social or emotional problems.

MYTH ■ People with special gifts or talents tend to be mentally unstable.

FACT ■ Those with special gifts or talents are about as likely to be well adjusted and emotionally healthy as those who do not have such gifts.

MYTH ■ We know that 3 to 5 percent of the population has special gifts or talents.

FACT ■ The percentage of the population that is found to have special gifts or talents depends on the definition of *giftedness* used. Some definitions include only 1 or 2 percent of the population; others, over 20 percent.

MYTH ■ Giftedness is a stable trait, always consistently evident in all periods of a person's life.

FACT ■ Some of the remarkable talents and productivity of people with special gifts develop early and continue throughout life; in other cases, a person's gifts or talents are not noticed until adulthood. Occasionally, a child who shows outstanding ability becomes a nondescript adult.

MYTH ■ People who have special gifts do everything well.

FACT ■ Some people who are characterized as having a special gift have superior abilities of many kinds; others have clearly superior talents in only one area.

MYTH ■ A person has special intellectual gifts if he or she scores above a certain level on intelligence tests.

FACT ■ IQ is only one indication of one kind of giftedness. Creativity and high motivation are as important as indications as general intelligence. Gifts or talents in some areas, such as the visual and performing arts, are not assessed by IQ tests.

MYTH ■ Students who have a true gift or talent for something will excel without special education. They need only the incentives and instruction that are appropriate for all students.

FACT ■ Some children with special gifts or talents will perform at a remarkably high level without special education of any kind, and some will make outstanding contributions even in the face of great obstacles to their achievement. But most will not come close to achieving at a level commensurate with their potential unless their talents are deliberately fostered by instruction that is appropriate for their advanced abilities.

530

People who have special gifts or the potential for gifted performance can go through life unrecognized. As Mark Twain pointed out (see p. 529), they might seem unremarkable to their closest associates. Sometimes the special talents or gifts of children and youths aren't discovered because their families and intimates place no particular value on their special abilities. And sometimes they aren't recognized because these young people are not given opportunities or training. Especially in the case of those who are poor or members of minority groups, students with extraordinary gifts or talents may be deprived of chances to demonstrate and develop their potential. How many more outstanding artists and scientists would we have if every talented child had the opportunity and the training necessary to develop his or her talents to the fullest possible extent? We know that we would have more, but we don't know how many.

Unlike disabilities, gifts and talents are abilities that nearly everyone believes should be fostered deliberately. Yet giftedness is not without risk of stigma and rejection. Many people have a low level of tolerance for those who eclipse ordinary individuals in some area of achievement, especially in areas of academic knowledge or achievement. Children who achieve far beyond the level of their average peers may be subjected to criticism, social isolation, or unhelpful social pressure by their parents, other children, or school personnel (Coleman & Cross, 2000; Freeman, 2005; Swiatek, 1998).

Some of the problems of giftedness parallel those of disabling conditions. For instance, defining and identifying children with special gifts or talents involve the same difficulties as defining and identifying intellectual disability or emotional or behavioral disorders (see Kauffman & Hallahan, 2005). But there's an underlying philosophical question regarding giftedness that makes us think differently about this exceptionality: Most of us feel a moral obligation to help people who are at some disadvantage compared to the average person, who have differences that prevent them from achieving ordinary levels of competence unless they are given special help. But we may not feel the same moral obligation to help people who have special gifts, who are already ahead of most of us, to become even better and distinguish themselves further by fulfilling their highest promise.

The desirability or necessity of helping the highest-achieving students to become even better is often questioned. Today, the emphasis is on programs to develop the talents of *all* students, with less special attention to those who might be identified as gifted or talented. As some researchers have noted, this trend toward downplaying or neglecting giftedness, especially as affected by the No Child Left Behind Act of 2002 (NCLB), might not be very wise (Colangelo, Assouline, & Gross, 2004a, 2004b; Gallagher, 2000b; Gentry, 2006; Goodkin, 2005; Mendoza, 2006; Kauffman & Konold, 2007; Van Tassel-Baska, 2006). DiGennaro (2007) describes the neglect of our most talented students as an ugly secret of contemporary American education policy.

Definition

Students with special gifts excel in some way compared to other students of the same age. Beyond this almost meaningless statement, however, there is little agreement about how giftedness should be defined. School systems have widely differing practices regarding the education of students with special gifts or talents, because the term *gifted* has no clear-cut definition. Disagreements about definition are due primarily to differences of opinion regarding the following questions:

1. *In what ways do students with a special gift or talent excel?* Do they excel in general intelligence, insight, creativity, special talents, and achievements in academic subjects or in a valued line of work, moral judgment, or some combination of such factors? Perhaps nearly everyone is gifted in some way or other. What kind of giftedness is most important? What kind of giftedness should be encouraged?

Video Homework Exercise

Gifted Students ● Go to the Homework and Exercises section in Chapter 15 of MyEducationLab and watch the video "Challenging Gifted Students."

Reading Homework Exercises

Teaching Gifted Students ● Go to the Homework and Exercises section in Chapter 15 of MyEducationLab to read the article "Teacher Says: Gifted Students."

2. *How is giftedness measured?* Is it measured by standardized tests of aptitude and achievement, teacher judgments, past performance in school or everyday life, or some other means? If it's measured in any one particular way, some individuals will be overlooked. If past performance is the test, giftedness is being defined after the fact. What measurement techniques are valid and reliable? What measurements will identify those students who have the potential to develop special gifts or talents?

3. *To what degree must a student excel to be considered to have a special gift or talent?* Must the student do better than 50 percent, 80 percent, 90 percent, or 99 percent of the comparison group? The number of individuals with special gifts will vary depending on the criterion (or criteria) for giftedness. What percentage of the population should be considered to have special gifts?

4. *Who should comprise the comparison group?* Should it be every student of the same chronological age, the other students in the same school, all students of the same ethnic or racial origin, or some other grouping? Almost everyone is the brightest or most capable in some group. What group should set the standard?

5. *Why should students with special gifts be identified?* What social or cultural good is expected to come from their identification? Is it important to meet individual students' educational needs? Are national economic or security issues at stake? Does identifying these individuals maintain an elite group or social power? By providing special educational opportunities for these students, will others reap personal or social benefits? What criteria will be used to judge whether identifying students with special gifts or talents pays off?

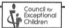

UNDERSTANDING THE STANDARDS AND PRINCIPLES Is there consensus about what giftedness means? Why or why not? (CEC Knowledge and Skill Standard GT1K5)

■ **Precocity**
Remarkable early development.

■ **Insight**
The ability to separate and/or combine various pieces of information in new, creative, and useful ways.

■ **Genius**
A word sometimes used to indicate a particular aptitude or capacity in any area; rare intellectual powers.

■ **Creativity**
The ability to express novel and useful ideas, to sense and elucidate new and important relationships, and to ask previously unthought of, but crucial, questions.

■ **Talent**
Ordinarily has been used to indicate a special ability, aptitude, or accomplishment.

Giftedness or *talentedness*, like *intellectual disability*, is whatever we choose to make it. Someone can be considered gifted (or intellectually disabled) one day and not the next, simply because an arbitrary definition has been changed. There is no inherent rightness or wrongness in the definitions that professionals use (Kauffman & Hallahan, 2005). Some definitions might be more logical, more precise, or more useful than others, but we are still unable to say that they are more correct in some absolute sense. We have to struggle with the concepts of gift and talent and the reasons for identifying individuals with gifts or talents before we can make any decisions about definition. Any definition of giftedness is shaped to a large extent by what the surrounding culture believes is most useful or necessary for its survival. Giftedness is defined, not discovered (see Gallagher, 2000a, 2000b, 2002; Heller, Monks, Sternberg, & Subotnik, 2000; Lohman, 2006).

Even the terminology of giftedness can be rather confusing. Besides the word *gifted*, a variety of other terms have been used to describe individuals who are superior in some way: talented, creative, insightful, genius, and precocious, for example.

- **Precocity** refers to remarkable early development. Precocious children develop gifts in such areas as language, music, or mathematics at a very young age.
- **Insight** may be defined as separating relevant from irrelevant information, finding novel and useful ways of combining relevant bits of information, or relating new and old information in a novel and productive way.
- **Genius** has sometimes been used to indicate a particular aptitude or capacity in any area. More often, it has been used to indicate extremely rare intellectual powers (often assumed to be indicated by IQ) or creativity.
- **Creativity** refers to the ability to express novel and useful ideas, to sense and elucidate novel and important relationships, and to ask previously unthought of, but crucial, questions.
- **Talent** ordinarily has been used to indicate a special ability, aptitude, or accomplishment.

Bill Gates dropped out of Harvard at age 19 to help form Microsoft Corp., now the world's largest producer of software for microcomputers. He and his wife Melinda established The Bill & Melinda Gates Foundation, one of the world's most prominent philanthropic organizations.

Bono is the charismatic lead singer for the Irish rock group U2, whose songs cover politics, religion, and social issues. Bono has dedicated a large part of his life to humanitarian efforts such as canceling the debt of impoverished third world nations, wiping out poverty—particularly in Africa—and expanding access to drugs that help control HIV.

Tiger Woods is a professional golfer whose achievements to date rank him among the most successful and highest paid golfers of all time. He is often credited with prompting a major surge of interest in the game of golf.

Julie Taymor is a renowned director of Broadway theatre and film. Her critically acclaimed work has garnered two Tony Awards, an Emmy Award, and an Academy Award nomination. Her work is noted for its visual innovation and highly creative costuming choices.

Mia Michaels is an American choreographer who has worked with Madonna, Prince, and Celine Dion. She is best known for her contemporary dance choreography, and has won an Emmy Award for her work on the television program *So You Think You Can Dance*.

Maria Sharapova is a professional tennis player and currently the fifth-ranked female player in the world. She has won two Grand Slam singles titles: the U.S. Open and Wimbledon.

Pehr Harbury, an associate professor in biochemistry at Stanford's School of Medicine, recently was named a MacArthur Fellow—a national honor frequently called the "genius grant." Harbury's most well-known research focuses on devising ways to use DNA molecules to create chemical compounds that may be useful in drug design.

David M. Carroll is a naturalist, artist, and author of acclaimed natural histories. He has earned awards from the U.S. Department of Agriculture and the International Society of Arboriculture, and also received an Environmental Merit Award from the Environmental Protection Agency.

James Randi is a magician and escape artist, but is best known as an investigator and debunker of paranormal and pseudoscientific claims. He has received numerous awards, including a Fellowship from the John D. and Catherine T. MacArthur Foundation.

Dr. Olufunmilayo Olopade is an oncologist who translates her basic research on individual and population cancer susceptibility into an effective clinical practice for treating breast cancer among African and African-American women.

■ **Giftedness**
Cognitive (intellectual) superiority, creativity, and motivation of sufficient magnitude to set the child apart from the vast majority of age peers and make it possible for the child to contribute something of particular value to society.

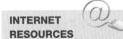

INTERNET RESOURCES

See ERIC Clearinghouse on Disabilities & Gifted Education, www.ericec.org

● **Giftedness**, as we use the term in this chapter, refers to cognitive (intellectual) superiority (not necessarily of genius caliber), creativity, and motivation in combination and of sufficient magnitude to set the child apart from the vast majority of age peers and make it possible for her or him to contribute something of particular value to society.

The lack of consensus about what giftedness means poses problems for government definitions. No federal law requires special education for students with special gifts or talents, although federal legislation encourages states to develop programs and support research. The federal mandate for special education applies only if the student has a disability in addition to giftedness (see Zirkel, 2003; Huefner, 2006). However, most states mandate programs, and the most common elements of state definitions are (1) general intellectual ability, (2) specific academic aptitude, (3) creative thinking ability, (4) advanced ability in the fine arts and performing arts, and (5) leadership ability.

Giftedness (or genius) appears to involve both quantitative and qualitative differences in thinking. "People who are gifted typically work really hard (i.e., they are highly motivated). Of course, quantity alone does not make one a genius. The quality of the quantity matters" (Shermer, 2001, p. 268). Gifted people might think and work more, but they also think and work better than most of us (Goldsmith, 2005; Heller et al., 2000).

The field of special education is beginning to appreciate the different ways in which giftedness can be expressed in various areas of human endeavor. Likewise, educators are starting to acknowledge the extent to which the meaning of giftedness is rooted in cultural values (Gallagher, 2002; Karnes & Bean, 2001; Lohman, 2006; Sternberg, 1998, 2000). There are many different abilities and many different ways of measuring them. What's considered giftedness and how it's measured depend to a large extent on what a culture values and believes. Most experts now acknowledge that intelligence isn't all there is to giftedness (Lohman, 2006).

Whereas the usual tests of intelligence assess the ability to think deductively and arrive at a single answer that can be scored right or wrong, tests of creativity suggest many different potential answers. Creativity is an extremely appealing topic of commentary and research (see Cramond, Matthews-Morgan, Bandalos, & Zuo, 2005; Feldhusen, 2005; Henshon, 2006; Hunsaker, 2005; Runco, 2005; Selby, Shaw, & Houtz, 2005; Treffinger & Isaksen, 2005). *American Psychologist* featured articles on the creative talents of writers John Irving (Amabile, 2001) and Stephen Donaldson (Ward, 2001), physicist Linus Pauling (Nakamura & Csikszentmihalyi, 2001), scientists Thomas Young (Martindale, 2001) and Charles Darwin (Gruber & Wallace, 2001), and painter Claude Monet (Stokes, 2001). McGreevy (2004) described the creative life of Joanne Kathleen Rowling, creator of the *Harry Potter* book series.

Recognizing the many facets of human intelligence has led to dissatisfaction with previous conceptualizations of general intelligence that reduced it to a single number (IQ) that was assumed to be unchangeable (Gould, 1996). Sternberg (1997) describes a theory of intelligence that suggests three main kinds of giftedness: analytic, synthetic, and practical.

● *Analytic giftedness* involves being able to take a problem apart—to understand the parts of a problem and how they are interrelated, which is a skill typically measured by conventional intelligence tests.

● *Synthetic giftedness* involves insight, intuition, creativity, or adeptness at coping with novel situations, skills that are typically associated with high achievement in the arts and sciences.

● *Practical giftedness* involves applying analytic and synthetic abilities to the solution of everyday problems, the kinds of skills that characterize people who have successful careers.

Children who are gifted may have superior cognitive abilities that allow them to compete with adults of average intellect.

Old stereotypes of giftedness die hard. For example, many people believe that those with special gifts or talents are superior in every way, comprising a distinct category of human beings. This myth may account in part for the public's fascination with particularly creative people and the tendency to fawn over those who distinguish themselves in glamorous lines of work. Another stereotype is that a gifted person knows everything (see Jacobs, 2004, for a very funny account of this idea). Still another mistaken idea is that ability and achievement are two completely different things (see Lohman, 2006).

A popular idea today is that there are "multiple intelligences" (Gardner & Hatch, 1989; see also Chan, 2006), although others argue that this theory is "scientifically untenable" (Lloyd & Hallahan, 2007, p. 251) and that the concept is simply unsupported by research (see Willingham, 2004 for a critique). The theory of multiple intelligences is widely held to be legitimate, but there are few, if any, proven applications of the theory to teaching (see Lloyd & Hallahan, 2007). This is not to say that intelligence can be reduced to a single score or performance, simply that the popular notion of *many* intelligences as described by Gardner and his colleagues with implications for teaching remains unproven.

Today, most experts in educating those with special gifts and talents suggest that giftedness refers to superior abilities in specific areas of performance, which may be exhibited under some circumstances but not others. Even though giftedness is believed to be a remarkable ability to do something that society values, it's not an inherent, immutable trait that a person necessarily carries for life. Moreover, having a special gift at one thing doesn't mean that a person is good at everything—or even that someone who is a good thinker about one thing is a good thinker about all things (see Kauffman, 2002). People get extraordinarily good at something only by developing their ability to do that particular thing. Ability is not "a mental tool that can be applied at will to different intellectual content . . . all cognitive tests measure developed abilities. There are no exceptions" (Lohman, 2006, p. 37).

Video Homework Exercise

Sternberg Definition • Go to the Homework and Exercises section in Chapter 15 of MyEducationLab and watch a video in which Dr. Sternberg provides his personal definition of intelligence.

INTERNET RESOURCES

For a sample of the controversy about multiple intelligences, go to http://www.hoover.org/ and input the search term "Willingham."

Reading Homework Exercise

Creativity ● Go to the Homework and Exercises section in Chapter 15 of MyEducationLab and read the article titled "Creativity, the Arts, and Madness."

UNDERSTANDING THE STANDARDS AND PRINCIPLES How are individuals with special gifts and talents different from the general population of learners? (CEC Knowledge and Skill Standard GT2K2)

Council for Exceptional Children

Another significant issue in reconceptualizing giftedness is recognizing that it, like beauty, is something that is defined by cultural consensus. Accordingly, Sternberg and Zhang (1995) proposed five criteria for judging whether someone exhibits giftedness:

1. *Excellence*: the individual must be superior to the peer group in one or more specific dimensions of performance.
2. *Rarity*: very few members of the peer group exhibit the characteristic or characteristics.
3. *Demonstrability*: the person must be able to actually exhibit the excellent and rare ability through some type of valid assessment (i.e., the person cannot just claim to have it or the potential for it).
4. *Productivity*: the person's performance must lead to or have the potential to lead to producing something.
5. *Value*: the person's performance is highly valued by society.

Sternberg and Zhang also suggest that most people intuitively believe that each of these five criteria is necessary and all five together are sufficient to define giftedness. Similar intuitive, consensual definitions appear to have existed in all cultures throughout history (see Hunsaker, 1995; Tannenbaum, 1993, 2000a). Some researchers have suggested that we should speak of people who exhibit gifted behavior, rather than of gifted people, because people typically demonstrate special gifts only under particular circumstances (Reis & Renzulli, 2001; Renzulli, 2005; Renzulli & Reis, 1997, 2000).

Prevalence

Federal reports and legislation have assumed that 3 to 5 percent of the U.S. school population could be considered to have special gifts or talents. The prevalence of giftedness is a function of the definition that is used; if giftedness is defined as the top x percent on a given criterion, the question of prevalence has been answered. Of course, if x percent refers to a percentage of a national sample, the prevalence of gifted pupils in a given school or cultural group may vary from that of the comparison group, regardless of the criteria that are used to measure performance (Gagne, 2000).

Origins of Giftedness

As defined today, giftedness isn't something that sets people apart in every way from people who are average. Instead, it refers to specific, valued, and unusual talents that people may exhibit during some periods of their lives. Therefore, the main factors that contribute to giftedness are really much the same as those that foster any type of behavior, whether typical or exceptional:

1. Genetic and other biological factors, such as neurological functioning and nutrition.
2. Social factors, such as family, school, the peer group, and community.

We are all combinations of the influences of our genetic inheritances and social and physical environments (see Gould, 1996; Heller et al., 2000; Pinker, 2002; Shermer, 2001; Simonton, 2005). What environments foster gifted performance? We can often change students' environments; we cannot change their genetic makeup.

Although giftedness may be determined in part by one's genetic inheritance, whatever genetic combinations are involved are exceedingly complex and not distributed according to race or social class. The idea that giftedness is entirely inherited is one of the worst ideas associated with gifted education (Gallagher, 2006). Genetic differences in abilities apply within various ethnic groups and social classes, not between them (see Gould, 1996; Plomin, 1997; Thompson & Plomin, 2000). However, children are not born with equal capabilities:

> There are some youngsters who are born with the capability to learn faster than others those ideas or concepts that modern societies value in children and adults. Such youngsters and their abilities are subject to many social influences and must interact with their environmental context. Therefore, it often becomes difficult to find students with these special talents in a multicultural society. (Gallagher, 2000b, p. 6)

Families, schools, peer groups, and communities have a profound influence on the development of giftedness. Stimulation, opportunities, expectations, demands, and rewards for performance all affect children's learning. For decades, researchers have found a correlation between socioeconomic level and IQ, undoubtedly in part because the performances measured by standard intelligence tests are based on what families, schools, and communities of the upper classes expect and teach.

How can families, schools, and the larger culture nurture children's giftedness? Research has shown that parents differ greatly in their attitudes toward and management of the giftedness of their children (Renzulli & Park, 2002; Silverman, 1997). Home and family are critically important, especially in the child's younger years (see Subotnik & Arnold, 1994; Muratori et al., 2006). In the families of highly successful persons:

- Someone in the family (usually one or both parents) had a personal interest in the child's talent and provided great support and encouragement for its development.

- The parents were role models (at least at the start of their child's development of talent), especially in terms of lifestyle.

- There was specific parental encouragement of the child to explore, to participate in home activities related to the area of developing talent, and to join the family in related activities. Small signs of interest and capability by the child were rewarded.

- Parents took it for granted that their children would learn in the area of talent, just as they would learn language.

- The family exhibited expected behaviors and values related to the talent, holding to clear schedules and standards for performance appropriate for the child's stage of development.

- Teaching was informal and occurred in a variety of settings. Early learning was exploratory and much like play.

- The family interacted with a tutor/mentor and received information to guide the child's practice—including specific tasks to be accomplished, information or specific points to be emphasized or problems to be solved, a set time by which the child could be expected to achieve specific goals and objectives, and the amount of time to be devoted to practice.

- Parents observed practice, insisted that the child put in the required amount of practice time, provided instruction where necessary, and rewarded the child for doing something especially well or meeting a standard.

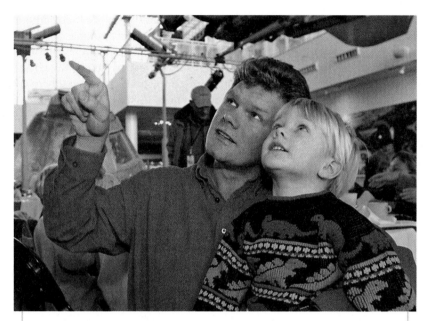

Research has shown that the home and family, especially in a child's younger years, are extremely important.

- Parents sought special instruction and special teachers for the child.
- Parents encouraged participation in events (recitals, concerts, contests, etc.) in which the child's capabilities were displayed in public.

How schools can nurture children's giftedness has received too little attention (Callahan & Miller, 2005; Cross & Coleman, 2005; Robinson, Shore, & Enersen, 2007). Yet the ways in which schools identify giftedness, group children for instruction, design curricula, and reward performance have profound effects on what the most able students achieve. When schools facilitate the performance of all students who are able to achieve at a superior level in specific areas, giftedness is found among children of all cultural and socioeconomic groups.

Identification of Giftedness

Measurement of giftedness is a complicated matter (Lohman, 2006). Some components cannot be assessed by traditional means; in addition, the particular definition of giftedness will determine how test scores are interpreted. But if it is indeed important to identify giftedness early to help children with special talents achieve self-fulfillment and aid them in developing their special potential to make a unique and valuable contribution to society, it is important to use appropriate methods.

The most common methods of identifying giftedness include IQ (based on group or individual tests), standardized achievement test scores, teacher nominations, parent nominations, peer nominations, self-nominations, and evaluations of student work or performance. In fact, strong arguments can be made not to disregard the traditional psychometric, test-score approach altogether (Robinson, 2005). Typically, some combination of several of these methods is used. Identification practices have been extremely controversial, and best practices have frequently been ignored.

In devising identification procedures that are fair to individuals from all cultural and ethnic groups and all social classes, educators must take into account the varied definitions of giftedness and recognize the effects of cultural variation on children's behavior (McCluskey, Baker, & McCluskey, 2005; Tomlinson, Ford, Reis, Briggs, & Strickland, 2004). In addressing multicultural differences, it's important to recognize the variations of socioeconomic status, language, and values that occur within various ethnic and cultural groups, not just between them. Hunsaker and Callahan (1995) propose eight general identification principles to help ensure fairness:

1. Assessments go beyond a narrow conception of talent.

2. Separate and appropriate identification strategies are used to identify different aspects of giftedness.

3. Reliable and valid instruments and strategies are used to assess talent.

4. Appropriate instruments are employed for underserved populations.

5. Each child is viewed as an individual, recognizing the limits of a single score on any measure.

6. A multiple-measure/multiple-criteria approach is followed.

7. Appreciation is shown for the value of the individual case study and the limitations of combinations of scores.

8. Identification and placement are based on individual students' needs and abilities rather than on the numbers who can be served.

The focus of identification methods should be on balancing concern for identifying only those students whose capabilities are markedly above average, with concern for including all who show promise for gifted performance (see Robinson, 2005).

Psychological and Behavioral Characteristics

Giftedness has been recognized in some form in every society throughout recorded history. In many societies, individuals with special gifts have been stereotyped in one of two ways: (1) as physically weak, socially inept, narrow in interests, and prone to emotional instability and early decline or, in the opposite direction, (2) as superior in intelligence, physique, social attractiveness, achievement, emotional stability, and moral character and immune to ordinary human frailties and defects. Although it might be possible to find a few individuals who seem to fit one stereotype or the other, the vast majority of people with special gifts or talents fit neither.

Nevertheless, stereotypes persist. A still-common misperception is that genius predisposes people to mental illness. For example, in the movie *A Beautiful Mind*, Russell Crowe plays the role of John Nash, a mathematician who had schizophrenia; one movie critic described the character as "one of those men both blessed and cursed by genius. It made him smart, it made him fragile" (Hunter, 2001, p. C1). The idea that giftedness and insanity are linked is one of the worst misconceptions of

Contrary to myth, most students who are gifted are not constantly bored with and antagonistic toward school, if they are given work that is challenging.

UNDERSTANDING THE STANDARDS AND PRINCIPLES What should teachers know about the psychological and behavioral characteristics of students with special gifts? (CEC Knowledge and Skill Standards GT3K3, GT3K4, & GT3K5)

Council for Exceptional Children

the field (Gallagher, 2006). Some people with special gifts and talents accomplish remarkable things in spite of, not because of, mental illness or physical disability (see Goldsmith, 2005).

Students with special gifts tend to be far ahead of their age peers in specific areas of performance. Many children carrying the label "gifted" learn to read easily, often before entering school—if they have been reared in a literature-rich environment. They may be far advanced in one area, such as reading or math, but not in another, such as penmanship or art (i.e., skills requiring manual dexterity). Contrary to popular opinion, most such students are not constantly bored with and antagonistic toward school if they are given work that is reasonably challenging for them (Gallagher & Gallagher, 1994; Neihart, Reis, Robinson, & Moon, 2002). Some, however, become uninterested in school and perform poorly in the curriculum or drop out (Renzulli & Park, 2002). Not surprisingly, they become upset and maladjusted when they are discriminated against and prevented from realizing their full potential. But such a reaction isn't unique to any group of children, whether exceptional or average along any dimension.

Perhaps it shouldn't be surprising that the majority of students who show giftedness enter occupations that demand greater-than-average intellectual ability, creativity, and motivation. Most find their way into the ranks of professionals and managers, and many distinguish themselves among their peers in adulthood. But not all such students enjoy occupational success in demanding jobs; some choose career paths that do not make use of their talents or otherwise fail to distinguish themselves (Manstetten, 2000).

The self-concepts, social relationships, and other psychological characteristics of students with special gifts or talents have been matters of considerable interest (Assouline & Colangelo, 2006; Robinson et al., 2007). Many of these students are happy, well liked by their peers, emotionally stable, and self-sufficient. They may have wide and varied interests and perceive themselves in positive terms. Nevertheless, some gifted students experience and are traumatized by bullying (Peterson & Ray, 2006).

Most gifted students appear to make internal as well as external comparisons of their performance—to see their own relative strengths and weaknesses and to see themselves as gifted only in their best or strongest area. "For example, a student with high mathematics achievement will probably have a high math self-concept, but her verbal self-concept may be depressed as a result—regardless of her verbal achievement" (Plucker & Stocking, 2001, p. 542).

Students with intellectual gifts are often acutely sensitive to their own feelings and those of others and highly concerned about interpersonal relationships, intrapersonal states, and moral issues. Using their advanced cognitive abilities appears to help many of these children develop at a young age the social and emotional adjustment strategies used by most adults. In short, many (but not all) students with high intellectual gifts are self-aware, self-assured, socially skilled, and morally responsible. Note that the prodigy Gregory Smith (described in our discussion of transition on page 558) is also very concerned about other children and issues of social justice.

However, assuming that gifted students never need education in morality is a terrible mistake. Students identified as gifted sometimes bully others (Peterson & Ray, 2006). Moreover, individuals can and have used their special gifts for nightmarish purposes, as Tannenbaum (2000b) has described. Therefore, it's important to recognize the enormous potential for both good and evil purposes to which special gifts and talents can be put and to help individuals who have such gifts and talents see the value of using them in the service of what is morally right.

Giftedness includes a wide variety of abilities and degrees of difference from average. Moreover, the nature and degree of an individual's giftedness may affect his or her social and emotional adjustment and educational and psychological needs. Consider, for example, that categorizing only people with IQs of 180 or higher as "gifted" is roughly like categorizing as "intellectually disabled" only those individuals with IQs of 20 or less. In fact, children who are exceptionally precocious—those whose talents are extremely rare—may constitute a group for which extraordinary adaptations of schooling are required (just as extraordinary adaptations are required for children with very severe intellectual disabilities; see Gross, 2000, 2002; von Karolyi & Winner, 2005).

Child prodigies are children whose development and accomplishments meet or exceed those of adults with extraordinary talent. Child prodigies often astonish others by their talent at an early age, and they often need opportunities that more typical students don't need and would find intimidating. (See the Personal Perspectives on page 542.) Burge (1998) describes Ayinde Jean-Baptiste (a gifted orator who first impressed adults as a four-year-old when he recited part of a sermon by Martin Luther King Jr. to his first-grade class), Carrie Shilyansk (a brilliant young scientist who began sitting in on neurobiology seminars at the California Institute of Technology when she was eleven), Chris Sharma (who won the World Cup in rock climbing at age fifteen), Jennifer Baybrook (who became the first female national yo-yo champion at age seventeen), Alexandra Nechita (who at age twelve showed her paintings in fifty galleries), Sara Chang (who at age eight was a guest violin soloist with Zubin Mehta and the New York Philharmonic), Emily Kumpel (who at age nine used her organizational and public relations savvy to collect thousands of books for school children in South Africa), Jason Crowe (who published a successful newspaper at age eleven), and Justin Miller (a globe-trotting gourmet who by age eight had cooked three times on David Letterman's show). Muratori et al. (2006) describe two prodigies in mathematics.

Cultural Values Regarding Students with Special Gifts and Talents and Their Education

In American culture, it's difficult to elicit sympathy and next to impossible to arrange sustained public support for education that meets the needs of children with special gifts, especially intellectual gifts (Clark, 1997; Gallagher, 2000a, 2002, 2004; Murray, 2005). This is not a peculiarly American problem, but there's something self-limiting, if not self-destructive, about a society that refuses to acknowledge and nourish the special talents of its children who have the greatest gifts (see Colangelo et al., 2004a; DiGennaro, 2007; De Hahn, 2000; Murray; Tannenbaum, 1993, 2000a). Hunsaker (1995) examined the perception and treatment of giftedness in traditional West African, Egyptian, Greco-Roman, Semitic, Chinese, Mesoamerican, and European Renaissance cultures. He found that few of these cultures used the term gifted. Nevertheless, as in contemporary American society, individuals with advanced abilities were viewed with ambivalence:

> They were considered exceptional because of the hopes people had that they would ensure the continued existence of their culture. Their ability was seen as a divine or inherited gift. Great efforts personally and societally were needed to develop their abilities, and special opportunities were generally not available to the socially disadvantaged. Finally, the exceptional were the objects of ambivalent feelings directed toward them as persons and toward their knowledge. Beliefs and feelings about individuals of exceptional ability have not changed a great deal from those we inherited from other cultures. (Hunsaker, 1995, pp. 265–266)

Gallagher (2000a) describes American society's ambivalence toward students with special gifts or talents. Our society loves the good things that people with extraordinary gifts produce, but it hates to acknowledge superior intellectual performance. Opponents of special education for students with special gifts argue that it's inhumane and un-American to segregate such students for instruction and to allocate special resources for educating those who are already advantaged. There is the danger of leaving some children out when only the ablest are selected for special programs. However, it seems

Personal PERSPECTIVES

Geoff Gallante: A Child Prodigy on Trumpet
First-grader blows away audiences

Geoff Gallante has played with Wynton Marsalis, jammed with Maynard Ferguson, played the National Anthem at numerous pro basketball games and on Sunday will join the University of Virginia Wind Ensemble for a rendition of "Trumpeter's Lullaby."

That's not a bad resume for a 6-year-old.

"It's pretty amazing, really," said William Pease, the wind ensemble's director. "It's not 'Carnival of Venice' but 'Trumpeter's Lullaby' is a good high school-level concerto and he's only 6."

Geoff, of Fairfax County, who has been featured in Washington newspapers and television broadcasts, is a bit of a rarity: He's a young child who plays a brass instrument well.

"You find child prodigies who play piano and violin and other stringed instruments but it's a lot different when you're talking about brass," Pease said, "It takes an enormous amount of air to play a brass instrument. If you change the amount of air you use when you're playing, you can actually change the note you're playing."

Add to that the complexities of brass embouchure—the position and use of lips and mouth on the instrument to create tone—and trumpet becomes a difficult instrument to play for most people under the age of 10.

"It's quite amazing when you see his size—he's small—and the size of the trumpet and then you hear him play," Pease said. "He has a very mellow sound, a dark and warm sound and that's good."

Geoff's playing has surprised people since he first picked the instrument up at the age of 4. He was at his grandmother's house, found his older brother's horn and took a quick lesson on lip placement from his mother.

"He made a sound with it and his eyes lit up," said his father, David Gallante. "He walked around with that trumpet blowing it for about a month or two. He'd put some CDs he owned in the [stereo] and try and play the trumpet with them."

Geoff Gallante began playing the trumpet at age 4. After two years of playing, he has racked up an impressive resume.

Gallante tried to convince trumpet teachers to teach his son, but most begged off.

"They thought I was crazy and totally dismissed it out of hand. They couldn't imagine that a 4-year-old could play a trumpet. They thought it would be a waste of time," said Gallante, who estimated that he approached eight teachers. "I finally convinced one to hear him play and he agreed to take Geoff as a student."

His first time at band camp, the pre-kindergarten Geoff auditioned with middle school students and was placed in the symphonic band, the band that plays the most difficult music. That's also where he met members of the UVa Wind Ensemble who served as camp counselors.

"They thought it would be fun for us to play with him," Pease said. "It is, too. It's amazing how good he sounds at his age."

Age: 6

Grade: First

Residence: Fairfax County

Age started playing trumpet: 4

Featured in: *The Washington Post, Downbeat Magazine,* various BBC radio broadcasts, CBS's "The Early Show," NBC's "Tonight Show with Jay Leno" and NBC's "Today" show

Played with: The Tonight Show Band, Arturo Sandoval, Phill Driscoll, Wynton Marsalis, Maynard Ferguson, Chuck Mangione and Doc Severinsen. He has also performed with The Washington Symphonic Brass, 257th Army Band, Metropolitan Jazz Orchestra, U.S. Army Blues Jazz Ensemble, George Mason University symphony orchestra and jazz ensemble. He has played the National Anthem for NBA games in Oakland, Phoenix, Salt Lake City, and Detroit.

Source: "First-grader blows away audiences" by Byran McKenzie. *Charlottesville Daily Progress,* Charlottesville, VA, February 24, 2007, p. A2. Reprinted with permission.

impossible to argue against special education for students with special gifts and talents without arguing against special education in general, because all special education involves recognizing and accommodating unusual individual differences (Kauffman & Hallahan, 2005).

Neglected Groups of Students with Special Gifts and Talents

Students who are disadvantaged by economic needs, racial discrimination, disabilities, or gender bias are often overlooked in programs for gifted and talented students. In fact, many groups of gifted learners are neglected in a diverse, multicultural society (Castellano, 2003). Two facts cannot be ignored:

1. Children from higher socioeconomic levels already have many of the advantages, such as more appropriate education, opportunities to pursue their interests in depth, and intellectual stimulation, that special educators recommend for those with special gifts or talents.

2. There are far too many individuals with special gifts or talents who are disadvantaged by life circumstances or disabilities and who have been overlooked and discriminated against, resulting in a tremendous waste of human potential.

Underachievers with Special Gifts and Talents

Monks and Katzko (2005) define underachievement as "a discrepancy between potential and achievement" (p. 189; see also Callahan & Miller, 2005; Davis & Rimm, 2004; Dixon & Moon, 2006; Reis & McCoach, 2002). Students can fail to achieve at a level consistent with their abilities for a variety of reasons, including low expectations, lack of motivation, family trauma, and other causes (Robinson et al., 2007). Many females achieve far less than they might because of social or cultural barriers to their selection or progress in certain careers. Students who are members of racial or ethnic minorities also are often underachievers because of bias in identifying or programming for their abilities. Likewise, students with obvious disabilities are frequently overlooked or denied opportunities to achieve.

Underachievement of children with special gifts or talents can result from any of the factors that lead to underachievement in any group, such as emotional conflicts or a chaotic, neglectful, or abusive home environment. A frequent cause is inappropriate school programs—schoolwork that is unchallenging and boring because these students have already mastered most of the material or because teachers have low expectations or mark students down for their misbehavior. A related problem is that underachievers with special gifts or talents often develop negative self-images and negative attitudes toward school. When a student shows negative attitudes toward school and self, any special abilities that she or he might have will likely be overlooked.

One way of preventing or responding to underachievement is allowing students to skip grades or subjects so that school becomes more nurturing and provides greater interest and challenge (see Colangelo et al., 2004a, 2004b). However,

Casebook Reflection

REFER TO THE CASE *Never Give Up* in your booklet. Ryan's case underscores the complexities for students who are gifted and talented. How and to what extent do you think Ryan's life experiences might have affected the way he behaved in school? How should life experiences be taken into consideration in devising a behavior management strategy? Do students who are gifted and talented need discipline? ●

Reading Homework Exercise

Gifted Debate ● Go to the Homework and Exercises section in Chapter 15 of MyEducationLab to access information about the debate over the best ways to instruct gifted students.

acceleration is not always appropriate, nor is it typically sufficient by itself to address the problems of the underachieving student with exceptional abilities. Counseling, individual and family therapy, and a variety of supportive or remedial strategies are possible alternatives or additions to acceleration.

Underachievement must not be confused with nonproductivity. A lapse in productivity doesn't necessarily indicate that the student is underachieving. Students with extraordinary ability should not be expected to be constantly producing something remarkable. But this highlights the difficulty in defining giftedness: How much time must elapse between episodes of creative productivity before we say that someone no longer exhibits giftedness or has become an underachiever? We noted earlier that giftedness is in the performance, not the person. Yet we know that the unrelenting demand for gifted performance is unrealistic and can be inhumane.

Students Low in Socioeconomic Status and Those Living in Remote Areas

Children who are reared in poverty might not have toys, reading materials, opportunities for travel and exploration, good nutrition and medical care, and many other advantages that more affluent families typically provide. Lack of basic necessities and opportunities for learning can mask intelligence and creativity. Families of children in inner-city areas don't have the financial resources to provide the opportunities and early experiences to foster talent. Yet support for gifted students from low-income families often appears to be an easy target for elimination in tight budgets (see Murray, 2005).

Children who live in remote areas might not have access to many of the educational resources typically found in more populated regions. Many of those who live in remote areas also experience economic deprivation and lack the advantages that affluent families have (Davis & Rimm, 2004).

UNDERSTANDING THE STANDARDS AND PRINCIPLES Why are some ethnic groups underrepresented in programs for gifted students? (CEC Knowledge and Skill Standards GT1K5, GT1K10, & GT3K2)

Council for Exceptional Children

Students with Special Gifts from Cultural- and Ethnic-Minority Groups

Some ethnic groups, such as many ethnic minorities from Asian countries, are included in programs for gifted students more often than would be suggested by their percentage of the general population. However, other ethnic groups, especially African Americans and Spanish-speaking students, are underrepresented in programs for gifted students.

Among the greatest challenges in the field today are identifying culturally diverse and disadvantaged students with special abilities and including and retaining these students in special programs (Moore, Ford, & Milner, 2005; Robinson et al., 2007). Some cultural and ethnic groups have been sorely neglected in programs for students with special gifts or talents. Many ethnic minority students with special gifts or talents remain underachievers, even if they recognize the importance of achievement in American society (Borland, 2004; Bridglall & Gordon, 2005; Lohman, 2005; Tomlinson et al., 2004).

Appropriate identification and programming for students with special gifts or talents can be assumed to result in approximately equal proportions of all ethnic groups. However, this proportionality will likely be achieved only if renewed efforts are made to do the following:

● Devise and adopt culturally sensitive identification criteria
● Provide counseling to raise the educational and career aspirations of students in underrepresented groups

- Make high-achieving models from all ethnic groups available
- Retain underrepresented ethnic students in programs for gifted students
- Adopt a workable system to ensure the inclusion of underrepresented groups
- Build relationships with the families of minority children

Ultimately, the larger social-environmental issue of making families and communities safe, as well as intellectually stimulating, for children and youths of all cultural and ethnic backgrounds must be addressed (Borland, 2004; Gallagher, 1998, 2000a; Gordon & Bridglall, 2005). Equal opportunity for development outside the school environment would help address the underrepresentation of minority students in programs for students with extraordinary abilities (see Davis & Rimm, 2004; Ford & Moore, 2006).

Students whose disabilities prevent them from speaking or physically expressing themselves may have potential that is not obvious through casual observation.

Students with Disabilities and Special Gifts and Talents

INTERNET RESOURCES

For additional information about children with disabilities who are also gifted or talented, see www.uniquelygifted.org

The education of students with both disabilities and special gifts or talents is emerging as a field. The idea that students can be "twice exceptional" (meaning that they have both a disability and a special gift or talent) is, as Gallagher (2006) notes, one of the best ideas in gifted education.

The major goals of special education for twice-exceptional students are identifying gifted and talented students with specific disabilities, research and development, preparing teachers and other professionals to work with such children and youths, improving interdisciplinary cooperation for the benefit of such children and youths, and preparing students for adult living. The full range of programs for gifted and talented students should be considered for those who are twice exceptional, including acceleration (Baum, Rizza, & Renzulli, 2006; Davis & Rimm, 2004; Moon & Reis, 2004). The Responsive Instruction on page 546 provides a summary of the early stages of the research on instructional strategies for twice exceptional students.

Our stereotypic expectations of people with disabilities frequently keep us from recognizing their abilities. For example, if a child lacks the ability to speak or to be physically active or presents a demeanor associated with intellectual dullness (e.g., drooling, slumping, dull eyes staring), we tend to assume that the child has intellectual disability. The fact is, students with physical characteristics typically associated with severe intellectual disabilities might be intellectually brilliant; unless this is acknowledged, however, the talents of students with cerebral palsy and other physical disabilities can be easily overlooked. Students with special gifts or talents and impaired hearing also can be overlooked if their communication skills are poorly developed, if their teachers are not looking for signs of talent, or if they are taught by teachers who have limited competence in communicating with people who are deaf.

Some students with learning disabilities or attention deficit hyperactivity disorder (ADHD) have extraordinarily high intellectual abilities, yet their talents will be missed if those abilities aren't properly assessed (Baum, Olenchak, & Owen, 1998; Kaufmann & Castellanos, 2000; Kaufmann, Kalbfleisch, & Castellanos, 2000; Moon, Zentall, Grskovic, Hall, & Stormont, 2001). Shaywitz and colleagues (2001) found

Meeting the Needs of Students with Special Gifts and Talents

Strategies for the Identification and Instruction of Twice Exceptional Students

WHO ARE "TWICE EXCEPTIONAL" STUDENTS?

The term *twice exceptional* refers to any student who is both gifted and has a disability, such as a learning disability or cerebral palsy. Unfortunately, the identification of gifts or talents can be challenging, as the "disability" characteristics often take center stage. Researchers have identified specific barriers to the identification of giftedness in populations of students with disabilities (Cline & Hegeman, 2001). Challenges can include:

- Focus on assessment of the disability without attention to possible talents
- Stereotypic expectations associated with physical or global intelligence expectations
- Developmental delays particularly evident in certain areas of cognitive ability such as abstract thinking or verbal ability
- Lack of worldly experiences due to disability limitations
- Narrow views of giftedness as global, high intelligence only
- Disability-specific concerns overshadowing possible gifts or talents

To overcome these barriers, these researchers recommend that (1) assessment batteries include information about participation in extracurricular activities, (2) patterns of strengths should be noted in addition to disability-specific reporting, (3) ability should be viewed in terms of experiential opportunities, (4) adaptations and accommodations should be made during testing (e.g., omitting questions about color for a blind student or allowing extended time for a student with learning disabilities), (5) comparisons should be made with other students with similar disabilities, and (6) areas unaffected by the disability should be weighed more heavily (Cline & Hegeman, 2001; Willard-Holt, 1999).

STRATEGIES FOR MEETING THE NEEDS OF TWICE EXCEPTIONAL STUDENTS

To address the issue of underidentification of giftedness in individuals with disabilities, schools need to become advocates for the identification of gifts in all populations of students. Parents, school personnel, and the community should take an active role in supporting the unique needs of students with gifts.

Instructional strategies to foster the development of gifts in twice exceptional students include the following:

- Focusing on the development of strengths, interests, and intellectual gifts
- Teaching and encouraging the use of compensatory strategies
- Reducing communication limitations and developing alternative means for communicating
- Helping students shape a healthy, realistic self-concept in which students acknowledge their strengths and weaknesses through open discussions
- Emphasizing high-level abstract thinking, creativity, and problem-solving approaches
- Providing for individual pacing in areas of giftedness and disability
- Establishing high expectations and promoting avenues for self-direction
- Offering instructional options that capitalize on students' strengths (Willard-Holt, 1999)

● *By Kristin L. Sayeski*

that boys with very high IQs and boys with learning disabilities exhibited similar types of behavior problems, strongly suggesting that gifted students are a very heterogeneous group.

Giftedness occurs in combination with disabilities of nearly every description. Personal Perspectives on page 548 tells the story of a Rhodes Scholar with dyslexia (a reading disability) and attention deficit disorder (ADD). Marie Curie, twice the winner of the Nobel Prize (physics and chemistry), suffered from profound depression (Goldsmith, 2005). Consider also Evelyn Glennie, a deaf percussionist, and Timothy Cordes, a blind medical student. They don't fit the stereotypes we hold. True, they are not typical of people with their disabilities—or of people who do not have their disabilities, for that matter. Fortunately, their disabilities were not allowed to preclude their pursuit of their areas of special talent.

We don't want to foster the myth that giftedness is found as often among students with disabilities as among those who do not have disabilities. But clearly, students with special gifts or talents and disabilities have been a neglected population. A key factor in meeting these students' needs is the collaboration of a variety of disciplines and institutions to provide appropriate technology and training.

Females with Special Gifts and Talents

Females comprise the largest group of neglected students with special gifts or talents. Females with extraordinary capabilities today have many opportunities for education and choice of careers that were denied to females a generation ago (see Goldsmith, 2005; Reis, 2005).

Cultural factors work against the development and recognition of females with special gifts or talents. Females simply have not had equal opportunity and motivation to enter many academic disciplines or careers that have by tradition been domi-

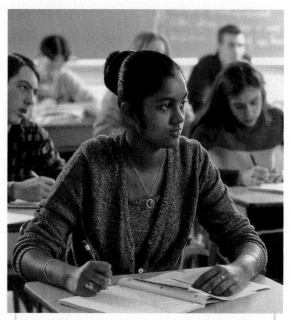

Cultural factors work against the development and recognition of females with special gifts and talents. Barriers to giftedness in females haven't always been recognized.

nated by males, such as chemistry, physics, medicine, and dentistry. When females have entered these fields, they have often been rewarded inappropriately (according to irrelevant criteria) for their performance. English literature has tended to portray females as wives, mothers, or "weaker" sisters, who are either dependent on males or sacrifice themselves for the sake of males. Such barriers to giftedness in females have only recently been brought forcefully to public attention (see Davis & Rimm, 2004; Reiss, 2006).

Females lag behind males in many measures of achievement and aptitude (e.g., professional and career achievement, standardized test scores, grades) and tend not to pursue courses of study or careers involving science, engineering, and math (Lubinski, Benbow, & Morelock, 2000). In short, they are underrepresented in many fields of advanced study and in professions and careers that carry high status, power, and pay. We can only presume to know the reasons for their underrepresentation (Kerr, 2000). Factors that have contributed to the situation might include lower parental expectations for females, overemphasis on and glamorization of gender differences, school and societal stereotypes of gender roles, and educational practices that are detrimental to achievement (e.g., less attention to high-achieving girls, expectations of less independence of girls).

Research suggests that the problems of neglect and underrepresentation of females with exceptional abilities are much more complex than was previously believed. Like underrepresentation of ethnic and cultural minorities, the problems involving females are closely tied to cultural, social, and political issues, and they do not have simple or easy solutions. Nevertheless, the education of females with special gifts or talents might be improved by encouraging females to take risks by enrolling in challenging courses, to make career choices appropriate for their abilities, and to explore avenues that break stereotypical female roles.

Casebook Reflection

REFER TO THE CASE *Filling Mr. K.'s Shoes—Not!!* in your booklet. How do you think Susan measures up as a teacher of high-achieving or gifted students? In what ways does she reflect what you believe are the ideal characteristics of a teacher of gifted students, and in what way(s) does she fall short? ●

Rhodes Scholar Overcomes Disabilities

Heather Long has dyslexia, ADD, and memory recall challenges. Learning to read was difficult for her, but special education during early elementary school, gifted classes in middle and high school, the support of dedicated parents, teachers, and tutors, plus her own hard work and determination helped Long overcome her disabilities and become a Rhodes Scholar.

How are you able to succeed when others with (or without!) similar challenges don't?

I was lucky that my parents got tutors for me as soon as they were alerted to [my challenges] when I was in first or second grade. And my mom stayed home and helped me with my schoolwork. It has not always been easy. Especially in college, there are so many distractions and so much going on that I stay up all night a lot of times, when it is quiet, to do my work. And I don't have a TV in my room.

Also, I have a natural passion for learning. I find that with a lot of gifted people and people with disabilities. It might not be in the traditional learning style, but we are really interested and intrigued in looking at the things around us in a different way.

What have you found most difficult?

Learning to read. I'm still not a speed-reader. This became very apparent when the last Harry Potter book came out. My friends in college were devouring the book in five hours and calling me about it, but it took me another day or two to get through it.

What strategies and accommodations do you use?

Part of it is scheduling—working in my room, not having distractions, working at night. When I was learning Old and Middle English, I went to the library and checked out tapes of people reading the Canterbury Tales and Beowulf. I also listened to audio books in elementary school, so my eyes couldn't slip around with the words I was reading or the spelling. I'm not really an auditory learner. I'm mostly visual, actually, but it helps me slow down visually when I listen to audio books and read along.

It's also knowing your limits. I want to challenge myself, but I know I can't take a course in which I have to read 1,000 page novels. I just read too slowly. But, I'm good at analyzing poetry.

What did teachers do that helped you?

I give a lot of credit to my second grade teacher. She kept telling the school counselor that "there was something wrong here." She was the first person who really pushed to identify specifically what was going on.

My second to fourth grade tutor, Mrs. Marti, used her creativity to help me learn. The only way to get me interested in spelling was to get out a can of shaving cream and let me use the shaving cream to spell the words. Then it was fun.

I also had a couple of teachers in elementary and middle school who pointed out my strengths—"Even though you are struggling in that area, you are gifted here." For instance, I was good in math but struggling with reading. I realized that, even though I felt I was behind some of my peers, I was not the worst student in the class at everything.

What advice do you offer other students who struggle with similar disabilities?

First, you have to realize it is not necessarily a "disability." There is so much stigma attached to that. You have to see some of your weaknesses as strengths.

Also, don't be afraid to seek help. There are times I wish I had sought help more often and been more open about [my challenges]. Often, you don't realize how many other people have these types of problems as well. I was stunned at the number of my friends who have ADD that I didn't find out about until last year. That was helpful, too—knowing I was not the only one.

What advice do you offer special and gifted education teachers?

It's integral for special education and gifted teachers to alert the regular curriculum teachers to ways they can make classroom settings and evaluations more conducive for varying types of learning. For instance, a college professor used to give really long essay tests—basically a regurgitation of information—until she had a child [of her own] with learning disabilities. Then she realized that might not be the best method of testing everyone. Teachers need to make sure they are not testing all students on the same skills but look at a wide variety.

There are different ways to show talents. Although a student may not be the best in her class at spelling, she may be the best at making a mobile about the book. We are really lucky in America, because we have a system that is evolving more and more to appreciate different ways of learning and incorporate the arts.

The biggest challenge now is to make the case that special and gifted education programs need to exist and to show how beneficial they are for both ends of the spectrum. It is important in a school to have a place where it is okay to do Odyssey of the Mind or Science Olympiad activities or just to do puzzles in the middle of the day.

Anything else you'd like to say?

I've benefited from both gifted and special education. I wish more school districts would recognize and fully fund these programs. These teachers really understand that students learn in different ways.

Source: CEC Today. (July–August–September 2004). "Rhodes Scholar Overcomes Disabilities. CEC, Arlington, VA. Reprinted with permission.

Educational Considerations

The focus of education is now on talent development across the full spectrum of abilities in particular areas of functioning (see Heller et al., 2000; Robinson et al., 2007; Tomlinson et al., 2002). However, this point of view includes the recognition that equity for many students with special gifts and talents may require special education. Although there is no federal requirement of special education for gifted students, the National Association for Gifted Children has published program standards that states and localities can use to assess the quality of their services (Landrum, Callahan, & Shaklee, 2001). Nevertheless, state and local policies are uneven and often inadequate (Van Tassel-Baska, 2006).

All students at all ages have relative talent strengths, and schools should help students to identify and understand their own best abilities. Those whose talents are at exceptionally higher levels than those of their peers should have access to instructional resources and activities that are commensurate with their talents (Davis & Rimm, 2004). The one-size-fits-all mentality that is at least partly an outgrowth of the inclusion movement reflects a mistaken view of human development. Highly talented young people suffer boredom and negative peer pressure in heterogeneous classrooms. Students at all ages and grade levels are entitled to challenging and appropriate instruction if they are to develop their talents fully. For some, like Noshua Watson, this instruction might be available only in a setting apart from her age mates. Read about Noshua's success in college courses in Success Stories on pages 550–551.

The belief that students with special gifts or talents don't need special education designed for their needs is, according to Gallagher (2006), one of the worst ideas of educators and works against talent development. "Such an idea justifies a 'Do Nothing' approach by educators. It encourages acceptance of such ideas as *inclusion* as doing no real mischief to gifted students and lowers the expectations for the performance of such students" (Gallagher, 2006, p. 10). As we noted earlier, family support plays a crucial role in the development of talent (Freeman, 2000). However, special school supports also are needed for many students if they are to achieve to their full potential. The consensus of leaders in the field is that special education for students with special gifts or talents should have three characteristics:

1. A curriculum designed to accommodate the students' advanced cognitive skills (see VanTassel-Baska & Stambaugh, 2006).

2. Instructional strategies consistent with the learning of students with extraordinary abilities in the particular content areas of the curriculum (see Davis & Rimm, 2004; Dixon & Moon, 2006).

3. Administrative arrangements facilitating appropriate grouping of students for instruction (see Callahan, 2000, 2001; Robinson et al., 2007; Tomlinson et al. 2002, 2004).

States and localities have devised a wide variety of plans for educating students with special gifts or talents. Generally, the plans can be described as providing **enrichment** (additional experiences provided to students without placing them in a higher grade) or **acceleration** (placing the students ahead of their age peers).

Many variations of enrichment and acceleration have been invented, however, ranging from general education placement with little or no assistance for the teacher to special schools offering advanced curricula in special areas such as science and mathematics or the arts. Between these extremes are consulting teacher programs, resource rooms, community mentor programs (in which highly talented students work individually with professionals), independent study programs, special classes, and rapid advancement of students through the usual grades, including early admission to high school or college.

Building Teaching Skills Lesson Planning Exercise

Do's & Don'ts ● Go to the Building Teaching Skills section in Chapter 15 of MyEducationLab to see a history lesson plan and related "Do's and Don't's" for gifted students.

■ **Enrichment**

An approach in which additional learning experiences are provided for students with special gifts or talents while the students remain in the grade levels appropriate for their chronological ages.

■ **Acceleration**

An approach in which students with special gifts or talents are placed in grade levels ahead of their age peers in one or more academic subjects.

Success Stories

Noshua excels in a residential acceleration program

Noshua: "I felt I could finally be myself!"

Eighteen-year-old Noshua Watson is enrolled in a Ph.D. program in economics at Stanford University. She completed high school and college through a residential acceleration program for gifted students.

These are the keys to her success:

- Intensive and accelerated programming,
- relentless, individualized, academic challenges,
- specific attention to personal growth and unique abilities.

At age thirteen, Noshua Watson enrolled in the Program for the Exceptionally Gifted, known as PEG, an acceleration program at Mary Baldwin College in Virginia. Combining high school and college, Noshua was challenged in a supportive environment that encouraged her personal growth. She thrived on campus activities, assisting with research and helping to teach an economics course during her senior year. Noshua credits her success to intensive, relentless, and specific instruction geared to her exceptional learning needs.

● **Intensive and Accelerated Programming** "Acceleration programs like PEG challenge our culture," says Celeste Rhodes, the program's director. "Parents and students must be courageous in their ability to accept uniqueness," she says. Rhodes describes the PEG program as an alternative for the motivated student who might have teenage interests but demonstrates a serious sense of purpose. "You see it in the interviews," she says. "There is an energy, a spark, a drive."

To Rhodes, giftedness is not defined narrowly by IQ but includes multiple measures including consistent achievement over time. "We are accelerating students by four years. That

requires a history of discipline, hard work, and high grades." Through a lengthy essay and interview process, an optimal match is sought between student and program. Says Rhodes, "Since we are residential, emotional stability is extremely important." Noshua agrees: "As PEG students, we were ready and eager for the academic rigors, but emotionally and physically, we were not as mature. We were still teenagers with a lot of special needs."

● **Relentless, Individualized, Academic Challenges** Noshua was supported by an individualized curriculum that matched her advanced cognitive skills. Small group instruction was combined with personal mentoring and alternatives such as independent study and accelerated pacing. Noshua was free to choose among the college's liberal arts offerings, but was required to take two PEG level courses—one in literature and one in mathematics. She also took study skills workshops taught by veteran PEG students designed to prepare novices for college-level learning and campus life. Says Noshua, "I was intellectually challenged, but I could socially mature at my own rate, and for me that was really key."

Not every community offers all possible options. In fact, there is great variation in the types of services that are offered within the school systems of given states and from state to state. As one might expect, large metropolitan areas typically offer more program options than small towns or rural areas. New York City, for example, has a long history of special high schools for students with extraordinary gifts and talents.

Some of the educational options for students with high ability, such as acceleration and inclusion, are extremely controversial. No single type of program option meets the needs of all students who have special gifts or talents. Ideally, assessment, identification, and instruction are closely linked, whether students have disabilities or special gifts and talents—or both. In including students with disabilities and special gifts and talents, it is important to use strategies that meet the needs of both types of students. Making It Work on page 553 provides a description of one such strategy, called fractured fairy tales.

● **Specific Attention to Personal Growth and Unique Abilities**
For her first two years, Noshua lived in a special dormitory for younger PEG students. Social activities were sponsored and friendships nurtured through residence life. Residential coordinators were sensitive to the needs of adolescents, and they also served as academic advisors. For her last two years, Noshua lived independently in a regular dorm, and her academic advisor was a faculty member in her chosen major of economics.

Selecting educational alternatives to meet her unique abilities is a familiar practice for Noshua and her family. As a youngster, she attended a magnet school and was described as an avid learner who was strong-willed and knew her own mind. She experienced gifted education for the first time in a regional public school program for third through fifth graders. Noshua's family moved in her sixth-grade year; there were no specialized programs for gifted students in her new district. Enrichment classes were held only before and after school, and transportation problems prevented Noshua from attending.

Junior high was not a positive experience. "I was frustrated academically because my guidance counselor said if I wanted to take both French and Spanish, I also had to take an honors math course one level beyond my grade. Socially, I was frustrated because most kids at school just wanted to 'hang out.' My parents wouldn't allow me to do this, and it was hard for me to relate. I guess you could say I was sort of a geek!" she says playfully.

Noshua felt that she could finally be herself after spending three happy summers at a residential camp for gifted students. In eighth grade, she and her parents looked for programs that offered alternatives to conventional high schools. "That's when I heard about PEG, and so did a fellow camper. We graduated from college together last June." As for starting graduate school, she says, "I just love being at Stanford. My life experience has been different, and I'm used to a lot more independence than other people my age."

CEC'S STANDARDS: PAVING THE WAY TO SUCCESS

ASSESS YOUR STEPS TO SUCCESS in meeting the CEC Knowledge and Skill Base for All Beginning Special Education Teachers of Students with Gifts and Talents. Use the following questions to reflect on the growth of your own professional knowledge, skills, and dispositions.

REFLECTING ON YOUR OWN PROFESSIONAL DEVELOPMENT

If you were Noshua's teacher . . .
- What are some areas about educating gifted students that you would need to know more about?
- What are some specific skills that would help you to address her advanced academic needs and social challenges?
- What personal dispositions do you think are most important for you to develop in teaching students with gifts and talents?

Using the CEC Standards
- What are some variations in beliefs, traditions, and values across and within cultures and their effects on relationships among individuals with gifts and talents, families, and schools? (GT3K2)
- What are some services, networks, and organizations for individuals with gifts and talents? (GT10K3)
- What procedures are used in your school system for screening and identifying individuals with gifts and talents? (GT8K4)

● *By Jean B. Crockett*

Advances in telecommunications, the presence of computers in the home and classroom, and the call for excellence in U.S. education are three developments with implications for educating the most able students. Telecommunications—including instructional television, telephone conferencing, and online sources—are technological means of facilitating the interaction of particularly able students and their teachers over wide geographical areas. These communication systems are important for extending appropriate education to students with special gifts or talents who live in rural and remote areas. The possible uses of computers for enhancing the education of extraordinarily high-performing students are enormous. Using software tutorials, accessing data banks, playing or inventing computer games that are intellectually demanding, writing and editing in English and foreign languages, learning computer languages, and solving advanced problems in mathematics are only a few of the possibilities (see Robinson et al., 2007; Sternberg & Davidson, 2005).

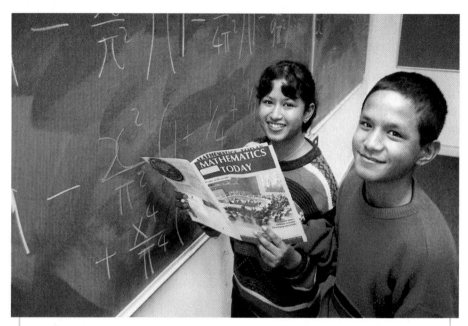

Accelerated educational programs, particularly in mathematics, have been evaluated favorably and may support early college entrance for some students who are gifted.

Acceleration

Acceleration involves moving a student ahead of her or his age peers in one or more areas of the curriculum. It might mean skipping one or more grades or attending classes with students in higher grades for one or a few specific subjects. Imagine trumpet prodigy Geoff Gallante's frustration if he were required to make music only with his age peers (see Personal Perspectives feature, p. 542). For him, acceleration in music was the only way to provide any semblance of challenge and excitement in music-making.

For high school students, acceleration may mean taking advanced placement (AP) courses (Callahan, 2003). Acceleration has not been used frequently, especially in rural areas. It has been used primarily with students who are extremely intellectually precocious (i.e., those who score 160 or higher on individually administered intelligence tests). Radical acceleration of extremely precocious students, combined with enrichment at each stage of their school careers, appears to offer many of these students the best social experiences as well as academic progress commensurate with their abilities (see Assouline & Lupkowski-Shoplik, 2003; Colangelo et al., 2004a, 2004b; Muratori et al., 2006). For a brief summary of research on acceleration, see Responsive Instruction on page 556.

Opponents of acceleration fear that children who are grouped with older students will suffer negative social and emotional consequences or that they will become contemptuous of their age peers, but this is seen by some experts as one of the worst ideas about gifted education (Gallagher, 2006). Proponents of acceleration argue that appropriate curricula and instructional methods are available only in special schools or in general education for students who are older than the child with special gifts or talents. Furthermore, proponents argue that by being grouped with other students who are their intellectual peers in classes in which they're not always first or correct, students acquire more realistic self-concepts and learn tolerance for others whose abilities are not as great as their own.

Research on the effects of acceleration clearly indicate that it typically has positive effects, although it doesn't clearly benefit the child in *every* case (but this is true of every approach; *nothing* works well in *every* case, although some things *usually* produce better

Collaboration and Co-Teaching of Students with Special Gifts and Talents

"How can I challenge him when half of my students have difficulty reading?"

Working with students with gifts and talents can be especially challenging for classroom teachers, considering the wide range of achievement levels in today's classrooms. Collaboration with a teacher of students with special gifts and talents can help general education teachers challenge all students.

WHAT DOES IT MEAN TO BE A TEACHER OF STUDENTS WITH SPECIAL GIFTS AND TALENTS?

The Council for Exceptional Children (2001) identifies the following skills as important for teachers of the gifted and talented:

1. Teach individuals to use self-assessment, problem solving, and other cognitive strategies.
2. Use procedures to increase the individual's self-awareness, self-management, self-control, self-reliance, self-esteem, and self-advocacy.
3. Create a safe, equitable, positive, and supportive learning environment in which diversities are valued.
4. Create an environment that encourages self-advocacy and increased independence.

SUCCESSFUL STRATEGIES FOR CO-TEACHING OR COLLABORATION

Instruction in a differentiated classroom is based upon student readiness and includes constant assessment of student skill and knowledge, varying activities or assignments for individuals, and the active exploration of topics at varying levels by individuals or groups of students (Tomlinson, 1995). Assignments vary, instructional support needs vary, and groupings vary. This can be quite difficult to manage as a single classroom teacher with between twenty and thirty students with a wide variety of skills. Teachers of students with gifts and talents can facilitate this process by helping to manage the classroom when groups and individuals are working, by helping to assess student progress, and by helping to collect resources. For example, the following lesson involving "fractured fairy tales" could be very successful with two teachers working together.

Using Fractured Fairy Tales to Explore Fiction

Fractured fairy tales are designed to be humorous by changing a familiar story in an unexpected way, such as altering the plot, a character, or setting. One student might decide to make Little Red Riding Hood a tough, strong girl, completely unafraid of the wolf and able to save her grandmother. Another student might select a fictional superhero and create a humorous flaw that causes problems when he or she has to save the day. When the teacher presents a fractured fairy tale, asking a series of questions helps the children to think through the changes and what they mean. Examples include: (1) What characters in this story differ from the original and how? (2) Which events occur in the new one that don't in the original? (3) How do the changes in characters and plot in the new version change the meaning and/or the way you feel about the characters? (4) How does this change the overall effect? When students are asked to change the nature of even a few characters in a fairy tale, they will discover that the smallest change can affect plot. If their changes remove the conflict and suspense from the story, the teacher can take them back to the original story. What moment in the story held the most tension for them? What kept them riveted to the story? This process can apply to the simplest stories as well as to the most advanced novels and plays. The key is to discuss the relationships across story elements and to examine what is gained or lost with each change (Smutny, 2001).

This lesson can be used with students of all achievement and grade levels; however, the instructional support necessary for all students to understand the lesson varies. For example, the collaborating teachers could split students into groups by their understanding of plot, conflict, resolution, and character and the two teachers could work with the groups to either help clarify these concepts and their application to creation of a new fairy tale or to help push students' thinking of perspective and the influence of small changes on these concepts. Together, the teachers can challenge all students to actively explore literature while providing the support that each needs to be successful—an often impossible task for a teacher working alone.

● *By Margaret P. Weiss*

results than other approaches). Acceleration appears to be a plan that can work very well but demands careful attention to the individual case and to specific curriculum areas—an important caveat for all of special education. Part of making acceleration work well is taking into consideration how superior the student's performance is compared to age mates and how radical the acceleration should be.

Enrichment

Renzulli and his colleagues developed an enrichment model based on the notion that children exhibit gifted behaviors in relation to particular projects or activities to which they apply their above-average ability, creativity, and task commitment (Reis & Renzulli, 2001; Renzulli, 2005; Renzulli & Reis, 2000). Students who are selected into a talent pool through case study identification methods are engaged in enrichment activities that involve individual or small group investigation of real-life problems; they become practicing pollsters, politicians, geologists, editors, and so on. The teacher (1) helps students to translate and focus a general concern into a solvable problem, (2) provides them with the tools and methods necessary to solve the problem, and (3) assists them in communicating their findings to authentic audiences (i.e., consumers of information). Students may stay in the enrichment program as long as they have the ability, creativity, and motivation to pursue productive activities that go beyond the usual curriculum for students their age. The model has become known as the schoolwide enrichment model. The purpose is to make special programming for students who have such abilities a more integral part of general education.

Tomlinson and colleagues (2002) developed a parallel curriculum designed to challenge all high-ability learners, in both homogeneous or heterogeneous classrooms. Their curriculum is a guide to ways to enrich the classroom for all learners and is based on the idea that intelligence should be more broadly and flexibly defined than it has been in the past.

Early Intervention

The giftedness of young children presents special problems of definition, identification, programming, and evaluation (Perleth, Schatz, & Monks, 2000; Porter, 2005; Robinson et al., 2007; Ruf, 2005). Although progress has been made in building model programs and providing better services for young children with special gifts, negative attitudes toward such efforts persist. Barriers inhibiting the development of better education for these children include lack of parental advocacy, lack of appropriate teacher training, an emphasis on older students of extraordinary ability, financial constraints, and legal roadblocks such as laws preventing early admission to school. The barriers to early identification and programming for students with special gifts or talents include school policies and ideologies that refuse to advance students in grade beyond their chronological age peers.

Ruf (2005) describes the early signs of giftedness and provides descriptions of children's typical abilities for each of her five levels of giftedness. Her descriptions are those of parents when their children were birth to nine years of age and older. Table 15.1 contains sample descriptions of one child at age four to five years from each level. In Ruf's classification scheme, Level One designates children who test between approximately the 90th and the 98th percentiles in general ability (meaning that they score higher than 90 to 98 percent of children taking the test). Each higher level in her system represents higher performance and a smaller percentage of the general population of children.

Many questions remain unanswered about the education of young children who have special gifts. Relatively little is known about how advantageous it is to identify and program for such children before they are in third or fourth grade or how best to train parents and teachers to work with preschoolers with special abilities. Young children with disabilities need the best possible early intervention to make sure that all of their

TABLE 15.1	Examples of gifted children at ages four to five years

Level One

Johnathan Truett—At four, Johnathan read *Hop On Pop* and other Dr. Seuss books that we'd read to him. He started sounding out simple words, so we read the text and stopped at words we thought he could recognize or figure out. He then did this with harder words.

Level Two

Debra Sund—At four, Debra read the label on the graham cracker box. Before she turned five, she read long words like "elevator." She didn't seem to learn to read by sounding out the letters. Instead, when she saw a word she didn't know, she would ask what it was. After she heard and saw the word once, she knew it on sight. At 4 1/2, while walking home from the park, Debra asked about wind and what we needed in order to live. Her father explained there was something in the air that we needed to breathe. Debra replied, "You mean oxygen?" Where she heard that is anyone's guess.

Level Three

Brennan Ahlers—Brennan started to read chapter books when he was about four. He did simple division and multiplication in his head at 4 1/2. When he started preschool, I didn't know enough to ask for any adjustments to be made for him. His teacher tried to keep him challenged, but he complained that it was boring. He was already reading and writing while many students couldn't write their names. He was puzzled at having to memorize his address and phone number, because it seemed so basic. He thought every kid knew that.

Level Four

Rebecca Renick—When she was four, Rebecca's babysitter played school with her and gave her addition and subtraction worksheets. Rebecca filled them out correctly. Her teacher said that she always had more complex and interesting ideas for play than the other kids. When she got frustrated that "they didn't get it," she went to the bookrack and read. She was really into jokes and told one joke after another to my mother on the phone. She also loved colored beads and made perfect geometric patterns with them.

Level Five

Jacob Jones—By the age of 4 1/2, we'd go to the library and Jacob would head to the section with computer manuals. Nobody imagined that he was really reading them, but he was. We allowed him access to any level book, which led to some interesting questions when this five-year-old was reading about human reproduction in a large book with pictures during church.

Source: Ruf, D. L. (2005). *Losing our minds: Gifted children left behind.* Scottsdale, AZ: Great Potential Press, pp. 63, 88, 113–114, 144, 178.

abilities, including any special gifts they might have, are not overlooked (see Odom & Wolery, 2006; Porter, 2005).

Although not a panacea, early admission to school and acceleration through grades and subjects offer significant advantages for some young students with special gifts or talents. What many young children with special abilities need most is the freedom to make full and appropriate use of school systems as they now exist. They need the freedom to study with older children in specific areas in which their abilities are challenged. Such children need to be able to get around the usual eligibility rules so that they can go through the ordinary curriculum at an accelerated rate. Unfortunately, relatively few preschoolers with special gifts receive the kind of educational programming appropriate for their abilities.

Preschoolers with special gifts or talents may be intellectually superior and have above-average adaptive behavior and leadership skills as well. Their advanced abilities in many areas, however, don't mean that their development will be above average across the board. Emotionally, they might develop at an average pace for their chronological

Meeting the Needs of Students with Special Gifts and Talents

Acceleration: A Nation Deceived Report

"Nothing is so unequal as the equal treatment of unequal people."

—*Thomas Jefferson*

WHAT THE RESEARCH SAYS

In 2004, *A Nation Deceived: How Schools Hold Back its Brightest Students* was released (Colangelo, Assouline, & Gross). This report summarized 50 years of research on the various forms of acceleration and came to the singular conclusion that acceleration, in many of its forms and under many different circumstances, benefits gifted students both academically and socially. Unfortunately, concern over ability tracking (an extreme form of ability grouping that sorts students based upon global measures such as IQ or GPA) has spilled over into concern about acceleration programs. Acceleration, not a form of tracking, is any educational program that moves students through at a faster rate or younger than typical age. Effective acceleration programs match the level and complexity of the curriculum to the readiness and motivation of the student (Colangelo et al., 2004).

The report dispels many myths associated with acceleration including the belief that the majority of students are not socially mature enough to advance grades, holding students to their grade-level is the "safer" educational route, and acceleration results in gaps in students' knowledge. The report touches upon the 18 types of acceleration found in schools today and reviews the relevant research associated with each practice. The types of acceleration are: early admission to kindergarten, early admission to first grade, grade-skipping, continuous progress, self-paced instruction, subject-matter acceleration/partial acceleration, combined classes, curriculum compacting, telescoping curriculum, mentoring, extracurricular programs, correspondence courses, early graduation, concurrent/dual enrollment, advanced placement, credit by examination, acceleration in college, and early entrance into middle school, high school, or college.

SUMMARY OF THE FINDINGS

A synthesis of the research highlights important aspects related to successful acceleration. Some of the main findings were:

1. Acceleration is more effective in raising student achievement than most successful school reforms;
2. Accelerated students are more likely than non-accelerated students to aspire to advanced educational degrees;
3. When the curriculum moves at a slow pace, boredom and discontent frequently ensue;

age. Sometimes, their uneven development creates special problems of social isolation, and adults might have unrealistic expectations for their social and emotional skills because their cognitive and language skills are so advanced (Porter, 2005). They might require special guidance by sensitive adults who not only provide appropriate educational environments for them, but also discipline them appropriately and teach them the skills required for social competence. They might need help, for example, in acquiring self-understanding, independence, assertiveness, sensitivity to others, friend-making skills, and social problem-solving skills (Perleth et al., 2000).

Transition to Adulthood

For students with special gifts or talents who are achieving near their potential and are given opportunities to take on adult roles, the transitions from childhood to adolescence to adulthood and from high school to higher education or employment are typically not very problematic. Particularly by adolescence, they tend to be aware of their relative strengths and weaknesses. This means that they might not see themselves as gifted in their areas of

4. Problems that stem from acceleration can frequently be traced to incomplete (poor) planning;

5. Almost *all* forms of acceleration result in academic growth (from a review of 380 studies);

6. Few early college entrants experience social or emotional difficulties—when difficulties do arise they are typically short-term and part of an overall adjustment period;

7. Gifted students tend to be socially and emotionally more mature than their same-age mates—thus, acceleration can provide a better personal maturity match;

8. The Iowa Acceleration Scale (IAS) is a proven instrument for making acceleration decisions; and

9. Many alternatives to full-time early college entrance are available today, including AP courses, dual-enrollment classes, distance education, and summer programs.

IOWA ACCELERATION SCALE

A consistent theme throughout the report is that the positive benefits of acceleration are associated with students who have been appropriately evaluated for the purposes of acceleration. One tool used to assess the "readiness" of students for grade-skipping acceleration is the Iowa Acceleration Scale (IAS). The IAS was designed for child-study teams to use to review objective data regarding a child's potential for successful acceleration. The survey includes 20 items divided into 4 subscales: (1) Academic Ability and Achievement, (2) School Information, (3) Interpersonal Skills; and (4) Attitude and Support. The Grand Total, a sum of the four subscales, translates into one of the following recommendations: (a) excellent candidate, (b) good candidate, (c) marginal candidate,

and (d) poor candidate. Studies that have examined the efficacy of the IAS find that it is a useful tool for schools and families (Assouline et al., 2003).

WHAT CAN SCHOOLS DO?

The report encourages school professionals to consider the following three questions when making acceleration decisions:

1. Have we assessed the student's ability correctly so that we know this child is ready for an advanced, fast-paced curriculum?

2. Given the results of our assessment, what might be the best form of acceleration for this child?

3. We know that in a few cases acceleration has not been effective. What can we do as a school to ensure success for the accelerated student? (Colangelo et al., 2004, p. 69)

The message of the report is clear—parents, teachers, administrators, and colleges of education need to be familiar with the research on acceleration to meet the needs of gifted students. Borland (1989) summarizes the current conundrum of resistance to acceleration when he stated:

Acceleration is one of the most curious phenomena in the field of education. I can think of no other issue in which there is such a gulf between what research has revealed and what most practitioners believe. The research on acceleration is so uniformly positive, the benefits of appropriate acceleration so unequivocal, that it is difficult to see how an educator could oppose it. (p. 185)

● *By Kristin L. Sayeski*

relative weakness even though they perform as well as or better than the majority of their age peers in those areas (Plucker & Stocking, 2001; Robinson et al., 2007).

In many ways, transitions for these youths tend to mirror the problems in transitions faced by adolescents and young adults with disabilities (see Kohler & Field, 2006). Not all adolescents and young adults with special gifts or talents take transitions in stride. Many need personal and career counseling and a networking system that links students to school and community resources (Herbert & Kelly, 2006; Neihart et al., 2002).

If there is a central issue in the education of adolescents with special gifts or talents, it is that of acceleration versus enrichment. Proponents of enrichment believe that these students need continued social contact with their age peers. They argue that such students should follow the curriculum of their age peers and study topics in greater depth. Proponents of acceleration believe that the only way to provide challenging and appropriate education for students with special gifts and talents is to let them compete with older students. These educators argue that because the cognitive abilities of such students are advanced beyond their years, these students should proceed through the curriculum at an accelerated pace.

Personal PERSPECTIVES

Child Prodigy Now U.Va. Grad Student

Gregory R. Smith completed one goal May 31 when he received his bachelor's degree from Randolph-Macon College at the age of 13. Now the child prodigy is aiming at another by jumping into the University's graduate studies program.

Smith started the first of two summer classes Tuesday, the day after his 14th birthday. He is pursuing a Ph.D. in mathematics, the first of several doctoral degrees he plans to obtain.

"The University of Virginia has been my first choice all along, Smith said in announcing his decision last week. "It has been my plan since I graduated from high school to apply to U.Va. for my graduate work. I am so excited to have this wonderful opportunity to study at one of our country's best universities."

U.Va. officials have been equally excited about Smith's selection. Gene Block, vice president and provost, said, "Greg will be a wonderful addition to our graduate studies program. His record of intellectual achievement, combined with his dedication to international service, fit well into the U.Va. tradition. We realize that it's important not only to challenge Greg academically but also to provide an environment where he feels at home among peers."

Smith has been recognized as a prodigy since early childhood. Born in West Reading, Pa., he was solving math problems at 14 months and reading by age 2. The family moved to Florida, where he completed his K-12 education in five years, then to Virginia, where at age 10 he enrolled at Randolph-Macon College in Ashland. He graduated cum laude with a degree in mathematics and was a member of Phi Beta Kappa and five other honor fraternities.

Along the way Smith has used the media attention generated by his blazing academic pace to become a vocal advocate for the pursuit of peace and for children's rights around the world. He founded International Youth Advocates and has served as youth ambassador for the Christian Children's Fund and youth spokesperson for World Centers of Compassion for Children. During the past year, he has traveled throughout the United States and visited six countries on four continents. Humanitarian aid efforts are benefiting orphans in East Timor and youth in Sao Paulo, Brazil, and Smith is helping people in Rwanda build their first public library.

He has met with presidents, including former President Bill Clinton and former Soviet Union President Mikhail Gorbachev, as well as Nobel Peace laureates, such as Ireland's Betty Williams and South Africa's Archbishop Desmond Tutu. His efforts have brought him before the United Nations Security Council and several state legislatures.

One of Smith's goals is to create an international symbol for the child, so that child-occupied buildings in conflict zones can be marked and protected. In addition, he hopes to create recognized safe havens in embattled areas so children will have shelters sanctioned by international law.

"I believe all children are born pure and innocent and only act with violence because we teach them hate and violence," he said. "There must be peaceful parenting to have a peaceful future. It is up to us to create an environment that makes it possible for children to resist the corruptions that take us down violent and immoral paths."

Nominated in 2002 and '03 for the Nobel Peace Prize, Smith has been tapped to co-chair the World of Children Awards with Muhammad Ali. He is among 43 students in the nation to receive scholarships up to $50,000 a year for six years from the Jack Kent Cooke Foundation for his graduate studies.

Source: Graves, L. (June 13, 2004). Child prodigy now U.Va. grad student. *Inside UVA.* Reprinted with permission.

Acceleration for adolescents with special gifts or talents can mean enrollment in advanced placement courses, early entrance to college, or enrollment in college courses while they are attending high school (see Callahan, 2003; Colangelo et al., 2004b; Muratori et al., 2006). Some of the most highly gifted students might even be admitted early to graduate study. In the case of the child prodigy who is now a graduate student at the University of Virginia (see Personal Perspectives above), radical acceleration seems to have been an obvious choice. It's difficult to argue against early admission to college and graduate school for an adolescent with Gregory Smith's very unusual intellectual gifts, social maturity, and moral commitments. Other students with special gifts or talents who are nonetheless less dramatically different from their age peers may not benefit from radical acceleration.

Acceleration programs, particularly in mathematics, have been evaluated very favorably (see Assouline & Lupkowski-Shoplik, 2003; Brody & Stanley, 2005; Muratori et al., 2006). In fact, early entrance to college on a full-time or part-time basis appears to work very well for adolescents, as long as it is done with care and sensitivity to the needs of individual students. It's important to provide counseling and support services for students who enter college early to ensure that they have appropriate, rewarding social experiences that enhance their self-esteem, as well as academic challenges and successes in the courses they take.

Beyond acceleration and enrichment, adolescents with special gifts or talents often need attention to social and personal development if they are to make successful and gratifying transitions to adulthood and careers (Assouline & Colangelo, 2006). Like other groups of students with special characteristics and needs, they may benefit from opportunities to socialize with and learn from other students who have similar characteristics and face similar challenges. They may be able to obtain particular benefit from reflecting on the nature and meaning of life and the directions they choose for themselves. Given proper supports, they can often make use of self-determination and survival skills (see Neihart et al., 2002).

Summary

How is giftedness defined?

▶ Students with special gifts excel in some way compared to others of the same age. However, there is little agreement about how giftedness should be defined. Disagreements about definition include:
  - What is to be measured
  - How it is to be measured
  - The degree to which one must excel
  - The comparison group
  - Reasons for identifying giftedness

▶ Giftedness is actually whatever we wish to make it.

▶ There may be different kinds of giftedness, such as analytic, synthetic, and practical intelligence.

▶ Giftedness may include the qualities of excellence, rarity, demonstrability, productivity, and value.

What is the prevalence of giftedness?

▶ Prevalence depends on definition; school systems across the nation typically identify about 3 to 5 percent of students as gifted.

What are the origins of giftedness?

▶ Both biological (primarily genetic) and social factors (e.g., family, school, peer group, community) are involved.
  - No one knows precisely how much each of these two factors contributes to giftedness, especially in the individual case.
  - We can alter many social factors but not genetic factors, and more attention needs to be given to how schools foster giftedness.

How is giftedness identified?

▶ Individual intelligence tests have been the traditional means of identifying giftedness.

▶ More attention is being given now to additional, culturally sensitive identification procedures, including nomination by peers, parents, teachers, and self as well as to interests and accomplishments.

What are the psychological and behavioral characteristics of students with special gifts and talents?

▶ Gifted students typically learn to read at an early age and achieve other developmental milestones earlier than most children.

▶ Gifted students are typically good at many things.

▶ Gifted students typically like school and like learning.

▶ Gifted students are subject to the same psychological and physical problems of other students.

How do cultural values affect the education of students with special gifts and talents?

▶ Throughout history, all cultures have had the concept of giftedness.

▶ American culture is ambivalent about giftedness, liking the good things that giftedness brings but disliking intellectual superiority and identifying individuals with intellectual gifts.

What groups of students with special gifts and talents are neglected?

▶ Underachievers are often overlooked.

▶ Students who are low in socioeconomic status and those living in remote areas are often unrecognized.

▶ Students from cultural- and ethnic-minority groups are often neglected.

▶ Those with disabilities are often not identified.

▶ Females are underrepresented.

What are the major educational considerations for students with special gifts and talents?

▶ Acceleration and enrichment are the two most common ways of accommodating gifted students; and both have advantages and disadvantages, proponents and opponents.
  ■ Acceleration involves moving a student ahead academically to be grouped with older students or those in advanced placement.
  ■ Enrichment involves adding to or altering the curriculum to be more challenging to those with special abilities.

What are the major problems of early intervention for children with special gifts and talents?

▶ Lack of research to indicate effective ways of identifying giftedness in young children (i.e., before third or fourth grade) is a major problem.

▶ Early admission to school or radical acceleration is a controversial practice that some adults fear results in psychological problems.

What provisions are made for transition of students with special gifts and talents?

▶ By adolescence, most gifted students can make an accurate estimate of their relative strengths and weaknesses.

▶ The problems of gifted adolescents tend to mirror those of students with disabilities of the same age, and many will need personal counseling about further education and career paths.

▶ Acceleration (including early admission to college) and enrichment (including advanced placement courses) are the two primary accommodations.

STANDARDS and PRINCIPLES in this Chapter*

SPECIAL EDUCATORS . . .

■ understand the similarities and differences in human development and the characteristics between and among individuals with and without exceptional learning needs (from CEC Content Standard #2).

■ possess a repertoire of evidence-based instructional strategies to individualize instruction for individuals with exceptional learning needs (from CEC Content Standard #4).

■ actively create learning environments for individuals with exceptional learning needs that foster cultural understanding, safety and emotional well-being, positive social interactions, and active engagement of individuals with exceptional learning needs (from CEC Content Standard #5).

ALL TEACHERS . . .

■ understand how children learn and develop, and can provide learning opportunities that support the intellectual, social, and personal development of each learner (INTASC Principle #2).

■ understand and use a variety of instructional strategies to encourage students' development of critical thinking, problem solving, and performance skills (INTASC Principle #4).

■ use an understanding of individual and group motivation and behavior to create a learning environment that encourages positive social interaction, active engagement in learning, and self-motivation (INTASC Principle #5).

*Also addressed in this chapter: CEC Standard #1, INTASC Principle #1.

Applying the STANDARDS and PRINCIPLES

■ HOW would you summarize what it means to be gifted? (CEC Content Standard #1 & #2; INTASC Principle #1 & #2)

■ HOW should teachers determine what instructional methods to use with students with special gifts and talents? (CEC Content Standard #4 & INTASC Principle #4)

■ DESCRIBE a learning environment in which students with special gifts and talents are likely to thrive. (CEC Content Standard #5 & INTASC Principle #5)

Now go to the Hallahan/Kauffman, Eleventh Edition MyEducationLab course at www.myeducationlab.com to:

- take a Pretest to assess your initial comprehension of the chapter content;
- study chapter content with your Individualized Study Plan;
- take a Posttest to assess your understanding of chapter content;
- engage in multimedia exercises to help you build a deeper and more applied understanding of chapter content.

Appendix
CEC Content Standards and INTASC Core Principles

CEC Special Education Content Standards for All Beginning Special Education Teachers

INTASC Core Principles for General and Special Education Teachers

CEC Special Education Content Standard #1

Foundations   Special educators understand the field as an evolving and changing discipline based on philosophies, evidence-based principles and theories, relevant laws and policies, diverse historical points of view, and human issues that have historically influenced and continue to influence the field of special education and the education and treatment of individuals with exceptional needs both in school and society. Special educators understand how these influence professional practice, including assessment, instructional planning, implementation, and program evaluation. Special educators understand how issues of human diversity can impact families, cultures, and schools, and how these complex human issues can interact with issues in the delivery of special education services. They understand the relationships of organizations of special education to the organization and functions of schools, school systems, and other agencies. Special educators use this knowledge as a ground upon which to construct their own personal understandings and philosophies of special education.

INTASC Principle #1

The teacher understands the central concepts, tools of inquiry, structures of the discipline(s) he or she teaches and can create learning experiences that make these aspects of subject matter meaningful for students.

CEC Special Education Content Standard #2

Development and Characteristics of Learners   Special educators know and demonstrate respect for their students first as unique human beings. Special educators understand the similarities and differences in human development and the characteristics between and among individuals with and without exceptional learning needs (ELN). Moreover, special educators understand how exceptional conditions can interact with the domains of human development, and they use this knowledge to respond to the varying abilities and behaviors of individuals with ELN. Special educators understand how the experiences of individuals with ELN can impact families, as well as individuals' ability to learn, interact socially, and live as fulfilled contributing members of the community.

INTASC Principle #2

The teacher understands how children learn and develop and can provide learning opportunities that support the intellectual, social, and personal development of each learner.

CEC Special Education Content Standard #3

Individual Learning Differences   Special educators understand the effects that an exceptional condition can have on an individual's learning in school and throughout life. Special educators understand that the beliefs, traditions, and values across and within cultures can affect relationships among and between students, their families, and the school community. Moreover, special educators are active and resourceful in seeking to understand how primary language, culture, and familial backgrounds interact with the individual's exceptional condition to impact the individual's academic and social abilities, attitudes, values, interests, and career options. The understanding of these learning differences and their possible interactions provide the foundation on which special educators individualize instruction to provide meaningful and challenging learning for individuals with ELN.

INTASC Principle #3

The teacher understands how students differ in their approaches to learning and creates instructional opportunities that are adapted to diverse learners.

CEC Special Education Content Standard #4

Individual Strategies   Special educators possess a repertoire of evidence-based instructional strategies to individualize instruction for individuals with ELN. Special educators select, adapt, and use these instructional strategies to promote challenging learning results in general and special curricula and to appropriately modify learning environments for individuals with ELN. They enhance the learning of critical thinking, problem solving, and performance skills of individuals with ELN and increase their self-awareness, self-management, self-control, self-reliance, and self-esteem. Moreover, special educators emphasize the development, maintenance, and generalization of knowledge and skills across environments, settings, and the life span.

INTASC Principle #4

The teacher understands and uses a variety of instructional strategies to encourage students' development of critical thinking, problem solving, and performance skills.

CEC Special Education Content Standards for All Beginning Special Education Teachers

INTASC Core Principles for General and Special Education Teachers

CEC Special Education Content Standard #5

Learning Environments and Social Interactions   Special educators actively create learning environments for individuals with ELN that foster cultural understanding, safety and emotional well being, positive social interactions, and active engagement of individuals with ELN. In addition, special educators foster environments in which diversity is valued and individuals are taught to live harmoniously and productively in a culturally diverse world. Special educators shape environments to encourage the independence, self-motivation, self-direction, personal empowerment, and self-advocacy of individuals with ELN. Special educators help their general education colleagues integrate individuals with ELN in regular environments and engage them in meaningful learning activities and interactions. Special educators use direct motivational and instructional interventions with individuals with ELN to teach them to respond effectively to current expectations. When necessary, special educators can safely intervene with individuals with ELN in crises. Special educators coordinate all these efforts and provide guidance and direction to paraeducators and others, such as classroom volunteers and tutors.

INTASC Principle #5

The teacher uses an understanding of individual and group motivation and behavior to create a learning environment that encourages positive social interaction, active engagement in learning, and self-motivation.

CEC Special Education Content Standard #6

Communication   Special educators understand typical and atypical language development and the ways in which exceptional conditions can interact with an individual's experience with and use of language. Special educators use individualized strategies to enhance language development and teach communication skills to individuals with ELN. Special educators are familiar with augmentative, alternative, and assistive technologies to support and enhance communication of individuals with exceptional needs. Special educators match their communication methods to an individual's language proficiency and cultural and linguistic differences. Special educators provide effective language models, and they use communication strategies and resources to facilitate understanding of subject matter for individuals with ELN whose primary language is not English.

INTASC Principle #6

The teacher uses knowledge of effective verbal, nonverbal, and media communication technologies to foster active inquiry, collaboration, and supportive interaction in the classroom.

CEC Special Education Content Standard #7

Instructional Planning   Individualized decision making and instruction is at the center of special education practice. Special educators develop long-range individualized instructional plans anchored in both general and special curricula. In addition, special educators systematically translate these individualized plans into carefully selected short-range goals and objectives taking into consideration an individual's abilities and needs, the learning environment, and a myriad of cultural and linguistic factors. Individualized instructional plans emphasize explicit modeling and efficient guided practice to assure acquisition and fluency through maintenance and generalization. Understanding of these factors, as well as the implications of an individual's exceptional condition, guides the special educator's selection, adaptation, and creation of materials, and the use of powerful instructional variables. Instructional plans are modified based on ongoing analysis of the individual's learning progress. Moreover, special educators facilitate this instructional planning in a collaborative context including the individuals with exceptionalities, families, professional colleagues, and personnel from other agencies as appropriate. Special educators also develop a variety of individualized transition plans, such as transitions from preschool to elementary school and from secondary settings to a variety of postsecondary work and learning contexts. Special educators are comfortable using appropriate technologies to support instructional planning and individualized instruction.

INTASC Principle #7

The teacher plans instruction based on knowledge of subject matter, students, the community, and curriculum goals.

CEC Special Education Content Standards for All Beginning Special Education Teachers	INTASC Core Principles for General and Special Education Teachers

CEC Special Education Content Standard #8

Assessment Assessment is integral to the decision making and teaching of special educators, and special educators use multiple types of assessment information for a variety of educational decisions. Special educators use the results of assessments to help identify exceptional learning needs and to develop and implement individualized instructional programs, as well as to adjust instruction in response to ongoing learning progress. Special educators understand the legal policies and ethical principles of measurement and assessment related to referral, eligibility, program planning, instruction, and placement for individuals with ELN, including those from culturally and linguistically diverse backgrounds. Special educators understand measurement theory and practices for addressing issues of validity, reliability, norms, bias, and interpretation of assessment results. In addition, special educators understand the appropriate use and limitations of various types of assessments. Special educators collaborate with families and other colleagues to assure nonbiased, meaningful assessments and decision making. Special educators conduct formal and informal assessments of behavior, learning, achievement, and environments to design learning experiences that support the growth and development of individuals with ELN. Special educators use assessment information to identify supports and adaptations required for individuals with ELN to access the general curriculum and to participate in school, system, and statewide assessment programs. Special educators regularly monitor the progress of individuals with ELN in general and special curricula. Special educators use appropriate technologies to support their assessments.

INTASC Principle #8

The teacher understands and uses formal and informal assessment strategies to evaluate and ensure the continuous intellectual, social, and physical development of the learner.

CEC Special Education Content Standard #9

Professional and Ethical Practice Special educators are guided by the profession's ethical and professional practice standards. Special educators practice in multiple roles and complex situations across wide age and developmental ranges. Their practice requires ongoing attention to legal matters along with serious professional and ethical considerations. Special educators engage in professional activities and participate in learning communities that benefit individuals with ELN, their families, colleagues, and their own professional growth. Special educators view themselves as lifelong learners and regularly reflect on and adjust their practice. Special educators are aware of how their own and others' attitudes, behaviors, and ways of communicating can influence their practice. Special educators understand that culture and language can interact with exceptionalities and are sensitive to the many aspects of diversity of individuals with ELN and their families. Special educators actively plan and engage in activities that foster their professional growth and keep them current with evidence-based best practices. Special educators know their own limits of practice and practice within them.

INTASC Principle #9

The teacher is a reflective practitioner who continually evaluates the effects of his or her choices and actions on others (students, parents, and other professionals in the learning community) and who actively seeks out opportunities to grow professionally.

CEC Special Education Content Standard #10

Collaboration Special educators routinely and effectively collaborate with families, other educators, related service providers, and personnel from community agencies in culturally responsive ways. This collaboration assures that the needs of individuals with ELN are addressed throughout schooling. Moreover, special educators embrace their special role as advocate for individuals with ELN. Special educators promote and advocate the learning and well being of individuals with ELN across a wide range of settings and a range of different learning experiences. Special educators are viewed as specialists by a myriad of people who actively seek their collaboration to effectively include and teach individuals with ELN. Special educators are a resource to their colleagues in understanding the laws and policies relevant to individuals with ELN. Special educators use collaboration to facilitate the successful transitions of individuals with ELN across settings and services.

INTASC Principle #10

The teacher fosters relationships with school colleagues, families, and agencies in the larger community to support students' learning and well being.

Sources: Council for Exceptional Children. (2003). *What every special educator must know: The international standards for the preparation and certification of special education* (5th ed.). Arlington, VA: Author; Council of Chief State School Officers. (1992). *Model standards for beginning teacher licensing, assessment, and development: A resource for state dialogue.* Washington, DC: Author. Available at www.ccsso.org/content/pdfs/corestrd.pdf.

Glossary

Acceleration An approach in which students with special gifts or talents are placed in grade levels ahead of their age peers in one or more academic subjects.

Accessible pedestrian signal (APSs) Devices for people who are blind to let them know when the "walk" signal is on at intersections; can be auditory, tactile, or both.

Accommodations Changes in the delivery of instruction, type of student performance, or method of assessment which do not significantly change the content or conceptual difficulty of the curriculum.

Acquired apraxia As in Developmental apraxia, there are problems in motor planning such that the child has difficulty in producing speech sounds and organizing words and word sounds for effective communication. However, the problem is known to be caused by neurological damage.

Acquired immune deficiency syndrome (AIDS) A virus-caused illness resulting in a breakdown of the immune system; currently, no known cure exists.

Acute A serious state of illness or injury from which someone often recovers with treatment.

Adaptive behavior Consists of social and practical intelligence that people have learned so that they can function in their everyday lives; along with intellectual functioning, are considered in making a determination of mental retardation/intellectual disability.

Adaptations Changes in curricular content or conceptual difficulty or changes in instructional objectives and methods.

Adapted signs Signs adapted for use by people who are deaf-blind; tactually based rather than visually based, such as American Sign Language for those who are deaf but sighted.

Adaptive behavior Social, and practical intelligence that people have learned so that they can function in their everyday lives; along with intellectual functioning are considered in making a determination of mental retardation/intellectual disability.

Adaptive devices Special tools that are adaptations of common items to make accomplishing self-care, work, or recreation activities easier for people with physical disabilities.

Adaptive skills Skills needed to adapt to one's living environment (e.g., communication, self-care, home living, social skills, community use, self-direction, health and safety, functional academics, leisure, and work); usually estimated by an adaptive behavior survey; one of two major components (the other is intellectual functioning) of the AAMR definition.

Adderall A psychostimulant for ADHD; its effects are longer acting than those of Ritalin.

Adventitiously deaf Deafness that occurs through illness or accident in an individual who was born with normal hearing.

Advocacy Action that is taken on behalf of oneself or others; a method parents of students with disabilities can use to obtain needed or improved services.

Affective disorder A disorder of mood or emotional tone characterized by depression or elation.

Aggression Behavior that intentionally causes others harm or that elicits escape or avoidance responses from others.

Aim Line Used in CBM; based on expected growth norms, a line drawn from the baseline data point to the anticipated end of instruction.

Americans with Disabilities Act (ADA) Civil rights legislation for persons with disabilities ensuring nondiscrimination in a broad range of activities.

Amniocentesis A medical procedure that allows examination of the amniotic fluid around the fetus; sometimes recommended to determine the presence of abnormality.

Anoxia Deprivation of oxygen; can cause brain injury.

Anxiety disorder A disorder characterized by anxiety, fearfulness, and avoidance of ordinary activities because of anxiety or fear.

Aphonia Loss of voice.

Applied behavior analysis (ABA) highly structured approach that focuses on teaching functional skills and continuous assessment of progress; grounded in behavioral learning theory.

Apraxia The inability to plan and coordinate speech.

Aqueous humor A watery substance between the cornea and lens of the eye.

Asperger syndrome One of five autistic spectrum disorders; a milder form of autism without significant impairments in language and cognition; characterized by primary problems in social interaction.

Assistance card A relatively small card containing a message that alerts the public that the user is deaf-blind and needs assistance in crossing the street.

Asthma A lung disease characterized by episodic difficulty in breathing, particularly exhaling, due to inflammation or obstruction of the air passages.

Astigmatism Blurred vision caused by an irregular cornea or lens.

Atonic Lack of muscle tone; floppiness.

Atresia Absence or closure of a part of the body that is normally open.

Attention deficit hyperactivity disorder (ADHD) A condition characterized by severe problems of inattention, hyperactivity, and/or impulsivity; often found in people with learning disabilities.

Audiologist An individual trained in audiology, the science dealing with hearing impairments, their detection, and remediation.

Audiometric zero The lowest level at which people with normal hearing can hear.

Auditory-verbal approach Part of the oral approach to teaching students who are hearing impaired; stresses teaching the person to use his or her remaining hearing as much as possible; heavy emphasis on use of amplification; heavy emphasis on teaching speech.

Augmentative or alternative communication (AAC) Alternative forms of communication that do not use the oral sounds of speech or that augment the use of speech.

Auricle The visible part of the ear, composed of cartilage; collects the sounds and funnels them via the external auditory canal to the eardrum.

Authentic assessment   A method that evaluates a student's critical-thinking and problem-solving ability in real-life situations in which he or she may work with or receive help from peers, teachers, parents, or supervisors.

Autism   One of five autistic spectrum disorders; characterized by extreme social withdrawal and impairment in communication; other common characteristics are stereotyped movements, resistance to environmental change or change in daily routines, and unusual responses to sensory experiences; usually evident before age of 3 years; a pervasive developmental disability characterized by extreme withdrawal, cognitive deficits, language disorders, self-stimulation, and onset before the age of 30 months.

Autism spectrum disorders   Five similar conditions: autism, Asperger syndrome, Rett syndrome, childhood disintegrative disorder, and pervasive developmental disorder not otherwise specified; all involve varying degrees of problems with communication skills, social interactions, and repetitive and stereotyped patterns of behavior.

Autistic regression   phenomenon whereby a child appears to progress normally until about 16 to 24 months of age and, then, begins to show signs of being autistic and ultimately is diagnosed as autistic.

Autistic savant   A person with severe autism whose social and language skills are markedly delayed but who also has advanced skills in a particular area, such as calculation or drawing.

Baby signs   A system developed to help hearing parents and their infants communicate with each other before spoken language develops; consists of signs from ASL as well as other gestures.

Basal ganglia   A set of structures within the brain that include the caudate, globus pallidus, and putamen, the first two being abnormal in people with ADHD; generally responsible for the coordination and control of movement.

Baseline Data Point   Used in CBM; the beginning score gathered before an intervention begins, e.g, the number of correct words per minute that a student reads before receiving a fluency intervention.

Behavior management   Strategies and techniques used to increase desirable behavior and decrease undesirable behavior. May be applied in the classroom, home, or other environment.

Behavior modification   Systematic control of environmental events, especially of consequences, to produce specific changes in observable responses. May include reinforcement, punishment, modeling, self-instruction, desensitization, guided practice, or any other technique for strengthening or eliminating a particular response.

Behavioral inhibition   The ability to stop an intended response, to stop an ongoing response, to guard an ongoing response from interruption, and to refrain from responding immediately; allows executive functions to occur; delayed or impaired in those with ADHD.

Behavioral phenotype   A collection of behaviors, including cognitive, language, and social behaviors as well as psychopathological symptoms, that tend to occur together in people with a specific genetic syndrome.

Bicultural-bilingual approach   An approach for teaching students with hearing impairment that stresses teaching American Sign Language as a first language and English as a second language and promotes the teaching of Deaf culture.

Braille bills   Legislation passed in several states to make braille more available to students with visual impairment; specific provisions vary from state to state, but major advocates have lobbied for (1) making braille available if parents want it, and (2) ensuring that teachers of students with visual impairment are proficient in braille.

Braille notetakers   Portable devices that can be used to take notes in braille, which are then converted to speech, braille, or text.

Braille   A system in which raised dots allow people who are blind to read with their fingertips; each quadrangular cell contains from one to six dots, the arrangement of which denotes different letters and symbols.

Cataracts   A condition caused by clouding of the lens of the eye; affects color vision and distance vision.

Catheterization   The insertion of a tube into the urethra to drain the bladder.

Caudate   A structure in the basal ganglia of the brain; site of abnormal development in persons with ADHD.

Center-based program   A program implemented primarily in a school or center, not in the student's home.

Central coherence   The inclination to bring meaning to stimuli by conceptualizing it as a whole; thought to be weak in people with ASD.

Cerebellum   An organ at the base of the brain responsible for coordination and movement; site of abnormal development in persons with ADHD.

Cerebral palsy (CP)   A condition characterized by paralysis, weakness, lack of coordination, and/or other motor dysfunction; caused by damage to the brain before it has matured.

CHARGE syndrome   A genetic syndrome resulting in deaf-blindness; characterized by physical anomalies, often including coloboma (abnormalities of the pupil, retina and/or optic nerve), cranial nerves, heart defects, atresia (absence or closure) of the chonae (air passages from nose to throat), retardation in growth and mental development, genital abnormalities, ear malformation and/or hearing loss.

Childhood disintegrative disorder   One of five autistic spectrum disorders; normal development for at least two and up to ten years, followed by significant loss of skills; much more prevalent in males.

Choanae   Air passages from the nose to the throat.

Choreoathetoid   Characterized by involuntary movements and difficulty with balance; associated with choreoathetoid cerebral palsy.

Chorionic villus sampling (CVS)   A method of testing the unborn fetus for a variety of chromosomal abnormalities, such as Down syndrome; a small amount of tissue from the chorion (a membrane that eventually helps form the placenta) is extracted and tested; can be done earlier than amniocentesis but the risk of miscarriage is slightly higher.

Chromosomal disorder   Any of several syndromes resulting from abnormal or damaged chromosome(s); can result in intellectual disabilities.

Chromosome   A rod-shaped entity in the nucleus of the cell; contains genes, which convey hereditary characteristics; each cell in the human body contains 23 pairs of chromosomes.

Chronic   A permanent condition; not temporary.

Chronological age   Refers to how old a person is; used in comparison to mental age to determine IQ. IQ = (mental age ÷ chronological age) × 100.

Classwide peer tutoring (CWPT)   An instructional procedure in which all students in the class are involved in tutoring and being tutored by classmates on specific skills as directed by their teacher.

Cleft palate   A condition in which there is a rift or split in the upper part of the oral cavity; may include the upper lip (cleft lip).

Closed head injury   Damage to the brain that occurs without penetration of the skull; might be caused by a blow to the head or violent shaking by an adult.

Coaching   A technique whereby a friend or therapist offers encouragement and support for a person with ADHD.

Cochlea   A snail-shaped organ that lies below the vestibular mechanism in the inner ear; its parts convert the sounds coming from the middle ear into electrical signals that are transmitted to the brain.

Cochlear implantation   A surgical procedure that allows people who are deaf to hear some environmental sounds; an external coil fitted on the skin by the ear picks up sound from a microphone worn by the person and transmits it to an internal coil implanted in the bone behind the ear, which carries it to an electrode implanted in the cochlea of the inner ear.

Cognition   The ability to solve problems and use strategies; an area of difficulty for many persons with learning disabilities.

Cognitive mapping   A nonsequential way of conceptualizing the spatial environment that allows a person who is visually impaired to know where several points in the environment are simultaneously; allows for better mobility than does a strictly sequential conceptualization of the environment.

Cognitive training   A group of training procedures designed to change thoughts or thought patterns.

Collaborative consultation   An approach in which a special educator and a general educator collaborate to come up with teaching strategies for a student with disabilities. The relationship between the two professionals is based on the premises of shared responsibility and equal authority.

Coloboma   A condition of the eye in which the pupil is abnormally shaped and/or there are abnormalities of the retina or optic nerve; can result in loss of visual acuity and extreme sensitivity to light.

Communication disorders   Impairments in the ability to use speech or language to communicate.

Communication   The process of sharing information.

Communicative function   Acts of communication, such as requesting, rejecting, commenting, arguing, and reasoning.

Communicative Intent   The need to communicate for social reasons; thought to be lacking in most children with autism.

Community residential facility (CRF)   A place, usually a group home, in an urban or residential neighborhood where about three to ten adults with intellectual disabilities live under supervision.

Comorbidity   Co-occurrence of two or more conditions in the same individual.

Competitive employment   A workplace that provides employment that pays at least minimum wage and in which most workers are nondisabled.

Comprehension monitoring   The ability to keep track of one's own comprehension of reading material and to make adjustments to comprehend better while reading; often deficient in students with learning disabilities.

Conduct disorder   A disorder characterized by overt, aggressive, disruptive behavior or covert antisocial acts such as stealing, lying, and fire setting; may include both overt and covert acts.

Conductive hearing impairment   A hearing impairment, usually mild, resulting from malfunctioning along the conductive pathway of the ear (i.e., the outer or middle ear).

Congenital   A characteristic or condition that is present at birth; might or might not be due to genetic factors.

Congenital anomaly   An irregularity (anomaly) that is present at birth; might or might not be due to genetic factors.

Congenital cytomegalovirus (CMV)   The most frequently occurring viral infection in newborns; can result in a variety of disabilities, especially hearing impairment.

Congenitally deaf   Deafness that is present at birth; can be caused by genetic factors, by injuries during fetal development, or by injuries occurring at birth.

Connexin-26 gene   A gene, the mutation of which causes deafness; the leading cause of congenital deafness in children.

Constant time delay   An instructional procedure whereby the teacher makes a request while simultaneously prompting the student and then over several occasions makes the same request and waits a constant period of time before prompting; often used with students with intellectual disabilites.

Content enhancement   The modification of curriculum materials to make them more salient or prominent, e.g., graphic organizers and mnemonics.

Contingency-based self-management   Educational techniques that involve having students keep track of their own behavior, for which they then receive consequences (e.g., reinforcement).

Continuous performance test (CPT)   A test measuring a person's ability to sustain attention to rapidly presented stimuli; can help in the diagnosis of ADHD.

Continuum of alternative placements (CAP)   The full range of alternative placements, from those assumed to be least restrictive to those considered most restrictive; the continuum ranges from general education classrooms in neighborhood schools to resource rooms, self-contained classes, special day schools, residential schools, hospital schools, and home instruction.

Cooperative learning   A teaching approach in which the teacher places students with heterogeneous abilities (for example, some might have disabilities) together to work on assignments.

Cooperative teaching   An approach in which general educators and special educators teach together in the general classroom; it helps the special educator know the context of the general education classroom better.

Cornea   A transparent cover in front of the iris and pupil in the eye; responsible for most of the refraction of light rays in focusing on an object.

Corpus callosum   a part of the brain, consisting of millions of fibers connecting the left and right hemispheres; responsible for communication between the two hemispheres; site of abnormal development in persons with ADHD.

Cortical visual impairment (CVI) A poorly understood childhood condition that apparently involves dysfunction in the visual cortex; characterized by large day-to-day variations in visual ability.

Co-teaching A special educator working side-by-side with a general educator in a classroom, both teachers providing instruction to the group.

Cranial nerves Twelve pairs of nerves that connect the brain with various muscles and glands in the body.

Creativity The ability to express novel and useful ideas, to sense and elucidate new and important relationships, and to ask previously unthought of, but crucial, questions.

Criterion-referenced testing Assessment wherein an individual's performance is compared to a goal or standard of mastery, differs from norm-referenced testing wherein an individual's performance is compared to the performance of others.

Cued speech A method to aid speechreading in people with hearing impairment; the speaker uses hand shapes to represent sounds.

Curriculum-based measurement (CBM) A formative evaluation method designed to evaluate performance in the curriculum to which students are exposed; usually involves giving students a small sample of items from the curriculum in use in their schools; proponents argue that CBM is preferable to comparing students with national norms or using tests that do not reflect the curriculum content learned by the students.

Cystic fibrosis An inherited disease affecting primarily the gastrointestinal (GI) tract and respiratory organs; characterized by thick, sticky mucous that often interferes with breathing or digestion.

Daily living skills Skills required for living independently, such as dressing, toileting, bathing, cooking, and other typical daily activities of nondisabled adults.

Deaf clubs Gathering spots where people who are deaf can socialize; on the decline in the United States.

Decibels Units of relative loudness of sounds; zero decibels (0 dB) designates the point at which people with normal hearing can just detect sound.

Decoding The ability to convert print to spoken language; dependent on phonemic awareness and understanding of the alphabetic principles; a significant problem for many people with reading disabilities.

Deinstitutionalization A social movement starting in the 1960s whereby large numbers of persons with intellectual disabilities and/or mental illness are moved from large mental institutions into smaller community homes or into the homes of their families; recognized as a major catalyst for integrating persons with disabilities into society.

Descriptive Video Service® A service for use of people with visual impairment that provides audio narrative of key visual elements; available for several public television programs and some videos of movies.

Developmental apraxia A disorder of speech or language involving problems in motor planning such that the child has difficulty in producing speech sounds and organizing words and word sounds for effective communication. The cause may be unknown.

Developmental delay A term often used to encompass a variety of disabilities of infants or young children indicating that they are significantly behind the norm for development in one or more areas such as motor development, cognitive development, or language.

Developmentally appropriate practice (DAP) Educational methods for young children that are compatible with their developmental levels and that meet their individual needs; coined by the National Association for the Education of Young Children.

Diabetic retinopathy A condition resulting from interference with the blood supply to the retina; the fastest-growing cause of blindness.

Direct Instruction (DI) A method of teaching academics, especially reading and math; emphasizes drill and practice and immediate feedback; lessons are precisely sequenced, fast-paced, and well-rehearsed by the teacher.

Differentiated instruction Instruction varied to meet the needs of all students.

Disability rights movement Patterned after the civil rights movement of the 1960s, this is a loosely organized effort to advocate for the rights of people with disabilities through lobbying legislators and other activities. Members view people with disabilities as an oppressed minority.

Dopamine A neurotransmitter, the levels of which may be abnormal in people with ADHD.

Doppler effect A term used to describe the phenomenon of the pitch of a sound rising as the listener moves toward its source.

Down syndrome A condition resulting from an abnormality with the twenty-first pair of chromosomes; the most common abnormality is a triplet rather than a pair (the condition sometimes referred to as trisomy 21); characterized by intellectual disabilities and such physical signs as slanted-appearing eyes, hypotonia, a single palmar crease, shortness, and a tendency toward obesity.

Dysarthria A condition in which brain damage causes impaired control of the muscles used in articulation.

Dysfluencies Hesitations, repetitions, and other disruptions of normal speech flow.

Early expressive language delay (EELD) A significant lag in the development of expressive language that is apparent by age 2.

Echolalia The parroting repetition of words or phrases either immediately after they are heard or later; often observed in individuals with autistic spectrum disorders.

Education for All Handicapped Children Act Also known as Public Law 94-142, which became law in 1975 and is now known as the Individuals with Disabilities Education Act (IDEA). Retitled in 1990 and reauthorized in 1997 and 2004.

Encephalitis An inflammation of the brain; can affect the child's mental development adversely.

Encopresis Bowel incontinence; soiling oneself.

Enrichment An approach in which additional learning experiences are provided for students with special gifts or talents while the students remain in the grade levels appropriate for their chronological ages.

Enuresis Urinary incontinence; wetting oneself.

Epilepsy A pattern of repeated seizures.

Episodic Occurring in episodes; a temporary condition that will pass but may recur.

Error analysis An informal method of teacher assessment that involves the teacher noting the particular kinds of errors a student makes when doing academic work.

Evoked-response audiometry A technique involving electroencephalograph measurement of changes in brain wave activity in response to sounds.

Executive functions The ability to regulate one's behavior through working memory, inner speech, control of emotions and arousal levels, and analysis of problems and communication of problem solutions to others; delayed or impaired in people with ADHD.

Expected growth norms Used with CBM; the rate at which the average student is expected to learn given typical instruction.

Expressive language Encoding or sending messages in communication.

External otitis An infection of the skin of the external auditory canal; also called swimmer's ear.

Externalizing Acting-out behavior; aggressive or disruptive behavior that is observable as behavior directed toward others.

Familiality studies A method of determining the degree to which a given condition is inherited; looks at the prevalence of the condition in relatives of the person with the condition.

Family activity settings Activities that families routinely engage in, such as mealtimes and seasonal celebrations; can be focal points for the implementation of PBSs.

Family-centered model A consumer-driven model that encourages the family to make its own decisions with respect to services while mobilizing resources and supports for the family's goals.

Family characteristics A component of the Turnbulls' family systems model; includes type and severity of the disability as well as such things as size, cultural background, and socioeconomic background of the family.

Family functions A component of the Turnbulls' family systems model; includes such things as economic, daily care, social, medical, and educational needs.

Family interaction A component of the Turnbulls' family systems model; refers to how cohesive and adaptable the family is.

Family life cycle A component of the Turnbulls' family systems model; consists of birth and early childhood, childhood, adolescence, and adulthood.

Family systems theory Stresses that the individual's behavior is best understood in the context of the family and the family's behavior is best understood in the context of other social systems.

Fetal alcohol effect (FAE) Abnormalities that are more subtle than those of FAS; caused by the mother drinking alcohol during pregnancy.

Fetal alchohol spectrum disorders (FASD) A range of disorders in children whose mothers consumed large quantities of alcohol during pregnancy.

Fetal alcohol syndrome (FAS) Abnormalities associated with the mother's drinking alcohol during pregnancy; defects range from mild to severe, including growth retardation, brain damage, intellectual disabilities, hyperactivity, anomalies of the face, and heart failure; also called alcohol embryopathy.

Fingerspelling Spelling the English alphabet by using various finger positions on one hand.

Formative assessment Measurement procedures used to monitor an individual student's progress; they are used to compare how an individual performs in light of his or her abilities, in contrast to standardized tests, which are primarily used to compare an individual's performance to that of other students.

Fragile X syndrome A condition in which the bottom of the X chromosome in the twenty-third pair of chromosomes is pinched off; can result in a number of physical anomalies as well as intellectual disabilities; occurs more often in males than females; thought to be the most common hereditary cause of intellectual disabilities.

Free appropriate public education (FAPE) The primary intent of federal special education law, that the education of all children with disabilities will in all cases be free of cost to parents (i.e., at public expense) and appropriate for the particular student.

Frontal lobes Two lobes located in the front of the brain; responsible for executive functions; site of abnormal development in people with ADHD.

Full inclusion All students with disabilities are placed in their neighborhood schools in general education classrooms for the entire day; general education teachers have the primary responsibility for students with disabilities.

Functional academics Practical skills (e.g., reading a newspaper or telephone book) rather than academic learning skills.

Functional Behavioral Assessment (FBA) Evaluation that consists of finding out the consequences (what purpose the behavior serves), antecedents (what triggers the behavior), and setting events (contextual factors) that maintain inappropriate behaviors.

Functional magnetic resonance imaging (fMRI) An adaptation of the MRI used to detect changes in the brain while it is in an active state; unlike a PET scan, it does not involve using radioactive materials.

Functional magnetic resonance spectroscopy (fMRS) An adaptation of the MRI used to detect changes in the brain while it is in an active state; unlike a PET scan, it does not involve using radioactive materials.

Functional vision assessment An appraisal of an individual's use of vision in everyday situations.

Gastrointenstinal Pertaining to the stomach, intestines, and/or other related organs.

Genius A word sometimes used to indicate a particular aptitude or capacity in any area; rare intellectual powers.

GeoLogger The GeoLogger is a multipurpose device for collecting detailed travel data including second-by-second position and speed data. This device works in concert with a GPS system; it has been used for assessment purposes to evaluate the orientation and mobility skills of persons with blindness or low-vision.

Giftedness Refers to cognitive (intellectual) superiority, creativity, and motivation of sufficient magnitude to set the child apart from the vast majority of age peers and make it possible for the child to contribute something of particular value to society.

Glaucoma A condition often, but not always, due to excessive pressure in the eyeball; the cause is unknown; if untreated, blindness results.

Globus pallidus A structure in the basal ganglia of the brain; site of abnormal development in people with ADHD.

Graphic organizers A way of enhancing content visual displays using lines, circles, and boxes to organize information.

Guardianship A legal term that gives a person the authority to make decisions for another person; can be full, limited, or temporary; applies in cases of parents who have children who have severe cognitive disabilities.

Guide dogs Dogs trained for the purpose of helping people who are blind navigate the environment; generally not recommended for children; they require extensive training for the user.

Gullibility An inclination to believe highly questionable statements or claims, despite scanty evidence; considered by some to be a key characteristic of persons with intellectual disabilities, especially those who are mildly intellectually disabled.

Handicapism A term used by activists who fault the unequal treatment of individuals with disabilities. This term is parallel to the term racism, coined by those who fault unequal treatment based on race.

Hand-over-hand guidance A tactile learning strategy for persons who are deaf-blind; the teacher places his or her hands over those of the person who is deaf-blind and guides them to explore objects.

Hand-under-hand guidance A tactile learning strategy for persons who are deaf-blind; the teacher places his or her hands underneath part of the student's hand or hands while the child is exploring objects.

Heritability studies A method of determining the degree to which a condition is inherited; a comparison of the prevalence of a condition in identical (i.e., monozygotic, from the same egg) twins versus fraternal (i.e., dizygotic, from two eggs) twins.

Herpes simplex A viral disease that can cause cold sores or fever blisters; if it affects the genitals and is contracted by the mother-to-be in the later stages of fetal development, it can cause mental subnormality in the child.

Hertz (Hz) A unit of measurement of the frequency of sound; refers to the highness or lowness of a sound.

Hidden curriculum The dos and don'ts of social interactions that most people learn incidentally or with little instruction but that remain hidden for those with Asperger syndrome.

History A patient's "story" of his or her functioning in life with respect to strengths and weaknesses; considered crucial by many physicians in the diagnosis of ADHD.

Home-based program A program delivered primarily in a student's home rather than in a school or center.

Home-note program A system of communication between the teacher and parents; the teacher evaluates the behavior of the student using a simple form, the student takes the form home, gets the parents' signatures, and returns the form the next day.

Homophenes Sounds that are different but that look the same with regard to movements of the face and lips (i.e., visible articulatory patterns).

Hydrocephalus A condition characterized by enlargement of the head because of excessive pressure of the cerebrospinal fluid.

Hyperactive child syndrome A term used to refer to children who exhibit inattention, impulsivity, and/or hyperactivity; popular in the 1960s and 1970s.

Hyperopia Farsightedness; vision for near objects is affected; usually results when the eyeball is too short.

In vitro fertilization The procedure of removing eggs from the mother, fertilizing them with the father's sperm in a laboratory, then returning them to the mother's uterus; used to help infertile couples conceive.

Inborn errors of metabolism Deficiencies in enzymes used to metabolize basic substances in the body, such as amino acids, car-

bohydrates, vitamins, or trace elements; can sometimes result in intellectual disabilities; PKU is an example.

Incus The anvil-shaped bone in the ossicular chain of the middle ear.

Individualized education program (IEP) IDEA requires an IEP to be drawn up by the educational team for each exceptional child; the IEP must include a statement of present educational performance, instructional goals, educational services to be provided, and criteria and procedures for determining that the instructional objectives are being met.

Individualized family service plan (IFSP) A plan mandated by PL 99-457 to provide services for young children with disabilities (under three years of age) and their families; drawn up by professionals and parents; similar to an IEP for older children.

Individuals with Disabilities Education Act (IDEA) The Individuals with Disabilities Education Act was enacted in 1990 and reauthorized in 1997 and 2004; it replaced PL 94-142, enacted in 1975. This federal law requires that to receive funds under the act, every school system in the nation must provide a free, appropriate public education for every child between the ages of three and twenty-one, regardless of how or how seriously he or she may be disabled.

Informal reading inventory (IRI) A method of assessing reading in which the teacher has the student read progressively more difficult series of word lists and passages; the teacher notes the difficulty level of the material read and the types of errors the student makes.

Inner speech An executive function; internal language used to regulate one's behavior; delayed or impaired in people with ADHD.

Insight The ability to separate and/or combine various pieces of information in new, creative, and useful ways.

Interim alternative educational setting (IAES) A temporary placement outside general education for students whose behavior is extremely problematic, but in which their education is continued.

Internalizing Acting-in behavior; anxiety, fearfulness, withdrawal, and other indications of an individual's mood or internal state.

IQ–achievement discrepancy Academic performance markedly lower than would be expected on the basis of a student's intellectual ability.

Iris The colored portion of the eye; contracts or expands, depending on the amount of light striking it.

Itinerant teacher services Services for students who are visually impaired in which the special education teacher visits several different schools to work with students and their general education teachers; the students attend their local schools and remain in general education classrooms.

Job coach A person who assists adult workers with disabilities (especially those with intellectual disabilities), providing vocational assessment, instruction, overall planning, and interaction assistance with employers, family, and related government and service agencies.

Juvenile rheumatoid arthritis A systemic disease with major symptoms involving the muscles and joints.

Kurzweil 1000 A computerized device that converts print into speech for persons with visual impairment; the user places the printed material over a scanner that then reads the material aloud by means of an electronic voice.

Language disorders Oral communication that involves a lag in the ability to understand and express ideas, putting linguistic skill behind an individual's development in other areas, such as motor, cognitive, or social development.

Language An arbitrary code or system of symbols to communicate meaning.

Language-based reading impairment A reading problem that is based on a language problem.

Large-print books Books having a font-size that is larger than the usual 10-point type; a popular size for large print books is 18-point type.

Larynx The structure in the throat containing the vocal apparatus (vocal cords); laryngitis is a temporary loss of voice caused by inflammation of the larynx.

Learned helplessness A motivational term referring to a condition in which a person believes that no matter how hard he or she tries, failure will result.

Least restrictive environment (LRE) A legal term referring to the fact that exceptional children must be educated in as normal an environment as possible.

Left temporal lobe An area on the left side of the brain; neuroimaging studies indicate it is responsible for speech, language, and reading abilities and is dysfunctional in persons with reading disabilities.

Legally blind A person who has visual acuity of 20/200 or less in the better eye even with correction (e.g., eyeglasses) or has a field of vision so narrow that its widest diameter subtends an angular distance no greater than 20 degrees.

Lens A structure that refines and changes the focus of the light rays passing through the eye.

Levels of support The basis of the AAIDD classification scheme; characterizes the amount of support needed for someone with intellectual disabilities to function as competently as possible as (1) intermittent, (2) limited, (3) extensive, or (4) pervasive.

Literary braille Braille symbols used for most writing situations.

Locus of control A motivational term referring to how people explain their successes or failures; people with an internal locus of control believe that they are the reason for success or failure, whereas people with an external locus of control believe that outside forces influence how they perform.

Long cane A mobility aid used by individuals with visual impairment, who sweep it in a wide arc in front of them; proper use requires considerable training; the mobility aid of choice for most travelers who are blind.

Low birth weight (LBW) Babies who are born weighing less than 5.5 pounds; usually premature; at risk for behavioral and medical conditions, such as intellectual disabilities.

Low vision A term used by educators to refer to individuals whose visual impairment is not so severe that they are unable to read print of any kind; they may read large or regular print, and they may need some kind of magnification.

Magnetic resonance imaging (MRI) A neuroimaging technique whereby radio waves are used to produce cross-sectional images of the brain; used to pinpoint areas of the brain that are dysfunctional.

Magnifying devices Often recommended for people with low vision; can be for close vision (e.g., handheld magnifier) or distance vision (e.g., monocular telescope or binocular telescope mounted on eyeglass frames).

Malleus The hammer-shaped bone in the ossicular chain of the middle ear.

Manifestation determination Determination that a student's misbehavior is or is not a manifestation of a disability.

Maternal serum screening (MSS) A method of screening the fetus for developmental disabilities such as Down syndrome or spina bifida; a blood sample is taken from the mother and analyzed; if it is positive, a more accurate test such as amniocentesis or CVS is usually recommended.

Meningitis A bacterial or viral infection of the linings of the brain or spinal cord; can cause a number of disabilities.

Mental age Age level at which a person performs on an IQ test; used in comparison to chronological age to determine IQ. IQ = (mental age ÷ chronological age) × 100.

Metacognition One's understanding of the strategies available for learning a task and the regulatory mechanisms needed to complete the task.

Microcephalus A condition causing development of a small, conical-shaped head; proper development of the brain is prevented, resulting in intellectual disabilities.

Mild mental retardation or intellectual disability A classification used to specify an individual whose IQ is approximately 50–70.

Milieu teaching A naturalistic approach to language intervention in which the goal is to teach functional language skills in a natural environment.

Minimal brain injury A term used to describe a child who shows behavioral but not neurological signs of brain injury; the term is not as popular as it once was, primarily because of its lack of diagnostic utility (i.e., some children who learn normally show signs indicative of minimal brain injury); a term used to refer to children who exhibit inattention, impulsivity, and/or hyperactivity; popular in the 1950s and 1960s.

Mirror neurons Neurons that fire when someone imitates or watches another person's behavior; malfunctioning in people with autism spectrum disorders; located deep within the brain in and around the amygdala.

Mixed hearing impairment A hearing impairment resulting from a combination of conductive and sensorineural hearing impairments.

Mnemonics The use of memory-enhancing cues to help one remember something; techniques that aid memory, such as using rhymes, songs, or visual images to remember information.

Moderate mental retardation or intellectual disabilities A classification used to specify and individual whose IQ is approximately 35–50.

Modifications Changes made in instruction or assessment to make it possible for a student with a disability to respond more normally.

Molecular genetics The study of the organization of DNA, RNA, and protein molecules containing genetic information.

Momentary time sampling An interval recording procedure used to capture a representative sample of a target behavior over a specified period of time.

Morphology The study within psycholinguistics of word formation; how adding or deleting parts of words changes their meaning.

Motor-speech disorder Loss or impairment of the ability to understand or formulate language because of accident or illness.

Multicultural education Aims to change educational institutions and curricula so they will provide equal educational opportunities to students regardless of their gender, social class, ethnicity, race, disability, or other cultural identity.

Muscular dystrophy A hereditary disease characterized by progressive weakness caused by degeneration of muscle fibers.

Mute Possessing no, or almost no, language; characteristic of many with autism.

Myopia Nearsightedness; vision for distant objects is affected; usually results when eyeball is too long.

Native-language emphasis An approach to teaching language-minority pupils in which the student's native language is used for most of the day and English is taught as a separate subject.

Natural supports Resources in person's environment that can be used for support, such as friends, family, co-workers.

Nemeth Code Braille symbols used for mathematics and science.

Neonatal intensive care unit (NICU) A special unit in a hospital designed to provide around-the-clock monitoring and care of newborns who have severe physical problems; staffed by professionals from several disciplines, such as nursing, social work, occupational therapy, respiratory therapy, and medicine; similar to an intensive care unit for older children and adults.

Neurotransmitters Chemicals involved in sending messages between neurons in the brain.

Newsline® A service allowing access via touch-tone phone to several national newspapers; available free of charge to those who are visually impaired.

Night blindness A condition characterized by problems in seeing at low levels of illumination; often caused by retinitis pigmentosa.

Nonverbal learning disabilities A term used to refer to individuals who have a cluster of disabilities in social interaction, math, visual-spatial tasks, and tactual tasks.

Norepinephrine A neurotransmitter, the levels of which may be abnormal in people with ADHD.

Normalization A philosophical belief in special education that every individual, even the most disabled, should have an educational and living environment as close to normal as possible.

Nuchal translucency sonogram A method of screening for Down syndrome; fluid from behind the fetus's neck and protein from the mother's blood are analyzed.

Nystagmus A condition in which there are rapid involuntary movements of the eyes; sometimes indicates a brain malfunction and/or inner-ear problems.

Obstacle sense A skill possessed by some people who are blind, whereby they can detect the presence of obstacles in their environments; research has shown that it is not an indication of an extra sense, as popularly thought; it is the result of learning to detect subtle changes in the pitches of high-frequency echoes.

Open head injury A brain injury in which there is an open wound in the head, such as a gunshot wound or penetration of the head by an object, resulting in damage to brain tissue.

Optic nerve The nerve at the back of the eye, which sends visual information back to the brain.

Oralism–manualism debate The controversy over whether the goal of instruction for students who are deaf should be to teach them to speak or to teach them to use sign language.

Orientation and mobility (O & M) skills The ability to have a sense of where one is in relation to other people, objects, and landmarks and to move through the environment.

Orthosis A device designed to restore, partially or completely, a lost function of the body (e.g., a brace or crutch).

Ossicles Three tiny bones (malleus, incus, and stapes) that together make possible an efficient transfer of sound waves from the eardrum to the oval window, which connects the middle ear to the inner ear.

Otitis media Inflammation of the middle ear.

Otoacoustic emissions Low-intensity sounds produced by the cochlea in response to auditory stimulation; used to screen hearing problems in infants and very young children.

Oval window The link between the middle and inner ears.

Paradoxical effect of Ritalin The now discredited belief that Ritalin, even though a stimulant, acts to subdue a person's behavior and that this effect of Ritalin is evident in people with ADHD but not in those without ADHD.

Paraplegia A condition in which both legs are paralyzed.

Partial participation An approach in which students with disabilities, while in the general education classroom, engage in the same activities as nondisabled students but on a reduced basis; the teacher adapts the activity to allow each student to participate as much as possible.

Peer confederates Peers who assist the teacher.

Peer tutoring A method that can be used to integrate students with disabilities in general education classrooms, based on the notion that students can effectively tutor one another. The role of learner or teacher may be assigned to either the student with a disability or the nondisabled student.

Peer-mediated instruction The deliberate use of a student's classroom peer(s) to assist in teaching an academic or social skill.

Perinatal causes of intellectual disabilities Causes at birth; some examples are anoxia, low birthweight, and infections such as syphilis and herpes simplex.

Perkins Brailler A system that makes it possible to write in braille; has six keys, one for each of the six dots of the cell, which leave an embossed print on the paper.

Perseveration A tendency to repeat behaviors over and over again; often found in people with brain injury, as well as those with ADHD.

Person-centered planning Planning for a person's self-determination; planning activities and services on the basis of a person's dreams, aspirations, interests, preferences, strengths, and capacities; a method of planning for people with disabilities that places the person and his or her family at the center of the planning process; a type of transition model; consumer-driven in that professionals are viewed as working for individuals.

Pervasive Developmental Disorder not Otherwise Specified (PDD-NOS) One of five autistic spectrum disorders; pervasive delay in development that does not fit into any of the other diagnostic categories.

Phenylketonuria (PKU) A metabolic genetic disorder caused by the inability of the body to convert phenylalanine to tyrosine; an accumulation of phenylalanine results in abnormal brain development.

Phonemic awareness One's ability to understand that words are made up of sounds or phonemes.

Phonological awareness The ability to understand that speech flow can be broken into smaller sound units such as words, syllables, and phonemes; lack of such awareness is generally thought to be the reason for the reading problems of many students with learning disabilities.

Phonological disorders A phonological disorder is a disorder that occurs in children who are younger than 9 years old. The disorder results in the impaired ability to produce sounds in his or her own language.

Phonology The study of how individual sounds make up words.

Play audiometry Use of a gamelike format to test hearing of young and hard-to-test children; the examiner teaches the child to respond to sounds.

Portfolio A collection of samples of a student's work done over time; a type of authentic assessment.

Positive behavior intervention plans A plan for changing behavior with an emphasis on positive reinforcement (rewarding) procedures.

Positive Behavioral Support (PBS) Positive reinforcement (rewarding) procedures intended to support a student's appropriate or desirable behavior.

Positive Behavioral intervention and Support (PBIS) Systematic use of the science of behavior to find ways of supporting desirable behavior rather than punishing the undesirable behavior; positive reinforcement (rewarding) procedures that are intended to support a student's appropriate or desirable behavior.

Positron emission tomography (PET) scans A computerized method for measuring bloodflow in the brain; during a cognitive task, a low amount of radioactive dye is injected in the brain; the dye collects in active neurons, indicating which areas of the brain are active.

Postlingual deafness Deafness occurring after the development of speech and language.

Postnatal Occurring in an infant after birth.

Postnatal causes of intellectual disabilities Causes occurring after birth; can be biological (e.g., traumatic brain injury, infections) or psychosocial (an unstimulating environment).

Practical intelligence Ability to solve everyday problems.

Prader-Willi syndrome Caused by inheriting from one's father a lack of genetic material on the fifteenth pair of chromosomes; leading genetic cause of obesity; degree of intellectual disabilities varies, but the majority fall within the mildly intellectually disabled range.

Pragmatics The study within psycholinguistics of how people use language in social situations; emphasizes the functional use of language rather than the mechanics.

Preacademic skills Behaviors that are needed before formal academic instruction can begin (e.g., ability to identify letters, numbers, shapes, and colors).

Precocity Remarkable early development.

Prefrontal lobes Two lobes located in the very front of the frontal lobes; responsible for executive functions; site of abnormal development in people with ADHD.

Prelingual deafness Deafness that occurs before the development of spoken language, usually at birth.

Prelinguistic communication Communication through gestures and noises before the child has learned oral language.

Prenatal causes of intellectual disabilities Causes occurring during fetal development; some examples include chromosomal disorders, inborn errors of metabolism, developmental disorders affecting brain formation, and environmental influences.

Prereferral teams (PRTs) Teams made up of a variety of professionals, especially general and special educators, who work with general education teachers to come up with strategies for teaching difficult-to-teach children. Designed to influence general educators to take ownership of difficult-to-teach students and to minimize inappropriate referrals to special education.

Primary language disorder A language disorder that has no known cause.

Profound mental retardation or intellectual disabilities A classification used to specify an individual whose IQ is below approximately 20.

Progressive A disease or condition that worsens over time and from which one seldom or never recovers with treatment.

Progressive time delay An instructional procedure whereby the teacher makes a request while simultaneously prompting the student and then over several occasions gradually increases the latency between the request and the prompt; often used with students with intellectual disabilities.

Progress monitoring Brief, frequent measures of performance used to determine whether a student is learning as expected; if student isn't learning as expected, the teacher can make changes to the instruction.

Prosthesis A device designed to replace, partially or completely, a part of the body (e.g., artificial teeth or limbs).

Psychoanalytic Related to psychoanalysis, including the assumptions that emotional or behavior disorders result primarily from unconscious conflicts and that the most effective preventive actions and therapeutic interventions involve uncovering and understanding unconscious motivations.

Psychostimulants Medications that activate dopamine levels in the frontal and prefrontal areas of the brain that control behavioral inhibition and executive functions; used to treat persons with ADHD.

Pull-out programs Special education programs in which students with disabilities leave the general education classroom for part or all of the school day (e.g., to go to a special class or resource room).

Pupil The contractile opening in the middle of the iris of the eye.

Pure-tone audiometry A test whereby tones of various intensities and frequencies are presented to determine a person's hearing loss.

Quadriplegia A condition in which all four limbs are paralyzed.

Raised dome detectable warnings Bumps in the pavement that are designed to alert people who are blind to unsafe areas.

Reading comprehension The ability to understand what one has read.

Reading fluency The ability to read effortlessly and smoothly; consists of the ability to read at a normal rate and with appropriate expression; influences one's reading comprehension.

Receptive language Decoding or understanding messages in communication.

Reciprocal teaching A cognitive teaching strategy whereby the student gradually assumes the role of co-instructor for brief periods; the teacher models four strategies for the students to use: (1) predicting, (2) questioning, (3) summarizing, and (4) clarifying; a method in which students and teachers are involved in a dialogue to facilitate learning.

Refraction The bending of light rays as they pass through the structures (cornea, aqueous humor, pupil, lens, vitreous humor) of the eye.

Resonance The quality of the sound imparted by the size, shape, and texture of the organs in the vocal tract.

Response-to-intervention (RTI) or response-to-treatment approach A way of determining whether a student has a learning disability; increasingly intensive levels of instructional intervention are delivered, and if the student does not achieve, at some point, he or she is determined to have a learning disability or is referred for special education evaluation.

Retina The back portion of the eye, containing nerve fibers connected to the optic nerve.

Retinitis pigmentosa A hereditary condition resulting in degeneration of the retina; causes a narrowing of the field of vision and affects night vision.

Retinopathy of prematurity (ROP) A condition resulting in abnormal growth of blood vessels in the eye; caused by factors related to premature birth, including the administration of an excessive concentration of oxygen at birth.

Rett syndrome A very rare autistic spectrum disorder, inherited; characterized by normal development followed by a severe regression of cognitive abilities.

Ritalin The most commonly prescribed psychostimulant for ADHD; its generic name is methylphenidate.

Rubella (German measles) A serious viral disease, which, if it occurs during the first trimester of pregnancy, is likely to cause a deformity in the fetus.

Scaffolded instruction A cognitive approach to instruction in which the teacher provides temporary structure or support while students are learning a task; the support is gradually removed as the students are able to perform the task independently.

Schizophrenia A disorder characterized by psychotic behavior manifested by loss of contact with reality, distorted thought processes, and abnormal perceptions.

Scoliosis An abnormal curvature of the spine.

Screening Quick measures administered to determine who may need further assessment.

Screen reader Software for computers that magnifies images on the screen and/or converts text on the screen to speech.

Secondary language disorder A language disorder that is caused by another disorder or disability, such as intellectual disabilities, hearing impairment, or brain injury.

Seizure (convulsion) A sudden alteration of consciousness, usually accompanied by motor activity and/or sensory phenomena; caused by an abnormal discharge of electrical energy in the brain.

Self-determination The ability to make personal choices, regulate one's own life, and be a self-advocate; a prevailing philosophy in education programming for people with intellectual disabilities; having control over one's life, not having to rely on others for making choices about one's quality of life; develops over one's life span.

Self-injurious behavior (SIB) Behavior causing injury or mutilation of oneself, such as self-biting or head-banging; usually seen in individuals with severe and multiple disabilities.

Self-instruction A type of cognitive training technique that requires individuals to talk aloud and then to themselves as they solve problems.

Self-monitoring A type of cognitive training technique that requires individuals to keep track of their own behavior.

Self-regulation Refers generally to a person's ability to regulate his or her own behavior (e.g., to employ strategies to help in a problem-solving situation); an area of difficulty for persons who are intellectual disabled.

Self-stimulation Any repetitive, stereotyped activity that seems only to provide sensory feedback.

Semantics The study of the meanings attached to words and sentences.

Sensorineural hearing impairment A hearing impairment, usually severe, resulting from malfunctioning of the inner ear.

Severe mental retardation or intellectual disabilities A classification used to specify an individual whose IQ is approximately 20–35.

Sheltered workshop A facility that provides a structured environment for people with disabilities in which they can learn skills; can be either a transitional placement or a permanent arrangement.

Sheltered-English approach A method in which language-minority students are taught all their subjects in English at a level that is modified constantly according to individuals' needs.

Short-term memory (STM) The ability to recall information after a short period of time.

Sibshops Workshops for siblings of children with disabilities; designed to help siblings answer questions about the disability and learn to adjust to having a sister or brother with a disability.

Sign language A manual language used by people who are deaf to communicate; a true language with its own grammar.

Signing English systems Used simultaneously with oral methods in the total communication approach to teaching students who are deaf; different from American Sign Language because the signs maintain the same word order as spoken English.

Slate and stylus A method of writing in braille in which the paper is held in a slate while a stylus is pressed through openings to make indentations in the paper.

Sleep apnea Cessation of breathing while sleeping.

Snellen chart Used in determining visual acuity; consists of rows of letters or Es arranged in different positions; each row corresponds to the distance at which a normally sighted person can discriminate the letters; does not predict how accurately a child will be able to read print.

Social intelligence Ability to understand and interpret people and social interactions.

Social support Emotional, informational, or material aid provided to a person or a family; this informal means of aid can be very valuable in helping families of children with disabilities.

Spasticity Characterized by muscle stiffness and problems in voluntary movement; associated with spastic cerebral palsy.

Specific language impairment (SLI) A language disorder with no identifiable cause; language disorder not attributable to hearing impairment, intellectual disabilities, brain dysfunction, or other plausible cause; also called specific language disability.

Speech The formation and sequencing of oral language sounds during communication.

Speech audiometry A technique that tests a person's detection and understanding of speech, rather than using pure tones to detect hearing loss.

Speech disorders Oral communication that involves abnormal use of the vocal apparatus, is unintelligible, or is so inferior that it draws attention to itself and causes anxiety, feelings of inadequacy, or inappropriate behavior in the speaker.

Speech reception threshold (SRT) The decibel level at which a person can understand speech.

Speechreading A method that involves teaching children to use visual information from a number of sources to understand what is being said to them; more than just lipreading, which uses only visual clues arising from the movement of the mouth in speaking.

Spina bifida A congenital midline defect resulting from failure of the bony spinal column to close completely during fetal development.

Standardized achievement assessment A method of evaluating a person that has been applied to a large group so that an individual's score can be compared to the norm, or average.

Stapes The stirrup-shaped bone in the ossicular chain of the middle ear.

Stereotypic behaviors Any of a variety of repetitive behaviors (e.g., eye rubbing) that are sometimes found in individuals who are autistic, blind, severely intellectually disabled, or psychotic; sometimes referred to as stereotypies or blindisms.

Strabismus A condition in which the eyes are directed inward (crossed eyes) or outward.

Strattera A nonstimulant medication for ADHD; affects the neurotransmitter norepinephrine.

Strauss syndrome Behaviors of distractibility, forced responsiveness to stimuli, and hyperactivity; based on the work of Alfred Strauss and Heinz Werner with children with intellectual disabilities.

Stuttering Speech characterized by abnormal hesitations, prolongations, and repetitions; may be accompanied by grimaces, gestures, or other bodily movements indicative of a struggle to speak, anxiety, blocking of speech, or avoidance of speech.

Subculture A culture that is associated with or part of a larger culture; a culture that is not the entire culture of a nation or other entity. Sometimes called "microculture," but a subculture is not necessarily small or a minority of a larger culture.

Supported competitive employment A workplace where adults who are disabled earn at least minimum wage and receive ongoing assistance from a specialist or job coach; the majority of workers in the workplace are nondisabled.

Supported employment A method of integrating people with disabilities who cannot work independently into competitive employment; includes use of an employment specialist, or job coach, who helps the person with a disability function on the job.

Supported living An approach to living arrangements for those with disabilities and/or intellectual disabilities that stresses living in natural settings rather than institutions, big or small.

Supports Resources and strategies that promote a person's development, education, interests, and personal well-being; critical to the AAIDD's conceptualization of intellectual disabilities.

Syntax The way words are joined together to structure meaningful sentences; grammar.

Syphilis A venereal disease that can cause mental subnormality in a child, especially if it is contracted by the mother-to-be during the latter stages of fetal development.

Systematic instruction Teaching that involves instructional prompts, consequences for performance, and transfer of stimulus control; often used with students with intellectual disabilities.

Tactile map An embossed representation of the environment that people who are blind can use to orient themselves to their surroundings.

Talent A special ability, aptitude, or accomplishment.

Task analysis The procedure of breaking down an academic task into its component parts for the purpose of instruction; a major feature of Direct Instruction.

Teratogens Agents, such as chemicals, that can disrupt the normal development of the fetus; a possible cause of learning disabilities and other learning and behavioral problems.

Text telephone (TT) A device connected to a telephone by a special adapter; allows communication over the telephone between people who are hearing impaired and those with hearing; sometimes referred to as a TTY (teletype) or TTD (telecommunication device for the deaf).

Theory of mind The ability to take another's perspective in a social exchange; the ability to infer another person's feelings, intentions, desires, etc.; impaired in those with ASD.

Thimerosal A preservative, that up until 1999, was used in vaccines as a preservative; contains small traces of mercury, which in higher doses is known to cause neurological defects.

Tiered assignment Assignments varying in difficulty but on a single topic.

Total communication approach An approach for teaching students with hearing impairment that blends oral and manual techniques.

Touch cues Tactual signals used to communicate with persons who are deaf-blind; can be used to signify a variety of messages.

Tourette's syndrome (TS) A neurological disorder beginning in childhood (about three times more prevalent in boys than in girls) in which stereotyped, repetitive motor movements (tics) are accompanied by multiple vocal outbursts that may include grunting noises or socially inappropriate words or statements (e.g., swearing).

Toxins Poisons in the environment that can cause fetal malformations; can result in cognitive impairments.

Transliteration A method used by most sign language interpreters in which the signs maintain the same word order as that of spoken English; American Sign Language (ASL) is also used by some interpreters.

Traumatic brain injury (TBI) Injury to the brain (not including conditions present at birth, birth trauma, or degenerative diseases or conditions) resulting in total or partial disability or psychosocial maladjustment that affects educational performance; may affect cognition, language, memory, attention, reasoning, abstract thinking, judgment, problem solving, sensory or perceptual and motor disabilities, psychosocial behavior, physical functions, information processing, or speech.

Traveling notebook A system of communication in which parents and professionals write messages to each other by way of a notebook or log that accompanies the child to and from school.

Trisomy 21 A type of Down syndrome in which the twenty-first chromosome is a triplet, making forty-seven, rather than the normal forty-six, chromosomes in all.

Tunnel vision A condition characterized by problems in peripheral vision, or a narrowing of the field of vision.

Tympanic membrane (eardrum) The anatomical boundary between the outer and middle ears; the sound gathered in the outer ear vibrates here.

Tympanometry A method of measuring the middle ear's response to pressure and sound.

Unified English Braille A combination of literary braille and braille codes for technical fields, such as the Nemeth Code for science and mathematics; not yet widely adopted.

Universal design The design of new buildings, tools, and instructional programs to make them usable by the widest possible population of potential users.

Universal Design for Learning (UDL) Designing lessons that are appropriate for all learners.

Usher syndrome An inherited syndrome resulting in hearing loss and retinitis pigmentosa, a progressive condition characterized by problems in seeing in low light and tunnel vision; there are three different types of Usher syndrome, differing with respect to when it occurs developmentally and the range of the major symptoms of hearing impairment, vision impairment, and balance problems.

Vestibular mechanism Located in the upper portion of the inner ear; consists of three soft, semicircular canals filled with a fluid; sensitive to head movement, acceleration, and other movements related to balance.

Video relay service (VRS) A service, using a sign language interpreter, a video camera or computer, and an internet connection, that allows persons who are deaf to communicate with those who are hearing.

Visual acuity The ability to see fine details; usually measured with the Snellen chart.

Visual efficiency A term used to refer to how well one uses his or her vision, including such things as control of eye movements, attention to visual detail, and discrimination of figure from background; believed by some to be more important than visual acuity alone in predicting a person's ability to function visually.

Vitreous humor A transparent, gelatinous substance that fills the eyeball between the retina and the lens of the eye.

Williams syndrome A condition resulting from deletion of material in the seventh pair of chromosomes; often results in mild to moderate intellectual disabilities, heart defects, and elfin facial features; people affected often display surprising strengths in spoken language and sociability while having severe deficits in spatial organization, reading, writing, and math.

Working memory (WM) The ability to remember information while also performing other cognitive operations.

Zero tolerance A school policy, supported by federal and state laws, that having possession of any weapon or drug on school property will automatically result in a given penalty (usually suspension or expulsion) regardless of the nature of the weapon or drug or any extenuating circumstances.

References

CHAPTER I

Bateman, B. D. (2007). Law and the conceptual foundations of special education practice. In J. B. Crockett, M. M. Gerber, & T. J. Landrum (Eds.), *Achieving the radical reform of special education: Essays in honor of James M. Kauffman* (pp. 95–114). Mahwah, NJ: Lawrence Erlbaum Associates.

Bateman, B. D., & Linden, M. A. (1998). *Better IEPs: How to develop legally correct and educationally useful programs* (3rd ed.). Longmont, CO: Sopris West.

Bateman, B. D., & Linden, M. A. (2006). *Better IEPs: How to develop legally correct and educationally useful programs* (4th ed.). Verona, WI: Attainment.

Board of Education of Hendrick Hudson v. Rowley 484 US 176 (1982).

Boardman, A. G., & Vaughn, S. (2007). Response to intervention as a framework for prevention and identification of learning disabilities: Which comes first, identification or intervention? In J. B. Crockett, M. M. Gerber, & T. J. Landrum (Eds.), *Achieving the radical reform of special education: Essays in honor of James M. Kauffman* (pp. 15–35). Mahwah, NJ: Lawrence Erlbaum Associates.

Bolger, K. E., & Patterson, C. J. (2001). Developmental pathways from child maltreatment to peer rejection. *Child Development, 72,* 549–568.

Carr, M. R. (2004, January 4). My son's disability, and my own inability to see it. *The Washington Post,* p. B5.

Council for Exceptional Children (1998). *What every special educator must know* (3rd ed.) Reston, VA: Author.

Council for Exceptional Children (2003). *What every special educator must know: Ethics, standards, and guidelines for special educators* (5th ed.). Arlington, VA: Author.

Crockett, J. B., & Kauffman, J. M. (1999). *The least restrictive environment: Its origins and interpretations in special education.* Mahwah, NJ: Lawrence Erlbaum.

Crockett, J. B., & Kauffman, J. M. (2001). The concept of the least restrictive environment and learning disabilities: Least restrictive of what? Reflections on Cruickshank's 1977 guest editorial for the Journal of Learning Disabilities. In D. P. Hallahan & B. K. Keogh (Eds.), *Research and global perspectives in learning disabilities: Essays in honor of William M. Cruickshank* (pp. 147–166). Mahwah, NJ: Lawrence Erlbaum.

Cruickshank, W. M. (1977). Guest editorial. *Journal of Learning Disabilities, 10,* 193–194.

Dupre, A. P. (1997). Disability and the public schools: The case against "inclusion." *Washington Law Review, 72,* 775–858.

Esquith, R. (2007). *Teach like your hair's on fire: The methods and madness inside room 56.* New York: Viking.

Finn, C. E., Jr., Rotherham, A. J., & Hokanson, C. R. Jr. (Eds.). (2001). *Rethinking special education for a new century.* New York: Thomas B. Fordham Foundation.

Fuchs, D., & Fuchs, L. S. (1994). Inclusive schools movement and the radicalization of special education reform. *Exceptional Children, 60,* 294–309.

Gelman, J. A., Pullen, P. L., & Kauffman, J. M. (2004). The meaning of highly qualified and a clear roadmap to accomplishment. *Exceptionality, 12,* 195–207.

Gibb, G. S., & Dyches, T. T. (2007). *Guide to writing quality individualized education programs* (2nd ed.). Boston: Allyn & Bacon.

Gliona, M. F., Gonzales, A. K., & Jacobson, E. S. (2005). Dedicated, not segregated: Suggested changes in thinking about instructional environments and the language of special education. In J. M. Kauffman & D. P. Hallahan (Eds.), *The illusion of full inclusion: A comprehensive critique of a current special education bandwagon* (2nd ed.) (pp. 135–146). Austin, TX: Pro-Ed.

Hallahan, D. P., & Kauffman, J. M. (1977). Labels, categories, behaviors: ED, LD, and EMR reconsidered. *Journal of Special Education, 11,* 139–149.

Hallahan, D. P. (2007). Learning disabilities: Whatever happened to intensive instruction? *LDA Newsbriefs, 42*(1), 1, 3–4, 24.

Hallahan, D. P., Lloyd, J. W., Kauffman, J. M., Weiss, M., & Martinez, E. (2005). *Introduction to learning disabilities* (3rd ed.). Boston: Allyn & Bacon.

Hart, B., & Risley, T. R. (1995). *Meaningful differences in the everyday experience of young American children.* Baltimore: Paul H. Brookes.

Hendrick, I. G., & MacMillan, D. L. (1989). Selecting children for special education in New York City: William Maxwell, Elizabeth Farrell, and the development of ungraded classes, 1900–1920. *Journal of Special Education, 22,* 395–417.

Heward, W. L. (2003). Ten faulty notions about teaching and learning that hinder the effectiveness of special education. *The Journal of Special Education, 36,* 186–205.

Hockenbury, J. C., Kauffman, J. M., & Hallahan, D. P. (1999–2000). What's right about special education? *Exceptionality, 8*(1), 3–11.

Holmes, M. S. (2004). *Fictions of affliction: Physical disability in Victorian culture.* Ann Arbor, MI: University of Michigan Press.

Howe, K. R., & Miramontes, O. B. (1992). *The ethics of special education.* New York: Teachers College Press.

Huefner, D. S. (1994). The mainstreaming cases: Tensions and trends for school administrators. *Educational Administration Quarterly,* 27–55.

Huefner, D. S. (2006). *Getting comfortable with special education law: A framework for working with children with disabilities* (2nd ed.). Norwood, MA: Christopher Gordon.

Hungerford, R. (1950). On locusts. *American Journal of Mental Deficiency, 54,* 415–418.

Itard, J. M. G. (1962). *The wild boy of Aveyron.* (G. Humphrey & M. Humphrey, Trans.). Englewood Cliffs, NJ: Prentice-Hall.

Kanner, L. (1964). *A history of the care and study of the mentally retarded.* Springfield, IL: Charles C. Thomas.

Kauffman, J. M. (1995). Why we must celebrate a diversity of restrictive environments. *Learning Disabilities Research and Practice, 10,* 225–232.

Kauffman, J. M. (1999a). Today's special education and its messages for tomorrow. *The Journal of Special Education, 32,* 244–254.

Kauffman, J. M. (1999b). How we prevent the prevention of emotional and behavioral disorders. *Behavioral Disorders, 65,* 448–468.

Kauffman, J. M. (1999–2000). The special education story: Obituary, accident report, conversion experience, reincarnation, or none of the above? *Exceptionality, 8*(1), 61–71.

Kauffman, J. M. (2005). Waving to Ray Charles: Missing the meaning of disability. *Phi Delta Kappan, 86*(6), 520–521, 524.

Kauffman, J. M. (2007). Conceptual models and the future of special education. *Education and Treatment of Children, 30*(4), 1–18.

Kauffman, J. M. (in press). 45: Special education. In T. L. Good (Ed.), *21st Century education: A reference handbook.* Thousand Oaks, CA: Sage.

Kauffman, J. M., & Hallahan, D. P. (1974). The medical model and the science of special education. *Exceptional Children, 41,* 97–102.

Kauffman, J. M. & Hallahan, D. P. (2005). *Special education: What it is and why we need it.* Boston: Allyn & Bacon.

Kauffman, J. M., & Hallahan, D. P. (2007). *Disability, habilitation, and choice: Confronting ethical dilemmas in an era of new possibilities.* Manuscript submitted for publication.

Kauffman, J. M., & Konold, T. R. (2007). Making sense in education: Pretense (including NCLB) and realities in rhetoric and policy about schools and schooling. *Exceptionality, 15,* 75–96.

Kauffman, J. M., & Landrum, T. J. (2007). Educational service interventions and reforms. In J. W. Jacobson, J. A. Mulick, & J. Rojahn (Eds.), *Handbook of intellectual and developmental disabilities* (pp. 173–188). New York: Springer.

Kauffman, J. M., Mock, D. R., Tankersley, M., & Landrum, T. J. (2008). Effective service delivery models. In R. J. Morris & N. Mather (Eds.), *Evidence-based interventions for students with learning and behavioral challenges* (pp. 359–378). Mahwah, NJ: Lawrence Erlbaum Associates.

Landrum, T. J., & Kauffman, J. M. (2006). Behavioral approaches to classroom management. In C. M. Evertson & C. S. Weinstein (Eds.), *Handbook of classroom management: Research, practice, and contemporary issues* (pp. 47–71). Mahwah, NJ: Lawrence Erlbaum Associates.

Metzler, I. (2006). *Disability in medieval Europe: Thinking about physical impairment during the Middle Ages, c. 1100–1400.* New York: Routledge.

Moore, T. (2007, January 19). Classroom distinctions. *The New York Times,* p. A27.

Rothstein, R., Jacobsen, R., & Wilder, T. (2006, November). *"Proficiency for all"—An oxymoron.* Paper presented at symposium on "Examining America's commitment to closing achievement gaps: NCLB and its alternatives." Teachers College, Columbia University, New York.

Simpson, R. L., & Kauffman, J. M. (in press). Inclusion of students with disabilities in general education. In J. Lopes & J. M. Kauffman (Eds.), *Educação especial: Crónica de uma morte anunciada/denunciada.* Braga, Portugal: Psiquilíbrios.

Stichter, J. P., Conroy, M. A., & Kauffman, J. M. (2008). *An introduction to students with high-incidence disabilities.* Upper Saddle River, NJ: Merrill-Prentice Hall.

Turnbull, H. R. (2007). A response to Professor Vitello. *Remedial and Special Education, 28,* 69–71.

U. S. Department of Education (1995). *Seventeenth annual report to Congress on the implementation of the Individuals with Disabilities Education Act.* Washington, DC: Author.

U. S. Department of Education (2002). *Twenty-fourth annual report to Congress on the implementation of the Individuals with Disabilities Education Act.* Washington, DC: Author. Retrieved July 19, 2004, from http://www.ed.gov/about/reports/annual/osep/2002/index.html

U.S. Department of Education. (2005). *Twenty-seventh annual report to Congress on implementation of the Individuals with Disabilities Education Act.* Washington, DC: Author.

Vitello, S. J. (2007). Shared responsibility reconsidered: A response to Professor Turnbull on IDEIA 2004 accountability and personal responsibility. *Remedial and Special Education, 28,* 66–68.

Walker, H. M., & Sprague, J. R. (2007). Early, evidence-based intervention with school-related behavior disorders: Key issues, continuing challenges, and promising practices. In J. B. Crockett, M. M. Gerber, & T. J. Landrum (Eds.), *Achieving the radical reform of special education: Essays in honor of James M. Kauffman* (pp. 37–58). Mahwah, NJ: Lawrence Erlbaum Associates.

Warnock, M. (2005). *Special educational needs: A new look. Impact No. 11.* London: Philosophy of Education Society of Great Britain.

Welch, E. M., Barton, E. R., Zhuo, J., Tomizawa, Y., Friesen, W. J., Trifillis, P., et al. (2007). PTC124 targets genetic disorders caused by nonsense mutations. Retrieved April 29, 2007, from www.nature.com/nature/journal/vaop/ncurrent/abs/nature05756.html

Yell, M. L. (2006). *The law and special education* (2nd ed.). Upper Saddle River, NJ: Prentice-Hall.

Zigmond, N. (2007). Delivering special education is a two-person job: A call for unconventional thinking. In J. B. Crockett, M. M. Gerber, & T. J. Landrum (Eds.), *Achieving the radical reform of special education: Essays in honor of James M. Kauffman* (pp. 115–137). Mahwah, NJ: Lawrence Erlbaum Associates.

CHAPTER 2

Abt Associates. (1976–1977). *Education as experimentation: A planned variation model* (Vols. 3A and 4). Cambridge, MA: Author.

Bateman, B. D. (2007). Law and the conceptual foundations of special education practice. In J. B. Crockett, M. M., Gerber, & T. J., & Landrum (Eds.), *Achieving the radical reform of special education: Essays in honor of James M. Kauffman* (pp. 95–114). Mahwah, NJ: Lawrence Erlbaum Associates.

Bateman, B. D., & Linden, M. A. (2006). *Better IEPs: How to develop legally correct and educationally useful programs* (4th ed.). Champaign, IL: Research Press.

Begeny, J. C., & Martens, B. K. (2007). Inclusionary education in Italy: A literature review and call for more empirical research. *Remedial and Special Education, 28,* 80–94.

Betts, G. (2004). Fostering autonomous learners through levels of differentiation. *Roeper Review, 26,* 190–191.

Boardman, A. G., & Vaughn, S. (2007). Response to intervention as a framework for prevention and identification of learning disabilities: Which comes first, identification or intervention? In J. B. Crockett, M. M. Gerber, & T. J. Landrum (Eds.), *Achieving the radical reform of special education: Essays in honor of James M. Kauffman* (pp. 15–35). Mahwah, NJ: Lawrence Erlbaum Associates.

Bradley, M. R. (2001). Positive behavior supports: Research to practice. *Beyond Behavior, 11*(1), pp. 3–26.

Brolin, D. E., & Loyd, R. J. (2004). *Career development and transition services: A functional life-skills approach* (4th ed). Upper Saddle River, NJ: Prentice Hall.

Browder, D. M., Wood, W. M., Test, D. W., Karvonen, M., & Algozzine, B. (2001). Reviewing resources on self-determination: A map for teachers. *Remedial and Special Education, 22,* 233–244.

Carolan, J., & Guinn, A. (2007). Differentiation: Lessons from master teachers. *Educational Leadership, 64*(5), 44–47.

Chambers, C. R., Wehmeyer, M. L., Saito, Y., Lida, K. M., Lee, Y., & Singh, V. (2007). Self-determination: What do we know? Where do we go? *Exceptionality, 15,* 3–15.

Cook, B. G. (2004). Inclusive teachers' attitudes toward their students with disabilities: A replication and extension. *The Elementary School Journal, 104,* 307–320.

Cook, B. G., Cameron, D. L., & Tankersley, M. (2007). Inclusive teachers' attitudinal ratings of their students with disabilities. *The Journal of Special Education, 40,* 230–238.

Cook, B. G., & Friend, M. (1998). Co-teaching: Guidelines for creating effective practices. In E. L. Meyen, G. A. Vergason, & R. J. Whelan (Eds.), *Educating students with mild disabilities: Strategies and methods* (2nd ed., pp. 453–479).

Cook, B. G, Semmel, M. I., & Gerber, M. M. (1999). Attitudes of principals and special education teachers toward the inclusion of students with mild disabilities. *Remedial and Special Education, 20,* 199–243.

Cook, B. G., Tankersley, M., Cook, L., & Landrum, T. J. (2000). Teachers' attitudes toward their included students with disabilities. *Exceptional Children, 67,* 115–135.

Crockett, J. B., & Kauffman, J. M. (1998). Taking inclusion back to its roots. *Educational Leadership, 56*(2), 74–77.

Crockett, J. B., & Kauffman, J. M. (1999). *The least restrictive environment: Its origins and interpretations in special education.* Mahwah, NJ: Lawrence Erlbaum.

Crockett, J. B., & Kauffman, J. M. (2001). The concept of the least restrictive environment and learning disabilities: Least restrictive of what? Reflections on Cruickshank's 1977 guest editorial for the Journal of Learning Disabilities. In D. P. Hallahan & B. K. Keogh (Eds.), *Research and global perspectives in learning disabilities: Essays in honor of William M. Cruickshank* (pp. 147–166). Mahwah, NJ: Lawrence Erlbaum.

Cronin, M. E. (2000). Instructional strategies. In P. L. Sitlington, G. M. Clark, & O. P. Kolstoe (Eds.), *Transition education and services for adolescents with disabilities* (3rd ed., pp. 255–283). Boston: Allyn & Bacon.

Cruickshank, W. M. (1977). Guest editorial. *Journal of Learning Disabilities, 10,* 193–194.

D'Agostino, D. (1997). Laughing out loud: Turning a deaf ear to comedy. *Exceptional Parent, 27*(3), 44–45.

Dettmer, P., Thurston, L. P., & Dyck, N. J. (2005). *Consultation, collaroration, and teamwork for students with special needs* (5th ed.). Boston: Allyn & Bacon.

Dobbs, M. (2004, April 22). "No child" law leaves schools' old ways behind. *The Washington Post,* pp. A1, A12–A13.

Dupre, A. P. (1997). Disability and the public schools: The case against "inclusion." *Washington Law Review, 72,* 775–858.

Dupre, A. P. (2000). A study in double standards, discipline, and the disabled student. *Washington Law Review, 75,* 1–96.

Earley, P. (2006). *Crazy: A father's search through America's mental health madness.* New York: Penguin.

Eisenman, L. T. (2007). Self-determination interventions: Building a foundation for school completion. *Remedial and Special Education, 28,* 2–8.

Evertson, C. M., & Weinstein, C. S. (Eds.). (2006). *Handbook of classroom management: Research, practice, and contemporary issues.* Mahwah, NJ: Lawrence Erlbaum Associates.

Fairbanks, S., Sugai, G., Guardino, D., & Lathrop, M. (2007). Response to intervention: Examining classroom behavior support in second grade. *Exceptional Children, 73,* 288–310.

Falk, K. B., & Wehby, J. H. (2001) The effects of peer-assisted learning strategies on the beginning reading skills of young children with emotional or behavioral disorders. *Behavioral Disorders, 26,* 344–359.

Fenning, P. A., & Bohanon, H. (2006). Schoolwide discipline policies: An analysis of discipline codes of conduct. In C. M. Evertson & C. S. Weinstein (Eds.), *Handbook of classroom management: Research, practice, and contemporary issues* (pp. 1021–1039). Mahwah, NJ: Lawrence Erlbaum Associates.

Finn, C. E., Jr., Rotherham, A. J., & Hokanson, C. R., Jr. (Eds.). (2001). *Rethinking special education for a new century.* New York: Thomas B. Fordham Foundation.

Fox, J. J., & Gable, R. A. (2004). Functional behavioral assessment. In R. B. Rutherford, M. M. Quinn, & S. R. Mathur (Eds.). *Handbook of research in emotional and behavioral disorders* (pp. 143–162). New York: Guilford.

Fuchs, D., & Fuchs, L. S. (1991). Framing the REI debate: Abolitionists versus conservationists. In J. W. Lloyd, N. N. Singh, & A. C. Repp (Eds.), *The regular education initiative: Alternative perspectives on concepts, issues, and models* (pp. 241–255). Sycamore, IL: Sycamore Publishing.

Fuchs, D., Fuchs, L. S., Thompson, A., Svenson, E., Yanb, L., Otaiba, S. A., et al. (2001). Peer-assisted learning strategies in reading: Extensions for kindergarten, first grade, and high school. *Remedial and Special Education, 22,* 15–21.

Fuchs, D., Mock, D., Morgan, P. L., & Young, C. L. (2003). Responsiveness-to-intervention: Definitions, evidence, and implications for the learning disabilities construct. *Learning Disabilities Research and Practice, 18,* 157–171.

Fulk, B. M., & King, K. (2001). Classwide peer tutoring at work. *Teaching Exceptional Children, 34*(2), 49–53.

Gallagher, P. A., Rhodes, C. A., & Darling, S. M. (2004). Parents as professionals in early intervention: A parent educator model. *Topics in Early Childhood Special Education, 2,* 5–13.

Gardner, R., Cartledge, G., Seidl, B., Woolsey, M. L., Schley, G. S., & Utley, C. A. (2001). Mt. Olivet after-school program: Peer-mediated interventions for at-risk students. *Remedial and Special Education, 22,* 22–33.

Gargiulo, R., & Kilgo, J. (2005). *Young children with special needs* (2nd ed.). Clifton Park, NY: Thompson.

Gelman, J. A., Pullen, P. L., & Kauffman, J. M. (2004). The meaning of highly qualified and a clear roadmap to accomplishment. *Exceptionality, 12,* 195–207.

Gliona, M. F., Gonzales, A. K., & Jacobson, E. S. (2005). Dedicated, not segregated: Suggested changes in thinking about instructional environments and the language of special education. In J. M. Kauffman & D. P. Hallahan (Eds.), *The illusion of full inclusion: A comprehensive critique of a current special education bandwagon* (2nd ed.) (pp. 135–146). Austin, TX: Pro-Ed.

Goin, M. K. (2007, July 8). The wrong place to treat mental illness. *The Washington Post,* p. B7.

Goodman, E. (2007, May 29). Wheels competing with feet. *The Charlottesville Daily Progress,* p. A8.

Greene, G., & Kochhar-Bryant, C. A. (2003). *Pathways to successful transition for youth with disabilities.* Upper Saddle River, NJ: Prentice Hall.

Greenwood, C. R., Arrega-Mayer, C., Utley, C. A., Gavin, K. M., & Terry, B. (2001). Classwide peer tutoring learning management system: Applications with elementary-level English language learners. *Remedial and Special Education, 22,* 34–47.

Grim, R. (2004, May 2). No rhyme, for no good reason. *The Washington Post,* p. B8.

Groopman, J. (2003, November 10). Annals of medicine: The Reeve effect. *The New Yorker,* pp. 82–93.

Guterman, B. R. (1995). The validity of categorical learning disabilities services: The consumer's view. *Exceptional Children, 62,* 111–124.

Hall, J. P. (2002). Narrowing the breach: Can disability culture and full educational inclusion be reconciled? *Journal of Disability Policy Studies, 13,* 144–152.

Hallahan, D. P., & Kauffman, J. M. (1994). Toward a culture of disability in the aftermath of Deno and Dunn. *The Journal of Special Education, 27,* 496–508.

Hallahan, D. P., Lloyd, J. W., Kauffman, J. M., Weiss, M., & Martinez, E. A. (2005). *Learning disabilities: Foundations, characteristics, and effective teaching* (3rd ed.). Boston: Allyn & Bacon.

Hoover, J. J., & Patton, J. R. (2004). Differentiating standards-based education for students with diverse needs. *Remedial and Special Education, 25,* 74–78.

Howard, V. F., Williams, B. F., & Lepper, C. (2005). *Very young children with special needs: A formative approach for today's children* (3rd ed.). Upper Saddle River, NJ: Prentice Hall.

Huefner, D. S. (2006). *Getting comfortable with special education law: A framework for working with children with disabilities* (2nd ed.). Norwood, MA: Christopher-Gordon.

Hughes, W., Wood, W. M., Konrad, M., & Test, D. W. (2006). Get a life: Students practice being self-determined. *Teaching Exceptional Children, 38*(5), 57–63.

Hyatt, K. J. (2007). Brain Gym®: Building stronger brains or wishful thinking? *Remedial and Special Education, 28,* 117–124.

Johns, B. H. (2003). NCLB and IDEA: Never the twain should meet. *Learning Disabilities: A Multidisciplinary Journal, 12*(3), 89–91.

Jones, M. (2006). Teaching self-determination: Empowered teachers, empowered students. *Teaching Exceptional Children, 39*(1), 12–17.

Kastor, E. (1997, June 19). Ready, willing, and disabled: Women at global forum turn the wheelchairs of progress. *The Washington Post,* p. D1.

Katsiyannis, A., & Maag, J. W. (2001). Manifestation determination as a golden fleece. *Exceptional Children, 68,* 85–96.

Kauffman, J. M. (1989). The regular education initiative as a Reagan-Bush education policy: A trickle-down theory of education of the hard-to-teach. *The Journal of Special Education, 2,* 256–278.

Kauffman, J. M. (1999a). Today's special education and its messages for tomorrow. *The Journal of Special Education, 32,* 244–254.

Kauffman, J. M. (1999b). How we prevent the prevention of emotional and behavioral disorders. *Behavioral Disorders, 65,* 448–468.

Kauffman, J. M. (1999–2000). The special education story: Obituary, accident report, conversion experience, reincarnation, or none of the above? *Exceptionality, 8*(1), 61–71.

Kauffman, J. M. (2002). *Education deform: Bright people sometimes say stupid things about education.* Landham, MD: Scarecrow Education.

Kauffman, J. M. (2003). Appearances, stigma, and prevention. *Remedial and Special Education, 24,* 195–198.

Kauffman, J. M. (2004). The president's commission and the devaluation of special education. *Education and Treatment of Children, 27,* 307–324.

Kauffman, J. M. (2005a). *Characterisftics of emotional and behavioral disorders of children and youth* (8th ed.) Upper Saddle River, NJ: Prentice-Hall.

Kauffman, J. M. (2005b). How we prevent the prevention of emotional and behavioural difficulties in education. In P. Clough, P. Garner, J. T. Pardeck, & F. K. O. Yuen (Eds.), *Handbook of emotional and behavioural difficulties in education* (pp. 366–376). London: Sage.

Kauffman, J. M. (2005c). Waving to Ray Charles: Missing the meaning of disability. *Phi Delta Kappan, 86,* 520–521, 524.

Kauffman, J. M. (2007). Labels and the nature of special education: We need to face realities. *Learning Disabilities: A Multidisciplinary Journal, 14*(4), 00–00.

Kauffman, J. M., Bantz, J., & McCullough, J. (2002). Separate and better: A special public school class for students with emotional and behavioral disorders. *Exceptionality, 10,* 149–170.

Kauffman, J. M., & Hallahan, D. P. (1993). Toward a comprehensive delivery system: The necessity of identity, focus, and authority for special education and other compensatory programs. In J. I. Goodlad & T. C. Lovitt (Eds.), *Integrating general and special education* (pp. 73–102). Columbus, OH: Merrill.

Kauffman, J. M., & Hallahan, D. P. (1997). A diversity of restrictive environments: Placement as a problem of social ecology. In J. W. Lloyd, E. J. Kame'enui, & D. Chard (Eds.), *Issues in educating students with disabilities* (pp. 325–342). Mahwah, NJ: Lawrence Erlbaum Associates.

Kauffman, J. M., & Hallahan, D. P. (2005a). *Special education: What it is and why we need it*. Boston: Allyn & Bacon.

Kauffman, J. M., & Hallahan, D. P. (Eds.) (2005b). *The illusion of full inclusion: A comprehensive critique of a current special education bandwagon*. (2nd ed.) Austin, TX: Pro-Ed.

Kauffman, J. M., & Hallahan, D. P. (2007). *Disability, habilitation, and choice: Confronting ethical dilemmas in an era of new possibilities*. Manuscript submitted for publication.

Kauffman, J. M., & Konold, T. R. (2007). Making sense in education: Pretense (including NCLB) and realities in rhetoric and policy about schools and schooling. *Exceptionality, 15*, 79–96.

Kauffman, J. M., & Landrum, T. J. (2005). Educational service interventions and reforms. In J. W. Jacobson & J. A. Mulick (Eds.), *Handbook of mental retardation and developmental disabilities*. New York: Kluwer.

Kauffman, J. M., & Landrum, T. J. (2006). *Children and youth with emotional and behavioral disorders: A history of their education*. Austin, TX: Pro-Ed.

Kauffman, J. M., & Landrum, T. J. (2007). Educational service interventions and reforms. In J. W. Jacobson, J. A. Mulick, & J. Rojahn (Eds.), *Handbook of intellectual and developmental disabilities* (pp. 173–188). New York: Springer.

Kauffman, J. M., Landrum, T. J., Mock, D. R., Sayeski, B., & Sayeski, K. L. (2005). Diverse knowledge and skills require a diversity of instructional groups: A position statement. *Remedial and Special Education, 26*, 2–6.

Kauffman, J. M., & Lloyd, J. W. (1995). A sense of place: The importance of placement issues in contemporary special education. In J. M. Kauffman, J. W. Lloyd, D. P. Hallahan, & T. A. Astuto (Eds.), *Issues in educational placement: Students with emotional and behavioral disorders* (pp. 3–19). Hillsdale, NJ: Lawrence Erlbaum.

Kauffman, J. M., Lloyd, J. W., Hallahan, D. P., & Astuto, T. A. (1995). Toward a sense of place for special education in the twenty-first century. In J. M. Kauffman, J. W. Lloyd, D. P. Hallahan, & T. A. Astuto (Eds.), *Issues in educational placement: Students with emotional and behavioral disorders* (pp. 379–385). Hillsdale, NJ: Lawrence Erlbaum.

Kauffman, J. M., McGee, K., & Brigham, M. (2004). Enabling or disabling? Observations on changes in the purposes and outcomes of special education. *Phi Delta Kappan, 85*, 613–620.

Kauffman, J. M., Mock, D. R., Tankersley, M., & Landrum, T. J. (2008). Effective service delivery models. In R. J. Morris & N. Mather (Eds.), *Evidence-based interventions for students with learning and behavioral challenges* (pp 359–378). Mahwah, NJ: Lawrence Erlbaum Associates.

Kauffman, J. M., Mostert, M. P., Trent, S. C., & Pullen, P. L. (2006). *Managing classroom behavior: A reflective case-based approach* (4th ed.). Boston: Allyn & Bacon.

Kauffman, J. M., & Sasso, G. M. (2006a). Toward ending cultural and cognitive relativism in special education. *Exceptionality, 14*, 65–90.

Kauffman, J. M., & Sasso, G. M. (2006b). Certainty, doubt, and the reduction of uncertainty: A rejoinder. *Exceptionality, 14*, 109–120.

Kauffman, J. M., & Wiley, A. L. (2004). How the President's Commission on Excellence in Special Education (PCESE) devalues special education. *Learning Disabilities: A Multidisciplinary Journal, 13*, 3–6.

Kavale, K. A., & Forness, S. R. (2000). History, rhetoric, and reality: Analysis of the inclusion debate. *Remedial and Special Education, 21*, 279–296.

Kavale, K. A., Kauffman, J. M., & Bachmeier, R. J. (2007). *The politics of response-to-intervention and reality surrounding the identification of specific learning disability*. Manuscript submitted for publication.

Kavale, K. A., Mostert, M. P., & Kauffman, J. M. (2008). Orthodoxy and dissent I: An introductory response to Gallagher et al. In M. P. Mostert, K. A. Kavale, & J. M. Kauffman (Eds.), *Challenging the refusal of reasoning in special education* (pp 00–00). Denver, CO: Love.

Klinger, J. K., Vaughn, S., Schumm, J. S., Cohen, P., & Forgan, J. W. (1998). Inclusion or pull-out: Which do students prefer? *Journal of Learning Disabilities, 31*, 148–158.

Kourea, L., Cartledge, G., & Musti-Rao, S. (2007). Improving reading skills of urban elementary students through total class peer tutoring. *Remedial and Special Education, 28*, 95–107.

Lamb, H. R., and Weinberger, L. E. (Eds.). (2001). *Deinstitutionalization: Promise and problems*. San Francisco: Jossey-Bass.

Landrum, T. J., & Kauffman, J. M. (2006). Behavioral approaches to classroom management. In C. M. Evertson & C. S. Weinstein (Eds.), *Handbook of classroom management: Research, practice, and contemporary issues* (pp. 47–71). Mahwah, NJ: Lawrence Erlbaum Associates.

Leahy, M. (2004, April 18). A job for Sarah: Can a mildly retarded young woman find success and independence greeting shoppers at Lowe's? *The Washington Post Magazine*, pp. 10–15, 20, 26–30.

Liaupsin, C. J., Jolivette, K., & Scott, T. M. (2004). Schoolwide systems of behavior support: Maximizing student success in school. In R. B. Rutherford, M. M. Quinn, & S. R. Mathur (Eds.). *Handbook of research in emotional and behavioral disorders* (pp. 487–501). New York: Guilford.

Lieberman, L. M. (1992). Preserving special education . . . for those who need it. In W. Stainback & S. Stainback (Eds.), *Controversial issues confronting special education: Divergent perspectives* (pp. 13–15). Boston: Allyn & Bacon.

Lindstrom, L., Doren, B., Metheny, J., Johnson, P., & Zane, C. (2007). Transition to employment: Role of family in career development. *Exceptional Children, 73*, 348–366.

Lloyd, J. W., & Hallahan, D. P. (2007). Advocacy and reform of special education. In J. B. Crockett, M. M., Gerber, & T. J., & Landrum (Eds.), *Achieving the radical reform of special education: Essays in honor of James M. Kauffman* (pp. 245–263). Mahwah, NJ: Lawrence Erlbaum Associates.

Longman, J. (2007, May 15). An amputee sprinter: Is he disabled or too-abled? *The New York Times*. Retrieved June 28, 2007 from http://www.nytimes.com/2007/05/15/sports/othersports/15runner.html?ex=1183176000&en=1a1cac2e919125c0&ei=5070

Maheady, L., Harper, G. F., & Mallette, B. (2001). Peer-mediated instruction and interventions with students with mild disabilities. *Remedial and Special Education, 22*, 4–14.

Martella, R. C., Nelson, J. R., & Marchand-Martella, N. E. (2003). *Managing disruptive behaviors in the schools: A schoolwide, classroom, and individualized learning approach*. Boston: Allyn & Bacon.

Martin, E. W. (1994). Case studies on inclusion: Worst fears realized. *The Journal of Special Education, 29*, 192–199.

Mathiason, C. S. (1997, February 15). *DPI advocates for a "disability-friendly" International Classification of Impairment, Disability and Handicap (ICIDH)*. Retrieved January 10, 2008, from http://www.dpa.org.sg/publication/dpipub/fall97/dpi8.htm.

McCarthy, M. R., & Soodak, L. C. (2007). The politics of discipline: Balancing school safety and rights of students with disabilities. *Exceptional Children, 73*, 456–474.

McLean, M., Wolery, M., & Bailey, D. B. (2004). Assessing infants and preschoolers with special needs (3rd ed.). Upper Saddle River, NJ: Prentice Hall.

Michalko, R. (2002). *The difference that disability makes*. Philadelphia: Temple University Press.

Miller, S. P. (2002). *Validated practices for teaching students with diverse needs and abilities*. Boston: Allyn & Bacon.

Mitchell, R. (2004, April 27). Dumbing down our schools. *The Washington Post*, p. A21.

Mock, D. R., & Kauffman, J. M. (2002). Preparing teachers for full inclusion: Is it possible? *The Teacher Educator, 37*, 202–215.

Mock, D. R., & Kauffman, J. M. (2005). The delusion of full inclusion. In J. W. Jacobson, J. A. Mulick, & R. M. Fuchs (Eds.), *Fads: Dubious and improbably treatments for developmental disabilities* (pp. 113–128). Mahwah, NJ: Lawrence Erlbaum Associates.

Moody, S. W., Vaughn, S., Hughes, M. T., & Fischer, M. (2000). Reading instruction in the resource room: Set up for failure. *Exceptional Children, 66*, 305–316.

Moon, M. S., & Inge, K. (2000). Vocational preparation and transition. In M. E. Snell & F. Brown (Eds.), *Instruction of students with severe disabilities* (5th ed., pp. 591–628). Upper Saddle River, NJ: Merrill.

Mostert, M. P., Kavale, K. A., & Kauffman, J. M. (Eds.). (2008). *Challenging the refusal of reasoning in special education.* Denver, CO: Love.

Mulick, J. A., & Butter, E. M. (2005). Positive behavior support: A paternalistic utopian delusion. In J. W. Jacobson, R. M. Foxx, & J. A. Mulick (Eds.), *Controversial therapies for developmental disabilities: Fad, fashion, and science in professional practice* (pp. 385–404). Mahwah, NJ: Lawrence Erlbaum Associates.

Nomani, A. Q. (2007, April 29). My brother's battle—and mine. *The Washington Post,* p. B2.

Noonan, M. J., & McCormick, L. (2006). *Young children with disabilities in natural environments: Methods and procedures.* Baltimore: Paul H. Brookes.

Odom, S. L. (2000). Preschool inclusion: What we know and where we go from here. *Topics in Early Childhood Special Education, 20,* 20–27.

Osborne, J. G. (2005). Person-centered planning: a *faux fixe* in the service of humanism? In J. W. Jacobson, J. A. Mulick & J. Rojahn (Eds.), *Handbook of intellectual and developmental disabilities* (pp. 313–329). New York: Springer.

Paley, A. R. (2007, April 5). Software's efficacy on tests in doubt: Study says tools don't raise scores. *The Washington Post,* pp. A1, A7.

Palmer, D. S., Fuller, K., Arora, T., & Nelson, M. (2001). Taking sides: Parent views on inclusion for their children with severe disabilities. *Exceptional Children, 67,* 467–484.

Palmer, S. B., & Wehmeyer, M. L. (2003). Promoting self-determination in early elementary school: Teaching self-regulated problem-solving and goal-setting skills. *Remedial and Special Education, 24,* 115–126.

Peck, S. (2004). Communication made easier: Facilitating transitions for students with multiple disabilities. *Teaching Exceptional Children, 36*(5), 60–63.

Pierangelo, R., & Giuliani, G. A. (2006). *Assessment in special education: A practical approach* (2nd ed.). Boston: Allyn & Bacon.

Pisha, B., & Coyne, P. (2001). Smart from the start: The promise of universal design for learning. *Remedial and Special Education, 22,* 197–203.

Powers, L. E., Garner, T., Valnes, B., Squire, P., Turner, A., Couture, T., et al. (2007). Building a successful adult life: Findings from youth-directed research. *Exceptionality, 15,* 45–56.

Pugach, M. C., & Warger, C. L. (2001). Curriculum matters: Raising expectations for students with disabilities. *Remedial and Special Education, 22,* 194–196.

Raspberry, W. (2004, May 3). No child's failure. *The Washington Post,* p. A21.

Rothstein, R., Jacobsen, R., & Wilder, T. (2006, November). *"Proficiency for all"—An oxymoron.* Paper presented at a symposium on "Examining America's commitment to closing achievement gaps: NCLB and its alternatives." New York: Teachers College, Columbia University.

Rueda, R., Gallego, M. A., & Moll, L. C. (2000). The least restrictive environment: A place or a context? *Remedial and Special Education, 21,* 70–78.

Saslow, E. (2007, April 12). In Maryland, a fight to the finish line: Wheelchair racer's quest for inclusion spurs debate. *The Washington Post,* pp. A1, A16.

Sasso, G. M. (2001). The retreat from inquiry and knowledge in special education. *The Journal of Special Education, 34,* 178–193.

Sasso, G. M. (2007). Science and reason in special education: The legacy of Derrida and Foucault. In J. B. Crockett, M. M. Gerber, & T. J. Landrum (Eds.), *Achieving the radical reform of special education: Essays in honor of James M. Kauffman* (pp. 143–167). Mahwah, NJ: Lawrence Erlbaum Associates.

Sasso, G. M., Conroy, M. A., Stichter, J. P., & Fox, J. J. (2001). Slowing down the bandwagon: The misapplication of functional assessment for students with emotional and behavioral disorders. *Behavioral Disorders, 26,* 269–281.

Saunders, R. R. (2007). Residential and day services. In J. W. Jacobson, J. A. Mulick. & J. Rojahn (Eds.), *Handbook of intellectual and developmental disabilities* (pp. 209–226). New York: Springer.

Schwartz, A. A., Jacobson, J. W., & Holburn, S. C. (2000). Defining person centeredness: Results of two consensus methods. *Education and Training in Mental Retardation and Developmental Disabilities, 35,* 235–249.

Scruggs, T. E., Mastropieri, M. A., & McDuffie, K. A. (2007). Co-teaching in inclusive classrooms: A metasynthesis of qualitative research. *Exceptional Children, 73,* 392–416.

Shogren, K. A., Wehmeyer, M. L., Palmer, S. B., Soukup, J. H., Little, T. D., Garner, N., et al. (2007). Examining individual and ecological predictors of the self-determination of students with disabilities. *Exceptional Children, 73,* 488–509.

Simpson, R. L., & Kauffman, J. M. (in press). Inclusion of students with disabilities in general education. In J. Lopes & J. M. Kauffman (Eds.), *Educação especial: Crónica de uma morte anunciada/denunciada.* Braga, Portugal: Psiquilíbrios.

Siperstein, G. N., Norins, J., & Mohler, A. (2007). Social acceptance and attitude change: Fifty years of research. In J. W. Jacobson, J. A. Mulick. & J. Rojahn (Eds.), *Handbook of intellectual and developmental disabilities* (pp. 133–154). New York: Springer.

Siperstein, G. N., Parker, R. C., Bardon, J. N., & Widaman, K. F. (2007). A national study of youth attitudes toward the inclusion of students with intellectual disabilities. *Exceptional Children, 73,* 435–455.

Sitlington, P. L., & Clark, G. M. (2006). *Transition education and services for students with disabilities* (4th ed.). Boston: Allyn & Bacon.

Sitlington, P. L., Clark, G. M., & Kolstoe, O. P. (2000). *Transition education and services for adolescents with disabilities* (3rd ed.). Boston: Allyn & Bacon.

Skiba, R. J., & Peterson, R. L. (2000). School discipline at a crossroads: From zero tolerance to early response. *Exceptional Children, 66,* 335–346.

Skiba, R. J., & Rausch, M. K. (2006). Zero tolerance, suspension, and expulsion: Questions of equity and effectiveness. In C. M. Evertson & C. S. Weinstein (Eds.), *Handbook of classroom management: Research, practice, and contemporary issues* (pp. 1063–1089). Mahwah, NJ: Lawrence Erlbaum Associates.

Smith, K., & Weitz, M. (2003). Problem solving and gifted education: A differentiated fifth-grade fantasy unit. *Gifted Child Today, 26*(3), 56–60.

Spooner, F., Baker, J. N., Harris, A. A., Ahlgrim-Delzell, L., & Browder, D. M. (2007). Effects of training in universal design for learning on lesson plan development. *Remedial and Special Education, 28,* 108–116.

Stainback, S., & Stainback, W. (1992). Schools as inclusive communities. In W. Stainback & S. Stainback (Eds.), *Controversial issues confronting special education: Divergent perspectives.* (pp. 29–43). Boston: Allyn & Bacon.

Stichter, J. P., Conroy, M. A., & Kauffman, J. M. (2008). *An introduction to students with high-incidence disabilities.* Upper Saddle River, NJ: Merrill-Prentice Hall.

Still failing the vulnerable: The District, "unmotivated" to help the retarded. (2007, February 26). *The Washington Post,* p. A14.

Strain, P. S. (2001). Empirically based social skills intervention: A case for quality of life improvement. *Behavioral Disorders, 27,* 30–36.

Strain, P. S., & Timm, M. A. (2001). Remediation and prevention of aggression: An evaluation of the Regional Intervention Program over a quarter century. *Behavioral Disorders, 26,* 297–313.

Stroman, D. F. (2003). *The disability rights movement: From deinstitutionalization to self-determination.* Lanham, MD: University Press of America.

Sugai, G., Sprague, J. R., Horner, R. H., & Walker, H. M. (2000). Preventing school violence: The use of office discipline referrals to assess and monitor school-wide discipline interventions. *Journal of Emotional and Behavioral Disorders, 8,* 94–101.

Switzer, J. V. (2003). *Disabled rights: American disability policy and the fight for equality.* Washington, DC: Georgetown University Press.

Thurlow, M. L. (2000). Standards-based reform and students with disabilities: Reflections on a decade of change. *Focus on Exceptional Children, 33*(3), 1–16.

Thurlow, M. L., Nelson, J. R., Teelucksingh, W., & Draper, I. L. (2001). Multiculturalism and disability in a results-based educational system: Hazards and hopes for today's schools. In C. A. Utley & F. E. Obiakor (Eds.), *Special education, multicultural education, and school reform: Components of quality education for learners with mild disabilities* (pp. 155–172). Springfield, IL: Charles C. Thomas.

Tomlinson, C. A. (1999). *The differentiated classroom: responding to the needs of all learners.* Alexandria, VA: Association for Supervision and Curriculum Development.

Tomlinson, C. A. (2001). *How to differentiate instruction in mixed-ability classrooms* (2nd ed.). Alexandria, VA: ASCD.

Tomlinson, C. A. (2004). Sharing responsibility for differentiating instruction. *Roeper Review, 26,* 188–189.

Torrey, E. F., & Zdandowicz, M. T. (1999, July 9). Deinstitutionalization hasn't worked: "We have lost effectively 93 percent of our state psychiatric hospital beds since 1955." *The Washington Post.* Retrieved February 25, 2007 from www.psychlaws.org/generalresources/article17.htm

Tregaskis, C. (2004). *Constructions of disability: Researching the interface between disabled and non-disabled people.* New York: Routledge.

University of Minnesota. (1999, October). Behavioral outcomes of deinstitutionalization for people with intellectual disabilities: A review of studies conducted between 1980 and 1999. *Policy Research Brief, 10*(1), 1–11.

U.S. Department of Education. (2007, April). *Measuring the achievement of students with disabilities: What families and schools need to know about modified academic achievement standards.* Washington, DC: Author.

Vaughn, S., Elbaum, B., & Boardman, A. G. (2001). The social functioning of students with learning disabilities: Implications for inclusion. *Exceptionality, 9,* 47–65.

Vaughn, S., & Fuchs, L. S. (2003). Redefining learning disabilities as inadequate response to instruction: The promise and potential problems. *Learning Disabilities Research and Practice, 18,* 137–146.

Vaughn, S., Moody, S. W., & Schumm, J. S. (1998). Broken promises: Reading instruction in the resource room. *Exceptional Children, 64,* 211–225.Walker, H. M., Ramsey, E., & Gresham, F. M. (2004). *Antisocial behavior in school: Strategies and best practices* (2nd ed.). Pacific Grove, CA: Brooks/Cole.

Walker, H. M., & Sprague, J. R. (2007). Early, evidence-based intervention with school-based behavior disorders: Key issues, continuing challenges, and promising practices. In J. B. Crockett, M. M. Gerber, & T. J. Landrum (Eds.), *Achieving the radical reform of special education: Essays in honor of James M. Kauffman* (pp. 37–58). Mahwah, NJ: Lawrence Erlbaum Associates.

Walsh, J. M., & Jones, B. (2004). New models of cooperative teaching. *Teaching Exceptional Children, 36*(5), 14–20.

Warnock, M. (2005). *Special educational needs: A new look. Impact No. 11.* London: Philosophy of Education Society of Great Britain.

Wehmeyer, M. L., Palmer, S. B., Soukup, J. H., Garner, N. W., & Lawrence, M. (2007). Self-determination and student transition planning knowledge and skills: Predicting involvement. *Exceptionality, 15,* 31–44.

Wehmeyer, M. L., & Powers, L. E. (2007). Self-determination. *Exceptionality, 15,* 1–2.

Wilson, R. A. (2003). *Special educational needs in the early years* (2nd ed.). New York: Routledge-Falmer.

Wolfensberger, W. (1972). *The principle of normalization in human services.* Toronto: National Institute on Mental Retardation.

Wormeli, R. (2006). Differentiating for tweens. *Educational Leadership, 63*(7), 14–19.

Yell, M. L. (2006). *The law and special education* (2nd ed.). Upper Saddle River, NJ: Prentice-Hall.

Yell, M. L., & Drasgow, E. (2005). *No child left behind: A guide for professionals.* Upper Saddle River, NJ: Merrill Prentice Hall.

Yell, M. L., Rozalski, M. E., & Drasgow, E. (2001). Disciplining students with disabilities. *Focus on Exceptional Children, 33*(9), 1–20.

Zigmond, N. (2003). Where should students with disabilities receive special education services? Is one place better than another? *The Journal of Special Education, 37,* 193–199.

Zigmond, N. (2007). Delivering special education is a two-person job: A call for unconventional thinking. In J. B. Crockett, M. M. Gerber, & T. J. Landrum (Eds.), *Achieving the radical reform of special education: Essays in honor of James M. Kauffman* (pp. 115–137). Mahwah, NJ: Lawrence Erlbaum Associates.

Zull, J. E. (2004). The art of changing the brain. *Educational Leadership, 62*(1), 68–72.

CHAPTER 3

Abedi, J., Hofstetter, C., & Lord, C. (2004). Assessment accommodations for English language learners: Implications for policy-based empirical research. *Review of Educational Research, 74,* 1–28.

Ahlberg, M. (2004). Concept maps: Theory, methodology, technology. *Proceedings of the First International Conference on Concept Mapping.* Pamplona, Spain.

Albus, D., Thurlow, M., Liu, K., & Bielinski, J. (2005). Reading test performance of English-language learners using an English Dictionary. *The Journal of Educational Research, 98,* 245–254.

Artiles, A. J., Rueda, R., Salazar, J. J., & Higareda, I. (2005). Within-group diversity in minority disproportionate representation: English language learners in urban school districts. *Exceptional Children, 71,* 283–301.

Artiles, A. J., Trent, S. C., Hoffman-Kipp, P., & Lopez-Torres, L. (2000). From individual acquisition to cultural-historical practices in multicultural teacher education. *Remedial and Special Education, 21,* 79–89, 120.

Associated Press. (2004, April 18). Gay teens harassed at school: Persecution leads to law. *Charlottesville Daily Progress,* p. A11.

Banks, J. A., & Banks, C. A. (2007). *Multicultural education: Issues and perspectives* (6th edition). Hoboken, NJ: Wiley.

Bateman, B. D. (1994). Who, how, and where: Special education's issues in perpetuity. *The Journal of Special Education, 27,* 509–520.

Bell, K. (2004). GLSEN in tough times: Training educators about LGBT issues in a challenging political, economic, and educational climate. *Beyond Behavior, 13*(2), 29–30.

Bennett, L. (2000). Equality by design: Three charter schools try new approaches to integration. *Teaching Tolerance, 17,* 43–49.

Calhoon, M. B., Al Otaiba, S., Greenberg, D., King, A., & Avalos, A. (2006). Improving reading skills in predominantly Hispanic Title 1 first-grade classrooms: The promise of peer-assisted learning strategies. *Learning Disabilities Research & Practice, 21,* 261–272.

Cartledge, G. (2004). Another look at the impact of changing demographics on public education for culturally diverse learners with behavior problems: Implications for teacher preparation. In L. M. Bullock & R. A. Gable (Eds.), *Quality personnel preparation in emotional/behavioral disorders: Current perspectives and future directions* (pp. 64–69). Denton, TX: Institute for Behavioral and Learning Differences at the University of North Texas.

Cartledge, G., & Loe, S. A. (2001). Cultural diversity and social skill instruction. *Exceptionality, 9,* 33–46.

Cho, S., Singer, G. H. S., & Brenner, M. (2000). Adaptation and accommodation to young children with disabilities: A comparison of Korean and Korean American parents. *Topics in Early Childhood Special Education, 20,* 236–249.

Chularut, P., & DeBacker, T. (2003). The influence of concept mapping on achievement, self-regulation, and self-efficacy in students of English as a second language. *Contemporary Educational Psychology, 29,* 248–263.

Cloud, N. (2002). Culturally and linguistically responsive instructional planning. In A. J. Artiles and A. A. Ortiz (Eds.), *English language learners with special education needs: Identification, assessment, and instruction.* McHenry, IL: Center for Applied Linguistics.

Collins, K. (2000). No place for bigotry: An anti-bias club changes the atmosphere at a suburban high school. *Teaching Tolerance, 17,* 26–27.

Colon, E. P., & Kranzler, J. H. (2007). Effects of instructions on curriculum-based measurement of reading. *Journal of Psychoeducational Assessment, 24,* 318–328.

Council for Exceptional Children. (2000). Improving results for culturally and linguistically diverse students. *Research Connections in Special Education, 7.*

Coutinho, M. J., & Oswald, D. P. (2000). Disproportionate representation in special education: A synthesis and recommendations. *Journal of Child and Family Studies, 9*, 135–156.

Cushner, K., McClelland, A., & Safford, P. (2006). *Human diversity in education: An interactive approach* (5th edition). Boston: McGraw Hill.

Dadurka, D. (2004, April 22). Ruffner's life, work honored. *Charlottesville Daily Progress*, p. A2.

De Melendez, W. R., & Beck, V. (2007). *Teaching young children in multicultural classrooms: Issues, concepts, and strategies*. Clifton Park, NY: Thomson Delmar.

Elksnin, L. K., & Elksnin, N. (2000). Teaching parents to teach their children to be prosocial. *Intervention in School and Clinic, 36*, 27–35.

Elliot, B. (2000). Finding my stride: A gay student takes the bold step of being true to himself. *Teaching Tolerance, 17*, 40–41.

Everston, C. M., & Weinstein, C. S. (Eds.). (2006). *Handbook of classroom management: Research, practice, and contemporary issues*. Mahwah, NJ: Lawrence Erlbaum Associates.

Fuchs, D., Fuchs, L. S., & Compton, D. L. (2004). Identifying reading disabilities by responsiveness to instruction: Specifying measures and criteria. *Learning Disabilities Quarterly, 27*, 216–227.

Fuchs, L. S., & Fuchs, D. (1997). Use of curriculum-based measurement in identifying students with disabilities. *Focus on Exceptional Children, 30*(3), 1–16.

Fuchs, L. S., Fuchs, D., Compton, D. L., Bryant, J. D., Hamlett, C. L., & Seethaler, P. M. (2007). Mathematics screening and progress monitoring at first grade: Implications for responsiveness to intervention. *Exceptional Children, 73*, 311–330.

Fujiura, G. T., & Yamaki, K. (2000). Trends in demography of childhood poverty and disability. *Exceptional Children, 66*, 187–199.

Fulk, B. M., & King, K. (2001). Classwide peer tutoring at work. *Teaching Exceptional Children, 34*(2), 49–53.

Gallucci, J. P. (2000). Signs of remembrance: A school for the deaf celebrates Dia de los Muertos. *Teaching Tolerance, 18*, 30–31.

Gelman, J. A., Pullen, P. L., & Kauffman, J. M. (2005). The meaning of highly qualified and a clear roadmap to accomplishment. *Exceptionality, 12*, 195–207.

Gersten, R., & Baker, S. (2000). What we know about effective instructional practices for English-language learners. *Exceptional Children, 66*, 454–470.

Gersten, R., Brengelman, S., & Jimenez, R. (1994). Effective instruction for culturally and linguistically diverse students: A reconceptualization. *Focus on Exceptional Children, 27*(1), 1–16.

Gersten, R., & Woodward, J. (1994). The language-minority student and special education: Issues, trends, and paradoxes. *Exceptional Children, 60*, 310–322.

Gollnick, D. M., & Chinn, P. C. (2006). *Multicultural education in a pluralistic society* (7th ed.). New York: Macmillan.

Good, R.H., & Kaminski, R.A. (Eds.) (2002). *Dynamic Indicators of Basic Early Literacy Skills* (6th ed.). Eugene, OR: Institute for the Development of Educational Achievement. Available: http://dibels.uoregon.edu

Greenwood, C. R., Arrega-Mayer, C., Utley, C. A., Gavin, K. M, & Terry, B. J. (2001). Classwide peer tutoring learning management system: Applications with elementary-level English language learners. *Remedial and Special Education, 22*, 34–47.

Gunn, B., Smolkowski, K., Biglan, A., Black, C., & Blair, J. (2005). Fostering the development of reading skill through supplemental instruction: Results for Hispanic and non-Hispanic students. *The Journal of Special Education, 39*, 66–85.

Hallahan, D. P., Lloyd, J. W., Kauffman, J. M., Weiss, M., & Martinez, E. (2005). *Introduction to learning disabilities* (3rd ed.). Boston: Allyn & Bacon.

Hammill, D. D. (2004). What we know about correlates of reading. *Exceptional Children, 70*, 453–468.

Heward, W. L. (2003). Ten faulty notions about teaching and learning that hinder the effectiveness of special education. *The Journal of Special Education, 36*, 186–205.

Hicks, M. A. (2005). Lessons from rental cars: The struggle to create seeing communities. *Educational Studies, 38*, 120–126.

Horwitz, S. (1998, April 5). Lessons in black and white; crossing color lines in room 406 with Miss Kay and her kids. *The Washington Post*, p. F1.

Hosp, J. L., & Reschly, D. J. (2004). Disproportionate representation of minority students in special education: Academic, demographic, and economic predictors. *Exceptional Children, 70*, 185–199.

Jones, C. J. (2001a). CBAs that work: Assessing students' math content-reading levels. *Teaching Exceptional Children, 34*(1), 24–28.

Jones, C. J. (2001b). Teacher-friendly curriculum-based assessment in spelling. *Teaching Exceptional Children, 34*(2), 32–38.

Kauffman, J. M. (2001). *Characteristics of emotional and behavioral disorders of children and youths* (7th ed.). New York: Merrill/Macmillan.

Kauffman, J. M. (2003). Appearances, stigma, and prevention. *Remedial and Special Education, 24*, 195–198.

Kauffman, J. M., Conroy, M., Gardner, R., & Oswald, D. (2008). Cultural sensitivity in the application of behavior principles to education. *Education and Treatment of Children*.

Kauffman, J. M., & Hallahan, D. P. (2005). *Special education: What it is and why we need it*. Boston: Allyn & Bacon.

Kauffman, J. M., & Konold, T. R. (2007). Making sense in education: Pretense (including NCLB) and realities in rhetoric and policy about schools and schooling. *Exceptionality, 15*, 75–96.

Kauffman, J. M., McGee, K., & Brigham, M. (2004). Enabling or disabling? Observations on changes in special education. *Phi Delta Kappa, 85*, 613–620.

Kauffman, J. M., Mostert, M. P., Trent, S. C., & Pullen, P. L. (2006). *Managing classroom behavior: A reflective case-based approach* (4th ed.). Boston: Allyn & Bacon.

Keogh, B. K. (2003). *Temperament in the classroom: Understanding individual differences*. Baltimore: Paul H. Brookes.

Klingner, J. K., & Edwards, P. A. (2006). Cultural considerations with response to intervention models. *Reading Research Quarterly, 41*, 108–117.

Lewis, A. C. (2004). Desegregation and degeneration. *Phi Delta Kappan, 85*, 643–644.

Linan-Thompson, S., Vaughn, S., Hickman-Davis, P., & Kouzekanani, K. (2003). Effectiveness of supplemental reading instruction of English language learners with reading difficulties. *Elementary School Journal, 103*, 221–238.

Linan-Thompson, S., Vaughn, S., Prater, K., & Cirino, P. T. (2006). The response to intervention of English language learners at risk for reading problems. *Journal of Learning Disabilities, 39*, 390–398.

MacSwan, J., & Rolstad, K. (2006). How language proficiency tests mislead us about ability: Implications for English language learner placement in special education. *Teachers College Record, 108*, 2304–2328.

McAfee, M. (2000). Welcome to Park Day School: A bay area teacher shares her independent school's commitment to community. *Teaching Tolerance, 18*, 24–29.

McCardle, P., & Leung, C. Y. Y. (2006). English language learners: Development and intervention. *Topics in Language Disorders, 26*, 302–304.

McCardle, P., McCarthy, J. M., & Leos, K. (2005). English language learners and learning disabilities: Research agenda and implications for practice. *Learning Disabilities Research & Practice, 20*, 68–78.

McCourt, F. (1996). *Angela's ashes*. New York: Scribner.

McDonnell, L. M., McLaughlin, M. J., & Morison, P. (Eds.). (1997). *Educating one and all: Students with disabilities and standards-based reform*. Washington, DC: National Academy Press.

McIntyre, T. (2007). *Are behaviorist interventions inappropriate for culturally different youngsters with learning and behavior disorders?* Retrieved April 14, 2007, from http://maxweber.hunter.cuny.edu/pub/eres/EDSPC715_MCINTYRE/CBehModR.html

Mostert, M. P. (2002). Useless eaters: Disability as handicap in Nazi Germany. *The Journal of Special Education, 36*, 155–168.

Mundy, L. (2002, March 31). A world of their own. *The Washington Post Magazine*, pp. 22–29, 38–43.

Nguyen, L., Huang, L. N., Arganza, G. F., & Liao, Q. (2007). The influence of race and ethnicity on psychiatric diagnoses and clinical characteristics of children and adolescents in children's services. *Cultural Diversity and Ethnic Minority Psychology, 13*, 18–25.

Novak, J. D., & Gowin, D. B. (1984). *Learning how to learn*. New York: Cambridge University Press.

Osher, D., Cartledge, G., Oswald, D., Sutherland, K. S., Artiles, A. J., & Coutinho, M. (2004). Cultural and linguistic competency and disproportionate representation. In R. B. Rutherford, M. M. Quinn, & S. R. Mathur (Eds.), *Handbook of research in emotional and behavioral disorders* (pp. 54–77). New York: Guilford.

Oswald, D. P., & Coutinho, M. J. (2001). Trends in disproportionate representation: Implications for multicultural education. In C. A. Utley & F. E. Obiakor (Eds.), *Special education, multicultural education, and school reform: Components of quality education for learners with mild disabilities* (pp. 53–73). Springfield, IL: Charles C. Thomas.

Pavri, S. (2001). Loneliness in children with disabilities: How teachers can help. *Teaching Exceptional Children, 33*(6), 52–58.

Peck, A., & Scarpati, S. (2004). Literacy instruction and research. *Teaching Exceptional Children, 36*(6), 71.

Pierce, R. L., Adams, C. M., Speirs Neumeister, K. L., Cassady, J. C., Dixon, F. A., & Cross, T. L. (2007). Development of an identification procedure for a large urban school corporation: Identifying culturally divers and academically gifted elementary students. *Roeper Review, 29*, 113–118.

Pollard-Durodola, S. D., Mathes, P. G., Vaughn, S., Cardenas-Hagan, E., & Linan-Thompson, S. (2006). The role of oracy in developing comprehension in Spanish-speaking English language learners. *Topics in Language Disorders, 26*, 365–384.

Pullen, P. L. (2004). *Brighter beginnings for teachers*. Lanham, MD: Scarecrow Education.

Ramirez, R., & Shapiro, E. S. (2006). Curriculum-based measurement and the evaluation of reading in Spanish speaking English language learners in bilingual education classrooms. *School Psychology Review,* 356–369.

Ravitch, D. (2003). *The language police: How pressure groups restrict what students learn*. New York: Knopf.

Reschly, D. J. (2001, July 13). *Overrepresentation, it's not what you think it is: Equal treatment studies*. Presentation at the Office of Special Education Programs Annual Research Project Directors' Conference, Washington, DC.

Reyna, V. F. (2004). Why scientific research? The importance of evidence in changing educational practice. In P. McCardle, & V. Chhabra (Eds.), *The voice of evidence in reading research* (pp. 47–58). Baltimore: Paul H. Brookes.

Rueda, R., & Kim, S. (2001). Cultural and linguistic diversity as a theoretical framework for understanding multicultural learners with mild disabilities. In C. A. Utley & F. E. Obiakor (Eds.), *Special education, multicultural education, and school reform: Components of quality education for learners with mild disabilities* (pp. 74–89). Springfield, IL: Charles C. Thomas.

Ruzic, R., & O'Connell, K. (2001). *Concept maps*. National Center on Accessing the General Curriculum. Retrieved May 10, 2007, from http://udl.cast.org/ncac/ConceptMaps1669.cfm

Shealey, M. W., & Callins, T. (2007). Creating culturally responsive literacy programs in inclusive classrooms. *Intervention in School and Clinic, 42*, 195–197.

Singh, N. N., Baker, J., Winton, A. S. W., & Lewis, D. K. (2000). Semantic equivalence of assessment instruments across cultures. *Journal of Child and Family Studies, 9*, 123–134.

Sleeter, C. E. (1999). *Making choices for multicultural education: Five approaches to race, class, and gender* (3rd ed.). New York: Wiley.

Sutphin, M. (2007, January). *Mapping concepts from the classroom to the computer: Instructors hope to combined concept maps and the Internet to test agriculture students*. Blacksburg, VA: Virginia Technical University College of Agriculture and Life Sciences. Retrieved May 12, 2007, from http://www.cals.vt.edu/news/pubs/innovations/jan2007/concepts.html

Takaki, R. (1994). Interview: Reflections from a different mirror. *Teaching Tolerance, 3* (1), 11–15.

Taylor, R. L. (1997). *Assessment of exceptional students: Educational and psychological procedures* (4th ed.). Boston: Allyn & Bacon.

Terwilliger, J. (1997). Semantics, psychometrics, and assessment reform: A close look at "authentic" assessments. *Educational Researcher, 26* (8), 24–27.

Thurlow, M. L., Nelson, J. R., Teelucksingh, W., & Draper, I. L. (2001). Multiculturalism and disability in a results-based educational system: Hazards and hopes for today's schools. In C. A. Utley &

F. E. Obiakor (Eds.), *Special education, multicultural education, and school reform: Components of quality education for learners with mild disabilities* (pp. 155–172). Springfield, IL: Charles C. Thomas.

Tyler, N. C., Yzquierdo, Z., Lopez-Reyna, N., & Flippin, S. S. (2004). Cultural and linguistic diversity and the special education workforce: A critical overview. *The Journal of Special Education, 38*, 22–38.

U.S. Department of Education. (2005). *Twenty-seventh annual report to Congress on the implementation of the Individuals with Disabilities Education Act*. Washington, DC: Author.

Utley, C. A., & Obiakor, F. E. (Eds.). (2001a). *Special education, multicultural education, and school reform: Components of quality education for learners with mild disabilities*. Springfield, IL: Charles C. Thomas.

Utley, C. A., & Obiakor, F. E. (2001b). Learning problems or learning disabilities of multicultural learners: Contemporary perspectives. In C. A. Utley & F. E. Obiakor (Eds.), *Special education, multicultural education, and school reform: Components of quality education for learners with mild disabilities* (pp. 90–117). Springfield, IL: Charles C. Thomas.

Utley, C. A., & Obiakor, F. E. (2001c). Multicultural education and special education: Infusion for better schooling. In C. A. Utley & F. E. Obiakor (Eds.), *Special education, multicultural education, and school reform: Components of quality education for learners with mild disabilities* (pp. 3–29). Springfield, IL: Charles C. Thomas.

Vaughn, S., Cirino, P. T., Linan-Thompson, S., Mathes, P. G., Carlson, C. D., Cardenas-Hagan, E., Pollard-Durodola, S. D., Fletcher, J. M., & Francis, D. J. (2006). Effectiveness of a Spanish intervention and an English intervention for English language learners at risk for reading problems. *American Educational Research Journal*.

Vaughn, S., Cirino, P., Linan-Thompson, S., Mathes, P. G, Carlson, C., Hagan, E. C., et al., (2006). Effectiveness of a Spanish intervention and an English intervention for English language learners at risk for reading problems. *American Educational Research Journal, 43*, 449–487.

Vaughn, S., Linan-Thompson, S., Mathes, P. G., Cirino, P. T., Carlson, C. D., Pollard-Durodola, S. D., et al. (2006). Effectiveness of a Spanish intervention for first-grade English language learners at risk for reading difficulties. *Journal of Learning Disabilities, 39* (1), 56–73.

Vaughn, S., Mathes, P., Linan-Thompson, S., Cirino, P., Carlson, C. Pollard-Durodola, S., et al. (2006). Effectiveness of an English intervention for first-grade English language learners at risk for reading problems. *The Elementary School Journal, 107*, 153–180

Vaughn, S., Mathes, P., Linan-Thompson, S., & Francis, D. (2005). Teaching English language learners at risk for reading difficulties to read in Spanish or English. *Learning Disabilities Research & Practice, 20* (1), 58–67.

Villegas, A. M., & Lucas, T. (2007). The culturally responsive teacher. *Educational Leadership, 64* (6), 28–33.

Walker, T. (2000). Street smart: Sidewalk libraries open a world of learning for urban youth. *Teaching Tolerance, 17*, 22–25.

Welsh, P. (2004, June 20). When the street and the classroom collide. *The Washington Post*, pp. B1, B4.

Wiesel, E. (2004, July 4). The America I love. *Parade*, pp. 4–5.

Williams, P. J. (1997). *Seeing a color-blind future: The paradox of race*. New York: Farrar, Strauss & Giroux, Inc.

CHAPTER 4

Alper, S., Schloss, P. J., & Schloss, C. N. (1996). Families of children with disabilities in elementary and middle school: Advocacy models and strategies. *Exceptional Children, 62*, 261–270.

Anderson, L., Larson, S., Lakin, C., & Kwak, N. (2002). Children with disabilities: Social roles and family impacts in the NHIS-D. *DD Data Brief, 4* (1), 1–11.

Bell, R. Q., & Harper, L. V. (1977). *Child effects on adults*. Hillsdale, NJ: Lawrence Erlbaum Associates.

Berry, J. O., & Hardman, M. L. (1998). *Lifespan perspectives on the family and disability*. Boston: Allyn & Bacon.

Blue-Banning, M., Summers, J. A., Frankland, H. C., Nelson, L. L., & Beegle, G. (2004). Dimensions of family and professional partnerships: Constructive guidelines for collaboration. *Exceptional Children, 70*, 167–184.

Bronfenbrenner, U. (1979). *The ecology of human development: Experiments by nature and design.* Cambridge, MA: Harvard University Press.

Bronfenbrenner, U. (1995). Developmental ecology through space and time: A future perspective. In P. Moen, G. H. Elder, & K. Luscher (Eds.), *Examining lives in context: Perspectives on the ecology of human development* (pp. 619–647). Washington, DC: American Psychological Association.

Brooks-Gunn, J., & Lewis, M. (1984). Maternal responsivity in interactions with handicapped infants. *Child Development, 55,* 858–868.

Bryan, T. H., Nelson, C., & Mathur, S. (1995). Homework: A survey of primary students in regular, resource, and self-contained classrooms. *Learning Disabilities Research & Practice, 10,* 85–90.

Bryan, T. H., & Sullivan-Burstein, K. (1997). Homework how-to's. *Teaching Exceptional Children, 29* (6), 32–37.

Burke, P. (2004). *Brothers and sisters of children with disabilities.* London: Jessica Kingsley.

Clay, V. (2006). Lessons from my brother. *Exceptional Parent, 36* (12), 24–25.

Collins, W., Maccoby, E., Steinberg, L., Hetherington, E. M., & Bornstein, M. (2000). The case for nature and nurture. *American Psychologist, 55,* 218–232.

Drotar, D., Baskiewicz, A., Irvin, N., Kennell, J., & Klaus, M. (1975). The adaptation of parents to the birth of an infant with a congenital malformation: A hypothetical model. *Pediatrics, 56,* 710–717.

Duis, S. S., Summers, M., & Summers, C. R. (1997). Parent versus child stress in diverse family types: An ecological approach. *Topics in Early Childhood and Special Education, 17,* 53–73.

Dunst, C. J. (2002). Family-centered practices: Birth through high school. *The Journal of Special Education, 36,* 139–147.

Epstein, M., Munk, D., Bursuck, W., Polloway, E., & Jayanthi, M. (1999). Strategies for improving home-school communication about homework for students with disabilities. *The Journal of Special Education, 33,* 166–176.

Featherstone, H. (1980). *A difference in the family: Life with a disabled child.* New York: Basic Books.

Ferguson, P. M. (2002). A place in the family: An historical interpretation of research on parental reactions to having a child with a disability. *The Journal of Special Education, 36,* 124–130.

Fox, L., Vaughn, B. J., Wyatte, M. L., & Dunlap, G. (2002). "We can't expect other people to understand": Family perspectives on problem behavior. *Exceptional Children, 68,* 437–450.

Fujiura, G. T., & Yamaki, K. (2000). Trends in demography of childhood poverty and disability. *Exceptional Children, 66,* 187–199.

Gallagher, P. A., Powell, T. H., & Rhodes, C. A. (2006). *Brothers & sisters: A special part of exceptional families* (3rd ed.). Baltimore: Paul H. Brookes.

Gavidia-Payne, S., & Stoneman, Z. (1997). Family predictors of maternal and paternal involvement in programs for young children with disabilities. *Child Development, 68,* 701–717.

Gerlach, E. K. (1999). *Just this side of normal: Glimpses into life with autism.* Eugene, OR: Four Leaf Press.

Hanline, M. F., & Knowlton, A. (1988). A collaborative model for providing support to parents during their child's transition from infant intervention to preschool special education public school programs. *Journal of the Division for Early Childhood, 12,* 116–125.

Harry, B. (2002). Trends and issues in serving culturally diverse families of children with disabilities. *The Journal of Special Education, 36,* 131–138.

Hastings, R. P., Daley, D., Burns, C., & Beck, A. (2006). Maternal distress and expressed emotion: Cross-sectional and longitudinal relationships with behavior problems of children with intellectual disabilities. *American Journal on Mental Retardation, 111,* 48–61.

Howell, A., Hauser-Cram, P., & Kersh, J. E. (2007). Setting the stage: Early child and family characteristics as predictors of later loneliness in children with developmental disabilities. *American Journal on Mental Retardation, 112,* 18–30.

Jayanthi, M., Sawyer, V., Nelson, J., Bursuck, W., & Epstein, M. (1995). Recommendations for homework-communication problems: From parents, classroom teachers, and special education teachers. *Remedial and Special Education, 16,* 212–225.

Kauffman, J. M., Mostert, M. P., Trent, S. C., & Pullen, P. L. (2006). *Managing classroom behavior: A reflective case-based approach.* Boston: Allyn & Bacon.

Kelley, M. L., (1990). *School-home notes: Promoting children's classroom success.* New York: Guilford Press.

Kelley, M. L., & McCain, A. P. (1995). Promoting academic performance in inattentive children. *Behavior Modification, 19,* 357–375.

Keogh, B. K., Garnier, H. E., Bernheimer, L. P., & Gallimore, R. (2000). Models of child-family interactions for children with developmental delays: Child-driven or transactional? *American Journal on Mental Retardation, 105,* 32–46.

Klingner, J., & Vaughn, S. (1999). Students' perceptions of instruction in inclusion classrooms: Implications for students with learning disabilities. *Exceptional Children, 66,* 23–37.

Lambie, R. (2000). *Family systems within educational contexts: Understanding at-risk and special-needs students.* Denver, CO: Love Publishing Co.

Lehmann, J. P., & Baker, C. (1995). Mothers' expectations for their adolescent children: A comparison between families with disabled adolescents and those with non-labeled adolescents. *Education and Training in Mental Retardation and Developmental Disabilities, 30,* 27–40.

Lenhard, W., Breitenbach, E., Ebert, H., Schindelhauer-Deutscher, H. J., Zang, K. D., & Henn, W. (2007). *Intellectual and Developmental Disabilities, 45,* 98–102.

Lessenberry, B. M., & Rehfeldt, R. A. (2004). Evaluating stress levels of parents with disabilities. (2004). *Exceptional Children, 70,* 231–244.

Lucyshyn, J. M., Horner, R. H., Dunlap, G., Albin, R. W., & Ben, K. R. (2002). Positive behavior support with families. In J. M. Lucyshyn, G. Dunlap, & R. W. Albin (Eds.), *Families and positive behavior support: Addressing problem behavior in family contexts* (pp. 3–43). Baltimore, MD: Paul H. Brookes.

Magana, S., Schwartz, S. J., Rubert, M. P., & Szapocznik, J. (2006). Hispanic caregivers of adults with mental retardation: Importance of family functioning. *American Journal on Mental Retardation, 111,* 250–262.

Mahoney, G., & Robenalt, K. (1986). A comparison of conversational patterns between mothers and their Down syndrome and normal infants. *Journal of the Division for Early Childhood, 10,* 172–180.

Mangelsdorf, S. C., & Schoppe-Sullivan, S. J. (2007). Introduction: Emergent family systems. *Infant Behavior & Development, 30,* 60–62.

Meadow-Orlans, K. P., Mertens, D. M., & Sass-Lehrer, M. A. (2003). *Parents and their deaf children: The early years.* Washington, DC: Gallaudet University Press.

Meyer, D. J., & Vadasy, P. F. (1994). *Sibshops: Workshops for siblings of children with special needs.* Baltimore: Paul H. Brookes.

Orsmond, G. I., & Seltzer, M. M. (2000). Brothers and sisters of adults with mental retardation: Gendered nature of the sibling relationship. *American Journal on Mental Retardation, 105,* 486–508.

Orsmond, G. I., Seltzer, M. M., Greenberg, J. S., & Krauss, M. W. (2006). Mother-child relationship quality among adolescents and adults with autism. *American Journal on Mental Retardation, 111,* 121–137.

O'Shea, D. J., & O'Shea, L. J. (2001). Why learn about students' families? In D. J. O'Shea, L. J. O'Shea, R. Algozzine, & D. J. Hammittee (Eds.), *Families and teachers of individuals with disabilities: Collaborative orientations and responsive practices* (pp. 5–24). Boston: Allyn & Bacon.

O'Shea, D. J., O'Shea, L. J., Algozzine, R., & Hammitte, D. J. (Eds.). (2001). *Families and teachers of individuals with disabilities: Collaborative orientations and responsive practices.* Boston: Allyn & Bacon.

O'Shea, D. J., & Riley, J. E. (2001). Typical families: Fact or fiction? In D. J. O'Shea, L. J. O'Shea, R. Algozzine, & D. J. Hammitte (Eds.), *Families and teachers of individuals with disabilities: Collaborative orientations and responsive practices* (pp. 25–50). Boston: Allyn & Bacon.

Osher, T. (1997). Advocacy in action: You can advocate for your child! *CEC Today, 4*(4), 4.

Parette, H. P., & Petch-Hogan, B. (2000). Approaching families: Facilitating culturally/linguistically diverse family involvement. *Teaching Exceptional Children, 33*(2), 4–10.

Polloway, E., Bursuck, W., Jayanthi, M., Epstein, M., & Nelson, J. (1996). Treatment acceptability: Determining appropriate interventions within inclusive classrooms. *Intervention in School and Clinic, 31*, 133–144.

Powell, T. H., & Gallagher, P. A. (1993). *Brothers & sisters—A special part of exceptional families* (2nd ed.). Baltimore: Paul H. Brookes.

Roach, M. A., Barratt, M. S., Miller, J. F., & Leavitt, L. A. (1998). The structure of mother-child play: Young children with Down syndrome and typically developing children. *Developmental Psychology, 34*, 77–87.

Rossiter, L., & Sharpe, D. (2001). The siblings of individuals with mental retardation: A quantitative integration of the literature. *Journal of Child and Family Studies, 10*, 65–84.

Scorgie, K., & Sobsey, D. (2000). Transformational outcomes associated with parenting children who have disabilities. *Mental Retardation, 38*, 195–206.

Singer, G. H. S. (2002). Suggestion for a pragmatic program of research on families and disability. *The Journal of Special Education, 36*, 148–154.

Singer, G. H. S. (2006). Meta-analysis of comparative studies of depression in mothers of children with and without developmental disabilities. *American Journal on Mental Retardation, 111*, 155–169.

Singer, G. H. S., Goldberg-Hamblin, S. E., Peckham-Hardin, K. D., Barry, L., & Santarelli, G. E. (2002). Toward a synthesis of family support practices and positive behavior support. In J. M. Lucyshyn, G. Dunlap, & R. W. Albin (Eds.), *Families and positive behavior support: Addressing problem behavior in family contexts* (pp. 155–183). Baltimore, MD: Paul H. Brookes.

Skinner, D., Bailey, D. B., Correa, V., & Rodriguez, P. (1999). Narrating self and disability: Latino mothers' construction of identities vis-à-vis their child with special needs. *Exceptional Children, 65*, 481–495.

Slonims, V., & McConachie, H. (2006). Analysis of mother-infant interaction in infants with Down syndrome and typically developing infants. *American Journal on Mental Retardation, 111*, 273–289.

Stoneman, Z., & Gavidia-Payne, S. (2006). Marital adjustment in families of young children with disabilities: Associations with daily hassles and problem-focused coping. *American Journal on Mental Retardation, 111*, 1–14.

Taylor, N. E., Wall, S. M., Liebow, H., Sabatino, C. A., Timberlake, E. M., & Farber, M. Z. (2005). Mother and soldier: Raising a child with a disability in a low-income military family. *Exceptional Children, 72*, 83–99.

Turnbull, A., & Turnbull, R. (2006). Fostering family-professional partnerships. In M. E. Snell & F. Brown (Eds.), *Instruction of students with severe disabilities* (6th ed.). Upper Saddle River, NJ: Merrill/Prentice Hall.

Turnbull, A., Turnbull, R., Erwin, E., & Soodak, L. (2006). *Families, professionals, and exceptionality: Positive outcomes through partnerships and trust.* Upper Saddle River, NJ: Merrill/Prentice Hall.

Warger, C. (2001, March). *Five homework strategies for teaching students with disabilities.* ERIC Clearinghouse on Disabilities and Gifted Education. Retrieved October 20, 2001 from www.ericec.org/digests/e608.html

CHAPTER 5

AAMR. (1999–2004). *Fact sheet: Frequently asked questions about mental retardation.* Retrieved June 4, 2004 from www.aamr.org/Policies/faq_mental_retardation.shtml

AAMR. (2000). *Self-determination policy statement* (Rev.). Retrieved September 23, 2007, from http://aamr.org/Policies/Pol_self_determination.shtml

AAMR Ad Hoc Committee on Terminology and Classification. (2002). *Mental retardation: Definition, classification, and systems of supports* (10th ed.). Washington, DC: American Association on Mental Retardation.

Abbeduto, L., Brady, N., & Kover, S. T. (2007). Language development and Fragile X syndrome: Profiles, syndrome-specificity, and within-syndrome differences. *Mental Retardation and Developmental Disabilities Research Reviews, 13*, 36–46.

Abbeduto, L., Keller-Bell, Y., Richmond, E. K., & Murphy, M. M. (2006). Research on language development and mental retardation: History, theories, findings, and future directions. *International Review of Research in Mental Retardation, 32*, 1–39.

Abbeduto, L., Murphy, M. M., Cawthon, S. W., Richmond, E. K., Weissman, M. D., Karadottir, S., et al. (2003). Receptive language skills of adolescents and young adults with Down or Fragile X syndrome. *American Journal on Mental Retardation, 108*, 149–160.

Abbeduto, L., Murphy, M. M., Richmond, E. K., Amman, A., Beth, P., Weissman, M. D., et al. (2006). Collaboration in referential communication: Comparison of youth with Down syndrome or Fragile X syndrome. *American Journal on Mental Retardation, 111*, 170–183.

Ager, A. K. (1990). *The Life Experiences Checklist.* Windsor, Ontario, Canada: NFER-Nelson.

Atkins v. State of Virginia, 536 U.S. 304 (2002).

Baumeister, A. A. (2006). Mental retardation: Confusing sentiment with science. In H. N. Switsky & S. Greenspan (Eds.), *What is mental retardation? Ideas for an evolving disability in the 21st Century* (Rev. ed. (pp. 95–126). Washington, DC: American Association on Mental Retardation.

Bebko, J. M., & Luhaorg, H. (1998). The development of strategy use and metacognitive processing in mental retardation: Some sources of difficulty. In J. A. Burack, R. M. Hodapp, & E. Zigler (Eds.), *Handbook of mental retardation and development* (pp. 382–407). New York: Cambridge University Press.

Beirne-Smith, M., Patton, J., & Kim, S. (2006). *Mental retardation: An introduction to intellectual disability* (7th ed). Upper Saddle River, NJ: Merrill/Prentice Hall.

Belser, R. C., & Sudhalter, V. (2001). Conversational characteristics of children with fragile X syndrome: Repetitive speech. *American Journal on Mental Retardation, 106*, 28–38.

Browder, D., Flowers, C., Ahlgrim-Delzell, L., Karvonen, M., Spooner, F., & Algozzine, R. (2004). The alignment of alternate assessment content with academic and functional curricula. *The Journal of Special Education, 37*, 211–223.

Brown, R. I., & Brown, I. (2005). The application of quality of life. *Journal of Intellectual Disability Research, 49*, 718–727.

Bush, A., & Beail, N. (2004). Risk factors for dementia in people with Down syndrome: Issues in assessment and diagnosis. *American Journal on Mental Retardation, 109*, 83–97.

Butterworth, J., & Strauch, J. D. (1994). The relationship between social competence and success in the competitive work place for persons with mental retardation. *Education and Training in Mental Retardation and Developmental Disabilities, 29*, 118–133.

Caballo, C., Crespo, M., Jenaro, C., Verdugo, M. A., & Martinez, J. L. (2005). Factor structure of the Schalock and Keith Quality of Life Questionnaire (QOL-Q): Validation on Mexican and Spanish samples. *Journal of Intellectual Disability Research, 49*, 773–776.

Campbell, F. A., Ramey, C. T., Pungello, E., Sparling, J., & Miller-Johnson, S. (2002). Early childhood education: Young adult outcomes from the Abecedarian Project. *Applied Developmental Science, 6*, 42–57.

Carr, J. (1994). Annotation: Long term outcome for people with Down's syndrome. *Journal of Child Psychology and Psychiatry, 35*, 425–439.

Carter, E. W., Hughes, C., Guth, C. B., & Copeland, S. R. (2005). Factors influencing social interaction among high school students with intellectual disabilities and their general education peers. *American Journal on Mental Retardation, 110*, 366–377.

Centers for Disease Control and Prevention. (2006, May 2). *Fetal alcohol spectrum disorders.* Retrieved September 23, 2007, from http://www.cdc.gov/ncbddd/fas/fasask.htm

Chapman, D. A., Scott, K. G., & Mason, C. A. (2002). Early risk factors for mental retardation: Role of maternal age and maternal education. *American Journal on Mental Retardation, 107*, 46–59.

Collodi, C. (1930). *Pinocchio: The adventures of a puppet.* (M. A. Murray, Trans.), New York: A. L. Burt Co. (Original work published 1883).

Conners, F. A. (2003). Phonological working memory difficulty and related interventions. In J. A. Rondal & S. Buckley (Eds.), *Speech and language intervention in Down syndrome* (pp. 31–48). London: Colin Whurr.

Council for Exceptional Children (2003). *What every special educator must know: Ethics, standards, and guidelines for special educators* (5th ed.). Arlington, VA: Author.

Cummins, R. A. (2005a). Instruments for assessing quality of life. In J. Hogg and A. Langa (Eds.). *Assessing adults with intellectual disabilities: A service provider's guide* (pp. 119–137). Malden, MA: Blackwell.

Cummins, R. A. (2005b). Issues in the systematic assessment of quality of life. In J. Hogg and A. Langa (Eds.). *Assessing adults with intellectual disabilities: A service provider's guide* (pp. 9–22). Malden, MA: Blackwell.

Davis, P. K., & Cuvo, A. J. (1997). Environmental approaches to mental retardation. In D. M. Baer & E. M. Pinkerston (Eds.), *Environment and behavior* (pp. 231–242). Boulder, CO: Westview Press.

Davis, S. (1997). *The Human Genome Project: Examining the Arc's concerns regarding the Human Genome Project's ethical, legal, and social implications.* Presentation at the DOE Human Genome Program Contractor-Grantee Workshop VI. Retrieved July 29, 2001, from www.ornl.gov/hgmis/resource/arc.html

Dimitropoulos, A., Feurer, I. D., Butler, M. G., & Thompson, T. (2001). Emergence of compulsive behavior and tantrums in children with Prader-Willi syndrome. *American Journal on Mental Retardation, 106,* 39–51.

Drew, C. J., & Hardman, M. L. (2004). *Mental retardation: A lifespan approach to people with intellectual disabilities* (8th ed.). Upper Saddle River, NJ: Merrill/Prentice-Hall.

Dykens, E. (2001). Introduction to special issue. *American Journal on Mental Retardation, 106,* 1–3.

Dykens, E. M., Hodapp, R. M., & Finucane, B. M. (2000). *Genetics and mental retardation syndromes: A new look at behavior and interventions.* Baltimore, MD: Paul H. Brookes.

Elliott, A. (Director) (2005). *The collector of Bedford Street* [Documentary short]. New York: Welcome Change Productions. (Available from New Day Films, 190 Route 17M, P.O. Box 1084, Harriman, NY 10926; www.Newday.com).

Evenhuis, H. M. (1990). The natural history of dementia in Down's syndrome. *Archives of Neurology, 47,* 263–267.

Fidler, D. J., Hepburn, S. L., Most, D. E., Philofsky, A., & Rogers, S. J. (2007). Emotional responsivity in young children with Williams syndrome. *American Journal on Mental Retardation, 112,* 194–206.

Fidler, D. J., Hodapp, R. M., & Dykens, E. M. (2002). Behavioral phenotypes and special education: Parent report of educational issues for children with Down syndrome, Prader-Willi syndrome, and Williams syndrome. *The Journal of Special Education, 36,* 80–88.

Frank, A. R., & Sitlington, P. L. (2000). Young adults with mental disabilities: Does transition planning make a difference? *Education and Training in Mental Retardation and Developmental Disabilities, 35,* 119–134.

Fraser, J., & Mitchell, A. (1876). Kalmuc idiocy: Report of a case with autopsy, with notes on sixty-two cases. *Journal of Mental Science, 22,* 161–179.

Fuchs, L. S., Fuchs, D., Compton, D. L., Bryant, J. D., Hamlett, C. L., & Seethaler, P. M. (2007). Mathematics screening and progress monitoring at first grade: Implications for responsiveness to intervention. *Exceptional Children, 73,* 311–330.

Glidden, L. M. (2006). An update on the label and definitional asynchrony: The missing *mental* and *retardation* in mental retardation. In H. N. Switsky & S. Greenspan (Eds.), *What is mental retardation? Ideas for an evolving disability in the 21st Century* (Rev. ed., pp. 39–49). Washington, DC: American Association on Mental Retardation.

Greenspan, S. (1999). What is meant by mental retardation? *International Review of Psychiatry, 11,* 6–18.

Greenspan, S. (2004). Why Pinocchio was victimized: Factors contributing to social failure in people with mental retardation. *International Review of Research in Mental Retardation, 28,* 121–144.

Greenspan, S. (2006a). Functional concepts in mental retardation: Finding the natural essence of an artificial category. *Exceptionality, 14,* 205–224.

Greenspan, S. (2006b). Mental retardation in the real world: Why the AAMR definition is not there yet. In H. N. Switsky & S. Greenspan (Eds.), *What is mental retardation? Ideas for an evolving disability in the 21st Century* (Rev. ed., pp. 165–183). Washington, DC: American Association on Mental Retardation.

Greenspan, S., Loughlin, G., & Black, R. S. (2001). Credulity and gullibility in people with developmental disorders: A framework for future research. *International Review of Research in Mental Retardation, 24,* 101–135.

Greenspan, S., & Switsky, H. N. (2006). Lessons from the *Atkins* decision for the next AAMR manual. In H. N. Switsky & S. Greenspan (Eds.), *What is mental retardation? Ideas for an evolving disability in the 21st Century* (Rev. ed., pp. 283–302). Washington, DC: American Association on Mental Retardation.

Guralnick, M. J., Connor, R. T., & Hammond, M. (1995). Parent perspectives of peer relationships and friendships in integrated and specialized programs. *American Journal on Mental Retardation, 99,* 457–476.

Hagerman, R. J. (2001). Fragile X syndrome. In S. B. Cassidy & J. E. Allanson (Eds.), *Management of genetic syndromes* (pp. 165–183). New York: Wiley-Liss.

Hardman, M. L., & Clark, C. (2006). Promoting friendship through Best Buddies: A national survey of college program participants. *Mental Retardation, 44,* 56–63.

Harrison, P. L., & Boney, T. L. (2002). Best practices in the assessment of adaptive behavior. In A. Thomas & J. Grimes (Eds.), *Best practices in school psychology IV* (pp. 1167–1179). Washington, DC: National Association of School Psychologists.

Hatton, D. D., Wheeler, A. C., Skinner, M. L., Bailey, D. B., Sullivan, K. M., Roberts, J. E., et al. (2003). Adaptive behavior in children with Fragile X syndrome. *American Journal on Mental Retardation, 108,* 373–390.

Heal, L. W., Gonzalez, P., Rusch, F. R., Copher, J. I., & DeStefano, L. (1990). A comparison of successful and unsuccessful placements of youths with mental handicaps into competitive employment. *Exceptionality, 1,* 181–195.

Hodapp, R. M., & Dykens, E. M. (2007). Behavioral effects of genetic mental retardation disorders. In J. W. Jacobson, J. A. Mullick, & J. Rojahn (Eds.), *Handbook of intellectual and developmental disabilities* (pp. 115–131). New York: Springer.

Hodapp, R. M., & Fidler, D. J. (1999). Special education and genetics: Connections for the 21st century. *Journal of Special Education, 33,* 130–137.

Hof, P. R., Bouras, C., Perl, D. P., Sparks, L., Mehta, N., & Morrison, J. H. (1995). Age-related distribution of neuropathologic changes in the cerebral cortex of patients with *Down's syndrome. Archives of Neurology, 52,* 379–391.

Horner, R. H., Albin, R. W., Sprague, J. R., & Todd, A. W. (2000). Positive behavior support. In M. E. Snell & F. Brown (Eds.), *Instruction of students with severe retardation* (5th ed., pp. 207–243). Upper Saddle River, NJ: Prentice-Hall.

Human Genome Project. (2006a, August 29). *Human Genome Project Information.* Retrieved June 24, 2007 from http://www.ornl.gov/sci/techresources/Human_Genome/home.shtml

Human Genome Project. (2006b, September 6). *Human Genome Project Information: Ethical, legal, and social issues.* Retrieved June 24, 2007 from http://www.ornl.gov/sci/techresources/Human_Genome/elsi/elsi.shtml

Kaiser, A. P., & Grim, J. C. (2006). Teaching functional communication skills. In M. E. Snell & F. Brown (Eds.), *Instruction of students with severe disabilities* (6th ed., pp. 447–488). Upper Saddle River, NJ: Prentice-Hall.

Kasari, C., & Bauminger, N. (1998). Social and emotional development in children with mental retardation. In J. A. Burack, R. M. Hodapp, & E. Zigler (Eds.), *Handbook of mental retardation and development* (pp. 411–433). New York: Cambridge University Press.

Kasari, C., Freeman, S. F. N., & Hughes, M. A. (2001). Emotion recognition by children with Down syndrome. *American Journal on Mental Retardation, 106,* 59–72.

Kaufman, A. S., & Kaufman, N. L. (1994). *Kaufman Functional Academic Skills Test (K-FAST).* Bloomington, MN: Pearson.

Kaufman, A. S., & Kaufman, N. L. (2004). *Kaufman Test of Educational Achievement (KTEA).* Bloomington, MN: Pearson.

Kaufman, S. Z. (1999). *Retarded isn't stupid, mom!* (Rev. ed.). Baltimore: Paul H. Brookes.

Kemp, C., & Carter, M. (2006). Active and passive task related behavior, direction following and the inclusion of children with disabilities. *Education and Training in Developmental Disabities, 41,* 14–27.

Kuna, J. (2001). The Human Genome Project and eugenics: Identifying the impact on individuals with mental retardation. *Mental Retardation, 39,* 158–160.

Lakin, K. C., Prouty, R., & Coucouvanis, K. (2006). Changing patterns in size of residential settings for persons with intellectual and developmental disability, 1977–2005. *Mental Retardation, 44,* 306–309.

Lenhoff, H. M., Wang, P. P., Greenberg, F., & Bellugi, U. (1997). Williams syndrome and the brain. *Scientific American, 277*(6), 68–73.

MacMillan, D. L., Gresham, F. M., Bocian, K. M., & Lambros, K. M. (1998). Current plight of borderline students: Where do they belong? *Education and Training in Mental Retardation and Developmental Disabilities, 33,* 83–94.

Mank, D., Cioffi, A., & Yovanoff, P. (2003). Supported employment outcomes across a decade: Is there evidence of improvement in the quality of implementation? *Mental Retardation, 41,* 188–197.

McDonnell, J. J., Hardman, M. L., & McDonnell, A. P. (2003). *An introduction to persons with moderate and severe disabilities* (2nd ed.). Boston: Allyn & Bacon.

Mechling, L. C., Gast, D. L., & Langone, J. (2002). Computer-based video instruction to teach persons with moderate intellectual disabilities to read grocery aisle signs and locate items. *The Journal of Special Education, 35,* 224–240.

Mervis, C. B., & Becerra, A. M. (2007). Language and communicative development in Williams syndrome. *Mental Retardation and Developmental Disabilities Research Reviews, 13,* 3–15.

Mervis, C. B., Klein-Tasman, B. P., & Mastin, M. E. (2001). Adaptive behavior of 4- through 8-year-old children with Williams syndrome. *American Journal on Mental Retardation, 106,* 82–93.

Meyer, G. A., & Batshaw, M. L. (2002). Fragile X syndrome. In M. L. Batshaw (Ed.), *Children with disabilities* (5th ed.). Baltimore, MD: Paul H. Brookes.

Moldavsky, M., Lev, D., & Lerman-Sagie, T. (2001). Behavioral phenotypes of genetic syndromes: A reference guide for psychiatrists. *Journal of the American Academy of Child and Adolescent Psychiatry, 40,* 749–761.

Morse, T. E., & Schuster, J. W. (2000). Teaching elementary students with moderate intellectual disabilities how to shop for groceries. *Exceptional Children, 66,* 273–288.

MR/DD Data Brief. (2001, April). *Characteristics of service use by persons with MR/DD living in their own homes or with family members: NHIS-D analysis.* Minneapolis, MN: University of Minnesota Research and Training Center on Community Living, Institute on Community Integration.

National Institute of Neurological Disorders and Stroke. (2007, February 13). *NINDS Microcephaly Information Page.* Retrieved June 27, 2007 http://www.ninds.nih.gov/disorders/microcephaly/microcephaly.htm

National Organization on Disability, & L. Harris & Associates. (2000). *National Organization on Disability/Harris Survey of Americans with Disabilities.* New York: Author.

Patton, J. P., & Keyes, D. W. (2006). Death penalty issues following *Atkins. Exceptionality, 14,* 237–255.

Prouty, R., Coucouvanis, K., & Lakin, K. C. (2007). State institution populations in 2006 less than 80% of 40 years earlier; "real dollar" per person costs more than 10 times greater. *Intellectual and Developmental Disabilities, 45,* 143–145.

Ramey, C. T., & Campbell, F. A. (1984). Preventive education for high-risk children: Cognitive consequences of the Carolina Abecedarian Project. *American Journal of Mental Deficiency, 88,* 515–523.

Ramey, C. T., & Campbell, F. A. (1987). The Carolina Abecedarian Project: An educational experiment concerning human mal-

leability. In J. J. Gallagher & C. T. Ramey (Eds.), *The malleability of children* (pp. 127–139). Baltimore, MD: Paul H. Brookes.

Reynolds, A. J., Temple, J. A., Robertson, D. L., & Mann, E. A. (2001). Long-term effects of an early childhood intervention on educational achievement and juvenile arrest. *Journal of the American Medical Association, 285,* 2339–2346.

Roberts, J. E., Price, J., Malkin, C. (2007). Language and communication development in Down syndrome. *Mental Retardation and Developmental Disabilities Research Reviews, 13,* 26–35.

Rosenquist, C. J., Conners, F. A., & Roskos-Ewoldsen, B. (2003). Phonological and visuospatial working memory in individuals with intellectual disabilities. *American Journal on Mental Retardation, 108,* 403–413.

Rueda, R., Monzo, L., Shapiro, J., Gomez, J., & Blacher, J. (2005). Cultural models of transition: Latina mothers of young adults with developmental disabilities. *Exceptional Children, 71,* 401–414.

Salzberg, C. L., Lignugaris/Kraft, B., & McCuller, G. L. (1988). Reasons for job loss: A review of employment termination studies of mentally retarded workers. *Research in Developmental Disabilities, 9,* 153–170.

Schalock, R. L., Brown, I., Brown, R. I., Cummins, R., Felce, D., Matikka, L., et al. (2002). Quality of life: its conceptualization, measurement, and application. A consensus document. *Mental Retardation, 40,* 457–470.

Schalock, R. L., & Keith, K. D. (1993). *Quality of life questionnaire.* Worthington, OH: IDA Publishing.

Shin, J., Deno, S. L., & Espin, C. (2000). Technical adequacy of the maze task for curriculum-based measurement of reading growth. *The Journal of Special Education, 34,* 164–172.

Sparrow, S. S., Chicchetti, D. V., & Balla, D. A. (2005). *Vineland Adaptive Behavior scales* (2nd ed.). Circle Pines, MN: American Guidance Service.

Spinath, F. M., Harlaar, N., Ronald, A., & Plomin, R. (2004). Substantial genetic influence on mild mental impairment in early childhood. *American Journal on Mental Retardation, 109,* 34–43.

Spinelli, C. G. (2006). *Classroom assessment for students in special and general education* (2nd ed.). Upper Saddle River, NJ: Pearson Prentice Hall.

Stancliffe, R. J., Abery, B. H., & Smith, J. (2000). Personal control and the ecology of community living settings: Beyond living unit size and type. *American Journal on Mental Retardation, 105,* 431–454.

Stecker, P. M., Fuchs, L. S., & Fuchs, D. (2005). Using curriculum-based measurement to improve student achievement: Review of research. *Pscychology in the Schools, 42,* 795–819.

Sugai, G., Horner, R., Dunlap, G., Lewis, T., Nelson C. M., Scott, T., et al. (2000). Applying positive behavior support and functional behavioral assessment in schools. *Journal of Positive Behavior Interventions, 2,* 131–143.

Switsky, H. N. (2006). The importance of cognitive-motivational variables in understanding the outcome performance of persons with mental retardation: A personal view form the early twenty-first century. *International Review of Research in Mental Retardation, 31,* 1–29.

Tansley, G. H., Burgess, B. L., Bryan, M. T., Su, Y., Hirsch-Reinshagen, V., Pearce, J., et al. (2007). The cholesterol transporter ABCG1 modulates the subcellular distribution and proteolytic processing of β-amyloid precursor protein. *Journal of Lipid Research, 48,* 1022–1034.

Taylor, H. G., Klein, N., Minich, N. M., & Hack, M. (2000), Middle-school-age outcomes in children with very low birthweight. *Child Development, 71,* 1495–1511.

Taylor, R. L., Richards, S. B., & Brady, M. P. (2005). *Mental retardation: Historical perspectives, current practices, and future directions.* Boston: Allyn & Bacon.

Thomas, C. L. (Ed.). (1985). *Taber's cyclopedic medical dictionary* (15th ed.). Philadelphia: F. A. Davis Co.

Tomporowski, P. D., & Tinsley, V. (1997). Attention in mentally retarded persons. In W. E. MacLean (Ed.), *Ellis' handbook of mental deficiency, psychological theory, and research* (pp. 219–244). Mahwah, NJ: Lawrence Erlbaum.

Venn, J. J. (2007). *Assessing students with special needs.* Upper Saddle River, NJ: Prentice Hall.

Wechsler, D. (2003). *Wechsler intelligence scale for children* (4th ed.). San Antonio, TX: Psychological Corporation.

Wehmeyer, M. L., Garner, N., Yeager, D., Lawrence, M., & Davis, A. K. (2006). Infusing self-determination into 18–21 services for students with intellectual or developmental disabilities: A multistage, multiple component model. *Education and Training in Developmental Disabilities, 41,* 1–13.

Wehymeyer, M. L., & Mithaug, D. E. (2006). Self-determination, causal agency, and mental retardation. *International Review of Research in Mental Retardation, 31,* 31–71.

Wehmeyer, M. L., Palmer, S. B., Agran, M., Mithaug, D. E., & Martin, J. E. (2000). Promoting causal agency: The self-determined learning model of instruction. *Exceptional Children, 66,* 439–453.

Wisniewski, H. M., Silverman, W., & Wegiel, J. (1994). Aging, Alzheimer disease, and mental retardation. *Journal of Intellectual Disability Research, 38,* 233–239.

Wolery, M., & Schuster, J. W. (1997). Instructional methods with students who have significant disabilities. *The Journal of Special Education, 31,* 61–79.

Woodcock, R. W., Schrank, F. A., Mather, N., McGrew, K. S (2007). *Woodcock-Johnson III Tests of Achievement.* Rolling Meadows, IL: Riverside Publishing.

Ysseldyke, J., & Olsen, K. (1999). Putting alternate assessments into practice: What to measure and possible sources of data. *Exceptional Children, 65,* 175–185.

CHAPTER 6

Adams, G. L., & Engelmann, S. (1996). *Research on direct instruction: 25 years beyond DISTAR.* Seattle: Educational Achievement Systems.

Al-Yagon, M. (2007). Socioemotional and behavioral adjustment among school-age children with learning disabilities: The moderating role of maternal personal resources. *The Journal of Special Education, 40,* 205–217.

American Psychiatric Association. (2000). *Diagnostic and statistical manual of mental disorders* (4th ed., rev.). Washington, DC: Author.

Arduini, R. G., Capellini, S. A., & Ciasca, S. M. (2006). Comparative study of the neuropsychological and neuroimaging evaluations in children with dyslexia. *Arquivos de Neuro-Psiquiatra, 64,* 369–375.

Bear, G. G., Kortering, L. J., & Braziel, P. (2006). School completers and noncompleters with learning disabilities: Similarities in academic achievement and perceptions of self and teachers. *Remedial and Special Education, 27,* 293–300.

Beichtman, J. H., Hood, J., & Inglis, A. (1992). Familial transmission of speech and language impairment: A preliminary investigation. *Canadian Journal of Psychiatry, 37,* 151–156.

Bender, W. N. (2004). *Learning disabilities: Characteristics, identification, and learning strategies* (5th ed.). Boston: Allyn & Bacon.

Bender, W. N., Rosenkrans, C. B., & Crane, M. K. (1999). Stress, depression, and suicide among students with learning disabilities: Assessing the risk. *Learning Disability Quarterly, 22,* 143–156.

Blachman, B. (2001). Phonological awareness. In D. P. Pearson (Ed.), *Handbook of reading research* (pp. 483–502). Mahwah, NJ: Lawrence Erlbaum Associates.

Blackorby, J., & Wagner, M. (1997). The employment outcomes of youth with learning disabilities: A review of findings from NLTS. In P. J. Gerber & D. S. Brown (Eds.), *Learning disabilities and employment* (pp. 57–74). Austin, TX: Pro-Ed.

Boada, R., & Pennington, B. F. (2006). Deficient implicit phonological representations in children with dyslexia. *Journal of Experimental Child Psychology, 95,* 153–193.

Brunswick, N., McCrory, E., Price, C. J., Frith, C. D., & Frith, U. (1999). Explicit and implicit processing of words and pseudowords by adult developmental dyslexics: A search for Wernicke's Wortschatz? *Brain, 122* (Part 10), 1901–1917.

Bryan, T., Burstein, K., & Ergul, C. (2004). The social-emotional side of learning disabilities: A science-based presentation of the state of the art. *Learning Disability Quarterly, 27,* 45–51.

Bryan, T. H., Donahue, M., Pearl, R., & Sturm, C. (1981). Learning disabled children's conversational skills—The "TV Talk Show." *Learning Disability Quarterly, 4,* 250–260.

Bryan, T. H., & Sullivan-Burstein, K. (1998). Teacher-selected strategies for improving homework completion. *Remedial and Special Education, 19,* 263–275.

Butler, D. L. (1998). Metacognition and learning disabilities. In B. Y. L. Wong (Ed.), *Learning about learning disabilities* (2nd ed., pp. 277–307). San Diego, CA: Academic Press.

Case, L. P., Harris, K. R., & Graham, S. (1992). Improving the mathematical problem-solving skills of students with learning disabilities. *The Journal of Special Education, 26,* 1–19.

Cawley, J. F., Parmar, R. S., Yan, W., & Miller, J. H. (1998). Arithmetic computation performance of students with learning disabilities: Implications for the curriculum. *Learning Disabilities Research & Practice, 13,* 68–74.

Clarizio, H. F., & Phillips, S. E. (1986). Sex bias in the diagnosis of learning disabled students. *Psychology in the Schools, 23,* 44–52.

Cobb, J. (2003). *Learning how to learn: Getting into and surviving college when you have a learning disability* (Rev. ed.). Washington, DC: Child & Family Press.

Cohen-Mimran, R., & Sapir, S. (2007). Deficits in working memory in young adults with reading disabilities. *Journal of Communication Disorders, 40,* 168–183.

Council for Exceptional Children (2003). *What every special educator must know: Ethics, standards, and guidelines for special educators* (5th ed.). Arlington, VA: Author.

Daniel, S. S., Walsh, A. K., Goldston, D. B., Arnold, E. M., Reboussin, B. A., & Wood, F. B. (2006). Suicidality, school dropout, and reading problems among adolescents. *Journal of Learning Disabilities, 39,* 507–514.

Danielson, L., Bradley, R., & Hallahan, D. P. (Eds.) (2002). *Identification of learning disabilities: Research to practice.* Mahwah, NJ: Lawrence Erlbaum Associates.

DeFries, J. C., Gillis, J. J., & Wadsworth, S. J. (1993). Genes and genders: A twin study of reading disability. In A. M. Galaburda (Ed.), *Dyslexia and development: Neurobiological aspects of extraordinary brains* (pp. 187–294). Cambridge, MA: Harvard University Press.

Deno, S. L. (1985). Curriculum-based measurement: The emerging alternative. *Exceptional Children, 52,* 219–232.

Deshler, D. D., Schumaker, J. B., Lenz, B. K., Bulgren, J. A., Hock, M. F., Knight, J., et al. (2001). Ensuring content-area learning by secondary students with learning disabilities. *Learning Disabilities Research & Practice, 16,* 96–108.

DeThorne, L. S., Hart, S. A., Petrill, S. A., Deater-Deckard, K., Thompson, L. A., Schatschneider, C., et al. (2006). Children's history of speech-language difficulties: Genetic influences and associations with reading-related measures. *Journal of Speech, Language, and Hearing Research, 49,* 1280–1293.

Ellis, A. (2001). *Research on educational innovations* (3rd ed.). Larchmont, New York: Eye On Education.

Elliot, S. N., & Marquart, A. M. (2004). Extended time as a testing accommodation: Its effects and perceived consequences. *Exceptional Children, 70,* 349–367.

Ellis, A. K., & Fouts, J. T. (1997). *Research on educational interventions.* Larchmont, NY: Eye on Education.

Ellis, E. S., & Howard, P. W. (2007, Spring). Graphic organizers: Power tools for teaching students with learning disabilities. *Current Practice Alerts, 13.* Retrieved July 26, 2007 from http://www.teachingld.org/pdf/alert13.pdf

Epstein, M. H., Munk, D. D., Bursuck, W. D., Polloway, E. A., & Jayanthi, M. (1998). Strategies for improving home-school communication about homework for students with disabilities. *Journal of Special Education, 33,* 166–176.

Fisher, S. E., & Francks, C. (2006). Genes, cognition and dyslexia: Learning to read the genome. *Trends in Cognitive Sciences, 10,* 250–257.

Fletcher, J. M., Lyon, G. R., Barnes, M., Stuebing, K. K., Francis, D. J., Olson, R. K., et al. (2002). Classification of learning disabilities: An evidence-based evaluation. In R. Bradley, L. Danielson, & D.590P. Hallahan (Eds.), *Identification of learning disabilities: Research to practice* (pp. 185–250). Mahwah, NJ: Lawrence Erlbaum.

Fletcher, J. M., Francis, D. J., Boudousquie, A., Copeland, K., Young, V., Kalinowski, S., et al. (2006). Effects of accommodations on high-stakes testing for students with reading disabilities. *Exceptional Children, 72,* 136–150.

Flowers, D. L. (1993). Brain basis for dyslexia: A summary of work in progress. *Journal of Learning Disabilities, 26,* 575–582.

Flowers, D. L., Wood, F. B., & Naylor, C. E. (1991). Regional cerebral blood flow correlates of language processes in reading disability. *Archives of Neurology, 48,* 637–643.

Foegen, A., Jiban, C. & Deno, S. (2007). Progress monitoring measures in mathematics: A review of the literature. *The Journal of Special Education, 41,* 121–139.

Forness, S. R., & Kavale, K. A. (2002). Impact of ADHD on school systems. In P. Jensen & J. R. Cooper (Eds.), *NIH consensus conference on ADHD.* Bethesda, MD: National Institutes of Health.

Frostig, M., & Horne, D. (1964). *The Frostig program for the development of visual perception: Teacher's guide.* Chicago: Follett.

Fuchs, D., & Fuchs, L. S. (2005). Peer-assisted learning strategies: Promoting word recognition, fluency, and reading comprehension in young children. *The Journal of Special Education, 39,* 34–44.

Fuchs, D., Fuchs, L., & Burish, P. (2000). Peer-Assisted Learning Strategies: An evidence-based practice to promote reading achievement. *Learning Disabilities Research & Practice, 15*(2), 85–91.

Fuchs, D., Fuchs, L. S., McMaster, K. L., Yen, L., & Svenson, E. (2004). Nonresponders: How to find them? How to help them? What do they mean for special education? *Teaching Exceptional Children, 37,* 72–77.

Fuchs, D., Mock, D., Morgan, P. L., & Young, C. L. (2003). Responsiveness-to-intervention: Definitions, evidence, and implications for the learning disabilities construct. *Learning Disabilities Research & Practice, 18,* 157–171.

Fuchs, L. S. (2003). Assessing intervention responsiveness: Conceptual and technical issues. *Learning Disabilities Research & Practice, 18,* 172–186.

Fuchs, L. S., Deno, S. L., & Mirkin, P. K. (1984). The effects of frequent curriculum-based measurement and evaluation of pedagogy, student achievement and student awareness of learning. *American Educational Research Journal, 24,* 449–460.

Fuchs, L. S., & Fuchs, D. (2007). A model for implementing responsiveness to intervention. *Teaching Exceptional Children, 39*(1), 14–20.

Fuchs, L. S., Fuchs, D., & Capizzi, A. (2005). Identifying appropriate test accommodation for students with learning disabilities. *Focus on Exceptional Children, 37,* 1–8.

Fuchs, L. S., Fuchs, D., Eaton, S., Hamlett, C. L. (2003). *Dynamic assessment of test accommodations.* San Antonio, TX: Harcourt Assessment.

Fuchs, L. S., Fuchs, D., Hamlett, C. L., Walz, L., & Germann, G. (1993). Formative evaluation of academic progress: How much growth should we expect? *School Psychology Review, 22,* 27–48.

Gajria, M., Jitendra, S., & Sacks, G. (2007). Improving comprehension of expository text in students with LD: A research synthesis. *Journal of Learning Disabilities, 40,* 210–225.

Galaburda, A. M., LoTurco, J., Ramus, F., Fitch, R. H., & Rosen, G. D. (2006). *Nature Neuroscience, 9,* 1213–1217.

Gathercole, S. E., Alloway, T. P., Willis, C., & Adams, A. M. (2005). Working memory in children with reading disabilities. *Journal of Experimental Child Psychology, 93,* 265–281.

Geary, D. C., Hoard, M. K., Byrd-Craven, J., Nugent, L., & Numtee, C. (2007). Cognitive mechanisms underlying achievement deficits in children with mathematical learning disability. *Child Development, 78,* 1343–1359.

Georgiewa, P., Rzanny, R., Hopf, J. M., Knab, R., Glauche, V., Kaiser, W. A., et al. (1999). fMRI during word processing in dyslexic and normal reading children. *Neuroreport, 10,* 3459–3465.

Gerber, P. J. (1997). Life after school: Challenges in the workplace. In P. J. Gerber & D. S. Brown (Eds.), *Learning disabilities and employment* (pp. 3–18). Austin, TX: Pro-Ed.

Gerber, P. J. (2006). Acceptable loss and potential gain: Self-disclosure and adults with learning disabilities. *Thalamus, 24,* 49–55.

Gerber, P. J., Ginsberg, R., & Reiff, H. B. (1992). Identifying alterable patterns in employment success for highly successful adults with learning disabilities. *Journal of Learning Disabilities, 25,* 475–487.

Goldstein, D. E., Murray, C., & Edgar, E. (1998). Employment earning and hours of high school graduates with learning disabilities through the first decade after graduation. *Learning Disabilities Research & Practice, 13,* 53–64.

Good, R. H., Simmons, D. C., & Kame'enui, E. J. (2001). The importance and decision-making utility of a continuum of fluency-based indicators of foundational reading skills for third-grade high-stakes outcomes. *Scientific Studies of Reading, 5,* 257–288.

Graham, S., & Harris, K. R. (2002). Prevention and intervention for struggling writers. In M. Shinn, G. Stoner, & H. Walker, H. (Eds.), *Interventions for academic and behavior problems: Vol. 2: Preventive and remedial techniques* (pp. 589–610). Washington, DC: National Association of School Psychologists.

Hagman, J. O., Wood, F., Buchsbaum, M. S., Tallal, P., Flowers, L., & Katz, W. (1992). Cerebral metabolism in adult dyslexic subjects assessed with positron emission tomography during performance on an auditory task. *Archives of Neurology, 49,* 734–739.

Hallahan, D. P. (1975). Comparative research studies on the psychological characteristics of learning disabled children. In W. M. Cruickshank & D. P. Hallahan (Eds.), *Perceptual and learning disabilities in children. Vol. 1: Psychoeducational practices* (pp. 29–60). Syracuse, NY: Syracuse University Press.

Hallahan, D. P. (1992). Some thoughts on why the prevalence of learning disabilities has increased. *Journal of Learning Disabilities, 25,* 523–528.

Hallahan, D. P., & Cruickshank, W. M. (1973). *Psychoeducational foundations of learning disabilities.* Englewood Cliffs, NJ: Prentice-Hall.

Hallahan, D. P., Lloyd, J. W., Kauffman, J. M., Weiss, M. P., & Martinez, E. A. (2005). *Learning disabilities: Foundations, characteristics, and effective teaching.* Boston: Allyn & Bacon.

Hallahan, D. P., & Mercer, C. D. (2002). Learning disabilities: Historical perspectives. In R. Bradley, L. Danielson, & D. P. Hallahan (Eds.), *Identification of learning disabilities: Research to practice* (pp. 1–67). Mahwah, NJ: Lawrence Erlbaum.

Hallgren, B. (1950). Specific dyslexia (congenital word blindness: A clinical and genetic study). *Acta Psychiatrica et Neurologica, 65,* 1–279.

Hammill, D. D. (1990). On defining learning disabilities: An emerging consensus. *Journal of Learning Disabilities, 23,* 74–84.

Hammill, D. D., & Larsen, S. (1974). The effectiveness of psycholinguistic training. *Exceptional Children, 41,* 5–15.

Hammill, D. D., & Larsen, S. C. (1996). *Test of written language* (3rded.). Austin, TX: Pro-Ed.

Hammill, D. D., Leigh, J. E., McNutt, G., & Larsen, S. C. (1981). A new definition of learning disabilities. *Learning Disability Quarterly, 4,* 336–342.

Helmuth, L. (2001). Dyslexia: Same brains, different languages. *Science, 291,* 2064.

Henderson, C. (1999). *1999 college freshmen with disabilities: A biennial statistical profile.* Washington, DC: American Council on Education HEALTH Resource Center.

Hitchings, W. E., Luzzo, D. A., Ristow, R., Horvath, M., Retish, P., & Tanners, A. (2001). The career development needs of college students with learning disabilities: In their own words. *Learning Disabilities Research & Practice, 16,* 8–17.

Hoeft, F., Hernandez, A., McMillon, G., Taylor-Hill, H., Martindale, J. L., Meyler, A., et al. (2006). Neural basis of dyslexia: A comparison between dyslexic and nondyslexic children equated for reading ability. *The Journal of Neuroscience, 26,* 10700–10708.

Hosp, M. K., Hosp, J. L., & Howell, K. W. (2007). *The abcs of CBM: A practical guide to curriculum-based measurement.* New York: Guilford.

Kavale, K. A. (1988). The long-term consequences of learning disabilities. In M. C. Wang, M. C. Reynolds, & H. J. Walberg (Eds.), *Handbook of special education: Research and practice. Vol. 2: Mildly handicapped conditions.* New York: Pergamon Press.

Kephart, N. C. (1971). *The slow learner in the classroom* (2nd ed.). Columbus, OH: Merrill.

Kibby, M. Y., & Hynd, G. W. (2001). Neurological basis of learning disabilities. In D. P. Hallahan & B. K. Keogh (Eds.), *Research and global perspectives in learning disabilities: Essays in honor of William M. Cruickshank* (pp. 25–42). Mahwah, NJ: Lawrence Erlbaum.

Kirk, S. A., & Kirk, W. D. (1971). *Psycholinguistic learning disabilities: Diagnosis and remediation*. Urbana: University of Illinois Press.

Kirk, S. A., McCarthy, J., & Kirk, W. D. (1967) *The Illinois test of psycholinguistic abilities*. Urbana, IL: University of Illinois Press.

Klingner, J. K., Vaughn, S., Hughes, M. T., Schumm, J. S., & Elbaum, B. (1998). Outcomes for students with and without learning disabilities in inclusive classrooms. *Learning Disabilities Research & Practice, 13*, 153–161.

Kotkin, R. A., Forness, S. R., & Kavale, K. A. (2001). Comorbid ADHD and learning disabilities: Diagnosis, special education, and intervention. In D. P. Hallahan & B. K. Keogh (Eds.), *Research and global perspectives in learning disabilities: Essays in honor of William M. Cruickshank* (pp. 43–63). Mahwah, NJ: Lawrence Erlbaum.

Kourea, L., Cartledge, G., & Musti-Rao, S. (2007). Improving the reading skills of urban elementary students through total class peer tutoring. *Remedial and Special Education, 28*, 95–107.

Kunsch, C. A., Jitendra, A. K., & Sood, S. (2007). The effects of peer-mediated instruction in mathematics for students with learning problems: A research synthesis. *Learning Disabilities Research & Practice, 22*, 1–12.

Lasley II, T. J., Matczynski, T. J., & Rowley, J. B. (2002). *Instructional models: Strategies for teaching in a diverse society*. Belmont, CA: Wadsworth/Thomas Learning.

Leinhardt, G., Seewald, A., & Zigmond, N. (1982). Sex and race differences in learning disabilities classrooms. *Journal of Educational Psychology, 74*, 835–845.

Levin, J. R. (1993). Mnemonic strategies and classroom learning: A twenty year report card. *Elementary School Journal, 27*, 301–321.

Lewis, B. A. (1992). Pedigree analysis of children with phonology disorders. *Journal of Learning Disabilities, 25*, 586–597.

Lewis, B. A., & Thompson, L. A. (1992). A study of development of speech and language disorders in twins. *Journal of Speech and Hearing Research, 35*, 1086–1094.

Lindstrom, L. E., & Benz, M. R. (2002). Phases of career development: Case studies of young women with learning disabilities. *Exceptional Children, 69*, 67–83.

Lloyd, J. W., Hallahan, D. P., Kauffman, J. M., & Keller, C. E. (1998). Academic problems. In G. Stoner, M. R. Shinn, & H. M. Walker (Eds.), *Intervention for achievement and behavior problems* (pp. 201–239). Silver Spring, MD: National Association of School Psychologists.

Maag, J. W., & Reid, R. (2006). Depression among students with learning disabilities: Assessing the risk. *Journal of Learning Disabilities, 39*, 3–10.

MacMillan, D. L., Gresham, F. M., & Bocian, K. M. (1998). Discrepancy between definitions of learning disabilities and school practices: An empirical investigation. *Journal of Learning Disabilities, 31*, 314–326.

MacMillan, D. L., & Siperstein, G. N. (2002). Learning disabilities as operationally defined by schools. In R. Bradley, L. Danielson, & D. P. Hallahan (Eds.), *Identification of learning disabilities: Research to practice* (pp. 287–333). Mahwah, NJ: Lawrence Erlbaum.

Maheady, L., Harper, G. F., & Mallette, B. (2003, Spring). Classwide peer tutoring. *Current Practice Alerts*. Retrieved July 26, 2007 from http://www.teachingld.org/pdf/PeerTutoring_rev1.pdf

Margalit, M. (2006). Loneliness, the salutogenic paradigm and learning disabilities: Current research, future directions, and interventional implications. *Thalamus, 24*, 38–48.

Mastropieri, M. A., & Scruggs, T. E. (1998). Constructing more meaningful relationships in the classroom: Mnemonic research into practice. *Learning Disabilities Research & Practice, 13*, 138–145.

Mastropieri, M. A., Scruggs, T. E., & Whedon, T. B. (1997). Using mnemonic strategies to teach information about U.S. Presidents: A classroom-based investigation. *Learning Disability Quarterly, 20*, 13–21.

Mastropieri, M. A., Sweda, J., & Scruggs, T. E. (2000). Putting mnemonics to work in an inclusive classroom. *Learning Disabilities Research & Practice, 15*, 69–74.

Mathes, M. Y., & Bender, W. N. (1997). The effects of self-monitoring on children with attention-deficit/hyperactivity disorder. *Remedial and Special Education, 18*, 121–128.

McCrory, E., Frith, U., Brunswick, N., & Price, C. (2000). Abnormal functional activation during a simple word repetition task: A PET study of adult dyslexics. *Journal of Cognitive Neuro-science, 12*, 753–762.

McGrady, H. J., Lerner, J. W., & Boscardin, M. L. (2001). The educational lives of students with learning disabilities. In P. Rodis, A. Garrod, & M. L. Boscardin (Eds.), *Learning disabilities and life stories* (pp. 177–193). Boston: Allyn & Bacon.

McGrath, L. M., Smith, S. D., & Pennington, B. F. (2006). Breakthroughs in the search for dyslexia candidate genes. *Trends in Molecular Medicine, 12*, 333–341.

McKenna, M. C., & Picard, M. C. (2006). Revisiting the role of miscue analysis in effective teaching. *The Reading Teacher, 60*, 378–380.

McMaster, K., & Espin, C. (2007). Technical features of curriculum-based measurement in writing: A review of the literature. *The Journal of Special Education, 41*, 68–84.

Meese, R. L. (2001). *Teaching learners with mild disabilities: Integrating research and practice* (2nd ed.). Stamford, CT: Wadsworth.

Montague, M., & Graves, A. (1992). Teaching narrative composition to students with learning disabilities. In M. Pressley, K. Harris, & J. T. Guthrie (Eds.), *Promoting academic competence and literacy in schools* (pp. 261–276). New York: Academic Press.

Morgan, P. L., & Fuchs, D. (2007). Is there a bidirectional relationship between children's reading skills and reading motivation? *Exceptional Children, 73*, 165–183.

Murawski, W. W., & Swanson, H. L. (2001). A meta-analysis of co-teaching research: Where are the data? *Remedial and Special Education, 22*, 258–267.

National Center for Children in Poverty. (2006, December). *Who Are America's Poor Children? The Official Story*. Retrieved July 19, 2007 from http://www.nccp.org/publications/pub_684.html

National Joint Committee on Learning Disabilities. (1989, September 18). *Modifications to the NJCLD definition of learning disabilities*. Letter from NJCLD to member organizations. Washington, DC: Author.

National Joint Committee on Learning Disabilities. (2006). *Learning Disabilities and Young Children: Identification and Intervention*. Retrieved July 27, 2007 http://www.ldonline.org/article/11511

Olson, R., Wise, B., Conners, F., Rack, J., & Fulker, D. (1989). Specific deficits in component reading and language skills: Genetic and environmental influences. *Journal of Learning Disabilities, 22*, 339–348.

Paulesu, E., Demonet, J. F., Fazio, F., McCrory, E., Chanonine, V., Brunswick, N., et al. (2001). Dyslexia: Cultural diversity and biological unity. *Science, 291*, 2165–2167.

Pelkey, L. (2001). In the LD bubble. In P. Rodis, A. Garrod, & M. L. Boscardin (Eds.), *Learning disabilities and life stories* (pp. 17–28). Boston: Allyn & Bacon.

Pennington, B. F. (1990). Annotation: The genetics of dyslexia. *Journal of Child Psychology and Child Psychiatry, 31*, 193–201.

Peterson (2003). *Colleges for students with learning disabilities or ADD (Peterson's colleges with programs for students with learning disabilities or attention deficit disorders)* (7th ed.). Princeton, NJ: Peterson's.

Petrill, S. A., Deater-Deckard, K., Thompson, L. A., DeThorne, L. S., & Schatschneider, C. (2006). Reading skills in early readers: Genetic and shared environmental influences. *Journal of Learning Disabilities, 39*, 48–55.

Phillips, S. E. (1994). High-stakes testing accommodations: Validity versus disabled rights. *Applied Measurement in Education, 7*, 93–120.

Plomin, R., & Kovas, Y. (2005). Generalist genes and learning disabilities. *Psychological Bulletin, 131*, 592–617.

Pullen, P. C. (2002, October 1). Expert connection: Phonological awareness. *TeachingLD.org*. Retrieved September 24, 2007, from http://TeachingLD.org/expert_connection/phonological.html

Pugh, K. R. Mencl, W. E., Shaywitz, B. A., Shaywitz, S. E., Fulbright, R. K., Constable, R. T., et al. (2000). Task-specific differences in functional connections within the posterior cortex. *Psychological Science, 11*, 51–56.

Queen, O. (2001). Blake Academy and the Green Arrow. In P. Rodis, A. Garrod, & M. L. Boscardin (Eds.), *Learning disabilities and life stories* (pp. 3–16). Boston: Allyn & Bacon.

Raskind, M. H., Goldberg, R. J., Higgins, E. L., & Herman, K. L. (1999). Patterns of change and predictors of success in individuals with learning disabilities: Results from a twenty-year longitudinal study. *Learning Disabilities Research & Practice, 14,* 35–49.

Raskind, W. H. (2001). Current understanding of the genetic basis of reading and spelling disability. *Learning Disability Quarterly, 24,* 141–157.

Reiff, H. B., Gerber, P. J., & Ginsberg, R. (1997). *Exceeding expectations: Successful adults with learning disabilities.* Austin, TX: Pro-Ed.

Reynolds, C. A., Hewitt, J. K., Erickson, M. T., Silberg, J. L., Rutter, M., Simonoff, E., et al. (1996). The genetics of children's oral reading performance. *Journal of Child Psychology and Psychiatry, 37,* 425–434.

Riccomini, P. J. (2005). Identification and remediation of systematic error patterns in subtraction. *Learning Disability Quarterly, 28,* 233–242.

Richards, T. L. (2001). Functional magnetic resonance imaging and spectroscopic imaging of the brain: Application of fMRI and fMRS to reading disabilities and education. *Learning Disability Quarterly, 24,* 189–203.

Rooney, K. J. (1998). *Independent strategies for efficient study.* Richmond, VA: Educational Enterprises.

Rourke, B. P. (1995). *Syndrome of nonverbal learning disabilities: Neurodevelopmental manifestations.* New York: Guilford Press.

Rumsey, J. M., Horwitz, B., Donohue, B. C., Nace, K. L., Maisog, J. M., & Andreason, P. (1999). A functional lesion in developmental dyslexia: Left angular gyral blood flow predicts severity. *Brain and Language, 70,* 187–204.

Salvia, J., & Ysseldyke, J. E.(2004). *Assessment* (9th ed.). Boston: Houghton Mifflin.

Schulte-Korne, G., Deimel, W., Muller, K., Gutenbrunner, C., & Remschmidt, H. (1996). Familial aggregation of spelling disability. *Journal of Child Psychology and Psychiatry, 37,* 817–822.

Schulte-Korne, G., Ziegler, A., Deimel, W., Schumaker, J., Plume, E., Bachmann, C., et al. (2006). Interrelationship and familiality of dyslexia related quantitative measures. *Annals of Human Genetics, 71,* 160–175.

Shalev, R. S. (2004). Developmental dyscalculia. *Journal of Child Neurology, 19,* 765–771.

Shaywitz, B. A., Skudlarski, P., Holahan, J. M., Marchione, K. E., Constable, R. T., Fulbright, R. K., et al. (2007). Age-related changes in reading systems of dyslexic children. *Annals of Neurology, 61,* 363–370.

Shaywitz, S. E., Shaywitz, B. A., Fletcher, J. M., & Escobar, M. D. (1990). Prevalence of reading disability in boys and girls: Results of the Connecticut Longitudinal Study. *Journal of the American Medical Association, 264,* 998–1002.

Shaywitz, S. E., Shaywitz, B. A., Pugh, K. R., Fulbright, R. K., Constable, R. T., Mencl, W. E., et al. (1998). Functional disruption in the organization of the brain for reading in dyslexia. *Neurobiology, 95,* 2636–2641.

Simos, P. G., Fletcher, J. M., Sarkari, S., Billingsley-Marshall, R., Denton, C. A., & Papanicolaou, A. C. (2007). *Journal of Learning Disabilities, 40,* 37–48.

Sireci, S. G., Li, S., & Scarpati, S. (2003). The effects of test accommodations on test performance: A review of the literature. *Center for Educational Assessment Research Report No. 485.* Retrieved June 17, 2007 from http://www.education.umn.edu/NCEO/Onlinepubs/TestaccommLitReview.PDF

Smith, S. D. (2007). Genes, language development, and language disorders. *Mental Retardation and Developmental Disabilities Research Reviews, 13,* 96–105.

Spekman, N. J., Goldberg, R. J., & Herman, K. L. (1992). Learning disabled children grow up: A search for factors related to success in the young adult years. *Learning Disabilities Research & Practice, 7,* 161–170.

Swanson, H. L. (2005). Memory and learning disabilities: Historical perspective, current status, and future trends. *Thalamus, 23,* 30–44.

Swanson, H. L., & Jerman, O. (2006). Math disabilities: A selective meta-analysis of the literature. *Review of Educational Research, 76,* 249–274.

Tarver, S. G. (1999, Summer). Direct instruction. *Current Practice Alerts, 2.* Retrieved July 26, 2007 from http://www.teachingld.org/pdf/Alert2.pdf

Torgesen, J. K., Wagner, R. K., & Rashotte, C. (1999). *Test of Word Reading Efficiency.* Pro-Ed Publishing.

Troia, G. A. (2004, Summer). A focus on phonological awareness acquisition and intervention. *Current Practice Alerts, 10.* Retrieved September 24, 2007, from http://www.dldcec.org/pdf/alert10.pdf

U.S. Department of Education. (2005). *Twenty-seventh annual report to Congress on the implementation of the Individuals with Disabilities Education Act.* Washington, DC: Author.

Vaughn, S., Elbaum, B., & Boardman, A. G. (2001). The social functioning of students with learning disabilities: Implications for inclusion. *Exceptionality, 9,* 47–65.

Vaughn, S., & Fuchs, L. S. (2003). Redefining learning disabilities as inadequate response to instruction: The promise and potential problems. *Learning Disabilities Research & Practice, 18,* 137–146.

Wax, I. F., & Kravets, M. (2003). *K & W guide to colleges for students with learning disabilities or attention deficit disorder* (7th ed.). New York: Princeton Review.

Werner, H., & Strauss, A. A. (1941). Pathology of figure-background relation in the child. *Journal of Abnormal and Social Psychology, 36,* 236–248.

Willows, D. M. (1998). Visual processes in learning disabilities. In H. L. Swanson (Ed.), *Handbook of assessment of learning disabilities: Theory, research, and practice* (pp. 147–175). Austin, TX: Pro-Ed.

Witte, R. H., Philips, L., & Kakela, M. (1998). Job satisfaction of college graduates with learning disabilities. *Journal of Learning Disabilities, 31,* 259–265.

Woodcock, R. W., McGrew, K. S., & Mather, N. (2001). *Woodcock-Johnson III Tests of Cognitive Achievement.* Itasca, IL: Riverside Publishing.

Woodward, J., & Baxter, J. (1997). The effects of an innovative approach to mathematics on academically low-achieving students in inclusive settings. *Exceptional Children, 63,* 373–388.

Worling, D. E., Humphries, T., & Tannock, R. (1999). Spatial and emotional aspects of language inferencing in nonverbal learning disabilities. *Brain and Language, 70,* 220–239.

CHAPTER 7

Abikoff, H. (2002). Matching patients to treatments. In P. Jensen & J. Cooper (Eds.), *Attention deficit hyperactivity disorder: State of the science, best practices* (pp. 15: 1–14). Kingston, NJ: Civic Research Institute.

American Psychiatric Association. (2000). *Diagnostic and statistical manual of mental disorders* (4th ed., rev.). Washington, DC: Author.

Barbaresi, W. J., Katusic, S. K., Colligan, R. C., Weaver, A. L., Leibson, C. L., & Jacobsen, S. J. (2006). Long-term stimulant medication treatment of ADHD: Results from a population based study. *Journal of Developmental and Behavioral Pediatrics, 27,* 1–10.

Barkley, R. A. (1997). Behavioral inhibition, sustained attention, and executive functions: Constructing a unifying theory of ADHD. *Psychological Bulletin, 121,* 65–94.

Barkley, R. A. (2000a). *A new look at ADHD: Inhibition, time, and self-control* [video manual]. Baltimore: The Guilford Press.

Barkley, R. A. (2000b). *Taking charge of ADHD: The complete, authoritative guide for parents* (rev. ed.). New York: The Guilford Press.

Barkley, R. A. (2006a). Associated cognitive, developmental, and health problems. In R. A. Barkley (Ed.), *Attention-deficit hyperactivity disorder: A handbook for diagnosis and treatment* (3rd ed., pp. 122–183). New York: The Guilford Press.

Barkley, R. A. (2006b). Etiologies. In R. A. Barkley (Ed.), *Attention-deficit hyperactivity disorder: A handbook for diagnosis and treatment* (3rd ed., pp. 219–247). New York: The Guilford Press.

Barkley, R. A. (2006c). History. In R. A. Barkley (Ed.), *Attention-deficit hyperactivity disorder: A handbook for diagnosis and treatment* (3rd ed., pp. 3–75). New York: The Guilford Press.

Barkley, R. A. (2006d). Primary symptoms, diagnostic criteria, prevalence, and gender differences. In R. A. Barkley (Ed.), *Attention-deficit hyperactivity disorder: A handbook for diagnosis and treatment* (3rd ed., pp. 76–121). New York: The Guilford Press.

Barkley, R. A. (2006e). A theory of ADHD. In R. A. Barkley (Ed.), *Attention-deficit hyperactivity disorder: A handbook for diagnosis and treatment* (3rd ed., pp. 297–334). New York: The Guilford Press.

Barkley, R. A., & Edwards, G. (2006). Diagnostic interview, behavior rating scales, and medical examination. In R. A. Barkley (Ed.), *Attention-deficit hyperactivity disorder: A handbook for diagnosis and treatment* (3rd ed., pp. 337–368). New York: The Guilford Press.

Barkley, R. A., & Murphy, K. R. (1998). *Attention-deficit hyperactivity disorder: A clinical workbook* (2nd ed.). New York: Guilford Press.

Barkley, R. A., & Murphy, K. R. (2007). Comorbid psychiatric disorders in adults with ADHD. *The ADHD Report, 15*(2), 1–7.

Bateman, B., Warner, J. O., Hutchinson, E., Dean, T., Rowlandson, P., Gant, C., et al. (2004). The effects of a double blind, placebo controlled, artificial food colourings and benzoate preservative challenge on hyperactivity in a general population sample of preschool children. *Archives of Disease in Childhood, 89,* 506–511.

Baumgaertel, A., Wolraich, M. L., & Dietrich, M. (1995). Comparison of diagnostic criteria for attention deficit disorders in a German elementary school sample. *Journal of the Academy of Child and Adolescent Psychiatry, 34,* 629–638.

Bener, A., Al Qahtani, R., & Abdelaal, I. (2007). The prevalence of ADHD among primary school children in an Arabian society. *Journal of Attention Disorders, 10,* 77–82.

Biederman, J., Faraone, S. V., Mick, E., Spencer, T., Wilens, T., Kiely, K., et al. (1995). High risk for attention deficit hyperactivity disorder among children of parents with childhood onset of the disorder: A pilot study. *American Journal of Psychiatry, 152,* 431–435.

Biederman, J., Wilens, T., Mick, E., Faraone, S. V., & Spencer, T., (1998). Does attention-deficit hyperactivity disorder impact the developmental course of drug and alcohol abuse and dependence? *Biological Psychiatry, 44,* 269–273.

Biederman, J., Wilens, T., Mick, E., Spencer, T., & Faraone, S. V. (1999). Pharmacotherapy of attention-deficit/hyperactivity disorder reduces risk for substance abuse disorder. *Pediatrics, 104,* 20.

Birch, H. G. (1964). *Brain damage in children: The biological and social aspects.* Baltimore: Williams & Wilkins.

Castellanos, F. X. (1997). Toward a pathophysiology of attention-deficit/hyperactivity disorder. *Clinical Pediatrics, 36,* 381–393.

Castle, L., Aubert, R. E., Verbrugge, R. R., Khalid, M., & Epstein, R. S. (2007). Trends in medication treatment for ADHD. *Journal of Attention Disorders, 10,* 335–342.

Chilcoat, H. D., & Breslau, N. (1999). Pathways from ADHD to early drug use. *Journal of the American Academy of Child and Adolescent Psychiatry, 38,* 1347–1354.

Christakis, D. A., Zimmerman, F. J., DiGiuseppe, D. L., & McCarty, C. A. (2004). Early television exposure and subsequent attentional problems in children. *Pediatrics, 113,* 708–713.

Cobb, B., Sample, P. L., Alwell, M., & Johns, N. R. (2006). Cognitive-behavioral interventions, dropout, and youth with disabilities. *Remedial and Special Education, 27,* 259–275.

Conners, C. K. (2001). *Conners' Rating Scales-Revised.* North Tonawanda, NY: Multi-Health Systems.

Conners, C. K., Erhardt, D., & Sparrow, E. (2000). *Conners' Adult ADHD Rating Scales.* North Tonawanda, NY: Multi-Health Systems.

Connor, D. F. (2006). Simulants. In R. A. Barkley (Ed.), *Attention-deficit hyperactivity disorder: A handbook for diagnosis and treatment* (3rd ed., pp. 608–647). New York: The Guilford Press.

Cooper, P. (1999). ADHD and effective learning: Principles and practical approaches. In P. Cooper & K. Bilton (Eds.), *ADHD: Research, practice and opinion* (pp. 138–157). London: Whurr.

Corkum, P., Andreou, P., Schachar, R., Tannock, R., & Cunningham, C. (2007). The telephone interview probe: A novel measure of treatment response in children with attention deficit hyperactivity disorder. *Educational and Psychological Measurement, 67,* 169–185.

Cox, D. J., Merkel, R. L., Kovatchev, B., & Seward, R. (2000). Effect of stimulant medication on driving performance of young adults with attention-deficit hyperactivity disorder. *Journal of Nervous and Mental Disease, 188,* 230–234.

Cruickshank, W. M., Bentzen, F. A., Ratzeburg, F. H., & Tannhauser, M. T. (1961). *A teaching method of brain-injured and hyperactive children.* Syracuse, NY: Syracuse University Press.

Cruickshank, W. M., Bice, H. V., & Wallen, N. E. (1957). *Perception and cerebral palsy.* Syracuse, NY: Syracuse University Press.

Davies, S., & Witte, R. (2000). Self-management and peer-monitoring within a group contingency to decrease uncontrolled verbalizations of children with attention-deficit/hyperactivity disorder. *Psychology in the Schools, 37,* 135–147.

DeRamirez, R. D., & Shapiro, E. S. (2005). Effects of student ethnicity on judgments of ADHD symptoms among Hispanic and White teachers. *School Psychology Quarterly, 20,* 268–287.

Diagnosis and Treatment of Attention Deficit Hyperactivity Disorder. NIH Consensus Statement Online 1998 Nov 16–18; *16*(2), 1–37, retrieved September 25, 2007 from http://consensus.nih.gov/1998/1998AttentionDeficitHyperactivityDisorder110html.htm

DuPaul, G., & Stoner, G. (2003). *ADHD in schools: Assessment and practice.* New York: Guilford.

DuPaul, G. J., Barkley, R. A., & Connor, D. F. (1998). Stimulants. In R. A. Barkley (Ed.), *Attention-deficit hyperactivity disorder: A handbook for diagnosis and treatment* (pp. 510–551). New York: Guilford Press.

DuPaul, G. J., & Eckert, T. L. (1997). The effects of school-based interventions for attention deficit hyperactivity disorder: A meta-analysis. *School Psychology Review, 26,* 5–27.

DuPaul, G. J., Eckert, T. L., & McGoey, K. E. (1997). Interventions for students with attention-deficit/hyperactivity disorder: One size does not fit all. *School Psychology Review, 26,* 369–381.

DuPaul, G. J., & Ervin, R. A. (1996). Functional assessment of behaviors related to attention-deficit hyperactivity disorder: Linking assessment to intervention design. *Behavior Therapy, 27,* 601–622.

DuPaul, G. J., Power, D. T. J., Anastopolos, A. D., & Reid, R. (1998). *ADHD Rating Scale-IV: Checklists, norms, and clinical interpretations.* New York: Guilford Press.

Erhardt, D., & Hinshaw, S. P. (1994). Initial sociometric impressions of attention-deficit hyperactivity disorder and comparison boys: Predictions from social behaviors and from nonbehavioral variables. *Journal of Consulting and Clinical Psychology, 62,* 833–842.

Ervin, R. A., DuPaul, G. J., Kern, L., & Friman, P. C. (1998). Classroom-based functional and adjunctive assessments: Proactive approaches to intervention selection for adolescents with attention deficit hyperactivity disorder. *Journal of Applied Behavior Analysis, 31,* 65–78.

Esser, G., Schmidt, M. H., & Woerner, W. (1990). Epidemiology and course of psychiatric disorders in school-age children—Results of a longitudinal study. *Journal of Child Psychology and Psychiatry, 31,* 243–263.

Evans, S. W., Pelham, W. E., Smith, B. H., Bukstein, O., Gnagy, E. M., Greiner, A. R., et al. (2001). Dose-response effects of methylphenidate on ecologically valid measures of academic performance and classroom behavior in adolescents with ADHD. *Experimental and Clinical Pharmacology, 9,* 163–175.

Fabiano, G. A., Pelham, W. E., Gnagy, E. M., Burrows-MacLean, L., Coles, E. K., Chacko. A., et al. (2007). The single and combined effects of multiple intensities of behavior modification and methylphenidate for children with attention deficit hyperactivity disorder in a classroom setting. *School Psychology Review, 36,* 195–216.

Faraone, S. V., & Doyle, A. E. (2001). The nature and heritability of attention-deficit/hyperactivity disorder. *Child and Adolescent Psychiatric Clinics of North America, 10,* 299–316.

Feingold, B. (1975). *Why your child is hyperactive.* New York: Random House.

Fergusson, D. M., Horwood, L. J., & Lynskey, M. T. (1993). Prevalence and comorbidity of DSM-III-R diagnoses in a birth cohort of 15 year olds. *Journal of the American Academy of Child and Adolescent Psychiatry, 32,* 1127–1134.

Fischer, M., Barkley, R. A., Smallish, L., & Fletcher, K. (2007). Hyperactive children as young adults: Driving abilities, safe driving behavior, and adverse driving outcomes. *Accident Analysis and Prevention, 39,* 94–105.

Forness, S. R., Kavale, K. A. (2002). Impact of ADHD on school systems. In P. Jensen & J. R. Cooper (Eds.), *Attention deficit hyperactivity disorder: State of the science; Best practices* (pp. 1–20). Kingston, NJ: Civic Research Institute.

Forness, S. R., Kavale, K. A., & Crenshaw, T. M. (1999). Stimulant medication revisited: Effective treatment of children with ADHD. *Journal of Emotional and Behavioral Problems, 7,* 230–235.

Frazier, T. W., Youngstrom, E. A., Glutting, J. J., & Watkins, M. W. (2007). ADHD and achievement: Meta-analysis of the child, adolescent, and adult literatures and a concomitant study with college students. *Journal of Learning Disabilities, 40,* 49–65.

Goldstein, K. (1936). The modification of behavior consequent to cerebral lesions. *Psychiatric Quarterly, 10,* 586–610.

Goldstein, K. (1939). *The organism.* New York: American Book Co.

Graetz, B. W., Sawyer, M. G., Hazell, P. L., Arney, F., & Baghurst, P. (2001). Validity of *DSM-IV* ADHD subtypes in a nationally representative sample of Australian children and adolescents. *Journal of the American Academy of Child and Adolescent Psychiatry, 40,* 1410–1417.

Hallahan, D. P., & Cottone, E. A. (1997). Attention deficit hyperactivity disorder. In T. E. Scruggs & M. A. Mastropieri (Eds.), *Advances in learning and behavioral disabilities, Vol. 11* (pp. 27–67). Greenwich, CT: JAI Press.

Hallowell, E. M., & Ratey, J. J. (2006). *Delivered from distraction: Getting the most out of life with attention deficit disorder.* New York: Ballentine Books.

Harris, K. R., Friedlander, B. D., Saddler, B., Frizzelle, R., & Graham, S. (2005). Self-monitoring of attention versus self-monitoring of academic performance: Effects among students with ADHD in the general education classroom. *The Journal of Special Education, 39,* 145–156.

Hoffmann, H. (1865). Die Geschichte vom Zappel-Philipp [The Story of Fidgety Philipp]. In *Der Struwwelpeter* [Shaggy Peter]. Germany: Pestalozzi-Verlag.

Horner, R. H., & Carr, E. G. (1997). Behavioral support for students with severe disabilities: Functional assessment and comprehensive intervention. *The Journal of Special Education, 31,* 1–11.

Hoza, B. (2007). Peer functioning in children with ADHD. *Journal of Pediatric Psychology, 32,* 655–663.

Jensen, P. S., Arnold, L. E., Swanson, J. M., Vitiello, B., Abikoff, H. B., Greenhill, L. L., et al. (2007). 3-year follow-up of the NIMH MTA Study. *Journal of the American Academy of Child and Adolescent Psychiatry, 46,* 989–1002.

Kanbayashi, Y., Nakata, Y., Fujii, K., Kita, M., & Wada, K. (1994). ADHD-related behavior among non-referred children: Parents' ratings of DSM-III-R symptoms. *Child Psychiatry and Human Development, 25* (1), 13–29.

Kavale, K. A., & Forness, S. R. (1983). Hyperactivity and diet treatment: A meta-analysis of the Feingold hypothesis. *Journal of Learning Disabilities, 16,* 324–330.

Kern, L., DuPaul, G. J., Volpe, R. J., Sokol, N. G., Lutz, G., Arbolino, L. A., et al. (2007). Multisetting assessment-based intervention for young children at risk for attention deficit hyperactivity disorder: Initial effects of academic and behavioral functioning. *School Psychology Review, 36,* 237–255.

Kessler, R. C., Adler, L., Barkley, R. A., Biederman, J., Conners, C. K., Demler, O., et al. (2006). The prevalence and correlates of adult ADHD in the United States: Results from the National Comorbidity Survey Replication. *American Journal of Psychiatry, 163,* 716–723.

Kohn, A. (1993). *Punished by rewards: The trouble with gold stars, incentive plans, A's, praise, and other bribes.* Boston: Houghton Mifflin.

Kroes, M., Kalff, A. C., Kessels, A. G. H., Steyaert, J., Feron, F. J. M., van Someren, A. J. W. G. M., et al. (2001). Child psychiatric diagnoses in a population of Dutch schoolchildren aged 6 to 8 years. *Journal of the American Academy of Child and Adolescent Psychiatry, 40,* 1401–1409.

Lambert, N. M., & Hartsough, C. S. (1998). Prospective study of tobacco smoking and substance dependencies among samples of ADHD and non-ADHD participants. *Journal of Learning Disabilities, 31,* 533–544.

Landau, S., Milich, R., & Diener, M. B. (1998). Peer relations of children with attention-deficit hyperactivity disorder. *Reading and Writing Quarterly: Overcoming Learning Difficulties, 14,* 83–105.

Lawrence, V., Houghton, S., Tannock, R., Douglas, G., Durkin, K., & Whiting, K. (2002). ADHD outside the laboratory: Boys' executive function performance on tasks in videogame play and on a visit to the zoo. *Journal of Abnormal Child Psychology, 30,* 447–462.

Leung, P. W. L., Luk, S. L., Ho, T. P., Taylor, E., Mak, F. L., & Bacon-Shone, J. (1996). The diagnosis and prevalence of hyperactivity in Chinese schoolboys. *British Journal of Psychiatry, 168,* 486–496.

Levy, F., & Hay, D. A. (2001). *Attention, genes, and attention-deficit hyperactivity disorder.* Philadelphia, PA: Psychology Press.

Levy, F., Barr, C., & Sunohara, G. (1998). Directions of aetiologic research on attention deficit hyperactivity disorder. *Australian and New Zealand Journal of Psychiatry, 32,* 97–103.

Lloyd, J. W., Hallahan, D. P., Kauffman, J. M., & Keller, C. E. (1998). Academic problems. In R. J. Morris & T. R. Kratochwill (Eds.), *The practice of child therapy* (pp. 167–198). Boston: Allyn & Bacon.

Lou, H. C., Henriksen, L., & Bruhn, P. (1984). Focal cerebral hypoperfusion in children with dysphasia and/or attention deficit disorder. *Archives of Neurology, 41,* 825–829.

Lou, H. C., Henriksen, L., Bruhn, P., Borner, H., & Nielsen, J. B. (1989). Striatal dysfunction in attention deficit and hyperkinetic disorder. *Archives of Neurology, 46,* 48–52.

Majewicz-Hefley, A., & Carlson, J. S. (2007). A meta-analysis of combined treatments for children diagnosed with ADHD. *Journal of Attention Disorders, 10,* 239–250.

Marshall, R. M., Hynd, G. W., Handwerk, M. J., & Hall, J. (1997). Academic underachievement in ADHD subtypes. *Journal of Learning Disabilities, 30,* 635–642.

Mayes, S. D., Calhoun, S. L., & Crowell, E. W. (2000). Learning disabilities and ADHD: Overlapping spectrum disorders. *Journal of Learning Disabilities, 33,* 117–124.

Milberger, S., Biederman, J., Faraone, S. V., Guite, J., & Tsuang, M. T. (1997). Pregnancy, delivery and infancy complications and attention deficit hyperactivity disorder: Issues of gene-environment interaction. *Biological Psychiatry, 41,* 65–75.

Molina, B. S. G., Flory, K., Hinshaw, S. P., Greiner, A. R., Arnold, L. E., Swanson, J. M., et al. (2007). Delinquent behavior and emerging substance use in the MTA at 36 months: Prevalence, course, and treatment effects. *Journal of the American Academy of Child and Adolescent Psychiatry, 46,* 1028–1040.

MTA Cooperative Group. (1999). A 14-month randomized clinical trial of treatment strategies for attention-deficit/hyperactivity disorder, *Archives of General Psychiatry, 56,* 1073–1086.

Murphy, K. R., & Barkley, R. A. (2007). Occupational functioning in adults with ADHD. *The ADHD Report, 15*(1), 6–10.

Neuman, R. J., Lobos, E., Reich, W., Henderson, C. A., Sun, L.-W., & Todd, R. D. (2007). Prenatal smoking exposure and dopaminergic genotypes interact to cause a severe ADHD subtype. *Biological Psychiatry, 61,* 1320–1328.

Nigg, J. T. (2006). *What causes ADHD? Understanding what goes wrong and why.* New York: The Guilford Press.

Pasamanick, B., Lilienfeld, A. M., & Rogers, M. E. (1956). Pregnancy experience and the development of behavior disorders in children. *American Journal of Psychiatry, 112,* 613–617.

Pfiffner, L. J., Barkley, R. A., & DuPaul, G. J. (2006). Treatment of ADHD in school settings. In R. A. Barkley (Ed.), *Attention-deficit hyperactivity disorder: A handbook for diagnosis and treatment* (3rd ed., pp. 122–183). New York: The Guilford Press.

Pinel, J. P. J. (2006). *Biopsychology* (5th ed.). Boston: Allyn & Bacon.

Reid, R., Casat, C. D., Norton, H. J., Anastopoulos, A. D., & Temple, E. P. (2001). Using behavior rating scales for ADHD across ethnic groups: The IOWA Conners. *Journal of Emotional & Behavioral Disorders, 9,* 210–218.

Reid, R., & Lienemann, R. O. (2006). Self-regulated strategy development for written expression with students with attention deficit/hyperactivity disorder. *Exceptional Children, 73,* 53–68.

Reid, R., Trout, A. L., & Schartz, M. (2005). Self-regulation interventions for children with attention deficit/hyperactivity disorder. *Exceptional Children, 71,* 361–377.

Richards, T. L., Deffenbacher, J. L., Rosen, L. A., Barkley, R. A., & Rodricks, T. (2007). Driving anger and driving behavior in adults with ADHD. *Journal of Attention Disorders, 10,* 54–64.

Richters, J. E., Arnold, L. E., Abikoff, H., Conners, C. K., Greenhill, L. L., Hechtman, L., et al. (1995). NIMH collaborative multisite multimodal treatment study of children with ADHD: Background and rationale. *Journal of the Academy of Child and Adolescent Psychiatry, 34,* 987–1000.

Rohde, L. A., Biederman, J., Busnello, E., Zimmerman, H., Schmitz, M., Martins, S., et al. (1999). ADHD in a sample of Brazilian adolescents: A study of prevalence, comorbid conditions, and impairments. *Journal of the Academy of Child and Adolescent Psychiatry, 38,* 716–722.

Rowland, A. S., Umbach, D. M., Catoe, K. E., Stallone, L., Long, S., Rabiner, D., et al. (2001). Studying the epidemiology of attention-deficit hyperactivity disorder: Screening method and pilot results. *Canadian Journal of Psychiatry, 46,* 931–940.

Rucklidge, J., Brown, D., Crawford, S, & Kaplan, B. (2007). Attributional styles and psychosocial functioning of adults with ADHD: Practice issues and gender differences. *Journal of Attention Disorders, 10,* 288–298.

Ryser, G., & McConnell, K. (2001). *Diagnostic assessment scale for attention/deficit hyperactivity disorder.* Austin, TX: Pro-Ed.

Schachar, R., Mota, V. L., Logan, G. D., Tannock, R., & Klim, P. (2000). Confirmation of an inhibitory control deficit in attention-deficit/hyperactivity disorder. *Journal of Abnormal Child Psychology, 28,* 227–235.

Schatz, D. B., & Rostain, A. L. (2007). ADHD with comorbid anxiety: A review of the current literature. *Journal of Attention Disorders, 10,* 141–149.

Schaughency, E. A., McGee, R., Raja, S. N., Freehan, M., & Silva, P. (1994). Self-reported inattention, impulsivity, and hyperactivity in ages 15 and 18 years in the general population. *Journal of the Academy of Child and Adolescent Psychiatry, 33,* 173–183.

Schnoes, C., Reid, R., & Marder, C. (2006). ADHD among students receiving special education services: A national survey. *Exceptional Children, 72,* 483–496.

Shapiro, E. S., DuPaul, G. J., & Bradley-Klug, K. L. (1998). Self-management as a strategy to improve the classroom behavior of adolescents with ADHD. *Journal of Learning Disabilities, 31,* 545–555.

Shelton, T. L., Barkley, R. A., Crosswait, C., Moorehouse, M., Fletcher, K., Barrett, M. S., et al. (2000). Multimethod psychoeducational intervention for preschool children with disruptive behavior: Two-year post-treatment follow-up. *Journal of Abnormal Child Psychology, 28,* 253–266.

Semrud-Clikeman, M., Steingard, R. J., Filipek, P., Biederman, J., Bekken, K., & Renshaw, P. F. (2000). Using MRI to examine brain-behavior relationships in males with attention deficit disorder with hyperactivity. *Journal of the American Academy of Child and Adolescent Psychiatry, 39,* 477–484.

Solanto, M. V. (1998). Neuropsychopharmacological mechanisms of stimulant drug action in attention-deficit hyperactivity disorder: A review and integration. *Behavioural Brain Research, 94,* 127–152.

Solanto, M. V. (2002). Dopamine dysfunction in AD/HD: Integrating clinical and basic neuroscience research. *Behavioural Brain Research, 130,* 65–71.

Still, G. F. (1902). Some abnormal psychical conditions in children. *The Lancet, 1,* 1008–1012, 1077–1082, 1153–1168.

Strauss, A. A., & Werner, H. (1942). Disorders of conceptual thinking in the brain-injured child. *Journal of Nervous and Mental Disease, 96,* 153–172.

Szatmari, P. (1992). The epidemiology of attention-deficit/hyperactivity disorder. In G. Weiss (Ed.), *Child and adolescent psychiatry clinics of North America: Attention deficit disorder* (pp. 361–372). Philadelphia: Saunders.

Tankersley, M. (1995). A group-oriented contingency management program: A review of research on the good behavior game and implications for teachers. *Preventing School Failure, 40,* 59–72.

Taylor, R. L. (2006). *Assessment of exceptional children: Educational and psychological procedures* 7th ed.). Boston: Allyn & Bacon.

Tercyak, K., Lerman, C., & Audrain, J. (2002). Association of attention-deficit/hyperactivity disorder symptoms with levels of cigarette smoking in a community sample of adolescents. *Journal of the American Academy of Child and Adolescent Psychiatry, 41,* 799–805.

Tripp, G., & Alsop, B. (2001). Sensitivity to reward delay in children with attention deficit hyperactivity disorder (ADHD). *Journal of Child Psychology and Psychiatry, 42,* 691–698.

U.S. Department of Education. (2005). *Twenty-seventh annual reports to Congress on the implementation of the Individuals with Disabilities Education Act.* Washington, DC: Author.

U. S. Department of Education, Office of Special Education and Rehabilitative Services, Office of Special Education Programs. (2004). *Teaching children with attention deficit hyperactivity disorder: Instructional strategies and practices.* Washington, DC: Author.

Vance, A., Silk, T. J., Rinehart, N. J., Bradshaw, J. L., Bellgrove, M. A., & Cunnington, R. (2007). Right parietal dysfunction in children with attention deficit hyperactivity disorder, combined type: A functional MRI study. *Molecular Psychiatry, 12,* 1–7.

Vaughn, S., Schumm, J. S., & Arguelles, M. E. (1997). The ABCDEs of Co-teaching. *Teaching Exceptional Children, 30* (2), 4–10.

Voeller, K. K. S. (2004). Attention-deficit hyperactivity disorder (ADHD). *Journal of Child Neurology, 19,* 798–814.

Volkow, N. D., Wang, G-J., Newcorn, J., Telang, F., Solanto, M. V., Fowler, J. S., et al. (2007). Depressed dopamine activity in caudate and preliminary evidence of limbic involvement in adults with attention-deficit/hyperactivity disorder. *Archives of General Psychiatry, 64,* 932–940.

Weiss, L. (1992). *Attention deficit disorder in adults.* Lanham, MD: Taylor Publishing Co.

Weiss, M., Hechtman, L., & Weiss, G. (2000). ADHD in parents. *Journal of the American Academy of Child and Adolescent Psychiatry, 39,* 1059–1061.

Werner, H., & Strauss, A. A. (1939). Types of visuo-motor activity in their relation to low and high performance ages. *Proceedings of the American Association on Mental Deficiency, 44,* 163–168.

Werner, H., & Strauss, A. A. (1941). Pathology of figure-background relation in the child. *Journal of Abnormal and Social Psychology, 36,* 236–248.

Weyandt, L. L., & DuPaul, G. (2006). ADHD in college students. *Journal of Attention Disorders, 10,* 9–19.

Whalen, C. K., Henker, B., Ishikawa, S. S., Jamner, L. D., Floro, J. N., Johnston, J. A., et al. (2006). An electronic diary study of contextual triggers and ADHD: Get ready, get set, get mad. *Journal of the American Academy of Child and Adolescent Psychiatry, 45,* 166–174.

Wilens, T. E., & Biederman, J. (1992). Pediatric psychopharmacology: The stimulants. *Pediatric Clinics of North America, 15* (1), 191–222.

Wilens, T. E., Biederman, J., & Spencer, T. J. (2002). Attention deficit/hyperactivity disorder across the lifespan. *Annual Review of Medicine, 53,* 113–131.

Willcutt, E. G., Chhabildas, N., & Pennington, B. F. (2001). Validity of the DSM-IV subtypes of ADHD. *ADHD Report, 9* (1), 2–5.

Willcutt, E. G., Pennington, B. F., Boada, R., Ogline, J. S., Tunick, R. A., Chhabildas, N. A., et al. (2001). A comparison of the cognitive deficits in reading disability and attention-deficit/hyperactivity disorder. *Journal of Abnormal Psychology, 110,* 157–172.

Wolraich, M. L., Wilson, D. B., & White, J. W. (1995). The effect of sugar on behavior or cognition in children: A meta-analysis. *Journal of the American Medical Association, 274,* 1617–1621.

Woodward, L. J., Fergusson, D. M., & Horwood, L. J. (2000). Driving outcomes for young people with attentional difficulties in adolescence. *Journal of the American Academy of Child and Adolescent Psychiatry, 39,* 627–634.

CHAPTER 8

Bandura, A. (1973). *Aggression: A social learning analysis.* Englewood Cliffs, NJ: Prentice-Hall.

Bandura, A. (1986). *Social foundations of thought and action: A social cognitive theory.* Englewood Cliffs, NJ: Prentice-Hall.

Bateman, B. D., & Chard, D. J. (1995). Legal demands and constraints on placement decisions. In J. M. Kauffman, J. W. Lloyd, D. P. Hallahan, & T. A. Astuto (Eds.), *Issues in educational placement: Students with emotional and behavioral disorders* (pp. 285–316). Hillsdale, NJ: Lawrence Erlbaum.

Bateman, B. D., & Linden, M. A. (2006). *Better IEPs: How to develop legally correct and educationally useful programs* (4th ed.). Verona, WI: Attainment.

Blake, C., Wang, W., Cartledge, G., & Gardner, R. (2000). Middle school students with serious emotional disturbances serve as social skills trainers and reinforcers for peers with SED. *Behavioral Disorders, 25,* 280–298.

Bowe, F. G. (2004). *Early childhood special education: Birth to eight* (3rd ed.). Clifton Park, NY: Delmar Learning.

Bower, E. M. (1981). *Early identification of emotionally handicapped children in school* (3rd ed.). Springfield, IL: Charles C. Thomas.

Bower, E. M. (1982). Defining emotional disturbance: Public policy and research. *Psychology in the Schools, 19,* 55–60.

Brigham, F. J., & Kauffman, J. M. (1998). Creating supportive environments for students with emotional or behavioral disorders. *Effective School Practices, 17* (2), 25–35.

Brolin, D. E., & Loyd, R. J. (2004). *Career development and transition services: A functional life-skills approach* (4th ed). Upper Saddle River, NJ: Prentice Hall.

Cheney, D., & Bullis, M. (2004). The school-to-community transition of adolescents with emotional and behavioral disorders. In R. B. Rutherford, M. M. Quinn, & S. R. Mathur (Eds.). *Handbook of research in emotional and behavioral disorders* (pp. 369–384). New York: Guilford.

Coleman, M., & Vaughn, S. (2000). Reading interventions for students with emotional/behavioral disorders. *Behavioral Disorders, 25,* 93–104.

Colvin, G. (2004). *Managing the cycle of acting-out behavior in the classroom.* Eugene, OR: Behavior Associates.

Cooper, P. (2005). Biology and behaviour: The educational relevance of a "biopsychosocial" perspective. In P. Clough, P. Garner, J. T. Pardeck, & F. K. O. Yuen (Eds.), *Handbook of emotional and behavioural difficulties in education* (pp. 91–105). London: Sage.

Costello, E. J., Egger, H., & Angold, A. (2005). 1-year research update review: The epidemiology of child and adolescent psychiatric disorders: I. Methods and public health burden. *Journal of the American Academy of Child and Adolescent Psychiatry, 44,* 972–986.

Costello, E. J., Foley, D., & Angold, A. (2006). 10-year research update review: The epidemiology of child and adolescent psychiatric disorders: II. Developmental epidemiology. *Journal of the American Academy of Child and Adolescent Psychiatry, 45,* 8–25.

Costenbader, V., & Buntaine, R. (1999). Diagnostic discrimination between social maladjustment and emotional disturbance: An empirical study. *Journal of Emotional and Behavioral Disorders, 7,* 1–10.

Coutinho, M. J., Oswald, D. P., Best, A. M., & Forness, S. R. (2002). Gender and socio-demographic factors and the disproportionate identification of minority students as emotionally disturbed. *Behavioral Disorders, 27,* 109–125.

Crockett, J. B., & Kauffman, J. M. (1999). *The least restrictive environment: Its origins and interpretations in special education.* Mahwah, NJ: Lawrence Erlbaum Associates.

Cullinan, D. (2004). Classification and definition of emotional and behavioral disorders. In R. B. Rutherford, M. M. Quinn, & S. R. Mathur (Eds.), *Handbook of research in emotional and behavioral disorders* (pp. 32–53). New York: Guilford.

Cullinan, D. (2006). *Students with emotional and behavior disorders: An introduction for teachers and other helping professionals* (2nd ed.). Upper Saddle River, NJ: Merrill/Prentice-Hall.

DiPerna, J. C. (2006). Academic enablers and student achievement: Implications for assessment and intervention in the schools. *Psychology in the Schools, 43,* 7–17.

DiPerna, J. C., & Elliott, S. N. (2000). *Academic competence evaluation scales.* San Antonio, TX: Psychological Corporation.

Donovan, M. S., & Cross, C. T. (Eds.). (2002). *Minority students in special and gifted education.* Washington, DC: National Academy Press.

Duke, D. L., Griesdorn, J., & Kraft, M. (1998, March). *A school of their own: A status check of Virginia's alternative high schools for at-risk students.* Charlottesville, VA: Thomas Jefferson Center for Educational Design.

Duncan, B. B., Forness, S. R., & Hartsough, C. (1995). Students identified as seriously emotionally disturbed in school-based day treatment: Cognitive, psychiatric, and special education

characteristics. *Behavioral Disorders, 20,* 238–252.

Dunlap, G., Strain, P. S., Fox, L., Carta, J. J., Conroy, M., Smith, B. J., et al. (2006). Prevention and intervention with young children's challenging behavior: Perspectives regarding current knowledge. *Behavioral Disorders, 32,* 29–45.

Edgar, E., & Siegel, S. (1995). Postsecondary scenarios for troubled and troubling youth. In J. M. Kauffman, J. W. Lloyd, D. P. Hallahan, & T. A. Astuto (Eds.), *Issues in educational placement: Students with emotional or behavioral disorders* (pp. 251–283). Hillsdale, NJ: Lawrence Erlbaum.

Epstein, M. H., & Sharma, J. (1997). *Behavioral and Emotional Rating Scale (BERS): A strength-based approach to assessment.* Austin, TX: Pro-Ed.

Falk, K. B., & Wehby, J. H. (2001). The effects of peer-assisted learning strategies on the beginning reading skills of young children with emotional/behavioral disorders. *Behavioral Disorders, 26,* 344–359.

Farmer, E. M. Z., & Farmer, T. W. (1999). The role of schools in outcomes for youth: Implications for children's mental health services research. *Journal of Child and Family Studies, 8,* 377–396.

Farmer, T. W. (2000). Misconceptions of peer rejection and problem behavior: Understanding aggression in students with mild disabilities. *Remedial and Special Education, 21,* 194–208.

Farmer, T. W., Farmer, E. M. Z., & Gut, D. (1999). Implications of social development research for school based intervention for aggressive youth with emotional and behavioral disorders. *Journal of Emotional and Behavioral Disorders, 7,* 130–136.

Farmer, T. W., Quinn, M. M., Hussey, W., & Holahan, T. (2001). The development of disruptive behavioral disorders and correlated constraints: Implications for intervention. *Behavioral Disorders, 26,* 117–130.

Forness, S. R., & Beard, K. Y. (2007). Strengthening the research base in special education: Evidence-based practice and interdisciplinary collaboration. In J. Crockett, M. Gerber, & T. Landrum (Eds.), *Achieving the radical reform of special education* (pp. 169–188). Mahwah, NJ: Lawrence Erlbaum Associates.

Forness, S. R., & Kavale, K. A. (1997). Defining emotional or behavioral disorders in school and related services. In J. W. Lloyd, E. J. Kame'enui, & D. Chard (Eds.), *Issues in educating students with disabilities* (pp. 45–61). Mahwah, NJ: Lawrence Erlbaum Associates.

Forness, S. R., & Kavale, K. A. (2001). Ignoring the odds: Hazards of not adding the new medical model to special education decisions. *Behavioral Disorders, 26,* 269–281.

Forness, S. R., Kavale, K. A., Sweeney, D. P., & Crenshaw, T. M. (1999). The future of research and practice in behavioral disorders: Psychopharmacology and its school implications. *Behavioral Disorders, 24,* 305–318.

Forness, S. R., & Knitzer, J. (1992). A new proposed definition and terminology to replace "serious emotional disturbance" in Individuals with Disabilities Act. *School Psychology Review, 21,* 12–20.

Fox, J., & Davis, C. (2005). Functional behavior assessment in schools: Current research findings and future directions. *Journal of Behavioral Education, 14* (1), 1–4.

Fuchs, D., Fuchs, L. S., Fernstrom, P., & Hohn, M. (1991). Toward a responsible reintegration of behaviorally disordered students. *Behavioral Disorders, 16,* 133–147.

Furlong, M. J., Morrison, G. M., & Jimerson, S. (2004). Externalizing behaviors of aggression and violence and the school context. In R. B. Rutherford, M. M. Quinn, & S. R. Mathur (Eds.), *Handbook of research in emotional and behavioral disorders* (pp. 243–261). New York: Guilford.

Furlong, M. J., Morrison, G. M., & Fisher, E. S. (2005). The influences of the school contexts and processes on violence and disruption in American schools. In P. Clough, P. Garner, J. T. Pardeck, & F. K. O. Yuen (Eds.), *Handbook of emotional and behavioural difficulties in education* (pp. 106–120). London: Sage.

Gargiulo, R., & Kilgo, J. (2005). *Young children with special needs* (2nd ed.). Clifton Park, NY: Thompson.

Godwin, R. (2004, February 2). In my father's footsteps: A thank-you to my big brother. *The Washington Post,* p. C10.

Gresham, F. M., & Kern, L. (2004). Internalizing behavior problems in children and adolescents. In R. B. Rutherford, M. M. Quinn,

& S. R. Mathur (Eds.), *Handbook of research in emotional and behavioral disorders* (pp. 262–281). New York: Guilford.

Gunter, P. L., Denny, R. K., & Venn, M. L. (2000). Modifications and adaptations of curricular materials for students with emotional and behavioral disorders. *Preventing School Failure, 44,* 116–121.

Hallenbeck, B. A., & Kauffman, J. M. (1995). How does observational learning affect the behavior of students with emotional or behavioral disorders? A review of research. *The Journal of Special Education, 29,* 45–71.

Harry, B., & Klingner, J. (2006). *Why are so many minority students in special education? Understanding race & disability in schools.* New York: Teachers College Press.

Harry, B., & Klingner, J. (2007). Discarding the deficit model. *Educational Leadership, 64*(5), 16–21.

Huefner, D. S. (2006). *Getting comfortable with special education law: A framework for working with children with disabilities* (2nd ed.). Norwood, MA: Christopher-Gordon.

Ialongo, N. S., Vaden-Kiernan, N., & Kellam, S. (1998). Early peer-rejection and aggression: Longitudinal relations with adolescent behavior. *Journal of Developmental and Physical Disabilities, 10,* 199–213.

Ishii-Jordan, S. R. (2000). Behavioral interventions used with diverse students. *Behavioral Disorders, 25,* 299–309.

Jolivette, K., Stichter, J. P., & McCormick, K. M. (2002). Making choices—improving behavior—engaging in learning. *Teaching Exceptional Children, 34*(3), 24–30.

Jones, V., Dohrn, E., & Dunn, C. (2004). *Creating effective programs for students with emotional and behavioral disorders.* Boston: Allyn & Bacon.

Jordan, D., Goldberg, P., & Goldberg, M. (1991). *A guidebook for parents of children with emotional or behavioral disorders.* Minneapolis: Pacer Center.

Kaiser, A. P. (Ed.). (2000). Special issue: Assessing and addressing problems in children enrolled in Head Start. *Behavioral Disorders, 26*(1).

Kamps, D. M., Tankersley, M., & Ellis, C. (2000). Social skills interventions for young at-risk students: A 2-year follow-up study. *Behavioral Disorders, 25,* 310–324.

Kaslow, N. J., Morris, M. K., & Rehm, L. P. (1997). Childhood depression. In R. J. Morris & T. R. Kratochwill (Eds.), *The practice of child therapy* (3rd ed., pp. 48–90). Boston: Allyn & Bacon.

Katsiyannis, A., & Archwamety, T. (1999). Academic remediation/achievement and other factors related to recidivism rates among delinquent youths. *Behavioral Disorders, 24,* 93–101.

Kauffman, J. M. (1999). How we prevent the prevention of emotional and behavioral disorders. *Exceptional Children, 65,* 448–468.

Kauffman, J. M. (2004). Foreword for H. M. Walker, E. Ramsey, & F. M. Gresham, *Antisocial behavior in school: Strategies and best practices* (2nd ed.) (pp. xix–xxi). Belmont, CA: Wadsworth.

Kauffman, J. M. (2005). How we prevent the prevention of emotional and behavioural difficulties in education. In P. Clough, P. Garner, J. T. Pardeck, & F. K. O. Yuen (Eds.), *Handbook of emotional and behavioural difficulties in education* (pp. 366–376). London: Sage.

Kauffman, J. M., Bantz, J., & McCullough, J. (2002). Separate and better: A special public school class for students with emotional and behavioral disorders. *Exceptionality, 10*(3), 149–170.

Kauffman, J. M., Brigham, F. J., & Mock, D. R. (2004). Historical to contemporary perspectives on the field of behavioral disorders. In R. B. Rutherford, M. M. Quinn, & S. R. Mathur (Eds.), *Handbook of research in emotional and behavioral disorders* (pp. 15–31). New York: Guilford.

Kauffman, J. M., & Hallenbeck, B. A. (Eds.). (1996). Why we need to preserve specialized placements for students with emotional or behavioral disorders [Special issue]. *Canadian Journal of Special Education, 11*(1).

Kauffman, J. M., & Landrum, T. J. (2006). *Children and youth with emotional and behavioral disorders: A brief history of their education.* Austin, TX: Pro-Ed.

Kauffman, J. M., & Landrum, T. J. (2009a). *Characteristics of emotional and behavioral disorders of children and youth* (9th ed.). Upper Saddle River, NJ: Prentice Hall.

Kauffman, J. M., & Landrum, T. J. (2009b). *Cases in emotional and behavioral disorders of children and youth* (2nd ed.). Upper Saddle River, NJ: Prentice Hall.

Kauffman, J. M., Landrum, T. J., Mock, D. R., Sayeski, B., & Sayeski, K. L. (2005). Diverse knowledge and skills require a diversity of instructional groups: A position statement. *Remedial and Special Education, 26,* 2–6.

Kauffman, J. M., Lloyd, J. W., Baker, J., & Riedel, T. M. (1995). Inclusion of all students with emotional or behavioral disorders? Let's think again. *Phi Delta Kappan, 76,* 542–546.

Kauffman, J. M., Lloyd, J. W., Hallahan, D. P., & Astuto, T. A. (Eds.). (1995). *Issues in educational placement: Students with emotional and behavioral disorders.* Hillsdale, NJ: Lawrence Erlbaum.

Kauffman, J. M., Mock, D. R., & Simpson, R. L. (in press). Problems related to underservice of students with emotional or behavioral disorders. *Behavioral Disorders.*

Kauffman, J. M., Mock, D. R., Tankersley, M., & Landrum, T. J. (2008). Effective service delivery models. In R. J. Morris & N. Mather (Eds.), *Evidence-based interventions for students with learning and behavioral challenges* (pp 359–378). Mahwah, NJ: Lawrence Erlbaum Associates.

Kauffman, J. M., Mostert, M. P., Trent, S. C., & Pullen, P. L. (2006). *Managing classroom behavior: A reflective case-based approach* (4th ed.) Boston: Allyn & Bacon.

Kauffman, J. M., & Pullen, P. L. (1996). Eight myths about special education. *Focus on Exceptional Children, 28*(5), 1–16.

Kavale, K. A., Forness, S. R., & Mostert, M. P. (2005). Defining emotional or behavioral disorders: The quest for affirmation. In P. Clough, P. Garner, J. T. Pardeck, & F. K. O. Yuen (Eds.), *Handbook of emotional and behavioural difficulties in education* (pp. 38–49). London: Sage.

Kazdin, A. E. (1995). *Conduct disorders in childhood and adolescence* (2nd ed.). Newbury Park, CA: Sage.

Kazdin, A. E. (1997). Conduct disorder. In R. J. Morris & T. R. Kratochwill (Eds.), *The practice of child therapy* (3rd ed., pp. 199–270), Boston: Allyn & Bacon.

Keogh, B. K. (2003). *Temperament in the classroom: Understanding individual differences.* Baltimore: Paul H. Brookes.

Kerr, M. M., & Nelson, C. M. (2006). *Strategies for addressing behavior problems in the classroom* (5th ed.). Upper Saddle River, NJ: Merrill/Prentice Hall.

Konopasek, D., & Forness, S. R. (2004). Psychopharmacology in the treatment of emotional and behavioral disorders. In R. B. Rutherford, M. M. Quinn, & S. R. Mathur (Eds.), *Handbook of research in emotional and behavioral disorders* (pp. 352–368). New York: Guilford.

Landrum, T. J. (2000). Assessment for eligibility: Issues in identifying students with emotional or behavioral disorders. *Assessment for Effective Intervention, 26*(1), 41–49.

Landrum, T. J., & Kauffman, J. M. (2003). Emotionally disturbed, education of. In J. W. Guthrie (Ed.), *Encyclopedia of education* (2nd ed., pp. 726–728). New York: Macmillan Reference.

Landrum, T. J., Tankersley, M., & Kauffman, J. M. (2003). What's special about special education for students with emotional and behavioral disorders? *The Journal of Special Education, 37,* 148–156.

Loeber, R., Green, S. M., Lahey, B. B., Christ, M. A. G., & Frick, P. J. (1992). Developmental sequences in age of onset of disruptive child behaviors. *Journal of Child and Family Studies, 1,* 21–41.

Maag, J. W., & Katsiyannis, A. (1998). Challenges facing successful transition for youths with E/BD. *Behavioral Disorders, 23,* 209–221.

Malmgren, K., Edgar, E., & Neel, R. S. (1998). Postschool status of youths with behavioral disorders. *Behavioral Disorders, 23,* 257–263.

Masia, C. L., Klein, R. G., Storch, E. A., & Corda, B. (2001). School-based behavioral treatment for social anxiety disorder in adolescents: Results of a pilot study. *Journal of the American Academy of Child and Adolescent Psychiatry, 40,* 780–786.

Merrell, K. W. (2002). *School social behavior scales* (2nd ed.). Eugene, OR: Assessment-Intervention Resources.

Miller, J. G. (1997). African American males in the criminal justice system. *Phi Delta Kappan, 79,* K1–K12.

Mueller, M. M., Edwards, R. P., & Trahant, D. (2003). Translating multiple assessment techniques into an intervention selection model for classrooms. *Journal of Applied Behavior Analysis, 36,* 563–573.

Nelson, C. M., & Kauffman, J. M. (1977). Educational programming for secondary school age delinquent and maladjusted pupils. *Behavioral Disorders, 2,* 102–113.

Nelson, C. M., Leone, P. E., & Rutherford, R. B., (2004). Youth delinquency: Prevention and intervention. In R. B. Rutherford, M. M. Quinn, & S. R. Mathur (Eds.), *Handbook of research in emotional and behavioral disorders* (pp. 282–301). New York: Guilford.

Noonan, M. J., & McCormick, L. (2006). *Young children with disabilities in natural environments: Methods and procedures.* Baltimore: Paul H. Brookes.

O'Mahony, P. (2005). Juvenile delinquency and emotional and behavioural difficulties in education. In P. Clough, P. Garner, J. T. Pardeck, & F. K. O. Yuen (Eds.), *Handbook of emotional and behavioural difficulties in education* (pp. 142–154). London: Sage.

Oswald, D. P., Coutinho, M. J., Best, A. M., & Singh, N. N. (1999). Ethnic representation in special education: The influence of school-related economic and demographic variables. *The Journal of Special Education, 32,* 194–206.

Patterson, G. R., Reid, J. B., & Dishion, T. J. (1992). *Antisocial boys.* Eugene, OR: Castalia.

Peacock Hill Working Group. (1991). Problems and promises in special education and related services for children and youth with emotional or behavioral disorders. *Behavioral Disorders, 16,* 299–313.

Presley, J. A., & Hughes, C. (2000). Peers as teachers of anger management to high school students with behavioral disorders. *Behavioral Disorders, 25,* 114–130.

Qi, C. H., & Kaiser, A. P. (2003). Behavior problems of preschool children from low-income families: Review of literature. *Topics in Early Childhood Special Education, 23,* 188–216.

Rhode, G., Jensen, W. R., & Reavis, H. K. (1992). *The tough kid book: Practical classroom management strategies.* Longmont, CO: Sopris West.

Rogers-Adkinson, D., & Griffith, P. (Eds.). (1999). *Communication disorders and children with psychiatric and behavioral disorders.* San Diego: Singular.

Sasso, G., Conroy, M., Stichter, J., & Fox, J. (2001). Slowing down the bandwagon: The misapplication of functional behavior assessment for students with emotional and behavioral disorders. *Behavioral Disorders, 26,* 282–296.

Schaffner, L. (2006). *Girls in trouble with the law.* New Brunswick, NJ: Rutgers University Press.

Shaw, D. S., Owens, E. B., Giovannelli, J., & Winslow, E. B. (2001). Infant and toddler pathways leading to early externalizing disorders. *Journal of the American Academy of Child and Adolescent Psychiatry, 40,* 36–43.

Sheras, P. L. (2001). Depression and suicide in adolescence. In C. E. Walker & M. C. Roberts (Eds.), *Handbook of clinical child psychology* (3rd ed., pp. 657–673). New York: Wiley.

Sitlington, P. L., & Clark, G. M. (2006). *Transition education and services for students with disabilities* (4th ed.). Boston: Allyn & Bacon.

Sprague, J., & Walker, H. (2000). Early identification and intervention for youth with antisocial and violent behavior. *Exceptional Children, 66,* 367–379.

Stein, M., & Davis, C. A. (2000). Direct instruction as a positive behavioral support. *Beyond Behavior, 10*(1), 7–12.

Stichter, J. P., Conroy, M. A., & Kauffman, J. M. (2008). *An introduction to students with high-incidence disabilities.* Upper Saddle River, NJ: Merrill-Prentice Hall.

Strain, P. S., McConnell, S. R., Carta, J. J., Fowler, S. A., Neisworth, J. T., & Wolery, M. (1992). Behaviorism in early intervention. *Topics in Early Childhood Special Education, 12*(1), 121–141.

Strain, P. S., & Timm, M. A. (2001). Remediation and prevention of aggression: An evaluation of the Regional Intervention Program over a quarter century. *Behavioral Disorders, 26,* 297–313.

Sugai, G., & Horner, R. H. (Ed.). (1999–2000). Special issue: Functional behavioral assessment. *Exceptionality, 8*(3).

Sutherland, K. S., & Wehby, J. H. (2001). Exploring the relationship between increased opportunities to respond to academic requests and the academic and behavioral outcomes of students with EBD. *Remedial and Special Education, 22,* 113–121.

Talbott, E., & Callahan, K. (1997). Antisocial girls and the development of disruptive behavior disorders. In J. W. Lloyd, E. J. Kame'enui, & D. Chard (Eds.), *Issues in educating students with disabilities* (pp. 305–322). Mahwah, NJ: Lawrence Erlbaum.

Tankersley, M., & Landrum, T. J. (1997). Comorbidity of emotional and behavioral disorders. In J. W. Lloyd, E. J. Kame'enui, & D. Chard (Eds.), *Issues in educating students with disabilities* (pp. 153–173). Mahwah, NJ: Lawrence Erlbaum.

Thomas, J. M., & Guskin, K. A. (2001). Disruptive behavior in young children: What does it mean? *Journal of the American Academy of Child and Adolescent Psychiatry, 40,* 44–51.

Timm, M. A. (1993). The Regional Intervention Program: Family treatment by family members. *Behavioral Disorders, 19,* 34–43.

Tolbin, T., & Sprague, J. (1999). Alternative education programs for at-risk youth: Issues, best practice, and recommendations. *Bulletin of the Oregon School Study Council, 42*(4).

U.S. Department of Education. (2005). *Twenty-seventh annual report to Congress on implementation of the Individuals with Disabilities Education Act.* Washington, DC: Author.

U.S. Department of Health and Human Services. (2001). *Report of the Surgeon General's Conference on Children's Mental Health: A national action agenda.* Washington, DC: Author.

Van Acker, R., Boreson, L., Gable, R. A., & Patterson, T. (2005). Are we on the right course? Lessons learned about current FBA/BIP practices in schools. *Journal of Behavioral Education, 14*(1), 35–56.

Wagner, M., Friend, M., Bursuck, W. D., Kutash, K., Duchnowski, A. J., Sumi, W. C., et al. (2006). Educating students with emotional disturbances: A national perspective on programs and services. *Journal of Emotional and Behavioral Disorders, 14,* 12–30.

Walker, H. M. (1995). *The acting-out child: Coping with classroom disruption.* Longmont, CO: Sopris West.

Walker, H. M., & Bullis, M. (1991). Behavior disorders and the social context of regular class integration: A conceptual dilemma? In J. W. Lloyd, N. N. Singh, & A. C. Repp (Eds.), *The regular education initiative: Alternative perspectives on concepts, issues, and models.* Sycamore, IL: Sycamore Publishing.

Walker, H. M., Forness, S. R., Kauffman, J. M., Epstein, M. H., Gresham, F. M., Nelson, C. M., et al. (1998). Macro-social validation: Referencing outcomes in behavioral disorders to societal issues and problems. *Behavioral Disorders, 24,* 7–18.

Walker, H. M., Kavanagh, K., Stiller, B., Golly, A., Severson, H., & Feil, E. G. (1998). First Step to Success: An early intervention approach for preventing school antisocial behavior. *Journal of Emotional and Behavioral Disorders, 6,* 66–80.

Walker, H. M., Ramsey, E., & Gresham, F. M. (2003–2004a). Heading off disruption: How early intervention can reduce defiant behavior—and win back teaching time. *American Educator, 27*(4), 6–21.

Walker, H. M., Ramsey, E., & Gresham, F. M. (2003–2004b). How disruptive students escalate hostility and disorder—and how teachers can avoid it. *American Educator, 27*(4), 22–27, 47.

Walker, H. M., Ramsey, E., & Gresham, F. M. (2004). *Antisocial behavior in school: Strategies and best practices* (2nd ed.). Pacific Grove, CA: Brooks/Cole.

Walker, H. M., & Severson, H. H. (1990). *Systematic screening for behavior disorders (SSBD): A multiple gating procedure.* Longmont, CO: Sopris West.

Walker, H. M., Severson, H. H., & Feil, E. G. (1994). *The early screening project: A proven child-find process.* Longmont, CO: Sopris West.

Walker, H. M., & Sprague, J. R. (2007). Early, evidence-based intervention with school-based behavior disorders: Key issues, continuing challenges, and promising practices. In J. B. Crockett, M. M. Gerber, & T. J. Landrum (Eds.), *Achieving the radical reform of special education: Essays in honor of James M. Kauffman* (pp. 37–58). Mahwah, NJ: Lawrence Erlbaum Associates.

Walker, H. M., & Stieber, S. (1998). Teacher ratings of social skills as longitudinal predictors of long-term arrest status in a sample of at-risk males. *Behavioral Disorders, 23,* 222–230.

Wehby, J. H., Dodge, K. A., & Valente, E. (1993). School behavior of first grade children identified as at-risk for development of conduct problems. *Behavioral Disorders, 19,* 67–78.

Weinstein, C. E., Palmer, D. R., & Schulte, A. C. (2002*). Learning and study strategies inventory* (2nd ed.). Clearwater, FL: H & H.

Wolf, M. M., Braukmann, C. J., & Ramp, K. A. (1987). Serious delinquent behavior as part of a significantly handicapping condition. *Journal of Applied Behavior Analysis, 20,* 347–359.

CHAPTER 9

American Speech–Language–Hearing Association. (1991, March). Guidelines for speech-language pathologists serving persons with language, socio-communicative, and/or cognitive-communicative impairments. *ASHA, 33,* 21–25.

American Speech–Language–Hearing Association. (1993). Definitions of communication disorders and variations. *ASHA, 35*(Suppl. 10), 40–41.

Anderson, N. B., & Shames, G. H. (2006). *Human communication disorders* (7th ed.). Boston: Allyn & Bacon.

Audet, L. R., & Tankersley, M. (1999). Implications of communication and behavioral disorders for classroom management: Collaborative intervention techniques. In D. Rogers-Adkinson & P. Griffith (Eds.), *Communication disorders and children with psychiatric and behavioral disorders* (pp. 403–440). San Diego: Singular.

Bauman-Waengler, J. (2000). *Articulatory and phonological impairments: A clinical focus.* Boston: Allyn & Bacon.

Bernthal, J. E., & Bankson, N. W. (1998). *Articulation and phonological disorders* (4th ed.). Boston: Allyn & Bacon.

Bernthal, J. E., & Bankson, N. W. (2004). *Articulation and phonological disorders* (5th ed.). Boston: Allyn & Bacon.

Calandrella, A. M., & Wilcox, M. J. (2000). Predicting language outcomes for young prelinguistic children with developmental delay. *Journal of Speech, Language and Hearing Research, 43,* 1061–1071.

Campbell, S. L., Reich, A. R., Klockars, A. J., & McHenry, M. A. (1988). Factors associated with dysphonia in high school cheerleaders. *Journal of Speech and Hearing Disorders, 53,* 175–185.

Cannito, M. P., Yorkston, K. M., & Beukelman, D. R. (Eds.). (1998). *Neuromotor speech disorders: Nature, assessment, and management.* Baltimore: Paul H. Brookes.

Catts, H., Adlof, S., Hogan, T., & Ellis Weismer, S. (2005). Are specific language impairment and dyslexia distinct disorders? *Journal of Speech, Language, and Hearing Research, 48,* 1378–1396.

Catts, H. W., Fey, M. E., Zhang, X., & Tomblin, J. (2001). Estimating the risk of future reading difficulties in kindergarten children: A research-based model and its clinical implications. *Language, Speech, and Hearing Services in Schools, 32,* 38–50.

Choudhury, N., & Benasich, A. A. (2003). A family aggregation study: The influence of family history and other risk factors on language development. *Journal of Speech, Language, and Hearing Research, 46,* 261–272.

Coggins, T., Olswang, L., Olson, H. C., & Timler, G. (2003). On becoming socially competent communicators: The challenge for children with fetal alcohol exposure. In L. Abbeduto (Ed.), *International review of research in mental retardation: Vol. 27. Language and communication in mental retardation* (pp. 121–150). San Diego, CA: Academic Press.

Conture, E. G. (2001). *Stuttering: Its nature, diagnosis, and treatment.* Boston: Allyn & Bacon.

Curlee, R. F., & Siegel, G. M. (Eds.). (1997). *Nature and treatment of stuttering: New directions* (2nd ed.). Boston: Allyn & Bacon.

Curlee, R. F., & Yairi, E. (1997). Early intervention with early childhood stuttering: A critical examination of the data. *American Journal of Speech-Language Pathology, 6,* 8–18.

Donahue, M. L., Hartas, D., & Cole, D. (1999). Research on interactions among oral language and emotional/behavioral disorders. In D. Rogers-Adkinson & P. Griffith (Eds.), *Communication disorders and children with psychiatric and behavioral disorders* (pp. 69–97). San Diego: Singular.

Fey, M. E., Catts, H. W., & Larrivee, L. S. (1995). Preparing preschoolers for academic and social challenges of school. In M. E. Fey, J. Windsor, & S. F. Warren (Eds.), *Language intervention: Preschool through the elementary years* (pp. 3–37). Baltimore: Paul H. Brookes.

Foundas, A. L. (2001). The anatomical basis of language. *Topics in Language Disorders, 21*(3), 1–19.

Goldstein, B., & Iglesias, A. (2004). Language and dialectical variations. In J. E. Bernthal & N. W. Bankson (Eds.), *Articulation and phonological disorders* (5th ed., pp. 348–375). Boston: Allyn & Bacon.

Graham, S., Harris, K. R., MacArthur, C., & Schwartz, S. (1998). Writing instruction. In B. Y. L. Wong (Ed.), *Learning about learning disabilities* (2nd ed., pp. 391–424). San Diego: Academic Press.

Guitar, B. (1998). *Stuttering: An integrated approach to its nature and treatment* (2nd ed.). Baltimore: Lippincott Williams & Wilkins.

Hadley, P. A., Simmerman, A., Long, M., & Luna, M. (2000). Facilitating language development for inner-city children: Experimental evaluation of a collaborative, classroom-based intervention. *Language, Speech, and Hearing in Schools, 31,* 280–295.

Hallahan, D. P., Lloyd, J. W., Kauffman, J. M., Weiss, M., & Martinez, E. (2005). *Introduction to learning disabilities* (3rd ed.). Boston: Allyn & Bacon.

Hammer, C. S., & Weiss, A. L. (2000). African American mothers' views of their infants' language development and language-learning environment. *American Journal of Speech-Language Pathology, 9,* 126–140.

Hart, B., & Risley, T. R. (1995). *Meaningful differences in the everyday experience of young American children.* Baltimore: Paul H. Brookes.

Hodson, B. W., & Edwards, M. L. (!997). *Perspectives in applied phonology.* Gaithersburg, MD: Aspen.

Hulit, L. M., & Howard, M. R. (2006). *Born to talk: An introduction to speech and language development* (4th ed.). Boston: Allyn & Bacon.

Justice, L. M. (2006). *Communication sciences and disorders: An introduction.* Upper Saddle River, NJ: Prentice Hall.

Justice, L. M., & Schuele, C. M. (2004). Phonological awareness: Description, assessment, and intervention. In J. E. Bernthal & N. W. Bankson (Eds.), *Articulation and phonological disorders* (5th ed., pp. 376–411). Boston: Allyn & Bacon.

Kaiser, A. P., Hemmeter, M. L., Ostrosky, M. M., Alpert, C. L., & Hancock, T. B. (1995). The effects of training and individual feedback on parent use of milieu teaching. *Journal of Childhood Communication Disorders, 16,* 39–48.

Kent, R. (2004). Normal aspects of articulation. In J. E. Bernthal & N. W. Bankson (Eds.), *Articulation and phonological disorders* (5th ed., pp. 1–62). Boston: Allyn & Bacon.

Klein, H. B., & Moses, N. (1999). *Intervention planning for adults with communication problems: A guide for clinical practicum and professional practice.* Boston: Allyn & Bacon.

Kohnert, K., Windsor, J., & Yim, D. (2006). Do language-based processing tasks separate children with language impairment from typical bilinguals? *Learning Disabilities Research and Practice, 21,* 19–29.

Koury, L. N. (2007). Service delivery issues in early intervention. In R. Lubinski, L. A. C. Golper, & C. M. Frattali (Eds.), *Professional issues in speech language pathology and audiology* (pp. 349–370). Clifton Park, NY, Thomson Delmar.

Lane, H. B., & Pullen, P. C. (2004). *Phonological awareness assessment and instruction: A sound beginning.* Boston: Allyn & Bacon.

Lazarus, S. S., Thurlow, M. L., Lail, K. E., Eisenbraun, K. D., & Kato, K. (2006). 2005 state policies on assessment participation and accommodations for students with disabilities (NCEO Synthesis Report 64). Minneapolis, MN: University of Minnesota, National Center on Educational Outcomes.

McCabe, P. C., & Marshall, D. J. (2006). Measuring the social competence of preschool children with specific language impairment: Correspondence among informant ratings and behavioral observations. *Topics in Early Childhood Special Education, 26,* 234–246.

McGregor, K. K. (2000). The development and enhancement of narrative skills in a preschool classroom: Towards a solution to clinician-client mismatch. *American Journal of Speech-Language Pathology, 9,* 55–71.

Mercer, C. D., & Pullen, P. C. (2009). *Students with learning disabilities* (7th edition). Upper Saddle River, NJ: Merrill Prentice Hall.

Mullen, R. (2003) National Outcomes Measurement System; (NOMS). *Audiology Online.* Retrieved from: http://www.audiologyonline.com/articles/article_detail.asp?article_id=422

Muter, V., Hulme, C., Snowling, M. J., & Stevenson, J. (2004). Phonemes, rimes, vocabulary and grammatical skills as foundations of early reading development: Evidence from a longitudinal study. *Developmental Psychology, 40,* 665–681.

Nelson, N. W. (1998). *Childhood language disorders in context: Infancy through adolescence* (2nd ed.) Boston: Allyn & Bacon.

Owens, R. E., Jr. (2004). *Language disorders: A functional approach to assessment and intervention* (4th ed.). Boston: Allyn & Bacon.

Owens, R. E., Jr., Evans, D. E., & Haas, B. A. (2000). *Introduction to communication disorders: A life span perspective.* Boston: Allyn & Bacon.

Owens, R. E., Metz, D. E., & Haas, A. (2007). *Introduction to communication disorders: A lifespan perspective.* Boston: Allyn & Bacon.

Plante, E., & Beeson, P. M. (2004). *Communication and communication disorders: A clinical introduction* (2nd ed.). Boston: Allyn & Bacon.

Prizant, B. M. (1999). Early intervention: Young children with communication and emotional/behavioral problems. In D. Rogers-Adkinson & P. Griffith (Eds.), *Communication disorders and children with psychiatric and behavioral disorders* (pp. 295–342). San Diego: Singular.

Raspberry, W. (2001, August 21). Bi-English education: Low-income children might benefit from early immersion in standards. *Charlottesville Daily Progress,* p. A6.

Robinson, R. L., & Crowe, T. A. (2001). Fluency and voice. In D. M. Ruscello (Ed.), *Tests and measurements in speech-language pathology* (pp. 163–183). Boston: Butterworth-Heinemann.

Rogers-Adkinson, D., & Griffith, P. (Eds.). (1999). *Communication disorders and children with psychiatric and behavioral disorders.* San Diego: Singular.

Sawyer, D. J. (2006). Dyslexia: A generation of inquiry. *Topics in Language Disorders, 26,* 95–109.

Silliman, E. R., & Scott, C. M. (2006). Language impairment and reading disability: Connections and complexities. *Learning Disabilities Research and Practice, 21,* 1–7.

Snow, C., Burns, M., & Griffin, P. (1998). Preventing reading difficulties in young children. Washington, DC: National Academy Press.

Snowling, M. J., & Hayiou-Thomas, M. E. (2006). The dyslexia spectrum: Continuities between reading, speech, and language impairments. *Topics in Language Disorders, 26,* 110–126.

Staskowski, M., & Nelson, N. W. (2007). Service delivery issues in educational settings. In R. Lubinski, L. A. C. Golper, & C. M. Frattali (Eds.), *Professional issues in speech language pathology and audiology* (pp. 329–348). Clifton Park, NY, Thomson Delmar.

Staskowski, M., & Nelson, N. W. (2007). Professional issues: From roots to reality. In R. Lubinski, L. A. C. Golper, & C. M. Frattali (Eds.). *Professional issues in speech language pathology and audiology* (pp. 3–45). Clifton Park, NY, Thomson Delmar.

Stothard, S., Snowling, M., Bishop, D., Chipchase, B., & Kaplan, C. (1998). Language impaired preschoolers: A follow-up into adolescence. Journal of Speech, Language and Hearing Research, 41, 407–418.

Throneburg, R. N., Calvert, L. K., Sturm, J. J., Paramboukas, A. A., & Paul, P. J. (2000). A comparison of service delivery models: Effects on curricular vocabulary skills in the school setting. *American Journal of Speech-Language Pathology, 9,* 10–20.

Timler, G. R., Olswang, L. B., & Coggins, T. E. (2005). "Do I know what I need to do?" A social communication intervention for children with complex clinical profiles. *Language, Speech, and Hearing in the Schools, 36,* 73–85.

Vellutino, F. R., Fletcher, J. M., Snowling, M. J., & Scanlon, D. M. (2004). Specific reading disability (dyslexia): What have we learned in the past four decades? *Journal of Child Psychology and Psychiatry, 45,* 2–40.

Vihman, M. M. (2004). Early phonological development. In J. E. Bernthal & N. W. Bankson (Eds.), *Articulation and phonological disorders* (5th ed., pp. 376–411). Boston: Allyn & Bacon.

Vinson, B. (2007). Language *disorders across the lifespan* (2nd ed.). New York: Thornson.

Walker, D., Greenwood, C., Hart, B., & Carta, J. (1994). Prediction of school outcomes based on early language production and socioeconomic factors. Child Development, 65, 606–621.

Warren, S. F., & Abbaduto, L. (1992). The relation of communication and language development to mental retardation. *American Journal on Mental Retardation, 97,* 125–130.

Williams, A. L. (2001). Phonological assessment of child speech. In D. M. Ruscello (Ed.), *Tests and measurements in speech-language pathology* (pp. 31–76). Boston: Butterworth-Heinemann.

Yairi, E. & Ambrose, N. (2004). Stuttering: Recent developments and future directions. *The AHSA Leader, 18,* 4–5, 14–15.

Yoder, P. J., & Warren, S. F. (2001). Relative treatment effects of two prelinguistic communication interventions on language development of toddlers with developmental delays vary by maternal characteristics. *Journal of Speech and Hearing Research, 44,* 224–237.

CHAPTER 10

Adams, M. (1990). *Beginning to read: Thinking and learning about print.* Cambridge, MA: MIT Press.

Aldersley, S. (2002). Least restrictive environment and the courts. *Journal of Deaf Studies and Deaf Education, 7,* 189–199.

Allinder, R. M., & Eccarius, M. A. (1999). Exploring the technical adequacy of curriculum-based measurement in reading for children who use manually coded English. *Exceptional Children, 65,* 271–288.

American Academy of Otolaryngology—Head and Neck Surgery. (2007). *Noise & Hearing Protection.* Retrieved May 24, 2007, from http://www.entnet.org/healthinfo/hearing/noise_hearing.cfm

American Academy of Pediatrics. (2007, March 5). *State summary statistics: Universal newborn hearing screening.* Retrieved May 25, 2007, from http://www.infanthearing.org/status/unhsstate.html

Andrews, J. F., Ferguson, C., Roberts, S., & Hodges, P. (1997). What's up, Billy Jo? Deaf children and bilingual-bicultural instruction in East-Central Texas. *American Annals of the Deaf, 142,* 16–25.

Andrews, J. F., Leigh, I. W., & Weiner, M. T. (2004). *Deaf people: Evolving perspectives from psychology, education, and sociology.* Boston: Allyn & Bacon.

Andrews, J. F., & Zmijewski, G. (1997). How parents support home literacy with deaf children. *Early Child Development and Care, 127,* 131–139.

Arnos, K. S. (2002). Genetics and deafness: Impacts on the Deaf community. *Sign Language Studies, 2,* 150–168.

Bornstein, M. H., Selmi, A. M., Haynes, O. M., Painter, K. M., & Marx, E. S. (1999). Representational abilities and the hearing status of child/mother dyads. *Child Development, 70,* 833–852.

Brashear, H., Henderson, V., Park, K-H., Hamilton, H., Lee, S., & Starner, T. (2006). American Sign Language recognition game development for deaf children. In *Proceedings of the 8th International ACM SIGACCESS Conference on Computers and Accessbility* (pp. 79–86). Portland, OR: ACM Press.

Brill, R. G., MacNeil, B., & Newman, L. R. (1986). Framework for appropriate programs for deaf children. *American Annals of the Deaf, 131,* 65–77.

Buchino, M. A. (1993). Perceptions of the oldest hearing child of deaf parents. *American Annals of the Deaf, 138,* 40–45.

Cambra, C. (1996). A comparative study of personality descriptors attributed to the deaf, the blind, and individuals with no sensory disability. *American Annals of the Deaf, 141,* 24–28.

Campbell, K. C. M., & Mullin, G. (2006, May 31). Otoacoustic emissions. *eMedicine.* Retrieved May 25, 2007, from http://www.emedicine.com/ent/topic372.htm

Campbell, R. & MacSweeney, M. (2004). Neuroimaging studies of crossmodal plasticity and language processing in deaf people. In G. A. Calvert, C. Spence, & B. E. Stein (Eds.), *The handbook of multisensory processing* (pp. 773–784). Cambridge, MA: MIT Press.

Charlson, E., Strong, M., & Gold, R. (1992). How successful deaf teenagers experience and cope with isolation. *American Annals of the Deaf, 137,* 261–270.

Cook, K. A., & Walsh, M. (2005, May 23). Otitis media. *eMedicine.* Retrieved May 26, 2007, from http://www.emedicine.com/EMERG/topic351.htm

Council for Exceptional Children (2003). *What every special educator must know: Ethics, standards, and guidelines for special educators* (5th ed.). Arlington, VA: Author.

Emmorey, K. (2002). *Language, cognition, and the brain: Insights from sign language research*. Mahwah, NJ: Lawrence Erlbaum Associates.

Feldman, H. M., Dollaghan, C. A., Campbell, T. F., Colborn, D. K., Janosky, J., Kurs-Lasky, M., et al. (2003). Parent-reported language skills in relation to otitis media during the first 3 years of life. *Journal of Speech, Language, and Hearing Research, 46,* 273–287.

Gallaudet Research Institute (December, 2005). *Regional and national summary report of data from the 2004–2005 Annual Survey of Deaf and Hard of Hearing Children and Youth*. Washington, DC: Author. Retrieved May 24, 2007, from http://gri.gallaudet.edu/ Demographics/2005_National_Summary.pdf

Goldin-Meadow, S. (2003). *The resilience of language: What gesture creation in deaf children can tell us about how all children learn language*. New York: Psychology Press.

Hanson, V. L. (1989). Phonology and reading: Evidence from profoundly deaf readers. In D. Shankweiler & I. Liberman (Eds.), *Phonology and reading disability: Solving the reading puzzle* (pp. 69–89). Ann Arbor, MI: University of Michigan Press.

Hanson, V. L., & Lichtenstein, E. (1990). Short-term memory decoding by deaf signers: The primary language hypothesis reconsidered. *Cognitive Psychology, 22,* 221–224.

Johnston, T. (2005). In one's own image: Ethics and the reproduction of deafness. *Journal of Deaf Studies and Deaf Education, 10,* 426–441.

Kegl J., Senghas A., & Coppola, M. (1999). Creation through contact: Sign language emergence and sign language change in Nicaragua. In M. DeGraff (Ed.), *Comparative grammatical change: The intersection of language acquisistion, creole genesis, and diachronic syntax* (pp. 179–237). Cambridge, MA: MIT Press.

Kluwin, T. N., Stinson, M. S., & Colarossi, G. M. (2002). Social processes and outcomes of in-school contact between deaf and hearing peers. *Journal of Deaf Studies and Deaf Education, 7,* 200–213.

Kyle, F. E., & Harris, M. (2006). Concurrent correlates and predictors of reading and spelling achievement in deaf and hearing school children. *Journal of Deaf Studies and Deaf Education, 11,* 273–288.

Lane, H. (1984). *When the mind hears: A history of the deaf*. New York: Random House.

Lane, H. (1992). *The mask of benevolence: Disabling the Deaf community*. New York: Knopf.

Lane, H., Hoffmeister, R., & Bahan, B. (1996). *A journey into the Deaf world*. San Diego, CA: Dawn Sign Press.

Ladd, P. (2003). *Understanding Deaf culture: In search of Deafhood*. Clevedon, England: Multilingual Matters.

Lazarus, S. S., Thurlow, M. L., Lail, K. E., Eisenbraun, K. D., & Kato, K. (2006). *2005 state policies on assessment participation and accommodations for students with disabilities* (Synthesis Report 64). Minneapolis, MN: University of Minnesota, National Center on Educational Outcomes. Retrieved June 7, 2007, from http:// education.umn.edu/NCEO/OnlinePubs/Synthesis64/

Lederberg, A. R., & Golbach, T. (2002). Parenting stress and social support in hearing mothers of deaf and hearing children: A longitudinal study. *Journal of Deaf Studies and Deaf Education, 7,* 330–345.

Lee, S., Henderson, V., & Brashear, H. (2005, June). *CopyCat: An ASL game for deaf children*. Paper presented at the meeting of the Rehabilitation Engineering & Assistive Technology Society of North America Student Design Competition, Atlanta, GA.

Luckner, J. L., & Bowen, S. (2006). Assessment practices of professionals serving students who are deaf or hard of hearing: An initial investigation. *American Annals of the Deaf, 151,* 410–417.

Marschark, M. (2002). *Language development in children who are deaf: A research synthesis*. Alexandria, VA: National Association of State Directors of Special Education (NASDE).

Marschark, M., Pelz, J. B., Convertino, C., Sapare, P., Arndt, M. E., & Seewagen, R. (2005). Classroom interpreting and visual information processing in mainstream education for deaf students: Live or Memorex®? *American Educational Research Journal, 42,* 727–761.

Marschark, M., Sapare, P., Convertino, C., & Seewagen, R. (2005). Access to postsecondary education through sign language interpreting. *Journal of Deaf Studies and Deaf Education, 10,* 38–50.

Marschark, M., Sapare, P., Convertino, C., Seewagen, R., & Maltzen, H. (2004). Comprehension of sign language interpreting: Deciphering a complex task situation. *Sign Language Studies, 4,* 345–368.

Mason, T. C. (2005). Cross-cultural instrument translation: Assessment, translation, and statistical applications. *American Annals of the Deaf, 150,* 67–72.

Meadow-Orlans, K. P. (1987). An analysis of the effectiveness of early intervention programs for hearing-impaired children. In M. J. Guralnick & F. C. Bennett (Eds.), *The effectiveness of early intervention for at-risk and handicapped children* (pp. 325–362). New York: Academic Press.

Meadow-Orlans, K. P. (1990). Research on developmental aspects of deafness. In D. F. Moores & K. P. Meadow-Orlans (Eds.), *Educational and developmental aspects of deafness* (pp. 283–298). Washington, DC: Gallaudet University Press.

Meadow-Orlans, K. P., Mertens, D. M., & Sass-Lehrer, M. A. (2003). *Parents and their deaf children: The early years*. Washington, DC: Gallaudet University Press.

Menchel, R. S. (1988). Personal experience with speechreading. *Volta Review, 90* (5), 3–15.

Mitchell, R. E., & Karchmer, M. A. (2004). Chasing the mythical ten percent: Parental hearing status of deaf and hard of hearing students in the United States. *Sign Language Studies, 4,* 138–163.

Mitchell, R. E., & Karchmer, M. A. (2005). Parental hearing status and signing among deaf and hard of hearing children. *Sign Language Studies, 5,* 231–244.

Moores, D. F. (2002). The law of unexpected consequences. *American Annals of the Deaf, 147,* 84–87.

Mundy, L. (2002, March 31). A world of their own. *The Washington Post Magazine*, pp. 22–31.

Musselman, C. (2000). How do children who can't hear learn to read an alphabetic script? A review of the literature on reading and deafness. *Journal of Deaf Studies and Deaf Education, 5,* 9–31.

Narr, R. A. F. (2006). Teaching phonological awareness with deaf and hard-of-hearing students. *Teaching Exceptional Children, 38* (4), 53–58.

National Center for Biotechnology Information. (2007, January 10). *Genes and disease: Ear, Nose, and Throat: Deafness*. Retrieved May 28, 2007, from http://www.ncbi.nlm.nih.gov/entrez/query.fcgi? cmd=Search&db=books&doptcm

National Institute on Deafness and Other Communication Disorders. (2006, May). *Cochlear implants*. Retrieved May 31, 2007, from http://www.nidcd.nih.gov/health/hearing/coch.asp

Nicaraguan sign language. (2007, May 11). Wikipedia. Retrieved May 28, 2007, from http://en.wikipedia.org/wiki/Nicaraguan_ Sign_Language

Nicholas, J. G., & Geers, A. E. (2006). Effects of early auditory experience on the spoken language of deaf children at 3 years of age. *Ear & Hearing, 27,* 286–297.

Oliva, G. A. (2004). *Alone in the mainstream: A deaf woman remembers public school*. Washington, DC: Gallaudet University Press.

Padden, C. A. (1996). Early bilingual lives of Deaf children. In I. Parasnis (Ed.), *Cultural and language diversity and the Deaf experience* (pp. 99–116). Cambridge, England: Cambridge University Press.

Padden, C., & Humphries, T. (2005). *Inside deaf culture*. Cambridge, MA: Harvard University Press.

Perfetti, C. A., & Sandak, R. (2000). Reading optimally builds on spoken language. Implications for deaf readers. *Journal of Deaf Studies and Deaf Education, 5,* 32–50.

Powers, S. (2003). Influences of student and family factors on academic outcomes of mainstream secondary school deaf students. *Journal of Deaf Studies and Deaf Education, 8,* 57–78.

Prinz, P. M., Strong, M., Kuntze, M., Vincent, M., Friedman, J., Moyers, P., et al. (1996). A path to literacy through ASL and English for Deaf children. In C. E. Johnson & J. H. V. Gilbert (Eds.), *Children's language* (Vol. 9, pp. 235–251). Mahwah, NJ: Lawrence Erlbaum Associates.

Punch, R., Creed, P. A., & Hyde, M. B. (2006). Career barriers perceived by hard-of-hearing adolescents: Implications for practice from a mixed-methods study. *Journal of Deaf Studies and Deaf Education, 11,* 225–237.

Punch, R., Hyde, M., & Creed, P. A. (2004). Issues in the school-to-work transition of hard of hearing adolescents. *American Annals of the Deaf, 149,* 28–38.

Quigley, S., Jenne, W., & Phillips, S. (1968). *Deaf students in colleges and universities.* Washington, DC: Alexander Graham Bell Association for the Deaf.

Reagan, T. (1990). Cultural considerations in the education of deaf children. In D. F. Moores & K. P. Meadow-Orlans (Eds.), *Educational and developmental aspects of deafness* (pp. 73–84). Washington, DC: Gallaudet University Press.

Reid, K. K., Hresko, W. P., Hammill, D. D., & Wiltshire, S. (1991). *Test of early reading ability—Deaf or hard of hearing (TERA-D/HH).* Austin, TX: ProEd.

Renaissance Learning (2006). *STAR early literacy assessment.* Wisconsin Rapids, WI: Author.

Sanghavi, D. M., (2006, December 5). Wanting babies like themselves, some parents choose genetic defects. *The New York Times.* Retrieved March 5, 2007, from www.nytimes.com/2006/12/05/health/05essa.html?ex=1322974800&en=9fbb1b0e738b55d1&ei=5088partner=rssnyt&emc=rss

Schick, B., Williams, K., & Kupermintz, H. (2006). Look who's being left behind: Educational interpreters and access to education for deaf and hard-of-hearing students. *Journal of Deaf Studies and Deaf Education, 11,* 3–20.

Schirmer, B. R. (2001). *Psychological, social, and educational dimensions of deafness.* Boston: Allyn & Bacon.

Schroedel, J. G., & Geyer, P. D. (2000). Long-term career attainments of deaf and hard of hearing college graduates: Results from a 15-year follow-up survey. *American Annals of the Deaf, 145,* 303–314.

Seal, B. C. (2004). *Best practices in educational interpreting* (2nd ed.). Boston: Allyn & Bacon.

Senghas, A. (2003). Intergenerational influence and ontogenetic development in the emergence of spatial grammar in Nicaraguan Sign Language. *Cognitive Development, 18,* 511–531.

Sheridan, M. (2001). *Inner lives of deaf children: Interviews and analysis.* Washington, DC: Gallaudet University Press.

Siegel, L. (2000). The educational and communication needs of deaf and hard of hearing children: A statement of principle on fundamental educational change. *American Annals of the Deaf, 145,* 64–77.

Spencer, P. E. (2004). Individual differences in language performance after cochlear implantation at one to three years of age: Child, family, and linguistic factors. *Journal of Deaf Studies and Deaf Education, 9,* 395–412.

Stinson, M. S., & Whitmire, K. (1992). Students' views of their social relationships. In T. N. Kluwin, D. F. Moores, & M. G. Gaustad (Eds.), *Toward effective public school programs for deaf students: Context, process, and outcomes* (pp. 149–174). New York: Teachers College Press.

Stokoe, W. C. (1960). *Sign language structure.* Silver Spring, MD: Linstok Press.

Stokoe, W. C., Casterline, D. C., & Croneberg, C. G. (1976). *A dictionary of American Sign Language on linguistic principles* (2nd ed.). Silver Spring, MD: Linstok Press.

Takruri, L. (2006, October 30). Gallaudet exposes debate over deafness. *The Washington Post.* Retrieved May 30, 2007, from http://www.washingtonpost.com/wp-dyn/content/article/2006/10/30/AR2006103000087.html

Tapper, J., & Sandell, C. (2006, May 10). *Is deaf university president not 'deaf enough'?* ABC News Internet Ventures. Retrieved May 30, 2007, from http://www.abcnews.go.com/WNT/story?id=1947073

Thompson, S. J., Johnstone, C. J., Thurlow, M. L., & Altman, J. R. (2005). *2005 State special education outcomes: Steps forward in a decade of change.* Minneapolis, MN: University of Minnesota, National Center on Educational Outcomes. Retrieved June 7, 2007, from http://education.umn.edu/NCEO/OnlinePubs/2005StateReport.htm/

Trezek, B. J., & Malmgren, K. W. (2005). The efficacy of utilizing a phonics treatment package with middle school deaf and hard-of-hearing students. *Journal of Deaf Studies and Deaf Education, 10,* 256–271.

Trezek, B. J., & Wang, Y. (2006). Implications of utilizing a phonics-based reading curriculum with children who are deaf or hard of hearing. *Journal of Deaf Studies and Deaf Education, 11,* 202–213.

U.S. Department of Education. (2005). *Twenty-seventh annual report to Congress on the implementation of the Individuals with Disabilities Education Act.* Washington, DC: Author.

U.S. Department of Education, National Center on Student Progress Monitoring. (2006). *Review of progress monitoring tools.* Retrieved June 12, 2007, from http://www.studentprogress.org/chart/chart.asp

Walker, L. A. (1986). *A loss for words: The story of deafness in a family.* New York: Harper & Row.

Waters, D., Campbell, R., Capek, C. M., Woll, B., David, A. S., McGuire, P. K., et al. (2007). Fingerspelling, signed language, text and picture processing in deaf native signers: The role of the mid-fusiform gyrus. *NeuroImage, 35,* 832–840.

Wechsler, D. (2002). *Wechsler Individual Achievement Test-Second Edition.* San Antonio, TX: Harcourt Assessment.

Wilbur, R. (2000). The use of ASL to support the development of English and literacy. *Journal of Deaf Studies and Deaf Education, 5,* 81–104.

CHAPTER 11

American Foundation for the Blind (2002, November 8). *Web developers—Tips & tricks to improve accessibility.* Retrieved February 15, 2004, from www.afb.org/info_document_view.asp?documentid=1453

American Printing House for the Blind. (2004). *What is CVI?* Retrieved July 3, 2006, from http://sun1.aph.org/cvi/define.html

Bailey, J. (2003). Surmounting the Braille reading speed plateau. *Braille Monitor, 46,* 323–325.

Barlow, J. M., Bentzen, B. L., & Bond, T. (2005). Blind pedestrians and the changing technology and geometry of signalized intersections: Safety, orientation, and independence. *Journal of Visual Impairment and Blindness, 99,* 587–598.

Barlow-Brown, F., & Connelly, V. (2002). The role of letter knowledge and phonological awareness in young Braille readers. *Journal of Research in Reading, 25,* 259–270.

Barraga, N. C., & Collins, M. E. (1979). Development of efficiency in visual functioning: Rationale for a comprehensive program. *Journal of Visual Impairment and Blindness, 73,* 121–126.

Berk, L. E. (2005). *Infants and children: Infants through middle childhood* (5th ed.). Boston: Allyn & Bacon.

Bishop, V. E. (2004). *Teaching visually impaired children* (3rd ed.). Springfield, IL: Charles S. Thomas.

Bolt, S. E., & Thurlow, M. L. (2004). Five of the most frequently allowed testing accommodations in state policy: Synthesis of research. *Remedial and Special Education, 25,* 141–152.

Brigance, A. (1999). *Brigance comprehensive inventory of basic skills–revised (CIBS-R).* North Billerica, MA: Curriculum Associates.

Capella-McDonnall, M. E. (2005). Predictors of competitive employment for blind and visually impaired consumers of vocational services. *Journal of Visual Impairment and Blindness, 99,* 303–315.

Castellano, C. (2005). *Making it work: Educating the Blind/VI student in the regular school.* Greenwich CT: Information Age Publishing.

Celeste, M. (2002). A survey of motor development for infants and young children with visual impairments. *Journal of Visual Impairment and Blindness, 96,* 169–174.

Celeste, M. (2006). Play behaviors and social interactions of a child who is blind: In theory and practice. *Journal of Visual Impairment and Blindness, 100,* 75–90.

Chen, D. (1996). Parent-infant communication: Early intervention for very young children with visual impairment or hearing loss. *Infants and Young Children, 9* (2), 1–12.

Chong, C. (2004). Appropriate use of the electronic notetaker in school. *Braille Monitor, 47,* 29–31.

Council for Exceptional Children (2003). *What every special educator must know: Ethics, standards, and guidelines for special educators* (5th ed.). Arlington, VA: Author.

D'Allura, T. (2002). Enhancing the social interaction skills of preschoolers with visual impairments. *Journal of Visual Impairment and Blindness, 96*, 576–584.

De l'Aune, W., Williams, M., Watson, G. R., Schuckers, P., & Ventimiglia, G. (2004). Clinical application of a self-report, functional independence outcomes measure in the DVA's blind rehabilitative service. *Journal of Visual Impairment and Blindness, 98*, 197–211.

Dobelle, W. H. (2000). Artificial vision for the blind by connecting a television camera to the visual cortex of the brain. *Journal of the American Society of Artificial Internal Organs, 46*, 3–9.

Edelman, S., Lashbrook, P., Carey, A., Kelly, D., King, R. A., Roman-Lantzy, C., et al. (2006). Cortical visual impairment: Guidelines and educational considerations. *Deaf-Blind Perspectives, 13* (3), 1–4.

Erin, J. N. (2006). Teaching social skills to elementary and middle school students with visual impairments. In S. Z. Sacks & K. E. Wolffe (Eds.), *Teaching social skills to students with visual impairments: From theory to practice* (pp. 364–404). New York: American Foundation for the Blind.

Faherty, J. (2006, June 1). Can't read this? *Arizona Living: Online Print Edition*. Retrieved June 3, 2006, from http://www.azcentral.com/arizonarebublic/arizonaliving/articles/060106

Farrell, M. (2006). *The effective teacher's guide to sensory impairment and physical disability: Practical strategies*. New York: Rutledge.

Fichten, C. S., Judd, D., Tagalakis, V., Amsel, R., & Robillard, K. (1991). Communication cues used by people with and without visual impairments in daily conversations and dating. *Journal of Visual Impairment and Blindness, 85*, 371–378.

Gabias, P. (1992, July). Unique features of guide dogs: Backtracking and homing. *Braille Monitor, 35*, 392–399.

Gillon, G. T., & Young, A. A. (2002). The phonological-awareness skills of children who are blind. *Journal of Visual Impairment and Blindness, 96*, 38–49.

Glaucoma Research Foundation. (2006, July 27). *What is glaucoma?* Retrieved July 27, 2006, from http://www.glaucoma.org/learn/what_is_glaucom.html

Greaney, J., Hill, E., & Tobin, M. J. (1998). *Neale analysis of reading ability: University of Birmingham braille version*. London: Royal National Institute for the Blind.

Groopman, J. (2003, September 29). Annals of Medicine: The bionic eye: Can scientists use electronic implants to help the blind see? *The New Yorker*, pp. 50–54, 67–68.

Hannan, C. K. (2007). Exploring assessment processes in specialized schools for students who are visually impaired. *Journal of Visual Impairment and Blindness, 101*, 69–79.

Hatlen, P. (1998). Goal 8: Educational and developmental goals, including instruction, will reflect the assessed needs of each student in all areas of academic and disability-specific core curricular. In A. L. Corn & K. M. Huebner (Eds.), *A report to the nation: The national agenda for the education of children and youths with visual impairments, including those with multiple disabilities* (pp. 50–52). New York: AFP Press.

Haymes, S. A., Johnston, A. W., & Heyes, A. D. (2001). Preliminary investigation of the responsiveness of the Melbourne Low Vision ADL Index to low-vision rehabilitation. *Optometry & Vision Science, 78*, 373–380.

Hill, A. (1997, April). Teaching can travel blind? *Braille Monitor, 40*, 222–225.

Hill, J., & Black, J. (2003). The Miniguide: A new electronic travel device. *Journal of Visual Impairment and Blindness, 97*, 655–656.

Houtenville, A. J. (2003). A comparison of the economic status of working-age persons with visual impairments and those of other groups. *Journal of Visual Impairment and Blindness, 97*, 133–148.

Huebner, K. M., & Wiener, W. (2005). Guest editorial. *Journal of Visual Impairment and Blindness, 99*, 579–583.

Hull, J. M. (1997). *On sight and insight: A journey into the world of blindness*. Oxford, England: Oneworld Publications.

Jernigan, K. (1992, June). Equality, disability, and empowerment. *Braille Monitor, 35*, 292–298.

Jernigan, K. (1994). *If blindness comes*. Baltimore: National Federation of the Blind.

Jindal-Snape, D. (2005). Self-evaluation and recruitment of feedback for enhanced social interaction by a student with visual impairment. *Journal of Visual Impairment and Blindness, 99*, 486–498.

Johns, J. (2005). *The basic reading inventory: Pre-primer through grade twelve & early literacy assessments*. Dubuque, IA: Kendall/Hunt Publishing Co.

Jolley, W. (2006, July). *Unified English Braille: A literacy bedrock in the digital age*. Paper presented at the International Council for Education of People with Visual Impairment Twelfth ICEVI World Conference, Kuala Lumpur. (Retrieved December 22, 2006, from http://www.iceb.org/ICEVI2006_UEB_Paper_Jolley.htm

Kilpatrick, J, Swafford, J, Findell, B (Eds.). (2001). *Adding It Up: Helping Children Learn Mathematics*. Washington, DC: National Academy Press.

Kirchner, C., & Smith, B. (2005). Transition to what? Education and employment outcomes for visually impaired youths after high school. *Journal of Visual Impairment and Blindness, 99*, 499–504.

Kleege, G. (1999). *Sight unseen*. New Haven, CT: Yale University Press.

Knott, N. I. (2002). *Teaching orientation and mobility in the schools: An instructor's companion*. New York: American Foundation for the Blind Press.

Koenig, A. J., & Holbrook, M. C. (2000). Ensuring high-quality instruction for students in braille literacy programs. *Journal of Visual Impairment and Blindness, 94*, 677–694.

Koenig, A. J., Sanspree, M. J., & Holbrook, M. C. (n.d.). Determining the reading medium for students with visual impairments. *D.V.I. Quarterly*. Retrieved June 13, 2007, from http://www.ed.arizona.edu/dvi/Postion%20Papers/determining_Read_med.htm

Kurson, R. (2005, June). Into the light. *Esquire*. Retrieved April 8, 2007, from http://www.esquire.com/print-this/ESQ0605BLIND_114.2

Kurson, R. (2007). *Crashing through: A true story of risk, adventure, and the man who dared to see*. New York: Random House.

Kuusisto, S. (2006). *Eavesdropping*. New York: W. W. Norton & Company.

Lansaw, J. (2000, December). Citizenship and the irony at the top of the world. *Braille Monitor, 43*, 963–965.

Lazurus, S. S., Thurlow, M. L., Lail, K. E., Eisenbraun, K. D., & Kato, K. (2006). *2005 state policies on assessment participation and accommodations for students with disabilities* (Synthesis Report 64). Minneapolis, MN: University of Minnesota, National Center on Educational Outcomes.

Lewis, S., & Iselin, S. A. (2002). A comparison of the independent living skills of primary students with visual impairments and their sighted peers: A pilot study. *Journal of Visual Impairment and Blindness, 96*, 335–344.

Lewis, V., & Klauber, J. (2002). [Image] [Image] [Image] [Link] [Link] [Link]: Inaccessible Web design from the perspective of a blind librarian. *Library Hi Tech, 20*, 137–140.

Lussenhop, K., & Corn, A. L. (2003). Comparative studies of the reading performance of students with low vision. *RE:view, 34*, 57–69.

Mangione, C. M., Phillips, R. S., Seddon, J. M., Lawrence, M. G., Cook E. F., Dailey, R., Goldman, L. (1992). Development of the Activities of Daily Vision Scale. A measure of visual functional status. *Med Care, 30*, 1111–1126.

Maurer, M. (2000, April). Blindness, quotas, and the disadvantages of civil rights. *Braille Monitor, 43*, 287–296.

Maurer, M. (2003). The Federation is attacked for seeking to enhance mobility and safety. *Braille Monitor, 46*, 1–5.

McHugh, E., & Lieberman, L. (2003). The impact of developmental factors on stereotypic rocking of children with visual impairments. *Journal of Visual Impairment and Blindness, 97*, 453–473.

Millar, D. (1996). A consumer's perspective. *Journal of Visual Impairment and Blindness, 90*, 9.

Miller, C. (1999). On the LOOK OUT for functional vision assessment/evaluation. *SEE/HEAR, 4*, No. 1. Retrieved February 20, 2004, from www.tsbvi.edu/Outreach/seehear/winter99/fva.htm

Morgan, S. K., & Bradley-Johnson, S. (1995). Technical adequacy of curriculum-based measurement for Braille readers. *School Psychology Review, 24*, 94–103.

National Eye Institute (2005, April). Retinopathy of prematurity. Retrieved July 28, 2006, from http://www.nei.nih.gov/health/rop/index.asp

National Federation of the Blind. (2006). NFB-NEWSLINE® Retrieved January 24, 2007, from http://www.nfb.org/nfb/Newspapers_by_Phone.asp?SnID=389319

Pare, J. G. (2005, June). Am I blind? *Braille Monitor, 48,* 412–414.

Perez-Pereira, M., & Conti-Ramsden, G. (1999). *Language development and social interaction in blind children.* East Sussex, England: Psychology Press, Ltd.

Pesudovs, K., Coster, D.J. (1998). Validation of a new tool for the assessment of subjective visual disability. *British Journal of Opthamology, 82,* 617–624.

Prevent Blindness America (2005). *Signs of possible eye trouble.* Retrieved July 27, 2006, from http://www.preventblindness.org/children/trouble_signs.html

Raeder, W. M. (2006, June/July). The case for braille. *Highlights.* Boston: National Braille Press. Retrieved December 27, 2006, from http://www.nbp.org/ic/nbp/braille/case_for_braille.html

Rapp, D. W., & Rapp, A. J. (1992). A survey of the current status of visually impaired students in secondary mathematics. *Journal of Visual Impairment and Blindness, 86,* 115–117.

Rex, E. J., Koenig, A. J., Wormsley, D., & Baker, R. (1994). *Foundations of braille literacy.* New York: American Foundation for the Blind.

Rodgers, M. D., & Emerson, R. W. (2005, October). Human factor analysis of long cane design: Weight and length. *Journal of Visual Impairment and Blindness, 99,* 622–632.

Rosel, J., Caballer, A., Jara, P., & Oliver, J. C. (2005). Verbalism in the narrative language of children who are blind and sighted. *Journal of Visual Impairment and Blindness, 99,* 413–425.

Rumrill, P. D., Roessler, R. T., Battersby-Longden, J. C., & Schuyler, B. R. (1998). Situational assessment of the accommodation needs of employees who are visually impaired. *Journal of Visual Impairment and Blindness, 92,* 42–54.

Rumrill, P. D., Schuyler, B. R., & Longden, J. C. (1997). Profiles of on-the-job accommodations needed by professional employees who are blind. *Journal of Visual Impairment and Blindness, 91,* 66–76.

Ryles, R. N. (1997). The relationship of reading skills on employment, income, education, and reading habits. *Journal of Visual Impairment & Blindness, 83,* 306–313.

Ryles, R. (2000). Braille as a predictor of success. In *Braille into the next millennium.* Washington, DC: National Library Service for the Blind and Physically Handicapped and Friends of Libraries for Blind and Physically Handicapped Individuals in North America.

Sacks, O. (1996). *An anthropologist on Mars: Seven paradoxical tales.* New York: Vintage Books.

Sacks, S. Z. (2006). The development of social skills: A personal perspective. In S. Z. Sacks & K. E. Wolffe (Eds.), *Teaching social skills to students with visual impairments: From theory to practice* (pp. 3–19). New York: American Foundation for the Blind.

Sauerburger, D. (2005). Street crossings: Analyzing risks, developing strategies, and making decisions. *Journal of Visual Impairment and Blindness, 99,* 659–663.

Schroeder, F. K. (2002). Research and future opportunities for the blind. *Braille Monitor, 45,* 581–586.

Spungin, S. J. (2003). Cannibalism is alive and well in the blindness field. *Journal of Visual Impairment and Blindness, 97,* 69–71.

Thompson, S. J., Johnstone, C. J., Thurlow, M. L., & Altman, J. R. (2005). *2005 state special education outcomes: Steps forward in a decade of change.* Minneapolis, MN: University of Minnesota, National Center on Educational Outcomes.

Thompson, S., & Thurlow, M. T. (2003). *2003 state special education outcomes: Marching on.* Minneapolis, MN: University of Minnesota, National Center on Educational Outcomes, University of Minnesota.

Thurber, R. S., Shinn, M. R., & Smolkowski, K. (2002). What is measured in mathematics tests? Construct validity of curriculum-based mathematics measures. *School Psychology Review, 31,* 498–513.

Ulrey, P. (1994). When you meet a guide dog. *RE:view, 26,* 143–144.

Warren, D. H. (1994). *Blindness and children: An individual differences approach.* New York: Cambridge University Press.

Webster, A., & Roe, J. (1998). *Children with visual impairments: Social interaction, language, and learning.* London: Routledge.

Weihenmayer, E. (2001). Touch the top of the world: A blind man's journey to climb farther than the eye can see. New York: Dutton.

Wolffe, K. E., Sacks, S. Z., Corn, A. L., Erin, J. N., Huebner, K. M., & Lewis, S. (2002). Teachers of students with visual impairments: What are they teaching? *Journal of Visual Impairment and Blindness, 96,* 293–303.

Wunder, G. (1993, March). Mobility: Whose responsibility is it? *Braille Monitor, 36,* 567–572.

Zebehazy, K., Hartmann, E., & Durando, J. (2006). High-stakes testing and implications for students with visual impairments and other disabilities. *Journal of Visual Impairment and Blindness, 100,* 598–601.

Zimmerman, G. J., Zebehazy, K. T., & Moon, M. L. (in press). Optics and low vision devices. In A. L. Corn & A. J. Koenig (Eds.), *Foundations of low vision: Clinical and functional perspectives* (2nd ed.). New York: AFB Press.

CHAPTER 12

Adreon, D., & Stella, J. (2001). Transition to middle and high school: Increasing the success of students with Asperger syndrome. *Intervention in School and Clinic, 36,* 266–271.

American Psychiatric Association. (2000). *Diagnostic and statistical manual of mental Disorders* (4th ed., text rev.). Washington, DC: Author.

Asperger, H. (1944). Die autistischen psychopathen im kindersalter. *Archiv für Psychiatrie und Nervenkrankheiten, 117,* 76–136. Translated by U. Frith in U. Frith (Ed.), *Autism and Asperger syndrome* (pp. 37–92). Cambridge, UK: Cambridge University Press, 1991.

Baron-Cohen, S., Leslie, A. M., & Frith, U. (1985). Does the autistic child have a "theory of mind"? *Cognition, 21,* 37–46.

Beale, A. J. (1998). Correspondence. *The Lancet, 351,* 906.

Bedford, H., Booy, R., Dunn, D., DiGuiseppi, C., Gibb, D., Gilbert, R., et al. (1998). Correspondence. *The Lancet, 351,* 907.

Bell, R. Q., & Harper, L. V. (1977). *Child effects on adults.* Hillsdale, NJ: Lawrence Erlbaum Associates.

Bellini, S., & Hopf, A. (2007). The development of the autism social skills profile: A preliminary analysis of psychometric properties. *Focus on Autism and Other Developmental Disabilities, 22,* 80–87.

Bettelheim, B. (1967). *The empty fortress.* New York: Free Press.

Bleuler, E. (1951). *Textbook of psychiatry* (A. A. Brill, Trans.). New York: Dover. (Original work published 1916).

Bock, M. A. (2002, April 30). *The impact of social behavioral learning strategy training on the social interaction skills of eight students with Asperger syndrome.* Paper presented at YAI National Institute for People with Disabilities 23rd International Conference on MR/DD, New York.

Bondy, A., & Frost, L. (2001). The picture exchange communication system. *Behavior Modification, 25,* 725–744.

Cadigan, K., & Estrem, T. (Fall/Winter, 2006/07). Identification and assessment of autism spectrum disorders. *Impact, 19* (3), 4–5.

Cannon, J. (2004, July 22). Youth uses Web to help others on "wrong planet." *Charlottesville Daily Progress.*

Charlop-Christy, M., Carpenter, M., Le, L., LeBlanc, L., & Kellet, K. (2002). Using the Picture Exchange Communication System (PECS) with children with autism: Assessment of PECS acquisition, speech, social-communicative behavior, and problem behavior. *Journal of Applied Behavioral Analysis, 35,* 213–231.

Chen, R. T., & DeStefano, F. (1998). Vaccine adverse events: Causal or coincidental? *The Lancet, 351,* 611–612.

Cohen, I. L., Schmidt-Lackner, S., Romanczyk, R., & Sudhalter, V. (2003). The PDD behavior inventory: A rating scale for assessing response to intervention in children with pervasive developmental disorder. *Journal of Autism and Developmental Disabilities, 33,* 31–45.

Cohen, I. L., & Sudhalter, V. (2005). *PDD Behavior Inventory (PDDBI).* Lutz, FL: Psychological Assessment Resources.

Constantino, J. N., & Gruber, C. P. (2005). *The social responsiveness scale (SRS).* Los Angeles: Western Psychological Services.

Courchesne, E., Carper, R., & Akshoomoff, N. (2003). Evidence of brain overgrowth in the first year of life in autism. *Journal of the American Medical Association, 290,* 337–344.

Courchesne, E., Karns, C. M., Davis, H. R., Ziccardi, R., Carper, R. A., Tigue, B. S., et al. (2001). Unusual brain growth patterns in early life in patients with autistic disorder. *Neurology, 57,* 245–254.

Crozier, S., & Sileo, N. (2005). Encouraging positive behavior with social stories: An intervention for children with autism spectrum disorders. *Teaching Exceptional Children, 37* (6), 26–31.

Dapretto, M., Davies, M. S., Pfeifer, J. H., Scott, A. A., Sigman, M., Bookheimer, S. Y., et al. (2006). Understanding emotions in others: mirror neuron dysfunction in children with autism spectrum disorders. *Nature Neuoscience, 9* (1), 28–30.

Eisenberg, L., & Kanner, K. (1956). Early infantile autism, 1943–1955. *American Journal of Orthopsychiatry, 26,* 556–566.

Fenson, L. (2007). *MacArthur-Bates Communicative Development Inventories (CDIs)* (3rd ed.). Balitmore: Paul H. Brookes.

Fenson, L., Marchman, V. A., Thal, D. J., Dale, P. S., Reznick, J. S., & Bates, E. (2003). *MacArthur-Bates Communicative Development Inventories (CDIs)* (2nd ed.). Baltimore: Paul H. Brookes.

Fombonne, E. (2001). Is there an autism epidemic? *Pediatrics, 107,* 411–412.

Fombonne, E. (2005). The changing epidemiology of autism. *Journal of Applied Research in Intellectual Disabilities, 18,* 281–294.

Fombonne, E., Roge, B., Claverie, J., Courty, S., & Fremoile, J. (1999). Microcephaly and macrocephaly in autism. *Journal of Autism and Developmental Disorders, 29,* 113–119.

Frith, U. (2003). *Autism: Explaining the enigma* (2nd ed.). Malden, MA: Blackwell Publishing.

Frost, L., & Bondy, A. (2002). *Picture exchange communication system training manual* (2nd ed.). Newark, DE: Pyramid Education Products.

Gerhardt, P. F. (2003). Transition support for learners with Asperger syndrome: Toward a successful adulthood. In R. W. Du Charme & T. P. Gullotta (Eds.). *Asperger syndrome: A guide for professionals and families* (pp. 157–171). New York: Kluwer Academic/Plenum Publishing.

Glaeser, B. C., Pierson, M. R., & Fritschmann, N. (2003). Comic Strip Conversations: A positive behavioral support strategy. *Teaching Exceptional Children, 36* (2), 14–19.

Grandin, T. (1995). *Thinking in pictures.* New York: Doubleday.

Grandin, T. (2002, May 6). First person: Myself. *Time,* 56.

Gray, C. A. (2004). Social Stories™ 10.1: The new defining criteria and guidelines. *Jension Autism Journal: Creative Ideas in Practice, 15* (4), 2–21.

Gray, K. M., Tonge, B. J., & Brereton, A. V. (2006). Screening for autism in infants, children, and adolescents. *International Review of Research in Mental Retardation, 32,* 197–227.

Guber, P. (Producer), & Levinson, B. (Director). (1988). *Rain Main* [Motion picture]. United States: United Artists.

Hallahan, D. P., Lloyd, J. W., Kauffman, J. M., Weiss, M. P., & Martinez, E. A. (2005). *Learning disabilities: Foundations, characteristics, and effective teaching* (3rd ed.). Boston: Allyn & Bacon.

Hermelin, B. (1976). Coding and the sense modalities. In L. Wing (Ed.), *Early childhood autism.* London: Pergamon.

Herschkowitz, N. (2000). Neurological bases of behavioral development in infancy. *Brain Development, 22,* 411–416.

Hewetson, A. (2002). *The stolen child: Aspects of autism and Asperger syndrome.* Westport, CT: Bergin & Garvey.

Hoekstra, R. A., Bartels, M., Verweij, C. J. H., & Boomsma, D. I. (2007). Heritability of autistic traits in the general population. *Archives of Pediatric and Adolescent Medicine, 161,* 372–377.

Hoopman, K. (2000). *Blue bottle mystery.* London: Jessica Kingsley Publishers.

Hoopman, K. (2001). *Of mice and aliens.* London: Jessica Kingsley Publishers.

Hoopman, K. (2002). *Lisa and the lacemaker.* London: Jessica Kingsley Publishers.

Hoopman, K. (2003). *Haze.* London: Jessica Kingsley Publishers.

Hoopman, K. (2006). *All cats have Asperger syndrome.* London: Jessica Kingsley Publishers.

Horner, R. H., Albin, R. W., Sprague, J. R., & Todd, A. W. (2000). Positive behavior support. In M. E. Snell & F. Brown (Eds.), *Instruction of students with severe retardation* (5th ed., pp. 207–243). Upper Saddle River, NJ: Prentice-Hall.

Individuals With Disabilities Education Improvement Act of 2004. (2004). 20 U.S.C. § 1400 *et seq.*

Institute of Medicine. (2004). Immunization safety review: Vaccines and autism. Washington, DC: National Academies Press.

Kanner, L. (1943). Autistic disturbances of affective contact. *Nervous Child, 2,* 217–250. Reprinted in L. Kanner, *Childhood psychosis: Initial studies and new insights* (pp. 1–43). Washington, DC: V. H. Winston, 1973.

Kuoch, H., & Mirenda, P. (2003). Social story interventions for young children with autism spectrum disorders. *Focus on Autism and Other Developmental Disabilities, 8,* 219–227.

Lainhart, J. E. (2003). Increased rate of head growth during infancy in autism. *Journal of the American Medical Association, 290,* 393–394.

Landa, R. J., Holman, K. C., & Garrett-Mayer, E. (2007). Social and communication development in toddlers with early and later diagnosis of autism spectrum disorders. *Archives of General Psychiatry, 64,* 853–864.

Lotter, V. (1966). Epidemiology of autistic conditions in young children: I. Prevalence. *Social Psychiatry, 1,* 124–137.

Luyster, R., Lopez, K., & Lord, C. (2007). Characterizing communicative development in children referred for autism spectrum disorders using the MacArthur-Bates Communicative Development Inventory (CDI). *Journal of Child Language, 34,* 623–654.

Luyster, R., Qiu, S., Lopez, K., & Lord, C. (2007). Predicting outcomes of children referred for autism using the MacArthur-Bates Communicative Development Inventory. *Journal of Speech, Language, and Hearing Research, 50,* 667–681.

Mesibov, G. B., Shea, V., & Adams, L. W. (2001). *Understanding Asperger syndrome and high functioning autism.* New York: Kluwer Academic/Plenum Publishing.

Mills, J. L., Hediger, M. L., Molloy, C. A., Chrousos, G. P., Manning-Courtney, P., Yu, K. F., et al. (2007). Elevated levels of growth-related hormones in autism and autism spectrum disorder. *Clinical Endocrinology, 67,* 230–237.

Minshew, N. J., Sweeney, J., & Luna, B. (2002). Autism as a selective disorder of complex information processing and underdevelopment of neocortical systems. *Molecular Psychiatry, 7* (Suppl. 2), S12–S15.

Mirenda, P. (2003). Toward functional augmentative and alternative communication for students with autism: Manual signs, graphic symbols, and voice output communication aids. *Language, Speech, and Hearing Services in Schools, 34,* 203–216.

Muller, R. A. (2007). The study of autism as a distributed disorder. *Mental Retardation and Developmental Disabilities Research Reviews, 13,* 85–95.

Murch, S. H., Anthony, A., Casson, D. H., Malik, M., Berelowitz, M., Dhillon, A. P., et al. (2004). Retraction of an interpretation. *The Lancet, 363,* 750.

Myles, B. S. (2003). Social skills instruction for children with Asperger syndrome. In R. W. Du Charme & T. P. Gullotta (Eds.). *Asperger syndrome: A guide for professionals and families* (pp. 21–42). New York: Kluwer Academic/Plenum Publishing.

Myles, B. S., & Simpson, R. L. (2001). Understanding the hidden curriculum: An essential social skill for children and youth with Asperger syndrome. *Intervention in School and Clinic, 36,* 279–286.

Myles, B. S., & Simpson, R. L. (2003). *Asperger syndrome: A guide for parents and teachers.* Austin, TX: Pro-Ed.

Naess, P. (Director), & Bass, R. (2005). *Mozart and the Whale* [Motion picture]. United States: Millennium Films, Inc.

National Research Council. (2001). *Educating children with autism.* Washington, DC: National Academy Press.

Norris, C., & Dattilo, J. (1999). Evaluating effects of social story intervention on a young girl with autism. *Focus on Autism and Other Developmental Disabilities, 14,* 180–186.

Ozonoff, S. (1997). Causal mechanisms of autism: Unifying perspectives from an information-processing framework. In D. J. Cohen

& F. R. Volkmar (Eds.), *Handbook of autism and pervasive developmental disorders* (pp. 868–879). New York: John Wiley.

Page, T. (2007, August 20). Parallel play: A lifetime of restless isolation explained. *The New Yorker*, pp. 36–41.

Piven, J. Arndt, S., Bailey, J., & Andreason, N. C. (1996). Regional brain enlargement in autism: a magnetic resonance imaging study. *Journal of the American Academy of Child and Adolescent Psychiatry, 35*, 530–536.

Piven, J., Arndt, S., Bailey, J., Havercamp, S., Andreason, N. C., & Palmer, P. (1995). An MRI study of brain size in autism. *American Journal of Psychiatry, 152*, 1145–1149.

Rogers, S. J. (2000). Diagnosis of autism before the age of 3. *International Review of Mental Retardation, 23*, 1–31.

Sacks, O. (1995). *An anthropologist on Mars*. New York: Knopf.

Sallows, G. O., & Graupner, T. D. (2005). Intensive behavioral treatment for children with autism: Four-year outcome and predictors. *American Journal on Mental Retardation, 110*, 417–438.

Scattone, D., Tingstrom, D. H., & Wilczynski, S. M. (2006). Increasing appropriate social interactions of children with autism spectrum disorders using Social Stories™. *Focus on Autism and Other Developmental Disabilities, 21*, 221–222.

Scattone, D., Wilczynski, S. M., Edwards, R. P., & Rabin, B. (2002). Decreasing disruptive behaviors of children with autism using social stories. *Journal of Autism and Developmental Disorders, 32*, 535–543.

Scheuermann, B., & Webber, J. (2002). *Autism: Teaching does make a difference*. Stamford, CT: Wadsworth Group.

Schopler, E., Reichler, R. J., & Ro, B. (1988). *Childhood autism rating scale (CARS)*. Los Angeles: Western Psychological Services.

Schuler, A. L. (1995). Thinking in autism: Differences in learning and development. In K. A. Quill (Ed.), *Teaching children with autism: Strategies to enhance communication and socialization* (pp. 11–32). New York: Delmar Publishers.

Schwartz, I., Garfinkle, A., & Bauer, J. (1998). The Picture Exchange Communication System: Communicative outcomes for young children with disabilities. *Topics in Early Childhood Special Education, 18*, 144–159.

Scott, J. (Producer), & Hicks, S. (Writer/Director). (1996). *Shine* [Motion picture]. Australia: New Line Cinema.

Sebat, J., Lakshmi, B., Malhotra, D., Troge, J., Lese-Martin, C., Walsh, T., et al. (2007). Strong association of de novo copy number mutations with autism. *Science, 316*, 445–449.

Shattuck, P. T. (2006). The contributions of diagnostic substitution to the growing administrative prevalence of autism in U. S. special education. *Pediatrics, 117*, 1028–1037.

Shore, S. (2003). My life with Asperger syndrome. In R. W. Du Charme & T. P. Gullotta (Eds.), *Asperger syndrome: A guide for professionals and families* (pp. 189–209). New York: Kluwer Academic/Plenum Publishing.

Simpson, R. L. (2004). Finding effective intervention and personnel preparation practices for students with autism spectrum disorders. *Exceptional Children, 70*, 135–144.

Simpson, R. L., de Boer-Ott, S. R., Griswold, D. E., Myles, B. S., Byrd, S. E., Ganz, J. B., et al. (2005). *Autism spectrum disorders: Interventions and treatments for children and youth*. Thousand Oaks, CA: Corwin Press.

Simpson, R. L., de Boer-Ott, S. R., & Smith-Myles, B. (2003). Inclusion of learners with autism spectrum disorders in general education settings. *Topics in Language Disorders, 23*, 116–133.

Stone, W. L., McMahon, C. R., Yoder, P. J., & Walden, T. A. (2007). Early social-communicative and cognitive development of younger siblings of children with autism spectrum disorders. *Archives of Pediatrics and Adolescent Medicine, 161*, 384–390.

Strock, M. (2004). *Autism spectrum disorders (pervasive developmental disorders)*. Bethesda, MD: U.S. Department of Health and Human Services, National Institutes of Health, National Institute of Mental Health. Retrieved August 9, 2004, from www.nimh .nih.gov/publicat/autism.cfm

Tammet, D. (2006). *Born on a blue day: A memoir of Asperger's and an extraordinary mind*. London: Hodder & Stoughton Ltd.

Thompson, S., & Thurlow, M. L. (2001). *2001 state special education outcomes: A report on state activities in the beginning of a new decade*. Minneapolis, MN: University of Minnesota, National Center on Educational Outcomes.

Travis, L. L., & Sigman, M. D. (2000). A developmental approach to autism. In A. J. Sameroff, M. Lewis, & S. M. Miller (Eds.), *Handbook of developmental psychopathology* (2nd ed., pp. 641–655). New York: Kluwer Academic/Plenum.

Treffert, D. A. (2006). *Extraordinary people: Understanding savant syndrome*. New York: Authors Guild Backprint Bookstore.

U.S. Department of Education. (2005). *Twenty-seventh annual report to Congress on the implementation of the Individuals with Disabilities Education Act*. Washington, DC: Author.

Vacca, J. J. (2007). Incorporating interests and structure to improve participation of a child with autism in a standardized assessment: A case study. *Focus on Autism and Other Developmental Disabilities, 22*, 51–59.

Volkmar, F. R., & Pauls, D. (2003). Autism. *The Lancet, 362*, 1133–1141.

Wakefield, A. J., Murch, S. H., Anthony, A., Linnell, J., Casson, D. M., Malik, M., et al. (1998). Illeal-lymphoid-nodular hyperplasia, non-specific colitis, and pervasive developmental disorder in children. *The Lancet, 351*, 637–641.

Wallin, J. (2004). Visual Supports: PECS. Retrieved August 2004 from the www.polyxo.com/visualsupport/pecs.html

Werner, E., & Dawson, G. (2005). Validation of the phenomenon of autistic regression using home videotapes. *Archives of General Psychiatry, 62*, 889–895.

Wing, L. (1981). Asperger syndrome: A clinical account. *Psychological Medicine, 11*, 115–129.

Wing, L., & Potter, D. (2002). The epidemiology of autistic spectrum disorders: Is prevalence rising? *Mental Retardation & Developmental Disabilities Research Reviews, 8*(3), 151–161.

CHAPTER 13

Aitken, S. (2000). Understanding deafblindness. In S. Aitken, M. Buultjens, C. Clark, J. T. Eyre, & L. Pease (Eds.), *Teaching children who are deafblind: Contact, communication, and learning* (pp. 1–34). London: David Fulton Publishers.

Ashley, M. J. (Ed.). (2004). *Traumatic brain injury: Rehabilitative treatment and case management* (2nd ed.). Boca Raton, FL: CRC Press.

Baldwin, V. (1994). *Annual Deaf-Blind Census. Monmouth: Teaching Research Division*. Monmouth, OR:DB-LINK Teaching Research Division.

Best, S. J., Heller, K. W., & Bigge, J. L. (2005). *Teaching individuals with physical or multiple disabilities* (5th ed.). Upper Saddle River, NJ: Prentice Hall.

Beukelman, D. R., & Mirenda, P. (1998). *Augmentative and alternative communication: Management of severe communication disorders in children and adults* (2nd ed.). Baltimore: Paul H. Brookes.

Beukelman, D. R., Yorkston, K. M., & Reichle, J. (Eds.). (2000). *Augmentative and alternative communication for adults with acquired neurologic disorders*. Baltimore: Paul H. Brookes.

Bodfish, J. W. (2007). Stereotypy, self-injury, and related abnormal repetitive behaviors. In J. W. Jacobson, J. A. Mulick, & J. Rojahn (Eds.), *Handbook of intellectual and developmental disabilities* (pp. 481–505). New York: Springer.

Bowe, F. G. (2004). *Early childhood special education: Birth to eight* (3rd ed.). Delmar, CA: Thompson Learning.

Boys Town National Research Hospital Genetics Department (2001, February 21). *The collaborative Usher syndrome project*. Retrieved May 15, 2001, from http://www.boystown.org/btnrh/genetics/ usher.htm

Bredekamp, S., & Rosegrant, T. (Eds.). (1992). *Reaching potentials: Appropriate curriculum and assessment for young children*. Washington, DC: National Association for the Education of Young Children.

Browder, D. M., & Bambara, L. M. (2000). Home and community. In M. E. Snell & F. Brown (Eds.), *Instruction of students with severe disabilities* (5th ed., pp. 543–589). Upper Saddle River, NJ: Merrill.

Brown, D. (1996, February). *CHARGE*. Retrieved May 15, 2001, from http://www.deafblind.com/chargedb.html

Cardona, G. W. (2000). Spaghetti talk. In M. Oken-Fried & H. A. Bersani (Eds.), *Speaking up and spelling it out: Personal essays on augmentative and alternative communication* (pp. 237–244). Baltimore: Paul H. Brookes.

Chen, D., Alsop, L., & Minor, L. (2000). Lessons from Project PLAI in California and Utah: Implications for early intervention services to infants who are deaf-blind and their families. *Deaf-Blind Perspectives, 7* 3), 1–8.

Chen, D., Downing, J., & Rodriguez-Gil, G. (2000/2001). Tactile learning strategies for children who are deaf-blind: Concerns and considerations from Project SALUTE. *Deaf-Blind Perspectives, 8* (2), 1–6.

Christensen, J. R. (1996). Pediatric traumatic brain injury. In A. J. Capute & P. J. Accardo (Eds.), *Developmental disabilities in infancy and childhood: Vol. I. Neurodevelopmental diagnosis and treatment* (2nd ed., pp. 245–260). Baltimore: Paul H. Brookes.

Council for Exceptional Children. (2001). Traumatic brain injury: The silent epidemic. *CEC Today, 7*(7), 1, 5, 15.

Crimmins, C. (2000). *Where is the mango princess?* New York: Knopf.

Cullen, C., & Mudford, O. C. (2005). Gentle teaching. In J. W. Jacobson, R. M. Foxx, & J. A. Mulick (Eds.), *Controversial therapies for developmental disabilities: Fad, fashion, and science in professional practice* (pp. 423–432). Mahwah, NJ: Lawrence Erlbaum Associates.

Dell Orto, A. E., & Power, P. W. (2000). *Brain injury and the family: A life and living perspective* (2nd ed.). Washington, DC: CRC Press.

DePompei, R., & Tyler, J. (2004). Children and adolescents: Practical strategies for school participation. In M. J. Ashley (Ed.), *Traumatic brain injury: Rehabilitative treatment and case management* (2nd ed., pp. 559–580). Boca Raton, FL: CRC Press.

Division for Early Childhood. (1993). DEC position statement on inclusion. *DEC Communicator, 19*(4), 4.

Families and Disability Newsletter. (2001, June). *Positive behavioral support (PBS)*. Lawrence, KS: University of Kansas Life Span Institute Beach Center on Families and Disability.

Ford, J., & Fredericks, B. (1995). Perceptions of inclusion by parents of children who are deaf-blind. In N. G. Haring & L. T. Romer (Eds.), *Welcoming students who are deaf-blind into typical classrooms: Facilitating school participation, learning, and friendships* (pp. 37–53). Baltimore: Paul H. Brookes.

Franklin, P., & Bourquin, E. (2000). Picture this: A pilot study for improving street crossings for deaf-blind travelers. *RE:view, 31,* 173–179.

Fraser, R. T., & Clemmons, D. C. (Eds.). (2000). *Traumatic brain injury rehabilitation: Practical, vocational, neuropsychological, and psychotherapy interventions*. Boca Raton, FL: CRC Press.

Gardner, W. I. (2007). Aggression in persons with intellectual disabilities and mental disorders. In J. W. Jacobson, J. A. Mulick, & J. Rojahn (Eds.), *Handbook of intellectual and developmental disabilities* (pp. 541–562). New York: Springer.

Gargiulo, R., & Kilgo, J. (2005). *Young children with special needs* (2nd ed.). Delmar, CA: Thompson Learning.

Gense, D. J., & Gense, M. (2004). *The importance of orientation and mobility skills for students who are deaf-blind*. Retrieved October 8, 2007, from http://dblink.org/lib/o&m.htm

Gerenser, J., & Forman, B. (2007). Speech and language deficits in children with developmental disabilities. In J. W. Jacobson, R. M. Foxx, & J. A. Mulick (Eds.), *Controversial therapies for developmental disabilities: Fad, fashion, and science in professional practice* (pp. 563–579). Mahwah, NJ: Lawrence Erlbaum Associates.

Green, P. M. (Producer), & Penn, A. (Director). (1962). *The Miracle Worker*. United States: Paramount Pictures.

Hall, B. D. (1979). Choanal atresia and associated multiple anomalies. *Journal of Pediatrics, 95,* 395–398.

Hembree, R. (2000). *National deaf-blind child count summary: December 1, 1999 count*. Monmouth, OR: National Technical Assistance Consortium for Children and Young Adults who are Deaf-Blind (NTAC), Teaching Research Division, Western Oregon University.

Hodges, L. (2000). Effective teaching and learning. In S. Aitken, M. Buultjens, C. Clark, J. T. Eyre, & L. Pease (Eds.), *Teaching children who are deafblind: Contact, communication, and learning* (pp. 167–199). London: David Fulton Publishers.

Horner, R. H., Albin, R. W., Sprague, J. R., & Todd, A. W. (2000). Positive behavior support. In M. E. Snell & F. Brown (Eds.), *Instruction of students with severe disabilities* (pp. 207–243). Upper Saddle River, NJ: Prentice-Hall.

Howard, V. F., Williams, B. G., & Lepper, C. (2005). *Very young children with special needs: A formative approach for today's children*. Upper Saddle River, NJ: Prentice Hall.

Individuals With Disabilities Education Improvement Act of 2004. (2004). 20 U.S.C. § 1400 *et seq.*

Jacobson, J. W., Foxx, R. M., & Mulick, J. A. (2005). Facilitated communication: The ultimate fad treatment. In J. W. Jacobson, R. M. Foxx, & J. A. Mulick (Eds.), *Controversial therapies for developmental disabilities: Fad, fashion, and science in professional practice* (pp. 363–383). Mahwah, NJ: Lawrence Erlbaum Associates.

Janssen, M. J., Riksen-Walraven, J. M., & van Dijk, J. P. M. (2004). Enhancing the interactive competence of deafblind children: Do intervention effects endure? *Journal of Developmental and Physical Disabilities, 16,* 73–94.

Kauffman, J. M. (2002). *Education deform: Bright people sometimes say stupid things about education*. Lanham, MD: Scarecrow Education.

Kauffman, J. M. (in press). 45: Special education. In T. L. Good (Ed.), *21st century education: A reference handbook*. Thousand Oaks, CA: Sage.

Kauffman, J. M., Conroy, M., Gardner, R., & Oswald, D. (in press). Cultural sensitivity in the application of behavior principles to education. *Education and Treatment of Children*.

Kauffman, J. M., & Hallahan, D. P. (2005). *Special education: What it is and why we need it*. Boston: Allyn & Bacon.

Kauffman, J. M., & Landrum, T. J. (2009). *Characteristics of emotional and behavioral disorders of children and youth* (9th ed.). Upper Saddle River, NJ: Merrill/Prentice Hall.

Kauffman, J. M., Mostert, M. P., Trent, S. C., & Pullen, P. L. (2006). *Managing classroom behavior: A reflective case-based approach* (4th ed.). Boston: Allyn & Bacon.

Keller, H. (1905). *The story of my life*. New York: Grosset & Dunlap.

Kennedy, C. H., Meyer, K. A., Knowles, T., & Shukla, S. (2000). Analyzing the multiple functions of stereotypical behavior for students with autism: Implications for assessment and treatment. *Journal of Applied Behavior Analysis, 33,* 559–571.

Lloyd, L. L., Fuller, D. R., & Arvidson, H. H. (Eds.). (1997). *Augmentative and alternative communication: A handbook of principles and practices*. Boston: Allyn & Bacon.

Loncke, F. (2001). Augmentative and alternative communication in the 21st century. *Augmentative and Alternative Communication, 17,* 61.

Marvin, C. A., Beukelman, D. R., Brockhaus, J., & Kast, L. (1994). "What are you talking about?" Semantic analysis of preschool children's conversational topics in home and preschool settings. *Augmentative and Alternative Communication, 10,* 75–86.

McLean, M. E., & Odom, S. L. (1996). Establishing recommended practices in early intervention/early childhood special education. In S. L. Odom & M. E. McLean (Eds.), *Early intervention/early childhood special education: Recommended practices* (pp. 1–22). Austin, TX: Pro-Ed.

Miles, B. (1998). *Overview of deaf-blindness*. Monmouth, OR: DB-LINK. Retrieved May 15, 2001, from www.tr.wou.edu/dblink/Overview2.htm

Miles, B. (1999, March 9). *Talking the language of the hands*. Retrieved June 1, 2001, from www.tr.wou.edu/dblink/hands2.htm

Miner, I., & Cioffi, J. (1999, October 25). *Usher syndrome in the school setting*. Retrieved May 15, 2001, from www.tr.wou.edu/dblink/usherfulltext.htm

Moon, M. S., & Inge, K. (2000). Vocational preparation and transition. In M. E. Snell & F. Brown (Eds.), *Instruction of students with severe disabilities* (5th ed., pp. 591–628). Upper Saddle River, NJ: Merrill.

Morris, R. J., & Mather, N. (Eds.) (2008). *Evidence-based interventions for students with learning and behavioral challenges*. London: Taylor & Francis.

Mostert, M. P. (2001). Facilitated communication since 1995: A review of published studies. *Journal of Autism and Developmental Disorders, 31,* 287–313.

Mostert, M. P., Kavale, K. A., & Kauffman, J. M. (Eds.). (2008). *Challenging the refusal of reasoning in special education.* Denver, CO: Love.

Mulick, J. A., & Butter, E. M. (2005). Positive behavior support: A paternalistic utopian delusion. In J. W. Jacobson, R. M. Foxx, & J. A. Mulick (Eds.), *Controversial therapies for developmental disabilities: Fad, fashion, and science in professional practice* (pp. 385–404). Mahwah, NJ: Lawrence Erlbaum Associates.

National Information Clearinghouse On Children Who Are Deaf-Blind. (2001, May 18). *State definitions of deaf-blindness.* Retrieved June 9, 2001 from www.tr.wosc.osshe.edu/dblink/data/definitions.htm

National Research Council. (2001). *Educating children with autism.* Washington, DC: National Academy Press.

Nelson, N. W. (1998). *Childhood language disorders in context: Infancy through adolescence* (2nd ed.). Boston: Allyn & Bacon.

Newsom, C., & Kroeger, K. A. (2005). Nonaversive treatment. In J. W. Jacobson, R. M. Foxx, & J. A. Mulick (Eds.), *Controversial therapies for developmental disabilities: Fad, fashion, and science in professional practice* (pp. 405–422). Mahwah, NJ: Lawrence Erlbaum Associates.

Nezu, C. M., Nezu, A. M., Klein, T. L., & Clair, M. (2007). Sex offending behavior. In J. W. Jacobson, J. A. Mulick, & J. Rojahn (Eds.), *Handbook of intellectual and developmental disabilities* (pp. 635–655). New York: Springer.

Noonan, M. J., & McCormick, L. (2006). *Young children with disabilities in natural environments.* Baltimore: Paul H. Brookes.

Oken-Fried, M., & Bersani, H. A. (Eds.). (2000). *Speaking up and spelling it out: Personal essays on augmentative and alternative communication.* Baltimore: Paul H. Brookes.

Oley, C. A. (2001). CHARGE association. In S. B. Cassidy & J. E. Allanson (Eds.), *Management of genetic syndromes* (pp. 71–84). New York: Wiley-Liss.

Osborne, J. G. (2005). Person-centered planning: A *faux fixe* in the service of humanism? In J. W. Jacobson, R. M. Foxx, & J. A. Mulick (Eds.), *Controversial therapies for developmental disabilities: Fad, fashion, and science in professional practice* (pp. 313–329). Mahwah, NJ: Lawrence Erlbaum Associates.

Pease, L. (2000). Creating a communicating environment. In S. Aitken, M. Buultjens, C. Clark, J. T. Eyre, & L. Pease (Eds.), *Teaching children who are deafblind: Contact, communication, and learning* (pp. 35–82). London: David Fulton Publishers.

Persel, C. S., & Persel, C. H. (2004). The use of applied behavior analysis: Traumatic brain injury rehabilitation. In M. J. Ashley (Ed.), *Traumatic brain injury: Rehabilitative treatment and case management* (2nd ed., pp. 403–453). Boca Raton, FL: CRC Press.

Rapp, J. T., Miltenberger, R. G., Galensky, T. L., Ellingson, S. A., & Long, E. S. (1999). A functional analysis of hair-pulling. *Journal of Applied Behavior Analysis, 32,* 329–337.

Savage, R. C. (1988). *Introduction to educational issues for students who have suffered traumatic brain injury. An educator's manual: What educators need to know about students with traumatic brain injury.* Southborough, MA: Author.

Scheetz, N. A. (2001). *Orientation to deafness* (2nd ed.). Boston: Allyn & Bacon.

Schlosser, R. W., & Raghenvendra, P. (2004). Evidence-based practice in augmentative and alternative communication. *Augmentative and Alternative Communication, 20,* 1–21.

Snell, M. E. (2004). What if your child lacks needed communication services and supports? *Exceptional Parent, 34* (2), 41–44.

Snell, M. E., & Brown, F. (2006). *Instruction of students with severe disabilities* (6th ed.). Upper Saddle River, NJ: Prentice Hall.

Stichter, J. P., Conroy, M. A., & Kauffman, J. M. (2008). *An introduction to students with high-incidence disabilities.* Upper Saddle River, NJ: Merrill-Prentice Hall.

Thompson, R. H., & Iwata, B. A. (2001). A descriptive analysis of social consequences following problem behavior. *Journal of Applied Behavior Analysis, 34,* 169–178.

Tyler, J. S., & Mira, M. P. (1999). *Traumatic brain injury in children and adolescents: A sourcebook for teachers and other school personnel* (2nd ed.). Austin, TX: Pro-Ed.

Wehmeyer, M. (1992). Self-determination and the education of students with mental retardation. *Education and Training in Mental Retardation, 27,* 303–314.

Westling, D. L., & Fox, L. (2000). *Teaching students with severe disabilities* (2nd ed.). Upper Saddle River, NJ: Merrill.

Worsdell, A. S., Iwata, B. A., Conners, J., Kahng, S. W. & Thompson, R. H. (2000). Relative influences of establishing operations and reinforcement contingencies on selfinjurious behavior during functional analysis. *Journal of Applied Behavior Analysis, 33,* 451–461.

Yoder, D. E. (2001). Having my say. *Augmentative and Alternative Communication, 17,* 2–10.

CHAPTER 14

Ainsa, P. (2000). *Teaching children with AIDS.* Lampeter, Ceredigion, Wales, UK: Edwin Mellen Press.

Andersson, C., & Mattson, E. (2001). Adults with cerebral palsy: A survey describing problems, needs, and resources, with special emphasis on locomotion. *Developmental Medicine and Child Neurology, 43,* 76–82.

Archibald, S. L., Fennema-Notestine, C., Gamst, A., Riley, E. P., Mattson, S. N., & Jernigan, T. L. (2001). Brain dysmorphology in individuals with prenatal alcohol exposure. *Developmental Medicine and Child Neurology, 43,* 148–154.

Arzimanoglou, A., Guerrini, R., & Aicardi, J. (2004). *Aicardi's epilepsy in children* (3rd ed.). Philadelphia: Lippincott Williams & Wilkins.

Auxter, D., Pyfer, J., & Huettig, C. (2005). *Principles and methods of adapted physical education and recreation* (10th ed.). New York: McGraw-Hill.

Avoli, M., Rogawski, M. A., & Avanzini, G. (2001). Generalized epileptic disorders: An update. *Epilepsia, 42,* 445–457.

Ayala, G. F., Elia, M., Cornaggia, C. M., & Trimble, M. M. (Eds.). (2001). Epilepsy and learning disabilities. *Epilepsia, 42* (Suppl. 1).

Barkovich, A. J. (2005). *Pediatric neuroimaging* (4th ed.). Philadelphia: Lippincott Williams & Wilkins.

Bartonek, A., & Saraste, H. (2001). Factors influencing ambulation in myelomeningocele: A cross-sectional study. *Developmental Medicine and Child Neurology, 43,* 253–260.

Batshaw, M. L. (Ed.). (2002). *Children with disabilities* (5th ed.). Baltimore: Paul H. Brookes.

Batshaw, M. L., & Tuchman, M. (2002). PKU and other inborn errors of metabolism. In M. L. Batshaw (Ed.), *Children with disabilities* (5th ed., pp. 333–345). Baltimore: Paul H. Brookes.

Battering and teen pregnancy: A connection too real to ignore. (2001, Fall). *Shelter News.* Charlottesville, VA: Shelter for Help in Emergency.

Bax, M. (2001). Editorial: What's in a name? *Developmental Medicine and Child Neurology, 43,* 75.

Besag, F. M. C. (1995). Epilepsy, learning, and behavior in children. *Epilepsia, 36,* 58–63.

Best, S. J., Heller, K. W., & Bigge, J. L. (2005). *Teaching individuals with physical or multiple disabilities* (5th ed.). Upper Saddle River, NJ: Prentice Hall.

Bottos, M., Feliciangeli, A., Sciuto, L., Gericke, C., & Vianello, A. (2001). Functional status of adults with cerebral palsy and implications for treatment of children. *Developmental Medicine and Child Neurology, 43,* 516–528.

Bullock, C. C., & Mahon, M. J. (2000). *Introduction to recreation services for people with disabilities: A person-centered approach.* Champaign, IL: Sagamore.

Cascio, J. (2007, June 13). *The Accidental Cyborg.* Retrieved October 8, 2007, from http://ieet.org/index.php/IEET/more/cascio20070613/

Closs, A. (Ed.). (2000). *The education of children with medical conditions.* London: David Fulton.

Conlon, C. J. (2002). Early intervention. In M. L. Batshaw (Ed.), *Children with disabilities* (5th ed., pp. 579–588). Baltimore: Paul H. Brookes.

Cowden, A. J., & Funkhouser, E. (2001). Adolescent pregnancy, infant mortality, and source of payment for birth: Alabama residential live births, 1991–1994. *Journal of Adolescent Health, 29,* 37–45.

DeAngelis, C. D. (Ed.). (2007). Chronic diseases of children. *Journal of the American Medical Association, 297* (24).

DeFord, S. (1998, July 26). High tech for the disabled. *The Washington Post Education Review, 4,* 30.

Earley, T. (2000). *Jim the Boy.* Boston: Little, Brown.

Giardino, A. P., Kohrt, A. E., Arye, L., & Wells, N. (2002). Health care delivery systems and financing issues. In M. L. Batshaw (Ed.), *Children with disabilities* (5th ed., pp. 707–724). Baltimore: Paul H. Brookes.

Goodman, E. (2007, May 29). Wheels competing with feet. *Charlottesville Daily Progress,* A8.

Gouvier, W. D., Brown, L. M., Prestholdt, P. H., Hayes, J. S., & Apostolas, G. (1995). A survey of common misconceptions about epilepsy *Rehabilitation Psychology, 40,* 51–59.

Hanson, M. J. (Ed.). (1996). *Atypical infant development* (2nd ed.). Austin TX: Pro-Ed.

Heller, K. W., Alberto, P. A., Forney, P. E., & Schwartzman, M. N. (1996). *Understanding physical, sensory, and health impairments: Characteristics and educational implications.* Pacific Grove, CA: Brooks/Cole.

Holmes, M. S. (2004). *Fictions of affliction: Physical disability in Victorian culture.* Ann Arbor, MI: University of Michigan Press.

Howe, M. (n.d.) *Born to run.* Retrieved October 8, 2007 from www.spectrum.ieee.org/print/2189

Leaman, O. (2000). Schools and death. In A. Closs (Ed.), *The education of children with medical conditions* (pp. 155–168). London: David Fulton.

Leet, A. I., Dormans, J. P., & Tosi, L. L. (2002). Muscles, bones, and nerves: The body's framework. In M. L. Batshaw (Ed.), *Children with disabilities* (5th ed., pp. 263–284). Baltimore: Paul H. Brookes.

Lerner, J. W., Lowenthal, B., & Egan, R. (1998). *Preschool children with special needs: Children at risk, children with disabilities.* Boston: Allyn & Bacon.

Levy, S. E., & O'Rourke, M. (2002). Technological assistance: Innovations for independence. In M. L. Batshaw (Ed.), *Children with disabilities* (5th ed., pp. 629–645). Baltimore: Paul H. Brookes.

Lindsey, J. E. (Ed.). (2000). *Technology and exceptional individuals* (3rd ed.). Austin, TX: Pro-Ed.

Liptak, G. (2002). Neural tube defects. In M. L. Batshaw (Ed.), *Children with disabilities* (5th ed., pp. 467–492). Baltimore: Paul H. Brookes.

Llewellyn, A., & Chung, M. C. (1997). The self-esteem of children with physical disabilities—Problems and dilemmas of research. *Journal of Developmental and Physical Disabilities, 9,* 265–275.

Longman, J. (2007, May 15). An amputee sprinter: Is he disabled or too-abled? *The New York Times.* Retrieved June 28, 2007, from http://www.nytimes.com/2007/05/15/sports/othersports/15runner.html?ex=1183176000&en=1a1cac2e919125c0&ei=5070

Magill-Evans, J., Darrah, J., Pain, K., Adkins, R., & Kratochvil, M. (2001). Are families with adolescents and young adults with cerebral palsy the same as other families? *Developmental Medicine and Child Neurology, 43,* 466–472.

Martin, S. (2006). *Teaching motor skills to children with cerebral palsy and similar movement disorders: A guide for parents and professionals.* Bethesda, MD: Woodbine House.

McGrath, B. (2007, July 30). Muscle memory: The next generation of bionic prostheses. *The New Yorker,* 40–45.

Metzler, I. (2006). *Disability in medieval Europe: Thinking about physical impairment during the Middle Ages, c. 1100–1400.* New York: Routledge.

Morningstar, M. E., Turnbull, H. R., Lattin, D. L., Umbarger, G. T., Reichard, A., & Moberly, R. (2001). Students supported by medical technology: Making the transition from school to adult life. *Journal of Developmental and Physical Disabilities, 13,* 229–259.

Murphy, D. A., Roberts, K., & Hoffman, D. (2002). Stigma and ostracism associated with HIV/AIDS children carrying the secret

of their mothers' HIV + serostatus. *Journal of Child and Family Studies, 11,* 191–202.

Nabors, L. A., & Larson, E. R. (2002). The effects of brief interventions on children's playmate preferences for a child sitting in a wheelchair. *Journal of Developmental and Physical Disabilities, 14,* 403–413.

Nabors, L. A., & Lehmkuhl, H. D. (2004). Children with chronic medical conditions: Recommendations for school mental health clinicians. *Journal of Developmental and Physical Disabilities, 16,* 1–19.

Navarro, M. (2007, May 13). 'This is who I am. If you have a problem with it, that's your problem.' *The New York Times,* Section 9, 1, 8–9.

Olrick, J. T., Pianta, R. C., & Marvin, R. S. (2002). Mother's and father's responses to signals of children with cerebral palsy during feeding. *Journal of Developmental and Physical Disabilities, 14,* 1–17.

Parra, J., Augustijn, P. B., Geerts, Y., & Boas, W. (2001). Classification of epileptic seizures: a comparison of two systems. *Epilepsia, 42,* 476–482.

Pellegrino, L. (2002). Cerebral palsy. In M. L. Batshaw (Ed.), *Children with disabilities* (5th ed., pp. 443–466). Baltimore: Paul H. Brookes.

Perrin, J. M., Bloom, S. R., & Gortmaker, S. L. (2007). The increase of childhood chronic conditions in the United States. *Journal of the American Medical Association, 297,* 2755–2759.

Robertson, C. M. T., Watt, M., & Yasui, Y. (2007). Changes in the prevalence of cerebral palsy for children born very prematurely within a population-based program over 30 years. *Journal of the American Medical Association, 297,* 2733–2740.

Rogers, A. S. (2001). HIV research in American youth. *Journal of Adolescent Health, 29* (Suppl. 3S), 1–4.

Saslow, E. (2007, April 12). In Maryland, a fight to the finish line: Wheelchair racer's quest for inclusion spurs debate. *The Washington Post,* A1, A16.

Sherman, E. M. S., Slick, D. J., & Eyrl, K. L. (2006). Executive dysfunction is a significant predictor of poor quality of live in children with epilepsy. *Epilepsia, 47,* 1936–1942.

Sherrill, C. (2004). *Adapted physical activity, recreation, and sport: Crossdisciplinary and lifespan* (6th ed.). New York: McGraw-Hill.

Singh, D. K. (2003). Families of children with spina bifida: A review. *Journal of Developmental and Physical Disabilities, 15,* 37–55.

Spiegel, G. L., Cutler, S. K., & Yetter, C. I. (1996). What every teacher should know about epilepsy. *Intervention in School and Clinic, 32,* 34–38.

Spiegel, H. M. L., & Bonwit, A. M. (2002). HIV infection in children. In M. L. Batshaw (Ed.), *Children with disabilities* (5th ed., pp. 123–139). Baltimore: Paul H. Brookes.

U.S. Department of Education. (2005). *Twenty-seventh annual report to Congress on implementation of the Individuals with Disabilities Education Act.* Washington, DC: Author.

Vig, S., & Kaminer, R. (2002). Maltreatment and developmental disabilities in children. *Journal of Developmental and Physical Disabilities, 14,* 371–386.

Vining, E. P. G., & Freeman, J. M. (1996). Epilepsy and developmental disabilities. In A. J. Capute & P. J. Accardo (Eds.), *Developmental disabilities in infancy and childhood: Vol. 2. The spectrum of developmental disabilities* (2nd ed., pp. 511–520). Baltimore: Paul H. Brookes.

Weinstein, S. (2002). Epilepsy. In M. L. Batshaw (Ed.), *Children with disabilities* (5th ed., pp. 493–523). Baltimore: Paul H. Brookes.

Welch, E. M., Barton, E. R., Zhuo, J., Tomizawa, Y., Friesen, W. J., Trifillis, P., et al. (2007, May 3). PTC124 targets genetic disorders caused by nonsense mutations. *Nature, 447,* 87–91. Retrieved April 29, 2007, from www.nature.com/nature/journal/vaop/ncurrent/abs/nature05756.html

White, P. H., Schuyler, V., Edelman, A., Hayes, A., & Batshaw, M. L. (2002). Future expectations: Transition from adolescence to adulthood. In M. L. Batshaw (Ed.), *Children with disabilities* (5th ed., pp. 693–705). Baltimore: Paul H. Brookes.

Willen, E. J. (2006). Neurocognitive outcomes in pediatric HIV. *Mental Retardation and Developmental Disabilities Research Reviews, 12,* 223–228.

Wolman, C., Garwick, A., Kohrman, C., & Blum, R. (2001). Parents' wishes and expectations for children with chronic conditions. *Journal of Developmental and Physical Disabilities, 13,* 261–277.

Zylke, J. W., & DeAngelis, C. D. (2007). Pediatric chronic diseases—stealing childhood. *Journal of the American Medical Association, 297,* 2765–2766.

CHAPTER 15

Amabile, T. M. (2001). Beyond talent: John Irving and the passionate craft of creativity. *American Psychologist, 56,* 333–336.

Assouline, S., & Lupkowski-Shoplik, A. (2003). *Developing mathematical talent: A guide for challenging and educating gifted students.* Waco, TX: Prufrock Press.

Assouline, S. G., & Colangelo, N. (2006). Social-emotional development of gifted adolescents. In F. A. Dixon & S. M. Moon (Eds.), *The handbook of secondary gifted education* (pp. 65–86). Waco, TX: Prufrock Press.

Baum, S. M., Olenchak, F. R., & Owen, S. V. (1998). Gifted students with attention deficits: Fact and/or fiction? Or, can we see the forest for the trees? *Gifted Child Quarterly, 42,* 96–104.

Baum, S. M., Rizza, M. G., & Renzulli, S. (2006). Twice-exceptional adolescents: Who are they? What do they need? In F. A. Dixon & S. M. Moon (Eds.), *The handbook of secondary gifted education* (pp. 137–164). Waco, TX: Prufrock Press.

Borland, J. H. (1989). *Planning and implementing programs for the gifted.* New York: Teachers College Press.

Borland, J. H. (2004). *Issues and practices in the identification and education of gifted students from under-represented groups.* Storrs, CT: National Research Center on the Gifted and Talented.

Bridglall, B. L., & Gordon, E. W. (2005, September). *Nurturing talent in underrepresented students: A study of the Meyerhoff Scholars program at the university of Maryland, Baltimore County* (RM05212). Storrs, CT: University of Connecticut, National Research Center on the Gifted and Talented.

Brody, L. E., & Stanley, J. C. (2005). Youths who reason exceptionally well mathematically and/or verbally. In R. J. Sternberg & J. E. Davidson (Eds.), *Conceptions of giftedness* (2nd ed., pp. 20–37). New York: Cambridge University Press.

Burge, K. (1998, April). Prodigies. *U.S. Airways Attache,* 80–87.

Callahan, C. M. (2000). Evaluation as a critical component of program development and implementation. In K. A. Heller, F. J. Monks, R. J. Sternberg, & R. F. Subotnik (Eds.), *International handbook of giftedness and talent* (2nd ed., pp. 537–548). New York: Pergamon.

Callahan, C. M. (2001). Evaluating learner and program outcomes in gifted education. In F. A. Karnes & S. M. Bean (Eds.), *Methods and materials for teaching the gifted* (pp. 253–298). Waco, TX: Prufrock Press.

Callahan, C. M. (2003). *Advanced placement and international baccalaureate programs for talented students in American high schools: A focus on science and mathematics.* Storrs, CT: National Research Center on the Gifted and Talented.

Callahan, C. M., & Miller, E. M. (2005). A child-responsive model of giftedness. In R. J. Sternberg & J. E. Davidson (Eds.), *Conceptions of giftedness* (2nd ed., pp. 38–51). New York: Cambridge University Press.

Castellano, J. A. (Ed.) (2003). *Special populations in gifted education: Working with diverse gifted learners.* Boston: Allyn Bacon.

Chan, D. W. (2006). Perceived multiple intelligences among male and female Chinese gifted students in Hon Kong: The structure of the Student Multiple Intelligences Profile. *Gifted Child Quarterly, 50,* 325–338.

Clark, B. (1997). *Growing up gifted: Developing the potential of children at home and at school* (5th ed.). Upper Saddle River, NJ: Prentice-Hall.

Colangelo, N., Assouline, S. G., & Gross, M. U. M. (2004a). *A nation deceived: How schools hold back America's brightest students. Vol. I.* Iowa City, IA: Connie Belin & Jacqueline N. Blank International Center for Gifted Education and Talent Development.

Colangelo, N., Assouline, S. G., & Gross, M. U. M. (Eds.). (2004b). *A nation deceived: How schools hold back America's brightest students. Vol. II.* Iowa City, IA: Connie Belin & Jacqueline N. Blank International Center for Gifted Education and Talent Development.

Coleman, L. J., & Cross, T. L. (2000). Social-emotional development and the personal experience of giftedness. In K. A. Heller, F. J. Monks, R. J. Sternberg, & R. F. Subotnik (Eds.), *International handbook of giftedness and talent* (2nd ed., pp. 203–212). New York: Pergamon.

Cramond, B., Matthews-Morgan, J., Bandalos, D., & Zuo, L. (2005). A report on the 40-year follow-up of the Torrence Tests of Creative Thinking: Alive and well in the new millennium. Gifted *Child Quarterly, 49,* 283–291.

Cross, T. L., & Coleman, L. J. (2005). School-based conception of giftedness. In R. J. Sternberg & J. E. Davidson (Eds.), *Conceptions of giftedness* (2nd ed., pp. 52–63). New York: Cambridge University Press.

Davis, G. A., & Rimm S. B. (2004). *Education of the gifted and talented* (5th ed.). Boston: Allyn & Bacon.

De Hahn, E. L. H. (2000). Cross-cultural studies in gifted education. In K. A. Heller, F. J. Monks, R. J. Sternberg, & R. F. Subotnik (Eds.), *International handbook of giftedness and talent* (2nd ed., pp. 549–561). New York: Pergamon.

DiGennaro, J. (2007, February 10). Gifted minds we need to nurture. *The Washington Post,* A17.

Dixon, F. A., & Moon, S. M. (Eds.). (2006). *The handbook of secondary gifted education.* Waco, TX: Prufrock Press.

Feldhusen, J. F. (2005). Giftedness, talent, expertise, and creative achievement. In R. J. Sternberg & J. E. Davidson (Eds.), *Conceptions of giftedness* (2nd ed., pp. 64–79). New York: Cambridge University Press.

Ford, D. Y., & Moore, J. L. (2006). Being gifted and adolescent: Issues and needs of students of color. In F. A. Dixon & S. M. Moon (Eds.), *The handbook of secondary gifted education* (pp. 113–136). Waco, TX: Prufrock Press.

Freeman, J. (2000). Families: The essential context for gifts and talents. In K. A. Heller, F. J. Monks, R. J. Sternberg, & R. F. Subotnik (Eds.), *International handbook of giftedness and talent* (2nd ed., pp. 573–586). New York: Pergamon.

Freeman, J. (2005). Permission to be gifted: How conceptions of giftedness can change lives. In R. J. Sternberg & J. E. Davidson (Eds.), *Conceptions of giftedness* (2nd ed., pp. 80–97). New York: Cambridge University Press.

Gagne, F. (2000). Understanding the complex choreography of talent development through DMGT-based analysis. In K. A. Heller, F. J. Monks, R. J. Sternberg, & R. F. Subotnik (Eds.), *International handbook of giftedness and talent* (2nd ed., pp. 67–79). New York: Pergamon.

Gallagher, J. J. (1998). Accountability for gifted students. *Phi Delta Kappan, 79,* 739–742.

Gallagher, J. J. (2000a). Changing paradigms for gifted education in the United States. In K. A. Heller, F. J. Monks, R. J. Sternberg, & R. F. Subotnik (Eds.), *International handbook of giftedness and talent* (2nd ed., pp. 681–693). New York: Pergamon.

Gallagher, J. J. (2000b). Unthinkable thoughts: Education of gifted students. *Gifted Child Quarterly, 44,* 5–12.

Gallagher, J. J. (2002). *Society's role in educating gifted students: The role of public policy.* Storrs, CT: National Research Center on the Gifted and Talented.

Gallagher, J. J. (2004). Public policy and acceleration of gifted students. In N. Colangelo, S. G. Assouline, & M. U. M. Gross (Eds.), *A nation deceived: How schools hold back America's brightest students. Vol. II* (pp. 39–45). Iowa City, IA: Connie Belin & Jacqueline N. Blank International Center for Gifted Education and Talent Development.

Gallagher, J. J. (2006). According to Jim: Best and worst of gifted education. *Roeper Review, 29,* 10.

Gallagher, J. J., & Gallagher, S. A. (1994). *Teaching the gifted child* (4th ed.). Boston: Allyn & Bacon.

Gardner, H., & Hatch, T. (1989). Multiple intelligences go to school: Educational implications of the theory of multiple intelligences. *Educational Researcher, 18* (8), 4–9.

Gentry, M. (2006). No Child Left Behind: neglecting excellence. *Roeper Review, 29,* 24–27.

Goldsmith, B. (2005). *Obsessive genius: The inner world of Marie Curie.* New York: Norton.

Goodkin, S. (2005, December 27). Leave no gifted child behind. *The Washington Post,* A25.

Gordon, E. W., & Bridglall, B. L. (2005). Nurturing talent in gifted students of color. In R. J. Sternberg & J. E. Davidson (Eds.), *Conceptions of giftedness* (2nd ed., pp. 120–146). New York: Cambridge University Press.

Gould, S. J. (1996). *The mismeasure of man* (Rev. ed.). New York: Norton.

Grazer, B. (Producer), & Howard, R. (Producer/Director). *A beautiful mind* [Motion picture]. United States: Universal Studios.

Gross, M. U. M. (2000). Issues in the cognitive development of exceptionally and profoundly gifted individuals. In K. A. Heller, F. J. Monks, R. J. Sternberg, & R. F. Subotnik (Eds.), *International handbook of giftedness and talent* (2nd ed., pp. 179–192). New York: Pergamon.

Gross, M. U. M. (2002). Social and emotional issues for exceptionally intellectually gifted students. In M. Neihart, S. M. Reis, N. M. Robinson, & S. M. Moon (Eds.), *The social and emotional development of gifted children. What do we know?* (pp. 19–29). Waco, TX: Prufrock Press.

Gruber, H. E., & Wallace, D. B. (2001). Creative work: The case of Charles Darwin. *American Psychologist, 56,* 346–349.

Heller, K. A., Monks, F. J., Sternberg, R. J., & Subotnik, R. F. (Eds.). (2000). *International handbook of giftedness and talent* (2nd ed.). New York: Pergamon.

Henshon, S. E. (2006). A journey through creativity as a writer and researcher: An interview with Jane Pirto. *Roeper Review, 29,* 5–9.

Herbert, T. P., & Kelly, K. R. (2006). Identity and career development in gifted students. In F. A. Dixon & S. M. Moon (Eds.), *The handbook of secondary gifted education* (pp. 35–64). Waco, TX: Prufrock Press.

Huefner, D. S. (2006). *Getting comfortable with special education law: A framework for working with children with disabilities* (2nd ed.). Norwood, MA: Christopher-Gordon.

Hunsaker, S. L. (1995). The gifted metaphor from the perspective of traditional civilizations. *Journal for the Education of the Gifted, 18,* 255–268.

Hunsaker, S. L. (2005). Outcomes of creativity training programs. *Gifted Child Quarterly, 49,* 292–299.

Hunsaker, S. L., & Callahan, C. M. (1995). Creativity and giftedness: Published instrument uses and abuses. *Gifted Child Quarterly, 39,* 110–114.

Hunter, S. (2001, December 21). Fragile genius of "A Beautiful Mind:" The human enigma within the known patterns of the universe. *The Washington Post,* C1, C5.

Jacobs, A. J. (2004). *The know-it-all: One man's humble quest to become the smartest person in the world.* New York: Simon & Schuster.

Karnes, M. B., & Bean, S. M. (Eds.). (2001). *Methods and materials for teaching the gifted.* Waco, TX: Prufrock Press.

Kaufmann, F. A., & Castellanos, F. X. (2000). Attention deficit/hyperactivity disorder in gifted students. In K. A. Heller, F. J. Monks, R. J. Sternberg, & R. F. Subotnik (Eds.), *International handbook of giftedness and talent* (2nd ed., pp. 621–632). New York: Pergamon.

Kaufmann, F., Kalbfleisch, M. L., & Castellanos, F. X. (2000). *Attention deficit disorders and gifted students: What do we really know?* Storrs, CT: National Research Center on the Gifted and Talented.

Kauffman, J. M. (2002). *Education deform: Bright people sometimes say stupid things about education.* Lanham, MD: Scarecrow Education.

Kauffman, J. M. & Hallahan, D. P. (2005). *Special education: What it is and why we need it.* Boston: Allyn & Bacon.

Kauffman, J. M., & Konold, T. R. (2007). Making sense in education: Pretense (including NCLB) and realities in rhetoric and policy about schools and schooling. *Exceptionality, 15,* 75–96.

Kerr, B. (2000). Guiding gifted girls and young women. In K. A. Heller, F. J. Monks, R. J. Sternberg, & R. F. Subotnik (Eds.), *International handbook of giftedness and talent* (2nd ed., pp. 649–658). New York: Pergamon.

Kohler, P. D., & Field, S. (2006). Transition-focused education: Foundation for the future. In B. G. Cook & B. R. Schirmer (Eds.), *What is special about special education? Examining the role of evidence-based practices* (pp. 86–99). Austin, TX: Pro-Ed.

Landrum, M. S., Callahan, C. M., & Shaklee, B. D. (Eds.). (2001). *Aiming for excellence: Gifted program standards.* Waco, TX: Prufrock Press.

Lloyd, J. W., & Hallahan, D. P. (2007). Advocacy and reform of special education. In J. B. Crockett, M. M. Gerber, & T. J. Landrum (Eds.), *Achieving the radical reform of special education: Essays in honor of James M. Kauffman* (pp. 245–263). Mahwah, NJ: Lawrence Erlbaum Associates.

Lohman, D. F. (2005, September). *Identifying academically talented minority students* (RM05216). Storrs, CT: University of Connecticut, National Research Center on the Gifted and Talented.

Lohman, D. F. (2006). Exploring perceptions and awareness of high ability. *Roeper Review, 29,* 32–40.

Lubinski, D., Benbow, C. P., & Morelock, M. J. (2000). Gender differences in engineering and the physical sciences among the gifted: An inorganic-organic distinction. In K. A. Heller, F. J. Monks, R. J. Sternberg, & R. F. Subotnik (Eds.), *International handbook of giftedness and talent* (2nd ed., pp. 633–648). New York: Pergamon.

Manstetten, R. (2000). Promotion of the gifted in vocational training. In K. A. Heller, F. J. Monks, R. J. Sternberg, & R. F. Subotnik (Eds.), *International handbook of giftedness and talent* (2nd ed., pp. 439–446). New York: Pergamon.

Martindale, C. (2001). Oscillations and analogies: Thomas Young, MD, FRS, genius. *American Psychologist, 56,* 342–345.

McCluskey, K. W., Baker, P. A., & McCluskey, A. L. A. (2005). Creative problem solving with marginalized populations: Reclaiming lost prizes through in-the-trenches interventions. *Gifted Child Quarterly, 49,* 330–341.

McGreevy, A. L. (2004). Under her spell: An analysis of the creativity of JK Rowling. *Gifted Education International, 19,* 34–40.

McKenzie, B. (2007, February 24). First-grader blows away audiences. *Charlottesville Daily Progress,* A2.

Mendoza, C. (2006). Inside today's classrooms: Teacher voices on No Child Left Behind and the education of gifted children. *Roeper Review, 29,* 28–31.

Monks, F. J., & Katzko, M. W. (2005). Giftedness and gifted education. In R. J. Sternberg & J. E. Davidson (Eds.), *Conceptions of giftedness* (2nd ed., pp. 187–200). New York: Cambridge University Press.

Moon, S. M., & Reis, S. M. (2004). Acceleration and twice-exceptional students. In N. Colangelo, S. G. Assouline, & M. U. M. Gross (Eds.), *A nation deceived: How schools hold back America's brightest students. Vol. II* (pp. 109–195). Iowa City, IA: Connie Belin & Jacqueline N. Blank International Center for Gifted Education and Talent Development.

Moon, S. M., Zentall, S., Grskovic, J. A., Hall, A., & Stormont, M. (2001). Emotional and social characteristics of boys with AD/HD and giftedness: A comparative case study. *Journal for the Education of the Gifted, 24,* 207–247.

Moore, J. L., Ford, D. Y., & Milner, H. R. (2005). Recruitment is not enough: Retaining African American students in gifted education. *Gifted Child Quarterly, 49,* 51–67.

Muratori, M. C., Stanley, J. C., Gross, M. U. M., Ng., L., Tao, T., & Ng., J., et al. (2006). Insights from SMPY's greatest former child prodigies: Drs. Terence ("Terry") Tao and Lenhard ("Lenny") Ng reflect on their talent development. *Gifted Child Quarterly, 50,* 307–324.

Murray, S. (2005, July 19). Grants for gifted children face major threat from budget ax. *The Washington Post,* A19.

Nakamura, J., & Csikszentmihalyi, M. (2001). Catalytic creativity: The case of Linus Pauling. *American Psychologist, 56,* 337–341.

Neihart, M., Reis, S. M., Robinson, N. M., & Moon, S. M. (Eds.). (2002). *The social and emotional development of gifted children. What do we know?* Waco, TX: Prufrock Press.

Odom, S. L., & Wolery, M. (2006). A unified theory of practice in early intervention/early childhood special education. In B. G. Cook & B. R. Schirmer (Eds.), *What is special about special education? Examining the role of evidence-based practices* (pp. 72–85). Austin, TX: Pro-Ed.

Perleth, C., Schatz, T., & Monks, F. J. (2000). Early identification of high ability. In K. A. Heller, F. J. Monks, R. J. Sternberg, & R. F. Subotnik

(Eds.), *International handbook of giftedness and talent* (2nd ed., pp. 297–316). New York: Pergamon.

Peterson, J. S., & Ray, K. E. (2006). Bullying among the gifted: The subjective experience. *Gifted Child Quarterly, 50*, 252–269.

Pinker, S. (2002). *The blank slate: The modern denial of human nature.* New York: Viking.

Plomin, R. (1997). Genetics and intelligence. In N. Colangelo & G. A. Davis (Eds.), *Handbook of gifted education* (2nd ed., pp. 67–74). Boston: Allyn & Bacon.

Plucker, J. A., & Stocking, V. B. (2001). Looking outside and inside: Self-concept development of gifted adolescents. *Exceptional Children, 67*, 535–548.

Porter, L. (2005). *Gifted young children: A guide for teachers and parents* (2nd ed.). Berkshire, England: Open University Press.

Reis, S. M. (2005). Feminist perspectives on talent development: A research-based conception of giftedness in women. In R. J. Sternberg & J. E. Davidson (Eds.), *Conceptions of giftedness* (2nd ed., pp. 217–245). New York: Cambridge University Press.

Reis, S. M., & Renzulli, J. S. (2001). The schoolwide enrichment model: Developing students' creativity and talents. In M. D. Lynch & C. R. Harris (Eds.), *Fostering creativity in children, K–8: Theory and practice* (pp. 15–39). Boston: Allyn & Bacon.

Reis, S. M., & McCoach, D. B. (2002). Underachievement in gifted students. In M. Neihart, S. M. Reis, N. M. Robinson, & S. M. Moon (Eds.), *The social and emotional development of gifted children. What do we know?* (pp. 81–91). Waco, TX: Prufrock Press.

Reiss, S. M. (2006). Gender, adolescence, and giftedness. In F. A. Dixon & S. M. Moon (Eds.), *The handbook of secondary gifted education* (pp. 87–112). Waco, TX: Prufrock Press.

Renzulli, J. S. (2005). The three-ring conception of giftedness: A developmental model for promoting creative productivity. In R. J. Sternberg & J. E. Davidson (Eds.), *Conceptions of giftedness* (2nd ed., pp. 246–279). New York: Cambridge University Press.

Renzulli, J. S., & Park. S. (2002). *Giftedness and high school dropouts: Personal, family, and school-related factors.* Storrs, CT: National Research Center on the Gifted and Talented.

Renzulli, J. S., & Reis, S. M. (1997). The schoolwide enrichment model: New directions for developing high-end learning. In N. Colangelo & G. A. Davis (Eds.), *Handbook of gifted education* (2nd ed., pp. 136–154). Boston: Allyn & Bacon.

Renzulli, J. S., & Reis, S. M. (2000). The schoolwide enrichment model. In K. A. Heller, F. J. Monks, R. J. Sternberg, & R. F. Subotnik (Eds.), *International handbook of giftedness and talent* (2nd ed., pp. 367–382). New York: Pergamon.

Robinson, A., Shore, B. M., & Enersen, D. L. (2007). *Best practices in gifted education: An evidence-based guide.* Waco, TX: Prufrock Press.

Robinson, N. M. (2005). In defense of a psychometric approach to the definition of academic giftedness: A conservative view from a die-hard liberal. In R. J. Sternberg & J. E. Davidson (Eds.), *Conceptions of giftedness* (2nd ed., pp. 280–294). New York: Cambridge University Press.

Ruf, D. L. (2005). *Losing our minds: Gifted children left behind.* Scottsdale, AZ: Great Potential Press.

Runco, M. A. (2005). Creative giftedness. In R. J. Sternberg & J. E. Davidson (Eds.), *Conceptions of giftedness* (2nd ed. pp. 295–311). New York: Cambridge University Press.

Selby, E. C., Shaw, E. J., & Houtz, J. C. (2005). The creative personality. *Gifted Child Quarterly, 49*, 300–314.

Shaywitz, S. E., Holahan, J. M., Freudenheim, D. A., Fletcher, J. M., Makuch, R. W., & Shaywitz, B. A. (2001). Heterogeneity within the gifted: Higher IQ boys exhibit behaviors resembling boys with learning disabilities. *Gifted Child Quarterly, 45*, 16–23.

Shermer, M. (2001). *The borderlands of science: Where sense meets nonsense.* New York: Oxford University Press.

Silverman, L. K. (1997). Family counseling with the gifted. In N. Colangelo & G. A. Davis (Eds.), *Handbook of gifted education* (2nd ed., pp. 382–397). Boston: Allyn & Bacon.

Simonton, D. K. (2005). Genetics of giftedness: The implications of an emergenic-epigenetic model. In R. J. Sternberg & J. E. Davidson

(Eds.), *Conceptions of giftedness* (2nd ed., pp. 312–326). New York: Cambridge University Press.

Sternberg, R. J. (1997). A triarchic view of giftedness: Theory and practice. In N. Colangelo & G. A. Davis (Eds.), *Handbook of gifted education* (2nd ed., pp. 43–53). Boston: Allyn & Bacon.

Sternberg, R. J. (1998). Abilities are forms of developing expertise. *Educational Researcher, 27* (3), 11–20.

Sternberg, R. J. (2000). Giftedness as developing expertise. In K. A. Heller, F. J. Monks, R. J. Sternberg, & R. F. Subotnik (Eds.), *International handbook of giftedness and talent* (2nd ed., pp. 23–54). New York: Pergamon.

Sternberg, R. J., & Davidson, J. E. (Eds.). (2005). *Conceptions of giftedness* (2nd ed.). New York: Cambridge University Press.

Sternberg, R. J., & Zhang, L. (1995). What do we mean by giftedness? A pentagonal implicit theory. *Gifted Child Quarterly, 39*, 88–94.

Stokes, P. D. (2001). Variability, constraints, and creativity: Shedding light on Claude Monet. *American Psychologist, 56*, 355–359.

Subotnik, R. F., & Arnold, K. D. (Eds.). (1994). *Beyond Terman: Contemporary longitudinal studies of giftedness and talent.* Norwood, NJ: Albex.

Swiatek, M. A. (1998). Helping gifted adolescents cope with social stigma. *Gifted Child Today, 21* (1), 42–46.

Tannenbaum, A. J. (1993). History of giftedness and "gifted education" in world perspective. In K. A. Heller, F. J. Monks, & A. H. Passow (Eds.), *International handbook of research and development of giftedness and talent* (pp. 3–27). New York: Pergamon.

Tannenbaum, A. J. (2000a). A history of giftedness in school and society. In K. A. Heller, F. J. Monks, R. J. Sternberg, & R. F. Subotnik (Eds.), *International handbook of giftedness and talent* (2nd ed., pp. 23–54). New York: Pergamon.

Tannenbaum, A. J. (2000b). Giftedness: The ultimate instrument for good and evil. In K. A. Heller, F. J. Monks, R. J. Sternberg, & R. F. Subotnik (Eds.), *International handbook of giftedness and talent* (2nd ed., pp. 447–466). New York: Pergamon.

Thompson, L. A., & Plomin, R. (2000). Genetic tools for exploring individual differences in intelligence. In K. A. Heller, F. J. Monks, R. J. Sternberg, & R. F. Subotnik (Eds.), *International handbook of giftedness and talent* (2nd ed., pp. 157–164). New York: Pergamon.

Tomlinson, C. A., Ford, D. Y., Reis, S. M., Briggs, C. J., & Strickland, C. A. (Eds.). (2004). *In search of the dream: Designing schools and classrooms that work for high potential students from diverse cultural backgrounds.* Washington, DC: National Association for Gifted Children.

Tomlinson, C. A., Kaplan, S. N., Renzulli, J. S., Purcell, J., Leppien, J., & Burns, D. (2002). *The parallel curriculum: A design to develop high potential and challenge high-ability learners.* Thousand Oaks, CA: Corwin.

Treffinger, D. J., & Isaksen, S. G. (2005). Creative problem solving: The history, development, and implications for gifted education and talent development. *Gifted Child Quarterly, 49*, 342–353.

Van Tassel-Baska, J. (2006). A content analysis of evaluation findings across 20 gifted programs: A clarion call for enhanced gifted program development. *Gifted Child Quarterly, 50*, 199–215.

Van Tassel-Baska, J., & Stambaugh, T. (2006). *Comprehensive curriculum for gifted learners* (3rd ed.). Boston: Allyn & Bacon.

von Karolyi, C., & Winner, E. (2005). Extreme giftedness. In R. J. Sternberg & J. E. Davidson (Eds.), *Conceptions of giftedness* (2nd ed., pp. 377–394). New York: Cambridge University Press.

Ward, T. B. (2001). Creative cognition, conceptual combination, and the creative writing of Sephen R. Donaldson. *American Psychologist, 56*, 350–354.

Willingham, D. T. (2004, Summer). Reframing the mind: Howard Gardner became a hero among educators simply by redefining talents as "intelligences" *Education Next,* 19–24.

Zirkel, P. A. (2003). *The law and gifted education.* Storrs, CT: National Research Center on the Gifted and Talented.

Author Index

Abbeduto, L., 159, 326
Abdelaal, I., 228
Abery, B. H., 174
Abikoff, H., 228, 251–252
Adams, C. M., 98
Adams, L. W., 437
Adams, M., 366
Adkins, R., 511
Adler, L., 254
Adlof, S., 312
Ager, A. K., 167
Ahlgrim-Delzell, L., 51
Aicardi, J., 500–501
Ainsa, P., 506
Aitken, S., 469, 471
Akshoomoff, N., 430
Al Otaiba, S., 101
Al Qahtani, R., 228
Al-Yagon, M., 201
Alberto, P. A., 504, 511, 514, 519
Albin, R. W., 133, 163, 439, 483–484
Albus, D., 100
Aldersley, S., 363
Algozzine, B., 50
Algozzine, R., 131, 162
Alloway, T. P., 200
Alpert, C. L., 327
Alsop, B., 236
Alsop, L., 474
Altman, J. R., 368, 411
Alwell, M., 246
Amabile, T. M., 534
Ambrose, N., 303
American Academy of Otolaryngology, 344
American Academy of Pediatrics, 344
American Federation for the Blind, 405
American Printing House for the Blind, 387
American Psychiatric Association, 282, 431, 437
American Speech-Language-Hearing Association, 322, 331
Amsel, R., 393
Anastopolos, A.D., 232
Andreason, N.C., 430
Andreason, P., 193
Andreou, P., 253
Angold, A., 269, 287
Anthony, A., 428–429
Apostolas, G., 501
Arbolino, L. A., 253
Archwamety, T., 290
Arganza, G. F., 95

Arguelles, M. E., 248
Arndt, S., 430
Arney, F., 228
Arnold, E. M., 201
Arnold, K. D., 537
Arnold, L. E., 228, 241, 251
Arnos, K. S., 347
Arora, T., 59
Arrega-Mayer, C., 64
Artiles, A. J., 95
Arvidson, H. H., 476, 478–479, 481
Arye, L., 495
Ashley, M. J., 459, 461
Asperger, H., 424
Assouline, S. G., 531, 541, 543, 552, 556–558
Astuto, T. A., 56, 287
Aubert, R. E., 250
Avanzini, G., 500

Bachmann, C., 194
Bacon-Shone, J., 231
Baghurst, P., 228
Bahan, B., 353, 358, 363, 369
Bailey, D. B., 73, 123, 159
Bailey, J., 396, 430
Baker, C., 130
Baker, J., 51, 99, 287
Baker, P. A., 539
Baker, R., 399
Baker, S., 93, 101, 104
Baldwin, V., 468
Balla, D. A., 167
Bambara, L. M., 489
Bandura, A., 279
Banks, C. A., 94, 102, 105, 108, 111
Bankson, N. W., 316
Bantz, J., 13, 16, 54, 286
Bardon, J. N., 56, 68
Barkley, R. A., 225, 227–228, 234–235, 237–238, 244–245, 250, 253–255
Barr, C., 235
Barratt, M. S., 130
Barrett, M. S., 253
Barry, L., 133
Bartels, M., 431
Barton, E. R., 5
Bateman, B. D., 16, 18, 24, 28, 30–32, 37, 54–55, 67, 110, 233
Bates, E., 445
Batshaw, M. L., 153, 504, 508, 519, 522
Bauer, J., 446
Baum, S. M., 545

Bauman-Waengler, J., 316
Baumeister, A. A., 147
Bauminger, N., 158
Bax, M., 499
Baxter, J., 199
Beale, A. J., 429
Bean, S. M., 534
Beard, K. Y., 272
Becerra, A. M., 153, 159
Beck, V., 88
Bedford, H., 429
Beeson, P. M., 321
Beirne-Smith, M., 151
Bell, K., 110
Ben, K. R., 133
Benasich, A. A., 311
Benbow, C. P., 547
Bender, W. N., 203, 218
Bennett, L., 103
Bentzen, B. L., 401
Benten, F. A., 241
Benz, M. R., 216
Berelowitz, M., 429
Berk, L. E., 412
Bernheimer, L. P., 120
Bersani, H. A., 480–481
Besag, F. M. C., 501
Best, A. M., 285
Bettelheim, B., 427
Betts, G., 61
Beukelman, D. R., 316, 480
Bice, H.V., 227
Biederman, J., 231, 234–236, 250, 254
Bielinski, J., 100
Bigge, J. L., 463, 467, 495, 500–504, 506, 508–509, 511–512, 514, 517, 519, 522
Biglan, A., 98
Billingsley-Marshall, R., 193
Birch, H. G., 227
Blacher, J., 173
Blachman, B., 196
Black, J., 406
Black, R. S., 158–159
Bleuler, E., 423
Bloom, S. R., 504
Blue-Banning, M., 126
Blum, R., 514
Boada, R., 235
Boardman, A. G., 58, 209
Bocian, K. M., 149, 192
Bodfish, J. W., 482–483
Bohanon, H., 78
Bond, T., 401
Bondy, A., 446
Boney, T. L., 167
Bonwit, A. M., 506
Bookheimer, S. Y., 430

Boomsma, D. I., 431
Boreson, L., 292–293
Borner, H., 234
Boscardin, M. L., 201
Bourquin, E., 476
Bowe, F. G., 72, 294, 486
Bowen, S., 367
Bower, E. M., 266, 295
Bradley, M. R., 79
Bradley-Johnson, S., 410
Bradley-Klug, K. L., 244, 246
Bradshaw, J. L., 234
Brady, M. P., 151, 153
Brady, N., 153, 159
Brashear, H., 363
Braukmann, C. J., 297
Braziel, P., 216
Breitenbach, E., 132
Brengelman, S., 105
Brenner, M., 103
Brereton, A. V., 431
Breslau, N., 241
Bridglall, B. L., 545
Brigance, A., 411
Brigham, F. J., 265
Brigham, M., 16, 58, 101
Brockhaus, J., 480
Browder, D.M., 51
Brown, D., 167, 255, 469
Brown, F., 459, 483, 488–489
Brown, I., 167
Brown, L. M., 501
Brown, R. I., 167
Bruhn, P., 234
Brunswick, N., 193
Buchino, M. A., 371
Bukstein, O., 250
Bulgren, J. A., 217
Bullis, M., 287, 296–297
Buntaine, R., 267
Burish, P., 207
Burke, P., 125
Burns, C., 122
Burns, D., 549
Burrows-MacLean, L., 251
Burstein, K., 201
Bursuck, W., 202, 293
Busnello, E., 231
Butler, D. L., 200
Butter, E. M., 482
Byrd, S. E., 439
Byrd-Craven, J., 200

Caballer, A., 388
Caballo, C., 167
Calhoon, M. B., 101
Calhoun, S. L., 252
Callahan, C. M., 549, 552, 558
Callahan, K., 270

Callins, T., 101
Cambra, C., 351
Cameron, D. L., 59
Campbell, F. A., 169
Campbell, R., 349
Capek, C. M., 349
Capella-McDonnall, M. E., 415
Capellini, S. A., 193
Cardenas-Hagan, E., 106
Cardona, G. W., 478
Carlson, C., 106
Carlson, J. S., 251
Carpenter, M., 446
Carr, E. G., 244
Carr, M. R., 8
Carta, J. J., 294
Carter, E. W., 165
Carter, M., 165
Cartledge, G., 64, 95–96, 109, 206, 290
Cascio, J., 513
Cassady, J. C., 98
Casson, D., 428–29
Castellano, C., 382, 397, 401
Castellano, J. A., 543
Castellanos, F. X., 234, 545
Casterline, D. C., 348
Catoe, K. E., 231
Catts, H., 312, 328, 330
Cawley, J. F., 199
Celeste, M., 388, 412
Chacko, A., 251
Chambers, C. R., 361
Chanonine, V., 193
Chard, D. J., 288
CHARGE Syndrome Foundation, 469
Charlop-Christy, M., 439
Chen, D., 412–413
Chhabildas, N. A., 235
Chicchetti, D. V., 167
Chinn, P. C., 96
Chong, C., 405
Christensen, J. R., 463
Chrousos, G. P., 430
Chung, M. C., 509
Ciasca, S. M., 193
Cioffi, A., 176
Cioffi, J., 476
Cirino, P., 98, 106
Clair, M., 482
Clark, B., 541
Clark, C., 165
Clark, G. M., 50–51, 74, 76–77, 296–297
Claverie, J., 430
Clemmons, D. C., 467
Closs, A., 514
Cobb, J., 217
Cohen, P., 57
Colangelo, N., 540, 559
Colarossi, G. M., 351, 363
Cole, D., 313

Coleman, L. J., 538
Coles, E. K., 251
Colligan, R. C., 250
Collins, K., 103
Collins, W., 118
Colvin, G., 279, 281, 286, 288
Compton, D. L., 98
Conlon, C. J., 520
Connelly, V., 391
Conners, C. K., 157, 228, 232, 252, 254
Conners, F., 157, 194
Connor, D. F., 241, 249–50
Connor, R. T., 165
Conroy, M., 6–8, 11–12, 24–25, 28, 37, 68, 76, 80, 93, 290–291, 293–294, 463, 487
Constable, R. T., 193
Conti-Ramsden, G., 388
Conture, E. G., 317–318
Convertino, C., 370
Cook, B. G., 59
Cook, E. F., 411
Cook, L., 59
Cooper, P., 242, 271
Copher, J. I., 175
Coppola, M., 350
Corda, B., 284
Corn, A. L., 400
Cornaggia, C. M., 502
Correa, V., 123
Coster, D. J., 411
Cottone, E. A., 240
Coucouvanis, K., 173
Council for Exceptional Children, 24, 365, 461, 463, 515, 553
Courchesne, E., 430
Courty, S., 430
Coutinho, M., 95–96, 109, 285
Couture, T., 30
Coyne, P., 51
Cramond, B., 534
Crawford, S., 255
Creed, P. A., 369
Crenshaw, T. M., 251, 272
Crespo, M., 167
Croneberg, C. G., 348
Cronin, M. E., 51
Cross, C. T., 270
Cross, T. L., 98, 531
Crosswait, C., 253
Crowe, T. A., 316–17
Crowell, E. W., 252
Cruickshank, W. M., 16, 54, 187, 195
Csikszentmihalyi, M., 534
Cullinan, D., 264–266, 269
Cummins, R., 167
Cunningham, C., 253
Cunnington, R., 234
Cutler, S. K., 501
Cuvo, A. J., 162

Dailey, R., 411
Dale, P. S., 445
Daley, D., 122
D'Allura, T., 412
Dapretto, M., 430
Darling, S. M., 70
Darrah, J., 511
Dattilo, J., 447
David, A. S., 349
Davidson, J. E., 551
Davies, M. S., 430
Davis, A. K., 172
Davis, C., 286, 293
Davis, H. R., 430
Dawson, G., 432
de Boer-Ott, S. R., 439, 448
DeAngelis, C. D., 495, 504, 507
Deater-Deckard, K., 194
Deffenbacher, J. L., 238
DeFord, S., 512
Deimel, W., 194
Demler, O., 254
Demonet, J. F., 193
Deno, S., 165, 209, 211
Deshler, D. D., 217
DeStefano, F., 428
DeStefano, L., 175
DeThorne, L. S., 194
Dhillon, A. P., 429
Diener, M. B., 239–240
Dietrich, M., 228
DiGennaro, J., 531, 541
DiGiuseppe, D. L., 233
DiPerna, J. C., 291
Dixon, F. A., 98
Dobbs, M., 67
Dobelle, W. H., 407
Dodge, K. A., 295
Donahue, M., 199
Doren, B., 74
Dormans, J. P., 503
Douglas, G., 235
Downing, J., 475
Doyle, A. E., 235, 254
Draper, I. L., 65, 97
Drasgow, E., 30, 65, 78
Drotar, D., 120
Duchnowski, A. J., 293
Dunlap, G., 133, 294–295
Dunst, C. J., 126
DuPaul, G., 244, 246, 253, 255
Dupre, A. P., 30, 55, 79
Durando, J., 411
Dyches, T. T., 32
Dykens, E., 151, 155, 159

Earley, P., 49–51
Eccarius, M. A., 364
Eckert, T. L., 244, 246–247
Edelman, A., 522
Edelman, S., 387
Edgar, E., 216, 297
Edwards, G., 231

Edwards, M. L., 316
Edwards, P. A., 98
Edwards, R. P., 291, 447
Egan, R., 509, 514
Egger, H., 269, 287
Eisenbraun, K. D., 326, 368, 411
Eisenman, L. T., 74
Elbaum, B., 58, 209
Elia, M., 502
Elksnin, N., 109
Ellingson, S. A., 482
Elliot, B., 110
Elliott, S. N., 293
Ellis, C., 294
Ellis Weismer, S., 312
Emerson, R. W., 401
Emmorey, K., 349
Enersen, D. L., 538, 540, 543–544, 549, 551, 554, 557
Epstein, M., 202, 286
Epstein, R.S., 250
Ergul, C., 201
Erhardt, D., 232
Erickson, M. T., 194
Erin, J. N., 391, 412
Ervin, R. A., 244
Erwin, E., 118, 128, 132
Espin, C., 165, 209
Esquith, R., 19
Evans, D. E., 318
Evans, S. W., 250
Eyrl, K. L., 502

Fabiano, G. A., 251
Faraone, S. V., 234, 241, 250
Farber, M. Z., 128
Farmer, E. M. Z., 278
Farmer, T. W., 263, 274, 278, 286
Farrell, M., 411
Fazio, F., 193
Featherly, C., 480
Feil, E. G., 276, 295
Feingold, B., 233
Felce, D., 167
Feldhusen, J.F., 534
Feliciangeli, A., 499
Fennema-Notestine, C., 505
Fenson, L., 445
Ferguson, C., 360
Ferguson, P. M., 122–123
Fergusson, D. M., 238
Fernstrom, P., 287
Feron, F. J. M., 228, 231
Fey, M. E., 312
Fidler, D. J., 159
Field, S., 557
Filipek, P., 236
Finn, C. E., Jr., 13
Finucane, B. M., 153, 159, 470
Fischer, M., 56, 59
Fisher, E. S., 273
Fisher, S. E., 13

Fletcher, J. M., 189, 193, 215, 312
Fletcher, K., 238, 253
Flippin, S. S., 101–102
Floro, J. N., 238
Flory, K., 241
Flowers, C., 162
Flowers, D. L., 193
Fombonne, E., 425–426
Ford, D. Y., 539, 544, 549
Forman, B., 476, 480
Forness, S. R., 56, 199, 266, 272, 285–286, 296
Forney, P. E., 504, 511, 514, 519
Foundas, A. L., 309
Fouts, J. T., 206
Fowler, J. S., 234
Fowler, S. A., 295
Fox, J., 80, 291, 293
Fox, L., 133, 294, 488–489
Foxx, R. M., 481
Francks, C., 194
Frankland, H. C., 126
Fredericks, B., 471
Freehan, M., 231
Freeman, J., 500, 531, 549
Fremoile, J., 430
Friedlander, B. D., 246
Friedman, J., 350
Friend, M., 63, 293
Friesen, W. J., 5
Friman, P. C., 244
Frith, U., 193, 423, 426, 437–438
Frizzelle, R., 246
Frost, L., 446
Fuchs, D., 62, 165, 191, 202
Fuchs, L.S., 18, 56, 62, 64, 98, 165, 191, 207, 209, 211, 214–215, 287
Fujii, K., 228
Fulbright, R. K., 193
Fulker, D., 194
Fuller, D. R., 476, 478–479, 481
Fuller, K., 59
Funkhouser, E., 507

Gabias, P., 402
Gable, R. A., 80, 292–293
Gajria, M., 205
Galaburda, A. M., 194
Gallagher, J. J., 531–532, 534, 537, 540–541, 545, 549, 552
Gallagher, S. A., 540
Gallaudet Research Institute, 342
Gallego, M. A., 54
Gallimore, R., 120
Gallucci, J. P., 110
Ganz, J. B., 439
Gardner, R., 93, 290, 487
Gardner, W. I., 64
Garfinkle, A., 446
Garner, N., 51, 74, 172

Garner, T., 30
Garnier, H. E., 120
Garrett-Mayer, E., 432
Garwick, A., 514
Gathercole, S. E., 200
Gavidia-Payne, S., 120
Geary, D. C., 200
Geers, A. E., 355
Gense, M., 476
Gentry, M., 531
Georgiewa, P., 193
Gerber, M. M., 59
Gerber, P. J., 216, 218
Gerhardt, P. F., 451–452
Gericke, C., 499
Gerlach, E. K., 121, 123
Gillis, J. J., 194
Ginsberg, R., 216
Giovannelli, J., 294
Giuliani, G. A., 67
Glauche, V., 193
Glaucoma Research Foundation, 386–387
Glidden, L. M., 146
Gliona, M. F., 55, 57
Glutting, J. J., 237
Gnagy, E. M., 250–251
Godwin, R., 285
Goin, M. K., 49
Golbach, T., 368
Goldberg, M., 272
Goldberg, P., 272
Goldberg, R. J., 216
Goldberg-Hamblin, S. E., 133
Goldin-Meadow, S., 349
Goldman, L., 411
Goldsmith, B., 534, 540, 546–547
Golly, A., 295
Gomez, J., 173
Gonzales, A. K., 16, 54, 56, 58
Gonzalez, P., 175
Goodman, E., 49, 512–513
Gordon, E. W., 544
Gortmaker, S. L., 504
Gould, S. J., 534, 536–537
Graham, S., 203, 246
Grandin, T., 434
Graupner, T. D., 442
Graves, A., 198
Gray, C. A., 447
Greenberg, D., 101
Greenberg, J. S., 118, 122
Greenhill, L. L., 228, 251
Greenspan, S., 147
Greenwood, C. R., 64, 101, 166
Greiner, A. R., 241, 250
Gresham, F. M., 69, 149, 192, 263, 270, 273–274, 276, 278–279, 281, 286, 288, 290, 294–295, 297
Grice, N., 403
Griesdorn, J., 297
Griffith, P., 278, 313

Grim, J. C., 163
Grim, R., 67
Griswold, D. E., 439
Groopman, J., 55, 407
Gross, M. U. M., 531, 541, 543, 552, 556–558
Grskovic, J. A., 545
Gruber, C. P., 446
Guardino, D., 62
Guerrini, R., 500–501
Guinn, A., 60
Guitar, B., 317
Gunn, B., 98
Gut, D., 278
Gutenbrunner, C., 194
Guterman, B. R., 57
Guth, C. B., 165

Haas, A., 303–304, 311, 315
Haas, B. A., 318
Hack, M., 154
Hagan, E. C., 106
Hagerman, R. J., 153
Hall, A., 545
Hall, B. D., 469
Hall, J. P., 56
Hallahan, D. P., 6–8, 11, 13, 15, 17–19, 22, 24, 26, 37, 45, 47–48, 53, 55–56, 59–61, 65, 67–68, 79–80, 90, 94, 107, 187, 192, 199, 203, 246, 287, 472, 531–532, 534, 543
Hallenbeck, B. A., 287
Hallgren, B., 194
Hamilton, H., 363
Hammill, D. D., 107, 186, 188, 367
Hammond, M., 165
Hancock, T. B., 327
Handwerk, M. J., 240
Hannan, C. K., 411
Hanson, M. J., 507, 514
Hanson, V. L., 366
Hardman, M. L., 118, 125, 131–132, 161, 175
Harlaar, N., 155
Harper, G. F., 64, 206
Harper, L. V., 118, 427
Harris, K. R., 198, 203, 324
Harris, M., 351
Harry, B., 132
Hart, S. A., 194
Hartas, D., 313
Hartmann, E., 411
Hartsough, C., 241, 296
Hastings, R. P., 122
Hatch, T., 534
Hatlen, P., 399
Hatton, D. D., 159
Hauser-Cram, P., 130
Havercamp, S., 430
Hay, D. A., 234
Hayes, A., 522
Hayes, J. S., 501

Hayiou-Thomas, M. E., 323
Hazell, P. L., 228
Hechtman, L., 228, 256
Hediger, M. L., 430
Heller, K. W., 463, 467, 495, 500–504, 506, 508–509, 511–512, 514, 517, 519, 522
Hembree, R., 467–469
Hemmeter, M. L., 327
Henderson, C., 217, 235
Henderson, V., 363
Henker, B., 238
Henn, W., 132
Henriksen, L., 234
Henshon, S. E., 534
Hepburn, S. L., 159
Herman, K. L., 216
Hermelin, B., 434
Hernandez, A., 193
Herschkowitz, N., 431
Heward, W. L., 6, 102
Hewetson, A., 427
Hewitt, J. K., 194
Heyes, A. D., 411
Higgins, E. L., 216
Hill, A., 402
Hill, E., 411
Hinshaw, S. P., 239, 241
Hoard, M. K., 200
Hock, M. F., 217
Hodapp, R. M., 153, 159, 470
Hodges, L., 467
Hodges, P., 360
Hoeft, F., 193
Hoffman, D., 506
Hoffman-Kipp, P., 95
Hoffmeister, R., 353, 358, 363, 369
Hofstetter, C., 100
Hogan, T., 312
Hohn, M., 287
Hokanson, C.R., Jr., 37, 65
Holahan, T., 263, 274, 286–287, 290, 295
Holbrook, M. C., 398–399
Holburn, S. C., 50
Holman, K. C., 432
Holmes, M. S., 6, 24, 495
Hood, J., 194
Hopf, A., 449
Hopf, J. M., 193
Horne, D., 187
Horner, R. H., 79, 133, 163, 291, 485
Horvath, M., 217–218
Horwitz, B., 193
Horwitz, S., 90
Horwood, L. J., 228, 238
Hosp, J. L., 209, 211
Houghton, S., 235
Houtenville, A. J., 415
Houtz, J. C., 534
Howell, K. W., 209, 211
Hoza, B., 238

Hresko, W. P., 367
Huang, L. N., 95
Huefner, D. S., 10, 12, 16, 24, 28, 30–32, 34, 67, 78, 291, 534
Huettig, C., 514, 516
Hughes, C., 165, 290
Hughes, M. T., 56, 59, 209
Hull, J. M., 388–89, 391
Hulme, C., 312
Humphries, T., 201, 340, 342, 352–353, 358, 363
Hungerford, R., 5
Hunsaker, S. L., 534, 536, 541
Hunter, S., 539
Hussey, W., 263, 274, 286–287, 290, 295
Hyatt, K. J., 61
Hyde, M., 369
Hynd, G. W., 193, 240

Iglesias, A., 306–307
Inge, K., 76–77, 489
Inglis, A., 194
Institute of Medicine, 429
Isaksen, S. G., 534
Iselin, S. A., 412
Ishii-Jordan, S. R., 285
Ishikawa, S. S., 238
Itard, J. M. G., 25
Iwata, B. A., 483

Jacobs, A. J., 534
Jacobsen, R., 30, 68
Jacobsen, S. J., 250
Jacobson, E. S., 16, 54, 56, 58
Jacobson, J. W., 50
Jamner, L. D., 238
Jara, P., 388
Jenaro, C., 167
Jenne, W., 370
Jensen, P. S., 251
Jensen, W. R., 288
Jerman, O., 199–200
Jernigan, K., 380, 415
Jernigan, T. L., 505
Jiban, C., 211
Jimenez, R., 105
Jimerson, S., 268, 270
Jindal-Snape, D., 391
Jitendra, A. K., 199
Jitendra, S., 205
Johns, B. H., 67
Johns, J., 410
Johns, N. R., 246
Johnson, P., 74
Johnston, A. W., 411
Johnston, J. A., 238
Johnston, T., 355
Johnstone, C. J., 368, 411
Jolivette, K., 78
Jolley, W., 395
Jones, B., 63
Jones, C. J., 98
Jones, M., 50

Judd, D., 393
Justice, L. M., 306, 315, 332

Kaiser, A. P., 294
Kaiser, W. A., 193
Kakela, M., 216
Kalbfleisch, M. L., 545
Kalff, A. C., 228, 231
Kaminer, R., 507
Kaminski, R. A., 101
Kanner, K., 427
Kanner, L., 25, 423, 427
Kaplan, B., 255
Kaplan, S. N., 549
Karchmer, M. A., 339, 351
Karnish, M. B., 518
Karns, C. M., 430
Karvonen, M., 50, 162
Kast, L., 480
Kastor, E., 55
Kato, K., 326, 368, 411
Katsiyannis, A., 296
Katusic, S. K., 250
Katz, W., 193
Kauffman, J. M., 6–8, 11–13, 16–19, 22–25, 27–28, 30–31, 37, 54–56, 58–59, 65, 68, 76, 80, 95, 192, 203, 246, 265, 285–88, 290, 296, 463, 481
Kaufman, N. L., 167
Kaufman, S., 145
Kavale, K. A., 56, 80, 199–200, 216, 240, 247, 251, 266, 271–272, 481
Kavanagh, K., 295
Kazdin, A. E., 271, 287, 295, 297
Keith, K. D., 167
Kellam, S., 278, 281, 295
Keller, C. E., 203, 246
Keller-Bell, Y., 157
Kellet, K., 446
Kelley, M. L., 135
Kelly, K. R., 557
Kent, R., 315
Keogh, B. K., 93, 272
Kephart, N. C., 187
Kern, L., 244, 253, 268, 285
Kersh, J. E., 130
Kessels, A. G. H., 228, 231
Kessler, R. C., 254
Khalid, M., 250
Kiely, K., 234
Kilgo, J., 69, 294, 486
Kim, S., 99
King, K., 64, 101
Kirk, S. A., 185
Kirk, W. D., 187, 195
Kita, M., 228
Klauber, J., 405
Kleege, G., 380
Klein, N., 154
Klein, R. G., 284
Klein, T. L., 482
Klim, P., 235

Klockars, A. J., 316
Knab, R., 193
Knight, J., 217
Knitzer, J., 264, 267
Knott, N. I., 389, 401
Knowles, T., 482
Knowlton, A., 131
Kochhar-Bryant, C. A., 50, 74
Koenig, A. J., 399
Kohn, A., 246
Kohrman, C., 514
Kohrt, A. E., 495
Kolstoe, O. P., 77
Konold, T. R., 8, 13, 18, 30, 55, 59, 66–68, 73, 89, 531
Konrad, M., 50
Kortering, L. J., 216
Kouzekanani, K., 106
Kovas, Y., 194
Kovatchev, B., 238
Kover, S. T., 153, 159
Kraft, M., 297
Kratochvil, M., 511
Krauss, M. W., 118, 122
Kravets, M., 217
Kroeger, K. A., 482
Kroes, M., 228, 231
Kuna, J., 150
Kuntze, M., 350
Kupermintz, H., 370
Kurson, R., 406–407
Kutash, K., 293
Kuusisto, S., 390
Kwak, N., 120

Ladd, P., 341–42, 352
Lainhart, J.E., 431
Lakin, C., 120
Lakshmi, B., 431
Lamb, H. R., 49
Lambie, R., 127
Landrum, T. J., 13, 19, 22, 24–25, 37, 47, 56, 59–60, 68, 80, 263–267, 269–270, 272–274, 277–278, 284, 286–288, 290, 482, 484
Lane, H., 342, 354–355, 371
Lansaw, J., 414
Larrivee, L. S., 328, 330
Larsen, S., 195, 213
Larson, E. R., 509
Larson, S., 120
Lathrop, M., 62
Lawrence, M., 74, 172, 411
Leahy, M., 76
Leaman, O., 519
Leavitt, L. A., 130
LeBlanc, L., 446
Lehmkuhl, H. D., 514
Leigh, I. W., 342, 355–356, 358
Leigh, J. E., 188
Lenz, B. K., 217
Leone, P. E., 270, 290, 296
Leos, K., 106
Lepper, C., 69, 486

Lerman-Sagie, T., 159
Lerner, J. W., 201
Lese-Martin, C., 431
Leslie, A. M., 438
Leung, C. Y., 106
Lev, D., 159
Levin, J. R., 207
Lewis, A.C., 89
Lewis, B. A., 194, 289
Lewis, D. K., 99
Lewis, M., 118
Liao, Q., 95
Lichtenstein, E., 366
Lida, K. M., 50
Lieberman, L., 59, 394
Lienemann, R. O., 246
Lilienfeld, A. M., 227
Linan-Thompson, S., 98, 106
Linden, M. A., 28, 32, 34–36, 78, 288
Lindsey, J. E., 512
Linnell, J., 428
Liptak, G., 502
Little, T. D., 51
Liu, J. K., 100
Lloyd, J. W., 6, 55–56, 61, 99, 192, 196, 198, 200, 202–203, 287, 324, 332
Lobos, E., 235
Loe, S. A., 109
Logan, G. D., 235
Lohman, D. F., 532, 534–535, 538, 544
Loncke, F., 481
Long, E. S., 482
Long, M., 331
Long, S., 231
Longden, J. C., 415
Longman, J., 49, 513
Lopez, K., 445
Lopez-Reyna, N., 101–102
Lopez-Torres, L., 95
Lord, C., 100, 445
Lotter, V., 425
LoTurco, J., 194
Loughlin, G., 158–159
Lowenthal, B., 509, 514
Loyd, R.J., 50, 74, 296–297
Lubinski, D., 325
Lucas, T., 101
Luhaorg, H., 157
Luk, S. L., 231
Luna, B., 431
Luna, M., 331
Lupkowski-Shoplik, A., 559
Lutz, G., 253
Luzzo, D. A., 217–218
Lynskey, M. T., 228

Maag, J. W., 79
MacArthur, C., 324
Maccoby, E., 118
MacMillan, D. L., 27
MacNeil, B., 340
MacSweeney, M., 349

Mahon, M. J., 514, 519
Malhotra, D., 431
Malik, M., 428–429
Malkin, C., 159
Mallette, B., 64, 206
Malmgren, K. W., 366
Maltzen, H., 370
Mangione, C. M., 411
Mann, E. A., 169
Manning-Courtney, P., 430
Manstetten, R., 540
Marchand-Martella, N. E., 78
Marchman, V. A., 445
Marder, C., 253
Margalit, M., 201
Marquart, A. M., 214
Marschark, M., 347
Marshall, D. J., 313
Martens, B. K., 55
Martin, E. W., 18, 58
Martin, J. E., 172
Martin, S., 498, 500, 522
Martindale, C., 534
Martindale, J. L., 193
Martinez, E. A., 6, 61, 99, 196,
     198, 200, 202–203, 324, 332
Martins, S., 231
Marvin, R. S., 510
Marx, E. S., 368
Mason, C. A., 155
Mastropieri, M. A., 63
Matczynski, T. J., 207
Mather, N., 167, 212, 486
Mathes, P. G., 106
Mathiason, C. S., 47
Matikka, L., 167
Mattson, E., 522
Maurer, M., 392, 413
McAfee, M., 103
McCain, A. P., 135
McCarthy, J., 106, 195
McCarty, C. A., 233
McClelland, A., 108
McCluskey, A. L. A., 539
McCoach, D. B., 543
McConachie, H., 118
McConnell, K., 253
McConnell, S. R., 295
McCormick, K. M., 286
McCormick, L., 69–70,
     72–73, 294, 486
McCrory, E., 193
McCullough, J., 13, 16,
     54, 286
McDonnell, A. P., 175
McDuffie, K. A., 63
McGee, K., 16, 58, 101
McGee, R., 231
McGoey, K. E., 244
McGrath, B., 512–513
McGreevy, A. L., 534
McGregor, K. K., 330
McGrew, K. S., 167, 212
McGuire, P. K., 349
McHenry, M. A., 316

McIntyre, T., 101
McLaughlin, M. J., 97
McLean, M., 72
McMahon, C. R., 431
McMaster, K. L., 191
McMillon, G., 193
McNutt, G., 188
Meadow-Orlans, K. P., 340, 368
Meese, R. L., 205
Menchel, R. S., 358
Mencl, W. E., 193
Mendoza, C., 531
Mercer, C. D., 193
Merkel, R. L., 238
Merrell, K. W., 292
Mertens, D. M., 127, 341
Metheny, J., 74
Metz, D. E., 303–4, 311, 315
Metzler, I., 6, 24, 495
Meyer, K. A., 482
Meyler, A., 193
Michalko, R., 55
Mick, E., 234, 241, 250
Miles, B., 468, 471, 474–475
Milich, R., 239–240
Millar, D., 402
Miller, E. M., 538, 543
Miller, J.F., 130
Miller, S. P., 64
Mills, J. L., 430
Milner, H. R., 544
Miltenberger, R. G., 482
Minich, N. M., 154
Minor, L., 474
Mira, M. P., 463, 467
Miramontes, O. B., 22
Mirenda, P., 446–447,
     476, 479, 481
Mitchell, R., 68
Mithaug, D. E., 172
Moberly, R., 522
Mock, D. R., 19, 47, 62, 265,
     269, 287
Mohler, A., 59
Molina, B. S. G., 241
Moll, L. C., 54
Molloy, C. A., 430
Monks, F. J., 532, 534, 536,
     549, 554, 556
Monzo, L., 173
Moon, M. L., 400
Moon, S. M., 540, 543, 549,
     557, 559
Moore, J. L., 545
Moore, T., 19
Moorehouse, M., 253
Moores, D. F., 355
Morelock, M. J., 547
Morgan, P. L., 62
Morison, P., 97
Morris, M. K., 284
Morrison, G. M., 268,
     270, 273
Moses, N., 330
Most, D. E., 159

Mostert, M. P., 23, 56, 77, 87,
     110, 134, 266, 274, 281,
     286–287, 290–291, 464,
     467, 481
Mota, V. L., 235
Moyers, P., 350
MTA Cooperative Group, 251
Mudford, O. C., 482
Mulick, J. A., 481
Muller, R. A., 428–29
Mullin, G., 344
Mundy, L., 94, 355
Munk, D., 202
Muratori, M. C., 559
Murch, S. H., 428–429
Murphy, K. R., 236–237, 255
Murphy, M. M., 157
Murray, C., 216
Murray, S., 541, 544
Musselman, C., 366
Musti-Rao, S., 64, 206
Myles, B. S., 439

Nace, K. L., 193
Nakata, Y., 228
National Center for Children in
     Poverty, 192
National Eye Institute, 387
National Federation of the
     Blind, 405
National Information
     Clearinghouse on Children
     Who Are Deaf-Blind, 468
National Institute of
     Neurological Disorders
     and Stroke, 154
National Institute on Deafness
     and Other Communication
     Disorders, 354
National Joint Committee on
     Learning Disabilities, 188
National Organization on
     Disability, 174
National Research Council, 12,
     426, 428, 437, 439, 449, 481
Navarro, M., 512
Naylor, C. E., 193
Neel, R. S., 297
Nelson, C. M., 286, 290
Nelson, J. R., 65, 78, 97
Nelson, M., 59
Nelson, N. W., 480
Newcorn, J., 234
Newman, L. R., 340
Nezu, A. M., 482
Ng., J., 537, 541, 552, 558
Nielsen, J. B., 234
Nigg, J. T., 232, 234–235
Nomani, A. Q., 50
Norins, J., 59

Obiakor, F. E., 97, 99–100,
     102, 111
Odom, S. L., 72, 486–87
Ogline, J. S., 235

Oley, C. A., 469
Oliva, G. A., 363
Oliver, J. C., 388
Olsen, K., 168
O'Mahony, P., 270
O'Rourke, M., 512
Osborne, J. G., 51, 488
O'Shea, L. J., 131
Oswald, D., 93, 96, 285, 487
Owens, E. B., 294
Owens, R. E., 306, 309, 319
Ozonoff, S., 438

Padden, C. A., 352
Painter, K. M., 368
Paley, A. R., 52
Palmer, D. R., 292
Palmer, P., 430
Palmer, S. B., 51, 74, 172
Papanicolaou, A. C., 193
Pare, J. G., 382
Parker, R. C., 56, 68
Park.S., 537, 540
Parmar, R. S., 199
Patterson, C. J., 6
Patterson, T., 292–293
Patton, J. R., 59, 65, 67
Paulesu, E., 193, 198
Pauls, D., 429, 431, 437
Peacock Hill Working Group,
     286, 295, 297
Pearl, R., 199
Pease, L., 471
Peck, S., 77
Pelham, W. E., 250–251
Pelkey, L., 185
Pellegrino, L., 498
Pennington, B. F., 194, 196, 235
Persel, C. H., 467
Pesudovs, K., 411
Peterson, J. S., 217
Peterson, R. L., 78
Petrill, S. A., 194
Pfeifer, J. H., 430
Philips, L., 216
Phillips, R. S., 411
Phillips, S., 192, 214, 370
Pianta, R. C., 510
Picard, M. C., 212
Pinel, J. P. J., 156, 234
Pinker, S., 536
Pisha, B., 51
Plomin, R., 155, 537
Plume, E., 194
Porter, L., 554–56
Potter, D., 426
Powell, T. H., 125
Power, D. T. J., 232
Power, P. W., 461, 463, 465, 467
Powers, L. E., 30, 50
Powers, S., 351
Prater, K., 98
Presley, J. A., 290
Prevent Blindness America, 384
Price, C. J., 193

Price, J., 159
Prinz, P. M., 350
Prizant, B. M., 330
Prouty, R., 173
Pugach, M. C., 65
Pugh, K. R., 193
Pullen, P., 23, 30, 65, 77, 95, 103, 110, 134, 196, 274, 281, 286–288, 290–291, 315, 324, 467
Pungello, E., 169
Purcell, J., 549
Pyfer, J., 514, 516

Qiu, S., 445
Queen, O., 201
Quinn, M. M., 263, 274, 286–287, 290, 295

Rabin, B., 447
Rabiner, D., 231
Raeder, W. M., 397
Raghenvendra, P., 480–481
Raja, S. N., 231
Ramey, C. T., 169
Ramp, K. A., 297
Ramsey, E., 69, 263, 270, 273–274, 276, 278–279, 281, 286, 288, 290, 294–295, 297
Ramus, F., 194
Rapp, A. J., 391
Rashotte, C., 213
Raskind, W. H., 194
Raspberry, W., 68, 307
Ratey, J. J., 254, 256–257
Rausch, M. K., 78
Ravitch, D., 89
Ray, K. E., 540
Reagan, T., 352
Reavis, H. K., 288
Rehfeldt, R. A., 122
Rehm, L. P., 284
Reich, A. R., 316
Reichler, R. J., 449
Reid, R., 201, 232, 253
Reiff, H. B., 216
Reis, S. M., 536, 539–540, 545, 554, 557, 559
Reiss, S. M., 547
Remschmidt, H., 194
Renaissance Learning, 366
Renshaw, P. F., 235–236
Renzulli, J. S., 536, 554
Reschly, D. J., 95–96
Reyna, V. F., 105
Reynolds, C. A., 194
Rhodes, C. A., 70, 125
Riccomini, P. J., 212
Richards, S. B., 151, 153
Richards, T. L., 27, 193
Richmond, E. K., 157
Richters, J. E., 228
Riedel, T. M., 287
Riksen-Walraven, J. M., 472
Rimm, S. B., 543–545, 547, 549

Risley, T. R., 6, 326
Roberts, J. E., 159
Roberts, K., 506
Roberts, S., 360
Robertson, D. L., 169
Robillard, K., 393
Robinson, N. M., 538–540, 557, 559
Rodricks, T., 238
Rodriguez, P., 123
Rodriguez-Gil, G., 475
Roe, J., 389
Roessler, R. T., 415
Rogawski, M. A., 500
Roge, B., 430
Rogers, A. S., 506
Rogers, M. E., 227
Rohde, L. A., 231
Rolstad, K., 97
Romanczyk, R., 446, 449
Ronald, A., 155
Rooney, K. J., 245
Rosegrant, T., 487
Roskos-Ewoldsen, B., 157
Rostain, A. L., 240
Rotherham, A. J., 13, 37, 65
Rourke, B. P., 201
Rowland, A. S., 231
Rowley, J. B., 207
Rozalski, M. E., 78
Rubert, M. P., 130, 132
Runco, M. A., 534
Rusch, F. R., 175
Rutherford, R. B., 270, 290, 296
Rutter, M., 194
Ryles, R., 398–399
Rzanny, R., 193

Sacks, O., 434
Sacks, S. Z., 391, 406, 412
Safford, P., 108
Sample, P. L., 246
Sandak, R., 366
Sandell, C., 353
Sanghavi, D. M., 355
Santarelli, G. E., 133
Sapare, P., 370
Sapir, S., 200
Saraste, H., 503
Saslow, E., 48, 503
Sass-Lehrer, M. A., 127, 341
Sasso, G. M., 80, 481
Sauerburger, D., 401
Saunders, R. R., 49
Savage, R. C., 463
Sawyer, D. J., 312
Sawyer, M. G., 228
Sayeski, B., 47, 287
Sayeski, K. L., 47, 287
Scanlon, D. M., 312
Scarpati, S., 107
Schaffner, L., 270
Schalock, R. L., 167
Schartz, M., 246
Schatschneider, C., 194

Schatz, T., 554, 556
Scheetz, N. A., 467
Schindelhauer-Deutscher, H. J., 132
Schirmer, B. R., 351, 360, 364, 369
Schloss, C. N., 137
Schloss, P. J., 137
Schmidt, M. H., 228
Schmidt-Lackner, S., 446, 449
Schmitz, M., 231
Schopler, E., 449
Schoppe-Sullivan, S. J., 118, 126
Schrank, F. A., 167
Schroeder, F. K., 397
Schuckers, P., 411
Schuele, C. M., 312
Schuler, A. L., 434
Schulte, A. C., 292
Schulte-Korne, G., 194
Schumaker, J., 194, 217
Schumm, J. S., 57, 209, 248
Schuster, J. W., 163
Schuyler, B. R., 415
Schuyler, V., 522
Schwartz, S., 130, 132, 324
Schwartzman, M. N., 504, 511, 514, 519
Scott, A. A., 430
Scott, C. M., 311–312
Scott, K. G., 155
Scott, T. M., 78
Scruggs, T. E., 206–207
Seal, B. C., 370
Sebat, J., 431
Seddon, J. M., 411
Seewagen, R., 370
Seewald, A., 192
Selmi, A. M., 368
Seltzer, M. M., 118, 122, 125
Semmel, M. I., 59
Senghas, A., 350
Severson, H. H., 276
Seward, R., 238
Shaklee, B. D., 549
Shalev, R. S., 194
Shames, G. H., 316, 325
Shapiro, E. S., 98, 231
Shapiro, J., 173
Sharma, J., 275
Sharpe, D., 125
Shattuck, P. T., 426
Shaw, E. J., 534
Shaywitz, B. A., 193, 545
Shaywitz, S. E., 193
Shea, V., 437
Shelton, T. L., 253
Sheras, P. L., 284
Sheridan, M., 339
Shermer, M., 534, 536
Sherrill, C., 514, 519
Shogren, K. A., 51
Shore, B. M., 538, 540, 543–544, 549, 551, 554, 557
Shore, S., 437

Shukla, S., 482
Siegel, G. M., 318
Siegel, L., 363
Siegel, S., 297
Sigman, M., 430
Silberg, J. L., 194
Sileo, N., 447
Silk, T. J., 234
Silva, P., 231
Silverman, L. K., 537
Simmerman, A., 331
Simonoff, E., 194
Simonton, D. K., 536
Simpson, R. L., 269, 433, 436–437, 439, 441–442, 450
Singer, G. H. S., 103, 122, 132
Singh, D. K., 510
Singh, N. N., 285
Singh, V., 50
Sitlington, P. L., 176
Skinner, M. L., 159
Sleeter, C. E., 101
Slick, D. J., 502
Smallish, L., 238
Smith, B., 250, 294, 415
Smith, J., 174
Smith, S. D., 24, 194
Smith-Myles, B., 448
Smolkowski, K., 98
Snell, M. E., 482
Snowling, M. J., 312
Sobsey, D., 123
Sokol, N. G., 253
Solanto, M. V., 234, 249
Sood, S., 199
Soodak, L., 77, 118, 128, 132
Soukup, J. H., 51
Sparrow, E., 232
Spencer, P. E., 355
Spencer, T., 231, 234, 241, 250
Spinelli, C. G., 168
Sprague, J. R., 6, 69–70, 79, 163, 294–295, 439, 483–484
Spungin, S. J., 412
Squire, P., 30
Stainback, W., 13, 53, 55
Stallone, L., 231
Stambaugh, T., 549
Stanley, J. C., 537, 541, 552, 558–59
Starner, T., 363
Steinberg, L., 118
Steingard, R. J., 235–236
Stella, J., 433
Sternberg, R. J., 532, 534, 536, 549
Stevenson, J., 312
Steyaert, J., 228, 231
Stichter, J., 80, 286, 291, 293
Stieber, S., 297
Still, G. F., 225, 227
Stinson, M. S., 351, 363
Stocking, V. B., 540, 557
Stokes, P. D., 534
Stokoe, W. C., 348

Stoneman, Z., 122
Stoner, G., 252
Storch, E. A., 284
Stormont, M., 545
Strain, P. S., 72, 294
Strauch, J. D., 175
Strauss, A. A., 193, 227
Strickland, C. A., 539, 549
Strock, M., 425, 428–429, 431
Stroman, D. F., 49
Strong, M., 350
Sturm, C., 199
Subotnik, R. F., 532, 534, 536, 549
Sudhalter, V., 445–446, 449
Sugai, G., 62, 164
Sullivan, K. M., 159
Sullivan-Burstein, K., 202
Sumi, W. C., 293
Summers, C. R., 122
Summers, J. A., 126
Summers, M., 122
Sun, L.-W., 235
Sunohara, G., 235
Swanson, H. L., 200, 209
Swanson, J. M., 241, 251
Sweda, J., 207
Sweeney, D. P., 272
Sweeney, J., 431
Swiatek, M. A., 531
Switsky, H. N., 158–159
Switzer, J. V., 55
Szapocznik, J., 130, 132
Szatmari, P., 231

Tagalakis, V., 393
Takaki, R., 102
Takruri, L., 353
Tallal, P., 193
Tammet, D., 435
Tankersley, M., 19, 47, 59, 246, 285, 287, 294, 330
Tannenbaum, A. J., 536, 540–541
Tanners, A., 217–218
Tannhauser, M. T., 241
Tannock, R., 201, 235, 253
Tao, T., 537, 541, 552, 558
Tarver, S. G., 206
Taylor, E., 231
Taylor, R. L., 99, 151, 153, 252–253
Taylor-Hill, H., 193
Teelucksingh, W., 65, 97
Telang, F., 234
Temple, J. A., 169
Terwilliger, J., 100
Test, D. W., 50
Thomas, C. L., 153
Thompson, L. A., 194
Thurlow, M., 65, 67, 100, 326, 368, 411, 449
Tigue, B. S., 430
Timm, M. A., 70, 295
Tingstrom, D. H., 447

Tinsley, V., 157
Tobin, M. J., 411
Todd, A. W., 439, 483–484
Todd, R. D., 235
Tomblin, J., 312
Tomizawa, Y., 5
Tomlinson, C. A., 60–61, 64, 544, 553–554
Tonge, B. J., 431
Tosi, L. L., 503
Trahant, D., 291
Treffert, D. A., 434
Tregaskis, C., 55
Trent, S. C., 23, 77, 95, 110, 134, 274, 281, 286–287, 290–291, 467
Trifillis, P., 5
Trimble, M. M., 502
Troge, J., 431
Troia, G. A., 196
Trout, A. L., 246
Tuchman, M., 508
Tunick, R. A., 235
Turnbull, H. R., 29, 522
Turnbull, R., 118, 128, 131–132
Turner, A., 30
Tyler, J., 463

Ulrey, P., 402
Umbach, D. M., 231
Umbarger, G. T., 522
University of Minnesota, 49
U.S. Department of Education, 11, 16, 20, 68, 207, 264, 269–270, 363, 366, 441
U.S. Department of Health and Human Services, 269
U.S. Office of Special Education Programs, 485
Utley, C. A., 64

Vacca, J. J., 449
Vadasy, P. F., 125
Vaden-Kiernan, N., 278, 281, 295
Valente, E., 295
Valnes, B., 30
van Dijk, J. P. M., 472
van Someren, A. J. W. G. M., 228, 231
van Tassel-Baska, J., 531, 549
Vaughn, B. J., 133
Vaughn, S., 18, 56–57, 59, 62–63, 98, 106, 209, 286
Venn, J. J., 167
Ventimiglia, G., 411
Verweij, C. J. H., 431
Vianello, A., 499
Vihman, M. M., 315
Vincent, M., 350
Vinson, B., 306, 327
Vitello, S. J., 29
Vitiello, B., 251
Voeller, K. K. S., 232

Volkow, N. D., 234
Volpe, R. J., 253

Wada, K., 228
Wadsworth, S. J., 194
Wagner, M., 215–216, 293
Wagner, R. K., 213
Wakefield, A. J., 428
Walden, T. A., 431
Walker, H. M., 79, 273, 286, 288, 295
Walker, L. A., 371
Walker, T., 92
Wall, S. M., 128
Wallace, D. B., 534
Wallen, N. E., 227
Walsh, A. K., 201
Walsh, M., 346
Walsh, T., 431
Wang, G-J., 234
Wang, W., 290
Wang, Y., 366
Ward, T.B., 534
Warger, C.L., 65
Warnock, M., 16, 18, 46–47, 53, 55–56, 59
Warren, D. H., 394
Warren, S. F., 328
Waters, D., 349
Watkins, M. W., 237
Watt, M., 499
Weaver, A. L., 250
Webber, J., 423, 433–434
Wechsler, D., 156
Wehby, J. H., 64, 286
Wehmeyer, M. L., 51
Wehmeyer, M., 50, 488
Weihenmayer, E., 415
Weinberger, L. E., 49
Weiner, M. T., 342, 355–356, 358
Weinstein, C. S., 77, 110
Weinstein, S., 500–501
Weiss, A. L., 327, 329
Weiss, G., 256
Weiss, M. P., 6, 61, 99, 196, 198, 200, 202–203, 324, 332
Weitz, M., 61
Welch, E. M., 5, 503
Wells, N., 495
Welsh, P., 94
Werner, H., 227
Whalen, C. K., 238
Wheeler, A. C., 159
White, J. W., 233
Whiting, K., 235
Widaman, K. F., 56, 68
Wiener, W., 401
Wiesel, E., 102
Wilbur, R., 360
Wilcox, M. J., 328
Wilczynski, S. M., 447
Wilder, T., 30, 68
Wilens, T., 234, 241, 250
Wiley, A. L., 13, 59, 66–68

Willcutt, E. G., 235
Willen, E. J., 506
Williams, A. L., 316
Williams, B. F., 69, 486
Williams, K., 370
Williams, M., 411
Willingham, D. T., 534
Willis, C., 200
Wilson, D. B., 233
Wilson, R. A., 72
Wiltshire, S., 367
Windsor, J., 311
Winner, E., 541
Winslow, E. B., 294
Winton, A. S. W., 99
Wise, B., 194
Witte, R., 244, 246
Woerner, W., 228
Wolery, M., 73, 295, 555
Woll, B., 349
Wolraich, M. L., 228
Wood, F. B., 193, 201
Wood, W. M., 50
Woodcock, R. W., 167
Woodward, J., 104
Woolsey, M. L., 64
Wormeli, R., 60
Wormsley, D., 399
Wyatte, M. L., 133

Yairi, E., 318
Yamaki, K., 92, 128
Yan, W., 199
Yasui, Y., 499
Yeager, D., 172
Yell, M. L., 28–29, 31, 67, 78
Yen, L., 191
Yetter, C. I., 501
Yim, D., 311
Yoder, D. E., 480–481
Yoder, P. J., 431
Yorkston, K. M., 316
Young, A. A., 391
Youngstrom, E. A., 237
Yovanoff, P., 176
Ysseldyke, J. E., 212
Yu, K. F., 430
Yzquierdo, Z., 101–102

Zane, C., 74
Zdandowicz, M. T., 49
Zebehazy, K. T., 400
Zentall, S., 545
Zhang, L., 536
Zhang, X., 312
Zhuo, J., 5
Ziccardi, R., 430
Ziegler, A., 194
Zigmond, N., 13, 17–18, 22, 24–25, 37, 52, 55–56, 59–60, 63–65, 67, 192
Zimmerman, F. J., 233
Zimmerman, H., 231
Zirkel, P. A., 534
Zmijewski, G., 368

Subject Index

AAC. *See* augmentative or alternative communication

AAMR. *See* American Association on Mental Retardation

ABA. *See* applied behavior analysis

Abilities, importance of, 6

Acceleration, 549, 552–554, 556–557

Accessible pedestrian signals, 412

Accommodations, 64

Acquired apraxia, 319

Acquired immune deficiency syndrome, 506

ADA. *See* Americans with Disabilities Act

Adaptability, 130

Adaptations, 64

Adapted signs, 475

Adaptive devices, 511–513

Adderall, 247

Adult service, integration into, 75t

Adventitiously deaf, 340

Advocacy, 137–138

Affective disorder, 267

Aggression, 279, 483

AIDS. *See* acquired immune deficiency syndrome

Alternative communication, 304, 440

Alzheimer's disease, 152

American Association on Mental Retardation, 145–146, 148

American Sign Language. *See* sign language

American Speech-Language-Hearing Association, 305

Americans with Disabilities Act, 28–30

Amniocentesis, 152

Analytic giftedness, 534

Anoxia, 154–155

Anxiety disorder, 267

Aphonia, 317

Applied behavior analysis, 442

Apraxia, 318–319

Aqueous humor, 383

Articulation disorders, 315–316

ASHA. *See* American Speech-Language-Hearing Association

Asperger syndrome, 425, 435–437
  transition programming, 450–452

Assistance cards, 476

Asthma, 504–505

Astigmatism, 384–385

At risk, defined, 18

Atonia, 499

Atresia, 470

Attention deficit hyperactivity disorder, 199, 222–259
  adaptive behavior, 237–238
  Barkley model, 235–237
  basal ganglia, 232–234
  behavioral disorders, 240
  behavioral inhibition, 235–236

caudate, 234

causal theories, 233

causes, 232–235
  areas of brain affected, 232–234
  hereditary factors, 234–235
  medical factors, 235
  neurotransmitters, 234
  toxins, 235

cerebellum, 232–34

cerebral palsy, 227

children with "defective moral control," Still, work of, 225–226

classroom structure, 241–242

coexisting conditions, 240–241

conduct disorder, 226

contingency-based self-management, 244

continuous performance test, 232

corpus callosum, 232–234

Cruickshank, work of, 227

diagnostic criteria, 229t

dopamine, 234

early intervention, 253

educational considerations, 241–247

emotional disorders, 240

executive functions, 236–237

family studies, 234

frontal lobes, 232–234

functional behavioral assessment, contingency-based self-management, 242–247

globus pallidus, 234

history, 225–228

hyperactive child syndrome, 227–228

identification, 231–232

inner speech, 237

learning disabilities, 240

medication, 247–251
  Adderall, 247
  cautions regarding medication, 250–251
  drug abuse, 250
  effectiveness, 250
  nonresponders, 250
  psychostimulants, 247
  research evidence, 250
  Ritalin, 247
    opposition to, 249–250
    paradoxical effect of, 247
  side effects, 250
  vs. behavior management, 251

minimal brain injury, 227–228

misconceptions, 224–225

molecular genetics, 234–235

neurotransmitters, 234

norepinephrine, 234

persistent goal-directed behavior, 237

prefrontal lobes, 234

prevalence, 228–231

problems socializing with peers, 238–240

progress assessment, 251–253

psychological/behavioral characteristics, 235–241

reinforcement, role of, 246–247

self-monitoring, 246

service delivery, 247

strattera, 249

Strauss syndrome, 227

substance abuse, 241

time awareness, management, 237

toxins, 235

transition to adulthood, 254–257
  coaching, 257
    importance of, 257
  diagnosis in adulthood, 254–255
  diagnostic criteria, 256t
  employment, 255–256
  marriage, family, 256–257

twin studies, 234

World War I brain-injured soldiers, Goldstein, work of, 226

Attitudes of general educators, 59

Audiologist, 344

Audiometric zero, 344–245

Auditory-oral approach, 356

Auditory-verbal approach, 356

Augmentative or alternative communication
  autism spectrum disorders, 440
  communication disorders, 304
  low-incidence, multiple, severe disabilities, 476–482
  multiple, severe disabilities, 476–482

Auricle, 342

Autism spectrum disorders, 12, 420–455, 432t, 433–435, 442–443t, 447–448
  abnormal sensory perceptions, 435
  alternative communication, 440
  applied behavior analysis, 442
  Asperger, work of, 424
  Asperger syndrome, 425, 435–437
    defined, 425
    transition programming, 450–452
  augmentative communication, 440
  autism, defined, 425
  autistic regression, 432
  autistic savant, 434
  behavior management, 439–440
  causes, 426–431
    causal theories, 428–431
    early causal theories, 427–428
    genetic basis of autism spectrum disorders, 431
    mirror neurons, 429
  central coherence, 438
  childhood disintegrative disorder, 432
  coaching, 441
  communicative intent, 433
  community residential facilities, 450

competitive employment, 450
definition, 424–425
direct instruction of skills, 439
early intervention, 449–450
early signs, 432t
echolalia, 424
educational considerations, 439–444
educational programming, 439–440
executive functions, 437–438
gastrointestinal, 428
hidden curriculum, 436
historic overview, 423–424
Hoopman, Kathy, 436
identification, 431–432
impaired cognition, 433–435
impaired communication, 433, 437
impaired social interaction,
        433, 435–437
instruction in natural settings, 440
Kannerm, work of, 423–424
misconceptions, 422–243
monitoring progress, 445–449
neurological basis, 429–431
outcome measures, 449
person-centered planning, 450
pervasive developmental disorder not
        otherwise specified, 432
picture exchange communication
        system, 446
pragmatics, 437
prevalence, 425–426
progress assessment, 444–449
psychoanalytic, 427
psychological/behavioral characteristics,
        433–438
repetitive behavior, 433
Rett syndrome, 426
schizophrenia, 424
service delivery, 441–444
social interpreting, 441
social skills, 440–441
stereotyped patterns of behavior, 433
stereotypic behaviors, 433
supported competitive employment, 450
supported living, 450
synesthesia, 435
testing accommodations, 449
theory of mind, 438
thimerosal, 428
transition programming, 450
transition to adulthood, 450–452
unifying theory, 437–438
vaccinations, autism and, 428–429
Autistic regression, 432
Autistic savant, 434
Autistic spectrum disorder, 12

Barkley model, attention deficit
        hyperactivity disorder, 235–237
Basal ganglia, 232–234
Behavioral disorders, 24, 269–299
affective disorder, 267
aggression, 279–285
anxiety disorder, 267

causes, 270–275
    biological factors, 271–272
    cultural factors, 274–275
    family issues, 272
    school factors, 272–274
classification, 268–269
commitment to sustained
        intervention, 287
comorbidity, 269
conduct disorder, 267
control, behavioral, 285–286
curriculum-based measurement, 292
definitions, 266–268
discipline, 290–291
early intervention, 294–296
educational considerations, 285–291
encopresis, 284
enuresis, 284
externalizing, 268
family factors, 273
federal definition, alternative
        to, 267–268
functional behavioral assessment, 291
identification, 275–276
instructional considerations, 288–290
integrated services, importance of, 286
intelligence, 149f, 277–278, 278f
internalizing, 268, 284–285
juvenile delinquents, needs of, 290
misconceptions, 262–264
multicomponent treatment, 286
new skills practice, 286
placements, 287–288
prevalence, 269–270
progress assessment, 291–294
    academic skills, 292–293
    monitoring progress, 291–293
    outcomes of behavioral interventions,
        291–292
    testing accommodations, 293–294
psychological/behavioral characteristics,
        277–285
schizophrenia, 269
service delivery, 287–288
social characteristics, 278–285
social skills, 290
strategies that work, 286–287
systematic, data-based
        intervention, 286
teachers, special challenges, 290
terminology, 264
transfer, maintenance,
        programming for, 287
transition to adulthood, 296–297
treatment matched to problem, 286
trends toward inclusion, 287
Behavioral phenotypes, 159
Bilingual students, 84–113
attitudes towards, 88–91
classwide peer tutoring, 101
cooperative learning, 109
cultural diversity, 91–94
curriculum-based measurement, 98
desegregation, 90

disabilities, identification, classification
        of, 97–98
ethnicity, 95t
instruction, 100–111
    family, working with, 103
    language instruction, 103–104
    reading instruction, 105–108
    socialization, 108–111
    teaching practices, 104–105
    tolerance, teaching of, 102–103
misconceptions, 86–88
mnemonics, 105
monitoring progress, 98–99
multicultural education, 87
native language, 100
progress assessment, 98–100
reciprocal teaching, 105
response to intervention, 97–98
scaffolded instruction, 105
sheltered-English approach, 105
subculture, 91
Bisexual students, 104
Blindness, 376–419, 395t, 413
academic achievement, 391
accessible pedestrian signals, 412
astigmatism, 384–385
Braille, 381, 395–400, 409
    Louis, 396
Braille bills, 398
Braille literacy instruction, 399
Braille notetakers, 405
cataracts, 387
causes, 384–387
cautions about technology, 408
cognitive mapping, 389
conceptual abilities, 388–389
cortical visual impairment, 387
de la Serre, Captain Charles Barbier, 396
Descriptive Video Service, 405
diabetic retinopathy, 387
Doppler effect, 389
early intervention, 412
educational considerations, 394–408
eye, anatomy, physiology of, 383
GeoLogger, 411
glaucoma, 386
guide dogs, 402
human guides, 404
hyperopia, 384–85
identification, 384
information access, 405–406
intellectual ability, 388–389
itinerant teacher services, 408
Kurzweil 1000, 405
language development, 388–389
large-print books, 400
legal blindness, 380
listening skills, 401
literary Braille, 395
long cane, 401–402
low vision, 381
magnifying devices, 400
misconceptions, 378–380
mobility, 389–391, 401–404, 406–407

Blindness (*Continued*)
monitoring progress, 410–411
myopia, 384–385
myth of sensory acuteness, 390–391
Nemeth code, 395
Newsline, 405
night blindness, 387
nystagmus, 387
obstacle sense, 389
optic nerve, 386
orientation, 389–391, 401–404
outcome measures, 411
performance on standardized
intelligence tests, 388
Perkins Brailler, 396
phonological awareness, 391
prevalence, 382–83
progress assessment, 410–411
psychological/behavioral
characteristics, 388–394
quality of life, 410–411
raised dome detectable warnings, 413
refraction, 384
remaining sight, use of, 400
retinitis pigmentosa, 387
retinopathy of prematurity, 387
screen readers, 405
service delivery models, 408–409
skills definition, 382
slate, 396
social adjustment, 391–394
societal discomfort with blindness,
391–393
stereotypic behaviors, 393–394
strabismus, 387
stylus, 396
subtle visual cues, 391
tactile maps, 403
technological aids, 404–408
testing accommodations, 411
transition to adulthood, 412–415
employment, 415
independent living, 412–415
tunnel vision, 387
unified English Braille, 395
Braille, 381, 395–400, 409, 475
Louis, 396
Braille bills, 398
Braille literacy instruction, 399
Braille notetakers, 405
Brain
areas of, 233*f*
left temporal lobe, 194*f*
structures of, 430*f*

CAP. *See* continuum of alternative
placements
Captioning, 361–362
Cataracts, 387
Catheterization, 503
Caudate, 234
CEC. *See* council for exceptional children
Center-based programs, 69
Cerebellum, 232–234

Cerebral palsy, 227, 319, 480, 496, 498–500
associated disabilities, 499–500
causes, types, 499
CHARGE syndrome, 468–469
Childhood disintegrative disorder, 432
Choanae, 469
Choreoathetoid, 499
Chorionic villus sampling, 152
Chromosomal disorders, 151–154
Chromosomes, 151
Classification, intellectual, developmental
disabilities, 149
Classwide peer tutoring, 64, 101, 206
Cleft palate, 317
Closed head injuries, 460
Co-teaching, 63
Coaching. *See* job coach
Cochlea, 343
Cochlear implant, 52, 354
debate, 354–355
Cognitive mapping, 389
Cognitive training, 203
Collaborative consultation, 63
Coloboma, 470
Communication, development of, 308*t*
Communication disorders, 300–335
acquired apraxia, 319
alternative communication, 304
American Speech-Language-Hearing
Association, 305
aphonia, 317
apraxia, 318
augmentative communication, 304
cerebral palsy, 319
cleft palate, 317
communication, development of, 308*t*
communication disorder, 304
communication variations, 306–307
communicative functions, 303
curriculum-based language, 325
decoding, 323
developmental apraxia, 319
dialects, 306
dynamic assessments, 325
dysarthria, 318
dysfluencies, 317
early expressive language delay, 312
early intervention, 326–330
delayed language development,
327–328
early development, 326–327
involvement of families, 328–330
educational considerations, 319–324
expressive language, 304
language
academic progress assessment, 324–326
development of, 308*t*
language-based reading impairment, 312
language disorders, 304, 307–314
classification of, 310–314
primary language disorders, 311–313
secondary language disorders, 313–314
larynx, 316
literacy, 323–324

milieu teaching, 328
misconceptions, 302–303
morphological disorder, 310
morphology, 304
morphosyntactic disorder, 310
phonological awareness, 312, 315
phonological disorder, 310
phonology, 304
pragmatic disorder, 310
pragmatics, 304–305
prelinguistic communication, 327
prevalence, 305–306
primary language disorder, 311
question-asking strategies, 320–322
receptive language, 304
resonance, 317
secondary language disorder, 311
semantic disorder, 310
semantics, 304
social use of language, 320
specific language impairment, 311
speech, development of, 308*t*
speech disorders, 304, 314–319
apraxia, 319
articulation disorders, 315–316
dysarthria, 319
fluency disorders, 317–318
motor-speech disorders, 318–319
phonological disorders, 314–315
voice disorders, 316–317
speech-language pathologist, 325
stuttering, 317
syntactical disorder, 310
syntax, 304
transition to adulthood, 330–332
written expression, 323–324
Community-based services, 49
Community employment, 75*t*
Community residential facilities,
173, 450, 489
Competitive employment, 176, 450, 487
Computer assisted instruction, 362–363
Conduct disorder, 226, 266
Conductive hearing impairment, 346
Conductive impairment, 346
Congenita, l48
Congenital cytomegalovirus, 347, 471
Connexin-26 gene, 347
Constant time delay, 163
Content enhancement, 205
Contingency-based self-management, 244
Continuous assessment and monitoring of
progress, 286
Continuous performance test, 232
Continuum of alternative placements, 54
Continuum of placements, 57–58
Convulsion, 500. *See also* seizure
Cooperative teaching, 63
Coordination problems, 199
Cornea, 383
Corpus callosum, 232–234
Cortical visual impairment, 387
Council for exceptional children,
development of profession, 27

CP. *See* cerebral palsy
CPT. *See* continuous performance test
Cranial nerves, 470
Creativity, 532
Cued speech, 357
Cultural diversity, 129
Culture, deaf, 351–352
Curricula, 63–64
Curriculum-based measurement, 98, 165, 190, 209, 252, 292, 325
CVI. *See* cortical visual impairment
CVS. *See* chorionic villus sampling
CWPT. *See* classwide peer tutoring
Cystic fibrosis, 5

Daily living skills, 488
DAP. *See* developmentally appropriate practice
de la Serre, Captain Charles Barbier, 396
Deaf-blindness, 467–476
    adapted signs, 475
    assistance cards, 476
    atresia, 470
    Braille, 475
    causes, 468–471
        genetic/chromosomal syndromes, 468–470
        postnatal conditions, 471
        prenatal conditions, 471
    CHARGE syndrome, 468
    choanae, 469
    coloboma, 470
    communication, 471–472, 474–475
    congenital cytomegalovirus, 471
    cranial nerves, 470
    direct teaching, importance of, 472
    Down syndrome, 468
    educational considerations, 472–476
    German measles, 471
    hand-over-hand guidance, 475
    hand-under-hand guidance, 475
    Howe, Samuel Gridley, 473
    information, problems accessing, 471
    meningitis, 471
    navigating environment, problems with, 472
    night blindness, 469
    orientation, mobility, 475–476
    postnatal, 471
    prenatal, 471
    prevalence, 468
    psychological, behavioral characteristics, 471–472
    retinitis pigmentosa, 469
    rubella, 471
    structured routines, importance of, 472–474
    touch cues, 475
    tunnel vision, 469
    Usher syndrome, 468, 470, 476
Deafness, 336–375. *See also* hearing impairment
    academic achievement, 350–351
    activism, 353–355

adventitiously deaf, 340
audiologist, 344
audiometric zero, 344–345
auditory-oral approach, 356–358
auditory-verbal approach, 356–358
auricle, 342
bicultural-bilingual approach, 355, 360
captioning, 361–362
causes, 346–347
cochlea, 343
cochlear implant, 354–355
computer assisted instruction, 362–363
conductive hearing impairment, 346
congenital cytomegalovirus, 347
congenital deafness, 340
connexin-26 gene, 347
criticisms of oral approach, 358
cued speech, 357
culture, deaf, concern for, 353
deaf culture, 351–352
decibels, 340
degrees, 348*t*
developmental milestones of sign language, 349
ear anatomy, physiology, 342–344
eardrum, 342
early intervention, 368–369
educational considerations, 355–364
evoked-response audiometry, 345
external otitis, 346
family issues, 371–372
fingerspelling, 358
Gallaudet, 353
genetic engineering, debate, 355
grammatical complexity of sign language, 348–349
hearing aids, 360–361
hertz, 344
homophenes, 358
identification, 344–345
incus, 343
inner ear, 343–344
intellectual ability, 349–350
internet, 363
malleus, 343
middle ear, 343
misconceptions, 338–339
mixed hearing impairment, 346
monitoring progress, 364–366
neurological foundations of sign language, 349
Nicaraguan sign language, 350
nonuniversality of sign language, 349
oral approaches, 356–58
oralism-manualism debate, 355
ossicles, 343
otitis media, 346
otoacoustic emissions, 344
outcome measures, 366–367
outer ear, 342–343
oval window, 343
phonics, 366–367
play audiometry, 345
postlingual deafness, 340

prelingual deafness, 340
prevalence, 341–342
progress assessment, 364–368
psychological/behavioral characteristics, 347–355
sensorineural hearing impairment, 346
service delivery, 363–364
sign language, 348–349
    interpreters, 371
signing English systems, 358
social adjustment, 351–355
speech development, 347–348
speechreading, 357
spoken language, 347–348
stapes, 343
technological advances, 360–363
telephone adaptations, 362
testing accommodations, 368
text telephones, 362
total communication, 355, 358–360
transition to adulthood, 369–372
    postsecondary education, 370–371
    sign language interpreters, 370–371
transliteration, 370
tympanic membrane, 342
tympanometry, 345
vestibular mechanism, 343
video relay service, 362
in vitro fertilization, 355
Decibels, 340
Decoding, 196, 323
Deinstitutionalization, 49–50
Descriptive Video Service, 405
Developmental apraxia, 319
Developmental delay, 69
Developmental disorders of brain formation, 153–154
Developmental milestones, 216*t*
Developmentally appropriate practice, 487
DI. *See* direct instruction
Diabetic retinopathy, 387
Dialects, 306
Differentiated instruction, 60
Direct instruction, 205
Disability
    vs. handicap, 6–7
    vs. inability, 7
Disability rights movement, 55
Dopamine, 234
Doppler effect, 389
Down syndrome, 5, 151–153, 468–469
Drug abuse, 250
Dysarthria, 318–319
Dysfluencies, 317
Dyslexia, 198

Ear anatomy, physiology, 342–344
    inner ear, 343–344
    middle ear, 343
    outer ear, 342–343
Eardrum, 342
Early expressive language delay, 312
Echolalia, 424

Education for All Handicapped
  Children Act, 28
EELD. *See* early expressive language delay
Effects of child with disability on family,
  119–125
  feelings, dealing with, 122
  guilt, role of, 120–121
  parental reactions, 120–122
  public, dealing with, 121
  stage theory approach, 120
Emotional disorders, 24, 149f, 240, 269–299,
  278f, 282–283, 286, 292–293
  affective disorder, 267
  aggression, 279–285
  alternative to federal definition, 267–268
  anxiety disorder, 267
  causes, 270–275
    biological factors, 271–272
    cultural factors, 274–275
    family issues, 272
    school factors, 272–274
  characteristics, emotional, 278–285
  classification, 268–269
  commitment to sustained
    intervention, 287
  comorbidity, 269
  conduct disorder, 266
  control, behavioral, 285–286
  current definitions, 266–268
  curriculum-based measurement, 292
  discipline, 290–291
  early intervention, 294–296
  educational considerations, 285–291
  encopresis, 284
  enuresis, 284
  externalizing, 268
  family factors, 273
  functional behavioral assessment, 291
  identification, 275–276
  instructional considerations, 288–290
  integrated services, importance of, 286
  intelligence, 149f, 277–278, 278f
  internalizing, 268, 284–285
  juvenile delinquents, needs of, 290
  misconceptions, 262–264
  multicomponent treatment, 286
  new skills practice, 286
  placements, 287–288
  prevalence, 269–270
  progress assessment, 291–294
    academic skills, 292–293
    outcomes of behavioral interventions,
      291–292
    testing accommodations, 293–294
  psychological/behavioral characteristics,
    277–285
  schizophrenia, 269
  service delivery, 287–288
  social characteristics, 278–285
  social learning, 285–286
  social skills, 290
  strategies that work, 286–287
  systematic, data-based intervention, 286
  teachers, special challenges, 290
  terminology, 264

transfer, maintenance, programming
  for, 287
transition to adulthood, 296–297
treatment matched to problem, 286
trends toward inclusion, 287
Encephalitis, 155–156
Encopresis, 284
Enrichment, 549, 554
Enuresis, 284
Environment, arrangement of, 26
Environmental influences, 154
Epilepsy, 500–502. *See also* seizure disorder
  first aid, 502
Error analysis, 212
Ethics, empirical evidence, distinguished, 56
Ethnicity, 84–113, 95t, 104, 108
  attitudes towards, 88–91
  classwide peer tutoring, 101
  cooperative learning, 109
  cultural diversity, 91–94
  curriculum-based measurement, 98
  desegregation, 90
  disabilities, identification, classification
    of, 97–98
  instruction, 100–111
    family, working with, 103
    language instruction, 103–104
    reading instruction, 105–108
    socialization, 108–111
    teaching practices, 104–105
    tolerance and appreciation, teaching
      of, 102–103
  misconceptions, 86–88
  mnemonics, 105
  monitoring progress, 98–99
  multicultural education, 87
  native language, 100
  progress assessment, 98–100
  reciprocal teaching, 105
  response to intervention, 97–98
  scaffolded instruction, 105
  sheltered-English approach, 105
  subculture, 91
Evoked-response audiometry, 345
Exceptional learners, educational
  definition of, 8–11
Exceptionality, 2–44
  abilities, importance of, 6
  Americans with Disabilities Act, 28–30
  autism, 12
  autistic spectrum disorder, 12
  behavioral disorders, 24
  council for exceptional children,
    development of profession, 27
  cystic fibrosis, 5
  disability
    vs. handicap, 6–7
    vs. inability, 7
  Down syndrome, 5
  Education for All Handicapped
    Children Act, 28
  emotional disorders, 24
  environment, arrangement of, 26
  exceptional learners, educational
    definition of, 8–11

expectations, 19–24
general education, special education,
  relationship between, 18
hydrocephalus, 6
immediate reward, 26
inclusion controversy, 18–19
individualized education programs,
  32–32t, 36t, 38t
individualized family service plan, 37
individualized instruction, 25
Individuals with Disabilities Education
  Improvement Act, 28–30
intent of special education law, 32–37
least restrictive environment, 15
legislation, 28–31
litigation, 28–31
mental retardation, 24
muscular dystrophy, 5
No Child Left Behind Act, 13, 28–30
parents, 27–28
phenylketonuria, 5
prevalence
  high-incidence, 11–12
  low incidence, 11–12
professional organizations, 27–28
progress of special education, 37–38
provision of special education, 13–17
referral, 21
retinopathy of prematurity, 5
at risk, defined, 18
roles of teacher, 17–24
Rowley court case, 30–31
senses, awakening of, 26
sequenced series of educational tasks, 26
special education
  definition of, 12–13
  history of, 24–28
stimulation, 26
students at risk, special education and, 18
traumatic brain injury, 12
tutoring, 26
Executive functions, 236–237, 502
Expectations, 19–24
Expressive language, 304
External otitis, 346
Externalizing, 268. *See also* aggression
Eye, anatomy, physiology of, 383

Families, 114–141
  advocacy, 137–138
  changing views, 118–119
  characteristics, 128
  cultural diversity, 129
  effects of child with disability, 119–125
    feelings, dealing with, 122
    guilt, role of, 120–121
    parental reactions, 120–122
    public, dealing with, 121
    stage theory approach, 120
  ethnicity, 132
  family activity settings, 133
  family-centered model, 126
  family systems theory, 127–132
  functions, 130–131
  guardianship, 131

home-note program, 135–136
homework, 135
individualized family service plan, 119
interaction of, 129–130
internet resources, 132
involvement, 125–138
life cycle, 131–132
linguistic diversity, 129
misconceptions, 116–118
parent centers, 132
parent-teacher conferences, 134, 136t
parental adjustment, 122–124
parental support groups, 132
positive behavioral intervention
        and support, 132–133
professionals, parents and, communication
        between, 133–137
sibling reactions, 124–125
    adjustment, 125
sibshops, 125
social support, 132
traveling notebooks, 136–137f
Family activity settings, 133
Family-centered model, 126
Family characteristics, 128
Family functions, 130
Family interactions, 129
Family life cycle, 131
Family systems theory, 127–132
FAS. See fetal alcohol syndrome
Fetal alcohol syndrome, 154–155, 194, 505
Fingerspelling, 358
Fluency disorders, 317–318
FMRI. See functional magnetic
        resonance imaging
Fragile X syndrome, 153
Franklin Pierce Frank, mnemonic, 207–207f
Free appropriate public education, 52
Frontal lobes, 232–234
Full inclusion, 53
Functional academics, 161
Functional behavioral analysis, defined, 79
Functional magnetic resonance imaging, 193
Functional vision assessment, 384

Gallaudet, 353
Gastrointestinal, 428
Gay Lesbian and Straight Education
        Network, 104
Gay students, 104
General education, special education,
        relationship between, 18
Genetic syndromes, 161t
    behavioral phenotypes, 158–161
Genius, 532
GeoLogger, 411
German measles, 154–155, 471
Gifted students, 528–561
    analytic giftedness, 534
    behavioral characteristics, 539–541
    creativity, 532
    cultural groups, 544–545
    cultural values, 541–543
    disabilities, 545–547
    educational considerations, 549–559

acceleration, 549, 552–554, 556–557
    early intervention, 554–556
    enrichment, 549, 554
ethnic-minority groups, 544–545
females, 547–548
genius, 532
giftedness, 534
identification of, 538–541
insight, 532
low socioeconomic status, 544
misconceptions, 530–531
neglected gifted students, 543–548
practical giftedness, 534
precocity, 532
prevalence, 536
psychological characteristics, 539–541
remote area-students, 544
synthetic giftedness, 534
talent, 532
transition to adulthood, 556–59
underachievers, 543–544
Giftedness, 534
Glaucoma, 386
Globus pallidus, 234
GLSEN. See Gay Lesbian and Straight
        Education Network
Graphic organizers, 205
Guardianship, 131
Guide dogs, 402
Gullibility, 158–159

Hand-over-hand guidance, 475
Hand-under-hand guidance, 475
Handicapism, 55
Hearing aids, 360–361
Hearing impairment, 336–75. See also
        deafness
    academic achievement, 350–351
    activism, 353–355
    adventitiously deaf, 340
    audiologist, 344
    audiometric zero, 344–345
    auditory-oral approach, 356–358
    auditory-verbal approach, 356–358
    auricle, 342
    bicultural-bilingual approach, 355, 360
    captioning, 361–362
    causes, 346–347
    cochlea, 343
    cochlear implant, 354
        debate, 354–355
    computer assisted instruction, 362–363
    conductive hearing impairment, 346
    congenital cytomegalovirus, 347
    congenital deafness, 340
    connexin-26 gene, 347
    criticisms of oral approach, 358
    cued speech, 357
    culture, deaf, concern for, 353
    deaf culture, 351–352
    decibels, 340
    degrees, 348t
    developmental milestones of sign
        language, 349
    ear anatomy, physiology, 342–344

inner ear, 343–344
    middle ear, 343
    outer ear, 342–343
eardrum, 342
early intervention, 368–369
educational considerations, 355–364
evoked-response audiometry, 345
external otitis, 346
family issues, 371–372
fingerspelling, 358
Gallaudet, 353
genetic engineering, debate, 355
grammatical complexity of sign
        language, 348–349
hearing aids, 360–361
hertz, 344
homophenes, 358
identification, 344–345
incus, 343
inner ear, 343–344
intellectual ability, 349–350
internet, 363
malleus, 343
middle ear, 343
misconceptions, 338–339
mixed hearing impairment, 346
monitoring progress, 364–366
neurological foundations of sign
        language, 349
Nicaraguan sign language, 350
nonuniversality of sign language, 349
oral approaches, 356–358
oralism-manualism debate, 355
ossicles, 343
otitis media, 346
otoacoustic emissions, 344
outcome measures, 366–367
outer ear, 342–343
oval window, 343
phonics, 366–367
play audiometry, 345
postlingual deafness, 340
prelingual deafness, 340
prevalence, 341–342
progress assessment, 364–368
psychological/behavioral characteristics,
        347–355
sensorineural hearing impairment, 346
service delivery, 363–364
sign language, 348–349
sign language interpreters, 371
signing English systems, 358
social adjustment, 351–355
speech development, 347–348
speechreading, 357
spoken language, 347–348
stapes, 343
technological advances, 360–363
telephone adaptations, 362
testing accommodations, 368
text telephones, 362
total communication, 355, 358–360
transition to adulthood, 369–372
    postsecondary education, 370–371
    sign language interpreters, 370–371

Hearing impairment (*Continued*)
   transliteration, 370
   tympanic membrane, 342
   tympanometry, 345
   vestibular mechanism, 343
   video relay service, 362
   in vitro fertilization, 355
Heritability studies, 194
Herpes simplex, 154–155
Hertz, 344
Hidden curriculum, 436
Home-based programs, 69
Home-note program, 135–136
Homework, 135
Homophenes, 358
Hoopman, Kathy, 436
Howe, Samuel Gridley, 473
Human genome project, 150
Human guides, 404
Human immunodeficiency virus, 506
Hydrocephalus, 6, 154
Hyperactive child syndrome, 227–228
Hyperactivity, 199–200
Hyperopia, 384–385
Hz. *See* Hertz

IEPs. *See* individualized education programs
IFSP. *See* individualized family service plan
Immediate rewards, 26
In vitro fertilization, 355
Inborn errors of metabolism, 153
Inclusion, 53–65, 72. *See also* full inclusion;
     integration/inclusion
   co-teaching, 63
   collaborative consultation, 63
   controversy, 18–19
   cooperative learning, 63
   differentiated instruction, 60–61
   full inclusion, 53–60
     arguments for/against, 54–59
   matching teaching to students, 60–61
   models of collaboration, 63–65
   prereferral teams and response to
     intervention, 61–63
   training general education teachers, 64–65
Incus, 343
Individualized education programs, 32–32*t*,
     36*t*, 38*t*, 71*t*, 488
Individualized family service plan, 37, 69,
     71*t*, 119, 514
Individualized instruction, 25
Individuals with Disabilities Education
     Improvement Act, 28–30, 51, 71*t*
Informal reading inventory, 211
Inner ear, 343–344, 346–347
Inner speech, 237
Insight, 532
Instructional strategies, 63–64
Integration/inclusion, 42–83
   accommodations, 64
   adaptations, 64
   adult service, integration into, 75*t*
   center-based programs, 69
   classwide peer tutoring, 64

co-teaching, 63
cochlear implant, 52
collaborative consultation, 63
community-based services, 49
community employment, 75*t*
congenita, l48
continuum of alternative placements, 54
cooperative learning, 63
cooperative teaching, 63
curricula, 63–64
deinstitutionalization, 49–50
developmental delay, 69
differentiated instruction, 60–61
disability rights movement, 55
early intervention, 69–73
   child-directed *vs.* adult-directed
     programs, 71–72
   consensus on, 70–72
   prevention, 72–73
free appropriate public education, 52
full inclusion, 53–60
   arguments for/against, 54–59
functional behavioral analysis, 79
handicapism, 55
home-based programs, 69
individualized education programs, 71*t*
individualized family service plan, 69, 71*t*
Individuals with Disabilities Education
     Improvement Act, 51, 71*t*
instructional strategies, 63–64
interim alternative educational setting, 79
job coach, 49
larger society, integration of people with
     disabilities into, 46–53
least restrictive environment, 54
manifestation determination, 78
matching teaching to students, 60–61
misconceptions about learners with
     disabilities, 44–46
models of collaboration, 63–65
modifications, 64
new technologies, use of, 52–53
No Child Left Behind Act, special
     education in context of, 67–68
   standards, 68
normalization, 47–49
   positives, negatives in, 47
partial participation, 64
peer confederates, 64
peer-mediated instruction, 64
peer tutoring, 64
person-centered planning, 50
positive behavioral intervention,
     support, 79
positive behavioral intervention plans, 79
positive behavioral support, 79
prereferral team, 61
prereferral teams, 61–63
progress assessments, 65–67
pull-out programs, 55
response to intervention, 61
responsibility, 50
self-determination, 50–51
spina bifida, 48

supported employment, 74
tiered assignments, 64
training general education teachers, 64–65
transitions to adulthood/
     employment, 73–77
   fit to need level, 76–77
   high-incidence disabilities, 76–77
   low-incidence disabilities, 76
trends overview, 80
universal design, 51–52
universal design for learning, 51–52
zero tolerance, 77–80
   functionality of supports, 79–80
   supports for desired behavior, 78–79
Intellectual, developmental disabilities,
     142–181
   adaptive behavior, 147–148, 157
   Alzheimer's disease, 152
   amniocentesis, 152
   anoxia, 154–155
   behavioral phenotypes, 159, 161*t*
   biological postnatal causes, 155
   causes, 150–156
   chorionic villus sampling, 152
   chromosomal disorders, 151–154
   chromosomes, 151
   chronological age, 156–157
   classification, 149
   classwide peer-tutoring, 166
   community residential facilities, 173
   competitive employment, 176
   constant time delay, 163
   curriculum-based measurement, 165
   Down syndrome, 151–152
   early intervention, 168–170
     to further development, 169–170
     prevention, 168–169
   educational considerations, 161–164
   encephalitis, 155–156
   fetal alcohol spectrum disorders, 154
   fetal alcohol syndrome, 154–155
   fragile X syndrome, 153
   functional academics, 161
   functional behavioral assessment, 163–164
   genetic syndromes, 161*t*
     behavioral phenotypes, 158–161
   gullibility, 158–159
   herpes simplex, 154–155
   human genome project, 150
   hydrocephalus, 154
   identification, 156–157
   inborn errors of metabolism, 153
   intellectual disabilities, improvement
     with, 148
   intelligence tests, 156–157
   job coach, 176
   learned helplessness, 172
   levels of support, 148
   low birthweight, 154–155
   maternal serum screening, 152
   meningitis, 155–156
   mental age, 156–157
   metacognition, 157
   microcephalus, 154

misconceptions, 144–145
natural supports, 145
nature/nurture controversy, 156
nuchal translucency sonogram, 152–153
perinatal, 150
perinatal causes, 151, 154–155
person-centered planning, 172
phenylketonuria, 153
postnatal, 150
postnatal causes, 151, 155
practical intelligence, 147
Prader-Willi syndrome, 153
prenatal causes, 151–154
progress assessment, 165–168
  academic skills, 165, 167
  adaptive behavior skills, 165–167
  monitoring progress, 165–167
  outcome measures, 167
  quality of life skills, outcome
    measures of, 167
  testing accommodations, 167–168
progress monitoring, 165
progressive time delay, 163
psychological/behavioral characteristics,
  157–161
psychosocial postnatal causes, 155
real-life settings, instruction in, 163
rubella, 154–155
scoliosis, 153
self-determination, 172–174
self-regulation, 157
service delivery models, 164–165
sheltered workshop, 176
sleep apnea, 153
social intelligence, 147
spina bifida, 152
supported competitive employment, 176
supported living, 174
syphilis, 154–155
systematic instruction, 162–163
transition to adulthood, 170–177
  community adjustment, 173–174
  employment, 174–176
  self-determination, 171–173
  sheltered workshops, 176
  supported competitive
    employment, 176
traumatic brain injury, 155–156
trisomy 21, 151
vs. mental retardation, 145–146
Williams syndrome, 152–153, 160
working memory, 157
Intent of special education law, 32–37
Interim alternative educational setting,
  defined, 79
Internalizing, 268
IQ-achievement discrepancy, 189
IRI. *See* informal reading inventory
Iris, 383
Itinerant teacher services, 408

Job coach, 49, 176, 488
Juvenile delinquents, needs of, 290
Juvenile rheumatoid arthritis, 503

Kurzweil 1000, 405

Labeling, 54–55
Language, development of, 308*t*
Language-based reading impairment, 312
Language disorders, 304, 307–314
  classification of, 310–314
  primary language disorders, 311–313
  secondary language disorders, 313–314
Large-print books, 400
Larger society, integration of people with
  disabilities into, 46–53
Larynx, 316
Learned helplessness, 172, 202
Learning disabilities, 182–221
  academic achievement, 195–199
  achievement-ability discrepancy, 189
  aim line, 209
  attention deficit hyperactivity
    disorder, 199
  baseline data point, 209
  causes, 193–195
    familiality studies, 194
    fetal alcohol syndrome, 194
    functional magnetic resonance
      imaging, 193
    genetic factors, 194
    heritability studies, 194
    left temporal lobe, 193
    magnetic resonance imaging, 193
    medical factors, 195
    positron emission tomography
      scans, 193
    teratogenic factors, 194–195
    teratogens, 194
  classwide peer tutoring, 206
  cognitive training, 203–205
  content enhancement, 205
  coordination problems, 199
  curriculum-based measurement, 190, 209
  decoding, 196
  developmental milestones, 216*t*
  direct instruction, 205–206
  dyslexia, 198
  early intervention, 214–215
  educational considerations, 202–209
  error analysis, 212
  expected growth norms, 209
  graphic organizers, 205
  hyperactivity, 199–200
  identification, 189–191
  informal reading inventory, 211
  interindividual variation, 195
  intraindividual variation, 195
  IQ-achievement discrepancy, 189
  learned helplessness, 202
  locus of control, 202
  memory, 200
  metacognition, 200
  metacognitive problems, 200
  minimal brain injury, 186
  misconceptions, 184–85
  mnemonics, 205–207

motivational problems, 202
National Joint Committee for
  Learning Disabilities
  definition, 187–188
nonverbal learning disabilities, 201
peer-assisted learning strategies, 207
peer tutoring, 206–207
perceptual-motor problems, 199
perceptual problems, 199
phonemic awareness, 196–197
phonological awareness, 196
phonology, 198
pragmatics, 199
prevalence, 191–192
  gender differences, 192
  increase in prevalence, 192
primary prevention, 190
progress assessment, 209–214
  curriculum-based measurement,
    209–211
  informal assessment, 211–212
  monitoring progress, 209–212
  outcome measures, 212–213
  testing accommodations, 213–215
progress monitoring, 190, 200
psychological/behavioral characteristics,
  195–202
reading, 196–197
reading comprehension, 197
reading fluency, 197
reciprocal teaching, 204–205
rejection, 201
response to intervention, 190
  treatment, 189–191
response-to-treatment approach, 190
scaffolded instruction, 204
secondary prevention, 190–191
self-instruction, 203
self-monitoring, 203
semantics, 198
service delivery, 207–209
short-term memory, 200
social-emotional problems, 201–202
spoken language, 198–199
standardized achievement
  assessment, 212
strategy deficits, 202
syntax, 198
task analysis, 205
tertiary prevention, 191
transition to adulthood, 215–218
  factors related to successful
    transition, 216–217
  postsecondary programming, 217–218
  secondary programming, 217
working memory, 200
written language, 197–198
Least restrictive environment, 15, 54
Left temporal lobe, 193
Legal blindness, 380
Legislation, 28–31
Lens, 383
Lesbian students, 104
Life cycle of family, 131–132

Lipreading. *See* speechreading
Literacy, 323–324
Literary Braille, 395
Litigation, 28–31
Locus of control, 202
Long cane, 401–402
Low birthweight, 154–155
Low-incidence, multiple severe disabilities, 456–491
    age-appropriate practices, 487
    aggression, 483
    alternative communication, 476–482
    augmentative communication, 476–482
    behavior problems, 482–484
    cerebral palsy, 480
    community residential facilities, 489
    community skills, 489
    competitive employment, 487
    cross-disciplinary collaboration, 487
    daily living skills, 488
        lack of, 483
    developmentally appropriate practice, 487
    domestic living skills, 489
    early intervention, 484–487
    family-centered practices, 486
    functional behavioral assessment, 483–484
    individualized education programs, 488
    job coach, 488
    misconceptions, 458–459
    multicultural perspective, 486–487
    natural supports, 488
    neonatal intensive care units, 484
    person-centered planning, 488
    principle of normalization, 487
    self-determination, 488
    self-injury, 482–483
    self-stimulation, 482
    sheltered workshop, 487
    sign language, 477
    tantrums, 483
    transition to adulthood, 487–489
    value-based practices, 486
    vocational programming, 488–489
Low vision, 376–419, 395*t*, 413
    academic achievement, 391
    accessible pedestrian signals, 412
    astigmatism, 384–385
    Braille, 381, 395–400, 409
        Louis, 396
    Braille bills, 398
    Braille literacy instruction, 399
    Braille notetakers, 405
    cataracts, 387
    causes, 384–387
    cautions about technology, 408
    cognitive mapping, 389
    conceptual abilities, 388–389
    cortical visual impairment, 387
    de la Serre, Captain Charles Barbier, 396
    Descriptive Video Service, 405
    diabetic retinopathy, 387

Doppler effect, 389
early intervention, 412
educational considerations, 394–408
eye, anatomy, physiology of, 383
GeoLogger, 411
glaucoma, 386
guide dogs, 402
human guides, 404
hyperopia, 384–385
identification, 384
information access, 405–406
intellectual ability, 388–389
itinerant teacher services, 408
Kurzweil 1000, 405
language development, 388–389
large-print books, 400
legal blindness, 380
listening skills, 401
literary Braille, 395
long cane, 401–402
low vision, 381
magnifying devices, 400
misconceptions, 378–380
mobility, 389–391, 401–404, 406–407
monitoring progress, 410–411
myopia, 384–385
myth of sensory acuteness, 390–391
Nemeth code, 395
Newsline, 405
night blindness, 387
nystagmus, 387
obstacle sense, 389
optic nerve, 386
orientation, 389–391, 401–404
outcome measures, 411
performance on standardized intelligence tests, 388
Perkins Brailler, 396
phonological awareness, 391
prevalence, 382–383
progress assessment, 410–411
psychological/behavioral characteristics, 388–394
quality of life, 410–411
raised dome detectable warnings, 413
refraction, 384
remaining sight, use of, 400
retinitis pigmentosa, 387
retinopathy of prematurity, 387
screen readers, 405
service delivery models, 408–409
skills definition, 382
slate, 396
social adjustment, 391–394
societal discomfort with blindness, 391–393
stereotypic behaviors, 393–394
strabismus, 387
stylus, 396
subtle visual cues, 391
tactile maps, 403
technological aids, 404–408
testing accommodations, 411

    transition to adulthood, 412–415
        employment, 415
        independent living, 412–415
    tunnel vision, 387
    unified English Braille, 395
LRE. *See* least restrictive environment

Magnetic resonance imaging, 193
Magnifying devices, 400
Malleus, 343
Manifestation determination, 78
Maternal serum screening, 152
Memory, 200
Meningitis, 155–156, 471
Mental age, 156–157
Mental retardation, 24
    vs. intellectual/developmental disabilities, 145–146
Metacognition, 157, 200
Methylphenidate. *See* Ritalin
Meticulous arrangement of environment, 26
Microcephalus, 154
Middle ear, 343, 346
Milieu teaching, 328
Minimal brain injury, 186, 227–228
Minority group, persons with disabilities as, 55–56
Mirror neurons, 429
Mixed hearing impairment, 346
Mnemonics, 105, 205–207
Molecular genetics, 234–235
Momentary time sampling, 252
Morphological and syntactical disorder, 310
Morphology, 304
Morphosyntactic disorder, 310
Motor-speech disorders, 318–319, 465
MRI. *See* magnetic resonance imaging
Multicomponent treatment, 286
Multicultural education, 87
Multicultural students, 84–113
    attitudes towards, 88–91
    classwide peer tutoring, 101
    cooperative learning, 109
    cultural diversity, 91–94
    curriculum-based measurement, 98
    desegregation, 90
    disabilities, identification, classification of, 97–98
    ethnicity, 95*t*
    instruction, 100–111
        family, working with, 103
        language instruction, 103–104
        reading instruction, 105–108
        socialization, 108–111
        teaching practices, 104–105
        tolerance and appreciation, teaching of, 102–103
    misconceptions, 86–88
    mnemonics, 105
    monitoring progress, 98–99
    multicultural education, 87
    native language, 100
    progress assessment, 98–100
    reciprocal teaching, 105

response to intervention, 97–98
scaffolded instruction, 105
sheltered-English approach, 105
subculture, 91
Multiple, severe disabilities, 476–489
    age-appropriate practices, 487
    aggression, 483
    alternative communication, 476–482
    augmentative communication, 476–482
    behavior problems, 482–484
    cerebral palsy, 480
    community residential facilities, 489
    community skills, 489
    competitive employment, 487
    cross-disciplinary collaboration, 487
    daily living skills, 488
        lack of, 483
    developmentally appropriate practice, 487
    domestic living skills, 489
    early intervention, 484–487
    family-centered practices, 486
    functional behavioral assessment, 483–484
    individualized education programs, 488
    job coach, 488
    multicultural perspective, 486–487
    natural supports, 488
    neonatal intensive care units, 484
    person-centered planning, 488
    principle of normalization, 487
    self-determination, 488
    self-injury, 482–483
    self-stimulation, 482
    sheltered workshop, 487
    sign language, 477
    tantrums, 483
    transition to adulthood, 487–489
    value-based practices, 486
    vocational programming, 488–489
Muscular dystrophy, 5, 503
Musculoskeletal disorders, 503–504
Muteness, 433
Myopia, 384–385

National Joint Committee for Learning
        Disabilities definition, 187–188
Native language, 100
Natural supports, 145, 488
Nature/nurture controversy, 156
NCLB. See No Child Left Behind Act
Nemeth code, 395
Neonatal intensive care units, 484
Neural tube defect, 502
Neuromotor impairments, 497–503
Neurotoxins, 508
Neurotransmitters, 234
New technologies, use of, 52–53
Newsline, 405
Nicaraguan sign language, 350
Night blindness, 387, 469
NJCLD. See National Joint Committee for
        Learning Disabilities
No Child Left Behind Act, 13, 28–30
    special education in context of, 67–68
Nonverbal learning disabilities, 201

Norepinephrine, 234
Normalization, 47–49
    positives, negatives in, 47
Nuchal translucency sonogram, 152–153
Nystagmus, 387

Occupational therapy, 518
Open head injuries, 460
Optic nerve, 383, 386
Oralism–manualism debate, 355
Orientation, 389, 475
Orthopedic disorders, 503–504
Orthotics, 511–513
Ossicles, 343
Otitis media, 346
Otoacoustic emissions, 344
Outer ear, 342–343, 346
Oval window, 343

PALS. See Peer-Assisted Learning Strategies
Paraplegia, 499
Parent centers, 132
Parent-teacher conferences, 134, 136t
Parental support groups, 132
Parents, 27–28, 114–141. See also families
    adjustment, 122–124
    advocacy, 137–138
    changing views, 118–119
    characteristics, 128
    cultural diversity, 129
    effects of child with disability, 119–125
        feelings, dealing with, 122
        guilt, role of, 120–121
        public, dealing with, 121
        reactions, 120–122
        stage theory approach, 120
    ethnicity, social support, 132
    family-centered model, 126
    family functions, 130
    family interactions, 129
    family life cycle, 131–132
    family systems theory, 127–132
    functions, 130–131
    guardianship, 131
    home-note program, 135–136
    homework, 135
    individualized family service plan, 119
    interaction, 129–130
    internet resources for parents, 132
    involvement, 125–138
    linguistic diversity, 129
    misconceptions, 116–118
    parent centers, 132
    parent-teacher conferences, 134, 136t
    parental support groups, 132
    positive behavioral intervention and
            support, 132–133
    professionals, parents and, communication
            between, 133–137
    sibling reactions, 124–125
    sibshops, 125
    social support, 132
    social support for families, 132
    traveling notebooks, 136–137f

Partial participation, 64
PBIS. See positive behavioral intervention
        and support
PDD-NOS. See pervasive developmental
        disorder not otherwise specified
PECS. See Picture Exchange
        Communication System
Pedestrian signals, accessible, 412
Peer-assisted learning strategies, 207
Peer confederates, 64
Peer-mediated instruction, 64
Peer tutoring, 64, 206–207
Perceptual-motor problems, 199
Perinatal causes of intellectual disabilities, 151
Perkins Brailler, 396
Person-centered planning, 50, 172, 450, 488
Pervasive developmental disorder not
        otherwise specified, 432
PET. See positron emission tomography scans
Phenylketonuria, 5, 153, 507
Phonemic awareness, 196–197
Phonics, 366–367
Phonological awareness, 196, 312, 315, 391
Phonological disorders, 310, 314–315
Phonology, 198, 304
Physical disabilities, 492–527
    academic achievement, 508–509
    adaptive devices, 511–513
    asthma, 505
    career, 523–524
    cerebral palsy, 496, 498–500
    early intervention, 520–522
    educational considerations, 513–520
    educational goals, 516–519
    educational placement, 514–516
    family reaction, 509–511
    individualized planning, 514
    misconceptions, 494–495
    musculoskeletal disorders, 503–504
    neuromotor impairments, 497–503
    occupational therapy, 518
    orthopedic disorders, 503–504
    orthotics, 511–513
    personality characteristics, 509
    placement, 517
    prevalence, 497
    prevention of physical disabilities, 507–508
    prosthetics, 511–513
    psychological/behavioral characteristics,
            508–511
    public reactions, 509
    seizure disorder, 500–502
    sociosexuality, 524
    spina bifida, 502–503
    spinal cord injuries, 502–503
    transition, 522–524
    traumatic brain injury, 497
Picture exchange communication system, 446
Pierce, Franklin, mnemonic, 207–207f
PKU. See phenylketonuria
Play audiometry, 345
Positive behavioral intervention and
        support, 79
    defined, 79

Positive behavioral support, defined, 79
Positron emission tomography scans, 193
Postlingual deafness, 340
Postnatal causes of intellectual
        disabilities, 151
Practical giftedness, 534
Practical intelligence, 147
Prader-Willi syndrome, 153
Pragmatic disorder, 310
Pragmatics, 199, 304–305, 437
Precocity, 532
Prefrontal lobes, 234
Prelingual deafness, 340
Prelinguistic communication, 327
Prenatal causes of intellectual disabilities, 151
Prereferral team, 61
Primary language disorder, 311
Professional organizations, 27–28
Profound mental retardation and
        intellectual disabilities, 149
Programming for transfer and
        maintenance, 287
Progress assessments, 65–67
    monitoring progress, 66
    outcome measures, 66
    testing accommodations, 66–67
Progress of special education, 37–38
Progressive time delay, 163
Prosthetics, 511–513
Provision of special education, 13–17
Psychoanalytic, 427
Psychostimulants, 247
Pull-out programs, 55
Pupil, 383
Pure-tone audiometry, 344

Quadriplegia, 499

Raised dome detectable warnings, 413
Reading comprehension, 197
Reading fluency, 197
Real-life settings, instruction in, 163
Receptive language, 304
Reciprocal teaching, 105, 204–205
Referral, 21
Refraction, 384
Rejection, 201
Remote area-students, 544
Repetitive behavior, 433
Resonance, 317
Response to intervention, 61
Responsibility, 50
Retina, 383
Retinitis pigmentosa, 387, 469
Retinopathy of prematurity, 5, 387
Rett syndrome, 426
Ritalin, 247
    opposition to, 249–250
    paradoxical effect of, 247
Roles of teacher, 17–24
ROP. *See* retinopathy of prematurity
Rowley court case, 30–31
RTI. *See* response to intervention
Rubella, 71, 154–155, 471

Scaffolded instruction, 105, 204
Schizophrenia, 269, 424
Scoliosis, 153
Screen readers, 405
Screening tests, 344
Secondary language disorder, 311
Seizure, epileptic, first aid, 502
Seizure disorder, 500–502
    causes, types, 500–501
    educational implications, 501–502
    epileptic seizures, first aid, 502
Self-determination, 50–51, 172–174, 488
Self-injury, 482–483
Self-instruction, 203
Self-monitoring, 203
Self-regulation, 157
Self-stimulation, 482
Semantic disorder, 310
Semantics, 198, 304
Senses, awakening of, 26
Sensorineural impairment, 346
Separate special education, 55
Sequenced series of educational tasks, 26
Sheltered-English, 105
Sheltered workshop, 176, 487
Short-term memory, 200
Sibling reactions to sibling with disability,
    124–125
Sibshops, 125
Sign language, 348–349, 477
    developmental milestones of, 349
    grammatical complexity of, 348–349
    interpreters, 370–371
    neurological foundations of, 349
    nonuniversality of, 349
Signing English systems, 358
Slate/stylus, 396
Sleep apnea, 153
SLI. *See* specific language impairment
Snellen chart, 384
Social intelligence, 147
Social learning, 285–286
Social use of language, 320
Sociosexuality, 524
Spasticity, 499
Special education, 2–44
    abilities, importance of, 6
    Americans with Disabilities Act, 28–30
    autism, 12
    autistic spectrum disorder, 12
    behavioral disorders, 24
    council for exceptional children,
        development of profession, 27
    cystic fibrosis, 5
    definition of, 12–13
    disability
        vs. handicap, 6–7
        vs. inability, 7
    Down syndrome, 5
    Education for All Handicapped
        Children Act, 28
    emotional disorders, 24
    environment, arrangement of, 26

    exceptional learners, educational
        definition of, 8–11
    expectations, 19–24
    general education, special education,
        relationship between, 18
    history of, 24–28
    hydrocephalus, 6
    immediate reward, 26
    inclusion controversy, 18–19
    individualized education programs,
        32–32*t*, 36*t*, 38*t*
    individualized family service plan, 37
    individualized instruction, 25
    Individuals with Disabilities Education
        Improvement Act, 28–30
    intent of legislation, 32–37
    least restrictive environment, 15
    legislation, 28–31
    litigation, 28–31
    mental retardation, 24
    muscular dystrophy, 5
    No Child Left Behind Act, 13, 28–30
    origins of, 24–28
    parents, 27–28
    phenylketonuria, 5
    prevalence, 11–12
    professional organizations, 27–28
    progress of, 37–38
    provision of, 13–17
    referral, 21
    retinopathy of prematurity, 5
    at risk, defined, 18
    roles of teacher, 17–24
    Rowley court case, 30–31
    senses, awakening of, 26
    sequenced series of educational tasks, 26
    stimulation, 26
    students at risk, special education and, 18
    traumatic brain injury, 12
    tutoring, 26
Specific language impairment, 311
Speech, 304
    development of, 308*t*
Speech audiometry, 345
Speech development, 347–348
Speech disorders, 304, 314–319
    apraxia, 319
    articulation disorders, 315–316
    dysarthria, 319
    fluency disorders, 317–318
    motor-speech disorders, 318–319
    phonological disorders, 314–315
    voice disorders, 316–317
Speech-language pathologist, 325
Speech reception threshold, 345
Speechreading, 357
Spina bifida, 48, 152, 502–503
    educational implications, 503
Spinal cord injuries, 502–503
    social implications, 503
SRT. *See* speech reception threshold
Standardized achievement assessment, 212
Stapes, 343
Stereotypic behavior, 393–394, 433

Stimulation, 26
STM. *See* short-term memory
Strabismus, 387
Strattera, 249
Strauss syndrome, 227
Students at risk, special education and, 18
Stuttering, 317
Stylus, 396
Subculture, 91
Substance abuse, 241
Supported employment, 74,
        176, 450, 523
Supported living, 174, 450
Synesthesia, 435
Syntactical disorder, 310
Syntax, 198, 304
Synthetic giftedness, 534
Syphilis, 154–155
Systematic, data-based intervention, 286
Systematic instruction, 162

Tactile maps, 403
Talent, 532
Tantrums, 483
Task analysis, 205
TBI. *See* traumatic brain injury
Teratogens, 194
Text telephone, 362
Theory of mind, 438

Thimerosal, 428
Tiered assignments, 64
Total communication, 355, 358–360
Touch cues, 475
Toxins, 235
Transgender students, 104
Transitions to adulthood/employment, 73–77
        fit to need level, 76–77
            high-incidence disabilities, 76–77
            low-incidence disabilities, 76
Transliteration, 370
Traumatic brain injury, 12, 155–156,
        460–467, 497
        behavior management, 466
        behavior modification, 466
        causes, 463
        closed head injuries, 460
        educational considerations, 463–467
        emotional problems, 466–467
        language disorders, 465–466
        motor-speech disorder, 465
        open head injuries, 460
        prevalence, 462–463
        social problems, 466–467
Traveling notebooks, 136–137*f*
Trends overview, 80
Trisomy 21, 151
TT. *See* text telephone
Tunnel vision, 387, 469

Tutoring, 26
Tympanic membrane, 342
Tympanometry, 345

Underachievers, 543–544
Unified English Braille, 395
Universal design for learning, 51–52
Usher syndrome, 468–470, 476

Vaccinations, autism and, 428–429
Vestibular mechanism, 343
Video relay service, 362
Vision impairment. *See* low vision
Visual acuity, 384
Visual efficiency, 384
Vitreous humor, 383
Voice disorders, 316–317

Williams syndrome, 152–153, 160
Working memory, 157, 200
World War I brain-injured soldiers,
        Goldstein, work of, 226
Written expression, 323–324

Zero tolerance, 46, 77–80, 82, 289
        emotional/behavioral disorders, 77–80
        functionality of supports, 79–80
        supports for desired behavior, 78–79
Zutter, Teresa, 280–281

Photo Credits